MW00365662

"It takes erudition, vision, and good taste to compile a good handbook of any field, even more so in the notoriously unruly field of pragmatics. Larry Horn and Gregory Ward have all of these. The editors have gathered together an excellent array of contributors to give us a handbook that will prove eminently useful to scholars and students within and outside pragmatics. Readers will find in it a reliable guide to the main pragmatic questions of the last three decades, which is insightful, up to date, authoritative, and accessible."

Mira Ariel, Tel Aviv University

Blackwell Handbooks in Linguistics

This outstanding multi-volume series covers all the major subdisciplines within linguistics today and, when complete, will offer a comprehensive survey of linguistics as a whole.

Already published:

The Handbook of Child Language
Edited by Paul Fletcher and Brian MacWhinney

The Handbook of Phonological Theory
Edited by John A. Goldsmith

The Handbook of Contemporary Semantic Theory
Edited by Shalom Lappin

The Handbook of Sociolinguistics
Edited by Florian Coulmas

The Handbook of Phonetic Sciences
Edited by William J. Hardcastle and John Laver

The Handbook of Morphology
Edited by Andrew Spencer and Arnold Zwicky

The Handbook of Japanese Linguistics
Edited by Natsuko Tsujimura

The Handbook of Linguistics
Edited by Mark Aronoff and Janie Rees-Miller

The Handbook of Contemporary Syntactic Theory
Edited by Mark Baltin and Chris Collins

The Handbook of Discourse Analysis
Edited by Deborah Schiffrin, Deborah Tannen, and Heidi E. Hamilton

The Handbook of Language Variation and Change
Edited by J. K. Chambers, Peter Trudgill, and Natalie Schilling-Estes

The Handbook of Historical Linguistics
Edited by Brian D. Joseph and Richard D. Janda

The Handbook of Language and Gender
Edited by Janet Holmes and Miriam Meyerhoff

The Handbook of Second Language Acquisition
Edited by Catherine J. Doughty and Michael H. Long

The Handbook of Bilingualism
Edited by Tej K. Bhatia and William C. Ritchie

The Handbook of Pragmatics
Edited by Laurence R. Horn and Gregory Ward

The Handbook of Applied Linguistics
Edited by Alan Davies and Catherine Elder

The Handbook of Speech Perception
Edited by David B. Pisoni and Robert E. Remez

The Blackwell Companion to Syntax, Volumes I–V
Edited by Martin Everaert and Henk van Riemsdijk

The Handbook of the History of English
Edited by Ans van Kemenade and Bettelou Los

The Handbook of English Linguistics
Edited by Bas Aarts and April McMahon

The Handbook of World Englishes
Edited by Braj B. Kachru; Yamuna Kachru, Cecil L. Nelso

The Handbook of Pragmatics

Edited by

Laurence R. Horn and Gregory Ward

Blackwell
Publishing

© 2004, 2006 by Blackwell Publishing Ltd

BLACKWELL PUBLISHING
350 Main Street, Malden, MA 02148-5020, USA
9600 Garsington Road, Oxford OX4 2DQ, UK
550 Swanston Street, Carlton, Victoria 3053, Australia

First published 2004 by Blackwell Publishing Ltd
First published in paperback 2006 by Blackwell Publishing Ltd

4   2008

Library of Congress Cataloging-in-Publication Data

The handbook of pragmatics / edited by Laurence R. Horn and Gregory
Ward.
    p. cm. — (Blackwell handbooks in linguistics ; 16)
    Includes bibliographical references.
    ISBN 978-0-631-22547-8 (alk. paper) – ISBN 978-0-631-22548-5 (paperback)
    1. Pragmatics. I. Horn, Laurence R. II. Ward, Gregory L. III. Series.
    P99.4.P72H35 2004
    306.44—dc22

                                                                    2003016284

A catalogue record for this title is available from the British Library.

Set in 10/12 pt Palatino
by Graphicraft Ltd, Hong Kong
Printed and bound in Singapore
by Fabulous Printers Pte Ltd

The publisher's policy is to use permanent paper from mills that operate a sustainable forestry
policy, and which has been manufactured from pulp processed using acid-free and elementary
chlorine-free practices. Furthermore, the publisher ensures that the text paper and cover board
used have met acceptable environmental accreditation standards.

For further information on
Blackwell Publishing, visit our website:
www.blackwellpublishing.com

Contents

List of Contributors   viii

Introduction   xi

I   The Domain of Pragmatics   1

1. Implicature   3
   LAURENCE R. HORN

2. Presupposition   29
   JAY DAVID ATLAS

3. Speech Acts   53
   JERROLD SADOCK

4. Reference   74
   GREGORY CARLSON

5. Deixis   97
   STEPHEN C. LEVINSON

6. Definiteness and Indefiniteness   122
   BARBARA ABBOTT

II   Pragmatics and Discourse Structure   151

7. Information Structure and Non-canonical Syntax   153
   GREGORY WARD and BETTY BIRNER

8. Topic and Focus   175
   JEANETTE K. GUNDEL and THORSTEIN FRETHEIM

9. Context in Dynamic Interpretation   197
   CRAIGE ROBERTS

10. Discourse Markers   221
     DIANE BLAKEMORE

11. Discourse Coherence   241
     ANDREW KEHLER

12. The Pragmatics of Non-sentences   266
     ROBERT J. STAINTON

13. Anaphora and the Pragmatics–Syntax Interface   288
     YAN HUANG

14. Empathy and Direct Discourse Perspectives   315
     SUSUMU KUNO

15. The Pragmatics of Deferred Interpretation   344
     GEOFFREY NUNBERG

16. Pragmatics of Language Performance   365
     HERBERT H. CLARK

17. Constraints on Ellipsis and Event Reference   383
     ANDREW KEHLER and GREGORY WARD

III **Pragmatics and its Interfaces**   **405**

18. Some Interactions of Pragmatics and Grammar   407
     GEORGIA M. GREEN

19. Pragmatics and Argument Structure   427
     ADELE E. GOLDBERG

20. Pragmatics and Semantics   442
     FRANÇOIS RECANATI

21. Pragmatics and the Philosophy of Language   463
     KENT BACH

22. Pragmatics and the Lexicon   488
     REINHARD BLUTNER

23. Pragmatics and Intonation   515
     JULIA HIRSCHBERG

24. Historical Pragmatics   538
     ELIZABETH CLOSS TRAUGOTT

25. Pragmatics and Language Acquisition   562
     EVE V. CLARK

26. Pragmatics and Computational Linguistics   578
     DANIEL JURAFSKY

IV Pragmatics and Cognition   **605**

27. Relevance Theory   607
     DEIRDRE WILSON and DAN SPERBER

28. Relevance Theory and the Saying/Implicating Distinction   633
     ROBYN CARSTON

29. Pragmatics and Cognitive Linguistics   657
     GILLES FAUCONNIER

30. Pragmatic Aspects of Grammatical Constructions   675
     PAUL KAY

31. The Pragmatics of Polarity   701
     MICHAEL ISRAEL

32. Abduction in Natural Language Understanding   724
     JERRY R. HOBBS

Bibliography   742
Index   820

Contributors

Barbara Abbott   Michigan State University, East Lansing, Michigan

Jay David Atlas   Pomona College, Claremont, California

Kent Bach   San Francisco State University, San Francisco, California

Betty Birner   Northern Illinois University De Kalb, Illinois

Diane Blakemore   University of Salford, Salford, UK

Reinhard Blutner   Humboldt University, Berlin Germany

Gregory Carlson   University of Rochester, Rochester, New York

Robyn Carston   University College, London, UK

Eve V. Clark   Stanford University, Stanford, California

Herbert H. Clark   Stanford University, Stanford, California

Gilles Fauconnier   University of California, San Diego, California

Thorstein Fretheim   Norwegian University of Science and Technology, Trondheim, Norway

Adele E. Goldberg   Princeton University, Princeton, New Jersey

Georgia M. Green   University of Illinois, Urbana, Illinois

Jeanette K. Gundel   University of Minnesota, Minneapolis, Minnesota

Julia Hirschberg   Columbia University, New York

Jerry R. Hobbs   Information Sciences Institute, University of Southern California, Los Angeles, California

Laurence R. Horn   Yale University, New Haven, Connecticut

Yan Huang   University of Reading, Reading, UK

Michael Israel   University of Maryland, College Park, Maryland

Daniel Jurafsky   Stanford University, Stanford, California

Paul Kay   University of California, Berkeley, California

Andrew Kehler   University of California, San Diego, California

Susumu Kuno   Harvard University, Cambridge, Massachusetts

Stephen C. Levinson   Max-Planck Institute, Nijmegen, the Netherlands

Geoffrey Nunberg   Stanford University, Stanford, California

François Recanati   Institut Jean Nicod (CNRS), Paris, France

Craige Roberts   Ohio State University, Columbus, Ohio

Jerrold Sadock   University of Chicago, Chicago, Illinois

Dan Sperber   CREA, Paris, France

Robert J. Stainton   University of Western Ontario, London, Ontario

Elizabeth Closs Traugott   Stanford University, Stanford, California

Gregory Ward   Northwestern University, Evanston, Illinois

Deirdre Wilson   University College, London, UK

Introduction

Pragmatics as a field of linguistic inquiry was initiated in the 1930s by Morris, Carnap, and Peirce, for whom syntax addressed the formal relations of signs to one another, semantics the relation of signs to what they denote, and pragmatics the relation of signs to their users and interpreters (Morris 1938). In this program, pragmatics is the study of those context-dependent aspects of meaning which are systematically abstracted away from in the construction of content or logical form.

The landmark event in the development of a systematic framework for pragmatics was the delivery of Grice's (1967) William James lectures, a masterful (if incomplete) program that showed how a regimented account of language use facilitates a simpler, more elegant description of language structure. Since then, a primary goal of pragmatics has been the one reflected in Bar-Hillel's celebrated warning (1971: 405): "Be careful with forcing bits and pieces you find in the pragmatic wastebasket into your favorite syntactico-semantic theory. It would perhaps be preferable to first bring some order into the contents of this wastebasket." More recently, work in pragmatic theory has extended from the attempt to rescue syntax and semantics from their own unnecessary complexities to other domains of linguistic inquiry, ranging from historical linguistics to the lexicon, from language acquisition to computational linguistics, from intonational structure to cognitive science.

In this Handbook, we have attempted to address both the traditional and the extended goals of theoretical and empirical pragmatics. It should be noted, however, that other traditions – especially among European scholars – tend to employ a broader and more sociological conception of pragmatics that encompasses all aspects of language use not falling strictly within formal linguistic theory; see for example the entries in Verschueren et al. (1995) and Mey (1998) and, for a more restricted view, Moeschler and Reboul (1994). For reasons of space and coherence of presentation, we have largely restricted our coverage to the more narrowly circumscribed, mainly Anglo-American conception of linguistic and philosophical pragmatics and its applications.

The Handbook is divided into four parts. Part I contains overviews of the basic subfields within pragmatic theory: implicature, presupposition, speech acts, reference, deixis, and (in)definiteness. The domain of discourse, and in particular the structuring of information within and across sentences, is the focus of the chapters in part II. The chapters in part III concentrate on the interfaces between pragmatics and other areas of study, while those in part IV examine the role of pragmatics in cognitive theory.

For centuries before the field had a label or identity, pragmatics as we now understand it has radiated outward from that aspect of human inferential behavior Grice calls implicature, the aspect of speaker meaning that distinguishes what is (strictly) said from what is (more broadly) meant. The character of conversational implicature is surveyed in Larry Horn's chapter, which explores the relation of implicature to propositional content and linguistic form.

In addition to implicature, the realm of pragmatic inference notably encompasses presupposition. While a semantic presupposition is a necessary condition on the truth or falsity of statements (Frege 1892, Strawson 1950; see also Beaver 1997 and Soames 1989), a pragmatic presupposition is a restriction on the common ground, the set of propositions constituting the ongoing discourse context. Its non-satisfaction results not in the emergence of truth-value gaps but in the inappropriateness of a given utterance in a given context (Karttunen 1974, Stalnaker 1974). In asserting p, I propose adding the propositional content of p to the common ground; in presupposing q, I treat q as already (and non-controversially) part of the common ground. But, as observed by Stalnaker (1974) and Lewis (1979), a speaker may treat q as part of the common ground even when it actually isn't, through the principle of accommodation. In his contribution to this volume, Jay Atlas focuses on accommodation and non-controversiality as the keys to the neo-Gricean theory of presupposition.

If pragmatics is "the study of linguistic acts and the contexts in which they are performed" (Stalnaker 1972: 383), speech act theory – elaborating the distinction between the propositional content and the illocutionary force of a given utterance – constitutes a central subdomain, along with the analysis of explicit performative utterances and indirect speech acts. Speech act theory has evolved considerably from the early work initiated by Austin and Searle, as is discussed in Jerry Sadock's chapter.

While speech acts and presuppositions operate primarily on the propositional level, reference operates on the phrasal level. Reference involves a speaker's use of linguistic expressions (typically NPs) to induce a hearer to access or create some entity in his mental model of the discourse. A discourse entity represents the referent of a linguistic expression, i.e. the actual individual (or event, property, relation, situation, etc.) that the speaker has in mind and is saying something about. The relation between the expressions uttered by a speaker (and the demonstrative gestures that may accompany them) and what they do or can denote presents a range of problems for semantics, pragmatics, and psychology. Greg Carlson's chapter on reference surveys this important domain, while other contributions to the Handbook (cf., for example, the chapters by Nunberg and by Kehler and Ward in part II) revisit specific aspects of the issues raised here.

One persistent complication for any theory of reference is the ubiquity of deictic or indexical expressions. From its inception, a central goal of pragmatics has been to "characterize the features of the speech context which help determine which proposition is expressed by a given sentence" (Stalnaker 1972: 383). The meaning of a sentence can be regarded as a function from a context into a proposition, where a proposition is a function from a possible world into a truth value; pragmatic aspects of meaning include the relation between the context in which an utterance is made and the proposition expressed by that utterance. Deixis characterizes the properties of expressions like *I*, *you*, *here*, *there*, *now*, *hereby*, tense/aspect markers, etc., whose meanings are constant but whose referents vary with the speaker and hearer, the time and place of utterance, and the style, register, or purpose of the speech act. This is explored in the chapter contributed by Steve Levinson, which examines in detail the nature of cross-linguistic variation within the deictic domain.

Another issue within the overall account of reference is the choice among referring expressions and in particular the notion of definiteness, which has been defined both as a formal marking of NPs and as an information status (see chapters in part II). The felicitous use of definite expressions has been pegged to the requirement that the referent of the NP be either familiar within the discourse or uniquely identifiable to the hearer. The other side of this coin is indefiniteness, which has typically been associated with novelty (as opposed to familiarity) or with non-uniqueness. These issues are investigated in Barbara Abbott's chapter, which concludes part I of the Handbook.

The chapters in part II focus on context-dependent aspects of meaning that arise within discourse, in particular the structuring of information within and across sentences. The starting point for work in this area is the now well-established principle that speakers structure their discourse by taking into account both the (assumed) belief states and attentional states of their addressees.

The lead-off chapter by Gregory Ward and Betty Birner examines the role that non-canonical syntactic constructions play in the construction and processing of a coherent discourse. One of the key factors contributing to the coherence of a discourse is the existence of informational links among utterances within the discourse. Ward and Birner show how speakers' use of non-canonical word order marks the information status of these links across sentences while at the same time facilitating discourse processing through the strategic placement of information in different syntactic positions.

At the heart of information structure since the seminal work of the Prague School in the 1930s are the interrelated notions of topic or theme (what a given statement is about) and focus or rheme (what is predicated about the topic). In their chapter, Jeanette Gundel and Thorstein Fretheim review the vast and often confusing literature on these notions across various frameworks. They take topic and focus to be essentially linguistic categories, irreducible to more general cognitive or social principles. Moreover, they argue, a crucial distinction must be made between those properties of topic and focus that are directly attributable to the grammar and those that follow from purely pragmatic principles. Distinguishing between the grammatical and extragrammatical properties of topic and focus is crucial to the formulation of theories of discourse and information structure and to a more adequate account of how the language system interacts with general pragmatic principles governing language production and understanding.

At the heart of any comprehensive theory of the relation of an utterance's meaning to its context is a precise characterization of the very notion of context itself. As Craige Roberts points out in her chapter, an adequate theory of discourse and discourse coherence requires that the relation holding between a linguistic expression and its context of utterance be appropriately modeled and continuously updated as the discourse unfolds. For Roberts, what is necessary in order to model and track this relation is information about the mutual intentions of the co-participants and how these intentions are interrelated. This information, coupled with an appropriate semantics and inference engine, provides the basis for our understanding how context affects (i.e. induces or constrains) utterance interpretation.

Diane Blakemore's chapter focuses on discourse markers (DMs), also known as discourse connectives or particles (*well, so, but*, and the like). DMs have been characterized both negatively, by the non-truth-conditionality of their contribution to meaning, and positively, by their role in highlighting coherence and connectivity among the units of a discourse. Blakemore sees the distribution and interpretation of such markers as informing our understanding of the semantics–pragmatics interface and of the distinction between conceptual and procedural meaning. After evaluating the accounts of DMs offered by speech act theory, traditional Gricean pragmatics, and argumentation theory, Blakemore argues for a relevance-theoretic analysis of the contribution of these expressions.

While Blakemore's chapter outlines the role that discourse markers play in establishing coherence, Andy Kehler's chapter analyzes discourse coherence in its own right. As Kehler observes, hearers do not generally interpret adjacent sentences within a discourse segment as independent and unrelated utterances. Rather, there is an expectation that statements are related in one of several ways that can be captured by a small number of coherence relations. Kehler categorizes these relations into three broad classes defined by basic cognitive principles: cause–effect, contiguity, and resemblance. Kehler illustrates the crucial role that coherence relations play in language by examining their influence on the interpretation of a wide range of disparate linguistic phenomena, including VP-ellipsis, gapping, extraction from conjoined clauses, and pronominal reference.

A long-standing challenge to sentence-based approaches to interpretation is the fact that a speaker whose utterances are syntactically and semantically subsentential may nevertheless manage to express complete propositions and perform fully felicitous speech acts by means of such expressions. The chapter by Rob Stainton on the pragmatics of non-sentences provides a cognitive-pragmatic analysis consisting of two processes: decoding and unencapsulated inference. According to Stainton, non-sentential utterances are first interpreted by the linguistic decoder, which produces a subsentential mental representation. This representation, in turn, is combined with another (non-decoder-derived) mental representation to yield a fully sentential mental representation, which, while not part of any natural language, nonetheless encodes the complete message as intended by the speaker.

Yan Huang's chapter investigates the extent to which the formal conditions of classical binding theory can be supplanted by pragmatic principles. Following earlier work by Reinhart, Dowty, and especially Levinson, he argues that the near-complementary distribution of pronominals and anaphors (i.e. reflexives and reciprocals) and the cross-linguistic patterns of long-distance anaphora and logophoric reference can best be accounted for if the syntax and semantics of binding interacts with neo-Gricean pragmatic theory. As Huang observes, the "soft constraints" built into the neo-Gricean analysis anticipates recent Optimality-theoretic approaches to anaphora.

Another challenge to the self-sufficiency of grammatical theory for explaining linguistic phenomena is offered in Susumu Kuno's chapter on empathy and perspective. Empathy is the degree to which a speaker identifies with, or takes the perspective of, a particular individual or entity referenced in a given utterance. In this way, the same propositional content can be presented from different points of view. Many apparently mysterious phenomena assumed to be purely syntactic can be successfully accounted for only by appeal to these quintessentially pragmatic notions. Kuno proposes that such perspectives interact with syntactic principles in predictable ways and that it is only through such an interaction of pragmatic and grammatical modes of explanation that a full account of such linguistic phenomena as anaphora, logophoricity, and passivization is possible.

Among the most creative but least well understood traits of colloquial discourse is the possibility of deferred reference, which occurs when an expression that conventionally picks out a given referent is used in a sufficiently rich context to refer instead to a discourse entity associated with that referent, as when a bartender refers to his customer as "the gin and tonic" or a doctor to her patient as "the kidney transplant in 317." In his chapter, Geoff Nunberg treats deferred reference as an instance of meaning transfer applied to the properties which linguistic expressions (NPs and predicates) supply. Nunberg explores some of the pragmatic and non-pragmatic factors that constrain and affect such transfers and figurative language more generally.

Herb Clark develops the (now uncontroversial) idea advanced by Grice, Lewis, and others that language is a fundamentally cooperative venture. In this chapter, Clark argues for a pragmatic theory of language performance drawing on two interrelated systems: a primary system of linguistic communication and a collateral system that draws heavily on Clark's notion of display. Speakers display various signals to addressees that serve to indicate the speaker, addressee, time, place, and content of the signal. The addressee, in turn, signals receipt of the display by conveying acceptance of these indications. Such feedback mechanisms are shown to be crucial to our understanding of the communicative process.

Rounding out part II is Andy Kehler's and Gregory Ward's chapter on event reference. Whereas most pragmatic accounts of the constraints associated with particular referring expressions focus on reference to entities (see e.g. Carlson's chapter in part I), Kehler and Ward argue that such accounts need to be revised and extended to account for event-level ellipsis and reference. Their examination of four different event-referring constructions suggests that an adequate model must ultimately appeal to a diverse set of properties that govern natural language syntax, semantics, and pragmatics.

Part III offers varied perspectives on the major interfaces of pragmatics. Linguists have long sought to rely on pragmatic theory to render their accounts of grammatical phenomena both simpler and more explanatory. In the early years of generative grammar, any appeal to pragmatics was seen as hand-waving, less of an explanation of the phenomenon in question than an excuse to avoid dealing with it. As our understanding of pragmatics has deepened, so has our recognition of the ways in which it interacts with other aspects of linguistic competence. Georgia Green's chapter addresses some of the more significant properties of the syntax–pragmatics interface, including the role of context (encompassing speakers' beliefs and intentions) in the description of grammatical constructions and in the formulation of constraints on grammatical processes.

Another investigation of the syntax–pragmatics interface is the chapter by Adele Goldberg on argument structure. Goldberg shows that pragmatic factors such as topic, focus, and information structure all play a crucial role in determining whether a particular argument (or adjunct) is realized in the syntax and, if so, where and in what form that argument appears. These pragmatic factors interact with language-specific grammatical principles to produce the variation in argument structure found cross-linguistically.

From the inception of the Peirce–Carnap–Morris trichotomy, one central issue in the study of meaning has been the semantics/pragmatics distinction and the proper treatment of the borderline defined by their interaction. This territory is explored in the chapters by François Recanati and Kent Bach. Recanati provides an overview of the domain, concentrating on the emergence of modern pragmatics from the crucible of the conflict between formal semanticists and ordinary language philosophers in the second half of the twentieth century. As Recanati shows, current disputes on the role of pragmatic processes in the determination of truth-conditional content and the treatment of unarticulated constituents can be traced to the different responses urged by Griceans and relevance theorists to the division of labor between semantics and pragmatics in the treatment of meaning in natural language.

Bach's chapter addresses two sets of problems: those for which the philosophy of language informs the study of pragmatics (e.g. the treatment of performatives, speech acts, and implicature) and those for which pragmatics informs the philosophy of language. In keeping with the Bar-Hillel wastebasket apothegm, Bach repositions the line of demarcation between semantics and pragmatics in a way that allows a significant range of traditional semantic problems in the areas of reference, presupposition, quantification, and ambiguity to be resolved – or at least clarified – by the application of independently motivated pragmatic, i.e. communication- or use-based, principles and processes.

The traditional syntax/semantics/pragmatics trichotomy extends from the analysis of sentences and discourse into the lexicon. While the study of the syntax and semantics of words (morphology and lexical semantics, respectively) are well-established disciplines, the last quarter century has witnessed the development of the new field of lexical pragmatics. Reinhard Blutner's chapter is devoted to this field, focusing on pragmatically based constraints on lexicalization (see also Horn's implicature chapter), the role of pragmatic strengthening, markedness asymmetries, and the non-monotonic character of word meaning. (The diachronic aspects of these questions are treated in Traugott's chapter.) As Blutner shows, there is a natural kinship between a neo-Gricean approach to the mental lexicon (dating back to McCawley 1978) and current developments in bidirectional Optimality Theory, in which the dialectic of speaker and hearer receives a natural representation.

As Julia Hirschberg points out in her chapter, intonational meaning is essentially pragmatic in nature, as its interpretation crucially depends on contextual factors. Hirschberg brings together research from linguistics, speech, computational linguistics, and psycholinguistics, applying a uniform notation to describe the prosodic variation discussed in this work. Intonation is shown to interact with syntax (attachment ambiguities), semantics (scope ambiguities, focus), and of course pragmatics (discourse and information structure, pronominal reference, and speech act interpretation).

The last quarter century has seen the study of pragmatic aspects of meaning change and lexicalization play an increasingly significant role within diachronic linguistics. Both corpus-based and theoretical investigations have been enriched by the recognition of the role of implicature in facilitating and constraining the set of possible and likely varieties of change. The application of neo-Gricean inference to lexical change is the focus of Elizabeth Traugott's chapter on historical pragmatics, which also explores the ways in which polysemy arises and the routes by which non-literal aspects of meaning tend to become frozen into the conventional value of a lexical expression.

Pragmatics plays a central role in ontogeny as well as phylogeny, as Eve Clark's chapter demonstrates. Clark explores the language learner's acquisition of the ability to tailor the form of utterances to the assumed requirements of one's conversational partners. In their application and eventual refinement of the principle of contrast, their familiarization with the interactional principles of politeness and common ground, and their first steps toward the development of a working knowledge of implicature from both speaker's and hearer's perspectives, children have set out on the road that will lead to full pragmatic competence.

No survey of the interfaces of pragmatics would be complete without a look at attempts to build machines that have the capacity to emulate human pragmatic competence. As Dan Jurafsky notes in his chapter, computational pragmatics is largely concerned with the modeling of the ability of humans to infer information not explicitly realized in an utterance. Jurafsky focuses on the interpretation and generation of speech acts as a case study of recent work in this area.

In keeping with other sections of the Handbook, part IV is organized thematically rather than doctrinally; the six papers it collects all deal with the relation between pragmatics and cognition, while encompassing a variety of distinct theoretical approaches. Deirdre Wilson, Dan Sperber, and Robyn Carston have been major advocates of relevance theory, an influential revision of the Gricean paradigm (Sperber and Wilson 1986a, Carston 2002b). Wilson and Sperber present a state-of-the-art overview of RT, focusing on the implications of this approach for communication, utterance interpretation, and the modular view of mental architecture, while also touching on the analysis of irony and metarepresentation more generally. In her chapter, Carston re-examines the classic Gricean distinction between what is said and what is implicated in the light of current developments in RT. She argues for a position in which "what is said," a central construct in neo-Gricean work, in fact plays no role within pragmatic theory, and in which the implicit/explicit distinction is reconstructed in terms of the relevance-theoretic notion of explicature, a pragmatically determined aspect of propositional content that (contrary to implicature) is germane to the determination of truth conditions.

A different model of the pragmatics of cognition underlies work by Gilles Fauconnier, the originator of the theory of mental spaces. In his chapter, Fauconnier examines the relation between literal and metaphorical interpretation, and concludes that a direct assignment of meaning to grammatical constructions offers a more insightful approach than one mediated by a two-stage Gricean analysis in which literal meaning serves as the input to metaphorical reanalysis. Fauconnier extends the theory of mental spaces to the analysis of opacity, presupposition, performatives, and scalar predication, surveying a variety of ways in which recent developments in cognitive science are relevant for research in pragmatics.

Another perspective on cognitive pragmatics is offered by Paul Kay, one of the founders of Construction Grammar. After demonstrating the complexity of the issues the hearer must sort out in the interaction of grammatical structure and context or common ground as a prerequisite to interpretation, Kay surveys a variety of domains in which pragmatic information influences grammatical constructions, including indexicals, scalar models, metalinguistic operators, hedges (*kinda, sorta, technically*), and speech acts.

In his chapter, Michael Israel investigates one such class of constructions, that comprising negative and positive polarity items. He shows how the lexical properties and grammatical distribution of such items are intricately tied to Kay's notion of scalar model and to the pragmatic asymmetry of negation and affirmation (Horn 1989). Like other essays in the volume, Israel's discussion also explores the important issue of how inherently pragmatic conditions become conventionalized into the lexicon and grammar.

A final look at the pragmatics/cognition interface is presented in the chapter by Jerry Hobbs on abductive reasoning. Abduction, originally identified by C. S. Peirce and more recently developed by researchers in artificial intelligence dealing with the non-monotonic nature of natural language inference, is applied by Hobbs to a variety of problems of a pragmatic nature, ranging from disambiguation and reference resolution to the interpretation of compound nominals and the nature of discourse structure.

We conclude our introductory remarks with a heartfelt appreciation for the efforts and perseverance of our contributors through the difficulties of the editorial process; without them there would be no *Handbook of Pragmatics*. In addition, we would like to thank Sarah Coleman and Tami Kaplan at Blackwell for their support and hard work on our behalf. Finally, we extend a special note of thanks to Kent Bach, Ann Bunger, and Bill Lachman for their editorial assistance.

Part I   The Domain of Pragmatics

1 Implicature

LAURENCE R. HORN

1 Implicature: Some Basic Oppositions

IMPLICATURE is a component of speaker meaning that constitutes an aspect of what is **meant** in a speaker's utterance without being part of what is **said**. What a speaker intends to communicate is characteristically far richer than what she directly expresses; linguistic meaning radically underdetermines the message conveyed and understood. Speaker S tacitly exploits pragmatic principles to bridge this gap and counts on hearer H to invoke the same principles for the purposes of utterance interpretation.

The contrast between the said and the meant, and derivatively between the said and the implicated (the meant-but-unsaid), dates back to the fourth-century rhetoricians Servius and Donatus, who characterized litotes – pragmatic understatement – as a figure in which we say less but mean more ("minus dicimus et plus significamus"; see Hoffmann 1987 and Horn 1991a). In the Gricean model, the bridge from what is said (the literal content of the uttered sentence, determined by its grammatical structure with the reference of indexicals resolved) to what is communicated is built through implicature. As an aspect of speaker meaning, implicatures are distinct from the non-logical inferences the hearer draws; it is a category mistake to attribute implicatures either to hearers or to sentences (e.g. *P and Q*) and subsentential expressions (e.g. *some*). But we can systematically (at least for generalized implicatures; see below) correlate the speaker's intention to implicate q (in uttering p in context C), the expression p that carries the implicature in C, and the inference of q induced by the speaker's utterance of p in C.

Subtypes of implicature are illustrated by (1a–c) (after Grice 1961: §3); the primed member of each pair is (in certain contexts) deducible from its unprimed counterpart:

(1)a. Even KEN knows it's unethical.
  a'. Ken is the least likely [of a contextually invoked set] to know it's unethical.

b.   [in a recommendation letter for a philosophy position]
     Jones dresses well and writes grammatical English.
b'. Jones is no good at philosophy.
c.   The cat is in the hamper or under the bed.
c'. I don't know for a fact that the cat is under the bed.

Unlike an entailment or logical presupposition, the inference induced by *even* in (1a, a') is irrelevant to the truth conditions of the proposition: (1a) is true if and only if Ken knows it's unethical. The inference is not CANCELABLE without contradiction (#*Even Ken knows it's unethical, but that's not surprising*), but it is DETACHABLE, in the sense that the same truth-conditional content is express-ible in a way that removes (detaches) the inference: KEN *knows it's unethical (too)*. Such detachable but non-cancelable aspects of meaning that are neither part of, nor calculable from, what is said are CONVENTIONAL implicatures, akin to pragmatic presuppositions (Stalnaker 1974). Indeed, along with con-nectives like *but*, the now classic instances of conventional implicature involve precisely those particles traditionally analyzed as instances of pragmatic pre-supposition: the additive component of adverbial particles like *even* and *too*, the "effortful" component of truth-conditionally transparent "implicatives" like *manage* and *bother*, and the existential component of focus constructions like clefts.

But in contrast with these non-truth-conditional components of an expres-sion's conventional lexical meaning,[1] the inferences induced by (1b, c) are NON-conventional, i.e. calculable from the utterance of such sentences in a particular context, given the nature of conversation as a shared goal-oriented enterprise. In both cases, the speaker's implicature of the corresponding primed proposition is cancelable (either explicitly by appending material inconsistent with it – "*but I don't mean to suggest that . . .*" – or by altering the context of utterance) but non-detachable (given that any other way of expressing the literal content of (1b, c) in the same context would license the same inference).[2] What distinguishes (1b) from (1c) is the generality of the circumstances in which the inference is ordinarily licensed. Only when the speaker of (1b) is evaluating the competence of the referent for a philosophy position will the addressee normally be expected to infer that the speaker had intended to convey the content of (1b'); this is an instance of PARTICULARIZED conversa-tional implicature.[3] In (1c), on the other hand, the inference – that the speaker does not know in which of the two locations the cat can be found – is induced in the absence of a special or marked context. The default nature of the trig-gering in (1c) represents the linguistically significant concept of GENERALIZED conversational implicature. But in both cases, as with conventional implicature, it is crucially not the proposition or sentence, but the speaker or utterance, that induces the relevant implicatum.

The significance of the generalized/particularized dichotomy has been much debated; cf. Hirschberg (1991) and Carston (1995) for skepticism and Levinson (2000a) for a spirited defense.[4] Whatever the theoretical status of the distinction, it is apparent that some implicatures are induced **only** in a special context (if Mr. Jones had been applying for a job as a personal secretary, Grice's remark in (1b) would have helped, rather than torpedoed, his candidacy), while others go through **unless** a special context is present (as in the utterance of (1c) as a clue in a treasure hunt). The contrast between particularized and generalized implicature emerges clearly in this scene from *When Harry Met Sally* (1989 screenplay by Nora Ephron). Harry (Billy Crystal) is setting up a blind date between his buddy Jess (Bruno Kirby) and his woman friend – but not (yet) girlfriend – Sally (Meg Ryan):

(2)   *Jess:*   *If she's so great why aren't YOU taking her out?*
    Harry: How many times do I have to tell you, we're just friends.
    Jess: *So you're saying she's not that attractive.*
    Harry: No, I told you she IS attractive.
    Jess: *But you also said she has a good personality.*
    Harry: She HAS a good personality.
    Jess: *[Stops walking, turns around, throws up hands, as if to say "Aha!"]*
    Harry: What?
→ *Jess:*   *When someone's not that attractive they're ALWAYS described as having a good personality.*
    Harry: Look, if you were to ask me what does she look like and I said she has a good personality, that means she's not attractive. But just because I happen to mention that she has a good personality, she could be either. She could be attractive with a good personality or not attractive with a good personality.
    Jess: *So which one is she?*
    Harry: Attractive.
⇒ *Jess:*   *But not beautiful, right?*

Jess's first arrowed observation incorrectly reanalyzes a particularized implicature (S, in describing X to H as having a good personality implicates that X is not attractive) as generalized, to which Harry responds by patiently pointing out the strongly context-dependent nature of the inference in question. To see that this is no isolated example, consider a parallel dialogue from an earlier film, *The Shop Around the Corner* (1940 Ernst Lubitsch screenplay). Kralik (James Stewart) is describing his epistolary inamorata to his colleague Pirovitch (Felix Bressart):

(3)   *Kralik:*   She is the most wonderful girl in the world.
    Pirovitch: *Is she pretty?*
    Kralik: She has such ideals, and such a viewpoint of things that she's so far above all the other girls that you meet nowadays that there's no comparison.
→ *Pirovitch:* *So she's not very pretty.*

Like Jess, Pirovitch (who, like Jess above, employs *so* to mark his pragmatic inference) misapplies the (here, tacit) inferential strategy to conclude from Kralik's impassioned (if unparsable) tribute to his love's virtues that she must be physically unprepossessing; in fact, Kralik believes (falsely) that he hasn't yet met her in the flesh, so no such implicature could have been made.

While the inferential step marked by the single arrows is indeed particularized and therefore context-dependent in the strong sense, the inference drawn by Jess at the double arrow is generalized, instantiating SCALAR IMPLICATURE, the upper-bounding of a weak predication ("X is attractive") to convey that the speaker was not in a position to assert any stronger counterpart ("X is beautiful"). The pattern exemplified by Jess's inference, and the reason why Jess is once again wrong to draw it, follow from our later discussion.

To conclude our brief taxonomy of implicature, we should note that despite extensive investigation in work culminating with Karttunen and Peters (1979), conventional implicature remains a controversial domain. While it continues to be invoked to handle non-truth-conditional aspects of lexical meaning, this tends to constitute an admission of analytic failure, a label rather than true explanation of the phenomenon in question. It has on occasion been maintained that conventional implicature is a myth (Bach 1999b), and even for the true believers, the domain in which such implicatures have been posited continues to shrink, eaten away on one side by an increasingly fine-grained understanding of truth-conditional meaning and entailment[5] (a trend begun in Wilson and Sperber 1979; see also Blakemore and Carston, this volume) and on the other by a more sophisticated employment of the tools of conversational implicature. While conventional implicature remains a plausible *faute de mieux* account of particles like *even* and *too*, whose contribution has not convincingly been shown to affect the truth conditions of a given utterance but is not derivable from general considerations of rationality or cooperation, the role played by conventional implicature within the general theory of meaning is increasingly shaky.

2   Speaker Meaning, Inference, and the Role of the Maxims

Whether generalized or particularized, conversational implicature derives from the shared presumption that S and H are interacting rationally and cooperatively to reach a common goal. A speaker S saying p and implicating q can count on her interlocutor to figure out what S meant (in uttering p at a given point in the interaction) from what was said, based on the assumption that both S and H are rational agents. Speakers implicate, hearers infer. While work as distinct as that of Levinson (2000a) and Sperber & Wilson (1986a) often appears to assimilate implicature to non-logical inference, the two phenomena were quite distinct for Grice (1989) (see Bach 2001a and Saul 2002 for discussion). While successful communication commonly relies on implicature, what a speaker implicates is often quite distinct from what her words imply or from what a hearer may be expected to take from them.

But it is S's assumption that H will draw the appropriate inference from what is said that makes implicature a rational possibility. The governing dictum is the Cooperative Principle: "Make your conversational contribution such as is required, at the stage at which it occurs, by the accepted purpose or direction of the talk exchange" (Grice [1967]1989: 26).[6] This general principle is instantiated by general maxims of conversation governing rational interchange (1989: 26–7):

(4) QUALITY: Try to make your contribution one that is true.
　　 1. Do not say what you believe to be false.
　　 2. Do not say that for which you lack evidence.
　　 QUANTITY:
　　 1. Make your contribution as informative as is required
　　　　 (for the current purposes of the exchange).
　　 2. Do not make your contribution more informative than is required.
　　 RELATION: Be relevant.
　　 MANNER: Be perspicuous.
　　 1. Avoid obscurity of expression.
　　 2. Avoid ambiguity.
　　 3. Be brief. (Avoid unnecessary prolixity.)
　　 4. Be orderly.

The fourfold set of macroprinciples has no privileged status, except as a nod to Kant's own categorical tetralogy. Note in particular that all maxims are not created equal. Following Grice himself –

> The maxims do not seem to be coordinate. The maxim of Quality, enjoining the provision of contributions which are genuine rather than spurious (truthful rather than mendacious), does not seem to be just one among a number of recipes for producing contributions; it seems rather to spell out the difference between something's being, and (strictly speaking) failing to be, any kind of contribution at all. False information is not an inferior kind of information; it just is not information.   (Grice 1989: 371)

– many (e.g. Levinson 1983, Horn 1984a) have accorded a privileged status to Quality, since without the observation of Quality, or what Lewis (1969) calls the convention of truthfulness, it is hard to see how any of the other maxims can be satisfied (though see Sperber and Wilson 1986a for a dissenting view).

But the role of the maxims is a more central problem. It is chastening to realize that for all the work inspired by the Gricean paradigm since the William James lectures first circulated in mimeo form among linguists and philosophers in the late 1960s, the nature of the enterprise stubbornly continues to be misunderstood. (See Green 1990 for an inventory of such misunderstandings.) Here is Exhibit A:

> Communication is a cooperative effort, and as such should conform to certain definite rules, or maxims of conversation, which Grice enumerates. The maxims presuppose an almost Utopian level of gentlemanly conduct on the part of a speaker and an old-fashioned standard of truthfulness that George Washington might have found irksome.[7] They remind one of the early Puritanism of the Royal Society. A speaker should give not too much but just enough information, hold his tongue about what he believes to be false, or for which he has insufficient evidence, be relevant, be brief and orderly, avoid obscurity of expressions and ambiguity. . . . Would we want to have dinner with such a person, such an impeccably polite maxim observer?   (Campbell 2001: 256)

This passage is taken from Jeremy Campbell's natural history of falsehood, a treatise hailed by reviewers as "carefully researched," "enlightening," and "thought-provoking," an "almost breathless exercise in intellectual synthesis." But it is not just the laity who are at fault; professional linguists and ethnographers, following Keenan (1976), have at times concluded that Grice's maxims are trivial, naïve to the point of simple-mindedness, and/or culture-dependent (if not downright ethnocentric), and that they fail to apply to phatic and other non-information-based exchanges.

But neither the Cooperative Principle nor the attendant maxims are designed as prescriptions for ethical actions or as ethnographic observations.[8] A more accurate approximation is to view them as default settings (or presumptions, à la Bach and Harnish 1979), the mutual awareness of which, shared by speech participants, generates the implicatures that lie at the heart of the pragmatic enterprise. Only if the speaker is operating, and presumes the hearer is operating, with such principles as defaults can she expect the hearer to recognize the apparent violation of the maxims as a source of contextual inference (see Grice 1989, Green 1996a, Levinson 2000a for elaboration). Further, as with presupposition (on the pragmatic account of Stalnaker 1974), conversational implicature operates through the mechanism of EXPLOITATION. Unlike syntactic and semantic rules, pragmatic principles and conventions do as much work when they are apparently violated – when speaker S counts on hearer H to recognize the apparent violation and to perform the appropriate contextual adjustment – as when they are observed or ostentatiously violated.

3   Scalar Implicature and Constraints on Lexicalization

For linguistic pragmatics, the core of the Gricean system is the first Quantity submaxim, which is systematically exploited to yield upper-bounding generalized conversational implicatures associated with scalar values (Horn 1972, 1989; Gazdar 1979; Hirschberg 1991). Under a variety of formulations, this principle and its explanatory potential have long been tacitly recognized, especially for the interpretation of quantified sentences. Sir William Hamilton (1860: 254) distinguishes two senses of *some*, the INDEFINITE (*at least some*) and the SEMI-DEFINITE (*some but not all*), taking the latter as basic: "Some, if not otherwise qualified, means some only – this by presumption." While acknowledging that such a presumption holds in "common language," De Morgan (1847) offers a proto-Gricean argument for rejecting Hamilton's thesis in favor of the standard practice of relegating the *some* → *not all* inference to an extra-logical domain, as does Mill (1867: 501):

> No shadow of justificaton is shown . . . for adopting into logic a mere sous-entendu of common conversation in its most unprecise form. If I say to any one, "I saw some of your children today", he might be justified in inferring that I did not see them all, not because the words mean it, but because, if I had seen them all, it is most likely that I should have said so: even though this cannot be presumed unless it is presupposed that I must have known whether the children I saw were all or not.

Similarly, while disjunctions are naturally taken exclusively – "When we say A is either B or C we imply that it cannot be both" – this too cannot be a logical inference: "If we assert that a man who has acted in a particular way must be either a knave or a fool, we by no means assert, or intend to assert, that he cannot be both" (Mill 1867: 512).

Notice Mill's epistemic rider in his *unless* clause: S's use of the weaker *some* implicates that **for all S knows** the strongest operator on the same scale, *all*, could not have been substituted *salva veritate*. Mill's tacit principle, with its epistemic condition, is independently invoked by later scholars:

> What can be understood without being said is usually, in the interest of economy, not said . . . A person making a statement in the form, "Some S is P", generally wishes to suggest that some S also is not P. For, in the majority of cases, if he knew that all S is P, he would say so . . . If a person says, "Some grocers are honest", or "Some books are interesting", meaning to suggest that some grocers are not honest or that some textbooks are not interesting, he is really giving voice to a conjunctive proposition in an elliptical way.
>
> Though this is the usual manner of speech, there are circumstances, nevertheless, in which the particular proposition should be understood to mean just what it says and not something else over and above what it says. One such circumstance is that in which the speaker does not know whether the subcontrary proposition is also true; another is that in which the truth of the subcontrary is not of any moment.   (Doyle 1951: 382)

The tacit principle to which Mill alludes, requiring S to use the stronger *all* in place of the weaker *some* when possible and licensing H to draw the corresponding inference when the stronger term is not used, later resurfaces within Grice's program as the first Quantity maxim, which is systematically exploitable to yield upper-bounding generalized conversational implicatures associated with scalar operators. Quantity-based scalar implicature – e.g. my inviting you to infer from my use of *some . . .* that for all I know *not all . . .* – is driven by our presumed mutual knowledge that I expressed a weaker proposition in lieu of an equally unmarked utterance that would have expressed a stronger proposition. Thus, what is said in the use of a weaker scalar value like those in boldface in the sentences of (5) is the lower bound (. . . *at least n . . .*), with the upper bound (. . . *at most n . . .*) implicated as a cancelable inference generated by (some version of) the first maxim of quantity. What is communicated in the default case is the TWO-SIDED UNDERSTANDING that combines what is said with what is implicated.

(5)

		ONE-SIDED →	TWO-SIDED
a.	Pat has **3** children.	"...at least 3..."	"...exactly 3..."
b.	You ate **some** of the cake.	"...some if not all..."	"...some but not all..."
c.	It's **possible** she'll win.	"...at least ◊..."	"...◊ but not certain..."
d.	He's a knave **or** a fool.	"...and perhaps both"	"...but not both"
e.	It's **warm**.	"...at least warm..."	"...but not hot"

The alternative view, on which each scalar predication in (5) is lexically ambiguous between one-sided and two-sided readings, is ruled out by the general metatheoretical consideration that Grice dubs the Modified Occam's Razor principle: "Senses are not to be multiplied beyond necessity" (1989: 47).

Negating such predications denies the lower bound: to say that something is not possible is to say that it's impossible, i.e. less than possible. When it is the upper bound that appears to be negated (*It's not possible, it's NECESSARY*), a range of syntactic, semantic, and prosodic evidence indicates the presence of the METALINGUISTIC or echoic use of negation, in which the negative particle is used to object to any aspect of an alternate (actual or envisaged) utterance, including its conventional and conversational implicata, register, morphosyntactic form or pronunciation (Horn 1989: Chap. 6; Carston 1996). If it's hot, it's (a fortiori) warm, but if I know it's hot, the assertion that it's warm can be echoed and rejected as (not false but) insufficiently informative:

(6)a.   It's not WARM, it's HOT!
   b.   You're right, it's not warm. It's HOT!

As seen in (6b), the metalinguistic understanding typically requires a second pass and the effect is typically that of an ironic "unsaying" or retroactive accommodation (Horn 1992).

The central role played by scalar implicature in natural language is illustrated by a systematic pattern of lexical gaps and asymmetries. Consider the post-Aristotelian square of opposition, defined by the logical relations definable between pairs of quantified expressions (ranging over non-empty sets):

(7)   Square of Opposition

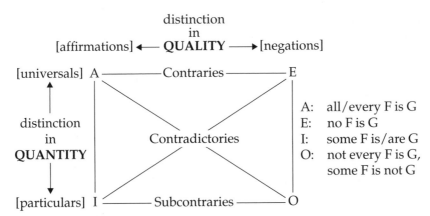

distinction
in
[affirmations] ◄— **QUALITY** —► [negations]

[universals] A ——————Contraries——————E

distinction
in
QUANTITY

Contradictories

[particulars] I ———— Subcontraries ————O

A: all/every F is G
E: no F is G
I: some F is/are G
O: not every F is G,
     some F is not G

(7′)   • Corresponding **A** and **E** statements are CONTRARIES; they cannot be simultaneously true (though they may be simultaneously false).
   • Corresponding **A** and **O** (and **I** and **E**) statements are CONTRADICTORIES; members of each pair cannot be true OR false simultaneously.
   • An **I** statement is the SUBALTERN of its corresponding **A** statement (and **O** of **E**); a subaltern is unilaterally entailed by its corresponding superaltern.
   • Corresponding **I** and **O** statements are SUBCONTRARIES and cannot be simultaneously false (though they may be simultaneously true).

Note in particular that the assertion of either of the two subcontraries Quantity-implicates the other. While what is said in *Some men are bald* and *Some men are not bald* is distinct, what is communicated is typically identical: *Some men are bald and some aren't.* Given that languages tend not to lexicalize complex values that need not be lexicalized, particularly within closed categories like quantifiers, we predict that *some . . . not* will not be lexicalized, and this is precisely what we find.

   In a wide variety of languages, values mapping onto the southeast, **O** corner of the square are systematically restricted in their potential for lexicalization (Horn 1972, 1989: 4.5). Thus alongside the quantificational determiners *all, some, no,* we never find an **O** determiner **nall;* corresponding to the quantificational adverbs *always, sometimes, never,* we have no **nalways* (= "not always," "sometimes not"). We may have equivalents for *both, one (of them), neither,* but never for **noth* (= "not both," "at least one . . . not"); we find connectives corresponding to *and, or,* and sometimes *nor* (= "and not"), but never to **nand* (= "or not," "not . . . and"). The story of **O* extends to the modals and deontics, as illustrated by the fact that the inflected negative in *He can't go* and the orthographic lexicalization in *He cannot go* only allows wide-scope (**E** vertex) negation, while the unlexicalized counterpart *He can not go* is ambiguous. The relation of mutual quantity implicature holding between positive and negative subcontraries results in the superfluity of one of the two subcontraries for lexical realization, while the functional markedness of negation assures that the unlexicalized subcontrary will always be **O**.

4   Q-based and R-based Implicature: Clash and Resolution

The earliest discussions of scalar quantity implicature were based on the informative content associated with values whose lexical semantics defined the relevant scale: *necessarily p* entails *possibly p* and not vice versa, whence the implicature from the utterance of the latter to the negation of the former. But as Fauconnier (1975b) and especially Hirschberg (1991) have eloquently shown, scales must be essentially pragmatic in nature. Indeed, Hirschberg has demonstrated that not just scales as such but any POSET (partially ordered set) can in principle define a quantity implicature in the right context. Thus if Robin is traveling westward from New York to California, my utterance *Robin has made it to Chicago* will implicate that Robin hasn't made it to Denver, but will not implicate that she hasn't yet reached Cleveland. As usual, such implicatures can be cancelled (*Not only has Robin made it to Chicago, but to Denver*). If Robin were traveling eastward, the facts would be reversed. (See Hirschberg 1991 for extensive elaboration.)

   M. Walker (1994) extends Hirschberg's results to show how quantity implicature functions to implicitly reject a proposition consistent with the context (cf. also Horn 1989: 410). Thus, in response to your question, "Is Smith honest and ambitious?" or to your assertion, "Smith is honest and ambitious," my assertion, "He's ambitious" will convey my belief that he's not honest; this proposition is, in Walker's terms, rejected by implicature. (See Ward and Hirschberg 1985, Horn 1989, and M. Walker 1994 on the role of intonation in such examples.) An attested example of the same phenomenon was provided in the exchange in (8) from the Senate investigation of President Clinton. Senator Ed Bryant is interrogating Monica Lewinsky on her affidavit in the Paula Jones case:

(8)   Mr. Bryant: "Were portions of it false?"
      Ms. Lewinsky: "Incomplete and misleading."

In implicating (but not saying) that no portions of her affidavit were technically false, Lewinsky, in the words of *New York Times* reporter Francis X. Clines (February 6, 1999), "exhibited a Clintonian way with the meaning of words."

   Other questions arising in early work on implicature concern the nature and scope of implicature. While the utterance of a weaker scalar value ... $p(i)$ ... tends to implicate that the speaker was not in a position to assert the correspondingly stronger value ... $p(j)$ ... (thereby implicating against the stronger value), this tendency is subject to a variety of constraints. The inheritance or projection properties of conversational implicata is a complex matter; it appears (Horn 1989: 234) that scalar implicature is blocked in precisely those environments where "scale reversal" applies, in the context of downward-entailing operators like negation and other negative polarity item (NPI) triggers, whence the disappearance of the upper-bounding implicature (*possible* +> *not certain*) in *If it's possible that it will rain I'll bring an umbrella*. (Chierchia 2001 argues from this correlation for the semantic status of scalar implicature; cf. Sauerland 2001.) Levinson (2000a: 80), on the other hand, has noted that if scale reversal is taken seriously, implicature need not be extrinsically blocked in such environments; rather, it will predictably be associated with the opposite scale, given the generalization that the negation of a weak positive value will constitute a strong value on the corresponding negative scale, and vice versa for the corresponding strong positive, for example (using the standard ⟨STRONGER-VALUE, WEAKER-VALUE⟩ notation), ⟨*certain, possible*⟩ vs. ⟨*not possible, not certain*⟩.

The significance of the first Quantity maxim for the form and function of natural language reflects its status as one of two cardinal principles regulating the economy of linguistic information. Setting Quality aside as unreducible, we can collapse the remaining maxims and submaxims into two fundamental principles corresponding to Zipf's "speaker's and auditor's economies" (1949: 20ff.; cf. Horn 1984a). The Q principle is a lower-bounding hearer-based guarantee of the sufficiency of informative content ("Say as much as you can, modulo Quality and R"); it collects the first Quantity maxim along with the first two "clarity" submaxims of manner and is systematically exploited (as in the scalar cases discussed above) to generate upper-bounding implicata. The R principle, by contrast, is an upper-bounding correlate of the Law of Least Effort dictating minimization of form ("Say no more than you must, modulo Q"); it collects the Relation maxim, the second Quantity maxim, and the last two submaxims of Manner, and is exploited to induce strengthening implicata.[9] Q-based implicature is typically negative in that its calculation refers crucially to what could have been said but wasn't: H infers from S's failure to use a more informative and/or briefer form that S was not in a position to do so. R-based implicature involves social rather than purely linguistic motivation and is exemplified by indirect speech acts and negative strengthening (including so-called neg-raising, i.e. the tendency for *I don't think that* ϕ to implicate *I think that not-*ϕ).

R-based implicata, while calculable, are often not calculated on line; a specific form of expression may be associated with a given pragmatic effect while an apparently synonymous form is not. Thus the question *Can you close the window?* is standardly used to convey an indirect request while *Are you able to close the window?* is not; *I don't guess that* ϕ allows a strengthened "neg-raised" understanding in a proper subset of the dialects for which *I don't think that* ϕ does. These are instances of SHORT-CIRCUITED CONVERSATIONAL IMPLICATURE or STANDARDIZED NON-LITERALITY (cf. Morgan 1978, Bach and Harnish 1979, Bach 1987b, Horn 1989).

The Zipfian character of the implicata generating indirect speech acts was recognized by Searle in his proposal for a condition on directives that "It is not obvious to both S and H that S will do A in the normal course of events":

> I think this condition is an instance of the sort of phenomenon stated in Zipf's law. I think there is operating in our language, as in most forms of human behaviour, a principle of least effort, in this case **a principle of maximum illocutionary ends with minimum phonetic effort**, and I think [this] condition is an instance of it.   (Searle 1965: 234–5, my emphasis)

Similar cost/benefit or minimax principles have been proposed by Paul, Zipf, and Martinet (see Horn 1993 for references and discussion) and by Carroll and Tanenhaus (1975: 51): "The speaker always tries to optimally minimize the surface complexity of his utterances while maximizing the amount of information he effectively communicates to the listener." Indeed, the interplay of perspicuity (or clarity) and brevity was a key issue for classical rhetoricians, who advanced their own minimax guidelines:

> If it is prolix, it will not be clear, nor if it is too brief. It is plain that the middle way is appropriate . . . , saying just enough to make the facts plain.   (Aristotle, *Rhetoric*, 3.12–3.16)

> *Brevis esse laboro; obscurus fio.* 'I strive to be brief; I become obscure'.   (Horace, *Ars Poetica*, l. 25)

> Personally, when I use the term brevity [*brevitas*], I mean not saying less, but not saying more than the occasion demands. (Quintilian, *Institutio Oratio*, iv.ii.41–43)

While the bilateral brevity of Quintilian may seem quirky, it is no more so than current redefinitions of relevance as a minimax equilibrium of effort and effect:

> Human cognitive activity is driven by the goal of maximizing relevance: that is . . . to derive as great a range of contextual effects as possible for the least expenditure of effort.   (Carston 1995: 231)

The two antinomic Q and R forces interact definitionally and dynamically, each referencing and constraining the other.[10] Grice himself incorporates R in defining the primary Q maxim ("Make your contribution as informative **as is required**" [here and below, emphasis added]), while Quantity$_2$ is constrained by Quantity$_1$[11] and essentially incorporates Relation: what could make a contribution more informative than required, except the inclusion of contextually irrelevant material? This interdependence was noted by Martinich (1980: 218), who urged collapsing Q_1 and Q_2 into a joint maxim dictating that the speaker "contribute as much as, but not more than, is required (for the current purposes of the exchange)," while rejecting the broader Relation as a "marauding maxim."

The role of relevance and clarity in constraining the informative strength of the Q principle emerges in its various incarnations, beginning with Strawson (1952: 178–9), who credits Grice for his "general rule of linguistic conduct": "One should not make the (logically) lesser, when one could truthfully (**and with greater or equal clarity**) make the greater claim." Grice's (1961: 132) own "first shot" at the relevant rule is bound by a similar rider – "One should not make a weaker statement rather than a stronger one **unless there is a good reason for so doing**" – as are later versions of the principle constructed in the wake of the maxim of quantity:

> Make the strongest possible claim **that you can legitimately defend**!
> RULE OF STRENGTH (Fogelin 1967: 20–2)

> Unless there are outweighing good reasons to the contrary, one should not make a weaker statement rather than a stronger one **if the audience is interested in the extra information that would be conveyed by the latter**.
> (O'Hair 1969: 45)

> Make the strongest relevant claim **justifiable by your evidence**.
> MAXIM OF QUANTITY-QUALITY (Harnish 1976: 362)

The "good reason" for avoiding the stronger scalar value thus may be either qualitative, constrained by truth (S doesn't know that the stronger value is applicable), or quantitative, where both relevance and brevity enter the picture (S doesn't believe the extra information is justified in terms of H's interests or S's own efforts in uttering it). Telling you that my wife is either in the kitchen or the bedroom, I will (*ceteris paribus*) Q-implicate that I don't know that she's in the kitchen – but I can tell you "The kitchen is a mess" without implicating that the bedroom isn't. If you tell me X is possibly true, I will infer you don't know it's true, but if you tell me X is true (e.g. that all bachelors are unmarried), I will not infer you don't know it's necessarily true. The use of a weak **I** or **O** proposition licenses the inference that the speaker was not in a position to use the basic unquantified, unmodalized proposition that unilaterally entails it, as the Q principle predicts, but the use of the basic propositional form does not Q-implicate the negation of its strong counterpart, **A** or **E** respectively. Since there is no quantity- or information-based distinction between these (sub)subalternations, we must seek the source of the asymmetry elsewhere.

The crucial distinction here relates not to the content (what is said) but to the form (how what is said is said). Because the basic forms are not only more informative but briefer than their **I/O** counterparts, the use of the latter will strongly implicate against the former. But the strong values, while more informative than their unmodified counterparts, are also more prolix, so Quantity is offset by Manner and potentially by Relation: the Q principle of informative sufficiency yields to the R principle of least effort. The richness of the pragmatic framework allows us to predict not just what can be implicated but what will be implicated in a given context.

When degree of lexicalization is not a factor, scalar implicature is normally generated. Thus, each of the ordered n-tuples of items in (9)

(9)   ⟨*always, usually, often, sometimes*⟩, ⟨*and, or*⟩, ⟨*certain, likely, possible*⟩, ⟨*cold, cool, lukewarm*⟩, ⟨*excellent, good, OK*⟩, ⟨*the, a*⟩

constitutes a Q-relevant scale in that the affirmation of any weak or intermediate value will implicate (*ceteris paribus*) that – for all the speaker knows – the value(s) on its left could not be substituted *salva veritate*.

But when the stronger value is less economical than the weaker one, no Q-implicature is triggered. Thus the apparent symmetry of the relevant scales – ⟨*x and y won, x won, x or y won*⟩, ⟨*a must be F, a is F, a may be F*⟩ – is misleading. This extends to non-quantitative "scales" of items differing in informative strength. Thus, while the use of *finger* typically conveys "non-thumb," it does not convey "non-pinky (finger)," nor does the use of *toe* convey "non-big toe," although the big toe is an analogue of the thumb. Crucial here is the status of *thumb* (as opposed to *pinky*) as a lexicalized alternative to *finger*. In the same way, *rectangle* conveys "non-square" (i.e. "non-equilateral rectangle") given the availability of the lexicalized alternative *square*, while *triangle* does not convey "non-equilateral triangle" – indeed, the prototype triangle IS equilateral – because of the non-existence of a lexicalized counterpart.

One robust linguistic phenomenon involving the interaction of Q and R principles is the DIVISION OF PRAGMATIC LABOR. Given two expressions covering the same semantic ground, a relatively unmarked form – briefer and/or more lexicalized – tends to be R-associated with a particular unmarked, stereotypical meaning, use, or situation, while the use of the periphrastic or less lexicalized expression, typically more complex or prolix, tends to be Q-restricted to those situations outside the stereotype, for which the unmarked expression could not have been used appropriately.[12] Thus consider the following pairs:

(10)a.   He got the machine to stop.
          He stopped the machine.
    b.   Her blouse was pale red.
          Her blouse was pink.
    c.   She wants her to win.
          She wants PRO to win.
    d.   I am going to marry you.
          I will marry you.
    e.   My brother went to the church (the jail, the school).
          My brother went to church (jail, school).
    f.   It's not impossible that you will solve the problem.
          It's possible that you will solve the problem.

    g.   That's my father's wife.
        That's my mother.

The use of the periphrastic causative in (10a) implicates that the agent achieved the effect in a marked way (pulling the plug, throwing a shoe into the machine), *pale red* in (10b) suggests a tint not pre-empted by *pink*, the choice of a full pronoun over null PRO in (10c) signals the absence of the coreferential reading associated with the reduced syntax, the periphrastic form blocks the indirect speech act function of promising conveyed by the modal in (10d), the full Det-N versions of (10e) imply literal motion toward the specified location without the socially stereotypic connection that is R-associated with the corresponding institution on the anarthrous version, the double contradictory negation in (10f) signals a rhetorical effect absent from the direct positive, and the more complex description in (10g) suggests that the more basic and lexicalized alternative could not have been used appropriately (the referent is probably the speaker's stepmother). When a speaker opts for a more complex or less fully lexicalized expression over a simpler alternative, there is a pragmatically sufficient reason, but which reason depends on the particular context. (See Horn 1991a, 1993, Levinson 2000a, and Blutner and Traugott, this volume, for references and related discussion.)

    A particularly rich explanatory vein lies in the realm of anaphora, in which the choice of an overt pronoun over controlled PRO in infinitivals in both English object raising (ECM) and Romance subjunctive constructions can be attributed to the division of pragmatic labor, as can switch-reference phenomena and the use of an overt subject in a pro-drop (null-subject) language like Turkish or Catalan, in which the overriding of "Avoid Pronoun" will often implicate change of topic. Valuable cross-linguistic studies of the neo-Gricean pragmatics of anaphora, with copious references, are provided in Levinson (2000a: Chapter 4) and Huang (2000a, this volume).

5   Implicature, Explicature, and Pragmatic Intrusion

Where the model we have been exploring retains two antinomic principles Q and R along with an unreduced maxim of Quality, and where the related model of neo-Gricean pragmatics urged by Levinson (2000a) contains the three Q, I, and M heuristics, a more radical simplification has been urged in the framework of relevance theory, in which a reconceptualized Principle of Relevance is taken to be the sole source of pragmatic inference.[13] At the heart of this program is a reworking of the architecture of the theory of logical form and utterance interpretation (Sperber and Wilson 1986a; cf. also Carston 1998b, this volume; Wilson and Sperber, this volume).

    Even for Grice, propositional content is not fully fleshed out until reference, tense, and other indexical elements are fixed. But, taking their lead from earlier work by Atlas (1979), relevance theorists have argued that the pragmatic reasoning used to compute implicated meaning must also be invoked to flesh out underspecified propositions in which the semantic meaning contributed by the linguistic expression itself is insufficient to yield a proper accounting of truth-conditional content. Thus, to take one example, when a pundit observed, as the jury retired to consider their verdict in the O. J. Simpson murder trial, that "It will take them some time to reach a verdict," the proposition he communicated (that it will take a long time) seems intuitively false, a fact hard to reconcile with a strict Gricean analysis on which the time communicated by S is merely an implicatum read off the underspecified content contributed by linguistic meaning alone, i.e. a trivially true existential proposition. Apparently the pragmatically strengthened communication contributes to, or intrudes upon, the propositional content.

A classic example of such apparent intrusion is illustrated by the temporal and causal asymmetry of conjoined event-denoting VPs and sentences. The logical "&" is a symmetric truth function; "p & q" is true if p and q are both true and false otherwise (as, of course, is "q & p"). Strawson (1952: 80) pointed to the apparent contrast in meaning exhibited by pairs like (11a, b)

(11)a.   They got married and (they) had a child.
    b.   They had a child and (they) got married.
    c.   They got married and then (they) had a child.

as prima facie counterexamples to this thesis, since the former appears to amount to the statement in (11c). (I add the parenthetical pronoun to render these sentences closer to the corresponding logical conjunctions, although that renders the asymmetric understanding less inevitable.) Similarly, Ryle (1954) famously observed that to get on one's horse and ride away is not the same as to ride away and get on one's horse. For Urmson (1956: 9–10), however, the truth-functional picture, while incomplete, is not ipso facto incorrect:

> In formal logic, the connectives "and" and "or" are always given a minimum meaning . . . such that any complex formed by the use of them alone is a truth-function of its constituents. In ordinary discourse the connectives often have a richer meaning; thus "he took off his clothes and went to bed" implies temporal succession and has a different meaning from "he went to bed and took off his clothes". Logicians would justify their use of the minimum meaning by pointing out that it is the common element in all our uses of "and."

For the classical Gricean approach, an assertion of the conjunction in (11a) will implicate (11c) by virtue of the Manner submaxim "Be orderly" (Grice 1981: 186). Indeed, Grice's approach was prefigured in the observation that "Events earlier in time are mentioned earlier in the order of words than those which occurred later," one of the eight "natural principles" that influence word order in the inventory of Dionysius of Halicarnassus, *Peri syntheseos onomaton* (*On the Juxtaposition of Words*), first century BC, cited in de Jonge (2001).

On this Dionysian/Gricean line, the distinction in meaning between (11a, b) need not be laid at the doorstep of an ambiguous *and* operator. For those who would semanticize temporal asymmetry, such a lexical ambiguity must be invoked for the fact that a non-sequential interpretation is available not only for non-eventive sentences (*They are tall and they are rich*) but even for (11a) in the appropriate context ("What stressed them out last year?"). Arguments against a lexical ambiguity for *and* ("and also" vs. "and then") include the following:

1   On the two-*and* theory, conjunction in (almost?) every language would just happen to be similarly ambiguous.
2   No natural language contains a conjunction *shmand* that would be ambiguous between "and also" and "and earlier" readings so that *They had a baby shmand they got married* would be interpreted either atemporally or as "They had a baby and, before that, they got married."
3   Not only temporal but causal asymmetry would need to be built in, as a variety of apparent strengthenings of the conjunction arise in different contexts of utterance.
4   The same "ambiguity" exhibited by *and* arises when two clauses describing related events are juxtaposed asyndetically (*They had a baby. They got married.*)

However, if conjuctions are semantically univocal while Manner- (or R-) implicating that the events occurred in the order in which they were described, the impossibility of the conjunction *shmand* can be attributed to the absence of any maxim enjoining the speaker to "Be disorderly." As with scalar implicature, the asymmetric implicatum may be canceled or suspended: *They had a baby and got married, but not necessarily in that order.*

But if the "and then" reading comes in only as an implicature, it is hard to explain its apparent contribution to truth-conditional meaning in embedded contexts, and in particular the non-contradictory nature of (12a–c) as pointed out by Cohen (1971) and Wilson (1975):

(12)a.   If they got married and had a child, their parents will be pleased, but if they had a child and got married their parents will not be pleased.
   b.   They didn't get married and have a child; they had a child and got married.
   c.   It's more acceptable to get married and have a child than to have a child and get married.

One possible conclusion is that while pragmatically derived, the enriched meaning is an EXPLICATURE, corresponding to what is said rather than to what is (merely) implicated[14] (see Carston, this volume); another is that we must revisit the architecture of Gricean theory to allow implicature to help determine propositional content (Levinson 2000a: chapter 3).

The explicature view also yields a re-evaluation of the traditional view of scalar predications, so that both one-sided and two-sided understandings of sentences in (5) will now be directly represented at the level of logical content. While such scalar predications are now all taken to be ambiguous, the ambiguity is situated not at the lexical but at the propositional level: what is **said** in an utterance is systematically underdetermined by the linguistic content of what is **uttered**. In particular, it does not seem possible to maintain the original Gricean line on the meaning of cardinal operators (lower-bounded by meaning, upper-bounded by implicature).

However, while a strong case can be made for an enrichment analysis of the meaning contribution of the cardinals, it does not generalize straightforwardly to the inexact scalar values. Evidence for this asymmetry (summarized in Horn 1992) comes from the contextual reversibility of cardinal scales and the non-implicating ("exactly n") reading of cardinals in mathematical, collective, and elliptical contexts, none of which applies to the scalar operators in, for example, (5b–e). Note also the contrast in the exchanges below:

(13) A: Do you have two children?   (14) A: Did many of the guests leave?
    B_1: No, three. B_1: ?No, all of them.
    B_2: ?Yes, (in fact) three. B_2: Yes, (in fact) all of them.

Further, a bare negative response to (13A) is compatible with an "exactly n" reading in an appropriate context (if B believes A is interested in precisely how many children B has, rather than in B's candidacy for a subsidy), while an unadorned negative response to (14A) can only be understood as conveying "fewer than many." In the same way, there is a sharp contrast between the "game-playing" nature of (15a), with ordinary scalar *like,* and the straightforward (15b), with cardinal values:

(15)a.   #Neither of us liked the movie – she adored it and I hated it.
   b.   Neither of us has three kids – she has two and I have four.

Similarly, if (5e) were truly propositionally ambiguous, there is no obvious reason why a *"No"* response to the question *"Is it warm?"* should not be interpretable as a denial of the enriched, two-sided content and thus as asserting that it's either chilly or hot, or why the comparative in *"It's getting warmer"* cannot denote "less hot" instead of "less cold." This suggests the need for a mixed theory in which cardinal values may well demand an enriched-content analysis, while other scalar predications continue to warrant a standard neo-Gricean treatment on which they are lower-bounded by their literal content and upper-bounded, in default contexts, by Q-implicature.

Standard critiques (e.g. Carston 1988, Recanati 1989) of traditional Gricean accounts of scalar implicature can be countered if this distinction between cardinals and other scalar values is maintained. Nor is it surprising to see the same distinction surfacing as significant in early childhood, as has been supported by recent work in developmental psycholinguistics (Papafragou and Musolino 2003).

6 Implicature vs. Impliciture: "What is said" Revisited

But are we really dealing with post-semantic implicature here in the original Gricean sense, or with a different aspect of what isn't said? The arguments we have been reviewing rest on the tacit assumption that whatever is communicated but not said must be implicated. Some (e.g. Levinson 2000a) have argued from this assumption that implicatures can affect ("intrude on") truth-conditional meaning after all, given cases like the asymmetric conjunction in (11); others have argued instead for the notion of explicature, i.e. pragmatically determined content. But what if not all implicit components of communicated meaning are implicatures? As stressed by Bach (1994a, 2001a), some aspects of speaker meaning need not be considered either part of what is implicated or of what is said. Thus consider the following utterances with the typically conveyed material indicated in curly brackets:

(16)a. I haven't had breakfast {today}.
   b. John and Mary are married {to each other}.
   c. They had a baby and they got married {in that order}.
   d. Robin ate the shrimp and {as a result} got food poisoning.
   e. Everybody {in our pragmatics class} solved the riddle.

In each case, the bracketed material contributing to what is communicated cannot be derived as a Gricean implicature (*pace* Levinson 2000a: chapter 3), given that it is truth conditionally relevant, but neither can it be part of what is said, since it is felicitously cancelable:

(17)a. John and Mary are married, but not to each other.
   b. They had a child and got married, but not necessarily in that order.

Bach has proposed that in such cases the enriched material may be regarded instead as an IMPLICITURE, an implicit weakening, strengthening, or specification of what is said. This permits an intuitive characterization of propositional content, a conservative mapping from syntactic structure to what is said, and an orthodox Gricean conception of implicature, albeit as a more limited construct than in much neo-Gricean work. While Levinson (2000a) bites the bullet and, accepting the relevance theorists' arguments for pragmatic intrusion into propositional content, concludes that implicatures must feed truth-conditional interpretation, Bach retains a neo-classically Gricean semantic characterization of what is said,[15] along with a post-semantic understanding of conversational implicature: it is implicItures, not implicAtures, that can determine the relevant truth conditions in such cases. Furthermore, it is misleading to take the expansions in (16) to be explicatures, since there is nothing explicit about them, and indeed the cancelability of such expanded understandings supports their status as implicit. At the same time, the standard view that every sentence expresses exactly one proposition must be abandoned, as it is typically and in some cases ONLY the impliciture – the expanded proposition that the speaker communicates but does not directly express – that is plausibly assessed for truth or falsity.[16]

Others have reached similar conclusions by different routes. Taylor (2001) stresses the role of beliefs about the world to explain why enrichment proceeds differently in contexts like *I haven't had breakfast* vs. *I haven't had sex*, although this too could (predictably) change in a culture in which it is expected that one has sex (but not necessarily breakfast) each morning. Saul (2002) has argued persuasively that the (neo-)Gricean and relevance theoretic conceptions of meaning are not as incompatible as it may appear, given that Grice's concerns lay in an account of speaker meaning (of which implicature constitutes a proper subpart), while relevance theorists have been primarily concerned with developing a cognitive psychological model of utterance interpretation, which does not address the question of how and why the speaker, given what she wants to convey, utters what she utters. Inevitably, the two goals must part company, as Saul demonstrates in some detail. While there is a natural tendency to characterize Grice's project in terms of the plausible interpretation of utterances (whence Levinson's 2000a depiction of generalized conversational implicatures as default inferences), it must be resisted, as Bach and Saul have argued.

As for pragmatic intrusion into propositional content and the determination of truth conditions, it should be noted that the Cohen-type argument for the intrusion of temporal asymmetry into the compositional meaning of conditionals (as in (18a) vs. (18b)) can be paralleled by other cases suggesting that all natural language epistemic conditionals are *ceteris paribus* claims; the statements in (19b–d) are no better candidates for valid inferences from (18a) than is (19a).

(18) a. If Annie got married and had a baby, her grandfather will be happy.
     b. If Annie had a baby and got married, her grandfather will not be happy.

(19)   If Annie got married and had a baby
    a. but in the opposite temporal order
    b. but her baby was born a week after the wedding
    c. but her husband was not the father of the baby
    d. but she married Sue and had the baby by artificial insemination her grandfather will be happy.

Similarly, consider the conditionals in (20), in which an explicature theorist would build the stronger (bilateral) meaning (e.g. *some but not all, warm but not very warm*) into what is said:

(20)a. If some of my friends come to the party, I'll be happy – but if all of them do, I'll be in trouble.
   b. If it's warm, we'll lie out in the sun. But if it's {very warm/hot}, we'll go inside and sit in front of the air-conditioner.
   c. If you're convicted of a felony, you'll spend at least a year in jail. And if you're convicted of murder, you'll be executed.
   d. If you're injured, the paramedics will take you to the nearest trauma center. But if you're fatally injured, you'll be taken to the morgue.

In each of these contexts, it's only when the stronger scalar is reached that the earlier, weaker one is retroactively accommodated, as it were, to incorporate an upper bound into its semantics, with, for example, "some" being REinterpreted as expressing (rather than merely communicating) "some but not all." This reinterpretation is facilitated by the obligatory focus on the relevant scalar operators (*some, warm,* etc.).

The same issues arise for other applications of the pragmatic intrusion argument. Thus, Levinson (2000a: 210) extends the classic Cohen–Wilson argument from conditionals like (18) to the *because* clauses of (21):

(21)a. Because he drank three beers and drove home, he went to jail.
   b. Because he earns $40,000, he can't afford a house in Palo Alto.
   c. Because he's such a fine friend, I've struck him off my list.
   d. Because the police recovered some of the missing gold, they will later recover it all.

But these examples are heterogeneous. (21a) sports the familiar temporal strengthening, while (21b) involves a cardinal, which as we have seen is plausibly reanalyzed as involving an adjustment of what is said. The example of "such a fine friend" in (21c), on the other hand, involves conventionalization of the sarcastic meaning; cf. *?Because he's so considerate, I fired him.* The *all* in the second clause of (21d) forces the reprocessing of the *some* in the first clause as "some but not all" (a reprocessing again triggered by the focal stress on *some*); in the other examples, the general context alone is sufficient to force the narrowed interpretation. Without the *all* or a similar context-forcing continuation, this narrowing appears to be impossible:

(22) Because the police recovered some of the gold, the thieves are expected to return later #(for the rest).

In general, such *because* cases are quite constrained, in particular for the non-cardinal scalar cases in which the implicated upper bound is taken to be the reason for the truth of the second clause (as in (22)) and in which no reprocessing is forced by the affirmation of a stronger value. Thus consider:

(23)a.   #Because it's warm out [i.e. because it's warm but not hot], you should
still wear a long-sleeved shirt.
   b.   #Because you ate some of your spinach [i.e. and not all], you don't get
dessert.

Of course, a move from *warm* or *some* to *only warm* or *just some* render these causals impeccable, but then the scales have been reversed.

7   Implicature, Cooperation, and Rationality

As we have seen, Paul Grice's pragmatic framework in general, and the elaboration of conversational implicature in particular, are founded on the Cooperative Principle. But while cooperation is a key notion, the role of an even more general principle has not always been fully appreciated. Describing the maxims of conversation, Grice cites the basis of rationality as the reason his program extends beyond communication to non-linguistic interchanges:

> As one of my avowed aims is to see talking as a special case or variety of
> **purposive, indeed rational behavior**, it may be worth noting that the specific
> expectations or presumptions connected with at least some of the foregoing
> maxims have their analogues in the sphere of transactions that are not talk
> exchanges.   (Grice 1989: 28; emphasis added)

As Smith (1999: 15) has noted, the Cooperative Principle need not be stipulated as an arbitrary convention (cf. Lewis 1969), but rather constitutes "a deduction from the general principle that we expect others to behave as best suits their goals."[17] The role of rationality in pragmatics has been stressed by Kasher (1982: 32), whose PRINCIPLE OF EFFECTIVE MEANS stipulates "Given a desired end, one is to choose that action which most effectively, and at least cost, attains that end, *ceteris paribus*." It will be noted that Kasher's principle incorporates the minimax of effort and cost that also underlies models as diverse as the apparently monoprincipled relevance theory (Sperber and Wilson 1986a), the dual Q- and R-based approach of Horn (1984a, 1993), and the tri-heuristic Q/I/M theory of Levinson (2000a).

In particular, the speaker's and hearer's joint (though tacit) recognition of the natural tendency to avoid unnecessary effort, and the inferences S expects H to draw from the former's efficient observance of this tendency, are more explicable directly from rationality than from cooperation as such. While Grice (1989: 28) describes how the maxims apply to cooperative ventures outside of language (baking a cake, fixing a car), collaboration need not be present, much less communication, at least for the quantity maxims. It seems plausible to assume that the generalized forms of both Q and R principles – "Do enough; Don't do too much" – govern ANY goal-oriented activity: a person brushing her teeth or working out a problem in the philosophy of language, a dog digging a hole to bury a bone. In this way, the maxim of quantity, in both its opposed (Q and R) subforms, is a linguistic instantiation of these rationality-based constraints on the expenditure of effort. Of course, as Grice recognized, the shared tacit awareness of such principles to generate conversational implicatures is a central property of speaker meaning within the communicative enterprise.

With a fuller understanding of the interaction of pragmatics and propositional content, we see that while the explanatory scope of conversational implicature may have been reduced from the heyday of the classical Gricean program, his framework and the pragmatic principles motivating it – rationality, common ground, and the distinction of implicit vs. explicit components of utterance meaning – continue to play a key role in the elaboration of dynamic models of context. As recent work on language acquisition (Noveck 2001, Chierchia et al. 2001, Papafragou and Musolino 2003)[18] and on lexical change (Traugott and Dasher 2002; Traugott, this volume) has further demonstrated, a suitably refined and constrained notion of conversational implicature remains at the heart of linguistic pragmatics.[19]

ACKNOWLEDGMENTS

Thanks to Barbara Abbott, Kent Bach, Betty Birner, Yasuhiko Kato, Benjamin Smith, J. L. Speranza, and Gregory Ward for helpful comments on some of this material.

NOTES

1 To say that an implicature (conventional or conversational) makes a non-truth-conditional contribution to an expression's meaning is not to say that the implicatum itself (= what is implicated) lacks truth conditions, but rather that the truth conditions of the original expression are not affected by the truth or falsity of the implicatum.

2 Beyond cancelability and non-detachability, another proposed criterion for conversational implicature is non-redundant reinforceability. Sadock (1978) argues that an inference can be non-redundantly reinforced just in case it can be canceled without contradiction, viz. when it is a conversational implicature (see also Morgan 1969, Horn 1972). Thus we

have the contrast between
(i) and (ii):

(i)a. Some men are chauvinists;
       indeed all are.
              [non-contradictory]
   b. Some but not all men are
       chauvinists.
              [non-redundant]
(ii)a. #It's odd that dogs eat cheese,
       and they don't.
              [contradictory]
    b. #It's odd that dogs eat cheese,
       and they do.   [redundant]

But concession/affirmation
structures *can* be felicitous even
when informationally redundant
provided the two clauses involved
are rhetorically opposed – whence
the adversative *but*:

(iii)a. It's (#not) odd that dogs eat
        cheese, but they do.
     b. I #(don't) know why I love
        you, but I do.

Thus, contra Sadock, and Hirschberg
(1991), semantically inferrable
(entailed or presupposed) material
may be felicitously reinforced.
(See Horn 1991b for details.)

3 Although the "Gricean letter of
   recommendation" in (1b) has
   become legendary, it appears not to
   be legal in the very state in which
   Grice taught:

> **If an employer chooses to provide
> a reference or recommendation, the
> reference giver must include factual
> negative information that may be
> material to the applicant's fitness
> for employment in addition to any
> positive information.** Campus
> managers and supervisors who
> provide employment references on
> current or former employees must be
> aware that untrue, incomplete or
> misleading information may cause a

different liability – negligent referral.
The court in Randi M. v. Livingston
Union School District, 1995 . . . found
that: **"A statement that contains only
favorable matters and omits all
reference to unfavorable matters is
as much a false representation as if
all the facts stated were untrue."**
[Emphasis added; *gratia* Bill Ladusaw]

4 For Davis (1998: 21), a particularized
   implicature reflects speaker
   implicature, while a generalized
   implicature is sentence implicature:
   "what speakers using the sentence
   with its regular meaning would
   commonly use it to implicate"
   (Davis 1998: 6). See Saul (to
   appear) for commentary.

5 Horn (to appear) argues for a
   distinction between what is entailed
   and what is asserted; entailed
   material that is not asserted (like
   the positive component of *Bush
   barely carried any northern states* or
   Only Chris has ever been to Bhutan)
   is ASSERTORICALLY INERT and plays
   no role in NPI licensing. On this
   account, scopal patterns taken to
   be diagnostic for conventional
   implicature or pragmatic
   presupposition are reanalyzed
   as diagnostics for non-assertion.
   See also Abbott (2000).

6 Grice (1989: 30–1) characterizes
   conversational implicature as
   follows: "A man who by saying that
   p has implicated that *q*, provided
   that (1) he is to be presumed to
   be observing the conversational
   maxims, or at least the Cooperative
   Principle; (2) the supposition that
   he is aware that, or thinks that,
   q is required in order to make his
   saying . . . *p* consistent with this
   presumption; and (3) the speaker
   thinks (and would expect the hearer
   to think that the speaker thinks) that
   it is within the competence of the
   hearer to work out, or grasp

intuitively, that the supposition mentioned in (2) is required." Many such implicatures will constitute non-literal or indirect speech acts overlaid on what is said; see Bach and Harnish (1979), Bach (this volume), and Sadock (this volume) for discussion, and Davis (1998) for vigorous critique.

7 Washington in fact promulgated his own set of maxims with close parallels to Grice's (see Horn 1990), but the father of his country did not account for his countrymen's ability to exploit these maxims to generate implicatures, while the father of pragmatics did.

8 As Smith (1999) points out, Keenan's central critique (1976: 79) that for Grice "the conversational maxims are not presented as working hypotheses but as social facts" should be reversed, with a twist: the maxims are indeed working hypotheses, but for the speaker (and indirectly the hearer), rather than for the philosopher, linguist, or anthropologist. Keenan's depiction of cases where the maxim of quantity is overridden by cultural taboos in fact supports rather than refutes the Gricean narrative, since her evidence shows that it is just when the maxims are predicted to be in operation that they can be exploited to generate implicata; cf. Prince (1983), Brown and Levinson (1987: 288–9) for further discussion.

9 In Levinson's work (Atlas and Levinson 1981; Levinson 1983, 2000a), the counterpart of the R principle is the I (for "Informativeness") heuristic; see Huang (this volume) for a definition and application to the characterization of anaphoric relations.

10 Recent work has incorporated the dialectic of Q- and R-based

implicature and the division of pragmatic labor into models of bidirectional Optimality Theory and game theory; cf. Blutner (1998; this volume) and van Rooy (to appear a).

11 Consider the boldened portion of the two submaxims of quantity –

1. Make your contribution **as informative as** is required (for the current purposes of the exchange).
2. Do **not** make your contribution **more informative than** is required.

– in light of the fact that (as noted in Horn 1972) an equative of the form *X is as A as Y* (e.g. *Robin is as tall as Sandy*) will Q_1-implicate that (for all I know) *X is not A-er than Y* (e.g. *Robin is not taller than Sandy*), given the ⟨more A than, as A as⟩ quantity scale. Thus, the utterance of Q_1 as stated will (auto-)implicate Q_2. As Gregory Ward points out, a similar auto-implicature can be detected in Martinich's duplex quantity maxim.

12 Levinson's (2000a) version of the Division of Pragmatic Labor involves not Q-narrowing but what he calls the M(anner) heuristic. He argues that the notion of minimalism involved in the inference from *some* to *not all* is defined in terms of an informational measure rather than complexity of production or processing; because of the apparent role of Manner in the latter case, Levinson refers to the Division of Labor as M-based (Q/M in Levinson 1987a), with Q reserved for pure scalar cases. As he acknowledges, however, the two patterns are related, since each is negatively defined and linguistically motivated: H infers from S's failure to use a more informative and/or briefer form that S was not in a

position to do so. R/I-based implicature is not negative in character and tends to be socially rather than linguistically motivated.

13   As noted above, relevance theory is predicated on a minimax or cost/benefit relation which takes the goal of communication as maximizing contextual effects while minimizing processing effort, and the Principle of Relevance is itself couched in terms of this trade-off of effort and effect. In this sense, relevance theory is a dialectic model as much as that of Horn (1984a, 1993), although the former model associates effort with the hearer rather than the speaker.

14   While (12b) may be attributed to metalinguistic negation (Horn 1989: 373), this analysis is unavailable for (12c).

15   Bach (2001a) adopts the SYNTACTIC CORRELATION CONSTRAINT, based on the position of Grice (1989: 87) that what is said must correspond to "the elements of [the sentence], their order, and their syntactic character"; typical aspects of enriched content that are not directly linked to the utterance cannot be part of what is said.

16   Those enrichments constituting necessary conditions for the expression of truth-evaluable propositions involve what Recanati (1989, 2002a) has called saturation. In such cases, there is a "bottom-up" process triggered by such linguistic elements as genitives (*John's car* – the one he owns? is driving? following? painting? repairing?), unspecified comparison sets (*Chris is tall* – for an adult (fe)male? adult American? human?) or other expressions with free variable slots: *Kim is ready* (for what?), *Robin is too short* (for what?). See Bach (1994a, 1994b) and Carston and Recanati (this volume) for related discussion.

17   Kent Bach points out the plausible invocation here of the reformulation of the Cooperative Principle (CP) as a communicative presumption: when people converse, they do so with an identifiable communicative intention (Bach and Harnish 1979: 7). The role of rationality and cooperation is also addressed in McCafferty (1987).

18   One interesting result from this work is that children may be more adept than adults at distinguishing the contributions to overall speaker meaning contributed by what is said vs. what is implicated.

19   Davis (1998) offers a wide-ranging attack on the theory of implicature; cf. Saul (to appear) for an assessment. See also R. Walker (1975), Wilson and Sperber (1981), Neale (1992), and Matsumoto (1995) for further critical commentary, and Levinson (2000a) for a conspectus and comprehensive bibliography.

2 Presupposition

JAY DAVID ATLAS

1 Frege on Semantical Presupposition

One of Frege's employments of the notion of presupposition occurs in a foot-note to a discussion of adverbial clauses in "On Sense and Reference" (1892). Frege (1892: 71) wrote:

> The sense of the sentence "After Schleswig-Holstein was separated from Denmark, Prussia and Austria quarreled" can also be rendered in the form "After the separation of Schleswig-Holstein from Denmark, Prussia and Austria quarreled". In this version it is surely sufficiently clear that the sense is not to be taken as having as a part the thought that Schleswig-Holstein was once separated from Denmark, but that this is the necessary presupposition in order for the expression "after the separation of Schleswig-Holstein from Denmark" to have a reference at all.

I shall call this notion of Frege's "referential presupposition." Since Frege took places, instants of time, and time intervals to be logical objects, to be desig-nated by singular terms, if there had been no event of Schleswig-Holstein's separating from Denmark, there could be no specification of a time at which Prussia and Austria quarreled as after the time of the alleged separation of Schleswig-Holstein from Denmark. The existence of a time at which Schleswig-Holstein separated from Denmark is required in order to give a reference to a singular term designating a time interval that would include a time or tem-poral subinterval at which Prussia and Austria quarreled. Thus, if the logical form of the main clause *Prussia and Austria quarreled* is:

(1) $\exists t Q(p, a, t)$
There is some time or time-interval at which Prussia and Austria quarreled.

one way to understand the semantical effect of a subordinate clause is for it to determine the relevant domain of temporal instants or intervals that fixes the truth conditions of the main clause. If the domain is restricted to times later than the time t_s of the separation of Schleswig-Holstein from Denmark, then the logical form of *Prussia and Austria quarreled after the separation of Schleswig-Holstein from Denmark* would be (2):

(2) $\exists t \, Q(p, a, t)$
      $t \in T$

where $T = \{t: t > t_s\}$. The truth of the clause *Schleswig-Holstein separated from Denmark at t_s* is then a **semantical determinant** of the truth conditions of the original sentence, since it specifies the domain of quantification T (Thomason 1973: 302). In such circumstances it is understandable that Frege (1892: 71) should write of someone who believes that it is false that Schleswig-Holstein was separated from Denmark, so that the domain of quantification of (2) is believed to be ill-defined:

> He will take our sentence . . . to be neither true nor false but will deny it to have any reference [on Frege's view, a truth value], on the ground of absence of reference for its subordinate clause.

It is clear that on Frege's semantical account of presupposition, on which the falsity of a presupposition entails the lack of truth value of the sentence with that presupposition, the negative sentence *Prussia and Austria did not quarrel after the separation of Schleswig-Holstein from Denmark* would have the logical form (3):

(3) $\neg \exists t \, Q(p, a, t)$
      $t \in T$

The negative sentence preserves the presupposition that there was a time at which Schleswig-Holstein was separated from Denmark, since the specification of the domain of quantification is antecedent to the assignment of truth conditions to the negative sentence. Thus the notion of a semantical presupposition as a semantical determinant of the truth value of the sentence possessing the presupposition offers one explanation of the preservation of the presupposition under ordinary, linguistic negation.

The invariance of presupposition under negation is also noted by Frege in an example sentence that contains a proper name and a one-place predicate, but his discussion of this example has features notably distinct from the example just discussed. It raises a number of questions about negation that recur in the discussion of presupposition.

2 The Alleged Ambiguity of Negation and the Contrasts among Presupposition, Assertion, and Direct Entailment

For Frege a logically perfect language would be one in which each well-formed singular term designates an object. In ordinary, logically imperfect languages, singular terms do not satisfy this requirement, e.g. *Vulcan* and *the cold-fusion reaction* are not guaranteed a reference merely by virtue of being singular terms in the language. Frege (1892: 69) claims:

> If anything is **asserted** there is always an obvious presupposition that the simple or compound proper names used have reference. If one therefore **asserts** "Kepler died in misery," there is a presupposition that the name "Kepler" designates something; but it does not follow that the sense of the sentence "Kepler died in misery" contains the thought that the name "Kepler" designates something. If this were the case the negation would have to run not:
> > Kepler did not die in misery
> but:
> > Kepler did not die in misery, or the name "Kepler" has no reference.
> That the name "Kepler" designates something is just as much a presupposition for the **assertion** [my emphasis]:
> > Kepler died in misery
> as for the contrary assertion.

In this passage Frege claims that the presupposition of an **assertion** and of its main-verb negation are the same, and he offers an argument to support it.

It is evident from his argument that the notion of ⟨*P* contains a thought *Q*⟩ was assumed by Frege to be representable by ⟨*P* contains a conjunct *Q*⟩ or by ⟨*P* directly entails *Q*⟩. (The angled-bracket quotation marks around "φ" in "⟨φ⟩" are Quine's (1951) quasi-quotation. The notion of "direct entailment" is, roughly, the entailment of a subformula; see Atlas (1991)). In the case of the negative assertion ⟨*Not P*⟩, it was obvious to him that the Fregean senses (the truth conditions) of ⟨*Not P*⟩ and ⟨*Not P* v *Not Q*⟩ were not the same, so long as ⟨*Not Q*⟩ did not entail ⟨*Not P*⟩. That condition would be guaranteed if " 'Kepler' has no reference" did not entail "Kepler did not die in misery." But what insures that this non-entailment obtains?

If the negative sentence "Kepler did not die in misery" is interpreted as an exclusion negation (van Fraassen 1971), paraphrased in English by "It is not true that Kepler died in misery," a vacuous singular term in the complement clause might be thought to yield for the statement the value TRUE (rather than no truth value at all as Frege might have thought, because "Kepler" would lack a reference). Since the exclusion negation ⟨¬φ⟩ of a statement φ is true in a valuation if and only if φ is not true, even if φ is not true because it is neither true nor false, ⟨¬φ⟩ will be true. But then there is an entailment of "Kepler did not die in misery" by " 'Kepler' has no reference," and Frege's argument, which supports the claim that statements and their main-verb negations that contain singular terms share the presupposition that the terms are referentially non-vacuous, fails!

Thus Frege's argument requires that the main-verb negation not be an exclusion negation, but a choice negation (van Fraassen 1971). The choice negation $\langle -\phi \rangle$ of a statement ϕ is true (false) in a valuation if and only if ϕ is false (true). If the choice negation is paraphrased in English by "Kepler didn't die in misery," but "Kepler" has no reference, one's intuition is that the choice negation is not true. So Frege's argument survives. But it survives on the assumption that the negative, ordinary-language sentence expresses a choice negation, typically a narrow-scope negation, not an exclusion negation, typically a wide-scope negation. The choice negation permits a failure of truth value for a sentence with a false (not-true) presupposition, but an exclusion negation will be true even though a presupposition is not true, as we have seen. For these reasons van Fraassen (1971) formalizes the semantical notion of presupposition using choice negation, but it commits a theorist of semantical presupposition to the lexical or scopal ambiguity of *not* in ordinary language.

Frege's argument also illustrates another aspect of presupposition. Since $\langle \text{Not } P \rangle$ is not equivalent to $\langle \text{Not } P \text{ v Not } Q \rangle$, P is not equivalent to $\langle P \text{ and } Q \rangle$. So Q is not contained in P. The thought that "Kepler" has a reference is not contained in the affirmative assertion. If the thought is not contained in the assertion, not asserted as part of it or directly entailed by it, Frege thought that it must be presupposed.

Here we have the contrast of presupposition with both assertion and direct entailment. If one asserts *Kepler died in misery* or asserts *Kepler did not die in misery*, one does not therein assert *"Kepler" has a reference*. Similarly, if one asserts these statements, the proposition " 'Kepler' has a reference" is not a subformula (or clausal constituent) of the asserted content. If "not" is understood as a choice negation, that "Kepler" has a reference will be semantically entailed by the negative sentence "Kepler did not die in misery" but not directly entailed by it, just as that "Kepler" has a reference will be semantically entailed by the affirmative sentence but not directly entailed by it. The difference between the affirmative statement entailing that "Kepler" has a reference and the negative statement not entailing that "Kepler" has a reference depends upon construing the negative statement as expressing an exclusion negation. Note that though the exclusion negation does not entail that "Kepler" has a reference, even the exclusion negation could be understood to have the referential presupposition that "Kepler" has a reference. It is just that if the name does have a reference, the exclusion negation will be equivalent to the choice negation. The point is that the exclusion negation can be true whether or not the name has a reference. Its truth value is unaffected by the obtaining of the referential presupposition. Hence it is not the case that in a use of the negative sentence understood as an exclusion negation a speaker cannot presuppose that the name has reference. But if the presupposition fails, the exclusion negation will be true, while the choice negation will be neither true nor false.[1]

In reconstructing Frege's argument I have implicated that not only is the English sentence "It's not true that Kepler died in misery" capable of expressing the exclusion negation of "Kepler died in misery" but that it is only capable of expressing the exclusion negation. This is a traditional linguistic assumption in twentieth-century logic and philosophy, e.g. in Whitehead and Russell (1910: 6), Frege (1919: 123), and Strawson (1952: 78).[2]

Frege's argument for the preservation of referential presupposition under main-verb negation will not succeed without the assumption that main-verb negation "not" (or "nicht" in his case) is semantically a choice negation, which allows for sentences that are neither true nor false. For other reasons, which I will not discuss here, Frege also accepts a negation that is a wide-scope, exclusion negation. So Frege, and, as is well known, Russell (1905, 1919) and Whitehead and Russell (1910) assume that "not" (or "nicht") sentences are ambiguous.[3]

3   Pragmatic Presupposition

In "Pragmatics" Stalnaker (1972: 387–8) wrote:

> To presuppose a proposition in the pragmatic sense is to take its truth for granted, and to presume that others involved in the context do the same. This does not imply that the person need have any particular mental attitude toward the proposition, or that he needs assume anything about the mental attitudes of others in the context. Presuppositions are probably best viewed as complex dispositions which are manifested in linguistic behavior. One has presuppositions in virtue of the statements he makes, the questions he asks, the commands he issues. Presuppositions are propositions implicitly *supposed* before the relevant linguistic business is transacted.

Karttunen (1973, 1974) and others took Stalnaker's notion to be a sincerity condition on the utterance by a speaker of a sentence in a context. Stalnaker's notion, in contrast with Frege's notion of pragmatic presupposition (Atlas 1975), requires that the suppositions of the speaker be assumed by him to be those of his audience as well. Stalnaker's presuppositions are what the speaker takes to be common background for the participants in the context. Grice (1967, 1981), Schiffer (1972), and Lewis (1969) had employed similar notions. Stalnaker (1974: 200) uses a Gricean formulation:

> A proposition *P* is a pragmatic presupposition of a speaker in a given context just in case the speaker assumes or believes that *P*, assumes or believes that his addressee assumes or believes that *P*, and assumes or believes that his addressee recognizes that he is making these assumptions, or has these beliefs.

4 The Introduction of Accommodation in Conditionals and Factives and the Neo-Gricean Explanation of Factive Presuppositions

Karttunen (1973), seconded by Atlas (1975, 1977a), had noted a weakness in Stalnaker's account. Karttunen pointed out that a counterfactual conditional like *If Bill had a dime, he would buy you a Coke* is sincerely uttered in some contexts in which the speaker does not assume that his audience assumes that Bill does not have a dime. One point of uttering the sentence is to inform the audience that Bill does not have a dime. On Stalnaker's (1972) account the proposition that Bill does not have a dime is not a pragmatic presupposition in that context, and, on Stalnaker's general principle that "any semantic presupposition of a proposition expressed in a given context will be a pragmatic presupposition of the people in that context," the proposition is not a semantic presupposition of the counterfactual conditional. That was a conclusion that Karttunen rejected, so he rejected Stalnaker's general principle.

Likewise Atlas (1975: 37) emphasized that "the assumption of common background knowledge is too strong to be applicable to speech-situations as universally as Stalnaker and others would like." I (1975: 40) noted that "there are two strategies of the Communication Game that are especially relevant to the problem of presupposition, the strategy of Telling the Truth and the complementary strategy of Being Informative."

Factive-verb statements, e.g. ⟨Geoffrey knows that *P*⟩, are said to presuppose ⟨*P*⟩. It is clear that there is an entailment of the complement from the affirmative factive-verb statement: *Geoffrey knows that P* ⊪ *P*, and of the object-language version of the referential presupposition: *Geoffrey knows that P* ⊪ *Geoffrey exists*. From an understanding of the negative statement, we may also infer these propositions.[4] For the neo-Gricean the question was how to explain the inferences from the negative statement by appeal to Grice's (1967) model of conversation as a rational, cooperative communication of information. If we take the Kiparskys' (1970) analysis of factive sentences seriously, we have, in effect, two referential presuppositions: "Geoffrey" has a reference; ⟨the fact that *P*⟩ has a reference; or, in the object-language: "Geoffrey exists," ⟨*P*⟩. According to Grice, when a speaker means more than he literally says and expects the hearer to recognize that he does, the speaker's expectations and the hearer's interpretation are governed by Grice's (1967) Maxims of Conversation. One particularly important pair, for our purposes, are the Maxims of Quantity: (a) Make your contribution as informative as is required by the current purposes of the exchange; (b) Do not make your contribution more informative than is required. The neo-Gricean account of a factive presupposition of a "know" statement can then be sketched as follows.

Negative sentences of the form ⟨Geoffrey does not know that *P*⟩ are not scope-ambiguous but rather semantically non-specific between presuppositional and non-presuppositional understandings (Atlas 1975: 42, n.23; Zwicky and Sadock 1975). On the semantical non-specificity view the negative sentence is not ambiguous; it is univocal, and the so-called wide-scope and narrow-scope "senses" are instead contextual specifications of the indeterminate literal meaning of the negative sentence. The literal meaning is neither the wide-scope nor the narrow-scope interpretation, but it is something to which contextual information is added to produce in the hearer a narrow-scope understanding of the speaker's utterance or a wide-scope understanding of the speaker's utterance in the context. On Frege's and Strawson's view the narrow-scope, choice negation will be true or false if $\langle P \rangle$ is true, and neither true nor false if $\langle P \rangle$ is not true. On the neo-Gricean view the truth of $\langle P \rangle$ is inferred by the hearer in order to construct a more informative understanding of the negative sentence than its indeterminate meaning. The syntax and meaning (the syntactical combination of its meaningful parts) of the sentence constrain, but do not alone specify, what a hearer understands a speaker to mean literally by an utterance of the sentence.

The specification of "not" as a choice or an exclusion negation is also made by the hearer in interpreting the speaker's utterance. The semantical indeterminacy of "not" in the sentence leaves it open to the hearer to make an inference to the best interpretation of the utterance (Atlas and Levinson 1981: 42).

The hearer's inference that "Geoffrey" has a reference is an interpretative one, in order to explain most plausibly the speaker's asserting *Geoffrey does not KNOW that P*, instead of the differently stressed utterance *GEOFFREY does not know that P – GEOFFREY doesn't exist*, and may be a real-time accommodation, taking the speaker at his word, viz. "Geoffrey," as referring to an actual individual.

I observed, like Karttunen in the case of conditionals, that speakers can make use of presuppositional sentences to Be Informative. The analysis was as follows (Atlas 1975: 42–3): If a speaker intends to be informative, in this case about Geoffrey's ignorance, the speaker must intend, and the hearer recognize, another understanding of the negative sentence (viz. one other than the non-presuppositional, exclusion negation understanding). This understanding is one in which the speaker presumes that the proposition expressed by the complement of "know" is true and hence a possible object of Geoffrey's knowledge. This presumption by the speaker is necessary whenever he intends his utterance to be informative (to the hearer about Geoffrey's ignorance). Likewise, the hearer presumes that the speaker intends to be informative, and so assumes that the speaker presumes that the complement is true. If the hearer does not know or believe, prior to the speaker's utterance, that the complement is true, his presumption, *ceteris paribus*, that the speaker's utterance is meant to be informative provides him with good reason to accept the complement as true. In this way, the speaker, by reporting Geoffrey's ignorance, can remedy the hearer's ignorance.

Thus was recognized, for conditionals (Karttunen 1973), and for factive-verb statements (Atlas 1975: 42–3), the possibility of unpresupposed "presuppositions," which were given a theoretical explanation as part of the strategy of Being Informative in the Communication Game.

Later the notion was given the name ACCOMMODATION by Lewis (1979) in his "Scorekeeping in a Language Game," and an earlier variant of the concept than Lewis's appeared in Ballmer (1972, 1978), and in the last few sentences of Strawson's (1950) "On Referring."

Stalnaker (1974: 206) had given an account of factive-verb statements that missed the significance of **accommodation**, and one that merely demonstrated the alleged infelicity of asserting ⟨*x* knows that *P*⟩ in a context in which speaker and hearer had not mutually acknowledged the truth of ⟨*P*⟩. (See my discussion of Stalnaker 1974 below.) Thomason (1984) gave a less detailed explanation of the factive-verb presuppositions but had recognized the importance of accommodation (see Thomason 1990). Accommodation, for them, is the repair of the alleged infelicity. I, by contrast, believe that there is no infelicity in asserting negative factive statements in these contexts.

5   Grice on Presupposition, Implicature, and the Ambiguity of Negation

In this section I shall compare the neo-Gricean treatment (Atlas 1975, 1978b, 1979, Atlas and Levinson 1981) of presupposition as a heterogeneous relation combining entailment and an extended concept of Grice's Generalized Conversational Implicature with that given independently by Grice (1981) himself in his essay "Presupposition and Conversational Implicature." Atlas, Levinson, and Grice agree that *There is a king of France* is entailed by *The king of France is bald*, though Grice takes the view, unlike myself, that the negative sentence "The king of France is not bald" is structurally ambiguous between a wide-scope and a narrow-scope "not." When a speaker asserts the (allegedly) ambiguous negative sentence, then, according to Grice (1981: 189), "without waiting for disambiguation, people understand an utterance of *The king of France is not bald* as implying (in some fashion) the unique existence of a king of France. This is intelligible," Grice continues, "if on one reading (the strong one), the unique existence of a king of France is entailed, on the other (the weak one), though not entailed, it is conversationally implicated. What needs to be shown, then, is a route by which the weaker reading would come to implicate what it does not entail." That was shown in Atlas (1975, 1979) and has been discussed above. (Similar, though not identical, approaches were taken by Kempson 1975 and Wilson 1975.)

The first striking difference between Grice (1981) and Atlas (1975 etc.) is Grice's claim that the negative sentence is ambiguous and Atlas's (1974, 1975) and Kempson's (1975, 1988) contrasting claim that the unambiguous negative sentence is semantically non-specific between the "weak" and "strong" understandings, which are not readings or senses. This subtle semantic difference has often been misunderstood, and its consequences underappreciated. Grice's

(1981) account allows us to see, in a more dramatic way than usual, the consequences of this apparently small difference in theory.

What is incoherent in Grice's (1981: 189) account is the remark that hearers somehow "without waiting for disambiguation . . . understand an utterance of *The king of France is not bald* as implying (in some fashion) the unique existence of a king of France." On Grice's own (1967, 1989) original discussion of conversational implicature, sentences were taken as disambiguated, so that statements had well-defined truth conditions, before the reasoning resulting in a conversational implicatum was applied to the statement in its context. But the intent of Grice's remark above is that on either sense of the negative sentence there will be an implication "in some fashion," an entailment from the strong sense and a conversational implicatum from the weak sense. The implication of the existence of a unique king of France is overdetermined; it is a double implication, the same from each sense but on semantic grounds for the first sense and on pragmatic grounds for the second sense.

What is incoherent about Grice's position is that if hearers really do not wait for disambiguation (and Grice's justification for that claim is an utter mystery), then there is no need to generate a conversational implicatum from the (alleged) weak sense. Prior to disambiguation all that can be required for there to be any implication at all is that there be an implication from some sense of the negative sentence – not from all senses of the negative sentence. Since the strong sense will entail the existence of a unique king of France, the implication, of some fashion, can be explained without appeal to any conversational implicature at all.

Grice (1981: 189) claims that the affirmative *The king of France is bald* logically implies the existence of a unique French king, and its ambiguous negative "The king of France is not bald" has a double implication, an entailment from its strong negative sense and a conversational implicatum from its weak negative sense.

By contrast the neo-Gricean claims that the affirmative statement *The king of France is bald* logically implies the existence of a unique French king or the existence of an individual that is the speaker's reference (see Abbott, this volume), and the semantically non-specific negative sentence *The king of France is not bald* may, when asserted, be understood by an addressee in a context to "implicate" – in the Atlas (1979, 1989) technical sense (see Levinson 2000a: 256–9) – distinct propositions constructed (or inferred) from the non-propositional, semantically non-specific literal meaning of the negative sentence. The strong implicatum in a context entails the existence of a unique French king (or an intended speaker's reference); the weak implicatum in a context does not. (I do not rule out a speaker misleading an addressee, or an addressee misunderstanding a speaker, by an addressee constructing both propositions in a context, analogous to what on the ambiguity account would be the addressee recognizing both (alleged) senses of the sentence. It is an empirical fact that for asserted sentences in most contexts addressees do not consciously recognize more than one of the alternative senses or consciously recognize more than one of the inferred alternative understandings.)

It is actually interesting how the philosopher who once proposed a Modified Occam's Razor, *Senses are not to be multiplied beyond necessity* (Grice 1989: 47), lands in this commitment to ambiguity. Sluga had pointed out to him (Grice 1981: 188, n.2 – an acknowledgment omitted from Grice 1989: 271) that one could treat *the king of France* either as a quantifier or as a primitive singular term. If the former, then the sentence would be open to scope ambiguities, like typical quantified sentences. But, Grice (1981: 188) notably observes, "if there were a clear distinction in sense (in English) between, say, *The king of France is not bald* and *It is not the case that the king of France is bald* (if the former demanded the strong reading and the latter the weak one), then it would be reasonable to correlate *The king of France is bald* with the formal structure that treats the iota operator [viz. Russell's definite description operator] like a quantifier. But this does not seem to be the case; I see no such clear semantic distinction."

I want to emphasize Grice's (1981: 188) last remark, a remark that may have been in the original lecture of 1970 that Grice delivered in the University of Illinois, Champaign–Urbana, since it was also made independently by Atlas (1974) and Kuroda (1977: 105), who also saw no such clear semantic distinction. But Atlas (1974) noted, contra Grice, that there was no scope ambiguity for these negative English sentences – they were semantically non-specific with respect to scope, which further suggested that the formalization of these English sentences in a formal language whose structure imposed a scope ambiguity would miss a semantically important feature of negative English sentences.

Rather than draw that conclusion, Grice (1981: 188) used his observation to motivate his choice of the formalization of the definite description as a logically primitive singular term and concluded, "We are then committed to the structural ambiguity of the sentence *The king of France is not bald*." As a result Grice's explanatory task was to show how, from an ambiguous negative sentence, Strawson's presupposition that there exists a unique French king (at the time of utterance) can be explained.

6   Grice's Reduction of Referential Presupposition to Implicature: the Evidence of Cancelability

Grice (1981: 187) had already correctly observed that "in the original version of Strawson's truth-gap theory, he did not recognize any particular asymmetry as regards the presupposition that there is a king of France, between the two sentences, 'The king of France is bald' and 'The king of France is not bald'; but it does seem to be plausible to suppose that there is such an asymmetry."

Grice then continues:

> I would have thought that the implication that there is a king of France is clearly part of the conventional force of *The king of France is bald*; but that this is not

clearly so in the case of *The king of France is not bald.* . . . An implication that there is a king of France is often carried by saying [*The king of France is not bald*], but it is tempting to suggest that this implication is not, inescapably, part of the conventional force of the utterance of ["The king of France is not bald"], but is rather a matter of conversational implicature.

Then, as did Atlas (1975, 1979), Boër and Lycan (1976), Atlas and Levinson (1981), among others, Grice argued that the so-called presupposition of the negative statement is (a) *cancelable*, (b) *non-detachable*, and (c) *calculable*, i.e. *justifiable by argument*, from Grice's Maxims of Conversation as a conversational implicatum (see Horn, this volume). (Roughly, this means that (a) one can assert the statement and deny the "presupposition" without inconsistency; that (b) other statements synonymous with this statement, but not differing wildly in manner, will carry the same "presupposition"; and that (c) the inference to the existence of a unique king of France is justifiable by principles governing rational, information exchange in conversation.) Grice argued that the proposition that there is a unique king of France is both explicitly cancelable (by outright denial) and contextually cancelable (by inconsistency with background information).

Grice offered the following support for those pragmatic features of the "presupposed" proposition. He (1981: 187) wrote: "if I come on a group of people arguing about whether the king of France is bald, it is not linguistically improper for me to say that the king of France is not bald, since there is no king of France." As I have mentioned earlier, speakers rarely notice the ambiguity of their utterances, and Grice is a case in point. He did not notice the ambiguity of his wording and placement of the comma in his indirect discourse sentence; he should have written in direct discourse: . . . for me to say *The king of France is not bald, since there is no king of France*. He also argued that the proposition was contextually cancelable. He (1981: 187) described an example as follows:

It is a matter of dispute whether the government has a very undercover person who interrogates those whose loyalty is suspect and who, if he existed, could be legitimately referred to as the loyalty examiner; and if, further, I am known to be very sceptical about the existence of such a person, I could perfectly well say to a plainly loyal person, *Well, the loyalty examiner will not be summoning you at any rate*, without, I would think, being taken to imply that such a person exists.

But the more compelling example is the one he then goes on to give:

Further, if I am well known to disbelieve in the existence of such a person, though others are inclined to believe in him, when I find a man who is apprised of my position, but who is worried in case he is summoned, I could try to reassure him by saying, *The loyalty examiner won't summon you, don't worry*. Then it would be clear that I said this because I was sure there is no such person.

Notice, as Atlas (1974) observed, clarity does not require Grice to have said *It's not the case that the loyalty examiner will summon you, don't worry*.

7   Non-detachability of Implicatures, Meaning, and the neo-Gricean Mechanism of Inference: Pragmatic Intrusion

The issue of non-detachability is more subtle. Here one looks for roughly synonymous ways of making an assertion in which differences of Manner are not so pronounced as to swamp the similarities of meaning. Levinson (2000a: 111) writes, "Most analysts hold that presupposition cannot be reduced to matters of implicature and that presuppositions are attached to their lexical or syntactic triggers (and are thus not detachable in Grice's sense . . .)," as if non-detachability were a problem for the neo-Gricean reduction. To the contrary, one expects generalized conversational implicata to be non-detachable. Syntactic triggers, like the syntactic structure of clefts, are accounted for on the neo-Gricean view if, as Atlas and Levinson (1981) show, the logical form of clefts, from which the implicata are generated, is distinct from that of the related simple declaratives, whose syntax does not trigger a "presupposition." As for lexical triggers, *knows that P* and *believes justifiably and non-accidentally the fact that P* will trigger the same "presupposition" ⟨*that P*⟩. Grice's (1981) and my arguments are designed to show that the neo-Gricean account "saves the phenomena" of presupposition.

For example, as suggested in Atlas (1974, 1975, 1977b), *The king of France is not bald* and *It's not the case that the king of France is bald* can have the same presupposition that there is a king of France, contrary to the tradition in philosophical logic that assumed the latter statement to express only the wide-scope or exclusion negation interpretation (e.g. Whitehead and Russell 1910: 6, Frege 1919: 123, Strawson 1952: 78). Grice (1981: 188) agrees with this linguistic judgment. But Grice holds that these sentences are semantically ambiguous and that the narrow-scope sense entails the existence of a king of France, while the wide-scope sense, when asserted, carries a generalized conversational implicature by the speaker that a king of France exists. Kempson (1975, 1988) and Atlas (1974, 1975, 1978a, 1978b, 1979) hold that these sentences are not ambiguous but univocal, semantically non-specific between the narrow-scope and wide-scope understandings. Thus the inferential mechanism of conversational implicature will map semantically non-specific, non-propositional semantic representations into narrow-scope or into wide-scope propositions depending on the context, as discussed in Atlas (1978a, 1979). As discussed in Atlas and Levinson (1981: 40–3), those singular terms in the statement that are Topic NPs are "non-controversially," by default, given status in the interpretations as referring terms.

The neo-Gricean account is non-Gricean, since the classical Gricean view took the semantic representation of sentence-types to be literal meanings incomplete only in contextual specification of the reference of singular terms, demonstratives, indexicals, tense, etc. and took the semantic representations of sentence-tokens (utterances) to be completed propositions, the content of "what is said." Thus I was committed to what later was labeled by Levinson (1988, 2000a) PRAGMATIC INTRUSION, the intrusion of pragmatically inferred content into the truth conditions of what Grice (1989) called "what is said."[5]

8   The Reduction of Presuppositions to Conversational Implicata: Accommodation, Calculability, and Common Ground

Grice (1981: 185) briefly characterizes the speaker's implicatum as the content that "would be what he might expect the hearer to suppose him to think in order to preserve the idea that the [conversational] maxims are, after all, not being violated." The neo-Gricean explanation (Atlas 1975, Atlas and Levinson 1981) of referential, factive, and cleft presuppositions depended on the hearer supposing the speaker not to be violating Atlas and Levinson's (1981: 40) Neo-Gricean Maxims of Relativity, which were refinements of Grice's Maxims of Quantity.

(4)   **Maxims of Relativity**
1.   Do not say what you believe to be highly noncontroversial, that is, to be **entailed** by the presumptions of the common ground.
2.   Take what you hear to be lowly noncontroversial, that is, **consistent with** the presumptions of the common ground.

The first maxim is a speaker-oriented production maxim; the second maxim is a hearer-oriented comprehension maxim. It is important that the production maxim is a prohibition, a "do not" maxim, and that the comprehension maxim is an obligation, a "must do" maxim. It is also important to note the difference between a sentence being **entailed** by a set of sentences in the common ground and a sentence being merely logically **consistent** with a set of sentences in the common ground. The consistency requirement was designed to permit the kind of informative statement **accommodation** for referential and factive presuppositions that I described in Atlas (1975, 1977a). If a singular term were introduced by its use in a statement that would be more informative under an interpretation requiring the singular term to be a referring term in that statement, and its having a reference was **consistent** with the previously established common ground, nothing in my maxim would stand in the way of such an informative interpretation, whether or not the existence of the reference of the singular term had already been established as part of the common ground. Atlas and Levinson's (1981) Maxims of Relativity were designed to accommodate accommodation.

It should also be noted that our Maxims of Relativity were couched in terms of **non-controversiality** and of **common ground**, constrained by a mini-theory of Non-controversiality. Among the axioms of that mini-theory were (Atlas and Levinson 1981: 40):

(5) **Axioms of Non-controversiality**
   a. If A(*t*) is "about" *t*, i.e. if ⟨*t*⟩ is a Topic NP in the statement A(*t*), then if ⟨*t*⟩ is a singular term, the proposition ⟨*t* exists⟩ is non-controversial.
   b. The obtaining of stereotypical relations among individuals is noncontroversial.

Embedded in our neo-Gricean account of referential and cleft "presuppositions" were the distinct notions **Topic NP, non-controversial proposition, common ground**, and **most informative interpretation of a statement**, the interpretation of which is consistent with the propositions of the common ground.

   What I showed in Atlas (1975) and Atlas and Levinson (1981) and have reviewed above was the reasoning by which the conversational implicatum *There is a king of France* could be reached from the **default** understanding of an assertion of *The king of France is not bald* (see (5a) above). The construction of reasoning to a default interpretation is required if Grice's third criterion for the existence of a conversational implicature is to be met, and the reasoning I constructed depended upon an elaboration and a revision of Grice's Maxims of Quantity (being as informative as is required).

   Grice (1981: 189) himself adopts a Russellian analysis of *The king of France is bald*, a conjunction of three independent clauses (cf. Strawson 1950: 5):

(6) *The king of France is bald.*
   (A) *There is at least one king of France.*
   (B) *There is not more than one king of France.*
   (C) *There is nothing which is a king of France and is not bald.*

The account of presupposition that Grice (1981: 190) gave of the presupposition of the negative statement *The king of France is not bald* depends upon a distinction between denied and undenied conjuncts:

> it would be reasonable to suppose that the speaker thinks, and expects his hearer to think, that some subconjunction of A and B and C has what I might call common-ground status and, therefore, is not something that is likely to be challenged. One way in which this might happen would be if the speaker were to think or assume that it is common knowledge, and that people would regard it as common knowledge, that there is one and only one [king of France].

Thus the speaker who asserts *The king of France is not bald* would be understood to deny only the third conjunct (C) {*Nothing that is a king of France is not bald, Whatever is a king of France is bald*}, since the argument just quoted was supposed to "show that, in some way, one particular conjunct is singled out" (Grice 1981: 190). Of course, if one takes it as common knowledge that there is a unique king of France, and then denies conjunct (C), as Grice proposes, one gets the conjunction (i) *There is a unique king of France and there is at least one king of France that is not bald*, which is supposed to be an interpretation of

(ii) *The king of France is not bald*. The (weak) denial, viz. the interpretation of *It's not the case that the king of France is bald* as ⟨¬ ((A and B) and C)⟩, conjoined with the common ground ⟨(A and B)⟩, is supposed to give ⟨((A and B) and ¬C)⟩ as the interpretation of *The king of France is not bald*. But the question is, WHY should the common ground intervene in utterance interpretation in this way? Grice believes that its commongroundedness is a sufficient and obvious explanation; I do not. A theory of how and why common ground enters into utterance interpretation is needed. Grice does not offer one; Atlas and Levinson (1981) do.

Sentence (i) entails *There is a unique king of France*, and an utterance of (ii), on Grice's (1981: 189) own showing, "without waiting for disambiguation," implies "(in some fashion) the unique existence of a king of France." Grice (1981: 189) has already remarked that "what needs to be shown is a route by which the weaker reading could come to implicate what it does not entail." But what Grice (1981: 190) has just shown is how the (weak) **denial** of *The king of France is bald*, in conjunction with the common ground, **entails** *There is a unique king of France*, which is what he has explicitly claimed a speaker **implicates** by the (weak) denial of *The king of France is bald* and that the (weak) denial does not entail without the common ground.

Does this mean that Grice reduces implicature to a context-relative entailment? If he were to do so, he would start to sound like a Sperber and Wilson (1986a) RELEVANCE theorist. But a common-ground-dependent entailment from the (weak) denial is merely a fact about context and the assertoric content of a weak negation. It is not a theory of an inference to the best interpretation of the negative utterance in the fashion of Atlas and Levinson (1981). Unlike me, Grice thinks the negative *sentence* already has an interpretation; it is the weak negation. (Levinson was classically Gricean about it in Atlas and Levinson (1981), though he (2000a) now takes a more favorable view of semantical non-specificity; see Atlas and Levinson 1981: 55, n.19). The question for Grice is, why should that interpretation generate the "implication" that there is a unique king of France? *Pace* Grice (1981: 190), the answer cannot be that the existential proposition is ALREADY ASSUMED in the context. The existence of a context-relative entailment is no explanation of "the route by which the weaker reading could come to implicate what it does not entail," since context-relative entailment does not possess the logical properties of implicature or presupposition. Even though the context provides premises, the relation is an entailment; it is monotonic, unlike implicature (which is non-monotonic, i.e. defeasible), and it is unlike presupposition (which is preserved under main-verb negation). Unlike an entailment an implicatum can also be cancelled (i.e. negated without a resulting contradiction).

The sources of these difficulties in Grice's (1981) analysis of *The king of France is not bald* are clear. The first source is his accepting the conjunction of three independent propositions as an analysis of *The king of France is bald* (for reasons that I have not discussed here) and his concomitant commitment to the scope ambiguity of *The king of France is not bald*. The ambiguity assumption leads Grice into an incoherent account in his attempt to derive the referential "presupposition" from his (weak) external negation reading of the negative sentence. It is here that ignoring the subtle difference between ambiguity and semantically non-specific univocality has devastating consequences for the success of Grice's (1981) attempt to reduce referential presupposition to implicature. And it is here that the Atlas's (1974, 1975, 1979) and Atlas and Levinson's (1981) analyses succeed where Grice's (1981) fails.

The second source is his appeal to **common ground** in the simple way he appeals to it, and the way that Stalnaker (1974) appeals to it in "Pragmatic Presuppositions." An explanation using speaker's presupposition is not equivalent to an account using conversational implicatures.

9   Common Ground and Context as the Source of Presuppositions: Stalnaker's "Pragmatic Presuppositions," the Problem of Accommodation, and the Concept of Non-controversiality

Grice's error was the tacit assumption that by putting *There is a unique king of France* into the common ground, its commongroundedness would explain its presuppositional – as contrasted with "assertoric" and with "entailed" – status in the interpretation of a speaker's assertion. But commongroundedness of a proposition can provide no such contrast with the assertoric status or entailments of a proposition. It matters not whether *There is a unique king of France* belongs to the speaker's and addressee's "common knowledge" if what needs to be explained is why and how Grice's weak reading of *The king of France is not bald*, if asserted, yields as an implicatum *There is a unique king of France*. Grice's attempted explanation by appeal to common knowledge of "There is a unique king of France" still results on his account in an entailment of "There is a unique king of France" from the common ground and the weak reading of *The king of France is not bald*, because it is entailed by the common ground alone.

What is missing is an account of why using the common-ground status of "There is a unique king of France" when combined with the weak negation interpretation of "The king of France is not bald" explains an inference to the presuppositional interpretation of the utterance *The king of France is not bald*, an inference to the token of the type *The king of France* having a reference, where the token's having a reference is neither entailed by the literal meaning of the utterance (on either my view or Grice's view of the literal meaning of the negative sentence) nor asserted in it.

If one needed more proof that "common knowledge" is not essential to explaining why people understand an utterance of *The king of France is not bald* to "imply (in some fashion)" the existence of a unique king of France, it is the existence of accommodation. And Grice (1981: 190), despite his own (misguided) attempt to explain presupposition as an implicatum somehow arising from common ground, understood what became known later as accommodation:

> it is quite natural to say to somebody, when we are discussing some concert, *My aunt's cousin went to that concert*, when one knows perfectly well that the person one is talking to is very likely not even to know that one had an aunt, let alone know that one's aunt had a cousin. So the supposition must be not that it is common knowledge but rather that it is noncontroversial, in the sense that it is something that you would expect the hearer to take from you (if he does not already know).

That is why the account in Atlas and Levinson (1981: 40–1) appealed to **non-controversiality** in stating the Maxims of Relativity, and why the referential "presuppositions" are expressed as Conventions of Extension, a subclass of Conventions of Non-Controversiality:

(7) If A(*t*) is "about" *t*, i.e. ⟨*t*⟩ is a Topic NP in a statement A(*t*), then:
    a. if ⟨*t*⟩ is a singular term, ⟨*t* exists⟩ is non-controversial;
    b. if ⟨*t*⟩ denotes a state of affairs or a proposition, ⟨*t* is actual⟩ and ⟨*t* is true⟩ are non-controversial.

and why a Convention of Intension among the Conventions of Non-Controversiality is the following:

(8) The obtaining of stereotypical relations among individuals is non-controversial.

If others were not as clear about the notion of non-controversiality as Grice was, others were clear about accommodation. In fact, as Larry Horn has reminded me, the Father of Accommodation is P. F. Strawson (1950: 27). In the last few sentences of "On Referring," Strawson writes:

> A literal-minded and childless man asked whether all his children are asleep will certainly not answer "Yes" on the ground that he has none; but nor will he answer "No" on this ground. Since he has no children, the question does not arise. To say this is not to say that I may not use the sentence, "All my children are asleep", with the intention of letting someone know that I have children, or of deceiving him into thinking that I have. Nor is it any weakening of my thesis to concede that singular phrases of the form "the so-and-so" may sometimes be used with a similar purpose. Neither Aristotelian nor Russellian rules give the exact logic of any expression of ordinary language; for ordinary language has no exact logic.

Lewis (1979) acknowledges Stalnaker's discussion of the phenomena of accommodation, and Stalnaker (1974: 202) is quite explicit:

a speaker may act as if certain propositions are part of the common background when he knows that they are not. He may want to communicate a proposition indirectly, and do this by presupposing it in such a way that the auditor will be able to infer that it is presupposed. In such a case, a speaker tells his auditor something in part by pretending that his auditor already knows it.

When a conversation involves this kind of pretense, the speaker's presuppositions, in the sense of the term I shall use, will not fit the definition sketched above. That is why the definition is only an approximation. I shall say that one actually does make the presuppositions that one seems to make even when one is only pretending to have the beliefs that one normally has when one makes presuppositions.

I shall return to the peculiarity of Stalnaker's account in the second paragraph of the quotation above. I merely want to note here the evident utility of the phenomena of accommodation in understanding a presupposition of an assertion, and distinguish the linguistic phenomena from Stalnaker's analysis of them as a pretended "speaker's presupposition." (In Stalnaker's (1974: 200) definition of a speaker's pragmatic presupposition in a context, "A proposition P is a pragmatic presupposition of a speaker in a given context just in case the speaker assumes or believes that P, assumes or believes that his addressee assumes or believes that P, and assumes or believes that his addressee recognizes that he is making these assumptions, or has these beliefs.")

The notion that is required to explain presupposition is not the common knowledge that is appealed to in Stalnaker's (1974: 200) definition of a speaker's pragmatic presupposition in a context. Common-ground status of a proposition for a speaker and addressee will in a speech-context be sufficient for a proposition to be non-controversial in that context, but common-ground status is not necessary for it to be non-controversial. The trouble with Stalnaker's analysis of accommodation is that accommodation supposedly occurs against a background of common knowledge in which, for example, the existence of Grice's aunt's cousin is established and in which an individual is identifiable as the reference of "my aunt's cousin." The point is that for purposes of a theoretical explanation of interpretations of assertions that carry presuppositions, common knowledge does not matter. The theoretically important notion, as Grice (1981) and Atlas and Levinson (1981) recognized, is non-controversiality.

The speaker's implicata that constitute the "presuppositions" of assertions can reinforce propositions already in the common ground of a conversation, or they can introduce propositions into the common ground, or they can be recognized and then dismissed, never even entering the common ground of a conversation, because they belong to a separate store of information that we characterize as non-controversial. This store of non-controversial information is accessible for use in a conversation; it need not be explicitly a part of the common ground, or part of mutual knowledge, for purposes of a particular conversation. But what is non-controversial on the occasion of an utterance need not have been stored at all. A speaker's expectation that an addressee will charitably take the speaker's word that a singular term ⟨*t*⟩ is non-vacuous is not the same as a speaker and addressee's expectations that they have in common the thought ⟨*t* exists⟩. What they linguistically have in common is not a background belief; it is a language-based practice or convention of inter-pretation that allows certain bits of language, e.g. singular terms, charitably to have a taken-for-granted semantic evaluation in the course of making and understanding assertions, but only if the singular terms are Topic Noun Phrases (see Davidson 1967, Grandy 1973, Atlas 1988, 1989).

Stalnaker (1974: 202), reflecting on accommodation, remarks that "Presup-posing is thus not a mental attitude like believing, but is rather a linguistic disposition – a disposition to behave in one's use of language as if one had certain beliefs, or were making certain assumptions." This is certainly closer to the truth than his notion of a speaker's pragmatic presupposition; it is his notion of a speaker's pretended pragmatic presupposition.

Is Grice (1981: 190) pretending to believe that his aunt has a cousin? Is he pretending, like Stalnaker, to believe that his addressee believes that Grice's aunt has a cousin? Is he pretending to believe that his addressee recognizes that he is pretending to believe that his aunt has a cousin? And what does any of this have to do with Grice's taking it for granted that his addressee will take it for granted that Grice's aunt has a cousin when Grice asserts *My aunt's cousin went to that concert*?

But, then, I am not saying anything that Stalnaker and Sadock have not already recognized. Stalnaker (1974: 202–3, n.3) reports a counterexample of Sadock's:

(9)   I am asked by someone whom I just met, "Are you going to lunch?" I reply, "No, I've got to pick up my sister."

Stalnaker admits that the I of the example "seems to *presuppose* that [he] has a sister even though [he] does not assume that the [first] speaker knows this. Yet the statement is clearly acceptable . . . ," which it would not be if Stalnaker's view were correct that, absent the mutual beliefs or assumptions, an assertion relying on them would be infelicitous. Stalnaker continues: "and it does not seem right to explain this in terms of pretense. . . ."

Indeed. The situation for Stalnaker's (1974) account of pragmatic presup-position is now this: first, "mutual knowledge" was seen to fail to account for accommodation; so, second, mutual knowledge was changed to pretended mutual knowledge; finally, pretended mutual knowledge was seen to fail to account for accommodation. What now?

Stalnaker (1974: 203, n.3) has two replies, in the first of which he appeals to a notion of Gricean implicature, the very notion that in his essay "Pragmatic Presuppositions" Stalnaker (1974: 212) proposes for explanatory purposes to replace by his notion of a speaker's presupposition in a context (see below)! Unfortunately this cannot rescue Stalnaker, since he glosses Grice's notion of implicature in terms of the notion of common background knowledge: "the addressee infers that the speaker accepts that *Q* from the fact that he says that

P because normally one says that *P* only when it is common background knowledge that *Q*," thus missing his own point about accommodation.

Stalnaker's second reply to Sadock's example is to consider the option of denying that there is a presupposition at all in the example, to claim that the example is an exception to the usual cases of referential presupposition, but Stalnaker refuses to undertake this strategy of dealing with Sadock's example, on the grounds of the complexity of accounting for both cases in which a speaker does presuppose the existence of a unique reference of a singular term and cases in which he does not; he fears the consequent loss of the simplicity of the generalization that "a speaker **always** presupposes the existence of a unique referent." (A falsehood is no loss. The falsity of Stalnaker's (1974) simple generalization follows from the Strawson–Grice Condition that a statement $\langle A(t)\rangle$ presupposes $\langle t$ exists$\rangle$ only if $\langle t\rangle$ is a Topic NP in $\langle A(t)\rangle$. See Strawson 1971: 92–5, Atlas 1988, 1989.)

10   The Context/Content Distinction

Stalnaker (1974: 212) describes his program in "Pragmatic Presuppositions" as follows:

> The contrast between semantic and pragmatic claims can be either of two things, depending on which notion of semantics one has in mind. First, it can be a contrast between claims about the particular conventional meaning of some word or phrase on the one hand, and claims about the general structure or strategy of conversation on the other. Grice's distinction between conventional implicatures and conversational implicatures is an instance of this contrast. Second, it can be a contrast between claims about the truth-conditions or *content* of what is said – the proposition expressed – on the one hand, and claims about the *context* in which a statement is made – the attitudes and interests of speaker and audience – on the other. It is the second contrast that I am using when I argue for a pragmatic rather than a semantic account of presupposition.

Atlas and Levinson's (1981) and Grice's (1981) claim is that no adequate theory of presupposition can maintain the contrast that Stalnaker proposes. PRAGMATIC INTRUSION (Levinson 2000a) and SEMANTICAL NON-SPECIFICITY (Atlas 1989), which I have discussed above, show that **the content/context distinction is just one more philosophical myth – another untenable dualism, like the figurative/literal distinction** (Atlas in press) **and the *a priori/a posteriori* distinction** (Putnam 1976).

As Sadock's example shows, Stalnaker's theory of context manifestly fails to save the presuppositional phenomena, and his only hope of responding to the counterexamples is the Gricean theory of conversational implicature that he wants his theory of context to supplant.

But there is an even simpler objection to Stalnaker's account of presupposition as a speaker's pragmatic presupposition. Consider the case of simple conditionals ⟨*If P then Q*⟩. Stalnaker's (1974: 211) account of conditionals is given briefly:

> we need first the assumption that what is explicitly *supposed* becomes (temporarily) a part of the background of common assumptions in subsequent conversation, and second that an *if* clause is an explicit supposition.

So, *If the king of France is a serial killer, his mother will be ashamed of him* now requires for its felicitous assertion that the speaker assume (temporarily) that there is a king of France, assume that his addressee assumes that there is a king of France, and assume that his addressee recognizes that the speaker is making these assumptions, and that the speaker assume (temporarily) that the king of France is a serial killer, assume that his addressee assumes that the king of France is a serial killer, and assume that his addressee recognizes that the speaker is making these assumptions. Note that the condition imposed by Stalnaker is not that one "entertains the thought," or "considers the consequences of," but rather that one is assuming as background . . . But are you? . . . assuming, I mean. I am not assuming, even temporarily, that there is a king of France when I reflect on the conditional *If the king of France is a serial killer, his mother will be ashamed of him*. And I am not assuming, even temporarily, that the king of France is a serial killer. I know that there is no king of France; why should I be assuming that he's a serial killer? Do I pretend to assume these things? No, I don't do that either. In fact in no pre-theoretical sense of "assumption" is the content of an *if*-clause being assumed. So what does Stalnaker mean by "assumption"?

   Might Stalnaker mean by "assuming" "taking it for granted"? I might take it for granted that there was a king of France if a speaker asserted the conditional, not myself knowing whether there was, but do I take it for granted that the king of France is a serial killer if a speaker asserts the conditional *If the king of France is a serial killer . . . ?* No, I don't, precisely because *the king of France is a serial killer* occurs in an *if* clause. I don't take the contents of *if* clauses for granted. So, on Stalnaker's theory of contexts, I cannot felicitously or appropriately assert *If the king of France is a serial killer, his mother will be ashamed of him*. Yet, surely, I can felicitously assert this conditional.

   What is worse, Stalnaker's position is inconsistent with his own view of conditionals. Consider for the moment that asserting ⟨*If P then Q*⟩ has the feature of requiring the common background assumptions that Stalnaker claims: the speaker temporarily assumes *P*, etc. Hence, according to Stalnaker, the speaker pragmatically presupposes *P*. But Stalnaker (1974: 208) writes, "if a speaker explicitly supposes something, he thereby indicates that he is not *pre*-supposing it, or taking it for granted. So when the speaker says 'if I realize later that *P*,' he indicates that he is not presupposing that he will realize later that *P*." So Stalnaker's (1974) account of the context of conditionals commits him to a speaker both presupposing and not presupposing the content of the *if* clause.

The fundamental problem with Stalnaker's analysis of the assertion of a conditional is that what motivates the analysis is the interesting but ultimately unsatisfactory view that an assertion of a conditional sentence is an assertion of the consequent $\langle B \rangle$ on the condition that $\langle A \rangle$ is true: $\langle \vdash (A \rightarrow B) \rangle$ is analyzed as $\langle A \vdash B \rangle$. If $\langle A \rangle$ is false, then there is no assertion. This is an obvious analogue of Strawson's view that when a presupposition is false, there is no true-or-false statement made. (Not surprisingly perhaps, it is the speech-act analogue to Stalnaker's (1968) account of the semantics of conditionals.) None of the attitudes of the speaker and addressee that Stalnaker has considered – believing, assuming, taking for granted – correctly characterizes the linguistic behavior or associated psychological states of speakers of a language, their attitudes toward what they say or hear. Stalnaker believed that in order to explain the presuppositions of assertions one should use the concept of "speaker's pretended presuppositions" to give a theory of linguistic contexts in which assertions are made. I believe, with Grice, that in order to explain the presuppositions of assertions, one should use the concept of "speaker's conversational implicata of an assertion." Stalnaker (1974: 202–3, n.3) never answered Sadock's counterexample to his theory of contexts.

11   Conclusion

It is peculiar that some of those who first noted the phenomena of accommodation have largely misunderstood their implications. The phenomena of accommodation show that the word "presupposition" misnames the linguistic facts. Referential *pre*suppositions are a special case of accommodations; accommodations are not a special case of presuppositions. What we want a logical and linguistic theory of is accommodation, not presupposition. Accommodations are linguistically primary; presuppositions are secondary – they are special cases in which $\langle t$ exists$\rangle$ is not merely accommodated as non-controversial for purposes of interpreting an assertion but also in which $\langle t$ exists$\rangle$ already belongs to the common ground. (The Newtonian motions that are primary and paradigmatic are those at constant speed in a straight line – at constant velocity – not those that require the application of a net force. Sadock's objection is to Stalnaker's account of presupposition as Galileo's objections are to Aristotle's account of motion.) A neo-Gricean theory of conversational implicature is a theory of one type of speaker's meaning; it is a theory of accommodation, or more broadly, as Levinson (2000a) has recently put it, of presumptive meanings. Non-controversiality, taking the speaker at his word, not commongroundedness, is the notion for understanding how the paradigm cases of assertions with "presuppositions" are interpreted by addressees.

According to the neo-Gricean account, the resources for an explanatory pragmatic theory of "presuppositional" inference consist in these elements: (a) the semantical non-specificity of *not*, non-specific between choice and exclusion negation understandings (see Atlas 1974, 1975, 1977b, Kempson 1975, 1988);

(b) a neo-Gricean mechanism for utterance-interpretation of semantically non-specific negative sentences (see Atlas 1979); (c) Atlas and Levinson's (1981) principles of non-controversial, default interpretations of statements containing singular terms that are Topic NPs; (d) a defensible Topic/Comment distinction for statements; (e) the Grice–Strawson Condition that permits a presuppositional inference to the referentiality of a singular term in a statement only if the term is a Topic NP (see Strawson 1964b: 92–5, Atlas 1988, 1989); and (f) (what I have not discussed here) the abandonment of theoretical preconceptions of the data that motivated the Projection Problem for Presupposition and presupposition cancellation by "metalinguistic" negation. (I have argued elsewhere (Atlas 1983, Atlas 2001) that so-called "presupposition canceling" data, e.g. *The king of France isn't bald – there is no king of France*, are not linguistically deviant or logically contradictory – as a matter of fact, they are consistent and linguistically normal and obviate the need for the "pragmatic ambiguity" of *not*.)

In this chapter I have argued for a shift in paradigm:

1 Accommodation is not a peripheral phenomenon of presupposition – it is the central phenomenon of presupposition.
2 Non-controversiality, not common knowledge, is the core notion that best describes the linguistic data of presuppositional assertions.
3 Pragmatic Intrusion (Levinson 1988, 2000) and Semantic Non-Specificity (Atlas 1974, 1975, etc.) show that the content/context distinction is a philosophical myth. It can do no philosophical work in the explanation of our linguistic knowledge of the presuppositions of assertions.[6]

This paper is dedicated to the memory of John Robert Purvis and to the memory of Karen Kossuth.

NOTES

1 So exclusion negation is not a presupposition "plug" in Karttunen's (1973) sense.
2 The assumption is, I have argued, false (see Atlas 1974, 1975, 1977b, 1978b, 1989; K. Bach 1987a; Kempson 1988; Horn 1989).
3 This assumption too, I have argued, is false. The free morpheme "not" does not create ambiguities in English. It is semantically non-specific with respect to scope or with respect to the logical difference between

exclusion and choice negation (see Zwicky and Sadock 1975; Atlas 1974, 1975, 1977b, 1978b, 1979, 1989; Kempson 1988, Horn 1989).

Happily the semantic non-specificity (generality) of "not" will not undermine Frege's argument, since he couched the argument in terms of **assertions** rather than **sentences**. A semantically negative **sentence** can be used to make a specific, choice negation **assertion**. Just so long as one treats **assertions** –

tokens of utterance-types in which a possible specification of a semantically non-specific sentence is achieved by the use of **collateral information** available to speakers and addressees (mutual "knowledge") in a **context** of utterance – as the carriers of presuppositions, Frege's argument for the preservation of referential presuppositions under main-verb negation in sentences of the form *Proper Name + Verb Phrase* will be sustained.

4   The proper explanation of the inference may appeal to entailment in some choice negation cases, e.g. *Geoffrey doesn't regret that P* $\Vdash$ *P*, but not in others; e.g. Horn (p.c. 2002) claims that entailment fails in the following case: *Geoffrey doesn't know for a fact that he can trust you* $\nVdash$ *Geoffrey can trust you*. I can hear Horn's example in both entailment and non-entailment ways. But the first-person, "quasi-performative" (Hunter 1990, Atlas 1995) version seems to me clearly a non-entailment:

I don't know for a fact that I can trust you $\nVdash$ *I can trust you*. So I shall distinguish the first-person, "know for a fact" sentences from the third-person "know that . . ." sentences.

5   The view of Atlas (1978a, 1979) bears a strong family resemblance, noted by Horn (1989: 433; 1992), to the views developed by the "London School," in their notions of "explicature" in Relevance Theory, and Kent Bach's notion of "impli*ci*ture"; see Kempson (1986, 1988), Sperber and Wilson (1986a), Carston (1988), Blakemore (1992), Recanati (1989, 1993), K. Bach (1994a), and papers in this volume by Bach, Carston, Horn, Recanati, and Wilson and Sperber. For early discusssions of Pragmatic Intrusion, see Katz (1972: 444–50) and Walker (1975).

6   I am indebted for comments on earlier drafts of this essay to Kent Bach, Laurence Goldstein, Larry Horn, Peter Ross, and Charles Young. They did the best they could to keep me from error.

3 Speech Acts

JERROLD SADOCK

When we speak we can do all sorts of things, from aspirating a consonant, to constructing a relative clause, to insulting a guest, to starting a war. These are all, pre-theoretically, speech acts – acts done in the process of speaking. The theory of speech acts, however, is especially concerned with those acts that are not completely covered under one or more of the major divisions of grammar – phonetics, phonology, morphology, syntax, semantics – or under some general theory of actions.

Even in cases in which a particular speech act is not completely described in grammar, formal features of the utterance used in carrying out the act might be quite directly tied to its accomplishment, as when we request something by uttering an imperative sentence or greet someone by saying "Hi!" Thus, there is clearly a conventional aspect to the study of speech acts. Sometimes, however, the achievement cannot be so directly tied to convention, as when we thank a guest by saying, "Oh, I love chocolates." There is no convention of English to the effect that stating that one loves chocolates counts as an act of thanking. In this case, the speaker's INTENTION in making the utterance and a recognition by the addressee of that intention under the conditions of utterance clearly plays an important role. Note that whether convention or intention seems paramount, success is not guaranteed. The person to whom the conventionalized greeting "Hi!" is addressed might not speak English, but some other language in which the uttered syllable means "Go away!," or the guest may not have brought chocolates at all, but candied fruit, in which cases these attempts to extend a greeting and give a compliment are likely to fail. On the other hand, failure, even in the face of contextual adversity, is also not guaranteed. Thus, one may succeed in greeting a foreigner who understands nothing of what is being said by making it clear through gesture and tone of voice that that is the intent. Much of speech act theory is therefore devoted to striking the proper balance between convention and intention.

Real-life acts of speech usually involve interpersonal relations of some kind: A speaker does something with respect to an audience by saying certain words to that audience. Thus it would seem that ethnographic studies of such relationships and the study of discourse should be central to speech act theory, but in fact, they are not. Such studies have been carried out rather independently of the concerns of those philosophers and linguists who have devoted their attention to speech acts. This is perhaps not a good thing, as Croft (1994) has argued, but since it is the case, anthropological and discourse-based approaches to speech acts will not be covered in this handbook entry.

1   Austin

The modern study of speech acts begins with Austin's (1962) engaging monograph *How to Do Things with Words*, the published version of his William James Lectures delivered at Harvard in 1955. This widely cited work starts with the observation that certain sorts of sentences, e.g., *I christen this ship the Joseph Stalin; I now pronounce you man and wife*, and the like, seem designed to **do** something, here to christen and wed, respectively, rather than merely to **say** something. Such sentences Austin dubbed PERFORMATIVES, in contrast to what he called CONSTATIVES, the descriptive sentences that until Austin were the principal concern of philosophers of language – sentences that seem, pretheoretically, at least, to be employed mainly for saying something rather than doing something.

While the distinction between performatives and constatives is often invoked in work on the law, in literary criticism, in political analysis, and in other areas, it is a distinction that Austin argued was **not** ultimately defensible. The point of Austin's lectures was, in fact, that every normal utterance has **both** a descriptive and an effective aspect: that saying something is also doing something.

1.1   Locutions, illocutions, and perlocutions

In place of the initial distinction between constatives and performatives, Austin substituted a three-way contrast among the kinds of acts that are performed when language is put to use, namely the distinction between locutionary, illocutionary, and perlocutionary acts, all of which are characteristic of most utterances, including standard examples of both performatives and constatives.

LOCUTIONARY ACTS, according to Austin, are acts **of** speaking, acts involved in the construction of speech, such as uttering certain sounds or making certain marks, using particular words and using them in conformity with the grammatical rules of a particular language and with certain senses and certain references as determined by the rules of the language from which they are drawn.

ILLOCUTIONARY ACTS, Austin's central innovation, are acts done **in** speaking (hence **il**locutionary), including and especially that sort of act that is the apparent purpose for using a performative sentence: christening, marrying, and so forth. Austin called attention to the fact that acts of stating or asserting, which are presumably illocutionary acts, are characteristic of the use of canonical constatives, and such sentences are, by assumption, not performatives. Furthermore, acts of ordering or requesting are typically accomplished by using imperative sentences, and acts of asking whether something is the case are properly accomplished by using interrogative sentences, though such forms are at best very dubious examples of performative sentences. In Lecture XXI of Austin (1962), the conclusion was drawn that the locutionary aspect of speaking is what we attend to most in the case of constatives, while in the case of the standard examples of performative sentences, we attend as much as possible to the illocution.

The third of Austin's categories of acts is the PERLOCUTIONARY ACT, which is a consequence or by-product of speaking, whether intended or not. As the name is designed to suggest, perlocutions are acts performed **by** speaking. According to Austin, perlocutionary acts consist in the production of effects upon the thoughts, feelings, or actions of the addressee(s), speaker, or other parties, such as causing people to refer to a certain ship as the Joseph Stalin, producing the belief that Sam and Mary should be considered man and wife, convincing an addressee of the truth of a statement, causing an addressee to feel a requirement to do something, and so on.

Austin (1962: 101) illustrates the distinction between these kinds of acts with the (now politically incorrect) example of saying "Shoot her!," which he trisects as follows:

Act (A) or Locution
  He said to me "Shoot her!" meaning by *shoot* "shoot" and referring by *her* to "her."

Act (B) or Illocution
  He urged (or advised, ordered, etc.) me to shoot her.

Act (C) or Perlocution
  He persuaded me to shoot her.

Though it is crucial under Austin's system that we be able to distinguish fairly sharply between the three categories, it is often difficult in practice to draw the requisite lines. Especially irksome are the problems of separating illocutions and locutions, on the one hand, and illocutions and perlocutions on the other, the latter being the most troublesome problem according to Austin himself.

Austin's main suggestion for discriminating between an illocution and a perlocution was that the former is "*conventional*, in the sense that at least it could be made explicit by the performative formula; but the latter could not" (Austin 1962: 103). This, however, is more a characterization of **possible** illocutionary act than a practicable test for the illocution of a particular sentence or an utterance of it. While the test can give direct evidence as to what is **not** an illocutionary act, it fails to tell us for sure what the illocution is. If, for example, someone says "The bull is about to charge," and thereby warns the addressee of impending danger, do we say that the speech act of warning is here an illocutionary act of warning because the speaker **could** have said "I warn you that the bull is about to charge"? Another reasonable interpretation would be that in this case, the warning of the addressee, i.e., the production of a feeling of alarm, is a perlocutionary by-product of asserting that the bull is about to charge. Many authors, such as Searle (1969, 1975a) and Allan (1998), seem to accept the idea that potential expression by means of a performative sentence is a sufficient criterion for the recognition of illocutions, while others, e.g. Sadock (1977), do not. Austin himself says that to be an illocutionary act it must also be the case that the **means** of accomplishing it are conventional.

Though a great many subsequent discussions of illocutions are couched within some version of Austin's theory that illocutionary acts are just those speech acts that could have been accomplished by means of an explicit performative, there are examples, such as threatening, that remain problematic. Nearly every authority who has touched on the subject of threats departs from the Austinian identification of illocutionary acts with potential performatives, since threatening seems like an illocutionary act but we cannot threaten by saying, for example, "I threaten you with a failing grade."

As for the distinction between the locutionary act of using particular words and constructions with particular meanings and the illocution performed in using that locution, Austin says that there is a difference between the locutionary MEANING and the illocutionary FORCE of the utterance. Without independent knowledge of the use of these two words in this context, however, the criterion seems circular. The contrast between locution and illocution is often intuitively clear, but problems and controversies arise in the case of performative sentences such as *I christen this ship the Joseph Stalin.* Is the performative prefix *I christen* to be excluded from the locutionary act or included within it? If it is included, is the primary illocutionary act that is done in uttering this sentence to **state** that one christens? Austin presumably would have said that to utter these words **is** to christen, not to state that one christens, but Allan (1998), for example, insists that the primary illocution is to state something.

There is a considerable literature on the validity and determination of the differences among locutions, illocutions, and perlocutions, some of which will be discussed or mentioned below.

1.2   The doctrine of infelicities

An important aspect of Austin's inquiry concerns the kinds of imperfections to which speech acts are prey. The motivation for this interest in the way things can go wrong is that, at first sight, it appears that constatives are just those utterances that are false when they fail, whereas failed performatives are not aptly described as false, but rather as improper, unsuccessful, or, in general, INFELICITOUS. If, for example, a passing inebriate picks up a bottle, smashes it on the prow of a nearby ship, and says, "I christen this ship the Joseph Stalin," we would not ordinarily say that he or she has said something false, whereas if I **describe** that event by saying, "The passerby christened the ship," I could properly be blamed for uttering a falsehood.

Austin distinguished three broad categories of infelicities:

A. Misinvocations, which disallow a purported act. For example, a random individual saying the words of the marriage ceremony is disallowed from performing it. Similarly, no purported speech act of banishment can succeed in our society because such an act is not allowed within it.

B. Misexecutions, in which the act is vitiated by errors or omissions, including examples in which an appropriate authority pronounces a couple man and wife, but uses the wrong names or fails to complete the ceremony by signing the legal documents. Here, as in the case of misinvocations, the purported act does not take place.

C. Abuses, where the act succeeds, but the participants do not have the ordinary and expected thoughts and feelings associated with the happy performance of such an act. Insincere promises, mendacious findings of fact, unfelt congratulations, apologies, etc. come under this rubric.

As interesting and influential on subsequent investigations as the doctrine of infelicities is, Austin concluded that it failed to yield a crucial difference between performatives and constatives. In the case of both there is a dimension of felicity that requires a certain correspondence with "the facts." With illocutionary acts of assertion, statement, and the like, we happen to call correspondence with the facts **truth** and a lack of it **falsity**, whereas in the case of other kinds of illocutions, we do not use those particular words. Acts of asserting, stating, and the like can also be unhappy in the manner of performatives when, for example, the speaker does not believe what he or she asserts, even if it happens to be true.

1.3 The performative formula

Austin investigated the possibility of defining performative utterances in terms of a grammatical formula for performatives. The formula has a first person singular subject and an active verb in the simple present tense that makes explicit the illocutionary act that the speaker intends to accomplish in uttering the sentence. Additionally, the formula can contain the self-referential adverb *hereby:*

(1) "I (hereby) verb-present-active X . . ."

Such forms he calls EXPLICIT PERFORMATIVES, opposing them with PRIMARY PERFORMATIVES (rather than with implicit or inexplicit performatives.) But as Austin shows, the formula is not a sufficient criterion, at least without the adverb *hereby*, since in general sentences that fit the formula can be descriptive of activities under a variety of circumstances, e.g., *I bet him every morning that it will rain*, or *On page 49 I protest against the verdict*. Nor is the formula a necessary criterion, since there are many forms that differ from this canon and nevertheless seem intuitively to be explicit performatives. There are, for example, passive sentences like *You are fired*, and cases in which the subject is not first person, e.g., *The court finds you guilty*. Austin therefore came to the conclusion that the performative formula was neither a necessary nor a sufficient condition for the recognition of those sentences we might want to call performatives.

There still are numerous clear cases of performative formulae, but the fact that explicit performatives seem to shade off into constatives and other non-performative sentence types greatly weakens their utility as a litmus for illocutionary force, since there are clear cases of illocutionary acts that **cannot** be accomplished in terms of an explicit performative formulae, e.g., **I fire you*. It can also be argued that the illocutionary act performed in uttering a sentence in one or another of the sentential moods (see below) cannot be accomplished by uttering a performative formula, since any such sentence will necessarily be more specific than what is accomplished by the use of the simpler sentence. For example, the illocutionary act that is accomplished by uttering *Come here!* can be reasonably taken to be not an order, request, command, suggestion, or demand, but some more general act of which all of these are more specific versions, a general act for which there is no English verb that can be used in the performative formula. (Compare Alston's notion of ILLOCUTIONARY ACT POTENTIAL discussed below.)

2   The Influence of Grice

Grice's influential articles (1957, 1967), while not dealing directly with the problems that occupied Austin, nevertheless have had a profound influence on speech act theory. In the earlier of these papers, Grice promulgated the idea that ordinary communication takes place not directly by means of convention, but in virtue of a speaker's evincing certain intentions and getting his or her audience to recognize those intentions (and to recognize that it was the speaker's intention to secure this recognition). This holds, Grice suggested, both for speech and for other sorts of intentional communicative acts. In his view, the utterance is not in itself communicative, but only provides clues to the intentions of the speaker.

A later part of Grice's program spelled out how various maxims of cooperative behavior are exploited by speakers to secure recognition of the speaker's intentions in uttering certain words under particular circumstances. Grice distinguished between what is SAID in making an utterance, that which determines the truth value of the contribution, and the total of what is communicated. Things that are communicated beyond what is said (in the technical sense)

Grice called IMPLICATURES, and those implicatures that depend upon the assumption that the speaker is being cooperative he called CONVERSATIONAL IMPLICATURES (see Horn, this volume).

2.1 Strawson's objection to Austin

Strawson (1971) criticized the Austinian view as wrongly identifying speech acts such as christening and marrying as typical of the way language works. He pointed out that such illocutionary acts ordinarily take place in highly formal, ritualistic, or ceremonial situations such as ship launchings and weddings. These do indeed involve convention, Strawson conceded, but what one says on such occasions is part of a formalized proceeding rather than an example of ordinary communicative behavior. He argued that for more commonplace speech acts, such as are accomplished by uttering declarative sentences of various sorts, the act succeeds by Gricean means – by arousing in the addressee the awareness that it was the speaker's intention to achieve a certain communicative goal and to get the addressee to reach this conclusion on the basis of his or her having produced a particular utterance.

Warnock (1973) and Urmson (1977) go one step farther than Strawson, arguing in essence that since the act of bidding in bridge, for example, is part of the institution of bridge, it does not even belong to the institution of (ordinary) language (see Bird 1994 for a criticism of this point of view).

2.2 Searle's defense of Austin

Searle 1969, a work that is second only to Austin's in its influence on speech act theory, presents a neo-Austinian analysis in which convention once again looms large, contra Grice and Strawson. While not denying the role of Gricean intentions in communication, Searle argued that such an account is incomplete because (1) it fails to distinguish communication that proceeds by using meanings of the kind that only natural languages make available, and (2) it fails to distinguish between acts that succeed solely by means of getting the addressee to recognize the speaker's intention to achieve a certain (perlocutionary) effect and those for which that recognition is "in virtue of (by means of) H[earer]'s knowledge of (certain of) the rules governing (the elements of) [the uttered sentence] T" (Searle 1969: 49–50). Searle labels these ILLOCUTIONARY EFFECTS.

Of the various locutionary acts that Austin mentions, Searle singled out the PROPOSITIONAL ACT as especially important. This, in turn, consists of two components: an ACT OF REFERENCE, in which a speaker picks out or identifies a particular object through the use of a definite noun phrase, and a PREDICATION, which Searle did not see as a separate locutionary act (or any other kind of speech act), but only as a component of the total speech act, which for him is the illocutionary force combined with the propositional content.

Searle (1969) observed that quite often the form of an utterance displays bipartite structure, one part of which determines the propositional act, and the other part the illocutionary act. The parts of an utterance that together are used by a speaker to signal the propositional act he symbolized as *p*. Formal features of the utterance that determine the literal illocutionary force (which are often fairly complex) he called the ILLOCUTIONARY FORCE INDICATING DEVICE (IFID), which he symbolized as *F*. The form of a complete utterance used to accomplish a complete speech act, including the propositional portion of the locution and the IFID, he therefore wrote as:

(2) $F(p)$.

Among Searle's arguments for the validity of this formula was the claim that negation can be either internal or external to the IFID, at least at the abstract level of grammatical analysis that Chomsky (1965) called deep structure. Thus, if *p* is (underlyingly) *I will come* and *F* is *I promise*, there are two negations, namely *I promise not to come* and *I do not promise to come*, the second of which Searle said must be construed as an illocutionary act of refusing to promise something, not as an illocutionary act of asserting, stating, or describing oneself as not making a certain promise.

A central part of Searle's program is the idea that "speaking a language is performing acts according to rules" (Searle 1969: 36–7), where by "rule" he means a conventional association between a certain kind of act and its socially determined consequences. These are CONSTITUTIVE RULES, he said, in the same sense that the rules of chess are constitutive of the game itself. To perform an illocutionary act, according to Searle, is to follow certain conventional rules that are constitutive of that kind of act. In order to discover the rules, Searle, following Austin, proposed to examine the conditions that must obtain for an illocutionary act to be felicitously performed. For each such condition on the felicitous performance of the act in question, he proposed that there is a rule to the effect that the IFID should only be uttered if that felicity condition is satisfied. The project was carried out in detail for promises, a kind of illocution that Searle described as "fairly formal and well articulated" (Searle 1969: 54), and from which "many of the lessons learned . . . are of general application" (Searle 1969: 54). For the illocutionary act of promising, the rules that he postulated are (Searle 1969: 63):

1   *Pr* (the IFID for promising) is to be uttered only in the context of a sentence (or larger stretch of discourse) T the utterance of which predicates some future act A of S.
2   *Pr* is to be uttered only if the hearer H would prefer S's doing A to his not doing A, and S believes hearer H would prefer S's doing A to his not doing A.
3   *Pr* is to be uttered only if it is not obvious to both S and H that S will do A in the normal course of events.
4   *Pr* is to be uttered only if S intends to do A.
5   The utterance of *Pr* counts as the undertaking of an obligation to do A.

Rule 1 Searle called the PROPOSITONAL CONTENT RULE; rules 2 and 3 are PRE-PARATORY RULES; rule 4 is a SINCERITY RULE; and rule 5 is the ESSENTIAL RULE. Searle found a similar set of rules to be operative in the case of other kinds of illocutions, as shown in the following table for assertion, thanking, and warning:

(3)

	Assert	*Thank (for)*	*Warn*
Propositional content	Any proposition *p*	Past act *A* done by *H*.	Future event or state, etc., *E*.
Preparatory	1. *S* has evidence (reasons, etc.) for the truth of *p*. 2. It is not obvious to both *S* and *H* that *H* knows (does not need to be reminded of, etc.) *p*.	*A* benefits *S* and *S* believes *A* benefits *S*.	1. *H* has reason to believe *E* will occur and is not in *H*'s interest. 2. It is not obvious to both *S* and *H* that *E* will occur.
Sincerity	*S* believes *p*.	*S* feels grateful or appreciative for *A*.	*S* believes *E* is not in *H*'s best interest.
Essential	Counts as an undertaking that *p* represents an actual state of affairs.	Counts as an expression of gratitude or appreciation.	Counts as an undertaking to the effect that *E* is not in *H*'s best interest.

Note that violations of Searle's preparatory conditions produce infelicities of Austin's type A, misinvocations. In a similar way, violations of the sincerity conditions correspond more or less directly to Austin's class Γ of infelicities, the abuses that do not nullify or vitiate the illocutionary act but nevertheless make it flawed. Neither the propositional content condition nor – importantly – the essential condition can be related very clearly to Austin's taxonomy of infelicities.

Two further features of Searle's (1969) theory deserve mention. First, he accepted Austin's idea that a sufficient test for illocutionary acts is that they **could** have been performed by uttering an explicit performative. Thus, he said that more than one illocutionary act can be accomplished by the utterance of a single, non-compound sentence, giving as an example the case of a wife who says at a party, "It's really quite late," and in doing so simultaneously performs the illocutionary act of stating a fact and the illocutionary act of making a suggestion equivalent to "I suggest that we go home." Elsewhere, Searle suggested that illocutionary acts can be cascaded, so to speak. Making a particular utterance may immediately accomplish one illocutionary act, e.g., stating something, which act, having been accomplished, may result in the accomplishment of a corollary illocutionary act, e.g., warning. Second, he observed that an illocutionary act is typically performed with a certain perlocutionary effect in mind, an effect that follows from the essential condition: "Thus requesting is, as a matter of its essential condition, an attempt to get the hearer to do something . . ." (Searle 1969: 71). Searle doubted that a reduction of illocutions to associated perlocutionary effects could be accomplished, but Austin's worry about the distinction between these two categories is highlighted by this possibility.

3   Illocutionary Act Potential

An important improvement on the view expressed by Austin and elaborated by Searle is developed in a number of works by Alston (see Alston 1964, 1994, and the works cited therein). If someone utters a declarative sentence like "This dog bites," one can, depending on the circumstances, be properly described as having asserted, warned, admitted, testified, rendered a finding, and so on. Insofar as any of these acts could have been made explicit in terms of an explicit performative such as *I assert that this dog bites*; *I warn you that this dog bites*; *I admit that this dog bites*; and so on, all of these should count as different illocutionary acts that can be performed by uttering one and the same sentence. Are we to say, then, that the sentence itself is multiply ambiguous with respect to illocutionary force? Should we postulate several (or perhaps many) different *F*s in the Searlean analysis $F(p)$, each corresponding to a specific illocutionary force? Given that the sentence has an invariable form and that the various specific illocutionary acts that are standardly accomplished by using it hardly seem like an arbitrary collection, an analysis in terms of ambiguity seems wrong. And yet, this case seems qualitatively different from the case of uttering "This dog bites," with the intent, perhaps perfectly clear in a given situation, of getting the addressee to put a muzzle on the dog, a case in which, once again, one might have said, "I request that you muzzle this dog because it bites" (see below under INDIRECT SPEECH ACTS).

Alston's suggestion was to recognize that the conventions of the language are such that a declarative sentence is suited to the production of a certain

range of illocutionary acts and not others. What particular illocutionary act is brought off ordinarily depends on the particular circumstances, as well as the form of the uttered sentence, but the sentence itself, standardly, because of rules of the language, has the potential, when uttered, to communicate some things and not others. It has, in other words, a single ILLOCUTIONARY ACT POTENTIAL that is closely and conventionally associated with its form.

3.1   *Strawson redux: Bach and Harnish (1979)*

Bach and Harnish (1979) completely rejected Searle's program for making constitutive rules central, and proposed to substitute a carefully worked-out version of Strawson's earlier, intention-centered theory. They followed Strawson in distinguishing between ceremonial acts like christening and marrying, for which convention is taken to be the primary illocutionary mechanism, and the case of non-ceremonial acts like asking and stating, which they label COMMUNICATIVE, and for which they assume that intention is crucial to the accomplishment of the illocutionary act. Their contribution was threefold: (1) to suggest a very general SPEECH ACT SCHEMA (SAS) for communicative illocutionary acts, (2) to show how inferences based on MUTUAL CONTEXTUAL BELIEFS (MCBs) play a role in communicative speech acts, and (3) to make detailed use of Grice's notion of conversational implicature in fleshing out the theory.

The most general form of SAS consists of the following ordered steps:

(4)a.   S is uttering *e*.
   b.   S means . . . by *e*.
   c.   S is saying so-and-so.
   d.   S is doing such-and-such.

In each phase of the interpretation, the derived inference follows from the previous conclusion plus general rules. Premise (4a) follows from hearing the speaker utter *e*, plus the hearer's knowledge of the language, and (4b) follows from (4a) plus the knowledge that in this language, *e* means . . . Then (4c) follows from (4b), supplemented with the assumption that S is speaking literally plus the knowledge that there are certain MCBs in the context in which *e* has been uttered. The reasoning to the conclusion (4d) – that S is doing such-and-such in uttering *e* – involves the previous conclusion, other MCBs, and what Bach and Harnish (1979: 7) call the COMMUNICATIVE PRESUMPTION:

> Communicative Presumption: The mutual belief in CL [the linguistic community] that whenever a member S says something in L to another member H, he is doing so with some recognizable illocutionary intent.

The way this works for Bach and Harnish is that the sentences of L belong, as a matter of locution, to a limited range of sentence types (see below) that are formally connected with the mood of the sentence, and that knowledge of *L* includes knowledge that the locutionary act of uttering a sentence of a certain sentence type is only compatible with the expression of certain sorts of feelings. Uttering a declarative sentence that expresses the proposition *p*, for example, is only compatible with a belief on the part of the speaker that *p*, and is therefore suitable only to illocutionary acts that fit with the speaker's having such a belief, e.g., asserting that *p*, stating that *p*, and so on.

Various additional assumptions are made to accommodate non-literal (e.g., sarcastic or metaphorical) speech acts, and still others are needed for INDIRECT SPEECH ACTS (see below). As with most theories that take inferencing to be a central notion in deriving the force of utterances, quite a few steps are needed to work out the illocution in Bach and Harnish's system.

3.2   *The classification of illocutionary acts*

In his last chapter, Austin (1962) presents a preliminary, intuitive, five-way taxonomy of illocutionary acts that Austin himself admitted was neither particularly well motivated nor always unambiguous in its application to particular examples. Since he believed that illocutionary acts could always be made explicit through the use of performative sentences, a taxonomy of illocutionary acts could therefore be couched in terms of an analysis of the various potentially performative verbs of English, which he estimated to number between 10^3 and 10^4. Austin's five classes, a brief explanation of each, and a few examples of each are as follows:

1   VERDICTIVES: acts that consist of delivering a finding, e.g., *acquit*, *hold* (as a matter of law), *read something as*, etc.
2   EXERCITIVES: acts of giving a decision for or against a course of action, e.g., *appoint, dismiss, order, sentence*, etc.
3   COMMISSIVES: acts whose point is to commit the speaker to a course of action, e.g., *contract, give one's word, declare one's intention*, etc.
4   BEHABITIVES: expressions of attitudes toward the conduct, fortunes, or attitudes of others, e.g., *apologize, thank, congratulate, welcome*, etc.
5   EXPOSITIVES: acts of expounding of views, conducting of arguments, and clarifying, e.g., *deny, inform, concede, refer*, etc.

The ungrounded nature, unclarity, and overlap of these classes has led to a sizable number of attempts to improve on Austin's taxonomy. Some of the more important of these, as well as discussions of the principles that might be used for classifying illocutionary acts, are to be found in Vendler (1972), Fraser (1974a), Searle (1975b), Katz (1977), McCawley (1977), Bach and Harnish (1979), Ballmer and Brennenstuhl (1981), Wierzbicka (1987), Croft (1994), Sadock (1994), and Allan (1998). It seems clear just from the length of this list and the fact that the efforts at classification continue apace that there is no firm agreement on the ultimate taxonomic system for illocutionary acts or performative verbs.

There seem in general to be two types of criteria that have been used to classify speech acts, namely formal/grammatical features and semantic/ pragmatic features.

Vendler (1972) and Fraser (1974a) based their respective arrangements on the grammatical properties of the complements that performative verbs take. Thus, verbs of promising and requesting generally take *for . . . to* complements (*I promise to retire early, I order you to desist*), whereas verbs of stating ordinarily do not (**I assert to retire early, *I explain you to be arrogant*). Verbs of inquiring take subordinate *wh*-complements (*I hereby ask you whether you own such a knife*), whereas verbs of promising do not (**I promise whether I will help you*), and so on. McCawley (1977) based his classification on such grammatical properties as whether verbs can occur as performatives in the passive and what sorts of expressions the verbs can be complements of. He observed, for example, that what he called advisories (a subclass of Austin's exercitives) occur comfortably in the passive (*You are hereby advised to resign*), whereas behabitives do not (**You are hereby apologized to*). His class of operatives (another subset of Austin's exercitives) do not occur performatively as complements of *would like to* (**I would like to baptise you Kimberly Ann, I would (hereby) like to sustain your objection*), whereas McCawley's class of advisories (yet another subclass of exercitives) do occur in this environment (*I would like to inform you that you are free to leave*).

Searle (1975b) presented a taxonomy of illocutionary acts based on a number of essentially pragmatic parameters, some of which are closely related to the felicity conditions of his earlier work, but some of which were introduced just for the purposes of classification. The most important of the added parameters is what Searle called DIRECTION OF FIT. This has to do with whether the words are supposed to fit the facts of the world or whether the world is supposed to come to fit the words. There are four values: words-to-world, world-to-words, neither, and both. Ballmer and Brennenstuhl (1981), as well as Wierzbicka (1987), are compendious treatments of the meta-vocabulary for speech acts classified largely on intuitively determined semantic similarities among the classes.

Some authors combine the two modes. Thus, Sadock (1994) sketched a system that is designed to conform to the formal properties of the basic sentence types (see below), but suggests that such a classification might be forthcoming from an examination of three cognitive dimensions that he called the REPRESENTATIONAL DIMENSION, the AFFECTIVE DIMENSION, and the EFFECTIVE DIMENSION. Harnish (1994) also has both formal and functional dimensions in his classificatory scheme for moods. For him, a mood is a conjunction of grammatical form, locution, and fit of the world to the locution.

In nearly all of these studies, there are many more dimensions than are needed to form a taxonomy with a small number of basic categories. Searle (1975b), for example, has a dozen different dimensions, each with several values, that would yield, in principle, tens of thousands of categories. It has therefore been up to the analyst to choose which dimensions to foreground so as to determine the larger groups and which to use only for the determination of finer divisions.

It is interesting to note that in almost all of the schemes that have been put forward, the imprint of Austin's original, highly intuitive compartmentalization is clearly visible. Austin's class of commissives, for example, seems to survive intact on everyone's list of basic illocutionary types.

3.3   Speech acts and grammar

Working within the framework of Transformational Grammar (TG), Katz and Postal (1964) proposed that a grammar of this kind should be constructed in such a way that transformational rules not change meaning. In a grammar that is constrained in this way, the deep structure would be all that is required for semantic interpretation. Obvious counterexamples to the proposal in the early TG literature included the rules that derived imperative and interrogative sentences from deep structures identical to those of the corresponding declarative sentences. Such transformations obviously change meaning, at least in a broad sense of the word that would count illocutionary force as a part of meaning. Katz and Postal proposed to eliminate these counterexamples by including markers of force in the deep structures of imperative and interrogative sentences. The transformations in question would apply only in the presence of these markers and would, therefore, not change meaning. In a footnote (Katz and Postal 1964: 149), they also considered the possibility that instead of an unanalyzed marker, the deep structures of interrogative and imperative sentences might include whole performative clauses. Thus the deep structure of *Go home!* would be similar to that of the explicit performative sentence *I request that you go home*, and the deep structure of *Did you go home?* would be similar to the performative *I ask you whether you went home*.

Ross (1970a), pursuing this idea within the framework of Generative Semantics, proposed to extend the proposal to declarative sentences as well, thus modeling, in grammatical terms, Austin's and Searle's suggestion that all normal sentences have both a locutionary and an illocutionary aspect. The underlying performative clause in Ross's proposal would correspond to Searle's illocutionary operator F, and its deep structure object clause would correspond to Searle's propositional content, p. Ross provided a number of arguments for the existence of such abstract performative clauses; some of these pointed to the existence of a higher verb of speaking, some to an element referring to the speaker, and some to an element referring to the addressee. Additional arguments of a similar sort were adduced by Sadock (1969, 1974), Davison (1973), and others.

The grammatical arguments for abstract performative clauses were generally of the following form:

(5)a.   P is a property characteristic of clauses that are subordinate to a higher clause of form F.

  b.   P', a special case of P, is found in main clauses.

   c.   P′ would be explained if in underlying structure, the main clause is subordinate to a higher clause of the form F′.

   d.   There exists an abstract performative clause of the form F′ that provides just the right environment for the occurrence of P′.

A typical instance of this argument from Ross (1970a) is this:

(6)a.   The reflexive pronoun in the sentence *Nancy claimed that the book was written by Fred and herself* requires coreference with the subject of a higher verb of speaking, cf. **Alfred claimed that the book was written by Fred and herself.*

   b.   First person reflexive pronouns of this kind can be found in main clauses: *This book was written by Fred and myself/*herself.*

   c.   This use of the reflexive would be explained if in deep structure the main clause were subordinate to a higher clause with a first person subject and a verb of speaking.

   d.   An abstract performative clause *I state that* provides just the right environment.

This PERFORMATIVE HYPOTHESIS, as it came to be called, was quickly and roundly condemned both on linguistic and on philosophical grounds.

Numerous problems with the syntactic arguments for the performative hypothesis were adduced by Anderson (1971a), Fraser (1974b), Leech (1976), and Mittwoch (1976, 1977), among others. For example, an argument that was intensively investigated in Davison (1973) has to do with the distribution of speech act adverbials like *frankly* in *Frankly, it's terrible.* Both the occurrence and interpretation of this adverbial are apparently explained if we assume that the non-performative form is derived from a performative like *I tell you frankly that it is terrible* (Sadock 1974). But Mittwoch (1977) pointed to the existence of sentences like (6), in which there is a similar use of *frankly* but postulating an abstract performative clause dominating the *because* clause is out of the question, since it would be at odds with the tenets of the performative hypothesis itself.

(7)   I won't eat any because, frankly, it's terrible.

McCawley (1985) responded to these syntactic challenges (and some of the semantic challenges discussed below) arguing that certain of these are not in fact problems and that the remainder, while real, only count as refutation if one is willing to give up entirely on making sense of the facts that the performative hypothesis does give an account of: "The problems [the performative hypothesis] was intended to deal with have not been solved so much as ignored" (McCawley 1985: 61).

Philosophically, the major objection is that the performative hypothesis seems to lead to an unresolvable contradiction with regard to truth conditions. The argument, with variations, is something like the following:

(8)a.   Either a performative clause is part of the semantics of a sentence or it is not.

   b.   If it is not part of the semantic form, then a performative sentence is not subject to judgments of truth or falsity, as Austin suggested.

   c.   But under the performative hypothesis, a simple declarative such as *It is raining* has a performative clause in deep structure and is therefore not subject to judgments of truth or falsity, which seems absurd.

   d.   If performative clauses are part of the semantics and are subject to judgments of truth and falsity, then a performative sentence such as *I christen this ship the Joseph Stalin* is true just in case the speaker succeeds in christening the ship by uttering the sentence.

   e.   But under the performative hypothesis, a simple declarative such as *It is raining* has a performative clause in deep structure and is therefore true just in case the speaker succeeds in asserting that it is raining by uttering the sentence, regardless of whether it is raining or not. This also seems absurd.

   f.   In either case we are led to an absurdity, and therefore, declarative sentences cannot be taken to be dominated by abstract performative clauses.

Boër and Lycan (1980) presented a detailed and sophisticated version of this argument based on the use of speech act adverbials of the kind discussed by Davison (1973) in arguing for abstract performatives. But Sadock (1985) rebutted these philosophical arguments on the grounds that they involved an equivocation on the notion of truth, sometimes taking this to be the abstract truth of a proposition and sometimes as the truth of an assertion made in uttering a sentence. The latter, said Sadock, can be understood as the truth of the complement of an overt or abstract assertive performative clause. Thus both *It is raining* and *I assert that it is raining* are used to assert that it is raining and are true, qua assertions, only if it is, in fact, raining. The controversy is discussed at length in Levinson (1983).

4   Indirect Speech Acts

As discussed above, Searle (1969) distinguished between effects that are achieved by getting the hearer to recognize that the rules governing the use of an illocutionary force indicating device are in effect, which he called illocutionary effects, and those effects that are achieved indirectly as by-products of the total speech act, for which he reserved the term perlocutionary effects. But the effect might be very similar and we might use the same words to describe it, whether it is an illocutionary or perlocutionary effect. A speaker might, for example, warn a hearer by uttering an explicit warning that a bull is about to charge, in which case we have an illocutionary effect of warning. Alternatively, a speaker might warn the addressee (in the sense of making him feel alarmed) by making a statement to the effect that the bull is about to charge, producing in the addressee an illocutionary effect of understanding that the speaker is stating that the bull is about to charge, which in turn, under the right circumstances, causes him or her to be warned. In this case, the effect of warning is a perlocutionary effect.

Sadock (1970, 1972) argued that, in certain cases, there was some conventional indication in the form of the utterance of what might be taken as an indirect, perlocutionary effect. The central sort of example is the utterance at a dinner table of an apparent question like "Could you pass the salt?" The utterance appears to be a question, but when produced at a dinner table, a commonly achieved effect is to arouse in the addressee a feeling of obligation to pass the salt. Sadock noticed that this sort of question can also include the word *please* sentence internally, which indicates clearly the intention of the speaker to produce the kind of effect that illocutionary acts of requesting typically do. It is important to notice that not all questions that can provoke such a feeling in the addressee can felicitously include this word. Thus *Isn't it cold in here* can, given the right circumstances, cause an addressee to feel obligated to close a window, light a fire in the fireplace, fetch a blanket, or the like. But even when intended to produce such results, one cannot say in idiomatic English **Isn't it please cold in here*. Sadock argued that examples of the former kind are conventionalized in a sense sufficient to justify analyzing the intended effect as directly illocutionary rather than as an indirect perlocutionary effect.

This idea soon came under attack. Gordon and Lakoff (1971) made the important observation that there is a high degree of systematicity connecting the apparent content of the utterance and the kind of speech act that can be indirectly accomplished through its utterance. Specifically, they observed that a common strategy for indirectly achieving an illocutionary effect is to assert a speaker-based sincerity condition governing that sort of illocutionary act or to question a hearer-based sincerity condition. Thus, an act of requesting has among its felicity conditions: (1) the requirement that the speaker desires the addressee to perform the requested action and (2) that the speaker believes that the hearer is able to carry out the action. The following are, therefore, rather ordinary ways of accomplishing the effect of a request without using an imperative:

(9) I'd like you to (please) take out the garbage.

(10) Can you (please) take out the garbage?

But while Gordon and Lakoff's scheme was fairly successful in predicting what the ordinary ways of accomplishing illocutionary effects indirectly could be, it said nothing about which particular **forms** could be used to do it, some of which, as Sadock had pointed out, are accompanied by grammatical peculiarities that even near paraphrases do not have. Thus while (9) and (10) comfortably accept the word *please* before the verb, neither of the following sounds nearly as good:

(11)   ?I desire for you to please take out the garbage

(12)   ?Are you able to please take out the garbage

The diminished acceptability of such examples cannot be due to the impossibility of their being used to get across the equivalent of a request; both of them can be so used, of course, since the illocutionary effect of any communicative speech act can be accomplished by practically any utterance, given the right external circumstances.

Several conceptually similar solutions to this grammatical problem have appeared. The approach shared by all of the opponents of the treatment of certain indirect speech acts as idioms makes use of some version of Grice's idea of conversational implicature, a special type of perlocutionary effect that relies for its success on principles of cooperativity of a very general sort. The Gricean chain of reasoning that can lead from the utterance of a question to the implication of a request might include something like the following steps:

(13)a.   The speaker has asked about a certain ability of mine.
   b.   It is clear that I have that ability.
   c.   Therefore, if the speaker is being cooperative, she must have intended something beyond a mere question concerning my abilities.
   d.   My being able to pass the salt is a prerequisite (a preparatory condition) to my actually passing it.
   e.   We are at the moment eating at the dinner table.
   f.   People often like to add salt to their food.
   g.   The speaker cannot add salt to her food unless she can reach it.
   h.   I see that she cannot reach the salt at the moment.
   i.   Therefore, by uttering *Can you pass the salt?* she is therefore requesting that I pass the salt to her.

Searle (1975a) suggested that, while not idioms, as Sadock (1972) claimed, the forms with special grammar are *idiomatic* ways of accomplishing a subsidiary illocutionary goal. Bach and Harnish (1979) set up a notion of illocutionary standardization for such cases, but handled the grammatical facts by drumming difficult examples out of the language. The perfectly acceptable examples (9) and (10) are taken by them to be not technically grammatical, a bold approach that has been resurrected by Bertolet (1994).

Morgan's (1978) important paper offered a synthesis of these proposals that has been taken up in one form or another by several researchers, e.g., Horn and Bayer (1984). Morgan distinguished between conventions of meaning and conventions of usage, arguing that idioms belong in the first category but standardized indirect speech acts belong in the latter. Since there is frequently a measure of conventionalization involved, even if it does not count as a convention of meaning but rather a convention about the use of the language, Morgan suggested that a pure Gricean account is inappropriate. The Gricean inference is, in his words, SHORT-CIRCUITED in such a case, and the addressee is not burdened with an actual calculation to the intended effect but can jump directly to it by means of the convention of use. As for the special grammatical properties that certain conventionalized usage displays, Morgan suggested that some formal features can be a function of conventional use, rather than the conventional meaning. Examples that do not present special formal properties would be treated by him as non-conventional, non-short-circuited implicatures.

4.1 Indirect speech acts and politeness

Most theories of indirect speech acts barely touch on the reasons for which speakers use indirect rather than direct forms, nor do they seek an explanation for which particular indirect forms will be used under which conditions. It takes little reflection, however, to notice that in most cases, some notion of politeness plays a role. Brown and Levinson (1987) include extensive investigations of how models of politeness can yield answers to these interesting questions. They assume – following R. Lakoff (1977) – that a fundamental rule of politeness (deriving from a need to preserve addressee's "face") is: *Don't impose*. Requests are, by definition, impositions, and the clash that they present with the rule of politeness is in need of resolution. The direct imposition can be ameliorated by avoiding a direct demand and instead asking whether the addressee is willing to or capable of carrying out the act. This gives the addressee the technical option of not carrying out the implied request without losing face. Hence *Would you pass the salt?* or *Can you pass the salt?* are more polite than *Pass the salt!* A rather similar account is offered by Leech (1976).

These studies of politeness have spawned a considerable interest in naturalistic studies of speech interaction, cross-cultural comparisons of indirection strategies, and intercultural communication. See, for example, the papers in Watts et al. (1992).

4.2 Mood and sentence type

In most languages, perhaps even all, sentences can be classified on the basis of formal features into a small number of sentence types, with each type associated with a certain illocutionary act potential (IAP). Thus in English, sentences can be classified as declarative, with IAP including acts of stating, asserting, claiming, testifying, and so on; interrogative, with IAP including asking, inquiring, querying, and so on; and imperative, with IAP including requesting, demanding, commanding, directing, and so on. To count as a type within such a system, the formal features defining the types must be mutually exclusive: A sentence cannot be simultaneously of the declarative and interrogative type, or of the interrogative and imperative type. Furthermore, every sentence should be of one or of another type according to the formal features that it displays.

Sadock and Zwicky (1985) studied sentence type systems in a typologically diverse range of languages from different linguistic stocks and found a remarkable similarity among such systems, a situation that is reminiscent of the similarities to be found in color-term vocabularies that were investigated by Berlin and Kay (1969). In general, we can expect a language to distinguish at least one declarative type, at least one interrogative type, and at least one imperative type. Within these broad types, some languages make further divisions. Thus, Hidatsa subdivides the declarative into several types depending on the source of the information: first hand (i.e., *I testify that . . .*), statements of others (i.e., *I pass on the information that . . .*), speaker's beliefs (i.e., *I think that . . .*), common knowledge (i.e., *It is said that . . .*), and a neutral type that does not commit the speaker to the truth of the proposition (i.e., *Perhaps . . .*). Some languages also have other types that are mutually exclusive with, and therefore at the same level as, the major types. Korean, for instance, has a propositive particle that occurs in the same sentence-final position as the declarative, interrogative, and imperative particles. Sentences ending with the propositive particle are used for proposing a course of action (i.e., *Let's . . .*) (Kim 1990).

Intuitive classifications of illocutionary acts and classifications based on philosophical principles often fail to jibe with the formal criteria that distinguish sentence types. Many authors agree, for example, that the interrogative should be viewed as a species of imperative – a request for information. But Sadock and Zwicky (1985), in a survey of approximately 40 diverse languages, failed to find a single case in which the interrogative was clearly aligned formally with the imperative. Another example of the divergence of philosophical and grammatical criteria is that interrogatives of all kinds would seem to belong together from an illocutionary point of view, but it is frequently the case that polarity questions, those that require a *yes* or *no* answer, form a class distinct from question-word questions, and often resemble declaratives. In German, for example, polarity questions begin with the finite verb, whereas questions with an interrogative word like *was, wo, wenn,* etc., begin with that element, with the finite verb immediately following. From a formal point of view, question-word questions like (14) are perfectly parallel to declarative sentences with a focal element like (15), rather than to polarity questions like (16):

(14)   Was hat er gekauft?
       "What did he buy?"

(15)   Ein Buch hat er gekauft.
       "(It was) a book he bought."

(16)   Hat er ein Buch gekauft?
       "Did he buy a book?"

Similarly, in a great many languages the polarity question has special, interrogative intonation, whereas the question-word question has the same intonation as the declarative. Bolinger (1982), however, argues that interrogative intonation has its own, quasi-illocutionary meaning. See also Pierrehumbert and Hirschberg 1990.

There are several divergent views as to the analysis of mood. The performative analysis reduces mood to performativity. Others, e.g., Karttunen (1977) and Hintikka (1976) for questions, and Han (2000), for imperatives, sought truth-conditional models of mood. Bach and Harnish (1979) take mood as the expression of an attitude toward the truth of a proposition, and Harnish (1994) treats the moods as sui generis, a device that directly determines the illocutionary force potential of a sentence.

5 Formal Approaches

Several attempts have been made to axiomatize aspects of speech act theory and produce an algebra of illocutionary forces, acts, etc., in which certain results can be proven concerning the relation of acts to acts, acts to intentions, acts to contexts, and so forth. Researchers in artificial intelligence have based their formalizations on the notions of plans, goals, intentions, and beliefs, hoping to derive some of the basic features of speech acts from these primitive notions. These include Perrault (1990), Cohen and Levesque (1990), and the numerous articles cited in those two works. Searle and Vanderveken (1985) and Vanderveken (1994), on the other hand, present a straightforward formalization of the informal ideas of Searle (1969, 1975b), with the idea of demonstrating the consistency and completeness of those ideas. Merin's (1994) novel approach to formalizing speech act theory takes dialogue as the central notion, with social acts such as the making of claims and the concession to or rejection of claims as primitives.

4 Reference

GREGORY CARLSON

1 The Phenomenon of Reference

In a paper evaluating animal communication systems, Hockett and Altmann (1968: 63–4) presented a list of what they found to be the distinctive character- istics which, collectively, define what it is to be a human language. Among the characteristics is the phenomenon of "aboutness," that is, in using a human language we talk **about** things that are external to ourselves. This not only includes things that we find in our immediate environment, but also things that are **displaced** in time and space. For example, at this moment I can just as easily talk about Tahiti or the planet Pluto, neither of which are in my imme- diate environment nor ever have been, as I can about this telephone before me or the computer I am using at this moment. Temporal displacement is similar: it would seem I can as easily talk about Abraham Lincoln or Julius Caesar, neither a contemporary of mine, as I can of former president Bill Clinton, or my good friend John, who are contemporaries of mine. This notion of aboutness is, intuitively, lacking in some contrasting instances. For example, it is easy to think that animal communication systems lack this characteristic – that the mating call of the male cardinal may be caused by a certain biological urge, and may serve as a signal that attracts mates, but the call itself is (putatively) not **about** either of those things. Or, consider an example from human behavior. I hit my thumb with a hammer while attempting to drive in a nail. I say, "Ouch!" In so doing I am saying this because of the pain, and I am communic- ating to anyone within earshot that I am in pain, but the word *ouch* itself is not about the pain I feel. If, on the other hand, I say, with unnatural calmness, "Pain is present in my thumb," then I am in this instance talking **about** pain.

Such intuitions have, for the most part, been extremely compelling, in fact so compelling that the CORRESPONDENCE THEORY OF MEANING has, since clas- sical times, in one form or another, been by far the most persistently pursued notion of how meaning in language is best characterized. Not to put too fine an edge on it, this is quite simply the idea that the significance or import of natural language utterances is found in the ways in which they correspond to facts and things in the world around us. In present times, this finds its clearest articulation in the framework of model-theoretic semantics. Yet not everyone finds these basic intuitions of aboutness quite so compelling as to base a theory of natural language meaning upon them. Most notably in the twentieth century, Wittgenstein is generally interpreted as articulating quite a different view of natural language meaning which, at best, treats "aboutness" as derivative or epiphenomenal (Wittgenstein 1953). Also, Chomsky (1981, 1992, 1995a), Hornstein (1984), Ludlow (2003) and others have articulated a similarly skeptical view about its centrality. Since this chapter is about (the notion of) reference, I set aside consideration of such alternatives and focus exclusively on work which does find this initial intuition most compelling.

The word *about(ness)* itself, however, is a folk notion that is too general and vague to really get at something fundamental about natural language. We may ask, quite sensibly, what is Beethoven's Third Symphony about, what is the relationship of a couple really about, what is a painting by Mondrian about, or what was the First World War all about, anyway? Even if we confine ourselves to linguistic utterances, we find ourselves with a slippery notion that is subject to all sorts of doubt and uncertainty. In saying to a person on the street "My garden is poor this year," I could very sensibly be talking about the cool weather, the lack of rain, the presence of pests, or a decision I made some time ago to plant a certain variety of tomatoes. I could be talking about any of these things, and more. However, the one thing that **is** clear that I am talking about in this instance that seems inescapable is quite simply that I am, in fact, talking about my garden. This is, obviously, because in uttering the sentence, I use the phrase *my garden*, whereas in this instance there is no particular mention of rain, weather, pests, or poor plant selection. To distinguish these two types of *aboutness*, the term REFERENCE is going to be used for those things overtly mentioned in the utterance of a sentence. Thus, I may be talking about the dry weather, but I am **referring to** my garden (and the current year as well).

This is helpful, in that it localizes and objectifies a certain type of aboutness in a reasonably clear and intuitive way. Yet, even here there is all manner of cause for question and uncertainty. For example, in the utterance above, might I also be referring to myself (by using *my*), gardens in general (by using *garden*), the quality of being poor, and so forth? Intuitively, these questions have sensible answers both yes and no. But it does remain a very solid intuition that I am referring to my garden, where an intuitively based denial would seem far less convincing. For this reason, the focus of a theory of reference has been on those elements of a sentence or utterance which most clearly display the intuitive phenomenon of reference, leaving aside the subsequent questions for resolution within a more precisely articulated theory. The types of words and phrases that canonically display reference (see Strawson 1950) include demonstrative and indexical words and phrases (e.g. *this table, that cat, I, this*), proper names (*Aristotle, Paris, Fred Smith*), and singular definite terms (*the woman standing by the table, my garden, the author of "The Republic"*). Phrases and words of these types, not only in English but where they appear in any other natural language, unequivocally "pick out" some particular, definite individual or object. The point is, if **these** things don't exhibit the phenomenon of "reference," then we should all close up shop on this particular topic and find something else to work on.

2   Semantic Reference

2.1   *Frege*

Reference, then, is a kind of verbal "pointing to" or "picking out" of a certain object or individual that one wishes to say something about. But what, then, is the connection between the meanings of the particular words of the language we use in order to accomplish this, and what is picked out as a consequence? In order to frame this question, let us consider what has been typically called the NAÏVE THEORY OF REFERENCE. This was by no means first articulated by Frege (1879) (one immediate precursor was Mill 1843), but Frege seems to have taken the idea and pursued it the furthest within a new conception of how to do things – using the tools of formal logic – that appears to have been a genuinely novel development on the intellectual scene. The basic notion is that the meaning of an entire (declarative) sentence of a natural language is intimately connected to its truth value, and the contributions of the words and phrases within a sentence to the meaning of the whole are determined by the contribution they make to the truth value of the whole. Or, as McGinn (1981) puts it: "Reference is what relates words to the world of objects on whose condition truth hinges."

If one then turns specifically to intuitively referential phrases and words and calculates the contribution they make to the truth value of the whole, one encounters an initially surprising result: that the truth value of sentences containing referential phrases is (in part) determined by what the phrases themselves refer to, and not by any other or further characteristics of the phrases themselves. From an intuitive point of view, if I say (falsely) that Ringo Starr wrote the novel *War and Peace* then the truth value of this sentence has not to do with any particular beliefs or conceptions I or anyone else might have about the world, but rather what Ringo himself, that guy out there, has and perhaps has not accomplished. Let ☺ be the person Ringo Starr. It is as if I am saying something to the effect that: ☺ wrote *War and Peace*.

Slightly more technically, and the success of this is easy to overlook, *any* phrase that has the reference ☺ will be **automatically** guaranteed to yield a sentence of the same truth value if placed in the same syntactic location in the sentence as the phrase *Ringo Starr*. Thus, supposing that the phrases *the most famous drummer for the Beatles, Jimmy Smits's boyhood hero*, and *that man over there* have, on an occasion of use, the reference of Ringo Starr, their contribution to the meaning of any sentence will be ☺ and nothing more. This will mean that all the following sentences are likewise guaranteed to be of the same truth value as "Ringo Starr wrote *War and Peace*"; as will, in fact, any other way whatsoever of referring to the particular man ☺, for this is the contribution any such phrase will make to the truth value of the whole:

(1)a. The most famous drummer for the Beatles wrote *War and Peace*.
   b. Jimmy Smits's boyhood hero wrote *War and Peace*.
   c. That man over there wrote *War and Peace*.

Thus we have an actual diagnostic for what is intended by the term *reference*, namely, preservation of truth value. Consider the following to see how this might go. I wonder if the word *someone* is a referring term, and on an occasion of use can be used to refer to Ringo. (This would seem intuitively plausible under certain circumstances. Suppose, for instance, I host a birthday party for Jimmy Smits and have invited Ringo as a surprise guest, and when Jimmy complains how the party is dragging I might say presciently, "Yes, but some-one has yet to arrive!") Now consider the contribution to the truth value of "someone" in the following:

(2) Someone wrote *War and Peace*.

The judgments here are not wholly secure, but most people who think about these things agree that what has been said here is, in fact, true, whereas if it were referential and had the value ☺, it would have to be false. Assuming these intuitions hold up, then *someone* is not a referential phrase (though see Fodor and Sag 1982 for a different point of view). It makes some other con-tribution to the meaning of the whole.

One might, thus far, look upon this discussion as a rearticulation of LEIBNIZ'S LAW of the intersubstitutability of indiscernibles *salva veritate*. But there are some objections to this that have been the source of continued inquiry to the present time, which Frege also tried to deal with, chiefly in Frege (1892). One objection, that I will mention and put to the side, is that one must not use examples where the use of a term is metalinguistic. Words and phrases func-tion as names of themselves occasionally in language. When so construed, they do not have reference to the "usual" objects and individuals, but to **different** objects, e.g. the linguistic objects themselves. Thus (3a) is not to be intersubstituted for (3b) (preserving truth):

(3)a. Ringo Starr is a stage-name.
   b. The most famous drummer of the Beatles is a stage-name.
   c. Richard Starkey's more famous alias is a stage-name.

However, any other phrase with the reference the name *Ringo Starr* will pre-serve truth value. Thus, (3c), unlike (3b), will have the same truth value as (3a), having the same reference.

While it is not always a straightforward matter to determine metalinguistic usage (e.g. consider the discussion of METALINGUISTIC NEGATION, Horn 1989), this particular objection has had primarily nuisance value in the development of a theory of reference. More telling is one type of intuitive objection and another based on failures of intersubstitutability. The intuitive objection can be simply illustrated thus. If the meaning of a word or phrase is its reference, and "Ringo Starr" and "the Beatles' most famous drummer" have the same reference, then they have the same meaning. This just plain is not so: these phrases have obviously different meanings. This objection has clear force. The other objection gets to the heart of the naïve theory of reference: that phrases with the same reference are not always intersubstitutable preserving truth value. This phenomenon has received a huge amount of attention in the literature. One facet of this objection comes from the behavior of propositional attitudes. The following pairs of sentence can easily diverge in truth value:

(4)a.   James believes that Ringo Starr is a solo singer.
   b.   James believes that the Beatles' most famous drummer is a solo singer.

Having followed sporadically the later stages of Ringo's career, and having no idea whatsoever of any connection he might have had to the Beatles, James could well be described as having the first belief, but not the second (he assumes any such drummer is a drummer and not a solo singer). The problem is, if reference, under the naïve theory, is all that contributes to truth value, then both sentences could (crudely again) have the following contents:

(5)a.   James believes that ☺ is a solo singer.
   b.   James believes that ☺ is a solo singer.

and so, being identical in content, have the same truth values. To object that there is, in fact, a reading of these sentences which does have this consequence – the *de re* reading where, intuitively, the speaker is the one taking responsibility for the contents of the referring phrases – does not adequately address this point. There is a reading (perhaps the more natural one) where identity of truth value is not the consequence, and on the purely naïve theory of reference discussed here this simply should not happen. This is traditionally called the *de dicto* reading, and if the theory thus far is correct there should be no such phenomenon.

The other major type of consideration is that of the contents of identity sentences, which are generally assumed to be successfully analyzed by the "=" relation. Such sentences do not appear to introduce operators giving rise to opaque or *de dicto* contexts, but nevertheless are a similar source of puzzlement. If the contribution to the meaning is the reference of the noun phrases in the following sentences, then both ought to have the same "cognitive value" (a phrase that will be somewhat clarified below).

(6)a. The Beatles' most famous drummer is Ringo Starr.
  b. Ringo Starr is Ringo Starr.

That is, both have the value:

(7) ☺ = ☺

But while the second is very obvious and can be known to be true a priori (assuming both instances of "Ringo Starr" are the same, see below for comments on this), the first seems to convey contingent information that may actually come as news to some people. This is a genuinely different kind of objection, because in fact "=" preserves truth value given identical referents. Whichever way one finds of referring to Ringo Starr, intersubstitution will in fact yield identical truth value.

Frege's proposed solution to these problems is well known and often written about, but is itself problematic. The proposal is that words and phrases, besides having a reference, also have something which, in English, is called a SENSE. This "sense" of a word or phrase is what distinguishes otherwise coreferential expressions. *Ringo Starr* and *the Beatles' most famous drummer* may have identical referents, but are distinguished by their senses. The sense contains the "mode of presentation" of a referent; it is an objective, and not a subjective, thing but it is what we psychologically "grasp" in understanding a word or phrase, and in so grasping enables us to find out the reference of the word or phrase. However, in Frege's view, it is not the psychological grasping itself that actually determines the reference, but rather the objective sense itself that is responsible for determining the reference. Thus, reference is determined indirectly from expressions of a language (this includes mathematical notation): a bit of language **expresses** a sense, which in turn **determines** a reference. This holds in the case of proper names as well – the names *Richard Starkey* and *Ringo Starr* (or *Hesperus* and *Phosphorus*, or *Cicero* and *Tully*, to revert to more traditional examples) have different senses associated with them despite common reference.

Frege's solution to the problem of *de dicto* meanings appears, initially at least, to work but strikes many people as unduly complex and counterintuitive (see, especially, Barwise and Perry 1983). In certain syntactically definable contexts such as embedded clauses, a referring expression does not have as its reference its "usual" one, but rather its sense. Thus, in the propositional attitude examples such as those above, the reference of *Ringo Starr* and *the Beatles' most famous drummer* is not the "usual" ☺, but rather the "customary" senses of each (we will call them S_1 and $S_{2)}$, which differ from one another, and it is these senses which now contribute to the meaning of the whole. And since the senses are different, one now has different propositions that can diverge in truth value:

(8)a. James believes that S_1 is a solo singer.
  b. James believes that S_2 is a solo singer.

There are two somewhat odd consequences of this solution. If the sense of an expression is, in these instances, its reference, and reference is determined by its sense, and since the reference determined by the senses S_1 and S_2 is ☺ in contexts such as those in (6), then there has to be *another* sense (S_3) that will determine S_1 and still another (S_4) that will determine S_2 as their references in examples such as those in (8). But, unlike the customary senses, we have no clear intuitive grasp of what these might be. Further, the claim is that referring phrases in *de dicto* contexts have as their meanings different things from what they have in *de re* contexts. Complicating things still further is that if you have a *de dicto* context embedded within another *de dicto* context (e.g. "John was surprised that the Queen of England believed the Beatles' drummer was Ringo Starr"), then in the most deeply embedded context, the reference of a referring expression is no longer its customary sense, but rather the sense that determines its customary sense, introducing a third-order sense that must determine that as its reference. This works recursively, so that if there are n embedded contexts in a single sentence, in the nth context there would have to be an nth+1 sense to determine the nth sense as *its* reference. (This is not an incoherent proposal. Within the formal framework of Montague 1973, for example, what correspond to such higher-level senses are recursively definable, though any sense beyond the customary one is a constant function.)

The oddness is compounded somewhat by Frege's view of sentence meanings. In ordinary contexts, such things do have a reference, which he takes to be a truth value, and a sense, which he takes to be a proposition of a "thought." In *de dicto* contexts, however, the same recursive piling up of senses occurs as with referential phrases, so that an embedded sentence ends up *meaning* something different from its unembedded counterpart, a doubly embedded sentence has still another meaning, and so on. This strikes many people, again, as a bit strange.

When we return to the issue of identity sentences, which do not involve *de dicto* contexts, it is a little hard to see how Frege's suggestions lead to a definite solution. For the phrases used have their customary reference, so all true identity sentences express a proposition of the form **a=a** (where **a** is some arbitrary referent), though within a belief context, for example, different senses will emerge to distinguish the (higher-level) propositions created.

Making use of the discussions to be found in McDowell (1977) and Dummett (1975), this is what may have been intended. From the point of view of one understanding an utterance, "grasping" the sense, which determines the reference, does not enable one to automatically grasp the reference itself. If this were so, and we happened on Smith foully murdered, all we would need to do is to hear someone utter the phrase (in a *de re* context) *Smith's murderer* and the identity of the murderer would be automatically known to us; but, obviously, it is not. Likewise, we would (in at least one uncharitable interpretation of Frege's framework) only have to understand a sentence in order to know its truth value. To check on how many copies of an article we need to submit to a journal for publication, we'd only need to hear someone go through a list

"*The Journal of Modern Fregean Studies* requires one copy . . . two copies . . . ,"
etc., until we hit on the reference "true."

But there has to be some kind of psychological connection between grasping
a sense and determining a reference (let's call this relation "finding" a reference, incorporating Russell's notion of "acquaintance" as a "direct cognitive
relation" (Russell 1910–11). Consider, for instance, your understanding of the
phrase "My sister's oldest daughter." If you can read this paper then you
clearly understand what this means – you "grasp" its sense – but it is very
doubtful you are antecedently familiar with that particular person. That is, the
reference is unknown to you. However, if you wanted to go to the time and
trouble to discover the identity of that person, the meaning of the phrase itself
provides you with some kind of clue about how you could go about finding
the reference. For instance, you could ask me who my sister is and how you
can reach her, and then ask her or whoever answers the door who her oldest
daughter is, and then go find her. On the other hand, if I used the phrase,
which you understand, "The best young salesperson at the Anthropologie
store located in downtown Seattle," to make reference to the same person,
you'd likely skip hunting up me and my sister and head for the manager of
that store in Seattle. In saying that understanding the contents provides one
with "some kind of clue" about how to find the reference, I am not implying
either that grasping the sense provides one with anything like a definite **procedure** for finding the reference, nor that it provides one with any guaranteed
means of making that identification. Furthermore, in this framework, the "clues"
are not the meaning of the phrase (for the meaning is an objective, not a
psychological matter), but rather psychological addenda that are intended to
elucidate further the notion of "mode of presentation."

Let us return to the point at hand, identity sentences. While in the Fregean
framework it appears one cannot make use of the notions of sense and reference directly to distinguish *de re* propositions with terms of identical reference,
the "cognitive values" will differ. In asserting, for example, that Plato is the
author of *The Republic*, different means of finding references are suggested by
the phrases *Plato* and *the author of "The Republic,"* and the information conveyed by asserting such an identity sentence is that the clues provided by each
via grasping their different senses will converge on the same reference. That
is, there is differing **psychological** information associated with the use of each
phrase, even if the contents of the proposition expressed is of the form **a=a**.

But, even if this view holds any validity, it generates a subsequent puzzle,
for what is the value in Frege's framework of grasping the sense of a proper
name? Beyond the fact that the reference is (at least occasionally) called by that
name, and in the normal case many people are (at least occasionally) called by
that same name who cannot be further distinguished, the sense of a proper
name seems largely if not entirely devoid of any "clues" about how to determine their referents. Nevertheless, the very fact that the names differ suggests
at least a partially distinguishing means of identification. We will see other
suggestions about this later.

There have been other problems and questions raised by the Fregean framework that have been pursued in subsequent work. Modal contexts, for example, have been noted as providing similar puzzles to those posed by propositional attitudes. A particularly knotty problem for the framework is posed by negative existential sentences, such as "The king of France does not exist." Let ☺ be the king of France. If this is so, then there is, in fact, some king of France, namely ☺. Thus, a proposition of the form ☺ *does not exist* would appear contradictory. Now suppose, as is currently the case, that there is no such ☺. The form of the proposition would appear to be an unsaturated proposition of the form __ *does not exist*, which is assigned no truth value since it lacks anything that the phrase *the king of France* contributes to the proposition.

2.2   *Russell*

There were two attempts in the same era intended to resolve this particular difficulty. One was the "bite the bullet" analysis of Meinong (1904), who made what some find the curious claim that, in fact, phrases like *the golden mountain*, *the square circle*, and similar phrases, including proper names like *Zeus*, do in fact have reference. It's just that they have the property of not existing, but such phrases can and do contribute a reference to the proposition. Such a solution strikes many as ontologically a bit bizarre, for if there is no such thing as a golden mountain, then surely "the golden mountain" has no reference, there being no such thing. This seems transparent reasoning. At least that seems the attitude of Russell (1905), who proposed instead a different, and what people at least for some time considered a much more clever, and more ontologically satisfactory, type of solution – his theory of definite descriptions. This theory addressed the problems of *de dicto* contexts, and of identity, so there was a lot of mileage to be gotten here.

The strategy Russell followed was, in effect, to deny that definite descriptions (and proper names were taken as a variety of definite descriptions) contributed anything like a reference to a proposition. In fact, definite noun phrases did not contribute to a proposition any identifiable single constituent of meaning at all. Rather, these were disguised existential statements, which were assertions of uniqueness. To illustrate, take the sentence "The Queen of England is dignified." This, setting aside analysis of the name *England*, cashes out as:

(9) $\exists x$ [Queen of England (x) and $\forall y$ [Queen of England (y) $\rightarrow$ y=x and dignified (x)]].

From there it is a short step to negative existential sentences, provided one has a syntactic means of according the negation widest scope. "The king of England does not exist" comes out as an unremarkable statement:

(10) $\neg\exists x$ [King of England (x) and $\forall y$ [King of England (y) $\rightarrow$ y=x]].

Proper names are taken as disguised definite descriptions and analyzed accordingly. Thus, *Pegasus* might have the contents of being a winged white horse of mythology, abbreviated as WWH, and "Pegasus does not exist" similarly comes out as:

(11)   ¬∃x [WWH (x) and ∀y [WWH(y) → y=x]].

There is no need for Meinongian non-existent objects, or any strange reference at all, since definite descriptions and names do not have reference in the first place.

Identity statements like "Hesperus is Phosphorus" become, on this view, unproblematic as well. Let the contents of *Hesperus* be ES and that of *Phosphorus* MS. Abbreviating by omitting the uniqueness clauses for the sake of simplicity, the identity statement comes out something like a fairly ordinary looking assertion:

(12)   ∃x ∃y [MS(x) and ES(y) and x=y].

And, finally, the problem of *de dicto* contexts receives a treatment that avoids the piling up of senses that is a consequence of the Fregean analysis, for the propositions expressed have different forms (RS abbreviates whatever descriptive contents the name *Ringo Starr* has, and, again, the uniqueness clauses are omitted for simplicity).

(13)a.   James believes that Ringo Starr is a solo singer.
   b.   James believes that the Beatles' most famous drummer is a solo singer.

(13')a.   James believes [∃x [RS(x) and solo singer (x)]].
    b.   James believes [∃x [most-famous-drummer (x) and solo singer (x)]].

The *de re* reading would simply accord the existential expressions widest scope.

In Russell's framework, then, did anything at all have reference value? He did admit of something called a logically proper name, which despite terminology is no proper name but would strike most as an indexical expression. This is exemplified by directly referring demonstratives without nominal contents such as *this* and *that* used in a context to make unmediated reference to some individual or object. Note that such instances do not, in fact, cause immediate difficulties for identity, or for negative existentials (e.g. "This (said, pointing at a table) does not exist" seems a blatant contradiction), or for *de dicto* contexts.

This would appear to be a significant improvement, but this theory too has been met by influential replies on two major fronts. One, articulated by Strawson (primarily, Strawson 1950) questions whether Russell's theory of descriptions might be missing something crucial. The other type of objection concerns the descriptive contents of proper names, discussed by Kripke (primarily, Kripke

1972), which gave rise to the idea of **direct reference** theories of names. (Though for an updated defense of Russell's position, see Neale 1990, and Ludlow and Neale 1991.)

3   Reference as Pragmatic

3.1   *Strawson*

The fundamental question Strawson raised is whether what we are calling "reference" is a matter of (linguistic) meaning. Both Frege and Russell expounded what we can call a "semantic" theory of reference, in the sense that a semantics characterizes the meanings of words and phrases of a language in a general sense. Any further meaning that results from producing and understanding the actual utterance of a sentence, which are types of human actions, is not characterizable within the semantics as there is no reference there to speakers and hearers, only words, phrases, syntactic categories, etc. Thus, Strawson argues, truth and falsity are not (semantic) properties of sentences of a language, but rather are a property of a **use** of a sentence (via an utterance) on a particular occasion. To illustrate his point, he presents the example of "I am hot." Now, he points out, it makes no sense to ask if this **sentence** is true or false; it is only when use is made of the sentence that we can so evaluate it. Thus, at this moment, if I pointlessly utter "I am hot" aloud, it's false, but said by another at this very moment it might be true. He points out, similarly, that a referring noun phrase like *the king of France* can only be evaluated for its reference value with respect to a use of the term via an utterance as well. It just so happened that Russell, writing in the early twentieth century, was writing at a time when there was no king of France; had he written two centuries earlier, there would have been and the phrase would have had a reference. But again, this is not a fact about the noun phrase meaning itself, but about a particular use of the noun phrase.

He further points out that the verbs *mention* and *refer* (he treats them as synonymous) are verbs of **doing**. This point is elaborated more clearly by Linsky (1963), who notes that the verb *refer* does not have only a general sense (e.g. as in "x refers to y"), but also a specific sense that may be applied to individuals, such as in saying, to use his example, "Who are you referring to when you say 'the Sultan of Swat'?", and receiving the reply "I am referring to Babe Ruth, of course." This more specific (non-stative, achievement verb) is not something we apply to language: it is strange to say " 'The Sultan of Swat' is referring to Babe Ruth." Linsky points out that the question, To what does x refer? is a different question from asking, What are you referring to in using x? Further, in most instances, definite descriptions cannot be said, in general, to have any reference at all, even if they have meaning. Thus, "the man with the gray hair" is and can be used to refer to some particular man on a given occasion, and another on another occasion, but the semantics of this phrase does not pick out some unique individual (there being many with gray hair) *simpliciter*.

To revert momentarily to the Fregean framework, we might reason thus: If the contribution to the meaning of a proposition is the reference of a phrase, and we determine the contribution some expression makes to the meaning of a proposition in terms of its contribution to the truth value of the sentence expressing it, and if the notion of truth value is something assigned to specific uses of a sentence via its utterance (and is therefore not a part of the semantics proper) – then, the notion of "reference" plays no (clear) role in the semantics proper but, rather, only in the use of a sentence on a given occasion.

Strawson points to another intuitive phenomenon that Russell's analysis provides no room for. If I were to say to you, right now, "The king of France is wise," on Russell's analysis I would have said something false (there being no such unique king). However, Strawson raised the point that it does not seem to be true or false *simpliciter*, but rather, there is something funny or strange about the utterance. His intuitions are, if asked if the sentence so used is true or false, he'd be at a loss. As he puts it, since there is no king of France, then the question of truth or falsity of the sentence simply does not arise. The use of the phrase *implies* that there is such a king, and in the absence of the validity of this implication one can make no sense of evaluating for truth or falsity. In more modern terms, this would be called PRESUPPOSITION FAILURE. Note, again, that this "implication" can hold or not hold depending upon when the sentence is used, so its holding or not is thus a matter of usage, not of semantics proper. Strawson holds that even in cases of presupposition failure, the **sentence** still has "significance" – it is not gibberish – but this significance is not grounded in evaluating for truth or falsity. Strawson also goes on to point out that the same phenomenon occurs with Russell's logically proper names, which behave in this respect just like definite descriptions, despite having a very different analysis in Russell's theory.

3.2 *Kripke and "direct reference"*

Kripke's critiques (Kripke 1972) focus on something quite different – the analysis of proper names that Russell presented (and also, though perhaps somewhat unfairly, Frege presented in according names senses), in which names were treated as disguised definite descriptions. His critiques more or less interweave with similar critiques of Putnam (1975), Barcan Marcus (1963), Donnellan (1972), Geach (1962), and Kaplan (1978). Kripke argued very persuasively that any such analysis will fail, and that another understanding of the nature of the reference of proper names is required in which names refer directly to their referents, without the mediation of any sense or descriptive contents (which is very similar to the "naïve" theory of reference). The arguments take a variety of forms, so I will present only a couple here to illustrate how this conclusion might be reached. An excellent summary may be found in Salmon (1989).

Suppose that we provide the name *Ringo Starr* with the content "(most famous) drummer for the Beatles," or something similar. The modal argument is that this would entail that no matter what the circumstances, the drummer for the Beatles would be Ringo Starr. This is, if Ringo had not passed his audition, and someone else had, then *that* person would be Ringo Starr, not the unemployed drummer wandering the streets of Liverpool. This type of argument rests on contrafactual thinking, but seems fairly persuasive. That Ringo Starr is the drummer for the Beatles is not a logical truth. The epistemological argument has a similar flavor; it rests on the possibility of mistakes. This works best for historical figures around whom legends have developed, where the proposed meaning of a name may contain all sorts of factual error, and identify either no one at all, or by chance someone else, which seems counterintuitive.

The strongest argument, though, seems to be the semantic argument, which does not deal in possibilia but relies upon our judgments about who or what a name does in fact refer to. Donnellan (1972) uses the example of a person named Thales, referred to by Aristotle and Herodotus, among others, as a philosopher who held that all was water. Now, suppose that Thales' view was, say, misinterpreted by these other philosophers (it happens!), and he in fact held a much more subtle view, which, in the end, could not be accurately so characterized. Imagine also that Thales had a not very good student who was a philosopher, about whom we know nothing whatsoever, who also misinterpreted his teacher and in fact did believe all was water. If the phrase "the ancient Greek philosopher who believed all was water" expresses the content of the name *Thales*, it does not pick out Thales but his student instead. Now, the question is whether the name *Thales* as used by Aristotle and Herodotus and passed along to us in fact refers to that obscure student. Manifestly, it does not (examine the discussion immediately above for clear evidence). It refers to, well . . . , Thales. The view that results from this general line of thought is that proper names are expressions which refer directly to their referents, and there is no mediating sense or meaning which is employed to necessarily determine reference. Further, this reference is RIGID, in that a name picks out the same individual in all possible worlds. Putnam (1975) has employed arguments that are similar in thrust to argue that natural kind terms, such as *tiger* or *gold*, lack extension-determining descriptive contents.

But this seems to leave us with the problems of identity sentences and the other issues Frege was struggling with. In partial answer, Kripke outlines an approach (which he himself does not characterize as a theory) that is critiqued subsequently by Evans (1973). This is the CAUSAL THEORY of names. The general idea is this: a speaker who uses a given name **A** will make successful reference to the individual it refers to ⊗ just in case there is a reference-preserving chain of usage of **A** that extends back to ⊗. Informally, at first there is some veridical naming or "dubbing" that initially fixes the reference of **A** as the individual ⊗. When one of the dubbers uses **A** in the presence of a further person Dr. X, then Dr. X's use of **A** will pick out ⊗ on the strength of the dubber's (secure) usage. This works transitively, so that if Dr. X talks to Professor Y and uses the name, Professor Y is thereby entitled to use **A** and will thereby refer to ⊗ as well, and so on.

Each name, including different names for the same individual or object, will appear in different utterances at different times, and almost certainly involve many people who are familiar with one name but not the other. That is, the usage of the names will distinguish different causal chains. Thus, what appear to be different senses attached to different names, like *Mark Twain* and *Samuel Clemens*, are not senses but causally determined chains of usage. And, roughly, in asserting that Mark Twain is Samuel Clemens the new information imparted is that the distinct causal chains associated with these two names will ultimately converge on one and the same person. The task of converting this line of thought into an actual theory, however, is daunting; Evans (1973) argues that the causal theory is problematic and resorts to a notion of communal knowledge about the use of a name and the intention to use the name in accordance with that communal knowledge. In some respects, this is similar to the causal theory, in that it does not accord proper names a semantic meaning, but rather reference is achieved via the mechanism of social practice.

Thus far, we have seen a communal line of thought in which the notion of reference has, in fits and starts, become increasingly removed from being a purely semantic notion, and increasingly a function of human action and interaction. At this point, though, I wish to step back and question the extent to which this particular direction is justified.

4 Semantic Reference and Pragmatic Reference

4.1 *Some issues*

One problem with talking about "reference" is that this word has an ordinary common meaning that we are trying to accord a consistently used technical meaning. Not only must we contend with this, but we also must contend with the extent to which translation decisions regarding Frege's use of *Sinn* and *Bedeutung* are best thought of as "Sense" and "Reference," when the German terms have no exact counterparts in English. Would things be different were these labeled "Concept" and "Designatum" instead? Perhaps – just perhaps – Frege was not even trying to talk about something called "reference" at all. We certainly want our discussions of reference to be substantive and not terminological. Thus far, we have been following the intuitive idea that the "reference" of a word or phrase is what contributes to the truth or falsity of a sentence (or a sentence in use). The strategy of fixing on those elements of language, such as names and definite descriptions, which most clearly are in line with our native understanding of the word, is an understandable and productive strategy. But what about all those other words and expressions in a sentence? Does a notion of "reference" fit them as well?

If we apply the notion, in slogan form: "reference determines truth," across the board, and consider all those other words and phrases in a sentence, it turns out that all of them play a role in determining truth and falsity. This, in very rough form, is what Church (1943) and Gödel (1944) quite independently noted about Frege's theory (see also Salmon 1981, 1986). The possibility of syncategorematic introduction of some words aside, what this means is that *all* words and *all* phrases within a sentence have a "reference" besides a "sense." If we examine, say, Montague's (1973) framework, which to a large extent can be thought of as one implementation of Frege's framework, at least in many important respects, most of the references of words and phrases turn out to be functions. This holds true as well for proper names (which turn out to be generalized quantifiers, that is, functions from properties to truth values) as well as definite descriptions (to which he gives a type of Russellian analysis). What then becomes of our naïve notions of "reference" that lead us to see the sense in focusing on names and definite noun phrases to the exclusion of everything else? Again, our naïve notion of reference brings us to the underlying intuition that reference is a "picking out" of a definite object, which we want to say something about. And the type of linguistic device that seems best suited for these purposes are (certain types of) noun phrases. An understanding of why this might be so might be gained from an analysis of the variety of noun phrase meanings.

Let us examine a proper name, within the Montague framework. Although its "reference" within a sentence is the set of properties that individual might have (an analysis suggested in Leibniz: Mates 1968), (nearly) any proposition in which this occurs is equivalent to another formally distinct proposition in which the individual itself appears as the subject (object, etc.) of predication. Thus, although the analysis of something like "John snores" is:

(14) $\lambda P[^{\vee}P(j)](^{\wedge}snore')$

which is semantically equivalent to:

(15)   snore' (j)

However, with quantificational noun phrases, which are not considered referential on the whole, no such similar reduction is possible. Since Montague chooses to represent definite descriptions in the Russellian manner, they too come out as quantified noun phrases. But updating the framework some, and allowing for presupposition failure with definite noun phrases, one can arrive at an interpretation which is of the form P(a), with a, as Russell might say, as the "logical subject" of the predication. In this way, we might begin to understand why certain types of noun phrases can be used "referentially," and others not. However, looking at things this way may seem to open the door once again to a semantic view of reference.

One view is discussed in McGinn (1981) and rests on an analogy. We do, in fact, make reference to things by uttering certain noises under certain

circumstances. However, consider the commonplace activity of buying something. This might at first sight seem to be a causal interaction describable in
such terms, but this doesn't seem correct (e.g. that we can buy things, and
often do, which do not exist at the moment of purchase). In making a purchase, we operate against a background of conventions and constructs, such
as the notion of money, ownership, legalities of exchange, and so forth.
These notions are not behaviors, but rather collectively define certain types
of economic relations between individuals and objects. In actually making a
purchase, we are in fact guided by perception and perform actions, but these
things are not part of the economic relations themselves. And we also have
considerable freedom of behavior in that there are many ways to make a
purchase. Rather, making a purchase results in a relation between us and
objects that we "get into" by doing certain things in concert with others.
Similarly, McGinn invites us to consider, reference is like this. Reference is
defined semantically by a relation between expressions and objects of the world,
but this relation is not defined in any way by actions or intentions. Rather, it is
a relation we can "get into" with an object by acting certain ways in a given
context.

There is also a concrete strategy for "semanticizing" reference. It is, basically, Kaplan's notion of how to accord a meaning to indexical expressions
(see also Levinson, this volume). Before doing this, though, we need to give a
bit of background on the notion of "truth."

The focus on truth and falsity as indicators of the reference of the use of a
phrase needs to be distinguished from the notion of giving truth **conditions**.
Let's approach it this way, within a possible worlds framework. In saying
something like "Larry is in Spain," I am expressing a proposition p. That
proposition p is a function in some theories from possible worlds (and times,
but I'll omit this) to truth values. That is, given a certain possible world w,
then $p(w)$ will yield either T or F. At the moment, I happen to know that who
I am referring to by using the name *Larry* is, in fact, not in Spain. That is, I
know that $p(w) = F$. Does this mean that, as a speaker, I know which possible
world w is? No, I do not. For instance, I do not know if this is among the
possible worlds in which Larry is in Spain *and* the rug in my office was installed in a month ending with *-ber*. I have no idea when it was installed. What
this means is this: I do not know which possible world is the actual world. Nor
does anyone else: no one is in command of all the statements that are true and
false in our world. This does not stop me from referring to it, indexically or by
description; it's just that the world we happen to inhabit as the actual one is
not identifiable to us as w^{338} rather than, say, w^{784}. We believe, of course, that
we can narrow down the host of candidates – this is not one of the worlds where
"Cleveland is the capital of France" is true, and a lot of other such things. This
would seem something of a step in the right direction, but this assumes none
of us hold any false beliefs about the world, nor that we hold any contradictory beliefs about the world, which only makes things worse for any kind of
psychological identification. In short, if we attempt a psychologization of the

possible worlds framework, our limitations prevent us from ever "homing in" on which world among them all we inhabit. This is not a quirky feature of a possible worlds point of view: any theory of intensionality leads to the same conclusion.

None of this means we can have no cognitive "grasp" of truth **conditions**, however. For any world w^n, $p(w^n)$ is true or false. We just don't happen to know if it's our world or someone else's.

4.2   *Kaplan's analysis*

Let us, in this setting, move on to Kaplan's notion of "character" of indexicals. There is a persistent intuition that although a noun phrase like *this woman* can be used on various occasions to refer to different women, and the class of women so referred to has nothing qualitatively in common (apart from being referred to in that way), nevertheless the phrase *this woman* has a constant meaning that transcends its particular uses.

Kaplan (1978, 1989a) proposed that indexical expressions such as *I* or *that man* are expressions which, due to their nature, are assigned extensions (or references) only when their interpretations take arguments that most other words (such as *man*) need not (though see below for some qualification). These arguments, or parameters of interpretation, are the CONTEXT: who is speaking, who is the addressee, where the speaker is located, who or what else is in the immediate environment, and so forth (see also Lewis 1979, Stalnaker 1978, and King 2001). The CHARACTER of an indexical expression, then, is that function from contexts to intensions; that is, from (say) world-time pairs to extensions (i.e. references, in the generalized Fregean sense of the term). What this buys us is a single meaning for indexical expressions, that is, as expressions which are characterizable by a single function.

What role, then, does context play in the case of expressions like *eat* or *man*? One can say that they are "insensitive" to contextual parameters, in which case they represent constant functions – that is, for any set of contextual parameters given a certain world-time pair, the result will be the same in all instances (Chierchia and McConnell-Ginet 2000). Or, one could propose that such expressions simply do not take such arguments. When we turn to indexical expressions, though, things become slightly more uncertain. Are they "insensitive" to world-time parameters of interpretation? It would seem in general that this is so – they have a rigid designation nature to them. But this is not always the case, it would appear.

(16)a.   Always do **today** what you could put off till **tomorrow**.
     b.   (Said, frustrated at where I put my glasses, again) Darn, they always seem to be over **there**, never over **here**!

Examples such as this seem to have natural interpretations that are at least time-dependent: always do things the day you're faced with them, and not the next; my glasses are always where I am not. If one takes these as serious data (some do not), then world-time pairs would appear to play a role in the case of at least some indexical expressions.

Is there a rationale for proposing that meanings have this two-stage nature to them? Is there any rationale for distinguishing between contextual parameters, and possible worlds (and times) in the construction of meaning? There may well be: one can be directly acquainted with the contextual parameters in a way that one cannot with worlds (and, I'd actually argue times as well, but have not). Context, unlike a possible world, is cognitively accessible.

4.3 *Pointing?*

There is another question about whether the nature of reference is found in human action. In Grice (1967) the notion of CONVERSATIONAL IMPLICATURE is introduced. There, he takes pains to point out that such implicatures are a special case of much more general principles appearing to govern human social interaction in general, verbal or non-verbal. A similar point is made in the case of speech acts (Austin 1962, Searle 1969): that the act of congratulating someone verbally, for example, can be alternatively accomplished non-verbally; one can equally well threaten verbally and non-verbally. From this perspective, we might ask the question, if reference is something we do, then how might we accomplish the same thing non-verbally? There is a fairly obvious potential answer, namely, the phenomenon of pointing.[1] But, does pointing constitute reference? Let us use the symbol ☞ to stand for the act of pointing at an object. It is quite clear that this gesture itself cannot function as a part of the meaning of a sentence the way a linguistic expression can, for something like "☞ is green" at best has a "word-play" nature to it, much like threatening to hit someone over the head with a newspaper and saying "I'm going to . . . (action of raising a rolled-up newspaper as if to strike the addressee in the head)," or the bumper stickers reading, "I ♥ my dog."

Another way of putting it is the question of whether pointing has semantic significance. Reimer (1991) argues contra Kaplan (1989a) that this is so, at least in cases where pointing is an accompaniment to the utterance of a demonstrative indexical; it is not just an attention-directing device. Reference is, Reimer notes, coupled with a certain intention on the part of the speaker to make reference. But the intention does not always determine what is said. For example, if there is a single dog sleeping among felines and there is no accompanying demonstration, the descriptive contents of the phrase *that dog* will be sufficient in the context to uniquely pick out (or discriminate) a unique reference, regardless of speaker's intentions. Likewise, if there are multiple dogs but one is especially salient in the context, say one wildly barking dog among other sleeping dogs, reference is again secured by uttering *that dog* in context. And again, the claim is, that reference would succeed independently of speaker's intentions; a pointing demonstration would be redundant. But suppose there are two equally salient dogs in a context, say both barking wildly. Here, pointing does have semantic significance in that it discriminates one dog from another. The dog pointed at is thereby the reference, and whatever is said of it is, truly or falsely, said of that individual, again regardless of speaker's intentions. If the speaker intends to point to refer to the white dog, but instead points at the black one, the black dog and not the white one determines the truth or falsity of what is said.

4.4   *Intentions*

Bach (1992) argues, on the other hand, that the "best of intentions" are good enough; that is, demonstrations do not have semantic significance. He considers a scenario where there are two (equally salient) sets of keys on a desk, and the speaker says, "These keys are mine," but by simple error grabs her office-mate's keys. Here, the mistaken demonstration (or, rather, what directs the listener's attention), it is argued, does not affect reference. The intentions of the speaker to refer to her own keys still holds. However, referential intentions are not just any intentions, but rather ones whose distinctive feature is that their fulfillment consists in their recognition. It involves also intending that one's audience identify something as the reference. This is the piece that is missing in the office keys example.

One's reference, in this case, is not fixed by one's beliefs; it is fixed by the intention to refer and the intention that it be recognized as such. Bach adduces the scenario (from Kaplan 1978) of a speaker sitting at her desk where behind her on the wall is normally placed a picture of Carnap. Unbeknownst to the speaker, someone has replaced it in the night with a picture of former US vice-president Spiro Agnew. In gesturing towards the picture and saying, "That is a picture of the greatest philosopher of the twentieth century," the speaker's belief is that the picture is one of Carnap, but the intention is to make reference to the picture (which is of Agnew) on the wall and the hearer is to recognize this intention via the gesture. The speaker has said something that is false, despite beliefs that she might have been saying something true (or at least less manifestly false). The intention to refer to a picture of Carnap is not the relevant intention here. It is instead the one that is made available and intended to be made available to the listener, which leads to the picture of Agnew which is in fact there. Since having intentions and intending are not a part of language itself, but a property of speakers and listeners that may be carried out or indicated by action, pointing has no semantic significance but functions as a highly reliable indicator of the right type of speaker intentions, which alone secure the reference. This is the thrust of Bach's argument.

This idea is at least partially supported by Donnellan (1966) in his article on definite descriptions. First of all, he distinguished between different meanings or uses (there is equivocation) of definite descriptions, the REFERENTIAL and ATTRIBUTIVE instances. The attributive uses seem to function in a way reminiscent of Russell's theory of descriptions. That is, the contents of the noun phrase determine the propositional content. This is clearest when the identity of the one referred to is unknown to both speaker and hearer, as in happening on a colleague murdered and saying something about Smith's murderer, whoever that may be. There is, however, the referential use which does not rely heavily (or maybe even at all?) on the contents of the noun phrase. This is most clearly the case when there is a mistake in the description. Donnellan asks us to imagine a circumstance where there is a man in a group of people at a party who has a drink in his hand, which is in fact water. But it looks like a martini to me, from this distance. If I say to someone: "The man holding the martini is a famous author," Donnellan argues, my reference to that particular man will be successful, and the truth or falsity of what I have just said will depend on whether that man, who is not holding a martini but a glass of water instead, is a famous author or not. My reference to that man was successful because the listener understood my intentions to refer to that person, whether cognizant of my misattribution or not. Further, suppose there is another man right next to this person who is holding what looks to me to be a malted milkshake, but suppose it's in fact a martini. Although my description would fit this other man, and attributively pick this other person out, the "referential" use that I intended does not, and it is my successfully executed intentions, recognized by the hearer, that determines propositional contents.

Birner (1989) questions whether the conclusion is appropriate. Imagine that Mr. Smith is brutally beaten, seriously but not life-threateningly. As he lies in an alley, along comes a kindly doctor who believes (falsely) that he cannot survive, takes pity on his suffering, and administers a lethal injection to end his pain. The doctor leaves, believing himself to be a good Samaritan, when in fact he has just committed murder. Along comes our person-in-the-street who utters the line: "Smith's murderer is insane." Now, to whom is the speaker referring?

Under Donnellan's account, this can't be a referential use because the speaker has no idea who did the beating. He means "whoever it was" who did the beating – the classic diagnostic for the attributive usage. But according to Donnellan, the attributive use would "pick out" the doctor as the referent, because the doctor is the one who satisfies the description. So there's no way a speaker can refer to whom he intends to refer to (i.e. the person who administered the beating) under Donnellan's account.

4.5 *Meaning imparted via usage*

Recall that on the direct reference theory of names, there is no propositional contribution of the interpretation of the name corresponding to a sense – there is only the reference. This left hanging, as noted above, the question of why we find "Sam Clemens is Mark Twain" different in content from "Mark Twain is Mark Twain." The causal theory was one attempt to begin to characterize this difference. Salmon (1991) takes this issue up in detail (along with propositional attitude contexts), and articulates a very interesting version of the "bite the bullet" approach. His view, stated broadly, is that using certain words or phrases not only gives us information about the contents of the expressions themselves – a proposition – but also about the intentions and beliefs of the speaker. There is a distinction between the information **contents** of a sentence, and the **information imparted** by its use in context. It is often observed that an utterance in context conveys information about a variety of matters that are characteristics of the act itself, and not part of literally what is said. Such things as distance from the listener, gender, emotional state, regional or foreign accents, etc. are a part of this information conveyed, as is illocutionary information: "I'll be there tomorrow" could be a prediction, a threat, a promise, an offer, depending on context. Some of this information is very hard to intuitively distinguish from what one might call core semantic contents. (The literature on scalar implicatures (Fauconnier 1975b) I believe illustrates this point quite well.)

What Salmon argues is that, yes, the propositional contents of names is just the object referred to itself, as direct-reference in its starkest form would demand. Thus, "Hesperus is Phosphorus" is in fact a proposition of the form **a=a**. Then why does it seem informative? This goes back to a fundamental criticism of Frege's notion of sense (*Sinn*). Frege thought (for the most part) that the sense would be that which determines the cognitive significance of an expression. He made no distinction, however, between the conceptual contents of an expression and how the reference (*Bedeutung*) of an expression is **secured**. This conflation, it is plausible to think, led to his attributing a sense to proper names (which was a change from an earlier more direct-reference view he held). However, once we make this separation, it becomes clear that "securing" the reference is a matter of how actions are carried out and the context in which they occur, and in particular by using certain words. In using a name, we also impart the information that use of that particular linguistic form can, in context, secure a particular reference. If we use a different name, even for the same object, then we are imparting a related but *different* type of information. Thus a sentence like "Samuel Clemens is Mark Twain" will impart information that "Mark Twain is Mark Twain" will not, even if the contents are identical. Soames (2001) mounts a substantial defense of (approximately) this point of view.

Perhaps, in the end, a notion of "reference" as a type of direct connection to objects in the world might well be appropriate for both a semantics and a pragmatics, as Kripke (1977) suggests, and that terminology could be modified to distinguish them.

5   What Can We Refer to?

Work on reference has, as noted above, tended to focus on what one might call the clearest cases. But the boundaries have been, for the most part, fairly limited. There remain a great number of questions and issues that the direct-reference theory raises. One particularly difficult issue that has received a great deal of attention, though, is the simple question: if a referring expression has no object for its reference, then can it have any content? That there should be some contents is intuitively clear from consideration of names of fictional characters. We need to distinguish cases of fictional reference from failure of reference. After all, Superman does, in fact, wear a cape, and the Lone Ranger a white hat, and decidedly not the other way around; however, at this moment, if I use the term *the giraffe in my office* and there is no such thing, this is simply reference failure. As there is no Superman or Lone Ranger, either, how can we attribute truth values to such sentences?[2] A number of answers have been suggested, such as Bertolet's (1984) notion that the content of such assertions is not the apparent subject, but that the myth or story (which is a part of the real world) exists and is structured in a certain way. In saying, for instance, that Pegasus does not exist, one presupposes that there is a story in which Pegasus figures, but asserts there is no real individual which the story is about. Hintikka (1983), on the other hand, takes a possible worlds approach and suggests that Pegasus, Superman, and the others are to be found as objects, but in other possible worlds from our own. So when we make reference to them, we are doing so in those worlds where they do exist, just not this one.

But "non-existent objects" are not limited by any means to fictional characters (Parsons 1980). There is the case of dreams and hallucinations, for instance, where we use referential terms to make something like successful reference. If, for instance, while in therapy I hallucinate that there is a wolf in the corner, the psychiatrist can ask me questions about it, such as what color it is and how big it is, and I can answer using the expression *the wolf*, even under circumstances where I know that I am hallucinating. We also, curiously, make reference to objects and events of the real world which very clearly do not exist. If I say "the earthquake is supposed to be here in three hours," there is no earthquake I am directly referring to, and there may never be one. Or, if we talk about the government's projected surplus, or the party planned for next Saturday, and none eventuate, what have we referred to? If I buy a bookshelf and a shelf is missing, I refer to the missing bookshelf but have no guarantee that one is, in fact, out there laying around somewhere. Maybe one was never manufactured in the first place.

Beyond this, there is the question of what types of things there are around that can be referred to. Let us ask, for example, about the limits of proper names. Quite obviously, we have names for people and pets, places (Antarctica) and buildings (Dewey Hall) and books and many works of art (*Pride and Prejudice*; *Venus de Milo*). Species names such as *Canis domesticus* also appear to exist. And if this is a name, what does it name that is a particular in the world (a species?), and then why wouldn't *the dog* (in the sense of "The dog is a mammal") also be a species name? Putnam and others have suggested that natural kind terms, like *gold*, directly refer to natural kinds; if so, would *honesty* be the name of a characteristic or property? Is *spring* the name of a season (after all, *August* would seem the name of a month)? The question here is, if a hallmark of proper names is that they name particulars that they take as their referents, then it is possible we have a lot more particulars around than we might have thought, or that things other than particulars can be made direct reference to. The same might be said of definite descriptions. If I talk about "the average French voter," which is no particular French person, am I making something we can meaningfully call *reference*? If, as Chomsky notes, there is a flaw in my argument, and I refer to the flaw later on (in correcting it, for instance), does this mean there are such things as flaws out there as particulars?

Finally, and this could be related to the question of fictional names, the use of referential-sounding expressions can be used for entities only discussed with respect to a particular stretch of discourse (Kamp and Reyle 1993 call this "spontaneous fiction"). Many instances of this can be found in the above discussion. Suppose there is a man at the door. *That man* knocks. I talk to **him**. **He** introduces **himself** as Steve. I ask **Steve** to leave. **The guy** was at the wrong door. What am I referring to in these instances? There is no such person, yet I have used what appears to be ordinary referential language to talk about him. The solution in the framework of Kamp and Reyle (1993) is to suggest that whenever we have (apparent) reference, we are in fact positing discourse markers and associating predicates with them. That is, the reference of language is not objects in the real world, but rather DISCOURSE ENTITIES. It is another stage of evaluation at which there is anything like a semantic mapping to the world (in this instance, models), where distinct discourse entities, for example, may or may not be mapped onto a single real individual. This is hardly a direct-reference way of looking at things, but it holds out interesting possibilities.

NOTES

1   By "pointing," I intend any means of indication of an object, whether one uses the index finger, an open hand, a sideways nod of the head, one's lips, chin, etc. What constitutes "pointing" is, like other gestures, subject to cultural variation.

2   It seems likely that no language distinguishes the fictional from the real in terms of reference. Gregory Ward notes that he made an inquiry on the Linguist List as to whether any known language formally distinguishes noun phrases making reference to fictional entities and real ones, and none was reported.

5 Deixis

STEPHEN C. LEVINSON

For those who treat language as a generative system for objectively describing the world, deixis is a big black fly in the ointment. Deixis introduces subjective, attentional, intentional and, of course, context-dependent properties into natural languages. Further, it is a much more pervasive feature of languages than normally recognized. This complicates a tidy treatment within formal theories of semantics and pragmatics. Deixis is also critical for our ability to learn a language, which philosophers for centuries have linked to the possibility of ostensive definition. Despite this theoretical importance, deixis is one of the most empirically understudied core areas of pragmatics; we are far from understanding its boundaries and have no adequate cross-linguistic typology of deictic expression.

This article does not attempt to review either all the relevant theory (see, e.g., the collections in Davis 1991, section III, or Kasher 1998, vol. III) or all of what is known about deictic systems in the world's languages (see, e.g., Anderson and Keenan 1985, Diessel 1999). Rather, I attempt to pinpoint some of the most tantalizing theoretical and descriptive problems, to sketch the way in which the subject interacts with other aspects of pragmatics, and to illustrate the kind of advances that could be made with further empirical work.

A word on terminology: I will use the terms DEIXIS and INDEXICALITY largely co-extensively – they reflect different traditions (see Bühler 1934 and Peirce in Buchler 1940) and have become associated with linguistic and philosophical approaches respectively. But I will make this distinction: indexicality will be used to label the broader phenomena of contextual dependency and deixis the narrower linguistically relevant aspects of indexicality.

1 Indexicality in Communication and Thought

Students of linguistic systems tend to treat language as a disembodied representational system essentially independent of current circumstances, that is, a system for describing states of affairs in which we individually may have no involvement. It is these linguistic properties that have been the prime target of formal semantics and many philosophical approaches – and not without good reason, as they appear to be the exclusive province of human communication. The communication systems of other primates have none of this "displacement," as Hockett (1958: 579) called it. For example, vervet monkeys produce four kinds of alarm calls, signaling snake, big cat, big primate, or bird of prey. But when the vervet signals BIG PRIMATE, it goes without saying that it means RIGHT HERE, RIGHT NOW, RUN! Indexicality is an intrinsic property of the signals, an essential part of their adaptive role in an evolutionary perspective on communication – animals squeak and squawk because they need to draw attention to themselves or to some intruder (Hauser 1997).

The question naturally arises, then, whether in studying indexicality in natural languages we are studying archaic, perhaps primitive, aspects of human communication, which can perhaps even give us clues to the evolution of human language. Jackendoff (1999) has argued that some aspects of language may be residues from ancient human communication systems, but he curiously omits deictics from the list. There would be reasons for caution, because indexicality in human communication has some special properties. For example, take the prototypical demonstrative accompanied by the typical pointing gesture – there seems to be no phylogenetic continuity here at all, since apes don't point (Kita in press). Secondly, unlike the vervet calls, demonstrative can referentially identify – as in *that* particular big primate, not *this* one. More generally, one can say that whereas other animals communicate **presupposing** (in a non-technical sense) the "here and now," as in vervet alarm calls, humans communicate by **asserting** the (non-)relevance of the "here and now." Thirdly, even our nearest animal cousins lack the complex, reflexive modeling of their partners' attentional states, which is an essential ingredient in selective indexical reference – this is why apes cannot "read" a pointing gesture (Povinelli et al. in press).

But if the phylogenetic continuities seem to be missing, perhaps the ontogenetic priority of deixis will be clear. Indeed, human infants invariably seem to point before they speak (see E. Clark 1978, Butterworth 1998, Haviland in press), although we have little cross-cultural evidence here. Philosophers have long taken indexicality as the route into reference – as John Stuart Mill argued, how could you learn a proper name except by presentation of the referent? The view was refined by Russell, who made the distinction between what he called logically proper names (*I, this*), which require such ostensive learning, and disguised descriptions, like *Aristotle*, which mercifully don't. Linguists have argued similarly that deixis is the source of reference, i.e. deictic reference is ontogenetically primary to other kinds (Lyons 1975). But the actual facts concerning the acquisition of deictic expressions paint a different picture, for the acquisition of many aspects of deixis is quite delayed (Tanz 1980, Wales 1986), and even though demonstratives figure early, they are often not used correctly (see Clark 1978). This is hardly surprising because, from the infant's point of view, deixis is as confusing as a hall of mirrors: my "I" is your "you," my "this" your "that," my "here" your "there," and so forth. The demonstratives aren't used correctly in English until well after the pronouns *I* and *you*, or indeed after deictic *in front of/in back of*, not until the age of about four (Tanz 1980: 145).

Apart from this oscillation of point of view, there's another reason that deixis in language isn't as simple as a vervet monkey call signaling BIG PRIMATE RIGHT HERE NOW! The deictic system in language is embedded in a context-independent descriptive system, in such a way that the two systems produce a third that is not reducible to either. To use Peirce's terminology, we have an intersection of the indexical plane into the symbolic one – it's a folding back of the primitive existential indexical relation into symbolic reference, so that we end up with something much more complex on both planes. On the one hand, symbolic reference is relativized to time, place, speaker, and so on, so that *John will speak next* is true now, not later, and on the other, indexical reference is mediated by symbolic meaning, so that *this book* can't be used to point to this mug.

The true semantical complexity of this emergent hybrid system is demonstrated by the well-known paradoxes of self-reference essentially introduced by indexical reference. Consider the liar paradoxes of the Cretan variety, as in *This sentence is false*, which is true only if it is false, and false only if it is true: the paradox resides in what Reichenbach called TOKEN-REFLEXIVITY, which he considered to be the essence of indexical expressions. There is still no definitive solution to paradoxes of this sort, which demonstrates the inadequacy of our current metalinguistic apparatus (but see Barwise and Etchemendy 1987 for a recent analysis invoking the Austinian notion of a proposition, which involves an intrinsic indexical component).

Indexical reference also introduces complexities into the relation between semantics and cognition – that is, between, on the one hand, what sentences mean and what we mean when we say them and, on the other hand, the corresponding thoughts they express. The idea that the relation between meaning and thought is transparent and direct has figured in many branches of linguistic inquiry, from Whorfian linguistics to Ordinary Language Philosophy. But as Frege (1918: 24) pointed out almost a century ago, indexicals are a major problem for this presumption. He was finally led to say that demonstratives, in particular the pronoun *I*, express thoughts that are incommunicable! Frege found that demonstratives introduced some special problems for the theoretical stance he wanted to adopt (see Perry 1977 for explication), but the general issue is easily appreciated.

The question is: what exactly corresponds in thought to the content of a deictically anchored sentence? For example, what exactly do I remember when I remember the content of an indexical utterance? Suppose I say, sweating it out in Clinton Hall at UCLA,

(1)   It's warm here now.

and suppose the corresponding thought is just plain "It's warm here now." When I recollect that thought walking in Murmansk in February, I will then be thinking something false, something that does not correspond to the rival Murmansk thought, namely "It's bone-chilling cold here now." So in some way the sentence meaning with its deictics must be translated into a deicticless UCLA-specific thought. A candidate would be:

(2)   It be warm (over 30 °C) at 3.00 p.m. on July 6, 2001 in room 327 in Clinton Hall on the UCLA campus.

Then when I inspect this thought in Murmansk in February it will look just as true as it did on July 6, 2001 in Clinton Hall. But unfortunately, this doesn't seem to correspond to the psychological reality at all – that's just not what I thought! I might not even know the name of the building, let alone the room number, and perhaps I have failed to adjust my watch for jet lag and so think it is July 7. So we cannot cash out indexicals into absolute space/time coordinates and retain the subjective content of the thought corresponding to the utterance (1). Well, what if the corresponding thought is just "It is warm here now" but somehow tagged with the time and place at which I thought it? Then walking in Murmansk I would think "In the first week of July somewhere on the UCLA campus I had the thought 'It is warm here now'." That seems subjectively on the right track, but now we are into deep theoretical water, because now the language of thought has indexicals, and in order to interpret THEM we would need all the apparatus we employed to map contexts into propositions that we need in linguistics but now reproduced in the *lingua mentalis*, with a little homunculus doing all the metalinguistic work. Worse, when we ultimately cash out the indexicals of thought into a non-indexical mental metalanguage of thought to get the proposition expressed, we will have lost the subjective content again (or alternatively, we will have an infinite regression of indexical languages). So we haven't reduced the problem at all.

So what does correspond to the thought underlying an indexical sentence? The source of the conundrum seems once again to be the peculiar hybrid symbolic/indexical nature of language – it seems easy enough (in the long run anyway) to model the objective content of symbolic expressions on the one hand and pure indexical signals like vervet monkey calls on the other, but something peculiar happens when you combine the two.

2   The Challenge of Indexicality

Deixis is the study of deictic or indexical expressions in language, like *you, now, today*. It can be regarded as a special kind of grammatical property instantiated in the familiar categories of person, tense, place, etc. In what follows, I adhere to this conservative division of the deictic field, because there is much to be said about how linguistic expressions build in properties for contextual resolution. But it is important to realize that the property of indexicality is not exhausted by the study of inherently indexical expressions. For just about any referring expression can be used deictically:

(3) *He* is my father (said of man entering the room)

(4) *Someone* is coming (said ear cocked to a slamming door)

(5) *The funny noise* is our antiquated dishwashing machine (said pointing chin to kitchen)

(6) What *a great picture*! (said looking at a picture)

For most such cases, some gesture or pointed gaze is required, and we may be tempted to think that a demonstration is the magic ingredient, as in the following cases where the demonstration replaces a linguistic expression:

(7) The editor's sign for "delete" is [followed by written demonstration]

(8) He is a bit [index finger to forehead, indicating "mad"]

But this is not a necessary feature:

(9) *The chairman* hereby resigns (said by the chairman)

(10) *He* obviously had plenty of money (said walking through the Taj Mahal). (after Nunberg 1993)

So what is the property of indexicality? With inherently deictic expressions like the demonstrative pronoun *this*, what is striking is that the referent is provided not by the semantic conditions imposed by the expression but by the context; for example, the speaker may be holding up a pen. It is the obvious semantic deficiency of *this* that directs the addressee's attention to the speaker's gesture. In a similar way, the semantic generality of *he* without prior discourse context (as in (3) or (10)) forces a contextual resolution in the circumstances of the speech event. In this respect, there is a close relation between exophora and anaphora. In both cases we have contextual resolution of semantically general expressions – in the physical space–time context of the speech event and in the ongoing discourse respectively (Levinson 2000a: 268ff.). Third-person referring expressions which are semantically deficient, in the sense that their descriptive content does not suffice to identify a referent, invite pragmatic resolution, perhaps by default in the discourse, and failing that in the physical context.

But semantic deficiency can't be the only defining characteristic of index-icality. After all, there is a cline of referring expressions like *he, the man, the short man, George, the President, the second President to be the son of a President* (see Abbott, this volume), and unambiguously identifying descriptions are the exception rather than the rule in natural language. Semantic deficiency or vacuity is resolved through the kind of mutual windowing of attention in which the speaker says *I just saw what's-his-name*, expecting the addressee to be able to guess who (for the mechanism see Schelling 1960 and H. Clark 1996). Although such a narrowing of possibilities relies on mutual attention to mutual knowledge in the context, to call such phenomena "deictic" or "indexical" would be to render the label too broad to be useful. Rather, the critical feature that picks out a coherent field is precisely the one that C. S. Peirce outlined, namely an existential relationship between the sign and the thing indicated – so that when *he* is said in the Taj Mahal, or *this* is said when holding a pen, the sign is connected to the context as smoke is to fire (although non-causally). How? The key is the direction of the addressee's attention to some feature of the spatio-temporal physical context (as in the case of *this*, said holding the pen), or the presumption of the prior existence of that attention (as in the *he*, said in the Taj Mahal). Indexicality is both an **intentional** and **attentional** phenomenon, concentrated around the spatial–temporal center of verbal interaction, what Bühler (1934) called the deictic *origo*.

This brings us to gesture, one obvious way of securing the addressee's attention. In philosophical approaches to language, ostension or gestural presentation has been thought crucial for acquisition (try teaching the word *ball* to a two-year-old with no ball in sight), but as both Wittgenstein and Quine have observed, pointing is hardly as self-explanatory as Mill imagined – when I point at a river and say *This is the Thames*, I could be pointing to one square kilometer of map-grid, or just the left bank, the sun sparkling on the ripples, or even the cubic meter of water just then flowing past my index finger on its way to the sea (Quine 1961: chapter 4, Wettstein 1984). Pointing works like inadequate descriptions, through the exercise of a Schelling coordination problem – I plan to pick out with a gesture just what I think you'll think I plan to pick out, given where we are and what we are doing. The reflexive phrasing here recalls Grice's (1957) theory of meaning, in which when I point and say *I mean that* I intend to invoke in you a referent-isolating thought by virtue of your recognizing that that is my intention.

In this way gesture – and arguably deixis in general – is crucially intentional: you cannot say "False!" to my utterance "I am referring to *that*." Deictic gestures do seem to be special; for example, they are made further from the body than other kinds of gesture (McNeill 1992: 91), and we now know something about their universal bases and cross-cultural variation (Kita in press). But the role of gesture is a much more complicated business than suggested by the philosophers, who imagine, for example, that demonstratives always require gestures (see e.g. Lewis's 1972: 175 coordinate for "indicated objects"). Not only can gestures be reduced to directed gaze or a nod (or in some cultures to a pursing of the lips – see Enfield 2002), they may be rendered unnecessary by the circumstances (consider "What was that?" said of a noise, or "This is wonderful" said of a room). As Fillmore (1997) points out, demonstratives typically have two uses – *this city* resists a gesture (symbolic usage), just as *this finger* requires one (gestural usage), while there are specific expressions (like presentatives or American *yea* in *yea big*) that always require gestures.

To sum up so far: indexicality involves what Peirce's "dynamical coexistence" of an indexical sign with its object of reference. It is normally associated with linguistic expressions that are semantically insufficient to achieve reference without contextual support. That support is provided by the mutual attention of the interlocutors and their ability to reconstruct the speaker's referential intentions given clues in the environment.

This does not, however, suffice to establish clear boundaries to the phenomena. One problem is what Bühler (1934) called *Deixis am Phantasma* ("deixis in the imagination"), in which one imagines oneself somewhere else, and shifts the deictic origo by a series of transpositions. Suppose I try to describe to you where I left a book, and I say, "Imagine this room were my office. The book would be right here [pointing to the edge of my desk]." As Fillmore (1975) observes, much deixis is relativized to text, as in reported speech or in the opening line of a Hemingway short story: "The door of Henry's lunchroom opened and two men came in," where, as Fillmore notes, the inside of Henry's lunchroom has become the deictic origo.

Then there is anaphora, which is so closely linked to deixis that it is not always separable, as in *I've been living in San Francisco for five years and I love it here* (where *here* is both anaphoric and deictic), bridged by the intermediate area of textual deixis (as in *Harry said "I didn't do that" but he said it in a funny way*, where *it* does not refer to the proposition expressed but to Harry's utterance itself). An additional boundary problem is posed by the fact that the class of indexical expressions is not so clearly demarcated. For example, in *Let's go to a nearby restaurant, nearby* is used deictically, but in *Churchill took De Gaulle to a nearby restaurant* it is not – is this deixis relativized to text, or does *nearby* simply presume some point of measurement? Suppose we yield *nearby* up to deixis, then what about *enemy* in *The enemy are coming*? *Enemy* seems to presume an implicit agonistic counterpart, which may be filled deictically but may not (as in *Hannibal prepared for the onslaught of the enemy*; see Mitchell 1986). There is no clear boundary here. Even more difficult, of course, is the point made above: indexicality exceeds the bounds of ready-made indexical expressions, i.e. deictics with in-built contextual parameters, as shown by the indexical use of third person pronouns and referring expressions.

3   Deictic Expressions in Semantic Theory

Let's return to relative terra firma, namely special-purpose deictic expressions – that is, linguistic expressions that require indexical resolution. The special semantic character of such expressions is an abiding puzzle in the philosophy of language. Expressions like *today* have a constant meaning, but systematically varying reference. In some ways they resemble proper names, since they often have little descriptive content (and hence resist good paraphrase), but in their constantly changing reference they could hardly be more different (Kaplan 1989a: 562). Above all, they resist eliminative paraphrase into non-indexical objective description – *I am Stephen Levinson* cannot be paraphrased as *Stephen Levinson is Stephen Levinson. The speaker of this utterance is Stephen Levinson* gets closer, but fails to eliminate the indexical component now shifted to *this* and introduces token-reflexivity.

So how should we think about the meaning of indexicals? What is clear is that any sentence with indexicals (and given person, tense, and spatial deixis, that means nearly every natural language sentence) cannot directly express a proposition, for a proposition is an abstract entity whose truth value is independent of the times, places, and persons in the speech event. If we think of propositions as mappings from worlds to truth values, then whereas we might be able to characterize the meanings of non-indexical expressions in terms of the part they play in such a mapping, there seems no such prospect for indexical expressions.

In philosophical approaches to semantics a consensus has now arisen for handling indexical expressions as a two-stage affair, a mapping from contexts into propositional contents, which are then a mapping from, say, worlds to truth values In Montague's (1970) early theory the content of deictic expressions was captured by mapping contexts (a set of indices for speakers, addressees, indicated objects, times, and places) into intensions. In Kaplan's (1989a) theory, all expressions have this characteristic mapping (their CHARACTER) from contexts into intensions (their proposition-relevant content). The meaning of *I* is its character, a function or rule that variably assigns an individual concept, namely the speaker, in each context (Kaplan 1978; cf. Carlson, this volume). Non-indexical expressions have constant character, but may (rigid designators) or may not (other referring expressions) have constant content.

Another influential version of the two-stage theory can be found in Situation Semantics (Barwise and Perry 1983). There, utterances are interpreted with respect to three situations (or states of affairs): the UTTERANCE SITUATION (corresponding to Montague's indices), the RESOURCE SITUATION (which handles other contextually determined reference like anaphora), and the DESCRIBED SITUATION (corresponding to the propositional content). Indexicals and other contextually parameterized expressions get their variables fixed in the utterance and/or resource situations, which are then effectively discarded – it is just the value of the variables, e.g. the referent of *I* or *that*, that is transferred to the described situation (e.g. *I gave him that* has the described content of "Stephen Levinson gave him that book"). Meaning is relational, the meaning of an indexical characterized as the relation between utterance/resource situations and described situations. This large improvement over the Montague theory no longer requires a complete pre-specification of relevant aspects of the context as in Montague's indices – other ad hoc factors can be picked up in the resource situation.

The central property of two-stage theories is that indexicals do not contribute directly to the proposition expressed, the content of what is said, or the situation described. Instead, they take us to an individual, a referent, which is then slotted into the proposition expressed or the situation described, or, as Nunberg (1993: 159) puts it: "The meanings of indexicals are composite functions that take us from an element of the context to an element of a contextually restricted domain, and then drop away."

This kind of treatment of indexicality falls far short of descriptive adequacy. First, the indexicals which have been the target of most philosophical approaches (sometimes called "pure indexicals" – expressions like *I*, *now*, or *here*), seem to have their semantico-pragmatic content exhausted by a specification of the relevant index (speaker, time, and place of speaking respectively; see Wettstein 1984). But closely related indexicals like *we*, *today*, *nearby* may also express additional semantic conditions (at least one person in addition to the speaker, the diurnal span which contains the coding time, a place distinct from here but close to here, respectively). So deictics may contain both descriptive properties and contextual variables in the one expression. Perhaps a more difficult problem for the view that deictics just deliver referents to the proposition expressed is the fact that they can in fact express quantified variables. For example, in *Every time a visiting soprano comes, we sing duets* the pronoun *we* denotes a set consisting of the speaker and a variable (Nunberg 1993). In addition, nearly all deictics are heavily dependent on pragmatic resolution – *Come here* may mean come to this sofa or come to this city according to context (see Levinson 2000a: 177ff.).

Secondly, the idea that the relevant contextual features can be fixed in advance (as is required by the Montague-style solution) is problematic. Suppose I say, "This is the largest walnut tree on the planet": I could be pointing to a tree some distance away, or we could just be standing underneath it, or I could be touching a picture in a book, or if you were blind I could be running your hand over the bark, or I could be telling you what we are about to see as we walk over the hill. The mode of demonstration just does not seem to be determined in advance (see Cresswell 1973: 111ff.). Thirdly, there are many aspects of the meaning of demonstratives that exceed any such specification by predetermined index. When Sheila says, "We have better sex lives than men," *we* doesn't just mean "speaker plus some other"; it denotes the set of women, including the speaker. Such usages exploit indexicality in the Peircean sense, that is, the direct connections between the situation of speaking (here, the fact that the speaker is female) and the content of what is communicated. Fourth, there is the problem that Quine called "deferred ostension," now familiar through the work of Nunberg (1977, 1993, this volume). Suppose we are listening to a program on a radio station and I say "CNN has just bought this" – I don't refer to the current jingle but the radio station. Or I point at a Coca-Cola bottle and say "That used to be a different shape" – what I refer to is not the current bottle, but the type of container of the holy liquid, and I assert that tokens used to be of a different shape. In these cases, the indicated thing is not the thing referred to, and the Montagovian or Creswellian mechanism will get us the wrong proposition. Fifth, these treatments of indexicality presuppose that there is a clear class of indexical expressions with a built-in variable whose value is instantiated in the context. But third-person, non-deictic expressions can have indexical uses, as when I say, pointing to a man in a purple turban, "He is Colonel Gaddafi's nephew."

There are then a formidable set of obstacles to the treatment of indexicals as simply a rule-governed mapping from contextual indices to intensions, or utterance-situations into individuals which can then play a role in described situations. The problems in essence are that the context offers Gibsonian AFFORDANCES, properties of the context which may be creatively exploited for communicative purposes.[1] Deictics have ATTENTIONAL, INTENTIONAL, and SUBJECTIVE features that resist this cashing out of their content in objective descriptions. The attentional and intentional features were mentioned in the previous section, but the subjective features are worth a special mention. Perry (1977), developing a character of Frege's, invites us to imagine an amnesiac, Rudolf Lingens, lost in the Stanford library, who discovers a complete biography of himself. So he knows everything there is to know about Rudolf Lingens, even that he is an amnesiac lost in the Stanford library, but he does not know that he himself is Rudolf Lingens. In this case, it is clear that when he says, "I am hungry," the corresponding Fregean thought is not "Rudolf Lingens is hungry." Were he to come to his senses and utter "Why, I am Rudolf Lingens!," the force of the realization would certainly not be captured by the proposition "Rudolf Lingens is Rudolf Lingens," or even "The speaker of this utterance is Rudolf Lingens" – for what he would have realized is not the identity of the subject of the sentence, but the identity of his subjective self.[2] Linguists have also noted a subjective quality to deixis, for example an overlap between the subjective aspects of modality and the objective aspects of tense – thus the French *Le premier ministre serait malade* codes both present tense and a lack of subjective certainty, as do grammaticalized evidentials in other languages (Lyons 1982: 111).

A final aspect of the semantic character of indexical expressions that should be mentioned is their special PROJECTION PROPERTIES, which follow from the fact that demonstratives and many other deictics have no substantial descriptive content, so that once the contextual parameters have been fixed they are "directly referential" (Kaplan 1989a). A true demonstrative remains transparent in an intensional context – in "Ralph said he broke that" *that* can only be the thing the speaker is now pointing at, not the thing Ralph pointed at – the speaker cannot withhold a gesture on the grounds that Ralph made it. Further, deictics do not generally fall under the scope of negation or modal operators: *That is not a planet* cannot be understood as "I am not indicating x and x is a planet" (Enç 1981). Deictics resist attributive or "semantic" readings; thus whereas *The man who can lift this sword is our king* has both a referential and attributive reading ("whoever can . . ."), *That man who can lift this sword is our king* has only a referential reading. In addition to the paradoxes of self-reference, there are sentences with indexicals which have the curious property of being at the same time contingently true or false, yet upon being uttered are automatically true or self-verifying, as in *I am here now* or *I am now pointing at that* (said pointing at something).

4 The Role of Pragmatics in the Resolution of Deictic Expressions: a Close Look at Demonstrative Systems

We have seen that indexicality exceeds the bounds of the built-in indexical expressions in any language. Moreover, the field of indexical expressions is not clearly delimited, because insofar as most referring expressions do not fully individuate solely by virtue of their semantic content but rather depend for success on states of mutual knowledge holding between discourse participants, the great majority of successful acts of reference depend on indexical conditions. Still, we may hope to make a distinction between expressions used indexically, and those – let us call them deictic – that necessarily invoke features of the context because of a contextual variable built into their semantic conditions. This distinction will also be plagued by borderline examples, as exemplified above by expressions like *nearby* or even *enemy*. Even if we decide that *local* as in *the local pub* is an expression with an unfilled variable that is preferentially filled by spatial parameters of the context of speaking, we would be loath to think that all quality adjectives are deictic just because they have a suppressed comparator as argument (as in *John is tall*, implying taller than the average reference population, as supplied by the context). Fuzzy borders to a phenomenon do not make categories useless (otherwise color terms would not exist), so in what follows we will proceed by focusing on deictic expressions which clearly involve inherent contextual variables.

The pragmatic character of indexicality is not the only central issue for a pragmatic theory of deictic expressions, for the organization of the semantic field of contrastive deictic expressions is often itself determined by pragmatic factors. As an illustration of this, we concentrate here on the cross-linguistic comparison of demonstrative systems, which have played a central role in philosophical and linguistic thinking about deixis. The analysis of demonstratives is much complicated by their multi-functional role in language – they are often used not only to point things out, but to track referents in discourse and more generally to contrast with other referring expressions. It has become traditional to distinguish amongst at least some of the uses (Levinson 1983, Diessel 1999) shown in figure 5.1.

The relations between these uses are probably more complex than this taxonomy suggests, but it is clearly not sufficient to distinguish simply between exophoric (deictic) and endophoric (non-deictic) at the highest branch as in Levinson (1983: 68) and Diessel (1999: 6), since discourse deixis is intra-text

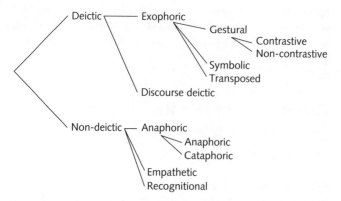

Figure 5.1   Distinct uses of demonstratives

but deictic, and empathetic and recognitional uses are extra-text but non-deictic. The following examples illustrate the distinctions involved:

(11)   "Give me **that** book" (exophoric: book available in the physical context)

(12)   "I hurt **this** finger" (exophoric gestural: requires gesture or presentation of finger)

(13)   "I like **this** city" (exophoric symbolic: does not require gesture)

(14)   "I broke **this** tooth first and then **that** one next" (gestural contrastive)

(15)   "He looked down and saw the gun: **this** was the murder weapon, he realized" (transposed)

(16)   "'You are wrong'. **That's** exactly what she said" (discourse deictic)

(17)   "It sounded like **this**: whoosh" (discourse deictic)

(18)   "The cowboy entered. **This** man was not someone to mess with" (anaphoric)

(19)   "He went and hit **that** bastard" (empathetic)

(20)   "Do you remember **that** holiday we spent in the rain in Devon?" (recognitional)

Exophoric, gestural, non-transposed uses of demonstratives have usually been considered basic. Diessel (1999) points out that exophoric gestural uses are the earliest in acquisition, the least marked in form, and the source of grammaticalization chains that run through the other uses. In what follows we shall concentrate on the exophoric gestural uses. Less well supported is the supposition that the basic semantic contrasts between sets of exophoric demonstratives are spatial in nature, encoding degrees of distance from speaker or addressee (cf. Anderson and Keenan 1985). There is no a priori reason why this should be the case, yet grammars of languages almost invariably describe demonstrative systems in this spatial way. There are two major kinds of paradigm: speaker-anchored distance systems, and speaker/addressee-anchored systems, as illustrated by Spanish and Quileute (Anderson and Keenan 1985):

(21) **Spanish** *Distance from speaker*
         –   (proximal) *este*
         +   (medial)   *ese*
        ++ (distal)   *acquel*

(22) **Quileute** *Close to speaker*   *Close to addressee*

+	–	*xo'ʔo*
–	+	*so'ʔo*
+	+	*sa'ʔa*
–	–	*á:ča'ʔa*

Although a few languages may have only one demonstrative pronoun or adjective, this is supplemented in probably most (Diessel (1999: 36) claims all) cases by a proximal/distal contrast in deictic adverbs ("here" vs. "there"). Three-term systems may be speaker-anchored (like two-term systems), speaker/addressee-anchored, or both. Systems with more than four terms combine other semantic dimensions, like visibility or vertical distance relative to the speaker, or shape of the referent.

A speaker-anchored distance system with three terms is often organized in terms of a binary opposition between proximal and distal, with the distal category permitting finer discrimination (McGregor argues for such an analysis for Warrwa, where the medial is the most marked form; see van Geenhoven and Warner 1999: 60). Some systems combine both speaker- and addressee-anchored systems, as with the Yélî Dnye demonstrative determiners:[3]

(23)   Speaker-based Addressee-based
    Proximal **ala**   **ye**
    Medial   **kî**   –
    Distal   **mu** (far from Speaker, can apply to objects close to Addressee)

Kî is the unmarked term here – it can refer freely, but if the speaker or addressee is actually holding something, the speaker- or addressee-centered term pre-empts it. Thus the medial interpretation is due entirely to pragmatic pre-emption from the more semantically specified forms. In this semantic generality, the Yélî Dnye medial contrasts with the marked Warrwa medial.

Yélî Dnye shows that there are actually at least three kinds of multi-term systems, not just the two posited in the literature – speaker-centered distance systems (with no addressee-centered forms) vs. person-based systems (with no medial-from-speaker forms, and where distal is interpreted as distal from both S[peaker] and A[ddressee]).

So far we have taken demonstratives to code spatial discriminations. But this may not always be so (cf. Hanks 1996, Himmelmann 1997). Two systems that have traditionally been treated as addressee-anchored distance systems have on close analysis proved to be less spatial than thought. Here is a typical analysis of Turkish and Japanese demonstratives:

(24) | | Turkish | Japanese |
| --- | --- | --- |
| "Near Speaker" | *bu* | *ko* |
| "Near Addressee" | *şu* | *so* |
| "Near neither Speaker nor Addressee" | *o* | *a* |

Close analysis of video-taped task-oriented communication shows that these glosses do not reflect real usage conditions (Özyürek and Kita 2002). For Turkish the correct analysis seems to be that *şu* presumes lack of joint attention and is used to draw the attention of the addressee to a referent in the context, while *bu* and *o* presume that the referents are already in the addressee's attentional focus, in which case *bu* is used for objects closer to the speaker and *o* for those distant from the speaker. A similar story can be told for Japanese: *so* has two functions – one simply to indicate that the referent is close to addressee, the other (as with Turkish *şu*) to draw the addressee's attention to a new referent. This latter usage is pre-empted by *ko* when the referent is very close to speaker, and by *a* when far from both speaker and addressee. A primary oppositions here involves not proximity to speaker vs. addressee, but rather shared vs. non-shared attentional focus.

This finding fits with the pre-theoretical ruminations above: indexicality crucially involves some link between utterance and context so that the context can be used as an affordance to find the intended reference. As noted, deictic expressions and gestures both do this by drawing the addressee's attention to some feature of the spatio-temporal environment (or of adjacent utterance). Also highlighted is the crucial role gesture plays in deixis, for gesture serves to direct the addressee's attention. The prototypical occurrence of demonstratives with gestures seems crucial to how children learn demonstratives, which are always amongst the first fifty words learned and often the first closed-class set acquired; the acquisition of the pointing gesture precedes that of the words (Clark 1978, Tanz 1980).

Finally, it is often suggested that definite articles are simply demonstratives unmarked for distance (Lyons 1977: 653–4, Anderson and Keenan 1985: 280), but this does not fit the fact, noted above, that many demonstrative systems themselves have unmarked members (like *that* in English), nor the fact that a number of languages (like German) have only one demonstrative that contrasts with a definite article. There certainly is close kinship between definite determiners and demonstratives, as shown by the frequent grammaticalization of the former from the latter. Both contrast with indefinites (see Diessel 1999), and both share a presumption of uniqueness within a contextually given set of entities (Hawkins 1991; Abbott, this volume). It is the focusing of attention on the physical context that is the special character of demonstratives in their basic use.

5   The Fields of Deixis

I turn now to a brief survey of deictic expressions in language. Linguists normally treat deixis as falling into a number of distinct semantic fields: person, place, time, etc. Since Bühler (1934), the deictic field has been organized around an **origo** or "ground zero" consisting of the speaker at the time and place of speaking. Actually, many systems utilize two distinct centers – speaker and addressee. Further, as Bühler noted, many deictic expressions can be transposed or relativized to some other origo, most often the person of the protagonist at the relevant time and place in a narrative (see Fillmore 1997).

We can make a number of distinctions between different ways in which deictic expressions may be used. First, many deictic expressions may be used non-deictically – anaphorically, as in *We went to Verdi's Requiem last weekend and really enjoyed that*, or non-anaphorically, as in *Last weekend we just did this and that*. Second, when used deictically, we need to distinguish between those used at the normal origo and those transposed to some other origo. It might be thought that the latter are not strictly speaking deictic (since they have been displaced from the time and place of speaking), but consider *He came right up to her and hit her like this here on the arm*, in which the speaker pantomimes the protagonists, so licensing the use of *come*, *this*, and *here*. Third, as noted, deictic expressions may be used gesturally or non-gesturally (*this arm* versus *this room*), while some like tense inflections may not occur with gestures at all. "Gesture" here must be understood in the widest sense, since pointing in some cultures (like the Cunha) is primarily with lips and eyes and not hands and since even vocal intonation can function in a "gestural" way (*Now hold your fire; wait; shoot NOW*, or *I'm over HERE*). Similarly, many languages have presentatives (like French *voila!*) requiring the presentation of something simultaneous with the expression, or greetings requiring the presentation of the right hand, or terms like *thus* requiring a demonstration of a mode of action.

The deictic categories of person, place, and time are widely instantiated in grammatical distinctions made by languages around the world (see Fillmore 1975; Weissenborn and Klein 1982; Anderson and Keenan 1985; Levinson 1983, chapter 2; Diessel 1999). Bühler's origo, the speaker and the place and time of her utterance, along with the role of recipient or addressee, recurs at the core of deictic distinctions in grammar after grammar. These are the crucial reference points upon which complex deictic concepts are constructed, whether honorifics, complex tenses, or systems of discourse deixis. They constitute strong universals of language at a conceptual level, although their manifestation is anything but uniform: not all languages have pronouns, tense, contrasting demonstratives, or any other type of deictic expression that one might enumerate.

Unfortunately, cross-linguistic data on deictic categories are not ideal. One problem is that the **meaning** of deictic expressions is usually treated as self-evident in grammatical descriptions and rarely properly investigated, and a second problem is that major typological surveys are scarce (but see Diessel 1999, Cysouw 2001). But despite the universality of deictic categories like person, place, and time, their expression in grammatical categories is anything but universal. For example, despite claims to the contrary, not all languages have first and second person pronouns (cf. "The first and second person pronouns are universal": Hockett 1961: 21), not all languages have spatially contrastive demonstrative pronouns or determiners (contra Diessel 1999, who suggests universality for such a contrast in demonstrative adverbs), not all languages have tense, not all languages have verbs of coming and going, bringing and taking, etc. Rather, deictic categories have a universality independent of their grammatical expression – they will all be reflected somewhere in grammar or lexis.

5.1   *Person deixis*

The grammatical category of person directly reflects the different roles that individuals play in the speech event: speaker, addressee, and other. When these roles shift in the course of conversational turn-taking the origo shifts with them (hence Jespersen's 1922 term SHIFTERS for deictic expressions): A's *I* becomes B's *you*, A's *here* becomes B's *there* and so forth.

The traditional person paradigm can be captured by the two semantic features of speaker inclusion (S) and addressee inclusion (A): first person (+S), second person (+A, –S), and third person (–S, –A), hence a residual, non-deictic category. Most languages directly encode the +S and +A roles in pronouns and/or verb agreement, and the majority explicitly mark third person (–S, –A). But there are clear exceptions to the alleged universality of first and second person marking; in Southeast Asian languages like Thai there are titles (on the pattern of "servant" for first person, "master" for second person) used in place of pronouns and there is no verb agreement (Cooke 1968). Many languages have no third person pronouns, often indirectly marking third person by zero agreement. Thus Yélî Dnye has the following pronoun paradigm (with different paradigms in possessive and oblique cases):

(25)   **Yélî Dnye nominative pronouns**

	Singular	Dual	Plural
1	*nê*	*nyo*	*nmo*
2	*nyi*	*dp:o*	*nmyo*
3	φ	φ	φ

The paradigmatic analysis of person marking, whether in pronouns or agreement, is a more complex area than one might at first suppose. Although the traditional notions first, second and third persons hold up remarkably well, there are many kinds of homophony, or different patterns of syncretism, across person paradigms (Cysouw 2001). Much of this complexity is due to the distinctive notions of plurality appropriate to this special paradigm: first person plural clearly does not entail more than one person in +S role, amounting to a chorus. "We" notions are especially troubling, since many languages distinguish such groups as: +S+A vs. +S+A+O (where O is Other, i.e. one or more third persons), vs. +S–A, vs. +S–A+O. In some pronominal systems "plural" can be neatly analyzed as augmenting a minimal deictic specification with "plus one or more additional individuals" (AUG). Thus the distinction between *I* and *we* might be analyzed as (+S, –AUG), (+S, +AUG). Additional motivation for such an analysis is the fact that a number of languages treat "I + you" – i.e. speech-act participants – as a singular pronominal package, which is then augmented to form a "I + you + other" pronoun. The following is the paradigm from Rembarrnga (Dixon 1980: 352):

(26) **Rembarrnga dative pronouns (after Dixon 1980)**

	Minimal	Unit augmented	Augmented
+S	ŋənə	yarrpparraʔ	yarrə
+S+A	yəkkə	ŋakorrparraʔ	ŋakorrə
+A	kə	nakorrparraʔ	nakorrə
–S–A masc	nawə	parrpparraʔ	parrə
–S–A fem	ŋatə		

Tamil, Fijian, and other languages distinguish INCLUSIVE from EXCLUSIVE *we*, i.e. (+S, +A) from (+S, –A, +AUG). A few languages (like Pirahã) do not mark plurality in the person paradigms at all (Cysouw 2001: 78–9).

One much studied phenomenon in person deixis is in the effect of reported speech on speakers' self-reference – where we say *John said he would come* many languages permit only in effect "John said 'I will come'." In Yélî Dnye thoughts and desires must also retain the correct subjective person: *John wants to come* must be rendered "John wants 'I come'." Then there is the phenomenon of honorifics, which typically make reference to speaking and recipient roles, dealt with separately below under the rubric of social deixis (section 5.5). Yet another important area is the special role that speaker and addressee roles play in typologically significant grammatical hierarchies; many languages have no dedicated reflexives in first and second person, and many treat first and second person as the topmost categories on an animacy hierarchy, governing case-marking, passivization, and other syntactic processes (see Comrie 1989).

In addition, although in the Bühlerian and the philosophical traditions the speaking role is given centrality, the importance of the addressee role is reflected in a number of special grammatical phenomena, e.g. vocative case and special forms for titles, kin-terms and proper names used in address.

Apart from its grammatical importance, person has a special significance because of its omnipresence – it is a grammatical category marked or implicit in every utterance, which inevitably indicates first, second or third person in nominal or verbal paradigms, either explicitly or by contrastive omission.

5.2   *Time deixis*

In Bühler's origo, the temporal "ground zero" is the moment at which the utterance is issued ("coding time" of Fillmore 1997). Hence *now* means some span of time including the moment of utterance, *today* means that diurnal span in which the speaking event takes place, and *is* predicates a property that holds at the time of speaking. Similarly we count backwards from coding time in calendrical units in such expressions as *yesterday* or *three years ago*, or forwards in *tomorrow* or *next Thursday*. In written or recorded uses of language, we can distinguish coding time from receiving time, and in particular languages there are often conventions about whether one writes "I am writing this today so you will receive it tomorrow" or something more like "I have written this yesterday so that you receive it today."

The nature of calendrical units varies across cultures. Yélî Dnye recognizes the day as a diurnal unit, has words for "yesterday" and "the day before," and special monomorphemic words for tomorrow, the day after tomorrow and so forth for ten days into the future, and thereafter a generative system for specifying days beyond that. It needs such a system because there is no concept of week, or any larger clockwork system of calendrical units that can be tied to coding time as in English *next March*. But most languages exhibit a complex interaction between systems of time measurement, e.g. calendrical units, and deictic anchorage through demonstratives or special modifiers like *next* or *ago*. In English, units of time measurement may either be fixed by reference to the calendar or not: thus *I'll do it this week* is ambiguous between guaranteeing achievement within seven days from utterance time, or within the calendar unit beginning on Sunday (or Monday) including utterance time. *This year* means the calendar year including the time of utterance (or in some circumstances the 365-day unit beginning at the time of utterance) but *this November* tends to mean the next monthly unit so named (or alternatively, the November of this year, even if past), while *this morning* refers to the first half of the diurnal unit including coding time, even if that is in the afternoon (see Fillmore 1975).

However, the most pervasive aspect of temporal deixis is tense. The grammatical categories called tenses usually encode a mixture of deictic time distinctions and aspectual distinctions, which are often hard to distinguish. Analysts tend to set up a series of pure temporal distinctions that correspond roughly to the temporal aspects of natural language tenses, and then catalogue the discrepancies (cf. Comrie 1985: 18ff.). For example, one might gloss the English present tense as specifying that the state or event holds or is occurring during a temporal span including the coding time, the past tense as specifying that the relevant span held before coding time, the future as specifying that the relevant span succeeds coding time, the pluperfect (as in *He had gone*) as specifying that the event happened at a time before an event described in the past tense, and so on. Obviously, such a system fails to capture much English usage (*The soccer match is tomorrow* (see Green, this volume), *John will be sleeping now*, *I wanted to ask you if you could possibly lend me your car*, etc.), but it is clear that there is a deictic temporal element in most tenses. Tenses are traditionally categorized as ABSOLUTE (deictic) versus RELATIVE (anterior or posterior to a textually specified time), so that the simple English past (*He went*) is absolute and the pluperfect (*He had gone*) is relative (anterior to some other, deictically specified point).

Absolute tenses may mark just, for example, past vs. non-past, or up to nine distinct spans of time counted out from coding time (Comrie 1985, chapter 4). Yélî Dnye has six such tenses, which – as in other Papuan and some Bantu languages – are interpreted precisely in terms of diurnal units. So counting back from the present, there is (in the continuous aspect) a tense specific to events that happened earlier today, another tense for yesterday, and yet another for any time before yesterday. In the other direction, there is a tense for later today, and a separate tense for tomorrow or later. Interestingly, the tense particles for tomorrow incorporate those for yesterday (and the word for "the day before yesterday" incorporates the word for "the day after tomorrow"), indicating a partial symmetry around coding time. Yélî Dnye, like a number of Amerindian languages (see Mithun 1999: 153–4), also has tensed imperatives, distinguishing "Do it now" from "Do it sometime later."

The interpretation of tenses often involves implicatures, so that e.g. *Believe it or not, Steve used to teach syntax* implicates that he no longer does so, but this is clearly defeasible as one can add *and in fact he still has to do so* (see Levinson 2000a: 95 for a relevant analytic framework and Comrie 1985 for the role of implicature in the grammaticalization of tense). Many languages in fact have no absolute deictic tenses (e.g. Classical Arabic; see Comrie 1985: 63), although they may pick up deictic interpretations by implicature. Yet other languages, e.g. Malay or Chinese, have no tenses at all. A specially interesting case in point is Yucatec, which not only lacks tenses but also lacks relative time adverbials of the "before" and "after" kind (cf. Bohnemeyer 1998). How on earth do speakers indicate absolute and relative time? By implicature of course. Bohnemeyer sketches how this can be done: for example, by the use of phasal verbs, so that *Pedro stopped beating his donkey and began walking home* implicates that he first stopped donkey-beating and then after that proceeded homewards.

However, for languages that have tense, this grammatical category is normally obligatory, and ensures that nearly all sentences (with the exception of tenseless sentences like *Two times two is four*) are deictically anchored with interpretations relativized to context. Although we tend to think of tenses as a grammatical category instantiated in predicates, some languages like Yup'ik tense their nouns as well, so one can say in effect "my FUTURE-sled" pointing at a piece of wood (Mithun 1999: 154–6). Note that even in English many nominals are interpreted through Gricean mechanisms as tensed; "John's piano teacher was a karate black-belt in his youth" suggests that the person referred to is currently John's piano teacher (Enç 1981). All of these factors conspire to hook utterances firmly to coding time.

It is clear that many deictic expressions in the temporal domain are borrowed from the spatial domain. In English, temporal prepositions and connectives like *in* (*the afternoon*), *on* (*Monday*), *at* (*5.00 p.m.*), *before* and *after* are all derived from spatial descriptions. The demonstratives in English follow the same pattern (cf. *this week*) and in many languages (like Wik Mungan, as described in Anderson and Keenan 1985: 298) "here" and "there" are the sources for "now" and "then." Many languages work with a "moving time" metaphor, so that we talk about *the coming week* and *the past year* – which is natural since motion involves both space and time. In general, the ways in which the spatial domain is mapped onto the temporal domain are quite intriguing, for as Comrie (1985: 15) notes, the temporal domain has discontinuities that the spatial one lacks (as in the discontinuity between past and future, unlike the continuity of places other than "here"), while space has discontinuities (like near speaker vs. near addressee) which the temporal one lacks (at least in the spoken medium, when "now" is effectively both coding and receiving time).

5.3   *Spatial deixis*

We have already examined two of the central kinds of place-deictic expressions, namely demonstrative pronouns and adjectives. But as we noted, there are one-term demonstrative (ad/pro)nominal systems unmarked for distance (German *dies* or *das* being a case in point, see Himmelmann 1997). Thus *here* and *there* may be the most direct and most universal examples of spatial deixis (Diessel 1999: 38). As a first approximation, English *here* denotes a region including the speaker, *there* a distal region more remote from the speaker. Languages with a speaker-anchored distance series of demonstrative pronouns will also have a speaker-centered series of demonstrative adverbs. It is clear that there is no necessary connection between the number of pronominal or adnominal demonstratives and demonstrative adverbs – German for example has one demonstrative pronoun (or rather no spatial distinction between *dies* and *das*) but two contrastive demonstrative adverbs. Malagasy has seven demonstrative adverbs, but only six demonstrative pronouns, apparently encoding increasing distance from speaker (Anderson and Keenan 1985: 292–4, although many commentators have suspected other features besides sheer distance). Speaker-centered degrees of distance are usually (more) fully represented in the adverbs than the pronominals, and it may be that no language has a person-based system in the demonstrative adverbs if it lacks one in the pronominal or adnominal demonstratives.

Very large paradigms of demonstratives usually involve many ancillary features, not all of them deictic. Yup'ik has three sets of demonstratives (31 in all) conventionally labeled "extended" (for large horizontal objects or areas or moving referents), "restricted" (for small, visible, or stationary objects), and "obscured" (for objects not in sight); cf. Anderson and Keenan (1985: 295), after Reed et al. (1977). Here the restricted condition is an additional non-deictic condition, but the other two sets involve a visibility feature that is deictic in nature (visible by the speaker from the place of speaking). Visibility is a feature reported for many North American Indian languages, and not only in demonstratives – in Kwakwa'la every noun phrase is marked for this deictic feature by a pair of flanking clitics (Anderson and Keenan 1985, citing Boas). But caution is in order with a gloss like "visibility"; Henderson (1995: 46) glosses the Yélî Dnye demonstratives *kî* and *wu* as "visible" and "invisible" respectively, but *wu* is more accurately "indirectly ascertained, not directly perceivable or not clearly identifiable to addressee," while *kî* is the unmarked deictic, pragmatically opposed to *wu* in one dimension and to the proximal/distal deictics in another.

Apart from visibility, deictics often contain information in an absolute frame of reference, that is, an allocentric frame of reference hooked to geographical features or abstract cardinal directions. Thus the large Yup'ik series of demonstratives has "upstream"/"downstream"/"across river" oppositions, West Greenlandic has "north"/"south" (Fortescue 1984), and languages used by peoples in mountainous areas of Australia, New Guinea, or the Himalayas often contain "uphill"/"downhill" oppositions (see Diessel 1999: 44–5 for references). Such languages are likely to use absolute coordinates unhooked from the deictic center (as in "north of the tree" (see Levinson 1996 for exposition)). In a cross-linguistic survey of demonstratives in 85 languages, Diessel (1999) attests, in addition to these deictic factors, such non-deictic properties of the referent as animacy, humanness, gender, number, and the boundedness of Eskimo languages mentioned above.

In many kinds of deictic expressions the deictic conditions are indeed back-grounded, and other semantic properties foregrounded. Thus if I say "He didn't come home," you are unlikely (absent contrastive emphasis on *come*) to read what I said as "He went home, but not toward the deictic center." Verbs of "coming" and "going" are not universal. In the first place, many languages do not have verbs encoding motion to or from the deictic center – they make do instead with "hither"/"thither" particles. Secondly, explicit verbs of "coming" and "going" vary in what they encode (Wilkins and Hill 1995, Wilkins et al. 1995). If someone comes toward me but stops short before he arrives at the tree over there, I can say "He came to the tree" in English, but not in Longgu or Italian, where we must say "He went to the tree." In fact we can distinguish at least four distinct kinds of "come" verbs, according to whether they are marked for telicity or require the goal to be the place of speaking, as exemplified below (Wilkins et al. 1995):

(27)   **Varieties of COME verbs**

	+telic	−telic (i.e. unmarked)
Goal is place of speaking	*Longgu*	*Italian*
Goal need not be place of speaking	*Ewe*	*Tamil*

Thus, it turns out there is no universal lexicalized notion of "come," although alignment with the place of speaking is a candidate for a universal feature. The notions underlying "go" may be somewhat more uniform because on close examination they generally do *not* encode anything about alignment of vectors with the deictic center (contra to, for example, Miller and Johnson-Laird 1976). Rather, "come" and "go" verbs tend to be in privative opposition, with "come" marked as having such an alignment, and "go" unmarked. Scalar implicature can then do the rest: saying "go" where "come" might have been used but wasn't implicates that the speaker is not in a position to use the stronger, more informative "come" because its conditions have not been met, and thus that the motion in question is not toward the deictic center.[4] Variants in "go" semantics should then be the mirror image of variants in "come" semantics, illustrating the point stressed in Levinson (2000a) that many Saussurean oppositions may be as much in the pragmatics as in the semantics.

Not all languages lexicalize the "toward the deictic center" feature in their verbs. Consider Yélî Dnye, which has a "hither" feature that can be encoded in variant forms of the verbal inflectional particles. Now there are irregular verbs that obligatorily take this feature, including a motion verb *pwiyé*. So it is tempting to gloss *pwiyé* "come," but in fact it is perfectly usable to encode motion away from the deictic center (one can say "He *pwiyé*-d off in that direction"), because it is just an irregular verb with meaning somewhat unrelated to its obligatory inflectional properties. So to say "Come here!" one can either use *pwiyé* or the unmarked "go" verb *lê*, but now marked with the "hither" particle. Note that Yélî Dnye has no "thither" particle – because by privative opposition it is not necessary: any motion verb unmarked for "hither" will be presumed to have a "thither" (or at least not-"hither") interpretation. Once again implicature provides the opposition.

5.4   *Discourse deixis*

In both spoken and written discourse, there is frequently occasion to refer to earlier or forthcoming segments of the discourse: *As mentioned before, In the next chapter*, or *I bet you haven't heard this joke*. Since a discourse unfolds in time, it is natural to use temporal deictic terms (*before, next*) to indicate the relation of the referred-to segment to the temporal locus of the moment of speaking or the currently read sentence. But spatial terms are also sometimes employed, as with *in this article* or *two paragraphs below*. Clearly, references to parts of a discourse that can only be interpreted by knowing where the current coding point or current reading/recording point is are quintessentially deictic in character.

A distinction is often made between textual deixis and general anaphora along the following lines. Whereas textual deixis refers to portions of the text itself (as in *See the discussion above* or *The pewit sounds like this: pee-r-weet*), anaphoric expressions refer outside the discourse to other entities by connecting to a prior referring expression (anaphora) or a later one (cataphora, as in *In front of him, Pilate saw a beaten man*). Insofar as the distinction between anaphoric and cataphoric expressions is conventionalized, such expressions have a clear conventional deictic component, since reference is relative to the point in the discourse. Thus Yélî Dnye has an anaphoric pronoun *yi*, which cannot be used exophorically and contrasts with the demonstratives that can be used cataphorically, looking backwards in the text from the point of reading like the English legalese *aforementioned*.[5] These expressions, with their directional specification from the current point in the text, demonstrate the underlyingly deictic nature of anaphora.

Many expressions used anaphorically, like third person pronouns in English, are general-purpose referring expressions – there is nothing intrinsically anaphoric about them, and they can be used deictically as noted above, or non-deictically but exophorically, when the situation or discourse context makes it clear (as in *He's died*, said of a colleague known to be in critical condition). The determination that a referring expression is anaphoric is itself a matter of pragmatic resolution, since it has to do with relative semantic generality. For this reason, *the ship* can be understood anaphorically in *The giant Shell tanker hit a rock, and the ship went down*, while resisting such an interpretation in *The ship hit a rock, and the giant Shell tanker went down* (see Levinson 2000a for a detailed Gricean analysis, and Huang 2000a, this volume for surveys of pragmatic approaches to anaphora).

An important area of discourse deixis concerns discourse markers, like *anyway, but, however*, or *in conclusion* (see Schiffrin 1987; Blakemore, this volume). These relate a current contribution to the prior utterance or text, and typically resist truth-conditional characterization. For this reason, Grice introduced the notion of conventional implicature, noting that *but* has the truth-conditional content of *and*, with an additional contrastive meaning which is non-truth conditional but conventional.

5.5 *Social deixis*

Social deixis involves the marking of social relationships in linguistic expressions, with direct or oblique reference to the social status or role of participants in the speech event. Special expressions exist in many languages, including the honorifics well known in the languages of Southeast Asia, such as Thai, Japanese, Korean, and Javanese. We can distinguish a number of axes on which such relations are defined (Levinson 1983, Brown and Levinson 1987):

(28)   **Parameters of social deixis**

Axis	Honorific types	Other encodings
(1) Speaker to referent	Referent honorifics	Titles
(2) Speaker to addressee	Addressee honorifics	Address forms
(3) Speaker to non-addressed participant	Bystander honorifics	Taboo vocabularies
(4) Speaker to setting	Formality levels	Register

The distinction between (1) and (2) is fundamental in that in (1) "honor" (or a related attitude) can only be expressed by referring to the entity to be honored, while in (2) the same attitude may be expressed while talking about unrelated matters. In this scheme, respectful pronouns like *vous* or *Sie* used to singular addressees are referent honorifics that happen to refer to the addressee, while the Tamil particle *nka* or Japanese verbal affix *–mas* are addressee honorifics that can be adjoined by the relevant rules to any proposition. The elaborate honorifics systems of Southeast Asia are built up from a mixture of (1) and (2) – for example, there are likely to be humiliative forms replacing the first person pronoun (on the principle that lowering the self raises the other) together with honorific forms for referring to the addressee or third parties (both referent honorifics), and in addition suppletive forms for such verbs as "eat" or "go," giving respect to the addressee regardless of who is the subject of the verb (see Brown and Levinson 1987, Errington 1988, Shibatani 1999).

The third axis is encoded in BYSTANDER HONORIFICS, signaling respect to non-addressed but present party. In Pohnpei, in addition to referent and addressee honorifics, there are special suppletive verbs and nouns to be used in the presence of a chief (Keating 1998). Many Australian languages had taboo vocabularies used in the presence of real or potential in-laws, or those who fell in a marriagable section for ego but were too close to marry (Dixon 1980: 58–65, Haviland 1979). Yélî Dnye has a similar, if more limited, taboo vocabulary for in-laws, especially parents and siblings of the spouse. The fourth axis involves respect conveyed to the setting or event. Most Germans use a system of address with *Du* vs. *Sie* and First Name vs. *Herr/Frau* + Last Name which is unwavering across formal or informal contexts; they find surprising the ease with which English speakers can switch from First Name to Title + Last Name according to the formality of the situation (Brown and Gilman 1960, Lambert and Tucker 1976). Many European languages have distinct registers used on formal occasions, where *eat* becomes *dine, home* becomes *residence*, etc., while Tamil has diglossic variants, with distinct morphology for formal and literary uses.

Systems of address of any kind – pronouns, titles, kin-terms – are guided by the social-deictic contrasts made by alternate forms. The contents of honorifics (see Shibatani 1999) should be taken to be conventional implicatures overlaid on the referential content (if any), for the deictic content is not cancelable and does not fall under the scope of logical operators (see Levinson 1979a).

6 Conclusions

This chapter has touched on a number of topics that establish deixis as a central subject in the theory of language. Indexicality probably played a crucial part in the evolution of language, prior to the full-scale recursive, symbolic system characteristic of modern human language. The intersection of indexicality and the symbolic system engenders a hybrid with complexities beyond the two contributing systems. These complexities are evident in the paradoxes of token-reflexivity and in the puzzles of the psychological content of indexical utterances. Deictic categories like person are universal (although variably expressed), demonstrating their importance to the fundamental design of language. Their special role in language learning and differential elaboration in the languages of the world makes a typology of the major deictic categories an important item on the agenda for future research.

NOTES

1 In opposition to classical perceptual theory, J. J. Gibson stressed the active nature of the perceiving animal and the way perception is geared to the features of the environment ("affordances") which encourage or inhibit certain actions. See Pick and Pick (1999).

2 For the further puzzles this raises for the subjective "thoughts" corresponding to sentences, see Stalnaker (1999: chapter 7).

3 Yélî Dnye is an isolate of the Papuan linguistic area spoken on Rossel Island (Henderson 1995, Levinson 2000b).

4 There is evidence suggesting a similar privative relation between *this* and *that*, with the former marked as [+proximal] and the latter unmarked for proximity, picking up its distal meaning by the Quantity maxim.

5 See Kehler and Ward (this volume) for a discussion of another anaphor – *do so* – that cannot be used exophorically.

6 Definiteness and Indefiniteness

BARBARA ABBOTT

1 Introduction

The prototypes of definiteness and indefiniteness in English are the definite article *the* and the indefinite article *a/an*, and singular noun phrases (NPs)[1] determined by them. That being the case, it is not to be predicted that the concepts, whatever their content, will extend satisfactorily to other determiners or NP types. However, it has become standard to extend these notions. Of the two categories definites have received rather more attention, and more than one researcher has characterized the category of definite NPs by enumerating NP types. Westerståhl (1985), who was concerned only with determiners in the paper cited, gave a very short list: demonstrative NPs, possessive NPs, and definite descriptions. Prince (1992) listed proper names and personal pronouns, as well as NPs with *the*, a demonstrative, or a possessive NP as determiner. She noted, in addition, that "certain quantifiers (e.g. *all*, *every*) have been argued to be definite" (Prince 1992: 299). This list, with the quantifiers added, agrees with that given by Birner and Ward (1998: 114). Ariel (1988, 1990) added null anaphoric NPs.

Casting our net widely, we arrive at the list in (1), ordered roughly from most definite or determined in some sense to least. Speaking loosely, we can see that each NP type listed in (1) is ordinarily used to refer to some particular and determinate entity or group of entities. Possessive NPs have been included in the table since they are almost universally considered to be definite. However Haspelmath (1999a) argued that possessives are not inherently definite but merely typically so. (See also Barker 2000).

Turning to indefinites, we can construct a parallel list, going in this case from intuitively least definite to most definite. The ordering here is very rough indeed, and (as with the ordering in (1)) specific details should not be taken to imply any serious claims – see (2):

(1)   **Preliminary list of definite NPs**

	NP type	More details	Examples
1	[NPe]	Control PRO; pro; other instances of ellipsis	*Mary tried e to fly*; *[on a pill packet] e contains methanol* [= Ariel 1988, ex. 7a]
2	Pronouns	the personal pronouns	*I, you, she, them*
3	Demonstratives	demonstrative pronouns; NPs with demonstrative determiners	*This, that, this chair over here*
4	Definite descriptions	NPs with *the* as determiner	*the king of France, the table*
5	Possessive NPs	NPs with genitive NPs as determiner	*my best friend's wedding, our house*
6	Proper names		
(a)	First name alone		*Julia*
(b)	Full proper name		*Julia Child*
7	∀ NPs	NPs with a universal quantifier as determiner	
(a)	*Each*		*Each problem*
(b)	*Every*		*Every apple*
(c)	*All*		*All (the) girls*
8	[DET Ø]	The null determiner understood generically	*Pencils [are plentiful/ made of wood], beauty [is eternal]*

(2)   **Preliminary list of indefinite NPs**

	Determiner type	Comments	Examples
1	[$_{\text{DET}}$ Ø]	"Bare" NPs understood existentially	*Children [are crying], snow [was piled high]*
2	*Any*		
(a)		Polarity sensitive *any*	*[hardly] any books*
(b)		"Free choice" *any*	*Any idiot [can lose money]*
3	*No*		*No thought(s), no music*
4	*Most*		*Most (of the) apples, most snow*
5	*A/an*		*A cook, an idea*
6	*Sm, some*	"*sm*" refers to unstressed occurrences with weak or cardinal interpretation. *Some* is the strong, or partitive, version (see section 4 below).	*Sm books, some (of the) space*
7	*Several, a few, many, few*	These determiners also are said to have weak and strong versions.	*Several (of the) answers, few (of the) athletes*
8	Indefinite *this*	Occurrences of this *this* can occur in existentials (see below).	*This weird guy [came up to me]*

These tables have been presented without explicit criteria or argument. In the remainder of this essay we look in turn at a series of properties – uniqueness, familiarity, strength, specificity – each of which is correlated with a range of grammatical phenomena and can lay some claim to expressing the essence of definiteness.[2,3]

2 Uniqueness

The classic "uniqueness" characterization of the difference between definite and indefinite NPs emerged in Russell's (1905) attempt to find the logical form of English sentences containing denoting phrases. A sentence with an indefinite NP as in (3) receives the logical analysis in (3a), which is paraphrasable back into semi-ordinary English as in (3b).

(3) A student arrived.
   a. $\exists x$ [Student(x) and Arrived(x)]
   b. There exists something which both is a student and arrived.

Viewed in this way, the NP *a student* has the same type of analysis as a clearly quantificational NP such as *every student*, whose standard logical analysis is shown in (4a).

(4) Every student arrived.
   a. $\forall x$ [Student(x) $\rightarrow$ Arrived(x)]
   b. Everything is such that if it is a student, then it arrived.

Notice that in neither case is the NP (*a student*, *every student*) translated as a constituent.[4] Instead these phrases only receive an analysis in the context of a complete sentence.

Definite descriptions (NPs with *the* as determiner) were the centerpiece of Russell's analysis. (4) receives the analysis in (5a).

(5) The student arrived.
   a. $\exists x$ [Student(x) and <u>$\forall y$[Student(y) $\rightarrow$ $y = x$]</u> and Arrived(x)]
   b. There is one <u>and no more than one</u> thing which is a student, and that thing arrived.

Comparing (3a) with (5a) it is clear that the clause distinguishing the two is the one underlined in (5a), which requires there to be only one student. Thus on this view the definite article expresses the idea that whatever descriptive content is contained in the NP applies uniquely, that is to at most one entity in the domain of discourse.

Uniqueness does seem to capture the difference between definite and indefinite descriptions in English when they contrast. This is brought out by examples such as the following:

(6) That wasn't A reason I left Pittsburgh, it was THE reason. [= Abbott 1999, ex. 2]

where the stress on each article brings forward a contrast between uniqueness vs. non-uniqueness. It also explains why the definite article is required when the descriptive content of the NP guarantees a unique referent.

(7)   The king of France is bald.

(8)   The youngest student in the class got the best grade.

(7) is Russell's most famous example.

  Russell's analysis as given applies only to singular NPs. However, it is relatively straightforward to extend Russell's concept (if not his formalization) to definite descriptions with plurals or mass heads (e.g. *the students, the sand*). In his classic treatment Hawkins (1978) proposed that the crucial concept is INCLUSIVENESS – reference to the totality of entities or matter to which the descriptive content of the NP applies. (Cf. also Hawkins 1991; Hawkins's analysis is actually more complex than this, in order to deal with the problem of incomplete descriptions. See below, section 2.3.) This aligns definite descriptions with universally quantified NPs.

  Russell's analysis of definite descriptions stood unchallenged for close to 50 years, but since that time a number of issues have arisen which have caused many to question or to reject it. Here we will mention three, in order of the seriousness of the challenge they present to Russell, from weakest to strongest: presuppositionality, referentiality, and incomplete descriptions.

2.1   The problem of presuppositionality

The first challenges to Russell's theory of descriptions were raised by P. F. Strawson in his classic 1950 article "On referring." One of the main points of this paper was to take issue with what Russell's analysis implied about what is asserted in the utterance of a sentence containing a definite description. Consider the Russellian analysis of (7):

(7)   The King of France is bald.
     a. $\exists x[\text{King-of-France}(x) \text{ and } \forall y[\text{King-of-France}(y) \rightarrow y = x] \text{ and } \text{Bald}(x)]$
     b.   There is one and only one entity who is King of France and he is bald.

Strawson argued that the first and second clauses of Russell's analysis (underlined in (7a) and (7b)), the clauses which contain the statements of existence and uniqueness of an entity meeting the descriptive content of the NP, have a different status from the baldness clause. He noted that were somebody to make an announcement using (7), we would not respond "That's false!," but would point out the speaker's confusion in making the utterance in the first place. Strawson argued that these two clauses would be PRESUPPOSED (the term is introduced in Strawson 1952) in a current utterance of (7) and that in the absence of a (unique) king "the question of whether it is true or false simply doesn't arise" (Strawson 1950: 330).

  It should be mentioned that some 60 years prior to Strawson's paper Frege had argued the same point in his classic paper "On sense and reference": "If anything is asserted there is always an obvious presupposition that the simple or compound proper names [roughly, definite noun phrases] used have reference" (Frege 1892: 69). Furthermore Frege included a specific argument: if the assertion were as given in (7b) then the negation of (7) should be:

(7)c.   Either the King of France is not bald, or the phrase "the King of France" has no reference.

However it seems obvious that the negation of (7) would not be (7c) but rather (7d):

(7)d.   The King of France is not bald.

which presupposes the existence of a King of France just as much as (7) does (cf. Frege 1892: 68f.). Frege's work, now considered fundamental, underwent a period of neglect during the middle part of the twentieth century.

Since the publication of Strawson's paper there has been fairly unanimous support for the intuitions he expressed, but less agreement on how best to give an account of these facts. One main parameter of disagreement has been whether presuppositions are best regarded as a semantic phenomenon affecting the truth conditions of utterances, as Strawson viewed them, or are instead better seen as pragmatic conditions on the appropriateness of an utterance. See Stalnaker (1974) and Boër and Lycan (1976) for discussion, and see Atlas (this volume).

A complicating factor is variation in strength of presuppositions, depending apparently on whether the triggering phrase is functioning as TOPIC of the sentence (see Gundel and Fretheim, this volume). (7e) seems not to presuppose the existence of a king, or not as strongly as (7), and seems to be simply false rather than lacking a truth value.

(7)e.   Bill had lunch with the King of France last week.

See Strawson (1964b) and McCawley (1979). See also Atlas (to appear), von Fintel (to appear), and the works cited there for discussion.

2.2   *The problem of referentiality*

The second important critique of Russell's theory was launched by Keith Donnellan in his 1966 classic "Reference and definite descriptions." Donnellan argued that definite descriptions have two uses, one of which, called by him the ATTRIBUTIVE use, corresponds to Russell's analysis but the other of which, termed REFERENTIAL, does not.

Donnellan's most famous example is given in (9):

(9)   Smith's murderer is insane.

As an example of the attributive use of the description in (9), consider a situation in which the police detective first views the crime scene where Smith, the sweetest and most lovable person imaginable, has been brutally murdered. The utterance in that case conveys: "Whoever murdered Smith is/must be insane," and the particular description used, *Smith's murderer*, is essential to the propositional content of the utterance, just as Russell's analysis suggests. However, we can imagine quite a different scenario, say at the trial of Jones, who everyone is convinced is the one who murdered Smith. Suppose that Jones is behaving very strangely while on trial – muttering constantly under his breath and throwing spitballs at the judge. A spectator might utter (9), perhaps with a nod in Jones's direction, in order to make a claim that the individual Jones is insane. This would be an example of Donnellan's referential use. While on the attributive use one says something about whoever or whatever fits the description used, on the referential use the description used is just a means to get the addressee to realize which entity is being spoken about, and in principle any other description or term which would have that result would do as well. Thus in the courtroom scenario the speaker might have said, instead of (9), *That guy is insane* or *He* [pointing] *is insane*.

Donnellan hedged a good bit on whether the distinction he was pointing out was semantic or pragmatic. One of his more controversial claims was that one could use a definite description referentially to make a true statement about somebody or something who did not fit the description – for instance in the example above, were Jones innocent of Smith's murder but insane. Kripke (1977) used this controversial claim in a rebuttal many have found persuasive. Kripke distinguished semantic reference from speaker's reference and argued that Donnellan's referential use was simply the latter and thus a purely pragmatic affair. On the other hand, many of Donnellan's defenders who have believed in the semantic relevance of his distinction have discarded this controversial aspect (see Kaplan 1978, Wettstein 1981, Wilson 1991, Reimer 1998b; cf. also Dekker 1998). Burge (1974) assimilated referentially used definite descriptions (as well as pronouns and, interestingly, tenses) to the category of demonstrative phrases. According to Burge what they all have in common is that they are used to "pick out an object without uniquely specifying it" (206f.). Burge proposed an analysis of demonstrative phrases according to which reference is determined, in part, by an act of referring on the part of the speaker, which accompanies the utterance of the demonstrative phrase. However the descriptive content of the NP must also apply to the referent on his account. (See Neale 1990 and Bach, to appear a, for extensive discussion of Donnellan's referential–attributive distinction, and see Carlson, this volume, on reference in general.)

2.3   The problem of incomplete descriptions

The kind of examples which appeared in Russell's 1905 paper, like (7) repeated here and (10),

(7)   The king of France is bald.

(10)   The author of *Waverley* is Scott.

are ones where the content of the description is such as to ensure a unique referent. Thus in a typical use of such sentences to make a true assertion the Russellian truth conditions would be satisfied: if (10), for example, is true then there is one and only one person who wrote *Waverley* and that person is Scott.

Perhaps the most intractable problem with Russell's analysis has been the existence of what are known as INCOMPLETE (or sometimes IMPROPER) descriptions.[5] These are examples in which the descriptive content of a definite NP does not apply uniquely to the intended referent, or to anything else. This problem was pointed out by Strawson in his 1950 critique, but only as a passing comment and not a major objection. Thus Strawson noted:

> Consider the sentence, "The table is covered with books." It is quite certain that in any normal use of this sentence, the expression "the table" would be used to make a unique reference, i.e. to refer to some one table. It is a quite strict use of the definite article. . . . Russell says that a phrase of the form "the so-and-so," used strictly, "will only have an application in the event of there being one so-and-so and no more." Now it is obviously quite false that the phrase "the table" in the sentence "the table is covered with books," used normally, will "only have an application in the event of there being one table and no more."   (Strawson 1950: 332)

Notice that in this passage Strawson did not object to the uniqueness aspect of Russell's analysis per se; rather his point is to distinguish referring uniquely from asserting that a description applies uniquely.

Strawson did not address the problem of how determinate reference is secured in the case of incomplete descriptions, but many others have. One possibility that might suggest itself is that incomplete definite descriptions are always used referentially, in Donnellan's sense. If that were so then an analysis such as that proposed by Burge and sketched above, for example, might solve this problem. However, it has long been clear that this is not the case. Peacocke (1975: 209) proposed the example of "two school inspectors visiting an institution for the first time: one may say to the other, on the basis of the activities around him, 'the headmaster doesn't have much control over the pupils.'" Here the description is clearly being used attributively in Donnellan's sense, although it is incomplete.

In Peacocke's example, how to fill in the missing constituent (*the headmaster [of this school]*) is fairly straightforward. If all cases of attributively used incomplete descriptions were of this type (as was suggested by Wettstein 1981), then the problem of incomplete descriptions might again be solved. However, Blackburn (1988) used one of Donnellan's own examples to argue that this hope, too, is forlorn.

> [I]n "Reference and Definite Descriptions," Donnellan imagines a speaker at a
> Temperance Union meeting saying "The man drinking a martini, whoever he is,
> is breaking the rules of our club." This is a Russellian [i.e. attributive] use of an
> incomplete description . . . but . . . [t]he speaker may be unable to say whether he
> means "the man *at this meeting* who is drinking a martini" or "the man *in our club*
> who is drinking a martini," or "the man *in this house* who is drinking a
> martini."   (Blackburn 1988: 276; emphasis in original)

Blackburn suggested that a person using an incomplete definite description is
actually tacitly alluding to a vague class of propositions determined by various ways of completing the incomplete description, and what the speaker says
is true if all of these, or perhaps a "weighted majority" (271), are true.

Neale (1990), citing a number of predecessors including Sellars (1954),
Sainsbury (1979), and Davies (1981), argued that the problem of incomplete
descriptions is not confined to definite descriptions but is faced equally by
(other) quantified NPs. Consider (11):

(11)   Everyone was sick.

uttered by Neale in response to a question about how his dinner party the
previous night had gone.

> Clearly I do not mean to be asserting that everyone in existence was sick, just
> that everyone *at the dinner party I had last night was*. . . . Similar examples can be
> constructed using "no," "most," "just one," "exactly eight," and, of course,
> "the". . . . Indeed, the problem of incompleteness has nothing to do with the use
> of definite descriptions *per se*; it is a quite general fact about the use of quantifiers
> in natural language.   (Neale 1990: 950; emphasis in original)

Neale's main concern was to defend Russell's quantificational analysis of
definite descriptions and it sufficed for that end to argue that the incomplete-
ness problem is general. In addition, however, following Sellars (1954) and
Quine (1940), Neale supported an approach on which incomplete NPs are seen
as elliptical for some fuller expression or expression content. There have been
many variations on this theme: see Stanley and Szabó (2000) and the works
cited there for examples. The main drawback has been discomfort at the fact
that the elided content must often be indeterminate, for both speaker and
addressee.

There are several other general lines of approach to the problem of incom-
pleteness currently on offer. One very popular one is to shrink the domain of
evaluation of the NPs in question, so that the descriptive content is satisfied
uniquely as intended. Barwise and Perry (1983) spoke in terms of RESOURCE
SITUATIONS, Westerståhl (1985) introduced CONTEXT SETS, Hawkins (1984, 1991)
invoked contextually supplied PRAGMATIC SETS or P-SETS, and Roberts (to
appear) postulated a concept of INFORMATIONAL UNIQUENESS, which is uniqueness relative to the discourse situation (cf. also Recanati 1996). Stanley and

Szabó (2000) proposed indexing nominals with functions from discourse entities to restricted sets.

McCawley (1979) used example (12) to argue that the relevant domains of nominal interpretation must be structured in terms of prominence:

(12) Yesterday **the dog** got into a fight with **a dog**. **The dogs** were snarling and snapping at each other for half an hour. I'll have to see to it that **the dog** doesn't get near **that dog** again. [= McCawley 1979, ex. 21]

Lewis (1979), citing McCawley's example, concluded: "The proper treatment of descriptions must be more like this: 'the *F*' denotes *x* if and only if *x* is the most **salient** *F* in the domain of discourse, according to some contextually determined salience ranking" (348; emphasis added); and he went on to argue that salience rankings could change in the course of a discourse. Finally, Bach (1994a, 2000) has argued for a more thoroughly pragmatic approach, where the content that would make an NP literally accurate is viewed as a conversational IMPLICITURE (as opposed to implic-a-ture) – something between what is literally expressed and what is conversationally implicated in Grice's sense (Grice 1967; see also Bach 1987b). This problem is still the subject of discussion; in addition to the works cited above, see Soames (1986), Reimer (1998a), Neale (to appear), Taylor (2001), and see Bach (this volume).

2.4 The problem of "non-unique" definite descriptions

A small group of problematic cases for Russell's analysis needs to be distinguished from instances of incomplete descriptions as described and discussed above. These are singular definite descriptions that are used to refer to entities which are typically or always NOT the only entity to which the descriptive content of the NP applies, even in a restricted domain of evaluation. Consider the examples in (13):

(13)a. Towards evening we came to <u>the bank of a river</u>. [from Christophersen 1939: 140]
  b. The boy scribbled on <u>the living-room wall</u>. [= Du Bois 1980, ex. 86]
  c. John was hit on <u>the arm</u>. [= Ojeda 1993, ex. 1]

Rivers always have two banks, rooms have more than one wall, and people have two arms, and there seems to be no reasonable way to reduce the context so as to exclude the other items falling under the description used without also excluding essential entities such as the river, the living room, and John, in the examples given. As pointed out by Birner and Ward (1994), in each of these examples the definite description gives a location. In other types of sentences these NPs are infelicitous:

(14)a. #<u>The bank of the Thames</u> is the personal property of the Queen.
  b. #Mary painted <u>the living room wall</u>.

(Of course the sentences in (14) would improve if placed in a context in which one particular bank of the river, or one particular wall of the room, were made salient in some way.)

Why are definite descriptions used in sentences like (13)? Du Bois made the interesting observation that in these cases, despite the non-uniqueness of potential referents, use of the indefinite article would be odd (cf. (15)):

(15)   #He scribbled on <u>a living-room wall</u>. [= Du Bois 1980, ex. 88]

Du Bois pointed out that (15) "gives the impression of being unnaturally precise" (Du Bois 1980: 233), and seems to carry the unwanted implication that the hearer might care which wall was being scribbled on.[6]

3   Familiarity

The chief competitor for the uniqueness approach to capturing the essence of definiteness has been an approach in terms of FAMILIARITY, or KNOWNNESS to use Bolinger's term (Bolinger 1977). The locus classicus of this approach within the tradition of descriptive grammars is Christophersen: "Now the speaker must always be supposed to know which individual he is thinking of; the interesting thing is that the *the*-form supposes that the hearer knows it too" (Christophersen 1939: 28). The concept of familiarity which Christophersen had in mind in this passage seems quite similar to Prince (1992)'s concept of HEARER-OLD information, which she aligned with the idea of information which is "in the permanent registry" (Kuno 1972), or "culturally copresent" (Clark and Marshall 1981). (Prince contrasted hearer-old information with the narrower category of DISCOURSE-OLD information, which includes only entities that have been mentioned in the previous discourse.) Prince noted that the category of definite NPs, defined in terms of form, correlates well with conveyers of hearer-old information, but that the correlation is not perfect: some NPs which are definite in form can introduce entities not assumed to be known to the addressee at the time of the utterance. She gave the examples in (16) (= Prince 1992, ex. 5).

(16)a.   There were <u>the same people</u> at both conferences.
   b.   There was <u>the usual crowd</u> at the beach.[7]
   c.   There was <u>the stupidest article</u> on the reading list.

The role of existential sentences, like those in (16), as a diagnostic for indefiniteness will be explored below in section 4.

3.1   *Heim's approach and donkey sentences*

The familiarity approach to definiteness received a major boost, especially among more formally inclined semanticists, with the appearance of Irene Heim's

(1982) University of Massachusetts dissertation "The semantics of definite and indefinite noun phrases" (see also Heim 1983a). A major concern of Heim's dissertation was a solution to the problem of what have come to be called DONKEY SENTENCES, after the example used by Peter Geach to introduce the problem to modern readers:

(17)   Any man who owns a donkey beats it.   [= Geach 1962: 117, ex. 12]

A central aspect of the problem created by such sentences is the interpretation of the phrase *a donkey*. Ordinarily the logical form of sentences with indefinite NPs is given with an existential quantifier, as shown in (3a), repeated here:

(3)   A student arrived.
  a. $\exists x$ [Student(x) and Arrived(x)].

If we do that in this case, we would assign (17) the logical form in (17a):

(17)a. $\forall x$ [Man(x) and $\exists y$[Donkey(y) and Own(x, y)] $\rightarrow$ Beat(x, y)].

But the final occurrence of the variable y escapes being bound by the existential quantifier in this formula, which thus expresses the thought "Any man who owns a donkey beats something" – not the intended interpretation.

As noted by Geach, we can assign (17) the logical form in (17b), which seems to give us the right truth conditions:

(17)b. $\forall x \forall y$[[Man(x) and Donkey(y) and Own(x, y)] $\rightarrow$ Beat(x, y)].

However, this is ad hoc. Furthermore the universal quantifier would not be appropriate in the case of (3): used there we would assign (3) the meaning "Every student arrived," which is definitely not correct. But if we use sometimes an existential quantifier and sometimes a universal, we suggest an ambiguity in indefinite NPs which is not felt.

Heim's elegant solution to this problem involved a novel approach to semantic interpretation called FILE CHANGE SEMANTICS. Drawing on prior work by Karttunen (1969, 1976), Heim took mini-discourses like that in (18) as illustrating prototypical uses of indefinite and definite NPs:

(18)   <u>A woman</u> sat with <u>a cat</u> on her lap. <u>She</u> stroked <u>the cat</u> and <u>it</u> purred.

On this view a major function of indefinite NPs is to introduce new entities into the discourse, while definite NPs are used to refer to existing discourse entities. Heim analyzed both indefinite and definite NPs as non-quantificational; instead their interpretation involves only a variable, plus whatever descriptive content may reside in the remainder of the NP. Following Karttunen (cf. also Du Bois 1980), Heim likened a discourse to the building up of a file, where the variables in question are seen as indexes on FILE CARDS representing discourse entities and containing information about them.

The difference between indefinite and definite NPs was expressed with Heim's NOVELTY and FAMILIARITY conditions, respectively. Indefinite NPs were required to introduce a new variable (corresponding to the act of getting out a new blank file card). On the other hand, definite NPs were required to be interpreted with a variable which has already been introduced, and (in the case of a definite description as opposed to a pronoun) whose corresponding file card contains a description congruent with that used in the definite NP. This explicates the idea that definite NPs presuppose existence of a referent, together with the idea that presuppositions are best seen as background information or as the common ground assumed in a discourse (see Stalnaker 1974, 1978; cf. Abbott 2000 for a contrary view).

On this approach an example like (3) (*A student arrived*) would receive an interpretation as in (3c):

(3)c.   Student(x) and Arrived(x).

The existential quantification needed for this example is introduced by a general discourse level rule, requiring that file cards match up with actual entities for the discourse to be true. However, if indefinite NPs fall within the scope of a quantified NP, as happens in donkey sentences, the variable they introduce is automatically bound by that dominating NP's quantifier. Thus Heim's File Change Semantics yielded an interpretation for (17) which is equivalent to that in (17b), but without requiring two different interpretations for indefinite NPs.[8]

3.2   *Unfamiliar definites and accommodation*

The familiarity approach to the definiteness–indefiniteness contrast seems to imply that any definite description must denote an entity which has been explicitly introduced into the discourse context or is common knowledge between speaker and addressee, but of course that is not always the case. Consider *her lap* in (18) (assumed to be a definite description). This possessive denotes an entity that has not been specifically introduced.

Heim's solution for this kind of case relied on a principle introduced in David Lewis's classic paper, "Scorekeeping in a language game" (Lewis 1979). In this paper Lewis compared the process of a conversation to a baseball game. One major DISanalogy is the fact that, while the score in a baseball game can only be changed by events on the field, the "conversational scoreboard" frequently undergoes adjustment just because the speaker behaves as though a change has been made. The relevant principle in this case is Lewis's RULE OF ACCOMMODATION FOR PRESUPPOSITIONS:

> If at time t something is said that requires presupposition P to be acceptable, and if P is not presupposed just before t, then – *ceteris paribus* and within certain limits – presupposition P comes into existence at t.   (Lewis 1979: 340)

As stated, and without cashing out the *ceteris paribus* clause, Lewis's rule of accommodation is extremely strong – strong enough to make familiarity virtually vacuous as a theory of definiteness (cf. Abbott 2000). Heim sought to rein in its power with a condition that accommodated entities be linked to existing discourse entities, in a move which explicitly recalled the phenomenon of BRIDGING (Clark 1977). The idea is that when entities have been explicitly introduced into a discourse, addressees will automatically make assumptions about entities associated with them, following our knowledge of the properties and relations things in a given category typically have. In the case of *her lap* in example (18), the link is obvious – once a seated person has been introduced, the existence of their lap may be inferred.

Despite the addition of a constrained accommodation rule, there remain difficult cases for the familiarity approach. Descriptions whose semantic content entails a unique referent, like those in (19), require the definite article, and this is difficult for familiarity views to account for.

(19)a.   Harold bought the/#a first house he looked at.
  b.   The instructor assigned the/#some most difficult exercises she could find.
  c.   In her talk, Baldwin introduced the/#a notion that syntactic structure is derivable from pragmatic principles.   [= Birner and Ward 1994, ex. 1a]

There are other examples where the referent of a definite description does not seem to be assumed to be familiar to the addressee, salient in the context, or otherwise already accessible in the discourse. Examples like those in (19) and (20) are sometimes called CATAPHORIC, since the uniquely identifying information follows the definite article.

(20)a.   What's wrong with Bill? Oh, <u>the woman he went out with last night</u> was nasty to him.   [= Hawkins 1978, ex. 3.16]
  b.   If you're going into the bedroom, would you mind bringing back <u>the big bag of potato chips that I left on the bed</u>?
       [= Birner and Ward 1994, ex. 1b]
  c.   Mary's gone for a spin in <u>the car she just bought</u>.
       [= Lyons 1999, ex. 18, p. 8]

One could argue that these are simply cases of accommodation, and point out that in each case the intended referent bears some relation to an entity which has already been introduced into the discourse context, but nevertheless they seem contrary to at least the spirit of the familiarity type of approach.

3.3   *Attempts at a synthesis*

In a sense the uniqueness and familiarity theories of definiteness are odd foes. Uniqueness of applicability of the descriptive content, as explicated in Russell's analysis, is a strictly semantic property while the assumption of familiarity to the addressee is discourse-pragmatic in nature. A priori one might have supposed the two to be complementary rather than at odds, and, indeed, there have been attempts to derive each from the other. Accepting both as correct in some sense, the idea of deriving familiarity from uniqueness is likely to strike one first since we generally suppose semantic properties to be arbitrary and pragmatic ones to be natural (if not inevitable) consequences of semantic facts plus the exigencies of the conversational situation. This was the approach sketched in, for example, Hawkins (1984) and Abbott (1999). However, with the development of "dynamic" theories like Heim's that embed sentence semantics into analyses of discourse, this old distinction became blurred. Heim raised familiarity to a principle of semantics, making it possible to suggest instead that the uniqueness requirement could be derived from it (cf. Heim 1982: 234ff.). Szabó (2000) and Roberts (to appear) have also taken this approach to unification.

Just as some have assumed that both uniqueness and familiarity are correct, others have argued in effect that neither is. Birner and Ward (1994) presented problematic examples for both approaches, some of which have been cited above, and concluded that neither gives a correct account of definite descriptions. Lyons (1999), too, reviewed existing theories in both camps and concluded that neither is synchronically correct.

Examples like those in (19) and (20) have led other authors to abandon familiarity (which implies prior acquaintance) in favor of a concept of IDENTIFIABILITY. The idea is that use of the definite conveys to the addressee that they ought to be able to determine a unique referent from the description used plus contextual or background information, whether or not they had prior acquaintance with it. Birner and Ward (1998) pointed out that the term "identify" suggests that an addressee is able to pick the referent out in the world at large. They argued instead that "what is required for felicitous use of the definite article (and most uses of other definites) is that the speaker must believe that the hearer is able to *individuate* the referent in question from all others within the discourse model" (Birner and Ward 1998: 122; italics in original). This is an idea that many have found attractive.

On the other hand, Lyons (1999) argued that definiteness is a GRAMMAT-ICALIZED category: originally definite NPs were understood to denote identifiable entities, but as a consequence of the category's becoming grammaticalized have acquired other uses. This is another way to attempt a synthesis between these two approaches, although there is a drawback in loss of ready formalizability.

Yet another way is to give up the idea that there is one particular property which applies in equal strength to all and only definite NPs. Bolinger (1977) suggested two moves in this direction. One is to distinguish grammatical definiteness from semantic definiteness (cf. also the remarks of Prince 1992 with respect to examples like (16) above). The other is to assert that definiteness, which Bolinger equates with "knownness," is a matter of degree. Bolinger distinguished five subcategories, from third person anaphoric pronouns (the most definite), through proper names, anaphoric NPs, cataphoric NPs, to the "indefinite superlative" as in Prince's example (16c) above. It could be argued that the last category is not semantically definite at all, and similar remarks would go for the "indefinite *this*" (Prince 1981b) as in (21)

(21)   There is <u>this huge boulder</u> sitting in the driveway.

Bolinger's graded concept of "knownness" may lie behind the intuitive ranking in the table in (1) above.

Others have also proposed a graded account. In the approach of Mira Ariel (Ariel 1988, 1990) the form of referential NPs marks the ACCESSIBILITY of their referent, where Accessibility in turn is a function of such factors as distance between antecedent and anaphor, competition with other potential referents, and salience, which is primarily determined by topichood. Third person pronouns and gaps are markers of a high level of Accessibility, demonstrative pronouns encode an intermediate level, and definite descriptions and proper names mark low Accessibility. Similarly Gundel et al. (1993) grouped NP types along an implicational hierarchy based on COGNITIVE STATUS – roughly, the degree to which an NP's referent is assumed to be known to the addressee (cf. also Gundel et al. 2001). Their GIVENNESS HIERARCHY is given below.

(22)   The Givenness Hierarchy   [= Gundel et al. 1993, ex. 1]:

In focus >	Activated >	Familiar >	Uniquely > identifiable	Referential >	Type identifiable
it	*that* *this* *this* N	*that* N	*the* N	indefinite *this* N	*a* N

Each status requires a certain degree of givenness as a minimal condition of use, with the weakest degree being TYPE IDENTIFIABILITY – i.e. familiarity with the category named by the noun (or common noun phrase) in question. Items to the left must meet that condition but also have additional requirements. Hence phrases to the right may be used in circumstances suitable for more highly ranked items, but Gricean conversational implicatures (Grice 1967) result from failure to use the most highly ranked item allowed in the context.

A problem with this type of approach, on which NP forms are held to **encode** degrees of Accessibility, is that it fails to recognize plausible **explanations** for the correlations between NP type and degree of accessibility – e.g. the more accessible a referent is, the less the descriptive information that needs to be included in the NP (see Bach 1998, and this volume, n. 36; and Abbott 2001, n. 2).

We turn now to two other semantic properties whose history is entwined with the definiteness–indefiniteness issue.

4 Existential Sentences and the Weak/Strong Distinction

In the early days of transformational grammar, the contrast shown in (23) attracted attention.[9]

(23)a. There is a wolf at the door.   [= Milsark 1977, ex. 5a]
    b. *There is the wolf at the door.   [= Milsark 1977, ex. 5b]

Sentences like (23a) are called EXISTENTIAL or *there*-insertion sentences. The initial diagnosis pointed to an unidentified problem with definite NPs in such sentences, and the term DEFINITENESS RESTRICTION or DEFINITENESS EFFECT came into common usage to reference this problem.

4.1 *Milsark's analysis*

Milsark (1974, 1977) provided the first thorough attempt within the Chomskyan linguistic tradition to find an explanatory analysis of the constraint just cited. He pointed out that the diagnostic of felicitous occurrence in an existential sentence served to categorize NPs in general, as seen in (24):

(24)a. There are some/several/many/few wolves at the door.
    b. *There are most/all/those/Betty's wolves at the door.

Noting a problem in extending the traditional terms "indefinite" and "definite" to other determiners, Milsark coined the terms WEAK and STRONG for those NPs which do and do not fit easily in existentials, respectively. The weak NPs, also termed CARDINAL, are those with determiners like *a/an, some, several, many*, and the "number determiners" (*one, two, three*, . . .). The strong NPs are those traditionally called "definite," i.e., definite descriptions, demonstratives, possessives, and pronouns, as well as NPs determined by universal quantifiers (*all, every, each*) or by *most*. Milsark's explanation for the "definiteness effect" was that (a) all of the strong determiners involve a quantificational element (hence the alternate term QUANTIFICATIONAL for the strong determiners) and (b) this quantificational element is incompatible with the existential quantification expressed by *there be*.

One subtle complication was observed by Milsark: his weak determiners in fact have two distinct uses – a weak one and a strong one. Compare the examples in (25) and (26).

(25)a.   I would like some ("sm") apple sauce.   [from Postal 1966: 204, n. 7]
   b.   There weren't many students in class this morning.

(26)a.   Some (of the) apple sauce was put in special bowls.
   b.   Many (of the) students objected to their grades after class.

It is a characteristic of weak determiners that, on their weak reading, they cannot occur with predications of relatively permanent properties – INDIVIDUAL-LEVEL properties in the sense of Carlson (1977). However, the strong senses of weak determiners can occur in such predications:

(27)a.   *Sm salesmen are intelligent.
   b.   Some (of the) salesmen (but not others) are intelligent.

   Carlson (1977) pointed out that the distinction in predication between individual-level properties and relatively ephemeral STAGE-LEVEL properties correlates with an even more dramatic difference in interpretation in "bare" NPs – NPs with plurals or mass nouns as head and no overt determiner:

(28)a.   Salesmen are intelligent.
   b.   Salesmen are knocking on the door.

(28a), with an individual-level predicate, can only mean that salesmen in general are intelligent. This is a quasi-universal reading. On the other hand, (28b) means that some particular salesmen are knocking on the door, an existential interpretation. Correspondingly in existential sentences bare NPs have only their existential readings, and weak NPs do not have a felicitous strong reading:

(29)a.   There are salesmen {knocking on the door/*intelligent}.
   b.   *There were some (of the) participants waiting outside.

(It should be noted, though, that (29a), with *intelligent*, is much worse than (29b), even on the strong partitive reading; some may in fact find the latter quite acceptable.)
   Although Milsark appeared to have proposed an elegant solution to the problem of the definiteness effect in existential sentences, it is not without problems. On the one hand, proper names, which are intuitively definite and pass Milsark's two tests for strength (infelicitous occurrence in existentials and ability to take individual-level predication), have traditionally been interpreted as logical constants, *not* quantificational expressions. On the other hand, with the appearance of Barwise and Cooper 1981, following Montague (1973), it became customary in some quarters to view *all* NPs as quantificational, more specifically as GENERALIZED QUANTIFIERS, or expressions denoting sets of sets.

This development obliterates Milsark's tidy distinction as well as his explanation for the definiteness effect.

4.2   *Barwise and Cooper's generalized quantifier approach*

Consider a simple sentence structure as in (30)

(30)a.   Det As are Bs.
    b.   Some/all/most activities are brainless.

On the generalized quantifier approach determiners are viewed as expressing relations between two sets – the one denoted by the common noun phrase (CNP) with which the determiner combines (the "A" set in (30a)) and the one denoted by the verb phrase (the "B" set). An equivalent alternative way of viewing determiners is as functions from sets (the CNP or "A" set) to sets of sets, the generalized quantifier interpretation of NPs. (NPs consisting of just a proper name also denote a set of sets.) The resulting set of sets is equivalent to another function taking sets (the VP, or "B" set) as argument and returning a truth value. Since both quantified NPs and proper names in natural language are constituents and appear in exactly the same kind of syntactic contexts, strict compositionality demands that they receive an interpretation of the same type, and this was Montague's main motivation in instituting generalized quantifiers. This was in marked contrast to the traditional logical treatment, following Russell, where (as noted above) quantified NPs are not even interpreted as constituents.

   Barwise and Cooper (1981) developed many consequences for the generalized quantifier approach to natural language, among them the weak/strong distinction. Barwise and Cooper borrowed Milsark's terms "weak" and "strong," but gave these terms their own formal definition. On this definition it turns out that the strong determiners are those for which sentences of the form *Det CNP exist(s)* is either a tautology or a contradiction in every world in which the sentence has a truth value. Consider the examples in (31):

(31)a.   Every unicorn exists.
    b.   Neither unicorn exists.

(31a) is vacuously true in the actual world, since there are no unicorns. It is also trivially true in any world in which there are unicorns. Thus *every* is a (positive) strong determiner. (31b), according to Barwise and Cooper, presupposes the existence of exactly two unicorns and so is undefined in the actual world. In any world in which this presupposition is satisfied, (31b) is false. *Neither* is (negative) strong. On the other hand (31c), with the weak determiner *many*,

(31)c.   Many unicorns exist.

is false in the actual world, but would be true in a possible world in which there were many unicorns. (Barwise and Cooper did not distinguish strong readings of weak NPs, in effect treating them as totally weak.)

If we accept Barwise and Cooper's assumptions, the explanation for the infelicity of strong NPs in existential sentences follows naturally. Existential sentences such as those in (32) (I follow Barwise and Cooper in assuming now that (32a, b) are infelicitous rather than ungrammatical)

(32)a.   #There is every unicorn.
  b.   #There is neither unicorn.
  c.   There are many unicorns.

assert propositions equivalent to those in (31) – namely they assert existence of a denotation for the post-verbal NP. With a strong determiner this assertion, if defined, is either tautological (32a) or contradictory (32b). Only with a weak determiner does an existential express something interesting.[10]

Although the Barwise and Cooper diagnosis of the definiteness effect in existential sentences has a lot of appeal, there are problems of a variety of sorts. First, it is necessary to their analysis that whatever follows *be* in an existential (what Milsark referred to as the CODA of an existential[11]) is a constituent, and in fact an NP. As they themselves noted, there are examples for which this analysis is implausible at best. (33a) is a fine existential, but (33b) argues that the coda is not an NP.

(33)a.   There is a girl who knows you interested in this problem.
      [= Barwise and Cooper 1981, ex. 5b, p. 206]
  b.   *I met a girl who knows you interested in this problem.
      [= Barwise and Cooper 1981, ex. 5a, p. 206]

Secondly, as Keenan (1987) has pointed out, while Barwise and Cooper's coverage of the data was adequate for the determiners they considered, there are others which they would classify wrongly. *Either zero or else more than zero*, for example, would be classified on Barwise and Cooper's account as positive strong, but it can occur felicitously in an existential:

(34)   Look, there were either zero or else more than zero students there at the time. Now which is it?   [= Keenan 1987, ex. 48a]

Finally, Keenan pointed out that Barwise and Cooper have no account for the difference in grammaticality or felicity in (35)

(35)a.   Every student exists.
  b.   #There is every student.

since the two sentence types are equivalent under their analysis.

4.3   Keenan's analysis

In his analysis of existential sentences Keenan broke up the coda into two constituents – the post-verbal NP and an additional phrase which can be of a variety of predicational types. Keenan defined a subcategory of NP which he called EXISTENTIAL, intended to capture those NPs which fit naturally in the post-verbal position in an existential sentence. Ignoring the formal details, the definition applies to those for which the equivalence in (36) holds:

(36)   Det As are Bs if and only if Det As who are Bs exist.

The fact that (37a) is equivalent to (37b), but (38a, b) differ, correctly classifies *some* as existential and *every* as not existential.

(37)a.   Some student is a vegetarian.
    b.   Some student who is a vegetarian exists.

(38)a.   Every student is a vegetarian.
    b.   Every student who is a vegetarian exists.

Keenan's explanation for the definiteness effect in existentials, then, was that it is only with existential NPs that existential sentences express a predication equivalent to the "exists" sentence.

    Keenan noted in a footnote (1987: 317, n. 1) that the property of being an existential NP as defined in (36) roughly coincides with two other semantic properties of determiners: SYMMETRY and INTERSECTIVITY, defined respectively in (39).

(39)a.   Det As are Bs if and only if Det Bs are As.   [symmetry]
    b.   Det As are Bs if and only if Det As who are Bs are Bs.   [intersectivity]

As Keenan's article is titled "A semantic definition of 'indefinite NP,'" presumably in his view all three definitions converge on this property. Speaking loosely, it is the property of having truth conditions depend solely on the intersection of the set denoted by the CNP with which the determiner combines (the "A" set in (36) and (39)) and the set denoted by the predicate (the "B" set). The non-existential NPs place additional requirements on the CNP denotation.

4.4   De Jong and Verkuyl and presuppositionality

De Jong and Verkuyl (1985) had another criticism of the Barwise and Cooper approach. Recall that Barwise and Cooper treated *every* and *neither* differently. For them, *every CNP* is always defined – in other words, it does not presuppose the existence of entities in the denotation of CNP. A consequence is that a sentence of the form *All As are Bs* where *A* denotes the empty set, will be true no matter what *B* denotes. Under these circumstances *All As* (e.g. *all unicorns*) is an IMPROPER generalized quantifier. Informally this means that it does not sort predicates into two non-empty classes – those which are true of the subject and those which are not. Instead the sentence is vacuously true for all predicates. On the other hand *neither CNP* does require a presupposition that the universe of discourse contain exactly two referents for the CNP, and is undefined when that is not the case, so *neither CNP* is always PROPER (some predicates will be true of it and some false).

De Jong and Verkuyl argued that Barwise and Cooper's decision on which determiners to treat as presuppositional and which to treat as non-presuppositional is arbitrary. De Jong and Verkuyl argued in particular that the universal quantifiers, which Barwise and Cooper analyzed as NON-presuppositional, are in fact presuppositional (and hence always proper). With this modification de Jong and Verkuyl could argue that strength consists in properness or presuppositionality.

There is much intuitive appeal in this approach. It also suggests a natural explanation for the "definiteness" effect in existential sentences which is slightly different from those proposed by Barwise and Cooper and by Keenan. If we assume, with most researchers, that existential sentences assert existence, then we might attribute the infelicity of a strong NP, or a weak NP on its strong reading, to a conflict between the assertion of existence of the *there be* construction and the presupposition of existence which constitutes the strength of a strong NP. This is an explanation which many have found appealing; cf., for example, Woisetschlaeger (1983), de Jong and Verkuyl (1985), de Jong (1987), Lakoff (1987), Lumsden (1988), Abbott (1993).[12]

So, should we conclude from this that presuppositionality – the assumption, rather than assertion, of existence of a certain set of entities denoted by the NP – is a candidate for the essence of definiteness? There are two problems in so doing. One is the cases noted above which are problematic for the familiarity approach to definiteness. If presuppositionality is understood as a prior condition on the context of utterance, then examples like those in (19) and (20) present a problem for this presuppositionality hypothesis.[13] The other problem is NPs which everyone would regard as indefinite, but which have uses which are strong or presuppositional. Recall that Milsark had pointed out strong uses of weak NPs, which do not occur felicitously in existential sentences (e.g. the difference between *sm apples* and *some (of the) apples*). Diesing (1992), Horn (1997), and others have argued that the crucial difference is exactly that the strongly used weak NPs presuppose the existence of their referents, yet these weak NPs (e.g. *some (of the) apples*) must still be regarded as indefinite in the traditional sense. Furthermore in Horn's view presuppositionality bifurcates tokens of universally quantified NPs: while ordinary examples like that in (40a) presuppose a non-empty extension for the CNP, those in law-like statements such as (40b) are non-presuppositional.

(40)a.   All of John's children are bald.
   b.   All trespassers will be prosecuted.   [= Horn 1997, ex. 39a]

We will return to this issue below, in the section on the specific/non-specific distinction.[14]

To summarize this section, it seems clear that the weak–strong distinction must be distinguished from the definite–indefinite distinction. The confounding of the two is probably a natural consequence of the early hasty identification of the class of NPs which are infelicitous in existential sentences as "definite," and the label for their infelicity as the "definiteness effect," which Milsark's careful coining of the terms "strong" and "weak" was not able to avert entirely.

5   Specificity

The discussion above touched on an ambiguity remarked by Milsark between weak and strong uses of weak NPs. This ambiguity is reminiscent of one noted by a number of linguists (Fillmore 1967, Karttunen 1969, Partee 1972), and described in the early days of transformational grammar as the SPECIFIC–NON-SPECIFIC distinction. However, there are indications that the two must be distinguished.

Observe the examples in (41), among the earliest used to introduce this distinction into the linguistics literature:

(41)a.   I talked with a logician.   [= Karttunen 1969, ch. 1, ex. 20a]
   b.   Some of my friends speak French.   [= Fillmore 1967, ex. 53]

Karttunen described (41a) as saying, on the specific reading, something about WHO the speaker talked with, but on the non-specific reading only something about the KIND of person the speaker talked with. Similarly, Fillmore noted that (41b) could be used to say of certain specific friends of mine that they speak French (the specific reading), or merely to assert that I have French-speaking friends (the non-specific reading).

Fillmore's description corresponds strikingly to a classic distinction which has recently been revived between CATEGORICAL and THETIC statements, respectively. Roughly speaking, categorical statements have a topic and express a thought about that topic – categorize it, much as Fillmore described the specific reading of (41b). On the other hand, thetic statements present a state of affairs as a whole, just as the non-specific reading of (41b) was described. While the usually cited founders of the categorical–thetic distinction are Brentano and his student Marty, the recent revival is due especially to Kuroda (1972), who sought to use this distinction to help explain the distinction in use between *wa* and *ga* in Japanese (see also Ladusaw 1994, Horn 1997, and the works cited there).

This ambiguity seems similar to the strong–weak ambiguity but there are several problems in making the identification. Note for one thing that Fillmore's example uses a partitive NP. Milsark used the partitive form to DISAMBIGUATE his examples, in favor of the strong reading, and de Hoop (1991, 1996), Enç (1991), Diesing (1992), and others have suggested that the strong readings are in some sense partitive in nature. Furthermore the predicate in Fillmore's example (*speak French*) is an individual-level rather than a stage-level property and this, according to Milsark, should require the subject to have a strong reading. Karttunen's example is problematic too – indefinite NPs with determiner *a/an* are supposed to be totally weak in Milsark's sense, i.e. not to allow a strong reading at all (see Ladusaw 1994).[15]

The literature in this area is filled with differences in terminology which may or may not correspond to differences in data. Thus Fodor and Sag (1982), citing Chastain (1975) and Wilson (1978), argued that indefinites have a REFERENTIAL reading in addition to their QUANTIFICATIONAL one, illustrating the distinction with (42).

(42)   A student in the syntax class cheated on the final exam.
       [= Fodor and Sag 1982, ex. 1]

They describe the difference in readings as follows:

> someone who utters [42] might be intending to assert merely that the set of students in the syntax class who cheated on the final exam is not empty; or he might be intending to assert of some particular student, whom he does not identify, that this student cheated.   (Fodor and Sag 1982: 356)

This description is very similar to those given by Fillmore and Karttunen, as well as Milsark, but note the difference in terminology: for Milsark, "quantificational" meant "strong" – specific in some sense; for Fodor and Sag "quantificational" here means NON-specific. Fodor and Sag gave new syntactic arguments for their referential reading; see King (1988) and Ludlow and Neale (1991) for replies.

Haspelmath (1997) distinguished nine distinct functions of indefinite pronouns. Most of these are confined to particular constructions or context types not at issue here. However, three of his functions are relevant, two of which he called "specific" and one "non-specific." The difference between the two "specific" functions cited by Haspelmath is whether or not the referent of the indefinite is known to the speaker. Now a common description of what is distinctive about the traditional specific–non-specific distinction is that it hangs on whether or not the speaker has a particular individual in mind.[16] That being the case, we might identify this feature as crucial for the traditional concept, as a way of distinguishing it from Milsark's concept of strength.

The traditional specific–non-specific distinction in indefinite NPs is quite parallel to the referential–attributive distinction in definite NPs discussed above in section 3.2. Compare Fodor and Sag's example (42) with Donnellan's famous example, repeated here as (43):

(43)   Smith's murderer is insane.

Uttered referentially (43) makes a statement about a particular person who is assumed to be the murderer. On the attributive use, on the other hand, a general statement is made.

Both the specific–non-specific distinction and the referential–attributive distinction must be distinguished from the various scope ambiguities that arise with NPs in clauses which are embedded under sentence operators such as modals, propositional attitude verbs, or other quantificational NPs. None of the sentences used above to illustrate these distinctions have had operators of this type. It should be noted, though, that the distinction in type of reading is very similar, as noted by Partee (1972). Thus (44):

(44)   John would like to marry a girl his parents don't approve of.
       [= Partee 1972, ex. 1]

has the traditional scope ambiguity. On the reading where the NP *a girl . . .* has wide scope with respect to the matrix clause, John has his girl picked out and it happens to be the case that his parents don't like her. On the reading where the NP *a girl . . .* has narrow scope, John apparently wants to offend his parents by finding someone they disapprove of to marry. Clearly on the former reading the interpretation is more specific than on the latter.

Partee pointed out that (45a) seems to have the same kind of ambiguity, and (45b) is not very different from (45a).

(45)a.   John succeeded in marrying a girl his parents don't approve of.
         [= Partee 1972, ex. 12]
     b.   John married a girl his parents don't approve of.
         [= Partee 1972, ex. 8]

However, one important difference between the embedded vs. the unembedded cases is whether the two interpretations can differ in truth value. In the case of sentences with sentence operators and indubitable scope ambiguities, like (44), there clearly is a difference in truth conditions: either of the two readings might be true in some circumstance without the other reading being true. However in the case of (45b) this is less clear. Which brings us to the question of how best to analyze the specific–non-specific distinction.

As with the referential–attributive distinction for definite NPs, the main issue in analyzing the specific–non-specific contrast is whether it should be regarded as semantic or pragmatic. Ludlow and Neale (1991) have argued most strongly that this distinction is a pragmatic one, just as in their view the referential–attributive distinction is pragmatic. Their analysis is similar to the one argued for by Kripke and sketched above in section 2.2, namely, that there is a single set of truth conditions for sentences like (45b), and the difference in construals consists only in whether the speaker has a particular individual in mind or not.

Those who believe the distinction to be semantic have the problem of providing an interpretation for the specific reading, assuming Russell's analysis is correct for the non-specific reading. Consider the following slightly modified version of Karttunen's example (41a):

(46) Mary talked to a logician.

For the specific reading what is needed is a particular logician for the sentence to be about. The problem is how to determine this individual. A natural suggestion is to let that be determined by the speaker's intention, as in the analyses of Kasher and Gabbay (1976) and Fodor and Sag (1982). However, then we would have to say (46) was false on the specific understanding that Mary did talk to a logician, but not the one the speaker had in mind.

This result seems to be a strong argument against this type of analysis. However, Dekker (1998) has put forward something of a compromise position. In Dekker's approach, utterances may be enriched by the addition of contextual information, and this is how the specific reading of indefinites, as well as the referential reading of definites, is obtained. More specifically, following an utterance of (46), if there is contextually available information that the speaker had intended to be talking about Mary's conversation with, say, Carnap, then the information that the logician in question was Carnap would be added, deriving the specific construal of (46). This contextually available information is what "licenses" specific utterances. Dekker noted that a sentence like (46) would be true as long as Mary had spoken with some logician or other, but it would not be true "as licensed."[17]

6   Concluding Remarks

We have examined a number of distinctions and attempts to characterize them with varying degrees of formality: uniqueness vs. non-uniqueness, familiarity vs. novelty, strength vs. weakness, specificity vs. non-specificity. Each has a foundation in intuition, as well as some degree of grammatical effect. However, it is not clear that any of them corresponds cleanly to formal categories. As so frequently seems to be the case, grammar is willfully resistant to attempts at tidy categorization.

ACKNOWLEDGMENTS

I am very grateful to the editors of this volume and to Kent Bach for their comments on a draft of this paper.

NOTES

1   "Noun phrase" and "NP" will be used to denote a category whose specifier is a determiner. It may be more accurate to speak in terms of determiner phrases (DPs), of which determiners are heads, but the more traditional category will be retained for this article.

2   Unfortunately we will be forced to confine our attention in this article to determiners and NP types in English. There are a number of excellent cross-linguistic studies available: Gundel et al. (1993) include data from five languages (English, Spanish, Russian, Mandarin Chinese, and Japanese); Lyons (1999) gives a broad cross-linguistic study of definiteness; and Haspelmath (1997) examines indefinite pronouns in 140 languages.

3   Predicate nominals will not be considered here, but see Graff (2001) for an interesting analysis, which she extends to NPs in argument positions.

4   This feature was essential to Russell's explanation of knowledge by description. However, it poses a problem for the compositional analysis of ordinary language, since quantificational NPs do not receive an interpretation by themselves. The use of restricted quantification (see e.g. McCawley 1981), while reducing the unsightly mismatch between the cumbersome formulas of first order logic and their counterpart sentences in English, does not by itself provide a semantic solution. That awaited Montague's (1973) introduction of generalized quantifiers. See below, section 4.2.

5   The distinction between complete and incomplete descriptions is similar to Löbner's (1985) distinction between semantic definites and pragmatic definites.

6   There are a few other types of non-unique definites. Abbott (2001) gives a fairly complete catalog, discussion, and further references.

7   For some speakers this example may be ambiguous, meaning roughly "there were the same people as usual at the beach" or "the beach was crowded, as usual." Prince (personal communication) has said that she intended the latter of the two readings.

8   Unfortunately this elegant solution to the donkey sentence problem eventually ran foul of several problems, and Heim herself later abandoned it (cf. Heim 1990). The donkey sentence problem continues to attract a stream of contributions to the literature while resisting satisfactory solution: cf. e.g. Kadmon (1990), Kanazawa (1994), Lappin and Francez (1994), Chierchia (1995), Dekker (1996).

9   I have asterisked (23b), as was customary at the time, although many would assume that this

example is infelicitous rather than downright ungrammatical (cf. the discussion of Barwise and Cooper 1981, below). The issue is complex: see Abbott (1993) and the works cited there for discussion.

10   Like Milsark, Barwise and Cooper distinguished the categories weak/strong from indefinite/definite, but unlike Milsark they also proposed a definition of definiteness, one which was motivated by an assumption that occurrence as the embedded NP in a partitive was a good diagnostic for definiteness. A definite on their definition is necessarily a proper principal filter (a set of sets with a non-empty intersection): this includes definite descriptions, proper names, and (presumably) demonstrative NPs (which Barwise and Cooper did not analyze). However, universally quantified NPs had to be excluded on a somewhat ad hoc basis: if we assume they are presuppositional (see below), there would be no way to exclude them. On the other hand, partitivity has been argued not to be a good diagnostic for definiteness anyway. See Ladusaw (1994), Abbott (1996), and Barker (1998) for discussion.

11   "Let us define the word <u>coda</u> to mean any and all material to the right of *be* in ES [existential sentences] . . ." (Milsark 1974: 8).

12   I am glossing over a number of difficult details in this brief summary. In particular, the relevant notion of existence should be discourse, rather than real-world,

existence; note that the contrast in (35) suggests that it is a different notion from the presumably real-world one expressed by the verb *exist*.

13   If presuppositions are regarded as non-assertions, as I have argued (Abbott 2000), then this problem would not arise. Cf. also Bach (1999a), Horn (to appear).

14   This discussion glosses over a possible distinction in presupposition types. A singular definite description like *the solution to the problem* presupposes not just that the set of solutions to the problem is non-empty but in addition that there is only one. For NPs like *all/some/several solutions* a mere presupposition of non-emptiness of the set of solutions is tantamount to guaranteeing a referent for the NP.

15   Horn (1997) assimilated Milsark's strength to presuppositionality and categoricality. If this is correct, and if, as suggested here, strength is different from traditional specificity, then we cannot align the traditional specific–non-specific distinction with the categorical–thetic distinction.

16   Cf. e.g. Quirk et al. (1985): "the reference is SPECIFIC, since we have in mind particular specimens" (265).

17   Another possible direction that may warrant pursuing is to regard the semantic values of specific indefinites (as well as referential definites) as constant individual concepts. This idea is similar to one suggested by Dahl (1988), as well as Abbott (1994).

Part II Pragmatics and Discourse Structure

7 Information Structure and Non-canonical Syntax

GREGORY WARD AND BETTY BIRNER

1 Introduction

One of the primary factors contributing to the coherence of a discourse is the existence of informational links between the current utterance and the prior context. These links facilitate discourse processing by allowing the hearer to establish and track relationships such as coreference between discourse entities. A variety of linguistic forms, in turn, mark these relationships. For example, the use of the definite article marks the referent of a noun phrase as being individuable within the discourse model (Birner and Ward 1994), and thereby cues the listener to the likelihood that the entity in question has been previously evoked and individuated; thus, the listener will look for an appropriate referent among his or her store of already evoked information rather than constructing a new discourse entity.

Similarly, speakers use a wide range of non-canonical syntactic constructions to mark the information status of the various elements within the proposition. These constructions not only mark the information status of their constituents, but at the same time facilitate processing through the positioning of various units of information. The speaker's choice of constructions, then, serves to structure the informational flow of the discourse. This dual function of structuring and marking the information in a discourse is illustrated in (1):

(1) Beds ringed the room, their iron feet sinking into thick *shirdiks* woven in colorful patterns of birds and flowers. *At the foot of each bed rested a stocky wooden chest*, festooned with designs of cranes and sheep, horses and leaves.   [D. L. Wilson, *I Rode a Horse of Milk White Jade*, 1998: 133]

Here, the NP *each bed* in the italicized clause has as its referent the set of beds already evoked in the first sentence; *the foot of each bed*, in turn, can be inferred on the basis of the generally known fact that a bed has a head and a foot. The inversion italicized here serves the dual function of, on the one hand, structuring the information so as to link up *the foot of each bed* with the previously mentioned *beds* for ease of processing and, on the other hand, marking the NP *the foot of each bed* as linked in this way, via its sentence-initial placement, so that the hearer knows to search for a previously evoked or inferrable entity rather than constructing a new entity for the beds.

The key factors that determine the structuring of information in English are the information's discourse-status and hearer-status (Prince 1992); additional factors include formal weight and the salience of particular "open propositions" (i.e., propositions containing an underspecified element) in the discourse. (All of these factors will be discussed below.) Because non-canonical constructions are used in consistent and characteristic ways to structure such information, formal features of a particular construction make it possible to infer the status of the constituents of the construction; in this way the choice of construction for information-packaging purposes simultaneously marks the information so packaged as to, for example, its discourse- and hearer-status. Thus, we can construct a typology of non-canonical syntactic constructions and the information status of their constituents (as will be shown in the table in (2) below).

Many languages tend to structure discourse on the basis of an "old/new" principle – that is, in any given sentence, information that is assumed to be previously known tends to be placed before that which is assumed to be new to the hearer.[1]

English is such a language; indeed, this principle can be seen to be at work in (1) above, in that *the foot of each bed*, inferrable from the previously evoked *beds*, is placed before the new and unpredictable *stocky wooden chest*. Extensive research, however, has failed to identify a unitary notion of "oldness" or "givenness" at work in all of the non-canonical constructions that are sensitive to givenness. Rather, some constructions are sensitive to the status that the information has in the discourse – whether it has been previously evoked or can plausibly be inferred from something that has been previously evoked – whereas others are sensitive to the status that the information has for the hearer – that is, whether the speaker believes it is already known to the hearer (not in the sense of "known to be true," but rather present in the hearer's knowledge store). Moreover, certain constructions are sensitive to the status of a single constituent, whereas others are sensitive to the relative status of two constituents.

The type of information status to which a particular English construction is sensitive is partly predictable from its form. As we will show below, PREPOSING constructions (that is, those that place canonically postverbal constituents in preverbal position) mark the preposed information as familiar within the discourse, while POSTPOSING constructions (those that place canonically preverbal constituents in postverbal position) mark the postposed information as new, either to the discourse or to the hearer. Finally, constructions that reverse the canonical ordering of two constituents (placing a canonically preverbal constituent in postverbal position while placing a canonically postverbal constituent in preverbal position) mark the preposed information as being at least as familiar within the discourse as is the postposed information.

Thus, the situation we find in non-canonical syntactic constructions is as follows:

(2)

Single argument	Information status
Preposed	Old
Postposed	New
Two arguments reversed	Preposed at least as old as postposed

This situation will be shown to hold for all constructions in English that involve the non-canonical placement of one or more constituents whose canonical position is not filled by a referential element (such as an anaphoric pronoun). It is traditional to think of such constructions as involving the "movement" of the preposed or postposed constituents from their canonical positions (hence the absence of a referential constituent in that position), but we will take no position on how these constructions are best analyzed syntactically. Our interest, rather, will be in their functional properties, and specifically in their use by speakers for the purpose of structuring information in a discourse.

2 Background and Definitions

Since the early Prague School work on syntax and discourse function (e.g. Firbas 1966), researchers have accrued evidence for a correlation between sentence position and givenness in the discourse. How to define the relevant notion of givenness, however, has been controversial. Prince (1981a) frames the issue in terms of ASSUMED FAMILIARITY, on the grounds that the speaker structures information in discourse based on his or her assumptions concerning the familiarity of the information to the hearer. Prince offers a preliminary taxonomy of types of givenness, ranging from brand-new information (either anchored to known information or not) through inferrable information (that which has not been evoked but can be inferred from the prior context or from a constituent contained within it) through "unused" information (not evoked in the current discourse but assumed to be previously known) to previously evoked information. Prince (1992) reframes this taxonomy in terms of a matrix of two cross-cutting distinctions – between, on the one hand, discourse-old and discourse-new information and, on the other hand, hearer-old and hearer-new information. Discourse-old information is that which has been explicitly evoked in the prior discourse, while hearer-old information is that which, regardless of whether it has been evoked in the current discourse, is assumed to be already known to the hearer. (See also Abbott, this volume, for a discussion of similar parameters with respect to definiteness.)

The resulting matrix corresponds to Prince's earlier formulations as shown in (3):

(3)

	Hearer-old	Hearer-new
Discourse-old	Evoked	(non-occurring)
Discourse-new	Unused	Brand-new
		Brand-new anchored

Thus, in an utterance like *The President gave a speech today, and in it he offered a new tax plan*, the NP *the President* represents information that is discourse-new but hearer-old, the NP *a speech* represents information that is both discourse-new and (assumed to be) hearer-new, and the pronoun *it* represents information that is both discourse-old and hearer-old. Information that is discourse-old but hearer-new is predicted not to occur, on the grounds that a speaker typically believes that the hearer is paying attention and thus that what has been evoked in the discourse is also known to the hearer.

Prince (1992) leaves the status of inferrable information unresolved, but later studies have shown that in those constructions sensitive to discourse-old status, inferrable information consistently patterns with discourse-old information (Birner 1994, Birner and Ward 1998). As will be demonstrated below, research has shown that the hearer- vs. discourse-status distinction is an important one for distinguishing among functionally distinct syntactic constructions, and it will form the basis of our functional typology of constructions.

In addition, many constructions require a particular open proposition to be salient in the discourse. An open proposition (OP) is a proposition in which a constituent is left OPEN or unspecified; thus, a question such as (4a) will render the OP in (4) salient.

(4)a.   Where are your mittens?
   b.   Your mittens are $X{:}X\varepsilon\{places\}$

That is, asking someone about the location of their mittens evokes the proposition that their mittens are in some location, i.e. some member of the set of places. Declarative statements likewise give rise to open propositions; for example, utterance of (5a) renders the OPs in (5b–d), among others, salient.

(5)a.   I found your mittens.
   b.   I found $X{:}X\varepsilon\{objects\}$
   c. $X{:}X\varepsilon\{people\}$ found your mittens
   d.   I did $X{:}X\varepsilon\{activities\}$

Uttering *I found your mittens* renders salient the notions that I found something, that someone found your mittens, and that I did something, inter alia (cf. Wilson and Sperber 1979). The felicitous use of certain constructions requires that a particular OP be salient in the discourse context, the classic example being clefts (Prince 1978, Delin 1995), as illustrated in (6)–(7):

(6)a.   Two sets of immigration bills currently before this session of Congress are giving observers both hope and worry. What is at stake are the immigration rights of gay people, and though gay legislation generally moves slowly, voting is expected soon.
[*Au Courant*]

   b.   Triggs is a lexicographer.
Over his desk hangs the 18th-century dictionary maker Samuel Johnson's ironical definition: "A writer of dictionaries; a harmless drudge that busies himself in tracing the original, and detailing the signification of words."
    What Triggs actually does is find alert readers who recognize new words or new usages for ordinary ones.
[*New York Times* News Service]

The *wh*-cleft in (6a), *what is at stake are the immigration rights of gay people*, is felicitous only in a context in which it is salient that something is at stake (i.e., the OP $X:X\varepsilon\{issues\}$ *is at stake* must be salient). Likewise, the *wh*-cleft in 4b, *what Triggs actually does is find alert readers who recognize new words or new usages for ordinary ones*, is felicitous only in a context in which it is salient that Triggs does something (i.e., the OP *Triggs does* $X:X\varepsilon\{activities\}$ must be salient). The contexts given in (6) clearly do render these OPs salient; conversely, if such an OP is not salient, the *wh*-cleft is infelicitous. Thus, compare (7a) and (7b), uttered in, say, a grocery store:

(7)a.   Hey, look! That's my friend Jeremy Triggs over there. He's a lexicographer. What he does is find alert readers who recognize new words or new usages for ordinary ones.

   b.   Hey, look! That's my friend Jeremy Triggs over there. #What he does is find alert readers who recognize new words or new usages for ordinary ones.

In (7a), the mention of Triggs's occupation gives rise to the issue of what he does, rendering the OP salient. In (7b), however, merely sighting a friend in a grocery store does not render the OP salient, and the *wh*-cleft is correspondingly infelicitous.

    The instantiation of the variable in the OP corresponds to the FOCUS, or NEW INFORMATION, of the utterance. In (7a), the focus is *find alert readers who recognize new words or new usages for ordinary ones,* corresponding to the instantiation of the OP. This packaging of information into an open proposition and a focus corresponds closely to the FOCUS/PRESUPPOSITION distinction of Chomsky (1971), Jackendoff (1972), and Rochemont (1978, 1986), inter alia (see also Vallduví (1992), Lambrecht (1994), Gundel and Fretheim (this volume)).

Finally, many constructions are sensitive to the formal weight of their constituents. That is, just as more informative (i.e. newer) information tends to appear late in the sentence, likewise longer or more syntactically complex constituents tend to appear late in the sentence. The correlation between the two, of course, is not coincidental. Information that has been previously evoked can frequently be identified on the basis of a relatively short phrase, with the limiting case being a pronoun or null argument for highly salient information; brand-new information, correspondingly, requires a sufficiently long or complex linguistic realization to enable the hearer to construct an appropriate discourse referent. Because formal weight is only tangential to the structuring of information, it will not be among our central concerns in this chapter.

3   Preposing

Following Birner and Ward (1998) and Ward (1988), a PREPOSING is a sentence in which a lexically governed, or subcategorized, phrasal constituent appears to the left of its canonical position, typically sentence-initially. Preposing is not restricted to any particular phrasal category, as illustrated by the examples of a preposed NP, PP, VP, and AP in (8) through (11), respectively:

(8)   NP

To illustrate with a simple analogy, consider a person who knows arithmetic, who has mastered the concept of number. In principle, he is now capable of carrying out or determining the accuracy of any computation. <u>Some computations he may not be able to carry out in his head</u>. Paper and pencil are required to extend his memory.
[N. Chomsky, *Rules and Representations*, 1980: 221]

(9)   PP

But keep in mind that no matter which type of equipment you choose, a weight-training regimen isn't likely to provide a cardiovascular workout as well. <u>For that, you'll have to look elsewhere</u>.
[*Philadelphia Inquirer*, 8/28/83]

(10)   VP

They certainly had a lot to talk about <u>and talk they did</u>.
[*The New Republic*, 4/23/84]

(11) AP

> Interrogative *do* should then be classed as a popular idiom. <u>Popular it may indeed have been</u>, but I doubt the different origin.
> [A. Ellegård, *The Auxiliary Do, the Establishment and Regulation of Its Use in English*, 1953: 168]

In each case, a single argument appears in preposed position and thus, following the generalization we outlined earlier, that argument is constrained to be old information. More specifically, felicitous preposing in English requires that the information conveyed by the preposed constituent constitute a discourse-old anaphoric link to the preceding discourse (see Reinhart 1981, Horn 1986, Vallduví 1992).

This information can be related to the preceding discourse in a number of ways, including such relations as type/subtype, entity/attribute, part/whole, identity, etc. These relations can all be defined as partial orderings (Hirschberg 1991) and, as we have argued (Ward 1988, Birner and Ward 1998), the range of relations that can support preposing are all of this type. Items (e.g. discourse entities) that are ordered by means of a partial ordering constitute partially ordered sets, or POSETS. Some typical partial orderings include, for example, type/subtype (*pie* and *desserts*), greater-than (*five* and *six*), and simple set inclusion (*apples* and *oranges*). The notion of a poset subsumes both coreferential links, where the linking relation between the preposed constituent link and the corresponding poset is one of simple identity, and non-coreferential links, where the ordering relation is more complex. Consider for example (12):

(12) *Customer*: Can I get a bagel?
      Waitress: No, sorry. We're out of bagels. <u>A bran muffin I can give you</u>.

Here, the link (*a bran muffin*) and the previously evoked *bagels* stand in a poset relation as alternate members of the inferred poset {breakfast baked goods}. However, note that the link could also have been explicitly mentioned in the prior discourse, as in (13):

(13) *A*: Can I get a bagel?
      B: Sorry – all out.
      A: How about a bran muffin?
      B: <u>A bran muffin I can give you</u>.[2]

Here, although the link *a bran muffin* is coreferential with the entity explicitly evoked in A's second query, the salient linking relation is not identity. Rather, the link is related via a type/subtype relation to the evoked poset {breakfast baked goods}, of which both bagels and bran muffins are members.[3]

Thus, both (12) and (13) illustrate preposings whose posets contain multiple set members. However, some types of preposing also permit links to posets containing only a single set member. Consider (14):

(14)   Facts about the world thus come in twice on the road from meaning to truth: once to determine the interpretation, given the meaning, and then again to determine the truth value, given the interpretation. <u>This insight we owe to David Kaplan's important work on indexicals and demonstratives, and we believe it is absolutely crucial to semantics.</u>   (J. Barwise and J. Perry, *Situations and Attitudes*, 1983: 11)

Here, the link *this insight* stands in a relation of identity to the evoked poset, consisting of a single member. By virtue of this poset relation, the link serves as the point of connection to the prior discourse.

   Another case of an identity link to the prior discourse is a type of preposing called PROPOSITION AFFIRMATION, illustrated in (15) (see Ward 1990; Birner and Ward 1998; Ward and Birner 2002):

(15)   With her new movie, called "Truth or Dare" in America, and "In Bed with Madonna" in Europe, Madonna provides pundits with another excuse to pontificate. And, on both sides of the Atlantic, <u>pontificate they have</u> – in reviews, essays, magazine features and on television chat shows.   (*The Economist*, July 27, 1991)

Here, the link *pontificate* is evoked in the immediately preceding sentence. Thus, as in (14), the relevant poset in (15) consists of a single member, evoked in the prior context and repeated in the link.

   In addition, preposing is a focus/presupposition construction involving a salient or inferrable open proposition in the discourse. Preposings can be classified into two major types based on their intonation and information structure: FOCUS PREPOSING and TOPICALIZATION. The preposed constituent of focus preposing contains the focus of the utterance, and bears nuclear accent; the rest of the clause is typically deaccented.[4] Topicalization, on the other hand, involves a preposed constituent **other than the focus** and bears multiple pitch accents: at least one on the preposed constituent and at least one on the (non-preposed) focus.[5] Nonetheless, both types of preposing require a salient or inferrable OP at the time of utterance for felicity.[6]

   Consider first the focus preposing in (16), where the focus is contained within the preposed constituent:

(16)   Colonel Kadafy, you said you were planning on sending planes – <u>M-16s I believe they were</u> – to Sudan.   (Peter Jennings on ABC's "World News Tonight")

The preposed constituent in this example, *M-16s*, contains the nuclear accent, which identifies it as the focus of the utterance.

   To construct the OP, the preposed constituent containing the focus is first placed in its canonical argument position. The focus is replaced with a variable representing a member of some contextually licensed poset (17a). (A gloss of the OP is provided in (17b).) The focus, provided in (17c), instantiates the variable in the OP.

(17) a. OP = The planes were of type X, where X is a member of the poset {types-of-military-aircraft}.
  b. The planes were of some type.
  c. Focus = M-16s

Here, *M-16s* serves as the link to the preceding discourse. It is a member of the poset {military aircraft}, which is part of the inferrable OP in (17a). In this example, the OP can be inferred on the basis of the prior context; from the mention of military planes, one is licensed to infer that those planes are of some type. While the anchoring poset {military aircraft} is discourse-old, the preposed constituent itself represents information that has not been explicitly evoked in the prior discourse. In the case of focus preposing, then, the related poset must be discourse-old while the link – as focus – is new. Thus, it follows that the poset must contain at least one other member in addition to the link.

The focus in a topicalization, on the other hand, is not contained in the preposed constituent but occurs elsewhere in the utterance. Intonationally, preposings of this type contain multiple accented syllables: (at least) one occurs within the constituent that contains the focus and (at least) one occurs within the preposed constituent, which typically occurs in a separate INTONATIONAL PHRASE (Pierrehumbert 1980). Consider (18):

(18) G: Do you watch football?
  E: Yeah. Baseball I like a lot BETTER.
  (G. McKenna to E. Perkins in conversation)

Here, it is the postverbal adverb *better* – and not the preposed NP *baseball* – that serves as the focus of the utterance. *Baseball* serves as the link to the poset {sports}, inferrable on the basis of the evoked set member *football*. Note that *baseball* is accented in (16) not because it is the focus but because it occurs in a separate intonational phrase.

The OP is formed in much the same way as for focus preposing, except that the poset member represented by the preposed constituent is replaced in the OP by the relevant poset, as in (19):

(19) a. OP = I like-to-X-degree {sports}, where X is a member of the poset {degrees}.
  b. I like sports to some degree.
  c. Focus = better

In (19a), the OP includes the variable corresponding to the focus, but note that the link *baseball* has been replaced by the set {sports}, i.e. the poset that includes both the previously evoked set member and the link. In other words, the OP that is salient in (18) is not that the speaker likes baseball per se, but rather that he likes sports to some degree.

Thus, the focus of a preposing may appear either in preposed or canonical position. However, in both cases the preposed constituent serves as the discourse-old link to the preceding discourse via a salient linking relation.

4.   Left-dislocation

Before we leave preposing, it is important to distinguish it from a superficially similar – but functionally distinct – construction with which preposing is often confused. Left-dislocation (LD) is superficially similar to preposing in that a non-subject appears in sentence-initial position, but in left-dislocation a coreferential pronoun appears in that constituent's canonical position. Consider (20):

(20)   One of the guys I work with, he said he bought over $100 in Powerball tickets.   (JM to WL, in conversation)

Here, a subject pronoun *he* – coreferential with the sentence-initial constituent – appears in canonical subject position; therefore, unlike preposing, there is no "empty" argument position. It is the presence of this coreferential pronoun that distinguishes LD from preposing in terms of sentence structure, and it is also what distinguishes the two constructions in terms of information structure. As we have seen, the preposed constituent of preposing uniformly represents discourse-old information in context. In the case of LD, however, it is possible for the initial constituent to be not only discourse-new, but even hearer-new, as in (20), where the guy in question is being mentioned for the very first time and therefore not linked in any way to the previous discourse.

Prince (1997) argues that there are three types of left-dislocation (LD), distinguishable on functional grounds. Type I LD is what Prince calls SIMPLIFYING LDs:

> A "simplifying" Left-Dislocation serves to simplify the discourse processing of Discourse-new entities by removing them from a syntactic position disfavored for Discourse-new entities and creating a separate processing unit for them. Once that unit is processed and they have become Discourse-old, they may comfortably occur in their positions within the clause as pronouns.   (1997: 124)

That is, LDs of this type involve entities that are new to the discourse and would otherwise be introduced in a non-favored (i.e. subject) position. Contrast (21a) with (21b–c):

(21)a.   Two of my sisters were living together on 18th Street. They had gone to bed, and this man, their girlfriend's husband, came in. He started fussing with my sister and she started to scream. <u>The landlady, she went up and he laid her out</u>.   (*Welcomat*, December 2, 1981)

  b. She had an idea for a project. She's going to use three groups of mine.
      One she'll feed them mouse chow. Just the regular stuff they make for
      mice. Another she'll feed them veggies. And the third she'll feed junk
      food.   [SH in conversation, 11/7/81 (=Prince 1997, ex. 9e)]

  c. That woman you were just talking to, I don't know where she went.

In (21a), the landlady is new to the discourse (and presumably to the hearer
as well); however, the speaker is introducing her via an NP in subject position
– a position disfavored for introducing new information. The dislocated NP
creates a new information unit and thus, according to Prince, eases processing.[7]
The other two types of LD – triggering a poset inference (21b) and amnestying
an island violation (21c) – typically do, according to Prince, involve discourse-
old information. This stands in stark contrast to true preposing constructions,
in which the preposed constituent must represent a discourse-old link to the
prior discourse.

5 Postposing

Whereas preposing constructions serve to place relatively familiar information
in preverbal position (via the preposing of a discourse-old link), postposing
constructions preserve the old-before-new information-structure paradigm by
presenting relatively unfamiliar information in postverbal position. That is,
when canonical word order would result in the placement of new information
in subject position, postposing offers a way of placing it instead toward the
end of the clause, in the expected position for new information. Nonetheless,
different postposing constructions serve this function in slightly different ways.
In this section we will discuss existential *there*, presentational *there*, and
extraposition. These postposing constructions will then be contrasted with
right-dislocation, which is structurally and functionally distinct.

   Two postposing constructions in English place non-referential *there* in subject position while placing what would be the canonical subject into postverbal
position. These constructions are illustrated in (22):

(22)a. In Ireland's County Limerick, near the River Shannon, there is a quiet
        little suburb by the name of Garryowen, which means "Garden of
        Owen". (Brown Corpus)

   b. After they had travelled on for weeks and weeks past more bays
       and headlands and rivers and villages than Shasta could remember,
       there came a moonlit night when they started their journey at evening,
       having slept during the day. (C. S. Lewis, *The Horse and His Boy*,
       (1954), p. 23)

Example (22a) presents an instance of existential *there*, defined by the presence of non-referential *there* occurring in subject position while the NP that would canonically appear in subject position instead appears postverbally, and finally by the presence of *be* as the main verb. Presentational *there*, as in (22b), is similar in that non-referential *there* appears in subject position while the NP that would canonically appear in that position instead appears postverbally; it differs, however, in having a main verb other than *be* (here, *came*). Note that (22a) also admits a second reading, in which *there* is referential; under this reading *there* receives an H* pitch accent (see Pierrehumbert 1980) and is coreferential with the previously evoked location in County Limerick. It is only the non-referential reading that concerns us here.

Both constructions constrain the postverbal NP (PVNP) to represent new information; in this way, both offer a way to preserve the given-before-new ordering of information in cases where canonical word order would violate this ordering. The specifics of the constraint, however, differ slightly in the two constructions: Existential *there* requires that the PVNP represent information that is hearer-new, while presentational *there* requires only that the PVNP represent information that is discourse-new. Thus, the constraint on presentational *there* is weaker than that on existential *there*, since it is possible for information to be new to the discourse while still being known to the hearer, and such information may felicitously occur in clauses containing presentational *there*. To see this, consider (23):

(23)a.   As soon as he laughed, he began to move forward in a deliberate way, jiggling a tin cup in one hand and tapping a white cane in front of him with the other. <u>Just behind him there came a child</u>, handing out leaflets. (Flannery O'Connor, *Wise Blood*, 1952)

    b.   . . . Just behind him there came the mayor, handing out leaflets.

Here we see that both the variant with a hearer-new PVNP (23a) and the variant with a hearer-old PVNP ((23b), where towns are known to have mayors) are acceptable, because in both cases the PVNP represents an entity that is new to the discourse. If we alter the discourse so that the PVNP is discourse-old, presentational *there* becomes infelicitous:

(24)   As they laughed, John and the mayor began to move forward in a deliberate way. John jiggled a tin cup in one hand and tapped a white cane in front of him with the other. #Just behind him there came the mayor, handing out leaflets.

Existential *there* is likewise felicitous with a hearer-new, discourse-new PVNP, as in (22a) above; however, consider the hearer-old, discourse-new PVNP in (25), modeled after the corresponding presentational-*there* variant in (23b):

(25) As soon as he laughed, he began to move forward in a deliberate way, jiggling a tin cup in one hand and tapping a white cane in front of him with the other. #Just behind him there was the mayor, handing out leaflets.

In this case, *the mayor* still represents hearer-old information, but unlike the presentational *there* in (23b), existential *there* in this sentence is infelicitous. That is, both constructions require a new PVNP, but the type of newness differs: presentational *there* requires only discourse-new status, whereas existential *there* also requires hearer-new status.

Notice that we cannot simply phrase the constraint in terms of definiteness; that is, the difference is not merely in whether the PVNP may be definite. Many authors (Milsark 1974, Safir 1985, Reuland and ter Meulen 1987, Lasnik 1992, inter alia) have assumed that there is a "definiteness effect" that prevents definite NPs from appearing in postverbal position in these sentences. However, as shown in Ward and Birner (1995) and Birner and Ward (1998), this illusion arises from the close similarity of the constraint on definiteness and that on the PVNP in a *there*-sentence. While the PVNP is constrained to be either discourse-new or hearer-new (depending on the construction), a definite NP in general is constrained to be, loosely speaking, identifiable; more specifically, it must be individuable within the discourse model (Birner and Ward 1994, 1998; cf. Gundel et al. 1990, 1993; Abbott 1993, this volume). While most referents satisfying the newness criterion for PVNP status will fail to meet this criterion for definiteness, the two sets are not totally distinct; thus there are a number of contexts in which a definite NP may appear in a *there*-sentence, as in, for example, hearer-new tokens of hearer-old (hence identifiable) types (26a), hearer-new entities with fully identifying descriptions that render them individuable (26b), and FALSE DEFINITES, which represent discourse-new, hearer-new information that does not in fact satisfy the usual criteria for definiteness (26c):

(26)a. The Woody Allen–Mia Farrow breakup, and Woody's declaration of love for one of Mia's adopted daughters, seems to have everyone's attention. <u>There are the usual sleazy reasons for that, of course</u> – the visceral thrill of seeing the extremely private couple's dirt in the street, etc. (*San Francisco Chronicle*, August 24, 1992)

   b. In addition, as the review continues, there is always the chance that we'll uncover something additional that is significant. (Challenger Commission transcripts, March 18, 1986)

   c. There once was this sharp Chicago alderman who also happened to be a crook. (*Chicago Tribune*; cited in Birner and Ward 1998: 139)

In (26a), the current set of sleazy reasons is hearer-new, but it represents an instance of a hearer-old type – the "usual" sleazy reasons for being interested in the troubles of celebrity couples. The hearer-new status of the current set of reasons justifies its postverbal placement in the existential, while the identifiability of the hearer-old type justifies the definite. In (26b), the definite is justified by the fact that the PVNP fully and uniquely individuates the chance in question, while its position in the existential is justified by the fact that this represents hearer-new information. Finally, in (26c), the NP *this sharp Chicago alderman* constitutes hearer-new information and hence is felicitous as a PVNP; in fact, this NP does not in any way represent identifiable or individuable information within the discourse model and hence is a "false definite" (Prince 1981b, Wald 1983, Ward and Birner 1995).

Notice that because the PVNPs in (26) are also discourse-new, they are equally felicitous in presentational *there* clauses:

(27) a.   The Woody Allen–Mia Farrow breakup, and Woody's declaration of love for one of Mia's adopted daughters, seems to have everyone's attention. There exist the usual sleazy reasons for that, of course – the visceral thrill of seeing the extremely private couple's dirt in the street, etc.

   b.   In addition, as the review continues, there always exists the chance that we'll uncover something additional that is significant.

   c.   There once lived this sharp Chicago alderman who also happened to be a crook.

In each case in (27), presentational *there* is licensed by the discourse-new status of the PVNP. Other cases in which a definite PVNP may occur in an existential or presentational *there*-sentence include hearer-old information treated as hearer-new, as with certain types of reminders, and hearer-old information newly instantiating the variable in an OP; see Ward and Birner (1995) for details.

The last type of postposing construction to be discussed is extraposition. In extraposition, a subordinate clause is postposed from subject position, while its canonical position is filled by non-referential *it*. Consider the canonical sentences in (28) and their variants with extraposition in (29):

(28) a.   <u>That a bloodthirsty, cruel capitalist should be such a graceful fellow</u> was a shock to me.   (Davis, *The Iron Puddler*; token courtesy of Philip Miller)

   b.   Yet <u>to determine precisely to what extent and exactly in what ways any individual showed the effects of Christianity</u> would be impossible. (Brown Corpus; token courtesy of Philip Miller)

(29) a.   It was a shock to me <u>that a bloodthirsty, cruel capitalist should be such a graceful fellow</u>.

b. Yet it would be impossible <u>to determine precisely to what extent and exactly in what ways any individual showed the effects of Christianity</u>.

In both (29a) and (29b), the clause appearing as an embedded subject in the canonical version is instead extraposed to the end of the matrix clause. As shown by Miller (2001), extraposition, like the other postposing constructions discussed above, serves to preserve an old-before-new ordering in the discourse. In particular, Miller shows that the canonical variant is felicitous only if the embedded subject clause represents familiar information; if it represents new information, it must be extraposed (cf. Horn 1986). To see this, consider the constructed examples in (30–31):

(30)a.   *A:*   Jeffrey didn't turn in his term paper until a week after the deadline.
         B: It's a miracle <u>that he turned in a term paper at all</u>.

   b.   *A:*   Jeffrey didn't turn in his term paper until a week after the deadline.
         B: <u>That he turned in a term paper at all</u> is a miracle.

(31)a.   *A:*   Jeffrey isn't a very good student.
         B: Yeah; #<u>that he turned in a term paper at all</u> is a miracle.

   b.   *A:*   Jeffrey isn't a very good student.
         B: Yeah, it's a miracle <u>that he turned in a term paper at all</u>.

In (30), the fact that Jeffrey turned in a term paper is discourse-old, having been presupposed in A's utterance, and both variants are felicitous. In (31), on the other hand, this fact is new to the discourse, and only the extraposed variant is felicitous. Notice that unlike each of the other constructions we have dealt with, in which the non-canonical version is subject to some constraint on its felicity, in the case of extraposition it is the canonical variant that is constrained; that is, the canonical variant is infelicitous when the embedded subject represents new information, and in such cases extraposition becomes obligatory.

Although Miller frames this constraint in terms of discourse-old vs. discourse-new status, it appears that in fact it is hearer-status that is relevant – i.e., that non-extraposed subject clauses are felicitous when they represent hearer-old information. Consider (32):

(32)   His act takes on lunatic proportions as he challenges female audience members to wrestling matches, falling in love with one while grappling it out on the canvas. <u>How he and feminist Lynne Margulies (Courtney Love) became life partners is anyone's guess.</u>   (*Man on the Moon* movie review; token provided by Rodney Huddleston)

Here the fact that the referent of *he* (comedian Andy Kaufman) and Lynn Margulies became life partners is treated as shared background knowledge, despite not having been evoked in the prior discourse. Hence it is hearer-old rather than discourse-old, yet the utterance is nonetheless felicitous. Thus, extraposition is required only when the embedded clause represents hearer-new information, and the extraposition in that case serves once again to preserve the ordering of old before new information within the utterance.

6   Right-dislocation

Just as left-dislocation is functionally distinct from preposing, so is right-dislocation functionally distinct from postposing, despite the fact that both constructions involve the rightward placement of information that would canonically appear earlier in the clause. In existential and presentational *there*-sentences, for example, the PVNP is required to represent information that is new, either to the discourse (for presentational *there*) or to the hearer (for existential *there*). For right-dislocation, no such requirement holds:

(33)   Below the waterfall (and this was the most astonishing sight of all), a whole mass of enormous glass pipes were dangling down into the river from somewhere high up in the ceiling! <u>They really were ENORMOUS, those pipes</u>. There must have been a dozen of them at least, and they were sucking up the brownish muddy water from the river and carrying it away to goodness knows where.   (R. Dahl, *Charlie and the Chocolate Factory*, 1964: 74–5)

Here, the pipes in question have been explicitly evoked in the previous sentence and therefore are both hearer-old and discourse-old; in fact, discourse-old status is not only permitted but indeed required:

(34)   Below the waterfall (and this was the most astonishing sight of all), a whole mass of enormous glass pipes were dangling down into the river from somewhere high up in the ceiling! #They really were ENORMOUS, some of the boulders in the river.

Here we see that when the right-dislocated NP represents discourse-new information, the utterance is infelicitous; thus, none of the requirements placed on postposing constructions (all of which permit or in fact require new information in postposed position) hold for right-dislocation. Notice, however, that the two are structurally distinct as well, paralleling the structural distinction seen above to hold between preposing and left-dislocation; specifically, whereas all of the above postposing constructions place a semantically empty element (*there* or *it*) in subject position while placing the canonical subject in postverbal position, right-dislocation instead places a coreferential pronoun in the right-dislocated NP's canonical position. That is, instead of non-referential *there* or *it*, we get the referential pronoun *they* in subject position in (33). This pronoun, like anaphoric pronouns in general, represents familiar information – and because the pronoun is coreferential with the dislocated constituent, that constituent too will therefore represent familiar information. In this way, the form of the right-dislocation – specifically, the presence of an anaphoric pronoun – constrains its information-packaging function.

7   Argument Reversal

We have seen how preposing places a single constituent to the left of its canonical position, where it is constrained to represent old information. We have also seen how postposing places a single constituent to the right of its canonical position, where it is constrained to represent new information. In this section, we examine argument reversal, a process that involves the displacement of **two** arguments and thus, we claim, imposes a relative rather than absolute constraint on the information status of the displaced constituents. Specifically, we have found that the preposed constituent must not represent information that is newer than that represented by the postposed constituent (Birner 1994, 1996, Birner and Ward 1998).

The English argument-reversing constructions we will consider are *by*-phrase passives and inversion, which we discuss in turn.

7.1   *Passives*

By-phrase passives are passive constructions with a *by*-phrase containing the logical subject, as in (35):

(35)   Connaught said it was advised that the Ciba-Geigy/Chiron offer would be increased to $26.51 a share from $25.23 a share if the company adopted a shareholder-rights plan that facilitated the Swiss and US firms' offer. <u>That offer was rejected by Connaught, which cited its existing pact with Institut Merieux.</u>   (*Wall Street Journal*, September 12, 1989)

Note that in this construction the canonical order of the two major NP constituents is reversed. As is the case with argument-reversing constructions in general, *by*-phrase passives are constrained in that the syntactic subject must not represent newer information within the discourse than does the NP in the *by*-phrase (Birner 1996).

We will restrict our discussion to passives with *by*-phrases containing the logical subject, as exemplified in (36):[8]

(36)   The mayor's present term of office expires January 1. <u>He will be succeeded by Ivan Allen Jr.</u> . . .   (Brown Corpus)

In referring to the preverbal NP in a *by*-phrase passive (e.g., *he* in (36)) as the syntactic subject, and to the postverbal NP (e.g., *Ivan Allen Jr.*) as the *by*-phrase NP, we break with the tradition of calling the *by*-phrase NP an "agent" and the construction itself an "agentive passive" (e.g., Siewierska 1984). Such terminology is misleading given that in many cases the *by*-phrase NP does not act as a semantic agent (in the sense of Fillmore 1968). In (36), for example, *Ivan Allen Jr.* is not an agent.

As an argument-reversing construction, this type of passivization requires that its syntactic subject represent information that is at least as familiar within the discourse as that represented by the *by*-phrase NP. Thus, when the information status of the relevant NPs is reversed, infelicity results. Consider again (36), as compared with (37):

(37)   Ivan Allen Jr. will take office January 1. #<u>The mayor will be succeeded by him</u>.

The subject *he* in (36) represents discourse-old information, while the *by*-phrase NP, *Ivan Allen Jr.*, represents discourse-new information, and the token is felicitous. In (37), on the other hand, the syntactic subject, *the mayor*, represents discourse-new information while the NP in the *by*-phrase, *him*, represents discourse-old information, and the passive is infelicitous. Thus, the subject NP in a *by*-phrase passive must not represent less familiar information within the discourse than does the NP within the *by*-phrase.

7.2   *Inversion*

Like *by*-phrase passives, the logical subject of inversion appears in postverbal position while some other, canonically postverbal, constituent appears in preverbal position (Birner 1994). As with preposing, any phrasal constituent can be preposed via inversion:

(38)   PP
       He, the publisher, is twenty-six. Born in Hungary, he emigrated to Canada after the revolution. He is as informal as the others. <u>On his lapel is a large "Jesus Loves You" button</u>; on his feet, sneakers. His dog scrounges about on a blanket in this inner office.   (S. Terkel *Working* (1974), p. 583)

(39)   AdjP
       Along US Route 6, overscale motels run by the national chains have started to supplant the quaint, traditional transients' cottages. <u>Typical of these new giants is the Sheraton Ocean Park at Eastham, which boasts an indoor swimming pool with cabanas in a tropic-like setting</u>. (*Philadelphia Inquirer*, p. 2-A, September 6, 1983, article "On Cape Cod, charm ebbs as numbers grow")

(40)   NP
       She's a nice woman, isn't she? <u>Also a nice woman is our next guest</u>.[9]
       (David Letterman, May 31, 1990)

(41)   VP
>   Discussion of the strategy began during this year's General Assembly and will conclude next year. <u>Dropped from consideration so far are the approaches of the past, which</u> *The Economist* <u>recently described as</u> <u>"based on the idea that the rules of orthodox economics do not hold in developing countries."</u>   (*New York Times Week in Review*, November 5, 1989, p. 2)

As with argument-reversal in general, felicitous inversion in English depends on the discourse-status of the information represented by the preposed and post-posed constituents. According to Birner (1994), the most common distribution of information is for the preposed constituent to represent discourse-old informa-tion while the postposed constituent represents discourse-new information, as in (42):

(42)   We have complimentary soft drinks, coffee, Sanka, tea, and milk. <u>Also complimentary is red and white wine</u>. We have cocktails available for $2.00.   (Flight attendant on Midway Airlines)

Here, the preposed AdjP *also complimentary* represents information previ-ously evoked in the discourse, while the postposed *red and white wine* is new to the discourse. In a corpus study of over 1,700 tokens, 78 percent of the tokens exhibited this distribution of information, while not a single example was found in which the situation was reversed – i.e., in which a preposed discourse-new element combined with a postposed discourse-old element.

Moreover, information that was merely inferrable (Prince 1981a) behaved as discourse-old, occurring in the same range of contexts as explicitly evoked information. Finally, the corpus study showed that among discourse-old infor-mation, that which has been mentioned more recently in general is treated as more familiar, in the sense of being more salient, than that which has been mentioned less recently.

It is not the case, however, that the preposed constituent need always be discourse-old, or that the postposed constituent need always be discourse-new. The pragmatic constraint on argument reversal disallows only a preposed constituent being *less* familiar in the discourse than the postposed constituent. Felicity is indeed possible when both constituents represent discourse-old in-formation. However, in these cases the preposed element is consistently the more recently mentioned of the two, as in (43):

(43)   Each of the characters is the centerpiece of a book, doll and clothing collection. The story of each character is told in a series of six slim books, each $12.95 hardcover and $5.95 in paperback, and in bookstores and libraries across the country. More than 1 million copies have been sold; and in late 1989 a series of activity kits was introduced for retail sale. <u>Complementing the relatively affordable books are the dolls, one for</u>

each fictional heroine and each with a comparably pricey historically accurate wardrobe and accessories . . .

(*Chicago Tribune* story on "American Girl" dolls)

Here, although the dolls have been evoked in the prior discourse, they have been evoked less recently than the books. Reversing the preposed and postposed constituents in the inversion results in infelicity:

(44)   Each of the characters is the centerpiece of a book, doll and clothing collection. The story of each character is told in a series of six slim books, each $12.95 hardcover and $5.95 in paperback, and in bookstores and libraries across the country. More than 1 million copies have been sold; and in late 1989 a series of activity kits was introduced for retail sale. #Complementing the relatively affordable dolls are the books, one for each fictional heroine. . . .

Thus, even in cases where both constituents have been previously evoked, the postposed constituent nonetheless represents less familiar information, where familiarity is defined by prior evocation, inferrability, and recency of mention. Therefore, what is relevant for the felicity of inversion in discourse is the relative discourse-familiarity of the information represented by these two constituents.

The relative (vs. absolute) information status to which argument reversal is sensitive, we argue, is a direct consequence of there being a displacement of two constituents. The transposition of arguments found in passivization and inversion imposes a relative constraint on the information status of those constituents, unlike the absolute constraint found for the non-canonical constructions that displace but a single constituent.

8   Conclusion

We have argued that discourse-status and hearer-status serve as key elements by which speakers structure their utterances, and in particular that non-canonical constructions are used in predictable ways in order to preserve a general old-before-new ordering of information in English. We have presented a general typology of non-canonical syntactic constructions based on the information status of their constituents, as shown above in (2). As shown in that table, whether a construction is sensitive to the absolute or relative status of its constituents is predictable from the number of non-canonically positioned constituents; and whether those constituents are constrained to represent old or new information is predictable from their position (preverbal or postverbal) in the construction. Whether it is discourse-status or hearer-status to which the constraint is sensitive, on the other hand, is an arbitrary fact associated with each construction. These generalizations have been shown to hold for non-canonical English constructions in which some constituent is placed in a non-canonical position, leaving its canonical position either empty or filled by a non-referential element, as in postposing, or a displaced argument, as in argument reversal. Crucially, this leaves out constructions like right- and left-dislocation, in which a constituent is similarly placed in a non-canonical position but its canonical position is filled by a referential pronoun. As predicted, such constructions place very different constraints on their non-canonically positioned constituents. Thus, we have found that preposing constructions are constrained to prepose only information that is discourse-old, while postposing constructions postpose information that is either discourse-new (for presentationals) or hearer-new (for existentials). Extraposition likewise serves to postpose hearer-new information, but there it is the canonical-word-order variant that is constrained; specifically, extraposition is obligatory where the embedded clause that would canonically appear in subject position represents hearer-new information.

Because both preposing and postposing involve only a single non-canonically positioned constituent, each of these constraints is an absolute constraint on that constituent's information status. In the case of passivization and inversion, on the other hand, the relative position of two arguments is reversed, and the constraint on these is a relative one: the preverbal argument must be at least as familiar within the discourse as is the postverbal argument. In each of the above cases, however, the non-canonical construction provides speakers with a way of ensuring that old information precede new; and just as importantly, we have shown that the constraints associated with these constructions are largely non-arbitrary, i.e. that information-packaging rules apply across a broad spectrum of constructions in predictable ways.

NOTES

1   This "given precedes new" principle of information structure may only apply to SV languages; at least some languages in which the verb canonically precedes the subject have been argued to display the reverse order, i.e. of new information preceding given (see Tomlin and Rhodes (1979, 1992), Creider and Creider (1983), Siewierska (1988), inter alia). For extension of the information-theoretic principles discussed here to other SV languages, see Birner and Ward (1998), inter alia.

2   We are glossing over important prosodic differences between the two renditions of *A bran muffin I can give you* in (12) and (13), e.g. the fall–rise contour that would naturally accompany the preposed constituent in (12) and the deaccenting of the verb in (13). However, these differences are not relevant to the point at hand.

3   See Ward and Birner (1988) for a more detailed discussion of links, linking relations, and posits as they relate to non-canonical syntax.

4   By ACCENT, we mean INTONATIONAL PROMINENCE in the sense of Terken and Hirschberg (1994): "a conspicuous pitch change in or near

the lexically stressed syllable of the word" (1994: 126); see also Pierrehumbert (1980).

5 Of course for both topicalization and focus preposing, other constituents may bear pitch accents. Intonationally speaking, the difference between focus preposing and topicalization is that only the former requires that the nuclear accent be on the preposed constituent.

6 As noted in Ward (1988) and Birner and Ward (1998), there is one preposing construction – locative preposing – that does not require a salient OP but does require a semantically locative element in preposed position.

7 Prince is not alone in claiming that at least some types of LD serve to introduce new entities into the discourse: Halliday (1967), Rodman (1974), and Gundel (1974, 1985) propose similar functions.

8 This restriction excludes such passives as that in (i):

(i) A car was stolen right outside our house yesterday.

9 Although the linear word order in this example (NP – *be* – NP) is the same as that of a canonical-word-order sentence, it is nonetheless an inversion, given that the postverbal NP (*our next guest*) represents the logical subject, of which the information represented by the preverbal NP (*a nice woman*) is being predicated. See Birner (1994) for discussion.

8   Topic and Focus

JEANETTE K. GUNDEL AND
THORSTEIN FRETHEIM

In his *Grammar of Spoken Chinese*, Chao (1968) notes a distinction between the grammatical predicate of a sentence and what he calls the "logical predicate." Chao points out that the two do not always coincide, illustrating this point with the following exchange between a guide (A) and a tourist (B):

(1)   A: We are now passing the oldest winery in the region.
      B: Why?

The source of the humor here is that the English sentence uttered by the guide has two possible interpretations. On one interpretation, the main predicate asserted by the sentence (Chao's logical predicate) coincides with the grammatical predicate, i.e., *are now passing the oldest winery in the region*. On the other interpretation, the logical predicate includes only the direct object. The tourist (B) seems to be questioning the first interpretation (we are passing the oldest winery in the region), but it is the second interpretation that the guide actually intended to convey (what we are passing is the oldest winery in the region).

Chao notes (1968: 78) that the humor would be absent in Chinese because "in general, if in a sentence of the form S-V-O the object O is the logical predicate, it is often recast in the form S-V *de shO* 'what S V's is O', thus putting O in the center of the predicate." In this case, the guide's intended message would be expressed in Chinese by a sentence which more literally translates as *The one we are passing now is the oldest winery in the region*.

Within the Western grammatical tradition, the idea that there is a distinction between the grammatical subject and predicate of a sentence and the subject–predicate structure of the meaning that may be conveyed by this sentence (its INFORMATION STRUCTURE) can be traced back at least to the second half of the nineteenth century, when the German linguists von der Gabelentz (1868) and Paul (1880) used the terms PSYCHOLOGICAL SUBJECT and PREDICATE for what Chao calls "logical subject" and "predicate" (or "topic" and "comment"), respectively. Work of the Czech linguist Mathesius in the 1920s (e.g. Mathesius

1928) initiated a rich and highly influential tradition of research in this area within the Prague School that continues to the present day (see Firbas 1966, Daneš 1974, Sgall et al. 1973, Sgall et al. 1986, inter alia). Also influential has been the seminal work of Halliday (1967) and, within the generative tradition, Kuroda (1965, 1972), Chomsky (1971), Jackendoff (1972), Kuno (1972, 1976b), Gundel (1974), and Reinhart (1981), inter alia. More recent work will be cited below.

Unless otherwise noted, we use the term FOCUS in this paper to refer roughly to the function described by Chao's notion of logical predicate, and we use the term TOPIC to refer to the complement of focus. Topic is what the sentence is about; focus is what is predicated about the topic. Our primary goals will be to clarify some of the major conceptual and terminological issues, to provide an overview of the phenomena that correlate with topic and focus across languages, and to review recent empirical and theoretical developments.

1   Conceptual and Terminological Issues

The literature on topic and focus is characterized by an absence of uniformity in terminology. Besides the earlier terms of psychological/logical subject and predicate, current terms for topic also include THEME and GROUND. In addition to focus, other terms for the complement of topic include COMMENT and RHEME. Most authors agree that these concepts, unlike purely syntactic functions such as subject and object, have a consistent semantic/pragmatic value. However, topic and focus are also sometimes defined directly on syntactic structures (e.g., Chomsky 1965, Halliday 1967, Kiss 1998). Consequently, topic, focus, and related terms have been used in a dual sense (sometimes by the same author) to refer to syntactic (and phonological) categories as well as their semantic/pragmatic interpretation. Below we address a few of the major conceptual issues.

1.1   Two given–new distinctions

The topic–focus distinction has been widely associated with the division between given and new information in a sentence. There has been disagreement and confusion, however, regarding the exact nature of this association. Some of the confusion has resulted from conflating two types of givenness–newness.[1] Following Gundel (1988, 1999a), we refer to these as REFERENTIAL GIVENNESS–NEWNESS and RELATIONAL GIVENNESS–NEWNESS.

Referential givenness–newness involves a relation between a linguistic expression and a corresponding non-linguistic entity in the speaker/hearer's mind, the discourse (model), or some real or possible world, depending on where the referents or corresponding meanings of these linguistic expressions are assumed to reside. Some representative examples of referential givenness concepts include existential presupposition (e.g. Strawson 1964b), various senses of referentiality and specificity (e.g. Fodor and Sag 1982, Enç 1991), the familiarity condition on definite descriptions (e.g. Heim 1982), the activation and identifiability statuses of Chafe (1994) and Lambrecht (1994), the hearer-old/new and discourse-old/new statuses of Prince (1992), and the cognitive statuses of Gundel et al. (1993). For example, the cognitive statuses on the Givenness Hierarchy in (2) represent referential givenness statuses that an entity mentioned in a sentence may have in the mind of the addressee.

(2)   **The Givenness Hierarchy** (Gundel et al. 1993)

in	uniquely	type
focus > activated > familiar > identifiable > referential > identifiable		

Relational givenness–newness, in contrast, involves a partition of the semantic/conceptual representation of a sentence into two complementary parts, X and Y, where X is what the sentence is about (the logical/psychological subject) and Y is what is predicated about X (the logical/psychological predicate). X is given in relation to Y in the sense that it is independent of, and outside the scope of, what is predicated in Y. Y is new in relation to X in the sense that it is new information that is asserted, questioned, etc. about X. Relational givenness–newness thus reflects how the informational content of a particular event or state of affairs expressed by a sentence is represented and how its truth value is to be assessed. Examples of relational givenness–newness pairs include the notions of logical/psychological subject and predicate mentioned above, presupposition–focus (e.g. Chomsky 1971, Jackendoff 1972), topic–comment (e.g. Gundel 1974), theme–rheme (e.g., Vallduví 1992), and topic–predicate (Erteschik-Shir 1997). Topic and focus, as we use these terms here, are thus relationally given and new, respectively.

Referential givenness–newness and relational givenness–newness are logically independent, as seen in the following examples (from Gundel 1980 and 1985, respectively):

(3)   *A*:   Who called?
      B: Pat said SHE[2] called.

(4)   *A*:   Did you order the chicken or the pork?
      B: It was the PORK that I ordered.

If *SHE* in (3) is used to refer to Pat, it is referentially given in virtually every possible sense. The intended referent is presupposed, specific, referential, familiar, activated, in focus, identifiable, hearer-old, and discourse-old. But, at the same time, the subject of the embedded sentence in this example is relationally new and, therefore, receives a focal accent. It instantiates the variable in the relationally given, topical part of the sentence, *x called*, thus yielding the new information expressed in (3). Similarly, in (4), the pork is referentially given. Its cognitive status would be at least activated, possibly even in focus, since it was mentioned in the immediately preceding sentence.[3] But it is new in relation to the topic of (4), what B ordered.

The two kinds of givenness–newness also differ in other respects. Both are properties of meaning representations. However, while relational givenness–newness is necessarily a property of linguistic representations, i.e., the meanings associated with sentences, referential givenness–newness is not specifically linguistic at all. Thus, one can just as easily characterize a visual or non-linguistic auditory stimulus, for example a house or a tune, as familiar or not, in focus or not, and even specific or not. In contrast, the topic-focus partition can only apply to linguistic expressions, specifically sentences or utterances and their interpretations.

Corresponding to this essential difference is the fact that referential givenness statuses, e.g., familiar or in focus, are uniquely determined by the knowledge and attention state of the addressee at a given point in the discourse. The speaker has no choice in the matter.[4] Relational givenness notions like topic, on the other hand, may be constrained or influenced by the discourse context (as all aspects of meaning are in some sense), but they are not uniquely determined by it. As Sgall et al. (1973: 12) notes, a sentence like *Yesterday was the last day of the Davis Cup match between Australia and Romania* could be followed either by *Australia won the match* or by *The match was won by Australia*. While the latter two sentences could each have an interpretation in which the topic is the Davis Cup match, or one in which the whole sentence is a comment on some topic not overtly represented in the sentence, it is also possible in exactly the same discourse context to interpret the first of these sentences as a comment about Australia and the second as a comment about the match. Which of these possible interpretations is the intended one depends on the interests and perspective of the speaker.

One place in which the linguistic context often seems to determine a single topic–focus structure is in question–answer pairs, which is why these provide one of the more reliable contextual tests for relational givenness–newness concepts. Thus, (5b) is judged to be an appropriate answer to the question in (5a) because the location of the prominent pitch accent is consistent with an interpretation in which the topic is who the Red Sox played and the focus is the Yankees. But (5c), for which the location of prominent pitch accent requires an interpretation in which the topic is who played the Yankees, is not an appropriate response to (5a).

(5)a.   Who did the Red Sox play?
   b.   The Red Sox played the YANKEES.
   c.   #The RED SOX played the Yankees.
   d.   #I love baseball.

The fact that the judgments here are sensitive to linguistic context has no doubt contributed to the widely held view that topic and focus are pragmatic concepts. However, as Gundel (1999b) points out, questions constrain other aspects of the semantic–conceptual content of an appropriate answer as well. All aspects of the meaning of a sentence have pragmatic effects in the sense that they contribute to a relevant context for interpretation. This much is determined by general principles that govern language production and understanding (Sperber and Wilson 1986a). Thus, (5d) is no more appropriate as an answer to (5a) than (5c) would be, though the exact reason for the inappropriateness is different. The fact that location of the prominent pitch accent has pragmatic effects thus does not itself warrant the conclusion that pitch accent codes a pragmatic concept, any more so than it would follow that the difference in meaning between (5b) and (5d) is pragmatic because the two sentences would be appropriate in different linguistic contexts.

1.2 *Referential properties of topic*

We noted in the previous section that topic–focus structure is associated with relational givenness–newness in the sense that topic is given in relation to focus and focus represents the new information predicated about the topic. This association is logically independent of referential givenness–newness, which is not necessarily connected to topic or focus at all. As we saw in examples (3) and (4), the focus (relationally new) part of the sentence can contain material that has a high degree of referential givenness. There is, however, a good deal of empirical evidence for an independent connection between topic and some degree of referential givenness. Virtually the whole range of possible referential givenness conditions on topics has been suggested, including presupposition, familiarity, specificity, referentiality, and focus of attention.

Some of the more well-known facts that indicate a connection between topicality and some kind of referential givenness have to do with the "definiteness" or "presupposition" effect of topics. For example, it has often been noted (e.g., in Kuroda 1965, Kuno 1972, inter alia) that the phrase marked by a topic marker in Japanese and Korean necessarily has a "definite" (including generic) interpretation. Thus, in (6), where the subject phrase is followed by the nominative marker *ga*, both the subject and the object can have either a definite or indefinite interpretation. But in (7), where the subject is followed by the topic marker *wa*, it can only be interpreted as definite.

(6) Neko ga   kingyo o   ijit-te ......
     cat   NOM goldfish OBJ play with-and
     "The/A cat is playing with the/a goldfish, and . . ."

(7) Neko wa   kingyo o   ijit-te
     cat   TOP goldfish OBJ play with-and
     "The/*A cat is playing with the/a goldfish, and . . ."

Similarly, in prototypical topic–comment constructions like those in (8)–(11), the topic phrase adjoined to the left of the clause is definite:

(8)   My sister, she's a high school teacher.

(9)   That book you borrowed, are you finished reading it yet?

(10) My work, I'm going crazy. (Bland 1980)

(11) The Red Sox, did they play the Yankees?

Indefinites are generally excluded from topic position unless they can be interpreted generically, as illustrated in (12) (from Gundel 1988):

(12)a. The window, it's still open.
     b. *A window, it's still open.[5]

Gundel (1985, 1988) proposes a condition on felicitous topics which states that their referents must already be familiar, in the sense that the addressee must have an existing representation in memory.[6] Since indefinites aren't generally used to refer to familiar entities (unless they are intended to be interpreted generically), the familiarity condition on topics provides a principled explanation for facts like those in (6)–(12).[7] It also captures, in more overtly cognitive terms, Strawson's (1964b) insight that only topical definites necessarily carry an existential presupposition.

The examples in (6)–(12) provide support for a familiarity condition on topics only to the extent that the constructions in question can be assumed to mark topics. These assumptions, though widely held, are not totally uncontroversial. For example, Tomlin (1995) proposes that Japanese *wa* is not a topic marker, but a new information marker. He argues that topics are associated with given information, but *wa* is typically used to mark noun phrases referring to entities that are newly introduced or reintroduced into the discourse. Tomlin's argument rests on the assumption that topics are referentially given in the sense of being the current focus of attention. Similar restrictions on topics are assumed by Erteschik-Shir (1997), who analyzes the left-dislocated phrase in constructions like (8)–(12) as a focus rather than a topic, since it is more likely to be something the speaker wants to call to the addressee's attention than something that is already in the focus of attention. Both Tomlin and Erteschik-Shir base their arguments on conceptions of topic that blur the distinction between relational and referential givenness by essentially equating topic with focus of attention.[8] Their notion of topic is thus closer to "continued topic" or to the backward-looking center of Centering Theory (see Walker et al. 1998). While some authors propose that topics are necessarily activated or even in focus because they have been mentioned recently in the discourse, others deny that topics must have any degree of referential givenness at all, including familiarity. For example, Reinhart (1981) proposes that topics only have to be referential. She notes that specific indefinites, whose referents are generally not familiar, can appear in dislocated topic position, as in the following example from Prince (1985):[9]

(13)   An old preacher down there, they augured under the grave where his
       wife was buried.

To sum up, topics are relationally given, by definition, in the sense that
they are what the sentence/utterance is about. They provide the context for
the main predication, which is assessed relative to the topic. The association
of topics with definiteness across languages suggests that topics must also
be referentially given (familiar or at least uniquely identifiable), and some
researchers define topics even more narrowly to include only entities with the
highest degree of referential givenness, the current center of attention. Others
propose to abandon any referential givenness condition on topics, citing the
possibility of indefinite topics as in (13).

1.3   *Information focus vs. contrastive focus*

As we saw in the previous section, topic is sometimes defined in terms of the
referential givenness status of entities, thus resulting in some conceptual confusion between two distinct, though orthogonal, interpretive categories: topic
as a relational category (the complement of focus/comment) and topic as the
current center of attention. There has been a similar confusion between two
conceptually distinct interpretative notions of focus: one of these is relational –
the information predicated about the topic; the other is referential – material
that the speaker calls to the addressee's attention, thereby often evoking a
contrast with other entities that might fill the same position. We refer to these
two senses as INFORMATION FOCUS and CONTRASTIVE FOCUS, respectively.[10]
According to Rooth (1985), evoking alternatives is the primary function of
focus (cf. Chafe 1976 for a similar position), and the contrast set evoked by the
focus provides the locus for focus-sensitive operators such as *only*, *even*, and
also. Other researchers (e.g. Horn 1981, Vallduví 1992) take information status
to be primary and treat contrast as secondary and derivative.

Both information focus and contrastive focus are coded by some type of
linguistic prominence across languages, a fact that no doubt has contributed to
a blurring of the distinction between these two categories. Information focus is
given linguistic prominence, typically (and possibly universally) by means of
some sort of prosodic highlighting, because it is the main predication expressed
in the sentence – the new information in relation to the topic. It correlates with
the questioned position in the relevant (implicit or explicit) *wh*-question or
alternative *yes-no* question that the sentence would be responsive to. Thus, in
both (14) and (15) below *Bill* expresses the information focus that identifies the
one who called the meeting (the topic) as Bill.

(14)   *A:*   Do you know who called the meeting?
       B1: BILL called the meeting.
       B2: It was BILL who called the meeting.

(15)   Every time we get together I'm the one who has to organize things, but this time BILL called the meeting.

But marking the information focus is not the only reason to call attention to a constituent. A constituent may also be made prominent because the speaker/writer does not think the addressee's attention is focused on some entity and for one reason or another would like it to be – for example, because a new topic is being introduced or reintroduced (topic shift) or because the meaning associated with some constituent is being contrasted, implicitly or explicitly, with something else.[11] The example in (16) illustrates a contrastive focus on the constituent referring to the topic (*that coat*). Example (17) has a contrastive focus on the constitutent referring to the topic (*the curry*) as well as on the information focus (*Bill*), thus showing that contrastive focus and information focus can coincide (see Gundel 1999a).

(16)   We have to get rid of some of these clothes. That COAT you're wearing I think we can give to the Salvation ARMY.

(17)   *A:*   Who made all this great food?
       B: BILL made the CURRY.

As seen in (14)–(17), both information focus and contrastive focus may be marked with a prominent pitch accent: Thus, (16) and (17) each have two positions of prominent pitch accent – one of these falls on the information focus, and the other falls on a contrastive topic.

It is widely assumed (though not uncontroversially) that in languages that use pitch accent to mark information focus, when a sentence contains only a single prominent pitch accent (as in (14) and (15) above) this will necessarily fall on the information focus (see Schmerling 1976, Gundel 1978, Selkirk 1984, Zacharski 1993, Vallduví and Vilkuna 1998, inter alia). Gundel (1999a) maintains that this is because all sentences have an information focus, as an essential part of the function of sentences in information processing, but not all sentences/utterances have a contrastive focus, the latter being determined primarily by a speaker/writer's intention to affect the addressee's attention state at a given point in the discourse. However, as Büring (1999) points out, a prominent pitch accent inside the constituent corresponding to the topic is obligatory in some discourse contexts. Büring, in fact, restricts the term "topic" to constituents that receive a prominent pitch accent (his S-topics). Topics for him are "simply an (improper) part of the non-focus" (Büring 1999: 145), and non-contrasted material that is not part of the information focus is called background. Thus, in (17), for example, *Bill* corresponds to the topic, *the curry* corresponds to the focus, and *made* represents the background.[12]

Similarly, both contrastive focus and information focus may be syntactically coded by placing the relevant constituent in a syntactically prominent position. This has resulted in some confusion in the literature, with the term "topicalization" being used to mark preposing of (contrastively focused) topics, as in (16) above, as well as preposing of information focus, as in (18).[13]

(18) A: Which of these clothes do you think we should give to the Salvation Army?
      B: That COAT you're wearing (I think we can give away).

The sentences in (16) and (18) are similar in that both have a prosodically prominent sentence-initial object (*that coat you're wearing*) that may be in contrast with other objects in some contextually relevant set. The information status of the preposed objects is different, however. In (16), the coat is a topic, possibly (though not necessarily) contrasting with other members of the set of clothes that are candidates for being disposed of and to which the predicate *we can give to the Salvation Army* would or would not apply. In (18), the coat is part of the information focus, the new information identifying objects that would be included in the set described by the topic (clothes that would be suitable to give away) and possibly contrasting with other clothes that could also be included in that set.[14] The type of pitch accent on the two preposed phrases is different as well, as will be discussed in section 2.

2   Phenomena

2.1   *Focus and intonation*

The association between prosodic prominence and focus has been shown to hold in a variety of typologically and genetically diverse languages, and is widely believed to be universal.[15] In some languages, there is no type of prosodic prominence that distinguishes information focus from contrastive focus (including contrastive topic). Thus, according to Vallduví and Vilkuna (1998: 89), information focus (their "rheme") and contrast (their "kontrast") are "associated with a single high tone accent" in Finnish, and the distinction between the two is coded syntactically rather than prosodically. Similarly, Fretheim (1987, 1992a, 1992b, 2001) argues that there is no particular pitch contour that encodes topic or focus in Norwegian. When a Norwegian unit contains two fundamental frequency maxima for maximum prosodic prominence, either one of them could be the information focus. Thus (19), with a prosodically prominent subject as well as a prosodically prominent direct object, could be a statement about Fred or a statement about the beans. There is no intonational phenomenon in Norwegian that enables the hearer to uniquely identify topic and focus in an utterance of (19). This must be determined by pragmatic inference alone.

(19) FRED spiste BØNNENE
      Fred ate   the beans
      "Fred ate the beans."

Similarly, the Norwegian sentence in (20) produced with the highest degree of prosodic prominence on *de bildene* ("those pictures") and on *etterpå* ("afterwards") means either (a) "Looking at those pictures [topic] is something you must postpone till some later time [focus]," or (b) "Afterwards [topic] you have to take a look at those pictures [focus]."

(20)   Du må   se   på de   BILDENE ETTERPÅ.
       you must look at those pictures   afterwards
       "You have to look at those pictures afterwards."

However, in some languages, information focus and contrastive focus are associated with distinct pitch accents. In English, for example, information focus is coded by what Bolinger (1961) and Jackendoff (1972) call an A accent (the simplex H* tone of Pierrehumbert 1980). A contrastive topic (and possibly contrast in general) is typically marked by what Bolinger and Jackendoff call a B accent (Pierrehumbert's complex L + H* tone), an accent pattern also used for functions not directly related to topic or focus.[16]

Elements within the prosodic domain of the H* accent are interpreted as part of the information focus and elements outside that domain are interpreted as part of the topic.[17] The projection of information focus to higher constituents results in topic–focus ambiguities. Thus, a sentence like (5b), with an H* pitch accent on the direct object, is an appropriate answer to the question in (5a) because it has a possible interpretation in which the information focus includes only the direct object. But the same sentence also has an interpretation in which the focus is the VP *played the Yankees*, as well as an interpretation in which the whole sentence is the focus, for example as an answer to *Did anything interesting happen today?* This latter interpretation corresponds to what Marty (1918) calls a thetic judgment (see also Kuroda 1972), and what Schmerling (1976) calls an "all-new" sentence. However, (5c), with an H* pitch accent on the subject, *Red Sox*, has a so-called narrow focus interpretation, in which the information focus includes only the subject.[18]

Lambrecht (1994: 133) provides an especially compelling example of the role of prosody in topic–focus interpretation. He notes that most people, when asked to interpret a written sentence like (21) in the absence of any contextual cues, would assign a generic interpretation in which the topic and focus coincide with the grammatical subject and predicate, respectively.

(21)   Nazis tear down antiwar posters.

One might imagine a context, for example, in which (21) is uttered during a discussion about Nazis, where Nazis is the topic and what is predicated about Nazis (the focus) is that they tear down antiwar posters. Another likely interpretation, which Lambrecht doesn't consider here, is one in which the whole sentence is the focus, for example as a newspaper heading, where the topic is simply what happened today. Both of these interpretations would be consistent with an H* accent on the direct object (ANTIWAR posters), the default (wide focus) accentual pattern that people normally assume when presented with written sentences in isolation. In fact, Lambrecht notes (1994: 133) that this sentence was "written with a felt pen across a poster protesting the war in Central America. The poster had been partly ripped down from the wall it had been glued onto." Provided with this additional contextual information, the interpretation of the sentence changes, as does the accentual pattern we assign to it. The prominent H* pitch accent now shifts to the subject and the interpretation is: people who tear down antiwar posters are Nazis. The situation here is reminiscent of Chao's exchange between the guide and the tourist in (1).

2.2   *Topic, focus, and syntactic structure*

Topic and focus have been associated with various syntactic structures across languages, especially ones in which a constituent has been "displaced" from its canonical position in a clause to occupy a syntactically more prominent position, as in the English examples in (22b–d):

(22)a.   Fred ate the beans.
    b.   The beans, Fred ate.
    c.   It was the beans that Fred ate.
    d.   The beans, Fred ate them.
    e.   Fred ate them, the beans.

However, as with pitch accent, the relation between surface syntactic form and topic–focus structure is complex and there is no simple one-to-one correlation between topic or focus and particular syntactic constructions, either across languages or even within particular languages. For example, as noted in section 1.3 (examples (16) and (18)), the sentence-initial constituent in an example like (22b) may refer either to the topic or to the information focus. The constituent *the beans* in (22b) could be a contrastive topic (e.g., as an answer to *What about the beans*? *Who ate them*?) or an information focus (e.g., as an answer to *What did Fred eat*?).[19] Corresponding to this distinction, as already noted, the sentence-initial phrase would also have two different pitch accents in English, but this would not be the case in Finnish or Norwegian, for example. In either case, non-canonical placement of constituents in sentence-initial position is not in itself uniquely associated with either topic or focus. Birner and Ward (1998: 95) argue that preposing in English is associated with the more general function of marking the preposed constituent as representing "information standing in a contextually licensed partially ordered set relationship with information invoked in or inferrable from the prior context." This contextually determined function is stated solely in terms of referential givenness, and is thus independent of the topic–focus distinction.

    The mapping between topic–focus structure and cleft sentences like those in (22c) is also less straightforward than has often been assumed. It is widely accepted that in canonical clefts with a single prominent pitch accent on the clefted constituent (here, *the beans*), the clefted constituent is the information focus and the open proposition expressed by the cleft clause (*Fred ate x*) is presupposed and topical.[20] Example (22c), with a prominent H* pitch accent on *beans*, would thus be an appropriate response to *What did Fred eat?*, for example. But it would be unacceptable as a response to *Who ate the beans?* or *Can you tell me something about the beans?* It is important to note, however, that the facts here follow independently from the assumption that a single H* pitch accent necessarily falls on the information focus (see section 2.1). It does not show that a clefted constituent necessarily codes an information focus or that a cleft clause necessarily codes the topic. In fact, not all clefts have only a single prominent pitch accent on the clefted constituent. In English, the H* accent associated with information focus may also fall within the cleft clause. Hedberg (1990, 2000) argues that the cleft clause is also the locus of the information focus in such "informative presupposition clefts" (Prince 1978).[21] When the information focus is on the whole sentence, it includes both the cleft clause and the clefted constituent, as in (23):

(23)   [Beginning of a newspaper article] **It was just about 50 years ago that Henry Ford gave us the weekend**. On September 25, 1926, in a somewhat shocking move for that time, he decided to establish a 40-hour work week, giving his employees two days off instead of one.   (*Philadelphia Bulletin*, cited in Prince 1978)

In other cases, Hedberg argues, the information focus includes only the material inside the clause, while the clefted constituent refers to the topic, as in (24):

(24)   The federal government is dealing with AIDS as if the virus was a problem that didn't travel along interstate highways and was none of its business. **It's this lethal national inertia in the face of the most devastating epidemic of the late 20th century that finally prompted one congressman to strike out on his own**.   (*Minneapolis Star and Tribune*, cited in Hedberg 1990)

It seems clear, then, that while clefts serve various information structural functions, there is no unique one-to-one mapping between the clefted constituent and the information focus of the sentence.

The structure most widely and consistently associated with topic marking is one in which a constituent referring to the topic of the sentence is adjoined to the left or right of a full sentence comment/focus. Such prototypical topic–comment constructions, exemplified in (22d, e) and in (8)–(11) above, are presumably found in all human languages, and are relatively unmarked structures in so-called topic-prominent languages like Chinese and Japanese (Li and Thompson 1976). Following a tradition that goes back to Ross (1967), we use the term LEFT-DISLOCATION here to refer to such constructions when a constituent is left-adjoined to a sentence containing a coreferential copy, as in (22d), and RIGHT-DISLOCATION when the constituent is right-adjoined, as in (22e).

In languages, like Japanese and Korean, that mark topics morphologically, such markers are typically associated with phrases that are adjoined to the left (and sometimes to the right) of a clause. The phrases so marked also exhibit referential properties, specifically definiteness effects, that have been associated with topics, as noted in section 1. Moreover, left- and right-dislocated phrases, unlike preposed phrases as in (22b), cannot carry the only high-pitched accent in the sentence, additional evidence that they mark topics.

Despite this evidence, serious empirical challenges to the assumption that dislocated phrases mark topics come from Prince and other researchers, who base their analyses on the distribution of these constructions in naturally occurring discourse. For example, Prince (1998) argues that left-dislocation does not consistently code topic. Rather, she proposes that this construction serves a variety of different functions, such as marking contrast and keeping phrases referring to a discourse-new entity out of subject position. However, as argued in Gundel (1999b), Prince's insights about why speakers might use left-dislocation in particular discourse contexts are in themselves not inconsistent with the grammatical claim that left- and right-dislocation partition a sentence into two syntactic constituents, a phrase that refers to the topic and an adjoined clause whose content is the comment/focus about that topic. On the contrary, such an analysis may help provide an explanation for some of the specific discourse functions that Prince posits.

A more serious challenge to the view that left-dislocation marks topics is posed by Prince's findings that non-referential, indefinite phrases may occupy left-dislocated position, as in (25) and (26).

(25)   Most middle-class Americans, when they look at the costs plus the benefits, they're going to be much better off.   (Prodigy 1993, cited in Prince 1998)

(26)   Any company, if they're worth 150 million dollars, you don't need to think of . . .   (Terkel 1974, cited in Prince 1998)

While there is still some controversy about the referential givenness properties of topics (see section 1.1), it is generally agreed that topics must be at least referential. There must be an individuated entity for the utterance, sentence, or proposition to be about, and in order for truth value to be assessed in relation to that entity. Gundel (1999b) argues, however, that sentences like those in (25) and (26) are not necessarily counterexamples to the view that left-dislocated phrases mark topics, if a distinction is made between topic as a syntactic category and topic as a semantic/pragmatic category. Gundel notes that dislocated phrases like those in (25) and (26) are strong NPs in the sense of Milsark (1977) and are pronounced with stress on the quantifier. As is well known, such phrases, which often have a partitive reading (which includes an overt or covert definite phrase), typically have the same presupposition effect as definite NPs. Gundel proposes that the semantic/pragmatic topic associated with dislocated phrases of this type is the entity that is quantified (i.e., the N-set), not the whole quantified phrase. Thus, (25) and (26) could be paraphrased as (25′) and (26′), respectively (see also Gundel 1974).

(25′)   (As for) Middle-class Americans, when most of them look at the costs plus the benefits, they're going to be much better off.

(26′)   (As for) Companies, if any one of them is worth 150 million dollars, you don't need to think of. . . .

Under such an analysis, the quantifier in (25) and (26) is part of the syntactic topic phrase, but it is not part of the semantic/pragmatic topic. If the topic of (25) is the middle-class Americans and the topic of (26) is companies, the topic of these sentences is not only referential; it is also familiar because the addressee can be assumed to have an existing representation of the intended referent in memory.[22]

Strong evidence for the topic-marking function of right-dislocation comes from Norwegian. In addition to canonical right-dislocation, exemplified by the English sentence in (22e), in which a full nominal phrase is right-adjoined to a clause that contains a coreferring pronoun, Norwegian, like other Scandinavian languages, also allows right-dislocation of a pronoun with a full coreferring nominal inside the clause (Fretheim 1995, 2001), as in (27).

(27)a.   ISKREMEN   har   JEG kjøpt.
          the.ice.cream have I   bought

   b.   ISKREMEN   har   JEG kjøpt,   den.
          the.ice.cream have I   bought it
          "I bought ice cream."

The existence of such constructions, which Fretheim (2001) notes are more frequent in spoken Norwegian than in Swedish and Danish, clearly shows that the right-dislocated phrase is not merely an afterthought, but possibly functions to help the addressee identify the intended referent of an intraclausal pronominal. Fretheim shows that such constructions, when they are associated with a particular prosodic pattern, function rather to encode the topic–focus structure of an utterance, since the dislocated pronoun necessarily refers to the topic.[23]

The topic-marking function of the construction exemplified in (27b) is crucial in disambiguating the topic–focus structure because, as noted in section 2.1, Norwegian does not have a pitch accent that is uniquely correlated with information focus. Thus, the "preposed" object *iskremen* in (27a) could be the topic (e.g., as a response to *I know Tor bought cake, but do we have ice cream?*) or it could be the focus (e.g., answering *What did YOU buy?*). Unlike in English, however, the type of pitch accent would not be different in the two cases. But (27b), with the dislocated pronoun *den* "it", can only have the former interpretation.

Right-dislocation of pronouns, and resulting topic–focus determination, can also play a role in disambiguating between two otherwise truth-conditionally distinct interpretations, as seen in (28) and (29).[24]

(28) SCOTT heter Glenn til ETTERNAVN.
      Scott is.named Glenn as surname
   a. "Scott's surname is Glenn."
   b. "Scott is the surname of Glenn."

(29)a. SCOTT heter Glenn til ETTERNAVN, han.
        Scott is.named Glenn as surname he
        "Scott's surname is Glenn."

   b. SCOTT heter Glenn til ETTERNAVN, det.
       Scott is.named Glenn as surname it
       "Scott is the surname of Glenn."

The Norwegian verb *hete* "be named" (cf. German *heissen*) takes two arguments. One of these, the subject, refers to an individual, and the other, the complement, refers to a name. Because Norwegian is a V2 language, (28) is ambiguous between the interpretation in (29a), in which Scott is the subject (literally, "Scott is named Glenn as a surname"), and the one in (29b), in which *Scott* is a preposed complement (literally "Scott Glenn is called as a surname"). This ambiguity is neutralized, however, in the examples in (29). Since the right-dislocated pronoun *han* "he" in (29a) can only refer to a person, (29a) must have an interpretation in which the topic is the person Scott. And since the right-dislocated pronoun *det* "it" in (29b) can only refer to the name, (29b) must have an interpretation in which the topic is the name Scott.[25]

2.3 *Meaning and truth-conditional effects of topic–focus structure*

The idea that topic–focus structure can affect truth conditions goes back at least to the work of Strawson (1950), who maintained that sentences (more specifically the statements made by sentences) lack a truth value when their presuppositions are not met. Strawson (1964b) argues that definite descriptions are associated with presuppositions only if they are topics. Thus, a sentence like (30a), in which the grammatical subject coincides with the topic, lacks a truth value if the subject has no existing referent; but (30b), in which the grammatical subject is the focus (and the topic is bald people) is simply false in that situation.

(30)a.   The King of France is BALD.
  b.   The King of FRANCE is bald.

The difference here is subtle, and Strawson's ideas have not been unanimously embraced by linguists or logicians (see Horn 1989 for detailed and insightful discussion). However, difference in topic–focus partition can have profound semantic effects, even if one doesn't assume a multi-valued logic. Some well-known examples taken from authors working in a variety of frameworks are given in (31)–(34):

(31)a.   DOGS must be carried.   (no dogless people allowed)
  b.   Dogs must be CARRIED.   (if you have a dog with you, you must carry it)
    [Halliday 1967]

(32)a.   Only voiceless OBSTRUENTS occur in word final position. (no final sonorants)
  b.   Only VOICELESS obstruents occur in word final position. (final sonorants ok)
    [G. Lakoff 1971a]

(33)a.   Clyde gave me the TICKETS by mistake.   (the tickets were a mistake)
  b.   Clyde gave ME the tickets by mistake.   (giving ME the tickets was a mistake)
    [Dretske 1972]

(34)a.   The largest demonstrations took place in PRAGUE in November [in] 1989.   (there were no larger demonstrations anywhere)
  b.   The largest demonstrations took place in Prague in NOVEMBER [in] 1989.   (there may have been larger demonstrations in Budapest at that time)
    [Partee 1991]

Gundel (1999a) maintains that in these and similar examples, it is location of information focus (her semantic focus), and not purely contrastive focus, that results in the truth-conditional effects. This is because information focus is a relational notion that determines the main predication in the sentence, that predication being assessed relative to the topic. Purely contrastive focus has no truth-conditional effects, as seen by comparing the sentences in (34) with (35) (small caps here indicate the L H* accent that marks contrast, including contrastive topics; large capital letters indicate the H* accent associated with information focus).

(35) The largest demonstrations took place in PRAGUE in NOVEMBER (in)
      1989.

Thus, (34a) would be false if the largest demonstrations in November of 1989
had been in one of the other cities under consideration, for example Budapest.
But both (35) and (34b) could still be true in this situation as long as the largest
demonstrations in Prague were in November 1989. This is so because the
topic–focus structure of (35) is the same as that of (34b): the topic is when the
largest demonstrations took place in Prague in 1989 and the focus/comment is
that this was in November. The topic of (34a), on the other hand, is the location of the largest demonstrations in November 1989, and the focus is that this
was in Prague. The only difference between (34b) and (35) is a contrastive focus
on Prague in (35), which explicitly evokes a contrast set of other cities that
Prague is being compared with, but this difference alone has no effect on truth
conditions.

3   Conclusion

As Reinhart (1981: 53) observes in the introduction to her classic paper on
topichood, (sentence) topics "are a pragmatic phenomenon which is specifically linguistic." Topic and focus are linguistic categories in the sense that their
expression and interpretation cannot be reduced to general principles governing
human interaction or to other cognitive/pragmatic abilities that are independent of language. While human languages differ in the manner and extent to
which topic and focus are directly and unambiguously encoded by linguistic
form (syntax, prosody, morphology, or some combination of these), all human
languages appear to have some means of coding these categories. Topic–focus
structure is thus constrained, and in this sense partly determined, by linguistic
form across languages. In addition, differences in topic–focus structure alone
sometimes correlate with profound differences in meaning, with corresponding truth-conditional effects. It is not surprising, then, that most accounts of topic
and focus have built these concepts into the grammar, as part of the syntax
and/or semantics (interpreted by the phonology in the case of prosody) or as
a separate information structural component.
     At the same time, however, it is evident that not all of the phenomena
associated with topic and focus can be directly attributed to the grammar.
Topic and focus are pragmatically relevant categories with clear pragmatic
effects, including the appropriateness/inappropriateness of sentences with
different possibilities for topic–focus interpretation in different discourse contexts. Indeed, the attempt to explain a speaker's ability to choose among various morphosyntactic and prosodic options and the corresponding ability of
speakers to judge sentences with different topic–focus structure as more or
less felicitous in different contexts has been one of the primary motivations for
introducing these categories into linguistic analysis and theory. Contrary to

what is sometimes assumed, however, the fact that topic and focus have pragmatic effects does not in itself make them essentially pragmatic. All aspects of
meaning (as well as aspects of linguistic form) have pragmatic effects in the
sense that they influence a speaker/hearer's ability to select a relevant context
for interpretation (see Sperber and Wilson 1986a).

The failure to clearly distinguish between properties of topic and focus that
are grammar-driven and those that are purely pragmatic is especially evident
in attempts at topic and/or focus identification, which typically involve taking
a sentence, or part of a sentence, and testing its appropriateness in a particular
discourse context. Such tests often fail to uniquely identify the topic or focus
of a given sentence, even in the simplest cases. Thus, the fact that the sentence
in (36b) would be an appropriate response to the *wh*-question in (36a) shows
that (36b) has a possible topic–focus structure in which the topic is Jane or
what Jane is doing and the focus/comment is that she is walking her dog.

(36)a.   What's Jane doing?
    b.   Jane's walking her DOG.
    c.   As for Jane, she's walking her DOG.

The fact that someone could report an utterance of (36b) (in any discourse
context) as *Someone said about Jane that she's walking her dog* (see Reinhart
1981) would provide further evidence for this analysis, as would the fact that
(37b) is an appropriate response to *What about Jane?* (see Gundel 1974). But
none of these tests necessarily show that Jane **must** be analyzed as the topic of
(36b). Even in this discourse context, (36b) could have an all-focus (thetic)
interpretation.

Similarly, the fact that (36c) is an appropriate response to (36a), and an
appropriate paraphrase of (36b), only when there is an alternative set that Jane
is contrasted with, does not mean that Jane can be the topic of either (36b) or
(36c) only under this condition. The failure of such tests to provide a foolproof procedure for identifying topics has led some authors to question the
linguistic relevance of this concept (cf. Prince 1998). But such tests were, in
fact, never intended to serve as necessary conditions for topic or focus. At best,
they can help to determine when a particular topic–focus analysis is possible.
Pragmatic tests can't be used for identifying linguistic categories because pragmatics is not deterministic.

Assuming a relevance-theoretic pragmatics (Sperber and Wilson 1986a),
Gundel (1999b) proposes that topic–focus structure is an essential component
of the semantic/conceptual representation associated with natural language
sentences by the grammar, since it is basic to the information processing function of language. This representation, and the expressed proposition which is
an enrichment of it, is a topic–focus structure in which the topic is what the
sentence is about and the comment/focus is the main predication about the
topic. Topic–focus structure is exploited at the grammar–pragmatics interface,
where information expressed in the proposition is assessed in order to derive

contextual effects, assessment being carried out relative to the topic. Within this framework, it is possible to reconcile the different positions concerning referential properties of topics (see section 1.1). A semantic/conceptual representation will be well-formed provided that the topic is referential, and thus capable of combining with a predicate to form a full proposition. This much is determined by the grammar and follows from what speakers know about the way sentence forms are paired with possible meanings in their language. Utterances with non-familiar topics may fail to yield adequate contextual effects, since assessment can only be carried out if the processor already has a mental representation of the topic. Such utterances are thus often pragmatically deviant, even if they are grammatically well-formed. So, while the referentiality condition on topics is a semantic, grammar-based restriction, the stronger familiarity condition on topics is pragmatic and relevance-based; it applies at the grammar–pragmatics (conceptual-intentional) interface.

The interesting question, then, is not whether topic and focus are basically grammatical or pragmatic concepts, but which of their properties are purely linguistic, i.e., grammar-driven, and which are derivable from more general pragmatic principles that govern language production and understanding.

NOTES

1 Lambrecht (1994) is a notable exception here.

2 Uppercase letters here and elsewhere in the paper indicate the location of a prominent pitch accent.

3 The relational notion of "focus" (as complement of topic) is not to be confused with the referential notion "in focus," which refers to the cognitive status of a discourse referent. See Gundel (1999a) for further discussion.

4 The speaker does of course choose what she wants to refer to, or whether she wants to refer at all; but once this choice is made, the referential givenness status of this choice is predetermined by the hearer's knowledge and attention state at the given point in the discourse.

5 Note that the unacceptability of (12b) cannot be attributed to the fact that the definite pronoun has an indefinite antecedent, since the following discourse is perfectly acceptable, with *A window* and *it* referring to the same entity: *We can't leave yet. A window is still open. It's the one in your bedroom.*

6 This is intended as a necessary, not a sufficient, condition on topics.

7 The referents of generics would always be familiar, or at least uniquely identifiable, since the addressee could be assumed to have a representation of the class/kind if he knows the meanings of the words in the phrase.

8 Tomlin's aim, in fact, is to argue that topic and focus are unnecessary linguistic constructs that can be reduced to the psychological notion of attention. For Erteschik-Shir, on the other hand, topic is a linguistic notion, defined in relational terms as

what the sentence is about (the complement to predication); however, she also assigns to topics the pragmatic value of instructing the addressee to "select a card from the top of the file," thus essentially building in the referential givenness condition that topics must refer to recently mentioned or otherwise salient entities (cf. also the definition of topic in terms of contextual boundedness in Rochemont 1986).

9 See also Davison (1984) inter alia for the view that specific indefinites can be topics.

10 The term INFORMATION FOCUS is used also by Vallduví and Vilkuna (1998), who use the term KONTRAST for contrastive focus.

11 See Zacharski (1993) and Vallduví and Zacharski (1994) for more detailed discussion of reasons for assigning phonological prominence.

12 The view that sentences may have either a bipartite or a tripartite information structure is shared also by some authors for whom topic and focus are primarily structural notions, defined on surface syntactic forms (e.g. Dik 1978, Vallduví 1992), though both the terminology and the conceptual details of the analyses differ.

13 Following Ward (1988), we use the term "preposing" here as a convenient label for constituents that appear to the left of their canonical position (involving a trace/gap in canonical position, and thus excluding left-dislocation as a type of preposing).

14 The two constructions exemplified by (16) and (18) also differ in other properties. For example, the referent of a preposed topic must already be familiar to the addressee and is thus typically definite or generic. But a preposed information focus has no

such restriction and can thus be definite or indefinite (Gundel 1974, Ward and Prince 1991, Birner and Ward 1998). Gundel (1999a) and Vallduví and Vilkuna (1998) provide further discussion and empirical support for a conceptual distinction between information focus (called semantic focus in Gundel 1999a) and contrastive focus.

15 Gundel (1988) notes, however, that one of the languages in the sample she surveyed, Hixkaryana (Derbyshire 1979, cited in Dooley 1982), was reported not to use prosody to mark focus.

16 It is widely assumed that the simplex H* accent specifically codes information focus, whereas L + H* also has other functions, including the marking of contrastive information. However, the exact distribution of the two pitch accents is still a matter of some controversy (see Zacharski 1993 and Vallduví and Zacharski 1994 for further discussion of some of these points). Resolution of the controversy awaits the results of detailed empirical studies investigating the relation between topic-focus structure and prosody in naturally occurring discourse (see, for example, Hedberg and Sosa 2001).

17 The identification of topic with material outside the domain of focus only holds if topic and focus are complementary relational categories, as we assume here. This position is not shared by all authors. For example, as noted in the previous section, Büring (1999) considers topic to be only a part of non-focal material. Others define topic positionally, for example as the first element in the sentence (Halliday 1967), independent of its focal status.

18 Focal accent on the subject can, however, project to the whole sentence with certain intransitive predicates, as in all-new sentences like *The DOOR's open*, *Her UNCLE died*, *My CAR broke down*, all of which would be appropriate responses to *What happened?* or *What's wrong?*, where the whole sentence is the focus and the topic is not overtly expressed at all. See Schmerling (1976), Ladd (1978), Selkirk (1984), and Zacharski (1993) for more detailed discussion.

19 Within the generative literature, the conflation of topic preposing and focus preposing can be traced back to the classic work of Ross (1967), who derives both by a single rule of topicalization. Gundel (1974) while (misleadingly) referring to the two constructions as topic topicalization and focus topicalization, proposes distinct analyses for the two, in which only topics occupy a topic position (see Ward 1988).

20 The equation of presupposition and topic again depends on an analysis such as the one we are assuming here that views topic and focus as complementary relational categories (cf. note 17). The equation does not require that the topic be construed as an open proposition rather than an entity (see Gundel 1985). But see Lambrecht (1994) for a different view of the relation between topic and presupposition.

21 According to Ball (1991), "informative presupposition" clefts are a relatively recent development in the history of English.

22 Treating the nominal in a phrase headed by a strong quantifier as potentially referring to a topic that doesn't include the quantifier also makes it possible to account straightforwardly for examples like those in (i) and (ii), discussed in Reinhart (1995), without giving up the generalization that topics must refer to familiar entities.
(i) Two American kings lived in New York.
(ii) There were two American kings who lived in New York.
Reinhart points out that a sentence like (i) is judged to be false by some speakers and neither true nor false by others, while (ii) is easily judged as simply false by all speakers. Her proposed explanation for such facts, based on Strawson's insight that only topics are associated with presupposition (because they are the locus of truth value assessment), is that *two American kings* in (i) may or may not be interpreted as the topic, depending on the context of utterance. The same phrase in (ii), however, can never be a topic because topics are excluded from postcopular position in existential sentences. Gundel (1999b) maintains that it is not *two American kings*, but only the phrase *American kings* which refers to the topic in (i), and that this is possible only under the partitive interpretation, when the quantifier is stressed. This is also the interpretation that yields the truth value gap.

23 Fretheim (2001) also notes a further referential givenness restriction on right-dislocated pronouns, and Norwegian right-dislocation in general, namely that the referent of the right-dislocated phrase must already be activated before the sentence is uttered. See Gundel (1988), Ziv and Grosz (1994), and Ward and Birner (this volume) for similar restrictions on right-dislocation.

24   For purposes of illustration, we
     assume prominent pitch accents
     here on *Scott* and *etternavn*.
     However, other intonation patterns
     would yield a similar ambiguity.
25   Fretheim (2001) discusses two
     other types of right-dislocated
     pronoun construction in Norwegian,
     with prosodic patterns different
     from the type discussed above,
     and suggests that these may have
     other functions unrelated to topic
     marking.

9 Context in Dynamic Interpretation

CRAIGE ROBERTS

1 Context, Semantics, and Pragmatics

The linguistic subfields of semantics and pragmatics are both concerned with the study of meaning. Semantics studies what Grice (1967) called the TIMELESS MEANING of a linguistic expression ϕ – the basic meanings of the words in ϕ composed as a function of the syntactic structure of ϕ. Formal semantics, especially since Montague (1973), attempts to develop an empirically adequate theory of semantics for a given language by developing rules that are clear and unambiguous in their application and effect, thereby making clear predictions about the possible meanings for a given expression. Semanticists assume that words do have basic meanings, and that a given syntactic structure corresponds with a determinate way of composing the meanings of its subparts.[1] Pragmatics, on the other hand, studies utterances of expressions like ϕ, attempting to explain what someone meant by saying ϕ on a particular occasion. The timeless meaning of ϕ often differs from what someone means by uttering ϕ on a given occasion. This difference arises because of the way that the context of utterance influences interpretation. We complain if someone quotes what we say out of context because this may distort our intended meaning. But what is a context of utterance, and how does it influence interpretation?

The problem of understanding contextual influences on interpretation is often stated in terms of the role of discourse context in interpretation. There are three general senses in which the notion of context is understood. The first is as the actual discourse event, a verbal exchange (or a monologue). This is associated with a very concrete situation including the speaker and addressee(s), the actual sound waves, a physical locale, and things pointed out (cf. Barwise and Perry 1983). The second sense is as the linguistic content of the verbal exchange – what's actually said. This may be characterized as a linguistic string under a **syntactic** analysis, with associated syntactic and prosodic structures, but more often it is represented as simple text (L. Carlson 1983, van Dijk

1985). The third sense is as a more abstract semantic notion – the structure of the information that is presupposed and/or conveyed by the interlocutors in an exchange. These three ways of characterizing discourse context – as an event of verbal exchange, the linguistic content of that exchange, or the structure of the information involved – are not mutually exclusive; there is no verbal exchange without linguistic content, and the linguistic content itself is one aspect of the abstract information structure of the exchange. Researchers approaching the problem from different directions, however, tend to focus on one of these to the exclusion of the others. Those interested in semantics from a truth-conditional perspective tend to regard the meaning of an utterance as the information it conveys about the world. In this case, it is convenient to characterize the context in which an utterance is made in terms of information structured in conventionally given ways and to study how that information structure interacts with the information contributed by the utterance itself to efficiently convey the intended meaning.

For example, Lewis (1979) uses the metaphor of a baseball scoreboard to characterize how context interacts with the content of an utterance in "a language game." There are different facets of the conversational score, and the different kinds of information shared by interlocutors have different functions in the game. Lewis differentiates, for example, among the set of presupposed propositions at a point in the conversation, the current ranking of relative degrees of salience of entities under discussion, and the current plans of the interlocutors. While the propositional information would play a clear role in satisfying, say, factive presuppositions, the ranked salient entities might serve to resolve anaphoric reference, and an interlocutor's global plans might reveal her local intention to perform a certain type of speech act. Organizing information in this rather abstract way makes it possible to say more clearly exactly what kind of information plays a particular role in interpretation. If we include in the score information about the actual situation of utterance and (at least temporarily) the form and sequence of the utterances, then context so conceived includes information about the two other notions of context. With this in mind, we will focus here on context as an abstract, structured object.

But what kinds of information does a context include, and how are these organized? In addressing this question I will adopt the strategy suggested for semantics by Lewis (1972): In order to say what a context of utterance IS, we will first ask what a context DOES in the course of semantic interpretation, and then find something that does that in a way that comports with our semantic theory. A pragmatic theory that approaches the rigor and predictive power of formal semantics would presuppose a theory of the linguistic structures (syntactic, morphological, prosodic) of an utterance. And it would include both a well-defined notion of linguistic context and a specification of how structure and context interact with semantic rules to yield the felicity of and interpretations for particular utterances. Such a theory would be capable of making clear predictions about the meanings conveyed by utterances in particular contexts.

In the following section, we will consider how context interacts with semantic interpretation. In section 3, we will consider the influential development within formal semantics of theories of dynamic interpretation, which involve a more sophisticated view of context and its role in interpretation than that found in earlier work. In section 4, we will consider the extension of such theories to account for a wider range of pragmatic phenomena. Section 5 presents some general conclusions.

2   What Context Does: Felicity and Context Update

Context interacts with the semantic content of an utterance in two fundamental ways: It is crucial in determining the proposition (or question, command, etc.) that a speaker intended to express by a particular utterance, and it is in turn updated with the information conveyed by each successive utterance. The first role – the context-dependence of interpretation – is most obvious when phenomena like anaphora, ellipsis, and deixis are involved. When these occur in an utterance, its semantic interpretation is essentially incomplete, and the intended truth conditions can only be determined on the basis of contextual clues.

The phenomenon of context dependence can be conceived more broadly in terms of felicity. The aptness of an utterance depends on its expressing a proposition that one could take to be reasonable and relevant given the context. We thus have to look at the context to determine what was expressed, either because the utterance was incomplete, as with anaphora or ellipsis, or because its prima facie interpretation would appear to be irrelevant or otherwise infelicitous. For example, knowledge of the context of utterance is crucial in figuring out which speech act a speaker intends to perform by the utterance of an imperative like *Hand me the rope*. Only by considering the relative status of the interlocutors and the information they share about where the rope is, whether the speaker needs or wants it, and what's to be done with it, can we form a hypothesis about whether this constitutes a request, a command, permission, or advice to the hearer. Otherwise, we cannot say what type of obligation the speaker urges the hearer to undertake, and, hence, we cannot understand the sense of the imperative.

Another reflex of felicity is the determination of intended reference, including anaphora resolution and deixis. Reference problems tied to context are often subtler than these paradigmatic reference problems, however, and may be encountered in non-pronominals as well.

(1)   Please hand me some lilacs.

If (1) is uttered in a florist shop, *some lilacs* will likely refer to the reproductive organs of plants cut for decorative use. But if the addressee is standing near some silk flowers with no organic flowers in view, the reference will generally be extended to include artificial lilacs. These two kinds of referential problems – anaphora and contextual suitability of reference – are often combined in definite descriptions, as pointed out by Nunberg (1977, this volume). We see this in the following discourse inspired by his examples:

(2)   A: Where's the ham sandwich?
        B: He's sitting at table 20.

   A definite description generally presupposes existence of some entity that is unique in satisfying the NP's descriptive content, and it has been argued that this entity is presupposed to be familiar to the interlocutors.[2] Carrying a presupposition puts a requirement on the context in which the relevant NP can be felicitously uttered. As in other cases involving definite descriptions, (2A) will only express a felicitous question when the context entails that there is a unique ham sandwich in the situation under discussion, which is familiar to the interlocutors.[3] If A is uttered in a kitchen, five minutes after one of the interlocutors has prepared an actual ham sandwich in full view of the other, *the ham sandwich* will be taken to refer to the one recently prepared. When uttered by a waitress standing at the kitchen door holding a ham sandwich and scanning the house, *the ham sandwich* will more likely be shifted to refer to the (unique) person who ordered the sandwich she's holding. In this context, someone might answer A with B. Since ham sandwiches don't generally take masculine pronouns, the familiarity presupposition associated with *he* will fail unless the meaning of the definite description has been shifted from the more literal denotation to the associated male customer. This leads the cooperative hearer to make the shift, guaranteeing the felicity of the utterance.
   Beyond reference and anaphora, interlocutors look to the context for the resolution of any presuppositions conventionally triggered by lexical items or constructions in an utterance.[4] Like pronominal anaphora, other sorts of presuppositions are often radically indeterminate, as we see with *too*:

(3)   [$_{Foc}$ I] ordered a ham sandwich, too.

The presupposition associated with *too* is the adjoined proposition with a variable substituted for the focus of *too* that must be satisfied in the context. (3) presupposes *x ordered a ham sandwich*, where *x* is someone other than the speaker of (3). In the restaurant context, this could be satisfied if the fellow at table 20 ordered a ham sandwich, an eventuality implied by the discourse in (2). Other types of presuppositions, e.g. factives, are more like definite descriptions in having a fairly rich descriptive content. That is, they are explicit enough that if they initially fail in the context of utterance, what is presupposed can often be reconstructed and hence, if the interlocutor is cooperative, accommodated (Lewis 1979, Atlas this volume). But when interlocutors cannot resolve such context-dependent elements of an utterance, as an out-of-the-blue utterance of (3), it is impossible to determine the proposition that the speaker intended to express.[5] Thus in the general case, presupposition failure – the inability to resolve the speaker's intended presupposition – results in a lack of truth value for the utterance.

Besides felicity, the other way that an utterance interacts with its context during interpretation is by inducing an update of that context. The fact of each utterance in a discourse and the content of the utterance itself is added to the information contextually available to the interlocutors. Cooperative interlocutors generally attempt to address current utterances. After the utterance of (1), unless the addressee rejects the speaker's implicit claim on her cooperation, she will be committed to handing him some of the relevant lilacs. Similarly, unless (2A) is rejected, saying something that doesn't address it would generally be taken as infelicitous or rude until the question has been answered. And in (2B) or (3), if the identity of the intended presupposition is contextually resolved, and the addressees (implicitly) accept its truth, then that proposition is added to their common information. In this way, requests or commands, questions, and assertions can contribute toward satisfying the presuppositions of subsequent utterances, hence making them felicitous.

I conjecture that all pragmatic phenomena pertain to these two ways of interacting with context: contextual felicity or context update. If so, any phenomena that hinge on felicity would place requirements on the types of information that context should provide to determine felicity. For example, deixis involves resolving the presuppositions of the deictic linguistic element; checking for felicitous use requires that the context provide information about the perceived environment of utterance, in particular, about what is being indicated by the speaker at the time of utterance. If we assume that resolution of deixis is one aspect of contextual felicity, then we must assume that the context of interpretation contains not only information conveyed by the linguistic text of the discourse, but also information about the physical situation of utterance (Roberts 2002). Another central problem in pragmatic analysis is Gricean conversational implicature. Several authors have argued that such implicatures may be explained as contextual entailments (McCafferty 1987, Thomason 1990, Welker 1994, Roberts 1996b). For example, if an utterance is prima facie irrelevant, then a metapresupposition of relevance and reasonable assumptions about the speaker's goals and intentions would lead us to infer that she meant more than she said. Felicity then drives the update of the context with the intended meaning beyond the proposition literally expressed. For this type of account to work, context must reflect that the interlocutors are committed to something like the Gricean maxims as well as containing information about the interlocutors' goals and intentions.

Grice's maxims can be seen as instances of a larger set of conventions – or metapresuppositions – governing the flow of information exchange in discourse. Just as one's utterances should be clear, unambiguous, and relevant to the topic under discussion and should contain the appropriate amount of information for the purposes of the interlocutors' current goals, in the interests of an orderly exchange we observe various conversational turn-taking conventions.

These can also be regarded as metapresuppositions about the well-formedness of the unfolding discourse. If someone fails to yield the floor at the appropriate point or overlaps with the current speaker, their contribution is as much in violation of the rules of discourse as a failed presupposition. The motivations for these different types of conventions and the consequences of their violation are different in character. The failure to resolve a presupposition leaves the interlocutors without an understanding of the proposition expressed, whereas overlapping with the speaker is more likely to irritate than to confuse. In both cases, however, the problem lies in a failure to make one's contributions accord with the evolving structure of the discourse context in a maximally cooperative way, as defined by the various conventions governing linguistic discourse. To capture these constraints on felicity, context must encode the rules of conversational turn-taking.

Another set of issues in pragmatics concerns matters of prominence and salience in discourse. Topic and Focus are argued to revolve around presuppositions about what was under discussion in the previous discourse, so the same notion of felicity can be argued to underlie the acceptability of, say, focus placement in the standard question/answer paradigm[6] or topicalization.[7] We would expect, then, that context would tell us what was under discussion in the relevant respects so that we could use that knowledge to determine whether a particular Focus or Topic is felicitous. Similarly, Centering Theory attempts to capture what makes certain potential pronominal antecedents more salient than others in a given discourse; again, it might be said that pronouns carry a presupposition of the salience of their antecedents, with salience taken to be a property of the context of utterance (Walker et al. 1998.) It seems clear, then, that the context must contain information about what is salient at any given point in the discourse.

Summarizing, a context stores various kinds of information shared in discourse. This information is used to determine discourse felicity, and is updated with the contributions of succeeding utterances. Several types of information have been mentioned here: propositional information, relevant for factive presuppositions and the like, information about the issues or questions under discussion, the entities under discussion, and the relative salience of these questions and entities all relevant for presupposition, Focus, Topic, and anaphora resolution. The context also encodes in some form various metaprinciples governing cooperative interchange, including Gricean maxims and the principles of conversational turn-taking. But there is one more constraint on context that has been the subject of considerable interest among semanticists over the past two decades: The information in the discourse context should be encoded so as to capture all the logical constraints on interpretation that have been explored in formal semantics, including entailments, the scope of operators and their potential for binding free pronominals and other variable-like elements, and a requirement on overall logical consistency. It is from the wedding of these logical constraints with the types of pragmatic factors just discussed that theories of dynamic interpretation were born.

3   Dynamic Theories of Interpretation

Context in the theories of Montague semanticists was captured as a set of indices, or contextual parameters, attached to the interpretive apparatus for a given sentence. These were pointers to specified sorts of contextual information, used to feed the relevant information into the process of compositional interpretation that yielded the proposition expressed by the sentence in the specified context. This limited set of indices typically included the world and time of utterance (for capturing facts about utterance situation and for interpreting tenses and utterances of words like *now*), the speaker and sometimes the addressee (for *I, we, you*, etc.), the location of the utterance (for *here, local,* etc.), and a function assigning values to free variables (the logical form counterparts of pro-forms). Additional indices were sometimes posited for elements like indicated objects (for deixis accompanying *this, that*), or even the relative status of the interlocutors (for Japanese honorifics, French *tu* vs. *vous*, etc.) and the level of formality of the discourse. However, it isn't clear that one could in principle specify a finite set of indices of this type that would be adequate for all the types of information relevant for capturing pragmatic influences on interpretation. Moreover, in the interpretation of a given utterance the values given by these indices were arbitrarily selected, without any mechanism for keeping track across the larger discourse of what was being talked about and how this might bear on the interpretation of utterances in that discourse. Finally, the notion of context in such theories was static, leaving no provision for capturing how interpretation of the first part of an utterance might influence interpretation of the rest.

Particular problems in anaphora resolution and the interpretation of tenses inspired the early work on what is now called DYNAMIC INTERPRETATION. Heim (1982) and Kamp (1981) focused on the so-called donkey sentences of Geach (1967), illustrated by the following:

(4)   If a farmer owns a donkey, he always uses it to plow his fields.

(5)   Most farmers that own a donkey use it to plow their fields.

Deceptively simple, these examples are semantically interesting because they show that the way we keep track of information across discourse, including possible anaphoric referents, must be sensitive to the presence of quantificational operators, here *always* and *most*, and that context must be updated sentence-internally. To see this, first note that the indefinite NP antecedent of *it* in both sentences occurs within a subordinate clause that restricts the domain of the quantificational operator. For example, in (4) we are not making a claim about just any kind of situation, but only those in which there is a farmer and a donkey he owns, and in (5), we're making a claim about the proportion of individuals involved in plowing their fields, but the class of individuals involved doesn't include all farmers, only those who own a donkey. But if we replace *a donkey* with a clearly quantificational NP like *every donkey*, the pronoun *it* becomes infelicitous, showing that the anaphoric relation in question isn't binding, and must instead be anaphora to some salient entity in prior discourse. But the antecedent in these examples, the indefinite *a donkey*, occurs in the same sentence, showing that if pronouns presuppose a familiar entity from prior discourse context as antecedent, discourse context must be updated even in the course of interpreting a single utterance. Moreover, although these examples show that the indefinite can serve as antecedent of a pronoun under the scope of the operator, it ceases to be accessible to pronouns in subsequent discourse. So, neither (4) nor (5) can be felicitously followed by (6):

(6)   It had to be fed extra grain during plowing season last spring.

The central feature of the theories proposed to account for such examples is that utterances are not interpreted in isolation. Instead, the meaning of an utterance is treated as a function from contexts (possible contexts of utterance) to contexts (those resulting from updating the context of utterance with the content of the utterance). Heim called this the utterance's CONTEXT CHANGE POTENTIAL. This notion of meaning is dynamic in that it changes continuously during interpretation. For example, the interpretation of utterances like (4) and (5) takes place in stages, corresponding in some respects to the two-sentence discourse in (7):

(7)a.   A farmer owns a donkey.
  b.   He uses it to plow his fields.

Interpreting (7) in a context *C*, we first update *C* with the information contributed by the utterance of (7a), as in (8):

(8)   Input context *C*:
      Propositional information shared by the interlocutors, including the
          proposition that a speaker *S* is speaking.
      A set of familiar entities, the discourse referents.
    Output context *C*+(7a):
      The propositional information in *C* plus the proposition that *S* uttered
          (7a) in *C* and (assuming no one questions *S*'s trustworthiness) the
          information that there is a farmer who owns a donkey.
      The set of discourse referents in *C* plus one for the farmer and one for
          the donkey.

We do much the same in the first stage of interpretation of (4) and (5), updating the initial context with the information in the subordinate adverbial clause or subject NP with its relative clause. We interpret (7b) taking the context of utterance to be *C*+(7a), the update of *C* with the information conveyed by (7a); after considering the gender of the pronouns we reasonably take the salient farmer to be the antecedent of *he* and the salient donkey owned by the farmer to be the antecedent of *it*. Similarly, in the remainder of (4) and (5), we use the entities made salient by the first part to resolve the anaphora. But there is a difference: We can follow (7) with (6), i.e. the update of C with (7a) (and (7b) subsequently) is a permanent update, but in (4) and (5), because of the operators, the update pertaining to the donkey is only temporary. Though there is a permanent effect – ruling out the existence of farmers who own a donkey but don't use it to plow – there is no particular salient donkey after interpretation because the indefinite was used under the scope of an operator to allude to the properties of any arbitrary donkey standing in the requisite relation to a farmer.

Hence, theories of dynamic interpretation treat meanings as functions on context and utilize techniques developed in formal semantics to capture logical constraints on interpretation, including quantifier scoping and entailment. Contexts are considered by some theorists to be representations of the contextual information in question, as in Discourse Representation Theories (Kamp and Reyle 1993), and by others to be more abstract structured information, as in Context Change Semantics (Heim 1982, 1992) and Dynamic Montague Grammar (Groenendijk and Stokhof 1989).[8] Dynamic Montague Grammar puts greater emphasis on the retention of compositionality as a methodological principle in interpretation, whereas Discourse Representation Theory tends to dismiss compositionality as uninteresting for natural language. There are significant differences as well in the proposed treatments of anaphora in these theories (cf. Chierchia 1995, Roberts to appear), but the general dynamic approach to the treatment of anaphora and several other types of pragmatic phenomena in discourse is now firmly established in the formal semantics tradition.

This approach offers a new dimension to earlier characterizations of an utterance as an ordered pair of a sentence and a context. On the dynamic view of interpretation, we might consider an utterance to be a pair consisting of a sentence under a linguistic analysis, e.g. its logical form, and an input context, the context just prior to utterance. Given that the logical form is conventionally correlated with a context change potential, this implies as well an output context, i.e. the value of the context change potential given the input context as argument. For example, (the logical form of) (7a) in the context C is an utterance, which results in the updated context C+(7a) given in (8).

What kinds of information are in the context in a dynamic theory? Heim takes context to be an elaboration of Stalnaker's common ground (CG), including not only the set of propositions that the interlocutors hold in common to be true (each proposition a set of possible worlds), but also a set of DISCOURSE REFERENTS, abstract entities-under-discussion. Such an entity may not actually exist – we can talk about hypothetical entities, even non-existent ones – but we nonetheless keep track of the information about each such entity across discourse. Heim characterizes a discourse referent informally as a file card; technically, it is an index, corresponding to the referential index on the NPs used to refer to this entity in the discourse. Keeping track of discourse referents permits a theory of the interpretation of pronouns and definite NPs like *the ham sandwich* in which such an NP carries a presupposition of familiarity; i.e. its utterance presupposes that there is a corresponding discourse referent in the input context of interpretation. Indefinites like *a donkey* are said to carry novelty presuppositions, requiring that in a context of interpretation there be no pre-existing corresponding discourse referent. Heim's context, then, is an abstract notion, a set with two kinds of information. Representations in Discourse Representation Theory contain variable-like elements that are analogous to Heim's discourse referents, as well as formulae that play much the same role as Heim's propositional component of CG, the representations contain similar semantic content by virtue of a model-theoretic interpretation. Differences aside, in both of these theories, as well as in other subsequent work on dynamic interpretation, most contextual information, apart from discourse referents, can be characterized directly or indirectly in propositional terms, where propositions are sets of possible worlds or situations.

Dynamic theories offer a number of advantages over the earlier index-based theories of context. Since most contextual information is basically propositional in the dynamic theories, information need no longer be characterized as a set of indices, with all the awkwardness of attempting to determine just how many indices, and of what character, are required. With no loss of theoretical elegance, there may be any number of different types of proposition in the context, influencing the interpretation of an utterance in as many different ways. Moreover, the context can contain information about both prior and current discourse, information that plays a central role in constraining the interpretation of anaphoric or deictic elements. Heim treats such elements as presuppositional, and in Heim (1983b) proposes an important extension of Context Change Semantics that includes a full theory of utterance presuppositions and of presuppositional felicity in context. In this extension, an utterance presupposition is taken to be a constraint on contexts of utterance. Technically, the context change potential corresponding to the utterance's logical form is undefined for any context of utterance that does not satisfy the presupposition in question. For example, in (3), we saw that the adverbial *too* in conjunction with the prosody of the utterance conventionally triggers the presupposition that someone other than the speaker has ordered a ham sandwich. The utterance is felicitous in the restaurant setting because this context resolves the utterance's presupposition; it entails that the fellow at table 20, who is not the speaker, ordered a ham sandwich. In dynamic terms, we say that the utterance meaning, a function over contexts, is defined in this particular context of utterance: we can update this context with (3) to yield a new context. This is what it means to be felicitous in such a theory. In another context C' that did not entail that someone else had ordered a ham sandwich, the same presupposition would fail, yielding infelicity – context update would be undefined for an utterance of (3) in C'.[9] Thus, dynamic theories of interpretation avoid the arbitrariness and disconnectedness of the earlier index-based theories; each utterance looks to the preceding context to resolve its presuppositions, and in turn updates that input context with the information contained in the utterance.

Such a theory realizes some facets of Lewis's (1979) discourse scoreboard. The score has two elements: a set of propositions and a set of familiar entities, i.e. discourse referents, and this information is updated dynamically, with each utterance corresponding to a move in the game. But will such a simple scoreboard suffice? The propositional content of this notion of context is well suited to help capture logical relations among utterances, including entailments associated with operators and constraints on operator scope of the sort noted in (4) and (5) above. But an unordered set of propositions fails to yield any insight into the notion of relevance so central in interpretation (Sperber and Wilson 1986a); relevance requires us to differentiate from among propositions in a discourse those that are more and less relevant to the purposes of the interlocutors at any given time. And although discourse referents are helpful in developing a theory of anaphora resolution, they fail to capture salience and so fall short of a full theory of anaphora. Given all that contexts do, it appears that we need more types of information and/or more structure in our dynamic scoreboard.

4 Intentions in Interpretation

Recently, several authors have begun to explore how to extend the notion of context developed in theories of dynamic interpretation to characterize a wider range of pragmatic phenomena. What would such a theory of context have to include to permit us to address all the issues mentioned in section 2? In keeping with the strategy of the earlier indexical theories, we could simply start adding additional sets to the two we already have, propositions in CG and discourse referents. For example, we could add a distinguished subset of the propositions, the topics under discussion; a subset of the discourse referents, the set of salient entities; another set of propositions characterizing Gricean maxims and other metaprinciples guiding discourse. But this seems rather arbitrary, and no more illuminating than the old set of indices. We want to know what is in these distinguished sets, how they are related to each other, and how they get updated. In addition, the theory we have sketched so far deals only with indicative mood, and so only with a very narrow range of speech act types. We need a more general theory, designed to deal as well with interrogatives, imperatives, and the full range of speech acts. Only then can we hope to have a basic framework within which to conduct pragmatic analysis incorporating the results of a formal semantic theory.

Perhaps the place to start in developing a more adequate theory of this type is with consideration of the interlocutors' intentions, following the general view of Grice (1957, 1989). Grice argued that our understanding of what it is for an agent to mean something depends on the prior recognition of certain types of intentions. Roughly, we take a speaker to mean φ only if we take her to intend that we recognize that she means to convey φ and to do so on the basis of her utterance. If this seems obvious, so much the better. Contrast this view of meaning something with the notion of spilling the beans: We cannot inadvertently mean φ, but we can certainly inadvertently spill the beans with the same informative outcome. This intentional theory of communication is supported by recent work in experimental psychology and psycholinguistics, strongly suggesting that recognition and tracking of interlocutors' intentions is crucial to how babies learn the meanings of their first words (Bloom 2000).[10] Grice's notion of mutually recognized intention depends on the assumption that interlocutors keep track of each other's intentions and assumptions. As briefly illustrated below, assuming that relations over intentions are the central organizing features of discourse gives us a conceptually simple and cohesive notion of context, which effectively facilitates interpretation and characterizes infelicity in discourse.

Many theorists argue that recognizing the role of goals and intentions must be central in the development of a theory of pragmatics.[11] Following Stalnaker (1978), I assume that the primary goal of discourse is communal inquiry – the intention to discover with other interlocutors "the way things are," to share information about our world. Drawing on Stalnaker's notion of COMMON GROUND and the related CONTEXT SET (i.e. the set of worlds in which all the propositions in CG are true), we can say that our goal is to reduce the context set to a singleton, the actual world. The linguistic counterpart of an inquiry is a question. Thus, we might take questions to be the formal objects that reflect interlocutors' intentions in conducting discourse. In that vein, Ginzburg (1996b) and Roberts (1996a) propose that interlocutors' discourse goals and intentions be encoded as the set of QUESTIONS UNDER DISCUSSION (QUDs) in the discourse, expanding the information in the discourse context to include a partially ordered set of such questions, as well as the propositions in the interlocutors' CG.

To understand how goals and intentions fit into the context of discourse, let us pursue Lewis's metaphor of the discourse context as a scoreboard and consider the character of the corresponding language game (cf. Carlson 1983, Roberts 1996a). The principal elements of a game are its goal(s), the rules that players follow, the moves they may make toward the goal(s), and the strategies they may pursue in making their moves, the last generally constrained by the first three and, above all, by rational considerations. The goal of discourse is to conduct inquiry by answering the QUDs. There are two types of RULES in the language game, both viewed as constraints on the interlocutors' linguistic behavior: conventional rules (syntactic, compositional, semantic, etc.) and conversational rules (e.g. Grice's maxims). The latter are not properly linguistic, but are given by rational considerations in view of the goal of the game. For example, the Cooperative Principle follows from the fact that playing the language game is a coordination problem, à la Lewis (1969); the Maxim of Quality from the fact that truth is the ultimate goal; and the first part of the Maxim of Quantity from the desire to maximize the payoff of a move (cf. the discussion in Sperber and Wilson 1986a of the Maxim of Relation and the second Maxim of Quantity).[12] There are two types of MOVES that players may make – linguistic behaviors that fall under the kinds of acceptable behavior defined by the rules and that are classified on the basis of their relationship to the goals of the game: what Carlson (1983) calls SET-UP MOVES, i.e. questions, and PAYOFF MOVES, i.e. assertions providing the answers to questions.[13] Moves here are not speech acts, but rather the semantic objects expressed in speech acts: A speech act is the act of proffering a move. I will return to discuss strategies of inquiry below.

I assume that there are two aspects to the interpretation of any given move, its PRESUPPOSED CONTENT and its PROFFERED CONTENT, which correspond to the two ways that context enters into interpretation. The presupposed content of an utterance constrains the types of context in which it may be felicitously uttered. The term PROFFERED is a cover term for what is asserted in an assertion and for the non-presupposed content of questions and commands; hence, this is that part of the content of an utterance that determines how the context of utterance will be updated. Lewis (1969) treats questions as a type of imperative: a question, if accepted, dictates that the interlocutors choose among the alternatives that it proffers.

Most contemporary semantic analyses regard a question as denoting or determining the set of propositions that are the possible answers (in some theories, the correct answers) to that question; these are the proffered alternatives. The acceptance of a question by the interlocutors commits them to a common goal: finding the answer. When interlocutors accept a question, they form an intention to answer it that is entered into CG.[14] A cooperative interlocutor who knows of this intention is committed to it. This is a particularly strong type of commitment, one that persists until the goal is satisfied or is shown to be unsatisfiable. Relevance, an organizing principle of discourse that supports coherence and hence facilitates the processing and storage of information, will lead her to attempt to answer it as soon as possible after it is asked. Grice's first maxim of Quantity, in view of the goals of discourse, makes a complete answer preferable to a partial one, all other things being equal.

Assertions are choices among alternatives, as for Stalnaker. If accepted, they are added to CG, thereby reducing the context set. For discourse to be coherent (i.e. adhere to Relevance), it must be clear which alternatives (corresponding to cells in a partition on the context set) a given assertion selects among. The relevant alternatives are those proffered by the question or topic under discussion. That's the sense in which assertions are payoff moves: they choose among the alternatives proffered by a set-up move/question, and thus further the goals of the game. Non sequiturs are assertions that don't bear on the QUD; even if they are informative, they reflect poor strategy and a lack of commitment to the immediate goals of the discourse, i.e. a lack of cooperation. Non sequiturs also fail to maximize payoff; good strategists make assertions that optimize the number of relevant inferences they will trigger, and it seems reasonable to assume that such inferences are facilitated by the discourse segmentation induced by the plan structure of the discourse (Grosz and Sidner 1986, Sperber and Wilson 1986a).

STRATEGIES OF INQUIRY are sequences of moves designed to (at least partially) satisfy the aims of the game while obeying its constraints. A reasonable strategy for answering the QUDs, which may themselves be quite difficult, will proceed by approaching subgoals (addressing subquestions) that are easier to achieve and that are logically related to each other in a way that facilitates achieving the main goal. We can define an entailment relation on questions, following Groenendijk and Stokhof (1984: 16): One interrogative Q_1 entails another Q_2 iff every proposition that answers Q_1 answers Q_2 as well. (This presupposes that we're talking about complete answers; otherwise the entailments can actually go the other way around.) For example, "What do you like?" entails "What food do you like?" We might call Q_1 in such a relation the SUPERQUESTION, and any Q_2 that it entails a SUBQUESTION. If we can answer enough subquestions, we have the answer to the superquestion. Answering a particular question may involve several steps: there may be better or worse ways of presenting information to maximize its inferential potential for our interlocutors, and determining the most effective of these is part of strategy development. Given the ultimate aim of discourse and the rationality of the participants, these types of relations are the principal factors that structure our moves.

Besides the discourse goal of inquiry in its most general sense, we usually have separate goals in the real world, our DOMAIN GOALS, and these goals, in the form of deontic priorities, generally direct the type of conversational inquiry that we conduct. We are, naturally, most likely to inquire first about those matters that directly concern the achievement of our domain goals. Once we've committed ourselves to a given question, we pursue it until either it is answered or it becomes clear that it isn't presently answerable. But the interlocutors' strategy in this pursuit may include the decision to pursue answers to subquestions; a series of related questions may realize a strategy to get at the answer to the most general, logically strongest question among them.

Thus, a strategy of inquiry will have a hierarchical structure based on a set of questions partially ordered by entailment. Relative to each such question in the resulting partial order, we pursue some rhetorical stategy to address that question. Things are actually more complex than this, as questions in an actual strategy may be logically related only in view of certain contextual entailments. But this is the basic nature of strategies, and in what follows I will assume that they have this idealized logical structure, relativized to context.

To get a general feeling for the character of strategies of inquiry, consider the following example from Asher and Lascarides (1998a):

(9)a.   A: I need to catch the 1:20 to Philadelphia.
  b.   Where's it leaving from?
  c.   B: Platform 7.
  d.   A: Where do I get a ticket?
  e.   B: From the booth at the far right end of the hall.

Informally, (10) gives the update dynamics of the discourse context in (9). At each stage, the context is a four-tuple, consisting of the set of discourse referents known by the interlocutors, the set of recognized domain goals, the set of QUDs, i.e. the accepted discourse goals, and the interlocutors' CG, a set of propositions. Propositions and questions are represented in italics; recall that these are abstract informational entities – sets of possible situations and sets of sets of possible situations, respectively – and not sentences of English or representations of such.

(10)   Dynamics of the Context for Discourse (9):
Input context C:

Discourse Referents:	empty of relevant entities
Domain Goals:	empty
QUD:	empty (nothing under discussion)
CG:	empty except for general world knowledge among strangers, including the information that to catch a train one needs to know where it leaves from and where to get a ticket for it, that tickets require payment, etc.

C+(9a):

Discourse Referents:	{x=1:20 train to Philadelphia}
Domain Goals:	{A catches x}
QUD:	⟨*how does one catch x?*⟩
CG:	general world knowledge among strangers + {*A needs to catch x*}

(C+(9a))+(9b):

Discourse Referents:	{x=1:20 train to Philadelphia}
Domain Goals:	{A catches x}
QUDs:	⟨*how does one catch x?, where is x leaving from?*⟩
CG:	general world knowledge among strangers + {*A needs to catch x, A inquired about where x is leaving from*}

((C+(9a))+(9b))+(9c):

Discourse Referents:	{x=1:20 train to Philadelphia. y=platform 7}
Domain Goals:	{A catches x}
QUD:	⟨*how does one catch x?*⟩
CG:	general world knowledge among strangers + {*A needs to catch x, A inquired about where x is leaving from, B asserted that x leaves from platform 7, x leaves from platform 7*}

(((C+(9a))+(9b))+(9c))+(9d):

Discourse Referents:	{x=1:20 train to Philadelphia. y=platform 7, z=ticket for x}
Domain Goals:	{A catches x}
QUDs:	⟨*how does one catch x?, where does A get z?*⟩

| CG: | general world knowledge among strangers + {*A needs to catch x, A inquired about where x is leaving from, B asserted that x leaves from platform 7, x leaves from platform 7, A inquired about where to get z*} |

(((((C+(9a))+(9b))+(9c))+(9d))+(9e):

Discourse Referents:	{x=1:20 train to Philadelphia. y=platform 7, z=ticket for x, u=the hall, w=booth at far right end of u}
Domain Goals:	{A catches x}
QUD:	empty
CG:	general world knowledge among strangers + {*A needs to catch x, A inquired about where x is leaving from, B asserted that x leaves from platform 7, x leaves from platform 7, A inquired about where to get z, B asserted that A could get z at w, A can get z at w, A knows how to catch x*}

At the outset, the interlocutors share little relevant information. A's utterance of (9a) is an assertion, and unless B objects, it is added to CG; the train itself becomes a familiar and salient discourse referent. It is also clear from the content of (9a) (via the meaning of *need*) that it expresses a goal for A, and unless B objects or is otherwise unhelpful, cooperative principles lead to the addition of that goal to the set of domain goals of the interlocutors. Henceforth, to be Relevant to the established domain goal, subsequent discourse must attempt to further it, directly or indirectly; this is reflected in the addition to the set of QUDs of the question of how to catch the train. (9b) poses a question that is Relevant in that it seeks information required to catch the train and hence represents a discourse goal that is part of a strategy to achieve the established domain goal. Given world knowledge about how to catch a train, this new question is a subquestion of the one already on the QUD stack, since knowing how to catch the train entails knowing where to get it. Again, unless B objects, the question is added to the QUD stack. B's reply in (9c) counts as a complete answer to the question at the top of the QUD stack, and so that question is removed from the stack when the answer is added to CG, along with the discourse referent for platform 7. A then initiates the next phase of his overall strategy to achieve the domain goal, introducing the discourse goal corresponding to the question in (9d). The treatment of this question/answer pair is parallel to that in (9b, c). In the end, the information in CG entails knowing how to catch the train, so the first question is also removed from the QUD stack, and the issues under discussion are resolved.

Not all discourses involve explicit QUDs, but all can be shown to address implicit questions, capturing the intuitive notion of topics under discussion. For example, consider examples (11)–(14) from Mann and Thompson (1986), illustrating various types of rhetorical relations that can generally be seen as types of strategies for pursuing goals in discourse:

(11)a.   I'm hungry.
   b.   Let's go to the Fuji Gardens.

(12)a.   We don't want orange juice.
   b.   We want apple juice.

(13)a.   I love to collect classic automobiles.
   b.   My favorite car is my 1899 Duryea.

(14)a.   Go jogging with me this afternoon.
   b.   You'll be full of energy.

The assertion in (11a) pertains to a particularly important human imperative, and hence suggests a domain goal: satisfying the speaker's hunger. As usual, suggesting a domain goal raises a corresponding topic for conversation – how to satisfy that goal. (11b) suggests an answer to that implicit question, going to eat at a particular restaurant. Mann and Thompson give this as an example of the rhetorical relation of SOLUTIONHOOD, since the second utterance proposes a solution to the problem posed by the first. This characterization is perfectly compatible with the intentional analysis just suggested.

(12) exemplifies the rhetorical relation Mann and Thompson call CONTRAST. This contrast would be reflected in the utterance of this discourse by placing narrow prosodic Focus on the direct object of *want* in each clause. Roberts (1996a) proposes a general theory of Focus interpretation in which the focal structure of an utterance presupposes the type of question it may address.[15] Here, the narrow focus on each utterance would presuppose that they both address the question of what the speaker and other individual(s) referred to by *we* want, contrasting two possible answers. If that (probably implicit) question weren't Relevant in the preceding discourse, then utterance of (12) would be infelicitous. While it seems correct to characterize this pair of utterances as standing in contrast, by itself this fails to predict the kinds of contexts in which they would be felicitously uttered. By looking at the discourse fragment while considering the presupposed QUD, however, we capture both the contrast and the felicity.

(13) illustrates the rhetorical relation Mann and Thompson call ELABORATION/SET-MEMBER. Again, there is no explicit QUD in this discourse fragment, but (13a) would be a relevant answer, to an implicit or explict question like "What are your hobbies?" The elaboration in (13b) would be warranted on the assumption by the speaker that the question was part of a larger strategy to find out what the speaker is like, what he likes and dislikes, etc., and, in this case, would actually be more helpful than the direct answer in (13a) alone. A cooperative interlocutor attempts to address what the query is really after rather than offering only the information literally requested.

(14) is of interest because the first utterance is an imperative rather than a question or assertion. Imperatives propose a domain goal to the addressee of making true the proposition expressed by the corresponding indicative with

the addressee as subject. So (14a) proposes that the addressee make it true that she jogs with the speaker on the afternoon in question. Whether the addressee accepts the proposed goal corresponding to an imperative depends on many things, including the relative power of speaker and addressee, degree of cooperativeness, reasonableness of the request, etc. When the speaker has little power to force adoption of the goal, she may attempt to motivate the addressee to accept it by addressing the potential response "Why should I?": (14b) is relevant to (14a) by virtue of addressing this question. This understanding is triggered by the need both to determine the Relevance of (14b) and to resolve the presupposition of a reference time for interpretation of the future tense: If the addressee does accept the proposal and go jogging, "after you do, you'll be full of energy." This account in terms of Relevance and QUDs is compatible with Mann and Thompson's characterization of this discourse fragment as illustrating the Rhetorical relation of MOTIVATION.

Hence, Relevance, Focus, and other presuppositions can be used to retrieve implicit QUDs. This illustrates a prevalent feature of the language game plan, modeled more abstractly in Planning Theory via Plan Inferencing Rules that permit one to infer interlocutors' plans from other information in CG plus what is actually said. Similarly, sometimes answers that are obviously entailed in a given context are not explicitly uttered, but are nonetheless entered into CG. These cases involve accommodation in the sense of Lewis (1979) and are quite normal in discourse: If it is clear that an interlocutor presupposes a question or assertion ϕ which is not yet commonly agreed upon, then if the interlocutors have no objection, they behave as if CG contained ϕ all along (see Atlas, this volume). The notion of a move in a discourse game is essentially semantic. A question is not necessarily realized by a speech act, but is only a question-denotation in the technical sense, a set of relevant alternatives that the interlocutors commit themselves to addressing. It indicates what the discourse is about at that particular point and, if we look at the strategy of questions in which it participates, where the discourse is going.

Let us summarize the picture of context and its role in the dynamic interpretation of a language game that we have developed to this point. I assume that a LINGUISTIC STRUCTURE is an ordered pair of a syntactic structure (with associated lexical items) and a prosodic structure. The interpretation of such a structure is its context-change potential, a function from contexts (potential contexts of utterance) to contexts (updated contexts resulting from their utterance). An UTTERANCE is then an ordered pair of a linguistic structure and a context of utterance. A context is a scoreboard, a way of keeping track of the various types of information being shared in discourse. Like a scoreboard, it is ideally public, but it isn't always the case that everyone has a clear view of the scoreboard. The types of information and the way in which they get updated by the proffering of various types of linguistic structure are constrained by the rules of the language game. Here are the facets of the score we have alluded to so far:[16]

(15)   **Context in Dynamic Interpretation**
At a given point in a discourse, the discourse context is an ordered n-tuple, with at least the following elements:
- a set of Discourse Referents, intuitively the set of entities under discussion;
- a set of sets of Domain Goals:
  - a set for each interlocutor, what that person is taken to be resolved to achieve, including goals suggested by imperative moves addressed to that person and subsequently accepted, and
  - a common set that the interlocutors are (at least ostensibly) committed to achieving together;
- the set of Moves made up to that point in the discourse, with a total order on them corresponding to the order in which they were proffered;
- the set of Questions under Discussion (QUDs) in the discourse: those interrogative moves that have been accepted by the interlocutors and have not yet been satisfactorily answered;[17]
- the set of propositions reflecting the interlocutors' Common Ground (CG).[18]

The rules of the language game constrain how different types of linguistic structures update the discourse context, with the following principal effects:[19]

(16)   **Pragmatics of Questions**
(a)   If a question is accepted by the interlocutors in a discourse, then it is added to the set of QUDs.
(b)   A member of the set of QUDs in a discourse is removed from that set iff its answer is entailed by CG or it is determined to be unanswerable.

(17)   **Pragmatics of Requests**
If a request is accepted by an addressee *i* in a discourse, the set of *i*'s goals is updated with the information expressed by the corresponding indicative, with *i* taken as the denotation of the subject.

(18)   **Pragmatics of Assertion** (following Stalnaker 1978)
If an assertion is accepted by the interlocutors in a discourse, it is added to CG.

The acceptance of a move of any type in the language game depends on its felicity in the context of utterance. If all of the move's presuppositions (in the extended sense suggested in section 2) are satisfactorily resolved and the move is accepted by the interlocutors, the context will be updated specific to that type of move. We can then capture Gricean maxims, rules of turn-taking, and other global constraints on well-formed discourse as metapresuppositions required to be satisfied for every move. For example, consider the following characterization of Relevance:[20]

(19)   A move m in a discourse game is RELEVANT to the question under discussion q iff m either introduces a partial answer to q (m is an assertion) or is part of a strategy to answer q (m is a question subordinate to q or an imperative whose realization would plausibly help to answer q).

Given that discourse is structured by intentions and the questions expressing them, we must guarantee that all the assertions in a discourse are at least partial answers to accepted questions, and that in fact each is a (partial) answer to the question under discussion at the time of utterance. This follows from the way that Relevance is defined in (19); cf. Grice's relativization of the maxims (1989: 26) to "the current purposes of the talk exchange." Without something like Relevance, it is hard to see how to predict that a given structure would be infelicitous in a given context. And without intentions and goals, it is hard to see how to define Relevance in a way that makes sense for dynamic interpretation. Adding a set of QUDs to the characterization of context gives us a way of capturing Relevance in a linguistically relevant way.

The above suggests that some notion of the intentions of interlocutors in discourse is crucial to capturing Relevance, and hence to adequately addressing several features of discourse context, felicity, and context update. There are various ways this approach might be extended to handle other types of pragmatic phenomena. For example, one can use the intentional structure represented by the QUDs to characterize the set of salient entities at that point in the discourse, as suggested in Grosz and Sidner 1986.[21] This would involve adding an ordered subset of the set of discourse referents, the SALIENT ENTITIES, to the types of information in (16), and modifying the context update rules to manage what was in the set of salient entities at a given time in discourse. One would also certainly want to implement some tactics for plan inferencing, in order to infer speech acts (Perrault 1990) and ultimately to draw conversational implicatures.

In addition to exploring such extensions, we might want to explore other ways of characterizing the intentions of interlocutors in discourse and the relationship of these intentions to questions and other sorts of speech act. In a series of recent papers, Asher and Lascarides (1994, 1998a, b) have discussed various facets of an ambitious project to model discourse processes within a version of Discourse Representation Theory. While their theory makes prominent use of information about interlocutors' intentions, it also makes crucial and extensive use of rhetorical relations, taken as primitives of the theory. And their theory does not make the types of connections between intentions and questions and between rhetorical relations and strategies of inquiry discussed above. Asher and Lascarides also go well beyond this discussion to propose certain principles for plan inferencing and to explore their interaction with the process of interpretation. A careful comparison of the two types of theory is beyond the scope of this chapter. However, such a comparison should ultimately prove useful in determining the extent to which the various structures and principles in discourse are independent of each other.

5 Conclusions

Developing an adequate characterization of the notion of discourse context is at the heart of a fully adequate, integrated theory of pragmatics. Other notions, including presuppositional relations, rhetorical relations, and other facets of discourse coherence (Halliday and Hasan 1976, Kehler, this volume) and felicity, can arguably best be captured in terms of an appropriately modeled relation between a linguistic expression and its context of utterance. In order to do so, however, it is crucial that we include among the types of information tracked in context information about the intentions of the interlocutors and general constraints on how these intentions are related to each other in felicitous discourse. Under these assumptions, the resulting model of context, appropriate rules for the semantic interpretation of particular structures and lexical items (drawing on contextually available information), and a suitable inference engine to generate contextual entailments will together yield a satisfactory theoretical account of how context influences interpretation.

Of course, in actual discourse interlocutors have to do a lot of guesswork to maintain control of a speaker's assumptions about context and, hence, about how particular utterances will be interpreted. In the theory of Hobbs et al. (1993) (cf. Hobbs, this volume), the fact that we must guess at the assumed context is captured by characterizing actual on-line interpretation in terms of abduction, a process whereby one figures out what the speaker must have assumed the context to be in order for her utterance to denote a true proposition.[22] Hobbs's theory is perfectly compatible with the claim made here that in the ideal discourse pragmatic enrichments of the timeless meaning of an utterance are, like presuppositions, contextual entailments. The basic theoretical task is to predict the particular interpretations that would be given to particular utterances by ideal hearers who had a **complete and mutually consistent understanding** of the context. The often incomplete and inconsistent character of actual interlocutors' information about contexts of utterance and the strategies they adopt to compensate for lack of omniscience in this respect – including redundancy[23] and abductive inference – are of considerable theoretical interest, but this should not obscure the basic abstract character of discourse context.

One interesting facet of contemporary work on dynamic interpretation and context dependence is its interdisciplinary character. Some of the best work in this area is being carried out within computational linguistics and artificial intelligence.[24] The domain of pragmatics includes phenomena at the edge of linguistics proper, the outcome of the interaction between purely linguistic structures (syntactic, phonological, etc.) and more general cognitive capacities and attitudes (inference, perception, belief, intentions, etc.). We cannot adequately characterize such interaction without taking into account this interaction and all the factors that play into it. Purely linguistic study of pragmatics will never yield as much insight as study that takes into account non-linguistic factors as well.

NOTES

1 While there are fascinating difficulties in maintaining these methodological assumptions, they have proven an excellent point of departure in theory building and make it possible to understand the productive character of our semantic competence. See Dowty (1979) and Partee (1984a).

2 The exact character of the presupposition associated with definite descriptions is disputed. See Russell (1905), Heim (1982), Kadmon (1990), Neale (1990), and Roberts (to appear) for a range of suggestions, and Abbott (this volume) for general discussion.

3 See Karttunen (1973), Stalnaker (1974), and Beaver (1997) for extensive discussion of presupposition satisfaction.

4 Kasper et al. (1999) provides an extended discussion of this idea and a sketch of its computational implementation within the framework for pragmatic analysis proposed in Roberts (1996a).

5 Kripke is said to have made this observation about *too* at a workshop on anaphora at Princeton University in 1990.

6 This approach goes back to Jackendoff 1972 in the generative literature and is explored (under a variety of theoretical assumptions) in more recent literature; e.g. Vallduví (1992), Roberts (1996a), Schwarzschild (1999), Gundel and Fretheim, this volume.

7 See Ward (1988).

8 There is a lot of variation even within one general approach. For an accessible introduction to File Change Semantics (Heim 1982) and Discourse Representation Theory (Kamp 1981, Kamp and Reyle 1993) and a comparison of the two theories, see Kadmon (2000). For a fairly accessible introduction to a theory close to the Dynamic Montague Grammar of Groenendijk and Stokhof (1990), see Chierchia (1995).

9 Of course, interlocutors might accommodate the failed presupposition, adding it to C', but then the accommodated context wouldn't be C', but its update as accommodated.

10 Note that this notion is compatible with the assumption of an innate Language Acquisition Device for phonology and syntax. Even with such an innate ability to acquire linguistic structures when exposed to particular languages, there remains the problem of grasping intended reference and comprehending the conventional extensions of kind-denoting expressions, etc.

11 See also Grosz and Sidner (1986), Pollack (1986), Litman and Allen (1990), and Thomason (1990).

12 Here and below, I capitalize the Gricean notion of Relation (Relevance) and the related formal notion to distinguish them from the ordinary English terms.

13 As we will see below, imperatives also establish goals, although of a different type than those established by accepted questions.

14 This is in distinction to Carlson's epistemic desideratum of a question, which has to do with increasing the knowledge of the questioner, and with the related views of Ginzburg (1996a). In my account, it is the CG, not the speaker, that is "informed", and it is mutual-belief-behavior, and not knowledge, that is sought. This permits a generalization over rhetorical questions, quiz questions, etc., which are problems for more solipsistic views of information in discourse.

15 See Roberts (1998b) for application of the theory to the comparative analysis of Hungarian and English, and Kadmon (2000) for comparison of this general approach to Focus with others in the contemporary literature.

16 See Roberts 1996a for a detailed formal proposal.

17 Questions ideally remain in the QUD until either answered or abandoned as practically unanswerable, at which time they are removed. So the QUD is non-monotonic, in the sense that information added to it at one point may be removed later.

18 Unlike the QUD, CG is ideally monotonic, so that once added, information does not get removed. Of course, sometimes interlocutors discover that they were wrong, and then CG must be corrected accordingly. However, this often involves difficult repair strategy, and is not the normal way of updating CG.

19 There will typically be additional effects. For example, if a question is asked, the fact that it is asked is entered into the CG, whether or not it is accepted, by virtue of the fact that the asking is a speech act performed in full knowledge of all the interlocutors and that such (non-linguistic) shared information is also represented in CG. If the question is accepted, then the interpretation of the question and the fact that it was added to the set of questions under discussion at that point also becomes part of CG, by virtue of the way that the character of the changing context is continuously reflected in CG.

20 A detailed comparison with Sperber and Wilson's (1986a) notion of Relevance is not possible here, but I will note two significant differences between their notion and that given in (19). First, Sperber and Wilson's Relevance reflects their reductionist program, since it is apparently intended to play the role of all of the original Gricean conversational maxims. (19) is not reductionist; e.g. it is not intended to account for Quantity implicatures. Second, Sperber and Wilson do not relativize their notion to the interlocutors' immediate intentions or goals (and in fact, they deny the very possibility of a common ground), so that the maximization of informativeness while minimizing processing cost is calculated absolutely. But the Relevance defined in (19) is crucially relativized by the interlocutors to the QUD, and, hence, given the pragmatic function of questions in information structure, to the interlocutors' goals.

21 Roberts (1998a) sketches how this might work in a version of Discourse Representation Theory.

22 I would add that the proposition must not only be true, but also Relevant.

23   See M. Walker (1993) for extended discussion of the frequency and function of redundancy in discourse.

24   In addition to work already cited, see the work by Johanna Moore, Richmond Thomason, Karen Lochbaum, and their associates, including Lochbaum (1993), Moore (1995), Thomason and Moore (1995), Moser and Moore (1996), and Thomason et al. (1996). Grosz (1997) presents a useful overview of the field, with extensive references. Thomason has an excellent bibliography on context available on his website: http://www.eecs.umich.edu/~rthomaso/bibs/context.bib.txt

10   Discourse Markers

DIANE BLAKEMORE

1   Introduction

The term DISCOURSE MARKER (DM) is generally used to refer to a syntactically heterogeneous class of expressions which are distinguished by their function in discourse and the kind of meaning they encode. This chapter aims to provide an overview of the issues that have arisen in the attempt to say what the function of these expressions is and how they should be accommodated in a theory of meaning. It does not, however, aim to provide a definitive list of DMs, for as Jucker (1993: 436) points out, research has not yielded a definitive list of DMs in English or any other language. Indeed, as Schourup (1999) observes, the use of this term by some writers (e.g. Blakemore 1987, 1996 and Unger 1996) is not intended to reflect a commitment to the existence of a class of DMs at all. Given this lack of agreement, it is not always possible to say that the range of alternative terms which have appeared in the growing literature in this area – for example, PRAGMATIC MARKER, DISCOURSE PARTICLE, DISCOURSE CONNECTIVE, DISCOURSE OPERATOR, CUE MARKER – are really labels for the same phenomenon.[1] At this stage, then, it is only possible to give examples of expressions which have been treated as DMs in a number of different languages. Thus English examples of DMs are *well*, *but*, *so*, *indeed*, *in other words*, *as a result* and *now*.[2]

In spite of these difficulties, it seems that we can say that the term DISCOURSE is intended to underline the fact that these expressions must be described at the level of discourse rather than the sentence, while the term MARKER is intended to reflect the fact that their meanings must be analyzed in terms of what they indicate or mark rather than what they describe. At the same time, however, it is acknowledged that DMs are not the only expressions that operate as indicators at the level of discourse: discourse adverbials like *frankly* or *reportedly* and expletives like *damn* and *good grief* are also described in these terms. The property generally considered to distinguish DMs from other discourse indicators is their function of marking relationships between units of discourse. Thus Levinson (1983) draws attention to words and phrases which not only have a "component of meaning which resists truth-conditional treatment" but also "indicate, often in very complex ways, just how the utterance that contains them is a response to, or a continuation of, some portion of the prior discourse" (1983: 197–8). A similar characterization is given by Fraser (1990, 1996), who sees them as a subclass of the class of expressions which contribute to non-truth-conditional sentence meaning distinguished from other such expressions by their role in signaling "the relationship of the basic message to the foregoing discourse" (1996: 186).

It is these two properties that have brought DMs into the center of pragmatics research. On the one hand, their non-truth-conditionality has meant that they play a role in discussions of the non-unitary nature of linguistic meaning and the relationship between semantics and pragmatics. On the other hand, their role in signaling connectivity in discourse has meant that they play a role in the discussion of how we should account for the textual unity of discourse. Given the theoretical divides that have emerged in the discussion of both these issues, it is not surprising that DM research has not yielded a single framework for the analysis of these expressions. The aim of this chapter is to review the main approaches that have been taken both to the question of what kind of meaning they express and the sense in which they can be said to connect units of discourse.

2   The Meaning of DMs

2.1   *DMs as conventional implicatures*

In this section I shall examine the role that DMs have played in the move toward a non-unitary theory of meaning. This move has not always been a move toward the same kind of distinction and, consequently, my task here is to tease these different distinctions apart and to locate DMs on the theoretical map that emerges.

For many writers, the significance of DMs lies in the role they have played in arguments for the existence of pragmatic meaning.[3] Underlying this approach is the view that semantics is the study of truth-conditional meaning while pragmatics is "meaning minus truth conditions" (cf. Gazdar 1979: 2). Given this view, DMs lie on the pragmatics side of the semantics–pragmatics border in virtue of the fact that they do not contribute to the truth-conditional content of the utterance that contains them. For example, it is generally agreed that although the suggestion of contrast in (1) is due to the linguistic properties of *but*, its truth depends only on the truth of the propositions in (2) (cf. Grice 1961). Similarly, the truth of (3) depends only on the propositions in (4) and not on whether the second is a consequence of the first.

(1)   Oscar is here but he has forgotten his calculator.

(2)a.   Oscar is here.

 b.   Oscar has forgotten his calculator.

(3)   They don't drink wine. So I have bought some beer and lemonade.

(4)a.   They don't drink wine.

 b.   I have bought some beer.

Even if there is no disagreement about these facts, there is disagreement about their significance.[4] While some writers (for example Fraser 1996) have adopted the classical view that truth-conditional semantics is a theory of sentence meaning and hence that expressions like *but* and *so* do not affect the truth conditions of sentences, others (for example, Carston 2000, Wilson and Sperber 1993, and Blakemore 1987, 1996, 2000) see having truth conditions as a property of mental representations rather than linguistic representations, and see the phenomena in (1) and (3) as examples of the way in which linguistic form does not contribute to the truth-conditional content of a conceptual representation. Either way, however, these expressions raise the same sort of question: If they don't contribute to truth conditions, what *do* they contribute to?

As we have already observed, DMs are not the only examples of non-truth-conditional meaning. This raises the question of whether the answer to this question is the same for all types of expressions which are said to encode non-truth-conditional meaning. Fraser (1990, 1996) has proposed that there are four different subtypes of expressions that contribute to non-truth-conditional meaning (called PRAGMATIC MARKERS): BASIC MARKERS, which indicate the force of the intended message (e.g. *please* and performatives like *I promise*); COMMENTARY MARKERS, which comment on the basic message (e.g. *frankly* and *allegedly*); PARALLEL MARKERS, which "encode an entire message . . . separate and additional to the basic and/or commentary message(s)" (1990: 387) (e.g. *damn*); and DISCOURSE MARKERS (e.g. *after all*, *but* and *as a result*) which, in contrast to commentary markers, do not contribute to REPRESENTATIONAL MEANING, but only have what Fraser calls PROCEDURAL MEANING, signaling how the basic message relates to the prior discourse.

In adopting this terminology Fraser claims to be following Blakemore (1987). However, Fraser's distinction between representational and procedural meaning is not equivalent to the cognitive distinction that has been developed in Relevance Theory (see section 2.3), since it appeals to the role that DMs play in the coherence of discourse. Not surprisingly, expressions that Fraser classifies as procedural (e.g., *as a result*) are not regarded as encoding procedural meaning in RT (Relevance Theory).

More generally, Fraser's framework for the analysis of non-truth-conditional meaning rests on the unexplained distinction between content or descriptive meaning and meaning which is signaled or indicated: an expression which functions as an indicator (or marker) does so simply on the grounds that it does not contribute to "content." As Rieber (1997) observes, Fraser is not alone in using the notion of an indicator without explaining it. It is, perhaps, odd that there is no reference in his work to Grice's (1967, 1989) notion of conventional implicature, which represents the first attempt to say something more about non-truth-conditional meaning other than the (obvious) fact that it is not truth-conditional.

According to Grice (1989), while some expressions communicate information about the CENTRAL or GROUND-FLOOR speech act performed by an utterance, DMs like *but* or *so* communicate information about a NON-CENTRAL or HIGHER LEVEL speech act which comments in some way on the interpretation of the central speech act.[5] For example, in (1) the speaker performs a ground-floor statement that Oscar is here and that he has forgotten his calculator, and at the same time a non-central speech act by which he indicates that he is drawing a contrast between the two conjuncts. The function of *but* is to signal the performance of this act and hence it does not affect the truth value of the utterance. Those aspects of linguistic meaning that contribute to the content of the ground-floor statement are said to contribute to WHAT IS SAID, while those aspects of meaning which signal information about the performance of a non-central act are said to contribute to what is CONVENTIONALLY IMPLICATED.

This speech act theoretic account of conventional implicature seems to assume that each DM corresponds to a speech act individuated by its content. Thus while *but* signals the performance of an act with the content presented schematically in (5), *so* signals the performance of an act with a content of the form in (6), and *moreover* signals the performance of an act whose content has the form in (7):

(5)   There is a contrast between the statement that P and the statement that Q

(6)   The statement that P is an explanation for the statement that Q

(7)   The statement that Q is additional to the statement that P

As Wilson and Sperber (1993) have observed, Grice's characterization of the meanings of these expressions fails to account for all of their uses. Consider, for example, the discourse initial use of *so* in (8) produced by a speaker who sees someone arrive home laden with parcels.

(8)   [the hearer has arrived home laden with parcels]
      So you've spent all your money.

Since there is no utterance which could be understood as an explanation for the ground-floor statement made by (8), one cannot characterize the meaning of *so* in terms of its role in signaling the performance of an act whose content has the form in (6). As Blakemore (1997) observes, it is even more difficult to see how a Gricean analysis could be applied in cases where DMs are used as fragmentary utterances, for example (9) and (10) (see also Stainton, this volume).

(9)   [speaker listens patiently to an account of why the carpenters have taken
       a whole day to put up three shelves]
       Still.

(10) [speaker and hearer are witnesses to a passionate speech followed by
       dramatic exit]
       Well.

It seems that underlying Grice's account is the assumption that corresponding to each DM there is a conceptual representation of a relation that holds
between two statements. Thus *but* encodes a conceptual representation of a
relation of contrasting, while *moreover* is linked to a conceptual representation
of the relation of adding. It has yet to be shown in detail how the meanings of
notoriously elusive DMs (*well*, for example) are analyzed along the lines given
in (5–7). Moreover, it is not clear how this sort of approach would distinguish
between DMs whose meanings, although closely related, are not identical –
but, *nevertheless* and *yet*, for example.[6]

These are questions about the content of the higher-order speech acts performed by speakers who use expressions like *but*. However, if a speaker who
uses *but* is performing a speech act, then it must also have an illocutionary
force, and it is not clear what this would be. It cannot be contrasting itself,
since this is not a speech act, at least not in the sense made familiar by classical
speech act theory (Austin 1962, Searle 1969). In any case, it seems that Grice
was looking for an analysis in which the information that the speaker is
drawing a contrast between emerges as a distinct proposition (a conventional
implicature). His idea seems to be that this proposition is a comment on the
central (ground-floor) act, and thus that the higher-order act is an act of
COMMENTING. The question, then, is how do we analyze commenting?

Rieber's (1997) modification of Grice's conventional implicature analysis
might seem to answer these questions. He argues that *but* is a parenthetical
TACIT PERFORMATIVE and that (11) should be analyzed as (12).

(11)   Sheila is rich but she is unhappy.

(12)   Sheila is rich and (I suggest that this contrasts) she is unhappy.

While this analysis does, as Rieber says, "get the truth conditions right" (1997:
54), it seems to raise the same sort of questions. His analysis is illuminating
only to the extent that we understand what it means to perform the speech act
of suggesting. Rieber himself is doubtful whether *suggest* is the most appropriate verb. However, this is not really the point, because it is clear that what he
has in mind is something like showing or indicating – which brings us back to
our original problem.

According to Rieber, the role of words like *but* is explained once it is recognized that not all communication consists in modifying the beliefs of the hearer.

In contrast with "ordinary communication," a speaker who is indicating or showing that something is the case is not standing behind her words, but simply inducing the hearer to notice something that he might have seen for himself (Rieber 1997: 61). In this way, using *but* is rather like pointing at an oncoming bus or opening the door of the fridge to show someone that there is no food. Pointing is, of course, a natural device rather than a linguistic one. The question is whether a linguistic expression points in this sense.

   According to Rieber, by using *but* in (11) the speaker is inducing the hearer to "see" that the second segment contrasts with the first – in other words, a hearer who understands an utterance containing *but* recovers the proposition in (13):

(13)   The state of affairs represented by the second segment contrasts with the state of affairs represented by the first segment.

Rieber gives no evidence that this is indeed the case. However, as we shall see in section 2.3, it is not clear that the recovery of this proposition is involved in the interpretation process for an utterance like (11). Thus according to Sperber and Wilson's (1986a) Relevance Theory a hearer will have understood (11) provided that he has recovered its intended explicit content and its intended implicit content (its implicatures). An assumption such as the one in (13) that identifies a relation between the two segments does not play a role in the interpretation process at all.

   Even if understanding (11) did involve the recovery of a distinct proposition whose truth is suggested by *but*, it is difficult to see how it could be the one in (13). Like Grice, Rieber does not explain what he means by "contrast." It would have to be extremely general to account for the full range of use of *but* (cf. Blakemore 2000, Iten 2000b), and as Iten (2000b) points out, no matter how generally it is defined, it is difficult to see how it could accommodate the use of *but* in (14):

(14)   That's not my sister but my mother.

At the same time, however, it would have to account for the differences in meaning between *but* and other so-called contrastive DMs such as *on the other hand*, *nevertheless*, and *although*.

   Bach (1999b) also analyzes *but* in terms of contrast. However, he proposes that the contrast it encodes must be pragmatically enriched on particular occasions of use. More importantly, in contrast with both Rieber and Grice, he rejects the idea that the analysis of non-truth-conditional DMs requires the postulation of a distinct proposition whose truth is suggested rather than asserted. Expressions which have been analyzed as carrying conventional implicatures, he argues, are either part of what is said or means for performing higher-order speech acts. *But* falls into the first category. His argument is as follows: since "the *that*-clause in an indirect quotation specifies what is said in the utterance

being reported" (1999b: 339), the fact that *but* can occur in an indirect quotation like (15) and, moreover, be understood as part of what is being reported,
means that it contributes straightforwardly to what is said.

(15)   Anne said that Sheila is rich but she is unhappy.

The fact that *but* appears not to contribute to the truth conditions of the utterances that contain it is, says Bach, the result of forced choice. Contrary to
popular opinion, Bach argues, an utterance may express more than one proposition. The fact that *but* does not seem to contribute to truth conditions is due
to the fact that it contributes to a proposition, which, while truth-conditional,
is "secondary to the main point of the utterance" (1999b: 328). This proposition
is not a conventional implicature whose truth is indicated by *but*. It is a proposition yielded when *but* combines with the rest of the sentence. In other words,
according to Bach, *but* is an operator which preserves the propositions expressed
while yielding a new one.

As Blakemore (2000) points out, there is a range of constructions and devices
which can be indirectly quoted in an embedded construction. These include
focal stress and expressions associated with vague stylistic effects (e.g. *the
bastard*). It is not easy to see how these could be analyzed as contributing to
something (propositional) with truth conditions. Moreover, as Iten (2000b)
observes, Bach's technical notion of saying is quite different from the natural
language "saying" that introduces indirect quotations, and consequently it is
not clear that his "IQ" (= indirect quotation) test is indeed the right diagnostic
for identifying "what is said" in the technical sense.

2.2   *Argumentation Theory*

Anscombre and Ducrot's (1977, 1989) Argumentation Theory (AT) begins,
as the speech act theoretic accounts of Grice and Rieber do, as an attempt
to accommodate non-truth-conditional meaning within a framework which
assumes that utterances have truth-conditional content. However, as Iten (2000a)
says, it ends up as a theory in which truth conditions play no role at all. This
means that the issues that the theory raises go beyond the concerns of this
chapter. On the other hand, since AT claims to provide an alternative answer
to the question of how we analyze the (non-truth-conditional) contribution of
DMs, and since their analysis of the French equivalent of *but* (that is, *mais*) has
been influential,[7] it cannot be ignored here.[8] I shall, however, restrict the discussion to those features of their analyses that distinguish the AT approach
from the conventional implicature approach to DMs (above) and the relevance-
theoretic approach (cf. section 2.3).

According to the original (1976) version of AT, utterances have not only
informational content, but also argumentative orientation. The role of argumentative potential in Anscombre and Ducrot's theory derives from their observation that two utterances with the same truth-conditional content cannot always

be used to support the same sort of conclusions (see Anscombre and Ducrot 1976: 10). This led them to develop a theory of *pragmatique integrée*, or in other words a theory of linguistically encoded non-truth-conditional meaning. For example, within this framework, *but* is an argumentative operator which constrains the argumentative orientation of the utterances that contain it. Thus according to Anscombre and Ducrot (1977), the speaker of (11) must be understood to be presenting the second segment as an argument that (a) is for a conclusion which contradicts the conclusion of an argument from the first segment, and (b) is a stronger argument than the argument from the first segment. The use of *but* in (14) imposes a different constraint: the second segment must be understood as a reason for rejecting the first segment, and the two segments have to represent the same kind of fact in ways that are incompatible with each other.

Anscombre and Ducrot's "arguments" are not captured by standard rules of logic, even in the early version of their theory, when the argumentative potential of an utterance is defined in terms of the conclusions it is used to support. Their revisions to the definition of argumentative strength, which features in the analysis of *but* (above), have led to a notion of argumentation which is even less recognizable from the point of view of standard logic, since it does not involve inferences from contents at all.[9] Because Anscombre and Ducrot (hereafter A and D) do not re-analyze *but* in terms of these revised definitions, one cannot say whether they yield an improved analysis.[10] However, it is difficult to see how a revised AT analysis of *but* would overcome the problems outlined by Iten (2000b). In particular, it is difficult to see how a revised analysis would enable A and D to account for the discourse initial and fragmentary uses of *but* discussed above.

On the other hand, it seems that A and D's move away from an analysis in which the meaning of *but* is a constituent of a proposition which isn't a truth condition (cf. Grice or Rieber) to one in which it is analyzed as a constraint on interpretation is a move in the right direction. Not only does it avoid the problems discussed above (section 2.1), but also it captures the elusiveness of expressions like *but*. Native speakers of English find it more difficult to pin down what *but* or *well* mean than to say how they are used. Similarly, it is difficult to say whether expressions like *but*, *nevertheless*, *yet*, and *although* are synonymous without investigating how they are used in context. As Wilson and Sperber (1993: 16) say, this is why A and D's analysis of *but* as a constraint on use is so insightful.

The question is, however, whether the meanings of all expressions which have been analyzed as DMs are elusive in this way, and hence whether A and D's analysis for *but* should be extended to all non-truth-conditional expressions. As I have said, A and D take a radical stand, arguing that no expression of language should be analyzed in terms of content. I do not wish to discuss the implications of this here. However, it is important to recognize that the agenda underlying AT has led to a tendency to see any theory which argues for the existence of non-truth-conditional meaning as being consistent with AT and hence to blur the AT conception of procedural meaning with other conceptions. In particular, it has led to a confusion between the AT approach to non-truth-conditional meaning and the relevance-theoretic one (see below) so that, for example, Moeschler (1999) analyzes expressions like *because*, which according to RT encodes conceptual meaning, as an example of procedural meaning in a framework which he describes as relevance-theoretic. It seems that Moeschler's use of the term "procedural" here owes more to the non-cognitive AT approach than to the cognitive RT approach outlined in the following section.

2.3 Relevance Theory

Within the framework of Sperber and Wilson's (1986a) Relevance Theory (RT), it has been argued that the speech act theoretic distinction between describing and indicating should be replaced by a cognitive distinction between two ways in which linguistic meaning can contribute to the inferential processes involved in utterance interpretation: either it may encode constituents of the conceptual representations that undergo these processes or it may encode procedural information or constraints on those processes (cf. Blakemore 1987, 1989, 1996, 1997, 2000). In contrast with AT (above), RT assumes that inferential comprehension involves the construction and manipulation of conceptual representations: hence the possibility of the RT distinction between conceptual and procedural meaning.

Bach (1999b: 361) has argued that this distinction is vacuous since "in some way or other anything one utters constrains the inferential phase of comprehension." It is indeed true that the inferences a hearer makes in the course of utterance interpretation depend on conceptual content in the sense that this is what interacts with the context in derivation of contextual effects. However, the effects derived also depend on the contextual assumptions used and the type of inferential computation performed. Thus (16b) can be interpreted either as evidence for the proposition that Stanley can open Oscar's safe, in which case it is functioning as a premise, or as a consequence of the assumption that Stanley can open Oscar's safe, in which case it is functioning as a conclusion.

(16)a. Stanley can open Oscar's safe.
   b. He knows the combination.
  [adapted from Hobbs 1979]

The claim that linguistic meaning can encode constraints on the inferential phase of comprehension means that there are linguistic expressions, *after all* and *so*, for example, which encode information about which of these inferential procedures yields the intended interpretation. (See Traugott, this volume.)

Within RT the fact that languages have developed means for encoding information about inferential processes can be explained in terms of the principle which, according to Sperber and Wilson, governs all communication. According to them, every act of ostensive communication comes with a guarantee of its own OPTIMAL RELEVANCE: that is, the speaker is communicating her belief, first, that the utterance is relevant enough to be worth processing and, second, that this level of relevance is the highest level she is capable of given her interests and preferences. Since the degree of relevance increases with the number of effects derived but decreases with the amount of processing effort required for their derivation, the use of an expression which encodes a procedure for identifying the intended contextual effects would be consistent with the speaker's aim of achieving relevance for a minimum cost in processing.[11]

The idea that linguistic meaning can encode constraints on relevance has been applied to the analysis of a range of non-truth-conditional DMs in a range of languages.[12] At the same time, however, further investigation of the role of linguistic meaning in interpretation has shown that the distinction between conceptual and procedural meaning is not after all equivalent to the distinction between truth-conditional and non-truth-conditional meaning, as Blakemore (1987) originally argued, and hence that the notion of procedural meaning does not provide the basis for an account of non-truth-conditional meaning. On the one hand, it has been shown that there are expressions – pronouns and mood indicators, for example – which encode procedures but which affect the truth conditions of the utterances that contain them (cf. B. Clark 1991, Wilson and Sperber 1993, Ziv 1998). On the other hand, it has been shown that there are non-truth-conditional expressions – for example, sentence adverbials like *frankly* and DMs like *in contrast, in other words, as a result* – which encode concepts rather than procedures (cf. Wilson and Sperber 1993, Ifantidou-Trouki 1993, Blakemore 1996, Iten 2000b).

This might seem to suggest that the procedural analysis outlined above is on the wrong track. However, this would be to assume that THE distinction between truth-conditional and non-truth-conditional meaning is *the* fundamental distinction in a cognitively grounded theory of linguistic meaning, and it is not at all clear that this is justified. Thus it has been argued by Sperber and Wilson (1986a) and Carston (1988, 2000, this volume) that the gap between linguistically encoded meaning and truth-conditional content means that linguistic decoding does not deliver representations with truth conditions, but conceptual representations which are developed by pragmatic inference into representations with truth conditions. This suggests that linguistic semantics is not concerned with the relation between linguistic form and the external world (as in Gazdar 1979) but with the relation between elements of linguistic form and the cognitive information they encode. In this picture, the question that matters is not whether a linguistic expression contributes to truth conditions but rather what kind of cognitive information it encodes – conceptual or procedural.

The research program suggested by this picture is one in which DMs feature as evidence not only for the distinction between conceptual and procedural meaning but also for a clearer understanding of what is meant for an expression to encode either a concept or a pragmatic procedure. Thus, following Wilson and Sperber (1993), Blakemore (1996, 1997), Rouchota (1998), and Iten (2000b) have explored the properties of a range of DMs in order to develop sharper tests for distinguishing conceptual non-truth-conditional meaning from procedural non-truth-conditional meaning. Some of this work has centered on the fact that in contrast with expressions that encode concepts – for example, *in contrast* – expressions that encode procedures do not undergo regular compositional semantic interpretation rules. Thus while the meaning of *complete* combines with the meaning of *in contrast* to create a new complex concept, the meaning of *but* cannot be modified in this way.

(17)   Stanley spends the whole day inside. In complete contrast, Oscar only comes in for meals.

As Rouchota (1998) and Blakemore (2000) have pointed out, although more than one procedural expression can be used in a single utterance, as in (18), it is not clear that the procedures they encode combine to form larger, more complex procedures.

(18)   Oscar has already eaten. But nevertheless I'll leave him some milk.

Other work (e.g. Blakemore 1996) has focused on the difference between the way procedural and conceptual DMs behave in fragmentary utterances (cf. (9–10)), demonstrating that the conceptual/procedural distinction offers an explanation for these differences not provided by (for example) Grice's conventional implicature approach.

More recently, attention has moved to the question of what it is that is encoded by expressions like *but* or *well*. Originally, procedural DMs were analyzed as encoding information about the inferential route involved in the derivation of the intended cognitive effects. For example, *but* was analyzed as encoding the information that the relevance of the utterance that contained it lay in the effect derived from following the route of contradiction and elimination (cf. Blakemore 1989). This raised the question of whether all procedural information is like this. As Blakemore (2000) and Iten (2000b) have shown, this narrow conception of procedural meaning cannot capture the differences between closely related but different DMs – *but*, *nevertheless, however, although*, for instance – and hence must be broadened to include all information about the inferential processes involved in utterance interpretation, including, for example, context selection. While the resulting analyses are unlikely to be the last word on these difficult expressions, it seems that they are capable of capturing the elusive and subtle distinctions not captured by the analyses of Grice, Rieber, or Bach (above) in a cognitively motivated theory of inference (cf. Argumentation Theory).

3   DMs and Coherence

It will be recalled that DMs are defined not only in terms of the kind of meaning they encode but also by their function in establishing connectivity in discourse. However, it would seem that this function does not feature in the RT research program just outlined, and hence that RT is unable to account for what many theorists take to be the primary role of DMs. In fact, the omission of discourse connectivity from this program is deliberate, deriving from a theoretical position in which discourse coherence is a derivative notion defined in terms of the search for optimal relevance. Thus the analysis of DMs is the center of the debate between RT and those theorists who see the connectivity of discourse as being central to utterance interpretation (see Kehler, this volume).[13]

As I have represented it, this debate is between RT and a united group of theorists who see connectivity as a primary function of DMs. In fact, as Schourup (1999) recognizes, this connectivity is conceived of in different ways. In this section, I shall attempt to tease these apart and then finally return to the general debate described above. This will not be a comprehensive or exhaustive account of the various accounts of discourse – it will, for example, focus on those accounts which see the unity of discourse in terms of relationships between adjacent units of text or discourse and ignore questions about the explanation of global coherence (cf. Samet and Schank 1984).[14]

3.1   Cohesion

As we have seen, for Fraser (1996) it is the connective role of DMs that distinguishes them from other discourse markers (e.g. illocutionary and attitudinal adverbials). Fraser conceives of connectivity as connectivity *between* textual units rather than *within* a textual unit. There is considerable disagreement about what exactly a textual unit is. Sometimes they are "units of talk" (Schiffrin 1987: 31). Sometimes they are utterances (e.g. Levinson 1983, Redeker 1991). And sometimes it is argued that language is produced in intonational units which reflect the organization of information (and do not necessarily correspond to syntactic units (cf. Chafe 1987)).[15] Fraser himself seems to assume that DMs connect utterances and that they are distinct from coordinators such as *and* or subordinators such as *because* or *although*, which encode connections within utterances. However, as Schourup (1999) observes, it is not clear that connectivity alone is sufficient for this distinction. Indeed, some writers who see DMs as encoding discourse relations do not wish to draw the distinction at all and list *and* and *because* as DMs alongside expressions like *as a result* and *however* (e.g. Halliday and Hasan 1976, Knott and Dale 1994).

The idea that DMs encode structural relations between units of text is inspired by Halliday and Hasan's (hereafter H and H) (1976) *Cohesion in English*. This seems odd when one remembers the assumption underlying their work, namely that "a text is a unit of language **in use**" (my emphasis) and not "a grammatical unit like a clause or sentence" (H and H 1976: 1–2). Given H and H's insistence that a text is not some kind of super-sentence, it is difficult to reconcile the Hallidayan commitment of writers (e.g. Hovy 1990) with their search for structural relations between units of text which are analogous to the hierarchical structure of sentences.

The explanation would seem to lie in the fact that although H and H do not regard a text as a grammatical unit, they do assume that there is a system of rules which relate linguistically determined patterns of connection – that is, COHESION – with texts in the same way that a grammar is said to pair sounds and meanings. Thus they argue that "although a text does not consist of sentences, it is REALIZED or encoded in sentences" (1976: 2).

Amongst the cohesive devices identified by H and H are a set which we would recognize as DMs but which H and H themselves call "conjunctive devices." They propose a complex taxonomy of conjunctions (cf. H and H 1976: 242–3) according to which the different types of conjunctive relations (additive, adversative, causal, temporal) can hold either at an "ideational" level, in which case they are relations between language and the world (e.g. (19)), or at an "internal" or "interpersonal" level, in which case they are defined in terms of a relation between language and the hearer/audience (e.g. (20)).

(19) She was never really happy here. So she's leaving.

(20) A: She'll be better off in a new place.
       B: So she's leaving?
      [H and H 1976: 241]

This idea that DMs can operate on different planes is developed in the work of theorists like Schiffrin (1987) and Redeker (1991). The idea that a research program involves the taxonomy of conjunctive or discourse relations is similarly pervasive. As we shall see in the following section, within the text representation frameworks of, for example, Mann and Thompson (1986, 1988), the classification of DMs follows from the assumption that they encode connections whose identification is necessary for utterance understanding. It is more difficult to see what kind of explanatory role H and H's taxonomies serve since they are not concerned with providing a theory of utterance understanding. But equally, it is not clear whether their classifications are descriptively adequate since they do not reflect the differences between the uses of related DMs. For example, while examples like (21) and (22) would seem to suggest that *but* and *nevertheless* fall into different categories, as H and H suggest, it is not clear how their subcategories "containing *and*" and "emphatic" contribute to an explanation of this contrast or, indeed, how the label "adversative 'proper'" contributes to an explanation of what these expressions have in common. At the same time, H and H's three-way sub-classification of expressions which encode "proper adversative connections" cross-cuts the contrast between (23), where the whole sequence is interpreted as communicating an attitude of (e.g.) outrage, which can be communicated implicitly in an *and* conjunction (cf. (24)), and the examples in (25–26), where the second segment receives a "denial of expectation" sort of interpretation (not recoverable from (24)).[16]

(21)   I have received the e-mail, but it's in Dutch.

(22)   I have received the e-mail. ?Nevertheless it's in Dutch.

(23)   Her husband is in hospital. Yet she's seeing other men.

(24)   Her husband is in hospital and she's seeing other men.

(25)   Her husband is in hospital. But she's seeing other men.

(26)   Her husband is in hospital. Nevertheless she's seeing other men.

It is now generally recognized that cohesion, as defined by H and H, is neither necessary nor sufficient for textual unity, and hence that cohesive devices are superficial symptoms of a deeper relation.[17] In the next section we shall see what role DMs have played in the analysis of this relation.

3.2   *Coherence and discourse representation*

In contrast with cohesion, coherence is a cognitive notion: it is a notion which, it is argued, people use when interpreting utterances: "coherence relations . . . should be thought of in psychological terms as a set of conceptual relations used by readers and writers when processing text" (Knott and Sanders 1998: 136). This hypothesis is based on the assumption that the hearer of a text constructs a representation of the information it contains which integrates the propositions expressed into a larger whole. Thus coherence relations are the various ways in which this integration takes place.

The question that has dominated research within this approach is: What is the set of coherence relations involved in this integration? As Hovy (1990) observes, there is a striking lack of consensus here: the number varies from two to over 100. This is largely due to differences between the way they have been conceived – for example, as propositional relations (cf. Hobbs 1979, Mann and Thompson 1988) or as intentional relations (cf. Grosz and Sidner 1990) – and recently there have been a number of attempts to resolve this issue.[18] However, there have also been attempts to show how DMs shed light on the classification of coherence relations. Thus the central idea of Knott and Dale's (1994) work is that, on the assumption that language is adapted to the communicative needs of its users, it is reasonable to suppose that a study of the means for signaling relations in language will yield (linguistic) evidence for the relations speakers of the language actually use.

Sanders et al. (1992) take a different approach to the classification of coherence relations. They argue that it is cognitively implausible that speakers have knowledge of all the relations that have been proposed, and that it is more attractive to generate the set of coherence relations by combining the members of a set of four primitive cognitive categories: (i) basic operation (CAUSAL or ADDITIVE); (ii) source of coherence (SEMANTIC or PRAGMATIC); (iii) polarity (NEGATIVE or POSITIVE); (iv) order of segments (BASIC or NON-BASIC). They argue that support for these primitives is provided by psycholinguistic experiments, including one in which Dutch-speaking subjects were asked to decide which of a given set of DMs should be used in a sample text. The assumption was that these markers "provided an experimental window on the relations being used by the subjects" (Knott and Sanders 1998).

Within this approach it is argued that since DMs make existing coherent relations explicit, not every connective can express every relation. However, at the same time, it seems that the distinctions that have been drawn between coherence relations do not reflect the (very subtle) distinctions between the meanings of certain connectives. For example, the differences between *but*, *nevertheless*, *although*, *however*, *whereas*, and *yet* are not captured in an analysis which links them to a contrastive or adversative relation.[19] Recently, Sanders and Noordman (2000) have argued that there is experimental evidence which supports the view that whereas coherence relations are part of the discourse representation itself, DMs merely "guide the reader in selecting the right relation" (Sanders and Noordman 2000: 56). While it seems correct to think of these expressions as mere guides to interpretation, in the sense that they encode a processing direction rather than an element of the interpretation derived, it would seem that in treating, say, *yet* as a guide for selecting the relation of contrast we would be failing to identify those aspects of its encoded meaning which distinguish its contribution to the interpretation of the utterances that contain it from that of, say, *but*. This suggests that either we accept that not every aspect of the contribution of these expressions can be explained in terms of the role they play in coherence or we conclude that each of the expressions just listed is linked to a different coherence relation. The first suggestion leaves us with the problem of saying what role these expressions play in interpretation in addition to the search for coherence, while the second leads to the proliferation of undefined coherence relations.

As we have seen, RT also views certain DMs as "guides" to interpretation. However, in contrast with Sanders and Noordman, there is no assumption that interpretation involves the identification of coherence relations. I shall return to this issue in the final section. First, let us take a non-cognitive detour and consider the approach to coherence underlying Schiffrin's (1987) analysis of DMs.

3.3 Coherence: functional approaches

Schiffrin's (1987) study of DMs is located on a theoretical map in which approaches to language are either structural (or formal) or functional (cf. Schiffrin

1994: 20–3). This distinction cross-cuts the distinction between cognitive approaches to language and non-cognitive approaches, with the (odd) result that Chomsky's mentalist theory of grammar is found on the structuralist side of the divide along with Harris (1951). It would also seem to mean that cognitive approaches to discourse representation (e.g. Sanders and Noordman 2000) and RT are to be aligned with the non-cognitive approaches to text structure of, for example, van Dijk (1977) or Hovy (1990). As we have seen, Sanders and Noordman do not regard discourse relations simply as tools for describing text structure (cf. Hovy 1990), but claim that these relations model cognitive mechanisms involved in processing text. We have also seen that for RT the object of study is neither discourse behavior (as for Schiffrin) nor discourse structure, but the cognitive processes involved in achieving communication through language, and that, in contrast with both the cognitive and the non-cognitive approaches to discourse, and indeed Schiffrin's own functional approach, it does not leave room for relations between segments of discourse at all.

Schiffrin's approach is firmly functionalist in the sense that her study of DMs is part of the study of actual behavior. She argues that DMs provide two kinds of "contextual co-ordinates within which an utterance is produced and designed to be interpreted" (1987: 315). First, they link utterances to the surrounding text and to the speaker/hearer. For example, she analyzes *but* as both returning a speaker to an earlier point of text and continuing a speaker's action. Second, they link utterances to different "planes of talk." Thus *but* locates the utterance within an ideational structure (since it marks contrasting ideas), an action structure (since it marks contrasting speech acts), and an exchange structure (since it can continue a turn). In this way DMs contribute toward the "integration of different components of talk" (1987: 330) or in other words to coherence.

It might be thought that by analyzing *but* as functioning on several planes of talk simultaneously Schiffrin is able to account for its wide range of uses in a single analysis. However, it seems that Schiffrin assumes that *but* is distinguished from other expressions that continue a turn by marking contrast either at an ideational or speech act level. As I have already indicated, this is explanatory only to the extent that the notion of contrast is itself explained. At the same time, it is not clear that *but*, or indeed any DM, actually *encodes* information about turn taking. It does seem to be true that DMs play different roles in turn taking so that while *but* and *and* are used in the continuation of a turn, *so* is used in relinquishing a turn (cf. Schiffrin 1987: 218). However, as Wilson (1994b) argues, these functions can be inferred from the encoded meaning of these expressions together with the assumption that the speaker has been optimally relevant. For example, "by saying *and*, the speaker will have put the hearer to gratuitous processing effort unless either she is allowed to complete the utterance, or the proposition she was about to express can be easily inferred" (Wilson 1994b: 22). This suggests that the multi-functionality of DMs should be revisited in the light of the distinction between linguistically encoded meaning and pragmatically inferred meaning.

3.4   *Conclusion: DMs, coherence, and relevance*

The assumption underlying Wilson's argument is that an account of the semantics of DMs is an account of what they encode. This view contrasts with the one outlined in section 2.1, where semantics is defined as a theory of truth conditions and DMs have no semantics but only a pragmatics. It is not difficult to see why DMs qualify for inclusion in this book on the latter view. However, it might seem that their presence in a book about pragmatics might need explanation if their contribution to the interpretation of the utterances that contain them is, as relevance theorists have argued, a matter for semantics. The question, then, is how does the information they encode have a bearing on pragmatic interpretation?

According to one approach, the answer is that they encode information about coherence relations, or, as Sanders and Noordman (2000) have argued, they encode directions for selecting the right coherence relation. On this approach, pragmatic interpretation is constrained by the search for coherence, in that pragmatic interpretation is a by-product of a theory of discourse acceptability, which is defined in terms of coherence.

RT has argued, however, that we should not see comprehension as a by-product of discourse acceptability (= coherence), but rather as the key to our intuitions about coherence. Thus for example, it is argued that the tendency to search for chronological and causal relations in a discourse is itself a consequence of a general principle grounded in human cognition which provides a guarantee that all ostensively communicated information comes with a guarantee of optimal relevance. As Blakemore and Carston (1999) have shown, while in some cases (e.g. (27)) the search for optimal relevance leads to an interpretation in which the discourse maps onto a cognitive unit or schema in which one event is a necessary precursor for another, in other cases (e.g. (28)) the search for relevance leads to a non-chronological interpretation.

(27)   Oscar knocked the vase and it broke.

(28)   A: Did Oscar break the vase?
       B: WELL | the VASE BROKE | and HE knocked it.
      [fall–rise nuclear tones in both clauses] (example due to Larry Horn)

(29)   A: All linguists can spell.
      B: STANLEY can't SPELL | and HE'S A LINGUIST
      [fall–rise nuclear tones in both clauses]

The fact that examples like (28) are highlighted by particular stress and intonation patterns indicate that in contrast with, for example, (27), they are not unmarked cases requiring the least effortful assumption of chronological progression.

Similarly, Blass (1990) has argued that while the search for optimal relevance may lead to a coherent interpretation in which the assumptions made accessible by the interpretation of one utterance are used in establishing the relevance of the next, there are cases in which neither the interpretation of the first segment of a discourse sequence nor the contextual assumptions used in deriving that interpretation play a role in the interpretation of the second. Consider, for example (30):

(30)   A: Where did you put my pen?
       B: Oscar's just brought in a mouse.

The suggestion, then, is that if a discourse sequence is coherent, then this is because the optimally relevant interpretation is one in which the assumptions made accessible by one segment are used in the interpretation of the next.[20]

It might be argued that DMs could still be markers of coherence in this framework, since they are used precisely in those cases in which the interpretation of one segment is used in the interpretation of the next. As we have seen, the fact that (16a) provides a highly accessible context for the interpretation of (16b) is consistent with (at least) two different interpretations.

(16)a.   Stanley can open Oscar's safe.
     b.   He knows the combination.
     [adapted from Hobbs 1979]

This would suggest that the role of *so* or *after all* would be to signal HOW the interpretation of (a) is used for interpreting (b) – or, in other words, how the segments are connected.

However, this would be to suggest that RT is simply arguing that the notion of discourse coherence should be replaced by relevance so that we can speak of the encoding of relevance relations rather than coherence relations. This would be to miss the point that discourse, whether it is construed in structural or interactional terms, is an artifact and that coherence is a property of that artifact. Relevance is not a property of discourse, but rather of a mentally represented interpretation derived through cognitive processes.[21]

Moreover, the suggestion that DMs are markers of coherence would not be able to account for the fact that some DMs can be used discourse initially. Recall (8):

(8)   [the hearer has arrived home laden with parcels]
      So you've spent all your money.

As Blakemore (1987) and Rouchota (1998) have argued, these examples can be accommodated in an account which analyzes DMs as encoding constraints on the relevance of the utterances that contain them rather than connections between discourse segments. Thus, according to Blakemore (1987), *so* encodes the information that the utterance it introduces is relevant as a contextual implication of a mutually manifest assumption. This means that the only difference between the use of *so* in (8) and the one in (31) is that the assumption from which *you've spent all your money* is derived is made mutually manifest through perception rather than verbal communication.

(31)   There's nothing in your wallet. So you've spent all your money.

At the same time, this analysis provides a framework for explaining why not all DMs can be used discourse initially (cf. Blakemore 1998).

If this is a gain, however, it is made at the expense of the loss of what many theorists have regarded as a useful category. For not all the expressions that have been classified as DMs can be analyzed as procedural constraints on relevance. For example, *besides*, *as a result*, and *in contrast* encode concepts and are constituents of propositional representations. This means that in adopting a relevance-theoretic approach we would lose not only a unified theory of non-truth-conditional meaning, but also a unified theory of the expressions that play a role in the way discourse is understood. For some this may be insupportable. On the other hand, given the conceptual confusion surrounding the notion of an indicator (cf. section 2.1) and the lack of agreement over what counts as a DM (cf. section 1), it may seem unsurprising, and perhaps even as progress.

The suggestion that the term "Discourse Marker" does not after all apply to a single class of expressions is not intended as a call to cease research on the expressions that have been given this label. On the contrary, as we have seen, these expressions have implications for many of the fundamental issues covered in this volume. In this chapter I have focused on the issues which derive from the two properties that are generally associated with expressions which are given the label "Discourse Marker," namely, their non-truth-conditionality and their role in the organization of discourse. This choice of focus has meant that I have ignored other issues, for example, issues surrounding the historical development of DMs, which, as Traugott (1982, 1995, this volume) and Schwenter and Traugott (2000) have shown, can be seen as part of the study of the process of grammaticalization. However, as Traugott's work shows, questions about the evolution of DMs cannot be answered without taking theoretical decisions about the domain of pragmatics, the relationship between linguistic form and pragmatic interpretation, and the nature of the principles constraining the interpretation of utterances in discourse. At the same time, these theoretical decisions must themselves be based on the kind of detailed synchronic and diachronic investigation of individual expressions that I have not been able to give in this chapter.

NOTES

1 For a discussion of alternative terminology, see Brinton (1996) and Fraser (1996); for a discussion of the relative merits of DISCOURSE MARKER and DISCOURSE PARTICLE, see Schourup (1999).

2 As Schourup (1999) says, there are issues concerning the extent to which generalizations about English DMs apply to other languages. However, note that there is a growing literature on DMs in languages other than English. See for example Anscombre and Ducrot (1977), Moeschler (1989), Hansen (1997) for French, Blass (1990) for Sissala, Pander Maat and Sanders (2000) and Sanders and Noordman (2000) for Dutch, Schwenter (1996) for Spanish, Takahara (1998) and Higashimori (1994) for Japanese, Park (1998) for Korean, and Ziv (1998) for Hebrew.

3 For a detailed discussion of the semantics–pragmatics distinction, see Recanati and Bach (this volume).

4 As we shall see, Bach (1999b) has taken issue with the idea that there is non-truth-conditional meaning.

5 For a comprehensive account of Grice's notion of implicature, see Horn (this volume).

6 Cf. Blakemore's (2000) and Iten's (2000b) relevance-theoretic accounts of the differences between *but, nevertheless, although.*

7 See, for example, König (1985), Winter and Rimon (1994).

8 For a fuller disucussion, see Moeschler and Reboul (1994), Iten (2000a, b).

9 Cf. Moeschler (1989), who suggests that questions about the nature of argumentation in AT can be

captured in a cognitively based theory of inference.

10 In fact Iten (2000b) argues that the revised definitions raise difficulties for the analysis of *but.*

11 For a more comprehensive introduction to Relevance Theory, see Blakemore (1992), Wilson (1994a, this volume), and Carston (this volume).

12 See for example, Gutt (1988), Blass (1990), Jucker (1993), Higashimori (1994), Rouchota (1998), Iten (2000b).

13 For a comprehensive account of this debate, see Giora (1997, 1998), Wilson (1998a), and Blakemore (2001).

14 This focus means that there will be no discussion of topic-based accounts of discourse coherence; see Giora (1997, 1998), Wilson (1998a).

15 For further discussion of this issue, see Unger (1996).

16 Examples (24–25) are due to Kitis (1995). For further discussion, see Blakemore and Carston (1999).

17 For further discussion, see Hobbs (1978, 1979), Blass (1990), Blakemore (2001).

18 E.g. see Sanders and Spooren (1999), Sanders and Noordman (2000).

19 As Iten (2000b) has shown, the distinction between "adversative" and "concessive" markers sheds little light on the differences between these expressions.

20 For further discussion, see Unger (1996), Blakemore (2000).

21 It should be noted that this departs from the position suggested in Blakemore (1987) and from the position suggested by the title of Blass's (1990) book, *Relevance Relations in Discourse.*

11 Discourse Coherence

ANDREW KEHLER

1 Introduction

While there are many aspects of discourse understanding that are poorly understood, there is one thing that we can be sure of: Discourses are not simply arbitrary collections of utterances. A felicitous discourse must instead meet a rather strong criterion, that of being COHERENT.[1]

Passages (1a–b) provide evidence for such a coherence constraint.

(1)a. George W. Bush wanted to satisfy the right wing of his party. He introduced an initiative to allow government funding for faith-based charitable organizations.

b. ?George W. Bush wanted to satisfy the right wing of his party. He smirked a lot.

Hearers do not generally interpret the two statements in passage (1a) as independent facts about Bush; they identify a causal relationship between the two that I, following Hobbs (1990), will call RESULT. The inference of Result requires that a presupposition be satisfied, specifically that government funding for faith-based charities is something that the right wing of Bush's party wants. Although this relationship is not actually asserted anywhere in passage (1a), a hearer would be well within his rights to question it if it did not accord with his beliefs about the world, say, with a response of the sort shown in (2).

(2) Actually, many on the right are against the initiative because they worry that government interference will affect the independence of religious organizations.

While passage (1a) does not explicitly contradict this statement, the inferences required to establish its coherence do, hence the felicity of the response.

The coherence of passage (1a) contrasts with the more marginal coherence of passage (1b). In this case, a hearer may attempt to establish a similar Result relationship, but it is less obvious how he could accommodate the presupposition that smirking a lot would please the Republican right into his beliefs about the world. Of course, he might nonetheless attempt to construct an explanation that would make passage (1b) coherent. For example, he might reason that smirking is a sign of confidence about winning the election – a form of rubbing it in to the previous Democratic administration – and that the right wing of the Republican party would appreciate such an outward show of confidence. The fact that hearers are driven to try to identify such explanations is itself evidence that coherence establishment is an inescapable component of discourse interpretation.

Of course, Result is not the only type of relation that can connect propositions in coherent discourse. Passage (3a) is coherent by virtue of a PARALLEL relation, licensed by the fact that similar properties are attributed to parallel entities Dick and George.

(3)a.   Dick is worried about defense spending. George is concerned with education policy.
   b.   ?Dick is worried about defense spending. George smirks a lot.

In contrast, passage (3b) seems to be less coherent due to the lack of a similar degree of parallelism. However, in a context that makes it clear that *Dick* refers to Vice President Dick Cheney and *George* refers to President George W. Bush, then the passage might become more coherent under the common topic of (roughly) *what high government officers are doing*. In fact, with this interpretation passage (3b) comes across as a joke at the expense of Bush, since the identification of parallelism between the clauses highlights the contrast between the importance and positive contribution of the activities attributed to the two men.

A third type of relation that can connect clauses in a coherent discourse has been called OCCASION, exemplified in passage (4a).

(4)a.   George delivered his tax plan to Congress. The Senate scheduled a debate for next week.
   b.   ?George delivered his tax plan to Congress. The Senate scheduled hearings into former President Clinton's pardon of Marc Rich.

Occasion allows one to describe a complex situation in a multi-utterance discourse by using intermediate states of affairs as points of connection between partial descriptions of that situation. As with the other examples discussed thus far, a hearer will normally make certain inferences upon interpreting passage (4a), for instance, that the scheduled Senate debate will center around George's tax proposal. On the other hand, it is harder to determine how the event described by the second sentence of (4b) can be seen as a natural follow-up to the event described by the first, which results in a less coherent passage under this relation. However, if the hearer already knew there to be an external set of factors that required the Senate to deal with the Marc Rich pardon before the tax proposal, then the passage would become more coherent. In this case, the second sentence can be interpreted as a precursor to debating the tax plan, placing the two events in a connected sequence.

In sum, what passages (1a, b), (3a, b), and (4a, b) all have in common is that they each contain two clauses which are independently well-formed and readily understood. The coherence of the (a) passages and relative incoherence of the (b) passages show that interpretation continues beyond this, however, as the hearer is further inclined to assume unstated information necessary to analyze the passage as coherent. These facts demonstrate that the need to establish coherence is a central facet of discourse understanding: Just as hearers attempt to recover the implicit syntactic structure of a string of words to compute sentence meaning, they attempt to recover the implicit coherence structure of a series of utterances to compute discourse meaning.

2   Perspectives on Coherence

In many respects, discourse coherence remains a relatively understudied area of language interpretation. This notwithstanding, it has received some degree of attention within several largely separate strands of research in the language sciences, a sample of which I briefly discuss here.

2.1   Theoretical linguistics perspectives

Theoretical linguists approaching coherence from a variety of perspectives have sought to categorize the different types of coherence relations that can serve to connect clauses, and in fact many of the resulting classifications bear a strong similarity to one another. Halliday and Hasan (1976), for instance, classify relations into four main categories: ADDITIVE, TEMPORAL, CAUSAL, and ADVERSATIVE. Longacre (1983) also distinguishes four categories, CONJOINING, TEMPORAL, IMPLICATION, and ALTERNATION, as does Martin (1992), in his case ADDITION, TEMPORAL, CONSEQUENTIAL, and COMPARISON. The first three categories in each analysis are quite similar, so the main difference lies with respect to the fourth category. Halliday and Hasan's Adversative category separates out relations based on contrast, Longacre's Alternation category distinguishes passages conjoined with *or*, and Martin's Comparison category differentiates comparative constructions. A case could be made that all of these are actually special cases of the Additive/Conjoining category, an idea that I endorse. Indeed, the agreement among the approaches with respect to the first three categories foreshadows the categorization that I will advocate later in this chapter.

Of course, other sets of relations (and categorizations thereof) have also been proposed, which leads us to the question of how competing proposals should be evaluated and compared.[2] Sanders et al. (1992) propose two criteria: DESCRIPTIVE ADEQUACY, the extent to which a relation set covers the diversity of naturally occurring data, and PSYCHOLOGICAL PLAUSIBILITY, the extent to which the relations are based on cognitively plausible principles. Whereas all proposals are undoubtedly informed by data analysis to some degree, some pursue the goal of descriptive adequacy to a greater extent than others. (One that considers it to be the primary motivating factor is Rhetorical Structure Theory, discussed briefly in the next section.) As pointed out by Knott and Dale (1994), however, without a priori constraints on relation definition one could easily define relations that describe incoherent texts. They suggest, for instance, the possibility of defining an INFORM-ACCIDENT-AND-MENTION-FRUIT relation that would cover example (5):

(5)   ?John broke his leg. I like plums.

Thus, an explanatory theory of coherence requires a set of externally driven principles to motivate and ultimately constrain the relation set.

A series of papers by Sanders and colleagues (Sanders et al. 1992, 1993, Sanders 1997) pursues a theory in which psychological plausibility is the primary motivating factor. They analyze relations as composites of more fine-grained features, of which they posit four: BASIC OPERATION (causal or additive), ORDER OF SEGMENTS (basic or non-basic), POLARITY (positive or negative), and SOURCE OF COHERENCE (semantic or pragmatic). By breaking down relations into more primitive features, Sanders et al. take a step toward a more principled and explanatory account of coherence than can be captured by simple lists of relations derived from corpus analysis. Although such an approach will not necessarily offer an exhaustive accounting of all the different coherence relations that researchers have proposed, the resulting set of relations is elegant and economic, and leaves open the possibility that other factors interact with these features to yield a more comprehensive set of distinctions. The more top-down derivational character to Sanders et al.'s analyses has received a more empirically grounded, bottom-up evaluation in several studies by Knott and colleagues (Knott and Dale 1994, Knott and Mellish 1996, Knott and Sanders 1998), which have examined the use and distribution of cue phrases in order to derive hierarchies of relations.

2.2   *Computational linguistics perspectives*

Computational linguists have also set out to characterize the set of coherence relations that can connect clauses, motivated by the need for computational models of both discourse interpretation and production. From the interpretation side, Hobbs (1979, 1990) provides definitions for a set of relations that are rooted in the operations of a computational inference system. In subsequent work, Hobbs et al. (1993) show how a proof procedure based on the unsound inference rule of ABDUCTION can be used to identify coherence in texts. See

Hobbs (this volume) for more details on the abductive approach. An alternative proof procedure based on non-monotonic deduction is used for establishing coherence in the DICE system of Asher and Lascarides (Lascarides and Asher 1993, Asher and Lascarides 1994, Asher and Lascarides 1995, Asher and Lascarides 1998a, inter alia); consult those works for further details.

On the discourse production side, analyses of coherence have been used as a basis for the automated generation of coherent text. The Rhetorical Structure Theory (RST) of Mann and Thompson (1986) has been a popular framework for this purpose. RST posits a set of 23 relations that can hold between two adjacent spans of text, termed the NUCLEUS (the more central text span) and SATELLITE (the span containing less central, supportive information).[3] RST relation definitions are made up of five fields: CONSTRAINTS ON NUCLEUS, CONSTRAINTS ON SATELLITE, CONSTRAINTS ON THE COMBINATION OF NUCLEUS AND SATELLITE, THE EFFECT, and LOCUS OF THE EFFECT. While RST is oriented more toward text description than interpretation, it has proven to be useful for developing natural language generation systems, since its relation definitions can be cast as operators in a text planning system that associates speaker intentions with the manner in which they can be achieved. In particular, a high-level communicative goal can be matched against the effect of an RST relation so as to break the problem down into the subgoals necessary to meet the constraints on the nucleus and satellite, which can be iterated until the level is reached at which these constraints can be met by generating single clauses. For further discussion of using RST for generation and for some of the obstacles such an approach presents, see Hovy (1991, 1993) and Moore and Paris (1993), inter alia. For a discussion of automated parsing of texts in terms of RST relations and its use for discourse summarization, see Marcu (2000).

2.3   *Psycholinguistics perspectives*

The processes that people use to establish coherence have also been studied from a psycholinguistic perspective; here I briefly mention just a few examples. One line of work has sought to identify which of a potentially infinite number of possible inferences are actually made during interpretation (Garnham 1985, McKoon and Ratcliff 1992, Singer 1994, Garrod and Sanford 1994, inter alia). Inferences are categorized in terms of being NECESSARY to establish coherence versus merely ELABORATIVE, the latter including those suggested by the text but not necessary for establishing coherence. These studies have yielded potentially contradictory results, as they appear to depend to a large degree on the experimental setup and paradigm (Keenan et al. 1990). One of the better known lines of psycholinguistic research into these questions and coherence in general is that of Kintsch and colleagues, who have proposed and analyzed a "construction-integration" model of discourse comprehension (Kintsch and van Dijk 1978, van Dijk and Kintsch 1983, Kintsch 1988, inter alia). They defined the concept of a TEXT MACROSTRUCTURE, which is a hierarchical network of propositions that provides an abstract, semantic description of the global content of the text. Guindon and Kintsch (1984) evaluated whether the elaborative inferences necessary to construct the macrostructure accompany comprehension processes in this framework. Consult these works for further details.

3   A Neo-Humean Analysis of Coherence and Its Application to Linguistic Theory

As the foregoing discussion might suggest, the majority of previous work on coherence relations has operated within the confines of the field of text coherence itself. As it may be tempting to believe that coherence establishment can only occur after all sentence-level interpretation issues have been resolved, theories of coherence rarely play a role in accounts of particular linguistic forms.[4] In this section, I briefly describe several of my own attempts to show that an analysis of coherence is in fact necessary to address outstanding problems in linguistics. I start by presenting my own categorization of a set of coherence relations, and then briefly summarize four linguistic analyses that rely on this categorization as a crucial component. Due to space limitations, I will not attempt to address all of the issues that these brief sketches might raise, and instead refer the reader to Kehler (2002) for more in-depth treatments.

3.1   *A neo-Humean classification of coherence relations*

In the introduction, I argued for the existence of coherence establishment processes by appealing to three pairs of examples – passages (1a, b), (3a, b), and (4a, b) – which are instances of the coherence relations Result, Parallel, and Occasion, respectively. In Kehler (2002), I argue that these relations can be seen as the canonical instances of three general classes of "connection among ideas," first articulated by David Hume in his *Inquiry Concerning Human Understanding*:

> Though it be too obvious to escape observation that different ideas are connected together, I do not find that any philosopher has attempted to enumerate or class all the principles of association – a subject, however, that seems worthy of curiosity. To me there appear to be only three principles of connection among ideas, namely *Resemblance*, *Contiguity* in time or place, and *Cause* or *Effect*. (Hume 1955: 32 [1748])

In the subsections that follow I analyze a set of coherence relations, many of which are taken and adapted from Hobbs (1990), as belonging to these three general categories.[5] I show that these categories differ systematically in two respects: in the type of arguments over which the coherence relation constraints are applied, and in the central type of inference process underlying this application. Although the details differ in several respects from the Sanders et al. (1992) classification, the two categorizations share the property that the relations are composites of more primitive, cognitively inspired features. The three classes of relations also, at least at a superficial level, show considerable overlap with the three categories that were common to the classifications of Halliday and Hasan, Longacre, and Martin discussed in section 2.

3.1.1   Cause–Effect relations

Establishing a Cause–Effect relation requires that a path of implication be identified between the propositions denoted by the utterances in a passage. The canonical case of a Cause–Effect relation is Result, which was exemplified in passage (1a).

Result: Infer P from the assertion of S_1 and Q from the assertion of S_2, where normally $P \rightarrow Q$.

The variables S_1 and S_2 represent the first and second sentences being related, respectively.

For example (1a), P corresponds to the meaning of the first clause, Q corresponds to the meaning of the second, and the implication that needs to be established is *if someone wants to satisfy the right wing of the Republican party, then it plausibly follows that that person would introduce an initiative to allow government funding for faith-based charitable organizations*. This constraint gives rise to the corresponding presupposition previously cited for example (1a), as well as the analogous one that is less readily satisfied in example (1b).

The definitions of other coherence relations in this category can be derived by simply reversing the clause order and optionally negating the second proposition in the conditional. All of the following examples require that the same presupposition cited above be met:

Explanation: Infer P from the assertion of S_1 and Q from the assertion of S_2, where normally $Q \rightarrow P$.

(6)   George introduced an initiative to allow government funding for faith-based charitable organizations. He wanted to satisfy the right wing of his party.

Violated expectation: Infer P from the assertion of S_1 and Q from the assertion of S_2, where normally $P \rightarrow \neg Q$.

(7)   George wanted to satisfy the right wing of his party, but he refused to introduce an initiative to allow government funding for faith-based charitable organizations.

Denial of preventer: Infer P from the assertion of S_1 and Q from the assertion of S_2, where normally $Q \to \neg P$.

(8)   George refused to introduce an initiative to allow government funding
for faith-based charitable organizations, even though he wanted to satisfy
the right wing of his party.

To sum, to establish a Cause–Effect relation the hearer identifies a path of
implication between the propositions P and Q denoted by the utterances.

3.1.2   Resemblance relations

Establishing a Resemblance relation is a fundamentally different process.
Resemblance requires that commonalities and contrasts among corresponding
sets of parallel relations and entities be recognized, using operations based on
comparison, analogy, and generalization. The canonical case of a Resemblance
relation is Parallel, which was exemplified in passage (3a).[6]

Parallel: Infer $p(a_1, a_2, \dots)$ from the assertion of S_1 and $p(b_1, b_2, \dots)$ from the
assertion of S_2, where for some vector of sets of properties $\vec{q}$, $q_i(a_i)$ and $q_i(b_i)$
for all i.

The phrase "vector of sets of properties" simply means that for each i, there is
a set of properties q_i representing the similarities among the corresponding pair
of arguments a_i and b_i. In example (3a), the parallel entities a_1 and b_1 are Dick
and George, respectively, the parallel entities a_2 and b_2 correspond to defense
spending and education policy, and the common relation p is roughly *what high
government officers are concerned about*. Note that p is typically a generalization
of the parallel relations expressed in the utterances.

Two versions of the CONTRAST relation can be derived by contrasting either
the relation inferred or a set of properties of one or more of the sets of parallel
entities.

Contrast (i):   Infer $p(a_1, a_2, \dots)$ from the assertion of S_1 and $\neg p(b_1, b_2, \dots)$
from the assertion of S_2, where for some vector of sets of properties $\vec{q}$, $q_i(a_i)$
and $q_i(b_i)$ for all i.

(9)   Dick supports a raise in defense spending, but George opposes it.

Contrast (ii):   Infer $p(a_1, a_2, \dots)$ from the assertion of S_1 and $p(b_1, b_2, \dots)$ from
the assertion of S_2, where for some vector of sets of properties $\vec{q}$, $q_i(a_i)$ and
$\neg q_i(b_i)$ for some i.

(10)   Dick supports a raise in defense spending, but George wants a raise in
education investment.

The EXEMPLIFICATION relation holds between a general statement followed by an example of it.[7]

Exemplification: Infer $p(a_1, a_2, \dots)$ from the assertion of S_1 and $p(b_1, b_2, \dots)$ from the assertion of S_2, where b_i is a member or subset of a_i for some i.

(11) Republican presidents often seek to put limits on federal funding of abortion. In his first week of office, George W. Bush signed a ban on contributing money to international agencies which offer abortion as one of their services.

The GENERALIZATION relation is similar to Exemplification, except that the ordering of the clauses is reversed.

Generalization: Infer $p(a_1, a_2, \dots)$ from the assertion of S_1 and $p(b_1, b_2, \dots)$ from the assertion of S_2, where a_i is a member or subset of b_i for some i.

(12) In his first week of office, George W. Bush signed a ban on contributing money to international agencies which offer abortion as one of their services. Republican presidents often seek to put limits on federal funding of abortion.

From the Exemplification and Generalization relations, negation can be added to derive two definitions for EXCEPTION, depending on the clause order.

Exception (i): Infer $p(a_1, a_2, \dots)$ from the assertion of S_1 and $\neg p(b_1, b_2, \dots)$ from the assertion of S_2, where b_i is a member or subset of a_i for some i.

Exception (ii): Infer $p(a_1, a_2, \dots)$ from the assertion of S_1 and $\neg p(b_1, b_2, \dots)$ from the assertion of S_2, where a_i is a member or subset of b_i for some i.

Examples in which these two definitions apply are given in (13) and (14) respectively:

(13) Republican presidents do not usually put limits on federal funding of abortion immediately upon entering office. Nonetheless, in his first week, George W. Bush signed a ban on contributing money to international agencies which offer abortion as one of their services.

(14) In his first week, George W. Bush signed a ban on contributing money to international agencies which offer abortion as one of their services. Nonetheless, Republican presidents do not usually put limits on federal funding of abortion immediately upon entering office.

Finally, the ELABORATION relation can be seen as a limiting case of Parallel, in which the two eventualities described are in fact the same.

Elaboration: Infer $p(a_1, a_2, \ldots)$ from the assertions of S_1 and S_2.

(15)   The new Republican president took a swipe at abortion in his first week of office. In a White House ceremony yesterday, George W. Bush signed an executive order banning support to international agencies which offer abortion as one of their services.

To sum, to establish a Resemblance relation the hearer identifies a relation p that applies over a set of entities $a_1, \ldots, a_n$ from the first sentence and a set of entities $b_1, \ldots, b_n$ from the second sentence, and performs comparison and generalization operations on each pair of parallel elements to determine points of similarity and contrast. These relations are therefore different than Cause–Effect relations, the arguments of which are simply the sentence-level propositions denoted by each utterance. Indeed, identifying the arguments to a Resemblance relation is considerably less straightforward, since it is not known a priori how many arguments there are; the common relation p to be inferred can have any number of arguments, including zero. Furthermore, in addition to identifying the appropriate sets of arguments from their respective utterances, it must also be determined which members of the first set are parallel to which members of the second. While the inference processes that underlie the establishment of Resemblance ultimately operate on semantic-level constructs, the process of argument identification and alignment likely utilizes the syntactic structure of the utterances, which would explain why many (but not all) passages standing in a Resemblance relation also display some degree of syntactic parallelism.

3.1.3   Contiguity relations

The third class of relation in my categorization is Contiguity. I place only one relation in this category, Occasion. Recall that Occasion allows one to express a situation centered around a system of entities by using intermediate states of affairs as points of connection between partial descriptions of that situation. An example of Occasion was given in passage (4a). Two definitions of Occasion, from Hobbs (1990), are given below:

Occasion (i):   Infer a change of state for a system of entities from S_1, inferring the final state for this system from S_2.

Occasion (ii):   Infer a change of state for a system of entities from S_2, inferring the initial state for this system from S_1.

Whereas the constraints for the other two types of relation and the types of inferential processes required for their establishment are at least somewhat understood, it is less straightforward to state the constraints imposed by

Occasion explicitly. Much of what makes for a coherent Occasion is based on knowledge gained from human experience and the granularity with which people conceptualize events and change resulting from them. Certain past treatments (e.g. Halliday and Hasan 1976, Longacre 1983) have equated this relation with temporal progression, the only constraint being that the events described in the discourse display forward movement in time. However, the additional information inferred in order to connect the events in passages like (4a), and the incoherence of passages such as (4b), show that temporal progression is not enough (Hobbs 1990: 86).

3.2 Linguistic case studies

Given the foregoing analysis of coherence relations and the inference processes used to establish them, one might ask whether coherence establishment could potentially affect the behavior and distribution of a variety of linguistic phenomena that operate at least in part at the discourse level. Using three case studies – VP-ellipsis, extraction from conjoined clauses, and pronominal reference – I will now argue that it in fact does.

3.2.1 VP-ellipsis
The first phenomenon I consider is verb phrase (VP) ellipsis, exemplified in sentence (16):

(16) George claimed he won the election, and Al did too.

The stranded auxiliary in the second clause (henceforth, the TARGET clause, following terminology introduced by Dalrymple et al. 1991) marks a vestigial verb phrase, a meaning for which must be determined from some contextually provided material – in this case, the first clause (henceforth, the SOURCE clause).

Past theories of VP-ellipsis interpretation can be largely classified into one of two categories: syntactic or semantic (Kehler 2000a). Inherent in syntactic accounts (Sag 1976, Williams 1977, Haïk 1987, Lappin 1993, Fiengo and May 1994, Hestvik 1995, Lobeck 1995, Lappin 1996, Kennedy 1997, inter alia) is the claim that VP-ellipsis is resolved at some level of syntactic structure. The evidence that proponents offer for this view includes the unacceptability of examples such as (24a–c).[8]

(17)a. #New York was won by Al, and Hillary did too. [won New York]
   b. #Al$_i$ blamed himself$_i$, and George did too. [blamed him$_i$]
   c. #George blamed Al$_i$ for losing, and he$_i$ did too. [blame Al$_i$ for losing]

The unacceptability of sentence (17a) is predicted by a syntactic account due to the mismatch in voice between the clauses. In particular, assuming that a process of SYNTACTIC RECONSTRUCTION copies the source VP to the site of the empty VP in the target representation, the syntactic structure representing the active voice VP *won New York* required in the target is not present in the source. Likewise, binding conditions (Chomsky 1981) predict that (17b–c) are unacceptable on the indicated readings. Specifically, CONDITION A, which requires that a reflexive pronoun have a c-commanding antecedent, predicts that (17b) does not have the strict reading in which George blamed Al. Likewise, CONDITION C, which prohibits coreference between a full NP and a c-commanding NP, predicts that sentence (17c) does not have the reading in which Al blamed himself.

In semantic accounts of VP-ellipsis interpretation (Dalrymple et al. 1991, Hardt 1992, Kehler 1993b, Hobbs and Kehler 1997, Hardt 1999, inter alia), on the other hand, VP-ellipsis is resolved at a purely semantic level of representation. The acceptability of sentences such as (18a–c) has been cited in support of this view:

(18)a.   In November, the citizens of Florida asked that the election results be overturned, but the election commission refused to. [overturn the election results] (adapted from Dalrymple 1991)
   b.   Bill is still a great campaigner, but he hasn't been allowed to this year, because Al doesn't want him to. [campaign] (adapted from Hardt 1993)
   c.   George expected Al$_i$ to win the election even when he$_i$ didn't. [expect Al$_i$ to win] (adapted from Dalrymple 1991)

VP-ellipsis is felicitous in sentence (18a), unlike (17a), even though the source clause is passivized. This is unanticipated in a syntactic account, since the syntactic structure for the active voice VP that would be required for syntactic reconstruction – *overturn the election results* – is not provided by the source. Likewise, sentence (18b) is at least marginally acceptable, even though the referent is evoked by a nominalization. Finally, sentence (18c) is felicitous despite the fact that Condition C predicts it to be unacceptable (cf. 17c).

The contrast between examples (17a–c) and (18a–c) is puzzling, since each set seems to offer strong evidence for its respective approach. There is an important difference between them, however. The examples that support syntactic theories (17a–c) participate in Resemblance relations, particularly Parallel. On the other hand, the examples that support semantic theories (18a–c) participate in Cause–Effect relations, particularly Violated Expectation (18a–b) and Denial of Preventer (18c). This suggests that the difference between (17a–c) and (18a–c) corresponds to a difference in the way that the inference processes used to establish these two types of coherence relation interact with the process of VP-ellipsis interpretation itself.[9]

There is plenty of evidence to suggest that VP-ellipsis interpretation is fundamentally an anaphoric process. For instance, it behaves like other forms of anaphora (e.g. pronominal reference) with respect to the circumstances in which it can be cataphoric (e.g. *If he$_i$ wants to* ϕ_j, *Al$_i$ [will contest the election]$_j$*) and the fact that it can access referents evoked from clauses other than the most immediate one (see Hardt 1993 for attested examples). Anaphora resolution is known to be a purely semantically mediated process, whereby referents are identified with respect to the hearer's knowledge state and mental model of the discourse. As such, it would be quite unexpected a priori if VP-ellipsis interpretation was associated with a process of syntactic reconstruction.

I claim that syntactic reconstruction is instead triggered by an aspect of the coherence establishment process, specifically, the need to recover the arguments to the coherence relation being established. In particular, reconstruction is triggered when the constituents corresponding to semantic representations necessary for coherence establishment have been elided from the syntactic structure. Whether or not reconstruction will be necessary therefore depends on what coherence relation is operative, because Cause–Effect and Resemblance relations differ with respect to the type of arguments they take. In the case of a Cause–Effect relation, such as those operative in (18a–c), reconstruction will not be required. As was indicated in section 3.1, the arguments to these relations are merely the sentence-level semantics of each utterance. Since the top-level sentence node is never elided (obviously), and its semantics will be complete once the meaning of the missing VP has been recovered through anaphora resolution, there will be no missing arguments that require reconstruction. On the other hand, the process of identifying the arguments to a Resemblance relation, as well as the correct parallel pairing among them, requires access to the structure and semantics of subsentential constituents within each utterance. Thus, for many cases in which a Resemblance relation is operative,[10] including (17a–c), certain of these arguments will have been elided in the target clause and reconstruction will be required. As such, the account explains why syntactic constraint violations appear for VP-ellipsis in the context of Resemblance relations, but not Cause–Effect relations.[11]

Other types of syntactic constraints that I have not yet addressed are also observed with VP-ellipsis, including those involving traces in antecedent-contained ellipsis (ACE). Haïk (1987) points out that the unacceptability of examples like (19) is predicted by the subjacency constraint in a syntactic analysis.

(19)   #John read everything which Bill believes the claim that he did. [read ϕ]

In Kehler (2000a, 2002), I suggest several ways that such violations could be addressed within the current proposal. First instance, an analysis in the spirit of Chao (1988) could be posited, in which the need to satisfy *wh*-trace dependencies in the target can also force the reconstruction of missing syntactic material. Alternatively, assuming a lexicalist theory of syntax capable of representing trace dependencies without movement or reconstruction (e.g. HPSG, LFG), a trace dependency represented at the elided VP node could be coordinated with a variable within the anaphorically resolved semantic representation (Mark Gawron, p.c., cf. Lappin 1999). Interestingly, cases like (19) contrast with ones involving traces in parasitic gap configurations (Fiengo and May 1994, Kennedy 1997, Lappin 1999); consider the unacceptability of (20a) versus the acceptability of its elided counterpart (20b), both from Rooth (1981).

(20)a.   *Which problem did you think John would solve because of the fact that Susan solved?
   b.   Which problem did you think John would solve because of the fact that Susan did? [solved the problem]

This example differs from examples (19) in that there is no dependency within the sentence that requires there to be a trace within the elided VP. Thus, assuming a semantic theory in which the representation of the missing VP in (20b) contains a bound variable (Dalrymple et al. 1991), the fact that a Cause–Effect relationship is operative in (20b) is consistent with its acceptability.[12]

3.2.2   *Extraction from conjoined clauses*

The second phenomenon I consider is extraction from conjoined clauses. As is well known, Ross (1967: 89) first proposed the Coordinate Structure Constraint (CSC) as a basic constraint in universal grammar:

> In a coordinate structure, no conjunct may be moved, nor may any element contained in a conjunct be moved out of that conjunct.

Grosu (1973) makes a convincing case that two components of the CSC should be differentiated: the CONJUNCT CONSTRAINT and the ELEMENT CONSTRAINT. The Conjunct Constraint bars the movement of whole conjuncts out of coordinate structures, ruling out sentences such as (21).

(21)   *This is the energy policy that George proposed the tax cut and.

The Conjunct Constraint is extremely robust, and has been argued to result from independently motivated constraints in several theories of grammar (but cf. Johannessen 1998).

The Element Constraint, which bars the movement of elements contained within a conjunct as opposed to the entire conjunct itself, has been more controversial, and hence will be my focus here. The Element Constraint rules out sentences such as (22a–b), because extraction of an NP has taken place out of a conjoined VP:

(22)a.   #What energy policy did George support and propose the tax cut?
   b.   #What energy policy did George propose the tax cut and support?

A very general class of counterexamples to the Element Constraint was first noticed by Ross (1967) himself, whereby extraction out of coordinate structures is possible when the same element is extracted "across the board" from all the conjuncts, as in sentence (23):

(23)   What energy policy did George propose and support?

Since Ross, the Element Constraint and the across-the-board exception has been taken by many syntactic theorists to be a valid generalization of the facts, and they have thus typically sought to explain it solely at the level of syntax (Schachter 1977b, Gazdar et al. 1985, Steedman 1985, Goodall 1987, Postal 1998). However, several other counterexamples that violate this generalization have been discussed in the literature.

For instance, Goldsmith (1985) points out that extraction out of a single conjunct can occur when the "nonetheless" use of *and* is operative between the conjuncts (which can be paraphrased as *and still, and nonetheless,* or *and yet*), as in example (24):

(24) How much can you drink and still stay sober?

G. Lakoff (1986) discusses the similar example given in (25), which he attributes to Peter Farley. In both (24) and (25), extraction has taken place out of the first conjunct but not the second.

(25) That's the stuff that the guys in the Caucasus drink and live to be a hundred.

Finally, Ross (1967) discusses examples of the sort shown in (26a), in which extraction has occurred only from the first and third conjuncts. Lakoff notes that unlike examples (24) and (25), extraction must take place out of the final conjunct in such cases, possibly along with certain other conjuncts that do not serve a scene-setting function. For instance, sentence (26b), which is the same as sentence (26a) but without the final (gap-containing) conjunct, is unacceptable.

(26)a. What did Harry buy, come home, and devour in thirty seconds?
     b. #What did Harry buy and come home?

The foregoing data pattern directly with the three classes of coherence relations I have proposed. First, the Resemblance relation Parallel holds between the conjoined VPs in sentences (22a, b) and (23). In these cases, any extraction must be across-the-board. Second, the Cause–Effect relations Violated Expectation and Result are operative in examples (24) and (25) respectively. In these cases, extraction from only one conjunct is permitted. Third, example (26a) is related by the Contiguity relation Occasion. These cases also allow extraction to occur out of only a subset of conjuncts, but appear to require extraction out of the final one (per 26b).

Viewing the data in light of this pattern, there does not appear to be much ground left on which to argue for the CSC as a purely syntactic constraint. In none of the three categories is extraction from within a conjunct barred entirely; instead, there appear only to be weaker constraints at play that differ with respect to the type of coherence relation. This fact suggests that the data would be better explained at the level of the syntax/pragmatics interface, rather than stipulated as a purely grammatical constraint.[13]

The factor that appears to be coming into play in these data is what Kuno (1976b, 1987) calls a TOPICHOOD CONDITION on extraction. Kuno cites sentences (27a–d) to support such a constraint:

(27)a.   I read a book about John Irving.
    b.   I lost a book about John Irving.
    c.   Who did you buy a book about?
    d.   ??Who did you lose a book about?

Whereas sentences (27a, b) are both perfectly acceptable, the extracted variants in sentences (27c, d) are not equally acceptable. Kuno says:

> In a highly intuitive sense, we feel that the fact that the book under discussion was on John Irving is much more *relevant* in [(27a)] than in [(27b)]. This is undoubtedly due to the fact that one buys books, but does not lose them, because of their content.   (Kuno 1987: 23)

Although the notion of topichood still lacks a concrete definition in the literature,[14] one can still ask how such a constraint might apply when extraction from coordinate clauses is considered. Indeed, as I describe in detail in Kehler (2002), one would expect that the constraints on what can serve as a topic of a conjoined set of clauses will depend on the operative coherence relation. Clauses related by a Resemblance relation are coherent by virtue of the very fact that they manifest a common topic (cf. R. Lakoff 1971b); the possibilities for topichood are thus provided by the properties shared by the corresponding elements over which the relation applies (at some, perhaps inferred, level of generalization). Syntactic constructions that involve extraction are thus felicitous only when a set of parallel elements that denote this topic can be extracted to a common topic-denoting position, which in most cases is possible only when the elements are identical, resulting in the "across-the-board" behavior.[15] In contrast, there is no similar property of Cause–Effect relations nor of the inference processes that underlie their establishment that would prohibit an element in one clause from serving as the topic of both; indeed, one would expect the topic of a clause expressing a cause to be relevant to one expressing its effect. Finally, the topic of a set of clauses related by Occasion need not be mentioned in every clause – in particular, coherent Occasions commonly contain scene-setting and similar types of clauses that do not mention, but also do not distract attention from, the discourse topic – so extraction need not take place out of all conjuncts. On the other hand, extraction must take place out of the conjuncts that do not serve this type of scene-setting function, including the final clause, insofar as a failure to do this would suggest that the extracted element is no longer the topic at that point in the passage.

3.2.3   *Pronominal reference*

Finally, I consider pronominal reference. Sure enough, three different types of approach can be found in the literature, each motivated by different types of examples. While the data that support each approach are often problematic for the others, a pattern emerges when the operative coherence relation is taken into account.

Hobbs (1979) presents what I will call a COHERENCE-DRIVEN theory, in which pronoun interpretation is not an independent process but instead a by-product of more general reasoning about the most likely interpretation of an utterance. Pronouns are modeled as free variables which become bound during these inference processes; potential referents of pronouns are therefore those which result in valid proofs of coherence. A typical example used to support a coherence-driven theory is given in sentence (28) with follow-ons (a) and (b), adapted from an example from Winograd (1972).

(28)   The city council denied the demonstrators a permit because
    a.   they *feared* violence.
    b.   they *advocated* violence.

Hearers appear to have little difficulty interpreting the pronoun *they* in each case, despite the fact that it refers to *the city council* in sentence (28a) and *the demonstrators* in sentence (28b). These different interpretations result even though the two sentence pairs have identical syntactic configurations. Indeed, the only difference between them is the verb in the second clause, suggesting that semantics is the key factor in determining the correct referents. In each case, the pronoun receives the assignment necessary to establish the Cause–Effect relation Explanation.

Contrasting with coherence-driven theories are what I will call ATTENTION-DRIVEN theories. Attention-driven theories treat pronoun interpretation as an independent process associated with its own interpretation mechanisms, rather than as a side-effect of more general interpretation mechanisms. Instances of this approach include Sidner's focusing framework (Sidner 1983) and Centering theory (Kameyama 1986, Brennan et al. 1987, Grosz et al. 1995), among others. Examples such as passage (29), from Grosz et al. (1995), have been used to support this type of approach.

(29)a.   Terry really goofs sometimes.
    b.   Yesterday was a beautiful day and he was excited about trying out his new sailboat.
    c.   He wanted Tony to join him on a sailing expedition.
    d.   He called him at 6 a.m.
    e.   He was sick and furious at being woken up so early.

This passage is perfectly acceptable until sentence (29e), which causes the hearer to be misled. Whereas commonsense knowledge would indicate that the intended referent for *He* is Tony, hearers tend to initially assign Terry as its referent, creating a garden-path effect. Such examples therefore provide evidence that there is more to pronoun interpretation than simply reasoning about semantic plausibility. In fact, they suggest that hearers assign referents to pronouns at least in part based on other factors (e.g. the grammatical role of the antecedent; cf. examples 28a, b) before interpreting the remainder of the sentence. In this example, the Contiguity relation Occasion is operative.

Finally, passages such as (30) and (31), from Sidner (1983) and Kameyama (1986) respectively, are potentially problematic for both types of approach:

(30)a. The green Whitierleaf is most commonly found near the wild rose.
   b. The wild violet is found near it too.

(31)a. Carl is talking to Tom in the Lab.
   b. Terry wants to talk to him too.

In these cases there is a strong bias for the pronoun to refer to its syntactically parallel referent (*the wild rose* in (30), and *Tom* in (31)). This fact poses a problem for attention-driven approaches that, as is typical, prefer referents evoked from subject position over those evoked from other grammatical positions (cf. example 29). Furthermore, there is no semantic basis to prefer one referent over the other in each case, since coherence could be established assuming either assignment. In these examples the Resemblance relation Parallel is operative.

While these three types of example offer contradictory evidence about the mechanisms that underlie pronoun interpretation, they pattern directly with the neo-Humian categorization of coherence relations I have proposed. Examples that offer specific support for interpretation preferences based on semantics and coherence, such as (28), tend to participate in Cause–Effect relations. Examples that directly support preferences based on a hierarchy of grammatical role, like (29), tend to be instances of Contiguity relations. And examples that support grammatical role parallelism preferences, such as (30) and (31), are typically instances of Resemblance. This pattern suggests that an adequate analysis will have to account for the differences among the inference processes that underlie the establishment of these different types of relations.

In Kehler (2002), I argue that these data can be explained by an analysis that shares characteristics of both coherence-driven and attention-driven approaches. As in attention-driven approaches, pronouns impose the requirement that their referents be highly attended to within the current discourse state. However, in contrast to the clause-by-clause discourse update mechanisms often found in such approaches, the discourse state changes on a rapid time scale as coherence establishment processes redirect the focus of attention as necessary during inferencing. The fact that different types of pronoun interpretation preferences appear to be in force when different coherence relations are operative is a result of the different types of reasoning underlying their recognition.

Recall, for instance, that the inference process associated with Resemblance first identifies pairs of parallel entities and relation from each clause, and then attempts to identify points of similarity and contrast among the members of each pair. When examples like (30) or (31) are interpreted, this process will pair each pronoun with its parallel element, placing the latter in focus. At that point, similarity can be established between the two by simply assuming coreference. The effect of attending solely to the pronoun's parallel element at that point during inferencing is so strong that it trumps even a strong world knowledge bias toward another referent. For instance, hearers universally assign Clinton as the referent of *her*[16] in (32a) even though world knowledge would strongly suggest Thatcher. Likewise, hearers even get confused by example (32b) due to the gender mismatch between *her* and Reagan, even though Thatcher is an otherwise perfectly suitable referent (cf. Oehrle 1981).

(32)a. Margaret Thatcher admires Hillary Clinton, and George W. Bush absolutely worships her.
   b. Margaret Thatcher admires Ronald Reagan, and George W. Bush absolutely worships her.

On the other hand, the inference process associated with Cause–Effect relations attempts to identify a chain of implication between the semantics representations of the clauses being related. As such, there would be no reason to expect a bias toward parallelism in such cases. Instead, an axiom used to create the implicational chain may bring into focus the pronominal referent that is necessary for that axiom to apply. As a result, examples that are ambiguous between Resemblance and Cause–Effect readings (for example) may display a corresponding ambiguity with respect to the interpretation of the pronoun, as in (33):

(33) Colin Powell defied Dick Cheney, and George W. Bush punished him.

If the Parallel relation is inferred then the pronoun must be interpreted to refer to its parallel element, Cheney. If a Result relation is inferred then Powell is the preferred referent, in accordance with our world knowledge about the relationship between defying and punishing.

Finally, the inference process associated with Contiguity attempts to draw the connections necessary to interpret the final state of one eventuality as being the initial state of the next. As such, at the time that a pronoun is encountered in a sentence like (29e), the referent most attended to should be the one that is most prominent with respect to the hearer's conceptualization of the end state of the previous eventuality. While this will often be the subject of the preceding sentence, this is not always so; consider examples (34a, b), from Stevenson et al. (1994).

(34)a.   John seized the comic from Bill. He . . .
    b.   John passed the comic to Bill. He . . .

In a set of psycholinguistic experiments, Stevenson et al. found that hearers are more likely to interpret *he* to refer to John in passage (34a) and to Bill in (34b), despite the fact that in (34b) Bill is mentioned from within a sentence-final prepositional phrase, a position which attention-driven theories typically consider to be much less salient than subject position. What these examples have in common is that the preferred referent occupies the Goal thematic role of its respective predication, which is presumably more central to the final state of the eventuality than the entity that occupies the Source thematic role.

To sum, by accounting for the different properties of the inference processes that underlie the establishment of the three types of coherence relations in the neo-Humean classification, facets of both coherence-driven and attention-driven theories can be integrated to account for pronominal reference behavior that is problematic for each in isolation.

4   Informational and Intentional Coherence

Thus far I have described an approach to establishing coherence based on making the inferences necessary to meet the constraints imposed by one of a set of coherence relations. Following the terminology of Moore and Pollack (1992), I will refer to this view as the INFORMATIONAL approach to coherence. Historically, this approach has been applied predominantly to monologues.

In contrast, other researchers (Grosz and Sidner 1986, inter alia), following work in speech act theory and plan recognition (e.g. Cohen and Perrault 1979, Allen and Perrault 1980), have argued that the role of the utterance in the overall plan underlying the speaker's production of the discourse is the determining factor of coherence. I will likewise follow Moore and Pollack and refer to this view as the INTENTIONAL approach. In this view, a hearer considers utterances as actions and infers the plan-based speaker intentions underlying them to establish coherence. The intentional approach has been applied predominantly to dialogues, such as the following interchange from Cohen et al. (1990):

(35) *Customer*:   Where are the chuck steaks you advertised for 88 cents per pound?
      Butcher: How many do you want?

A more appropriate information-level response to the customer's question would be *behind the counter*. However, the butcher recognizes the customer's higher-level goal of purchasing the steaks and responds with a question that is designed to address and ultimately satisfy that goal, hence the coherence of the response with respect to the speaker's intentions.

In the intentional approach of Grosz and Sidner (1986), each discourse segment has a corresponding DISCOURSE SEGMENT PURPOSE, or DSP. In contrast to the large set of relations commonly found in informational analyses, there are only two relations that can hold between discourse segments: DOMINANCE, in which the satisfaction of the DSP of one discourse segment is intended to provide part of the satisfaction of the DSP of another segment, and SATISFACTION-PRECEDENCE, in which the DSP of one segment must be satisfied as a prerequisite to satisfying the DSP of another.

The relationship between these two conceptions of coherence has been a topic of some debate (Moore and Pollack 1992, Moore and Paris 1993, Asher and Lascarides 1994, Hobbs 1997, inter alia). Moore and Pollack (1992) argued that in fact both levels of analysis must co-exist, illustrating the point with passage (36):

(36)a. George Bush supports big business.
   b. He's sure to veto House Bill 1711.

Passage (36) can be analyzed from either the intentional or informational perspective. At the intentional level, the speaker may be trying to convince the hearer of the claim being made in sentence (36b), and offering sentence (36a) as evidence to support it. At the informational level, she intends that the hearer recognize a Result relationship between the fact expressed in sentence (36a) and the event expressed in sentence (36b). This duality is not surprising, since one way to provide evidence for a proposition is to show that it follows as a consequence of another proposition that the hearer already believes.

Moore and Pollack demonstrate that this connection may allow a hearer to recognize a relation at one level from the recognition of a relation at the other level. For instance, if the hearer knows that House Bill 1711 imposes strong environmental controls on manufacturing processes, but does not know the intentions of the speaker a priori, he can infer the intention of providing evidence from having recognized the informational Result relation. Alternatively, if the hearer has no knowledge of the content of House Bill 1711, but has prior reason to believe that the speaker is attempting to provide evidence for the proposition in (36b), he may infer that a Result relation holds, and from this that House Bill 1711 must place undesirable constraints on businesses. As such there is reason to suggest that both levels co-exist, with links between the two to enable the recognition of relationships on one level from the recognition of relationships on the other.

5 Conclusion

In this chapter, I have attempted to convince the reader that coherence establishment is not only a fundamental aspect of discourse interpretation, but that it needs to be accounted for in analyses of a variety of linguistic phenomena that operate across clauses. I categorized a set of coherence relations with respect to Hume's three types of connection among ideas, and demonstrated how differences among the inference processes that underlie the establishment of such relations affect the distribution and behavior of three different linguistic phenomena. Given the centrality of coherence establishment to language interpretation, it would perhaps have been surprising if it were found that these processes did not affect the behavior of such phenomena.

I again refer the reader to Kehler (2002) for considerably more detailed treatments. I also address two other linguistic phenomena in that work, gapping and tense interpretation. The treatment of gapping accounts for the fact that conjoined clauses that are compatible with Resemblance and Cause–Effect interpretations lose the latter after gapping has applied (Levin and Prince 1986). This prediction falls out from the theory of VP-ellipsis summarized in this paper, along with the fact that the gapping, unlike VP-ellipsis, is not anaphoric. The treatment of tense shows how the temporal constraints imposed by coherence relations interact with the anaphoric properties of tense to predict data that are problematic for past analyses, including approaches that treat the simple past as anaphoric (Partee 1984b, Hinrichs 1986, Nerbonne 1986, Webber 1988, inter alia), as well as one that resolves temporal relations involving both simple (e.g. the past) and complex (e.g. the past perfect) tenses purely as a by-product of coherence establishment processes (Lascarides and Asher 1993).

Much remains to be accomplished before we have a fully adequate analysis of discourse coherence. We have only scratched the surface with respect to understanding the answers to many questions: the detailed workings of the inference mechanisms that underlie relation establishment; how a preferred interpretation emerges from a set of alternative proofs of coherence; the manner in which these mechanisms operate during on-line, left-to-right processing; in what contexts a discourse connective is necessary, optional, or even redundant; what the basic principles of coherence are and how they interact with the large set of connectives that a language makes available; how deeply embedded these basic principles are not only with respect to discourse but also at the levels of the lexicon and clause; and many, many others. It is hoped that this chapter has inspired some new interest in these questions.

ACKNOWLEDGMENTS

This research was supported in part by National Science Foundation Grant IIS-9619126. I would like to thank Gregory Ward, Larry Horn, and two anonymous reviewers for extensive comments on a draft.

NOTES

1 In the majority of this chapter, I will focus almost solely on coherence in monologue, specifically with respect to relationships that hold between adjacent clauses and their implications for sentential interpretation. I will not address coherence among larger segments of discourse here, and I speak only briefly about dialogue in section 4.

2 Indeed, a common objection to theories of coherence is that the proposed relations have a laundry-list quality, with no rationale given for why they constitute the correct set. The unwieldiness of the situation is demonstrated in Hovy (1990), who compiled over 350 previously proposed relations from 26 researchers. After merging redundancies, a hierarchy with 63 relations resulted.

3 I am oversimplifying a bit here, since there is a small set of relations which are multi-nuclear and can relate more than two spans of text (e.g. the JOINT relation).

4 Notable exceptions include Hobbs's (1979) approach to resolving pronouns in the context of coherence establishment and Lascarides and Asher's (1993) similar approach to tense interpretation.

5 Hobbs (1990: 101–2) was the first to point out that Hume's principles could be used as a basis for categorizing coherence relations, but he did not pursue such a classification in depth, opting instead for a different basis for categorizing relations.

6 For ease of exposition, I will treat Parallel as if it always relates only two clauses, whereas in reality it can operate over longer sequences.

7 While not directly stated in this definition of Exemplification, the subset relationship can also hold between the relations expressed instead of one or more pairs of entities (or both). The same is true for the Generalization and Exception relations, discussed below.

8 Here and elsewhere in the paper, my analyses suggest that various examples commonly considered to be ungrammatical are actually pragmatically infelicitous. As such, I will typically indicate unacceptability with a hash mark (#) rather than an asterisk, except in a few instances that I still consider to be ungrammatical.

9 The situation with respect to Contiguity relations is less clear, and will not be discussed further here. See Kehler (2002) for discussion.

10 The situation is more complicated for comparative and temporal subordination constructions, which, despite being instances of Resemblance, readily violate Binding Theory constraints:

(i)a. Al$_i$'s lawyer defended him$_i$ better than he$_i$ did. [defend him$_i$]

b. Al claimed that George$_i$ won before he$_i$ did. [claimed that George$_i$ won]

However, these constructions still require that the source and target VPs be parallel; consider the infelicity of the following voice mismatches:

(ii)a. #Al was defended by Joe more competently than Bill did. [defend Al]

b.   #CNN announced Al as the winner before George was. [announced as the winner]

I argue in Kehler (2000a, 2002) that the process of establishing the coherence of such constructions only requires VP-level parallelism, which would account for these facts.

11   Kennedy (in press), who advocates a syntactic reconstruction account, criticizes my analysis by stating that:

> there is a third, more general problem with a mixed approach such as Kehler's. If a purely semantic analysis is available in some examples, then it ought to be in principle available in all examples, even if a syntactic analysis is preferred.

In actuality, my analysis specifically predicts that this is not the case. This prediction comes about because the relevant syntactic and semantic constraints originate from different recovery processes. To reiterate, the meaning of the elided VP is always recovered anaphorically (i.e. semantically), regardless of the coherence relation. In no case is syntactic reconstruction performed out of a need to recover the meaning of an elided VP. Syntactic reconstruction is instead necessitated only by the independent need to recover elided arguments to a coherence relation. Thus, while a "semantic analysis" is in fact available for all examples, some examples have the *additional* constraint of requiring a syntactic antecedent that can be reconstructed. Hence there is no respect in which my analysis is "mixed" with respect to the mechanism used for

recovering the meaning of an elided VP.

There are two other respects in which Kennedy criticizes my account. One pertains to the status of Condition B violations in Cause–Effect relations – e.g. *Joe has to take care of Al$_i$ because he$_i$ won't* – which I find acceptable and he does not. The other pertains to certain examples involving trace violations, which space precludes addressing here. I refer the reader to Kennedy's discussion and the relevant discussions in Kehler (2000a, 2002).

12   But cf. Kennedy (1997), who presents a syntactic analysis in which reconstructed target VPs in examples such as these contain a pronoun rather than the expected trace, utilizing the VEHICLE CHANGE proposal of Fiengo and May (1994).

13   Per footnote 8, I have marked the unacceptable extraction examples (except 21) as infelicitous rather than ungrammatical, as my analysis implies that none of these are unacceptable on purely syntactic grounds. Although this may contradict the intuitions of some with respect to examples like (22a, b), it can hardly be any other way. As Lakoff (1986) points out, if one allows an autonomous syntactic module to generate sentences such as (24), (25), and (26a), then it must also be able to generate (22a, b), leaving the task of filtering out (22a, b) to semantic or pragmatic constraints. The converse – keeping the CSC and adding a semantic or pragmatic condition to allow (24), (25), and (26a) – is not an option, since such conditions could not turn an ungrammatical sentence into a grammatical one.

14   In lieu of such a definition, Kuno (1976b) offers a "Speaking of X"

test for a potential sentence topic X (see also Reinhart 1981), in which this phrase is placed at the beginning of the sentence and the mentions of X pronominalized:

(i)a. Who did you buy a book about?

b. Speaking of John Irving, I just bought a book about him.

c. ??Who did you lose a book about?

d. ??Speaking of John Irving, I just lost a book about him.

15 Actually, it is possible to extract more than one element from a conjoined clause when a RESPECTIVE READING is operative, as in the following example (Postal 1998):

(i) What book and what magazine did John buy and Bill read, respectively?

In fact, Gawron and Kehler (2000) show that similar examples are felicitous even when the "extracted" elements are denoted as a group by a single noun phrase, posing a challenge for theories that account for extraction by movement or that otherwise require coreference between the gap site and the constituent on which it is dependent. Both predict only an across-the-board reading for example (ii):

(ii) I finally met Susan, Marilyn, and Lucille yesterday. They are the three sisters that Bob married, John is engaged to, and Bill is dating (respectively).

16 This assumes that the pronoun remains unaccented, of course.

12 The Pragmatics of Non-sentences

ROBERT J. STAINTON

1 The Appearances

I want to begin by describing some appearances. The word "appearances" is important – as will emerge at length below, these appearances might be misleading. That warning being issued, it appears that ordinary speakers routinely utter non-sentences, and in so doing perform full-blown speech acts.

In saying this, I don't mean that they appear to produce non-linguistic gestures and such, thereby performing speech acts. (How could something be a speech act, and be non-linguistic?) Nor do I mean that they utter ungrammatical sentences and yet succeed in asserting, or asking, or ordering. It seems plausible that speakers do the latter, but that isn't the issue I will be discussing. Instead, what I mean is that speakers appear to utter, consciously and by design, fully grammatical expressions which happen to be less-than-sentential: nouns and NPs, adjectives and AdjPs, as well as PPs, VPs, and so on. That is, speakers routinely utter bare words and phrases not syntactically embedded in any sentence, and they thereby perform speech acts like asserting, asking, commanding, and so on. Again, so it appears.

That bare words/phrases can be so used might seem obvious. Many would grant, for example, that a hearer may answer a question with a mere word or a phrase. For instance, Tracy says, "Where do you live?", and Isaac replies, "London." There are also examples of correction (repairs): Tracy says, "I think we met in London," and Isaac responds, "Paris, actually." Not everyone would grant that such cases are, in fact, subsentential; some will insist that in such cases the answers are actually elliptical sentences. But, even if these are subsentential, they aren't the sort of cases I want to emphasize here.[1] Rather, I want to focus on examples in which it is not prior linguistic context but non-linguistic context that somehow "completes" what is asserted, asked, commanded, etc.

Here are some examples of the kind of thing I want to discuss. A woman could enter a room, and Leah could say to Anita, looking at the woman in the doorway: "Sam's mom." Here, Leah says about the woman entering the room that she is Sam's mom, but what she utters is not a sentence. Instead, she utters an NP.[2] What's more, it's not an NP that answers an interrogative, nor is it an NP that corrects a previously spoken sentence. Similarly, Anita and Sheryl could be looking at a tote board, watching the progress of shares in Acme Internet. As the stock rises, Anita could say, "Moving pretty fast!" In this example, Anita appears to utter a bare VP, not a sentence. And, here again, it's not a VP that answers an interrogative, nor is it a VP that corrects a previously spoken sentence (I'll exclude this qualification in what follows), yet Anita still succeeds in making a statement. Other examples abound: pick up any magazine, leaf through the ads, and you will find carefully edited (and hence, surely grammatical) copy of the following sort:

(1)   America's most frequent service to Asia

(2)   Fast relief for arthritic pain

(3)   From the sun-soaked mountains of Colombia

Let me describe the appearances a bit more formally. In doing so, I'll make use of some non-obvious theoretical machinery, so in that sense what follows goes beyond "obvious appearances." But it will, I hope, clarify the phenomenon being discussed. The generalization at the level of syntax, first formulated by Barton (1990 and elsewhere), seems to be that speakers can utter not just sentences, but any MAXIMAL PROJECTION. This emphatically does include maximal projections whose GRAMMATICAL HEAD is a lexical item: a noun, an adjective, a preposition, etc. It is uses of these LEXICAL PROJECTIONS that are precisely the cases of interest here.[3] As for the semantics of the things used in such cases, it does not seem to matter what content is assigned to the expression in the language. It can stand for an object, a property, or even a function from a property to a truth value, and yet still be used to make a statement, or ask a question, or issue an order. In the notation of Montague grammar, the point can be put this way: an expression need not be of SEMANTIC TYPE $\langle t \rangle$ to be used to perform a speech act; it can be of type $\langle e \rangle$, or $\langle e, t \rangle$, or $\langle \langle e, t \rangle, t \rangle$, etc.[4] Thus, returning to an earlier example, the phrase *moving pretty fast* does not express a proposition. It doesn't even do so after reference is assigned to indexicals and such, there being none. Put differently, the phrase type *moving pretty fast* is not synonymous with the sentence type *That is moving pretty fast*, as it would have to be if the contextualized meaning of the former were to be a proposition – and this lack of synonymy of the types obtains even if one can make an assertion by tokening either type. (Notational aside: the word "type" unfortunately refers to two quite different things in semantic theorizing. There is the TYPE versus TOKEN distinction, which is in play in the preceding sentence, and there is the distinction between various semantic categories in Montague grammar: semantic types $\langle e \rangle$, $\langle e, t \rangle$, $\langle t \rangle$, etc. Where there is a risk of confusion,

I will use "expression type/phrase type/sentence type" for the former, and "Montagovian semantic type" for the latter.) The complete sentence *That is moving pretty fast*, despite containing context-sensitive elements, is indeed of Montagovian semantic type ⟨t⟩. But the phrase *moving pretty fast* is not of type ⟨t⟩: its semantic type is ⟨e, t⟩. This becomes evident when the phrasal expression is embedded. What *moving pretty fast* contributes to the complete sentence *That stock is moving pretty fast*, once reference has been assigned to indexicals and such, is not a proposition, but a property: that property shared by things which are moving pretty fast. Thus, when a speaker utters *Moving pretty fast* on its own, it appears that she utters an expression that, even after it is contextualized, means a property, not a proposition. Similarly, the phrase *Sam's mom*, even contextualized, does not express a proposition. The same can be said of the expressions in (1)–(3). And yet, it appears that these expression types, which purportedly have both the syntax and the semantics of ordinary phrases, can be used to make statements. Indeed, it appears that they can be used to perform speech acts of many kinds. For instance, one could ask about a displayed letter, "From Colombia?" Or one could issue a command to one's child by saying, "To your bedroom. Right now."

Notice too that, whereas it's sometimes supposed that complete sentence meanings contain FORCE INDICATORS that account for the kind of act the sentences are typically used to perform, bare word and phrase meanings are assumed not to contain such things. This is still another (apparent) difference in content. Let me explain. One view of the difference in meaning between the sentences (4a–c) is that, though they share the same propositional content, viz. that-John-is-running, (4a–c) exhibit distinct force indicators.

(4)a.   John is running
   b.   Is John running?
   c.   Run, John!

That is, their content is bipartite: part of it is a proposition, the other part is a force indicator. The first sentence, the syntactic type, has as its non-propositional content an assertoric force indicator; the second sentence type has an interrogatival force indicator as part of its context-insensitive content; and the third has an imperatival force indicator. Notice that force indicators are considered here to be part of content of the expression type: they are (at least in English) syntactically carried by the MOOD of the sentence. Mood is a constant feature of syntax, and thus force indication is a matter of context-invariant content. It is the presence of force indicators, encoded by mood, that helps explain why one makes an assertion by uttering (4a) but one asks a question by uttering (4b).

Under these assumptions, then, the phrase type *moving pretty fast* surely does not contain a force indicator as part of its context-invariant content. Clearly it has no mood as part of its syntax, neither declarative nor any other. Its constant content, then, is just a property of things, not a property/force pair.

We thus have another apparent difference between the sentence type *That is moving pretty fast* and the phrase type *moving pretty fast* – a difference that extends beyond the fact that they are of distinct Montagovian semantic types.

To clarify this difference, it will help to say a word about expression types, speech acts, and force. I don't deny that speech acts performed using subsentences exhibit force; indeed, it's part of my description of the appearances that they do so. It may even be true that there are sound pattern types – consisting of the sound of a lexical phrase, though modulated by a special intonation pattern – that have illocutionary force. For instance, the type *From Colombia?* said with rising intonation might be claimed to have interrogatival force. Be that as it may, the point I'm making here is that the force of such things – the speech acts or the phrase-intonation pairs – is not inherited from the syntax and semantics of the phrase type itself, since that phrase type does not syntactically encode a force indicator. Suffice it, then, to say that the syntax of complete sentences apparently (often) encodes a force indicator, via mood, but the syntax of lexical projections does not appear to encode this. That is another apparent difference.

There is then – or at least, there appears to be – a significant mismatch in non-sentential speech between what the expression type means in the language and what the speaker of it means. Now, cases of speaker meaning that outpace (contextualized) expression meaning are very familiar in pragmatics. For instance, in CONVERSATIONAL IMPLICATURE (see Horn, this volume), the speaker means something different than (or in addition to) what his words mean, even once reference has been assigned to context-sensitive elements. As Grice would say, "what is said" in such cases does not (wholly) capture what is meant. Recall, for instance, the delightful sort of case imagined by Grice (1989: Chap. 2). Professor Koorb writes a letter of reference for a student that says only:

(5)   Mr. Tonstain has neat handwriting, and he usually arrives on time for class. Yours, J. A. Koorb.

Here what the speaker means goes well beyond what his words mean. What he means is something like: This student is appallingly bad; don't even dream of hiring him. But that is not what his words, even in context, mean. Similarly in non-sentence cases, it appears that what the speaker means, which is a proposition, is quite different from what her words mean, which is not a proposition but an object, or property, or something along those lines.

Interestingly, however, though there is this mismatch between what the expression uttered means in the context (i.e. an object, or property, etc.), and what the speaker of it meant (i.e. a complete proposition), this does not appear similar to cases of non-literal communication. Of course, there are special cases in which one can speak metaphorically or ironically while using a subsentence: Richard could utter "The next Nobel Laureate" while pointing at a notoriously brainless politician, thereby **saying** that the politico is the next

Nobel Laureate – but **meaning** that he is a buffoon.[5] But not all uses of subsentences are non-literal. For instance, recalling Leah and Anita, if Leah knew perfectly well that the person coming through the doorway was not Sam's mother, but she wanted to convince Anita otherwise, she would have lied in uttering "Sam's mother." Leah could not later say, "Oh I didn't tell Anita that she was Sam's mother. In fact, I made no literal statement at all about the woman. Anita just drew her own conclusions." To the contrary, Leah did make a statement: she strictly and literally said, about the woman at the door, that she was Sam's mother. Unlike in the Gricean case of Professor Koorb described above, in speaking non-sententially it doesn't look like Leah merely suggested, or implicated, a proposition: what Leah does looks very much like assertion, and very much unlike non-literal speech – despite the mismatch between expression meaning and speaker meaning.

To sum up so far: speakers utter ordinary words and phrases, with the syntax and semantics of ordinary words and phrases, and thereby perform speech acts. More formally put, they produce projections of lexical items – which, seen semantically, are not of semantic type $\langle t \rangle$ and contain no force indicator – and yet they thereby make assertions, ask questions, etc. Since there is an assertion of something of semantic type $\langle t \rangle$, what the speaker means in these cases extends beyond what her words mean. And yet, this mismatch is not strikingly similar to metaphor, or conversational implicature, or speaker's reference, or other clearly non-literal speech acts. Rather, one seems to have perfectly literal communication in these cases. As I stressed at the outset, this is how things appear. (Or anyway, how they appear to me.)

There are, of course, two possible responses to such appearances. One is to say that what I've just described are only appearances. That is, one possibility is to deny that there are genuine cases of non-sentential speech acts of the sort just introduced. One must then go on to explain away the appearances. The other possibility is to say that the reason people appear to use subsentential things to perform speech acts is because that's what they really do. (Compare: "The reason the car over there looks purple is because it is purple." This certainly accounts for the appearances.) Taking this second route, the burden is not to "explain away," but to "explain how." Specifically, to explain how speakers manage to do this – a non-trivial task since, as just noted, if the phenomenon is genuine there is an important gap between the meaning of the things used and the nature and content of the act itself. Much of this chapter will be dedicated to exploring these two responses to the just-described appearances.[6]

2   Rejecting the Appearances: Introducing the Options

In this section, I consider a number of attempts to explain away the appearances.

2.1   Not a genuine speech act

Notice that what appears to be the case is a conjunction: it appears that, in some cases anyway, speakers produce non-sentences and in so doing they perform a speech act. One obvious maneuver in resisting the appearances is to go after the second conjunct: to deny that a genuine speech act is ever performed when something less-than-sentential is produced. Let's explore this option. (Doing so will also help clarify what the second conjunct actually commits one to.)

It would be difficult to maintain that speakers and writers only utter complete sentences, even allowing for performance errors, slips of the tongue, and outright grammatical mistakes. To give just a few obvious examples, book titles are often single words or phrases: *Symbolic Logic*, *Language*, etc. And, of course, there are signs that simply say *Exit* and *Fire extinguisher*. In addition, borrowing an example from Shopen (1973), we affix phrasal labels to objects, e.g. *strawberry jam*. There are spoken cases too: if someone really wanted to, she surely could stand on a street corner and just repeat the word *cymbidium*. (According to my dictionary, this word refers to some kind of orchid.) It's hopeless to insist that in all these cases there is a sentence employed: people surely can, and they surely do, produce plain old words and phrases. The conjunction above requires more than this, however. It requires not only that words and phrases be uttered, but also that such utterances sometimes result in the speaker having performed a speech act: a conventional linguistic act like naming a ship or making a promise, a request, or an assertion, etc. But notice that when the *Exit* sign is posted there is no assertion made. No question is asked by the person who constantly repeats the word *cymbidium*. No promise is issued by the book title. It seems reasonable to say that in these cases there is simply no ILLOCUTIONARY ACT at all: there might be language use, but there is no speech act properly so called. Having noticed cases of non-sentential speech in which no speech act is made, the next step would be to argue that whenever a mere word or phrase is uttered, no speech act results (putting aside, as noted at the outset, answers to questions, repairs, and the like). True enough, goes this line of thought, people utter mere words in isolation – but they do not thereby "make a move in the language game," to use Wittgenstein's famous phrase. Put otherwise, the path of less resistance for the theorist who wishes to reject the appearances is to simply deny that a speech act is performed in subsentential speech of the kind here under consideration.

Unfortunately for those who want to explain away the appearances in this way, this line of argument seems unlikely to succeed. There may be cases that initially look like speech acts but in which one can make the case that appearances mislead. Stanley (2000) gives the example of a thirsty man, emerging parched and sunburned from the desert, who scratchily utters, "water." Stanley says that this isn't determinately a request, or an assertion, or an order; as such, it might be written off as subsentential but not genuinely a speech act. Maybe that's right. On the other hand, there are lots of cases, like Leah's utterance to Anita, that are lie-prone, and hence really are assertions. And there are lots of non-sentential utterances that are clearly questions. And others which are promises. And so on.[7] So, while this strategy might allow one to explain away some apparent cases of non-sentential speech acts – e.g. an utterance of *water* by the thirsty man – it cannot on its own explain away the appearances described in section 1.

2.2   Three senses of "ellipsis"

The next obvious means of explaining away the appearances is to suppose that whenever a genuine speech act is performed, the speaker actually uses a sentence. To account for the appearances, specifically the sound produced by the speaker, one would then have to claim that the thing used was an ELLIPTICAL SENTENCE. This despite the fact that the utterance is not an answer to an explicit question, or a repair. This questions not the second conjunct, but the first: there are genuine speech acts being performed, in the cases at hand, but they aren't in fact performed using non-sentences – because elliptical sentences are a kind of sentence. So, if this maneuver works, what appears to be non-sentential speech is really sentential after all.

Now, there are lots of things that might be meant by the word "ellipsis." It's not possible to canvass them exhaustively here (but see Huang, this volume). Instead, I'll introduce two promising possibilities.[8] Before I do so, however, I want to issue a warning. One might say "That's ellipsis" about an apparently non-sentential speech act, and simply mean: The speaker produced words that mean less than the complete thought that she communicated. Thus, put pretheoretically, she "spoke elliptically." To anticipate: I think that this is true, but that it doesn't help to reject the appearances. To explain why, consider a comparison. If I say "Postal, Ross, Lakoff, et al.," one might describe me as "speaking elliptically" about early Generative Semanticists. Or, I if say, "John has finished," meaning that he has finished eating dinner, I do not explicitly say what it is that he has finished – hence one might again describe this, pretheoretically, as "speaking elliptically." But in neither of these cases is it imagined that somehow, under my breath as it were, I really uttered more linguistic material than what one hears on the surface. I did not utter the phrase *early Generative Semanticists*, nor did I utter the phrase *eating dinner*. The only sense in which I spoke elliptically is that I let the hearer fill in contextually available information for herself – I did not produce a special "elliptical" expression.

But now, if this sort of thing is all that is meant by the term *ellipsis*, then one cannot explain away the appearances described in section 1 by appealing to ellipsis. Instead, in saying "That's ellipsis," one is at best redescribing those appearances, using alternative vocabulary. No doubt the agent "spoke elliptically" in this extremely weak sense: the very description of the appearances highlights (1) the content "mismatch" between the expression used and the complete thought that the speaker of that expression meant; and (2) the key role of non-linguistic context in filling the resulting gap between expression-meaning and speaker-meaning. But to capture this fact by saying that the agent "spoke elliptically" is not to grant that the appearances are mere appearances. In particular, saying this is not to deny that the agent really did produce a word/phrase and really did not produce a sentence; on the contrary, it's to presuppose that the appearances reflect what is genuinely going on, in that a word/phrase was produced. Here is the warning, then: In what follows I will never use the term *ellipsis* in the extremely weak sense of a speaker meaning more than her words mean.[9] Thus, both varieties of ellipsis described below are designed to explain away non-sentential speech acts by not granting the existence of genuinely non-sentential speech acts.

Having issued my warning, now consider what I'll call "the fundamental feature of ellipsis." In ellipsis, the sound produced by the speaker is abbreviated *vis-à-vis* the message encoded, but the hearer can recover the complete message because the abbreviated sound somehow linguistically encodes that message. Thus, when a speaker means more than what his words mean that isn't a case of ellipsis, as intended here – essentially because the "more" that he meant is not linguistically encoded; instead, it is supplied by other means. Given the fundamental feature – i.e. abbreviated sound produced with complete meaning encoded – an issue that immediately arises is: how can this occur? There are at least two ways, as I'll now explain. (Readers already familiar with linguistic theories of ellipsis may wish to merely skim what follows.)

It is a truism of linguistic theory that sound patterns don't directly correspond to meanings. Rather, there is an intermediate level, syntax, the level at which words combine to make phrases, and phrases combine to make sentences.[10] What a sound pattern immediately corresponds to, on this view, is a syntactic structure; that syntactic structure, in its turn, corresponds to a semantic content. That is:

(6) Sound pattern → Syntactic structure → Semantic content

Given this tri-level picture, it's easy to see the two ways that a sound pattern can end up seeming "abbreviated" *vis-à-vis* the complete message linguistically encoded. There can be something irregular about the sound/syntax correlation, giving rise to the apparent shortening, or there can be something irregular about the syntax/semantics correlation. This yields two quite different notions of ellipsis, namely SYNTACTIC ELLIPSIS and SEMANTIC ELLIPSIS, respectively. Put in terms of (6), on one view ellipsis has to do with abbreviation occurring between level one (sound pattern) and level two (syntactic structure): this is syntactic ellipsis. (Some might equally call it "phonological ellipsis," but I'll use the more traditional term.) On the other view, ellipsis has to do with abbreviation occurring between level two (syntactic structure) and level three (semantic content): this is semantic ellipsis.

On the first kind of ellipsis, the correspondence between the sound produced and the syntactic structure of the utterance is not perfectly ordinary, in the sense that a comparatively "short" sound gets mapped onto a comparatively "long" syntactic structure (but the subsequent mapping from syntax to semantics is perfectly normal). VP-ellipsis is typically considered to be an example of this. Thus when a speaker pronounces the sound pattern /*John wants a dog, but Jane doesn't*/, this is short when compared with the corresponding syntactic structure, which (as a first pass) one might represent as in (7):

(7) $[_{S1}[_{S2}$ John $[_{I'}[_{VP}$ wants $[_{NP}$ a dog]]]] but $[_{S3}$ Jane $[_{I'}$ doesn't $[_{VP}$ want [a dog]]]]]

Specifically, (7) contains two VPs, whereas the corresponding sound contains a sound pattern for only one of them; the second VP is simply not pronounced.[11]

According to the second notion of ellipsis, the correspondence between the sound and the associated syntactic structure is perfectly ordinary, but the mapping from syntax to semantics is non-standard in that the comparatively short syntactic structure gets mapped onto a comparatively long semantic content. An example of such semantic ellipsis might be the word *cheers*. It is simply a word – specifically the noun $[_{N}$ cheer] in the plural form – pronounced in the usual way. This ordinary word could be used in a sentence as follows: *I heard cheers coming from the stadium, but I didn't know why*. But, someone might say, this perfectly ordinary plural noun, with its perfectly standard pronunciation, sometimes exhibits a special meaning – for instance, when it is said in a pub as glasses are raised. (What is produced in that circumstance might be called the "one-word sentence" *Cheers!*) Still, they could add, what the sound maps onto syntactically speaking is a plain old word. So, goes this line of thought, the connection between level one and level two is perfectly ordinary: what's odd is the mapping from level two, the plain old word, to level three – the special meaning.

One might wonder: if the speaker has simply used a word, with its ordinary pronunciation, what is meant by calling it elliptical? Just that, semantically speaking, this ordinary syntactic item "has a special meaning," here in the sense of being conventionally assigned a special use. (One might be tempted to claim similar things about *Out!* as uttered by a baseball umpire.)

How is semantic ellipsis different from syntactic ellipsis? Here is a heuristic for seeing the difference. As Sylvain Bromberger pointed out to me (in conversation), it doesn't make sense to ask about utterances of *Cheers!*: "What verb was uttered? What was the subject of the sentence?" There patently was no verb – and there was no grammatical subject. The sound that the drinkers produced corresponded to an ordinary word, *cheers*. Compare, however, the previous example of VP-ellipsis: "What was the second VP in the utterance of *John wants a dog, but Jane doesn't*?" is a perfectly reasonable question. The answer is fairly straightforward as well: the second VP was $[_{VP}$ want a dog].

Let me sum up this section. I began by considering whether a genuine speech act is performed when someone speaks subsententially. It seemed likely that, at least in many instances, that is the case. Given this, one cannot reject the appearances by saying that speakers who speak subsententially never perform speech acts. I then considered various senses of "ellipsis." I put aside an extremely weak notion, in which the agent "speaks elliptically." It is of course true that the appearances presented in section 1 involve the agent "speaking elliptically." But to say this is not to reject the appearances: it is not being denied that the agent produced only a subsentence; nor is it denied that a genuine speech act resulted. (For example, as I described the case, Leah made an assertion of a complete proposition, even though her words encoded neither a force indicator nor a semantic content of type $\langle t \rangle$. Thus, she meant more than what her words, even contextualized, meant.) If the appearances are to be rejected by appeal to ellipsis, a much stronger notion of ellipsis is required, one according to which the thing produced is actually, in some sense, genuinely a sentence after all. There are, I noted, two possibilities. Either the thing produced is syntactically a sentence (with the associated meaning of a sentence), though it doesn't sound like a sentence, or it is not syntactically a sentence, but the subsentential expression produced nevertheless has the content of a sentence. These two may be summarized as follows:

(8)   SYNTACTIC ELLIPSIS: Using an abbreviated sound pattern that corresponds to what is syntactically a more complete structure, which structure then linguistically encodes the complete message recovered.

(9)   SEMANTIC ELLIPSIS: Using an abbreviated sound pattern that corresponds to an equally abbreviated syntactic structure, but where that syntactic structure somehow linguistically encodes the complete message recovered.

Notice that both options respect what I called the "fundamental feature" of ellipsis. According to both, the sound pattern produced by the speaker is abbreviated *vis-à-vis* the complete message linguistically encoded. Where they differ has to do with how (i.e. where) the abbreviation occurs: the former has a non-standard mapping from sound to syntactic structure (but a standard mapping from syntax to meaning), the latter has a non-standard mapping from syntactic structure to meaning (but a standard mapping from sound to syntax). Having these two options on the table, we must now consider whether they successfully "reject the appearances" described in section 1 by explaining them away.

3   Challenges to the Ellipsis-based Rejection of the Appearances

Recall two of the examples introduced in section 1. Leah used *Sam's mom* on its own to say about the woman entering the room that she is Sam's mom. And Anita used *Moving pretty fast* in isolation to assert that a certain stock was moving quickly, in terms of its rising price. The syntactic ellipsis story, applied to these examples, would proceed as follows: Leah and Anita did indeed perform genuine speech acts, specifically, each made an assertion, but they did not perform genuine non-sentential speech acts because in both cases what they produced were sentences, reduced via syntactic ellipsis. What the sounds corresponded to, the proponent of syntactic ellipsis could say, were the full syntactic structures:

(10)   [$_S$ That [$_I'$ is [$_{NP}$ Sam's mom]]]

(11)   [$_S$ That stock [$_I'$ is [$_{VP}$ moving pretty fast]]]

And, of course, these structures linguistically encode the complete propositions asserted by Leah and Anita, respectively. So this explains both why the message recovered was fully propositional, and why it appeared that the speakers had produced mere phrases. (It appeared that way because the utterances did indeed **sound** just like phrases.)

The syntactic ellipsis gambit looks initially promising, but it is an open empirical question both whether it is a correct view of the cases at hand and whether it can be extended to handle a broader range of (apparently) non-sentential speech. My own view – argued for in Stainton (1997b, 1998a, to appear), as well as in Elugardo and Stainton (2001a, to appear) – is that it cannot. My aim in this paper, however, is simply to introduce the issue of non-sentential speech, and not to settle all the outstanding disputes. So I will rest content with explaining the syntactic ellipsis approach and noting a couple of the obstacles that it faces.

There are clear disanalogies between, say, VP-ellipsis and the sort of speech described in section 1. In particular, VP-ellipsis requires the presence of explicitly spoken linguistic material in prior discourse.[12] Indeed, this prior material must be such as to allow a purely grammatical reconstruction of the elided material.[13] Notice, for instance, that the elliptical sentence *Jane doesn't* typically cannot be used in DISCOURSE INITIAL POSITION. Nor can it be used in the middle of a discourse but without appropriate prior material. (Thus, imagine that Mary-Liz shows Paul a photograph of her daughter, in which the daughter, Karen, is smoking. Mary-Liz says, "Karen at school," and sighs. Paul cannot grammatically reply with *My daughter doesn't*, though he might well get his message across by so speaking. The reason is that there is some prior linguistic material, namely *Karen at school*, but there isn't the right sort of material – the sort that would allow a straightforward grammar-driven reconstruction of *My daughter doesn't smoke*.) VP-ellipsis is not a matter of the agent "guesstimating," on an all-things-considered basis, which material was omitted. Rather, it is a highly constrained algorithmic process that uses the "fragment" spoken and appropriate prior linguistic material to recover the source from which the fragment was derived. In contrast, as Barton (1990) first stressed, prior linguistic material is not required for the use of non-sentences. (Notice, in this regard, that both Leah and Anita's speech acts initiated a conversation in the examples described at the outset.) And understanding what is meant is very much a matter of the agent, drawing on all her relevant resources, "figuring out" from the non-linguistic context what the speaker might be talking about. It is not a wholly grammatical process, and it is very flexible about the sorts of linguistic material (if any) that precede it.

Another disanalogy is this: In VP-type ellipsis, the elided element is always a SYNTACTIC CONSTITUENT. One cannot choose to omit any old sequence, up to recoverability of the intended meaning. But look again at (10) and (11), the purported sources for Leah and Anita's utterances. What would have to be left out of them are, in each case, non-constituents – specifically *That is* and *That stock is*. Similarly, in familiar kinds of syntactic ellipsis, the remnant expression reflects the GRAMMATICAL CASE that the words would have had in the full sentence. This is not, however, a true generalization for non-sentential speech: e.g. in English one says "Me, me!" to get across that one wants a free T-shirt, though the corresponding sentence is not "Me want a free T-shirt" but rather "I want a free T-shirt." (Similar points apply to more richly case-marked languages such as German and Korean. See Stainton, in press, for extended discussion.)

There is, at present, no consensus about whether syntactic ellipsis can explain away the appearances. It does seem that if syntactic ellipsis is occurring, the variety of ellipsis in play is not one that can be assimilated to other, better understood, varieties of ellipsis. For example, it would be quite unlike VP-ellipsis (*Juan doesn't__*), sluicing (*I wonder why__*), or gapping (*Lucia lives in Spain and Alain __ in France*). Still, there are many possible moves that a proponent of syntactic ellipsis could make.[14] Rather than pursue the question further here, however, I will turn to how a semantic ellipsis account might work.

The idea, recall, is that the sound–syntax correspondence is perfectly normal, so that when it sounds like the agent has produced what is syntactically a word/phrase, that is precisely what she has produced. However, the syntax–semantics mapping is non-standard, since the word/phrase has a special meaning. This is why the message encoded is a complete proposition, even though the sound produced is abbreviated *vis-à-vis* that encoded proposition. Applied to the (apparent) non-sentence cases noted above, the idea would be that when Leah produces the sound /*sam's mother*/, she really did produce an NP. No subject, no auxiliary verb, no tense here: syntactically, what Leah uttered was just a single phrase. But this NP has a non-standard meaning. It is of semantic type $\langle t \rangle$, not of type $\langle e \rangle$.[15] Hence, in this crucial sense, the thing uttered wasn't really non-sentential; semantically at least, it was sentential. (Optionally, it might be added that the NP had, as part of its content, a force indicator.) Similarly, the proponent of semantic ellipsis will say that Anita really did utter the bare VP [$_{VP}$ moving pretty fast] but that this VP was assigned a non-standard meaning, namely a sentential meaning. This is what explains both what was asserted, namely the propositional content of the one-phrase sentence, and why it sounded like a mere phrase – because it was a mere phrase, though only syntactically speaking. This explanation shows, then, that what appeared to be non-sentential speech acts, though they are speech acts, aren't really non-sentential.

How promising is this approach? Well, appealing to semantic ellipsis may allow one to explain away certain isolated cases of apparently non-sentential speech. For instance, when the baseball umpire yells "Out," he clearly performs a speech act. But one can, it seems, reasonably reject this as a case of a non-sentential speech act – by noting that *out* here has a special meaning. What the umpire produced was syntactically a particle, the story would go, but it doesn't have the same meaning as when it appears embedded in complete sentences. Similarly for *Exit* signs, or cries of "Fire!" in crowded theaters: in each of these cases it's at least plausible to suppose that there is a special convention that establishes a special use, and hence a special meaning (including even a force indicator). However, it surely isn't plausible that every phrase in the language has two meanings, one that it exhibits embedded and one that it exhibits when used on its own, unembedded. As will emerge below, this would be far more meanings than one really needs to explain the speech observed. But such a duplication of meanings is precisely what the semantic ellipsis approach re-quires, if it is to be a general solution. After all, performance limitations aside – e.g. eventually speakers run out of breath – any NP can, in the right circum-stances, be used to perform a speech act. Ditto for every VP, PP, and so on. So each of them would have to have (at least) two meanings.

Let me stress: what would have to be postulated is a genuine ambiguity, rather than mere context sensitivity. Everyone grants that *She is a professor* can be used to make quite distinct statements, but it would be naïve indeed to conclude from this that the sentence type is ambiguous. What happens in this latter case is just that the meaning of the type – its character, to use David Kaplan's phrase – gets completed by having reference assigned to the index-ical *she*. Notice, however, that the sentence-type *She is a professor* is such that the meaning of each token is always a proposition. No token ever stands for an object, or for a property. What varies is simply who the resulting proposi-tion is about. This is not a difference in logical structure. Similarly then, if the phrase-type *moving pretty fast* were univocal, all tokens of it would share the same logical structure: they would all express properties. So if some token of *moving pretty fast* expresses a proposition, this must be because the expression type is ambiguous.

Here is a comparison. There is a rock band called *Better than Ezra*, and so one can say things like, "Better than Ezra will be playing the hockey stadium on Friday." Given this, some tokens of the (sound) type /*better than ezra*/ actually denote an object, namely the rock band, while others express the property shared by all things that are better than Ezra. As a result of this naming, the expression itself became not just context sensitive, in the sense in which *She is a professor* is context sensitive, but ambiguous: it became both a complex name and a one-place predicate, exhibiting both semantic type $\langle e \rangle$ and semantic type $\langle e, t \rangle$. Now, in the same vein, suppose that the sound /*better than ezra*/ also corresponded to what is semantically a sentence, as per the semantic ellipsis hypothesis now being considered. (This would account for why, for example, one may point at a surfer, exclaim /*better than ezra*/, and thereby say of that surfer that she is a better surfer than Ezra.) To capture this in the same way that we capture the use of /*better than ezra*/ as a name, the sound type /*better than ezra*/ would have to exhibit a third kind of meaning, a propositional meaning. Here is why. The proposition about the surfer could not result merely from filling in any indexical slots in the character of the one-place predicate [$_{AdjP}$ better than Ezra], since that would always yield a property, not a proposition; nor could slot-filling applied to the band-name version, [$_{NP}$ Better than Ezra], result in this proposition. Such slot-filling would (vacuously) yield the rock band as referent. Thus, if slot-filling is to yield a proposition, then the sound must have as one of its meanings something of type ⟨t⟩. That is, it must share the semantics of the sentence type *He/she/it is better than Ezra*. Thus the sound type would need to have three conventionalized meanings on this proposal.

Returning to the original cases, it really isn't plausible that *moving pretty fast* and *Sam's mom* have two standardized meanings, one of type ⟨t⟩ and the other **not** of type ⟨t⟩. (Where it is the latter, subpropositional meaning that the word contributes to the truth conditions of larger wholes, e.g. in *Sam's mom is in her car, and it is moving pretty fast*. Clearly **here** neither *Sam's mom* nor *moving pretty fast* contribute a proposition, even once contextualized.) So this method of rejecting the appearances is quite unpromising. Though, to repeat, it may allow one to explain away some apparent cases: *Out* as said by the umpire, for example.

Some theorists remain hopeful that the above strategies, possibly taken in combination, will allow one to "reject the appearances." Stanley (2000), for instance, proposes (very roughly) to treat some cases as not genuinely speech acts, some as syntactically elliptical, and some as semantically elliptical. He expresses the hope that such a divide-and-conquer approach will ultimately cover all cases of apparently subsentential speech acts. Others think this hope is in vain (see for example Clapp 2001). Unfortunately, the issue is too complex, and the relevant empirical questions too unsettled, to know for sure who is right, so I leave the issue here.

4 Accepting the Appearances

Suppose, for the sake of argument, that neither special syntax nor special semantics is enough to account for the appearances. It would, then, surely fall to pragmatics to explain how subsentential communication can succeed. (Notice that, for the pragmaticist, the aim would be to explain how, not to explain away.) The general strategy should be obvious: The person who speaks subsententially cannot be trying to assert an object, or a property, or a property-of-properties, or anything else non-propositional. Even if we could make sense of what that would be, doing it would not carry forward the talk exchange in an acceptable way. Thus, the hearer would inevitably recognize that the speaker must mean more than what his words mean (and the speaker will presumably intend for the hearer to recognize this, and so on). The hearer will, therefore, use all the evidence at her disposal to find out what the speaker likely did mean.

This general story seems plausible, at least to me. The question is, what exactly happens during this process? In what follows, I sketch one possible story.[16] It is uncomfortably speculative, but it gives a sense of the sort of tale a cognitively oriented pragmaticist might tell. To tell the story, however, I need to sketch by way of background two quite different conceptions of linguistic interpretation.

According to one way of thinking about language, a language is a system of shared rules – a complex algorithm – that, in advance of occasions of interpretation, determines the meaning of utterances. True, the algorithm needs to take as inputs not just the form of the thing uttered, but also a (quite limited) set of CONTEXTUAL PARAMETERS. But once speaker, addressee, time, and place are specified, employing a language is simply applying the algorithm in question: the speaker employs the algorithm, and nothing else, to "encode" her thought; the hearer employs the self-same algorithm, applying it to the form of the thing uttered and the contextual parameters, to decode the thought. End of story. Because the algorithm assigns meanings compositionally, and because the composition is recursive, knowing it explains the ability of speaker and hearer to interpret an (in principle) unlimited number of novel utterances in a systematic way. Taking a leaf from Davidson (1986: 437–8), who later came to have serious reservations about this approach, the idea is this:

> You might think of this system as a machine which, when fed an arbitrary utterance (and certain parameters provided by the circumstances of the utterance), produces an interpretation. One model for such a machine is a theory of truth, more or less along the lines of a Tarski truth definition. It provides a recursive characterization of the truth conditions of all possible utterances of the speaker, and it does this through an analysis of utterances in terms of sentences made up from the finite vocabulary and the finite stock of modes of composition. I have frequently argued that command of such a theory would suffice for interpretation.

It's worth stressing that "an interpretation" here means, at a minimum, an assignment of truth-evaluable content, at least in the case of declarative speech. So what the "machine" does is to take in sounds (plus some highly restricted set of contextual parameters for assigning reference to explicit indexical elements – i.e. speaker, addressee, time of utterance, place of utterance) and output something propositional. For ease of reference, let's call this the ALGORITHM IS SUFFICIENT (AIS) conception. On the AIS conception, employing a language emphatically is not a process of "guesstimating" what a specific utterance literally means. Guessing may play a role in understanding metaphor and conversational implicature, but it has no place in literal comprehension. True enough, it is creative – in the sense of being generative – but it is not creative in the sense of requiring cleverness and imagination.

A rather different way of thinking about language, a way that I personally find much more plausible, goes like this: A language is indeed a system of shared rules, a complex algorithm. Moreover, here too the algorithm is considered to be compositional and recursive. But the algorithm, though it is necessary, is not anything like sufficient for interpretation: the algorithm does not, in advance of occasions of interpretation, determine the meaning of literal utterances all on its own. Specifically, the algorithm often does not – even given the aforementioned contextual parameters – inevitably assign something propositional to the utterance. Rather, it (often) assigns something that must be COMPLETED or ENRICHED to arrive at something truth-evaluable. Thus, although knowing English is required for understanding English speech, it isn't enough – not even when supplemented by knowledge of the highly constrained contextual factors like addressee, time of utterance, etc. It is this second non-AIS conception of interpretation that will play a key role in the positive, pragmatics-based story about how subsentential communication works that I will present at the end.[17]

Employing a language, so conceived, involves not only the process of applying the algorithm, but some other process as well. It is the second process that does the enriching. Of particular interest recently is the idea that the additional process is one of drawing general-purpose inferences to arrive at all-things-considered judgments about what the utterance meant. (The idea being not that all things have been considered, which is impossible given the time constraints, but that anything that the person knows is relevant in principle.) Employing a language would thus involve two quite distinct processes, neither of which is individually sufficient for discovering the meaning of the utterance. The first process is algorithmic, but the second is not: It is non-deterministic inference. (Both processes are "creative," but in quite different senses: the former is creative in the sense of involving a generative procedure; the second is creative in the sense in which an artistic creation is.)

One way of thinking about the different conceptions is psychologically. (I expect, however, that proponents of the AIS conception would not themselves think of the difference this way.) The second conception is MODULAR, in something like the sense of Fodor (1983). In particular, the psychological concomitant of the non-AIS-conception goes like this: There is a language-specific subfaculty, in which the algorithm is stored; and there is another component of the mind-brain, call it the "Central System," where inferences get drawn; and both of these subfaculties play a role in both the production and comprehension of speech. (The second subfaculty plays a role in much else besides, of course, including the interpretation of non-linguistic communication. It is, I repeat, not language-specific.) In contrast, the psychological concomitant of the first conception would have to be either that there are not mental subfaculties at all or that there are such subfaculties, but that exactly one is employed in speech and interpretation. This would be the way of cashing out the idea that there is only one process at play – be it in "the mind as a whole" (the no-subfaculties version) or in exactly one subfaculty thereof. Put in COMPETENCE–PERFORMANCE talk, the two conceptions would see things this way: For the non-AIS-conception, more than one mental competence plays a causal role in yielding observed performance; for the AIS-conception, exactly one competence yields performance. (This may, in fact, lead one to prefer doing away with the competence–performance distinction altogether.)[18] In a nutshell, on the non-AIS-conception the psychology looks like this: there is a specifically linguistic process of decoding the signal to arrive at a representation of its meaning. This process has to do with what the expression spoken – the expression type, that is – means. That decoding is carried out by a task-specific module called the language module. On the other hand, there is a process of general-purpose inference, drawing in principle on all the information at the disposal of the agent (not, to repeat, in the sense of the agent actually accessing all of her information; rather, in the sense of all of it being in principle relevant). This second process is crucial not only for determining what the speaker meant, above and beyond what he said, but also for determining what the speaker literally asserted/stated/said.

Having drawn the contrast, I now want to apply the non-AIS conception to the understanding of non-sentential speech. Let's start with the complete sentence case, by way of introduction. On the picture I am assuming here, when a complete sentence is spoken, the linguistic decoder does not typically yield a truth-evaluable mental representation. Two processes, decoding and inference, are required even here. Still, when given a complete sentence the decoder does yield something – let's call them PROPOSITIONAL FORM SCHEMAS – which, once "fleshed out," are truth-evaluable. What "fleshing out" means here is: all indexical slots are filled, all vague terms are sorted out, and all ambiguities are resolved – but nothing more. That is, the process in the complete sentence case is as follows: the decoder outputs a propositional form schema, the Central System then fleshes out this schema (i.e. assigns reference to indexical slots, disambiguates, and sorts out vague terms), and these two processes together yield a propositional form.

Crucially, this is not what occurs in subsentential speech, or so I have argued elsewhere. In non-sentence cases, what the decoder yields is not even a propositional form schema, let alone a propositional form. Instead, it outputs a representation that, even after fleshing out, represents an object, or property, or property-of-properties. (For instance, in the *Sam's mother* case, we might suppose that what decoding-plus-fleshing-out provides is a mental representation that applies uniquely to the person who is the mother of the contextually salient Sam.) The mental representation produced by the decoder in subsentential speech cases must be altered to arrive at something which is truth-evaluable – i.e. to arrive at a propositional form; this much is the same. But the kind of "alteration" is importantly different: the decoded representation is not altered merely by fleshing it out, i.e. by assigning reference to existing slots, disambiguating, and sorting out vagueness. Rather, it is altered by **conjoining the bit got from decoding-plus-fleshing-out with another representation entirely**. This is what is distinctive about subsentential communication.

Where does that other representation come from? The sources don't seem any different than in the case in which a referent must be assigned to an indexical. Thus, the representation may come from long-term memory, from short-term memory, from the imagination, from a perceptual module, etc. What's different is how the sources are employed: they don't just help to assign a referent to a pre-existing natural language expression; rather they provide a whole new, not-in-spoken-language piece of the whole mental representation. Thus, returning to the original case, Leah and Anita could both see the woman in the doorway. Anita could, therefore, combine a mental representation from the visual faculty, which denotes the woman, with the mental representation resulting from the decoding/fleshing out. This would yield a sentential mental representation – not a sentence of English, mind you, but a propositional form in a mental language. In different examples, the "other representation" could come from memory or many other sources. The key point is that it does not come from the language module. This isn't so surprising, when all is said and done – at least once it's agreed that linguistic interpretation involves not one process (e.g. an algorithm that blindly takes structure-plus-contextual-factors to interpretation), but two processes, where the second process involves drawing inferences using all information available to the agent. If linguistic interpretation works like this, it is understandable that the inferential process could bridge the gap to pragmatically yield a complete proposition.

Notice, in conclusion, that this story does indeed treat the appearances as reflecting what is really going on. Speakers do indeed routinely produce subsentential expressions – nouns and NPs, verbs and VPs, PPs, etc. – and that is precisely what the hearer decodes. Moreover, the expression types produced are not just syntactically subsentential, but semantically subsentential as well: they are not of Montagovian semantic type $\langle t \rangle$, and they do not have force indicators as part of their content. And yet, in speaking subsententially, speakers really do perform fully propositional speech acts. This is possible because the hearer can understand the proposition meant by employing not only information got from linguistic decoding, but also information from a host of other possible sources.

Let me end this section with some questions. They are, I think, among the most pressing issues facing the pragmaticist who wishes to explain, in this sort of way, how subsentential speech works. The questions are:

1 How precisely does the representation of the object/property/etc., which doesn't come from linguistic decoding, get combined with the part that does? For example, how does the hearer know which object/property/etc. representation to use from memory, vision, etc.?
2 What is the representational format like, such that it is conducive to the combination of (i) something from linguistic decoding and (ii) a non-linguistic representation – retrieved from memory, or created in the Central System, or deriving from a perceptual module?

3   How do perceptual and other non-linguistic representations get into this integration-conducive format?

These questions are pressing, not just because they are inherently interesting, but because if they cannot be answered, then one is pushed back toward the "reject the appearances" approach. Depending on how one takes them, these questions either indicate directions for exciting further research, or they pose possibly devastating objections. It will be noticed, for instance, that these sorts of questions either do not arise, or are easily answered, on the ellipsis approaches. Some attempt to address these questions within a non-AIS conception can be found in Carberry (1989), Stainton (1994), and Elugardo and Stainton (in press). I leave them open here.

5   Summary

I began the paper with a couple of examples of non-sentential speech, also providing a more general description of what appeared to be going on in such examples. What appeared to be going on was this: Speakers utter things that are, both syntactically and semantically, subsentential, but they nevertheless manage to perform genuine speech acts (e.g. asserting) in so speaking. (And this isn't a matter of replying to an interrogative, or repairing a prior utterance.)

Having described the appearances, I presented two broad strategies for rejecting them. The first was to deny that a genuine speech act was being performed. This might work for some isolated cases, but it seems unpromising as a general approach. The second broad strategy was to deny that the speech episodes in question really were non-sentential. To make this latter idea plausible, it was necessary to introduce the notion of "ellipsis." I thus described three senses of ellipsis. Only two of them were robust enough to actually support the rejection of the appearances, however; the weak sense of ellipsis, it will be recalled, was essentially a redescription of the appearances, rather than a rejection of the reality of non-sentential speech acts.

The first "strong" variant, syntactic ellipsis, involved treating (apparently) subsentential speech as rather like VP-ellipsis. The second variant, semantic ellipsis, involved positing the existence of "one-word sentences" and the like with special propositional meanings (and, optionally, force indicators). Both variants of the ellipsis strategy, it emerged, face important obstacles, and only further research will tell us whether some version of the ellipsis story can succeed.

After exploring a few avenues for rejecting the appearances, I briefly sketched a pragmatics-based approach that accepts that the phenomenon is genuine. The key background presupposition for this cognitive-pragmatic approach was that there are two processes involved in speech-understanding, namely decoding and unencapsulated inference. Because of the latter, mental representations from many different sources can be brought together with mental representations derived from linguistic decoding. On this story, then, what occurs in subsentential speech cases is this: The linguistic decoder works on the (genuinely) subsentential utterance; it outputs a subsentential mental representation; and this gets combined with another (non-decoder-derived) mental representation to yield a sentential mental representation, which is not in any natural language. This latter encodes the complete message meant by the speaker.[19]

NOTES

1 For discussion of "completing fragments" of this sort, see Morgan (1973c) and Shapley (1983).

2 Actually, according to some recent syntactic theories *Sam's mom* is not an NP. Rather, it is a Determiner Phrase (DP), whose grammatical head is not a noun but a determiner. I'll ignore such issues for present purposes. For an early discussion of the use of NPs in isolation, see Yanofsky (1978).

3 If the jargon is unfamiliar, the following gloss will do: Speakers may utter any phrase, including in particular phrases whose "core" is an ordinary word. These latter are the lexical projections. Such phrases contrast with items whose "core" is a tense marker or an agreement feature, the latter two being the "core" of sentences. Examples of lexical projections include $[_{NP}$ a dog], $[_{PP}$ from Brazil], $[_{AdjP}$ red], etc.

4 This notation is introduced and explained in detail in Dowty et al. (1981: Chap. 4). For present purposes, however, the following will do: Once reference is assigned to all indexicals, an expression of semantic type $\langle e \rangle$ denotes an individual; an expression of semantic type $\langle e, t \rangle$ denotes a function from an individual to a truth value (equivalently, a set of individuals); an expression of semantic type $\langle t \rangle$ denotes a truth value; and an expression of semantic type $\langle \langle e, t \rangle, t \rangle$ denotes a function from a set to a truth value (equivalently, a set of sets of individuals). Note that, for the sake of simplicity, I am ignoring intensions throughout.

5 My thanks to Rebecca Kukla for the point, and for the example.

6 There are many possible implications of subsentential speech, implications about Frege's (1884) context principle, the domain of logical form, external determinants of content, the relationship between thought and "inner speech," the pragmatic determinants of what is said, etc. For extensive discussion of these possible implications, see: Dummett (1973, 1981, 1993); Stainton (1995, 1997a, 1997b, 1998a, 1998b, in press); Carstairs-McCarthy (1999); Kenyon (1999); Stanley (2000); Clapp (2001); and Elugardo and Stainton (in press).

7 For instance, imagine Leah is often late for dinner. Randy is giving Leah a familiar nasty look, as the latter goes out the door. She responds: "Seven o'clock. Without fail." Here Leah seemingly makes a promise to Randy to be home by seven o'clock.

8 Work on ellipsis exists in a host of distinct frameworks. For examples, see: Shopen (1973); Halliday and Hasan (1976); Sag (1976); Williams (1977); Chao (1988); Carberry (1989);

Dalrymple et al. (1991); Stainton (1995, 1997b, in press); Fiengo and May (1996); Lappin (1996); Lappin and Benmamoun (1999).

9   It's worth noting that some contributors to the literature do use "ellipsis" in this very weak way. One example is Carberry (1989). She thinks of the issues in terms of "understanding elliptical fragments," but she clearly means "elliptical" in the weak sense noted here, since her solution to the problem is not to explain it away (by appeal to elliptical sentences), but rather to explain how speakers/ hearers, using pragmatic information about discourse goals and the speaker's plans, manage to communicate using genuine subsentences.

10 It might be more accurate to speak of MORPHOSYNTAX here, since morphology is part of the "intermediate" level too. However, to simplify the exposition I will continue to speak of syntactic structure.

11 Actually, there are several quite different accounts of how the mapping between "short" sound and "long" syntactic structure is achieved. In particular, some accounts introduce not an unorthodox mapping, but rather an unorthodox resulting structure – one which contains, say, elements that have no pronunciation. (That is, the posited elements are in this respect like big PRO, or trace, in Chomsky's Government and Binding Theory.) Thus, regarding the present example, such a theorist might suggest that the corresponding syntactic structure is not (7) but:

(i) $[_{S1}[_{S2}$ John $[_{I'}[_{VP}$ wants $[_{NP}$ a dog of his own]]]] but $[_{S3}$ Jane $[_{I'}$ doesn't $[_{VP}\Delta [_{NP}\Delta]]]]]$

where Δ has no pronunciation at all. Williams (1977) offers a theory of this sort. For a useful survey of theories of ellipsis, see Chao (1988) and Lappin (1996). Good collections on ellipsis include Berman and Hestvik (1992) and Lappin and Benmamoun (1999).

12 Some apparent counterexamples can be found in Hankamer and Sag (1976) and Sag and Hankamer (1977). They discuss the sort of case in which, for example, a woman walks up to a cliff, and someone else says, "She won't." This looks like genuine ellipsis without appropriate prior material. For discussion of the implications of such cases for subsentential speech, see Stanley (2000) and Stainton (in press). The latter paper also goes into much greater depth about the nature of syntactic ellipsis and how it differs from non-sentence use.

13 In fact, the constraint is usually taken to be that deletion of material may only occur when the **identical** material occurs in the immediately preceding discourse. Put otherwise, only identical material counts as "appropriate prior discourse." For an early statement of the identity constraint, see Shopen (1973). Arguments for it, and refinements on the notion of "identical material," are provided in Sag (1976). But see note 12 for some possible hedges to this constraint.

14 For instance, it would be worth examining closely fragments apparently created by phonological deletion of initial material – especially of determiners, subjects, and auxiliaries. Examples include *Paper boy's here*, in which the determiner is left out, *Seems suspicious*, and *Guess I should be more careful*, in which subjects are omitted, and *Find what you were*

looking for? in which both the subject and the auxiliary are left out. For discussion of this interesting phenomenon, see Schmerling (1973) and Napoli (1982). They take it to be a quite superficial process, occurring at the interface of syntax and phonology, of the same sort that derives *'sgusting* from *disgusting.* Clearly not all subsentence cases could be assimilated to deletion of this sort, since what would need to be omitted would very often not be **initial** material, but some apparent cases of subsentential speech might be explained away in this fashion.

15 Or, if one wishes to be more of a Montagovian, the expression is not of type $\langle\langle e, t \rangle, t \rangle$. (Montague himself thought that all NPs, including proper names, actually stood for generalized quantifiers.)

16 A positive, pragmatics-based story is offered in rather more detail, and with supporting empirical evidence, in Elugardo and Stainton (in press); see also Carberry (1989) and Stainton (1994).

17 The AIS and non-AIS conceptions are not the only possibilities, of course: there are intermediate positions that assign the language-specific algorithm more or less weight in linguistic interpretation. The motivation for introducing the contrast this starkly is that it highlights how the accept-the-appearances strategy fits into a comprehensive view about language interpretation.

18 I realize that some will balk at reading psychological commitments into these conceptions, especially the first one. But, as I've repeatedly noted, I am not interested in exegesis here. My aim, rather, is to highlight a contrast by drawing

it starkly. Hence, I will not try to pin the two conceptions, or their psychological concomitants, on particular philosophers. On the other hand, it's only fair to give credit where credit is due, so let me note that I have gleaned the non-AIS-conception of interpretation quite directly from conversations with, and readings of, Sperber and Wilson and other Relevance Theorists; see Sperber and Wilson (1986a) and Carston (1988). See also Recanati (1989) for related discussion. Speaking of giving credit where it is due, it is also worth noting that Strawson anticipated the possibility of stating something with a subsentential expression some 50 years ago. He writes, in "On Referring":

> There is nothing sacrosanct about the employment of separable expressions for these two tasks [i.e., the tasks of forestalling the question "What (who, which one) are you talking about?" and the task of forestalling the question "What are you saying about it (him, her)?"]. Other methods could be, and are, employed. There is, for instance, the method of uttering a single word or attributive phrase in the conspicuous presence of the object referred to; or that analogous method exemplified by, e.g., painting of the words "unsafe for lorries" on a bridge, or the tying of a label reading "first prize" on a vegetable marrow. (Strawson 1950: 303)

19 I am very grateful to the following for comments on an earlier draft: Ash Asudeh, Andrew Carstairs-McCarthy, Ray Elugardo, Rebecca Kukla, Zoltan Gendler Szabo, and Gregory Ward.

13 Anaphora and the Pragmatics–Syntax Interface

YAN HUANG

ANAPHORA can be defined as a relation between two linguistic elements, in which the interpretation of one (called an anaphor) is in some way determined by the interpretation of the other (called an antecedent).[1] In terms of syntactic category, anaphora falls into two main groups: (i) NP-, including N-, anaphora, and (ii) VP-anaphora. From a truth-conditional, semantic point of view, anaphora can be divided into five types: (i) referential anaphora, (ii) bound-variable anaphora, (iii) E[vans]-type anaphora, (iv) anaphora of "laziness," and (v) bridging cross-reference anaphora (cf. Huang 2000a: 2–7).

Anaphora is at the center of research on the interface between syntax, semantics, and pragmatics in linguistic theory. It is also a key concern of psycho- and computational linguistics, and of work on the philosophy of language and on the linguistic component of cognitive science. It has aroused this interest for a number of reasons. In the first place, anaphora represents one of the most complex phenomena of natural language, the source of fascinating problems in its own right. Secondly, anaphora has long been regarded as one of the few "extremely good probes" (Chomsky 1982b: 23) in furthering our understanding of the nature of the human mind, and thus in facilitating an answer to what Chomsky (e.g. 1981, 1995c) considers to be the fundamental problem of linguistics, namely, the logical problem of language acquisition – a special case of Plato's problem. In particular, certain aspects of anaphora have repeatedly been claimed by Chomsky (e.g. 1981) to present evidence for the argument that human beings are born equipped with some internal, unconscious knowledge of language, known as the language faculty. Thirdly, anaphora has been shown to interact with syntactic, semantic, and pragmatic factors. Consequently, it has provided a testing ground for competing hypotheses concerning the relationship between syntax, semantics, and pragmatics in linguistic theory.

Anaphora clearly involves syntactic, semantic, and pragmatic factors. Although it is generally acknowledged that pragmatic factors play an important role in discourse anaphora, it is equally widely held that only syntactic and semantic factors are crucial to intrasentential anaphora. In this article, I shall concentrate on that type of referential, NP-anaphora known as BINDING in the linguistics literature. In the spirit of an ongoing debate about the interaction and division of labor between syntax and pragmatics, I shall first discuss the two main generative approaches to binding. I shall then examine some earlier neo-Gricean pragmatic analyses of anaphora. Finally, I shall present a revised neo-Gricean pragmatic theory of anaphora as developed in Levinson (1987b, 1991, 2000a) and Huang (1989, 1991, 1994, 1995, 2000a, b).

1   Generative Approaches to Binding

Two generative approaches to binding can be identified: (i) syntactically oriented, and (ii) semantically oriented.

1.1   *The syntactic/geometric approach*

The syntactic or geometric approach is formulated predominantly in configurational terms, appealing to structural concepts such as c-command, government, and locality. This approach is best represented by Chomsky's (1981, 1995c) binding conditions (see also Chomsky 1995c: 211 for the interpretative version of these conditions within the minimalist framework).

(1)   Chomsky's (1995c: 96) binding conditions
    A.   An Anaphor must be bound in a local domain.[2]
    B.   A pronominal must be free in a local domain.
    C.   An R expression must be free.

(2)   Chomsky's (1995c: 41) typology of overt NPs
    a.   [+anaphor, −pronominal]   reflexive/reciprocal
    b.   [−anaphor, +pronominal]   pronoun
    c.   [+anaphor, +pronominal]   −
    d.   [−anaphor, −pronominal]   name

1.2   *The semantic/argument-structure approach*

In contrast to the syntactically based approach, the semantically oriented approach attempts to give an account of binding primarily in argument-structure terms. Reinhart and Reuland's (1993) theory of reflexivity belongs to this camp.

(3)   Reinhart and Reuland's (1993: 678) binding conditions
    A.   A reflexive-marked syntactic predicate is reflexive.
    B.   A reflexive semantic predicate is reflexive-marked.[3]

(4)   Reinhart and Reuland's (1993: 659) typology of overt NPs

	SELF	SE	pronoun
Reflexivizing function	+	−	−
Referential independence	−	−	+

SELF = a morphologically complex reflexive
SE = a morphologically simplex reflexive

The paradigmatic patterns for binding are illustrated from English in (5):

(5)a.   Handel$_1$ admired himself$_1$.
   b.   Handel$_1$ admired him$_2$.
   c.   Handel$_1$ admired Handel$_2$.

1.3   Problems for both approaches

Cross-linguistically, both approaches are problematic. Let us take the binding condition A pattern first. To begin with, many languages in the world systematically allow long-distance reflexives – reflexives that are bound outside their local syntactic domain, and even across sentence boundaries into discourse. These include most East, South, and Southeast Asian languages (e.g. Chinese, Kannada, and Malay), some mainland and insular Scandinavian languages (e.g. Norwegian, Swedish, and Icelandic), some non-Scandinavian Germanic and Romance languages (e.g. Dutch, Italian, and Old Provençal), some Slavonic languages (e.g. Czech, Polish, and Russian), and others (e.g. Greek, KiNande, and Northern Pomo). The following is an example from Chinese:

(6)   (Chinese)
      Xiaoming$_1$ yiwei Xiaohua$_2$ xihuan ziji$_{1/2}$.
      Xiaoming think Xiaohua like   self
      "Xiaoming$_1$ thinks that Xiaohua$_2$ likes him$_1$/himself$_2$."

   In recent years, two general strategies have been established in generative grammar to tackle the problems posed by long-distance reflexivization for Chomsky's binding theory: (i) to deny that binding condition A is violated by claiming that a long-distance reflexive is not a true anaphor, and (ii) to modify the standard version of binding theory in such a way as to allow long-distance reflexivization to be accommodated by binding condition A. Under the first strategy, there are three ways to pursue such an escape route: (i) to argue that a long-distance reflexive is a (bound) pronominal; (ii) to treat a long-distance reflexive as a pronominal Anaphor; and (iii) to claim that a long-distance reflexive is an Anaphor of a special kind. Under the second strategy, there are also three tacks: (i) to parameterize the notion of local domain; (ii) to postulate movement at LF; and (iii) to relativize antecedents for long-distance reflexives (see also Cole et al. 2001).

However, as I have argued in Huang (1996, 2000a), none of these proposals really works. Let us start with the first generative strategy. First, what syntactic evidence there is shows that a long-distance reflexive is an Anaphor rather than a pronominal in the Chomskyan sense. Unlike a real pronoun, a long-distance reflexive cannot undergo topicalization, cannot be co-indexed with a non-c-commanding NP, and cannot be bound to an object. Secondly, if a long-distance reflexive were a pronominal Anaphor, we would expect it to be illicit in a syntactic position which constitutes both its Anaphoric and pronominal binding domain. One such position is the object position of an embedded clause. But this is clearly not the case, as can be evidenced by the grammaticality of (6) above. Finally, the distribution of such long-distance reflexives as *ziji* in Chinese, *zibun* in Japanese, and *caki* in Korean poses serious problems for the Anaphor in a special kind of analysis. On the one hand, these long-distance reflexives may be bound within their local domain, and on the other hand, they need not be bound in their matrix sentence.

What, then, about the second generative strategy? In the first place, as mentioned above, a long-distance reflexive need not even be bound in the root sentence. This would make any attempt to expand and parameterize the syntactically definable binding domain a very dubious enterprise. Next, contrary to the predictions of the LF movement analysis, there is no direct correlation between either locality and the X-bar status, or the domain properties and the antecedent properties, of reflexives. Finally, under the relativized antecedent account, the class of so-called anti-local reflexive in some South Asian languages remains unexplained (see Huang 2000a: 90–126 for detailed argumentation).

A second type of counter-evidence to condition A is presented by the distribution of certain morphologically simplex reflexives in such languages as Dutch and Norwegian. It has been observed (e.g. in Reinhart and Reuland 1993) that there is a contrast in the use of this type of reflexive between intrinsic and extrinsic reflexivization contexts: whereas a morphologically simplex reflexive can be locally bound in the former, as in (7a), it cannot be locally bound in the latter, as in (7b).

(7) (Dutch)
  a. Rint schaamt zich.
      Rint shames self
      "Rint is ashamed."
  b. *Rint veracht zich.
      Rint despises self
      "Rint despises himself."

There is thus evidence that, cross-linguistically, the distribution of reflexives violates Chomsky's binding condition A in both directions: on the one hand, a reflexive can be bound outside its local domain, and on the other, it may not be bound within its local domain.

How, then, does the cross-linguistic distribution of reflexives fit with Reinhart and Reuland's theory of reflexivity? Given (3) and (4), the ungrammaticality of (7b) ceases to require an explanation. This is because since (7b) contains a semantic predicate, it must be reflexive-marked in order to cohere with Reinhart and Reuland's binding condition B. But the SE-anaphor is not a reflexivizer and, as a consequence, cannot reflexive-mark the predicate, hence the ungrammaticality of (7b). However, the theory per se has nothing to say about long-distance reflexivization, given that on this account, binding is defined on the co-arguments of a predicate.

We move next to the binding condition B pattern. Once again, evidence from various languages casts serious doubts on both Chomsky's binding condition B and Reinhart and Reuland's theory of reflexivity. First, many languages in the world have no reflexives, and consequently utilize pronominals as one of the means to encode reflexivity. These include some Low West Germanic languages (e.g. Old and Middle Dutch, Old English, Old Frisian, and perhaps West Flemish and Modern Frisian), Bamako Bambara, biblical Hebrew, Isthmus Zapotec, the majority of Australian languages (e.g. Gumbaynggir, Jiwarli, and Nyawaygi), some Austronesian languages (e.g. Chamorro, Kilivila, and Tahitian), some Papuan languages (e.g. Harway), and many pidgin and creole languages (e.g. the Spanish-based Palenquero, and perhaps Bislama, Chinook Jargon, the French-based Guadeloupe, the Arabic-based KiNubi, Kriyol, Martinique Creole, and Negerhollands). An example from Fijian is given below.

(8)   (Fijian, cited in Levinson 2000a)
        Sa   va'a-.dodonu-.ta'ini 'ea   o   Mika.
        ASP correct   3SG-OBJ ART Mika.
        "Mike corrected himself/him."

Secondly, there are languages that lack first- and/or second-person reflexives. In these languages, first- and second-person personal pronouns double for use as bound Anaphors. Some Germanic (e.g. Danish, Dutch, and Icelandic) and Romance (e.g. French and Italian) languages, for instance, belong to this type.

(9)   (German)
        Du denkst immer nur an dich.
        you think always only of you
        "You always think only of yourself."

Thirdly, the use of a locally bound third-person personal pronoun in syntactic structures where its corresponding, third-person reflexive is not available is attested in a range of languages. This can be illustrated from Piedmontese in (10). Similar examples can be found in, for example, Catalan, French, Galician, Portuguese, Rumanian, Russian, Sardinian, Spanish, and Tsaxur.

(10) (Piedmontese, Burzio 1991)
      Giuanin a parla   sempre d' chiel.
      Giuanin CL-speak always of him
      "Giuanin always talks about himself."

All this shows that the use of a pronoun as an Anaphor in the world's languages is not highly marked, as Reinhart and Reuland (1993) claim. Consequently, neither Chomsky's binding condition B nor Reinhart and Reuland's theory of reflexivity can be correct. This is because given Chomsky's binding condition B, a pronominal is not allowed to be bound within its local domain, and by Reinhart and Reuland's binding condition B, a pronominal, being a non-reflexivizer, is not permitted to reflexive-mark a predicate.

Next, given the standard formulation of Chomsky's binding conditions A and B, it is predicted that Anaphors and pronominals should be in strict complementary distribution; that is, Anaphors can occur only where pronominals cannot, and vice versa. This is because the two binding conditions are precise mirror images of each other.

This predicted distributional complementarity between Anaphors and pronominals, however, seems to be a generative syntactician's dream world. Even in a "syntactic" language like English, it is not difficult to find syntactic environments where the complementarity breaks down. Well-known cases (cf. e.g. Kuno 1997) include (i) "picture" NPs (11a), (ii) adjunct PPs (11b), (iii) possessive NPs (11c), and (iv) emphatic NPs (11d).

(11)a. George W. Bush$_1$ saw a picture of himself$_1$/him$_1$ in *The New York Times*.
   b. Yan$_1$ is building a wall of pragmatics books around himself$_1$/him$_1$.
   c. [Pavarotti and Domingo]$_1$ adore each other's$_1$/their$_1$ performances.
   d. Pavarotti$_1$ said that tenors like himself$_1$/him$_1$ would not sing operas like that.

Worse still, when we take a look at a wider range of languages, we find that the total distributional complementarity entailed by Chomsky's binding conditions A and B stands on softer ground. First, as we have remarked above, there are long-distance reflexivization languages – languages that systematically allow a reflexive to be bound outside its local domain. In these languages, there is frequently a systematic syntactic distributional overlap between Anaphors and pronominals, as can be exemplified in (12).

(12) (Malay)
      Fatimah$_1$ mengadu bahawa Ali$_2$ mengecam dirinya$_1$/nya$_1$.
      Fatimah complain that   Ali criticize   self-3SG/3SG
      "Fatimah$_1$ complains that Ali$_2$ criticizes her$_1$/himself$_2$."

Secondly, following in part a suggestion by Burzio (1996), languages can be grouped into three types with respect to bound possessive anaphora: (i) those allowing Anaphors but not pronominals (e.g. Basque, Chechen, Danish, Gimira, Hindi/Urdu, and Mundani); (ii) those permitting pronominals but not Anaphors (e.g. Akan, English, German, Guugu Yimidhirr, and Spanish); and (iii) those permitting both Anaphors and pronominals (e.g. Japanese, Malay, Malayalam, Sinhala, Tamil, and Tuki). In the first type, the possessive and the antecedent are "near" enough to allow only a reflexive but not a pronoun, as in (13). In the second, because either there is no possessive reflexive in the language or the possessive reflexive cannot be used, only a pronoun is permitted, as in (14). Finally, in the third type, the possessive and the antecedent are both "close" enough to allow a reflexive and at the same time "distant" enough to permit a pronoun as well, as in (15).

(13)   (Ingush, Nichols 2001)
       Muusaaz$_1$ shii$_1$/cyn$_2$ bierazhta
       Muusaaz-ERG 3SG-REFL-GEN/3SG-GEN children-DAT
       kinashjka   icaad.
       book   bought
       "Muusaaz$_1$ bought self's$_1$/his$_2$ children a book."

(14)   (Akan, Faltz 1985)
       John$_1$ praa   ne$_{1/2}$ 'fie.
       John swept 3SG-POSS house
       "John$_1$ swept his$_{1/2}$ house."

(15)   (Oriya, Ray 2000)
       raama$_1$ nija$_1$/taa$_1$ bahi paDhilaa.
       Rama   self's his book read
       "Rama$_1$ read self's$_1$/his$_1$ book."

While Chomsky's binding conditions A and B make correct predications for the distribution of possessive anaphora in "Anaphors only" and perhaps also in "pronominals only" languages, depending on how the binding domain is defined, they certainly make wrong predictions for "both Anaphors and pronominals" languages.

Thirdly, still another type of distributional overlap is found cross-linguistically. This involves certain emphatic contexts. Emphatics can be either morphologically simplex or complex. Morphologically complex emphatics are usually in the form of "pronoun/reflexive + adjunct/modifier," with the adjunct/modifier having the meaning of "self," "same," "body," "head," "eye," "soul," "marrow," "seed," or – in the case of possessives – "own" (cf. Levinson 1991, Baker 1995, König and Siemund 2000). These morphologically complex emphatics can alternate with pronouns.

(16) Pronoun versus pronoun + "self"
      (Chinese)
      Feng xiansheng shuo gongyuan li   you ta/taziji   sheji
      Feng Mr   say park   LOC exist 3SG/3SG-self design
      de   baota.
      REL pagoda
      "Mr Feng says that in the park there is a pagoda he/he himself designed."

(17) Pronoun versus pronoun + "same"
      (French)
      François pense   que Viviane aime Pierre plus
      François believes that Viviane loves Pierre more
      que lui/lui-même.
      than him/him-same
      "François believes that Viviane loves Pierre more than him/himself."

(18) Pronoun versus pronoun + "own"
      (Italian, Burzio 1991)
      Gianni legge il   suo/il (suo) proprio libro.
      Gianni reads the his/the his   own   book
      "Gianni reads his/his own book."

We can thus conclude that the strict distributional complementarity between Anaphors and pronominals dictated by Chomsky's binding conditions A and B cannot be maintained.

In contrast, on Reinhart and Reuland's theory of reflexivity, the distributional overlap between Anaphors and pronominals is allowed in these cases. This is because the Anaphor and its antecedent, being non-co-arguments of the same predicate, are not subject to Reinhart and Reuland's binding conditions A and B. Put another way, in these cases, binding conditions A and B are met trivially by not applying. But whether this is a matter of design or accident is not clear.[4]

We come finally to the binding condition C pattern. Following Chomsky (1981), Lasnik (1989) argues that binding condition C be split into two sub-conditions, to be called binding conditions C_1 and C_2. Furthermore, he claims that while binding condition C_1 is subject to parametric variation, binding condition C_2 is universal.

(19) Lasnik's (1989: 154) binding condition C (my phrasing)
      C_1 An R expression is R-expression-free everywhere.
      C_2 An R expression is pronoun-free everywhere.

Binding condition C_1 says that an R expression cannot be bound by another R expression anywhere in the sentence, while binding condition C_2 dictates that an R expression cannot be bound by a pronoun anywhere in the sentence.

But this way of looking at binding condition C is not seriously tenable. Take binding condition C_1 first. It can easily be frustrated cross-linguistically, especially in some East, South, and Southeast Asian languages such as Chinese, Bangla, Hindi/Urdu, Malayalam, Sinhala, Vietnamese, and Thai.

(20)   (Tamil, Annamalai 2000)
      kumaaree$_1$ kumaarukku$_1$ ediri.
      Kumar-EMPH Kumar to   enemy
      "Kumar$_1$ is enemy to Kumar$_1$."

Next arises the question of whether or not binding condition C_2 can be maintained universally. The answer is again negative, as the following classic example from English (Evans 1980) shows.

(21)   Everyone has finally realized that Oscar$_1$ is incompetent.
      Even he$_1$ has finally realized that Oscar$_1$ is incompetent.

In (21), the R expression in the second sentence is preceded and c-commanded by the pronoun in the matrix clause of the same sentence, yet it is bound by the pronoun, contra binding condition C_2. One proposal to accommodate counterexamples of this kind is to reinterpret binding theory as a theory of referential dependency, along the lines of Evans (1980). On this view, the reference of the pronoun in (21) has to be antecedently assigned in the previous sentence, and consequently, the pronoun can be accidentally co-indexed with the relevant R expression, in conformity with binding condition C_2. Such an escape mechanism, however, both over- and undergenerates. In the case of (22a), non-referential dependence between the pronoun and the second instance of *Oscar* should be possible, since there is a possible antecedent in the previous discourse. But this is not the case. On the other hand, in the case of (22b), the R expression should not be co-indexed with the preceding and c-commanding pronoun without invoking a previous context. But it is.

(22)a.   *Oscar$_1$ is sad. He$_1$ thinks that Oscar$_1$ is incompetent.
      b.   He$_1$'s doing what John$_1$ always does.

This indicates that Evans's proposal may not be valid in explaining away such counterexamples as (21). If this is the case, then there is no avoiding the conclusion that binding condition C_2 can also be falsified.

2   A Revised Neo-Gricean Pragmatic Theory of Anaphora

In the last section, I have shown that both Chomsky's binding conditions and Reinhart and Reuland's theory of reflexivity are inadequate to account for the binding patterns. In this section, I shall first outline a general neo-Gricean pragmatic theory. I shall then proceed to discuss some earlier pragmatic analyses of anaphora within this theoretical framework. Finally, I shall present a revised neo-Gricean pragmatic theory of anaphora.

2.1 Inferential principles in a neo-Gricean pragmatic theory

On a general Gricean account of meaning and communication, there are two theories: a theory of meaning$_{-n[on]-n[atural]}$ and a theory of conversational implicature (cf. Grice 1989). In the theory of MEANING$_{-nn}$, Grice (1989: 213–23) emphasizes the conceptual relation between natural meaning in the external world and the non-natural, linguistic meaning of utterances. He develops a reductive analysis of meaning$_{-nn}$ in terms of the speaker's intention.

In his theory of conversational implicature, Grice proposes that there is an underlying principle that determines the way in which language is used maximally efficiently and effectively to achieve rational interaction in communication (see also Horn, this volume). He calls this governing dictum the co-operative principle and subdivides it into nine maxims classified into four categories. The co-operative principle and its component maxims ensure that in an exchange of conversation, the right amount of information is provided and the interaction is conducted in a truthful, relevant, and perspicuous manner.

One recent advance on the classical Gricean account is the neo-Gricean pragmatic theory put forward by Levinson (1987b, 1991, 2000a). Aside from the unreducible maxim of Quantity, Levinson proposes that the original Gricean program be reduced to three neo-Gricean pragmatic principles, which he dubs the Q[uantity], I[nformativeness], and M[anner] principles (see also Horn 1984a, 1989, 1993 for a two-principle system).

(23) Levinson's (2000a: 76, 114–15, 136–7) Q, I, and M principles
    a. The Q principle
        Speaker's maxim:
        Do not provide a statement that is informationally weaker than your knowledge of the world allows, unless providing a stronger statement would contravene the I principle.
        Recipient's corollary:
        Take it that the speaker made the strongest statement consistent with what he knows, and therefore that:
        (i) if the speaker asserted $A(W)$, where A is a sentence frame and W an informationally weaker expression than S, and the contrastive expressions $\langle S, W \rangle$ form a Horn scale (in the prototype case, such that $A(S)$ entails $A(W)$), then one can infer that the speaker knows that the stronger statement $A(S)$ (with S substituted for W) would be false (or $K{\sim}(A(S))$);

    (ii)   if the speaker asserted $A(W)$ and $A(W)$ fails to entail an embedded sentence Q, which a stronger statement $A(S)$ would entail, and $\langle S, W \rangle$ form a contrast set, then one can infer the speaker does not know whether Q obtains or not (i.e., $\sim K(Q)$ or equally $\{P\,(Q),\, P\!\!\sim\!\!(Q)\}$).

  b. The I principle
Speaker's maxim: the maxim of minimization
"Say as little as necessary," that is, produce the minimal linguistic information sufficient to achieve your communicational ends (bearing the Q principle in mind).
Recipient's corollary: the rule of enrichment.
Amplify the informational content of the speaker's utterance, by finding the most specific interpretation, up to what you judge to be the speaker's m-intended point, unless the speaker has broken the maxim of minimization by using a marked or prolix expression.
Specifically:

    (i)   Assume the richest temporal, causal, and referential connections between described situations or events, consistent with what is taken for granted.

    (ii)   Assume that stereotypical relations obtain between referents or events, unless this is inconsistent with (a).

    (iii)   Avoid interpretations that multiply entities referred to (assume referential parsimony); specifically, prefer **coreferential** readings of reduced NPs (pronouns or zeros).

    (iv)   Assume the existence or actuality of what a sentence is about if that is consistent with what is taken for granted.

  c. The M principle
Speaker's maxim:
Indicate an abnormal, non-stereotypical situation by using marked expressions that contrast with those you would use to describe the corresponding normal, stereotypical situation.
Recipient's corollary:
What is said in an abnormal way indicates an abnormal situation, or marked messages indicate marked situations.
Specifically:
Where S has said p containing a marked expression M, and there is an unmarked alternate expression U with the same denotation D which the speaker might have employed in the same sentence frame instead, then where U would have I-implicated the stereotypical or more specific subset d of D, the marked expression M will implicate the complement of the denotation of d.

The basic idea of the metalinguistic Q principle is that the use of an expression (especially a semantically weaker one) in a set of contrastive semantic alternates Q-implicates the negation of the interpretation associated with the use of another expression (especially a semantically stronger one) in the same set. The effect of this inferential strategy is to give rise to an upper-bounding conversational implicature: from the absence of an informationally stronger expression, we infer that the interpretation associated with the use of that expression does not hold. Using the symbol +> to mean "conversationally implicate," we can represent the Q implicature schematically in (24).

(24)   Q/Horn scale: $\langle x, y \rangle$
       $y +>_Q \sim x$

(25)a. $Q_{\text{-scalar}}$: $\langle \text{all, some} \rangle$
         Some of my friends love Christmas carols.
         +> Not all of my friends love Christmas carols
    b. $Q_{\text{-clausal}}$ $\langle \text{know that } p, \text{ believe that } p \rangle$
         I believe that John loves Christmas carols.
         +> John may love Christmas carols or he may not love Christmas carols – I don't know which

Next, the central idea of the I principle is that the use of a semantically general linguistic expression I-implicates a semantically specific interpretation. The operation of the I principle induces an inference to a proposition that accords best with the most stereotypical and explanatory expectation given real-world knowledge. Schematically:

(26)   I scale: $[x, y]$
       $y +>_I x$

(27)a.   (Conjunction buttressing; see, however, Carston 1995, 1998b)
         p and q +> p and then q
                         +> p and therefore q
                         +> p in order to cause q
         John pressed the spring and the drawer opened.
         +> John first pressed the spring and then the drawer opened
         +> John pressed the spring and therefore the drawer opened
         +> John pressed the spring in order to cause the drawer to open

    b.   (Conditional perfection)
         if p then q +> iff p then q
         If you let me have a free Beethoven, I'll buy five Mozarts.
         +> If and only if you let me have a free Beethoven, will I buy five Mozarts

Finally, the basic idea of the metalinguistic M principle is that the use of a marked expression M-implicates the negation of the interpretation associated with the use of an alternative, unmarked expression in the same set. In other words, from the use of a marked expression, we infer that the stereotypical interpretation associated with the use of an alternative, unmarked expression does not hold (see also the Division of Pragmatic Labor in Horn 1984a, 1993, this volume). Schematically:

(28)   M scale: {x,y}
       y +>$_M$~x

(29)a.   The train comes frequently
         +> The train comes, say, every ten minutes
    b.   The train comes not infrequently
         +> The train comes not as frequently as the uttering of (a) suggests –
         say, every half an hour

Taken together, the I and M principles give rise to complementary interpretations: the use of an unmarked expression tends to convey an unmarked message, whereas the use of a marked expression tends to convey a marked message. Furthermore, potential inconsistencies arising from the Q, I, and M principles are resolved by an ordered set of precedence.

(30)   Resolution schema (Levinson 2000a)
       a.   Level of genus: Q > M > I
       b.   Level of species: e.g. Q$_{-clausal}$ > Q$_{-scalar}$

This is tantamount to saying that genuine Q implicatures tend to override I-implicatures, but otherwise I implicatures take precedence until the use of a marked expression triggers a complementary M implicature to the negation of the applicability of the pertinent I implicatures (see e.g. Huang 1991, 1994, 2000a: 205–12 for further discussion).

2.2   Some earlier neo-Gricean pragmatic analyses of anaphora

2.2.1   The Dowty–Reinhart analysis
Dowty (1980) represents the first attempt to partially reduce Chomsky's binding conditions to Gricean pragmatics within the context of modern linguistics, though the essential insights may go back at least as far as Lees and Klima (1963). He proposes a neo-Gricean pragmatic principle of ambiguity avoidance.

(31)   Dowty's (1980: 32) AVOID AMBIGUITY principle
       If a language has two (equally simple) types of syntactic structures A and B, such that A is ambiguous between meanings X and Y while B has only meaning X, speakers of the language should reserve structure A for

communicating meaning Y (since B would have been available for communicating X unambiguously and would have been chosen if X is what
was intended).

In the case of binding, what (31) basically says is that given the binding condition A pattern, the complementary binding condition B pattern can be derived
pragmatically.

This central idea of Dowty's is elaborated in Reinhart (1983). Reinhart (1983:
150ff.) maintains that a distinction must be made between bound-variable
anaphora and unbounded coreference. She further argues that while the former
should fall under the scope of sentence grammar, the latter should lie within
the province of pragmatics. Thus, on this account, bound-variable binding is
effected by a single co-indexing rule, which applies to both quantificational
and definite NPs and which incorporates both Chomsky's binding conditions
A and B. On the other hand, the mirror-image unbound coreference is left to
a Dowty-type, ambiguity avoidance pragmatic principle. Within the Gricean
framework, Reinhart puts forward a manner submaxim of explicitness and
formulates an "avoid ambiguity" strategy:

(32)   Reinhart's (1983: 167) submaxim of explicitness
       Be as explicit as the conditions permit.

(33)   Reinhart's (1983: 167) "avoid ambiguity" pragmatic strategy
       Speaker's strategy:
       Where a syntactic structure you are using allows bound-anaphora inter-
       pretation, then use it if you intend your expressions to corefer, unless
       you have some reasons to avoid bound anaphora.
       Hearer's strategy:
       If the speaker avoids the bound-anaphora options provided by the struc-
       ture he is using, then, unless he has reasons to avoid bound anaphora,
       he did not intend his expressions to corefer.

The pragmatic strategy in (33) operates roughly as follows. Given the co-
indexing rule, any speaker who intends a bound-variable reading will use the
pertinent syntactic structures, otherwise he or she will be in violation of the
submaxim of explicitness. If, on the other hand, the syntactic forms that are
required to encode a bound-variable interpretation are not employed, but
some other syntactic structures are used instead, then a pragmatic inference is
generated, namely that the bound-variable interpretation is not intended. Thus,
the Dowty–Reinhart analysis has laid the initial foundation for Levinson and
Huang to develop a more systematic neo-Gricean pragmatic theory of anaphora
(see also Horn 1984a: 23–25).[5]

2.2.2   *The Levinson–Huang analysis*
Building on the insights of Dowty, Reinhart, and Horn, Levinson (1987b,
1991) and Huang (1989, 1991, 1994) put forward the first explicit neo-Gricean

pragmatic theory of anaphora. In this theory, it is assumed that the general pattern of anaphora, stated in (34) and illustrated in (35) and (36), is largely an instantiation, in the realm of linguistic reference, of the systematic interaction of the Q, I, and M principles, mentioned above.

(34)   The general pattern of anaphora
       Reduced, semantically general anaphoric expressions tend to favor locally **coreferential** interpretations; full, semantically specific anaphoric expressions tend to favor locally **non-coreferential** interpretations.

(35)a.   Handel$_1$ adored his$_{1/2}$ music.
    b.   He$_1$ adored Handel's$_2$ music.

(36)a.   The rose$_1$ on the windowsill has come to blossom.
         The flower$_1$ is beautiful.
    b.   The flower$_1$ on the windowsill has come to blossom.
         The rose$_2$ is beautiful.

Returning to binding, Levinson (1987b) argues that if we accept Chomsky's binding condition A as a basic rule of grammar, binding conditions B and C can then be partially reduced to pragmatics by the use of the Q principle, on what he calls the A-FIRST analysis. In somewhat simplified terms, this can be achieved in the following way. If binding condition A is taken to be grammatically specified, binding condition B is then the direct result of the application of the Q principle. The use of a semantically weaker pronoun where a semantically stronger reflexive could occur will induce a classic Q implicature to the negation of the more informative, coreferential interpretation associated with the use of the reflexive. On the other hand, where a reflexive cannot occur, the use of a pronoun will I-implicate a preferred, more informative, coreferential interpretation. By the same token, binding condition C is then the direct outcome of the application of both the Q and M principles, the former applied to binding condition A and the latter applied to binding condition B. Whenever a reflexive could occur, the use of a semantically weaker R expression will Q-implicate the non-applicability of the more informative, coreferential interpretation. On the other hand, the use of a more marked R expression where a reflexive could not occur, and thus where a pronoun would normally fall under the I principle, will invite an M implicature to the effect that the otherwise I-implicated coreferential interpretation does not obtain.

However, as I have pointed out in Huang (1989, 1991, 1994: 123–4), there are some difficulties with the A-first analysis. One central problem is that it fails to account for long-distance reflexivization. This is attributable to the fact that the A-first analysis depends crucially on the acceptance of binding condition A as a basic rule of grammar, thus presupposing that reflexives and pronouns are always in complementary distribution on a given interpretation. Clearly, as we have seen in section 1.3 above, this is not the case with long-distance reflexivization languages. In attempting to tackle this and other problems raised by the A-first analysis, Levinson (1991), following in the spirit of proposals by Farmer and Harnish (1987) and Huang (1989), develops an alternative, B-FIRST analysis within the same theoretical framework. In this alternative, the pattern predicted by binding condition B is taken to be the basic pattern, from which the patterns regulated by binding conditions A and C can then be derived for free by the systematic interaction of the I and M principles. The argument goes roughly like this: assuming that the pattern characterized by binding condition B is the basic pattern of anaphoric interpretation and that reflexives and R expressions are prolix, marked expressions (as opposed to pronouns and zero anaphors), the use of a reflexive or R expression where a pronoun or zero anaphor could have been used will M-implicate the negation of the interpretation associated with the use of the pronoun or zero anaphor.

But the B-first analysis is also problematic, especially when applied to languages such as Chinese, Japanese, and Korean. For example, the analysis makes wrong predictions for both the binding condition A and C patterns of a certain type in these East Asian languages (see e.g. Huang 1989, 1991, 1994: 125–7 for detailed discussion relating to Chinese).

Finally, synthesizing his A-first and B-first analyses, Levinson (1991) puts forward his third and final analysis, which he terms the "B THEN A" analysis. As the term suggests, in this analysis it is assumed that, historically, reflexives derive from emphatic pronouns, and A-first systems are developed out of B-first ones. Subsuming Farmer and Harnish's (1987) DISJOINT REFERENCE PRESUMPTION in (37) under the I principle, the synthesis can be summed up in (38).

(37) Farmer and Harnish's disjoint reference presumption (DRP):
The arguments of a predicate are intended to be disjoint, unless marked otherwise.

(38) Levinson's (1991, 2000a: 346) "B then A" analysis:
(i) Presume clausemate co-argument disjointness, the DRP, a stereotypical presumption that can be attributed to the I-principle.
(ii) Establish a scalar Q-implicature contrast between reflexives and pronouns, based on the differential semantic strength of the reflexive and the pronoun, the former being necessarily referentially dependent, the latter only optionally so; the former suggesting subjective perspective and emphasis, the latter lacking such suggestions.

Now, given this account, where the anaphor and its antecedent are the co-arguments of the same predicate, the I-presumptive DRP will ensure that there is always a contrast in reference. Outside these positions, the Q presumption will ensure that a long-distance reflexive is contrastive, but not necessarily contrastive in reference.

While the "B then A" analysis undoubtedly constitutes an advance upon the previous two analyses, it is not without problems. For one thing, given that

⟨reflexive, pronoun⟩ forms a Q or Horn scale, the interpretation of a pronoun is parasitic on that of the pertinent reflexive. However, how long-distance reflexives themselves are interpreted in this theory is not clear. A second problem is that unless ⟨R expression, pronoun⟩ is taken as forming a Q/Horn scale, R expressions would remain uninterpreted, since there is no longer an M-principle in this system. But to posit ⟨R expression, pronoun⟩ as forming a Q/Horn scale would violate both the entailment and the equal lexicalization constraints on Q/Horn scales.

As an alternative, and based on a thorough investigation of anaphora in Chinese, Huang (1989, 1991, 1994) develops another analysis within the same theoretical framework. The basic intuition behind this account is that in languages like Chinese, Japanese, and Korean, except in cases where the anaphor and its antecedent are the co-arguments of the same predicate, there is simply a stronger preference for coreference than for non-coreference. In this theory, we assume that there is a distinction of referential dependence between reflexives on the one hand and other types of anaphoric expression on the other, and we attribute this to semantics. The interpretation of anaphora can then be largely determined by the systematic interaction of the M and I principles (in that order of priority), constrained by a world knowledge-based DRP and general consistency conditions on conversational implicature. In addition, a set of information saliency constraints are proposed to curtail the excessive power of the mechanism in some cases.

2.3   A revised neo-Gricean pragmatic account of anaphora

Having discussed some earlier pragmatic analyses, I now proceed to present a revised neo-Gricean pragmatic theory of anaphora, based on Levinson (1987b, 1991, 2000a) and Huang (1989, 1991, 1994, 1995, 2000a, b).

As I have emphasized in Huang (1989, 1991, 1994, 2000a: 212–14), the pragmatic theory of anaphora I have been advancing does not deny the existence of distinct syntactic, semantic, and pragmatic levels and modes of explanation in linguistic theory. On the contrary, it presumes the independence of an irreducible grammatical stratum for pragmatically motivated constraints: calculation of pragmatic inferences of the Gricean sort has to be made over a level of independent syntactic structure and semantic representation. What I have been arguing is that syntax interacts with pragmatics to determine many of the anaphoric processes that are thought to be at the very heart of grammar. If this is the case, then a large part of the burden of linguistic explanation concerning anaphora currently sought in grammatical terms may be shifted to pragmatics. The resultant division of labor between syntax and pragmatics may be summarized in a Kantian slogan: pragmatics without syntax is empty; syntax without pragmatics is blind (Huang 1994: 259, 2000a: 213).[6] What pragmatics does here is to provide a set of complementary explanatory principles that constrain the interpretation or production of an utterance whose linguistic representation has already been antecedently cognized. But these are important and indispensable principles for linguistic explanation, for as Horn (1988: 115) has pointed out, "an independently motivated pragmatic theory (or several such theories, on the compartmentalized view) should provide simplification and generalization elsewhere in the overall description of language."

The central idea underlying our revised neo-Gricean pragmatic theory is that the interpretation of certain patterns of anaphora can be made utilizing pragmatic inference, dependent on the language user's knowledge of the range of options available in the grammar, and of the systematic use or avoidance of particular anaphoric expressions or structures on particular occasions. Put slightly differently, anaphoricity is not a property of specific lexical items (as can be seen by the fact that binding conditions cannot be formulated as constraints on particular lexical items), but on uses of lexical items (see also Levinson 2000a: 270).

Applying the Q, I, and M principles, sketched in section 2.1 above, to the domain of anaphoric reference, we can derive a general neo-Gricean pragmatic apparatus for the interpretation of various types of anaphoric expression. Assuming the hierarchy of referentiality for different kinds of anaphoric expression in (39), along the lines of Burzio (1991, 1996), Levinson (1991, 2000a), and Huang (1991, 1994, 2000a), this pragmatic apparatus can be presented in (40), with a revised DRP given in (41).

(39)   A hierarchy of referentiality for different types of anaphoric expression:
       Anaphors < pronominals < R expressions
       (Anaphors are less referential than pronominals, and pronominals are less referential than R expressions.[7])

(40)   A revised neo-Gricean pragmatic apparatus for anaphora:
       (a)   Interpretation principles
             (i)   The use of an anaphoric expression x I-implicates a local coreferential interpretation, unless (ii) or (iii).
             (ii)   There is an anaphoric Q/Horn scale $\langle x, y \rangle$, where informally x is semantically stronger than y, in which case the use of y Q-implicates the complement of the I implicature associated with the use of x, in terms of reference.
             (iii) There is an anaphoric M scale $\{x, y\}$, where informally x is unmarked with respect to y or simpler than y, in which case the use of y M-implicates the complement of the I-implicature associated with the use of x, in terms of either reference or expectedness.
       (b)   Consistency constraints
             Any interpretation implicated by (a) is subject to the requirement of consistency with
             (i)   The revised DRP (see (41) below).
             (ii)   Information saliency, so that

(a)   implicatures due to matrix constructions may take precedence over implicatures due to subordinate constructions,
and

(b)   implicatures to coreference may be preferred according
to the saliency of antecedent in line with the hierarchy
topic > subject > object, etc.; and

(iii)   General implicature constraints, i.e.

(a)   background assumptions

(b)   contextual factors

(c)   meaning$_{-nn}$, and

(d)   semantic entailments.

(41)   The revised DRP
The co-arguments of a predicate are intended to be disjoint, unless one
of them is reflexive-marked.

There is good reason to believe that the revised DRP is not syntactic or
semantic, but pragmatic in nature: what it describes is essentially a usage
preference (see e.g. Huang 1991, 1994 for supporting evidence from Chinese).
On the other hand, however, the principle could be equally strongly argued to
be based on world knowledge, since the fact that one entity tends to act upon
another could be due largely to the way the world stereotypically is. The
advantage of attributing it to world knowledge is that it will automatically
either prevent any inconsistent pragmatic implicature from arising or cancel it
without violating the hierarchy Q > M > I.

At this point, it is useful to draw the reader's attention again to the distinction
of whether or not an anaphor and its antecedent are the co-arguments of a
predicate. If they are, then the predicate may be reflexive-marked. As I have
noted in Huang (2000a: 163–4, 216–18), a reflexive predicate can in general
be reflexive-marked in three distinct ways: (i) lexically, by the use of an inherently reflexive verb as in (7a) above; (ii) morphologically, by the employment
of a reflexive affix attached to the verb as in (42); or (iii) syntactically, by the
use of a reflexive nominal as in (5a) above or a grammaticalized lexeme typically denoting human body parts (including the body itself) as in (43).

(42)   (Kalkatungu, Lidz 1996)
marapai   karri-ti-mi   thupu-ngku.
woman-NOM wash-REFL-FUT soap-ERG
"The woman will wash herself with soap."

(43)   (Kabuverdiano, Schladt 2000)
Manel feri se   cabeca.
Manuel hurt 3SG-POSS head
"Manuel hurt himself."

Furthermore, the choice of one particular reflexivizing strategy over another in a language is in part determined by the semantics/pragmatics of the reflexive predicate in question. The meaning of the predicate can roughly be divided into two types here: self-directed and other-directed. By self-directed is meant that the action (or attitude) denoted by the predicate is typically performed by a human agent on him- or herself, whereas in the case of other-directed, the action denoted by the predicate is typically directed toward others. Evidently, events such as grooming, change of body posture, and some emotions such as being ashamed/frightened/proud are typical examples of self-directed action/attitude. By way of contrast, communication, violent actions and emotions such as love, hate, and being angry with/jealous of/pleased with fall standardly under the category of other-directed action or attitude (cf. König and Siemund 2000; see also Haiman 1985: 120–30, 168–74).

Now, of particular interest is that if we take a careful look at the relationship between the meaning of a reflexive predicate and the various reflexivizing devices a language has, a cross-linguistic, iconic correlation emerges (adapted from König and Siemund 2000):

(44) The predicate meaning/reflexivizing strategy correlation:
      The more "marked" a reflexivizing situation (e.g. other-directed) is, the more "marked" (i.e. more complex) a reflexivizing strategy will be used to encode it.

What (44) basically states is this: if a language has more than one reflexivizing strategy/form, we would expect that the simplex ones be employed for inherently reflexive predicates and other self-directed situations, but the complex ones be utilized for other-directed situations. Different languages, of course, may afford their speakers different means to conform to this correlation. In some languages (e.g. Modern Hebrew, Russian, and Turkish), we find a choice between verbal and nominal strategies as in (45); in others (e.g. English, Kannada, and Spanish), the opposition is between zero and non-zero anaphors as in (46); in yet others (e.g. Dutch, Norwegian, and Swedish), there is an opposition between morphologically simplex and complex reflexives as in (7) above, or between the morphologically simplex pronouns and morphologically complex reflexives, as in (47); or the choice may be between the use of simple versus non-simple emphatics (e.g. in Lezgian, Tsakhur, and Turkish) as in (48) (Huang 2000a: 219–20, König and Siemund 2000).

(45) (Russian)
      a. Milicioner umyvaet-sja.
          policeman washes-REFL
          "The policeman is washing (himself)."
      b. Milicioner zastrelil sebja.
          policeman shot   self
          "The policeman shot himself."

(46)   (Kannada, Lidz 1996)
    a. hari-yu   kannu-gaL-annu tere-d-a.
         Hari-NOM eye-PL-ACC   open-PAST-3SG-M
         "Hari opened his eyes."
    b. hari-yu   kannu-gaL-annu tere-du-koND-a.
         Hari-NOM eye-PL-ACC   open-PP-REFL-PAST-3SG-M
         "Hari opened his eyes (not in a natural way, e.g. with his hands)."

(47)   (Frisian)
    a. Rint skammet him
         Rint shames   him
         "Rint is ashamed."
    b. Rint hatet himsels
         Rint hates himself
         "Rint hates himself."

(48)   (Turkish, König and Siemund 2000)
    a.   yak-mak
          wash
          "wash"
    a'. yak-n-mak
          wash-EMPH
          "wash oneself"
    b.   vur-mak
          beat
          "beat"
    b'. (Ø) kendi kendi-si-ni   vur-du.
         3SG self   self-3SG-ACC beat-PAST-3SG
         "He beat himself."

Clearly, this distribution is explainable in terms of our M principle: to convey a marked message, use a marked linguistic expression.

With all this in place, we can now give a revised neo-Gricean pragmatic account of intrasentential anaphora. I shall begin with cases where the anaphor and its antecedent are the co-arguments of the same predicate. Consider (5). Since (5a) contains a reflexive predicate and reflexivity is marked in the overt syntax by a reflexive, the revised DRP is not applicable. Consequently, the interpretation of the reflexive is subject to the I principle, which induces a local coreferential interpretation. Next, the binding condition B effect of (5b) can be obtained by the operation of both the Q principle and the revised DRP. By the referentiality hierarchy (39) and the I principle, a reflexive will be chosen if coreference is intended, because the reflexive is referentially most economical. This has the consequence that if the reflexive is not employed but a pronoun is used instead, a Q implicature will arise, namely that no coreference is intended. In other words, we have a Q/Horn scale ⟨reflexive, pronoun⟩ here, such that the use of the semantically weaker pronoun Q-implicates that the use of the semantically stronger reflexive cannot be truthfully entertained, that is, the coreferential reading associated with the use of the reflexive should be avoided. Reflexives are semantically stronger than pronouns in that (i) syntactically, they typically need to be bound in some domain, and (ii) semantically, they are normally referentially dependent. On the other hand, since the pronoun encodes a co-argument of a potentially reflexive predicate which is not reflexive-marked, it is also subject to the revised DRP. Thus, the potential local coreferential interpretation encouraged by the I-principle is ruled out twice, first by the rival Q principle (Q > M > I) and then by the revised DRP. Finally in the case of (5c), by the same reasoning, the R expression will again be read first by the Q principle and then by the revised DRP as preferably being disjoint in reference with the local subject.

One advantage of our pragmatic approach over both Chomsky's binding theory and Reinhart and Reuland's theory of reflexivity can be seen in accommodating those binding patterns where a pronoun is happily bound in its local domain. This is the case with (8), (9), and (10) above. Given the referentiality hierarchy (39), the pronoun becomes the most favored choice for encoding reflexivity in these examples. Since the revised DRP is not at work here, because reflexivity is marked by the pronoun in the overt syntax, the preference for a local coreferential interpretation induced by the I principle (as given in (40)) will go through unblocked. Thus, unlike Reinhart and Reuland's analysis, our theory allows reflexivity to be marked by a lower-ranked anaphoric expression (such as a pronoun) if its immediately higher-ranked counterpart (such as a reflexive) is not available, an analysis that is empirically more accurate.

But what is more interesting, from a pragmatic point of view, is the interpretation of cases where an anaphor and its antecedent are not the co-arguments of a predicate, about which neither Chomsky's binding theory nor Reinhart and Reuland's theory of reflexivity has anything to say. Regarding the reflexive/pronoun distribution in these cases, three types can be identified: (i) those permitting reflexives but not pronouns as in (49), (ii) those allowing pronouns but not reflexives as in (50), and (iii) those warranting both as in (12) above and (51) below.

(49) (Russian, cited in Burzio 1996)
      On$_1$ dal ej   umyt' sebj$_1$/ego$_{(*1/2)}$.
      he   let her wash self/him
      "He$_1$ let her wash himself$_1$/him$_{*1}$."

(50) John$_1$ said that *heself$_1$/he$_1$ is a basketball fan.

(51) (Korean)
      Pavarotti$_1$-un   caki$_1$/ku$_1$-kasalang-ey ppacyessta-ko malhayssta.
      Pavarotti$_1$-TOP self/he-NOM love-in fell-COMP   said
      "Pavarotti$_1$ said that self$_1$/he$_1$ was in love."

Note that in all these cases, the revised DRP is irrelevant, the anaphor and its antecedent being non-co-arguments of the same predicate. Now, in the case of (49), the interpretation of the reflexive falls under the I principle, which engenders a local coreferential reading. The interpretation of the pronoun is then due to the working of the Q principle. The use of a semantically weaker pronoun where a semantically stronger reflexive could occur elicits a classical Q implicature, to the effect that a local coreferential interpretation is not available. The same can be said of the "Anaphors only" cases of possessive anaphora in (13) above. Next, in the case of (50), because no reflexive is available as a possible candidate to indicate coreferentiality, by the referentiality hierarchy (39) a pronoun is used instead. Consequently, there is no Q/Horn scale ⟨reflexive, pronoun⟩ to prevent the pronoun from falling under the I principle, which gives rise to a local coreferential interpretation. The same is just as true of the "pronominals only" cases of possessive anaphora in (14).

Finally, of particular interest to us is (51), where there is a distributional overlap between the reflexive and the pronoun. Given the referentiality hierarchy (39), one question arises: why should there be such an overlap? One plausible view, due to Burzio (1996), is that this may be the result of a conflict between the "Anaphors first" condition (induced by the I-principle in our theory), which favors the use of a reflexive, and the locality condition, which goes against the use of a reflexive and therefore indirectly facilitates the use of a pronoun. Regardless of whether or not this explanation is on the right track, within the proposed neo-Gricean pragmatic framework (51) can be interpreted along the following lines. Both the reflexive and the pronoun are subject to I-implicated coreference. However, since the grammar allows the unmarked pronoun to be used to encode coreference, the speaker will use it if such an interpretation is intended. This gives rise to the question as to why the marked reflexive can also be used. Put another way, a question may be raised as to whether or not there is any systematic semantic/pragmatic contrast between the reflexive on the one hand and the pronoun on the other. The answer is certainly yes. Intuitively, the use of a reflexive in these locations indicates some sort of unexpectedness (Edmondson and Plank 1978). Examined in a more careful way, this unexpectedness turns out to be mainly of two types: (i) logophoricity, and (ii) emphaticness/contrastiveness.

2.4 Unexpectedness

2.4.1 Logophoricity

LOGOPHORICITY refers to the phenomenon in which the perspective of an internal protagonist of a sentence or discourse, as opposed to that of the current, external speaker, is being reported by some morphological and/or syntactic means. The term PERSPECTIVE is used here in a technical sense and is intended to encompass words, thoughts, knowledge, emotion, perception, and space-location. The concept of logophoricity was introduced in the analysis of African languages like Aghem, Efik, and Tuburi, where a separate paradigm of logophoric pronouns is employed. Cross-linguistically, logophoricity may be morphologically and/or syntactically expressed by one or more of the following mechanisms: (i) LOGOPHORIC PRONOUNS (e.g. Babungo, Mundani, and Yulu) as in (52); (ii) LOGOPHORIC ADDRESSEE PRONOUNS (e.g. Angas, Mapun, and Tikar) as in (53); (iii) LOGOPHORIC VERBAL AFFIXES (e.g. Ekpeye, Gokana, and Ibibio) as in (54); and (iv) LONG-DISTANCE REFLEXIVES (e.g. Chinese, Icelandic, and Turkish) as in (51) (see Huang 2000a: 172–204, and Huang 2002 for detailed discussion; see also Sells 1987, Zribi-Hertz 1989, Stirling 1993).

(52)   (Donno Sɔ, Culy 1994)
       Oumar Anta inyemeñ   waa be   gi.
       Oumar Anta LOG-ACC seen AUX said
       "Oumar$_1$ said that Anta$_2$ had seen him$_1$."

(53)   (Mapun, Frajzyngier 1985)
       n- sat n-wur   taji   gwar dim n   Kaano.
       I   say BEN-3SG PROHB ADDR go   PREP Kano
       "I told him$_1$ that he$_1$ may not go to Kano."

(54)   (Hyman and Comrie 1981)
       aè kɔ   aè dɔ – è.
       he said he fell-LOG
       "He$_1$ said that he$_1$ fell."

   The use of long-distance reflexives in examples like (51) can be accounted for in terms of our M principle. Since the grammar allows the unmarked pronoun to be used to encode coreference, the speaker will use it if such an interpretation is intended. On the other hand, if the unmarked pronoun is not used but the marked long-distance reflexive is employed instead, then an M implicature will be licensed. The implicature is that not only coreference but logophoricity as well is intended.

2.4.2   Emphaticness/contrastiveness

A second dimension of unexpectedness arising from the use of a long-distance reflexive involves emphaticness or contrastiveness. The use of an emphatic is in general subject to certain semantico-pragmatic conditions, such as those proposed by Baker (1995), and typically produces a number of effects: (i) contrariety to expectation, (ii) availability of a natural negative gloss of the sort "and not anyone else", (iii) inducing a particular anaphoric/referential interpretation, (iv) contrastiveness, and (v) the emergence of a particular scope reading (e.g. Edmondson and Plank 1978, and especially Levinson 1991). Witness (55):

(55)   (Chinese)

      Zhuxi   zongshi yiwei ta/ziji/taziji   dui, bieren dou bu dui.
      chairman always think 3SG/self/3SG-self right other all   not right
      "The chairman$_1$ always thinks that he$_1$ is right, but others are all wrong."

The use of *bieren* "others" is a clear indication that (55) conveys an emphatic/contrastive message. This seems to explain why, intuitively, the use of *ziji* and *taziji* sound slightly more natural than *ta* on the indexed interpretation. Furthermore, *taziji* is intuitively felt to be more emphatic/contrastive than *ziji*. On our account, the emphaticness/contrastiveness associated with the use of a long-distance reflexive again falls out naturally from the M principle: it is because the use of a reflexive in these contexts would carry an emphatic/contrastive message that would not be conveyed by the use of either a pronoun or zero anaphor that it is chosen. Furthermore, the fact that the use of *taziji* is more emphatic/contrastive than that of *ziji* can also be explained by the M principle. Given this principle, it is predicted that the use of a more prolix expression tends to give a more marked message, hence a more emphatic/contrastive reading for *taziji*.

Looked at from a slightly different vantage point, an iconicity principle is also in operation here, namely, the more coding material present, the more emphatic/contrastive the message. This analysis can be extended to the use of the morphologically complex emphatics in (16)–(18) and the "both Anaphors and pronominals" cases of possessive anaphora in (15). Furthermore, the repetition of the R expression in (20) may also be given a similar account, for it also seems to carry a contrastive, emphatic message " . . . but not anyone else." All this indicates that our revised neo-Gricean pragmatic theory can account for a range of facts relating to intrasentential anaphora that have always embarrassed both Chomsky's binding conditions and Reinhart and Reuland's theory of reflexivity (see Huang 2000a, b for an extension of this analysis to discourse anaphora). Another main advantage of our theory is that since conversational implicatures are cancelable, we can always arrive at an interpretation that is best in keeping with our knowledge about the world (see Huang 1991, 1994, 2000a for detailed discussion).

3   Concluding Remarks

In this chapter, I have discussed both Chomsky's syntactic and Reinhart and Reuland's semantic accounts of binding. I have reviewed some earlier neo-Gricean pragmatic analyses and presented a revised neo-Gricean pragmatic theory of anaphora. In recent years, this theory has generated other pragmatic analyses of anaphora (e.g. Kim 1993 on Korean, Blackwell 2000, 2001 on Spanish, and Demirci 2001 on the acquisition of binding of English reflexives by Turkish L2 learners), and significant progress can confidently be anticipated in the near future. Further, it is encouraging that recent versions of generative grammar seem to be moving toward the view of the pragmatics–syntax interface being advocated in this chapter. In the case of the minimalist program, given that the syntax/computational system is neither a phonological nor a semantic component, a large amount of current syntactic explanation has to be shifted to the LF and PF interfaces. As a consequence, syntax has inevitably to interact with semantics and pragmatics in a much more extensive way to link it to the mental world of cognition (e.g. Chomsky 1995c: 219–20). This holds, of course, for the study of anaphora. Similarly, the basic notions of Optimality-theoretic syntax are very much in the spirit of the revised neo-Gricean pragmatic theory I have advocated here. In fact, some of the insights central to an Optimality syntactic analysis such as competition, hierarchy and soft constraints (cf. Legendre et al. 2001) have already been independently developed in our pragmatic approach (see Huang 2000a for comments on some Optimality-theoretical analyses of anaphora). All this, I hope, will open the way for a more interactive approach between the I [internalized and intensional]- and E [externalized and extensional]-models of language study (Chomsky 1995c: 15–17) to be pursued in the search for a better understanding of anaphora.

ACKNOWLEDGMENT

I am grateful to Larry Horn for his comments on an earlier version of this article.

ABBREVIATIONS

ACC, accusative; ADDR, addressee pronoun; ART, article; ASP, aspect; AUX, auxiliary; CL, clitic; COMP, complementizer; DAT, dative; EMPH, emphatic; ERG, ergative; FUT, future; GEN, genitive; LOC, locative; LOG, logophor; M, masculine; NOM, nominative; OBJ, object; PL, plural; POSS, possessive; REFL, reflexive; REL, relative marker; TOP, topic; 3SG, third-person singular personal pronoun.

NOTES

1 There are at least two other distinct senses of anaphora/anaphor: (i) as an NP with the features [+anaphor, –pronominal] versus pronominal as an NP with the features [–anaphor, +pronominal] in generative grammar, and (ii) as "backward" versus cataphor as "forward." In what follows, I shall use capitalized *Anaphor* to refer to "anaphor" in the generative sense.

2 α binds β if and only if (i) α is in an A-position, (ii) α c-commands β, and (iii) α and β are coindexed (Chomsky 1981, 1995c: 93).

3   (i) A predicate is REFLEXIVE if and only if two of its arguments are co-indexed. (ii) A predicate (formed of P) is REFLEXIVE-MARKED if and only if either P is lexically reflexive or one of P's arguments is a SELF anaphor (Reinhart and Reuland 1993: 678).

4   But this does not mean that Reinhart and Reuland's theory of reflexivity does not have its own problems. As I have pointed out in Huang (2000a: 159–67), one of the crucial problems is that its central prediction that only a reflexive predicate can and must be reflexive-marked is falsified in both directions.

5   Chomsky has never put forward any systematic pragmatic theory of anaphora. However, in his work on binding, we can find occasional reference to pragmatic principles. One such principle is the "avoid pronoun" principle (Chomsky 1981: 65). Another is the general discourse principle (Chomsky 1981: 227) that allows binding condition C to be overridden given the appropriate context under certain circumstances, though the relevant conditions have never been spelled out by Chomsky.

In more recent work on the minimalist program, Chomsky (1995c: 138–43, 145–6, 150) has argued that both derivation and representation are subject to a kind of least effort guideline: there are no superfluous steps in derivation and there are no superfluous symbols in representation. The economy of derivation and representation is considered to be the functional driving force behind certain innate grammatical rules such as the last resort constraint on movement and the Full Interpretation Principle. Furthermore, on a more global level, this principle is linked to some notion of cost in relation to U[niversal]G[rammar] principles and language-specific rules. UG principles are less costly than language-particular rules; therefore, they obtain wherever possible, with language-specific rules employed only if they are not applicable. Chomsky considers the least effort principle of this kind specific to the human language faculty, but more compelling evidence is needed before such a claim can be substantiated.

6   Cf. Kant's original apothegm from his *Critique of Pure Reason*: "Concepts without percepts are empty; percepts without concepts are blind" (75B, in the Norman Kemp Smith translation).

7   Regarding the referentiality of empty categories or gaps, some can be grouped with pronominals, and others with Anaphors.

14 Empathy and Direct Discourse Perspectives

SUSUMU KUNO

1 Introduction

This paper discusses two functional perspectives – the EMPATHY PERSPECTIVE and the DIRECT DISCOURSE PERSPECTIVE – that are indispensable for the study of syntactic phenomena in natural language. These perspectives, like other discourse-based perspectives, such as PRESUPPOSITION and THEME/RHEME, that interact closely with syntactic constructions, help us distinguish what is non-syntactic from what is syntactic and guard us from mistakenly identifying as syntactic the effects of non-syntactic factors on the construction under examination.

2 The Empathy Perspective

2.1 The Empathy Principles

Assume that John and Bill, who share a dormitory suite, had an argument, and John ended up hitting Bill. A speaker, observing this event, can report it to a third party by uttering (1a–c) or (2a–b), but not (2c):

(1)a.   Then John hit Bill.
   b.   Then John$_i$ hit his$_i$ roommate.
   c.   Then Bill$_j$'s roommate hit him$_j$.

(2)a.   Then Bill was hit by John.
   b.   Then Bill$_j$ was hit by his$_j$ roommate.
   c.   ??/*Then John$_i$'s roommate was hit by him$_i$.

These sentences are identical in their logical content, but it is generally felt that they are different with respect to the speaker's attitude toward the event, or toward the participants of the event. It is intuitively felt that in (1b), the speaker has taken a perspective that places him/her closer to John than to Bill, whereas in (1c), the speaker is closer to Bill than to John. The notion of EMPATHY was proposed in Kuno (1975), Kuno and Kaburaki (1977), and Kuno (1987) to formalize this intuitive feeling and thus to account for the unacceptability of (2c) and many other related phenomena.

The following definitions, assumptions, and hypotheses are in order:

(3)a.   EMPATHY: Empathy is the speaker's identification, which may vary in degree, with a person/thing that participates in the event or state that he/she describes in a sentence.

b.   Degree of Empathy: The degree of the speaker's empathy with x, E(x), ranges from 0 to 1, with E(x) = 1 signifying his/her total identification with x and E(x) = 0 signifying a total lack of identification.

c.   DESCRIPTOR EMPATHY HIERARCHY: Given descriptor x (e.g. *John*) and another descriptor f(x) that is dependent upon x (e.g. *John's roommate*), the speaker's empathy with x is greater than that with f(x):

$$E(x) > E(f(x))$$

d.   SURFACE STRUCTURE EMPATHY HIERARCHY: It is easier for the speaker to empathize with the referent of the subject than with that of any other NP in the sentence:

$$E(subject) > E(other NPs)$$

e.   TOPIC EMPATHY HIERARCHY: Given an event or state that involves A and B such that A is coreferential with the topic of the present discourse and B is not, it is easier for the speaker to empathize with A than with B:

$$E(topic) \geq E(nontopic)$$

f.   SPEECH ACT EMPATHY HIERARCHY: The speaker cannot empathize with someone else more than with himself/herself:

$$E(speaker) > E(others)$$

g.   HUMANNESS EMPATHY HIERARCHY: It is more difficult for the speaker to empathize with a non-human animate object than with a human, and more difficult to empathize with an inanimate object than with an animate object:

$$E(human) > E(non\text{-}human\ animate) > E(inanimate)$$

h.   TRANSITIVITY OF EMPATHY RELATIONSHIPS: Empathy relationships are transitive.

i.   BAN ON CONFLICTING EMPATHY FOCI: A single sentence cannot contain logical conflicts in empathy relationships.

j.   MARKEDNESS PRINCIPLE FOR DISCOURSE RULE VIOLATIONS: Sentences that involve marked (or intentional) violations of discourse principles are unacceptable. On the other hand, sentences that involve unmarked (or unintentional) violations of discourse principles go unpenalized and are acceptable.

The Descriptor Empathy Hierarchy (EH) states that, given two descriptors *John* and *John's/his roommate* in (1b), the speaker's empathy with John is greater than that with his roommate. The Surface Structure EH says that, given *John* in subject position and *his roommate* in non-subject position, the speaker's empathy with John is greater than that with his roommate. Since these two empathy relationships are consistent, the sentence does not violate the Ban on Conflicting Empathy Foci, hence the acceptability of the sentence. I will schematize the above two relationships and the resulting conclusion in the following way:

(4)(1b)   Then John$_i$ hit his$_i$ roommate.
   Descriptor EH   E(John$_i$) > E(his$_i$ roommate=Bill)
   Surface Structure EH   E(subj=John$_i$) > E(non-subj=his$_i$ roommate=Bill)
   E(John) > E(Bill) [no conflict]

The acceptability of (1c), on the other hand, is accounted for in the following fashion. According to the Descriptor EH, the use of the descriptor *Bill* to refer to Bill, and of *Bill's roommate* to refer to John shows that the speaker's empathy with Bill is greater than that with John. However, the Surface Structure EH says that the speaker's empathy with the referent of the subject (i.e. *Bill's roommate* = John) should be greater than that with the referent of the non-subject (i.e. *him* = Bill). Therefore, there is a logical conflict between these two empathy relationships. This conflict has been created non-intentionally, however, by placing the agent NP *Bill's roommate* in subject position and the theme NP *him* (=*Bill*) in object position, as dictated by the subcategorization requirement of the transitive verb *hit*. That is, there is no intentional/marked violation of the Ban on Conflicting Empathy Foci. Hence, there is no penalty for the violation. The above explanation is schematically summarized in (5):

(5)   Then Bill$_j$'s roommate hit him$_j$. (=1c)
   Descriptor EH: E(Bill) > E(Bill's roommate = John)
   Surface Structure EH: E(subject=Bill's roommate=John) > E(him=Bill)
   Transitivity: *E(Bill) > E(John) > E(Bill)
   Markedness Principle for Discourse Rule Violations: The above violation is unintentional ⇒ no penalty

Now we can account for the marginality or unacceptability of (2c):

(6)   ??/*Then John$_i$'s roommate was hit by him$_i$. (=2c)
   Descriptor EH: E(John) > E(John's roommate = Bill)
   Surface Structure EH: E(subject = John's roommate = Bill) > E(him=John)
   Transitivity of Empathy Relationships: *E(John) > E(Bill) > E(John) [a violation of the Ban on Conflicting Empathy Foci]
   Markedness Principle for Discourse Rule Violations: The above violation has been created by the speaker's intentional use of a marked construction (i.e. the passive sentence construction) ⇒ a penalty

Note that the Markedness Principle for Discourse Rule Violations penalizes (2c) because the violation of the Ban on Conflicting Empathy Foci that the sentence contains is intentional. That is, the conflict in empathy foci has been created by the speaker's intentional use of the passive sentence construction, which didn't have to be used.

The marginality or unacceptability of sentences with a first-person *by-*agentive, as in (7b), illustrates the working of the Speech Act EH:

(7)a.   Then I hit John.

    Speech Act EH   E(speaker=I) > E(John)
    <u>Surface Structure EH</u>   <u>E(subject=I) > E(non-subject=John)</u>
    E(speaker) > E(John) [no conflict]

  b.   ??/*Then John was hit by me.

    Speech Act EH   E(speaker=I) > E(John)
    <u>Surface Structure EH</u>   <u>E(John) > E(me=speaker)</u>
    Transitivity: *E(speaker) > E(John) > E(speaker)
    Markedness Principle: The above conflict has been created by the speaker's intentional use of the passive sentence construction ⇒ a penalty

The marginality or unacceptability of discourses such as (8b) illustrates the importance of the role that the Topic EH plays in the Empathy Perspective:

(8)a.   Mary had quite an experience at the party she went to last week. √She slapped a drunken reporter on the face.

    Surface Structure EH   E(she=Mary) > E(a drunken reporter)
    <u>Topic EH</u>   <u>E(she=Mary) > E(a drunken reporter)</u>
    E(Mary) > E(a drunken reporter) [no conflict]

  b.   Mary had quite an experience at the party she went to last night. *A drunken reporter was slapped on the face by her.

    Surface Structure EH   E(a drunken reporter) > E(her=Mary)
    <u>Topic EH</u>   <u>E(she=Mary) > E(a drunken reporter)</u>
    Transitivity: *E(a drunken reporter) > E(Mary) > E(a drunken reporter)
    Markedness Principle: The above conflict has been created by the speaker's intentional use of the passive sentence construction ⇒ a penalty

Thus, (8b) is unacceptable because Passivization, which is an optional process, has been used intentionally to create a conflict in empathy relationships.[1]

Observe now the next discourse fragments:

(9)   Mary had quite an experience at the party she went to last night.
    a.   She met a *New York Times* reporter.
    b.   *A *New York Times* reporter met her.
    c.   A *New York Times* reporter asked her about her occupation.

Both (9b) and (9c) have a non-topic NP in subject position and a topic NP in non-subject position, but while there is nothing wrong with (9c), (9b) is totally unacceptable in the given context. The Empathy Principle accounts for this fact by attributing it to the fact that *meet* is a reciprocal verb. If two people (say, John and Mary) met, the speaker has the following four alternatives in reporting this event using *meet*:

(10)a. John and Mary met.
   b. Mary and John met.
   c. John met Mary.
   d. Mary met John.

The relationship that (10c, d) have with (10a, b) is similar to the one that passive sentences have with their active counterparts in that they involve the speaker's intentional choice of *John* and *Mary* in subject position, and *Mary* and *John* in non-subject position in (10c, d), respectively. That is, (10c, d) can be characterized as the passive versions of (10a, b) and thus constitute marked constructions. In contrast, if John asks Mary about her occupation, the subcategorization requirement of the verb *ask* automatically places the agent NP *John* in subject position and the theme NP *Mary* in object position. This difference between *meet* and *ask* accounts for the contrast between the unacceptable (9b) and the acceptable (9c). More schematically, the acceptability status of the three sentences in (9) is accounted for in the following fashion:

(11)a. She met a *New York Times* reporter. (=9a)
   Topic EH   E(she=Mary) ≥ E(a *NY Times* reporter)
   Surface Structure EH   E(she=Mary) > E(a *NY Times* reporter)
   E(Mary) > E(a *NY Times* reporter) [no conflict]

   b. *A *New York Times* reporter met her. (=9b)
   Topic EH   E(she=Mary) ≥ E(a *NY Times* reporter)
   Surface Structure EH   E(a *NY Times* reporter) > E(her=Mary)
   Transitivity: *E(Mary) ≥ E(a *NY Times* reporter) > E(Mary)
   Markedness Principle: The above conflict has been created by the speaker's intentional choice of a non-topic NP as subject of *meet* ⇒ a penalty

   c. A *New York Times* reporter asked her about her occupation. (=9c)
   Topic EH   E(she=Mary) ≥ E(a *NY Times* reporter)
   Surface Structure EH   E(a *NY Times* reporter) > E(her=Mary)
   Transitivity: *E(Mary) ≥ E(a *NY Times* reporter) > E(Mary)
   Markedness Principle for Discourse Rule Violations: The above violation is unintentional ⇒ no penalty

Observe next the following sentences:

(12)a.   John told Mary that Jane was seriously sick.
   b.   Mary heard from John that Jane was seriously sick.

(13)a.   John sent Mary a Valentine's Day present.
   b.   Mary received from John a Valentine's Day present.

Hear from in (12b) and *receive from* in (13b) are marked verbs in the sense that they place non-agent NPs in subject position and agent NPs in non-subject position. That is, they are like passive verbs in that they represent the speaker's intentional choice of non-agent NPs in subject position. This fact accounts for the acceptability status of the following sentences:

(14)a.   I told Mary that Jane was seriously sick.
   b.   ??Mary heard from me that Jane was seriously sick.

(15)a.   I sent Mary a Valentine's Day present.
   b.   ??Mary received from me a Valentine's Day present.

(14b) and (15b) are marginal out of context because they contain a conflict in empathy relationships just as (7b) does, which conflict has been created by the speaker's use of the marked verbs *hear from* and *receive from*.[2]
   Now, we can account for the acceptability status of the following sentences:

(16)a.   John$_i$ told Mary$_j$ what she$_j$ had told him$_i$ two days before.
   b.   John$_i$ told Mary$_j$ what he$_i$ had heard from her$_j$ two days before.
   c.   Mary$_j$ heard from John$_i$ what she$_j$ had told him$_i$ two days before.
   d.   ??Mary$_j$ heard from John$_i$ what he$_i$ had heard from her$_j$ two days before.[3]

I give below the empathy relationships represented by the main clause and the embedded clause of each of (16a–d). I use the notation "E(x) m> E(y)" if the empathy relationship is derived from the Surface Structure EH due to the use of **marked** patterns (e.g. the passive construction and special verbs such as *meet, hear from,* and *receive from*).

(17)a.   John$_i$ told Mary$_j$ what she$_j$ had told him$_i$ two days before. (=16a)
      Surface Structure EH
         Main Clause: E(John) > E(Mary)
         Embedded Clause: E(she=Mary) > E(him=John)
      Transitivity: *E(John) > E(Mary) > E(John)
      Markedness Principle: No marked patterns are used ⇒ no penalty

   b.   John$_i$ told Mary$_j$ what he$_i$ had heard from her$_j$ two days before. (=16b)
      Surface Structure EH
         Main Clause: E(John) > E(Mary)
         Embedded Clause: E(he=John) m> E(her=Mary)
                                   No conflict

c.   Mary$_j$ heard from John$_i$ what she$_j$ had told him$_i$ two days before. (=16c)
     Surface Structure EH

Main Clause:	E(Mary) m> E(John)
<u>Embedded Clause:</u>	<u>E(she=Mary) > E(him=John)</u>
	No conflict

d.   ??Mary$_j$ heard from John$_i$ what he$_i$ had heard from her$_j$ two days before. (=16d)
     Surface Structure EH

Main Clause:	E(Mary) m> E(John)
<u>Embedded Clause:</u>	<u>E(he=John) m> E(her=Mary)</u>

Transitivity: *E(Mary) m> E(John) m> E(Mary)
Markedness Principle: The above conflict has been created by the intentional use of the marked verb *hear from* ⇒ penalty

The Markedness Principle for Discourse Rule Violations states that conflicts in empathy relationships attributable to the speaker's intentional use of marked constructions result in unacceptability, but when there is a good reason for using such a construction, an ensuing conflict in empathy relationships does not result in a penalty. Observe, for example, the following exchange:

(18) A: John says he hasn't met you before.
      B: That's not correct. He met me last year at Mary's party.
          Empathy Relationships for "He met me last year . . ."

Speech Act EH	E(speaker=me) > E(non-speaker=he)
<u>Surface Structure EH</u>	<u>E(subj=he) m> E(non-subj=me)</u>

          Transitivity: *E(I) > E(he) m> E(I)

The sentence *he met me last year at Mary's party* in Speaker B's answer involves the use of the marked verb *meet*, and therefore, there should be a penalty for the conflict in the empathy relationships that the sentence contains. In spite of this fact, the sentence is perfectly acceptable in the given context. I attribute this to the application of the following principle:

(19) THE CORRECTIVE SENTENCE PATTERN REQUIREMENT: In correcting a portion of a sentence uttered by someone else maintain the same sentence pattern and change only that portion of the sentence that needs to be corrected, together with necessary tense and personal pronoun switches.

Speaker B wants to correct Speaker A's remark that "he [John] hasn't met you before." In accordance with the Corrective Sentence Pattern Requirement, Speaker B maintains the same sentence pattern, keeping *he* (*John*) in subject position, but switching *you* in object position to *me* referring to the speaker himself/herself. Thus, the conflict in empathy relationships contained in Speaker B's answer in (18) is not by design, but is required by the Corrective Sentence

Pattern Requirement. Thus there is no intentionality in the conflict, and hence there is no penalty for the conflict.

There is another discourse principle that makes sentences involving empathy relationship conflicts acceptable. Observe first the following sentences:

(20)a.   John read *War and Peace* last night.
   b.   ??/*War and Peace* was read by John last night.

The unacceptability of (20b) is due to the fact that an inanimate NP is in subject position in a passive sentence construction:

(21)   Empathy Relationships for (20b)
       Humanness EH   E(John) > E(*War and Peace*)
       Surface Structure EH   E(*War and Peace*) m> E(John)
       Transitivity: *E(John) > E(*War and Peace*) m> E(John)
       Markedness Principle: The above conflict has been created by the speaker's intentional use of the passive sentence construction ⇒ a penalty

The above accounting for the unacceptability of (20b) predicts that the following sentences should be as marginal or unacceptable as (20b), but these sentences are perfectly acceptable:

(22)a.   *War and Peace* was written by Tolstoy.
   b.   *War and Peace* has been read by millions of people all over the world.
   c.   *War and Peace* has been read even by Bill.

The difference between the unacceptable (20b) and the acceptable (22a–c) lies in the fact that while the latter sentences characterize what kind of book *War and Peace* is, the former does not have such a characterizational property. That is, the fact that Tolstoy wrote *War and Peace* gives a robust characterization of the novel. The fact that millions and millions of people all over the world have read the novel says what kind of book it is. Likewise, the fact that even Bill – apparently someone who doesn't ordinarily read books – has read the book implicates that many other people have read it, and characterizes what kind of book it is. In contrast, (20b) cannot be interpreted as a characterizational sentence: a single event of John's reading the novel doesn't characterize what kind of book it is.

Given that passive sentences with inanimate subjects and human *by*-agentives are acceptable if they robustly characterize the referents of the subject NPs, we still need to explain why the empathy relationship conflicts created by the use of the marked sentence pattern (i.e. Passivization) that (22a–c) contain do not make them unacceptable. It seems that this is due to the fact that sentences that characterize or define the referent of an NP are the most felicitous when that NP is placed in subject position. For example, observe the following sentences:

(23)a.   Whales are mammals.
  b.   Mammals include whales.

The above sentences are logically identical, but they are different in respect to what they characterize or define. That is, (23a) is a sentence that characterizes or defines whales, whereas (23b) is a sentence that characterizes or defines mammals. This observation leads to the following hypothesis:

(24)   SUBJECT PREFERENCE FOR CHARACTERIZING SENTENCES: Sentences that characterize/define X are most felicitous if X is placed in subject position. (Kuno 1990: 50)

We can now account for the acceptability of (22a–c) by saying that the empathy relationship conflicts that these sentences contain have been forced by the Subject Preference for Characterizing Sentences, and thus have not been created intentionally by the speaker.

There is another discourse phenomenon that seems to be explained in a principled way only by the Empathy Perspective. When two NPs are conjoined, they must be arranged in a fixed order if the descriptor for one NP is dependent on the descriptor for the other. Observe, for example, the following sentences:

(25)a.   John$_i$ and his$_i$ brother went to Paris.
  b.   *John$_i$'s brother and he$_i$/John$_i$ went to Paris.

This fact can be accounted for by hypothesizing the following empathy principle:

(26)   WORD ORDER EMPATHY HIERARCHY: It is easier for the speaker to empathize with the referent of a left-hand NP in a coordinate NP structure than with that of a right-hand NP.
    E(left-hand NP) > E(right-hand NP)

Considering the fact the left-hand position in a coordinate structure is more prominent than the right-hand position, and considering the fact that, given the subject and non-subject NPs, the former is the more prominent position, the Surface Structure EH and the Word Order EH can be considered to be two different manifestations of the same principle:

(27)   SYNTACTIC PROMINENCE EMPATHY HIERARCHY: Give syntactic prominence to a person/object that you are empathizing with.

The Surface Structure EH deals with the manifestation of syntactic prominence in terms of structural configuration, while the Word Order EH deals with the manifestation of syntactic prominence in terms of linear order.

Let us examine some more examples relevant to the Word Order EH:

(28)a.   I saw John and a policeman walking together yesterday.
   b.   ??I saw a policeman and John walking together yesterday.

(29)a.   I saw you and a policeman walking together yesterday.
   b.   ??I saw a policeman and you walking together yesterday.

(30)a.   John and someone else will be there.
   b.   *Someone else and John will be there.

The marginality of (28b) and (29b) arises from the conflict between the Word Order EH and the Topic EH. The unacceptability of (30b) arises from the conflict between the Word Order EH and Descriptor/Topic Empathy Hierarchies. Note that *someone else* in the sentence is a descriptor that is dependent upon *John*.

Recall now that I mentioned previously that since *meet* is a reciprocal verb, if John and Mary met, there are four ways to describe this event:

(10)a.   John and Mary met.
   b.   Mary and John met.
   c.   John met Mary.
   d.   Mary met John.

I have already explained the difference between (10c) and (10d) by saying that the former involves the speaker's intentional placement of *John* in subject position, while the latter involves his/her intentional choice of *Mary* in that position. The Word Order EH can account for the difference between (10a) and (10b): the speaker's empathy with John is greater than that with Mary in (10a), and the speaker's empathy with Mary is greater than that with John in (10b).

The Word Order EH interacts in an interesting way with a "modesty" principle taught in prescriptive grammar. For example, observe the following sentences:

(31)a.   ??I and John are good friends.
   b.   John and I are good friends.

(31b)   involves the following empathy hierarchy conflicts:

(32)   Empathy Relationships of (31b):
       Speech Act EH   E(I) > E(John)
       Word Order EH   E(John) m> E(I)
       Transitivity: *E(I) > E(John) m> E(I)
       Markedness Principle: The above conflict is intentional because the speaker has intentionally placed *John* in the left-hand position, and *I* in the right-hand position ⇒ a penalty

That is, from the point of view of the Empathy Perspective, (31b) should be unacceptable, and (31a) acceptable. However, prescriptive grammar says that the first person nominative pronoun should be placed at the end of a list. I will refer to this artificial rule as the Modesty Principle:

(33)   THE MODESTY PRINCIPLE: In the coordinate NP structure, give the least prominence to the first person pronoun.

We can now account for the acceptability of (31b) by stating that the choice of the expression *John and I*, which is instrumental in creating an empathy relationship conflict, is not intentional, but is forced on the speaker by the Modesty Principle. Therefore, there is no penalty for the violation.[4]

2.2   *More on the Markedness Principle for Discourse Rule Violations*

The contrast in the acceptability status of the following two sentences seems to be unexplainable without resorting to the Markedness Principle for Discourse Rule Violations:

(34)a.   *At the gate were John$_i$'s brother and John$_i$/he$_i$ smiling at me.
   b.   At the top of the rank list were John$_i$'s brother and John$_i$ in that order.

Both (34a) and (34b) contain a conflict between the Descriptor EH (i.e. E(John) > E(John's brother)) and the Word Order EH (i.e. E(John's brother) > E(John)). (34a) is unacceptable because the placement of *John's brother* to the left of *John* in the NP coordination is by the speaker's design. In contrast, (34b) is acceptable because the placement of *John's brother* to the left of *John* has been forced on the speaker by the relative ranking of the two siblings. That is, the empathy relationship conflict that (34b) involves was forced upon the speaker and was not intentional, and therefore, there is no penalty for the violation.
   Observe next the following sentences:

(35)a.   John gave a book to the girl.
   b.   John gave the book to a girl.

(36)a.   John gave the girl a book.
   b.   ??John gave a girl the book.

(35a, b) are examples of the periphrastic dative sentence pattern, whereas (36a, b) are examples of the incorporated dative sentence pattern. What needs to be explained is the marginality of (36b). It is reasonable to assume that (36b) is marginal because it violates the well-known discourse principle given below:[5]

(37)   FROM-OLD-TO-NEW PRINCIPLE: In languages in which word order is relat-
       ively free, the unmarked word order of constituents is old, predictable
       information first and new, unpredictable information last.

Let us assume that the above principle applies to English in places where there
is freedom of word order. In (36b), *a girl*, which represents new information,
appears before *the book*, whose anaphoric nature marks that it represents old
information. Therefore, the marginality or unacceptability of (36b) can be
attributed to its violation of the *From-Old-To-New Principle*. However, once one
adopts this approach to account for the marginality of (36b), the acceptability
of (35a), repeated below, becomes a puzzle:

(35)a.   √John gave a book to the girl.
                     New   Old

(36)b.   ??John gave a girl   the book.
                     New   Old

As shown above, (35a) violates the From-Old-To-New Principle as much as
(36b) does.
    The above dilemma can be resolved by assuming that the periphrastic dative
pattern represents the underlying pattern for giving verbs, and that the incorporated dative pattern is derived by applying DATIVE INCORPORATION to the
underlying periphrastic dative pattern.[6] According to this hypothesis, the violation of the From-Old-To-New Principle that (35a) involves is non-intentional
because the speaker simply used the underlying sentence pattern, and placed
the theme NP *a book* in verb object position and the goal NP *the girl* in prepositional object position. Therefore, there is no penalty for the violation. In contrast,
the violation of the Principle that (36b) involves is intentional because the
speaker has chosen to apply Dative Incorporation, an optional transformation.
Therefore, the resulting violation of the From-Old-To-New Principle cannot go
unpenalized, and the unacceptability of the sentence results.[7]

2.3   *Empathy and reflexive pronouns*

There are languages (e.g. Japanese, Korean, and Chinese) that require that the
antecedents of reflexive pronouns be animate and, most preferably, human. This
suggests that the reflexive pronoun, at least in these languages, requires a high
degree of the speaker's empathy with its referent. The fact that sentences such
as (38b) below are acceptable might give a false impression that English reflexives are free from such a requirement, but the fact that (39b) is unacceptable
shows that they are subject to an empathy requirement, albeit to a lesser degree.

(38)a.   John criticized himself.
     b.   Harvard overextended itself in natural sciences in the sixties.

(39)a. John wrote to his friends about himself.
   b. *Harvard wrote to its alumni about itself.[8]

The unacceptability of (39b) shows that English reflexive pronouns in oblique case position require a high degree of the speaker's empathy with their referents. (39b) is unacceptable because it is not possible for the speaker to empathize to a high degree with inanimate objects like Harvard University.

Empathy factors influence the interpretation of reflexive pronouns even when their referents are human. Observe first the following sentences:

(40)a. John talked to Mary about himself.
   b. √/?/??Mary talked to Bill about himself.

While all speakers accept (40a), some speakers consider (40b) awkward or marginal. This fact can be explained by assuming that a sentence containing a reflexive pronoun in oblique position is most felicitous when the referent of the reflexive receives the highest degree of empathy in the sentence. There is no problem with (40a) because the subject NP is the sentence's unmarked empathy focus (cf. the Surface Structure EH) and the reflexive pronoun has that NP as its antecedent. In contrast, (40b) is problematic in that the antecedent of the reflexive pronoun is not the highest-ranked candidate in the empathy hierarchy on the unmarked interpretation of the sentence. Likewise, observe the following sentences:

(41)a. √/?/??Mary talked to Bill about himself. (=40b)
   b. ?/??/*I talked to Bill about himself.

There are many speakers who consider (41b) less acceptable than (41a). This can be attributed to the fact that the subject NP in (41b), because it is a first person pronoun, is even stronger than *Mary* in (41a) in its qualification as the focus of the speaker's empathy, and hence as the antecedent of the reflexive. This makes the *Bill* of (41b) less qualified to be the antecedent of a reflexive pronoun than the *Bill* in (41a), and makes (41b) less acceptable than (41a).

Observe next the following sentences:

(42)a. √/?/??John talked to Mary about herself.
   b. *John talked about Mary to herself.

The fact that (42a) (and (40b)) is acceptable or nearly so for many speakers has been a problem in the framework of Chomsky's (1981) theory of grammar because the reflexive pronoun is not c-commanded by its intended antecedent *Mary*. According to Chomsky's binding theory, a reflexive must be c-commanded by a co-indexed NP in a local context.[9] Chomsky (1981) circumvented this problem by claiming that *talk to* in (42a) is reanalyzed as a single V, with a resulting loss of the PP node dominating *to Mary*. Thus, *Mary* becomes the direct object of the V, and it c-commands the reflexive pronoun. Chomsky argued that (42b) is unacceptable because reanalysis of *talk about* does not take place, apparently because *about Mary* is not base-generated next to *talk*.

There is, however, a serious problem with the above account of the acceptability of (42a) and the unacceptability of (42b). Observe the following sentence:

(43)   ??/*John discussed Mary with herself.

There is no doubt that the reflexive pronoun in the above sentence is c-commanded by a co-indexed NP (i.e. *Mary*) in its local domain. In spite of this fact, (43) is marginal or unacceptable. Observe, however, that (43) and (42b) are more or less synonymous. Therefore, the unacceptability of (42b) seems to be a non-syntactic phenomenon, rather than a syntactic one. In comparing the acceptable (42a) with the unacceptable (42b), we note that while the antecedent of the reflexive pronoun in the former is Mary as a human being, the antecedent of the reflexive in (42b) and (43) is semantically inanimate; that is, the antecedent is what Mary is or what she has done. Thus, the unacceptability of (43) is automatically accounted for in the framework of the Empathy Perspective via the requirement that the referents of the antecedents of the reflexive pronouns in oblique position in English must receive a high degree of the speaker's empathy. That is, (42b) and (43) are unacceptable because *Mary*, the antecedent of the reflexive pronouns, cannot receive a high degree of the speaker's empathy because it is semantically inanimate.

Finally, observe the following picture-noun sentences involving reflexive pronouns:

(44)a.   Mary cost John a picture of himself in the paper.
         Intended Interpretation: "In order to impress Mary, John paid for a picture of himself to be printed in the newspaper." or "John was adversely affected by the fact that what Mary had done caused his picture to appear in the newspaper."
     b. *Mary cost John a picture of herself in the paper.
         Intended Interpretation: "In order to impress Mary, John paid for her picture to be printed in the newspaper."

Note that in these sentences *John* is semantically human because it represents the experiencer of the cost or damage, whereas *Mary* is semantically inanimate because it represents notions such as "what Mary had done," "(John's) desire to impress Mary," and so on. These sentences also show that reflexive pronouns in picture nouns are also empathy expressions, and as such require a high degree of the speaker's empathy with their referents. There are several other factors that conspire to produce the acceptability judgments for these sentences; see Kuno 1987: Chap. 4.5) for details.

3   Direct Discourse Perspective

3.1   *Logophoric NP constraint*

Observe the following sentences:

(45)a.   John said, "I am a genius."
  b.   John$_i$ said that he$_i$ was a genius.

(46)a.   John said to Mary, "You are a genius."
  b.   John said to Mary$_j$ that she$_j$ was a genius.

(47)a.   John said about Mary$_j$, "Mary$_j$/She$_j$ is a genius."
  b.   John said about Mary$_j$ that she$_j$ was a genius.

(45a), (46a), and (47a) contain direct discourse quotations, whereas (45b), (46b), and (47b) contain indirect discourse clauses. In the indirect discourse clauses in (45b), (46b), and (47b), the pronouns are coreferential with main-clause NPs. However, there is a significant difference between the pronouns in (45b) and (46b) and the pronoun in (47b). That is, in the former, the pronouns correspond to the first and second person pronouns in the corresponding direct quotations: they cannot correspond to non-pronominal NPs because the following sentences are unacceptable:[10]

(48)a.   *John$_i$ said, "John$_i$ is a genius."
  b.   *John said to Mary$_j$, "Mary$_j$ is a genius."

Let us refer to saying and asking verbs as LOGOPHORIC VERBS (abbreviated as LogoV), and to their complement clauses as LOGOPHORIC COMPLEMENTS (abbreviated as LogoComp). Given a sentence with a logophoric complement, I will use the term Logo-1 NP (or the abbreviation Logo-1) to refer to the NP in the main clause that refers to the speaker of the utterance represented by the logophoric complement. Likewise, I will use the term Logo-2 NP (or the abbreviation Logo-2) to refer to the hearer of the utterance. These terms are illustrated in (49):

(49)   John$_i$ said to Mary$_j$ that she$_j$ was a genius.
       Logo-1 LogoV Logo-2   LogoComp

I assume that even sentences with complements that do not have direct discourse counterparts are logophoric complements if they represent the thoughts, feelings, or realization of the referent of the main-clause Logo-1 or Logo-2 NP:

(50)a.   John   thinks   that he is a genius.
         Logo-1 LogoV LogoComp
  b.   Hypothetical Structure: [John thinks, "[I am a genius.]"]

(51)a.   John   heard from Mary   that she was sick.
         Logo-2 LogoV   Logo-1 LogoComp
     b.   Hypothetical Structure: [John heard from Mary, "[I am sick]"]

I will refer to an analytical framework that makes use of the notions described
above as a direct discourse perspective, or alternately as a LOGOPHORIC
PERSPECTIVE.

Kuno (1987: Chap. 3) has shown that an NP in a logophoric complement (in
an extended sense, as shown above) that is intended to be coreferential with
the main-clause Logo-1 or Logo-2 NP behaves very differently from those NPs
that are not coreferential with either of them. I will illustrate this difference
by using a few examples from (Kuno 1987) and add a new set of data from
Kuno (1997) that further illustrates the importance of the direct discourse
perspective. Observe, first, the following sentences:

(52)a.   The remark that Churchill$_i$ was vain was often made about him$_i$.
     b.   *The remark that Churchill$_i$ was vain was often made to him$_i$.

While (52a) is acceptable on the interpretation in which the non-pronominal
full NP *Churchill* in the embedded clause is coreferential with the pronoun *him*
in the main clause, such an interpretation is ruled out for (52b). This contrast
can be explained only by paying attention to who said what. I will represent
what was said using a direct discourse representation:

(53)a.   [People often made about Churchill the remark "[Churchill is vain]"]
         Logo-1   -Logo-1/2
     b.   [People often made to Churchill the remark "[You are vain]"]
         Logo-1   Logo-2

Observe that *Churchill* in the matrix clause of (53a) is marked as -Logo-1/2
because it is neither the speaker NP nor the hearer NP of the proposition
represented by the direct discourse quotation. The subject of the direct discourse
quotation is *Churchill*, and not *you*, because, again, Churchill was not the hearer
of the remark. In contrast, *Churchill* in the matrix clause of (53b) is marked as
Logo-2 because it is the hearer NP of the direct discourse quotation, which has
you, and not *Churchill*, in subject position. The fact that (52a) is acceptable but
(52b) is not suggests that a full NP (i.e. a non-reflexive and non-pronominal
NP) in the direct discourse representation of a logophoric complement can
remain as a full NP if other conditions are met, as in (52a), but a second person
pronoun in the direct discourse representation of a logophoric complement
cannot be realized as a full NP. That is, a second person pronoun *you* must
remain pronominal in indirect discourse formation.

Likewise, observe the following sentences:

(54)a.   The allegation that John$_i$ was a spy was vehemently denied by him$_i$.
     b.   *The claim that John$_i$ was a genius was made by him$_i$.

While (54a) is acceptable on the interpretation whereby the full NP *John* in the embedded clause is coreferential with the pronoun *him* in the main clause, such an interpretation is ruled out for (54b). This contrast can also be explained by observing the direct discourse representation of what was said by whom:

(55)a. [John denied the allegation "[John is a spy]"]
   b. [John made the claim "[I am a genius]"]

Note that John was neither the "speaker" nor necessarily the hearer of the allegation. This explains why *John*, and not *I* or *you*, appears in subject position of the direct discourse representation in (55a).[11] In contrast, John was necessarily the "speaker" of the claim, and therefore, the subject of the direct discourse representation in (55b) must be a first person pronoun. The fact that (54b) is unacceptable suggests that a first person pronoun in the direct discourse representation of a logophoric complement cannot be realized as a full NP in the derived surface sentences. That is, the first person "I" in a direct discourse representation has to remain pronominal in indirect discourse formation. I should hasten to add that if Passivization does not apply to (52a) and (54a), there is no way to pronominalize the main clause NPs *Churchill* and *John* and keep *Churchill* and *John* in the embedded clause unpronominalized:

(56)a. *People often made about him$_i$ the remark that Churchill$_i$ was vain.
   b. *He$_i$ vehemently denied the allegation that John$_i$ was vain.

But the unacceptability of (56a, b) can be attributed to violation of Principle C (see section 3.2 of this paper) of my version of the Binding Theory, which says that an R-expression (a full NP) cannot be c-commanded by a co-indexed NP (with PP nodes not counting for the purpose of delimiting the c-command domain of a given node).

   Let us depart from the account given above, which is based on the direct discourse representation of logophoric complement clauses, and move to one which assumes that indirect discourse logophoric complements are base-generated as such. In that framework, the constraint that we have observed above can be restated in the following manner:

(57) LOGOPHORIC NP CONSTRAINT: Given a sentence with a matrix Logo-1/2 NP and a logophoric complement attributable to that Logo-1/2 NP, a full NP in the logophoric complement cannot be coreferential with the Logo-1/2 NP in the main clause.   (cf. Kuno 1987: 109)

According to this constraint, the acceptability status of the sentences in (52) and (54) can be accounted for in the following manner:

(58)a. The remark that [Churchill$_i$ was vain] was often made about him$_i$.
                    LogoComp   -Logo-1/2

b.   *The remark that [Churchill$_i$ was vain] was often made to him$_i$.
        LogoComp   Logo-2

(59)a.   The allegation that [John$_i$ was a spy] was vehemently denied by him$_i$.
            LogoComp   -Logo-1/2
     b.   *The claim that [John$_i$ was a genius] was made by him$_i$.
            LogoComp   Logo-1

(58a) and (59a) are acceptable because full NPs in their logophoric complements are co-indexed with main clause NPs that represent neither the speaker nor the hearer of the propositions that the logophoric complements represent. In contrast, (58b) and (59b) are unacceptable because full NPs in their logophoric complement clauses are co-indexed with the main clause hearer/speaker NPs that the logophoric complements are attributable to.
   Observe next the following sentences:

(60)a.   *The claim [$_{LogoComp1}$ that John$_i$ said [$_{LogoComp2}$ that Bill$_j$ was a spy]] was
            made by him$_i$.
            cf. John made the claim: *"I said that Bill is a spy."*
     b.   *The claim [$_{LogoComp1}$ that John$_i$ said [$_{LogoComp2}$ that Bill$_j$ was a spy]] was
            made by him$_j$.
            cf. Bill made the claim: *"John said that I am a spy."*

The fact that the sentence is unacceptable on the *him = Bill* interpretation shows that the Logophoric NP Constraint applies between a full NP (e.g. *Bill* in (60b)) in a logophoric complement and a Logo-1/2 NP (e.g. *him* in (60b)) in a higher clause, even if there is an intervening Logo-1/2 NP (e.g. *John* in (60b)) between the two.
   There are many phenomena that can be accounted for only in the Logophoric Perspective. They are discussed in detail in Kuno (1987: Chap. 3).

3.2   *The Logophoric NP Constraint and the Binding Theory*

I will now show that the Logophoric NP Constraint can resolve the puzzle given in (61) that has defied attempts at explanation by scholars working in the framework of Chomsky's BINDING THEORY (see also Huang, this volume).

(61)a.   *Which claim that John$_i$ was asleep was he$_i$ willing to discuss?
            (Chomsky 1993)
     b.   Which claim that John$_i$ made did he$_i$ later deny? (Lebeaux 1992)

The problem here is at what stage the unacceptability of these sentences can be captured as involving a violation of Principle C of the Binding Theory:

(62) Principle C: An R-expression cannot be co-indexed with a c-commanding NP.[12]

   C-command: A c-commands B iff the branching node α_1 most immediately dominating A either dominates B or is immediately dominated by a node α_2 that dominates B, and α_2 is of the same category type as α_1. (Reinhart 1976)

For those readers who are not familiar with the notion of c-command and Chomsky's Binding Theory, it is sufficient for the purpose of this paper to interpret Principle C in a much more limited sense as meaning that, given a sentence with NP_1 in subject position and NP_2 elsewhere in the same sentence, NP_2 cannot be interpreted as coreferential with NP_1, as illustrated below:

(63)a. *John$_i$/*He$_i$ hates *John$_i$*'s mother.
   b. *John$_i$/*He$_i$ hated the man that *John$_i$* shared an office with.
   c. *John$_i$/*He$_i$ thinks that *John$_i$* is a genius.

The above sentences are all unacceptable because the italicized *John* is intended to be coreferential with the main clause subject, in violation of Principle C.

   Returning to (61a), it has been assumed that Principle C applies to the open sentence portion of the abstract representation (called the LF representation) of the structure of the sentence informally shown in (64):

(64) LF representation of (61a):
   [Which x [he was willing to discuss [x claim that John was asleep]]]
   {_____Open sentence _____}

That is, it has been assumed, in essence, that the LF representation given in (64) is illicit on the coreferential interpretation of *he* and *John* because it violates Principle C in the same way that the following sentence does:

(65) *He$_i$ was willing to discuss which claim that John$_i$ was asleep.

   The above account of the unacceptability of (61a) immediately runs into difficulty, however, because it predicts that (61b) should also be unacceptable because it violates Principle C in the same way that (67) does:

(66) LF representation of (61b):
   [Which x [he did later deny [x claim that John made]]]

(67) *He$_i$ did later deny the claim that John$_i$ made.

   Attempts have been made in the framework of the Minimalist Program (Freidin 1986, 1994, 1997; Lebeaux 1988, 1992, 1995; Chomsky 1993) to resolve the above puzzle and account for the acceptability of (61b) and the unacceptability of (61a) by attributing it to the difference in the ways that complements and adjuncts are introduced into sentence structures. Noting that the embedded clause in (61a) is a complement clause of the noun *claim*, whereas the embedded clause in (61b) is an adjunct relative clause of the noun, minimalist theorists have claimed that the contrast in acceptability status between these two sentences can be accounted for by assuming the following:

(68)(i)   The introduction of complements into sentence structures must be cyclic.

(ii)   The introduction of adjuncts into sentence structures can be cyclic or non-cyclic.

Thus, they have assumed that Principle C applies to the LF representations that are informally shown below:

(69)a.   LF representation of (61a):
[Which claim that John was asleep [he was willing to discuss {which claim that John was asleep}]]
b.   LF representation of (61b)
[Which claim that John made [he was willing to discuss {which claim}]]

In the above LF representations, the copy of a fronted *wh*-expression is shown in curly brackets. Note that the complement clause *that John was asleep* in (69a) is adjoined to the noun *claim* before the syntactic fronting of the *wh*-expression, whereas the adjunct clause *that John made* in (69b) is adjoined to the fronted *which claim*, and not to the expression before *wh*-movement takes place. Principle C disallows the co-indexing of the full NP *John* with the c-commanding *he* in the open sentence part (i.e. *[he was willing to discuss {which claim that John was asleep}]*). In contrast, Principle C does not apply to the open sentence portion of the LF representation in (69b) because there is no full NP there. Principle C does not apply to *John* in the fronted *wh*-expression because it is not in the open sentence part of the LF representation (and *he* does not c-command *John* anyway).

The above account of the contrast between (61a) and (61b) appears to be credible when coupled with the contrast between (70a) and (70b), which also appears to show an ARGUMENT/ADJUNCT ASYMMETRY:

(70)a.   ??/*Which pictures of John$_i$ did he$_i$ like? (Lebeaux 1992)
b.   Which pictures near John$_i$ did he$_i$ look at? (Lebeaux 1992)

Observing that *of John* in (70a) is a complement of *pictures*, but *near John* in (70b) is an adjunct, Lebeaux (1992) attempts to account for the marginality/unacceptability of (70a) and the acceptability of (70b) on the coreferential interpretation of *John* and *he* in the following way:

(71)a. LF representation of (70a)
     [Which pictures of John [he did like {which pictures of John}]]
   b. LF representation of (70b):
     [Which pictures near John [he did look at {which pictures}]]

The introduction of *of John* in (70a) takes place before the fronting of the *wh*-expression *which pictures* because it is a complement of *pictures*. Therefore, a copy of the fronted *wh*-expression *which pictures of John* is in the object position of the verb *like*, as shown in (71a). Thus, Principle C disallows the co-indexing of *John* with the c-commanding *he*. This explains the unacceptability of (70a) on the coreferential interpretation of *John* and *he*. In contrast, the introduction of *near John* in (70b) can take place after the *wh*-movement of *which pictures* because it is an adjunct, not a complement, of *pictures*. Therefore, the copy of *John* is absent in the open sentence part of the LF representation of the sentence, as shown in (71b). Principle C is inapplicable to the open sentence part of (71b), and hence Principle C does not mark (70b) unacceptable on the coreferential interpretation of *John* and *he*.

The above account of the contrast between (61a) and (61b) and between (70a) and (70b), based on the claimed asymmetry in the ways that arguments and adjuncts are introduced into sentence structures, does not go far beyond these four sentences, however. Once the database of sentences with the same patterns is only slightly extended, it becomes clear that the claimed asymmetry is an illusion. Observe the following sentences:

(72)a. Whose allegation that John$_i$ was less than truthful did he$_i$ refute vehemently?
   b. Whose opinion that Weld$_i$ was unfit for the ambassadorial appointment did he$_i$ try to refute vehemently?
   c. Whose claim that the Senator$_i$ had violated the campaign finance regulation did he$_i$ dismiss as politically motivated?
   d. Which psychiatrist's view that John$_i$ was schizophrenic did he$_i$ try to get expunged from the trial records?

The embedded clauses in the above sentences are all complement clauses. Therefore, a Minimalist analysis based on argument/adjunct asymmetry predicts that they should all be unacceptable. In spite of this prediction, however, most speakers consider these sentences acceptable, and even those speakers who judge them as less than acceptable report that they are far better than (61a).

The argument/adjunct asymmetry-based analysis of the contrast between (70a) and (70b) fares as poorly, as witnessed by the acceptability of sentences such as the following:

(73)a. Which witness's attack on John$_i$ did he$_i$ try to get expunged from the trial records?
   b. Which artist's portrait of Nixon$_i$ do you think he$_i$ liked best?
   c. Whose criticism of John$_i$ did he$_i$ choose to ignore?

(74)a.   Which doctor's evaluation of John$_i$'s physical fitness did he$_i$ use when he$_i$ applied to NASA for space training?

b.   Which psychiatrist's evaluation of John$_i$'s mental state did he$_i$ try to get expunged from the trial records?

The PPs in the above sentences are all complements of the nouns (i.e. *attack, portrait, criticism, evaluation*) and therefore, Freidin (1986), Lebeaux (1988) and Chomsky (1993) all predict that their LF representations violate Principle C. But these sentences are all perfectly acceptable. The acceptability of the sentences in (72)–(74) shows not only that an argument/adjunct-asymmetry-based account of the contrast between (61a) and (61b) and between (70a) and (70b) is untenable, but also that to the extent that the account is derived from the theoretical framework of the Minimalist Program, there is something wrong with the theory itself.

3.3   Logophoric analysis

Observe now the contrast in acceptability status of the following sentences:

(75)a.   *Which claim that John$_i$ had helped develop new technologies did he$_i$ make at last year's national convention?

b.   Which claim that John$_i$ made did he$_i$ later deny? (Lebeaux 1992)

The Logophoric NP Constraint can automatically account for the contrast between these two sentences: (75a) involves a logophoric complement that is attributable to the matrix subject NP *he*. The sentence violates the Logophoric NP Constraint because a full NP (i.e. *John*) in the logophoric complement is co-indexed with the matrix Logo-1 NP (i.e. *he*). (75b), in contrast, does not involve a logophoric complement, and therefore, the Logophoric NP Constraint has nothing to do with this LF representation, hence the acceptability of this sentence.

The acceptability of the sentences in (72) can be accounted for in the same fashion. For example, observe the following:

(72)a.   Whose allegation that John$_i$ was less than truthful did he$_i$ refute vehemently?

The above sentence has a logophoric complement (i.e. *that John was less than truthful*), but the Logo-1 NP of this complement is not *he* (= *John*), but *whose*. Therefore, the Logophoric NP Constraint does not disallow the co-indexing of *John* and *he*.

Now let us re-examine (61a), the sentence that Chomsky, Lebeaux, and Freidin have all considered unacceptable:

(61)a.   *Which claim that John$_i$ was asleep was he$_i$ willing to discuss? (Chomsky 1993)

It seems that the sentence is potentially ambiguous with respect to whether the claim that John was asleep is to be interpreted as John's claim or someone else's claim. As must be clear to the reader by this time, the Logophoric NP Constraint predicts that the sentence is unacceptable if the claim is interpreted as John's, but acceptable if it is interpreted as someone else's claim. This prediction is consistent with the judgments that most, if not all, native speakers make about the sentence.

The above observations show that the account of the contrast between (61a) and (61b) that is based on argument/adjunct asymmetry is untenable. That is, there is no justification for assuming that arguments and adjuncts are different with respect to when they must or must not be introduced into sentence structures. Let us assume that they are both introduced cyclically. According to this hypothesis, (72a), (61b), and (75a) have the structures shown below:

(76)a. LF representation of (72a)
        [Whose allegation that John was less than truthful [he did refute vehemently {whose allegation that John was less than truthful}]]
    b. LF representation of (61b)
        [Which claim that John made [he did later deny {which claim that John made}]]
    c. LF representation of (75a)
        [[Which claim that John had helped develop new technologies] [he did make {which claim that John had helped develop new technologies} at last year's national convention]]

The way that the Binding Theory (cf. Chomsky 1981) is organized, Principle C applies to the open sentence part of these LF representations, and marks them as unacceptable. But (72a) and (61b) are perfectly acceptable. Therefore, the Binding Theory needs to be re-examined to see if it has been properly organized. The problem with its current organization is that it is based on the assumption that since there are three types of NPs (i.e. anaphors, pronominals, and R-expressions), there should be one rule for each NP type. I have proposed a different organization of the binding theory in Kuno (1987). I show below first the overall difference in organization and then present revised binding principles:

(77) Chomsky's Organization of the Binding Theory
    a. anaphors in a local domain [coreference]
    b. pronominals in a local domain [disjoint reference]
    c. R-expressions in all domains [disjoint reference]

(78) Kuno (1987)'s Organization of the Binding Theory
    a. anaphors in a local domain [coreference]
    b. non-anaphors (pronominals and R-expressions) in a local domain [disjoint reference]
    c. R-expressions in all domains [disjoint reference]

(79)   Kuno (1987)'s Binding Principles

Principle A':   An anaphor may receive a coreferential interpretation only with a c-commanding NP within its local domain. N.B. An LF representation that contains an anaphor which is not interpreted coreferentially with any NP in it is unacceptable.

Principle B':   A non-anaphor (pronominal or R-expression) is obligatorily assigned disjoint indexing *vis-à-vis* a c-commanding NP within its local domain.

Principle C':   An R-expression is barred from receiving coreferential interpretation *vis-à-vis* a c-commanding non-anaphor NP in either A- or A'-position.[13] N.B. Principle C' does not apply to the reconstructed portion of the LF representation. (That is, in a theoretical framework in which the binding theory applies to syntactic structures rather than to LF representations, Principles A' and B' apply cyclically, and Principle C' applies post-cyclically.)

C-command: A c-commands B iff the non-PP branching node α_1 most immediately dominating A either dominates B or is immediately dominated by a node α_2 that dominates B, and α_2 is of the same category type as α_1.

With the above revised binding theory, (76a–c) pose no problem. In these LF representations, since the non-anaphor *John* is in the embedded clause and the c-commanding NP *he* in the main clause (that is, since *he* is not in *John*'s local domain), Principle B' does not apply. Therefore, they are not assigned disjoint indexing. Furthermore, Principle C' does not apply to an R-expression which is in the reconstructed portion of the LF representation, and therefore, it is not assigned disjoint indexing *vis-à-vis* the c-commanding *he*. (The *John* in the fronted portion of the LF representation is not assigned disjoint indexing with *he* either, because the latter does not c-command the former.) Thus, there are no binding principles that block the coreferential interpretation of *he* and *John*. The Logophoric NP Constraint does not apply to (76a) because *he* is not the Logo-1 NP of the complement clause. It does not apply to (76b), either, because that sentence does not involve a logophoric complement at all. Hence the acceptability of (72a) and (61b). On the other hand, the Logophoric NP Constraint applies to (76c) because *he* is the Logo-1 NP of the complement clause and disallows a coreferential interpretation of *he* and *John*, hence the unacceptability of (75a).

The above revised binding principles can also account for the contrast among the following three sentences:

(70)a.   ??/*Which pictures of John did he like? (Lebeaux 1992)

(73)a.   Which witness's attack on John did he try to get expunged from the
trial records?

(70)b.   Which pictures near John did he look at? (Lebeaux 1992)

These sentences have the following LF representations:

(80)a.   LF representation of (70a)
[Which pictures of John [*he* did like {which pictures of *John*}]]
 b.   LF representation of (73a)
[Which witness's attack on John [*he* did try to get {which witness's
attack on *John*} expunged from the trial records]]
 c.   LF representation of (70b)
[Which pictures near John [*he* did look at {which pictures near *John*}]]

Note in (80a) that the non-anaphor *John* is c-commanded by *he* in its local
domain. Therefore, Principle B′ obligatorily assigns disjoint indexing to *he* and
John. Hence the unacceptability of (70a). In contrast, in (80b), *John* is not c-
commanded by *he* in its local domain because *John*'s local domain is *which
witness's attack on John*. Hence Principle B′ does not assign disjoint indexing to
he and *John*. Principle C′ does not apply to *John* in the reconstructed portion of
the LF representation. (It applies to *John* in the fronted *wh*-expression, but it is
not c-commanded by *he*, and thus no disjoint indexing takes place.) Therefore,
there is no binding principle that disallows the co-indexing of *he* and *John*.
Furthermore, the Logophoric NP Constraint does not apply to *he* and *John*
either, because no logophoric complement is involved. Therefore, it does not
disallow the co-indexing of the two NPs, hence the acceptability of (73a).
Finally, in (80c), the c-commanding *he* is not in *John*'s local domain because
there is a clause boundary between *he* and *John*, as witnessed by the fact that
John is not in a reflexive context:

(81)a.   *He looked at pictures near himself.
 b.   *[He did look at [pictures [PRO near himself]]]

(82)a.   *Mary talked with people angry about herself.
 b.   *[Mary talked with people [PRO angry about herself]]

Therefore, Principle B′ does not apply to (80c), and consequently, there is no
obligatory disjoint-indexing of *he* and *John* by Principle B′. Principle C′ does
not apply to *John* in the reconstructed portion of the LF. (It applies to *John* in
the fronted *wh*-expression, but since that is not c-commanded by *he*, it does not
bar co-indexing of the two NPs.) The Logophoric NP Constraint does not
apply because the sentence does not contain a logophoric complement. Thus,

there is no rule that disallows the co-indexing of the two NPs, hence the acceptability of (80c).

4   Concluding Remarks

In this paper, I have examined various syntactic constructions in English and shown how syntactic and non-syntactic constraints interact with one another to produce the acceptability status of sentences that employ those constructions. Given a contrast in acceptability status like the one in (61), the linguist who is unaware of the existence of various non-syntactic factors that interact with syntax assumes that the contrast is due to syntactic factors and proposes syntax-based hypotheses to account for it. In contrast, the linguist who is aware of various non-syntactic factors that closely interact with syntax begins his/her analysis bearing in mind that the contrast might be due to one or more such non-syntactic factors. I hope I have amply demonstrated in this paper which approach is more productive in arriving at the correct generalizations on such constructions.

ACKNOWLEDGMENTS

I am indebted to Karen Courtenay, Nan Decker, Tatsuhiko Toda, and Gregory Ward for their numerous invaluable comments on earlier versions of this paper. I am also greatly indebted to Bill Lachman for providing me with the phrase structure representation in note 9.

NOTES

1   It is possible for a speaker to take a detached view of an event involving the referent of a topic NP. This is why the Topic EH E(topic) ≥ E(non-topic) has "≥" rather than ">".

2   Sentences of the same pattern as (14b) are acceptable if they are used as corrective sentences:

   (i)   Speaker A: Mary heard from Bill that Jane was seriously sick.
   Speaker B: No, she heard it from ME.

I will discuss empathy principle violations in corrective sentences later in this section.

Likewise, sentences of the same pattern as (15b) become acceptable if placed in contexts in which the time and location of the receipt of the thing the speaker sent are at issue. For example, observe the following sentence:

   (ii)   When Bill *received from me* a package containing a maternity dress for his wife, they had already broken up.

Note that (ii) is not synonymous with (iii):

(iii)   When *I sent* Bill a package containing a maternity dress for his wife, they had already broken up.

It is clear that while the mailing-out time of the package is at issue in (iii), the receipt time of the package is at issue in (ii). That is, the speaker's use of the marked expression *receive from* in (ii) has been forced on the speaker because of the necessity to refer to the receipt time rather than the mailing-out time. Therefore, there is no intentionality in the speaker's use of the expression *receive from* in (ii), nor is there a penalty for the conflict in empathy relationships that the sentence contains.

3   (16d) is acceptable if the pronouns are stressed, as shown in (ib) below. But note that (ii), which has the same relative order of full names and pronouns, is acceptable without stress on the pronouns.

(i)a.   ?? Mary$_i$ heard from John$_j$ what he$_j$ had heard from her$_i$ two days before. (=16d)
   b.   Mary$_i$ heard from John$_j$ what HE$_j$ had heard from HER$_i$ two days before.
   c.   Mary$_i$ told John$_j$ what he$_j$ had told her$_i$ two days before.

The above phenomenon is similar to the pronominalization phenomenon with possessive NPs as antecedents. First note that (ii) is perfectly acceptable:

(ii)   Bill$_i$'s brother is visiting him$_i$.

But when two such sentences are juxtaposed as in (iiia), unacceptability results:

(iii)a.   *Bill$_i$'s brother is visiting him$_i$, and John$_j$'s uncle is visiting him$_j$.
    b.   Bill$_i$'s brother is visiting HIM$_i$, and John$_j$'s uncle is visiting HIM$_j$.
    c.   Bill$_i$ is visiting his$_i$ brother, and John$_j$ is visiting his$_j$ uncle.

The right-hand pronoun, if unstressed, cannot be interpreted as coreferential with *John* – it must be interpreted as coreferential with the left-hand pronoun – but if stressed, it is interpreted as coreferential with *John*. This contrasts with the fact that (iiic), which has the same relative order of full names and pronouns, is acceptable without requiring the stressing of the pronouns.

In Kuno (1975: 289), the unacceptability of (iiia) with the pronouns unstressed was attributed to the following constraint:

(iv)   THE CONSTRAINT ON PRONOMINALIZATION WITH GENITIVE ANTECEDENT: The coreference linkage between a noun phrase in the genitive case and a pronoun is weak unless they are coreferential with the discourse topic.

According to the above hypothesis, (ii) is acceptable because it is easy to assume that Bill is the topic of the preceding discourse, but (iiia) is unacceptable because the assumption needed to obtain the specified coreferential interpretation for the latter half of the sentence (i.e. the assumption that John should be the topic of the preceding discourse) is contradicted by the first part of the sentence.

The fact that (iiia) becomes acceptable if the pronouns are stressed suggests that the following principle applies (cf. G. Lakoff 1971b, Hirschberg and Ward 1992):

(v)   THE FUNCTION OF STRESSED PRONOUNS: The stressing of pronouns signals that they are coreferential with NPs that they are not expected to refer to according to the normal set of rules in operation.

The above principle can account for the contrast between (via) and (vib) below (cf. Lakoff 1971b):

(vi)a.   John$_i$ hit Bill$_j$, and then he$_{i/*i}$ hit Tom.
    b.   John$_i$ hit Bill$_j$, and then HE$_{*i/j}$ hit Tom.

If the pronoun *he* is unstressed, it is coreferential with *John*. We can attribute this interpretation to the general principle that says, given coordinated clauses, try to assign parallel interpretations to the clauses as much as possible (G. Lakoff 1971b, Hirschberg and Ward 1992). In contrast, if the pronoun is stressed, it must be interpreted as coreferential with *Bill*. Thus, the stress on the pronoun signals to the hearer not to follow the parallel interpretation principle, but to look for a different antecedent, hence arises the *HIM = Bill* interpretation of (vib).

Returning now to (iiib), the stress on the pronouns in the sentence signals that the pronouns refer to NPs that the Constraint on Pronouns with Genitive Antecedents would otherwise ban them from referring to, hence the specified coreferential interpretation of the sentence. Likewise, the stress on the pronouns in (ib) signals that they refer to NPs that the Empathy Principles would otherwise ban

them from referring to, hence the acceptability of the sentence with the specified coreferential interpretation.

4   There are many speakers who prefer (i) to (31b):

(i)   Me and John are good friends.

The above pattern violates both the artificial Modesty Principle and the prescriptive Nominative Case Marking Rule for subject NPs. There are fewer speakers who say:

(ii)   John and me are good friends.

What this seems to suggest is that the acquisition of the Modesty Principle and of the Nominative Case Marking Rule go together.

5   This principle was first proposed by Mathesius (1939) and became the central theme of Prague School linguistics. See also Firbas (1964), Daneš (1970) and Gundel and Fretheim (this volume).

6   There are several pieces of evidence that support this assumption, but there is no space to present them here.

7   As far as I know, Olga Yokoyama (personal communication, 1975) was the first to observe the marginality of sentences of the pattern of (36b) and to attribute it to the violation of the From-Old-To-New Principle caused by application of optional Dative Incorporation.

8   The non-reflexive counterpart of (39b) is also unacceptable:

(i)   *Harvard$_i$ wrote to its alumni about it$_i$.

9   There are several different definitions of c-command, but for the purpose of the present discussion, the following definition will suffice:

(i)   C-command: Node A c-commands node B if the first branching node that dominates A also dominates B, and A does not dominate B. (Reinhart 1976)

Let us assume that (iia) has the structure shown in (iib):

(ii)a.   John talked to Mary about himself.

b.

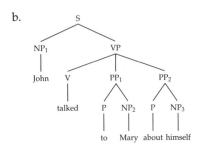

In (iib), NP$_1$ c-commands NP$_3$ because S, the first branching node that dominates it, also dominates NP$_3$, and NP$_1$ does not dominate NP$_3$. Furthermore, NP$_1$ and NP$_3$ are in the same local domain (i.e. in the same simplex S). Therefore, the reflexive pronoun *himself* satisfies Principle A of the binding theory:

> Principle A: An anaphor (a reflexive or reciprocal pronoun) must be co-indexed with a c-commanding NP in a local domain.

In contrast, NP$_2$ does not c-command NP$_3$ in (iib) because PP$_1$, the first branching node that dominates NP$_2$, does not dominate NP$_3$. Therefore, co-indexation of

Mary with the reflexive pronoun *herself* in (42a) constitutes a violation of Principle A, and the sentence is predicted to be unacceptable, which it is not for many speakers.

10   It goes without saying that (48a, b) are acceptable if *John/Mary is a genius* is what John actually said. In this connection, note the following sentence, which is perfectly acceptable because Ali used to say "Ali is the greatest":

(i)   Mohammed Ali$_i$ used to say, "Ali$_i$ is the greatest."

11   If the alleger had made the allegation directly to John, the direct discourse representation of what the alleger said would have a second person pronoun in subject position:

(i)   [John denied the allegation "[You are a spy]"]

The above representation would not yield (54a) because *you* must remain pronominal in indirect discourse formation.

12   An R(eferring)-expression is a non-reflexive/non-reciprocal NP or a trace of a moved NP.

15   Observe the following sentences:

(i)a.   *Him$_i$, John$_i$'s father dislikes.
   b.   *Him$_i$, John$_i$'s mother thinks Mary is in love with.

The unacceptability of these setences can be captured only if Principle C' is allowed to apply to *John*, with the c-commanding co-indexed *him* in A'-position. See Kuno (1987: Chap. 2) for details.

15 The Pragmatics of Deferred Interpretation

GEOFFREY NUNBERG

1 Deferred Interpretation

By deferred interpretation (or "deference") I mean the phenomenon whereby expressions can be used to refer to something that isn't explicitly included in the conventional denotation of that expression. The interest in these phenomena stretches back to Aristotelian discussions of metaphor, and while the study of the mechanisms of deference has made considerable progress in the interval, that (literally) classical framework still underlies a lot of the assumptions that people bring to the phenomena. So it will be useful to address some of these legacies from the outset.

Traditional approaches tend to regard figuration (and by extension, deference in general) as an essentially marked or playful use of language, which is associated with a pronounced stylistic effect. For linguistic purposes, however, there is no reason for assigning a special place to deferred uses that are stylist-ically notable – the sorts of usages that people sometimes qualify with a phrase like "figuratively speaking." There is no important linguistic difference between using *redcoat* to refer to a British soldier and using *suit* to refer to a corporate executive (as in, "A couple of suits stopped by to talk about the new products"). What creates the stylistic effect of the latter is not the mechanism that generates it, but the marked background assumptions that license it – here, the playful presupposition that certain executives are better classified by their attire than by their function. Those differences have an undoubted cultural interest, but they don't have any bearing on the more pedestrian question of how such usages arise in the first place.[1]

This assumption about the stylistic role of figuration is closely linked to a second assumption of traditional approaches, the idea that deference is exclus-ively a pragmatic phenomenon. For example, Grice (1967) treats metaphor as a kind of conversational implicature that arises from a violation of the maxim of quality; on his view, metaphorical utterances invariably have a literal reading to which a truth value (usually, false) can be assigned and which constitutes the input to some inferential schema that generates a "secondary" figurative reading. The assumption is that deference is somehow inconsistent with conventionalization, so that we can say that a word has distinct lexical meanings only when the connections that once licensed its multiple uses have been somehow obscured or forgotten. That is what often leads people to characterize polysemy in diachronic terms and to talk about figurative meanings that have been lexicalized as "dead" or "frozen" metaphors. As Ravin and Leacock (2000) put it: "polysemes are etymologically and therefore semantically related, and typically originate from metaphorical usage." But statements like this are better thought of as origin myths than as analytic hypotheses.[2] In fact, our assumption that such-and-such a usage is lexicalized is very often based on no more than an intuitive sense of its stylistic effects or an observation of its frequency, rather than on any strict analytical criteria.

But from a linguistic point of view, there's no reason to distinguish between the mechanisms that operate within the lexicon to produce meaning extensions and those that operate in a purely pragmatic way. Figuration doesn't necessarily cease to be figurative just because it is subject to some conventionalized restrictions. What leads us to say that the processes that produce multiple uses of expressions are lexicalized is not that they are no longer transparent (they may very well be), but only that the language constrains or enriches their use over and above what could be predicted on pragmatic grounds alone. Conventionalization should not be confused with absolute arbitrariness; it makes more sense to think of deference as a process that is orthogonal (or more accurately, heterogonal) to the pragmatic mechanisms that give rise to deferred readings, analogous to other productive derivational processes. And conversely, the mere fact that a particular usage is both frequent and stylistically unremarkable doesn't necessarily mean that it is lexicalized (even if that criterion may lead lexicographers to include it in their dictionaries).

A further problem with the traditional view of deference is in the way it classifies the deferred uses of expressions, according to the conceptual relations or correspondences that they manifest. Synecdoche, for example, is defined by the third edition of the *American Heritage Dictionary*, in part, as "a figure of speech in which a part is used for the whole." Over and above the obvious category mistake here – what the dictionary means, of course, is that synecdoche involves using the *names* of parts in place of the *names* of wholes – there are reasons for keeping these relations distinct from the purely linguistic mechanisms that exploit them. For one thing, a single mechanism may exploit several distinct figures. There may be no purely linguistic reason, for example, for distinguishing a traditional synecdoche like *blade* for "sword" from a metonymy like *crown* for "monarch" or a metaphor like *wolf* for "rapacious person."[3] And conversely, a single conceptual correspondence might figure in two distinct kinds of deferred interpretation. For example, the perceived relation between newspaper publishers and their products makes possible two interpretations of the objects in (1) and (2):

(1)   Murdoch bought a newspaper last week.

(2)   (pointing at a newspaper) Murdoch bought that last week.

Still, there are reasons for believing that (1) and (2) involve different linguistic mechanisms, the first affecting the use of descriptive terms and the second the use of demonstratives and indexicals. Finally, we will see that linguistic mechanisms of transfer are subject to certain constraints which aren't necessarily implicit in the conceptual relations they depend on, but which require the introduction of independent principles.

2   Meaning Transfers

With this as background, we can turn to the linguistic mechanisms that license the deferred uses of expressions. In this article, I will concentrate on the mechanism I will refer to as MEANING TRANSFER, which underlies what we ordinarily describe as the metaphorical and metonymic uses of names and descriptions. I will start by discussing meaning transfer as a purely pragmatic process, then turn to the way it is implicated in various lexicalized rules and schemas, and then finally discuss its application to some long-standing questions in syntax.

Meaning transfer is the process that allows us to use an expression that denotes one property as the name of another property, provided there is a salient functional relation between the two.[4] These relations can obtain in virtue of a direct correspondence between properties, when one property calls up another that it resembles (as in metaphor) or evokes (as in synaesthesias like *a blue mood*). When we use the word *horseshoe* to refer to a logical operator shaped like a horseshoe, for example, we exploit a relation that can be characterized without reference to the circumstances of any particular horseshoes or any particular typographical marks. Or the relation can be mediated by relations between the bearers of the properties. This is what underlies transfers involving metonymy and synecdoche, such as when we use the word *novel* or the name of a particular novel to refer to the film rights to a work, as in "Spielberg bought the novel for $1 million." In that case we exploit a correspondence that holds between distinct instances of film rights and distinct novels: there is exactly one of the former for each of the latter. In what follows I will be mostly talking about the second sort of transfer, but everything I say will apply with appropriate modifications to transfers of the first kind as well.

Meaning transfers can apply to predicates of any kind, whether lexical or phrasal, and whether used attributively or predicatively. By way of developing some of the features of the process, let's consider (3):

(3)   I am parked out back.

One might be tempted to say that the transfer in (3) applies to the subject *I*, in a sort of "driver for car" metonymy. But there are a number of reasons for assuming that the transfer here applies to the conventional meaning of the predicate. For example, if the speaker has two cars, he wouldn't say:

(4)   We are parked out back.

though of course this would be an appropriate utterance if there were two people who were waiting for the car.[5] Note, moreover, that we can conjoin any other predicate that describes the speaker, but not always one that literally describes the car:

(5)   I am parked out back and have been waiting for 15 minutes.

(6)   *I am parked out back and may not start.

For both these reasons, we assume that the predicate *parked out back* in (3) carries a transferred sense, which contributes a property of persons whose cars are parked out back.

Meaning transfer operates not just on the meanings of predicates or verb phrases, but on the meanings of common nouns, as well, whether they appear in predicate position or referring position. Take (7), as uttered by a restaurant waiter:

(7)   Who is the ham sandwich?

The process of transfer is straightforward here; from the point of view of the waiter, at least, customers acquire their most usefully distinctive properties in virtue of their relations to the dishes they order. But in this case, unlike the "parked out back" examples, the relevant property is expressed by a common noun, which can equally well be used as the content of an NP in referential position in a sentence like (8):

(8)   The ham sandwich is at table seven.

In (8), the predicate *ham sandwich* has a transferred meaning, where it contributes a property of people who have ordered ham sandwiches.[6]

3   Conditions on Meaning Transfer

As I noted earlier, meaning transfer is possible when there is a salient correspondence between the properties of one thing and the properties of another, in which case the name of the first property can be used to refer to the second. With an utterance like *I am parked out back*, for example, we begin with a functional correspondence between the locations of cars in a lot and the properties of the owners or drivers of these cars. When two property domains

correspond in an interesting or useful way – of which more in a moment – we
can schematize the operation of predicate transfer as follows:

(9)   Condition on Meaning Transfer
      Let P and P′ be sets of properties that are related by a salient function
      g_t: P → P′. Then if F is a predicate that denotes a property P ∈ P, there
      is also a predicate F′, spelled like F, that denotes the property P′, where
      P′ = g_t (P).[7]

A correspondence of this sort can hold in either of two cases. Sometimes there
is a direct functional relation between two sets of properties, as in cases of
metaphor and synaesthesia – for example in the relation between grades of
temperature (cold, cool, warm, hot) and the affects they bring to mind. In
other cases, though, the correspondences between properties are mediated by
correspondences between their bearers, which is what underlies metonymic
and synecdochic transfers. There is no direct correspondence between the
property of being parked out back and the distinguishing property of any
particular person, save via the relation between a person and the thing that
has that property. We can represent this particular case of meaning transfer as
follows:

(10)   Metonymic Transfers
       Let h be a salient function from a set of things A to another (disjoint) set
       of things B. Then for any predicate F that denotes a property P that
       applies to something in A, we can represent the meaning of a derived
       predicate F′, spelled like F, as in either a or b:

       a. $\lambda P. \lambda y (\forall x_{[dom\ h]}. h(x) = y \rightarrow P(x))$
       b. $\lambda P. \lambda y (\exists x_{[dom\ h]}. h(x) = y$ and $P(x))$

Note that this entails that predicates of this type are in fact ambiguous between
"universal" and "existential" readings, depending on whether all or only some
of the bearers of the original property are in the inverse image of h for a given
value. And in fact both types of reading are generally available. In cases like
"I am parked out back," we would normally assume that the speaker means
to say that all the (relevant) cars he is looking for are parked out back, as in
(10a).[8] By contrast, when a painter says, "I am in the Whitney," she doesn't
imply that all her paintings or even all her relevant paintings are in the Whitney,
but only that something she painted is in the Whitney, as in (10b). And when
an accountant says of her firm, "We are in Chicago," she might intend either
interpretation, depending on whether she's talking about all of the firm's offices
or merely about one of them. Still, it is more useful to think of these two types
of readings as two ways of instantiating the general schema given in (9), rather
than as two distinct conditions that license predicate transfer. Meaning transfer
is a single linguistic process.

4   The Criterion of Noteworthiness

The schemas in (9) and (10) do a reasonable job of representing the truth conditions associated with utterances like "I am parked out back" and "I'm in the Whitney," but they miss some important pragmatic conditions on the use of such utterances. For example, suppose my car was once driven by Yogi Berra. Then according to the conditions in (10), I should be able to use the name of this property to describe the property that I acquire in virtue of my relationship to my car. But it would be odd for me to say:

(11)   ?I was once driven by Yogi Berra.

even in a context in which it might be relevant to say, "My car was once driven by Yogi Berra." By the same token, a painter might say with reference to one of her paintings, "I'm in the Whitney Museum," but not, ordinarily:

(12)   ?I'm in the second crate on the right.

Intuitively, the difference is this: when a painting goes into a museum its creator acquires a significant or notable property, whereas when it goes into a crate she doesn't, at least not usually.[9]

Let me describe this condition by saying that predicate transfer is only possible when the property contributed by the new predicate is "noteworthy," which is to say one that is useful for classifying or identifying its bearer relative to the conversational interests. In this sense noteworthiness is equivalent to what Downing (1977) meant when she said that novel noun–noun compounds must be "appropriately classificatory," and to the conditions that Clark and Clark (1979) observed on the zero-derivation of English verbs from nouns. The fact that the criterion is applicable here demonstrates that the transfer process creates new predicates with new meanings, just as other derivational processes do.[10]

It is important to bear in mind that noteworthiness is not the same thing as relevance, though it is clearly a related notion. In this connection, consider (13) and (14), adapted from Jackendoff (1992):

(13)   Ringo was hit in the fender by a truck when he was momentarily distracted by a motorcycle.

(14)   ?Ringo was hit in the fender by a truck two days after he died.

Let's assume that these utterances exemplify transfers of the meanings of the relevant relational expressions – that is, that *Ringo* denotes the singer rather than his car.[11] The difference between the two cases is that when a truck hits Ringo's car while he is driving it, the event will probably have important consequences for him as well: he is likely to have been startled, or annoyed, or put to trouble and expense. Whereas once Ringo is dead, the things that happen to his car don't generally invest him with any properties worth mentioning.[12] But while the distinction is intuitively clear, our ability to characterize it formally requires that we be able to distinguish between the relevance of a proposition (e.g. that Ringo's car was hit) and the relevance of its trivial entailments (e.g. that Ringo has the property of having had his car hit). It may be that a suitable version of relevance theory will be able to clarify this distinction, but for the present purposes we can just take noteworthiness in an intuitive way.[13]

5   Predicate Transfer in Systematic Polysemy

The availability of transfer for common nouns, adjectives, and other lexical categories is what underlies the patterns of lexical alternation that have been described using such terms as "regular polysemy" (Apresjan 1973), "deferred reference" (Nunberg 1979), "semantic transfer rules" (Leech 1974), "sense transfer" (Sag 1981), "connectors" (Fauconnier 1985), "sense extensions" and "logical metonymies" (Pustejovsky 1991, 1995, Copestake and Briscoe 1995), "lexical networks" (Norvig and Lakoff 1987), "subregularities" (Wilensky 1991), and "lexical implication rules" (Ostler and Atkins 1991) – not to mention just plain "metonymy" and "metaphor" (see, among many others, Lakoff 1987). Needless to say, there are many differences among these approaches, both formally and in the data they are invoked to explain. But they all involve the same type of generalizations, which can be phrased as implicational statements of the form: "If an expression has a use of type U, it also has a use of type U'." For example, the name of a writer can be used to refer to his or her works, a word that denotes a periodical publication or kind of periodical publication can be used to refer to the organization that publishes it; and a word that denotes a kind of plant or animal can refer to its meat or substance (this latter is the rule called "grinding").

(15)   Proust is on the top shelf.

(16)   The *Chronicle* (the newspaper) opposed the highway project.

(17)   We were eating chicken on tables made of oak.

Many of these rules are much more general in their application than the examples we have been discussing, and require no specialized context to license them. The correspondence between the properties of dishes and customers provides a useful means of identification only in the domain of a restaurant, and then only relative to the interests of waiters – we could think of usages like these as examples of Clark and Clark's (1979) "contextual expressions." In general, we don't think of these as involving lexical senses of the items in question: their number is too open-ended, and their use tends to be restricted to particular types of contexts or subcommunities of speakers.[14]

But the property correspondences that license the transfers in (15)–(17) hold across a wider range of situations, and provide a more context-independent way of classifying the bearers of derived properties. In these cases we may very well want to say that the transferred predicate represents a lexical sense of the item in question, or at least deserves listing in a dictionary.[15] To a certain extent, this is a relative matter. For example standard dictionaries often assign the word *white* a sense like "In chess, the person playing white." They do this because even though the correspondence between a color and a role is context-specific, the derived predicates *white* and *black* are much more generally useful for classifying chess players than the property of having ordered a ham sandwich as a means of classifying restaurant customers, since so many relevant things follow from which color a player takes.

As usages become progressively more useful and less specialized, we come to the more general patterns of lexical alternation that are commonly described by means of the formula "x for y," as in "artist for work" or the alternation sometimes described as "portioning," as in "I spilled a couple of beers." In the extreme case we can talk about very general patterns of alternation like the systematic polysemy of abstract nouns like *obstinacy* or *vanity*, which can refer either to a quality or to the extent of its instantiation in a particular case (see Aronoff 1976):

(18)   Obstinacy is usually a mistake.

(19)   Her obstinacy surprised us.

6   Semantics or Pragmatics?

At this point we can ask in what ways the alternations created by meaning transfer should be treated as semantic (that is to say, conventionalized), rather than being derived by purely pragmatic processes. As I noted earlier, this is not a simple matter of a privative opposition: the mere fact that an alternation is in some way conventionalized does not mean that it no longer has any pragmatic basis. In the extreme case, of course, alternations may be preserved in the lexicon as the *disjecta membra* of transfers that no longer have any productive role in the language, whether because the background assumptions that originally licensed them are no longer valid, or because the items have acquired specialized meanings over the years. We may still perceive a certain relation among the uses of *cell* to refer to small rooms, organizational units, and the structural units of biology, but no one would seriously propose that these could all be generated from some core sense via purely pragmatic inferences – over the years the senses have been enriched with lexically specific material (a political cell, for example, is necessarily clandestine). At the other end of the scale, there are uses like those in the *ham sandwich* cases that are obviously extralexical – that is, as generated exclusively by pragmatic principles, with no need of any lexical specification. In the middle, however, lies a very broad range of productive alternations whose status is less clear.

There are several factors that militate for a semantic treatment of certain alternations. In the first place, alternations are sometimes subject to language-specific restrictions that don't seem to have any obvious pragmatic explanations. For some reason or another, for example, the English rule of grinding seems not to apply to yield the names of liquids:

(20)   ?We fried the chicken in safflower (olive, corn, etc.).

(21)   ?I enjoy a glass of orange (pear, apple, etc.) with my breakfast.

The meaning that *safflower* would have in (20) is clear enough – what else would you fry things in, if not an oil? – and it may very well be that in some kitchens cooks routinely use *safflower* in this way, but this is not the general practice. Analogously, in English we use the names of painters to refer to their works, and of designers to refer to their clothes, but we don't do this with the names of composers, and we do it with the names of novelists and film-makers only when they produce genre fiction or genre films:

(22)   She owns two Picassos and a Renoir.

(23)   The sale racks at the store were full of Jill Sanders.

(24)   ?We listened to a lovely Scarlatti (?Steven Sondheim).

(25)   I love to curl up with a good Agatha Christie (Simenon, ?Italo Calvino, ?Dostoyevsky).

(26)   One of my favorite Hitchcocks (?Renoirs) is playing at the Bijou.

There may very well be some subtle ethnoaesthetic explanation for these patterns, but it is by no means obvious what it could be – certainly it can't be argued that the interpretation of *a Dostoyevsky* would be any harder to figure out than the interpretation of *an Agatha Christie*. On the face of things, this is just a fact of English.[16]

The rule of portioning provides similar examples. As Copestake and Briscoe (1995) observe, the rule is highly productive: we can say, "I drank two beers," "I drank two Michelobs," and so forth. But for some reason the rule doesn't apply to the names of wines. "I drank two Sauternes last night" can only involve reference to two types of wine, not two glasses. It may be that this difference has a connection with a difference in the way beer and wine were historically sold, but in the wine-bar-saturated context of modern London or San Francisco, it certainly feels like an arbitrary constraint.

We can make a similar point about the use of words like *cheerful* and *sad* to apply to places or circumstances that evoke certain emotional responses. We speak of *a cheerful room* or *a sad turn of affairs*, but the alternation doesn't extend to items like *afraid* and *frightened*; we don't speak of *an afraid house*, for example. Pustejovsky (1995) has noted that this behavior correlates with the fact that *sad*-type predicates do not take prepositional objects except by adjunction (e.g. *sad about the loss*), whereas passive participles like *frightened* do (e.g. *frightened of the bear*). The observation seems sound, but it is hard to see how we could get from this syntactic property to a purely pragmatic explanation of which predicates allow this alternation.

Similar patterns emerge when we look at systematic polysemy cross-linguistically. For example, there seems to be no salient cultural reason why French-speakers should use the names of fruits to refer to the brandies made from them (*une prune, une poire*) whereas English-speakers do not.[17] Apresjan (1973) notes that in Russian you can use the name of an organ to denote a disease of that organ, as in "She has a kidneys." But this usage is not common in English, though it would be comprehensible enough.

More generally, languages can differ not just in the particular alternations that they permit, but in the general tolerance of polysemous processes. According to Jerrold Sadock (personal communication), Greenlandic Eskimo permits few types of systematic polysemy; for example, it does not allow grinding of animal names to produce mass terms for either meat or fur, though you can apply grinding to tree names to get terms for wood. So you can't say, "He eats walrus" or "He wears walrus," but you can say "His boat is made of oak." Here too, we seem to be dealing with arbitrary lexical restrictions, though in this case we would want to cast them as very general principles.

But even when there are strong arguments that militate for treating a given pattern of systematic polysemy as lexicalized, there may still be reasons for looking to pragmatics to explain the intricacies of its application. There are various exceptions to general patterns of polysemous alternation that can be explained only by reference to the noteworthiness criterion that I described earlier. For example, the name of a publication can be used to refer to a publisher only when the publication is one that is usually produced by an organization dedicated to that task – a newspaper or travel guide, say, but not a cookbook or Latin grammar. Only in those circumstances would there be an identificationally useful correspondence between the distinctive properties of the publication and those of its publisher. Clearly, though, this isn't the sort of property that would be specified in the lexical entries for items like *newspaper* and *cookbook*: the essential properties of those types of publications are independent of the particular economic structures in which they are produced.[18] In the same way, while we saw that the application of the rule of grinding is subject to various lexical constraints, it answers to pragmatic considerations as well. We don't ordinarily use the names of breeds to refer to the meat of animals, for example, but we sometimes use them to refer to their hides or fleeces: we say *She wears angora* but not *We don't eat angora*. But this isn't a matter of lexical meanings, and it would take only a slight modification of culinary or sartorial practices to change the pattern.

A similar point could be made about the well-studied phenomena involving verb-class alternations. For example, Dowty (2000) has pointed out that the criterion of noteworthiness is relevant to determining when predicates permit the "*swarm* alternation" exemplified by (27) and (28):

(27)   Bees are swarming in the garden.

(28)   The garden is swarming with bees.

Dowty points out that like other derivational processes, such as noun–noun compounding, new predicates formed on the model of (28) are felicitous only if they contribute "the property a place or space has when it is 'characterized' by an activity taking place within it – that is, when the extent, intensity, frequency, and/or perceptual salience of [the] activity [that] takes place there is sufficient to characterize the Location in a way that is relevant for some purpose in the current discourse" (2000: 122). So while there is no question that the *swarm* alternation is a lexicalized construction of English, its application is nonetheless subject to broadly pragmatic conditions on meaning transfer.

7   Transfer in Composition

The observations about noteworthiness that we've made here help to shed some light on compositional processes, as well. It's well known, for example, that adjectives can exhibit a considerable flexibility as regards the relation of their conventional meaning to their heads. Following Leech (1974), Fillmore (1978) has noted that the adjective *topless* can be used in any of the following ways:

(29)a.   *topless swimsuit*, "swimsuit without a top."
   b.   *topless dancer*, "dancer who wears a swimsuit without a top."
   c.   *topless bar*, "bar featuring dancers who wear swimsuits without a top."
   d.   *topless district*, "district containing bars featuring dancers who wear swimsuits without a top."
   e.   *topless legislation*, "legislation regulating bars featuring dancers who wear swimsuits without a top."

As Fillmore points out, there are two ways of analyzing examples like these: we can assume either that the adjective has a transferred meaning in (29b)–(29e) or that the adjective retains its literal meaning and the looser connection between it and the noun meaning is made possible constructionally in one way or another.

Pustejovsky (1991) opts for a constructional approach in connection with the analogous example of *a fast motorway*, which has a meaning equivalent to "a motorway permitting fast driving." On his analysis, this interpretation arises when the adjective is applied in its conventional meaning to an event embedded in the telic structure of the noun *motorway*, which yields an interpretation as in (30):

(30)   ... *Telic* = λe[*drive on* (e, people) and *fast* (e)]

This line of analysis could in theory be applied to examples like:

(31)   *fast food*, "food intended for rapid service and consumption."

(32)   *free-range chicken* (*eggs*), "chicken meat (eggs) derived from free-range chickens."

There are reasons, though, for thinking that the multiple readings here arise from lexical transfers rather than from constructional vagueness or ambiguity. Note that only certain adjectives can appear in these constructions:

(33)   A fast (?drunken) motorway.

(34)   Fast (?rude) food.

(35)   Free-range (?beheaded) chicken.

(36)   Topless (?Speedo) bars.

   These observations can be explained by appeal to the criterion of note-worthiness: the property of motorways that permits fast driving is significant to classifying them, and for this reason we can derive a new adjective *fast′* to denote this property. But the property of motorways that permits drunken driving has no particular classificatory usefulness, and hence the conventional meaning of *drunken* does not correspond to a noteworthy property of motorways. Analogously, we can usefully classify foods according to whether they are characteristically eaten or served quickly, but not according to whether they are eaten or served in a rude manner. And while the way a chicken was nourished corresponds to a noteworthy property of its meat, the fact that it was killed by beheading does not. Finally, we may find it useful to single out a class of bars whose dancers wear topless garments, but people to date have not demonstrated an interest in distinguishing classes of bars according to the brand of swimsuit that their dancers wear.[19]
   Note that this is not to say that postulating a deferred meaning for an expression is always preferable to offering a constructional solution or to assigning the expression a more general monosemous meaning. For example, consider examples like (37)–(39):

(37)   We enjoyed the movie.

(38)   We enjoyed the book.

(39)   We enjoyed the talk.

In principle, we could understand the objects in (37)–(39) as having transferred senses that enable them to refer, respectively, to the processes of watching a movie, reading a book, and listening to a talk. But there seems to be no criterion of noteworthiness associated with this construction – the object of *enjoy* can be just about any noun that can be associated with some kind of process that could evoke pleasure, from a radio to a thermos bottle to a printing press.[20] It seems preferable, then, to assume that the interpretations of (37)–(39) are supplied constructionally, possibly following the proposals of Pustejovsky (1991) and Copestake and Briscoe (1995).[21]

8   Noteworthiness as a Diagnostic

The examples we've been discussing show how the criterion of noteworthiness provides a useful diagnostic for determining whether and where meaning transfer is present. Consider sentence (40), from Copestake and Briscoe (1995):

(40)   The south side of Cambridge voted Conservative.

On the face of things, we might analyze (40) in either of two ways: either the description within the subject NP has a transferred meaning that describes a group of people, or the VP has a transferred meaning in which it conveys the property that jurisdictions acquire in virtue of the voting behavior of their residents. In this connection, Briscoe and Copestake observe that not all geographical descriptions can be used in constructions like these:

(41)   Three villages/three villages south of the river/?three villages built of stone voted for the proposed ban on timber production.

Briscoe and Copestake note that "it appears that only modifiers which might apply to the group of people, or which are locational (*the south side of Cambridge*) are fully acceptable" (1996: 45). We might put this by saying that geographical expressions can have transferred meanings in which they apply to groups of people only when the property they denote correlates usefully with a distinguishing characteristic of those groups. This property need not necessarily be locational – one might say, for example, *Villages with large numbers of detached single-family houses tend to vote Conservative*, since the kinds of housing a village has may correlate with some distinctive properties of people who live there.

But the restrictions on this type of transfer make clear that the transfers in (40) and (41) is on the interpretation of the subject NP. An analogous point could be made about a sentence like (42):

(42)   The huge (?domed) stadium rose as one to cheer the team.

The size of a stadium correlates with an important property, the magnitude, of the group of people who fill it; its architectural features do not. Again, this supports the analysis of (42), in which the subject has a deferred interpretation.[22]

Note, by contrast, that other words that denote places or physical locations can be used without restriction to refer to the people who frequent or inhabit them. Consider the difference between (43)–(44) and (45)–(46), after some examples suggested by Cruse (2000):

(43)   The factory is out on strike.

(44)   ?The factory rose as one to cheer the contract.

(45)   The school is taking a day off.

(46)   The school rose as one to cheer the football team's victory.

Factory behaves like *village* – it can have a transferred sense in which it applies to people just in case it provides a noteworthy property of the group. But *school* seems to have a single lexical meaning that allows it to denote both a building and the people who use or run it. Following Pustejovsky (1995), we could say that *school* has a "dot object" structure, which provides for its use to refer to things of different types, though nothing turns on this particular form of analysis.[23] But whether we can postulate a univocal analysis of a word depends on how and whether the criterion of noteworthiness comes into play in determining its uses.

9   Syntactic Consequences: "Sortal Crossings"

On the basis of the examples I gave by way of introducing the notion of predicate transfer, like *I am parked out back*, it might be thought that the process is generally confined to highly context-particular situations, particularly as it affects phrasal constituents. In fact, though, the mechanism is applied very widely and usually passes without notice. This point has a particular relevance to the syntactic phenomena that we can think of as "sortal crossings," as in (47), suggested by Jackendoff, and (48):

(47)   Ringo squeezed himself into a narrow space.

(48)   Yeats did not like to hear himself read in an English accent.

On the standard way of thinking about these phenomena, the reflexives in these examples present a problem, since they seem not to be coreferential with their antecedents. In (47), the subject *Ringo* refers to a person, whereas the reflexive appears to refer to his car. In the heyday of imperial syntax, there were proposals to handle sentences like this one by means of syntactico-semantic operations like "car deletion" or with other formal devices of roughly equivalent effects, and other people have suggested various semantic and pragmatic approaches.

But approaches like these all have the same failing, in presuming that the reflexive is not strictly coreferential with the subject. In fact we might better think of a sentence like (47) as involving a transfer in which *squeeze into a narrow space* has a meaning that applies to persons – it denotes the relation that people enter into in virtue of the maneuvers they perform with their car. In this case the reflexive and its antecedent are coreferential in a strict sense. And by the same token, for (48) we can assume that people who read Yeats's poetry aloud are doing something to him as well. But here again, the transfer is only available when the derived property or relation provides some useful or noteworthy information about its bearer, in accord with modern assumptions about authorship. So we wouldn't ordinarily say:

(49)   ?Yeats wrote a lot of himself in sprung rhythm.

When Yeats writes a poem in a particular metrical pattern, that is, he is not performing an operation on himself, in the way that someone who reads his poetry aloud is also doing something to him.

All of this leads to a strong hypothesis: natural language permits no sortal crossings in any of the rules or constructions that ordinarily impose conditions of identity – not just with reflexives, but with pronouns, relative constructions, and so forth. In a sentence like (50), for example, we can assume that the content of the clause *was featured in a Madonna video* has a deferred meaning in which it contributes the property that newspaper companies acquire in virtue of the exposure given their publications:

(50)   The newspaper that Mary works for was featured in a Madonna video.

But not everything that happens to a newspaper copy confers a noteworthy property on its publisher, of course:

(51)   ?The newspaper that Mary works for fell off the table.

Stallard (1993) suggests an analogous example:

(52)   No airlines that fly to Denver are based on the East Coast.

In this case the predicate in the relative clause contributes the noteworthy property that an airline acquires from the activities of the flights it operates. But other activities of flights don't have these consequences for the airlines that operate them:

(53)   ?The airline disappeared behind a mountain.

A related hypothesis would stipulate that there need be no relaxing of the coordinate structure constraint to deal with sentences like:

(54)   Roth is Jewish and widely read.

Instead, we will interpret both *Jewish* and *widely read* as predicates that contribute properties of persons. In this way we can honor the intuitions that originally motivated semanticists to appeal to zeugma as a way of determining whether a word has one or more senses.[24]

ACKNOWLEDGMENTS

Versions of this material can be found in Nunberg (1979, 1995) and Nunberg and Zaenen (1992). For comments on these articles, I am grateful to Sue Atkins, Ted Briscoe, Cleo Condoravdi, Ann Copestake, Lauri Karttunen, James Pustejovsky, Ivan Sag, Tom Wasow, and Annie Zaenen. I am grateful to Gregory Ward for comments on this article.

NOTES

1   The study of the cultural and cognitive implications of the belief systems that underlie various forms of deferred use has been an important theme in the program of cognitive linguistics; see, among many others, Johnson (1987), Lakoff (1987), Lakoff and Turner (1989), Sweetser (1990).

2   The view of polysemes and idioms as "dead metaphors" is mostly wishful, when you think about it, since there is no evidence that most such usages were ever "live" in the sense that they were transparent and optimal ways expressing certain meanings. Despite the earnest efforts of armchair philologists to find the "true story" behind figures like *pull the wool over someone's eyes* or *rob Peter to pay Paul*, there's no reason to believe that these expressions were ever completely transparent – that there was a time when everybody had a particular Peter and Paul in mind.

3   Another reason for distinguishing between types of figuration and the linguistic processes that exploit them is that the same relations that

underlie metaphor, metonymy, and the rest can be used in non-linguistic systems of communication, such as the icons on a computer desktop.

4 I am speaking here of properties, but everything I say will generalize to relations and other types.

5 By the same token, in Italian the predicate adjective agrees with the subject, so in (i), with "my father" as subject, we would express the transferred meaning using a masculine adjective *parcheggiato* for "parked," even though the word for "car" is a feminine, *la macchina*:

(i) Mio padre è parcheggiato (*parcheggiata*, fem. sing.) in dietro. "My father is parked out back."

6 In some discussions, examples like (8) have been analyzed as involving a kind of "reference transfer" or "deferred reference," with the implication that an actual ham sandwich must figure in the interpretation of the utterance – that is, that the transfer operates on the NP interpretation. But there are a number of reasons for concluding that the transfer here takes place on the common noun meaning – that is, that this is a case of meaning transfer, rather than reference transfer. One way to make this point is to consider the interpretation of the determiner in the phrase *the ham sandwich*, which doesn't presuppose the existence of a unique ham sandwich (think of a waiter in a fast-food restaurant who is standing in front of a table piled with ham sandwiches), but does presuppose the existence of a unique ham-sandwich orderer. Or we can consider some examples involving anaphor. Fauconnier (1985) gives examples (i) and (ii):

(i) The mushroom omelet was eating with chopsticks.
(ii) *The mushroom omelet was eating itself/himself with chopsticks.

The use of a reflexive in (ii) would presume that the object of *eat* was introduced by the subject NP – that is, that the subject NP actually referred to a mushroom omelet on the route to its ultimate interpretation. But inasmuch as the transfer actually takes place at the level of the common noun, which contributes only a property of persons, the example is ill formed.

Gregory Ward (personal communication) has observed that it is in fact possible to say things like:

(iii) The ham sandwich is complaining because the bread is soggy.

where it might be argued that it is only in virtue of the introduction of a ham sandwich as a discourse referent that we can infer the uniqueness of the bread. I agree that utterances like (iii) are more felicitous than the referentially equivalent (iv):

(iv) The customer at table 7 is complaining because the bread is soggy.

It can be argued, though, that the relative felicity of (iv) is due more to the mode of presentation of the reference (i.e., as a ham-sandwich orderer) than in virtue of the introduction of any actual ham sandwich as a discourse referent. By analogy, consider how we sometimes take advantage of the nominal root of a derived adjective to establish the definiteness of some other thing that's associated with the reference of that root:

(v)   I don't much like Italian food but I'd like to learn the language.
(vi) ?I don't much like the kind of food they serve at Mario's Grotto but I'd like to learn the language.

In neither (v) nor (vi) is Italy itself an element of the discourse, but the country is made salient by the mode of presentation of a certain kind of food in (v).

7   The "salience" of a function depends on a number of factors. Among other things, the properties in the domain of the function (here, car locations) have to be discriminable, and the relation itself has to be manifestly familiar to participants. These conditions are schematized at some length in Nunberg (1995), though in that paper these transfer functions were defined over domains of individuals rather than properties, and no distinction was made between predicate transfer and what I call DEFERRED INDEXICAL REFERENCE, the operation that explains how you can point at a set of keys and say "That is parked out back."

8   Ordinarily, of course, a single parking-lot patron is interested in only a single car, but we can imagine cases in which a single person has come with more than one car – or, more plausibly, we can take an author's utterance of a sentence like "I'm published by Knopf," which on its most likely reading is equivalent to "All of my books are published by Knopf."

9   Of course the noteworthiness of a property depends among other things on the conversational interests, and you could fiddle with the utterance or the context in such a way as to make most of these examples acceptable. A painter who feels she is being slighted in favor of other painters in her gallery, for example, might say:

(i)   Those daubers get one-person shows while I'm relegated to a crate in the basement.

The most we can say, then, is that certain derived properties are canonically or stereotypically more noteworthy than others, a difference that will be important when we come to talk about the lexicalization of predicate transfer.

10   The requirement of noteworthiness is one feature that distinguishes meaning transfer from the process of deferred indexical reference that I mentioned in connection with (2), an utterance of *Murdoch bought that*, accompanied by demonstration of a newspaper. This follows from the fact that deferred indexical reference exploits correspondences between individual things, not the properties associated with lexical meanings – it does not create new predicates (or any predicates at all). For example, the name of a publication can't be used to refer to a publisher unless there is a salient functional relation between the distinctive properties of the first and the distinctive properties of the second, which usually obtains because the publishing organization is constituted to produce only that work. That explains why we can say *She works for a newspaper* but not *She works for a cookbook*. But if the identity of a publisher is evident in the appearance of a particular cookbook, we can point at it and say *She works for them*. I will not

take up the phenomenon of deferred indexical reference in this article; for a discussion, see Nunberg (1993).

11   Jackendoff analyzes these as involving transfer of the sense of *Ringo*, rather than of the relational expressions, but we've seen that there are a number of reasons for rejecting this approach.

12   Of course one could say, "Picasso had to wait until after he died to get into the Louvre." But in this case the transferred predicate here applies to the personage, who survives the person.

13   See Sperber and Wilson (1995) and the large body of literature on relevance theory that has grown out of their work.

14   From the linguistic point of view, perhaps, the most interesting forms of transfer involve the multiple uses of functors and grammatical categories – prepositions, for example, or simple verbs of motion. I won't have anything to say about these types of transfer here, simply because the subject is too vast.

15   This doesn't necessarily mean that the senses have been conventionalized. Dictionaries often assign separate senses to the common metaphorical uses of words, for example, even though these might be predictable. To take an example suggested by Fillmore and Atkins (2000), the fact that dictionaries assign the word *crawl* a sense "to act or behave in a servile manner" doesn't mean that people couldn't come up with this use of the word in the absence of a convention. Dictionaries are more concerned with recording what is conventional in the loose sense of the word (i.e. as opposed to what is unconventional) than in its strict sense (as opposed to what is non-conventional).

16   I would be happier with this conclusion if the same regularities didn't show up in more-or-less the same form in a number of other languages.

17   In French, one can use the expression *une menthe* to refer to a syrup made from mint, but one cannot use *une* (or *un*) *pomme* to refer to a juice made from apples. This last example shows that these are not simple cases of ellipsis of the head noun, which in the case of syrups (*un syrop*) would be masculine.

18   It could easily happen that cookbook publishing should become the province of dedicated organizations, as dictionary publishing is, in which case it would make sense to say "John works for a cookbook." But the lexical meaning of *cookbook* would not have changed in the process.

19   Though, as one of the editors points out to me, people do sometimes have an interest in distinguishing bars according to the material worn by their patrons – e.g. leather.

20   Copestake and Briscoe (1995) suggest that the sentence *We enjoyed the dictionary* is odd because dictionary is not lexically associated with a process. But it's easy to imagine a context in which this sentence could be used, and more generally, there is no requirement that the relevant process be explicit in the lexical meaning of the noun. When someone says, for example, *I enjoy the beach*, the understanding is that the speaker enjoys the activity of sitting around or walking at the beach, but there is nothing in the meaning of the word that specifies these processes.

21   There is no reason to assume that meaning transfer is involved in all processes of type-shifting, for

example when a verb like *consider* coerces a predicate interpretation of its complement. In contrast to the cases we have been talking about, criteria of noteworthiness seem to play no role here: there is no constraint on what NP can be substituted for *x* in the frame "I consider it an x."

22 One thing we should note is that in some cases transfers can apply either to a subject or to a predicate in such a way that it can be difficult to tell which element has the transferred reading. In a sentence like *Stevens is challenging*, for example, we might assume either that a transfer occurs on the noun *Stevens* to enable it to contribute the property of a body of literary work, or that *challenging* has a transferred meaning that contributes a property that writers acquire in virtue of the properties of their works. Note that we could elaborate this sentence with either an animate or an inanimate pronoun:

(i) Many people find Stevens challenging, but we sell a lot of it.
(ii) Many people find Stevens challenging, but he regarded his poems as simple.

In (i), transfer occurs on the noun *Stevens*; in (ii), on the predicate *challenging*.

23 Cruse would presumably explain this distinction by saying that *school* and *factory* are both monosemous, but would highlight different "facets" of lexical meaning. This is similar, I believe, to what Langacker (1984, 1987) is getting at when he talks about "active zones," this in connection with examples like (i) and (ii):

(i) We heard the bugle.
(ii) I finally blinked.

In (i), what we heard was **the sound** of a bugle; on Langacker's view this reading is created when the verb emphasizes a certain substructure of lexical meaning. In one form or another, this kind of analysis is certainly justified for many words that denote complex objects, but it is an empirical question whether we want to apply it in any given case, as opposed to postulating a meaning transfer. One reason for supposing that it may not be the right tack in (i) is that *bugle* can often designate a disembodied sound, as in:

(iii) The bugle floated faintly in the still night air.

But this form of analysis certainly seems plausible for (ii), as an alternative to supposing a transfer from persons to eyelids. In the end, of course, the choice between a monosemous analysis and one involving meaning transfer can't always be cleanly resolved – there is no magic way to resolve the long-standing lexicographical debates between "splitters" and "lumpers" of word-senses. For an appreciation of just how complicated these issues can become when one tries to resolve them in full lexicographical detail, see Fillmore and Atkins (2000).

24 Note that sortal crossings of this sort are not possible when the transfers are metaphorical rather than metonymic; that is, when they involve a direct relationship between properties rather than one mediated by relations among their bearers. For example, we can't say (i):

(i) ?The second line of the proof begins with the horseshoe that's hanging on the wall of Deb's room.

In this and similar cases, the particular things in the range of the transfer function don't acquire properties from anything that happens to the things in its domain – that is, nothing that happens to any real horseshoe has any consequences (noteworthy or otherwise) for any particular horseshoe-shaped symbol.

16 Pragmatics of Language Performance

HERBERT H. CLARK

1 Introduction

Language seems orderly when it is found in novels, plays, and news broadcasts, but much less so when it is heard in cafés, classrooms, and offices. Take this exchange between two British academics:

(1) Peter: And he's going to go to the top, is he?
     Reynard: Well, Mallet said he felt it would be a good thing if Oscar went.

This is an example worthy of a playwright, but what Peter and Reynard actually produced was this:[1]

(2) Peter: and he's going to . go to the top, is he?
     Reynard: well, . I mean this . uh Mallet said Mallet was uh said something about uh you know he felt it would be a good thing if u:h . if Oscar went,   (1.2.370)

In his answer, Reynard decides what to say as he goes along. He takes first one direction ("Mallet said something about") and then another ("he felt it . . ."). Along the way he replaces phrases, makes clarifications (with *I mean* and *you know*), and introduces delays (with *uh*). Reynard's utterance looks anything but orderly, and yet he succeeds in coordinating with Peter on what he wanted to say. How do they manage?

Pragmatics traditionally has focused on the PREPLANNED, NON-INTERACTIVE language of novels, plays, and news broadcasts. The pioneers in the field (e.g. Austin 1962, Lewis 1969, Searle 1969, 1975a, Bach and Harnish 1979, Sperber and Wilson 1986a, Grice 1989) all worked from clean, invented examples.[2] But if pragmatics is the study of language in use, it must also account for the SPONTANEOUS, INTERACTIVE LANGUAGE of cafés, classrooms, and offices. Language evolved, after all, before people could read or write, attend plays, or watch television. Even today, the primary setting for language use is conversation. Accounting for the features of (2) that are absent from (1) will require principles beyond those needed for preplanned, non-interactive language.

This chapter is about communicative acts that are needed in the performance of language. The argument is this (H. Clark 1996, 1999): Spontaneous, interactive language has its origins in joint activities. When people do things together in cafés, classrooms, and offices, they need to coordinate their individual actions, and they use a variety of communicative acts to achieve that coordination. These constitute the PRIMARY SYSTEM of communication – the official business of their discourse. But communicative acts are themselves joint actions that require coordinating, and people have a special class of communicative acts for this coordination – including many of Reynard's actions in (2). These constitute the COLLATERAL SYSTEM of communication. The goal here is to characterize the collateral system and the pragmatic principles by which it works.

2   Saying and Displaying

In using language, speakers make communicative choices of many types. Consider an exchange between two academics in a British university common room:

(3)   Nancy: I acquired an absolutely magnificent sewing-machine, by foul means, <u>did I tell you about that,</u>
       Julia: no.

Nancy utters the sentence *Did I tell you about that?* as a signal to Julia. A SIGNAL here is any action by which one person MEANS something for another person in the sense of Grice (1989). Nancy performs her utterance to ask Julia a question and, in turn, to gain her consent to tell her a story.

Signals, however, are Janus-faced objects. One face is CONTENT, the choice of *what* to signal. Nancy, for example, chooses to seek Julia's permission to tell a story; she chooses to do that by asking a question; to ask the question, she selects the English sentence *Did I tell you about that?*; and so on. The other face is PERFORMANCE, the choice of *how* to realize the signal. Nancy, for example, chooses to direct her voice, face, and gestures at Julia. She does this to designate herself as speaker, and Julia as addressee. She chooses to initiate her utterance at that precise moment – not earlier or later – to designate the now of her signal (e.g. for the interpretation of *did*) and its relation to her previous phrases (e.g. for the interpretation of *that*). Nancy's very realization of the sentence *Did I tell you about that?* designates the content of her signal.

Speakers make choices not only in WHAT they say, but in HOW they say it. They perform what they say IN A PARTICULAR TIME, PLACE, AND MANNER – at the right moment, for the right duration, originating from and directed to the right locations, at the right amplitude, with the right gestures. In the terminology adopted here, they DISPLAY their signals to others in order to designate such things as the speaker, addressee, time, place, and content of their signals. What speakers mean by a signal, then, is determined by their choice of both content and display. Schematically:

signal = content + display

Both parts are necessary to the whole. Speakers cannot express the content of their signal without displaying it, nor can they form a display without content to display. And both parts require interpretation *à la Grice*.

2.1   *Displays as indicative acts*

Displays, in this view, are communicative acts of INDICATING. The prototype of indicating is pointing. When June asks, "Which car is yours?" and David points at a nearby Honda, David indicates the Honda as "his car." His act of pointing is an *index* to the car. An index, according to C. S. Peirce (Buchler 1940), signifies its object, its referent, by means of an INTRINSIC CONNECTION – a spatial or causal connection – between the index and the object. David's pointed finger has a spatial connection to the car. The problem is that his pointed finger also has intrinsic connections to his fingernail, his right arm, and the left front door of the Honda, and so brute pointing isn't enough. June is to recognize the connection David intends by inferring his purpose against their current common ground. As a response to her question, he must be indicating the Honda as his car.

Nancy's display of "Did I tell you about that?" has intrinsic connections to a number of SITUATION INDIVIDUALS, and these allow Nancy to use her display to indicate, or point to, these individuals. So in the very realization of her display, Nancy creates a set of PERFORMANCE INDEXES:

- PRODUCER (abbreviated p): Nancy uses the index p to indicate herself as producer of the signal. She creates p through the source and distinctive quality of her voice. Let us denote Nancy's index as p ("did I tell you about that"), which is to be read: the index to the producer of the display of "did I tell you about that."
- RECIPIENT (r): Nancy uses index r to indicate Julia as the recipient of the signal. She creates r by gazing at Julia and directing her voice in Julia's direction at an amplitude appropriate for a person 1.5 meters away.
- TIME (t): Nancy uses index t to indicate the current moment as the now of the signal. She creates t by producing her utterance over that precise interval.
- LOCATION (l): Nancy uses index l to indicate the current location as where she is posing her question. She creates this index by the source of her voice and gestures and by the placement of her body.

- CONTENT (*c*): Nancy uses index *c* to indicate what she is realizing as the content of her signal to Julia.

These are not the only indexes Nancy can create, and each can be analyzed further.

Content *c*, in particular, is a complex index. In traditional accounts, the content of a signal has several levels (Austin 1962, Searle 1969, Bach and Harnish 1979). When Nancy produces "Did I tell you about that," she performs a PHONETIC ACT (producing certain speech sounds), an ILLOCUTIONARY ACT (asking a question), and a PERLOCUTIONARY ACT (getting Julia to agree to answer it), among others.

These accounts, however, assume that speakers act independently of their addressees, and vice versa, and the assumption is clearly false (H. Clark 1996). In their dialogue, Nancy and Julia work together to assure (1) that Julia attends to Nancy's vocalizations and gestures; (2) that Julia identifies Nancy's words and gestures; (3) that Julia figures out what Nancy means by her words and gestures; and (4) that Julia considers what Nancy is proposing. The two of them engage in joint actions at the four levels shown in the table in (4), with A as speaker and B as addressee. These form a ladder of actions that run from Level 1 to Level 4. A and B perform their joint actions at Level 2 by means of their joint actions at Level 1, and so on up the ladder (see Goldman 1970).

(4)   Four levels of joint action in communicative acts

Level	Speaker A's action	Addressee B's action
1.	A makes sounds, gestures for B	B attends to A's sounds, gestures
2.	A presents a signal for B	B identifies what A's signal is
3.	A means something for B	B understands what A means
4.	A proposes a joint project to B	B considers A's proposal

Nancy's display of "Did I tell you about that?" then indexes at least four levels of content: Nancy's sounds and movements; Nancy's phrases and gestures; what Nancy means; and Nancy's proposal. We can denote the index to what she means (Level 3), for example, as *c3* ("Did I tell you about that?"). When Nancy indicates what she means with this index, she expects Julia to identify the referent of the index – namely, what she means by "Did I tell you about that?" If Julia were to say, "What did you mean by that?" she would be using *that* to refer to that content.

In this scheme, therefore, speakers use the display of a signal – the time, place, and manner of its performance – to indicate situational individuals that are essential to the interpretation of the signal. It is as if the producer were saying to the recipient, "In displaying this signal to you, I hereby indicate myself as producer, you as recipient, now as the time of the signal, here as my location, and this sentence, among other things, as the content of the signal."

Without these indexes, Nancy has no way of establishing that she is addressing Julia there and then with the content of her utterance.

2.2 Uses of performance indexes

The most obvious use of displays is to fix the referents of INDEXICAL EXPRESSIONS such as *I, you, here, now, this,* and *that.* For Nancy to ask Julia, "Did I tell you about that?" she must specify the individual people, objects, and times she is referring to with *I, you, that,* and *did.* She does this by indicating them with the display of her utterance – with performance indexes *p, r, l,* and *t.*

Consider the word *I,* which means "the person producing this word." This meaning doesn't by itself specify the referent. It takes *p* ("I") to complete the specification. In (3), then, Nancy's use of *I* indexes *p* ("I"), and it is *p* ("I") that indexes Nancy herself. Even with the display, it isn't always easy for speakers to get addressees to identify the producer. When a student in a large class yells, "I do" in answer to the question, "Does anyone need a syllabus?" the professor may need to ask, "Who said that?" to fix the student's identity. The same holds for other indexical expressions.

Performance indexes have other purposes, too. When June sees David across the street and yells "Hey," she indicates him as his addressee by means of *r* ("hey"), based on the amplitude and direction of her voice and the direction of her gaze and waving hand. When June asks David in a dark room, "Where are you?" and he answers, "Yo," he uses *l* ("yo") to indicate his location at the moment indicated by *t* ("yo") . When a race official says "Ready . . . set . . . go!" he uses *t* ("go") as the starting time of the race. June, David, and the race official use these indexes to fix speakers, addressees, times, locations, and content even when there are no indexical expressions.

The point is especially clear with interjections (see Wilkins 1992). When June calls David on the telephone and says, "Hello," she is performing an illocutionary act whose basic meaning, crudely put, is "I hereby greet you here now." Unlike the paraphrase, June's utterance ("Hello") makes no explicit reference to the speaker, addressee, time, location, or content of that utterance. She indicates these individuals through her display of *hello,* creating *p, r, t, l,* and *c* to bind the arguments associated with *greet.* These is nothing special about interjections. Speakers create the same indexes whenever they display signals to other people.

In all these examples, performance indexes are being used in the primary system of communicative acts – for the official business of the discourse. They are also essential to the collateral system, the topic we turn to next.

3   Coordinating on the Use of Language

Language is ordinarily used for coordinating people's participation in joint activities. Consider Alan and Barbara assembling a TV stand from its parts, as captured on videotape.³ The two of them proceed by agreeing on which pieces to connect at which moments, how to orient each piece, who will hold a piece while the other attaches the screws, and so on. They reach these agreements, or JOINT COMMITMENTS, by means of language and other signals.

What are these agreements about? To engage in any joint activity – from assembling TV stands to negotiating contracts – people must become jointly committed, explicitly or tacitly, to certain REQUISITES, including these:

- Participants: What individuals are to participate in the joint activity?
- Roles: In what roles?
- Content: What actions are they to perform, and what conditions are they to adopt?
- Timing: When are the actions to take place and the conditions to take effect?
- Location: And where?

In assembling the TV stand, Alan and Barbara begin by agreeing to be the participants, as co-builders, in assembling a TV stand at that time and location. Later, as they go along, they agree to more specific content, timing, and locations.

A common way to reach joint commitments is with what I will call PROJECT-IVE PAIRS. A projective pair consists of two actions, by two people, in which (a) the first person PROPOSES a joint project to the second, and (b) the second person TAKES UP that proposal in some way. The classic form is the ADJACENCY PAIR (Schegloff and Sacks 1973), as in this exchange in assembling the TV stand:

(5)   Alan: Now let's do this one [picking up the top-piece]
       Barbara: Okay.

In turn 1, Alan makes a proposal to Barbara, and in turn 2, she takes it up, establishing the joint commitment to do the top-piece next. In adjacency pairs, however, both parts must be spoken actions, and in many situations, one or both actions are non-linguistic, as in this example:

(6)   Barbara: [Extends hand with screw] So you want to stick the screws in?
       Alan: [Extends hand to take screw]

Here Alan takes up Barbara's request, but with a gestural signal. The term *projective pair* is intended to cover both types of pairs.

Using language, however, is itself a joint activity, which requires its own coordination. As noted earlier, communicative acts consist of joint actions at four levels, so in dialogue the participants have to manage who talks when, whether they are attending to, hearing, and understanding each other as intended, and so on. If so, then the participants should have to agree on the same five requisites for each signal. For Alan to suggest to Barbara, "Now let's do this one," they must agree on the participants (Alan and Barbara), their roles (speaker and addressee), the timing of the signal (starting with Alan's "now"), the location (there), and the content of his signal (all four levels). These, of course, are just the elements indicated by the five performance indexes of Alan's display – producer, recipient, time, place, and four levels of content.

Using language, in short, requires speakers and addressees to work together to establish the intended producer, recipient, time, place, and four levels of content.

3.1 *Grounding*

To communicate is, etymologically, to "make common" – to establish something as part of common ground. But what is it that speakers try to make common? The obvious answer is what they are saying – for example, Alan's suggestion in (5) that he and Barbara do the top-piece next. But to do that, they have to make common all five requisites – not only content, but also participants, roles, timing, and place.

The process of establishing something as common ground is called GROUNDING (H. Clark and Marshall 1981, H. Clark and Wilkes-Gibbs 1986, H. Clark and Schaefer 1989, H. Clark and Brennan 1991). Take Alan's suggestion in (5). To succeed at Level 3, the two of them must establish the mutual belief that Barbara has understood what Alan means by "Now let's do this one." They don't need to establish this mutual belief for certain, but only WELL ENOUGH FOR CURRENT PURPOSES. To ground something, therefore, is to establish it as part of common ground well enough for current purposes.

In dialogue, people ground many signals in the very course of their official business. Consider this exchange:

(7) Kenneth: how how was the wedding, –
     Fran: oh it was it was really good,   (7.31.1441)

In the first turn, Kenneth invites Fran to tell him about a wedding. He does this by getting her attention, getting her to identify the sentence *how was the wedding,* getting her to understand what he means, and getting her to consider his invitation. But is he successful? Fran gives him evidence that he is by responding with an appropriate reply. With it, she shows that she has attended, identified his sentence, grasped his invitation, and considered telling him about the wedding. That evidence is just what they need to reach the mutual belief that they have established all four levels of content well enough for current purposes. It is also evidence for the mutual belief that they have established the speaker, addressee, timing, and location as well.

Other forms of grounding work by a different logic. Fran and Kenneth continue the dialogue in (7) as follows:

(8) Fran: it was uh it was a lovely day,
     Kenneth: <u>yes,</u>
     Fran: and . it was a super place, . to have it . of course,
     Kenneth: <u>yes, –</u>

The first two lines may appear to form a standard adjacency pair, but they do not. In line 2, Kenneth does not mean "Yes, it was a lovely day." He has no idea whether the day was lovely or not. What he means is, "Yes, I *understand*, or *see*, what you mean by 'it was uh it was a lovely day.'" And in line 4, he means, "Yes, I *understand*, or *see*, what you mean by 'and it was a super place to have it of course.'" His *yes*'s are not about the content itself, but about his IDENTIFICATION of that content. The first projective pair is really this:

(8') Fran: Have you identified *c* ("it was uh it was a lovely day")?
      Kenneth: yes,

The *yes*'s in (8) are ACKNOWLEDGMENTS.[4] They are also called CONTINUERS. As Schegloff (1982) noted, when Kenneth says "yes" in (8), he is signaling Fran to continue, as if he were saying, "Go on." The BASIC MEANING of *yes* in these positions is "Yes, I understand (well enough for current purposes)," and speakers can use that basic meaning via Grice's Maxim of Relevance to implicate "Please continue." In English, the commonest acknowledgments are *uh-huh, yes, yeah, m-hm, m,* and head nods, which are all possible *yes* answers to yes/no questions. *Yes* answers are also used as acknowledgments in languages ranging from German (*ja* and *m-hm*) and French (*oui*) to Japanese (*hai*) and Mandarin (*shì*). All this is evidence that *yes* is an acknowledgment first ("Yes, I hear or understand") and a continuer by implicature.

Speakers and addressees, however, often run into problems establishing performance indexes, and when they do, they exploit a variety of techniques. One such technique is the SIDE SEQUENCE (Jefferson 1972, Schegloff 1972). In the following exchange, Maggie and Julie have a problem establishing index *c3*:

(9) Maggie: you fancy it yourself do you? –
     Julia: <u>what, the men's doubles?</u>
     Maggie: <u>yeah,</u>
     Julia: well more than the singles, yes, – (7.3e.278)

Julia seems unsure of what Maggie meant by "it," so she initiates a side sequence to ground *c3* ("it"). In turn 2, Julia asks, in effect, "By *c3* ('it'), do you mean *c3* ('the men's doubles')?" and in turn 3, Maggie answers "yeah." With that collateral issue resolved, they return to the official business of their conversation. Side sequences can be used to establish all levels of content as well as other performance indexes. A potential addressee, for example, could initiate a side sequence about index *r* with "Are you talking to me?"

3.2   *Performance indexes in dialogue*

In dialogues, people use performance indexes not only to INTRODUCE new producers, recipients, times, locations, and content, but to MAINTAIN the current ones. In ongoing discourse, it is often easy to specify p and r because the potential producers and recipients are limited. When there are two participants, p predictably becomes r, and r becomes p, with every change in speaker. At the start-up of a discourse, people need to establish the initial set of participants, perhaps using a summons (e.g. "Hey, Barbara") or ringing someone on the telephone (Schegloff 1968, 1979).

Introducing new bindings for displays can occur even within an utterance. In the following example, John produces and utterance in three increments, each with a different addressee (Goodwin 1981: 160):

(10)   John: I gave, I gave up [gazing at Don] smoking cigarettes:
      Don: Yeah,
      John: I-uh: [turning gaze to Beth] one-one week ago toda:y. [turning gaze to Ann] actually,

As John speaks, he moves his gaze from Don to Beth to Ann. He designs the first increment ("I gave up smoking cigarettes") as new information for Don. But since his own wife Beth already knows this, he designs the second increment ("one week ago today") to remind her of the one-week anniversary of his achievement. He designs the third increment ("actually") for Don's wife to acknowledge that all this is new to her. John designs each increment for each addressee, indicating these bindings with his display.

Coordinating on the use of language, in short, requires coordinating on each signal's performance indexes – producer, recipient, timing, location, and content. Speakers and their addressees, indeed, work to make this information common through the process of grounding.

4   Collateral Signals

Coordinating on performance indexes cannot always succeed with PRIMARY SIGNALS alone, that is, with signals that refer to the official business of the discourse. In cafés, classrooms, and offices, people often start before they know what they want to say and then change their minds. They normally start speaking before they have selected every word or phrase and are therefore often delayed in coming up with later words and phrases (Levelt 1989).

To deal with these problems, speakers and addressees often deploy COLLATERAL SIGNALS, this is, signals that refer to the *local, ongoing performance* of those primary signals.[5] The distinction between primary and collateral signals is nicely illustrated, in different terminology, in Goffman's (1981) analysis of radio talk. As he noted, radio announcers are expected "to produce the effect of a spontaneous, fluent flow of words – if not a forceful, pleasing personality – under conditions that lay speakers would be unable to manage" (p. 198). As good as they are, they still run into problems, and when they do, they often add parenthetical asides to correct, poke fun at, apologize for, or otherwise explain the problems. Take the following example:

(11)   Announcer: Seventy-two degrees Celsius. <u>I beg your pardon</u>. Seventeen degrees Celsius. <u>Seventy-two would be a little warm</u>. [Continues]

The announcer's official business is to report the weather, which he does with "seventy-two degrees Celsius" and "Seventeen degrees Celsius." But to present himself as knowing and attentive, he inserts an apology and brief joke as commentaries on his performance. These we recognize to be his personal actions and distinct from his official business, the weather report.

Collateral signals take many forms besides parenthetical asides. They fall into four main categories, each with its own properties:

- Inserts: signals that are achieved by INTERPOSING linguistic expressions between two parts of a primary utterance or between two primary utterances.
- Modifications: signals that are achieved by MODIFYING part or all of the display of a primary utterance.
- Juxtapositions: signals that are achieved by displaying one primary utterance JUXTAPOSED against another.
- Concomitants: signals that are displayed at the same time as, but separate from, a primary signal.

These signals differ in form, but they all refer to the local, ongoing performance, and that makes them collateral signals.

4.1   Inserts

Inserts are parenthetical comments or exchanges interposed within the official business of a discourse. They may be side exchanges, side moves, or simple asides.

Side exchanges. These are projective pairs interposed within or between utterances to deal with local, ongoing performance. The most common are side sequences. In (9), for example, Maggie and Julia interpose an exchange between Julia's question and Maggie's answer:

(12)   Julia: what, the men's doubles?
       Maggie: yeah,

Julia asks "what, the men's doubles?" to clarify what Maggie meant, and Maggie takes Julia up with her answer "yeah." The entire exchange is interposed within their primary talk.

Side moves. These consist of the interposition of the second part of a project-ive pair within or between utterances. Consider the acknowledgment in (8'), repeated here:

(13) Fran: it was uh it was a lovely day,
      Kenneth: yes,

Fran refers to the content of what she is saying with *c* ("it was uh it was a lovely day"), which Kenneth takes up with "yes [I understand *c*]." The second part gets inserted within the ongoing talk as a side move.[6] Side moves can also originate much deeper within an utterance, as here (see also (17) below):

(14) Susan: they still talk about rubbish tins, which is the American
            the Australian
      Jean: <u>m yeah,</u>
      Susan: expression, . for that thing you put all the . stuff in at the back
            gate, you know?   (1.10.388)

When Susan corrects "the American" to "the Australian," Jean acknowledges the correction with "m" and verifies it with "yeah" before Susan goes on. The projective pair "the Australian" plus "m yeah" occurs not merely mid-utterance, but mid-noun phrase (*the Australian expression*).

Asides. These are expressions that speakers interpose within their own utterances to comment on their local, ongoing performance.

Speakers tend to produce utterances one parcel of speaking at a time. By PARCEL OF SPEAKING, I mean a continuous fluent stretch of an intonation unit in the target utterance. Consider Reynard's utterance in (2). In the following, it is annotated with left curly brackets to mark points of suspension of fluent speech and right curly brackets to mark points of resumption of fluent speech. Each pair of brackets encloses a HIATUS, which may contain other speech, a pause, a gesture, or nothing. The hiatuses are lined up on the right:

(15) well,   {. I mean}
      this   {. uh}
      Mallet said   { }
      Mallet was   {uh}
      said something about   {uh you know}
      he felt it would be a good thing if   {u:h .}
      if Oscar went,

Here Reynard produces thirteen parcels. Seven belong to his primary utterance, and six come in hiatuses: *I mean*, *you know*, and four instances of *uh*. These six are all asides.

Asides are inserted to help explain features of local performance. In line 5, Reynard introduces *you know* to say he is adding a clarification to what he had already started to say. It is as if he had said, "Instead of 'Mallet said something about' what I mean more specifically is 'he felt it would be . . .'" *I mean* and *you know* are both clarifying asides, but they contrast in meaning (Levelt 1983, 1989, Erman 1987, Fox Tree and Schrock 2002).

The commonest asides are the FILLERS *uh* and *um*. Speakers use *uh* and *um* to announce "I am initiating at *t* (filler) what I expect to be a minor or major delay in speaking" (Fox Tree 2001; H. Clark and Fox Tree 2002). They use *uh* to announce minor delays, and *um*, major delays. By introducing these at the right moments, speakers can also create implicatures, via Grice's Maxim of Relevance, that range from "I am now searching for a word" to "I now invite you to speak." All these signals are addressed to issues of performance.

Speakers often introduce asides to comment on *why* they are doing what they are doing locally. It is common to comment on self-repairs (Schegloff et al. 1977; Levelt 1983), as in this example:

(16)   Robert: or do they only know about thi:y {.} practical, {. excuse me} experimental aspects, of reading,   (2.4.736)

Robert begins with *practical*, thinks better of it, and replaces it with *experimental*. He introduces *excuse me* to apologize for misleading his addressee, if only for one word.

Expressions such as *I mean, you know, excuse me, well, oh, like, ah, now, uh*, and *um* have been classified under many names. These include editing expressions (Levelt 1983), discourse markers (Schiffrin 1987), discourse particles (Schourup 1985), pragmatic expressions (Erman 1987), disjunct markers (Jefferson 1978), discourse operators (Polanyi 1985, Redeker 1986, 1990), clue words (Reichman 1978), cue words (Grosz and Sidner 1986), and cue phrases (Hirschberg and Litman 1987). Some of these schemes, such as Schiffrin's discourse markers, classify a wide range of expressions, whereas others, such as Levelt's editing expressions, are restricted to one or two functions. It remains to be seen how these schemes deal with the contrast between the primary and collateral systems.

4.2   *Modifications*

Another way to signal a local problem in performance is to MODIFY a current word or phrase. Among the common modifications in English are try markers, non-reduced vowels, and prolongations, but there are many others.

Try markers. When speakers present a name or description they aren't sure is correct or comprehensible, they can mark it with what Sacks and Schegloff (1979) have called a TRY MARKER, a rising intonation followed by a slight pause. With this modification, speakers initiate a projective pair to get their partners to confirm or correct the constituent before the speakers go on, as in (17):

(17) Alan: so I wrote off to {.} Bill, {. uh} who had presumably disappeared
                    by this time, certainly, a man called <u>Annegra?</u> {–}
      Barbara: {<u>yeah, Allegra</u>}
      Alan: Allegra, {uh} replied, {. uh} and I {.} put {.} two other people,
                    who'd been in for {.} the BBST job {.} with me . . .   (3.2a.59)

Alan apparently is uncertain about the name *Annegra*, so he presents it with
rising intonation and a slight pause. Barbara responds "yeah" to confirm she
knows who he is referring to, then corrects the name to *Allegra*. Alan accepts
the correction by repeating *Allegra* and continuing. All of this happens
mid-sentence.

The try marker in (17) is an INTONATIONAL modification of the word *Annegra*
that points to, or flags, a problem associated with the word itself, roughly, "Do
you understand who I'm referring to with the word *Annegra*?" It also projects
an immediate response. So Alan's try marker functions as the first part of a
projective pair, which Barbara takes up with the side move "yeah, Allegra."

Non-reduced vowels. Speakers ordinarily pronounce *the*, *a*, and *to* with
reduced vowels (schwas) which I will write *thuh monastery, uh gravel company*,
and *tuh regulate*. On occasion, speakers produce these vowels in a marked
NON-REDUCED form, which I will write *thiy, ei*, and *tuw* (rhyming with *see, day*,
and *glue*). Here is an example for *thiy*:[7]

(18) Kate: it's <u>thiy</u> {.} thuh monastery, {– you know} thuh very Gothic
           monastery, with all <u>thi:y</u> {–} wedding-cake, {– –} I – it's a special
           kind of Gothic architecture, which is even more decorated than
           Decorated.   (2.13.664)

Speakers often use *thiy* in place of *thuh* to signal that they are suspending
speech immediately after the word *the*, as Kate does twice in (18) (Fox Tree
and H. Clark 1997). In signaling a suspension, they implicate that they are
having a problem that prevents them from continuing immediately. We find
similar examples with *a* and *to* in (19) and (20):

(19) Roger: we are <u>ei</u> {um – –} <u>ei</u> gravel company (2.11b.1063)

(20) Albert Gore: not be <u>tuw</u> um regulate (televised debate, October 17,
                      2000, St. Louis, Missouri).

Non-reduced vowels can also combine with *uh* or *um* to form complex
modification-plus-asides (H. Clark and Fox Tree 2002). Gore's *to um* in (20)
was pronounced *tu.wum*, a trochee with the syllable boundary (marked by the
period) before the *w* in *tuw*. Likewise, *the uh* is often pronounced *thi.yuh*, and
a uh as *ei.yuh* – trochees with syllable boundaries before the *y* in *thiy* and *ei*. So
when Gore uttered "not be tu.wum regulate," he was signaling not just a
suspension at the end of *to*, but the initiation of a delay at the beginning of *um*.

Prolongations. Speakers often prolong words mid-utterance as they plan what to say next. Take this excerpt from a narrative about picking pears (Chafe 1980: 308):[8]

(21)   A—nd u—m [3.35] he's just picking them, he comes off of the ladder, [.35] a—nd he— u—h [.3] puts his pears into the basket.

In (21), the narrator prolongs *and, um, and, he,* and *uh*. With these prolongations, he slows down the initial parts of two clauses, but then produces the remaining parts fluently.

Prolongations are used to signal the CONTINUATION of a delay in progress (H. Clark and Fox Tree 2002). They contrast with *uh* and *um*, which mark the INITIATION of a delay. Also, prolonged words belong to the primary utterance, whereas *uh* and *um* do not. Speakers often want to advance the primary utterance – or give the appearance of doing so – even when they cannot really go on. They can do that with prolongations, but not with *uh* or *um*.

4.3   *Juxtapositions*

Juxtapositions are signals achieved by juxtaposing the display of one primary utterance against the display of another. The two displays may be produced by the same or different speakers. Here are three techniques that exploit juxtaposition.

Replacement. The commonest way to repair a word or phrase is to juxtapose a new display directly against what it is to replace (see Levelt 1983). Consider (22):

(22)   Peter: there was {u:m .} w- {} what is {.} has happened since then, is that there has been another meeting of the executive committee, (1.2.80)

Treated literally, Peter's utterance is ungrammatical (even ignoring *um*): *there was w-what is has happened since then* . . . Peter surely isn't trying to be ungrammatical, and yet he produces each word deliberately, not in error (except perhaps *w-*), as a part of what he wants to say at that moment. It is just that he changes his mind several times, and he uses juxtapositions to let his addressee know *how* he is changing his mind.

In (22), Peter replaces (1) *there was* with *what has happened since then*, (2) *w-* with *what has happened since then*, and (3) *is* with *has*. He signals each replacement by displaying the replacing words adjacent to, or JUXTAPOSED AGAINST, his display of the original words. What Peter means by these juxtapositions is this: "Give the juxtaposed display PRECEDENCE over a final continuous part of the original display." This way speakers can use replacements to substitute new elements for old ones, as in (22), or to add or delete elements (see H. Clark 1996: 264).

Repetition. In spontaneous speech, people often repeat words like *the, in, if,* and *I,* as in (23):

(23)   Reynard: well, I̲ {uh} I̲ wouldn't be surprised at that,   (1.1.278)

Treated literally, Reynard's utterance, like Peter's in (22), is ungrammatical: *I I wouldn't be surprised at that.* And yet he produces the two tokens of *I* as part of what he wanted to say at the moment. Repeating *I* is a violation of Grice's Maxim of Manner, namely "Be brief (avoid unnecessary prolixity)," so why does Reynard do it?

The two tokens of repeated words serve distinct purposes (H. Clark and Wasow 1998). The first token is often, though not always, used to make a PRELIMINARY COMMITMENT to what speakers are about to say but cannot yet produce. Reynard produces the first *I* to signal that he intends to produce a clause that begins with *I.* The second token is used to RESTORE CONTINUITY, or fluency, to the current phrase or clause. With the second *I,* Reynard restores continuity to the clause he has just committed himself to (*I wouldn't be surprised at that*). So the second *I* is a type of repair, but what Reynard is repairing is the continuity of his display of the clause.

Overlap. Speakers can do a variety of collateral chores by producing a display juxtaposed against what another speaker is currently displaying (see H. Clark 1996: 278–82). Consider the overlap in the last line of this exchange:

(24)   Wendy: and as long as I'm in my own {–} little nit, and nobody's telling me what to do,
         Ken: yes,
         Wendy: there doesn't really seem *anything*
         Ken: *but how* long do you think it'll take then, {–} to finish?

Ken times his display "but how long . . ." to begin before Wendy is finished, juxtaposing his primary utterance against hers. He does this, apparently, to ask Wendy for the floor, and one word later she accedes to his request. That is, he uses the juxtaposition of his utterance against hers as a STRATEGIC INTER-RUPTION, a collateral signal for requesting the floor. Another type of juxtaposition, the RECYCLED TURN BEGINNING, is used by a second speaker to claim the next turn (Schegloff 1987).

4.4   Concomitants

When people talk face to face, they rely not only on speech, but on gestures – manual, facial, ocular, postural, and vocal gestures. When June asked David, "Where is your car?" and he pointed at the nearby Honda, he used his gesture as a primary signal – as part of their official business. But speakers also use gestures for collateral signals, performing them at the same time as, or in parallel with, the primary utterances. In this case, gesture and speech are concurrent, even coordinated, but not composite signals. Collateral signals of this type will be called CONCOMITANTS.

Gestures that depict what they refer to are called ICONIC GESTURES (see, e.g., Schegloff 1984, McNeill 1992). Most are parts of composite signals in primary utterances. In the following example (from Kendon 1980), Fran is telling a friend about a scene from the Billy Wilder movie *Some Like it Hot*:

(25) Fran: they wheel a big table in, with a big with a big [1.08 sec] cake on
              it, and the girl, jumps up.

Fran uses one gesture to depict the height and movement of the table, the gesture peaking at the word *table*. She uses a second gesture to depict the size and shape of the cake during "[1.08 sec]," and she uses a third to depict the vertical movement of the girl jumping during *girl*. Her phrase *a big cake* plus her circular gesture depicting the cake form a composite signal – a unified description of a cake of a particular size and shape.

Other iconic gestures are used instead to refer to features of performance. One example is what Goodwin and Goodwin (1986; Goodwin 1987) called a THINKING FACE:

(26) Arthur: He pu:t uhm, (0.7) tch! Put *crab*meat on th'bo:dum

Arthur apparently has trouble finding the word *crabmeat*. Beginning at *uhm* and ending at *tch!* he turns from his addressee and, with a distant look in his eyes, puts on a stereotyped facial gesture of someone thinking hard – a thinking face. The thinking face is an iconic gesture speakers use (a) to assert that they are thinking hard, hence (b) to implicate that they are searching for the next word. In (26) Arthur ended the thinking face when he went on to say *crabmeat*. In other examples, speakers end the thinking face by turning to gaze at their addressees to request help in finding the elusive word. The thinking face and the return gaze are both concomitant signals.

Collateral gestures like this appear to fall into four broad classes (see also Cassell and McNeill 1991, Bavelas et al. 1992, Bavelas 1994):[9]

- DELIVERY GESTURES, as when speakers "hand over" to addressees new information relevant to their main point;
- CITING GESTURES, as when speakers point at addressees to indicate "as you said earlier;"
- SEEKING GESTURES, as when speakers gaze at addresses as if to say "Can you give me the word for . . . ?"
- TURN GESTURES, as when speakers "hand over" the turn to addressees.

These gestures take many forms. Some are so-called EMBLEMS (e.g. head nods, head shakes, thinking faces); others are indicative gestures (eye gaze, pointing); and still others are iconic gestures (smiles). What is common to them all is that they are displayed concurrently with the primary utterances and deal with issues of performance.

5 Summary

People use language primarily to coordinate activities they are doing jointly – from assembling TV stands to negotiating contracts. They use both linguistic and non-linguistic signals to reach joint commitments on who is participating, in what roles, with what content, and at what time and location. These signals constitute the primary system of communication. But using language is itself a joint activity and requires the same joint commitments. The signals used in that process constitute the collateral system of communication.

The collateral system relies on two main devices. The first is displays – the time, place, and manner with which a signal is performed. Speakers design each display to indicate the producer, recipient, content, timing, and location of the signal. But for speakers to be sure their addressees have identified who and what they are indicating, they ordinarily work with their addressees to ground each signal. The second main device is collateral signals, which refer to the local, ongoing performance. In spontaneous speech, people add these to their primary signals in the form of inserts, modifications, juxtapositions, and concomitants. It is these that give the language of cafés, classrooms, and offices its spontaneous character.

What, then, about novels, plays, and news broadcasts? Writers, actors, and radio announcers do indeed display their utterances, but their displays are limited, and they have no way of grounding what they say. Nor do they have recourse to most collateral signals. They can only hope and pray that they will succeed. So, for language in general, we must go to cafés, classrooms, and offices, for it is there that we find the primary and collateral systems of communication in their fullest form.

ACKNOWLEDGMENTS

I am grateful to the Max Planck Institute for Psycholinguistics, Nijmegen, the Netherlands, for their hospitality while I worked on the issues in this chapter. I am especially indebted to David P. Wilkins for many discussions. I also thank Adrian Bangerter, Eve V. Clark, Laurence Horn, Teenie Matlock, and Gregory Ward for constructive comments.

NOTES

1 Most of the examples in this chapter are taken from the London–Lund corpus (Svartvik and Quirk 1980). In the notation retained here, a period (".") marks a brief pause, a dash ("–") a unit pause, a colon (":") a prolongation, a question mark ("?") an intonation unit ending in a rising intonation, and a comma (",") an intonation unit ending in any other intonation. The examples are numbered by conversation (e.g. 1.2) and line number (e.g. 370).

2 Many in pragmatics have since turned to spontaneous language for evidence, but others reject it as a proper subject for pragmatic theories.

3 I am indebted to Julie Heiser and Barbara Tversky for videotapes of this example.

4 They are often called BACK CHANNEL RESPONSES (Yngve 1970), but that term includes other phenomena too.

5 Most (but not all) collateral signals may be described as metalinguistic, though not all metalinguistic techniques are collateral signals.

6 The same goes for INSTALLMENT UTTERANCES, as in the transfer of telephone numbers, addresses, and instructions (Goldberg 1975, H. Clark and Schaefer 1987, 1989), and for certain LEFT DISLOCATIONS (Geluykens 1987, 1988, 1992).

7 In most dialects of English, when *the* is cliticized onto a word that begins with a vowel, it is an unstressed version of *thiy* with a reduced vowel. So *the egg* is pronounced *thi.yegg* (where the syllable boundary is marked by a period). The version of *thiy* at issue here has a non-reduced stressed vowel, as in the trochee *thi.yum* (Fox Tree and H. Clark 1997).

8 In Chafe's transcripts, prolongations are marked with dashes, and silences are given in seconds in parentheses.

9 Bavelas and her colleagues called these INTERACTIVE GESTURES, which they contrasted with TOPICAL GESTURES, which are composite parts of primary utterances.

17 Constraints on Ellipsis and Event Reference

ANDREW KEHLER AND GREGORY WARD

1 Introduction

Natural languages provide speakers with a wide variety of linguistic devices with which to refer to things. Speakers do not select among these referential options randomly, however, since the linguistic system imposes constraints, both formal and functional, on the use of these expressions (see also Carlson, this volume). For instance, the felicity of a particular choice might depend on whether the speaker believes that the hearer has prior knowledge of the referent, whether it had been mentioned previously in the discourse, or whether it is situated in the immediate surroundings of the discourse participants.

As with reference to entities, we also find a range of options with respect to reference to eventualities[1] in discourse. Four options that we address in this chapter are GAPPING, VERB PHRASE ELLIPSIS, SO ANAPHORA, and PRONOMINAL EVENT REFERENCE, illustrated in (1a–d) respectively.

(1)   George claimed he won the electoral vote, and . . .
    a.   Al, the popular vote.
    b.   Al did too.
    c.   Al did so too.
    d.   Al did it too.

These constructions are similar in one crucial respect: The interpretation of the eventuality expressed in the second clause requires the recovery of a predication expressed in the first. In recognition of this similarity, Dalrymple et al. (1991) suggest that their mechanism for recovering relations from antecedent clauses in verb phrase ellipsis applies equally to the other three constructions (among others). For expository convenience, we will follow their terminology and refer to the antecedent clause in all of these constructions as the SOURCE clause, and the clause containing the elliptical or referential form (the second clause in 1a–d) as the TARGET clause.

There are many respects in which these four constructions differ, however. For instance, they have quite distinct syntactic properties. In the case of gapping (1a), all but two (and in some cases, more than two) stranded constituents are elided from the target clause, none of which is an auxiliary.[2] In verb phrase ellipsis (1b), on the other hand, the target clause contains a stranded auxiliary verb that stands proxy for a missing verb phrase. There is less agreement about the syntactic structure of *do so* (1c); while some authors (Lakoff and Ross 1966, Fu et al. 2001, inter alia) have treated it as an idiosyncratic form of ellipsis, Kehler and Ward (1999) argue that it consists instead of an intransitive use of the main verb *do* (vs. auxiliary *do*) coupled with a referential use of *so* canonically found in preverbal position (cf. *so doing*). Pronominal event reference (1d) is like *do so* in that there is no ellipsis, but different in that it contains the transitive main verb *do*. The referential properties of pronominal event reference derive from those of the pronoun itself.

This range of syntactic properties is matched by an equally varied set of referential properties, which serve as the focus of this chapter. To provide a framework for our analysis, we begin by describing and situating several previous accounts of the constraints on the use of referring expressions in discourse. We then show that the referential behaviors of the four constructions illustrated in (1a–d) reveal several ways in which these analyses need to be revised and extended if we are to have a fully adequate account of reference in discourse. This result in turn suggests several interesting avenues for future research.

2   Constraints on Reference in Discourse

The use of referring expressions is constrained by several sources of information. One of these sources consists of the speaker's beliefs about the KNOW-LEDGE OF THE HEARER, a factor which is likely to dictate whether the speaker selects a definite or indefinite form of reference (Hawkins 1978, Clark and Marshall 1981, Prince 1992). A second source pertains to the speaker's beliefs about the state of the hearer's DISCOURSE MODEL (Karttunen 1976, Webber 1978), that is, the hearer's model of the discourse that represents the entities and eventualities that have been introduced and the relationships that hold among them. A third source is the SITUATIONAL CONTEXT of the discourse, which includes entities and eventualities currently within the interlocutors' perceptual sphere. Thus, any complete theory of reference will have to account for two aspects of discourse understanding: the process of modeling these sources of information (which, particularly the discourse model, are continually changing as the discourse progresses), and the constraints governing the use of referring expressions with respect to these knowledge sources.

There are several properties that can be distinguished when analyzing such constraints; in this chapter we will focus on three.[3] First, a distinction can be drawn based on LEVEL OF REPRESENTATION, that is, whether a particular referential expression requires the availability of an antecedent of a particular syntactic form, or merely a semantic referent. Second, with respect to semantic referents, those that are OLD with respect to (the speaker's beliefs about) the hearer's beliefs about the world and/or the hearer's discourse model can be distinguished from those that are NEW. Finally, with respect to those semantic referents that are old, the relative levels of SALIENCE OR ACTIVATION (Chafe 1976, Prince 1981a, Lambrecht 1994, inter alia) associated with each at a given point in the discourse can be differentiated. In what follows, we discuss three analyses that, in turn, address each of these three properties.

2.1   An initial distinction: deep and surface anaphora

The notion that referring expressions impose constraints on the level of representation of their referents was addressed in a classic paper by Hankamer and Sag (1976, henceforth H&S), who argued for a categorical distinction between DEEP and SURFACE anaphora. Surface anaphors are SYNTACTICALLY CONTROLLED, in that they require a linguistic antecedent of a particular syntactic form. Examples of surface anaphora include gapping, verb phrase ellipsis, and *do so* (1a–c, respectively). Deep anaphors, on the other hand, do not require an antecedent of a particular syntactic form, but only a referent that is of the appropriate semantic type. Indeed, deep anaphoric reference may be PRAGMATICALLY CONTROLLED, whereby the referent is evoked situationally without any linguistic introduction. Pronominal event referential forms like *do it* (1d) and *do that* are among the forms in this category.[4]

These two types of anaphora are illustrated in (2a–c).[5]

(2)   A peace agreement in the Middle East needs to be negotiated.
 a.   An agreement between India and Pakistan does too.   [verb phrase ellipsis (surface)]
 b.   #Colin Powell volunteered to.   [verb phrase ellipsis (surface)]
 c.   Colin Powell volunteered to do it.   [event anaphora (deep)]

H&S's account predicts that (2a) is acceptable because the antecedent – the syntactic representation of *needs to be negotiated* – is a surface verb phrase in the propositional representation of the source clause. By the same token, (2b) is unacceptable because the putative antecedent *negotiate a peace agreement* is not a surface verb phrase in the source propositional representation. On the other hand, (2c) is acceptable because *do it* is a deep anaphor, and is therefore interpreted with respect to a discourse model, in which there presumably exists a purely semantic representation for *negotiate a peace agreement*.

In H&S's dichotomy, the requirement that there be a syntactic antecedent for surface anaphora implies that the antecedent must be linguistic; that is, surface anaphora is not compatible with situationally evoked referents. The unacceptability of verb phrase ellipsis with situationally evoked referents is illustrated in (3a), in contrast to the acceptability of *do it* anaphora in the same context shown in (3b).

(3)   [Hankamer attempts to stuff a 9-inch ball through a 6-inch hoop. Sag says:]
  a.   #It's not clear that you'll be able to.   [surface]
       (=Hankamer and Sag 1976, ex. 3)
  b.   It's not clear that you'll be able to do it.   [deep]
       (=Hankamer and Sag 1976, ex. 4)
  c.   #I don't think you can do so.   [surface]
       (=Hankamer and Sag 1976, ex. 86)

Likewise, *do so* (3c) is also infelicitous with situationally evoked referents, a topic to which we return in section 3.3.

To summarize, surface anaphora requires an antecedent of an appropriate syntactic form, which in turn implies that its referent must be linguistically evoked. In contrast, deep anaphora only requires a semantic referent of the appropriate type, and allows for such referents to be situationally evoked.

2.2   A second distinction: old vs. new

Having distinguished between syntactically mediated and semantically mediated reference, additional distinctions can be drawn within the latter category.[6] One of these pertains to whether or not an entity is known to the hearer at the time the referring expression is uttered, that is, whether the referent is OLD or NEW. Prince (1992) describes two ways in which a referent may be old or new, particularly with respect to its HEARER-STATUS and DISCOURSE-STATUS. From the speaker's perspective, the hearer status of an entity depends on whether the speaker believes it is known or unknown to the hearer at the time of reference; entities that are believed to be known to the hearer are HEARER-OLD, otherwise they are HEARER-NEW. For instance, by using the indefinite *a book* in (4a), the speaker conveys that the hearer is not already familiar with the book being referred to (i.e., it is hearer-new), and hence the hearer is induced to create a new representation for it in his discourse model.[7] On the other hand, the use of a proper name, as in (4b), conveys that the speaker believes *The Handbook of Pragmatics* is hearer-old, i.e. already familiar to the hearer.

(4)a.   I bought a book at the bookstore today.
   b.   I bought *The Handbook of Pragmatics* at the bookstore today.

Unlike hearer-status, the discourse-status of an entity depends only on whether the entity has already been introduced into the discourse at the time of reference (and is thus presumably already in the hearer's discourse model); an entity that has been so introduced is DISCOURSE-OLD, otherwise it is DISCOURSE-NEW. Thus, produced discourse initially, both *a book* in (4a) and *The Handbook of Pragmatics* in (4b) represent discourse-new referents. In contrast, the referent of *the book* in (5) is discourse-old, since it was previously introduced.

(5)   I bought a book at the bookstore today. The book had been marked down
       to 99 cents.

Considering hearer- and discourse-status together, entities can thus have one
of three INFORMATION STATUSES: hearer-old/discourse-old (e.g. the referent of
the book in (5)), hearer-new/discourse-new (e.g. the referent of *a book* in (4a)
and (5)), and hearer-old/discourse-new (e.g. the referent of *The Handbook of
Pragmatics* in (4b)). An entity cannot be both hearer-new and discourse-old, as
any entity already introduced into the discourse will presumably be known to
the hearer from that point on.
     Prince claims that the use of a definite NP in English signals that its referent
is hearer-old, whereas use of an indefinite signals that the referent is hearer-
new. These markings, however, do not directly encode discourse-status; for
instance, definites are used for referents that are either discourse-old (e.g. the
referent of *the book* in (5)) or discourse-new (e.g. the referent of *The Handbook of
Pragmatics* in (4b)). Prince in fact claims that, in English at least, "there is virtually no marking of an NP with respect to the Discourse-status of the entity it
represents" (1992: 304). However, she then cites pronouns as a possible exception:

> Pronouns indicate that the entities they represent are salient, i.e. appropriately in
> the hearer's consciousness . . . at that point in the construction of the discourse
> model. Therefore, they are presumably already in the discourse model. Therefore,
> they are Discourse-old. However, at any point in (discourse) time, only a subset,
> usually proper, of the entities already evoked are salient and hence representable
> by a pronoun.   (Prince 1992: 304)

The issue of pronouns and the relative salience of referents leads us to the
third distinction that we address.

2.3   A third distinction: salience

Thus far we have distinguished between forms of reference whose interpretation is sensitive to the form of a particular syntactic antecedent and those whose
interpretation is dependent on the presence of a semantic referent. Among
those referents in the latter category, we have also distinguished between
those which are old and those which are new, with respect to the speaker's
beliefs about both the hearer's knowledge and his discourse model. Among
the referents that are old, a further distinction can be drawn with respect to
their degree of salience in the discourse context.
     Salience has been a prominent factor in accounts of the COGNITIVE STATUS[8]
of referents (Chafe 1976, Prince 1981a, Ariel 1990, Gundel et al. 1993, Lambrecht
1994, inter alia). Consider, for example, the analysis of Gundel et al. (1993), who
propose a GIVENNESS HIERARCHY containing six possible cognitive statuses
that a referent may have. Below each cognitive status are the (English) referential
expressions that encode it.

in		uniquely		type
focus >	activated > familiar >	identifiable >	referential >	identifiable
it	*that* *that* N	*the* N	indef *this* N	*a* N
	this			
	this N			

The statuses REFERENTIAL and TYPE IDENTIFIABLE will not concern us here, since entities referred to with indefinites are (usually) hearer-new. The remaining four categories distinguish the relative levels of salience that license different forms of definite reference: IN-FOCUS referents, which license pronouns; ACTIVATED referents, which license demonstratives; FAMILIAR referents, which can be hearer-old but discourse-new, e.g. *That national debt sure is getting large* spoken discourse-initially; and UNIQUELY IDENTIFIABLE referents, which license definite lexical noun phrases, and may be (contra Prince) hearer-new. The particular details of Gundel et al.'s analysis and the ways in which they differ with the other analyses cited above need not concern us here. The important point is that any such theory must have some way of distinguishing referents on the basis of their (contextually determined) salience, since the felicitous use of definite referring expressions appears to be sensitive to it.

3   Reference to Eventualities

To summarize thus far, we have classified referents with respect to three properties: (i) the level at which they are represented in the discourse model, that is, syntax or semantics; (ii) in the case of semantic referents, the information status associated with them, that is, old or new; and (iii) in the case of (hearer-)old referents, their relative level of salience.

We now consider the four forms of reference to eventualities discussed in section 1. We will show that, in light of the referential behavior of these expressions, previous accounts such as those discussed in the previous section must be revised and extended.

3.1 *Gapping*

The first form we consider is the gapping construction, exemplified in (1a) and repeated below in (6).

(6)   George won the electoral vote, and Al, the popular vote.

Evidence from both syntax and discourse supports H&S's categorization of gapping as a form of surface anaphora. The syntactic basis for its interpretation has been widely argued for, based on its sensitivity to various syntactic constraints that we will not cover here (Ross 1970b, Jackendoff 1971, Hankamer 1971, Stillings 1975, Sag 1976, Neijt 1979, Chao 1988, Steedman 1990, 2000, inter alia). Likewise, the data show that gapping fails to pattern with deep anaphora in terms of its referential behavior; for instance, it is more constrained than pronominal reference with respect to referents evoked from clauses other than the most immediate one.

(7)a. Al was declared to have won Florida, and George, Texas.
   b. #Al was declared to have won Florida, but then the networks rescinded their projection, and George, Texas.
   c. Al was declared to have won Florida, but then the networks rescinded their projection, and he had no option but to wait for the votes to be counted.

Whereas (7a) is perfectly acceptable, the insertion of an additional clause between the source and target clauses renders (7b) unacceptable. In contrast, the pronoun *he* in (7c) is felicitously used to refer to an entity (Al) evoked two clauses prior. Similarly, as with other surface-anaphoric forms, gapping cannot refer to situationally evoked referents:

(8) [Hankamer produces an orange, proceeds to peel it, and just as Sag produces an apple, says:]
   #And Ivan, an apple. (=Hankamer and Sag 1976, ex. 50)

The surface anaphoric account captures these facts.

   This analysis leaves one fact about gapping unaccounted for, however, which was originally noticed by Levin and Prince (1986, henceforth, L&P) and discussed in greater detail in Kehler (2000a, 2002). Briefly, L&P note that pairs of conjoined sentences as in (9a) are ambiguous between a SYMMETRIC reading, in which the two events are understood as independent, and an ASYMMETRIC reading, in which the first event is interpreted as the cause of the second event.

(9)a. Sue became upset and Nan became downright angry.
       (=Levin and Prince 1986, ex. 3a)
   b. Sue became upset and Nan ϕ downright angry.

That is, under a symmetric interpretation, (9a) describes a situation in which Sue and Nan both expressed independent emotions that may have (but not necessarily) resulted from the same provocation, whereas under an asymmetric interpretation it describes a situation in which Nan became angry because of Sue's becoming upset. L&P point out that the gapped counterpart of (9a), given in (9b), has only a symmetric reading; the reading in which Nan's anger is caused by Sue's becoming upset is unavailable.

   The characterization of gapping as surface anaphora does not explain why gapping is inconsistent with asymmetric readings. As such, L&P offer an account that also incorporates a pragmatic component. They base their analysis on the ORDERED ENTAILMENT framework of Wilson and Sperber (1979), in which processing a sentence results in an ordered set of foreground and background entailments. The background entailments are those OPEN PROPOSITIONS resulting from applying constituent-to-variable replacement rules on focused constituents; the FIRST BACKGROUND ENTAILMENT (FBE) is the open proposition resulting from replacing a minimal tonically stressed (or clefted) constituent with a variable. For instance, (10a), with the indicated stress on *Bill*, has as its FBE (10b), along with the other background entailments (10c) and (10d).

(10)a. BILL's father writes books.
   b. Someone's father writes books.
   c. Someone writes books.
   d. Someone does something.

L&P then posit a DISCOURSE FUNCTION OF GAPPING rule, which states that all conjuncts in a gapped sentence must share a single open proposition as their FBE. This open proposition consists of the representation of the material deleted in the conjuncts in which gapping has applied, with variables replacing (the representation of) the constituents remaining in those conjuncts. This principle accounts for the symmetric reading of example (9b) because the corresponding elements in both the source and target clauses are contrastively accented. As such, the two clauses share the FBE given in (11).

(11) Someone became something. [open proposition: X BECAME Y]

According to L&P, however, two FBEs are required for causal implicature. For example, the FBEs for the two clauses in (9a) could be those provided in (12a–b), respectively:

(12)a. Something happened.
   b. Nan did something.

L&P claim that since gapping requires that all conjuncts share a single FBE, their analysis accounts for the lack of a causal reading in examples like (9b).

  Kehler (2000a) presents an alternative account that is based on the inferential processes that operate during discourse comprehension. This analysis incorporates the common assumption in the syntax literature that the interpretation of gapping is made possible by the reconstruction of the source syntactic material at the target site (but cf. Steedman 1990, 2000). Unlike syntactic accounts, however, this reconstruction process is not triggered by a (surface) anaphoric interpretation process, but instead only by the need to recover the (elided) arguments of certain kinds of COHERENCE RELATIONS. In particular, reconstruction will occur for those relations that Kehler categorizes in the RESEMBLANCE category, an instance of which is the PARALLEL relation operative in the symmetric reading of (9a–b). In contrast, no reconstruction occurs for CAUSE–EFFECT relations, an instance of which is the RESULT relation operative in the asymmetric reading of (9a). With no mechanism for recovering the antecedent syntactic material, gapping is predicted to be infelicitous under asymmetric interpretations.

While Kehler's account differs from L&P's in various respects, they both address the facts by appealing to principles that apply at the syntax/pragmatics interface, rather than syntax alone. Since we are aware of no independent evidence that the two readings of (9a) are associated with different syntactic structures, it would appear that such an appeal is necessary.

3.2   Verb phrase ellipsis

We now turn to verb phrase ellipsis, exemplified in (13):

(13)   George claimed he won the election, and Al did too.

Note that the pronoun in the source clause leads to two possible interpretations for the target clause: either Al claimed that George won the election (the STRICT reading), or Al claimed that Al won the election (the SLOPPY reading).

Recall that H&S (1976) categorized verb phrase ellipsis as a form of surface anaphora, which is licensed only when an antecedent of an appropriate syntactic form is available. Indeed, there is evidence to support this categorization; consider (14a–c)[9]:

(14)a.   #The aardvark was given a nut by Wendy, and Bruce did too.
        [gave the aarvark a nut] (=Webber 1978, ch. 4, ex. 40)
     b.   #Al$_i$ blamed himself$_i$, and George did too.   [blamed Al]
     c.   #James defended George$_i$ and he$_i$ did too.   [defended George]

The unacceptability of (14a) is predicted by the surface-anaphoric account because the source clause is in the passive voice. As such, the syntactic structure representing the active voice verb phrase *give the aardvark a nut* that is required in the target representation is not present in the source clause. Likewise, binding conditions (Chomsky 1981) predict that sentences (14b–c) lack the indicated readings on the assumption that the source verb phrase is reconstructed at the target site.[10] That is, CONDITION A, which requires that a reflexive have a c-commanding antecedent, predicts the lack of a strict interpretation for (14b). Similarly, CONDITION C, which disallows coreference between a full noun phrase and a c-commanding pronoun, rules out the interpretation in which George defended himself in (14c).

However, several researchers (Dalrymple et al. 1991, Dalrymple 1991, Hardt 1992, Kehler 1993a, inter alia) have provided numerous examples in which verb phrase ellipsis is felicitous despite the fact that no appropriate syntactic antecedent is available. Consider the examples in (15a–c):

(15)a. In November, the citizens of Florida asked that the election results be overturned, but the election commission refused to. [overturn the election results] (adapted from Dalrymple 1991, ex. 15a)

  b. Al$_i$ defended himself$_i$ because Bill wouldn't. [defend Al] (adapted from Dalrymple 1991, ex. 75a)

  c. George expected Al$_i$ to win the election even when he$_i$ didn't. [expect Al to win the election] (adapted from Dalrymple 1991, ex. 75c)

Verb phrase ellipsis is felicitous in (15a), unlike (14a), despite the fact that the source clause is passivized, and thus the syntactic structure for the putative elided active voice verb phrase required by syntactic analyses – *overturn the election* – is not available. Likewise, sentence (15b) is acceptable even though a syntactic account would predict a Condition A violation, as in (14b). Finally, (15c) is felicitous despite a violation of Condition C (cf. 14c).

   The fact that neither syntax nor semantics alone can account for the full range of verb phrase ellipsis data suggests that additional pragmatic and/or discourse factors may be at play. Kehler (2000a, 2002) offers an analysis in which these data are explained by the interaction between the properties of verb phrase ellipsis itself and those of the inference processes that underlie the establishment of coherence in discourse (see also Kehler, this volume). The crucial distinction between (14a–c) and (15a–c) is that the former three participate in Resemblance coherence relations (in particular, Parallel), whereas the latter three participate in Cause–Effect relations (VIOLATED EXPECTATION, EXPLANATION, and DENIAL OF PREVENTER, respectively). Kehler argues that two different recovery processes interact to produce this pattern: the anaphoric interpretation of verb phrase ellipsis, and the syntactic reconstruction mechanism posited in the analysis of gapping summarized in section 3.1.

   Unlike gapping, verb phrase ellipsis displays the property of being anaphoric, which is demonstrated by its behavioral similarity to pronominal reference. First, as is well known, verb phrase ellipsis and pronouns may be cataphoric in similar circumstances, as shown in (16a–d) (G. Lakoff 1968, Jackendoff 1972):

(16)a. #George will ϕ_i, if Al [makes a statement claiming the election]$_i$.

  b. #He$_i$ will make a fool of himself, if Al$_i$ makes a statement claiming the election.

  c. If George will ϕ_i, Al [will make a statement claiming the election]$_i$.

  d. If he$_i$ makes a statement claiming the election, Al$_i$ will make a fool of himself.

In (16a–b), but not (16c–d), the ellipsis and pronominal anaphors c-command their respective antecedents, and therefore coreference is disallowed. Second, verb phrase ellipsis and pronominal anaphora may both access referents evoked from clauses other than the most immediate one; Hardt (1993) reports that 15 out of 315 instances (5 percent) of verb phrase ellipsis he found in the Brown corpus (Francis 1964) have a referent evoked from at least two sentences prior.

The anaphoricity of verb phrase ellipsis predicts the insensitivity to syntactic form found in examples (15a–c). The remaining question, therefore, is why such a sensitivity is found in examples (14a–c). In section 3.1, we argued that elliptical expressions may be subject to a syntactic reconstruction mechanism. Crucially, this mechanism is not invoked by the need to recover the meaning of the missing material, but instead by the need to recover missing arguments to the coherence relation that is operative. Because this need only arises when the relation is of the Resemblance type, a sensitivity to syntactic form is found only in (14a–c). Thus, while verb phrase ellipsis may take on the superficial appearance of a surface anaphor in the presence of this type of relation, this sensitivity to syntactic form is **not** a result of its anaphoric properties – which to this point pattern more closely with deep anaphora – but instead is a result of the fact that verb phrase ellipsis also involves omitted syntactic material.

Given its apparent patterning with deep anaphora, we are led to ask whether verb phrase ellipsis allows situationally evoked referents. Schachter (1977a) provides a number of felicitous examples of such ellipsis, including (17a–b):

(17)a. [John tries to kiss Mary. She says:]
         John, you mustn't.   (=Schachter 1977a, ex. 3)
    b.   [John pours another martini for Mary. She says:]
         I really shouldn't.   (=Schachter 1977a, ex. 4)

Based on such examples, Schachter argues for a proform theory of verb phrase ellipsis, as have others since (Chao 1988, Hardt 1992, Lobeck 1999). However, Hankamer (1978) argues that such cases are, in his terms, either formulaic or conventionalized, occurring only as ILLOCUTIONALLY CHARGED EXPRESSIONS and not generally as declarative statements or informational questions. For instance, the elliptical expressions in (18a–b) are infelicitous, even though the contexts are the same as for Schachter's examples:

(18)a. [John tries to kiss Mary. She says:]
         #John, you're the first man who ever has.   (=Hankamer 1978, 7a')
    b.   [John pours another martini for Mary. She says:]
         #John, are you aware that no one else has?   (=Hankamer 1978, 7b')

Based on these data, Hankamer argues that the possibility of situationally evoked referents does not extend to verb phrase ellipsis in general.

Although we maintain that the interpretation of verb phrase ellipsis is a semantic process, we agree with Hankamer that the possibility of situationally evoked referents is extremely restricted. We therefore argue, contra Hankamer and Sag (1976), that the questions of whether a given expression requires an antecedent of a particular syntactic form and whether it can be used for situationally evoked referents need to be kept separate in a general theory of anaphora. We will see in the following section that verb phrase ellipsis is not the only form of anaphora that provides support for this claim.

In sum, verb phrase ellipsis is not strictly categorizable with respect to H&S's distinction between deep and surface anaphora. We have argued that it is similar to deep anaphora in that its anaphoric behavior renders it insensitive to the syntactic form of the referent. The fact that an apparent sensitivity to syntactic form is manifest when a Resemblance relation is operative is due to factors independent of a theory of anaphora. On the other hand, verb phrase ellipsis patterns with surface anaphora in not generally tolerating situationally evoked referents. Thus, an adequate theory of anaphora must incorporate distinctions beyond those associated with deep and surface anaphora.

3.3   So *anaphora*

In this section we consider *so* anaphora. The particular form of anaphoric *so* that concerns us here can appear in preverbal position as in (19a), or postverbally as part of the *do so* construction, as in (19b):

(19)a.   "... and with complete premeditation resolved that His Imperial Majesty Haile Selassie should be strangled because he was head of the feudal system." He was *so strangled* on Aug. 26, 1975, in his bed most cruelly.   (*Chicago Tribune*, 12/15/94)

   b.   Section 1 provides the examples to be derived by Gapping, and a formulation of Gapping capable of *doing so*.   [=deriving the examples] (from text of Neijt 1981)

H&S treat the anaphor *so*, and consequently the form *do so*, as a surface anaphor. This classification is motivated by the fact that *do so* disallows situationally evoked referents, as illustrated by the unacceptability of example (3c), repeated as (20):

(20)   [Hankamer attempts to stuff a 9-inch ball through a 6-inch hoop. Sag says:] #I don't think you can do so.   [=3c]

This restriction appears to be especially strong with *so*. Recall from section 3.2 that there has been some controversy regarding the possibility of situationally evoked referents with verb phrase ellipsis, given Schachter's purported counterexamples. Although we have seen (per Hankamer's (1978) arguments) that such cases are highly restricted, it is worth noting that *so* is unacceptable even in these limited cases in which verb phrase ellipsis is licensed. This is demonstrated by the infelicity of examples (21a–b), which differ from (17a–b) only in that they employ *do so* anaphora rather than verb phrase ellipsis.

(21)a.   [John tries to kiss Mary. She says:] #John, you mustn't do so. (cf. 17a)

   b.   [John pours another martini for Mary. She says:] #I really shouldn't do so. (cf. 17b)

The same restriction applies to preverbal uses of *so*, as seen in (22):

(22)   [A and B together have just witnessed Haile Selassie being murdered by strangulation]
       A: # He was so strangled most cruelly.

Thus, *so* – whether preverbal, or postverbal as part of the *do so* construction – patterns with surface anaphora in disallowing reference to situationally evoked referents.

However, *so* does not satisfy the other criterion for surface anaphora; that is, it imposes no requirement for a syntactically parallel antecedent. First, as exemplified by (19b), repeated below as (23a), *do so* can be felicitous in cases in which the voice between the source and target clauses is mismatched; in this case, there is no active voice syntactic representation for the verb phrase *deriving the examples* available in the source clause. Additional examples are provided in (23b–c).

(23)a.   Section 1 provides the examples to be derived by Gapping, and a formulation of Gapping capable of *doing so*. [=deriving the examples] [=19b]
   b.   As an imperial statute the British North America Act could be amended only by the British Parliament, which *did so* on several occasions. [amended an imperial statute] (*Groliers Encyclopedia*)
   c.   It is possible that this result can be derived from some independent principle, but I know of no theory that *does so*. [derives this result from some independent principle] (from text of Mohanan 1983, p. 664, cited by Dalrymple 1991)

Likewise, examples (24a–b) show that *do so* can be felicitous when its referent is evoked from a nominalization:

(24)a.   The defection of the seven moderates, who knew they were incurring the wrath of many colleagues in *doing so*, signaled that it may be harder to sell the GOP message on the crime bill than it was on the stimulus package. [defecting] (*Washington Post*)
   b.   For example, in the dialogue of Figure 2, the purpose of the subdialogue marked (3) is to support the agents' successful completion of the act of removing the pump of the air compressor; the corresponding SharedPlan, marked (P3) in Figure 3, specifies the beliefs and intentions that the agents must hold to *do so*. [successfully complete the act of removing the pump of the air compressor] (from text of Lochbaum 1994)

Finally, other form mismatches between the source and target clauses are attested as well, as illustrated in (25a–b):

(25)a.   There was a lot more negativity to dwell on, if anyone wished to *do so*. [=dwell on more negativity] (*Wall Street Journal*)
   b.   With or without the celebration, Belcourt is well worth seeing, and you can *do so* year round. [=see Belcourt] (*Wall Street Journal*)

The related preverbal *so* construction also does not require a syntactically-parallel antecedent. In fact, it can be used even in cases in which the intended referent must be inferred, as in (26):

(26)   Regarding a possible Elvis Presley stamp, Postmaster General Frank notes that anyone so honored must be "demonstrably dead" for 10 years.   (*Wall Street Journal*)

Here, the use of the phrase *so honored* signals to the reader that there is an "honoring" event recoverable from the discourse. In the absence of such an event being explicitly introduced, the hearer is induced to infer one from what **has** been said. In this case, the referent, which can be paraphrased roughly as "issuing a stamp with a particular person's picture on it," can be inferred under the presupposition that such an action would constitute an honoring. While the interpretation of this passage may seem effortless, upon closer analysis one finds a non-trivial chain of inference that must be carried out to arrive at the intended interpretation.

Thus, *so* anaphora patterns with surface anaphora with respect to disallowing situationally evoked referents, but patterns with deep anaphora with respect to its insensitivity to the syntactic form of the antecedent expression. It is therefore not categorizable within the H&S dichotomy and, like certain examples of verb phrase ellipsis discussed in the previous section, shows that a simple two-way distinction between deep and surface anaphora cannot be maintained.

Kehler and Ward (1999) present an analysis of anaphoric *so* that captures precisely these properties. Briefly, *so* serves as an information status marker for the verb phrase it modifies; in particular, it signals a dependency between the event denoted by this verb phrase and other salient, discourse-old information. This treatment provides a unified account of *so doing* and its variant *do so* in which they are analyzed compositionally as forms of hyponymic reference to a previously evoked "doing," the most general of event types (see also Miller 1990).[11] The claim that these expressions are interpreted with respect to semantic representations in a discourse model explains why they do not require an antecedent of a certain syntactic form.

With a minor modification to the notion of discourse-old (Prince 1992), the analysis also captures the fact that anaphoric *so* cannot access situationally evoked referents. Recall from section 2.2 that Prince considers all salient entities to be discourse-old. Because pronouns are indicators of salience, it follows that pronouns mark their referents as discourse-old, which includes referents that achieve salience solely from situational evocation such as in (27a–b).

(27)a.   [Norman sees a copy of *The Handbook of Pragmatics* on a table]
           Fred says to Norman: It's a wonderful book.
     b.   [Hankamer attempts to stuff a 9-inch ball through a 6-inch hoop.]
           Sag says:
           It's not clear that you'll be able to do it. [=3b]

We differ from Prince in that we consider only those entities that have been explicitly (that is, linguistically) introduced into the discourse to be discourse-old. That is, at the moment at which the pronoun is encountered in (27a), *The Handbook of Pragmatics* is highly salient, yet it is discourse-new because there has yet to be a linguistic mention of it. (Of course, this entity becomes discourse-old after the use of this referring expression.) This change in what counts as discourse-old allows for a straightforward articulation of the difference between the referential properties of pronouns and *so* anaphora: We can now simply say that pronouns require that their referents be salient (or IN FOCUS in the sense of Gundel et al. 1993) without further qualification as to the manner of evocation. Thus, not only is it the case that pronouns do not directly mark discourse status (*pace* Prince), they imply nothing with respect to it. On the other hand, *so* anaphora not only encodes the constraint that its referent be salient, but also that it be discourse-old in our sense. Prince's two-dimensional account of information status, as modified, is better equipped to incorporate these constraints, as there is no obvious way to distinguish those referents that achieve salience via (linguistic) introduction into the discourse in unidimensional frameworks such as that of Gundel et al. (1993).

In sum, as with the other phenomena we have considered thus far, the anaphoric use of *so* demonstrates the need to extend or revise current theories of constraints on anaphora. On the one hand, it cannot be categorized within H&S's distinction between deep and surface anaphora, whereas on the other it illustrates the need to extend unidimensional theories of cognitive status to account for the different manners in which entities can achieve salience. It also suggests that Prince's bidimensional framework be revised such that salience does not necessarily imply the status of discourse-old.

3.4   *Pronominal event reference*

Finally, we consider cases of pronominal event reference, such as *do it*, *do this*, and *do that*, exemplified in (28a–c), respectively:[12]

(28)a.   As they said about Ginger Rogers: "She did everything Fred Astaire did, and she *did it* backwards and in high heels."
     b.   Writing is a passion, and a film about the genesis of a writer should delve into the mind and heart of its subject. That "Becoming Colette" tries to *do this* is irrelevant, because it doesn't succeed.
     c.   So off he goes, writing in his diary the whole 3 day trip and complaining about the food and the runs I suppose, like all English people do

> when they go abroad, but he writes very well considering he's riding
> on a bumpy train, I mean he never even smears his ink *once*   (I'm
> bitter. I can't *do that* with *my* fountain pens . . .).

As we mentioned in section 1, these forms are distinct from both verb phrase
ellipsis and *do so* anaphora in a number of respects. Unlike verb phrase
ellipsis, but like *do so* anaphora, the verb *do* in these constructions is a main
verb and not an auxiliary. However, unlike the *do* of *do so*, this verb is transitive.
Finally, unlike verb phrase ellipsis (but again like *do so*), these forms are full
verb phrases from which nothing has been elided. The anaphoric properties of
these expressions derive from the pronoun that occupies the object position,
which is constrained to specify an event by the transitive main verb *do*. As one
would expect, these pronouns can be used in any grammatical position to
refer to events.

Thus, these expressions are uncontroversially forms of deep anaphora, and
as such they do not require an antecedent of a particular syntactic form.
Indeed, in some cases it is even difficult to precisely identify the linguistic
material that gives rise to the referent; this is the case in (28c), for instance, in
which we take the referent of *that* to be paraphrased roughly by "write without smearing my ink once while riding on a (bumpy) train." Likewise, as we
have already established, such forms readily allow for situationally evoked
referents, as in (29):

(29)   [Hankamer attempts to stuff a 9-inch ball through a 6-inch hoop. Sag says:]

It's not clear that you'll be able to do $\begin{Bmatrix} \text{it} \\ \text{this} \\ \text{that} \end{Bmatrix}$.

However, much more remains to be said about the referential behavior of
these expressions. For instance, Webber (1991) illustrates the wide variety of
different types of referents to which *that* can be used to refer, as shown in the
following examples (adapted from Webber 1991, ex. 5).

(30)   Hey, management has reconsidered its position. They've promoted Fred
       to second vice president.
       a.   *That's* my brother-in-law.
       b.   *That's* a lie.
       c.   *That's* false.
       d.   *That's* a funny way to describe the situation.
       e.   When did *that* happen?

The referents in each case are: (a) an entity; (b) a speech act; (c) a proposition;
(d) an expressed description; and (e) an event. Thus, while the referent of *that*
may be constrained in terms of its accessibility within the discourse context,
the TYPE of referent involved appears to be relatively unconstrained. This

behavior poses interesting questions regarding the time at which representations of such referents are constructed in the discourse model and the means by which they are created.

Webber also points out that *that* is often used to access a referent that is constructed from information communicated in more than one clause. She discusses a variety of such examples, including (31):

(31)   It's always been presumed that when the glaciers receded, the area got very hot. The Folsum men couldn't adapt, and they died out. *That's* what's supposed to have happened. *It's* the textbook dogma. But *it's* wrong. They were human and smart. They adapted their weapons and culture, and they survived.   (=Webber 1986, ex. 10)

In this example, *that* is used to refer to the sequence of events described in the first two sentences: the glaciers receding, the area getting hot, the Folsum men's failure to adapt, and their dying out (but – crucially – not the presuming). To model this behavior, Webber (1986) appeals to a process of CIRCUM-SCRIPTIVE REFERENCE that identifies this collection of discourse entities and creates a new entity that represents them as a unit. This newly–created entity is then available for subsequent reference, hence the felicitous use of the pronoun *it* in the two sentences that follow.

The existence of a process that creates representations of such referents on the fly raises additional questions regarding the constraints on the use of referring expressions since, strictly speaking, the referent is not available at the time the referring expression is used. As it is, Gundel et al.'s claim (for instance) that referents of *this* and *that* are ACTIVATED is somewhat under-constraining, and the space of possibilities that arise when one considers examples like (31) compound the problem. In a subsequent paper, however, Webber (1991) proposes a specific constraint. She argues that it is not the case that any arbitrary sequence of clauses can give rise to the referent of a demonstrative pronoun, but only those sequences that constitute DISCOURSE SEGMENTS. Furthermore, only certain discourse segments qualify – those whose contribution to the discourse model is currently IN FOCUS.[13]

Webber offers an algorithm that represents the structure of a discourse as a tree, on which a set of insertion operations apply for building discourse structure. (See also Webber et al. (1999) for a system that utilizes a discourse-level version of Lexicalized Tree Adjoining Grammar.) Only those segments on the RIGHT FRONTIER of a tree are in focus at a given time. She provides the following example (her ex. 8):

(32)a.   For his part in their term project, John built a two-armed robot.
  b.   He had learned about robotics in CSE391.
  c.   For her part, Mary taught it how to play the saxophone.
  d.   *That* took her six months.
  d'.   *That* earned them both A's.

Sentences (32a–b) together form a discourse segment, which then combines with (32c) to form a larger one. In sentence (32d), *that* is used to refer to the event evoked by the immediately preceding clause (32c), which is by defini-tion always on the right frontier. In contrast, *that* in (32d') is used to refer to the set of events evoked by the next larger segment on the right frontier, sentences (32a–c). Whereas both of these references are felicitous, it is hard to imagine an example in which *that* can felicitously be used to refer to a complex referent formed only from material in the non-segment (32b–c), or from the (inaccessible) discourse segment formed by (32a–b), as predicted by Webber's account. As such, the right frontier condition can be seen as a constraint on the use of Webber's notion of circumscriptive reference.

Of course, it is possible for a single discourse segment to give rise to more than one potential referent. Webber (1991) illustrates this point with the fol-lowing examples:

(33)a.   Segal, however, had his own problems with women: he had been trying to keep his marriage of seven years from falling apart; when *that* became impossible . . .   (=Webber 1991, ex. 7a)

   b.   Segal, however, had his own problems with women: he had been trying to keep his marriage of seven years from falling apart; when *that* became inevitable . . .   (=Webber 1991, ex. 7b)

In (33a), *that* is used to refer to Segal's keeping his marriage from falling apart, whereas in sentence (33b) *that* is used to refer only to Segal's marriage falling apart. This minimal pair is particularly interesting in that the passages differ only with respect to the adjective following the demonstrative. These examples demonstrate the crucial role that semantic information can play in determin-ing the referent of *that*, including information that is encountered after the referring expression itself. Of course, the fact that both referents may be activ-ated in Gundel et al.'s sense does not help differentiate among these possible interpretations.

Up to this point we have focused primarily on the nominal demonstrative *that*. We now consider the demonstrative *this*, which shares many traits with *that*. In many contexts the two forms can be interchanged with only subtle differences in meaning; consider (34):

(34)   Using microscopes and lasers and ultrasound, he removes tumors that are intertwined with children's brain stems and spinal cords. There is only the most minute visual difference between the tumors and normal tissue. Operations can last 12 hours or more. The tiniest slip can kill, paralyze or leave a child mentally retarded. *This* is the easy part of his job.   (*New York Times*, 8/11/90; cited by Webber 1991, ex. 2)

Replacing *this* with *that* in the final sentence does not significantly alter the meaning of the passage. One could in fact consider Gundel et al.'s placement of these two forms in the same category as an acknowledgment of this commonality. However, there are also important differences between them. For instance, *this* can be used cataphorically, whereas *that* cannot. Consider the following example:[14]

(35)   But wait! After this, more stuff happens! Now get *this* – you'll never believe *it*: as it happens (and purely by chance) our two very white firemen bumble into the middle of the execution and get both Ice-T, Ice Cube, and all their very black cronies more than a little miffed at them – especially after they take Ice-T's brother hostage. Thus is the stage set for great drama and tragedy, just as the Bard might have *done it* several hundred years ago.

In the third sentence, *this* is used cataphorically to refer to a complex situation that is about to be described, followed by another mention using *it*. In this case, the demonstrative *that* could not be felicitously used in place of *this*. As an aside, note also that *done it* in the final sentence is used to felicitously refer to an event – which can be paraphrased as *set the stage for great drama and tragedy* – that was evoked by a syntactically mismatched antecedent, in accordance with it being a form of deep anaphora.

This difference between nominal *this* and *that* may be a result of the oft-noted property that *this* encodes proximity of the referent to the speaker in terms of some cognitive dimension (spatial, temporal, perspective, and so forth), whereas *that* indicates distance (Fillmore 1997, inter alia). If hearer-status is viewed as one of these dimensions, then the cataphoricity of *this* could be seen to result from the fact that, at the time of utterance, the referent is "proximal" only to the speaker (i.e., known to the speaker but hearer-new), whereas *that* is appropriate only when the referent is hearer-old. It is less clear, however, what the relationship is between the proximal/distal distinction and the apparent interchangeability of *this* and *that* in passages such as (34).

In sum, the referential behavior of various pronominal forms of reference to eventualities challenges current theories of information status, particularly regarding the constraints on their use and the manner in which their referents are identified – and perhaps even dynamically constructed – in the discourse model.

4   Conclusion

Existing theories of cognitive status and reference in discourse will need to be revised and extended in order to account for the behavior of a variety of types of ellipsis and reference to eventualities. Indeed, the data presented here suggest that a comprehensive model capable of accounting for the distribution of these forms will, at a minimum, require an appeal to principles relating to syntax, semantics, pragmatics, reference, inference, salience, cognitive status, and discourse coherence. The distinctions made in existing theories are simply too coarse to account for the richness of the data that characterize these forms.

One must therefore fight the temptation to be overly reductionist when developing models of discourse processing and reference. In many respects, the full complexity of the integration among the aforementioned areas of language processing needs to be understood before we can arrive at a satisfactory account of reference. On the other hand, the very fact that natural languages offer us so many different ways to refer to things provides important clues to this end.

ACKNOWLEDGMENTS

The authors thank Larry Horn for extensive comments on a previous draft. Kehler was supported in part by National Science Foundation Grant IIS-9619126.

NOTES

1   Following Bach (1986), we use the term EVENTUALITIES to refer to events, processes, and states.

2   Gapping is therefore distinguished from PSEUDO-GAPPING, in which an auxiliary is left behind, as in (i):

 (i)   George claimed he won the electoral vote before Al did the popular vote.

3   For discussion of additional constraints and the issues related thereto, see Carlson, this volume, and the papers in Part II (especially those by Abbott, this volume, Gundel and Fretheim, Huang, Kehler, Roberts, and Ward and Birner.)

4   In Sag and Hankamer (1984), this dichotomy was revised to distinguish between two types of anaphoric processes: ELLIPSIS (their earlier surface anaphora) and MODEL-INTERPRETIVE ANAPHORA, or MIA (their earlier deep anaphora). The former process derives antecedents from PROPOSITIONAL REPRESENTATIONS that maintain some degree of syntactic constituent structure. On the other hand, MIA operates with respect to purely semantic representations in a discourse model. In some respects the ellipsis/MIA distinction more adequately characterizes the difference between these two types of contextual dependence; the process of recovering a missing syntactic representation is arguably not a form of anaphora at all. However, following standard practice in the literature, we will nonetheless continue to use H&S's original and more familiar "surface" and "deep" terminology.

5   Authors vary as to whether they consider unacceptable examples of surface anaphora to be syntactically ungrammatical (identified as such

with a "*") or pragmatically infelicitous (identified with a "#"). The difference is a crucial one in that it reflects whether anaphora and ellipsis are taken to be governed by principles of syntax or semantics/pragmatics. In light of the crucial role that context plays in judging the acceptability of such examples, however, we shall uniformly mark all unacceptable examples of anaphora and ellipsis with the mark of pragmatic infelicity.

6   Again, we refer the reader to the other papers in Part II of this volume.

7   Of course, it could turn out that the hearer was already familiar with a referent that was introduced indefinitely:

(i)   I saw a guy on the subway today. He turned out to be your roommate Joe!

In such a case, the hearer will associate the newly created representation for the guy introduced in the first sentence with that of Joe upon interpreting the second sentence.

8   Gundel et al. (1993) use the term COGNITIVE STATUS, whereas Prince (1992) uses the term INFORMATION STATUS. We will use these terms interchangeably.

9   See also Kehler, this volume, for a discussion of data like these.

10   We should note that not all informants agree that (14b–c)

are unacceptable under the intended interpretation, and in fact judgments for examples involving verb phrase ellipsis and binding theory violations are notorious for being subject to a great deal of idiolectal variation. See Kitagawa (1991), inter alia, for discussion.

11   Note that while *so doing* and *do so* are variants, they are distinct from forms such as *so do(es)* and *so did*, which contain auxiliary *do*. As such, other auxiliaries can be used in these latter constructions (i) but not in the former ones (ii):

(i)   George will/may/can claim victory, and so will/may/can Al.

(ii)   #George will/may/can claim victory, and will/may/can so Al.

Moreover, only the auxiliary constructions are compatible with stative antecedents as shown in (iii) and (iv):

(iii)   George intends to claim victory, and so does Al.

(iv)   #George intends to claim victory, and Al does so too.

12   Examples (28a–c) were collected from an on-line corpus of movie reviews.

13   Webber's use of the term IN FOCUS should not be confused with that of Gundel et al. (1993).

14   Example (35) was also collected from an on-line corpus of movie reviews.

Part III Pragmatics and its Interfaces

18   Some Interactions of Pragmatics and Grammar

GEORGIA M. GREEN

It has been recognized in generative grammar since the 1960s[1] that the acceptability of sentences depends on the referential and predicative intents imputed to the speaker. Of course, this fact has not always been represented in those baldly pragmatic terms; for a long time it was (and in some quarters still is) socially or tactically unwise to refer to speakers' mental states in describing syntactic knowledge, so the problem was reframed in terms of the properties of the syntactic or semantic properties of the sentence (see e.g. Karttunen 1977, Karttunen and Peters 1979). Now, however, a deeper understanding of the relation of knowledge of grammar and lexicon to knowledge of the principles of language use, both universal (e.g. Grice's (1967) Cooperative Principle[2]) and language particular (cf. e.g. Morgan 1978), allows a direct and straightforward description of linguistic competence (Green 2000). The problem is not an isolated one restricted to a few troublesome constructions. Many or most of the constraints that have been proposed by generative grammarians (e.g. binding constraints, constraints on the reference of unexpressed subjects of infinitives) must either be stated in ultimately pragmatic terms or describe constructions whose use conveys pragmatic information about the beliefs of the speaker – beliefs about the world (presuppositions), about the propositional attitudes of the addressee, or about the structure of the ongoing discourse.[3] This chapter reviews a broad selection of syntactic phenomena that have been observed to have pragmatic values, and sketches the properties of a description of competence that straightforwardly reflects them.

1   What Kind of Information is Pragmatic?

In a sense, all pragmatic information is ultimately indexical information, that is, related to indices for speaker, hearer, time, and location of an act of uttering something that the sign represents (Bar-Hillel 1954, Nunberg 1993, Levinson this volume). It is important to be clear that it is not linguistic forms (words, morphemes, expressions) that carry pragmatic information (though informal descriptions often suggest this, in formulations like "this form expresses/marks the speakers belief/intention that . . ."), but the facts of their utterance. Pragmatic information is information about the relation between the user of the form and the **act** of using the form. First and foremost, pragmatic information is information about mental models: speaker's and addressee's mental models of each other. Linguistic pragmatics irreducibly involves the speaker's model of the addressee, and the hearer's[4] model of the speaker (potentially recursively). For George to understand Martha's utterance of "Xxx" to him, he must not only recognize (speech perception, parsing) that she has said "Xxx," he must have beliefs about her which allow him to infer what her purpose was in uttering "Xxx," which means that he has beliefs about her model of him, including her model of his model of her, and so on, as illustrated in figure 18.1. Thus, when Martha says "Xxx" to George, meaning by it "*p*", she does so believing that George believes "not *p*". And when George hears her speak to him, he recognizes that she has said *Xxx*, and understands that she believed that he believed the negation of what she meant by it. Any of these beliefs could be incorrect at one level of detail or another. That is why, in figure 18.1, we see that George's image of Martha, and his of her, as well as his belief about what she meant, are not quite accurate. Martha's image of George as having less, longer, and straighter hair than we can see he has, and his image of her as being smaller and having longer hair than she in fact does are visual metaphors for the fact that we have imperfect knowledge of each other. Significantly, the participants' images of each other are also successively less detailed, illustrating that their knowledge of each other is incomplete as well as not quite accurate. And most important, illustrated by the different fonts for the letter "p" that represents Martha's meaning, what Martha meant by *Xxx* is distinct from what George believes she meant. As a *New Yorker* cartoon caption once had it: "I know you believe you understand what you thought I said, but I'm not sure that you realize that what you heard was not what I meant." Since acts are interpreted at multiple levels of granularity, this built-in indeterminacy or margin of error is present for acts involved in choosing words and construction types, as well as for acts of uttering sentences containing or instantiating them.

These are background assumptions against which all discussion of linguistic pragmatics must take place, and which in fact motivate a pragmatic load for both "meaningless" discourse particles like *um, well*, and *like* (Schourup 1985, Kose 1997, Schwenter and Traugott 2000, Green 2001, Fukada-Karlin (in preparation), Blakemore this volume) and truth-conditionally equivalent alternative constructions to express the same proposition.

2   Some Illustrative Phenomena

In English and probably all other natural languages, there are truth-conditionally equivalent alternatives to practically every describable construction, and

Figure 18.1   Illustration of speaker's and addressee's mental models of each other

to the extent that this is true, the alternatives turn out to have different prag-matic values.[5] Horn (1984a, 1993) offers a detailed and convincing explanation of why this is inevitable.

The factors which might enter into the choice between or among truth-conditionally equivalent constructions are numerous. To take one of the most familiar examples, choosing a passive construction over an active counter-part might be motivated by an intention to represent the patient as the topic, and/or defer information about the agent to the end of the sentence, as in (1a), where it will be more perceptually prominent, naturally receiving sentence stress. On the other hand, using the passive allows expression of the agent to be entirely suppressed, enabling a speaker to accommodate the fact that it is unknown (1b) or irrelevant (1c) who the agent is, or to just avoid saying who the agent is, even if he does know, as in (1d).

(1)a. The bank was robbed by two young men with extensive facial scars.
  b. My bike was taken between 3:00 and 5:30 on Monday.
  c. Over 20,000 copies of the book were sold before it was discovered that pages 285 and 286 were missing.
  d. [Do you know where the February *Scientific American* is?] It was thrown out.

Using a passive also commonly implies a belief that the event described had a particular effect on some contextually salient sentient individual (R. Lakoff 1971a, Davison 1980, Fukada 1986). Often the affected individual is the subject (as in (2a, 2b)), but it can be any contextually salient legal person, including, but not limited to, the speaker or addressee, as in (2c, 2d).

(2)a. He was interrogated for three hours.
  b. He was awarded a Pulitzer Prize for that photograph.
  c. The evidence was destroyed in the fire.
  d. This idea has been attacked as simplistic and naïve.

The effect can be negative, as in (2a), or positive, as in (2b); only the details of the context in which the sentence is uttered could tell us which it is in (2c). The jarring effect of (3a) is attributable to the fact that the referent of a term is clearly affected, but the construction does not represent that term as a subject (cf. 3b).

(3)a. #A car hit your dog, but he's OK now.
  b. Your dog was hit by a car this afternoon, but he's OK now.

There is even suggestive evidence that details of complementizer choice have pragmatic implications associated with them (cf. Bolinger 1972a, Borkin 1974, Riddle 1975, 1978), reflecting different assumptions of the speakers as in (4) and (5), where the (b) examples imply a stronger conviction on the part of the subject.

(4)a. He expects that he will win.
  b. He expects to win.

(5)a. I know that it's raining.
  b. I know it's raining.

In the cases that are the focus of this chapter, the connection between the way something is said and what is intended to be conveyed is automatic, suggesting an analysis as fossilized conversational implicature, according to the following logic. Since implicatures exploit (assumed) literal meanings, with "live" conversational implicature, and even with short-circuited conversational implicature (Morgan 1978), it is often reasonable to deny that an implicature was intended. Thus, denying the causal implicature of the embedded conjunction in (6) is acceptable.

(6) The committee money disappeared from the safe that day, and Lee came home with a new jacket that night, but I don't believe or intend to imply that the two events have anything to do with each other.

In contrast, the cases discussed here involve use conditions which refer to beliefs or attitudes of the speaker and amount to presuppositions; they are so strongly linked to a syntactic construction that it sounds irrational to use that construction and then deny that the conditions hold. For example, the present tense can be used to refer to future time as long as the event referred to is assumed to be prearranged, and there is an adverbial expression indicating a future time indicated explicitly or in ellipsis (G. Lakoff 1971b, Prince 1982). Thus, (7a) can be used in many of the same situations as (7b).

(7)a. The Celtics play the Bucks tomorrow.
   b. The Celtics are going to play the Bucks tomorrow.

If the event is not (mutually) understood to be prearranged or scheduled, simple present tense cannot be used for future time, so using (8) would imply that the speaker (and the addressee, in the speaker's estimate) either (a) knew that the game was fixed, or (b) had a firm belief in predestination, and believed that the speaker had an inside line on the Omnipotent's plans for basketball games.

(8) The Celtics crush the Bucks tomorrow.

The time adverbial can be either explicit as in (7) and (9a), or implicit, as in (9b).

(9)a. Sandy arrives tomorrow, so we'll have to clean up the guest-room.
   b. A: What's on the docket for tomorrow?
       B: Well, Sandy arrives, so I have to go to the airport.

But when a shared presumption that the event is scheduled cannot be assumed, as in (10), people won't use a present tense form to refer to a future event.

(10) A: What's new?
      B: #My sister comes in from Seattle, so I'm getting ready to go to the airport.

The bizarreness of (11a) shows that this belief requirement cannot be denied like a conversational implicature, but can be suspended, like a presupposition (11b).

(11)a.   #The Celtics win tomorrow, but it's not preordained or fixed; there's an off chance the Pistons might beat them.

   b.   The Celtics win tomorrow, if Benny got the fix in and explained to the players on the other team what would happen to them if they didn't lose.

The main focus of this chapter is how the construction used to say something reflects the speaker's attitude toward and beliefs about the topics and referents in the ongoing discourse. Other aspects of how what is said is said that have been shown to affect what is conveyed include intonational choices (Schmerling 1976, Cutler 1977, Olsen 1986, Ward 1988, Hirschberg 1991) and more segmental phonological choices (e.g. sarcastic nasalization, Cutler 1974: 117), as well as the choice of which language to use (Gumperz 1976, Burt 1994). In the cases to be discussed, the focus is more on what the speaker intends (or is content) to convey than on an appreciation of the addressee's limitations in processing language "on-line," though of course, a rational speaker will take the hearer's needs into consideration in deciding how to say what must be said. This topic is addressed briefly in section 5. However, a primary goal of this chapter is to draw attention to a variety of cases where potential inferences from the way something is said are grammaticalized as part of the syntactic repertoire. The following sections describe a selection of other constructions that differ from their truth-conditionally equivalent counterparts in various ways. Most reflect different beliefs about or attitudes toward referents of linguistic expressions that are part of the utterance. Of course, truth-conditionally equivalent sentences may also differ from each other in rhetorical function (i.e., in what gets asserted and what is presupposed), and these are treated in section 3. Section 4 treats syntactic devices that reflect the speaker's assumptions about the structure of the discourse. Section 5 addresses processing-related issues: syntactic constructions that enable a speaker to compensate for (perceived) difficulties in producing or parsing a complex utterance. Many of the constructions have more than one use or function, and show up in more than one category.

3   Belief/Attitude/Value Cases

Another instance of "stylistic variants" exhibiting a difference in rhetorical value involves constructions with sentential complements as in (12) and (13), or adjuncts as in (14). The (a) sentences in these sets differ from the (b) sentences in that the italicized subordinate clause represents a presupposed or otherwise subordinate proposition in the (a) sentences, but has its own declarative illocutionary force in the (b) sentences.

(12)a.   I bet *it'll float if you throw it in the lake.*
   b.   It'll float if you throw it in the lake, I bet. [SLIFTING][6]

(13)a.   That *Sandy thought it was Tuesday* is obvious/clear.
   b.   It's obvious/clear that Sandy thought it was Tuesday. [EXTRAPOSITION]

(14)a.   Someone *who said the girls were supposed to bring two quarts of potato salad* called.
   b.   Someone called who said the girls were supposed to bring two quarts of potato salad. [RELATIVE CLAUSE EXTRAPOSITION]

Thus, depending on the sense intended for *bet* in (12a), (12a) is either a wager or a speculation, but (12b) can only be a speculation – *bet* does not have a performative interpretation in that construction (Ross 1975, Horn 1986). And while both (13a) and (13b) could be used to assert something about the claim that Sandy had some belief about the identity of a day, only (13b) could be used to **make** the claim that Sandy had that belief (Morgan 1975b, Horn 1986). In the case of (14), the (a) sentence reports who called, while the (b) sentence reports what someone said the girls were supposed to bring (Ziv 1976).

Other constructions reflect particular kinds of beliefs speakers have about the objects of their discourse. For example, use of the INTERNAL DATIVE construction (Green 1974) in (15b) implies that the speaker believes that the referents of the subject and beneficiary noun phrases were alive at the same time.

(15)a.   Win this one for the Gipper/me.
   b.   Win me/#the Gipper this one.

Wierzbicka has argued (1986) that use of the internal dative construction reflects more generally the speaker's greater interest in the referent of the indirect object noun phrase.

The RAISED SUBJECT constructions in (16b, d–f) (Borkin 1974, Postal 1974, Steever 1977, Schmerling 1978) reflect the speaker's assumption of the possibility of interaction between the (implied) experiencer (MacArthur in (16b)), or agent (Eks in (16d–f)) and the referent of the raised subject (Caesar, Sandy, Dale) at the time referred to by the raising verb.

(16)a.   It seemed to MacArthur that Patton/Julius Caesar was the greatest general in history.
   b.   Patton/#Julius Caesar seemed to MacArthur to be the greatest general in history.
   c.   Eks asked that Sandy leave.
   d.   Eks asked Sandy to leave.
   e.   Eks allowed Dale to examine Dana.
   f.   Eks allowed Dale to be examined by Dana.

A similar construction with finite complements and predicates including *looks like* and *appears as if* (Rogers 1971, Postal 1974: 356–68) has related properties, so that sentences like (17a) provide no information about the nature of the evidence for the claimed resemblance, while ones like (17b) reflect the speaker's ability to perceive the referent of the subject displaying the predicated property at the time of the speech act.

(17)a.   It looks like Stalin's been dead for years.
   b.   #Stalin looks like he's been dead for years.

R. Lakoff (1969a) and Horn (1971, 1978b, 1989) have described the NEGATIVE TRANSPORTATION phenomenon illustrated in (18a) where, with a certain class of verbs and adjectives, a negative occurs one or more clauses above the clause it conversationally negates. Thus (18a) would communicate what (18b) straightforwardly asserts, and (19a) would be conversationally ambiguous between a report that Dana lacks the desire to wash dishes, and a report like (19b) that Dana desires not to wash dishes.

(18)a.   I don't think Sandy will arrive until Monday.
   b.   I think Sandy won't arrive until Monday.

(19)a.   Dana doesn't want to wash dishes.
   b.   Dana wants to not wash dishes.

The difference between the (a) sentences and the (b) sentences in (18–19) is that the (a) sentences, with transported negatives, are hedged – they represent weaker claims, apparently by implicating rather than asserting the relevant negative proposition (cf. Horn 1978b: 131–6, 177–216 and Horn 1989, Chapter 5 for discussion). A similar phenomenon is evident in the fact that the morphologically incorporated negative in (20b) is pragmatically stronger than the unincorporated negative in (20a) (Sheintuch and Wise 1976), though of course, as (20a,b) are truth-conditionally identical, they have the same entailments.

(20)a.   I didn't see anyone there.
   b.   I saw no one there.

The use of *some* or *any* described by R. Lakoff (1969b) provides a very clear reflection of speakers' attitudes. As Lakoff showed, in the class of interrogative, conditional, and hypothetical constructions where *some* and *any* are truth-conditionally equivalent, the use of *some* indicates a positive attitude toward the situation described by the proposition it is part of, while *any* reflects a neutral or negative attitude. Thus, the condition in (21a) is satisfied by the same state of affairs as the one in (21b), but (21b) implies an assumption that it is likely that there are no apples on the table.

(21)a.   if there are some apples on the table
    b.   if there are any apples on the table

Similarly, the question in (22a) reflects the hope that Bill wants spinach, while (22b) may reflect the hope that he does not.

(22)a.   Does Bill want some spinach?
    b.   Does Bill want any spinach?

In the same vein, (23a) could be a bribe, intended to get the addressee to eat bread (treating cooking hamburgers all week as a reward), while (23b) would be a threat, intended to keep the addressee from eating bread (and treating cooking hamburgers all week as an undesirable event).

(23)a.   If you eat some bread, I'll cook hamburgers all week.
    b.   If you eat any bread, I'll cook hamburgers all week.

A whole host of other NEGATIVE POLARITY ITEMS (cf. Baker 1970, Horn 1971, 1989, Schmerling 1971a, Israel this volume) reflect attitudes similar to those which *any* reflects (Ladusaw 1980). The examples in (24) expose the speaker's suspicion that Bo spent, ate, and knew nothing, and did not bother to RSVP, respectively.

(24)   Do you think Bo ⎰ spent a red cent on that?
                     ⎪ ate a bite?
                     ⎱ knows bupkes? ("nothing" [⟨Yid.⟩])
                       bothered to RSVP?

In addition to the negative polarity sensitivity of syntax illustrated just above, languages may display sensitivity to ignorance. Both the inversion of subject and auxiliary verb in embedded questions that is common in many dialects of English and truncation of embedded questions (SLUICING) imply that the individual to whom the answer is implied or assumed to be relevant is in fact ignorant of the answer. Thus the (a) sentences in (25) and (26) are more acceptable than the (b) sentences, which have contradictory implications which their acceptable and uninverted or unreduced (c) counterparts lack (cf. Ross 1975).

(25)a.   She wants to know who did I appoint.
    b.   #She already knows who did I appoint.
    c.   She already knows who I appointed.

(26)a.   John broke something, but he won't say what.
    b.   #John broke something, and he said what.
    c.   John broke something, and he said what he broke.

This property of subject–auxiliary inversion and sluicing explains why the examples in (27) induce the implicature that the speaker does not know the answer to the question.

(27)a. It never occurred to me to wonder who did she appoint.
    b. John went somewhere with my car, and you know where.

Although the examples cited here are all from English, it would be surprising to find a language where custom didn't link beliefs or attitudes to the use of particular words or constructions. Sakakibara (1995) and Kose (1997) give detailed examples of the speaker beliefs associated with the use of Japanese long-distance reflexives and sentence-final particles, respectively; cf. Huang (this volume) for additional discussion of the pragmatics of anaphora.

4 Reflections of Discourse Structure

Language scholars have long recognized that there are correlations between the order of syntactic constituents in a sentence and the discourse function of the information which a particular constituent references (Mathesius 1928, Firbas 1964, Halliday 1967, Kuno 1972, Gundel and Fretheim, this volume; Ward and Birner, this volume, inter alia).[7] In general, and all other things being equal, the first phrase in a sentence tends to be intended to denote familiar (or TOPICAL, or GIVEN, or OLD, or presupposed, or predictable, or THEMATIC) material, while phrases toward the end of the sentence tend to denote NEW (or FOCUSED, or asserted, or RHEMATIC) material. Other things are not always equal, however. Sentence stress or intonational accent (higher pitch which falls off rapidly and is perceived as louder) also correlates with information being treated as new (Schmerling 1976), and new information may be expressed in phrases that occur toward or at the beginning of a sentence if they bear the main sentence stress, as in (28) (Olsen 1986).

(28) *John* ate the cookies.

Furthermore as Prince (1981a) demonstrated, *familiar, predictable, given, old, theme*, and *sentence topic* do not denote interchangeable notions, and different writers have used the same term to refer to rather different categories. Still, the various writers seem to have been addressing the same point, summarized by Horn's (1986) observation that the initial slot in a sentence tends to be reserved for material taken to refer to the discourse theme or sentence topic (i.e., what the sentence is about). Typically, this is material that the speaker (reflexively) assumes to be familiar to the addressee, and preferentially, it is material which is either salient (assumed by the speaker to be in the addressee's consciousness) or presupposed (taken as non-controversial) (Horn 1986: 171). It is not surprising, then, that syntactic rules of languages provide for numerous alternative constructions which differ in the order of phrases while preserving truth-conditional semantics and illocutionary force. This is true even in a "fixed word order" language like English,[8] as illustrated by the incomplete list of options for English declarative sentences given in examples (29–32):

(29)a.　Eks delivered a rug to Aitchberg.

　　b.　A rug was delivered to Aitchberg by Eks. [PASSIVE]

　　c.　There was a rug delivered (to Aitchberg) (by Eks). [THERE-INSERTION]

　　d.　A rug, Eks delivered to Aitchberg. [TOPICALIZATION]

　　e.　It was a rug that Eks delivered to Aitchberg. [CLEFT]

　　f.　What Eks delivered to Aitchberg was a rug. [PSEUDO-CLEFT]

　　g.　...and deliver a rug to Aitchberg, Eks did. [VERB PHRASE PREPOSING]

(30)a.　Finding typographical errors is never simple.

　　b.　It is never simple to find typographical errors. [EXTRAPOSITION]

　　c.　Typographical errors are never simple to find. [TOUGH-MOVEMENT]

　　d.　Simple to find, typographical errors are not. [ADJECTIVE PHRASE PREPOSING]

(31)a.　Eks met a woman who said she was the Princess Anastasia's governess at Treno's.

　　b.　At Treno's, Eks met a woman who said she was the Princess Anastasia's governess. [ADVERB PREPOSING]

　　c.　Eks met at Treno's a woman who said she was the Princess Anastasia's governess. [HEAVY NP SHIFT]

　　d.　Eks met her at Treno's, that woman who said she was the Princess Anastasia's governess. [RIGHT DISLOCATION]

　　e.　That woman who said she was the Princess Anastasia's governess, Eks met her at Treno's. [LEFT DISLOCATION]

(32)a.　The little bunny scampered into its hole.

　　b.　Into its hole, the little bunny scampered. [LOCATIVE PREPOSING]

　　c.　Into its hole scampered the little bunny. [INVERSION]

Of course, old information does not tend to go first just because it is old, or become old just because it is first. Sometimes none of the material in a sentence represents "old information," and as noted above, new information sometimes goes first; generally speakers have more particular reasons (not necessarily conscious reasons) for making a particular constituent first or last in a sentence (cf. Green 1982a). Such functions of word order have been explored in some detail for a number of constructions. Two are described below.

4.1 Preposing

Ward's (1988) analysis of preposings like those in (29d), (29g), and (30d) indicated that while they may serve a variety of discourse functions, which he described in detail, they have two properties in common. In Ward's terminology, they first of all mark the preposed element as referring to an entity which is related in a certain way (as a BACKWARD LOOKING CENTER) to entities previously evoked in the discourse (the set of FORWARD LOOKING CENTERS).[9] Second, they mark the presupposed open proposition of the unstressed part of the sentence as salient in the discourse. Viewed from a different perspective, the referent of the presupposed element must function as a backward-looking center and the open proposition must be salient in the discourse for the utterance of a sentence with a preposed phrase to be acceptable in its context. Thus, a sentence like (29d) might be used in a context like (33), where the referent of *one of these rugs* is very obviously in a subset relation to the previously mentioned set {rugs to be given as rewards} and the open proposition is "Eks deliver a rug to someone".

(33).   An Eastern bloc embassy official gave Eks six full-size oriental rugs, and directed him to give them to the senators who had been most cooperative. One of these rugs Eks delivered to Sen. Aitchberg.[10]

It might also be used in a context like (34), where *one of these rugs* is a member of the set {rugs concealing cocaine}, and the open proposition "Eks delivered something to Aitchberg" is salient in the discourse.

(34).   FBI agents suspected both Eks and Aitchberg of trafficking in cocaine, and had been tailing them for months. In March, they learned from an informant that six oriental rugs concealing 20 pounds of cocaine each had come through JFK airport, and as Exhibit B indicates, one of these rugs Eks delivered to Aitchberg.

But a sentence like (29d) could not be used in a context like (35), where neither of these conditions holds.

(35).   Eks and Aitchberg played golf together regularly. ??An oriental rug Eks delivered to Aitchberg one day.

4.2   *Main-verb inversion*

English is graced with a number of inversion constructions which, as in (32c), allow the subject noun phrase to appear after the main verb instead of before it (Green 1980, 1982b, 1985, Birner 1992, 1994, Ward and Birner, this volume). The inversions begin with a preposed adjective phrase, participial phrase, or locative or directional adverbial phrase. Because of this, they can be used to serve any of a number of functions which exploit that phrase order (Green 1980, Birner 1992, 1994). For example, a writer[11] may use an inversion with a preposed phrase which refers to a previously established or implied referent to describe how information following it relates to previous discourse, as in the examples in (36), where the initial phrase contains something explicitly ((36a,b)) or implicitly ((36c)) anaphoric to something preceding in the discourse.

(36)a.   [... new license ...] Attached to it, as always, is an application blank for next year's license.

  b.   Jerome and Rita Arkoff and Tom and Fanny Irwin were in the front row ... Back of the Arkoffs and Irwins were William Lesser and Patrick Degan, and between them and slightly to the rear was Saul Panzer. [Rex Stout, *Might as Well Be Dead*, p. 180. (New York: Viking Books, 1956)]

  c.   At issue is Section 1401(a) of the Controlled Substances Act.

In other instances, what is exploited is the fact that the inversion construction puts what would otherwise be a subject noun phrase in the sentence final position, which is typically reserved for focused, new information. This enables a writer to introduce a new discourse element (e.g. an important character or object or an element of the setting) in a focused position, as in (37).[12] Travelog-style descriptions exploit this extensively, as in (37c).

(37)a.   In a little white house lived two rabbits. [Dick Bruna, *Miffy*. (New York: Two Continents, 1975)]

  b.   Competing with the screamers for popularity are the phone-in programs, an adaptation of two rural American pastimes – listening in on the party-line and speaking at the town meeting. [Robert Dye, "The Death of Silence," *Journal of Broadcasting*, 12, 3 (1968). Reprinted in *Subject and Strategy*, ed. Paul Escholz and Alfred Rosa, 169–72, p. 170. (New York: St. Martins, 1978)]

  c.   The grounds were lavishly furnished with ceramic, stone, and wrought-metal sculpture. There were an enormous stainless steel frog and two tiny elves in the foyer of the guest house, and outside stood a little angel.

A related use of inversions is to describe an event or locative relationship which resolves a salient indeterminacy in a narrative as it has been established up to that point. It might be the whereabouts of an important character, as in the second inversion in (38a), or the identity of the previously unknown agent of some significant action, as in (38b), or an event significant in the protagonist's execution of his plans, as in the second inversion in (38c) (the first introduces a new discourse element).

(38)a.   Then at the darkest hour dawned deliverance. *Through the revolving doors swept Tom Pulsifer.* [S. J. Perelman, "The Customer is Always Wrong," *The Most of S. J. Perelman*, p. 227. (New York: Simon and Schuster, 1958)]

b.   One night there was a tap on the window. Mrs. Rabbit peeped through the window. *Outside stood a little angel.*
[Bruna]

c.   Dumble vanished and in his place rose a dark, angry cloud of bees. They flew straight at the soldiers' faces, and *from the soldiers came yells of anguish, of sorrow, and of despair.*
[Jay Williams, *The King with Six Friends* (New York: Parents' Magazine Press, 1968)]

The particular discourse values of several other of the constructions in (29–31) have been explored in some detail.[13] For Japanese, Makino (2001) describes the conditions on the use of the formal nouns *no* and *koto.*

5   Reflections of Perceived Difficulty

Finally, speakers may take advantage of constructions like EXTRAPOSITION (39b) and HEAVY NP SHIFT (40b), which allow a constituent to appear at the end of the sentence to put the longest or most conversationally significant constituent last.

(39)a.   Whether Kim will visit museums in France and Dana will go to concerts in Vienna, or Dana will visit museums in France and Kim will go to concerts in Vienna is unclear.

b.   It is unclear whether Kim will visit museums in France and Dana will go to concerts in Vienna, or . . .

(40)a.   Dana attributed a poem in which intuitions were compared to anemones and academic theories were described as battlements to Coleridge.

b.   Dana attributed to Coleridge a poem in which intuitions were compared to anemones and academic theories were described as battlements.

It is not clear whether this option serves to make the sentence easier to articulate (cf. Olsen 1986) or simply easier to keep track of, or whether the motivation is altruistic – accommodating the addressee's likely strategies or difficulties in parsing, or some combination of these. Length and discourse significance seem to be at least partially independent factors. Longer postposed noun phrases tend to sound better, as in (41a), even if they have no more semantic content, as in (41b), but of two noun phrases of equal length the more significant-sounding sounds better, as (41c) shows. (See Arnold et al. 2000 for related discussion.)

(41)a.   But they attributed to Blake *The Rise and Fall of the Roman Empire/ ?Typee.*

b. The district attorney considers indictable Montgomery J. Jingleheimer-Smith III/?Rose Budd.

c. The committee has attributed to Margaret Thatcher an extraordinary poem/?the 27-line poem.

6 Representing the Pragmatic Value of Syntactic Constructions

In the early years of generative grammar, the distribution of linguistic expressions in sentences was taken to be an exclusively formal matter, and the relevant notion of identity among expressions was assumed to be identity of form. However, as early as 1965, attempts were made to incorporate various kinds of pragmatic conditions into the framework then available for syntactic description. For example, G. Lakoff (1965), assuming that restrictions on distribution were all syntactic in nature, claimed that the unacceptability of *beware* in certain constructions (e.g. in (42)) reflected the fact that *beware* bore a syntactic RULE FEATURE which indicated that auxiliary inversion could not apply in clauses where *beware* was the main verb.

(42) #Did you beware of John?

Of course, Lakoff's system would break down when confronted with the fact that pragmatic factors influence the acceptability of using syntactic constructions, such as inversion in embedded interrogatives. It cannot be claimed that *know* has a (different) rule feature which precludes its complement from appearing inverted, to account for the unacceptability of (25b), because inversion is fine in the complement of *know* in (25a). Lakoff (1965) also proposed STRUCTURAL DESCRIPTION FEATURES to constrain a structure from meeting the structural description of a transformational rule, but these would be equally inadequate to the task of excluding (43a), while allowing (43b).[14]

(43)a. #We need a registrar who can beware of phony addresses.
   b. We need a registrar who will beware of phony addresses.

At the same time, addressing other issues, Chomsky (1965) proposed indexing nodes in constituent structure trees for coreference so that the kind of identity required for personal and relative pronouns could be represented as syntactic information.[15]

Approaches to accommodating other kinds of pragmatic conditions into syntactic descriptions involved representing contingent assumptions about real-world relations among situations as syntactic information (e.g. Green 1968). For example, to distinguish between the appropriateness of (44a) and (44b), one would have to have access to the proposition that being interested in sports (but not being interested in knitting) entails or implies the ability to tell a zone press from a fast break.

(44)a.   Jo isn't interested in sports, and Bo couldn't tell a zone press from a
         fast break either.
    b.   #Jo isn't interested in knitting, and Bo couldn't tell a zone press from a
         fast break either.

This proposal was taken seriously despite the fact that it clearly required
making the rules of the grammar (insertion of the particles *too* and *either*)
sensitive to properties of speakers (specifically, to whether they believed that
some proposition implied some other proposition), and this involves a gross
category error. A later proposal (Green 1973) to encode the implication as part
of the deep structure – as was then being done at every turn to account for
the syntactic constraints imposed by various illocutionary forces (e.g. R. Lakoff
1968, Ross 1970a) – was equally doomed. Morgan (1973a) showed that this
approach led to theory-internal logical contradictions.

   Meanwhile, linguists' interpretation of Grice's paper "Logic and Conversation" (Grice 1989: Chapter 2), which had been circulating underground for
several years, prompted them to begin to describe relations between grammaticality and usage. Although Morgan (1975b) had demonstrated that making
a strict separation in grammatical descriptions between constraints on form
and constraints on usage wasn't going to be as simple as it looked, given the
fact that certain forms (like those in (45)) induced implicatures which are not
induced by semantically equivalent forms (cf. (46)), this warning went largely
unheeded.

(45)a.   *Do you have any idea* how much that cost?
    b.   *Why* paint your house purple?

(46)a.   *Any idea* how much that cost?
    b.   *Why do you* paint your house purple?

Gordon and Lakoff (1971) had interpreted Grice's proposal as sanctioning
the codification of likely implicatures into "conversational postulates" and the
incorporation of speech act participants' beliefs and intentions into syntactic
derivations in the guise of constraints on derivations that referred to other
possible derivations (a sort of precursor of today's optimality syntax (e.g.
Grimshaw 1997) and pragmatics (Blutner, this volume)). Gordon and Lakoff
claimed that a rule of *you*-TENSE DELETION derived sentences like (45a) from
structures similar to that of (46a) if and only if the logical structure L of (46a),
taken in conjunction with Con_{I}, a class of contexts, and the set of conversational
postulates entails (47).

(47)   Unless you have some good reason for doing VP', you should not
       do VP'.

Gordon and Lakoff's Con_{I} encoded speakers' intentions and beliefs as if they
were semantic matters of truth. But that obscures the fact that the relation

between the use of a form and its interpretation in context depends on the speaker's and addressee's beliefs and intentions about each other's beliefs and intentions (Cohen and Perrault 1979, Cohen and Levesque 1990, 1991, Green 1996a) and not on any other kinds of contingent facts.

An approach that is more consistent with these facts and with the better understanding of implicature now available to us will minimize the number of grammatical constraints on the syntactic combination of grammatical categories and unify them with lexical and syntactic constraints on their semantics, and with construction-specific pragmatic constraints of the sorts discussed here. Such an approach would be, in effect, a complex function on a theory of communication which entailed the integration of such more or less universal principles as Grice's Cooperative Principle and the strategies of relevance and quantity (cf. Horn 1984a) that derive from it (strategies for referring, predicating, focusing, etc.), with culture-specific interpretations (or implementations) of politeness principles (cf. Brown and Levinson 1987, Green 1993b). All of these aspects of pragmatics refer directly to language users' intentions and beliefs, linking them to the conventions of usage (Morgan 1978) that the construction-specific constraints encode. Such a treatment, in contrast to known predecessors, would not claim that sentences like (25b) are ungrammatical.

(25)b.   #She already knows who did I appoint.

Rather, it would predict (a) that the use of such sentences will cause hearers to make certain inferences about their speaker, (b) that some of these may result in the sentence being considered inappropriate, given what else the hearer knows about the speaker and the subject matter, or contradictory, or ineffective for the purpose the hearer imputes to the speaker, or, in plain language, dumb, and (c) that the speaker is aware at some level of (a) and (b).

Thus, while the approach of the 1960s entailed claiming that a sentence like (25b) was ungrammatical because the auxiliary-inversion rule had applied in the complement of a verb constraining it from applying there, and the approach of the 1970s entailed claiming such a sentence was ungrammatical because inversion in the complement implied that the speaker believed that the referent of the subject of the embedding verb didn't know the answer to the evoked question, contradicting the assertion of the whole sentence (that the referent of the subject has it figured out, and does know), the approach sketched here claims that sentences like (25b) are perfectly grammatical: they conform in every respect to the rules of syntactic combination that comprise the grammar. It claims that such sentences are nonetheless inappropriate, ineffective, or dumb because of the contradiction between what is asserted and what is implicated by the choice to use an inversion in an interrogative complement.

Pollard and Sag (1994) take a first step toward such an approach, treating speaker's presuppositions and other categories of propositional attitudes as part of the representation for lexical and phrasal expressions. As discussed in

Green (1994, 2000), such representations might be very detailed, incorporating much of the same sort of information as might be expressed in a Discourse Representation Theory representation (Kamp 1981, Kamp and Reyle 1993). One concern of Pollard and Sag (1994: 332–5), however, is that while background presuppositions have to be projected from lexical items to phrases containing them, it has been known since the early 1970s that the projection is not a function of tree geometry (Morgan 1973b, Karttunen and Peters 1979), or even of the semantic class of predicates and operators in the structural projection path. Morgan showed that neither the problem nor the solution is strictly linguistic, but depends instead on beliefs attributed by the interpreter to the speaker and agents and experiencers of propositional attitude verbs in the sentence. Morgan's account, and Gazdar's (1979) formalization of it, show that conversational implicatures of the utterance of the sentence limit the presuppositions of a sentence uttered in context to the subset of presuppositions associated with the lexical items in it that are consistent with the speaker's assumptions and intended implicatures.

Conversational implicature, of course, is a function of a theory of human behavior generally, not something specifically linguistic (Grice 1989, Green 1993a), because it is based on inference of intentions for actions generally, not on properties of the artifacts (sentence and utterance tokens) that are the result of linguistic actions. Conversational implicatures arise from the assumption that it is reasonable (under the particular circumstances of the speech event in question) to expect the addressee to infer that the speaker intended the addressee to recognize the speaker's intention from the fact that the speaker uttered whatever the speaker uttered. Thus, it would be naïve to anticipate that the filtering in the projection of presuppositions or other associated propositional attitudes could be represented as a constraint or set of constraints on values of some attribute of linguistic expressions and therefore as of the same character as, say, the constraints on the projection of agreement or subcategorization or unbound dependency information, precisely because conversational implicature is inherently indeterminate (Morgan 1973b, Gazdar 1979, Grice 1989).

This does not necessarily mean that a projection principle for pragmatic information is logically impossible. Background propositions of a phrase can be computed as a conjunction of the background propositions of all the daughters, along the lines suggested by Pollard and Sag (1994: 333) and Wilcock (1999). This sort of context inheritance principle would be completely consistent with the inherently indeterminate character of Gricean conversational implicature. If that conjunction should happen to contain predications that are inconsistent with each other, or predications that are inconsistent with what is predicated by the sentence as a whole, that does not pose a logical problem, or a problem for a formal theory. It is not even a linguistic problem. It is a practical sort of problem for a human being who wants to construe the speaker's behavior in uttering the sentence as rational.[16] Doing that requires using knowledge of principles of sense and/or reference transfer (Nunberg 1995, this volume) and lexical rules, as well as beliefs about what is sensible and what is silly. For example, one way of resolving a conflict involving lexical presuppositions would be to interpret one or more of the presupposition-bound phrases involved as figuratively intended in a way that allows propositions intended to be conveyed to be regarded as all true. In any case, the resolution of such contradictions is precisely what the Cooperative Principle was invented for (Grice 1989, Green 1996b) and what the computation of implicatures is about, as Morgan and Gazdar have demonstrated.

ACKNOWLEDGMENT

This work owes much to Jerry Morgan, whose deep understanding of these issues has influenced my articulation of them in uncountable ways. Some of the discussion in this chapter is reworked from material that has appeared elsewhere (e.g. Green 1982a, 1996a, 2000).

NOTES

1 Cf. Lees and Klima (1963).
2 Cf. Green (1990, 1996a) for discussion.
3 An extensive, and still incomplete, catalog may be viewed at http://mccawley.cogsci.uiuc.edu/~green.
4 The choice of *addressee* and *hearer* in this sentence is not accidental. Speakers plan speech with a particular audience in mind, but everyone who hears it has access to the same rules for interpreting it.
5 There are also well-known cases where the number agreement morpheme on a verb with an apparently plural subject induces inferences from the fact that one choice was made rather than another, inferences that, in fact, affect the truth conditions, not just "mere" pragmatic differences (Morgan 1972a, 1972b, Pollard and Sag 1994). Thus, (i) would be used to extol the virtues of two foods,

while (ii) is about a single unusual concoction.

(i) Pickles and ice cream taste good.
(ii) Pickles and ice cream tastes good.

6 The construction names in SMALL CAPITALS are those familiar in modern generative grammar. See Green and Morgan (2001: Appendix) for further references.
7 For some more recent treatments, see Prince (1981a), Zaenen (1982), and Horn (1986).
8 It has generally not been claimed that the Old Information First principle is a universal principle, though it may be a universal tendency driven by the interpersonal nature of discourse. Most of the illustrations have come from Czech, English, French, and Japanese.

9   Specifically, the backward-looking center must stand in a salient scalar relation to the partially ordered set constituting the forward-looking centers. A partially ordered set is a set whose members are all related by some ordering relation which is transitive, and either reflexive and antisymmetric, like "is as tall as or taller than," or irreflexive and asymmetric, like "is taller than" (cf. Ward 1988 52ff., Hirschberg 1991). Salient scalar relationships include any where one element is higher or lower than another on some scale, or they are incomparable alternative values, but there are values higher or lower than both. Some examples are the set/subset relation, part/whole, type/subtype, entity/attribute, and of course, *greater than* and *less than*.

10   The example is adapted from a passage in Nixon's *Six Crises* cited by Ward (1988: 57).

11   Or speaker; cf. Green (1982b) for discussion of the genres and registers where these constructions are found.

12   This common function of inversions may be what has misled some writers (e.g. Longuet-Higgins 1976) into thinking that inversions after directional phrases must describe a character coming into (the narrator's) view. Inversions have other uses, and we do find such inversions as (i)–(iii), which describe a character going out of view.

(i)   Then off marched the little tailor, cocky as could be, with his thumbs thrust through his boasting belt.

(ii)   Into the forest ran the four, and soon they could be seen no more.

(iii)   Off across the grass ran the three little girls.

Examples (i) and (iii) are from children's books whose exact titles I cannot locate.

13   Cf. for example Prince 1981c, 1984 (TOPICALIZATION and LEFT DISLOCATION); Prince 1978 (CLEFT and PSEUDO-CLEFT); Milsark 1977, Napoli and Rando 1978, Aissen 1975 (THERE-INSERTION). Further references may be found in Green and Morgan (2001: Appendix).

14   The pragmatic condition on *beware*, still mysterious, seems to involve (not all that surprisingly, given its meaning) reference to awareness of a threat. Cf. Green (1981) for some preliminary observations. The absence of inflected forms explains the unacceptability of such forms as *We bewore of the bandersnatch, *We bewared of the dog.

15   McCawley (1968) argued that referential indices have the structure of sets rather than being discrete units; Postal (1967) outlines some reasons to be skeptical about Chomsky's notion. Morgan (1968, 1970) provided early demonstrations that the kind of identity required varies from syntactic construction to syntactic construction.

16   Obviously, it is also a practical problem of enormous dimensions for any automated natural language processing system that seeks to interpret natural language input, if for no other reason than its inescapable dependence on the encyclopedic knowledge that human natural language users take for granted.

19 Pragmatics and Argument Structure

ADELE E. GOLDBERG

1 What is Argument Structure?

ARGUMENT STRUCTURE has been used to refer to various things in the literature. In the logical tradition, argument structure refers to the number and type of arguments that are associated with a predicate (e.g. a verb). The argument structure of *give* is a three-place predicate, requiring an agent, a theme, and a recipient argument. On this view, then, one and the same argument structure is expressed by the ditransitive and dative patterns, as in (1) and (2):

(1) She gave him an apple.   Ditransitive

(2) She gave an apple to him.   Dative

In recent syntactic theories, on the other hand, argument structure is often taken to refer to a level of purely formal abstraction, devoid of any semantics. On this view, (1) and (2) may be understood to represent two different argument structures, or only one if the first is assumed to be syntactically derived from the second. My use of the term in what follows is a hybrid of these approaches, in which the argument structure of a clause is defined as the surface syntactic form together with the overall event-interpretation of a clause. The examples in (1) and (2), therefore, illustrate two different argument structures insofar as they differ in form. As described below, they differ in their semantics as well. Examples of argument structure patterns include the transitive, the ditransitive, the resultative, the sentential clause complement construction, etc.

Most verbs readily appear in more than one argument structure pattern. A question that has been gaining attention, and that we focus on here, is: What determines which argument structure pattern will actually be used? A related question is: Why do languages provide alternative ways to express similar meanings? A great deal of work has noted semantic differences between rough paraphrases (e.g. Partee 1965, Fillmore 1968, Anderson 1971b, Borkin 1974, Levin

1993, Goldberg 1995). For example, the ditransitive or double object construction requires that its goal be animate, whereas the dative construction does not:

(3)a.   Chris sent them a package.   Ditransitive
   b.   *Chris sent that place a package.

(4)   Chris sent a package to them/to that place.   Dative

Slight differences in meaning such as this are clearly one factor that distinguishes between alternate argument structure patterns. They allow speakers to choose which pattern to use on the basis of differing semantics, thereby offering speakers of a language more expressive power. Less studied, however, is the role of pragmatics in differentiating among argument structure possibilities.

2   What is Pragmatics?

For present purposes we distinguish two types of pragmatics – non-conventional and conventional.

NON-CONVENTIONAL PRAGMATICS involves the effects of the comprehension or production of sentences in particular contexts of use by actual language users having the type of processing and cognitive abilities and preferences that humans do. These effects are expected to be universal, given that languages are products of human beings. CONVERSATIONAL PRAGMATICS (Grice 1967, Horn 1984a) is perhaps the best known example of non-conventional pragmatics, and the one that is focused on here.

CONVENTIONAL PRAGMATICS is the conventional association of certain formal properties of language with certain constraints on pragmatic contexts. Effects of conventional pragmatics are non-necessary effects, and so we would expect to find some degree of language variation, at least in degree of conventionalization.[1] As pertains to clause structure, conventional pragmatics largely corresponds to ways in which languages choose to package INFORMATION STRUCTURE (Halliday 1967, Chafe 1976, Lambrecht 1994, Ward and Birner this volume).

Two notions that play a central role in the packaging of information structure are TOPIC and FOCUS, which we can define as follows (see Gundel and Fretheim (this volume) for a more in-depth discussion): a sentence topic can be defined as a "matter of [already established] current interest which a statement is about and with respect to which a proposition is to be interpreted as relevant" (Lambrecht 1994: 119). On focus, we follow Halliday (1967: 204), who writes: "Information focus is one kind of emphasis, that whereby the speaker marks out a part (which may be the whole) of a message block as that which he wishes to be interpreted as informative." Similarly Lambrecht (1994: 218) defines the focus relation as relating "the pragmatically non-recoverable to the recoverable component of a proposition [thereby creating] a new state of information in the mind of the addressee."

Other notions that are often used in discussions of information structure describe whether particular arguments within a discourse have been previously mentioned: that is, whether the arguments are DISCOURSE-OLD (GIVEN) or DISCOURSE-NEW (Prince 1992). The correlations between focus and topic on the one hand, and discourse-old/given or -new on the other are complicated, but some rough generalizations can be made. Continuing topics are given in that they have to have been mentioned in order to be continuing as topics (e.g. *she* in (5a) below); even newly established topics tend to be accessible or anchored in the discourse as opposed to brand new, insofar as they appear with a definite determiner or are explicitly related to a discourse-old entity by means of a possessive determiner or relative clause (e.g. *her mother* in (5b); see Francis et al. 1999). Focal arguments are often discourse-new (*a snake* in (5d)); discourse-old elements can serve as foci only if they are accented (*her* in (5c)).

(5)

	Discourse-old (given)	Discourse-new
topic	(a) *She* hit a pole.	(b) *Her mother* feared snakes.
focus	(c) George said they called *HER*.	(d) She saw *A SNAKE*.

Since all of the cells of the matrix are instantiated, it is clear that the notions of topic and focus cannot be reduced to the notions of discourse-old and -new, as is sometimes assumed. Still, it is clear that most commonly, topics are discourse-old (e.g. (5a)), because most topics are continuing topics. Focal elements tend to be discourse-new, since asserting information most commonly occurs via the mention of a new entity (e.g. (5d)). These common correlations are important to keep in mind when we try to relate proposals, such as many of the ones discussed below, that are couched exclusively either in terms of topic vs. focus or in terms of given/old vs. new.

3 Information Structure and Argument Structure

A simple transitive argument structure pattern can appear in a cleft construction, a left-dislocation construction, or a topicalization construction:

(6) It was a giraffe that the mouse saw.   *It*-cleft

(7) The giraffe, the mouse saw it.   Left-dislocation

(8) The giraffe, the mouse saw.   Topicalization

It is generally recognized that sentence-level constructions such as those represented in (6)–(8) are associated with their own information structure properties.

For example, in an extensive analysis of the Switchboard corpus of spoken language, Gregory and Michaelis (to appear) document the functions of the left-dislocation and topicalization constructions, finding subtle distinctions between them. The fronted NPs in the left-dislocation construction are not previously mentioned and yet do persist as topics. The fronted NPs in the topicalization construction display the opposite tendency: the majority are previously mentioned and do not persist as topics. Thus, the left-dislocation construction is topic establishing, whereas the topicalization construction tends to be used for moribund topics.

It is not immediately obvious that argument structure, which has to do with the semantic relation between a verb and its arguments, should have any direct relationship to conventional pragmatics. As Lambrecht (1994: 159) observes, "the independence of semantic and pragmatic roles is an obvious consequence of the fact that information structure has to do with the use of sentences, rather than the meaning of propositions." Nonetheless, on the view that different syntactic complement arrays reflect different argument structures, we will see below that argument structure patterns are indeed associated with information structure generalizations.

4   Preferred Argument Structure

Du Bois (1987) proposed a Preferred Argument Structure for the way argument structures are actually used in discourse. Assuming Dixon's (1972) system for classifying core arguments, intransitive clauses have only one core argument, the subject or S, and transitive clauses have two core arguments: the actor or A and the object or O. In English sentences like *The vase broke* or *The boy ran*, "the vase" and "the boy" are S's; in a sentence such as *The giraffe spotted the owl*, "the giraffe" is an A and "the owl" is an O.

Du Bois (1987) analyzed the distribution of lexical A, S, and O in elicited, on-going discourse in the ergative language of Sacapultec Maya. The corpus study revealed that only 2.8 percent of transitive clauses involved two lexical NPs. Moreover, only 3.2 percent of A's represented discourse-new entities, expressed by lexical NPs. On the other hand, 22.5 percent of S's and 24.7 percent of O's represented such discourse-new entities. Du Bois posits two constraints: (1) a QUANTITY GENERALIZATION: "avoid more than one new argument per clause" (Du Bois 1987: 819; see also Dixon 1972, Givón 1975, Chafe 1987); and (2) the GIVEN A GENERALIZATION: "avoid new A's." These two constraints are jointly taken to define the Preferred Argument Structure cross-linguistically.

These findings have been replicated again and again in many unrelated languages, including English (Iwasaki 1985), German (Schuetze-Coburn 1987), French (Lambrecht 1987), Hebrew (Smith 1996), Mam (England 1983), Malay (Hopper 1988), Quechua (Payne 1987), child Inuktitut speech (Allen and Schroder to appear), Papago (Payne 1987), and Tzeltal (Brown to appear). S and O both easily accommodate discourse-new elements. The A slot is distinct in that it strongly prefers old or given elements.[2] This split between S and O on one hand and A on the other is what generally defines ergativity, whether it is morphologically marked or syntactically expressed. It is the discourse properties, Du Bois (1987) argues, that form the basis for the categorization that results in all types of ergativity.

It is worth asking whether the Quantity and Given A generalizations are both independently required. One question that arises is whether the Given A generalization is ultimately just an effect of a correlation between animates and topicality. That is, the A argument of transitive clauses strongly favors animate entities, and animates are good candidates for topic status simply because human beings like to talk about other human beings (Osgood 1980). A's are likely to be topical, and ongoing topics are necessarily given: therefore, A's are likely to be given – thus, the Given A generalization. There is, however, a consideration that mediates against this idea that the Given A generalization is simply epiphenomenal. Languages strongly favor introducing new animate entities via an intransitive clause whenever new animate entities are introduced. Du Bois (1987: 831) suggests that speakers opt for "intransitive introduction followed by transitive narration." That is, humans may be likely to make animate entities topics, but that is not sufficient to explain why the A slot is avoided when animates are not topical. Thus it seems that the Given A constraint does not follow directly from the prevalence of animate topics.

A second question that arises is whether the two constraints could possibly be conflated into one. Other than A, there is only one other argument available in the nuclear clause (either S or O), so the Quantity generalization (avoid more than one new argument per clause) would seem to follow from the Given A generalization. But the Quantity generalization may help to motivate why it should be that new animate entities are often introduced via an intransitive rather than transitive clause, which again, is the one aspect of the Given A constraint that does not follow from the discourse frequency of animate topics. Of course the Quantity constraint could be satisfied in one of two ways in discourse contexts in which a new animate participant is introduced: either an intransitive clause could be used **or** a transitive clause with a given O could be used. In fact, as discussed below, the admittedly rare transitive expressions with non-given A's do tend to have given O's. Thus, there is evidence that the Quantity constraint is not a consequence of the Given A constraint. Moreover, a possibly related type of Quantity generalization seems to be operative in accounting for object omission with normally transitive verbs, as is discussed below.

Can the Given A constraint be derived completely from the Quantity generalization together with the general tendency for animates to be ongoing topics and therefore given? The fact just noted, that languages apparently prefer the intransitive mention of new animates rather than the transitive mention with given O's, even though the Quantity constraint is satisfied equally well in either way, provides one piece of evidence that the Given A constraint is not simply epiphenomenal. Moreover, languages differ in the degree to which the Given A generalization holds (Van Valin and LaPolla 1997, Lambrecht 2001).

For example, the constraint is near absolute in spoken French insofar as subject arguments cannot be focal and non-focal subjects tend to be given (Lambrecht 1995), whereas English allows new, focal A's in certain circumstances (discussed below). Thus it seems that the Quantity and Given A generalizations are both required to describe the data.

The Given A and Quantity generalizations seem to be accurate cross-linguistically, and their existence is likely motivated, if not predicted, by process-ing and discourse factors. The Quantity generalization may be based on some kind of ease of processing generalization, although the specific explanation has not yet been identified. As noted above, the Given A generalization goes beyond the conversational tendency to make humans topical; still, the motivation for the generalization undoubtedly lies in this tendency. In fact, the tendency for humans to make other animate beings topics results in a tendency for both A and S to be topical more often than O in many languages. Thus, sentences in which the logical subject represents the topic and the predicate represents the comment or assertion about that topic represent the most frequent pattern and can, therefore, be considered the canonical or unmarked construction type (Kuno 1972, Horn 1986, Chafe 1994, Lambrecht 1994).

5   Sentence Focus Constructions

Languages typically have special constructions that allow for non-canonical packaging of information. Lambrecht (1994) defines SENTENCE FOCUS (SF) CONSTRUCTIONS as constructions that are formally marked as expressing a prag-matically structured proposition in which both the subject and the predicate are in focus. As Lambrecht (1995) notes, the function of SF constructions is presentational – namely, to present an entity or an event into the discourse (cf. also Sasse's (1987) entity-central vs. event-central thetic sentences). An Eng-lish SF construction that introduces an event into the discourse is characterized by having pitch accent only on the logical subject, and not on the predicate phrase, as in (9).

(9)   What happened?
    a.   Her SON is sick.
    b.   Her BIKE broke down.
    c.   My SHOULDER hurts.
    d.   ZACH called.
    e.   Her HUSBAND left her.

Lambrecht (1994) observes as well that the subject in this construction is not topical and cannot be pronominal. For example, (10) can only be interpreted with a narrow focus on the subject argument (an ARGUMENT FOCUS reading) and does not permit a sentence focus interpretation:

(10)   HE is sick. (possible context: A: Is she sick? B: No, HE is sick)

The predicate in the SF construction typically has semantics that are compatible with presentation, with SF constructions cross-linguistically favoring certain unaccusative verbs such as *arrive, come, die,* and *disappear.* SF expressions are rarely transitive, consistent with the Given A generalization, since the focal intransitive subject is an S and not an A. When SF expressions are transitive (e.g. (9e)), the object nominal strongly tends to be pronominal (Lambrecht 1995), in accord with the Quantity generalization.

In sections 4 and 5, we have seen that information structure properties motivate the existence of a dominant argument structure type cross-linguistically, the specific properties of which are conventionalized differently and to different extents in different languages. The need for a full range of expressive power motivates the existence of marked construction types such as the SF construction.

The ditransitive construction, as seen in (1) above, can be used to illustrate the potentially far-reaching role of information structure in the grammar of argument structure.

6   Information Structure and the Ditransitive

In both corpus and experimental studies, Arnold et al. (2000) found that both newness and heaviness play a role in determining the choice of the ditransitive over the dative construction, where heaviness is determined by number of words, and newness by lack of previous mention in the discourse[3] (see also Givón 1979, 1984, Dryer 1986, Thompson 1990). For present purposes, we will interpret these generalizations as implying that the recipient argument must be topical, not focal:

(11)   Subj V   Obj1(topical) Obj2
       She kicked him   the ball

The idea that the ditransitive constrains the recipient argument to be non-focal may ultimately help account for certain interesting facts about how the ditransitive construction interacts with long-distance dependency constructions and the passive construction in English. In particular, notice that the recipient argument of the ditransitive cannot readily appear in a long-distance dependency relation:

(12)   ??Who did Chris give the book?

(13)   ?*It is that girl that Chris gave the book.

whereas the patient argument can appear in such relations:

(14)   What did Pat give Chris?

(15)   It is that book that Pat gave Chris.

Conversely, the recipient argument can passivize, as in (16), but the patient argument resists passivization, as in (17):

(16)   Pat was given the book by Chris.

(17)   ??The book was given Pat by Chris.

Erteschik-Shir (1979) suggests that these facts can be explained by appealing to the difference in discourse function of the two arguments and the two types of constructions. Long-distance dependency constructions typically require that the fronted element be focused. Thus the infelicitous sentences (12) and (13) result, she argues, from a clash in information structure: the recipient argument, which is constrained to being topical, cannot appear in the focus position of a long-distance dependency construction. The recipient argument can readily appear as the subject of a passive, however, because subjecthood is compatible with topicality.

This account is quite provocative in that it predicts that the recipient argument can appear as the dependent element in a topicalization construction. As noted above, topicalization tends to be used for elements that have been topical in the discourse (and which are likely to cease continuing to be topics). Therefore, topicalization of the recipient argument of the ditransitive should present no clash. As expected, we find the following acceptable example:[4]

(18)   She had an idea for a project. She's going to use three groups of mice. One, she'll feed them mouse chow, just the regular stuff they make for mice. Another she'll feed them veggies. And *the third, she'll feed junk food.* [Prince 1997: 129]

Here "the third" is clearly topical in that it refers to the last of three groups of mice under discussion. It does not, therefore, present a clash of discourse constraints to topicalize this recipient argument, and as predicted, the sentence is acceptable. It remains to be seen whether this type of discourse-based explanation can explain the full range of facts,[5] but research on the role of pragmatics in motivating constraints on long-distance dependencies in a general way represents an exciting trend in syntactic theory (e.g. Erteschik-Shir 1998).

7   Discourse-conditioned Argument Omission

Cross-linguistically, focal elements must be expressed. This follows from the fact that they are not predictable: they must be expressed in order to be identified. On the other hand, there is a clear motivation from conversational pragmatics for leaving topical arguments unexpressed, e.g., Horn's (1984a) R Principle or Grice's (1967) Maxim of Quantity: say no more than you must. Since topical arguments are fully recoverable, there is no need to utter them.

While omissibility generalizations are motivated by non-conventional pragmatics in this way, omissibility and non-omissibility of arguments is clearly
conventional in that languages differ in whether or not recoverable arguments
can be omitted. In Hindi, all continuing topics and backgrounded information
can be dropped (Butt and King to appear). In Hebrew, discourse topics, whether
subjects or objects, can be omitted, but other recoverable arguments cannot
generally be (Uziel-Karl and Berman 2000). In Brazilian Portuguese, a combination of discourse and lexical semantic factors seem to be at play in argument
omission: for example, omitted objects must be topics and are predominantly
inanimate or third person animate, that is, first or second person objects are
not readily omitted, even when they are topical (Farrell 1990). English generally requires all arguments to be overtly expressed, unless lexically specified
for object omission (e.g. Fillmore 1986).

   Interestingly enough, all languages allow omitted arguments in certain circumstances. An illustrative case comes from English, in which a particular
confluence of discourse properties can result in object omission, even for verbs
that are normally strictly transitive. The following examples illustrate this
phenomenon:

(19)a.   The chef-in-training chopped and diced all afternoon.
    b.   Tigers only kill at night.
    c.   Pat gave and gave, but Chris just took and took.

As in all cases of argument omission, the semantic requirement of recoverability
must be satisfied. In addition, a further discourse condition seems to be necessary to license these examples:

(20)   Principle of Omission under Low Discourse Prominence
       Omission of the patient argument is possible when the patient argument
       is construed to be de-emphasized in the discourse vis à vis the action.
       That is, omission is possible when the patient argument is not topical (or
       focal) in the discourse, and the action is particularly *emphasized*. (Goldberg
       2000)

"Emphasis" is intended as a cover term for several different ways in which an
action is construed to be especially prominent in the discourse. The following
examples illustrate the phenomenon with various types of emphasis labeled
on the right:[6]

(21)   Pat gave and gave but Chris just took
       and took.   Repeated action

(22)   He was always opposed to the idea of murder,
       but in the middle of the battlefield, he had no
       trouble killing.   Discourse topic

(23)   She picked up her carving knife and began
        to chop.   Narrow focus

(24)   Why would they give this creep a light prison
        term!? He murdered!   Strong affective stance

(25)   "She could steal but she could not rob." (from
        the Beatles' song "She Came in Through the
        Bathroom Window")   Contrastive focus

The generalization in (20) is paralleled by Brown's (to appear) finding that children and adult speakers of Tzeltal realize the O argument lexically less often when the verb is semantically rich than when it is semantically general. For example, object arguments are more often omitted for verbs like *k'ux* "eat mush stuff" than for verbs like *tun* "eat (anything)."[7] That is, if the verbal predicate is emphasized in some way, the object argument is more likely to be omissible. This finding is reminiscent of the Quantity generalization (only one new mention per clause) proposed independently by Givón (1975), Chafe (1987), and Du Bois (1987): in both cases, there is a trade-off in terms of how much is expressed per clause. However, unlike the facts motivating the Quantity generalization, it is not clear that emphasizing a predicate makes it preferable to omit the object, only that it makes it possible.

7.1 Grammatical omissibility hierarchy?

Many have proposed that there is asymmetry in which arguments can be omitted, with subjects being the most likely candidates in both child and adult speech (Bloom 1970, Chomsky 1982a, Hyams 1986, Jaeggli and Hyams 1988, Uziel-Karl and Berman 2000). We have seen that topical arguments are good candidates for ellipsis, and that the subject argument is topical and not focal in the unmarked case. As might be expected, then, many languages allow topical subject arguments to be unexpressed.

On the other hand, among the languages that allow subject arguments to be omitted, many display subject agreement properties on the verb (e.g. ASL, Brazilian, Inuktitut, Italian). It has been proposed that the agreement morphology should be understood to represent the subject argument in these so-called "pro-drop" languages (Bresnan and Mchombo 1986, Lambrecht 1994). On this view, the apparent omission of the subject argument should not be counted as such. Most languages that allow null subjects and that do not have verbal agreement marking on the verb also allow null objects and oblique arguments (when these arguments are topical in the discourse), including Chinese, Japanese, Korean and Mauritian Creole.[8] In these languages, objects and oblique arguments can be omitted as well as subjects as long as the omitted argument is recoverable and non-focal (including non-contrastive). Examples from Korean with both subject and object omitted are given in (26) and (27).

(26) A: [I ran across a big fat rat in the kitchen this morning]
    B: kulayse, cwuki-ess-e?
        So,   kill-PAST-SententialEnding
        "So, did [you] kill [it]?"

(27) A: Ani, tomanka-key   naypelie twu-ess-e
        No, run away-comp   leave let-PAST-SententialEnding
        "No, [I] let [it] run away."

                                    (Woo-hyoung Nahm, personal commun-
                                    ication, 2/16/99)

Thus, it may not seem clear that an asymmetry exists at all. There do exist, however, rare instances of languages that have no subject agreement and yet still only allow subjects and not other arguments to be omitted, for example, Lezgian (see Haspelmath 1993). Also, it has been observed that a higher percentage of subjects than objects are omitted in children's early speech (e.g. Mazuka et al. 1986, Allen 2000). The reason for this (subtle) asymmetry is likely pragmatic, and it is not clear that a grammatical relation hierarchy is required to explain the data. That is, Allen (2000) carefully demonstrates that it is the frequent status of subjects as predictable or topical elements that accounts for their advantage in omissibility. To summarize, discourse factors strongly motivate the phenomena of argument ellipsis, although it is clear that languages conventionally allow ellipsis under different circumstances and to different extents.

Below we will see that conversational pragmatics also underlies the phenomenon of "obligatory" adjuncts.

8 Discourse-conditioned Obligatory Adjuncts

It is generally assumed that it is only arguments (and not adjuncts) that are ever obligatorily expressed. What do we make, then, of the existence of obligatory phrases that appear to be adjuncts? For example, when uttered in "neutral" contexts, an adjunct is required in (28a) and (29a) in order to avoid a sense of anomaly:

(28)a. #The house was built.
    b. The house was built last year.

(29)a. #The car drives.
    b. The car drives like a boat/easily/365 days a year/only in the summertime.

Focusing on (28a), certain changes in tense or aspect (30), modality (31), or polarity (32) and emphatic uses of the auxiliary (33) can obviate the need for an adjunct.

(30)a.   The house will be built.
   b.   The house has been built.

(31)a.   The house might be built.
   b.   The house should be built.

(32)   The house wasn't built.

(33)   The house WAS built.

    Goldberg and Ackerman (2001) argue that conversational pragmatics accounts for the apparent existence of obligatory adjuncts. Their explanation for the oddness of (28a) is that without a special context, the utterance is not informative in the Gricean sense. That is, a clause with a definite subject presupposes the existence of the subject referent (Strawson 1964b); in this case, the fact that the house exists is presupposed. It is possible to infer, therefore, that, at some point in the past, the house was created. Nothing informative is being said that cannot be calculated by knowing how the lexical meanings of *house* and *build* work in conjunction with the presuppositions that are evoked by definite NP subjects. Thus, an utterance asserting that a house is built simply states what is already known to normal participants in a conversation. Moreover, while superficially uninformative utterances can be acceptable because they evoke informative or relevant inferences, no obvious inferences can be drawn simply from the fact that an artifact was created in the usual way.

    When a contrastive context is invoked, as in (33) where there is stress on "was," we assume that what is asserted is that the house was in fact actually built, and no adjunct is required. In this case, there is an implicit contrast with a negative proposition, and the positive polarity of the copula verb provides new information for the clause. For this same reason, contrastive focal stress on the subject argument or on the verb can also, as expected, render bare passives felicitous:

(34)a.   The HOUSE was built (not the garage).
   b.   The house was BUILT (not just designed).

    There are various other ways of providing a meaningful assertion in simple sentences. For example, if the method of creation is somehow unusual, then a verb of creation can itself provide a meaningful assertion without emphatic stress or an obligatory adjunct, as in (35) and (36):

(35)   This cake was microwaved.

(36)   These diamonds were synthesized.

Likewise, various tenses or aspects other than the simple past serve to inform the listener that the creation took place before, after, or during a particular reference time (cf. (30)).

As for the sentences in (29), the English middle construction, as has frequently been observed, often requires some type of adjunct (e.g. Jackendoff 1972, Ernst 1984, van Oosten 1984, Fellbaum 1985).[9] As is evident from (29b), a wide variety of adjuncts can be used to rescue middles from infelicity. Several researchers have observed that negated middles (37) or middles that are overtly emphasized (38) often attenuate the need for an adjunct (Keyser and Roeper 1984, Fellbaum 1985, Dixon 1991, Rosta 1995).

(37)   That car doesn't drive.

(38)   These red sports cars DO drive, don't they? [Dixon 1991: 326].

Suggesting a pragmatic account of obligatory adjuncts with middles, Fellbaum (1985) notes that the negation serves to supply non-given information, and the emphasized verb serves to indicate unexpectedness (see also Iwata 1999). That is, the change in polarity or emphasis makes the expression informative and therefore acceptable. Our default assumption is that cars can be driven, so asserting that they cannot be, as in (37), is informative; in (38), the emphasized auxiliary is used to convey the idea that the cars drive really well or fast or easily.

Positing a pragmatic explanation for obligatory adjuncts allows us to explain why certain middles, like certain short passives with verbs of creation, do not require an adjunct. For example:

(39)   A: How do you close this purse?
       B: It snaps/It zips/ It buttons.

(40)   A: Where do we enter the secret passageway?
       B: The bookshelf opens.

In a context in which it is informative to assert that people should be able to perform a given action on the subject argument as in (39) and (40), no adjunct is required.

This discussion raises the question of how to treat cases of **"subcategorized" adverbs** (Jackendoff 1972, McConnell-Ginet 1982). Consider the following examples (judgments of # and * are clarified below):

(41)a.   #Pat dresses.
     b.   Pat dresses stylishly.

(42)a.   *Pat behaved to Chris.
     b.   Pat behaved badly to Chris.

Several researchers have suggested that the adjuncts only appear to be required because the verbs themselves do not normally convey enough information (Dinsmore 1981, Ernst 1984, Iwata 1999). However, only certain of these verbs display the sort of contextual variability that we saw was the hallmark of "obligatory" adjuncts, required because of conversational principles. As Ernst (1984) points out, *dress* is clearly such a case. Example (41a) is acceptable, for example, if Pat lives on a remote island where only some people wear clothing. One could also felicitously utter:

(43)a.   Pat DRESSES! (to mean that Pat dresses up and looks good)
   b.   Pat doesn't dress.
   c.   Pat dresses first thing in the morning/in the middle of the night/only on Tuesdays.

That is, as long as the utterance is made informative, via contrastive context, emphasis (43a), negation (43b), or any type of adjunct (43c), *dress* can appear without a modifying adverb. The case of *behave to* is quite different, however. Notice that none of the following contexts rescues (42a):

(44)a.   *Pat behaved to Chris, but not to Sam.   Contrastive
   b.   *Pat BEHAVED TO Chris.   Emphasis
   c.   *Pat doesn't behave to Chris.   Negation
   d.   *Pat behaves to Chris first thing in the morning/
         in the middle of the night/only on Tuesdays.   Other adjuncts

Thus, in the case of *behave to* (also *treat* with a meaning like that of *behave to*), a manner adverb is indeed subcategorized for by the verb (McConnell-Ginet 1982). In this way it is quite different from the other instances of "obligatory" adjuncts, in that it is required by more than conversational pragmatics.

9   Conclusion

Returning to the question we posed at the outset, why do languages provide alternative ways to express similar meanings? We have seen that alternative choices of argument structures are conditioned in part by pragmatic differences; alternations often provide different ways of packaging information. Patterns of usage of simple clauses and patterns of omission are also strongly influenced by pragmatic factors. Information structure may play a role in explaining how argument structure patterns combine with other syntactic constructions and give rise to constraints on long-distance dependencies. Therefore, despite the fact that it is often ignored, the pragmatics of argument structures is rife with explanatory power.

ACKNOWLEDGMENTS

I wish to thank Knud Lambrecht, Laura Michaelis, Masha Polinsky, and Sujin Yang for helpful discussions.

NOTES

1 At the same time, non-conventional pragmatics often gives rise to conventional pragmatic properties of language through a process of grammaticalization (Horn 1984a, Traugott 1988, Hopper and Traugott 1993). That is, if the same structures are repeated often enough because of some general human preference, the language may conventionalize those structures. This recalls Du Bois's assertion that "grammars code best what speakers do most" (Du Bois 1987: 851).

2 Oblique arguments pattern with S and O in easily accommodating new information.

3 Semantic differences between the two constructions were controlled for by considering only uses of the verb *give*, a verb that largely neutralizes the semantic differences between the two constructions (Goldberg 1995).

4 It is also possible for the recipient argument to appear as the dislocated element in a left-dislocation construction (as in *One, she'll feed them mouse chow*). This is expected since the left-dislocation construction is not generally subject to long-distance dependency constraints

(Ross 1967, Gregory and Michaelis forthcoming).

5 The pragmatic account leaves certain questions unanswered. For example, why is it that recipients can appear in a long-distance dependency if they are the passive subjects of a ditransitive, as in (i):

   (i) Who was given the book by Chris?

6 I thank Christiane Fellbaum and Knud Lambrecht for suggesting several of these examples.

7 Cacoullous and Hernandez (1999) likewise document the use of Mexican Spanish *le* as an intensifier, which they describe as emphasizing the verb by de-emphasizing the object argument. See also Lemmens (1998).

8 Hindi is another language in which verb agreement is not necessary for all persons, and in which objects as well as subjects can be omitted.

9 The middle construction is one that includes an implicit actor argument and that prototypically appears in the simple present tense with a generic interpretation (Roberts 1985, Hale and Keyser 1987, Iwata 1999).

20 Pragmatics and Semantics

FRANÇOIS RECANATI

Around the middle of the twentieth century, there were two opposing camps within the analytic philosophy of language. The first camp – IDEAL LANGUAGE PHILOSOPHY, as it was then called – was that of the pioneers: Frege, Russell, Carnap, Tarski, etc. They were, first and foremost, logicians studying formal languages and, through them, "language" in general. They were not originally concerned with natural language, which they thought defective in various ways;[1] yet in the 1960s, some of their disciples established the relevance of their methods to the detailed study of natural language (Montague 1974, Davidson 1984). Their efforts gave rise to contemporary FORMAL SEMANTICS, a very active discipline developed jointly by logicians, philosophers, and grammarians.

The other camp was that of so-called ORDINARY LANGUAGE PHILOSOPHERS, who thought important features of natural language were not revealed but hidden by the logical approach initiated by Frege and Russell. They advocated a more descriptive approach and emphasized the pragmatic nature of natural language as opposed to, say, the formal language of *Principia Mathematica*. Their own work[2] gave rise to contemporary pragmatics, a discipline which, like formal semantics, has been developed successfully within linguistics over the past 40 years.

Central in the ideal language tradition had been the equation of, or at least the close connection between, the meaning of a sentence and its truth conditions. This truth-conditional approach to meaning is perpetuated to a large extent in contemporary formal semantics. On this approach a language is viewed as a system of rules or conventions, in virtue of which (i) certain assemblages of symbols count as well-formed sentences, and (ii) sentences have meanings which are determined by the meanings of their parts and the way they are put together. Meaning itself is patterned after reference. The meaning of a simple symbol is the conventional assignment of a worldly entity to that symbol: for example, names are assigned objects, monadic predicates are assigned properties or sets of objects, etc. The meaning of a sentence, determined by the meanings of its constituents and the way they are put together, is equated with its truth conditions. For example, the subject–predicate construction is associated with a semantic rule for determining the truth conditions of a subject–predicate sentence on the basis of the meaning assigned to the subject and that assigned to the predicate. On this picture, knowing a language is like knowing a theory by means of which one can deductively establish the truth conditions of any sentence of that language.

This truth-conditional approach to meaning is something that ordinary language philosophers found quite unpalatable. According to them, reference and truth cannot be ascribed to linguistic expressions in abstraction from their use. In vacuo, words do not refer and sentences do not have truth conditions. Words–world relations are established through, and are indissociable from, the use of language. It is therefore misleading to construe the meaning of a word as some worldly entity that it represents or, more generally, as its truth-conditional contribution. The meaning of a word, insofar as there is such a thing, should rather be equated with its use-potential or its use-conditions. In any case, what must be studied primarily is speech: the activity of saying things. Then we will be in a position to understand language, the instrument we use in speech. Austin's theory of speech acts and Grice's theory of speaker's meaning were both meant to provide the foundation for a theory of language, or at least for a theory of linguistic meaning.

Despite the early antagonism I have just described, semantics (the formal study of meaning and truth conditions) and pragmatics (the study of language in use) are now conceived of as complementary disciplines, shedding light on different aspects of language. The heated arguments between ideal language philosophers and ordinary language philosophers are almost forgotten. Almost, but not totally: as we shall see, the ongoing debate about the best delimitation of the respective territories of semantics and pragmatics betrays the persistence of two recognizable currents or approaches within contemporary theorizing.

1   Abstracting Semantics from Pragmatics: the Carnapian Approach

The semantics/pragmatics distinction was first explicitly introduced by philosophers in the ideal language tradition. According to Charles Morris, who was influenced by Peirce, the basic "semiotic" relation is triadic: a linguistic expression is used to communicate something to someone. Within that complex relation several dimensions can be isolated:

> In terms of the three correlates (sign vehicle, designatum, interpreter) of the triadic relation of semiosis, a number of other dyadic relations may be abstracted for study. One may study the relations of signs to the objects to which the signs are applicable. This relation will be called the *semantical dimension of semiosis* . . . The study of this dimension will be called *semantics*. Or the subject of study may be the relation of signs to interpreters. This relation will be called the *pragmatical*

dimension of semiosis, . . . and the study of this dimension will be named *pragmatics* . . . The formal relation of signs to one another . . . will be called the *syntactical dimension of semiosis*, . . . and the study of this dimension will be named *syntactics*. (Morris 1938: 6–7)

Carnap took up Morris's distinction and introduced an order among the three disciplines, based on their degree of abstractness. In semantics we abstract away from more aspects of language than we do in pragmatics, and in syntax we abstract away from more aspects than in semantics:

> If in an investigation explicit reference is made to the speaker, or, to put it in more general terms, to the user of a language, then we assign it to the field of pragmatics. . . . If we abstract from the user of the language and analyze only the expressions and their designata, we are in the field of semantics. And if, finally, we abstract from the designata also and analyze only the relations between the expressions, we are in (logical) syntax.   (Carnap 1942: 9)

In the theorist's reconstruction of the phenomenon, we start with the most abstract layer (syntax) and enrich it progressively, moving from syntax to semantics and from semantics to pragmatics. Syntax provides the input to semantics, which provides the input to pragmatics.

In what sense is it possible to separate the relation between words and the world from the use of words? There is no doubt that the relations between words and the world hold only in virtue of the use which is made of the words in the relevant speech community: meaning supervenes on use.[3] That is something the logical empiricists fully admitted. Still, a distinction must be made between two things: the conventional relations between words and what they mean, and the **pragmatic basis** for those relations. Though they are rooted in, and emerge from, the use of words in actual speech situations, the conventional relations between words and what they mean can be studied in abstraction from use. Such an abstract study constitutes semantics. The study of the pragmatic basis of semantics is a different study, one which belongs to pragmatics or (as Kaplan puts it) METASEMANTICS:

> The fact that a word or phrase *has* a certain meaning clearly belongs to semantics. On the other hand, a claim about the *basis* for ascribing a certain meaning to a word or phrase does not belong to semantics. . . . Perhaps, because it relates to how the language is used, it should be categorized as part of . . . *pragmatics* . . . , or perhaps, because it is a fact *about* semantics, as part of . . . *Metasemantics*. (Kaplan 1989b: 574)

In the same Carnapian spirit Stalnaker distinguishes between DESCRIPTIVE semantics and FOUNDATIONAL semantics:

> "Descriptive semantics" . . . says what the semantics for the language is, without saying what it is about the practice of using that language that explains why that

semantics is the right one. A descriptive-semantic theory assigns *semantic values* to the expressions of the language, and explains how the semantic values of the complex expressions are a function of the semantic values of their parts.... Foundational semantics [says] what the facts are that give expressions their semantic values, or more generally, ... what makes it the case that the language spoken by a particular individual or community has a particular descriptive semantics.   (Stalnaker 1997: 535)[4]

The uses of linguistic forms on which their semantics depends, and which therefore constitute the pragmatic basis for their semantics, are their **past** uses: what an expression means at time *t* in a given community depends upon the history of its uses before *t* in the community. But of course, pragmatics is not merely concerned with past uses. Beside the past uses of words (and constructions) that determine the conventional meaning of a given sentence, there is another type of use that is of primary concern to pragmatics: the current use of the sentence by the speaker who actually utters it. That use cannot affect what the sentence conventionally means, but it determines another form of meaning which clearly falls within the province of pragmatics: what **the speaker** means when he says what he says, in the context at hand. That is something that can and should be separated from the (conventional) meaning of the sentence. To determine "what the speaker means" is to answer questions such as: Was John's utterance intended as a piece of advice or as a threat? By saying that it was late, did Mary mean that I should have left earlier? Like the pragmatic basis of semantics, dimensions of language use such as illocutionary force (Austin, Searle) and conversational implicature (Grice) can be dealt with in pragmatics without interfering with the properly semantic study of the relations between words and their designata. So the story goes.

There are two major difficulties with this approach to the semantics/ pragmatics distinction – the Carnapian approach, as I will henceforth call it. The first one is due to the fact that the conventional meaning of linguistic forms is not exhausted by their relation to designata. Some linguistic forms (e.g. *goodbye,* or the imperative mood) have a "pragmatic" rather than a "semantic" meaning: they have use-conditions but do not "represent" anything and hence do not contribute to the utterance's truth conditions. Because there are such expressions – and because arguably there are many of them and every sentence contains at least one – we have to choose: either semantics is defined as the study of conventional meaning, or it is defined as the study of words–world relations. We can't have it both ways. If, sticking to Carnap's definition, we opt for the latter option, we shall have to acknowledge that "semantics," in the sense of Carnap, does not provide a complete (descriptive) account of the conventional significance of linguistic forms.

The second difficulty is more devastating. It was emphasized by Yehoshua Bar-Hillel, a follower of Carnap who wanted to apply his ideas to natural language. Carnap explicitly said he was dealing "only with languages which contain *no expressions dependent upon extra-linguistic factors*" (Carnap 1937: 168).

Bar-Hillel lamented that this "restricts highly the immediate applicability" of Carnap's views to natural languages since "the overwhelming majority of the sentences in these languages are *indexical*, i.e. dependent upon extra-linguistic factors" (Bar-Hillel 1970: 123; see Levinson, this volume for more on indexicality). In particular, Carnap's view that words–world relations can be studied in abstraction from use is no longer tenable once we turn to indexical languages; for the relations between words and their designata are mediated by the (current) context of use in such languages.

> The abstraction from the pragmatic context, which is precisely the step taken from descriptive pragmatics to descriptive semantics, is legitimate only when the pragmatic context is (more or less) irrelevant and defensible as a tentative step only when this context can be assumed to be irrelevant.   (Bar-Hillel 1970: 70)

Since most natural language sentences are indexical, the abstraction is illegitimate. This leaves us with a number of (more or less equivalent) options:

1   We can make the denotation relation irreducibly triadic. Instead of saying that words denote things, we will say that they denote things "with respect to" contexts of use.
2   We can maintain that the denotation relation is dyadic, but change the first relatum – the *denotans*, as we might say – so that it is no longer an expression-type, but a particular occurrence of an expression, i.e. an ordered pair consisting of an expression and a context of use.
3   We can change the second relatum of the dyadic relation: instead of pairing expressions of the language with worldly entities denoted by them, we can pair them with functions from contexts to denotata.

Whichever option we choose – and, again, they amount to more or less the same thing – we are no longer doing "semantics" in Carnap's restricted sense. Rather, we are doing pragmatics, since we take account of the context of use. Formal work on the extension of the Tarskian truth-definition to indexical languages has thus been called (FORMAL) PRAGMATICS, following Carnap's usage (Montague 1968). As Gazdar (1979: 2–3) pointed out, a drawback of that usage is that there no longer is a contrast between "semantics" and "pragmatics," as far as natural language is concerned: there is no "semantics" for natural language (and for indexical languages more generally), but only two fields of study: syntax and pragmatics.

2   Meaning and Speech Acts

Can we save the semantics/pragmatics distinction for natural language? At least we can try. Following Jerrold Katz, we can give up Carnap's definition of semantics as the study of words–world relations, and define it instead as the study of the conventional, linguistic meaning of expression-types. "Pragmatic phenomena," Katz says, are "those in which knowledge of the setting or context of an utterance plays a role in how utterances are understood"; in contrast, semantics deals with "what an ideal speaker would know about the meaning of a sentence when no information is available about its context" (Katz 1977: 14). This view has been, and still is, very influential. Semantics thus understood does not (fully) determine words–world relations, but it constrains them (Katz 1975: 115–16).

Because of indexicality and related phenomena, purely linguistic knowledge is insufficient to determine the truth conditions of an utterance. That much is commonly accepted. What semantics assigns to expression-types, independent of context, is not a fully-fledged content but a linguistic meaning or CHARACTER that can be formally represented as a function from contexts to contents (Kaplan 1989a, Stalnaker 1999, part 1). Thus the meaning of the pronoun *I* is the rule that, in context, an occurrence of *I* refers to the producer of that occurrence.

Insofar as their character or linguistic meaning can be described as a rule of use, indexical expressions are not as different as we may have thought from those expressions whose meaning is purely "pragmatic." What is the meaning of, say, the imperative mood? Arguably, the sentences "You will go to the store tomorrow at 8," "Will you go to the store tomorrow at 8?", and "Go to the store tomorrow at 8" all have the same descriptive content. The difference between them is pragmatic: it relates to the type of illocutionary act performed by the utterance. Thus the imperative mood indicates that the speaker, in uttering the sentence, performs an illocutionary act of a DIRECTIVE type. To account for this non-truth-conditional indication we can posit a rule to the effect that the imperative mood is to be used only if one is performing a directive type of illocutionary act. This rule gives **conditions of use** for the imperative mood. By virtue of this rule, a particular token of the imperative mood in an utterance *u* "indicates" that a directive type of speech act is being performed by *u*. This reflexive indication conveyed by the token follows from the conditions of use which govern the type. The same sort of USE-CONDITIONAL analysis can be provided for, for example, discourse particles such as *well, still, after all, anyway, therefore, alas, oh*, and so forth, whose meaning is pragmatic rather than truth-conditional (see Blakemore, this volume).

There still is a difference between indexical expressions and fully pragmatic expressions such as the imperative mood. In both cases the meaning of the expression-type is best construed as a rule of use. Thus *I* is to be used to refer to the speaker, just as the imperative mood is to be used to perform a certain type of speech act. By virtue of the rule in question, a use *u* of *I* reflexively indicates that it refers to the speaker of *u*, just as a use *u* of the imperative mood indicates that the utterer of *u* is performing a directive type of speech act. But in the case of *I* the token does not merely convey that reflexive indication: it also contributes its referent to the utterance's truth-conditional content. In contrast, the imperative mood does not contribute to the truth-conditional (or, more generally, descriptive) content of the utterances in which it occurs. In general, pragmatic expressions do not contribute to the determination of the content of the utterance, but to the determination of its force or of other aspects of utterance meaning external to descriptive content.

It turns out that there are (at least) three different types of expression. Some expressions have a purely denotative meaning: their meaning is a worldly entity that they denote. For example, *square* denotes the property of being square. Other expressions, such as the imperative mood, have a purely pragmatic meaning. They have conditions of use but make no contribution to content. Finally, there are expressions which, like indexicals, have conditions of use but contribute to truth conditions nevertheless. (The expression-**type** has conditions of use; the expression-**token** contributes to truth conditions.)

This diversity can be overcome and some unification achieved. First, we can generalize the content/character distinction even to non-indexical expressions like *square*. We can say that every linguistic expression is endowed with a character that contextually determines its content. Non-indexical expressions will be handled as a particular case: the case in which the character is "stable" and determines the same content in every context. Second, every expression, whether or not it contributes to truth-conditional content, can be construed as doing basically the same thing – namely, helping the hearer to understand which speech act is performed by an utterance of the sentence. A speech act typically consists of two major components: a content and a force (Searle 1969; see also Sadock, this volume). Some elements in the sentence indicate the force of the speech act which the sentence can be used to perform, while other elements give indications concerning the content of the speech act. Unification of the two sorts of elements is therefore achieved by equating the meaning of a sentence with its speech act potential.

On the view we end up with – the speech-act theoretic view – semantics deals with the conventional meaning of expressions, the conventional meaning of expressions is their contribution to the meaning of the sentences in which they occur, and the meaning of sentences is their speech act potential. Pragmatics studies speech acts, and semantics maps sentences onto the type of speech act they are designed to perform. It follows that there are two basic disciplines in the study of language: syntax and pragmatics. Semantics connects them by assigning speech act potentials to well-formed sentences, hence it presupposes both syntax and pragmatics. In contrast to the Carnapian view, according to which semantics presupposes only syntax, on the speech-act theoretic view semantics is not autonomous with respect to pragmatics:

> There is no way to account for the meaning of a sentence without considering its role in communication, since the two are essentially connected . . . Syntax can be studied as a formal system independent of its use . . . , but as soon as we attempt to account for meaning, for semantic competence, such a purely formalistic approach breaks down, because it cannot account for the fact that semantic competence is mostly a matter of knowing how to talk, i.e. how to perform speech acts. (Searle, "Chomsky's Revolution in Linguistics," cited in Katz 1977: 26)

There are other possible views, however. We can construe semantics as an autonomous discipline that maps sentences to the type of thought they express or the type of state of affairs they describe. That mapping is independent from the fact that sentences are used to perform speech acts. Note that communication is not the only possible use we can make of language; we can also use language in reasoning, for example. Be that as it may, whoever utters a given sentence – for whatever purpose – expresses a thought or describes a state of affairs, in virtue of the semantics of the sentence (and the context).[5] Let us assume that the sentence is uttered in a situation of communication. Depending on the audience-directed intentions that motivate the overt expression of the thought or the overt description of a state of affairs in that situation, different speech acts will be performed. Those audience-directed intentions determine the force of the speech act, while the thought expressed by the sentence or the state of affairs it describes determines its content. In this framework, pragmatic indicators like the imperative mood can be construed as conventional ways of making the relevant audience-directed intentions manifest. Their meaning, in contrast to the meaning of ordinary words like *square*, will be inseparable from the speech act the sentence can be used to perform. It is therefore not the overall meaning of the sentence that must be equated with its speech act potential. The major part of linguistic meaning maps linguistic forms to conceptual representations in the mind or to things in the world in total independence from communication. It is only a small subset of linguistic expressions, namely the pragmatic indicators and other expressions (including indexicals) endowed with use-conditional meaning, whose semantics is essentially connected with their communicative function.

Whichever theory we accept, semantics (the study of linguistic meaning) and pragmatics (the study of language use) overlap to some extent (see figure 20.1). That overlap is limited for the theories of the second type: the meaning of a restricted class of expressions consists in conditions of use and therefore must be dealt with both in the theory of use and the theory of meaning. According

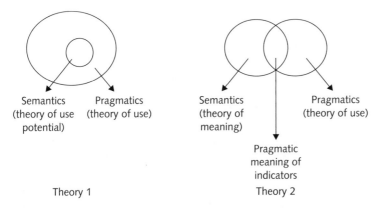

Figure 20.1   Diagram showing the overlap of semantics and pragmatics

to the first type of theory, there is more than partial overlap: every expression has a use-conditional meaning. Since, for that type of theory, the meaning of a sentence is its speech act potential, semantics is best construed as a subpart of speech act theory.

3   Literal Meaning vs. Speaker's Meaning

Let us take stock. The view discussed in section 1 was based on the following assumptions:

(i)   semantics and pragmatics are two complementary, non-overlapping disciplines;
(ii)   pragmatics deals with the use of language;
(iii)   semantics deals with content and truth conditions.

Since words–world relations in natural language (hence content and truth conditions) cannot be studied in abstraction from use, those assumptions form an inconsistent triad – or so it seems. Semantics cannot be legitimately contrasted with pragmatics, defined as the theory of use, if semantics itself is defined as the study of words–world relations.

In section 2 we entertained the possibility of giving up (iii). Following Katz, we can retreat to the view that semantics deals with the conventional meaning of expression-types (rather than with content and truth conditions). But we have just seen that the meaning of at least some expressions is best construed as a convention governing their use. It follows that the theory of meaning and the theory of use are inextricably intertwined, in a manner that seems hardly compatible with (i). Be that as it may, most semanticists are reluctant to give up (iii). For both philosophical and technical reasons, they think the denotation relation must be the cornerstone of a theory of meaning. As David Lewis wrote in a famous passage, "semantics with no treatment of truth conditions is not semantics" (Lewis 1972: 169). I will return to that point below (section 4).

An attempt can be made to save the triad, by focusing on the distinction between LITERAL MEANING and SPEAKER'S MEANING. What a sentence literally means is determined by the rules of the language – those rules that the semanticist attempts to capture. But what the speaker means by his utterance is not determined by rules. As Grice emphasized, speaker's meaning is a matter of intentions: what someone means is what he or she overtly intends (or, as Grice says, "M-intends") to get across through his or her utterance. Communication succeeds when the M-intentions of the speaker are recognized by the hearer.

This suggests that two distinct and radically different processes are jointly involved in the interpretation of linguistic utterances. The process of SEMANTIC INTERPRETATION is specifically linguistic. It consists in applying the tacit theory that speaker-hearers are said to possess, and that formal semantics tries to make explicit, to the sentence undergoing interpretation. By applying the theory, one can deductively establish the truth conditions of any sentence of the language. To do so, it is argued, one does not need to take the speaker's beliefs and intentions into account: one has simply to apply the rules. In contrast, the type of competence that underlies the process of PRAGMATIC INTERPRETATION is not specifically linguistic. Pragmatic interpretation is involved in the understanding of human action in general. When someone acts, whether linguistically or otherwise, there is a reason why he does what he does. To provide an interpretation for the action is to find that reason, that is, to ascribe to the agent a particular intention in terms of which we can make sense of the action.

Pragmatic interpretation thus construed is characterized by the following three properties:

- CHARITY. Pragmatic interpretation is possible only if we presuppose that the agent is rational. To interpret an action, we have to make hypotheses concerning the agent's beliefs and desires, hypotheses in virtue of which it can be deemed rational for the agent to behave as she does.
- NON-MONOTONICITY. Pragmatic interpretation is defeasible. The best explanation we can offer for an action given the available evidence can always be overridden if enough new evidence is adduced to account for the subject's behavior.
- HOLISM. Because of its defeasibility, there is no limit to the amount of contextual information that can in principle affect pragmatic interpretation. Any piece of information can turn out to be relevant and influence the outcome of pragmatic interpretation.

The three features go together. Jointly they constitute what we might call the HERMENEUTIC character of pragmatic interpretation. It strikingly contrasts with the algorithmic, mechanical character of semantic interpretation.

It is important to realize that, on this view (which I will shortly criticize), semantic competence involves more than the ability to determine the context-independent meaning of any well-formed expression in the language. It also involves the ability to assign values to indexical expressions in context. Those assignments are themselves determined by linguistic rules, which linguistic rules constitute the context-independent meaning of indexical expressions. In virtue of its linguistic meaning, an indexical expression like *I* tells you three things: (i) that it needs to be contextually assigned a value; (ii) which aspect of the situation of utterance is relevant to determining that value; and (iii) how the value of the indexical can be calculated once the relevant feature of the context has been identified. If one adds to one's knowledge of the language a minimal knowledge of the situation of utterance – the sort of knowledge which is available to speech participants qua speech participants – one is in a position to assign contextual values to indexicals, hence to determine the truth conditions of the utterance.

From what has been said, it follows that the context of use plays a role both in semantic and in pragmatic interpretation. But it plays very different roles in each, and it can even be denied that there is a single notion of "context" corresponding to the two roles. According to Kent Bach, there are two notions of context: a narrow and a broad one, corresponding to semantic and pragmatic interpretation respectively.

> Wide context concerns any contextual information relevant to determining the speaker's intention and to the successful and felicitous performance of the speech act . . . Narrow context concerns information specifically relevant to determining the semantic values of [indexicals] . . . Narrow context is semantic, wide context pragmatic.[6]

In contrast to the wide context, which is virtually limitless in the sense that any piece of information can affect pragmatic interpretation, the narrow context is a small package of factors involving only very limited aspects of the actual situation of utterance: who speaks, when, where, to whom, and so forth. It comes into play only to help determine the reference of those few expressions whose reference is not fixed directly by the rules of the language but is fixed by them only "relative to context." And it does so in the algorithmic and non-hermeneutical manner which is characteristic of semantic interpretation as opposed to pragmatic interpretation. The narrow context determines, say, that *I* refers to John when John says *I* quite irrespective of John's beliefs and intentions. As Barwise and Perry write, "even if I am fully convinced that I am Napoleon, my use of 'I' designates me, not him. Similarly, I may be fully convinced that it is 1789, but it does not make my use of 'now' about a time in 1789" (Barwise and Perry 1983: 148).

The view I have just described is very widespread and deserves to be called the Standard Picture (SP). It enables the theorist to maintain the three assumptions listed at the beginning of this section. Semantics and pragmatics each has its own field of study. Semantics deals with literal meaning and truth conditions; pragmatics deals with speech acts and speaker's meaning. To be sure, the "context" plays a role in semantic interpretation, because of the context-dependence of truth-conditional content. But that is not sufficient to threaten assumption (i). Because of context-dependence, semantics cannot deal merely with sentence-types: it must deal with OCCURRENCES or sentences-in-context. But this, as Kaplan writes, "is not the same as the notion, from the theory of speech acts, of an utterance of an expression by the agent of a context" (Kaplan 1989b: 584):

> An occurrence requires no utterance. Utterances take time, and are produced one at a time; this will not do for the analysis of validity. By the time an agent finished uttering a very, very long true premise and began uttering the conclusion, the premise may have gone false . . . Also, there are sentences which express a truth in certain contexts, but not if uttered. For example, "I say nothing". Logic and semantics are concerned not with the vagaries of actions, but with the verities of meanings.   (Kaplan 1989b: 584–5)

Moreover, as we have seen, the context which is appealed to in semantic interpretation differs from the "wide" context which features in pragmatic interpretation. Semantics deals with occurrences, narrow contexts, and literal meaning; pragmatics deals with utterances, wide contexts, and speaker's meaning. Appearances notwithstanding, the two types of study do not overlap.

4   Semantic Underdetermination

Even though it is the dominant view, SP has come under sustained attack during the last 15 years, and an alternative picture has been put forward: TRUTH-CONDITIONAL PRAGMATICS (TCP). From SP, TCP inherits the idea that two different sorts of competence are jointly at work in interlocution: a properly linguistic competence in virtue of which we access the meaning of the sentence, and a more general-purpose competence in virtue of which we can make sense of the utterance much as we make sense of a non-linguistic action. What TCP rejects is the claim that semantic interpretation can deliver something as determinate as a truth-evaluable proposition. As against SP, TCP holds that full-blown pragmatic interpretation is needed to determine an utterance's truth conditions.

Recall that, on the Standard Picture, the reference of indexicals is determined automatically on the basis of a linguistic rule, without taking the speaker's beliefs and intentions into consideration. Now this may be true of some of the expressions that Kaplan (1989a) classifies as PURE INDEXICALS (e.g. *I, now, here*) but it is certainly not true of those which he calls DEMONSTRATIVES (e.g. *he, she, this, that*). The reference of a demonstrative cannot be determined by a rule like the rule that *I* refers to the speaker. It is generally assumed that there is such a rule, namely the rule that the demonstrative refers to the object which happens to be demonstrated or which happens to be the most salient, in the context at hand. But the notions of "demonstration" and "salience" are pragmatic notions in disguise. They cannot be cashed out in terms merely of the narrow context. Ultimately, a demonstrative refers to **what the speaker who uses it refers to by using it**.

To be sure, one can make that into a semantic rule. One can say that the character of a demonstrative is the rule that it refers to what the speaker intends to refer to. As a result, one will incorporate a sequence of "speaker's intended referents" into the narrow context, in such a way that the nth demonstrative in the sentence will refer to the nth member of the sequence. Formally that is fine, but philosophically it is clear that one is cheating. We pretend that we can manage with a limited, **narrow** notion of context of the sort we need for handling pure indexicals, while in fact we can only determine the speaker's intended referent (hence the narrow context relevant to the interpretation of the utterance) by resorting to pragmatic interpretation and relying on the **wide** context.

We encounter the same problem even with expressions like *here* and *now*, which Kaplan classifies as **pure** indexicals (as opposed to demonstratives).

Their semantic value is said to be the time or place of the context respectively. But what counts as the time and place of the context? How inclusive must the time or place in question be? It depends on what the speaker means, hence, again, on the wide context. We can maintain that the character of *here* and *now* is the rule that the expression refers to "the" time or "the" place of the context – a rule that automatically determines a content, given a (narrow) context in which the time and place parameters are given specific values; but then we have to let a pragmatic process take place to fix the values in question, that is, to determine *which* narrow context, among indefinitely many candidates compatible with the facts of the utterance, serves as argument to the character function. On the resulting view, the (narrow) context with respect to which an utterance is interpreted is not **given**, not determined automatically by objective facts like where and when the utterance takes place, but it is determined by the speaker's intention and the wide context. Again we reach the conclusion that, formal tricks notwithstanding, pragmatic interpretation has a role to play in determining the content of the utterance.

The alleged automaticity of content-determination and its independence from pragmatic considerations is an illusion due to an excessive concern with a subclass of "pure indexicals," namely words such as *I, today*, etc. But they are only a special case – the end of a spectrum. In most cases the reference of a context-sensitive expression is determined on a pragmatic basis. That is true not only of standard indexical expressions, but also of many constructions involving something like a free variable. For example, a possessive phrase such as *John's car* arguably means something like "the car that bears relation R to John". The free variable R must be contextually assigned a particular value; but that value is not determined by a rule and it is not a function of a particular aspect of the narrow context. What a given occurrence of the phrase *John's car* means ultimately depends upon what the speaker who utters it means. It therefore depends upon the wide context. That dependence upon the wide context is a characteristic feature of semantically indeterminate expressions, which are pervasive in natural language. Their semantic value varies from occurrence to occurrence, yet it varies not as a function of some objective feature of the narrow context but as a function of **what the speaker means**. It follows that semantic interpretation by itself cannot determine what is said by a sentence containing such an expression: for the semantic value of the expression – its own contribution to what is said – is a matter of speaker's meaning, and can only be determined by pragmatic interpretation.

Once again, we find that semantics by itself cannot determine truth conditions. Content and truth conditions are, to a large extent, a matter of pragmatics. That is the gist of TCP. Consequently, most advocates of TCP hold a view of semantics which is reminiscent of that put forward by Katz. According to Sperber and Wilson (1986a) and other relevance theorists (see Wilson and Sperber, this volume; Carston, this volume), semantics associates sentences with semantic representations which are highly schematic and fall short of determining truth-conditional content. Those semantic representations, which they call LOGICAL FORMS, are transformed into complete, truth-evaluable representations (which they call PROPOSITIONAL FORMS) through inferential processes characteristic of pragmatic interpretation. (Chomsky holds a similar view, based on a distinction between the logical form of a sentence, determined by the grammar, and a richer semantic representation associated with that sentence as a result, in part, of pragmatic interpretation. See Chomsky 1976: 305–6.)

This view of semantics is one most semanticists dislike. In contrast to Katz, leading semanticists like Lewis, Cresswell, and Davidson hold that "interpreting" a representation is NOT a matter of associating it with another type of representation (whether mental or linguistic). "Semantic interpretation [thus construed] amounts merely to a translation algorithm"; it is "at best a substitute for real semantics" (Lewis 1972: 169). Real semantics maps symbols to worldly entities – things that the representations may be said to represent.

Relevance theorists apparently bite the bullet. They accept that linguistic semantics (which maps sentences to abstract representations serving as linguistic meanings) is not real semantics in the sense of the model-theoretic tradition descended from Frege, Tarski, Carnap, and others. But, they argue, there is no way to do real semantics directly on natural language sentences. Real semantics comes into play only after "linguistic semantics" has mapped the sentence onto some abstract and incomplete representation which pragmatics can complete and enrich into a fully-fledged propositional form. It is that propositional form which eventually undergoes truth-conditional interpretation. As Carston writes,

> Since we are distinguishing natural language sentences and the propositional forms [i.e. the thoughts] they may be used to express as two different kinds of entity, we might consider the semantics of each individually. Speakers and hearers map incoming linguistic stimuli onto conceptual representations (logical forms), plausibly viewed themselves as formulas in a (mental) language. The language ability – knowing English – according to this view, is then precisely what Lewis and others have derided . . . : it is the ability to map linguistic forms onto logical forms . . . In theory this ability could exist without the further capacities involved in matching these with conditions in the world. A computer might be programmed so as to perform perfectly correct translations from English into a logical language without, as Lewis and Searle have said, knowing the first thing about the meaning (= truth conditions) of the English sentence. Distinguishing two kinds of semantics in this way – a translational kind and the truth-conditional – shows . . . that the semantic representation of one language may be a syntactic representation in another, though the chain must end somewhere with formulas related to situations and states of the world or possible worlds.   (Carston 1988: 176–7)

There was a time when practitioners of model-theoretic semantics themselves thought their apparatus could not be transplanted from artificial to natural languages. Tarski thought so, for example. Following Davidson,

Montague, and others, it has become widely accepted that Tarskian methods are applicable to natural languages after all. Now it seems that pragmaticists are saying that that conclusion was premature: truth-conditional semantics, they hold, is applicable to the language of thought, but not, or not directly, to natural language sentences. Because of context-sensitivity, there must be an intermediary step involving both translational semantics and pragmatic interpretation before a given natural language sentence can be provided with a truth-conditional interpretation. "Linguistic semantics" and pragmatics together map a natural language sentence onto a mental representation which model-theoretic semantics can then (and only then) map to a state of affairs in the world.

The general picture of the comprehension process put forward by relevance theorists may well be right. But it is a mistake to suggest that the model-theoretic approach to natural language semantics and TCP are incompatible. Even if, following Lewis and Davidson, one rejects translational semantics in favor of "direct" truth-conditional semantics, one can still accept that pragmatic interpretation has a crucial role to play in determining truth conditions.

First, it should be noted that referential semantics, as Lewis calls the model-theoretic approach, can and must accommodate the phenomenon of context-sensitivity. Because of that phenomenon, we cannot straightforwardly equate the meaning of a sentence with its truth conditions: we must retreat to the weaker view that sentence meaning **determines** truth conditions. As Lewis writes, "A meaning for a sentence is something that determines the conditions under which the sentence is true or false" (Lewis 1972: 173). That determination is **relative to** various contextual factors. Hence the meaning of a sentence can be represented as a function from context to truth conditions. Since meaning is characterized in terms of reference and truth, this still counts as referential semantics.

In this framework, the role pragmatic interpretation plays in the determination of truth-conditional content can be handled at the level of the contextual factors on which that determination depends. For example, if the truth conditions of an utterance depend upon who the speaker means by *she*, then the speaker's intended referent can be considered as one of the contextual factors in question. To be sure, the speaker's referent can be determined only through pragmatic interpretation. That fact, as we have seen, is incompatible with the Standard Picture, according to which semantic interpretation by itself assigns truth conditions to sentences. But it is not incompatible with referential semantics per se. From the role played by pragmatic interpretation in fixing truth conditions, all that follows is that **truth-conditional semantics has to take input from pragmatics**. That is incompatible with the claim that semantics is autonomous with respect to pragmatics (as syntax is with respect to semantics). But this claim is not essential to referential semantics. Several theorists in the model-theoretic tradition have rejected it explicitly (see e.g. Gazdar 1979: 164–8 for an early statement). As Levinson (2000a: 242) writes, "there is every reason to try and reconstrue the interaction between semantics and pragmatics as the intimate interlocking of distinct processes, rather than, as traditionally, in terms of the output of one being the input to the other."

I conclude that referential semantics and TCP are compatible. We can maintain both that semantics determines truth conditions and that, in order to do so, it needs input from pragmatics. The two claims are compatible provided we give up the assumption that semantics is autonomous with respect to pragmatics. If, for some reason, we insist on keeping that assumption, then we must indeed retreat to a translational view of semantics. Thus Carston (1988: 176) writes: "Linguistic semantics IS autonomous with respect to pragmatics; it provides the input to pragmatic processes and the two together make propositional forms which are the input to a truth-conditional semantics." But this view, which distinguishes two kinds of semantics, is not forced upon us by the simple fact that we accept TCP. We need to posit a level of **translational** semantics distinct from and additional to standard truth-conditional semantics only if, following Katz, we insist that linguistic semantics must be autonomous with respect to pragmatics.

5   Varieties of Meaning

Meaning comes in many varieties. Some of these varieties are said to belong to the field of semantics, others to the field of pragmatics. What is the principle of the distinction? Where does the boundary lie? Before addressing these questions, let us review the evidence by actually looking at the varieties of meaning and what is said about them in the literature on the semantics/pragmatics distinction.

As we have seen, there are several **levels** of meaning. When an utterance is made, the sentence-type that is uttered possesses a linguistic meaning (level 1). More often than not, that meaning is not a complete content: to get a complete content, one must resolve indeterminacies, assign values to indexical expressions, etc. The richer meaning thus determined is the literal content of the occurrence, which depends not merely upon the conventional significance of the expression-type, but also on features of the context of use (level 2). At level 3, we find aspects of meaning that are not part of the literal content of the utterance. Those aspects of meaning are not aspects of what is said. Rather, the speaker manages to communicate them indirectly, BY saying what she says. Conversational implicatures and indirect speech acts fall into that category. This division into three levels – linguistic meaning, literal content, and conveyed meaning – is incomplete and very rough, but it will do for my present purposes.

Besides the division into levels, there is a further distinction between two types of meaning: descriptive meaning and pragmatic meaning. Both types of meaning can be discerned at the three levels listed above. At the first level, descriptive meaning maps linguistic forms to what they represent; pragmatic meaning relates to their use and constrains the context in which they can occur.

At the next level, this corresponds to the distinction between the descriptive content of the utterance (the state of affairs it represents) and its role or function in the discourse. Something similar can often be found at the third level, since what is conveyed may itself be analyzable into force and content. This gives us six aspects of meaning, corresponding to the six cells in (1):

(1)

	Descriptive meaning	Pragmatic meaning
Linguistic meaning	A	B
Literal content	C	D
Conveyed meaning	E	F

In what follows I will briefly consider the six aspects in turn. Of each aspect I will ask whether, according to the literature, it pertains to semantics, to pragmatics, or to both.

In cell A, we find the descriptive meaning of expression-types (e.g. the meaning of words like *square* or *table*). That is clearly and unambiguously part of the domain of semantics. No one will disagree here. When we turn to cell B things are less clear. The pragmatic meaning of indicators pertains to semantics insofar as semantics deals with linguistic meaning. Many people hold that view. Some theorists insist on excluding that sort of meaning from semantics, because it is not relevant to truth conditions (Gazdar 1979). Even if one is convinced that semantics with no treatment of truth conditions is not semantics, however, it seems a bit excessive and unnatural to hold that semantics deals only with truth conditions. Still, the meaning of pragmatic indicators is best handled in terms of conditions of use or in terms of constraints on the context, and that provides us with a positive reason for considering that it belongs to the field of pragmatics. This does not necessarily mean that it does not belong to semantics, however. It is certainly possible to consider that the meaning of pragmatic indicators is of concern to both semantics and pragmatics (section 2).

Let us now consider the aspect of meaning that corresponds to cell D. In context, the meaning of pragmatic indicators is fleshed out and made more specific. For example, an utterance of an imperative sentence will be understood specifically as a request or as a piece of advice. Or consider the word *but*, which carries what Grice (1967) calls a CONVENTIONAL IMPLICATURE, that is, a non-truth-conditional component of meaning conventionally associated with the expression. The word *but* in the sentence type "He is rich, but I like beards" signals an argumentative contrast between "he is rich" and "I like beards," but that contrast cannot be specified *in vacuo*. To understand the contrast, we must know which conclusion the antecedent "he is rich" is used to argue for, in the context at hand. According to Ducrot (1972: 128–31), *but* indicates that the following conditions are contextually satisfied: the first clause *p* supports a certain conclusion *r*, while the second clause *q* provides a stronger argument against that very same conclusion. (As a result, the whole conjunction argues against *r*.) Just as one must assign a referent to the third-person pronoun in order to understand the literal content of "he is rich," in order to grasp the literal content of the conjunction "He is rich but I like beards" one must assign a value to the free variable *r* which is part and parcel of the meaning of *but*, e.g. ". . . so I won't marry him." Yet the indication thus fleshed out remains external to the utterance's truth-conditional content: it belongs only to the "pragmatic" side of literal content. Because that is so, and also because the specific indication conveyed by *but* heavily depends upon the context (which provides a value for the free variable), it does not feel natural to say that that aspect of the interpretation of the utterance is semantic. Many theorists hold that the conventional meaning of *but* (cell B) belongs to semantics (as well as, perhaps, to pragmatics), but many fewer would be willing to say the same thing concerning the specific suggestion conveyed by a contextualized use of *but*. In the case of the imperative sentence which, in context, may be used either to request or to advise, the contrast is even more dramatic. As far as I can tell, no one is willing to say that the specific illocutionary force of the utterance belongs to semantics, even among those who consider the meaning of moods (cell B) as semantic.

What about the descriptive side of literal content (cell C)? That, as we have seen, belongs both to semantics and to pragmatics. Pragmatics determines the value of indexicals and other free variables, and semantics, with that input, determines truth-conditional content. Most theorists think the literal truth conditions of an utterance fall on the semantic side of the divide, however, even though pragmatics plays a crucial role. The reason for that asymmetry is that it is the words themselves which, in virtue of their conventional significance, make it necessary to appeal to context in order to assign a semantic value to the indexicals and other free variables. In interpreting indexical sentences, we go beyond what the conventions of the language give us, but that step beyond is still governed by the conventions of the language. In that sense pragmatics is subordinated to semantics in the determination of truth-conditional content.

That conclusion can be disputed, however. According to TCP, the pragmatic processes that play a role in the determination of literal content (PRIMARY pragmatic processes, as I call them) fall into two categories. The determination of the reference of indexicals and, more generally, the determination of the content of context-sensitive expressions is a typical BOTTOM-UP PROCESS, i.e. a process triggered (and made obligatory) by a linguistic expression in the sentence itself. But there are other primary pragmatic processes that are not bottom-up. Far from being triggered by an expression in the sentence, they take place for purely pragmatic reasons. To give a standard example, suppose someone asks me, at around lunchtime, whether I am hungry. I reply: "I've had a very large breakfast." In this context, my utterance conversationally implicates that I am not hungry. In order to retrieve the implicature, the interpreter must first understand what is said – the input to the SECONDARY pragmatic process responsible for implicature generation. That input is the proposition that the speaker has had a very large breakfast . . . when? No time is specified in the sentence, which merely describes the posited event as past. On the other hand, the implicature that the speaker is not hungry could not be derived if the said breakfast was not understood as having taken place on the very day in which the utterance is made. Here we arguably have a case where something (the temporal location of the breakfast event on the day of utterance) is part of the intuitive truth conditions of the utterance yet does not correspond to anything in the sentence itself.[7] If this is right, then the temporal location of the breakfast event is an UNARTICULATED CONSTITUENT of the statement made by uttering the sentence in that context.

Such unarticulated constituents, which are part of the statement made even though they correspond to nothing in the uttered sentence, are said to result from a primary pragmatic process of FREE ENRICHMENT – "free" in the sense of not being linguistically controlled (see Carston, this volume). What triggers the contextual provision of the relevant temporal specification in the above example is not something in the sentence but simply the fact that the utterance is meant as an answer to a question about the speaker's present state of hunger (a state that can be causally affected only by a breakfast taken on the same day). While the assignment of values to indexicals is a bottom-up, linguistically controlled pragmatic process, free enrichment is a top-down, pragmatically controlled pragmatic process. Both types of process are primary since they contribute to shaping the intuitive truth conditions of the utterance, the truth conditions that in turn serve as input to secondary pragmatic processes.

Since the pragmatic processes that come into play in the determination of truth-conditional content need not be linguistically triggered, pragmatics is not subordinated to semantics in the determination of truth-conditional content. Hence truth-conditional content (cell C) is as much a matter of pragmatics as a matter of semantics, according to TCP.

In order to reconcile the two views, some theorists are willing to distinguish two sorts of literal content. The first type of literal content is "minimal" in the sense that the only pragmatic processes that are allowed to affect it belong to the bottom-up variety. That minimal content is semantic, not pragmatic. Pragmatic processes play a role in shaping it, as we have seen, but they remain under semantic control. In our example, the minimal literal content is the proposition that the speaker has had a large breakfast (at some time in the past). The other notion of literal content corresponds to what I have called the "intuitive" truth conditions of the utterance. Often – as in this example – that includes unarticulated constituents resulting from free enrichment. That content is not *as* literal as the minimal content, but it still corresponds to "what is said" as opposed to what the utterance merely implies. (In the example, what the speaker implies is that he is not hungry; what he says, in the non-minimal sense, is that he's had a large breakfast **that morning**.) What is said in that non-minimal sense is what relevance theorists call the EXPLICATURE of the utterance.

Even if we accept that there are these two sorts of content, one may insist that the intuitive (non-minimal) content also is semantic, simply because it is the task of semantics to account for our truth-conditional intuitions. So there is no consensus regarding cell C. As for cells E and F, if they host only meanings that are indirectly conveyed and result from secondary pragmatic processes, there is general agreement that they fall on the pragmatic side of the divide. On the other hand, if we insist that the non-minimal content talked about above is properly located in cell E, while only the minimal content deserves to remain in cell C, then there will be disagreement concerning the semantic or pragmatic nature of the aspect of meaning corresponding to cell E. There may also be disagreement regarding the phenomenon of **generalized** conversational implicature, which belongs to semantics, according to some authors, to pragmatics according to others, and to an "intermediate layer," according to still others (Levinson 2000a: 22–7; the "semantic" approach is argued for in Chierchia 2001).

From all that, what can we conclude? The situation is very confused, obviously, but it is also very clear. It is clear that the semantics/pragmatics distinction as it is currently used obeys several constraints simultaneously. Something is considered as semantic to the extent that it concerns the conventional, linguistic meaning of words and phrases. The more contextual an aspect of meaning is, the less we are tempted to call it semantic. The difference of treatment between cells B and D provides a good illustration of that. At the same time, something is considered as semantic to the extent that it concerns the truth conditions (or, more generally, the descriptive content) of the utterance. The less descriptive or truth-conditional an aspect of meaning is, the less we are tempted to call it semantic. On these grounds it is clear why there is no disagreement regarding cells A and D. A-meaning is both descriptive and conventional; D-meaning is both non-descriptive and contextual. Those aspects of meaning unambiguously fall on the semantic and the pragmatic side respectively. B and C raise problems because the relevant aspects of meaning are conventional but not truth-conditional, or truth-conditional but not conventional (or not conventional enough).

The semantics/pragmatics distinction displays what psychologists call "prototypicality effects." It makes perfect sense with respect to Carnapian languages: languages in which the conventional meaning of a sentence can be equated with its truth conditions. Such languages constitute the prototype for the semantics/pragmatics distinction. As we move away from them, the distinction becomes strained and less and less applicable. Natural languages, in particular, turn out to be very different from the prototype – so different that it is futile to insist on providing an answer to the twin questions: What is the principled basis for the semantics/pragmatics distinction? Where does the boundary lie? Answers to these questions can still be given, but they have to rely on stipulation.

NOTES

1   There are a few exceptions. The most important one is Reichenbach, whose insightful "Analysis of Conversational Language" was published in 1947 as a chapter – the longest – in his *Elements of Symbolic Logic*.

2   The most influential authors were Austin, Strawson, Grice, and the later Wittgenstein. Grice is a special case, for he thought the two approaches were not incompatible but complementary.

3   "The relations of reference which are studied in semantics are neither directly observable nor independent of what men do and decide. These relations are in some sense themselves established and 'upheld' through human behavior and human institutions . . . In order to understand fully the basis of semantics, we are thus led to inquire into the uses of our symbols which bring out the ways in which the representative function of our language comes about" (Hintikka 1968: 17–18).

4   David Lewis makes a similar distinction. A language, Lewis says, is "a set-theoretic abstraction which can be discussed in complete abstraction from human affairs" (1983: 176). More precisely it is "a set of ordered pairs of strings (sentences) and meanings" (1983: 163). On the other hand, language (as opposed to "a language") is "a social phenomenon which is part of the natural history of human beings; a sphere of human action, wherein people utter strings of vocal sounds, or inscribe strings of marks, and wherein people respond by thought or action to the sounds or marks which they observe to have been so produced" (1983: 164). When we observe the social phenomenon, we note regularities, some of which are conventions in the sense of Lewis (1969). To provide a proper characterization of the linguistic conventions in force in the community we need the abstract notion of language: we need to be able to abstractly specify a certain language L in order to characterize the speech habits of a community by saying that its members are using that language and conforming to conventions involving it.

5   Because of indexicality, a sentence expresses a complete thought or describes a complete state of affairs only with respect to a particular context; but that determination is independent from issues concerning illocutionary force.

6   From the handout of a talk on "Semantics vs Pragmatics", delivered in 1996 and subsequently published as Bach 1999a. See also Bach (this volume).

7   This is debatable. In Recanati (1993: 257–8), I suggest a possible bottom-up treatment of that example.

21 Pragmatics and the Philosophy of Language

KENT BACH

During the first half of the twentieth century, philosophy of language was concerned less with language use than with meanings of linguistic expressions. Indeed, meanings were abstracted from the linguistic items that have them, and (indicative) sentences were often equated with statements, which in turn were equated with propositions. As Austin complained, it was assumed by philosophers that "the business of a [sentence] can only be to 'describe' some state of affairs, or to 'state some fact,' which it must do either truly or falsely" (1962: 1). Here he also had in mind the early Wittgenstein's picture-theory of meaning. Austin observed that there are many uses of language which have the linguistic appearance of fact-stating but are really quite different. Explicit performatives like "You're fired" and "I quit" are not used to make mere statements. And Wittgenstein himself swapped the picture metaphor for the tool metaphor and came to think of language not as a system of representation but as a system of devices for engaging in various sorts of social activity; hence, "the meaning of a word is its use in the language" (1953, §43: 20).

Here he went too far, for there is good reason to separate the theory of linguistic meaning (semantics) from the theory of language use (pragmatics), not that they are unconnected. We can distinguish sentences, considered in abstraction from their use, and the acts speakers (or writers) perform in using them. We can distinguish what sentences mean from what speakers mean in using them. Whereas Wittgenstein adopted a decidedly anti-theoretical stance toward the whole subject, Austin developed a systematic, though largely taxonomic, theory of language use. And Grice developed a conception of meaning which, though tied to use, enforced a distinction between what linguistic expressions mean and what speakers mean in using them.[1]

An early but excellent illustration was provided by Moore's paradox (so called by Wittgenstein 1953: 190). If you say, "Pigs swim but I don't believe it," you are denying that you believe what you are asserting. This contradiction seemed paradoxical because it is not logical in character. That pigs swim (if they do) does not entail your believing it, nor vice versa, and there's no contradiction in MY saying, "Pigs swim but you don't believe it." Your inconsistency arises not from what you are claiming but from the fact that you are claiming it. That's what makes it a **pragmatic** contradiction.

The phenomena to be considered in section 1, including performatives, illocutionary acts, communicating, and implicating, are essentially pragmatic. As explained in section 2, whereas semantic information is carried by linguistic items themselves, pragmatic information is generated by, or at least made relevant by, the act of uttering them. And the approach to various philosophical issues discussed in section 3 exploit the semantic–pragmatic distinction, illustrating that apparent matters of linguistic meaning are often really matters of use.

1   Speech Acts and Communication

Here we will take up relationships between speech acts and the linguistic means used to perform them, the distinctive character of communicative intentions, and various basic distinctions pertaining to speech acts.

1.1   *Performatives and illocutionary force*

Paradoxical though it may seem, there are certain things one can do just by saying that one is doing them. One can apologize by saying "I apologize," promise by saying "I promise," and thank someone by saying "Thank you." These are examples of EXPLICIT PERFORMATIVE utterances, statements in form but not in fact. Or so thought their discoverer, J. L. Austin (1962), who contrasted them with CONSTATIVES. Performatives are utterances whereby we make explicit what we are doing. Austin challenged the common philosophical assumption (or at least pretense) that indicative sentences are necessarily devices for making statements. He maintained that, for example, an explicit promise is not, and does not involve, the statement that one is promising. It is an act of a distinctive sort, the very sort (promising) named by the performative verb. Of course one can promise without doing so explicitly, without using the performative verb *promise*, but if one does use it, one is, according to Austin, making explicit what one is doing but not stating that one is doing it.

Austin came to realize that explicit constatives function in the same way. After all, a statement can be made by using a phrase like "I assert ..." or "I predict ... ," just as a promise can be made by means of "I promise ..." So he replaced the distinction between constative and performative utterances with one between locutionary and illocutionary acts, and included among illocutionary acts assertions, predictions, reports etc. (he still called them "constatives"), along with promises, requests, apologies, etc. The newer nomenclature recognized that illocutionary acts need not be performed explicitly – you don't have to use "I suggest ..." to make a suggestion or "I apologize ..." to apologize.

Even so, it might seem that because of their distinctive self-referential character, the force of explicit performatives requires special explanation. Indeed, Austin supposed that illocutionary acts in general should be understood on the model of explicit performatives, as when he made the notoriously mysterious remark that the use of a sentence with a certain illocutionary force is "conventional in the sense that at least it could be made explicit by the performative formula" (1962: 91). This is not a genuine sense of "conventional," but presumably he thought that explicit performative utterances are conventional in some more straightforward sense. Since it is not part of the meaning of the word "apologize" that an utterance of "I apologize . . ." count as an apology rather than a statement, perhaps there is some convention to that effect. If there is, presumably it is part of a general convention that covers all performative verbs. But is such a convention needed to explain performativity?

Strawson (1964a) argued that Austin was overly impressed with institution-bound cases, where there do seem to be conventions that utterances of certain forms (an umpire's "Out!," a legislator's "Nay!," or a judge's "Overruled!") count as the performance of acts of certain sorts. Likewise with certain explicit performatives, as when under suitable circumstances a judge or clergyman says, "I pronounce you husband and wife," which counts as joining a couple in marriage. In such cases there are specific, socially recognized circumstances in which a person with specific, socially recognized authority may perform an act of a certain sort by uttering words of a certain form. But Strawson argued that most illocutionary acts involve not an intention to conform to an institutional convention but an intention to communicate something to an audience. An act is conventional just in case it counts as an act of a certain sort because, and only because, of a special kind of institutional rule, what Searle (1969) called a CONSTITUTIVE RULE, to that effect. However, in contrast to the special cases Austin focused on, utterances can count as requests, apologies, or predictions, as the case may be, without the benefit of such a rule. For example, it is perfectly possible to apologize without using the performative phrase "I apologize . . ." That is the trouble with Austin's view of speech acts – and for that matter Searle's – which attempts to explain illocutionary forces by means of constitutive rules for using FORCE-INDICATING DEVICES, such as performatives. These theories can't explain the presence of illocutionary forces in the absence of such devices.[2] There is a superficial difference between apologizing explicitly (by saying, "I apologize") and doing it inexplicitly, but there is no theoretically important difference. Performativity requires no special explanation, much less a special sort of convention. Being standardized for a certain use provides a precedent that serves to streamline the hearer's inference.[3]

1.2 Types of speech acts

Here we will spell out Austin's distinction between locutionary, illocutionary, and perlocutionary acts, classify types of illocutionary acts, and draw the further distinction between direct, indirect, and nonliteral illocutionary acts.

This taxonomizing will serve to pinpoint the locus and role of communicative intentions in the total speech act.

1.2.1   *Locutionary, illocutionary, and perlocutionary acts*

When one acts intentionally, generally one has a set of nested intentions. For instance, having arrived home without one's keys, one might move one's finger in a certain way with the intention not just of moving one's finger in that way but with the further intentions of pushing a certain button, ringing the doorbell, arousing one's spouse, . . . and ultimately getting into one's house. The single bodily movement involved in moving one's finger comprises a multiplicity of actions, each corresponding to a different one of the nested intentions. Similarly, speech acts are not just acts of producing certain sounds.

Austin identifies three distinct levels of action beyond the act of utterance itself. He distinguishes the act of saying something, what one does **in** saying it, and what one does **by** saying it, and dubs these the LOCUTIONARY, the ILLOCUTIONARY, and the PERLOCUTIONARY act, respectively. Suppose, for example, that a bartender utters the words, "The bar will be closed in five minutes," reportable with direct quotation. He is thereby performing the locutionary act of saying that the bar (the one he is tending) will be closed in five minutes (from the time of utterance). What he says, the content of his locutionary act, is reported by indirect quotation (notice that it is not fully determined by the words he is using, for they do not specify the bar in question or the time of the utterance). In saying this, the bartender is performing the illocutionary act of informing the patrons of the bar's imminent closing and perhaps also the act of urging them to order a last drink. Whereas the upshot of these illocutionary acts is their understanding on the part of the audience, perlocutionary acts are performed with the intention of producing a further effect, in this case of causing the patrons to believe the bar is about to close and of getting them to order one last drink. He is performing all these speech acts, at all three levels, just by uttering certain words.

1.2.2   *Classifying illocutionary acts*

Utterances are generally more than just acts of communication. They have more than illocutionary force. When you apologize, for example, you may intend not merely to express your regret but also to seek forgiveness. Seeking forgiveness is to be distinguished from apologizing, even though the one utterance is the performance of an act of both types. As an apology, the utterance succeeds if it is taken as expressing regret for the deed in question; as an act of seeking forgiveness, it succeeds if forgiveness is thereby obtained. Speech acts, being perlocutionary as well as illocutionary, generally have some ulterior purpose, but they are distinguished primarily by their illocutionary type, such as asserting, requesting, promising, and apologizing, which in turn may be distinguished by the type of attitude expressed. The perlocutionary act is essentially a matter of trying to get the hearer to form some correlative attitude. Here are some typical examples:

ILLOCUTIONARY ACT	ATTITUDE EXPRESSED	INTENDED HEARER ATTITUDE
• statement	• belief that p	• belief that p
• request	• desire for H to D	• intention to D
• promise	• firm intention to D	• belief that S will D
• apology	• regret for D-ing	• forgiveness of S for D-ing

These illustrate the four major categories of communicative illocutionary acts, which may be called CONSTATIVES, DIRECTIVES, COMMISSIVES, and ACKNOWLEDGMENTS.[4] Here are some further examples of each type:

- **Constatives**: affirming, alleging, announcing, answering, attributing, claiming, classifying, concurring, confirming, conjecturing, denying, disagreeing, disclosing, disputing, identifying, informing, insisting, predicting, ranking, reporting, stating, stipulating
- **Directives**: admonishing, advising, asking, begging, dismissing, excusing, forbidding, instructing, ordering, permitting, requesting, requiring, suggesting, urging, warning
- **Commissives**: agreeing, betting, guaranteeing, inviting, offering, promising, swearing, volunteering
- **Acknowledgments**: apologizing, condoling, congratulating, greeting, thanking, accepting (acknowledging an acknowledgment)

Conventional illocutionary acts, the model for Austin's theory, succeed not by recognition of intention, but by conformity to convention. That is, an utterance counts as an act of a certain sort by virtue of meeting certain socially or institutionally recognized conditions for being an act of that sort. They fall into two categories, EFFECTIVES and VERDICTIVES, depending on whether they effect an institutional state of affairs or merely make an official judgment as to an institutionally relevant state of affairs.[5] Here are some examples of each:

- **Effectives**: banning, bidding, censuring, dubbing, enjoining, firing, indicting, moving, nominating, pardoning, penalizing, promoting, seconding, sentencing, suspending, vetoing, voting
- **Verdictives**: acquitting, assessing, calling (by an umpire or referee), certifying, convicting, grading, judging, ranking, rating, ruling

To appreciate the difference, compare what a judge does when he convicts someone and when he sentences them. Convicting is the verdictive act of officially judging that the defendant is guilty. Whether or not he actually committed the crime, the judge's determination that he did means that the justice system treat this as being the case. However, in performing the effective act sentencing him to a week in jail, the judge is not ascertaining that this is his sentence but is actually making this the case.

1.2.3   *Direct, indirect, and non-literal illocutionary acts*

Generally speaking, different illicutionary acts can be performed in uttering a given sentence. Just as in shaking hands we can, depending on the circumstances, introduce ourselves, greet each other, seal a deal, congratulate, or bid farewell, so we can use a sentence with a given locutionary content in various ways. For example, we could use "I will call a lawyer" to make a promise or a warning, or just a prediction. Moreover, we can perform an illocutionary act (1) directly or indirectly, by way of performing another illocutionary act; (2) literally or non-literally, depending on how we are using our words; and (3) explicitly or inexplicitly, depending on whether we fully spell out what we mean.

These three contrasts are distinct and should not be confused. The first two concern the relation between the utterance and the illocutionary act(s) thereby performed. In INDIRECTION a single utterance is the performance of one illocutionary act by way of performing another. For example, we can make a request or give permission by way of making a statement, say by uttering "It's getting cold in here" or "I don't mind," and we can make a statement or give an order by way of asking a question, such as "Is the Pope Catholic?" or "Can you open the door?" When an illocutionary act is performed indirectly, it is by way of performing another one directly. With NON-LITERALITY, we mean not what our words mean but something else instead. What one is likely to mean in uttering, "My mind got derailed" or "You can stick that in your ear" is not predictable just from linguistic meaning. Sometimes utterances are both non-literal and indirect. One might utter, "I love the sound of your voice" to tell someone non-literally (ironically) that she can't stand the sound of his voice and thereby indirectly to ask him to stop singing.

Non-literality and indirection are two well-known ways in which the semantic content of a sentence can fail to determine the full force and content of the illocutionary act being performed in using the sentence. They rely on the same sorts of processes that Grice (1967) discovered in connection with CONVERSATIONAL IMPLICATURES. Some of his examples illustrate non-literality, e.g. "He was a little intoxicated," but most are indirect statements, e.g. "There is a garage around the corner," used to tell someone where to get gas, and "Mr. X's command of English is excellent, and his attendance has been regular," used to give a weak recommendation. These are all examples in which what is meant is not determined by what is said. However, Grice overlooks a different kind of case, marked by the third contrast listed above.

There are many sentences whose standard uses are not strictly determined by their meanings but are not oblique (implicature-producing) or figurative uses either. For example, if one's spouse says, "I will be home later," she is likely to mean that she will be home later that night, not merely at some time in the future. In such cases what one means is what I call (Bach 1994a) an EXPANSION of what one says, in that adding more words (*tonight*, in the example) would have made what was meant fully explicit. In other cases, like "Jack is ready" and "Jill is late," the sentence does not express a complete proposition.

It is not specified what Jack is being claimed to be ready for and or what Jill is being claimed to be late to. Here what one means is a COMPLETION of what one says. In both sorts of case, no particular word or phrase is being used non-literally and there is no indirection. Both exemplify what I call conversational IMPLICITURE, since part of what is meant is communicated not explicitly but implicitly, by way of expansion or completion. Completion and expansion are both processes whereby the hearer supplies missing portions of what is otherwise being expressed explicitly. With completion a propositional radical is filled in, and with expansion a complete but skeletal proposition is fleshed out.

1.3   Communication and speech acts

The taxonomy laid out above assumes that Strawson was right to claim that most illocutionary acts are performed not with an intention to conform to a convention but with an audience-directed communicative intention. But why are illocutionary acts generally communicative, and what exactly is a communicative intention?

1.3.1   Communicative speech acts

Pre-theoretically, we think of an act of communication, linguistic or otherwise, as an act of expressing oneself. This rather vague idea can be made more precise if we become more specific about what is expressed. Take the case of an apology. If you utter, "[I'm] sorry I forgot your birthday" and intend this as an apology, you are expressing regret, in this case for forgetting the person's birthday. An apology just **is** the act of (verbally) expressing regret for, and thereby acknowledging, something one did that might have harmed or at least bothered the hearer. It succeeds as an act of communication if it is taken as expressing that attitude, in which case one has made oneself understood, achieving what Austin called UPTAKE. Any further result, such as being accepted or even being taken as sincere, is not essential to its being an apology. Accordingly, we need to distinguish the success of a speech act as an illocutionary and as a perlocutionary act. Notice that an utterance can succeed as an act of communication even if the speaker doesn't possess the attitude he is expressing, and even if the hearer doesn't take him to possess it.[6] Communication is one thing, sincerity another. Sincerity is actually possessing the attitude one is expressing.

1.3.2   Communicative intentions

As Strawson argued, illocutionary acts, other than those performed in special institutional contexts, are performed not with an intention to conform to a convention but with a communicative intention. But what sort of intention is that? The success of most acts has nothing to do with anyone's recognizing the intention with which the act is performed. You won't succeed in standing on your head because someone recognizes your intention to do so. But an act of communication is distinctive in this respect. It is successful if the intention with which it is performed is recognized by the audience: its fulfillment consists in its recognition. Indeed, as Grice (1957) discovered, a communicative intention is distinctively REFLEXIVE, since the speaker intends "to produce some effect in an audience by means of the recognition of **this intention.**"[7] The intention includes, as part of its content, that the audience recognize this very intention by taking into account the fact that they are intended to recognize it. Accordingly, the hearer is to take into account **that** he is intended to figure out the speaker's communicative intention. The meaning of the words uttered provides the input to this inference, but what they mean does not determine what the speaker means (even if he means precisely what his words means, they don't determine **that** he is speaking literally). What is loosely called CONTEXT, i.e. a set of MUTUAL CONTEXTUAL BELIEFS (Bach and Harnish 1979: 5), encompasses whatever other considerations the hearer is to take into account in ascertaining the speaker's intention, partly on the basis that he is intended to do so.

When Grice characterized meaning something as intending one's utterance "to produce some effect in an audience by means of the recognition of this intention," he wasn't very specific about the kind of effect to be produced. But since meaning something (in Grice's sense) is communicating, the relevant effect is, as both Strawson (1964a) and Searle (1969) recognized, understanding on the part of the audience. Moreover, an act of communication, as an essentially overt act, just **is** the act of expressing an attitude, which the speaker may or may not actually possess. Since the condition on its success is that one's audience infer the attitude from the utterance, it is clear why the intention to be performing such an act should have the reflexive character pinpointed by Grice. Considered as an act of communication rather than anything more, it is an attempt simply to get one's audience to recognize, partly on the basis of being so intended, that a certain attitude is being expressed. One is, as it were, putting a certain attitude on the table. The success of any further act has as its prerequisite that the audience recognize this attitude. Communication aims at a meeting of the minds not in the sense that the audience is to think what the speaker thinks but only in the sense that a certain attitude toward a certain proposition is to be recognized as being put forward for consideration. What happens beyond that is more than communication.[8]

1.3.3   *Intention, inference, and relevance*

Communication succeeds if the hearer identifies the speaker's communicative intention in the way intended. Since what the speaker says, the content of his locutionary act, does not determine the force or content of the illocutionary act(s) the speaker is performing, i.e. what the speaker is trying to communicate, figuring that out requires inference on the part of his audience. Now to describe the general character of communication is not to explain how it succeeds in particular cases. As Sperber and Wilson (1986a: 20, 69–70) have rightly pointed out, Grice and his followers have not supplied much in the way of psychological detail about how the process of understanding utterances works (or, I would add, about the process of producing utterances). Providing such detail would require a general theory of real-world reasoning and a theory of salience in particular. Research in the psychology of reasoning has identified many sorts of limitations in and constraints on human reasoning and AI models of well-demarcated tasks have been developed, but a general predictive and explanatory theory is not even on the horizon.

Grice made progress in explaining what this ability involves, as in his account of conversational implicature (see Horn, this volume),[9] such as when one says of an expensive dinner, "It was edible," and implicates that it was mediocre at best. Grice proposed a Cooperative Principle and several maxims which he named, in homage to Kant, Quantity, Quality, Relation, and Manner (Kant's Modality).[10] His account of implicature explains how ostensible violations of them can still lead to communicative success. Although Grice presents them as guidelines for how to communicate successfully, I think they are better construed as presumptions (they should not be construed, as they often are, as sociological generalizations). Nor should it be supposed, as it commonly is, that they come into play only with implicatures. They are operative even when the speaker means precisely what he says, since even that is a matter of intention and inference.

Because of their potential clashes, these maxims or presumptions should not be viewed as comprising a decision procedure.[11] Rather, they provide different dimensions of considerations that the speaker may reasonably be taken as intending the hearer to take into account in figuring the speaker's communicative intention. A speaker can say one thing and manage to mean something else, as with "Nature abhors a vacuum," or something more, as with "Is there a doctor in the house?", by exploiting the fact that he may be presumed to be cooperative, in particular, to be speaking truthfully, informatively, relevantly, and otherwise appropriately. The listener relies on this presumption to make a contextually driven inference from what the speaker says to what he means. If taking the utterance at face value is incompatible with this presumption, one may suppose that he intends one to figure out what he does mean by searching for an explanation of why he said what he said.

These maxims or presumptions do not concern what should be conveyed at a given stage of a conversation. When someone says something to you, you do not consider what, among everything possible, is the most relevant and informative thing he could have said consistent with what he has strong evidence for. Nor should you. Unless information of a very specific sort is required, say in answer to a *wh*-question, there will always be many things any one of which a speaker could have tried to convey which would have contributed more to the conversation than what he was in fact trying to convey. Rather, these maxims or presumptions frame how the hearer is to figure out what the speaker is trying to convey, **given** the sentence he is uttering and what he is saying in uttering it. What could he have been trying to convey given that? Why did he say *believe* rather than *know*, *is* rather than *seems*, *soon* rather than *in an hour*, *warm* rather than *hot*, *has the ability to* rather than *can*?

Sperber and Wilson (1986a) offer Relevance Theory as an alternative to Grice's inferential account (see Wilson and Sperber's and Carston's chapters in this volume). They eschew such allegedly problematic notions as reflexive intention, mutual belief, and maxims of conversation. They suggest that the principle of relevance and the presumption of optimal relevance can pick up the slack, where "relevance" is a matter of maximizing contextual effects and minimizing processing effort. Interestingly, however, when they take up specific examples in detail, they rely on considerations about what the speaker might reasonably be expected to intend, given that he said what he said. At times they slide from relevance in their technical sense, which is a property of propositions relative to contexts, to relevance in the ordinary sense. Such considerations and relevance in the ordinary sense are central to the Gricean picture of the hearer's inference. And the inference to the speaker's communicative intention essentially involves the supposition that this intention is to be recognized. That's what makes relevance relevant.

On the other hand, Sperber and Wilson are right to complain that reconstructions of hearers' inferences, however much they ring true, will inevitably appear ad hoc in the absence of an explanation of how it is that certain information emerges as mutually salient so that it might be exploited by the hearer. For that very reason, to suggest that processing takes place only if it is worth the effort and is a matter of settling on the first hypothesis that satisfies the principle of relevance (Sperber and Wilson 1986a: 201), does not say much about how this hypothesis is arrived at.[12] Equally, to say that inference is to the first plausible explanation of the speaker's communicative intention (Bach and Harnish 1979: 92) is not to say how **that** is arrived at. They speak of optimizing relevance and we speak of default reasoning, but to speak of either is not to say with any specificity how these processes work. Nor is it to explain how or why certain thoughts, such as hypotheses about speakers' intentions, come to mind when they do. No one is prepared to explain that.

1.4   Saying

Several important issues pertain to the act of saying (the locutionary level of speech act) and the correlative notion of what is said: the need for the notion of locutionary act, the question of how much is included in what is said, and the category of conventional implicature, which complicates Grice's account of saying.

1.4.1   What is said and what isn't

The notion of saying is needed for describing three kinds of cases: where the speaker means what he says and something else as well (implicature and indirect speech acts generally), where the speaker says one thing and means something else instead (non-literal utterances), and where the speaker says something and doesn't mean anything.[13] What is said, according to Grice, is "closely related to the conventional meaning of the . . . sentence . . . uttered" and must correspond to "the elements of [the sentence], their order, and their syntactic character" (1989: 87). Although what is said is limited by this SYNTACTIC CORRELATION CONSTRAINT, because of ambiguity and indexicality it is not identical to what the sentence means. If the sentence is ambiguous, usually only one of its conventional (linguistic) meanings is operative in a given utterance (*double entendre* is a special case). And linguistic meaning does not determine what, on a given occasion, indexicals like *she*, *this*, and *now* are used to refer to (see Levinson, this volume). If someone utters "She wants this book," he is saying that a certain woman wants a certain book, even though the words do not specify which woman and which book. So, along with linguistic information, the speaker's semantic (disambiguating and referential) intentions are needed to determine what is said.

Grice may have given the impression that the distinction between what is said and what is implicated is exhaustive. However, it seems that irony, metaphor, and other kinds of non-literal utterances are not cases of implicature, since they are cases of saying one thing and meaning something else instead, rather than saying and meaning one thing and meaning something else as well. Moreover, he overlooked the phenomenon of IMPLICITURE (roughly what Sperber and Wilson call EXPLICATURE). How does what is said fit in with that? In impliciture the speaker means something that goes beyond sentence meaning (ambiguity and indexicality aside) without implicating anything or using any expressions figuratively. For example, if your child comes crying to you with a minor injury and you say to him reassuringly, "You're not going to die," you don't mean that he will never die but merely that he won't die from that injury. And if someone wants you to join them for dinner and you say with regret, "I've already eaten," you mean that you have eaten dinner that evening, not just at some time previously. In both cases you do not mean precisely what you are saying but something more specific.[14]

Now several of Grice's critics have pointed out that implicitures (this is my term, not theirs) are not related closely enough to conventional meaning to fall under Grice's notion of what is said but that they are too closely related to count as implicatures. Recanati (1989) suggests that the notion of what is said should be extended to cover such cases, but clearly he is going beyond Grice's understanding of what is said as corresponding to the constituents of the sentence and their syntactic arrangement. The syntactic correlation constraint entails that if any element of what the speaker intends to convey does not correspond to any element of the sentence he is uttering, it is not part of what he is **saying**. Of course it may correspond to what he is asserting, but I am not using *say* to mean "assert." In the jargon of speech act theory, saying is locutionary, not illocutionary. Others speak of implicitures as the "explicit" content of an utterance. Sperber and Wilson's neologism "explicature" (1986a: 182) for this in-between category is rather misleading in this respect. It is a cognate of *explicate*, not *explicit*, and explicating, or making something explicit that isn't, isn't the same thing as making something explicit in the first place.

That's why I prefer the neologism "impliciture," since in these cases part of what is meant is communicated only implicitly.[15]

1.4.2   Conventional implicature

Grice is usually credited with the discovery of conventional implicature, but it was actually Frege's (1892) idea – Grice (1967) merely labeled it. They both claimed that the conventional meanings of certain terms, such as *but* and *still*, make contributions to the total import of a sentence without bearing on its truth or falsity. In "She is poor **but** she is honest," for example, the contrast between being poor and being honest due to the presence of *but* is, according to Grice (1961: 127), "implied as distinct from being stated." Frege and Grice merely appeal to intuition in suggesting that the conventional contributions of such terms do not affect what is said in utterances of sentences in which they occur. Grice observes that conventional implicatures are detachable but not cancelable, but this cannot serve as a test for their presence. It does distinguish them from conversational implicatures, which are cancelable but not detachable (except for those induced by exploiting the maxim of Manner, which depend on how one puts what one says), and from entailments, which are neither cancelable nor detachable. However, detachability is not an independent test. If a supposed implicature really were part of what is said, one could not leave it out and still say the same thing. To use *and* rather than *but*, for example, would be to say less.

In my opinion (Bach 1999b), the category of conventional implicature needlessly complicates Grice's distinction between what is said and what is implicated. Indeed, apparent examples of conventional implicature are really instances of something else. There are two kinds of case. The first involves expressions like *but* and *still*. If we abandon the common assumption that indicative sentences express at most one proposition, we can see that such expressions do contribute to what is said. With "She is poor but she is honest," the main proposition is that she is poor and she is honest, and the additional proposition is that being poor precludes being honest. The intuition that the utterance can be true even if this secondary proposition is false is explained by the fact that the intuition is sensitive only to the main proposition. But what is said includes both.

Grice also suggested that conventional implicature is involved in the performance of "non-central" speech acts (1989: 122). He had in mind the use of such expressions as these: *after all, at any rate, besides, by the way, first of all, frankly, furthermore, however, if you want my opinion, in conclusion, indeed, in other words, moreover, now that you mention it, on the other hand, otherwise, strictly speaking, to digress, to oversimplify, to put it mildly.*[16] These are used to comment on the very utterance in which they occur – its force, point, character, or the role in the discourse. However, I see no reason to call these second-order speech acts **implicatures**. In uttering, "Frankly, the dean is a moron," for example, you are not **implying** that you are speaking frankly, you are **saying** something about (providing a gloss or commentary on) your utterance. As a result, the contribution of an utterance modifier does not readily figure in an indirect report of what someone said, e.g. "He said that (*frankly) the dean is a moron." Utterance modifiers are in construction syntactically but not semantically with the clauses they introduce.

2   The Semantic–Pragmatic Distinction

Historically, the semantic–pragmatic distinction has been formulated in various ways.[17] These formulations have fallen into three main types, depending on which other distinction the semantic–pragmatic distinction was thought most to correspond to:

- linguistic (conventional) meaning vs. use;
- truth-conditional vs. non-truth-conditional meaning;
- context independence vs. context dependence.

In my view, none of these distinctions quite corresponds to the semantic–pragmatic distinction. The trouble with the first is that there are expressions whose literal meanings are related to use, such as the utterance modifiers mentioned above. It seems that the only way to specify their semantic contribution (when they occur initially or are otherwise set off) is to specify how they are to be used. The second distinction is inadequate because some expressions have meanings that do not contribute to truth-conditional contents. Paradigmatic are expressions like "Alas!," "Good-bye," and "Wow!," but utterance modifiers also illustrate this, as do such linguistic devices as *it*-clefts and *wh*-clefts, which pertain to information structure, not information content. The third distinction neglects the fact that some expressions, notably indexicals, are context-sensitive as a matter of their meaning.

A further source of confusion is a clash between two common but different conceptions of semantics. One takes semantics to concern the linguistic meanings of expressions (words, phrases, sentences). On this conception, sentence semantics is a component of grammar. It assigns meanings to sentences as a function of the meanings of their semantically simple constituents, as supplied by lexical semantics, and their constituent structure, as provided by their syntax. The other conception takes semantics to be concerned with the truth-conditional contents of sentences (or, alternatively, of utterances of sentences) and with the contributions expressions make to the truth-conditional contents of sentences in which they occur. The idea underlying this conception is that the meaning of a sentence, the information it carries, imposes a condition on what the world must be like in order for the sentence to be true.

Now the linguistic and the truth-conditional conceptions of semantics would come to the same thing if, in general, the linguistic meanings of sentences determined their truth conditions, and they all had truth conditions. Many sentences, though, are imperative or interrogative rather than declarative. These do not have truth conditions but compliance or answerhood conditions instead.

Even if only declarative sentences are considered, often the linguistic meaning of a sentence does not uniquely determine a truth condition. One reason for this is ambiguity, lexical or structural. The sentence may contain one or more ambiguous words, or it may be structurally ambiguous. Or the sentence may contain indexical elements. Ambiguity makes it necessary to relativize the truth condition of a declarative sentence to one or another of its senses, and indexicality requires relativization to a context. Moreover, some sentences, such as *Jack was ready* and *Jill had enough*, though syntactically well-formed, are semantically incomplete. That is, the meaning of such a sentence does not fully determine a truth condition, even after ambiguities are resolved and references are fixed (Sperber and Wilson 1986a, Bach 1994a). Syntactic completeness does not guarantee semantic completeness.

2.1   Drawing the semantic–pragmatic distinction

A semantic–pragmatic distinction can be drawn with respect to various things, such as ambiguities, implications, presuppositions, interpretations, knowledge, processes, rules, and principles. I take it to apply fundamentally to types of information. Semantic information is information encoded in what is uttered – these are stable linguistic features of the sentence – together with any extralinguistic information that provides (semantic) values to context-sensitive expressions in what is uttered. Pragmatic information is (extralinguistic) information that arises from an actual act of utterance, and is relevant to the hearer's determination of what the speaker is communicating. Whereas semantic information is encoded in what is uttered, pragmatic information is generated by, or at least made relevant by, the act of uttering it.[18] This way of characterizing pragmatic information generalizes Grice's point that what a speaker implicates in saying something is carried not by what he says but by his saying it and perhaps by his saying it in a certain way (1989: 39).

It could easily be maintained that disputes about the semantic–pragmatic distinction are merely terminological.[19] The main thing is to choose coherent terminology and apply it consistently. So, as illustrated above, clearly there are aspects of linguistic meaning (semantics) that pertain to use. Does this threaten our conception of the semantic–pragmatic distinction? Not at all. These aspects of linguistic meaning, like any others, are encoded by linguistic expressions – they just don't contribute to the truth-conditional contents of sentences in which they occur. But the fact that they pertain to use does not make them pragmatic. As aspects of linguistic meaning, they belong to expressions independently of whether those expressions are used. Of course, when such an expression is used, its presence contributes to what the speaker is doing in uttering the sentence containing it.

In order to apply the semantic–pragmatic distinction coherently, it is necessary to be clear on the notions and roles of context. It is a platitude that what a sentence means generally doesn't determine what a speaker means in uttering it. The gap between linguistic meaning and speaker meaning is said to be filled by "context": what the speaker means somehow "depends on context," or at least "context makes it clear" what the speaker means. But there are two quite different sorts of context, and they play quite different roles. What might be called WIDE CONTEXT concerns any contextual information that is relevant to determining, in the sense of **ascertaining**, the speaker's intention. NARROW CONTEXT concerns information specifically relevant to determining, in the sense of **providing**, the semantic values of context-sensitive expressions (and morphemes of tense and aspect). Wide context does not literally determine anything.[20] It is the body of mutually evident information that speaker and hearer exploit, the speaker to make his communicative intention evident and the hearer, presuming he's intended to, to identify that intention.[21]

2.2 Some consequences of the semantic–pragmatic distinction

The formulation has certain interesting theoretical implications, which can only be sketched here. For one thing, it helps explain why what Grice called GENERALIZED conversational implicature is a pragmatic phenomenon, even though it involves linguistic regularities of sorts. They are cancelable, hence not part of what is said, and otherwise have all the features of PARTICULARIZED implicatures, but are characteristically associated with certain forms of words. So special features of the context of utterance are not needed to generate them and make them identifiable. As a result, they do not have to be worked out step by step as particularized implicatures have to be. Nevertheless, they can be worked out. A listener unfamiliar with the pattern of use could still figure out what the speaker meant. This makes them standardized but not conventionalized.[22]

Also, the semantic–pragmatic distinction as understood here undermines any theoretical role for the notion of presupposition, whether construed as semantic or pragmatic (see Atlas, this volume). A SEMANTIC PRESUPPOSITION is a precondition for truth or falsity. But, as argued long ago by Stalnaker (1974) and by Boër and Lycan (1976), there is no such thing: it is either entailment or pragmatic. And so-called PRAGMATIC PRESUPPOSITIONS come to nothing more than preconditions for performing a speech act successfully and felicitously, together with mutual contextual beliefs taken into account by speakers in forming communicative intentions and by hearers in recognizing them. In some cases they may seem to be conventionally tied to particular expressions or constructions, e.g. to definite descriptions or to clefts, but they are not really. Rather, given the semantic function of a certain expression or construction, there are certain constraints on its reasonable or appropriate use. As Stalnaker puts it, a "pragmatic account makes it possible to explain some particular facts about presuppositions in terms of general maxims of rational communication rather than in terms of complicated and ad hoc hypotheses about the semantics of particular words and particular kinds of constructions" (1974/1999: 48).

Finally, our formulation of the semantic–pragmatic distinction throws a monkey wrench into the conception of the semantic content of a sentence as its

CONTEXT-CHANGE POTENTIAL. This conception, adopted by many formal semanticists (e.g. Heim 1983a), treats semantic content dynamically, as the ability of
a sentence, when uttered, to alter the context in which it is uttered (or, where
what Lewis 1979 calls "accommodation" is required, to change the context
retroactively). In my view, however, this conception conflates semantic content
with pragmatic effect. It is in virtue not just of what the speaker says but of the
fact that he says it that the (wide) context is changed in a certain way. Context
change is the combined effect of what is said **and** saying it in the context.

These examples illustrate not only the importance of the semantic–
pragmatic distinction but the import of Grice's pragmatic strategy of trying to
explain linguistic phenomena in as general a way as possible, of appealing to
independently motivated principles and processes of rational communication
rather than to special features of particular expressions and constructions.

3   Applied Pragmatics

Here we will take up a few philosophically important expressions and problems
whose treatment is aided by pragmatic considerations. Needless to say, the
issues here are more complex and contentious than our discussion can indicate.
But at least these examples will illustrate how to implement what Stalnaker has
aptly described as "the classic Gricean strategy: to try to use simple truisms
about conversation or discourse to explain regularities that seem complex and
unmotivated when they are assumed to be facts about the semantics of the
relevant expressions" (1999: 8).

3.1   The speech act and assertion fallacies

The distinction between what an expression means and how it is used had
a direct impact on many of the claims made by so-called Ordinary Language
philosophers. In ethics, for example, it was (and sometimes still is) supposed
that sentences containing words like *good* and *right* are used to express affective
attitudes, such as approval or disapproval, hence that such sentences are not
used to make statements and that questions of value and morals are not matters
of fact. This line of argument is fallacious. As Moore points out, although
one expresses approval (or disapproval) by making a value judgment, it is
the act of making the judgment, not the content of the judgment, that does
this (1942: 540–5). Sentences used for ethical evaluation, such as "Loyalty is
good" and "Cruelty is wrong," are no different in form from other indicative
sentences, which, whatever the status of their contents, are standardly used
to make statements. This leaves open the possibility that there is something
fundamentally problematic about their contents. Perhaps such statements are
factually defective and, despite syntactic appearances, are neither true nor false.
However, this is a metaphysical issue about the status of the properties to
which ethical predicates purport to refer. It is not the business of the philosophy

of language to determine whether or not goodness or wrongness are real properties (or whether or not the goodness of loyalty and the wrongness of cruelty are matters of fact).

The fallacious line of argument exposed by Moore commits what Searle calls the SPEECH ACT FALLACY (1969: 136–41). Searle gives further examples, each involving a speech act analysis of a philosophically important word. These analyses claim that because *true* is used to endorse or concede statements (Strawson), *know* to give guarantees (Austin), and *probably* to qualify commitments (Toulmin), those uses constitute the meaning of these words. In each case the fallacy is the same: identifying what the word is typically used to do with its semantic content.

Searle also exposes the ASSERTION FALLACY (1969: 141–6), which confuses conditions on making an assertion with what is asserted. Here are two examples: because you would not assert that you believe something if you were prepared to assert that you know it, knowing does not entail believing; similarly, because one would not be described as trying to do something that involves no effort or difficulty, trying entails effort or difficulty. Grice (1961) identified the same fallacy in a similar argument, due to Austin, about words like *seems*, *appears*, and *looks*: since you would not say that a table looks old unless you (or your audience) doubted or were even prepared to deny that the table was old, the statement that the table looks old entails that its being old is doubted or denied. This argument is clearly fallacious, since it draws a conclusion about entailment from a premise about conditions on appropriate assertion. Similarly, you wouldn't say that someone tried to stand up if doing it involved no effort or difficulty, but this doesn't show that trying to do something entails that there was effort or difficulty in doing it. You can misleadingly imply something without its being entailed by what you say.

3.2 *Logical expressions*

In "Logic and Conversation," undoubtedly the philosophy article with the greatest impact on pragmatics, Grice (1967) introduces his theory of conversational implicature by considering whether the semantics of logically important expressions, such as certain sentential connectives and quantificational phrases, are captured by the logical behavior of their formal counterparts. For example, are the terms *and* and *or* adequately represented by "&" and "∨"? Applying Grice's theory to these terms suggests that apparent difficulties with their usual logical renderings can be explained away pragmatically.

3.2.1 and
Pragmatic considerations exploit the fact that in ordinary speech not just what a sentence means but the fact that someone utters it plays a role in determining what its utterance conveys. For example, there is a difference between what is likely to be conveyed by utterances of (1) and (2), and the difference is due to the order of the conjuncts.

(1)   Henry had sex and got infected.

(2)   Henry got infected and had sex.

Yet *and* is standardly symbolized by the conjunction "&," and in logic the order of conjuncts doesn't matter. However, it seems that (1) and (2) have the same semantic content and that it is not the meaning of *and* but the fact that the speaker utters the conjuncts in one order rather than the other that explains the difference in how each utterance is likely to be taken. But then any suggestion of temporal order, or even causal connection, is not a part of the literal content of the sentence but is merely implicit in its utterance (Levinson 2000a: 122–7). One piece of evidence for this is that such a suggestion may be explicitly canceled (Grice 1989: 39). One could utter (1) or (2) and continue, "but not in that order" without contradicting what one has just said. One would be merely canceling any suggestion, due to the order of presentation, that the two events occurred in that order.

However, it has been argued that passing Grice's cancelability test does not suffice to show the difference between the two sentences above is not a matter of linguistic meaning. Cohen (1971) and Carston (1988) have appealed to the fact that the difference is preserved when the conjunctions are embedded in the antecedent of a conditional, as here (my example, not theirs):

(3)a.   If Henry had sex and got infected, he needs a doctor.
   b.   If Henry got infected and had sex, he needs a lawyer.

Also, the difference is apparent when the two conjunctions are combined:

(4)   It's worse to get infected and have sex than to have sex and get infected.

However, these examples do not show that the relevant differences are a matter of linguistic meaning. A simpler hypothesis, one that does not ascribe temporal or causal meanings to *and*, is that these examples, like the simpler (1) and (2), involve conversational impliciture, in which what the speaker means is an implicitly qualified version of what he says. Likely utterances of (1) and (2) are made as if they included an implicit *then* after *and*, and are likely to be taken accordingly (with (1) there is also likely to be an implicit *as a result*). The speaker is exploiting Grice's maxim of Manner in describing events in their order of occurrence, and the hearer relies on the order of presentation to infer the speaker's intention in that regard. On the pragmatic approach, *and* is treated as unambiguously truth-functional, without having additional temporal or causal senses.

3.2.2   or

Even though it is often supposed that in English there is both an inclusive *or* and an exclusive *or*, in the propositional calculus *or* is symbolized with just the inclusive "∨." A disjunction is true just in case at least one of its disjuncts is true. Of course, if there were an exclusive *or* in English, it would also be truth-functional – an exclusive disjunction is true just in case exactly one of its disjuncts is true – but the simpler hypothesis is that the English *or* is unambiguously inclusive, like "∨." But does this comport with an example like this?

(5)   Max is in Miami or he's in Palm Beach.

An utterance of (5) is likely to be taken as exclusive. However, this is not a consequence of the presence of an exclusive *or* but of the fact that one can't be in two places at once. Also, it might seem that there is an epistemic aspect to *or*, for in uttering (5), the speaker is implying that he doesn't know whether Max is in Miami or in Palm Beach. Surely, though, this implication is not due to the meaning of the word *or* but rather to the presumption that the speaker is supplying as much relevant and reliable information as he has.[23] The speaker wouldn't be contradicting himself if, preferring not to reveal Max's exact whereabouts, he added, "I know where he is, but I can't tell you."

The case of (6) requires a different story, because it raises a different issue.

(6)   Max is in Miami or Minnie (his wife) will hire a lawyer.

Here it is the order of the disjuncts that matters, since an utterance of "Minnie will hire a lawyer or Max is in Miami" would not be taken in the way that (6) is likely to be. Because the disjuncts in (6) are ostensibly unrelated, its utterance would be hard to explain unless they are actually connected somehow. In a suitable context, an utterance of (6) would likely be taken as if it contained *else* after *or*, i.e. as a conditional of sorts. That is, the speaker means that if Max is **not** in Miami, Minnie will hire a lawyer, and might be implicating further that the reason Minnie will hire a lawyer is that she suspects Max is really seeing his girlfriend in Palm Beach. The reason that order matters in this case is not that *or* does not mean inclusive disjunction but that in (6) it is intended as elliptical for *or else*, which is not symmetrical.

3.2.3   *Quantificational phrases and descriptions*

There are discrepancies between ordinary uses of quantificational phrases and how they are represented in logic. For example, although "$(\exists x)(Fx \text{ and } Gx)$" is logically compatible with "$(\forall x)(Fx \supset Gx),$" ordinarily when you say, for example, "Some politicians are honest," you imply that not all politicians are honest. But clearly this is a (generalized) conversational implicature: you would not say what you said if you were in a position to assert that **all** politicians are honest. Also, in standard logical systems "$(\forall x)(Fx \supset Gx)$" does not entail "$(\exists x)(Fx)$". Nevertheless, if you were to say, for example, "All of Venus's moons are small," you would imply that Venus has moons. But again, this discrepancy between ordinary use and logical representation can be explained away pragmatically: normally you wouldn't say what you said if you thought Venus had no moons.

Another issue concerns the domain of quantificational phrases. If you said to a group you invited to a potluck dinner, "Everyone should bring something," you would mean that everyone who comes to the dinner should bring something to eat. Similarly, when Yogi Berra said, speaking of a certain restaurant, "Nobody goes there any more – it's too crowded," he meant that nobody important goes there any more. It is sometimes supposed that these restrictions on the "universe of discourse" or "domain of quantification" are provided contextually as values of covert quantifier domain variables.[24] However, it is not necessary to transpose these technical notions from logic to natural language. Instead we may suppose instead that these examples are but special cases of impliciture. A speaker who uses a quantified noun phrase with a certain intended restriction could have made that restriction explicit by modifying with it with an adjective, prepositional phrase, or relative clause.

Philosophers commonly distinguish referring terms from quantificational phrases. They generally, though not universally, treat proper names, indexicals, and demonstratives (see Levinson, this volume) as referring terms and definite and indefinite descriptions as quantificational phrases.[25] The relevant difference between the two types of noun phrase consists in whether they contribute objects or quantificational structure to the contents of sentences in which they occur. As Russell puts it, a referring term serves "merely to indicate what we are speaking about; [it] is no part of the fact asserted . . . : it is merely part of the symbolism by which we express our thought" (1919: 175). Sentences containing quantificational phrases express general propositions, and particular objects do not enter into their contents. This is true even in the case of definite and indefinite descriptions, although they may seem to refer when used to refer.

According to Russell's (1905) famous theory of descriptions, a subject-predicate sentence of the form "The F is G" does not express a singular proposition of the form "a is G" but a general, existential proposition of the form (in modern notation) "$(\exists x)((\forall y)(Fy \equiv y=x)$ and $Gx)$" (or in less misleading form, using restricted quantifier notation, "$[\text{the } x: Fx] \ Gx$"), in which the object that is the F does not appear. So, for example, "The queen of England loves roses" does not express a proposition about Elizabeth II. It means what it means whether or not she is queen of England and, indeed, whether or not England has a queen. As a quantificational phrase, "the queen of England" does not refer to Elizabeth II (Russell would say it "denotes" her, but for him denotation was a semantically inert relation). It can, of course, be **used** to refer to her. This might suggest that definite descriptions phrases are semantically ambiguous, a possibility Donnellan (1966) raised with his well-known distinction between referential and attributive uses and posed as a threat to Russell's theory of descriptions (see Abbott, this volume). However, as Kripke (1977) forcefully argued, with later support from Bach (1987b: Chap. 5), Neale (1990), and Salmon (1991), referential uses of definite descriptions can be understood in pragmatic terms. Ludlow and Neale (1991) have given a similarly pragmatic account of referential uses of indefinite descriptions.

Although quantificational phrases are not referring terms, some can be used to refer. Even so, because of their distinct logical and semantic role, they should not be assimilated to referring terms. Take the case of indefinites. Suppose Jack says, "A woman wants to marry me," he is not referring to any woman – even if he has a particular woman in mind. For there is no woman that the listener must identify in order to understand the utterance (this is so even if the hearer recognizes that the speaker has some unspecified woman in mind, perhaps because the speaker uses the specific indefinite form "a certain woman"). To see this point, one must distinguish the content of the utterance from a fact that makes it true. So, for example, even if Jill wants to marry Jack, he is not saying that Jill wants to marry him, although this fact about her is what makes his utterance true – it would be true even if she wanted to marry someone else. Also, suppose that after saying "A woman wants to marry me," Jack adds, "But she doesn't love me." Even if Jack were using *she* to refer to the woman who (he believes) wants to marry him (actually, it seems that he is merely alluding to her), this would not show that *a woman* referred to that woman. Although it is often said, following Karttunen (1976), that indefinites introduce DISCOURSE REFERENTS, that is to use the term "referent" loosely.

This point is clear when the indefinite is used without any implication of uniqueness and is followed by a singular pronoun. Suppose someone says,

(7)   Phil took a pill last night at 11 p.m., and it relieved his migraine.

Assume that Phil took several pills at that time and that the speaker has no particular pill in mind but that exactly one relieved his migraine. Then it may seem that (7) is true. However, I suggest, this is illusory: its second conjunct does not have a determinate truth condition with respect to the assumed circumstances, because the anaphoric pronoun *it* does not pick out a determinate pill. For what if no pill relieved Phil of his migraine? Presumably, what the second conjunct of (7) says is the same whether or not it is true. But what could it say if it is not true, since then there is no pill that the speaker is mistakenly saying relieved Phil's migraine? So if there is such a pill, the illusion that the second conjunct of (7) is true arises because it doesn't matter which pill makes it true. We confuse what (7) says with the proposition that Phil took a pill (last night at 11 p.m.) that cured his headache. That is not what (7) says because *a pill* does not bind *it*, which is outside its binding domain. So *it* can only be what Neale calls a D-TYPE PRONOUN, one which "goes proxy for a definite description" (1990: 67). In this case the description is "the pill that Phil took," but since he took more than one pill, this description does not denote some one pill. This kind of example again illustrates the force of a pragmatic explanation for what might otherwise be a mysterious semantic phenomenon, in this case the illusion that a pronoun refers even though it has no determinate reference.

In this section we have sampled a variety of philosophically significant types of expressions that seem give rise to ambiguities and other semantic complications. Economy and plausibility of explanation are afforded by heeding the semantic–pragmatic distinction. Rather than attribute needlessly complex properties to specific linguistic items, we proceeded on the default assumption that uses of language can be explained by means of simpler semantic hypotheses together with general facts about rational communication. In this way, we can make sense of the fact that to communicate efficiently and effectively people rarely need to make fully explicit what they are trying to convey. Most sentences short enough to use in everyday conversation do not literally express things we are likely ever to mean, and most things we are likely ever to mean are not expressible by sentences we are likely ever to utter.

NOTES

1   This distinction is compatible with Grice's conviction that linguistic meaning can be reduced to (standardized) speaker's meaning. However, this reductive view has not gained wide acceptance, partly because of its extreme complexity (see Grice 1969 and Schiffer 1972) and partly because it requires the controversial assumption that language is *essentially* a vehicle for communicating thoughts. Even so, many philosophers would grant that mental content is a more fundamental notion than linguistic meaning. This issue will not be taken up here.

2   So it would seem that an account of explicit performatives should not appeal, as Searle's (1989) elaborate account in "How Performatives Work" does, to any special features of the performative formula. In "How Performatives Really Work," Bach and Harnish (1992) argue that Searle's account is based on a spurious distinction between having a communicative intention and being committed to having one and on a confusion between performativity and communicative success.

3   There are all sorts of other forms of words which are standardly used to perform speech acts of certain types without making explicit the type of act being performed, e.g. "It would be nice if you ..." to request, "Why don't you ... ?" to advise, "Do you know ... ?" to ask for information, "I'm sorry" to apologize, and "I wouldn't do that" to warn. Even in the case of hedged and embedded performatives, such as "I can assure you ...," "I must inform you ...," "I would like to invite you ...," and "I am pleased to be able to offer you ...," in which the type of act is made explicit, the alleged conventions for simple performative forms would not apply. For discussion of hedged and embedded performatives, see Fraser (1975) and Bach and Harnish (1979: 209–19).

4   We develop a detailed taxonomy in Bach and Harnish (1979: Chap. 3). We borrow the terms "constative" and "commissive" from Austin and "directive" from Searle. We adopt the term "acknowledgment" rather than Austin's "behabitive" or Searle's "expressive" for

apologies, greetings, thanks, congratulations, etc.

5 This distinction and the following examples are drawn from Bach and Harnish (1979: Chap. 6).

6 The difference between expressing an attitude and actually possessing it is clear from the following definition: To express an attitude in uttering something is reflexively to intend the hearer to take one's utterance as reason to think one has that attitude (Bach and Harnish 1979: 15). This reason need not be conclusive and if in the context it is overridden, the hearer will, in order to identify the attitude being expressed, search for an alternative and perhaps non-literal interpretation of the utterance. For discussion see Bach and Harnish (1979: 57–9, 289–91).

7 Partly because of certain alternative wordings and perhaps indecision (compare his 1969 with his 1957 article), Grice's analysis is sometimes interpreted as defining communicative intentions iteratively rather than reflexively, but this not only misconstrues Grice's idea but leads to endless complications (see Strawson 1964a and especially Schiffer 1972 for good illustrations). Recanati (1986) has pointed to certain problems with the iterative approach, but in reply I have argued (Bach 1987a) that these problems do not arise on the reflexive analysis.

8 If the hearer thinks the speaker actually possesses the attitude he is expressing, in effect she is taking him to be sincere in what he is communicating. But there is no question about his being sincere in the communicative intention itself, for this intention must be identified before the question of his sincerity (in having that attitude) can even arise.

9 For a review of earlier approaches to what used to be called "contextual implication," see Hungerland (1960).

10 See Horn, this volume. Also, see Harnish (1976/1991: 330–40), for discussion of Grice's maxims, their weaknesses, and their conflicts, and Levinson (2000a) for extensive discussion and adaptation of them to various types of generalized conversational implicature.

11 See Bach and Harnish (1979: 62–5). We replace Grice's Cooperative Principle with our own CP, the COMMUNICATIVE PRESUMPTION.

12 There is also the question of how costs (of effort) and benefits are to be measured, as well as, because of the trade-off between cost and benefit, the problem that a given degree of relevance can be achieved in various ways. For all Sperber and Wilson say, their principle of relevance is not equipped to distinguish much benefit at much cost from little benefit at little cost. So their principle has little predictive or explanatory power. Besides, it disregards the essentially reflexive character of communicative intentions and instead assumes that speakers are somehow able to gear their utterances to maximize relevance.

13 That is why the notion of locutionary acts is indispensable, as Bach and Harnish (1979: 288–9) argue in reply to Searle (1969).

14 In Bach (2001b) I describe such utterances as cases of *sentence* non-literality, because the words are being used literally but the sentence as a whole is being used loosely. Compare the sentences mentioned in the text with the similar sentences, "Everybody is going to die" or "I've already been

in the Army," which are more likely to be used in a strictly literal way.

15 Recanati (1989) and I (Bach 1994a) have debated whether intuition or syntax constrain what is said, and we have renewed the debate in Recanati (2001) and Bach (2001a).

16 I classify these and many other utterance modifiers in Bach (1999b: sec. 5).

17 For a collection of sample formulations, see the Appendix to Bach (1999a). (See also Recanati, this volume.)

18 In Bach (1999a), I develop and defend this conception of the distinction and contrast it with alternatives.

19 To the extent that the debate about the semantic–pragmatic distinction isn't entirely terminological, perhaps the main substantive matter of dispute is whether there is such a thing as "pragmatic intrusion," whereby pragmatic factors allegedly contribute to semantic interpretation (see Carston and Recanati, this volume). Various linguistic phenomena have been thought to provide evidence for pragmatic intrusion, hence against the viability of the semantic–pragmatic distinction, but in each case, in my opinion (Bach 1999a), this is an illusion, based on some misconception about the distinction. Levinson (2000a: Chap. 3) argues that many alleged cases of pragmatic intrusion are really instances of generalized conversational implicature, which he thinks is often misconstrued as a purely semantic phenomenon.

20 For this reason, I do not accept Stalnaker's contention that "we need a single concept of context that is both what determines the contents of context-dependent expressions, and also what speech acts act upon" (1999: 4)

21 For more on the notions of context and context dependence, and on their abuse, see Bach (to appear b).

22 Levinson (2000a) describes them as "default meanings," but he does not mean sentence meanings. He thinks of them as comprising an "intermediate layer" of meaning, of "systematic pragmatic inference based not on direct computations about speaker-intentions but rather on general expectations about how language is normally used, . . . which give rise to presumptions, default inferences, about both content and force" (2000a: 22). In my view, this does not demonstrate an intermediate layer of meaning – there is still only linguistic meaning and speaker meaning – but rather that speakers' communicative intentions and hearers' inferences are subject to certain systematic constraints based on practice and precedent. See Bach (1995).

23 This sounds like a combination of Grice's Quantity and Quality maxims, or what Harnish proposed as the "Maxim of Quantity-Quality: Make the strongest relevant claim justifiable by your evidence" (1976/1991: 340; see also note 46, pp. 360–1).

24 Stanley and Szabó (2000) have offered some ingenious arguments for the claim that quantified noun phrases have domain variables associated with them. I have replied to these arguments in Bach (2000).

25 There is considerable uncertainty about the status of demonstrative descriptions (Neale 1993, Braun 1994). But see King (2001). As for proper names, it is widely held, thanks largely to Kripke (1980) but originally to Mill (1872), that they are referring and not, as Russell claimed, "truncated" definite descriptions. I have rebutted

Kripke's anti-descriptivist arguments as they apply to the metalinguistic version of descriptivism, or what I call the "nominal description theory," on which a name "N" occurring as a stand-along noun phrase is semantically equivalent to the definite description "the bearer of 'N'." I use pragmatic considerations to explain away the "illusion of rigidity". Ironically, Millians (other than Braun 1998) use similar considerations to explain away Frege's (1892) puzzles (see Salmon 1986), not realizing that they can be used to undermine the support for Millianism itself, which is what gives rise to Frege's puzzles in the first place. See Bach (1987b: Chaps. 7 and 8, and 2002).

22 Pragmatics and the Lexicon

REINHARD BLUTNER

1 Introduction

In the view of Katz and Fodor (1963: 176) the scope of a language description covers the knowledge of a fluent speaker "about the structure of his language that enables him to use and understand its sentences." The scope of a semantic theory is then the part of such a description not covered by a theory of syntax. There is a second aspect which Katz and Fodor make use of in order to bound the scope of semantics. This is the pragmatic aspect of language and it excludes from the description any ability to use and understand sentences that depends on the "setting" of the sentence. Setting, according to Katz and Fodor (1963), can refer to previous discourse, sociophysical factors and any other use of "non-linguistic" knowledge. A nice demonstration of the essence of "non-linguistic" knowledge in the understanding of sentences was provided by psychologists in the 1970s (e.g. Kintsch 1974). Let's consider the following utterance:

(1)   The tones sounded impure because the hem was torn.

I suggest we do not really understand what this sentence means until we know that this sentence is about a bagpipe. It is evident that this difficulty is not due to our insufficient knowledge of English. The syntax involved is quite simple and there are no unknown words in the sentence. Instead, the difficulty is related to troubles in accessing the relevant conceptual setting. The idea of bagpiping is simply too unexpected to be derived in a quasi-neutral utterance context. The example demonstrates that we have to distinguish carefully between the linguistic aspects of representing the (formal) meaning of sentences and the pragmatic aspects of utterance interpretation (speaker's meaning).

In this contribution I restrict myself to the semantics of lexical units and intend to explain the interaction of lexical meaning with pragmatics. Katz and Fodor (1963) already have stressed the point that a full account of lexical meaning has to include more information than that which allows one to discriminate the meanings of different words. In one of their examples they argue that "take back" is used in very different ways in the sentences (2a, b), although the relevant lexical entries are semantically unambiguous.

(2)a.   Should we take the lion back to the zoo?
   b.   Should we take the bus back to the zoo?

An obvious difference between these sentences is that the lion is the object taken back to the zoo in (2a), but the bus is the instrument that takes us back to the zoo in (2b). The problem for the pragmatic component of utterance interpretation is to explain the difference in terms of different conceptual settings, starting from a lexicon that doesn't discriminate the two occurrences of *take back* semantically and from a syntax that is completely parallel for the two sentences.[1]

As another introductory example let's consider the perception verbs of English (cf. Sweetser 1990). If Saussure is right, there is an essential arbitrary component in the association of words or morphemes with what they mean. Consequently, the feature of arbitrariness could be taken at least as a sufficient condition for the presence of semantic information. It is certainly an arbitrary fact of English that *see* (rather than, say, *buy* or *smell*) refers to visual perception when it is part of the utterance (3a). Given this arbitrary association between a phonological word and its meaning, however, it is by no means arbitrary that *see* can also have an epistemic reading as in (3b).

(3)a.   I see the tree.
   b.   I see what you're getting at.

Moreover, it is not random that other sensory verbs such as *smell* or *taste* are not used to express an epistemic reading. Sweetser (1990) tries to give an explanation for such facts and insists that they have to do with conceptual organization. It is our knowledge about the inner world that implicates that vision and knowledge are highly related, in contrast to, say, smelling and knowledge or taste and knowledge, which are only weakly related for normal human beings. If this claim is correct, then the information that *see* may have an epistemic reading but *smell* and *taste* do not must no longer be stipulated semantically. Obviously, this can be formalized by language-independent, universal preferences. In specific languages, these preferences can be over-ridden – consider the "ingestive" verbs in languages of India, or even English "I can't swallow that" = "can't believe". Instead, this information is pragmatic in nature, having to do with the utterance of words within a conceptual setting, and can be derived by means of some general mechanism of conceptual interpretation.

Considerations of this kind raise a standard puzzle for lexical semantics when we ask how to separate the (mental) lexicon from the (mental) encyclopedia.

How should we separate information about the meaning of words from information about the (supposed) reality associated with these words? Admittedly, it may be rather difficult to distinguish these two kinds of information. Tangible, theory-independent empirical tests simply don't exist. There are two principal possibilities for dealing with this situation. First, the distinction between the lexicon and the encyclopedia is said to be illusory (as has sometimes been suggested by proponents of Cognitive Semantics, e.g. G. Lakoff 1987). In this case all the relevant information has to be put into the lexicon. It will be argued in what follows that this view leads to a highly non-compositional account of meaning projection. The second possibility is to take the distinction as an important one. As a consequence, we are concerned with two different types of mechanisms:

- a mechanism that deals with the combinatorial aspects of meaning;
- a pragmatic mechanism that deals with conceptual interpretation.

Once we have adopted such theoretical mechanisms, the problem of discriminating lexical semantic information from encyclopedic information need no longer look so hopeless, and we really may profit from a division of labor between semantics and pragmatics. It is the position of this contribution to argue in favor of the second option.

From a Gricean perspective, two different ideas of how to overcome the divergences between (formal) meaning and natural language interpretation come to mind. The first one uses conventional implicatures as an enlargement of the classical information entries. The second idea uses conversational implicatures as a method to overcome the divergences. While I believe that modern semantic theories (which usually are characterized as dynamic, epistemic, and non-monotonic) make the conception of conventional implicature superfluous as an addendum to the semantic component, I do not think the same is true of conversational implicature. In fact, in this chapter I will argue that the proper use of conversational implicature will resolve some of the problems of lexical interpretation that remain unsolved otherwise.

The conceptual core of the theory I want to propose demands a straight formulation of conversational implicature. Paired with the idea of (radical) semantic underspecification in the lexicon and an appropriate representation of contextual and encyclopedic knowledge, this conception avoids unmotivated lexical ambiguities as well as the need for expansive reinterpretation and coercion mechanisms.

There are two basic aims of this chapter. First, I want to demonstrate some general problems we are confronted with when trying to analyze the utterance of words within concrete conceptual and contextual settings and to go beyond the aspects of meaning typically investigated by a contrastive analysis of lexemes within the Katz–Fodor tradition of semantics. This may help to develop a sensitive feeling for what kind of problems may be approached by means of the division of labor between lexical semantics and pragmatics. Second, I would like to argue in favor of a particular account of the interaction between lexical semantics and pragmatics, one that combines the idea of (radical) semantic underspecification in the lexicon with a theory of pragmatic strengthening (based on conversational implicature). It is illustrated that this view conforms with recent attempts to extend the framework of optimality theory (originally proposed by Prince and Smolensky 1993) for the purpose of natural language interpretation.

The organization of this chapter is as follows. In the next section I will emphasize some important consequences of the traditional view of (lexical) semantics. In the third section some phenomena are collected that have a prima facie claim on the attention of linguists, and I will show that most of these phenomena conflict with the theoretical assumptions made by the traditional view. In the fourth section I introduce a particular way of combining (radical) semantic underspecification with a theory of pragmatic strengthening. Finally, the fifth section shows that this view can be expressed very naturally by using a (bidirectional) optimality theory of interpretation.

2   The Standard View of (Lexical) Semantics

In this section I will remain neutral about what sort of thing a semantic value should be taken to be: an expression in some language of thought, a mental structure as applied in cognitive semantics or a model-theoretic construct. To be sure, there are important differences between conceptualistic accounts à la Katz and Fodor and realistic accounts as developed within model-theoretic semantics. These differences become visible, first of all, when it comes to substantiate the relationship between individual and social meaning (see Gärdenfors 1993). For the purpose of the present paper, however, the question of whether semantics is realistic or conceptualistic doesn't matter. In the following I will concentrate on some general features that can be ascribed to both accounts in their classical design. These features are not intended to completely characterize the family of theories representing the "standard view" in any sense. Rather, their selection is intended to emphasize several properties that may become problematic when a broader view of utterance meaning is taken. In sections 4 and 5, I will use these features for marking out the borderline between semantics and pragmatics.

2.1   *Systematicity and compositionality*

One nearly uncontroversial feature of our linguistic system is the systematicity of linguistic competence. According to Fodor and Pylyshyn (1988: 41–2), this feature refers to the fact that the ability to understand and produce some expressions is intrinsically connected to the speaker's ability to produce and understand other semantically related expressions. The classical solution to account for the systematicity of linguistic competence crucially makes use of the principle of compositionality. In its general form, tracing back at least to Frege (1892), this principle states the following:

(4) The meaning of a complex expression is a function of the meanings of its parts and their syntactic mode of combination.

In an approximation that is sufficient for present purposes, the principle of compositionality states that "a lexical item must make approximately the same semantic contribution to each expression in which it occurs" (Fodor and Pylyshyn 1988: 38). As a simple example consider adjective–noun combinations such as *brown cow* and *black horse*. Let's take absolute adjectives (such as *brown* and *black*) as one-place predicates. Moreover, non-relational nouns are considered as one-place predicates as well. Let's assume further that the combinatorial semantic operation that corresponds to adjectival modification is the intersection operation. Fodor and Pylyshyn (1988) conclude that these assumptions may explain the feature of systematicity in the case of adjectival modification. For example, when a person is able to understand the expressions *brown cow* and *black horse*, then she should understand the expressions *brown horse* and *black cow* as well. Note that it is the use of the intersection operation that is involved in explaining the phenomenon, not compositionality per se. Nevertheless the principle of compositionality is an important guide that helps us to find specific solutions to the puzzle of systematicity.

Lexical semantics is concerned with the meanings of the smallest parts of linguistic expressions that are assumed to bear meaning. Assumptions about the meanings of lexical units are justified empirically only insofar as they make correct predictions about the meanings of larger constituents. Consequently, though the principle of compositionality clearly goes beyond the scope of lexical semantics, it is indispensable as a methodological instrument for lexical semantics. I state the principle of compositionality as the first feature characterizing the standard view of (lexical) semantics.

2.2   *The monotonicity of inferential competence*

The SYSTEMATICITY OF INFERENCE is another important feature of the standard view that was emphasized by Fodor and Pylyshyn (1988). Having in mind the logical vocabulary of natural language, the authors stress the common claim that these elements trigger systematic inferential competences. To be accurate, the systematicity feature of inference refers to the structure-sensitivity of the inferential relation. This contrasts with ASSOCIATIONS, which are not seen as structure-sensitive. As a standard example take the rule of SIMPLIFICATION in natural deduction, which is one of two rules connected with logical conjunction:

(5)   P and Q
  ∴ P

In a conditional proof, the constituent structure of the rule proves essential. In example (5) the constituent symbols P and Q function as place holders or variables, without having any intrinsic content. This trait allows different instantiations in one and the same actual proof. For instance, when starting with the premise p&q&r, we can infer p, q, and r, inter alia, by applying the same rule (5) different times.

Why does the **content** of the premises not affect the inferences drawn? I claim that the answer to this question has to do with the more general idea of the MONOTONICITY OF INFERENTIAL COMPETENCE. Tarski (1930, 1935) was the first to state the idea of monotonicity as one of three conditions that aimed to reflect the minimal requirements which a deductive inferential relation must fulfill if it is truly to be a logical relation. In informal terms, the condition says that old theorems remain valid when the system of axioms (definitions, meaning postulates, factual knowledge) has been augmented by adding some new axioms.[2]

For the sake of illustration, assume that the "content" of the elementary expressions p, q, and r is partially described by some additional premises Π. If we add Π to the original expression p&q&r, then we expect that the "old" inferences p, q, and r remain valid – due to the monotonicity of our inferential competence. Otherwise, we could not be sure that the old inferences survive, and the content of the constituent expressions p, q, r would affect the inferential potential of the logical conjunction – a rather absurd idea. Hence, the idea that logical inferences respect this pattern of monotonicity is so natural that it may appear to be unavoidable.

We conclude that the systematicity of inferential competence is intrinsically connected with the monotonicity restriction of the inferential relation. Without this restriction the systematicity of inference can become lost for the most part. However, what is good for mathematics must not necessarily conform to the laws of cognition in the general case. The monotonicity restriction is an empirical issue concerning our inferential competence. As such it has to be carefully checked.

2.3   *The monotonicity of the lexical system*

Another general characteristic of the standard view is connected with the idea of analyzing the meanings of lexical items as a complex of more primitive elements. The main motivation for such a COMPONENTIAL ANALYSIS is connected with the explanation of such semantic relations as antonymy, synonymy, and semantic entailment. If the meaning of a lexical item were not analyzable into components, the lexical system of grammar would have to simply enumerate the actually realized relations as independent facts. This procedure would be descriptively uneconomical. More important, it would miss the point that these facts are NOT independent from each other. The componential approach can be found both in theories of meaning in generative semantics (cf. Fodor

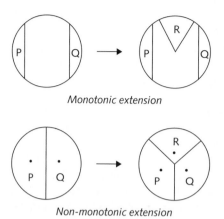

Monotonic extension

Non-monotonic extension

Figure 22.1   Monotonic and non-monotonic extensions of a (lexicalized) system of concepts

1977) and in model-theoretic based (especially Montagovian) semantic work (cf. Dowty 1979).

Defining the meaning of lexical items in terms of a repertoire of more primitive elements leads to a second-order property which I will call the MONOTONICITY OF THE LEXICAL SYSTEM. In short, this monotonicity restriction refers to the fact that we can incrementally extend the lexical system (by adding some definitions for new lexical material) without influencing the content of elements already defined.

At first glance, the monotonicity of the lexical system looks quite natural as a constraint within formal semantics. Of course, it would be very surprising if the content of . . . *is a bachelor* were to change if the system learns what a *spinster* is (by acquiring the corresponding definition). Similarly, the meaning of *prime, even, odd (number)* should be independent of whether the system knows the meaning of *rational number* or *perfect number*.[3]

It should be stressed that it is not the idea of decomposition (definition) per se that leads to the monotonicity feature of the lexical system. Instead, it is its classical treatment within a formal metalanguage that exhibits all features of a deductive system in the sense of Tarski. In this vein, the monotonicity of the lexical system can be seen as a specific realization of the more general aspect of the monotonicity of our inferential competence.

Figure 22.1 illustrates the difference between monotonic lexical systems and non-monotonic ones in a schematic way. The picture simplifies matters by identifying meanings with extensions (represented by Venn diagrams). In the case of a monotonic system, the addition of a new predicate R doesn't change the extensions of the old predicates P and Q. However, the same doesn't hold in the case of a non-monotonic system. In this case we have **field**-effects: there seem to be attracting and repelling **forces** that shift the extensions of old predicates in a particular way when new lexical material comes into play.

2.4 The persistence of anomaly

Lexical semantics has to account for semantic contradictions such as *married spinster*, *female bachelor*, *reddish green* and for other types of semantic anomalies as exemplified by the famous *Colorless green ideas sleep furiously*. Usually, SEMANTIC ANOMALY of an expression is defined as logical incompatibility of (some part of) the formal translation of the expression taken in union with a given system Γ of definitions and/or meaning postulates (e.g. McCawley 1971). Explicating incompatibility in terms of inconsistency and inconsistency in terms of contradictory entailments makes it possible to derive a second-order property which I call the PERSISTENCE OF ANOMALY.

The persistence of anomaly comes in two variants:

- if we add some new axioms to Γ, then any former anomaly persists;
- if a (propositional) formula is anomalous, then every other formula that implies it is anomalous as well.

Both varieties seem to be satisfied empirically. It would be very surprising if the anomaly of *married bachelor* could be canceled by learning the meaning of several new words. Once an anomaly is established it seems to persist when the system is extended. In a similar sense it would be perplexing if the anomaly of the expression *the idea sleeps* did not persist when the expression is made more specific, e.g. *the new idea sleeps*.

It is straightforward that the notion of semantic anomaly can be converted into a notion of pragmatic anomaly if the system Γ of axioms is assumed to include other sources of knowledge, such as conceptual and ontological knowledge. Not surprisingly, the persistence of anomaly remains in this case.

3 Challenging the Standard View

In this section, I will present several phenomena that may raise some doubts about the validity of the four principles just sketched. These phenomena suggest that we take a broader perspective on meaning and include various aspects of utterance interpretation. The examples address the whole spectrum of information shared between lexicon and encyclopedia.

3.1 The principle of compositionality

In section 2.1 we have taken adjectives like *red, interesting,* or *straight* as INTERSECTIVE adjectives, and I have illustrated how this fairly simple analysis brings together systematicity and compositionality. Unfortunately, the view that a large range of adjectives behaves intersectively has been shown to be questionable. For example, Quine (1960) notes the contrast between *red apple* (red on the outside) and *pink grapefruit* (pink on the inside), and between the different colors denoted by *red* in *red apple* and *red hair*. In a similar vein, Lahav (1989, 1993) argues that an adjective such as *brown* doesn't make a simple and fixed contribution to any composite expression in which it appears.

> In order for a cow to be brown most of its body's surface should be brown, though not its udders, eyes, or internal organs. A brown crystal, on the other hand, needs to be brown both inside and outside. A book is brown if its cover, but not necessarily its inner pages, are mostly brown, while a newspaper is brown only if all its pages are brown. For a potato to be brown it needs to be brown only outside . . . Furthermore, in order for a cow or a bird to be brown the brown color should be the animal's natural color, since it is regarded as being 'really' brown even if it is painted white all over. A table, on the other hand, is brown even if it is only painted brown and its 'natural' color underneath the paint is, say, yellow. But while a table or a bird are not brown if covered with brown sugar, a cookie is. In short, what is to be brown is different for different types of objects. To be sure, brown objects do have something in common: a salient part that is wholly brownish. But this hardly suffices for an object to count as brown. A significant component of the applicability condition of the predicate 'brown' varies from one linguistic context to another.   (Lahav 1993: 76)

Some authors – for example, Keenan (1974), Partee (1984a), Lahav (1989, 1993) – conclude from facts of this kind that the simplistic view mentioned above must be abolished. As suggested by Montague (1970), Keenan (1974), Kamp (1975), and others, there is a simple solution that addresses such facts in a descriptive way and obeys the principle of compositionality. This solution considers adjectives essentially to be adnominal functors. Such functors, for example, turn the properties expressed by *apple* into those expressed by *red apple*. Of course, such functors have to be defined disjunctively in the manner illustrated in (6):

(6)   **RED(X)** means roughly the property
    a.   of having a red inner volume if X denotes fruits whose inside only is edible;
    b.   of having a red surface if X denotes fruits whose outside is edible;
    c.   of having a functional part that is red if X denotes tools.

Let us call this the FUNCTIONAL VIEW. It should be stressed that the functional view describes the facts mentioned above only by enumeration. Consequently, it doesn't account for any kind of systematicity concerning our competence to deal with adjective–noun combinations in an interesting way. Another (notorious) problem with this view has to do with the treatment of predicatively used adjectives. In that case the adjectives must at least implicitly be supplemented by a noun. Various artificial assumptions are necessary which make such a theory inappropriate. We may conclude that compositionality doesn't necessarily lead to systematicity.

There is a third view about treating the meanings of adjectives, which I call the FREE VARIABLE VIEW. In a certain sense, this view can be seen as preserving the advantages of both the simplistic as well as the functional view, but as overcoming their shortcomings. The free variable view has been developed in considerable detail for the gradable adjectives (see Bierwisch 1989 and the references given therein). It is well known that the applicability conditions of restricting adjectives that denote gradable properties, such as *tall, high, long, short, quick, intelligent* vary depending upon the type of object to which they apply. What is high for a chair is not high for a tower and what is clever for a young child is not clever for an adult. Oversimplifying, I can state the free variable view as follows. Similar to the first view, the meanings of adjectives are taken to be one-place predicates. But now we assume that these predicates are complex expressions that contain a free variable. Using an extensional language allowing λ-abstraction, we can represent the adjective *long* (in its contrastive interpretation), for example, as λx LONG(x, X), denoting the class of objects that are long with regard to a comparison class, which is indicated by the free variable X. At least on the representational level the predicative and the attributive use of adjectives can be treated as in the first view: *The train is long* translates (after λ-conversion) to LONG(**t**, X) and *long train* translates to λx [LONG(x, X) $\wedge$ T(x)]. In these formulas **t** is a term denoting a specific train and T refers to the predicate of being a train.

Free variables are the main instrument for forming underspecified lexical representations. To be sure, free variables simply have the status of place holders for more elaborated subpatterns and expressions containing free variables should be explained as representational schemes. Free variables stand not only as place holders for a comparison class X as just indicated. The view can be generalized to include other types of free variables as well, for example a type of variable connected with the specification of the dimension of evaluation in cases of adjectives such as *good* and *bad* or a type of variable connected with the determination of the object-dependent spatial dimensions in cases of spatial adjectives such as *wide* and *deep*.

Of course, it is not sufficient to postulate underspecified lexical representations and to indicate what the sets of semantically possible specifications of the variables are. In order to grasp natural language interpretation ("conceptual interpretation"), it is also required to provide a proper account of contextual enrichment, explaining how the free variables are instantiated in the appropriate way. Obviously, such a mechanism has to take into consideration various aspects of world and discourse knowledge.

In some particular cases the instantiation of free variables may be done by using ordinary (monotonic) unification. If that works successfully, it may be concluded that the mechanism of contextual enrichment has the feature of compositionality. In other words, the principle of compositionality stated for semantic representations can be transferred to the level of contextually enriched forms. In Blutner (1998), I consider some examples that demonstrate that monotonic unification doesn't suffice for contextual enrichment.

There are a variety of other examples that demonstrate that our comprehension capacities have salient non-compositional aspects. The most prominent class of examples may be found within the area of SYSTEMATIC POLYSEMY. This term refers to the phenomenon of one lexical unit being associated with a whole range of senses which are related to each other in a systematic way. The phenomenon has traditionally been thought intractable, and in fact it IS intractable when considered as a problem of lexical semantics in the traditional sense. Related problems with compositionality arise when considering word formation in general (e.g. Aronoff 1976, Bauer 1983) and the interpretation of compounds in particular (e.g. Wu 1990).

3.2   *The non-monotonicity of invited inferences*

It was the evident divergence between the formal devices ~, ∧, ∨, ⊃, (∀x), (∃x) (in their standard two-valued interpretation) and their natural language counterparts that was the starting point of Grice's "logic of conversation" (Grice 1967; see Bach and Horn, this volume). In subsequent work these divergences were investigated carefully from an empirical and a theoretical point of view, sometimes adopting Grice's conceptual framework and sometimes rejecting it. For example, Geis and Zwicky (1971) introduced and discussed the inference scheme they dubbed CONDITIONAL PERFECTION, the notorious tendency to "perfect" an *if* conditional into the corresponding biconditional (*if and only if, iff*). As an example, the utterance of (7a) was claimed to invite the inference of (7b), thus conveying the utterance meaning of (7c).

(7)a.   If you mow the lawn, I'll give you \$5.
  b.   If you don't mow the lawn, I won't give you \$5.
  c.   If and only if you mow the lawn, I'll give you \$5.

In order to account for such inferences, it may be appealing to use rules in the style of natural deduction. For example, we could introduce an inference rule like the following:

(8)   if (P, Q)
   ∴ if(~P, ~Q)

Obviously, (8) can be seen as instantiating the inference from (7a) to (7b). However, in contrast to inference rules like **modus ponens** or **simplification**, the structure-sensitivity of which is never violated (see section 2.2), the same doesn't hold for the schema (8). This was demonstrated by many authors (for a recent survey see Horn 2000a). The following examples show situations where the corresponding inferences cannot be drawn:

(9)a.   If John quits, he will be replaced.
  b.   If John doesn't quit, he won't be replaced.
  c.   If and only if John quits, he will be replaced.

(10)a.   If you're in Toronto, you are in Canada.
   b.   If you're not in Toronto, you're not in Canada.
   c.   If and only if you're in Toronto, you are in Canada.

There are at least three different strategies for dealing with this observation. The first one is to assume a lexical ambiguity of *if* stipulating two readings: the standard reading and the biconditional reading. The second strategy is to doubt that the tendency of drawing invited inferences in the sense of Geis and Zwicky is a real one, and it aims to reduce the relevant observation exclusively to language-independent factors. The third strategy accepts the reality of these inferences, and, at the same time, acknowledges the non-monotonicity of (parts of) our inferential competence. After pointing out that all three strategies are represented in the literature, Horn (2000a) demonstrates that the third strategy is the most promising one. What's more, he suggests clarifying the strategy in terms of a non-monotonic operation of pragmatic strengthening[4] – a suggestion I want to follow in the theoretical part of this chapter (sections 4 and 5.)

Negation in natural language is a rich source of a variety of non-logical inferences (see Horn 1989). Standard examples are SCALAR IMPLICATURES (*Not all of the students came* ≈> *Some of them came*). Others are collected under the term NEGATIVE STRENGTHENING.[5] The latter are concerned with the effect of preferred interpretations that occurs when certain sentence types are negated. In section 5 they are used to explain the basic mechanisms of pragmatic strengthening.

One instance of the phenomenon of negative strengthening arises in connection with gradable adjectives typically occurring as antonyms, such as {*good, bad*}, {*large, small*}, {*happy, unhappy*}. Semantically, the elements of antonym pairs are CONTRARIES, that is, they are mutually inconsistent but do not exhaust the whole spectrum, permitting a non-empty middle ground.

What are the effects of negating gradable adjectives? For the sake of explicitness let's consider the gradable antonyms *happy* and *unhappy*, and assume three possible states of happiness – iconized by ☺, ☹, and ☺. Not unexpectedly, we want to take *happy* as referring to the first state, *unhappy* as referring to the second state, and *neither happy nor unhappy* as referring to the third state.

Let's consider first the effect of negating positive adjectives, starting with a sentence like (11a). Obviously, the preferred interpretation of this sentence is (11c); this corresponds to a logical strengthening of the content of (11a), which is paraphrased in (11b). The discourse (11d) shows that the effect of strengthening (11c) is defeasible. This indicates that the inferential notion that underlies the phenomenon of strengthening ought to be non-monotonic.

(11)a.   I'm not happy
   b.   It isn't the case that I'm happy   **(Entailment)** ☹ ☺
   c.   I'm unhappy   **(Implicature)** ☹
   d.   I'm not happy and not unhappy   **(Defeasibility)**

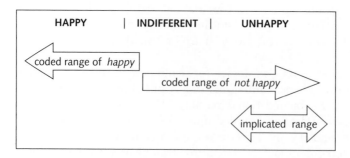

Figure 22.2   Negative strengthening as implicated contraries

Following Levinson (2000a), the effect of negative strengthening for positive adjectives can be illustrated as shown in figure 22.2. It describes the effect of negative strengthening as implicating contraries from contradictions.

The illustrated shape of negative strengthening is restricted to the positive (unmarked) element of an antonym pair. When considering negative adjectives, deviations from this pattern may be found. The deviations are rather obvious for adjectives with incorporated affixal negation. This leads us to the well-known case of double negation (*litotes*):

(12)a.   I'm not unhappy
    b.   It isn't the case that I'm unhappy   **(Entailment)** ☺ ☹
    c.   I'm neither happy nor unhappy   **(Implicature)** ☹
    d.   I'm rather happy (but not quite as happy as   **(proper Implicature)**
        using the expression "*happy*" would suggest)
    e.   I'm not unhappy, in fact I'm happy   **(Defeasibility)**

Admitting only three states on the happiness scale allows only a rather rough approximation of the interpretational effects. The simplest approximation describes negative strengthening as a preference for the middle ground. This is what (12c) expresses. A more appropriate formulation of the effect is given in (12d). For the sake of precision, we had to introduce intermediate states between ☺ and ☹ (on the scale of happiness). In figure 22.3 a more adequate

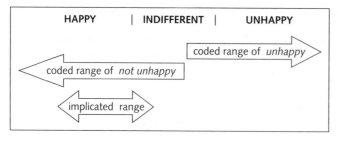

Figure 22.3   Litotes: when two negatives don't make a positive

illustration of the basic pattern is presented (as described in Horn 1989, 1991a, Levinson 2000a.) As in the case discussed before, the effect of negative strengthening proves defeasible, a fact that requires the underlying inferential notion to be non-monotonic.

The theoretical discussion of the phenomenon of negative strengthening is postponed until section 5, where the inspirational ideas of Horn and Levinson will be outlined and a formal account of their ideas will be given in terms of optimality theory.

3.3 The non-monotonicity of the lexical system

Another general problem that lexical semantics has to address is the phenomenon of LEXICAL BLOCKING. This phenomenon has been demonstrated in a number of examples, where the appropriate use of a given expression formed by a relatively productive process is restricted by the existence of a more "lexicalized" alternative to this expression. One case in point was provided by Householder (1971). The adjective *pale* can be combined with a great many color words: *pale green, pale blue, pale yellow*. However, the combination *pale red* is limited in a way that the other combinations are not. For some speakers *pale red* is simply anomalous, and for others it picks up whatever part of the pale domain of red *pink* has not pre-empted. This suggests that the combinability of *pale* is fully or partially blocked by the lexical alternative *pink*.

Another standard example is the phenomenon of blocking in the context of derivational and inflectional morphological processes. Aronoff (1976) has shown that the existence of a simple lexical item can block the formation of an otherwise expected affixally derived form synonymous with it. In particular, the existence of a simple abstract nominal underlying a given *-ous* adjective blocks its nominalization with *-ity*:

(13) a.   curious – curiosity
           tenacious – tenacity
  b.   furious – *furiosity – fury
           fallacious – *fallacity – fallacy

While Aronoff's formulation of blocking was limited to derivational processes, Kiparsky (1982) notes that blocking may also extend to inflectional processes and he suggests a reformulation of Aronoff's blocking as a subcase of the ELSEWHERE CONDITION: special rules block general rules in their shared domain. However, Kiparsky cites examples of PARTIAL BLOCKING in order to show that this formulation is too strong. According to Kiparsky, partial blocking corresponds to the phenomenon that the special (less productive) affix occurs in some restricted meaning and the general (more productive) affix picks up the remaining meaning (consider examples like *refrigerant – refrigerator, informant – informer, contestant – contester*). To handle these and other cases Kiparsky (1983) formulates a general condition which he calls AVOID SYNONYMY: "The output of a lexical rule may not be synonymous with an existing lexical item."

Working independently of the Aronoff–Kiparsky line, McCawley (1978) collects a number of further examples demonstrating the phenomenon of partial blocking outside the domain of derivational and inflectional processes. For example, he observes that the distribution of productive causatives (in English, Japanese, German, and other languages) is restricted by the existence of a corresponding lexical causative. Whereas lexical causatives (e.g. (14a)) tend to be restricted in their distribution to the stereotypic causative situation (direct, unmediated causation through physical action), productive (periphrastic) causatives tend to pick up more marked situations of mediated, indirect causation. For example, (14b) could be used appropriately when Black Bart caused the sheriff's gun to backfire by stuffing it with cotton.

(14)a.   Black Bart killed the sheriff.
    b.   Black Bart caused the sheriff to die.

The phenomenon of blocking can be taken as evidence demonstrating the apparent non-monotonicity of the lexical system. This becomes pretty clear when we take an ontogenetic perspective on the development of the lexical system. Children overgeneralize at some stage while developing their lexical system. For example, they acquire the productive rule of deriving deverbal adjectives with *-able* and apply this rule to produce *washable, breakable, readable,* but also *seeable* and *hearable*. Only later, after paired forms like *seeable/visible* and *hearable/audible* have coexisted for a while, will the meanings of the specialized items block the regularly derived forms. Examples of this kind suggest that the development of word meanings cannot be described as a process of accumulating more and more denotational knowledge in a monotonic way. Instead, there are highly non-monotonic stages in lexical development. At the moment, it is not clear whether this ontogenetic feature must be reflected in the logical structure of the mental lexicon. Rather, it is possible that pragmatic factors (such as Gricean rules of conversation) play an important role in determining which possible words are actual and what they really denote (McCawley 1978, Dowty 1979, Horn 1984a).

3.4   The non-persistence of (pragmatic) anomaly

Take the well-known phenomenon of CONCEPTUAL GRINDING, whereby ordinary count nouns acquire a mass noun reading denoting the stuff the individual objects are made of, as in *Fish is on the table* or *Dog is all over the street*. There are several factors that determine whether grinding may apply, and, more specifically, what kind of grinding (meat grinding, fur grinding, universe grinding, . . .) may apply. Some of these factors have to do with the conceptual system, while others are language-dependent (cf. Nunberg and Zaenen 1992, Copestake and Briscoe 1995).

One of the language-dependent factors affecting the grinding mechanism is lexical blocking. For example, in English the specialized mass terms *pork, beef, wood* usually block the grinding mechanism in connection with the count nouns *pig, cow, tree*. This explains the contrasts given in (15).

(15)a. I ate pork/?pig
   b. Some people do not eat beef/?cow
   c. The table is made of wood/?tree

The important point is the observation that blocking is not absolute but may be canceled under special contextual conditions. That is, we find cases of DEBLOCKING. Nunberg and Zaenen (1992) consider the following example:

(16) Hindus are forbidden to eat cow/?beef

They argue that "what makes *beef* odd here is that the interdiction concerns the status of the animal as a whole, and not simply its meat. That is, Hindus are forbidden to eat beef only because it is cow-stuff." (Nunberg and Zaenen 1992: 391). Examples of this kind strongly suggest that the blocking phenomenon is pragmatic in nature. Furthermore, these examples suggest that (pragmatic) anomaly does not necessarily persist when specific contextual information is added. Copestake and Briscoe (1995) provide further examples that substantiate this claim.

4 Conversational Implicature and Lexical Pragmatics

For Griceans, conversational implicatures are those non-truth-functional aspects of utterance interpretation which are conveyed by virtue of the assumption that the speaker and the hearer are obeying the COOPERATIVE PRINCIPLE of conversation, and, more specifically, various CONVERSATIONAL MAXIMS of quantity, quality, relation, and manner. While the notion of conversational implicature doesn't seem hard to grasp intuitively, it has proven difficult to define precisely. An important step in reducing and explicating the Gricean framework has been made by Atlas and Levinson (1981) and Horn (1984a). Taking Quantity as a starting point they distinguish between two principles, the Q principle and the I principle (termed the R principle by Horn 1984a). Simple informal formulations of these principles are as follows:

Q principle:
- Say as much as you can (given I) (Horn 1984a: 13)
- Make your contribution as informative (strong) as possible (Matsumoto 1995: 23)
- Do not provide a statement that is informationally weaker than your knowledge of the world allows, unless providing a stronger statement would contravene the I principle (Levinson 1987b: 401)

I principle:
- Don't say more than you must (given Q) (Horn 1984a: 13)
- Say as little as necessary, i.e. produce the minimal linguistic information sufficient to achieve your communicational ends (bearing the Q principle in mind) (Levinson 1987b: 402)
- Read as much into an utterance as is consistent with what you know about the world (Levinson 1983: 146–7)

Obviously, the Q principle corresponds to the first part of Grice's quantity maxim (*Make your contribution as informative as required*), while it is argued (cf. Horn 1989, 1993) that the countervailing I principle collects the second part of the quantity maxim (*Do not make your contribution more informative than is required*), the maxim of relation and at least two of the manner submaxims, "Be brief" and "Be orderly." As Horn (1984a) seeks to demonstrate, the two principles can be seen as representing two competing forces, one force of *unification* minimizing the Speaker's effort (I principle), and one force of *diversification* minimizing the Auditor's effort (Q principle).

Conversational implicatures which are derivable essentially by appeal to the Q principle are called Q-based implicatures. Standard examples are scalar implicatures and clausal implicatures. I-based implicatures, derivable essentially by appeal to the I principle, can be generally characterized as enriching what is said via inference to a rich, stereotypical interpretation (cf. Gazdar 1979, Atlas and Levinson 1981, Horn 1984a, Levinson 2000a).

In my opinion, the proper treatment of conversational implicature crucially depends on the proper formulation of the Q and the I principle. The present explication (cf. Blutner 1998) rests on the assumption that the semantic description of an utterance is an underspecified representation f determining a wide range of possible enrichments m, one of which covers the intended content. There are different possibilities to make explicit what possible enrichments are: the idea of abductive specification may be useful (e.g. Hobbs et al. 1993), and likewise the idea of non-monotonic unification (e.g. Lascarides et al. 1995). Both mechanisms make use of the notion of *common ground*, which informally can be introduced as an information state containing all the propositions shared by several participants, including general world and discourse knowledge. I will not be very specific about the device that generates possible enrichments. For the sake of convenience, I simply assume a function **Gen** that determines for each common ground σ what the possible enrichments of f are. In other words,

(17) $\langle f, m \rangle$ is called a **possible enrichment pair** (or *pep*) iff $\langle f, m \rangle \in \mathbf{Gen}_\sigma$, i.e. m can be generated from f by means of a common ground σ.

The other important component that is necessary to reconstruct the essence of conversational implicature is the evaluation component. It evaluates *peps* and typically is defined by a cost function $\underline{c}(f, m)$ (cf. Blutner 1998). For example, in weighted abduction (Hobbs et al. 1993) this function reflects the *proof* cost for deriving an interpretation *m* from the underspecified form f.[6] For the present aims it is not necessary to have the numerical values of this cost function. What is sufficient is an ORDERING RELATION > (*being more harmonic, being more economical*) defined on the *peps*.[7] To be sure, the concrete realization of this ordering relation relates to a variety of different graded factors such as informativity, relevance, and effort, and is a matter for empirical investigation (cf. Ducrot 1972, Merin 1999, van Rooy 2000, 2004a)

In Blutner (1998) it is pointed out that the effect of the Gricean maxims is simply to constrain the relation defined by **Gen** in a particular way. In short, the Q and the I principle can be seen as conditions constraining possible enrichment pairs ⟨*f*, *m*⟩. The precise formulation assumes the availability of the (partial) ordering > and formulates a two-way optimization procedure:

(18)a. ⟨*f*, *m*⟩ satisfies the Q principle iff ⟨*f*, *m*⟩ ∈ **Gen**$_\sigma$ and there is no other pair ⟨*f'*, *m*⟩ such that ⟨*f'*, *m*⟩ > ⟨*f*, *m*⟩

b. ⟨*f*, *m*⟩ satisfies the I principle iff ⟨*f*, *m*⟩ ∈ **Gen**$_\sigma$ and there is no other pair ⟨*f*, *m'*⟩ such that ⟨*f*, *m'*⟩ > ⟨*f*, *m*⟩[8]

In this (rather symmetrical) formulation, the Q and the I principle constrain the *peps* in two different ways. The I principle constrains them by selecting the most economic/harmonic enrichments, and the Q principle constrains them by blocking those enrichments which can be grasped more economically/harmonically by an alternative linguistic input *f'*. Obviously, it is the Q principle that carries the main burden in explaining the blocking effects discussed in section 3.2.

The important definitions of pragmatic anomaly and conversational implicature can be stated as follows, making use of an auxiliary notion called PRAGMATIC LICENSING:

(19)a. A *pep* ⟨*f*, *m*⟩ is called **pragmatically licensed** (in a common ground σ) iff ⟨*f*, *m*⟩ satisfies the Q and the I principle and *m* is consistent with σ.

b. An utterance that corresponds to the (underspecified) semantic form *f* is called **pragmatically anomalous** (in σ) iff there is no pragmatically licensed *pep* ⟨*f*, *m*⟩.

c. A proposition *p* is called a **conversational implicature** of *f* (in σ) iff *p* is a classical consequence of σ∪*m* for each *m* of a pragmatically licensed *pep* ⟨*f*, *m*⟩.

It is not difficult to see how the general mechanism of conversational implicature introduced in (19) reflects the four features/phenomena repeated here for convenience:

- the non-compositional aspect of utterance interpretation;
- the non-monotonicity of conversational implicature;
- the phenomena of blocking and deblocking;
- the general fact that pragmatic anomalies usually don't persist.

First, let's consider compositionality. Almost everything in the formulation of conversational implicature has a non-compositional character: the formulation of both the Q principle and the I principle is *holistic* in addressing a wide range of alternative expressions; the conceptions of informativeness, surprise (measured in terms of conditional probability), and linguistic complexity are non-combinatorial and cannot be reduced to the corresponding properties of the parts of an expression (cf. Blutner 1998).

Next, our system deals with non-monotonicity by basing the notion of conversational implicature on preferred interpretations (via the optimization of *peps*). It is the old insight of McCarthy (1980), Shoham (1988), and others that the idea of preferred interpretations establishes a non-monotonic (cumulative) inferential relation.

Third, our system deals with blocking and deblocking. The crucial mechanism involved is due to the Q principle. In the same way, the present system captures the field effects, which are very important if the extensions of lexical concepts are considered.

The fourth and last point concerns the persistence of anomalies. The general definition of pragmatic anomaly doesn't simply define this notion as some kind of inconsistency. Instead, non-representational parameters (such as surprise, cue validity, relevance, frequency of use, etc.) are crucially involved in controlling the selection and suppression of possible enrichments. Within this setting, typically some kind of garden-path effect may arise. This constitutes pragmatic anomaly (Blutner 1998).

5   Optimality Theory and Lexical Pragmatics

The situated meanings of many words and simple phrases are combinations of their lexical meanings proper and some superimposed conversational implicatures. In the previous sections we have suggested representing lexical meanings by means of underspecified forms and taking compositionality, monotonicity, and the persistence of anomaly as bounding the domain of semantics proper. On the other hand, a mechanism of pragmatic strengthening was suggested which crucially makes use of non-representational parameters that are described by a certain ordering relation. It is the use of an optimization procedure that gives pragmatics its holistic flourish, systematically destroys the listed features, and relegates them to the level of semantics proper.

Before we come to the treatment of examples, we will show the close relationship between the formulation of pragmatic strengthening given in the previous section and recent developments in OPTIMALITY THEORY (OT).

5.1 *Bidirectional OT and pragmatic strengthening*

OT is a linguistic framework that is not only of interest to phonologists but has likewise attracted students of morphology, syntax, and natural language interpretation. As pointed out by Anttila and Fong (2000), current work in optimality theoretic syntax and semantics has been concerned with two closely related questions:

- OT syntax: Given a semantic input, what is its optimal expression?
- OT semantics: Given a syntactic input, what is its optimal interpretation?

OT syntax takes the point of view of the speaker (the EXPRESSIVE perspective): given a semantic input, the goal is to select the optimal syntactic expression for this input among a well-defined set of candidate expressions (see e.g. Grimshaw 1997, Bresnan 2001). OT semantics takes the point of view of the hearer (the INTERPRETIVE perspective): given a syntactic input, the goal is to select the optimal semantic interpretation among a set of candidate interpretations (see e.g. de Hoop and de Swart 1998, Hendriks and de Hoop (2001), de Hoop 2000). In Blutner (1999) I argue that this design of OT – taking the different perspectives isolated from each other – is inappropriate and too weak in a number of cases. What I proposed is bidirectional optimization, where both types of optimization are carried out simultaneously.

The formulation of the Q and I principle in (18) makes it quite clear that a bidirectional optimality framework – integrating expressive (Q) and interpretive (I) optimization – is an appropriate tool to reconstruct the Gricean mechanism of pragmatic strengthening.[9] Consider the following conception of OPTIMAL form-meaning pairs, which is a straightforward reformulation of (18). It is dubbed the STRONG version of bidirectional OT.

(20) **Bidirectional OT** (strong version)
A form-meaning pair $\langle f, m \rangle$ is called **optimal** iff $\langle f, m \rangle \in \textbf{Gen}_\sigma$ and

    (Q)   there is no other pair $\langle f', m \rangle$ such that $\langle f', m \rangle > \langle f, m \rangle$
    (I)   there is no other pair $\langle f, m' \rangle$ such that $\langle f, m' \rangle > \langle f, m \rangle$

The crucial notion of PRAGMATICALLY LICENSED *pep*s (19a) now transforms into

(19)a′.   A *pep* $\langle f, m \rangle$ is called **pragmatically licensed** (in a common ground σ) iff $\langle f, m \rangle$ is optimal and m is consistent with σ.

At first glance, using the bidirectional competition technique can be seen as just establishing the very same ideas presented in Blutner (1998) by means of a more broadly acknowledged and more well-known basis. However, that is not the whole story. We have to acknowledge that the framework of OT gives us a much wider perspective for relating natural language comprehension, language acquisition (Tesar and Smolensky 2000), and language change (e.g. Haspelmath 1999b). Furthermore, there are important explorations concerning the concrete realization of the (harmonic) ordering relation (e.g. Zeevat 1999a, b, Aissen 2000, Beaver 2000). Taking the broader perspective and the more rigorous formalization, the use of OT may give the enterprise of Radical Pragmatics in general, and Lexical Pragmatics in particular, a new impulse.

In standard OT the ordering relation between elements of the generator is established via a system of ranked constraints. These constraints are typically assumed to be output constraints, i.e. they may be either satisfied or violated by an output form. In the bidirectional framework changing perspectives are possible. This means that an output under one perspective can be seen as an input under the other perspective. Therefore, it is plausible to assume output AND input constraints. Seeing the input as a linguistic form that conveys phonological, syntactic, and semantic information, constraints on inputs are typically markedness conditions evaluating the HARMONY of forms. On the other hand, the output (i.e. the result of contextual enriching) is evaluated by constraints that determine its coherence and informativeness (with regard to a context σ).

I will now give a very schematic example in order to illustrate some characteristics of bidirectional OT. Assume that we have two forms f_1 and f_2 which are semantically equivalent. This means that **Gen** associates the same meanings with them, say m_1 and m_2. We stipulate that the form f_1 is less complex (marked) than the form f_2 and that the interpretation m_1 is less complex (marked) than the interpretation m_2. From these differences of markedness with regard to the levels of syntactic forms/semantic interpretations, the following ordering relation between form-meaning pairs can be derived:

(21) a. $\langle f_1, m_1 \rangle > \langle f_2, m_1 \rangle$
   b. $\langle f_1, m_2 \rangle > \langle f_2, m_2 \rangle$
   c. $\langle f_1, m_1 \rangle > \langle f_1, m_2 \rangle$
   d. $\langle f_2, m_1 \rangle > \langle f_2, m_2 \rangle$

Using Dekker's and van Rooy's (1999) notation, a bidirectional OT diagram can be construed, nicely representing the preferences between the pairs (the arrows point to the preferred pair.) More importantly, such diagrams give an intuitive visualization for the optimal pairs of (strong) bidirectional OT: they are simply the hollows if we follow the arcs.[10] The optimal pairs are marked with the symbol ✌ in the diagram.

(22)

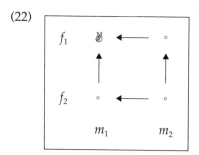

The scenario just installed describes the case of **total** blocking, where some forms (e.g. **furiosity*, **fallacity*) do not exist because others do (*fury, fallacy*). However, as noted in section 3.3, blocking is not always total but may be **partial**, in that only those interpretations of a form are ruled out that are pre-empted by a "cheaper" competing form.

Cases of total and partial blocking are not only found in morphology, but in syntax and semantics as well (cf. Atlas and Levinson 1981, Horn 1984a, Williams 1997). The general tendency of partial blocking seems to be that "unmarked forms tend to be used for unmarked situations and marked forms for marked situations" (Horn 1984a: 26) – a tendency that Horn terms the DIVISION OF PRAGMATIC LABOR (see Horn, this volume).

We have seen that the strong form of bidirectionality describes total blocking and doesn't account for partial blocking. There are two principal possibilities for avoiding the fatal consequences of total blocking. The first possibility is to make some stipulations concerning **Gen** in order to exclude equivalent semantic forms. The second possibility is to weaken the notion of (strong) optimality in a way that allows us to derive Horn's division of pragmatic labor in a principled way by means of a sophisticated optimization procedure.

In Blutner (1998, 1999) I argue that the second option is much more practicable and theoretically interesting. I proposed a recursive variant of bidirectional optimization (also called WEAK bidirection), which was subsequently simplified by Jäger (2000). Here is Jäger's formulation:

(23) **Bidirectional OT** (weak version)
      A form-meaning pair $\langle f, m \rangle$ is called **super-optimal** iff $\langle f, m \rangle \in$ **Gen**$_\sigma$ and

      (Q)   there is no other super-optimal pair $\langle f', m \rangle : \langle f', m \rangle > \langle f, m \rangle$
      (I)   there is no other super-optimal pair $\langle f, m' \rangle : \langle f, m' \rangle > \langle f, m \rangle$

Under the assumption that $>$ is transitive and well-founded, Jäger (2000) proved that (23) is a sound recursive definition and he showed its equivalence with the formulation in Blutner (1998, 1999). In addition, he proved that each pair that is **optimal** (strong bidirection) is **super-optimal** (weak bidirection) as well, but not vice versa. Hence, weak bidirection gives us a chance to find additional super-optimal solutions. For example, weak bidirection allows marked expressions to have an optimal interpretation, although both the expression and the situations they describe have a more efficient counterpart. To make this point clear, consider again the situation illustrated in (22), but now applying the weak version of bidirectional optimization as demonstrated in the diagram (24). In order to make things more concrete we can take f_1 to be the lexical causative form (14a), f_2 the periphrastic form (14b), m_1 direct (stereotypic) causation and m_2 indirect causation.

(24)

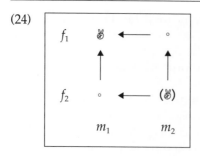

The solution $\langle f_1, m_1 \rangle$ comes out as the strong solution and can be taken as the initial point of recursion. The pairs $\langle f_1, m_2 \rangle$ and $\langle f_2, m_1 \rangle$, respectively, are both blocked by this solution.

We have seen that the **strong** version cannot explain why the marked form f_2 has an interpretation. The **weak** version, however, can explain this fact. Moreover, it explains that the marked form f_2 gets the atypical interpretation m_2. This comes out since the pair $\langle f_2, m_2 \rangle$ is **super-optimal** according to definition (23): It is never blocked by another super-optimal pair.[11] In this way, the weak version of bidirection accounts for Horn's "division of pragmatic labor." Jäger (2000) has shown that this pattern can be generalized to systems where more than two forms are associated by **Gen** with more than two interpretations. In the general case, we start by determining the optimal pairs. Then we drop the rows and columns corresponding to the optimal pair(s) and apply the same procedure to the reduced tableau.[12]

5.2   *Negative strengthening*

In section 3.2 a concise description of the phenomenon of negative strengthening was given. Now I will bring this phenomenon into play in order to illustrate the general mechanism of pragmatic strengthening, which is formulated by using the method of bidirectional optimization.

In the analysis of Horn (1989) and Levinson (2000a) there are some types of negative strengthening that are obviously attributable to the I/R principle. A clear case is the negation of positive adjectives, which was described in connection with example (11). Here the I/R principle leads to a pragmatic strengthening effect excluding the middle ground and implying the contrary.

The situation is not so clear in the case of adjectives with incorporated affixal negation such as in example (12). Whereas Horn (1984a, 1989) attributes the observed effect of negative strengthening to the interaction between Q and R, Levinson stipulates a third pragmatic principle, the M(anner) principle: "what's said in an abnormal way, isn't normal; or marked message indicates marked situation" (Levinson 2000a: 33). Obviously, this principle expresses the second half of Horn's division of pragmatic labor (see also Horn 1991a on double negation and the division of pragmatic labor).[13]

Let's see now how bidirectional OT accounts for the effects of negative streng-thening. The bidirectional tableau (28) shows the competing candidate forms in the left column. (Take the candidate entries as shortcuts for complete sen-tences; for example take *happy* as abbreviating *I'm happy*, etc.). The other columns are for the three possible states of happiness considered in this simplified analysis. The gray areas in the tableau indicate which form-interpretation pairs are excluded by the compositional mode of truth-functional semantics. For example, *I'm not unhappy* is assumed to exclude the state iconized by ☹.

(25)

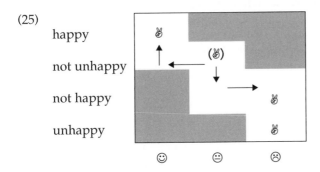

The preferences between the form-interpretation pairs are due to marked-ness constraints for forms and markedness constraints for interpretations, respectively.

With regard to the forms, we simply assume that the number of negation morphemes is the crucial indicator. The corresponding preferences are indic-ated by the vertical arrows. (Note that *not happy* and *unhappy* aren't differen-tiated in terms of markedness – a rough simplification, of course.)

With regard to the states, we assume that they are decreasing in marked-ness towards both ends of the scale, assigning maximal markedness to the middle ground. Although this assumption seems not implausible from a psycholinguistic perspective, I cannot provide independent evidence for it at the moment. In (25), the corresponding preferences are indicated by the horizontal arrows.

Now it is a simple exercise to find out the optimal solutions – indicated by ✌. One optimal solution pairs the sentence *I'm not happy* with the interpreta-tion ☹. This solution corresponds to the effect of negative strengthening that is attributable to the I/R principle. The other two optimal solutions reflect the truth conditions of *I'm happy/unhappy*.

Most interesting, there is an additional super-optimal solution, indicated by (✌). It pairs the sentence *I'm not unhappy* with the interpretation ☺. This corres-ponds to the effect of negative strengthening in the case of LITOTES, normally attributed to Levinson's (2000a) M principle or Horn's division of pragmatic labor (cf. Horn 1991a). As already stressed, this solution comes out as a natural consequence of the weak form of bidirection, which can be seen as a formal way of describing the interactions between Q and I/R.

It's an interesting exercise to introduce more than three states of happiness and to verify that the proper shape of implicature, as indicated in figure 22.3, can be approximated. More importantly, in the context of litotes it seems necessary to account for the effect of gradient acceptability and continuous scales. Using a stochastic evaluation procedure, Boersma (1998) and Boersma and Hayes (2001) did pioneering work in this field, which should be exploited in the present case.

The other prominent class of examples that exhibit the effect of negative strengthening concerns the phenomenon of neg-raising, i.e. the tendency for negative main sentences with subordinate clauses to be read as negations of the subordinate clause (cf. Horn 1989, Levinson 2000a). It seems fruitful to analyze the phenomenon using the same technique as described above.

6   Conclusions

Investigating the interactions between the (mental) lexicon and pragmatics, we have pointed out that situated meanings of many words and simple phrases are combinations of their lexical meanings proper and some superimposed conversational implicatures. In particular, we have suggested representing lexical meanings by means of underspecified forms and using compositionality, monotonicity, and the persistence of anomaly for demarcating the borderline between semantics proper and pragmatics. A mechanism of pragmatic strengthening was suggested which crucially makes use of "non-representational" parameters that are described by preferential relations, such as information scales or salience orderings. The basic pragmatic mechanism can be expressed within the framework of bidirectional OT.

This approach may provide a principled account of several lexical-pragmatic phenomena that are currently being investigated: negative strengthening for graded antonym pairs (Horn 1989, Levinson 2000a), the effects of neg-raising (Horn 1989), the pragmatics of adjectives (Lahav 1993, Blutner 1998), the distribution of lexical and productive causatives (McCawley 1978, Horn 1984a), the pragmatics of dimensional designation (Blutner and Solstad 2000), the interpretation of compounds (Meyer 1993) and many phenomena presently discussed within the framework of Cognitive Semantics.

The main advantage of bidirectional OT is that it helps us to put in concrete terms what the **requisites** are for explaining the peculiarities of negative strengthening, neg-raising, and the other phenomena under discussion. What are the relevant cognitive scales? How do we measure morpho-syntactic markedness? How do we measure the values of probabilistic parameters that control and organize conceptual knowledge (salience, cue validity)? The latter proves essential when it comes to considering word formation and the investigation of different types of polysemy.

An important challenge for the present view is the work done in relevance theory (e.g. Sperber and Wilson 1986a, Carston 1998b, 1999, this volume).

Although I prefer a variant of Atlas's, Levinson's, and Horn's frameworks, that doesn't mean that I am taking a stand against relevance theory. Rather, it seems desirable and possible to integrate the major insights from relevance theory into the present view. As a kind of meta-framework, optimality theory can help to realize this integrative endeavor and to bring the two camps closer to each other. Recently, van Rooy (2000, 2004b) has taken the first important steps in this direction.

NOTES

1   This is arguable, depending on the nature and depth of the syntax involved; note that they are discriminated by passive: *The {lion/ #bus} was taken back to the zoo.* In Relational Grammar, *the lion* is an initial 2 but *the bus* is not.

2   According to Tarski (1930, 1935), a logical consequence relation $\models$ has to satisfy the following principles (here Γ and Γ' range over sets of formulas and ϕ over isolated formulas of a formal language L):

   a. Reflexivity: $\Gamma \models \Gamma$
   b. Cut: if $\Gamma \models \Gamma'$ and $\Gamma \cup \Gamma' \models \phi$, then $\Gamma \models \phi$
   c. Monotonicity: if $\Gamma \models \phi$, then $\Gamma \cup \Gamma' \models \phi$

3   A perfect number is a natural number that is identical to the sum of its true divisors; e.g. $6 = 1 + 2 + 3$ or $28 = 1 + 2 + 4 + 7 + 14$.

4   This contrasts with the view of Geis and Zwicky (1971), who insist that their "invited inferences" are notably different from "conversational implicatures" in the sense of Grice.

5   For excellent discussions of the phenomenon of negative strengthening see Horn (1989: Chap. 5) and Levinson (2000a).

6   Roughly, this cost is correlated with the surprise that the particular enrichment m has for an agent confronted with the underspecified representation f.

7   Obviously, the cost function can be used to define the ordering, but not vice versa. The connection, of course, is as follows: $\langle f', m \rangle \, \text{C⃪} \, \langle f, m \rangle$ iff $\underline{c}(f', m) < \underline{c}(f, m)$.

8   Being more pedantic, we should write $>_\sigma$ in order to indicate the dependence on the actual context σ. We can drop the index because here and in the following we assume the actual context to be fixed.

9   In fact the ideas of Horn, Atlas, and Levinson were the original inspiration for developing my version of bidirectional OT.

10   It should be noted that Dekker and van Rooy (1999) give bidirectional OT a game-theoretic interpretation, where the optimal pairs can be characterized as so-called NASH EQUILIBRIA (cf. van Rooy to appear a).

11   In the diagram, optimal *peps* are marked ✍; the remaining super-optimal pairs are marked by (✍).

12   The recursive notation of bidirection accounts for the interaction between Q and I/R that is informally expressed already in Horn (1984a). The advantage of the present formalization is that it allows us

to PROVE the general pattern of iconicity (subsuming Horn's division of pragmatic labour, Wurzel's (1998) constructional iconicity, and Levinson's (2000a) M principle – the latter expressing the second half of the pattern only).

13   In my opinion, Levinson (2000a) tries to turn a plausible heuristic classification scheme based on the three principles Q, I, and M into a general theory by stipulating a ranking Q > M > I. Accepting the heuristic classification schema, I see problems for this theory, which is burdened with too many stipulations. Not unlike Horn, I prefer to see the M principle as an epiphenomenon that results from the interaction of Zipf's two "economy principles" (1949) (Q and R in Horn's terminology).

23 Pragmatics and Intonation

JULIA HIRSCHBERG

1 Introduction

There is a long tradition of research on the role of prosodic variation in the interpretation of a wide variety of linguistic phenomena (Ladd 1980, Bolinger 1986, 1989, Ladd 1996). Whether a speaker says (where "|" is read as a prosodic boundary and capitals denote emphasis) *John only introduced MARY to Sue* or *John only introduced Mary to SUE; Bill doesn't drink | because he's unhappy* or *Bill doesn't drink because he's unhappy* **can**, in the appropriate context, favor different interpretations of the same sentence. Since the interpretation of such intonational variations is indeed dependent upon contextual factors, we will define intonational "meaning" as essentially pragmatic in nature.

In this chapter, we will provide an overview of various types of intonational variation and the interpretations such variation has been found to induce. While the very large literature on intonational meaning from the linguistics, computational linguistics, speech, and psycholinguistic communities makes it impossible to provide an exhaustive list of relevant research efforts on the topic, examples of such work will be provided in each section. In section 2, we will first describe the components of intonational variation that will be addressed in this chapter, employing as a framework for intonational description the ToBI system for representing the intonation of standard American English. In section 3, we will survey some of the ways intonation can influence the interpretation of syntactic phenomena, such as attachment. In section 4 we will examine intonational variation and semantic phenomena such as scope ambiguity and association with focus. In section 5, we will turn to discourse-level phenomena, including the interpretation of pronouns, the intonational correlates of several types of information status, the relationship between intonational variation and discourse structure, and the role of intonational variation in the interpretation of different sorts of speech acts. A final section will point to future areas of research in the pragmatics of intonation.

2   Intonation: Its Parts and Representations

To discuss prosodic variation usefully, one must choose a framework of intonational description within which to specify the dimensions of variation. The intonational model we will assume below is the ToBI model for describing the intonation of standard American English (Silverman et al. 1992, Pitrelli et al. 1994).[1] The ToBI system consists of annotations at four, time-linked levels of analysis: an ORTHOGRAPHIC TIER of time-aligned words; a TONAL TIER, where PITCH ACCENTS, PHRASE ACCENTS and BOUNDARY TONES describing targets in the FUNDAMENTAL FREQUENCY (f0) define intonational phrases, following Pierrehumbert's (1980) scheme for describing American English, with some modifications; a BREAK INDEX TIER indicating degrees of junction between words, from *0* "no word boundary" to *4* "full INTONATIONAL PHRASE boundary," which derives from Price et al. (1990); and a MISCELLANEOUS TIER, in which phenomena such as disfluencies may be optionally marked (ordered from top to bottom in figure 23.1).

Break indices define two levels of phrasing: minor or INTERMEDIATE PHRASE (in Pierrehumbert's terms) (level 3); and major or INTONATIONAL PHRASE (level 4), with an associated tonal tier that describes the phrase accents and boundary tones for each level. Level 4 phrases consist of one or more level 3 phrases,

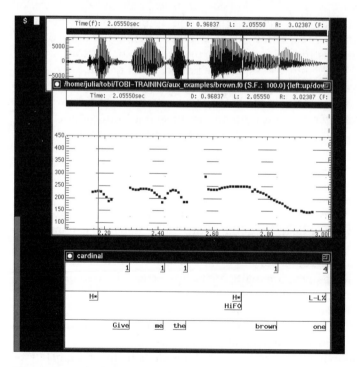

Figure 23.1   A H* L-L% contour

plus a high or low boundary tone (**H%** or **L%**) at the right edge of the phrase. Level 3 phrases consist of one or more pitch accents, aligned with the stressed syllable of lexical items, plus a PHRASE ACCENT, which also may be high (**H-**) or low (**L-**). A standard declarative contour, for example, ends in a low phrase accent and low boundary tone, and is represented by **L-L%**; a standard yes-no-question contour ends in **H-H%**. These are illustrated in figures 23.1 and 23.2, respectively.[2]

Differences among ToBI break indices can be associated with variation in f0, PHRASE-FINAL LENGTHENING (a lengthening of the syllable preceding the juncture point), glottalization ("creaky voice") over the last syllable or syllables preceding the break, and some amount of pause. Higher-number indices tend to be assigned where there is more evidence of these phenomena. Phrasal tone differences are reflected in differences in f0 target.

Pitch accents render items intonationally prominent. This prominence can be achieved via different tone targets, as well as differences in f0 height, to

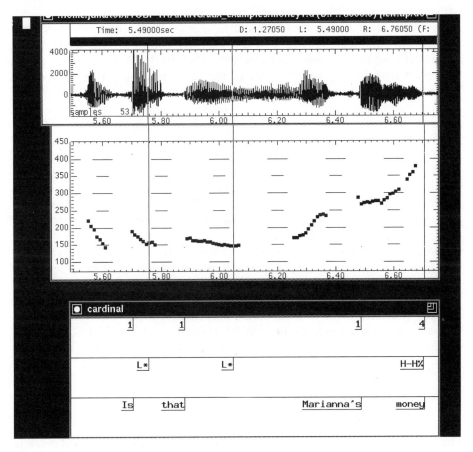

Figure 23.2   A L* H-H contour

convey different messages (Campbell and Beckman 1997, Terken 1997). So, items may be accented or (DEACCENTED (Ladd 1979)) and, if accented, may bear different tones, or different degrees of prominence, with respect to other accents. In addition to f0 excursions, accented words are usually louder and longer than their unaccented counterparts. In addition to variation in type, accents may have different levels of prominence; i.e. one accent may be perceived as more prominent than another due to variation in f0 height or amplitude, or to location in the intonational phrase. Listeners usually perceive the last accented item in a phrase as the most prominent in English. This most prominent accent in an intermediate phrase is called the phrase's NUCLEAR ACCENT or NUCLEAR STRESS. Constraints on nuclear (sometimes termed sentence) stress are discussed by many authors, including Cutler and Foss (1977), Schmerling (1974, 1976), Erteschik-Shir and Lappin (1983), and Bardovi-Harlig (1983b). Despite Bolinger's (1972b) seminal article on the unpredictability of accent, attempts to predict accent placement from related features of the uttered text continue, especially for purposes of assigning accent in text-to-speech systems, for example (Altenberg 1987, Hirschberg 1993, Veilleux 1994).

Five types of pitch accent are distinguished in the ToBI scheme for American English: two simple accents **H*** and **L***, and three complex ones, **L*+H**, **L+H***, and **H+!H***. As in Pierrehumbert's system,[3] the asterisk indicates which tone is aligned with the stressed syllable of the word bearing a complex accent. Differences in accent type convey differences in meaning when interpreted in conjunction with differences in the discourse context and variation in other acoustic properties of the utterance. The **H*** accent is the most common accent in American English. It is modeled as a simple peak in the f0 contour, as illustrated in figure 23.1 above; this peak is aligned with the word's stressable syllable.

H* accents are typically found in standard declarative utterances; they are commonly used to convey that the accented item should be treated as NEW information in the discourse, and is part of what is being asserted in an utterance (Pierrehumbert and Hirschberg 1990). **L*** accents are modeled as valleys in the f0, as shown in figure 23.2 above.

These accents have been broadly characterized as conveying that the accented item should be treated as **salient** but not part of what is being asserted (Pierrehumbert and Hirschberg 1990). As such, they typically characterize prominent items in *yes-no* question contours. In addition to this use, they are often employed to make initial prepositions or adverbs prominent or to mark DISCOURSE readings of CUE PHRASES (see section 5.3 below). **L+H*** accents can be used to produce a pronounced "contrastive" effect, as in (1a).

(1) The Smiths aren't inviting anybody important.

    a.   They invited **L+H*** Lorraine.
    b.   They invited **L*+H** Lorraine.

This complex accent, where the high tone is aligned with the stressed syllable and the f0 rise is thus rapid, can serve to emphatically contradict the initial

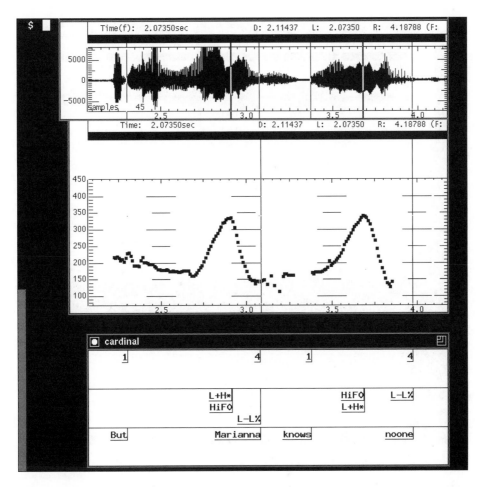

Figure 23.3 A **L+H*** pitch accent

claim that Lorraine is unimportant and is illustrated in figure 23.3. A similarly shaped accent with slightly but crucially different alignment, the **L*+H** accent, can convey still other distinctions. For example, **L*+H** pitch accent on *Lorraine* in (1b), where the low tones is aligned with the stressed syllable, can convey uncertainty about whether or not Lorraine is an important person. This type of accent is shown in figure 23.4. And **H+!H*** accents, realized as a fall onto the stressed syllable, are associated with some implied sense of familiarity with the mentioned item. An example of a felicitous use of **H+!H*** is the "reminding" case in (2) and the accent is illustrated in figure 23.5.

(2)   A: No German has ever won the Luce Prize.
       B: **H+!H*** Joachim's from Germany.

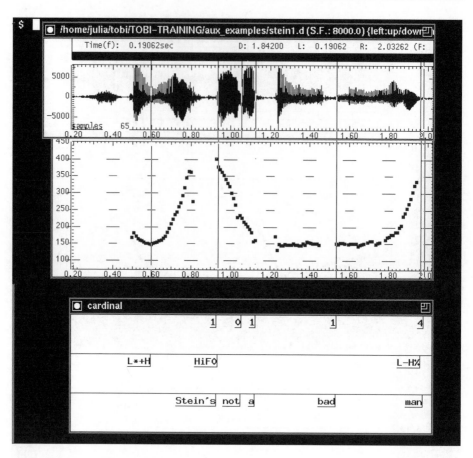

Figure 23.4 A **L*+H** pitch accent

By way of summary, table 23.1 provides a schematic representation of the possible contours in Standard American English, in the ToBI system.

3 Intonation in the Interpretation of Syntactic Phenomena

There has been much interest among theorists over the years in defining a mapping between prosody and syntax (Downing 1970, Bresnan 1971, Cooper and Paccia-Cooper 1980, Selkirk 1984, Dirksen and Quené 1993, Prevost and Steedman 1994, Boula de Mareüil and d'Alessandro 1998). Intuitively, prosodic phrases, whether intermediate or intonational, divide an utterance into meaningful "chunks" of information (Bolinger 1989); the greater the perceived phrasing juncture, the greater the discontinuity between segments or constituents. While many researchers have sought to identify simple syntactic

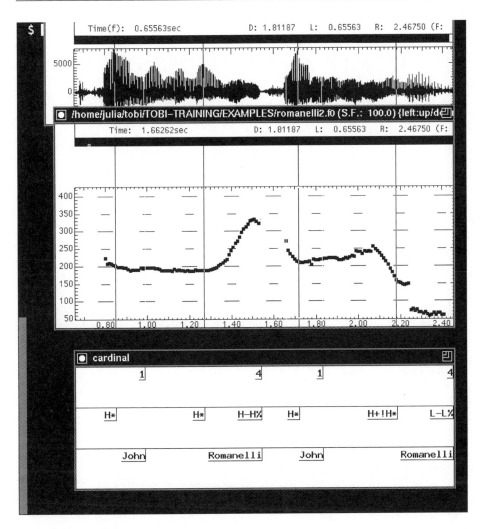

Figure 23.5 A H+!H* pitch accent

constraints on phrase location (Crystal 1969, Cooper and Paccia-Cooper 1980, Selkirk 1984, Croft 1995), especially for parsing (Marcus and Hindle 1990, Steedman 1991, Oehrle 1991, Abney 1995), more empirical approaches have focused upon discovering the circumstances under which one sort of phrasing of some syntactic phenomenon will be favored over another by speakers and perhaps differently interpreted by hearers. Corpus-based studies (Altenberg 1987, Bachenko and Fitzpatrick 1990, Ostendorf and Veilleux 1994, Hirschberg and Prieto 1996, Fujio, et al. 1997) and laboratory experiments (Grosjean et al. 1979, Wales and Toner 1979, Gee and Grosjean 1983, Price et al. 1990, Beach 1991, Hirschberg and Avesani 1997) have variously found that the discontinuity indicated by a phrase boundary may serve to favor various differences in

Table 23.1   ToBI contours for Standard American English

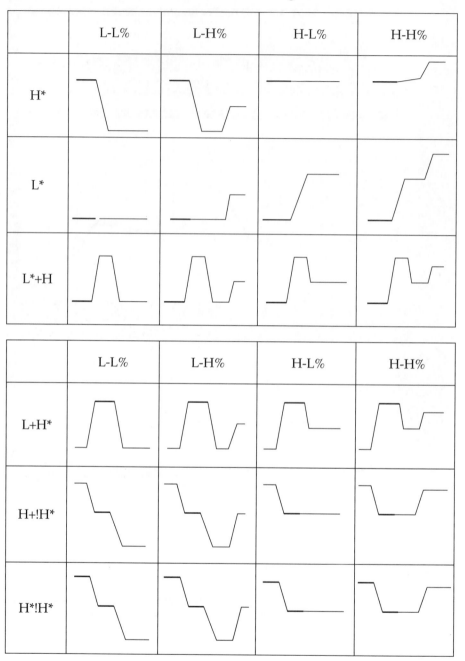

	L-L%	L-H%	H-L%	H-H%
H*				
L*				
L*+H				

	L-L%	L-H%	H-L%	H-H%
L+H*				
H+!H*				
H*!H*				

the interpretation of syntactic attachment ambiguity, for phenomena such as prepositional phrases, relative clauses, adverbial modifiers. Moreover, it has been found that the presence or absence of a phrase boundary can distinguish prepositions from particles and can indicate the scope of modifiers in conjoined phrases. Some examples are found in (3)–(11), where boundaries are again marked by "|":

(3) Anna frightened the woman | with the gun.
     [VP-attachment: Anna held the gun]
     Anna frightened | the woman with the gun.
     [NP-attachment: the woman held the gun]

(4) Mary knows many languages you know.
     [Complementizer: Mary knows many languages that you also know]
     Mary knows many languages | you know.
     [Parenthetical: as you are aware, Mary knows many languages]

(5) The animal that usually fights the lion is missing.
     [the lion's normal opponent is missing]
     The animal that usually fights | the lion | is missing.
     [Appositive: the lion is missing]

(6) My brother who is a writer needs a new job.
     [Restrictive relative clause: I have at least one other brother but I am not speaking of him]
     My brother | who is a writer | needs a new job.
     [Non-restrictive relative clause: I may or may not have other brothers]

(7) John laughed | at the party.
     [Preposition: John laughed while at the party]
     John laughed at | the party.
     [Particle: John ridiculed the party]

(8) If you need me | when you get there call me.
     [Attachment to main clause VP: if you need me, call me when you arrive]
     If you need me when you get there | call me.
     [Attachment to antecedent clause VP: if you need me when you arrive, call me]

(9) This collar is dangerous to younger | dogs and cats.
     [Conjunction modification: the collar may be dangerous to younger dogs and younger cats]
     This collar is dangerous to younger dogs | and cats.
     [Single conjunct modification: the collar may be dangerous to younger dogs and all cats]

(10)   Stir in rice wine | and seasonings.
       [Compound noun: stir in two ingredients]
       Stir in rice | wine | and seasonings.
       [List interpretation: stir in three ingredients]

(11)   We only suspected | they all knew that a burglary had been committed.
       [Simple complement: we only suspected that they all knew that a bur-
       glary had been committed]
       We only suspected | they all knew | that a burglary had been committed.
       [Parenthetical: they all knew that we only suspected that a burglary had
       been committed]

Prosodic variation other than phrasing can also influence disambiguation of
syntactic ambiguity. For example, range and rate can also distinguish phenomena such as parenthetical phrases from others (Kutik et al. 1983, Grosz and
Hirschberg 1992): parentheticals like that in (11) are generally uttered in a
compressed pitch range and with a faster speaking rate than other phrases.
And the location of pitch accent can cue the right node raising reading of the
sentence uttered in (11), as in (12) (Marcus and Hindle 1990).

(12)   WE only SUSPECTED | THEY all KNEW | that a BURGLARY had been
       committed.
       [we suspected but they in fact knew that a burglary had been committed]

Pitch accent location is also a well-known factor in conveying the structure
of complex nominals (Liberman and Sproat 1992, Sproat 1994) and in distinguishing among part-of-speech ambiguities, as is evident from the examples
in (13) and (14):

(13)   GERMAN teachers
       German TEACHERS

(14)   LEAVE in the LIMO
       leave IN the REFERENCE

In (13), accent on the modifier or head signals the different interpretations:
"teachers of German" vs. "teachers who are German." And differences in accent
location distinguish prepositions from VERBAL PREPOSITIONS as in (14). But
note that prepositions may also be accented, to convey focus or contrast, as
illustrated in (15).

(15)   I didn't shoot AT him, I shot PAST him.

So, the relationship between accent and part of speech is also dependent upon
context.

And, while intonational variation **can** serve all these functions, evidence that it does so reliably is mixed (Wales and Toner 1979, Cooper and Paccia-Cooper 1980, Nespor and Vogel 1983, Schafer et al. 2000). Speakers routinely violate all of the distinctions illustrated above, perhaps because they do not recognize the potential ambiguity of their utterances or because context disambiguates. Even when explicitly asked to disambiguate, they may choose different methods of disambiguation.

4   Intonation in the Interpretation of Semantic Phenomena

There is a long and diverse tradition of research on the role of accent in the interpretation of semantic phenomena, centering around the interpretation of FOCUSED constituents (G. Lakoff 1971b, Schmerling 1971b, Jackendoff 1972, Ball and Prince 1977, Enkvist 1979, Wilson and Sperber 1979, Gussenhoven 1983, Culicover and Rochemont 1983, Rooth 1985, Horne 1985, Horne 1987, Baart 1987, Rooth 1992, Dirksen 1992, Zacharski 1992, Birch and Clifton 1995). Changing the location of nuclear stress in an utterance can alter the interpretation of the utterance by altering its perceived focus. An utterance's focus may be identified by asking "To what question(s) is the utterance with this specified accent pattern a felicitous answer?" (Halliday 1967, Eady and Cooper 1986). For example, (16b) is a felicitous response to the question *Whom did John introduce to Sue?*, while (16c) is an appropriate response to the question *To whom did John introduce Mary?* In each case the focused information is the information being requested, and is the most prominent information in the utterance.

(16)a.   John only introduced Mary to Sue.
    b.   John only introduced MARY to Sue.
    c.   John only introduced Mary to SUE.

In (16b), Mary is the only person John introduced to Sue; in (16c), Sue is the only person John introduced Mary to. (16b) is false if John introduced Bill, as well as Mary, to Sue; (16c) is false if John introduced Mary to Bill, as well as to Sue. This variation in focus takes on an added dimension when FOCUS-SENSITIVE OPERATORS, such as *only*, are present (Halliday 1967, Jackendoff 1972, Rooth 1985, Sgall et al. 1986, Partee 1991, Rooth 1992, Vallduví 1992, Selkirk 1995, Schwarzschild 1999, Büring 1999). In (16), the focus-sensitive operator *only* interacts with the intonational prominence of pitch accents to produce the different interpretations of the sentence discussed above. Other such operators include other quantifiers (*all, most, some*), adverbs of quantification (*sometimes, most often*), modals (*must*), emotive factives/attitude verbs (*It's odd that*), and counterfactuals. With prominence on *night*, for example, (17a) is felicitous, with the meaning "it is at night that most ships pass through the lock."

(17)a. Most ships pass through the lock at night.
    b. When do ships go through the lock?
        Most ships pass through the lock at NIGHT.
    c. What do ships do at night?
        Most ships pass through the LOCK at night.

However, with prominence on *lock*, the same sentence becomes a felicitous answer to a different question, as illustrated in (17c): passing through the lock is what most ships do at night. Temporal quantification behaves similarly, as illustrated in (18). Other temporal quantifiers include *frequently, rarely, sometimes, occasionally*, and so on.

(18)a. Londoners *most often* go to Brighton.
    b. Who goes to Brighton?
        LONDONERS most often go to Brighton.
    c. Where do Londoners go on vacation?
        Londoners most often go to BRIGHTON.

The well-known example in (19a) was originally observed on a sign on a British train by Halliday (1967), who was startled to learn that every train rider was commanded to carry a dog, under the reading induced by (19b).

(19)a. Dogs must be carried.
    b. DOGS must be carried.
    c. Dogs must be CARRIED.

A more likely interpretation of the sentence in the railway context would be favored by the accent pattern represented by (19c): if you bring a dog on the train, then you must carry it. Other modals which associate with focus in a similar way include *can, should, may*.

Other focus-sensitive operators that also appear to identify the scope of the operator within the utterance are illustrated in (20)–(21):

(20)a. It's ODD that Clyde married Bertha.
    b. It's odd that CLYDE married Bertha.
    c. It's odd that Clyde MARRIED Bertha.
    d. It's odd that Clyde married BERTHA.

Depending upon whether *odd*, the operator itself, or one of its potential foci (*Clyde, married*, or *Bertha*) bears nuclear stress, what is "odd" may vary considerably. The entire proposition that Clyde married Bertha is odd. The fact that it was Clyde and not someone else who married Bertha is odd. What is odd is that what Clyde did with respect to Bertha was to marry her. Or it is the fact that the person Clyde chose to marry was indeed Bertha that is strange. And in (21), a listener would be likely to draw very different inferences depending upon the speaker's location of nuclear stress.

(21)a.   This time HARRY didn't cause our defeat.
    b.   This time Harry didn't CAUSE our defeat.
    c.   This time Harry didn't cause our DEFEAT.

Someone else caused our defeat, not Harry (21a); Harry didn't actually cause our defeat though he may have, for example, contributed to it (21b); Harry didn't cause our defeat but rather he caused something else (21c).

Although most research on the role of intonation in semantic interpretation has concentrated on pitch accent variation, variation in phrasing can also change the semantic interpretation of an utterance, again though with considerable variation in performance. For example, the interpretation of negation in a sentence like (22) is likely to vary, depending upon whether it is uttered as one phrase (22a) or two (22b).

(22)a.   Bill doesn't drink because he's unhappy.
    b.   Bill doesn't drink | because he's unhappy.

In (22a) the negative has wide scope: Bill does indeed drink – but the cause of his drinking is not his unhappiness. In (22b), it has narrow scope: Bill's unhappiness has led him **not** to drink. However, like other interpretations that may be favored by intonational variation, if context itself can disambiguate a potentially ambiguous sentence, speakers sometimes produce intonational phrasings that do not obey these likelihoods. For example, an utterance of *Bill doesn't drink because he's unhappy* as a single phrase may be interpreted with the narrow scope of negation as well as the wide (Hirschberg and Avesani 2000); interestingly, *Bill doesn't drink | because he's unhappy* is less likely to be interpreted with wide-scope negation. Such cases where a particular intonational pattern may be interpreted in several ways – but its contrast is less likely to – give rise to the notion of "neutral" intonation, a notion whose evidence is probably more persuasive for phrasing variations than for accent variation.

5   Intonation in the Interpretation of Discourse Phenomena

Intonational variation has been much studied in its role in the interpretation of numerous discourse phenomena. Pronouns have been found to be interpreted differently depending upon whether they are prominent or not, in varying contexts. Different categories of information status, such as THEME/RHEME distinctions, GIVEN/NEW status, and contrast, are believed to be intonationally markable (Schmerling 1976, Chafe 1976, Lehman 1977, Gundel 1978, Allerton and Cruttenden 1979, Fuchs 1980, Nooteboom and Terken 1982, Bardovi-Harlig 1983a, Brown 1983, Fuchs 1984, Terken 1984, 1985, Kruyt 1985, Fowler and Housum 1987, Terken and Nooteboom 1987, Horne 1991a, b, Terken and Hirschberg 1994, Prevost 1995, Cahn 1998). Variation in overall discourse structure has been found to be conveyed by intonational variation, whether in the production of DISCOURSE MARKERS or in larger patterns of variation in pitch range, pausal duration, speaking rate, and other prosodic phenomena. Finally, variation in tune or contour has been widely associated with different SPEECH ACTS in the literature. Other correlations between features such as contour, pausal duration, and final lowering with TURN-TAKING phenomena have also been studied (Sacks et al. 1974, Auer 1996, Selting 1996, Koiso et al. 1998). And the role of intonation in conveying affect, or emotional state, is an important and still open question (Ladd et al. 1985, Cahn 1989, Murray and Arnott 1993, Pereira and Watson 1998, Koike et al. 1998, Mozziconacci 1998).

The relation between the relative accessibility of information in a discourse and a number of observable properties of utterances has been broadly explored in theories of COMMUNICATIVE DYNAMISM, ATTENTIONAL FOCUSING and CEN-TERING in discourse (Chafe 1974, Grosz 1977, Sidner 1979, Grosz 1981, Sidner 1983, Grosz et al. 1983, Grosz and Sidner 1986, Kameyama 1986, Brennan et al. 1987, Asher and Wada 1988, Hajicova et al. 1990, Gordon et al. 1993, Gundel et al. 1993), and in models of sentence production (Bock and Warren 1985). The available evidence supports the notion that the relative accessibility of entities in the discourse model is a major factor in the assignment to grammatical role and surface position, and in the choice of the form of referring expressions: highly accessible entities tend to be realized as the grammatical subject, to occur early in the utterance, and to be pronominalized. Furthermore, available evidence from studies on comprehension shows that accessibility is also an important factor in the way the listener processes the incoming message (Kameyama 1986, Gordon et al. 1993). Much research on pitch accent in discourse stems from questions of accessibility.

5.1   The interpretation of pronouns

While corpus-based studies have found that, on the whole, pronouns tend to be deaccented, they can be accented to convey various "marked" effects – that is, an interpretation identified in some sense as less likely. In (23), the referents of the pronouns *he* and *him* will be different in (23a) and (23b), because the accenting is different (G. Lakoff 1971b).

(23)a.   John called Bill a Republican and then he insulted him.
    b.   John called Bill a Republican and then HE insulted HIM.

In (23a), *he* and *him* are deaccented, and the likely interpretation will be that John both called Bill a Republican and subsequently insulted him. In (23b), with both pronouns accented, most hearers will understand that John called Bill a Republican (which was tantamount to insulting him) and that Bill in return insulted John.

In another case of interaction between pitch accent and BOUND ANAPHORA, the interpretation of one clause can be affected by the intonational features of the preceding one, as in (24).

(24)a.   John likes his colleagues and so does Sue.
    b.   John likes HIS colleagues and so does Sue.

However, this interpretation appears more clearly dependent upon the underlying semantics of the sentence and the larger context. In perception studies
testing the role of accent in the STRICT/SLOPPY interpretation of ellipsis
(Hirschberg and Ward 1991), subjects tended to favor a "marked" or less likely
interpretation of sentences uttered with a pitch accent on the anaphor than
they proposed for the sentence in a "neutral" (read) condition. That is, if a
sentence like (24a) were likely to be interpreted with the strict reading (John
likes his colleagues and Sue also likes John's colleagues), then in the spoken
variant in which *his* is accented, listeners tended to favor the sloppy reading,
"John likes his own colleagues and Sue likes her own colleagues".

    Terken (1985) found that, in task-oriented monologues, speakers used
deaccented, pronominal expressions to refer to the local topic of discourse,
and accented, full NPs otherwise, even though many of these NPs referred to
entities which had already been mentioned in the previous discourse. Pitch
accent on pronouns has also been found to be correlated with changes in
attentional state in studies by Cahn (1995) and by Nakatani (1997). What the
conversation is "about" in terms of its topic or discourse BACKWARD-LOOKING
CENTER (Grosz et al. 1995) can be altered, it is proposed, by the way pronouns
are produced intonationally. For example, in (25), it has been suggested (Terken
1995) that the accented pronoun in the fourth line of (25) serves to shift the
topic to Betsy from Susan, who had previously been the pronominalized subject
and backward-looking center of the discourse.

(25)   Susan gave Betsy a pet hamster.
       She reminded her such hamsters were quite shy.
       She asked Betsy whether she liked the gift.
       And SHE said yes, she did.
       She'd always wanted a pet hamster.

5.2   *The given/new distinction*

It is a common generalization that speakers typically deaccent items that
represent old, or given information in a discourse (Prince 1981a). Mere repeated
mention in a discourse is, however, clearly an inadequate definition of givenness
and thus a fairly inaccurate predictor of deaccentuation. Halliday has argued
that an expression may be deaccented if the information conveyed by the
expression is situationally or anaphorically recoverable on the basis of the
prior discourse or by being salient in the situation (Halliday 1967). Chafe
proposed that an expression may be deaccented if the information is in the
listener's consciousness (Chafe 1974, 1976). But it seems likely that not all
items which have been mentioned previously in a discourse of some length
are recoverable anaphorically or are in the listener's consciousness. What is
also clear is that there is no simple one-to-one mapping between givenness

and deaccenting, even if givenness could be more clearly defined. Among the factors which appear to determine whether a given item is accented or not are: (1) whether or not a given item participates in a complex nominal; (2) the location of such an item in its prosodic phrase; and (3) whether preceding items in the phrase are "accentable" due to their own information status, the grammatical function of an item when first and subsequently mentioned.

For example, consider (26a) in the discourse below:

(26)a. The SENATE BREAKS for LUNCH at NOON, so I HEADED to the CAFETERIA to GET my STORY.
   b. There are SENATORS, and there are THIN senators.
   c. For SENATORS, LUNCH at the cafeteria is FREE. For REPORTERS, it's not.
   d. But CAFETERIA food is CAFETERIA food.

(26a) shows a simple pattern of unaccented function words and accented "content words." However, in (26b), while speakers are likely to accent the content word *senators* on first mention, they are less likely to accent it on subsequent mention, when it represents given information. But in (26c), while *senators* still represents given information, speakers are likely to accent it, to contrast *senators* with *reporters*. *Cafeteria* in this utterance is likely to be deaccented, since it represents given information and is **not** being contrasted with, say, another location. But in (26d), this same given item, *cafeteria*, is likely to be accented, in part because of the stress pattern of the COMPLEX NOMINAL *cafeteria food* of which it is a part, and in part because all items in the utterance appear to be in some sense given in this context and something must bear a pitch accent in every phrase.

Brown (1983) found that all expressions used to refer to items which had been mentioned in the previous discourse were deaccented, but that expressions used to refer to inferrable items were usually accented. And Terken and Hirschberg (1994) found that differences in grammatical function of previously mentioned items with their function in the current utterance was a major factor in whether they were accented or not. It is also unclear whether what is given for a speaker, should also be treated as given for his/her illocutionary partner (Prince 1992) – and thus, potentially deaccentable. Empirical results from the Edinburgh Map tasks dialogs (Bard 1999) suggest that such clearly given items are rarely deaccented across speakers. And there are other studies of repeated information where it is clear that simple prior mention should not be taken as evidence of givenness for the listener, who may repeat prior data to confirm or question it (Shimojima et al. 2001).

5.3 Topic structure

Rate, duration of inter-phrase pause, loudness, and pitch range can also convey the topic structure of a text (Lehiste 1979, Brown et al. 1980, Silverman 1987,

Avesani and Vayra 1988, Ayers 1992, Grosz and Hirschberg 1992, Passoneau and Litman 1993, Swerts et al. 1994, Hirschberg and Nakatani 1996, Swerts 1997, Koiso et al. 1998, van Donzel 1999). In general, it has been found that phrases beginning new topics are begun in a wider pitch range, are preceded by a longer pause, are louder, and are slower, than other phrases; narrower range, longer subsequent pause, and faster rate characterize topic-final phrases. Subsequent variation in these features then tends to be associated with a topic shift.

One of the features most frequently mentioned as important to conveying some kind of TOPIC STRUCTURE in discourse is PITCH RANGE, defined here as the distance between the maximum of the FUNDAMENTAL FREQUENCY (f0) for the vowel portions of accented syllables in the phrase, and the speaker's BASELINE, defined for each each speaker as the lowest point reached in normal speech overall. In a study of speakers reading a story, Brown et al. (1980) found that subjects typically started new topics relatively high in their pitch range and finished topics by compressing their range; they hypothesized that internal structure within a topic was similarly marked. Lehiste (1975) had reported similar results earlier for single paragraphs. Silverman (1987) found that manipulation of pitch range alone, or range in conjunction with pausal duration between utterances, could enable subjects to reliably disambiguate utterances that were intuitively potentially structurally ambiguous; for example, he used a small pitch range to signal either continuation or ending of a topic or quotation, and an expanded range to indicate topic shift or quotation continuation. Avesani and Vayra (1988) also found variation in range in productions by a professional speaker which appear to correlate with topic structure, and Ayers (1992) found that pitch range appears to correlate more closely with hierarchical topic structure in read speech than in spontaneous speech. Swerts et al. (1992) also found that f0 scaling was a reliable indicator of discourse structure in spoken instructions, although the structures tested were quite simple.

Duration of pause between utterances or phrases has also been identified as an indicator of topic structure (Lehiste 1979, Chafe 1980, Brown et al. 1980, Silverman 1987, Avesani and Vayra 1988, Swerts et al. 1992, Passoneau and Litman 1993), although Woodbury (1987) found no similar correlation. Brown et al. (1980) found that longer, TOPIC PAUSES (0.6–0.8 sec.) marked major topic shifts. Passoneau and Litman (1993) also found that the presence of a pause was a good predictor of their subjects' labeling of segment boundaries in Chafe's pear stories. Another aspect of timing, speaking rate, was found by Lehiste (1980) and by Butterworth (1975) to be associated with perception of text structure: both found that utterances beginning segments exhibited slower rates and those completing segments were uttered more rapidly.

Amplitude was also noted by Brown et al. (1980) as a signal of topic shift; they found that amplitude appeared to rise at the start of a new topic and fall at the end. Finally, contour type has been mentioned as a potential correlate of topic structure (Brown et al. 1980, Hirschberg and Pierrehumbert 1986, Swerts et al. 1992). In particular, Hirschberg and Pierrehumbert (1986) suggested that so-called DOWNSTEPPED contours[4] commonly appear either at the beginning or the ending of topics. Empirical studies showed that "low" vs. "not-low" boundary tones were good predictors of topic endings vs. continuations (Swerts et al. 1992).

FINAL LOWERING, a compression of the pitch range during the last half second or so of an utterance, can also convey structural information to hearers, by signaling whether or not a speaker has completed his/her TURN. Pitch contour and range as well as timing have also been shown to correlate with turn-final vs. turn-keeping utterances – and distinguishing the former from discourse boundaries – as well as marking backchannels in dialogue (Sacks et al. 1974, Geluykens and Swerts 1994, Auer 1996, Selting 1996, Caspers 1998, Koiso et al. 1998).

Grosz and Hirschberg (1992) and Hirschberg and Nakatani (1996) have also investigated the acoustic-prosodic correlates of discourse structure, inspired by the need to test potential correlates against an independent notion of discourse structure, as noted by Brown et al. (1980), and to investigate spontaneous as well as read speech. They looked at pitch range, aspects of timing and contour, and amplitude to see how well they predicted discourse segmentation decisions made by subjects using instructions based on the Grosz and Sidner (1986) model of discourse structure. They found statistically significant associations between aspects of pitch range, amplitude, and timing with segment beginnings and segment endings both for read and spontaneous speech.

Accent can also disambiguate potentially ambiguous words such as DISCOURSE MARKERS, or CUE PHRASES – words and phrases such as *now, well, in the first place*. These cue phrases can function as explicit indicators of discourse structure (a discourse use) or can have a sentential reading, often as adverbials. Variation in intonational phrasing and pitch accent are correlated with the distinction between these discourse and sentential uses (Hirschberg and Litman 1993). Tokens interpreted as discourse uses are commonly produced either as separate phrases (27a) or as part of larger phrases; in the latter case they tend to be deaccented or uttered with a L* accent. However, when cue phrases are produced with high prominence, they tend to be interpreted as temporal adverbs. So (27a)–(27b) are likely to be interpreted as starting a new subtopic in a discourse, while (27c) is likely to be interpreted as a temporal statement: *Now Bill is a vegetarian, although he wasn't before*. And (27a) and (27b) convey no such assertion.

(27)a.   Now, Bill is a vegetarian.
    b.   Now Bill is a vegetarian.
    c.   NOW Bill is a vegetarian.

5.4   *Speech acts*

There is a rich linguistic tradition characterizing variation in overall pitch contour in many different ways: as conveying syntactic mood, speech act, speaker attitude, or speaker belief or emotion (O'Connor and Arnold 1961, Bolinger 1986, 1989, Ladd 1980, 1996). Some inherent meaning has often been sought in particular contours – though generally such proposals include some degree of modulation by context (Liberman and Sag 1974, Sag and Liberman 1975, Ladd 1977, 1978, Bing 1979, Ladd 1980, Bouton 1982, Ward and Hirschberg 1985, Grabe et al. 1997, Gussenhoven and Rietveld 1997). And more general attempts have been made to identify compositional meanings for contours within various systems of intonational analysis (Gussenhoven 1983, Pierrehumbert and Hirschberg 1990). Efforts have been made to define "standard" contours for declaratives, *wh*-questions, *yes-no* questions as a method for beginning the study of intonation in a particular language. As noted in section 2, for example, the ToBI representation of the "standard" declarative for standard American English is **H* L-L%**, with *wh*-questions also **H* L-L%** and *yes-no* questions **L* H-H%**. The "intrinsic meaning" of other intonational contours remains, however, both more controversial and more elusive. However, below we will mention a few of the contours which have been studied by way of example.

The CONTINUATION RISE contour, which is represented by a low phrase accent and high boundary tone (**L-H%**), is generally interpreted as conveying that there is "more to come" (Bolinger 1989), as in (28).

(28)a. The number is L-H%: 555–1212.
  b. Open the carton L-H%. Now remove the monitor carefully.

Continuation rise appears to be associated with turn-keeping phenomena, as is variation in final lowering. Internal intonational phrase boundaries in longer stretches of read speech are often realized with **L-H%**. Elements of a list, for example, are often realized as **H* L-H%** phrases.

Another contour often used in list construction is the PLATEAU contour (**H* H-L%**). However, unlike the rather neutral lists produced with continuation rise, the plateau contour conveys the sense that the speaker is talking about an "open-ended set," as in (29):

(29) The Johnsons are solid citizens.
    They **H*** pay their **H*** taxes **H-L%**.
    They **H*** attend **H*** PTA meetings **H-L%**.
    They're just good people.

That is, that the enumeration is for illustrative purposes only and far from complete. **H* H-L%** more generally seems to convey a certain sense that the hearer already knows the information being provided and only needs reminding – that the speaker is simply going through the motions of informing. However, this contour has received little formal study.

Much more popular among students of intonation has been the RISE-FALL-RISE contour (represented in the ToBI framework as one or more **L*+H** accents plus a low phrase accent and high boundary tone but characterized variously in other schemas), see Ladd (1980). In its more recent interpretations, it has been found to indicate either uncertainty or incredulity, depending upon the speaking rate and pitch range (see section 2) (Ladd 1980, Ward and Hirschberg 1985, Hirschberg and Ward 1992). In (30a), **L*+H L H%** is produced to indicate uncertainty; in (30b), it is produced to convey incredulity.

(30) Did you finish those slides?
  a. **L*+H** Sort of **L-H%**. (Gloss: I did MOST of them; is that good enough?)
  b. **L*+H** Sort of **L-H%**. (Gloss: What do you mean, "sort of"? They were due yesterday!)

Variation in aspects of pitch range and voice quality appear to be the significant factors in triggering this change in interpretation (Hirschberg and Ward 1992), although differences can also be observed in rate and amplitude of the two readings. "Uncertainty" interpretations have a narrower pitch range and are softer and slower than "incredulity" readings. Note that range variation can also convey differences in degree of speaker involvement, or communicate the topic structure of a text (Hirschberg and Pierrehumbert 1986, Pierrehumbert and Hirschberg 1990). So this type of prosodic variation can be several ways ambiguous.

L* accents can also be combined with H* accents to produce the so-called SURPRISE-REDUNDANCY contour (Sag and Liberman 1975), as in (31); in ToBI representation, the phrase accent and boundary tone are both low.

(31) The **L*** blackboard's painted **H*** orange.

This contour has been interpreted as conveying surprise at some phenomenon that is itself observable to both speaker and hearer (hence, the notion of "redundancy"). Both this contour and a set of DOWNSTEPPED contours discussed below, might profitably be re-examined in light of currently richer resources of labeled corpora.

  The downstepped contours all exhibit patterns of pitch range compression following complex pitch accents, reflected in a sequence of increasingly compressed pitch peaks in the f0 contour. In Pierrehumbert's original system, all complex pitch accents trigger downstep: **H*+L, H+L*, L*+H** and **L+H***; downstep is indicated in ToBI, however, by an explicit "!" marking on the **H** component of a downstepped pitch accent, e.g. **H* !H* !H***. . . . None of the downstepped contours have been seriously studied in terms of their "meanings," although proposals have been made that **H* !H* L L%** in particular is felicitously used to open or close of a topic, especially in didactic contexts, such as academic lectures, as in (32a), or cooking classes, as in (32b).

(32)a. **H*** Today we're **!H*** going to **!H*** look at the **!H*** population of **!H*** Ghana **L-L%**.
  b. **H*** This is **!H*** how you **!H*** heat the **!H*** soup **L-L%**.

In addition to investigations of contour meaning, studies have also been done on the disambiguating role various contours may play in distinguishing between DIRECT and INDIRECT speech acts – between what might be taken as the "literal meaning" of a sentence and some other illocutionary use of that sentence by a speaker (Searle 1969). For example, a sentence with the form of a *yes-no* question, such as (33),

(33) A: Can you tell me the time?
      B1: Yes.
      B2: It's four o'clock.

in its literal interpretation requests a simple *yes* or *no* – is the hearer capable of providing such information? In its more customary use, however, it may be interpreted as a request to perform some action – and actually inform the questioner of the time.

Many accounts have been provided of how hearers are able to distinguish between these possible interpretations and there is considerable evidence that intonational variation can play an important role. For example, it is possible to turn a sentence with the form of a declarative into a *yes-no* question, simply by using a rising contour, as in (34):

(34)a. I like grapefruit.
     b. I like grapefruit?

Most plausibly, (34a) states a fact, while (34b) seems to question a prior assertion of that fact. Perception studies performed by Sag and Liberman (1975) examined whether in fact *yes-no* questions interpreted as **direct** speech acts – requests for a simple *yes* or *no* – differed from those interpreted as **indirect** speech acts – requests to perform an action – in terms of the speaker's intonation, for sentences such as (35a). They also investigated intonational conditions under which *wh*-questions were interpreted as simple requests for information vs. those in which they were interpreted as suggestions or criticisms or denials, in sentences such as (35):

(35)a. Would you stop hitting Gwendolyn?
     b. Why don't you move to California?

In preliminary findings, they reported that subjects did tend to interpret sentences like (35a) as direct speech acts when uttered with a classic interrogative contour (**L* H-H%** in ToBI notation). And productions of such sentences that were **least** likely to be interpreted as direct speech acts were uttered with a high-level PLATEAU contour, e.g., (35a) uttered with the ToBI contour **H* H-L%**. *Wh*-questions such as (35b) that were interpreted as simple requests for information were often uttered with a high-low-high pattern, e.g. probably **H* L-H%** in ToBI annotation. But those interpreted as indirect speech acts

– suggestions or denials – were uttered with other intonational patterns, usually falling at the end of the phrase, such as uttered as a simple declaration (**H* L-L%**). Since **H* L-L%** is thought to be the most common pattern for *wh*-questions in English, these latter findings are somewhat puzzling.

In a corpus-based study focusing on intonational features of *yes-no* questions, Steele and Hirschberg (1987) examined recordings of modal second-person *yes-no* questions (of the form, *Can you X?*) in recordings from a radio financial advice show. They found that tokens uttered with **L* H-H%** tended to be interpreted as requests for a simple *yes* or *no*. Tokens uttered with a standard declarative contour (**H* L-L%**) were **also** interpreted as direct speech acts – and generally answered with a simple *yes* or *no*. Utterances interpreted as indirect requests, on the other hand, tended to be those that were uttered with continuation rise (**L-H%**) or with a plateau contour (**H* H-L%**). Additionally, the modal *can* in tokens interpreted as direct was more likely to be reduced than was the modal in tokens interpreted as indirect speech acts.

Following up on this study, Nickerson and Chu-Carroll (1999) found somewhat different results in a series of production experiments. Their analysis showed that utterances realized with a low boundary tone (**L%**) were more likely to be used to convey an indirect reading (73% of tokens ending in L% were used in indirect contexts) and that those with a high boundary tone (**H%**) were slightly more likely to be used to convey a direct *yes-no* question reading (54% were used in direct contexts). So, while various studies have indeed found differences between productions of direct vs. indirect speech acts that are linked to intonational variation, the exact nature of that difference is open to further study.

Other corpus-based studies on the role of intonational variation in identifying DIALOGUE ACTS has been targeted toward speech recognition applications, but is also of some theoretical interest. Work on the DARPA Switchboard corpus (Shriberg et al. 1998) and the Edinburgh Map Task corpus (Taylor et al. 1998) has sought to associate particular intonational and lower-level prosodic features with utterances hand-labeled as, inter alia, "statements" or "acknowledgments" or BACKCHANNELS. Work on the Verbmobil corpus particularly at Erlangen (Nöth et al. 2002) has also investigated the use of prosodic features such as prominence and phrasing to improve performance in speech understanding.

6   Intonational Meaning: Future Research Areas

While there has been increasing interest in intonational studies in recent years, fueled in part by advances in the speech technologies, concern for modeling greater "naturalness" in speech synthesis (text-to-speech), and a desire to make use of whatever additional evidence intonation can provide to improve automatic speech recognition performance, much remains to be done. Corpus-based studies of all aspects of intonational meaning are still at an early stage, due to the large amount of hand labor involved in developing labeled corpora to serve as a basis for research. Study of the contribution of intonational contours to overall utterance interpretation has so far been confined to a few contours – and such common contours as continuation rise or **H* !H* L-L%** remain relatively unexamined. While there have been numerous empirical studies of accent and the given/new distinction, other forms of information status such as theme/rheme, topic/comment, and contrast could benefit from more attention. While corpus-based studies have provided some significant exceptions, most studies of intonation have examined monologue; the cross-speaker characteristics of intonation in dialogue systems offer rich prospects for investigation. And cross-language comparisons of intonational variation are also relatively scarce. In short, we still have much to learn about the pragmatics of intonation.

NOTES

1   A fuller description of the ToBI systems may be found in the ToBI conventions document and the training materials available at http://ling.ohiostate.edu/tobi. Other versions of this system have been developed for languages such as German, Italian, Japanese, and Spanish.

2   The examples in figures 23.1–23.5 are taken from the ToBI training materials, prepared by Mary Beckman and Gail Ayers, and available at http://ling.ohiostate.edu/tobi.

3   Pierrehumbert's **H+L*** corresponds to the ToBI ʺ+ !H*. Her **H*+L** is included in the simple **H*** category, and may be distinguished contextually from the simple **H*** by the presence of a following down-stepped tone. Otherwise the systems are identical.

4   Contours in which one or more pitch accents which follow a complex accent are uttered in a compressed range, producing a "stairstep" effect.

24 Historical Pragmatics

ELIZABETH CLOSS TRAUGOTT

1 The Field

During the last two decades, the study of meaning change based in theoretical pragmatics has come to play an important part in our understanding not only of semantic change and lexicalization, but also of the relationship between structure and use in general, most especially the nature of contextual meaning.[1]

Historical pragmatics is a usage-based approach to language change[2] which came to be identified and institutionalized as a field of study largely owing to the work represented in Jucker (1995) and in the *Journal of Historical Pragmatics*. Jacobs and Jucker (1995) present an overview of historical pragmatics from various perspectives, and characterize it as being essentially of two types, which correspond roughly to the distinction between "external" and "internal" language change. The first they call "pragmaphilology." This is a primarily a "macro-approach" (Arnovick 1999), and the focus is on the changing social conditions in which linguistic change occurs, for example changes in the "aims, motives, interests, public and private behaviour, institutions, formulae and rituals" (Jacobs and Jucker 1995: 5). The prime data are text types that are written or spoken: monologues, conversations, etc. seen in terms of religious, legal, pedagogical, and other norms of text production and reproduction. Research along these lines poses anthropological and cross-cultural or intercultural questions. Jacobs and Jucker call the second type of work on historical pragmatics "diachronic pragmatics." This approach is typically a "micro-approach." The focus is on the interface of linguistic structure and use, and on "what types of rules, conditions, and functions of social acts were effective in earlier stages or processes of language change" (1995: 5). Data are textual evidence for the development of, for example, honorifics, focus particles, discourse markers, or performative uses of locutionary verbs. Within diachronic pragmatics, Jacobs and Jucker further distinguish two well-known approaches that will be important in discussion below (for fuller details see Geeraerts

1997: 17–18). One involves "form-to-function mapping" and is "semasiological." The dominant question is: What are the constraints on ways in which a meaning can change while form remains constant (*modulo* independent phonological changes)? For example, what are the constraints on the ways in which *may* developed polysemies over time? The other approach involves "function-to-form mapping" and is "onomasiological." The dominant question is: What constraints are there on recruitment of extant terms to express a semantic category? For example, what constraints are there on development of lexical resources for expressing epistemic possibility?

Although some very important theoretical work has been based on dictionaries, claims made by scholars like Bréal (1900) and Ullmann (1959), or introspection (see especially Horn 1984a et passim), much recent historical pragmatics is based in textual data. Some text-based work has investigated changes in patterns of foregrounding and backgrounding of material in the narrative story-line (e.g. Hopper 1979, Fleischman 1990) or of markers that signal narrative structure (e.g. Brinton 1996). Hardly surprisingly, there is considerable overlap between text-based historical pragmatics and historical discourse analysis; whether there is any significant difference between the two is debatable. Brinton (2001) provides a threefold classification of historical discourse analysis: HISTORICAL DISCOURSE ANALYSIS PROPER, DIACHRONICALLY ORIENTED DISCOURSE ANALYSIS, and DISCOURSE-ORIENTED HISTORICAL LINGUISTICS. These distinctions are based primarily on the methodological perspective of the work. According to Brinton, historical discourse analysis proper is essentially synchronic: the study of pragmatic factors such as orality, text type, or narrative markers, at a particular language stage; for example, the use of narrative markers in Middle English (this mode of work include aspects of what Jacobs and Jucker call PRAGMAPHILOLOGY). Diachronically oriented discourse analysis examines the evolution of forms or systems that have a discourse function, such as the development of particular adverbials or verbal phrases into narrative markers, or changes in the systems of narrative marking over time. Discourse-oriented historical linguistics is an approach to historical linguistics that seeks to find the origins of or motivations for change in discourse, for example the origins of semantic change in the conventionalizing of implicatures.

The present essay will discuss issues primarily from the perspective of diachronic pragmatics and diachronically oriented discourse analysis, taking pragmatics to be non-literal meaning that arises in language use. Section 2 outlines some proposals regarding discourse pragmatic origins and motivations for semantic and lexical change from a primarily synchronic "neo-Gricean" perspective, since this has been the most influential and widely used theoretical approach in historical pragmatics. Data used from this perspective are usually presented out of context, as individual lexical items, or constructions. Section 3 introduces proposals embedded in historical linguistics and based on textual data from historical corpora. Section 4 provides a case study using data of this type.

2   From the Synchronic Perspective on Pragmatics

Much historical pragmatics builds on work in the early 1970s. An early and seminal suggestion was made in a short paper by Geis and Zwicky:

> It seems to be the case that an invited inference can, historically, become part of semantic representation in the strict sense; thus, the development of the English conjunction *since* from a purely temporal word to a marker of causation can be interpreted as a change from a principle of invited inference associated with *since* (by virtue of the temporal meaning) to a piece of the semantic content of *since*. (Geis and Zwicky 1971: 565–6)

In this idea they echo Grice (1967), who tentatively remarked, "it may not be impossible for what starts life, so to speak, as a conversational implicature to become conventionalized" (Grice 1989: 39; for an early follow-up see Brown and Levinson 1987 on the development of honorifics).

Two questions have been of central concern since the mid-1970s:

1   Do different conversational maxims motivate different types of semantic change?
2   Does Grice's distinction between particularized and generalized conversational implicatures help account for how semantic change occurs?

A further question has been posed primarily within historical linguistics:

3   Are there additional important factors that need to be considered in accounting for frequently observed types of semantic change?

The first two questions are the topic of the next subsections, the third of section 3.

2.1   The role of conversational maxims in semantic change

A central issue in the debate around Gricean pragmatics has been discussion of the validity of his maxims. These were reconceptualized by Horn as "principles." Levinson further reconceptualized them as design features of communication or "heuristics," available to speakers and hearers when they attempt to solve the problem of converting thought into speech ("heuristics" is the term adopted here).[3] In neo-Gricean pragmatics, as exemplified by, for example, Atlas and Levinson (1981), Horn (1984a) and later works, some kind of division of labor has been maintained between what Grice initially identified as Quantity$_1$: "Make your contribution as informative as is required (for the current purposes of the exchange)" and Quantity$_2$ ("Do not make your contribution more informative than is required") (Grice 1989: 26). Among reasons given in Horn (1984a) and Levinson (2000a) for retaining the division of labor, despite objections from other research paradigms, especially Relevance Theory (e.g. Sperber and Wilson 1986a), is semantic change.

Since Horn's and Levinson's proposals, although related, suggest slightly different issues for semantic change, I treat each separately.

2.2   *Horn's proposals*

Invoking Zipf's (1949) recognition that much of language use can be accounted for in terms of the competing forces of speaker economy vs. hearer economy, Horn collapsed Grice's Maxims into two principles, Q(uantity) and R(elation):

(1)a.   **The Q Principle** (hearer-based):
MAKE YOUR CONTRIBUTION SUFFICIENT (cf. Quantity$_1$). SAY AS MUCH AS YOU CAN (given R).
Lower-bounding principle, inducing upper-bounding implicata.

b.   **The R Principle** (speaker-based):
MAKE YOUR CONTRIBUTION NECESSARY (cf. Relation, Quantity$_2$, Manner).
SAY NO MORE THAN YOU MUST (given Q).
Upper-bounding principle, inducing lower-bounded implicata (Horn 1984a: 13).

Q-based implicature is "typically negative in that its calculation [by the hearer] refers crucially to what could have been said, but wasn't," and is therefore linguistically motivated, as exemplified by scalar implicatures such as hold between the members of the pair ⟨all, some⟩. On the other hand, R-based implicature "typically involves social rather than purely linguistic motivation," as exemplified by indirect speech acts (Horn 1996a: 313). Nevertheless, as discussed below, since the division of labor between Q and R principles often concerns lexical distribution of less vs. more complex forms, R-based implicature is often also linguistically motivated.

Horn relates the Q- and R-based implicatures to two types of semantic change that are well known from the work of Bréal and Ullmann: broadening and narrowing. He suggests that broadening is always uniquely R-based, e.g. *xerox, kleenex* (Horn 1984a: 35). In the case of *xerox*, a salient exemplar of a wider class, e.g. copy-machines, is generalized to denote that wider class. This is a case of form-to-function or semasiological change.

Where narrowing is concerned, the issues are more complex. Horn (1984a) mentions various types of semasiological narrowing in which a superordinate term comes to be interpreted as the complement of a hyponym, e.g. in certain circumstances, *finger* is interpreted to exclude its hyponym *thumb* (e.g. when one says *I hurt my finger*), or *rectangle* is interpreted to exclude *square*. He calls this AUTOHYPONYMY. As he argues in Horn (1984b: 117), contra Kempson (1980), such narrowings tend to be highly irregular ("an ornery array of disparate cases"). The examples appear to be motivated by euphemism (cf. *stink – smell*), restriction of technical terms (e.g. *rectangle*), association with particular contexts (e.g. *drink* "alcoholic beverage"), and no generalization seems possible other than: "Diachronically, implicated autohyponymy leads to systematic polysemy" (Levinson 2000a: 103).

The second type of narrowing is not semasiological but onomasiological since it involves alignments among the meanings of lexical resources given a pre-existing set of "closely related meanings." Synchronically there is often a "briefer and/or more lexicalized" form that coexists with a "linguistically complex or more prolix" expression (Horn 1996a: 314). The pair will typically reflect a pragmatic division of labor: "Given two co-extensive expressions, the more specialized form – briefer and/or more lexicalized – will tend to become R-associated with a particular unmarked, stereotypical meaning, use, or situation, while the use of the periphrastic or less lexicalized expression, typically (but not always) linguistically more complex or prolix, will tend to be Q-restricted to those situations outside the stereotype, for which the unmarked expression could not have been used appropriately" (Horn 1996a: 314). The less complex term is synchronically narrowed by R-based inferencing that crystallizes "unmarked" meanings such as *kill*, or *will* (future). By contrast, the more complex term is Q-restricted: *cause to die* implicates that direct causation does not obtain, or that the speaker does not have adequate information to vouch for it (Horn 1984a, 1996a, citing McCawley 1978; see also e.g. Langacker 1987, vol. 2); *be going to* "blocks the indirect speech act function of promising" conveyed by *will* (Horn 1996a: 314).

Horn's claim about the division of labor is understood as motivating the principles variously referred to as BLOCKING (Aronoff 1976) or the PRINCIPLE OF CONTRAST (E. Clark 1993). It appears to be generally, perhaps universally, true that there are no true synonyms[4] (see Haiman 1980a on iconic isomorphism), and that in general, given two or more semantically related lexemes, the more complex form (morphologically derived or periphrastic) represents the more specialized or less stereotypical meaning. From a historical point of view, meaning change and the development of new lexical resources are clearly constrained by "Avoid Synonymy" (Kiparsky 1982, Horn 1996a) and the principle of the division of labor. We see this repeatedly in grammaticalization, the stereotypic examples of which involved the recruitment of a prolix expression (often a construction such as *be going to*) into an extant lexical field in certain highly constrained contexts, followed by a realignment of the members of the extant set, and often the replacement of the earlier by the later construction (see Hopper and Traugott 1993). We also see it when synonymous lexemes appear or are borrowed (even though semantically synonymous the latter will always be pragmatically differentiated, precisely because they are borrowings).

Before looking at some striking cases of diachronically operative constraints on lexicalization that have been argued to be motivated by the division of labor between more marked and less marked members of a lexical pairing, several caveats deserve mention:

1   As Horn has often pointed out, the principles are tendencies only. Indeed this is expected, given that change is never wholly predictable.
2   Discussions of synonymy-avoidance tend to be made in terms of pairs, e.g. *cook–cooker, drill–driller, kill–cause to die*. However, these pairs have been extrapolated from a larger lexical set, making "synonymy-avoidance" less easy to pinpoint. In a recent study of the complexities of investigating the meanings of competing forms for various types of theft in Old and Middle English, Roberts (2001) shows that in Old English there was a large set of words for what we now think of as robbery (involving violence) and theft (not involving violence). These included several lexemes based on *stal-* "steal," *ðief-* cf. "thief," *reaf* cf. "rape." When *rob-* forms (< Lat. *robaria* "robbery") appeared in Middle English around 1200, they were apparently used synonymously with native forms, but over the next 300 years *ðief-* forms gradually narrowed, *stal-*forms were restricted to e.g. *stealth*, and a variety of other lexical alignments took place. Lexical pairs are, therefore, often only part of a larger, complex story, in which competition, collocation, and specialized (in this case legal) use may play a part, clouding the attractiveness of claims about Q vs. R-narrowing made out of the context of the whole lexical field in question.
3   What "synonymy" is may be theory dependent. To what extent should *driller* or *cooker* really be considered to be "affixally derived form[s] **synonymous** with" (Horn 1984a: 25, my emphasis) the simple forms *drill* and *cook*?
4   Although "different form implies (partially) different meaning" is often regarded as crucial to an explanation of how the lexicon is constructed and maintained or realigned, its complement "same form implies (partially) same meaning" is often treated differently. Such a principle is often regarded with suspicion, and has been interpreted either as evidence for monosemy (one core meaning – see Relevance Theoretic approaches), or homonymy (see generative theories of semantics). However, from a historical perspective, a theory of semantics encompassing polysemy is crucial if an adequate account is to be given of semasiological change. Once the validity of polysemy is accepted, then we begin to see that some of the examples cited as "synonymy-avoidance," such as the development of *cooker* beside *cook*, *driller* beside *drill*, may be thought of from a historical perspective as avoidance of polysemy across noun-verb doublets, i.e. innovation to construct contrast, rather than as synonymy-avoidance. However, this is a very weak tendency, as can be seen from productivity of noun-verb doublets with no morphological or stress pattern difference between them such as *blanket, butcher, sanction*.

5   A "simple" form may historically derive from a complex one by loss of morphological and semantic compositionality or grammaticalization (development of grammatical out of lexical or constructional meaning), with the
result that over time what was originally complex and marked will become
the unmarked term, and a new marked one will enter the system. For
example, *will*, itself originally a marked periphrastic future that developed
to signal future meaning in Middle English, is being replaced by *be gonna*
at least in spoken language (Krug 2000).

6   The productivity of sets of related lexical items as well as the meanings
associated with them may change over time, as may the extent to which there
is evidence for division of labor. An example is the development of full
lexical verb vs. "light verb" + deverbal noun (e.g. *advise/give advice, help/give
help, answer/give an answer*) (Brinton and Akimoto 1999). Old English (*c*.600–
1150) provides relatively little evidence for such pairings. The few examples
that exist are firmly based in larger lexical sets and appear to show only
part of the division of labor found in Modern English (primarily correlation
with transitive–intransitive, e.g. *cyðan* "to make X known" – *cyððe habban*
"have knowledge"; *wrecan* "to avenge X" – *wracu don* "exact revenge").
During Middle English (*c*.1150–1500) periphrastic constructions of various
types developed, e.g. prepositional phrases, complex verbal phrases (pre-
auxiliaries + main verb constructions), and also article + noun phrase; all
these syntactic changes together with borrowings from French correlated
with increasing expansion of the lexicon, and by Early Modern English
(*c*.1500–1700) the pairings in question had not only become highly productive
but were also developing new semantic significance. In Modern English
"the complex verb is an important means of making situations telic, that is,
of converting activities into accomplishments or achievements, yet without
the necessity of stating an explicit goal (e.g. *dream/have a dream, nibble/have
a nibble* . . .)" (Brinton and Akimoto 1999: 6). R-based narrowing of the
simple form appears to have occurred only after the complex form became
entrenched in competition with the simpler one.

7   Semantic and lexical change have sometimes been considered to be the
same thing (see Householder 1992) and Horn and Levinson appear to equate
them. Unquestionably there is considerable overlap: word formation involves
meaning. This truism does not, however, entail that all word formation
involves change in the same way. When speakers semanticized the causal
implicature from temporal *since*, they developed a new polysemy; this
had distributional consequences for the older lexeme, only secondarily
for the lexical field of causal connectives. But when speakers innovated
cooker, they developed a new form and also a new meaning that had consequences for the lexical field of instruments for cooking, only secondarily
for the lexeme *cook*. The distinction being made here is once again the
distinction between semasiological and onomasiological change. Because
the consequences of these innovations are different, inferences do not
necessarily function in the same way on the two dimensions.

All these caveats aside, the hypothesis that Q- vs. R-based inferencing motivates lexicalization is a powerful one. Horn (1989: chapters 5 and 6; this volume) makes a particularly interesting hypothesis regarding the relevance of the Q principle in an attempt to predict the (near) universal lack of lexical items that denote the negation of the weaker member of a scaled pair. He points out that in the logical square of oppositions O ("particular negative") is typically not lexicalized as a monomorphemic form, although periphrastic expressions may occur. Thus we find *some, all, none,* and *not all,* but not **nall.* Likewise there is no **nalways,* or **noth of them.* Horn proposes that the reason for such structural gaps is the conventionalization of (defeasible) scalar implicatures. The generalization is that historically a lexicalized expression of negative scalar O will not occur since I and O co-implicate each other and pre-existing I blocks O.

Horn has also shown that the lexicalization of modals has similar restrictions: alethic (or in natural language, more properly epistemic) modality typically allows only complex forms in the O position. For example, in contemporary English there is no monomorphemic form meaning "possible not" or "permit not" in the O corner, and in American English no reduced form *mayn't* occurs for "permit not." Instead, we find *may not,* or more complex forms yet, e.g. *You are not allowed to go.* However, the constraints are considerably weaker than in the case of quantifiers (or logical conjunctions, cf. *not and* for **nand*). In modals O can in fact be expressed (cf. *needn't,* British English *mayn't*) and older forms may acquire polysemies by R-narrowing to E. In other words, diachronically there is an attested drift from O → E: "The outer negation associated with a necessity predicate often seems to develop an inner negation reading" (Horn 1989: 261, citing Tobler 1882).

In a study of 29 languages of Europe and India, van der Auwera (2001) confirmed that while quantifiers and conjunctions do not lexicalize negative O, or appear in reduced form, modals sometimes do. Like Horn, he hypothesized that "implicatures can conventionalize, make the expression vague between the original literal meaning and the conventionalizing implicature and later oust the original meaning" (van der Auwera 2001: 32). One of the factors that motivates the frequent renewal and sometimes reduction of the negative modal O, according to him, is the fact that there is a great deal of vagueness in the modal domain.

In sum, Horn's approach provides valuable insights into the ways in which pragmatic principles may give rise to change, especially in the realm of lexicalization and the onomasiological realignments associated with it. It remains to be seen, however, to what extent some of his findings (and equally those of Levinson, to be discussed immediately below) depend on the artifact of selecting pairs from larger lexical sets.

2.3 *Levinson's proposals*

A related but somewhat different neo-Gricean account of Q- and R-based phenomena appears in some detail in Levinson (2000a). He cites Horn's work at considerable length on Q- and R-based inferencing, but does not restrict the division of labor to two principles. Instead, he works with three "heuristics" (2000a: 35–9; cf. Huang, this volume):

1   THE Q HEURISTIC: "What isn't said, isn't."
2   THE I HEURISTIC: "What is expressed simply is stereotypically exemplified" (the "I" stands for "informativeness").
3   THE M HEURISTIC: "What's said in an abnormal way isn't normal").[5]

He suggests that where inconsistent implicatures arise, they are (synchronically) "systematically resolved by an ordered set of priorities" (2000a: 39), among them:

(2)   Q > M > I (read > as "defeats inconsistent") (Levinson 2000a: 39)

Levinson proposes that Q and M have priority over I because I inferences are "based primarily on stereotypical presumptions about the world" and Q and M can be used to show that these I-inferences do not hold (2000a: 40). I implicatures are *grosso modo* Horn's R implicatures, but Relation is downplayed in favor of Information. Levinson goes on to say that "Q relies on sets of alternates of essentially similar form with contrastive content, whereas M relies on sets of alternatives that contrast in form but not in inherent semantic content" (40); in other words, Q operates on contrasting sets of lexemes of similar morphological complexity (e.g. *all*, *some*), M operates on word-form(ation)s (e.g. *drill–driller*, *advise–give advice*). Therefore Q and M implicatures overlap with Horn's Q implicatures and in particular his Division of Pragmatic Labor.

To what extent can (2) be projected onto historical pragmatics? As Levinson has pointed out for over two decades: "One major source for new grammatical constructions is what we have called I-implicatures" (2000a: 263), e.g. in the development of *be going to*, or of morphological markers of honorification in Japanese; I implicatures are also the major source for new polysemies, e.g. the temporal and causal polysemies of *since*. According to Levinson, M implicatures "seem to be essentially parasitic on corresponding I implicatures: whatever an unmarked expression U would I-implicate, the marked alternative (denotational synonym) will implicate the *complement* of U's denotation" (2000a: 137; italics original). Historically, examples are said to include autohyponyms like Horn's examples of *rectangle* and *informant*. Q-based implicatures affect semantic change primarily in the very restricted domains of the negation of quantifiers, logical connectives and modals, most particularly as they enter into the relationships postulated to exist in the Aristotelian square of oppositions. Given the complementarity of the domains of M- and Q-based heuristics in Levinson's system, the need for both heuristics is unclear synchronically. Diachronically it is unnecessary (see Traugott, in press). Rather than invoke the M heuristic, it would appear to be preferable to invoke a general heuristic of the type called PRINCIPLE OF CONTRAST, a constraint that appears to be strong for children

(E. Clark 1993), but weak for adults, who presumably innovated such forms as *cooker, driller, informant,* etc. For adults the principle operates primarily on already extant competing forms, but is no doubt also drawn on when new words are deliberately constructed, e.g. by advertising agencies, or are deliberately restricted, e.g. by practitioners of professional discourse.

Levinson's major contribution to historical pragmatics is that, having earlier suggested that the development of honorifics is the result of the conventionalizing of conversational implicatures (see Brown and Levinson 1987), he further proposed that "it is possible to argue that there is a sequence from particularized through generalized conversational implicatures to conventional implicatures" (Levinson 1979a: 216). The argument for the importance of distinguishing token implicatures that arise on the fly in conversation (particularized conversational implicatures or PCIs) from preferred type-implicatures (generalized conversational implicatures or GCIs) was expanded in Levinson (1995 and especially 2000a). It can be abbreviated as (3), where SM means conventionalized or "semanticized" (i.e. coded) meaning:

(3) PCI → GCI → SM (read → as "may become")

The key claims may be stated as follows:

1 PCIs are highly context-dependent, and are not stably associated with any linguistic form.
2 GCIs are normally, even stably, associated with certain linguistic forms.

Both types are defeasible in the sense that they can be defeated by the addition of premises.

From a historical point of view, provided we have a rich enough database, we can see how virtually every example of semasiological innovation (whatever its heuristic base) must have started with a PCI, i.e. a possible meaning in context. Typically the numbers of examples that qualify are minimal (one or two within a number of texts at a particular time or in a particular author's work). Over time the number of eligible readings increases, perhaps at differential rates in different text types, and can be hypothesized to have become a preferred, if not default, reading, as the result of the operation of appropriate heuristics. Eventually this preferred reading may become conventionalized, or "semanticized," as a polysemy of the item in question. Levinson gives the example of the development of the reflexive marker -*self* in English. Originally used as an emphatic as in *Hi hiene selfne gefengon* "They captured even him" (lit. "They him himself captured"), it could on occasion be construed reflexively; by Middle English, it came to be used reflexively with dramatically increasing frequency, and eventually became grammaticalized as a (largely) obligatory pronoun under specific binding conditions (Levinson 2000a: 338–59 and references therein; see also Huang, this volume for more on neo-Gricean approaches to anaphora).[6]

Despite Levinson's insights that token meanings develop by pragmatic inferencing into type meanings, and ultimately may become semanticized, and that the "engine" for many of these changes is I-inferencing. (Levinson 2000a: 370), we are left with a problem: that of directionality of change. Honorifics develop out of non-honorifics, not the other way round, and addressee honorifics out of referent honorifics, not the other way round (Brown and Levinson 1987: 276–7). Reflexives arise out of emphatics and not the other way around (Faltz 1989, Kemmer 1993). Subsequent work in a large number of domains has pointed to more and more examples of unidirectionality in semantic change, e.g. from part to whole (Wilkins 1996), from deontic to epistemic (Traugott 1989, Bybee et al. 1994), from conditional to concessive (König 1985), from meanings based in the concrete sociophysical world to those based in the world of the speech event (Traugott 1982, Sweetser 1990). Additional ingredients are therefore needed to account for semantic change.

3   From the Perspective of Language Change

In Horn and Levinson's work, a historical perspective on pragmatics is called upon primarily as additional support for synchronic analysis. In much recent historical work on semantic change, the role of pragmatics plays center stage. For a historical linguist key questions concern what the "path" of change is, what motivates it, and what the mechanism for the change is.[7] The first of these questions has been called the TRANSITION question. Mechanisms and motivations are part of the ACTUATION question (Weinreich et al. 1968).

With respect to mechanisms of change, from the beginning of the twentieth century on, two have been recognized as being of crucial importance in the field of morphosyntax: reanalysis and analogy (see e.g. Meillet 1912, Harris and Campbell 1995); a third is borrowing. Reanalysis modifies underlying representations, whether semantic, syntactic, or morphological. For example, the development of auxiliaries is a case of reanalysis (category, and hence distributional status, changes). In semantics we may think of reanalysis as involving change in the status of implicatures associated with lexemes. Studies of a large number of instances of grammaticalization (e.g. Fleischman 1982 on the development of future markers in Romance languages, Traugott 1982 on the development of connectives in English, Bybee et al. 1994 on the development of tense, aspect, and modality in the languages of the world) and of semantic change independent of grammaticalization (e.g. Traugott 1996, on the development of *promise* and *threaten*), led to the hypothesis that the shift in (3) is one, perhaps the most important, way in which reanalysis operates in semasiological change. By contrast, in the domain of lexicalization by innovative word-formation, this shift does not appear to be a factor. For example, in cases of zero-derivation such as are found in the creation of denominal verbs in English, e.g. *calendar* (n) → *to calendar* "enter in one's calendar" (v), or in the creation of deverbal nominals in Latin, e.g. *praelud-* (v) "play before" → *praelud-* (n) "prelude," the reanalysis occurs instantaneously, with entirely predictable semantic consequences for the new word formation in question (a denomin-alized verb acquires event-structure, for example). Word formation by overt derivation, such as *driller* and *cooker*, is likewise instantaneous. Such changes may have consequences for the semantics of the root form and certainly for newly contrasting members of the same lexical field, but (3) is not at issue.

With respect to motivations, two are most frequently mentioned in the literature: language acquisition and strategic interaction by speakers/writers (SP/Ws) and addressees/readers (AD/Rs) in the dyadic speech event. Innova-tion of a new meaning, once replicated by the innovator, by definition involves acquisition of the innovation. Replication by others, i.e. spread to others, also by definition involves acquisition. In this process of acquisition, the prime type of reasoning has been shown to be ABDUCTION (see Andersen 1973, Anttila 1992, Levinson 2000a, Hobbs this volume). Abduction is "common-sense reason-ing" by which language acquirers infer something to be the case, based on observation of data and invoking a regularity, e.g. hearing *cooker*, and know-ing that in English *-er* usually marks an animate agent, the hearer might con-clude that it meant "one who cooks" until further evidence showed that *cook* already exists in that meaning. While much of the generative literature on syntactic and phonological change has assumed that restructuring in grammar occurs as a result of child language learning (e.g. Halle 1964, Lightfoot 1979 et passim), there is growing evidence that attention needs to be paid to language learners of any age (see e.g. Andersen 1973, Ravid 1995, Eckert 1999). When the data for historical linguistics comes from periods prior to recording, claims about acquisition can be only speculative, since it is impossible to access evid-ence of child (or adult) language acquisition in any detail from written records of the past. In the case of historical pragmatics, we can only say that we are coming to understand that children pay attention to pragmatic factors from a very early age (e.g. E. Clark 1999, 2002a), but they are of course also learning which strategies to pay attention to (Slobin 1994). To date we regrettably have no firm empirical evidence for the extent to which small children, young adults, or older adults actually bring change about through innovations motivated by inferencing.

We can, however, observe strategic interaction by the SP/W–AD/R dyad in various discourse situations, such as conversations, legal and medical inter-views, etc. Since we have written textual evidence for a variety of genres, including interactive genres as represented by drama, we have more adequate evidence for motivations in this area than in acquisition. By hypothesis, SP/ Ws and AD/Rs interacted in similar ways drawing on similar heuristics across time, at least within the 3,000-year history of languages known to us (such as Indo-European, Chinese, and Japanese). We assume therefore that interlocutors draw and have drawn on a number of cognitive abilities. One is the ability to maximize Relation/Relevance to that situation. Another is the ability to use vari-ous kinds of rhetorical strategies like METAPHOR, METONYMY, and SYNECDOCHE[8] (see Nerlich and Clarke 1992, 1999). Metaphor can be thought of as a cognitive process involving associations mainly of the "equivalence" or "paradigmatic" type: "a mapping of a domain onto another domain, both being conventionally and consciously classified as separate domains" (Barcelona 2000: 9), e.g. body part, space and time, emotion. Metonymy can be thought of as a cognitive process in which "one conceptual entity ... provides access to another conceptual entity ... within the same domain" (Kövecses and Radden 1998: 38). While metonymy has until recently been given little attention, its importance is coming to be increasingly recognized as "probably even more basic [than metaphor] to cognition" (Barcelona 2000: 4). Metonymies of this kind are typically conceptual and can be construed as including the implicatures associated with linguistic expressions (Traugott and König 1991). The existence at a moment in time of culturally accepted and salient metonymies and metaphors, as well as cognitively more general ones without doubt both motivates and constrains change. However, the actual process of the development of conventionalized metonymies and metaphors ("metaphorization" and "metonymization") is crucially tied up with the mechanisms of reanalysis in the case of metonymization, and with analogy in the case of metaphorization. Anttila (1992) usefully pairs metonymy with indexicality and syntagmatic relationships, metaphor with iconicity and paradigmatic relationships.[9] Here I discuss only the kinds of semantic changes that arise out of regularly recurring metonymic inferencing in the syntagmatic flow of speech.

One of the strongest metonymies is attraction of meaning to the metalinguistic domain of the SP/W–AD/R dyad, a process that has been variously identified as the development of "expressive," "subjective," "metatextual," "procedural," or "speech act" meanings over time (e.g. Traugott 1982, 1989, Sweetser 1990, Nicolle 1998); as a historical process deriving from pragmatic inferencing it is widely known as SUBJECTIFICATION (e.g. papers in Stein and Wright 1995). Subjectivity as a synchronic (and partially diachronic) phenomenon plays a role in Bréal's work (1900: Chap. 25) and was later elaborated on in several works including Kuroda's (1973) classic study of Japanese expressions of physical sensation. The concept is, however, most frequently associated with Benveniste, who distinguished "sujet d'énoncé"/"syntactic subject" and "sujet d'énonciation"/"speaking subject" (Benveniste 1958). In Lyons's words: "The term subjectivity refers to the way in which natural languages, in their structure and their normal manner of operation, provide for the locutionary agent's expression of himself and his own attitudes and beliefs" (Lyons 1982: 102). This "expression of self" may be instantiated lexically or grammatically, for example, by deictics, performative uses of speech act verbs, choice of aspect, or of discourse markers like *after all*.

As a historical pragmatic phenomenon, subjectification is the mechanism whereby meanings tend to become increasingly based in the SP/W's subjective belief state or attitude toward what is being said and how it is being said.[10] It is metonymic to the SP/W–AD/R dyad, in other words, to the communicative situation, and strongly suggests that R-based inferencing (using the heuristic of Relation/Relevance, not just Informativeness) is crucial to semantic change. On the assumption that the basic problem of communication is the mismatch between speaker's thinking and articulation of that thought (speaking), then SP/W has a significantly more difficult task than AD/R. This task will encourage exploitation of R heuristics as meanings are used in novel utterances, since it minimizes production effort ("Say no more than you must," in Horn's terms). Since the pragmatic cues given and inferred are contextually negotiated in terms of "the accepted purpose or direction of the talk exchange" (Grice 1989: 26), the R relation will be construed with reference to the speech situation and the dyad in it. AD/R is not excessively burdened by the innovation and the violation of M heuristics, because experimental innovations on the semasiological dimension are typically introduced in ways that are harmonic with other meanings already available in the context, and are therefore informationally minimally problematic. This will be demonstrated in section 4. If AD/R does not interpret the cue or interprets but does not replicate it, then the experiment will remain just that. If AD/R does interpret it and replicate it, then he or she will do so as SP/W, and over time relatively normative and stable generalized implicatures may arise that are enrichments of earlier meanings.

Once a lexeme has undergone subjectification it may be further grounded in the communicative dyad and intersubjectification may occur. That is, meanings may develop that encode intersubjectivity: awareness of each participant by the other (see Benveniste 1958). As a historical mechanism, intersubjectification motivates the semasiological shift of meanings over time to encode or externalize implicatures regarding SP/W's attention to the "self" of AD/R. Although honorifics might seem to exemplify intersubjectification only, in fact, the changes in meaning that a lexeme or construction undergoes if it is pre-empted to honorific function always involve some degree of subjectification. This is because honorifics index social status from the point of view of SP/W. One example of such a shift is pre-tenth-century Old Japanese non-honorific *samoraFu* "wait on/for, be in attendance" → eleventh-century humiliative referent honorific *saburahu* "HUMIL-be" (indexing SP/Ws assessment that the subject referent is lower in social status than some other referent) → thirteenth-century addressee honorific "polite" *saburahu/soorau*, indexing AD as being socially superior to SP (Traugott and Dasher 2002: §6.5.1).

Some of the changes outlined here involve primarily social-cultural motivation, for example the kinds of euphemisms that Horn and Levinson discuss; examples tend to be nominal, or to involve nominals (e.g. *go to the bathroom*), but some are verbal (e.g. *sleep with*) (see Horn 2000a); all have clearly referential properties. Many other changes involve primarily linguistic motivation, e.g. space to time, temporal to causal, conditional to concessive, deontic to epistemic; examples tend to be expressed by demonstratives, verbs, adverbials or connectives, and to defy referential interpretation. In so far as subjectification and intersubjectification involve the SP/W–AD/R dyad and crucially influence interpretation of deixis, modals, etc., they are on the interface between social and grammatical meaning. It is therefore not the case that R-based implicatures "typically involve social rather than purely linguistic motivation," as suggested by Horn (1996a: 313; see also Levinson 2000a on I implicatures), except in the broadest sense that all implicatures arise in the speech event situation, which is a social phenomenon. Most R-based implicatures involve both social and linguistic motivation.

3.1   *The Invited Inference Theory of Semantic Change*

An attempt to provide a fuller account of the pragmatic factors involved in semantic change than is proposed in the work discussed in section 2 is the Invited Inferencing Theory of Semantic Change (IITSC) (e.g. Traugott 1999, Traugott and Dasher 2002). The term INVITED INFERENCE is borrowed from Geis and Zwicky (1971) but has been extended to conversational implicatures; it is not considered to be a "special class of 'implicatures'" distinct from conversational implicatures as in that work (1971: 565). "Invited inferences" is preferred over "implicatures" in that it highlights the dual role of SP/Ws and AD/Rs in the dyadic speech event: SP/Ws strategically use implicatures and invite AD/Rs to infer a meaning. Therefore, in this model PCIs are renamed Invited Inferences (IINs), and GCIs are renamed "Generalized Invited Inferences" (GIINs). (3) is restated as (4):

(4)   IIN → GIIN → SM

Implicatures are considered to be R-based rather than I-based, because of the widespread development of meanings based in the interactive dyad, not exclusively in information. They are also assumed to be motivated largely by linguistic rather than social factors.

The IITSC focuses on schemas that represent types of semasiological reanalysis that language-specific lexemes may (but do not have to) undergo, constrained by larger cross-linguistic and onomasiological conceptual categories such as causal, conditional, future epistemic, animate, etc. It also focuses on the way in which stereotypes emerge, a perspective missing in most work discussed in section 2. Wherever semantic change is of the type in (4), the IIN is by definition not (yet) stereotypic. As IINs become more salient in the community, i.e. as they become GIINs, the stereotype is actually being created for the form with which they are associated; it does not pre-exist. For example, while it may be that inferences from emphatic *-self* could be made to anaphoric identity with a prior NP, so long as this inference was unusual and only contextually accessible, it was not yet a stereotype; the stereotype inference to the anaphor developed over time.

In the IITSC the assumption is that every innovation at the GIIN stage (if not before) has the potential for violating the Manner maxim "be orderly," insofar as that may be interpreted as pertaining to maintenance of norms. As we shall see in the case study below, most GIINs become crystallized in contexts where the new meaning is redundant with other elements in the sentence, and so violation of "avoid ambiguity" is probably relatively minimal in context, albeit large-seeming out of context. However, when a new polysemy is semanticized, redundancy of context is no longer in play, and ambiguity can occur more readily. In many cases the new polysemy is distributionally different from the old one and a reanalysis has therefore occurred, e.g. epistemic *must* is available in past tense and stative contexts in a way in which the older deontic *must* is not, *evidently* as a sentential epistemic adverbial is available in clause-initial position which the older manner adverbial (meaning "clearly") is not. These new polysemies, particularly if they are modal or connective, may be used to signal that there is some doubt is being cast on the proposition, and so can function to warn that a special interpretation is necessary, i.e. as violations of "avoid prolixity."

4   A Case Study: *after all*[11]

I turn now to a brief case study exemplifying an approach to historical pragmatics based on corpora: the development of *after all*. A methodologically useful way to begin such a study is to investigate the synchronic situation after a set of polysemies has come into existence and then to seek evidence in a historical corpus for the transition from an earlier stage to the synchronic one studied, all the while watching for developments that may have dead-ended. Such dead-ended developments frequently show incipient conventionalization of a meaning that is not replicated, or not replicated for any considerable length of time, whereas it may become a highly salient meaning in another language. For example, there is some sporadic evidence of incipient "because"-meanings for *while* in Middle English; this IIN never became a GIIN in English, but it did for the cognate *weil* in German.

Since most of the material for historical linguistics is written, it is important to use corpora in the same mode, if not genre. This means that contemporary spoken language can be used as a comparison only with spoken material from an earlier era; and constructed data may be helpful in highlighting areas of inquiry but they need to be used with great caution since they cannot be verified by native speakers in earlier periods.

After all has been discussed in terms of Relevance Theory by Blakemore (1987, this volume), Blass (1990), Carston (1993), and others as a prime example of a non-truth-conditional PROCEDURAL MARKER. It has also been variously called a "discourse marker" (Schiffrin 1987), "pragmatic marker" (Fraser 1996), "connector," "(discourse) connective," and in much European work "argumentative operator" (e.g. Jakobson 1957, Ducrot 1972, Anscombre and Ducrot 1989). Using constructed examples of the type in (5):

(5)a.   He is brave; he is <u>after all</u> an Englishman.
   b.   Tom has left. <u>After all,</u> his wife is not here.

Blakemore proposes that *after all* in *p after all q* constructions provides evidence to the hearer for the truth of *p* and serves as a reminder of *q* (Blakemore 1987: 81–2). Blass adds that *q* is known to the hearer (Blass 1990: 129). These accounts assume unitary meanings that are contextually interpreted. They are also primarily MONOLOGIC, in that they assume perspectival continuity between the clauses represented by *p* and *q*. Other approaches have, however, been very different. Roulet (1990), for example, highlights the multiplicity of uses of French *après tout* and its English counterpart *after all* (he says they behave identically), as a concessive ("nevertheless"), and as a connective meaning "of course" in some contexts, "because" in others. He points out that it is often used "dans une contexte refutative" ("in a refutational context") (Roulet 1990: 342). On this account adverbial *after all* is strongly "dialogic" and "polyphonic" in some of its uses: it involves "crystallized" dialogues, and "incompatible viewpoints" (Nølke 1992: 191, Schwenter 1999a).[12]

The following account of the history of *after all* builds on these prior analyses, especially Roulet's, to suggest a methodology for text-based historical pragmatics.

4.1   *The present-day situation*

The following account of contemporary *after all* is based on a computerized corpus of top stories issued by United Press International (UPI) in the years 1990–2; these stories contain quotations of speeches and also newspaper reporting. In this corpus there are 45 tokens of *after all*; the usages appear to be entirely characteristic of American English.

Of the 45 tokens of *after all*, 10 involve the preposition *after* followed by *all NP*; together they form a temporal adverbial construction, as in *after all these years*, which is to be understood literally and compositionally.

Four tokens have connective adverbial properties that are epistemic, that is, they concern SP/W's assessment of the truth of the proposition that follows (*q*). These four tokens are oriented away from some aspect of the prior discourse (*p*) and are therefore adversative. Two of them are concessive adverbials meaning "however, nonetheless, despite what was expected" by some locutor, who could be a third person, SP/W in another (dialectic) role, or (hypothetically) AD/R, as in (6):

(6)   The federal fund that finances presidential campaigns should have enough money to pay for the 1992 race <u>after all</u>, but by 1996 the coffer could be depleted, a new report said Wednesday.
      The Federal Election Commission issued a new projection on how much money will be available to finance the 1992 primaries . . . that is more optimistic than some previous estimates.   (UPI, August 14, 1991)

This example, which occurs at the beginning of the news story, has no antecedent *p*, but *after all* evokes one (*there won't be enough money to pay for the 1992 race*), and confirms it in the second paragraph. The concessive introduces an argument *q* (the proposition), and invites the conclusion *r* that *p* (which is implicit in this case) is not true, i.e. it is backward-looking and epistemic.

There are two other epistemic examples that share some of the features of (6), but they are not restricted to final position. Like the concessive, they signal epistemic counter-expectation, but they are more complex (both positive and negative aspects of *p* are brought into focus), and the logical connection between *p* and *q* is less obvious. An example is (7):

(7) Grodin [an actor] also captures the movie star's obsessive concern with his image, which is, <u>after all</u>, what he has to sell.   (UPI, June 19, 1990)

In (7) *q* (*his image is what he has to sell*) must be understood to be not only plausible but acceptable in a social world of norms. Rather than involving "locutor or addressee did not believe/expect *q* to be true," *after all* invokes "locutor or addressee might not have thought of *q* because of some aspect *a* of *p* (*obsessive*)." On this view, *after all* marks *q* as an argument to the conclusion *r*: "so you shouldn't be concerned about the star's obsessive worries". This use of *after all* is often associated with an implicature of reminder, because appeal is made to obvious, interpersonally recoverable, societal norms or known situations.

By far the most common use in contemporary American English of *after all* is as a different kind of adverbial connective: one in which the conclusion is oriented toward *p*. This is a true discourse marker (DM) in the sense of Fraser (1988), a "deictic discourse marker" (Schiffrin 1990) that is metatextual in function and signals the speaker's discourse strategy. It serves as "a comment specifying the type of sequential discourse relationship that holds between the current utterance – the utterance of which the discourse marker is a part – and the prior discourse" (Fraser 1988: 21–2). The purpose of such markers is to "combine viewpoints into structure" (Nølke 1992: 197) and to express the discourse relationship intended by the speaker between two utterances. While richer than the constructed example (5a), this type of *after all* has some of its flavor. (There are no examples resembling (5b)).

There are 26 examples in the corpus of uses like (8):

(8) The notion that bombs can strike military targets without killing and maiming innocent women and children is absurd. If there is war, the Iraqi dictator can be expected to employ chemical weaponry. <u>After all</u>, he killed his own people, including Kurdish women and children, with poison gas.   (UPI, October 8, 1990)

This kind of DM use has been said (see Blakemore 1987, Blass 1990) to serve to signal that *q* is a justification for *p*: the speaker's reason for saying *p*. Although partially correct, this characterization misses an important point. The justification is actually not of *p*, but of some particular expression in the prior discourse of the speaker's subjective attitude (typically expressed by negation, epistemic modality, or an evaluative lexeme). In (8) *after all* points back anaphorically to the evaluative lexeme *absurd*, as well as the modal *can be expected*, at the same time as signaling cataphorically that *q* is a justification of those two evaluations. Thus while DM *after all* has some epistemic properties (it signals SP/W's belief) and adversative properties (it rejects aspects of *p*), it is different from epistemic adversative *after all* in that it is anaphoric as well as cataphoric, and in that it elaborates on the attitudinal components of *p*. Also, although DM *after all* may conversationally imply that information in *q* is known to the addressee, the strongest invited inference is "You might have thought of this in relation to *p*."

An additional characteristic of DM *after all* is that it is a disjunct and follows an intonational break (reflected by a comma in writing). *q* is therefore syntactically paratactic, and pragmatically an "add-on," conveying a sense of superiority and condescension, even dismissiveness or verbal play on SP/W's part, either to the point of view expressed in *p* (minus the evaluation to be justified), or to AD/R ("Despite the fact that you can't put these two things together, I can!" and "Aren't I being funny/clever/cute?"), or both. These are among factors that differentiate it from *because* and *since*, which can be substituted for it but which convey none of the subjective attitude or metatextual stance of *after all*.

4.2   The diachronic development

I turn now to the question of how these uses came into being (for related studies see Traugott 1989, Powell 1992, Brinton 1996, Rossari 1996, Jucker 1997 among others).

After was a spatial ("behind") and temporal ("later") preposition in Old English. In the context of certain nouns it could indicate "in conformity with" as in example (9) from Middle English:

(9)   Hou that men schal the wordes pike <u>after</u> the forme of eloquence
      "How people shall pick the words according to the form of eloquence"
      (*c*.1393 Gower, *Confessio Amantis* 4.2651 [MED <u>after</u> 8])

The first example in my database of *after all* as an adverbial is from the sixteenth century and it is temporal:

(10) [about the funeral of the Bishop of Winchester] and my lord bysshope
      Bonar of London did syng masse of requiem, and doctur Whyt bysshope
      of Lynkolne dyd pryche at the sam masse; and <u>after all</u> they whent to his
      plasse to dener.

      "and my lord Bishop Bonar of London sang a requiem mass, and
      Dr. White, Bishop of Lincoln, preached that Mass; and after it was all
      over they went to his place to dinner."   (*c*.1560 Machyn, *Diary*, p. 97)

This non-adversative meaning of "finally," "on top of all that" occurs sporadically in the data, with reference not only to time but to sequences of argument, but is always preceded by *and*. There is an implicature of normative sequence or "natural order," perhaps derived or at least supported by *and*. A striking early example of *after all* being used in reference to a sequence of arguments comes from a long "apology" by Dryden concerning a play that he feels was misunderstood. He shows how earlier criticism of the play had been addressed, and goes on to say that the most recent charge is that one of the characters, Almanzor, "performs impossibilities." After a summary of the plot Dryden finally claims:

(11) but, 'tis far from being impossible. Their King had made himself contemptible to his people, as the History of Granada tells us. And . . . <u>And, after all</u>, the greatness of the enterprise consisted only in the daring: for, he had the King's guards to second him.   (1672 Dryden, Dedication, *Conquest of Granada*, p. 30)

Here *and, after all*, can only mean "and in the end" (in terms of the plot) or "finally" (in terms of Dryden's argument). There may be a conversational implicature of adversativity from *after all*, but it is derived largely from the general discourse strategy and is an IIN from the argument that "'tis far from impossible."

By the beginning of the seventeenth century a few uses can be found of the temporal preposition *after* followed by NP, in which the sequence of events can be interpreted as implying that the expected order of events has been violated and that the outcome is not normative:

(12)a. [The Duke has disguised himself to test Angelo, and has said treasonable things about himself]

    Lucio: Do you remember what you said of the Duke? . . . was the Duke a flesh-monger, a fool, and a coward, as you then reported him to be? . . .

    Duke: I protest I love the Duke as I love myself.

    Angelo: Hark how the villain would close now, <u>after</u> his treasonable abuses!

                 (1604 Shakespeare, *Measure for Measure*, v.i.330)

   b. Really, Madam, says Robin, I think 'tis hard you should Question me upon that Head, <u>after all I have said</u>.

                 (1722 Defoe, *Moll Flanders*, p. 54)

There is little evidence that the new meanings in (12a) and (12b) were stereotypic at the time, or that there were any significant sociocultural changes in the community to which they could be tied. Rather, the examples in (12) appear to have been experiments with IINs arising from the temporal expression. Such IINs (and later GIINs) arise fairly frequently cross-linguistically (see Rudolph 1996). Indeed, the use of *after all*, with its generalized quantifier *all* and temporal *after* has lexical properties in common with two of the major cross-linguistic sources[13] for concessives identified by König (1985: 10–11); cf. English *al-be-it, although, however, nevertheless*. From a temporal perspective, the move is from "at the end" to "in the end"; the quantifier specifies "re-examination" of all that preceded, not just the immediately prior *p* (Rossari 1994: 20).

Over the course of the seventeenth century, the kind of dialogic, adversative use of *after all* in (12) develops from a contingent conversational implicature into a generalized one. By the end of the century we find a conventionalized concessive sentential adverbial use as in (13) (see Modern English (6)). It is no longer contextually supported by the construction . . . *that is said and done*, but rather stands alone in a set with *despite everything*.

(13)   [Mrs. Fainell, Lady Wishfort's daughter, has been falsely accused]
     Mrs. Fainell: I know my own innocence, and dare stand a trial. [*Exit*]
     Lady Wishfort: Why, if she should be innocent, if she should be wronged
                 after all? I don't know what to think.
                           (1700 Congreve, *The Way of the World*, Act v)

This dialogic clause-final concessive meaning became entrenched, and the bare temporal adverbial ceased to be used.

At the same time as the clause-final concessive arose we also find *after all* used as an epistemic adversative much like adversative, *actually, in fact* (see (7)). Unlike the clause-final concessive, it is first used in a construction with an adversative connective such as *but*, as in:

(14)   I have not made it my business either to quit or follow any authority in
     the ensuing discourse: Truth has been my only aim . . . Not that I want
     ["lack"] a due respect to other men's opinions; but, <u>after all</u>, the greatest
     reverence is due to truth.
                        (1690 Locke, *Essay Concerning Human Understanding*,
                                   bk. 1, chapter 4, section 23)

Here *after all* is harmonic with, indeed redundant to, *but* and is strongly motivated by the dialogic context in which opposing positions are presented, including negative propositions (*I have not made it my business . . . Not that I want respect*). Early examples like (14) are more strongly truth-oriented than many later ones, which are weakened, partly by generalization to non-negative contexts.

Justification also appears in the seventeenth century, again contextually derived, this time in the context of *and* or *for* "because" preceded by a negative as in:

(15) You need not be much concerned at it; for <u>after all</u>, this way of explaining
      things, as you called it, could never have satisfied any reasonable man.
                                        (1713 Berkeley, *Dialogue*, 2, p. 210)

When, at the beginning of the eighteenth century, justificational *after all*
can occur clause-initially without a preceding connective, it has become
conventionalized.

Blass (1990: 129) suggested that the concessive and justificational *after all's*
derive from *after all that has been said and done*. Examples like (12b) show that
such constructions are indeed likely sources of the concessive. However, since
Blass cites the construction out of context, her proposal gives no insight into
the strongly adversative discourse context that motivated the conventionalization of the adverbial. Furthermore, there is no obvious or natural connection in
terms of implicatures between the temporal and the justificational meanings of
after all. Since justification requires potential adversativity, it is implausible
that it derives directly from the temporal construction. Although temporal
sequence can give rise to causal conjunctions (cf. *since*), and, as we have seen,
quantified temporals are well known to be the source of concessives, they do
not give rise directly to metatextual justification markers. The corpus data
shows that adversative *after all* arises in strongly adversative, largely dialogic
contexts. Justificational *after all* does not emerge until *after all* had come to be
associated with an adversative GIIN.

When we consider the changes outlined here in terms of Horn's and
Levinson's proposals about pragmatic bases for semantic change, we see that
each change involved initial experimentation with IINs in redundant contexts;
the hypothesis in (4) is supported. With respect to the differing roles attached
to Q, M, and R(= Levinson's I), we see that R-based enrichment is central, with
Relation to the SP/W–AD/R dyad, especially SP/W's subjective rhetorical
purposes motivating the shift to adversative procedural meaning. Insofar as
I-based enrichment is "information-based" and not linked to any particular
aspect of the communicative interaction, it accounts less well than R-based
enrichment for the direction of change evidenced by *after all* and the many
other expressions like it. Each change violates the M heuristic in some respect
– the new meanings engendered competition with extant members of the same
conceptual set (e.g. in (13) *after all* competes with *despite everything*, in (14) with
indeed, actually; and the new syntactic positions in which the expression came
to be used violate norms of use. Apparently, however, such M violations (in
the sense of violations of norms and orderliness) did not trigger new restrictions on the pre-existing lexemes as the innovations were taking place. Insofar
as it is prolix (three syllables long) it certainly is more informative than the
but and *for* with which the adversative and then the justificational *after all* co-
occurred, but its presence does not appear to have triggered new restrictions
on them. The eventual loss of clause-final temporal *after all* does not appear to
have been triggered by the M heuristic either: it was lost to the full prepositional phrase with a determiner and noun, e.g. *after all these months*. Insofar as
Levinson's Q implicatures operate on scalar particles, they are not relevant to

the development under discussion here. The main principle at work appears to be the principle of contrast that motivates the maintenance of distinctions from other lexical items within the same general semantic space, but also allows some readjustments over time within it.

The historical data show that the contexts in which new uses of old form-meaning pairs arise are clearly linguistic, not primarily "sociocultural": the new meanings (new token exploitation of implicatures) are reinforced by juxtaposition with connectives that sharply constrain the implicatures. Where individual lexemes or constructions are concerned, implicatures that arise in on-line verbal utterances or writings (IINs) are initially recruited redundantly to extant linguistic contexts for discourse purposes. Once the new usage has been accepted by the community (i.e. has become a GIIN), such redundant cues may be reduced or allowed to be less directly explicit, in which case conventionalization (semanticization) may occur. Absent direct collocation with redundant cues signaled by other connectives or DMs they "actively help to construct that very context" (Hansen 1996: 108); however, as we have seen from the contemporary data on *after all*, redundant cues tend to be very much part of the fabric of the discourse and of the context in which interpretation is to occur. Eventually some DMs like *so*, *because*, *indeed* have come to serve a whole turn (at least in conversation); those that can do so are relatively old; newer ones cannot do this.[14]

5   Conclusion

Historical pragmatics can yield results that bear on fundamental claims in pragmatic theory as well as semantic and lexical change. In answer to question (1) posed in section 2, "Do different conversational maxims motivate different types of semantic change?," the answer is clearly "Yes." The R heuristic (and R inferences from it) accounts for most regularly attested semantic change, in the sense outlined here, excluding word-formation. The Q and M heuristics account primarily for constraints on word formation and realignments of meanings among lexical items, for example in the domain of Aristotelian squares. With respect to question (2), "Does Grice's distinction between particularized and generalized conversational implicatures help account for how semantic change occurs?," again the answer is "Yes." Particularized conversational implicatures are factors in semasiological change only if they become generalized; only generalized implicatures play a role in regular semasiological change. Finally, with respect to question (3), "Are there additional important factors that need to be considered in accounting for frequently observed types of semantic change?," once more the answer is "Yes." R inferences to the SP/W–AD/R dyad in the speech event are prime motivators of change. Furthermore, historical pragmatics requires going beyond decontextualized examples of semantic change, and paying attention to the discourse contexts in which the changes occur. To achieve a full picture, a macro-approach taking external factors such as cultural changes into consideration is, of course, also necessary.

NOTES

1   Thanks to David Beaver and members of his Winter 2001 seminar on radical pragmatics at Stanford for discussion of some of the points in this paper, and to Eve V. Clark and David Beaver for comments on an earlier draft. Larry Horn made many helpful suggestions.

2   Recent broad-based frameworks for usage-based approaches to language change can be found in Keller (1994) and Croft (2000); however, neither focuses on historical pragmatics.

3   See also Keller (1994) for a proposed modified set of maxims of action to account for language change.

4   Except perhaps in a very strict truth-conditional sense of denotational synonymy that is rarely in effect in language use.

5   Levinson (2000a: 41) provides a useful table summarizing corresponding terminologies in Grice, Horn, and Levinson.

6   In a detailed study of the development of *-self* reflexives in the history of English, with attention to anti-synonymy, Keenan (to appear) suggests that Levinson's assumption that non-marking of pronouns will necessarily implicate disjoint reference (2000a: 348–9) is questionable for Old English. Reflexive marking may have been an opportunistic reanalysis based on the emphatic once the latter had spread to non-subject arguments.

7   "Path" or "trajectory" of change is only a metaphor for the linguist's analysis, a metalinguistic way of referring to changes of the type A → A ~ B (→ B), not to any kind of hard-wiring in the brain.

8   Nerlich and Clarke (1999) define "synecdoche" in terms of moving up and down taxonomic space, i.e. as the issue of change of hyponym to super-category (hyperonym) status and vice versa.

9   Despite the differences between them, however, metaphor and metonymy sometimes blend; see Goossens (1995).

10   "Subjectification" has been construed in another line of research, associated with Langacker (1990, 1999), as perspectival shifts from a "syntactic subject" to "speaking subject," as evidenced by the development of raising constructions from control verbs such as *promise, be going to do X* (directional movement for a purpose).

11   An earlier version of this section was presented at the 10th International Congress of Linguistics, Paris, July 1997. Thanks to Regina Blass and Scott Schwenter for comments on that paper.

12   For the distinction between "dialogic" and "monologic" uses of language and approaches to them, see Bakhtin (1981), Ducrot (1984), Roulet (1984) among others.

13   The others are: conditionals (Gm. *ob-gleich*), expressions of co-existence or similarity in space or time, (Fr. *tout de même*, Turk. *bununla beraber* "together with this"), or obstinacy, spite (*de-spite*, Arab. *ragman* from "compel").

14   This shows that DMs like *so*, *therefore, whereas* that can initiate discourses should not be considered of a different type from those that cannot, contra e.g. Rouchota (1996).

25 Pragmatics and Language Acquisition

EVE V. CLARK

The main function of language is not to express thought, . . . but rather to play an active pragmatic part in human nature.

Bronislaw Malinowski (1935)

Do children focus first on forms and later on uses, or do they acquire both together as they master a first language? Consider the exchange in (1) between preverbal Jordan (aged 1;2) and his mother, with Jordan in his highchair looking toward a counter in the kitchen (Golinkoff 1983: 58).[1]

(1) Jordan (vocalizes repeatedly until his mother turns around)
    Mother (turns around to look at him)
    Jordan (points to one of the objects on the counter)
    Mother: Do you want this? (holds up milk container)
    Jordan (shakes his head "no")
      (vocalizes, continues to point)
    Mother: Do you want this? (holds up jelly jar)
    Jordan (shakes his head "no") (continues to point)
    [two more offer–rejection pairs]
    Mother: This? (holds up sponge)
    Jordan (leans back in highchair, puts arms down, tension leaves body)
    Mother (hands Jordan sponge)

This child was intent on communicating something, and managed to do so without words. He first had to establish joint attention with his mother; he achieved this by getting her attention (with vocalization) then pointing at the counter. But the counter had several objects on it, and without words to pick out the one he wanted, he had to rely on his mother's being willing to offer each one in turn until she reached the right one. He consistently rejected unwanted objects with a head-shake while continuing to point and vocalize until his mother hit on the thing he wanted. This exchange is far from unusual. Children communicate remarkably well, even when their linguistic resources are still very limited. They persist in expressing their intentions and adults cooperate in trying to arrive at appropriate interpretations (Werner and Kaplan 1963, Bates 1976, Carter 1978, de León 1998).

How do children manage this? First, they make use of what they know, in context, to make inferences about the intentions of others. Take the episode in (2) (from E. Clark, diary data).

(2)   D (1;11.28, talking at breakfast, as his father tapped the edge of D's bowl with a spoon):   *Herb hitting* [ə] *bowl.*
      Father: Why was I hitting your bowl? Why was I hitting your bowl?
      D (grinning, as he picked up his spoon):   [ə] *eat* [ə] *cornflakes.*

This child drew on his experience of past mealtimes when he typically talked a lot and ate rather little. One- and two-year-olds generally appear to rely on their knowledge about events in deciding how to treat requests (e.g. Shatz 1978). And by age two, for example, they readily treat negated *why* questions as requests for action (Ervin-Tripp 1970: 82), as shown in (3):

(3)   *Mother*:   Why don't you put it in the wastebasket?
      Sally (2;0):   *Throw away?*

By age three, they can sometimes offer explicit analysis of a situation as well, as in (4) (Ervin-Tripp 1977: 182):

(4)   *Mother* (in car):   I'm cold.
      Child (3;3):   *I already shut the window.*

In short, children express their own intentions and make inferences about the intentions of others from an early age.

What kinds of pragmatic knowledge can children draw on as they acquire communicative skills? In this chapter, I take up some aspects of pragmatic development and the evidence that children are attending to speaker intentions on the one hand, and to what the addressee already knows on the other. Attending to these two factors in an exchange requires that children make use of common ground, updating it as needed; it also requires that they take note of speech acts, and learn which inferences to draw from what speakers do and don't say (see Austin 1962, Levinson 1983, Horn 1996a).

1   Joint Attention

In the exchanges just cited, the children's inferences seemed to be based on their own experience and licensed by what was in common ground. Common ground restricts the possible inferences, whether these concern the speaker's intentions, the meaning of a new word or construction, or what is implicated by what the speaker said.

To make use of common ground, speakers must first establish joint attention; then they can draw on that along with physical and conversational
co-presence (H. Clark 1996). Consider the exchange in (5) where a parent
establishes joint attention with a young one-year-old in order to show him an
unfamiliar object. Joey's mother tries six times to get his attention before
succeeding. She uses his name twice, then touches his cheek, then uses his
name again. She then switches to *look*, then combines *look* with an endearment
as she moves her gaze to the target object. Only at this point did the child look
at the object and so give evidence of joint attention.[2]

(5)   *Joey* (1;5.3; being introduced to a small plastic crocodile)
      child looking at door, 0secs–4secs
      parent <u>looks</u> at child, 0secs–7.03secs
      (a)   Parent: *Joe.* (0.25secs–)
      (b)   Parent: *Joey.* (2secs–)
            parent <u>touches</u> J's cheek, 3.1secs–
      (c)   Parent: *Joey.* (3.25secs–)
      child looks off at camera, 4.2secs–8.23secs
      (d)   Parent: *Look!* (5.25secs–)
      (e)   Parent: *Look!* (7.1secs–)
      (f)   Parent: *Honey – look at this.* (7.15secs–)
            parent <u>looks</u> at toy crocodile, 7.25secs–
      child looks at crocodile, 8.25secs–16.22secs
            parent <u>presents</u> crocodile, 9.05secs–
      (g)   Parent: *Look at this.* (9.2secs–)

As children get older, they appear to monitor adults more closely, and are
able to switch their attention more quickly to whatever the adult is attending to. Consider the exchange in (6) between Cathy (1;9.4) and her mother.
Within one second of her mother's simultaneously picking up and looking
at the (unfamiliar) measuring-spoon, Cathy switched her gaze to the spoon
too.[3]

(6)   Cathy (1;9.4, being introduced to a measuring-spoon)
      parent <u>picks</u> up measuring-spoon, 0secs–
      parent <u>looks</u> at measuring-spoon, 0secs–
      child looks at measuring-spoon, 1sec–7.3secs
      parent holds out spoon, 2.05secs–
      (a)   Parent: *This is a spoon.* (2.95secs–)
            parent <u>looks</u> at child, 3.8secs–
      (b)   Parent: *It's a measuring-spoon.* (4.05secs–)

The parents of one-year-olds get their children's attention with gesture and
gaze on the one hand and with language on the other (Moore and Dunham

1995, Schmidt 1996). They look at the child and the target object; they point to the object, hold it out, pick it up, tap it, and point to properties like teeth, wheels, or spots. And they may also demonstrate how an object moves or works (e.g. pushing a toy truck across the table, putting sunglasses on) (see also Shatz 1978, Zukow 1986, Mervis and Mervis 1988, Gogate et al. 2000). They use deictic terms in introductory utterances (e.g. *this, that, see, here*), names, and formulaic utterances to engage the child's attention. For their part, one-year-olds indicate when they are attending: they look at the focus of attention; they reach for the target object, touch it, or manipulate it. As they get older, they also repeat the term the adult has offered for it (E. Clark 2001b).

Once parents and young children achieve joint attention, they can count as *grounded* whatever object or action is at the focus of shared attention. This grounding restricts the candidate referents for any new words on that occasion, and so places limits on children's hypotheses about the meanings of unfamiliar words.

2   Common Ground

Adults offer children extensive pragmatic information about language use, especially about word use (E. Clark and Wong 2002). They offer conventional terms for objects, properties, relations, and activities, and in so doing, place the referents of these terms in common ground. They offer information about how an unfamiliar term differs from and is related to other words in the same domain. They often point out distinguishing properties of the referents of new words, e.g. characteristic noises, activities, or details of appearance (E. Clark 2001a, E. Clark and Chouinard, in preparation). Consider the exchange in (7):

(7)   *Mo* (looking at a picture of some owls in a book with child):   what are these? those are birdies.
  Ch (1;7.19):   *birdies.*
  Mo: and the name of these kinds of birdies they call owls.
    (mother points at the picture)
  Mo: and they say "hoo-hoo."
  Ch: *hoo.*   [NEWENG:NE20:0191, line 1432+]

Notice that the mother here first offers the word *birdies*, which is immediately repeated by the child. She then offers *owls* and goes straight on to offer a distinguishing sound, *hoo*. This too is taken up by the child.

The child's utterances suggest that she has probably made three inferences here: that the objects pictured belong to the category of birds (*birdies*), and to the subcategory owls (*owls*), and that this subcategory of bird says "hoo" (*hoo*) (see E. Clark 2001a).

Some adult offers are tacit repairs of what the child has just proposed, as in (8), where the child takes up the adult term and makes use of it seconds later.

(8)   D (2;8.14, with a toothbrush in his hand):   *An' I going to tease.*
        Mother (puzzled):   Oh. Oh, you mean you're going to *pretend* to do your teeth?
        Child: Yes.
        (then, as father came by a minute later)
        Father: Are you going to do your teeth?
        Child: No, I was pretending.   [E. Clark, diary data]

Both direct and indirect offers depend on joint attention combined with the physical co-presence of the target object or action, plus conversational co-presence (the word for the target referent). Because, together, these factors restrict the domain of possible meanings, they limit the inferences children can make about a new word (E. Clark 2001a).

Adults also connect new words to known ones: they relate them through inclusion ("X is a kind of Y"), parts ("X is part of Y"), properties ("Xs have Ys"), and function ("X is used for doing Y"); they also give definitions and provide lists of entities or actions from the same domain (E. Clark and Wong 2002). All this information is introduced within conversational exchanges. By supplying conventional terms and relating them to others already known, adults offer children more general "maps" of how words represent the world. What these metalanguage directions convey is an important ingredient in adult–child conversations. They provide words and their connections, as shown in (9) and (10).

(9)   *Sarah* (3;6.6) looking at a picture of a nest with eggs in it, with her mother)
        Mo: that's a nest.
        Sarah: a nest.
        Mo: um. that's where the birdies live. that's a birdie house. they call it a nest.

                                        [Brown: Sarah064, line 345+]

(10)   D (3;9.18, at the airport; watching as a mechanic put two chocks by the plane wheels):   *Why did he put two loggers?*
        Mother: Oh, they're called chocks and they keep the wheels from moving.
        Child: Why did he put the chocks?   [E. Clark, diary data]

With each offer of a word, adults add to common ground. And children often ratify these offers explicitly by repeating them. Whenever adults add further information about a new term, this too is added to common ground. With these directions about use, then, adults both provide new words and connect them to their semantic neighbors.

3   Convention and Contrast

Users of language observe two general pragmatic principles. The first assumes conventionality in the system they are using. If a particular meaning is conventionally associated with a particular form, speakers typically use that form for that meaning. They can then be sure their addressees will understand them as intended. If they don't use the expected form, their addressees assume they must mean something else (E. Clark and H. Clark 1979, Horn 1984a, E. Clark 1987, 1990, 1993). Conventionality can be defined as follows:

> *Conventionality*:   For certain meanings, speakers assume that there is a conventional form that should be used in the language community.

For a conventional system to be most effective, speakers will give priority to already-established, conventional forms for particular meanings.

This principle goes hand-in-hand with a second. It assumes that different forms differ in meaning. If a speaker uses two distinct forms, he must intend two different things. And if he uses a form different from the one anticipated, he must intend something else. This is the principle of Contrast, defined as follows:

> *Contrast*:   Speakers assume that any difference in form signals a difference in meaning.

Conventionality and Contrast interact: speakers are expected to use conventional forms. When they don't (when they coin new terms, for instance), their addressees infer that they are trying to express some other meaning, one *not* captured by a conventional term (E. Clark and H. Clark 1979). For example, the speaker who first coined *to winterize* (meaning "to make winter-proof") made clear by using an unfamiliar form that his meaning differed from that of the established verb from the same stem, *to winter* ("spend the winter"). Conventionality confers consistency over time for speakers denoting object- and event-types. This stability in conventional meanings, along with the contrasts among them, is what makes languages effective for communication (Lewis 1969, H. Clark 1996).

Children appear to grasp these principles at an early age (E. Clark 1983, 1993). They take as targets in producing words the conventional forms they hear from adults. Where there are discrepancies between adult and child productions, they repair their own pronunciations in the direction of adult forms, from age one onwards. They treat different words as having different meanings from the start, and rely on this as they build up semantic domains. In summary, they use both Conventionality and Contrast as they make inferences about new words.

Children rely on Conventionality more generally when they receive corrections from adults. Adults often reformulate erroneous child utterances, providing a conventional way to express the child's apparent intention: they correct mispronounced words (e.g. *fish* for *fis*, *jump* for *dup*); they correct morphological errors, changing *her* to *she*, and *comed* to *came*; they offer the conventional word where children have chosen another term (e.g. *peel* for *fix*, *logger* for *chock*, or *gardener* for *plant-man*); and they correct children's syntactic errors, fixing word-order or switching to the appropriate construction. In short, adult reformulations generally offer children the conventional forms for what they seem to be saying (Chouinard and E. Clark 2001, E. Clark and Chouinard 2000).

Adults often offer such reformulations in side-sequences as they try to establish what the child meant, as in (11), where the child's father, in reformulating, initially misunderstood him:

(11)   *Abe* (2;5.7):   *the plant didn't cried.*
        Father: the plant cried?
        Abe: *no.*
        Father: Oh, the plant didn't cry.
        Abe: uhhuh.   [Kuczaj, Abe 3:163]

And children generally acknowledge these reformulations. They repeat the words or constructions proposed by the adult, as in (12):

(12)   *Abe* (2;5.10):   *I want butter mine.*
        Father: Ok, give it here and I'll put butter on it.
        Abe: *I need butter on it.*   [Kuczaj, Abe 4:66]

They acknowledge the adult's reformulation, with *yes*, *uhhuh*, or even *no*, within side-sequences, as in (11). Or they tacitly accept the reformulation by simply continuing on with their next turn in the exchange, much as adults do (H. Clark 1996).

When adults reformulate children's utterances, they offer the conventional form for the meaning intended. By reformulating the child's utterance with any changes called for, they offer an utterance that contrasts directly with what the child just said. By doing this, they implicate that *this* is how to say what the child apparently intended. Just as in adult exchanges (Walker 1996), these reformulations (or repeats with corrections) signal to children that there is some question about either what they said or how they said it. In summary, children become aware early on that adult reformulations signal that there is something awry with how they said what they said.

Children start to master the general conditions on conversations (how to start up, how to take turns, what to infer from certain kinds of contributions) fairly early. But what goes on in conversation cannot always be generalized to other situations. The pragmatic inferences applicable to questions, for instance, don't always hold for test settings where children often have a hard time working out what the adult wants, and may at first take into account factors that are irrelevant (Donaldson 1971). Consider a conservation task where children are shown two sticks the same length, aligned in parallel, and asked *Are they the same?* They typically answer correctly with *Yes.* But if the experimenter then moves one of the sticks so the ends are no longer aligned and repeats the same question, three-, four-, and even five-year-olds now (wrongly) answer *No.* They take the change of position for the two sticks as relevant to the adult's repeat question. When trained to ignore irrelevant or accidental changes, children do better (e.g. Gelman 1969, McGarrigle and Donaldson 1975).

If children interpret a repeated question as a direction to *alter* their initial answer (and therefore their judgment), they should manage better in such conservation tasks when questioned only once, right after they have observed a change designed to test whether they can conserve a property like length. When four-, five-, and six-year-olds are given tasks where they are asked either one or two questions about conservation of number, those who get a one-question task first, produce a larger number of conservation responses in later standard two-question versions, than children who get the standard task first and then the one-question version (59 percent versus 19 percent) (Siegal 1997). Initial experience with the one-question task helps make clearer to the children what the experimenter wants in asking questions.

Studies like these show that children construe questions according to the usual conversational practices. When such practices fail to hold, younger children may misread the adult speaker's intentions. This can then result in mis-assessments of what children actually know. To succeed in many test situations, children must learn to suspend their assumptions about conversational practice and invoke additional pragmatic rules just for test settings.

4   Speech Acts

In any conversation, participants need to assess the current speaker's intention. Is this a request for action or for information? Is this an offer awaiting acceptance or rejection? Is this a promise or a threat? Is he marking a social exchange with a greeting, an apology, a thank-you? Is this an action co-extensive with the utterance, as in *You're it, I resign,* or *I name this ship the Nereid*? (see Austin 1962, H. Clark 1996).

Between nine and 12 months of age, infants start to make active efforts to attract adult attention to what interests them or what they want. Sometimes these efforts involve actively enlisting adult attention, as when they hold on to adult clothing and pull in the direction of something they wish to have opened, or something they want reached down off a shelf. They indicate with pointing gestures, typically an index finger extended and the remaining fingers curled into a fist. Pointing contrasts with a different kind of gesture, less fixed in form, that marks desire rather than just interest. Infants this age persistently reach towards what they want. Pointing and reaching, typically present before the first words, have been documented by many researchers, and are generally

viewed as proto-versions of the speech acts of asserting (points) and requesting (reaches) (Werner and Kaplan 1963, Bates et al. 1975, Bruner 1975). Early
points and reaches are combined first with single words and later with combinations of words as children become more skilled with language. Their persistence in seeking adult acknowledgment – attending to assertions of interest
or acceding to requests – offers further evidence that they use gestures and
gesture–word combinations to express different intentions.

To further assess speaker intentions, children must work out which utterances can be used to perform which functions.[4] Since a single construction can
often be used with several functions, children have to infer what the speaker's
intention is in terms of what they know about form/function relations, what is
physically co-present on each occasion, and what is conversationally co-present
– the linguistic content of the utterance in the current context.

Children must learn how to take factors like these into account in assessing
the speaker's intent, and hence the speech act being used. For instance, when
asked to identify offers and requests, three-year-olds can distinguish some of
the conditions for each speech-act type. Which features best identify the speaker's
intention? Reeder (1980) set up contexts where children heard variants of
"Would you like to do A?" and then had to judge whether this utterance was
equivalent to either "I want you to do A" (requests), or "I'll let you do A"
(offers). On each trial, children heard a sentence followed by the variants to be
judged, as in (13):

(13)   *Would you like to play on the train?*
       (a)   I want you to play on the train.
       (b)   I'll let you play on the train.

Children's judgments were elicited in scenes with a Speaker (S), an Addressee
(H), and the target toy. In offer trials, H stood near the toy and S stood at a
neutral distance. In request trials, S stood near the toy with H at a neutral
distance. These scenarios, Reeder argued, licensed the pragmatic inferences
needed to distinguish offers (14) from requests (15):

(14)   OFFER   O1 H wants to do act A
                   O2 No indication that S wants H to do A
                   O3 No indication that S objects to H doing A

(15)   REQUEST   R1 S wants H to do A
                   R2 No indication that H wants to do A
                   R3 No indication that H objects to doing A

At 2;6, children generally chose the "let" variant (13b) for offers (69 percent of
the time), but they didn't yet show a significant preference for the "want"
variant (13a) for requests. By age three, they chose the appropriate variants most
of the time for both offers and requests. How were the children identifying the

speech act at issue? They could have been using simple inferences of the following type: when the Hearer is close to the train, he wants to play with it; and when the Speaker is closer, he can let the Hearer play. Both require that children keep track of the speaker's location and draw the appropriate inference.

As children get older, they add to their repertoire of speech acts and to the range of forms used to convey each one. Grimm (1975) set up a series of scenarios designed to elicit specific speech acts from five- and seven-year-olds. She included acts of asking, ordering, forbidding, and allowing (all directives), and of promising (a commissive). A sample scenario is given in (16):

(16)   To get a child to <u>ask</u> for something:
       "You're at the playground with Felix [a large toy cat]. He's sitting on the swing and you're on the slide. Now you'd like Felix to let you swing too. What do you say to him?"

In each scenario, the experimenter made Felix refuse to cooperate at least three times. This compelled the child to reiterate the targeted speech act at least four times. Consider the exchange between a seven-year-old and Felix the cat (his voice was supplied by the experimenter), in (17):

(17)   *Child*:   *Felix, will you let me swing too, just once, please?*
       Felix: *I don't want you to swing.*   [refusal 1]
       Child: *But then you can slide down the slide.*
       Felix: *I'd rather not let you swing.*   [refusal 2]
       Child: *I'd like to swing just once, not you all the time.*
       Felix: *I'd still rather not let you swing.*   [refusal 3]
       Child: *But you must!*

Five-year-olds found it easier to ask, order, and forbid than to allow or promise. Seven-year-olds did well on all four of the directives, but knew less about how to promise. Overall, children seem to find it easier to produce speech acts that require addressees to act than ones where the obligation remains with the speaker (see also Read and Cherry 1978, Bernicot 1992). But in tasks like these, the speech acts produced are second-order ones since the children are either making a judgment about a speech act or taking on a specific role themselves; they are not expressing their own intentions directly.

5   Speaker Intentions

Can children understand the intentions behind an utterance? How consistent are they in their inferences about what adults say to them? To what extent do their responses show they have understood the speaker and are attempting to respond appropriately? The ability to make inferences in context appears critical because it affords children a basis for interpreting the speaker even when their knowledge of language is still minimal. It also provides a basis for any coping strategies that children rely on in the earlier stages of mapping meanings onto words (E. Clark 1997), and so helps them accumulate information across contexts as they start to fill in details about meanings for different words and constructions.

Children begin to participate in conversation very early in acquisition. While the earliest "turns" in preverbal infants are imposed by adults who count hand-waves, smiles, burps, and babbles as turns in babies (Snow 1977), one-year-olds can often take a more deliberate role in contributing to conversation. They contribute one-word utterances both in response to adult prompts and questions, and in initiating exchanges with adults. In fact, young children initiate some two-thirds of adult–child exchanges (Bloom et al. 1996).

If children can follow the speaker's intention, they should be able to deal with repairs to that intention. There is good evidence that they can. As young as two, they are aware that they need to discard information that has been repaired, and replace it by the speaker's more recent offering. For example, in one study young two-year-olds were taught a new word for an unfamiliar object-type, then, after the learning trials were completed, the experimenter made an explicit repair such as "Oops, these aren't X's; they're Y's" and then proceeded to teach a second new word (Y) as the term for the same objects (E. Clark and Grossman 1998). When tested, nearly all the children knew that they did *not* know what the first term (X) meant. (They all knew the second term that had replaced it.) Similarly, children this age are able to distinguish intended from accidental actions performed in the course of an adult's teaching them a new word for an object or an action. Verbal signals marking accidental actions (*uhoh*, *oops*, etc.) effectively lead two-year-olds to ignore those events in favor of others (Tomasello and Barton 1994, Carpenter et al. 2000). Finally, two-year-olds take account of what the speaker is attending to in talking about unfamiliar, unseen objects. They assume that any new word introduced refers to whatever the speaker is attending to, and not to what they were attending to themselves (Baldwin 1993).

By age two, children are already quite skilled at tracking the speaker's intentions in a variety of settings. These intentions may be obscured for young children by language that is too complex, but in tasks where children are focused on the activity at hand, they show good understanding of the pragmatic consequences of speaker repairs. They are also responsive to requests for clarification, whether from peers (Garvey 1979) or adults (e.g. Corsaro 1977, Gallagher 1977). These requests help the interaction run smoothly and repair disruptions by clearing up misunderstandings that result from not hearing or from misinterpreting what a child said. In responding to such requests, children may repeat themselves, repair words that were poorly pronounced, reword what they are saying, or speak more loudly. Much of the time, their repair zeroes in on what led the adult interlocutor to ask for clarification in the first place (see also Chouinard and E. Clark 2001).

6 Taking Account of the Addressee

To what extent do children take into account what their addressees know? Such an ability is important for establishing and updating common ground, and even two-year-olds appear to keep quite careful track of what adults know on occasion. For instance, O'Neill (1996) gave two-year-olds (2;7) a game where she told them their parents would help them. She then showed them a toy that she placed in one of two containers (a box or a cup), on a shelf out of the child's reach. The child's task was to get the toy in order to drop it into another container. The parent, meanwhile, was either in the room, watching, or else outside the room or seated with eyes closed and so unable to see where the toy was put. What happened? These two-year-olds provided significantly more information about where the toy was when the parent did *not* know its location (parents who had been outside or had had their eyes closed) than when the parent *did* know it (parents who had been present and watching while the object was put into one of the containers).

In a second game, O'Neill had younger children enlist parental help to retrieve stickers dropped into one of two identical opaque containers, out of reach. Again, on some trials the parent was visibly watching; on others, the parent sat with eyes closed and ears covered. The children (aged 2;3) took into account what their parents knew. They supplied information about location more often when parents had *not* seen which container was used than when they had (see also Maratsos 1976).

Children are quite skilled by age four at distinguishing among addressees on other grounds as well, and they adjust the way they speak according to the age of their addressee (Shatz and Gelman 1973). For instance, when offering instructions to adults about a toy, four-year-olds used longer utterances, few imperatives, and no attention-getters, compared to their speech to two-year-olds. Their speech to other four-year-olds didn't differ from their speech to adults. Distinguishing among addressees by age is consistent with children's growing skill in "doing voices" for different characters. Sachs and Devin (1976) recorded four children (aged 3;9 to 5;5) talking to an adult, a peer, a baby, and a baby-doll, as well as role-playing "a baby just learning how to talk." The speech addressed to adults and peers versus babies replicated earlier findings. Children distinguished younger addressees by shortening their utterances, using attention-getters, and modifying their speech significantly along a number of dimensions.

Children also talk differently to mothers and fathers (Andersen 1990). This may be a function of the time each parent spends with the child. The more familiar parent is usually addressed less formally (and less politely) than the less familiar parent. This matched the differences in status and sex that showed up in Andersen's children's role-play (see also Newcombe and Zaslow 1981).

7 Taking Turns

One way to assess children's skill in conversation is to look at whether they offer pertinent information when they take a turn in an ongoing exchange. This has been studied from several perspectives: answering questions and eliciting responses; joining in conversations between other family members; and contributing to conversations between a parent and older sibling. What children say on such occasions is generally relevant to the topic, and they add new information. But they may often come in late, perhaps a reflection of their lack of skill in production (E. Clark 2002c), so what they have to say may not be as relevant as it would have been a couple of seconds earlier.

One measure of turn-taking is how successful younger versus older children are at taking over from the current speaker. In a detailed study of three two-year-olds and five four-year-olds, Ervin-Tripp (1979) found that, having interrupted an ongoing turn, two-year-olds then produced delayed responses from 27 percent to 55 percent of the time, compared to four-year-olds who produced delayed follow-up utterances between 9 percent and 20 percent of the time.

Children get better at timing the placement of their interpolated turns as they get older (Ervin-Tripp 1979). Those under 4;6 entered at syntactic or prosodic boundaries 25 percent of the time with a single speaker, but got the timing right only about 12 percent of the time when they interrupted a dyad to take a turn. Their slowness in getting out what they wanted to say led them to overlap with the next turn, which was often no longer relevant to what they wanted to say. Older children (4;6 to 6;0) did better, with 27 percent appropriate timing, regardless of whether they were interrupting a single speaker or a dyad. The younger children were probably not yet as good at processing an ongoing conversation and, at the same time, planning their own turns, so that when they took a turn, they were often late and therefore judged to be saying something irrelevant.

8 Politeness

What are the social rules behind choices of polite forms? To make appropriate use of politeness, children must master several different dimensions of use. They need to know the linguistic forms for marking different degrees of politeness. They must identify the pragmatic conditions on greetings and requests, for instance, according to the status, age, and sex of their co-participants. And they need to learn what the costs and benefits are of gaining (or losing) face in relation to others (Brown and Levinson 1987).

Take the case of requests. What do young children know about the forms available, and how polite each form is? Bates (1976) looked at spontaneous requests in the speech of Italian children and identified three early stages of use. Up until age four, children rely mainly on direct questions and imperatives. As they get older, they add expressions like *please*, they give reasons, they add softeners of various kinds, and they start to state their wishes in generic form. By age six, they can produce a range of syntactic forms, but do not yet modulate their requests appropriately. By age seven or so, they can vary both form and content in making polite requests. These findings are consistent with children's judgments of politeness (Garvey 1975, Bates 1976, Bates and Silvern 1977).

Children are politer, by adult norms, when they produce positive requests (for someone to do something) than when they produce negative ones (for someone not to do something). And they are generally politer to older addressees: they are politer to adults to peers, and politer to peers than to younger children. One measure of this appears in their uses of *please*: it occurs in 84 percent of requests to adults, but in only 37 percent of requests to two-year-olds (James 1978).

What criteria do children themselves use in judging whether a request is polite? When asked to classify spontaneous requests, not until age nine did children make adult-like judgments (Axia and Baroni 1985). Do children recognize the "cost" of requests for speaker versus addressee? To study this, Axia and Baroni devised a game where children needed to ask for help. Adults used two forms of "resistance" to the children's requests: (a) turning a deaf ear, so as to elicit a further request, and (b) motivated refusals, also designed to elicit further requests where children were forced to infer from context what to do, namely, ask again more politely.

First requests tended to be as impolite for nine-year-olds as for younger children (five- and seven-year-olds). After encountering resistance, the two older groups generally produced requests that were more polite. After deaf-ear refusals, five-year-olds simply asked again more loudly; older children opted for politer forms. After motivated refusals, five-year-olds gave very few polite requests; seven-year-olds gave more, and nine-year-olds gave the most. The older children also added expressions of deference (mitigators, *please*, and use of question-forms) (see also Axia and Baroni 1985).

Studies of younger children report similar findings. Newcombe and Zaslow (1981) looked at the requests two-year-olds use to adults. In transcripts from 11 children, they found both hints and questions serving as requests. When the adult didn't comply with the initial request, children persisted 82 percent of the time, repeating their original utterance in a variant that was also a hint or question (83 percent), or else producing a more explicit directive (17 percent). This suggests that even very young children have quite an extensive repertoire for making requests (see also Read and Cherry 1978).

Other studies suggest that not until age seven do children become more polite when trying to get their addressee to comply with a request. In one study of small groups of six-year-olds reading in the classroom, Wilkinson et al. (1982) found that children this age tended to use direct forms to their peers in requests for action or information, and that they more often aggravated than mitigated any follow-up requests. (Aggravation usually meant repetition of the same form, with a rise in pitch and more accompanying gestures.) The form of Annie's request to another six-year-old in (18) is typical:

(18)   Annie: *Judy. Judy, what's this word?*
Judy. Judy. Judy. Judy, what's this word?
Judy, Judy, Judy, Judy. Judy, Judy, Judy, Judy, Judy.
What's this word?
   Judy: *"Only."*

Children this age use some mitigations, e.g. *I can't get it. Why don't you read this page too, please?* and also offer reasons for compliance, e.g. *Michelle, can I have the pen? I need the eraser for it. I did something wrong* (Wilkinson et al. 1982: 170–1). In summary, many six-year-old requests to peers are unsuccessful, and they make little use of politer forms in repeat requests.

At the same time, children as young as four or five are aware that greater status calls for more politeness. In their role-play with puppets, children who do the voices for younger and less powerful roles (e.g. *a child* talking to an adult, *a woman* talking to a man, or *a nurse* talking to a doctor) made requests that were more polite than those they made for the voices in more powerful roles in each dyad. In their role-play, children made doctors less polite to nurses, men less polite to women, and adults less polite to children, than the reverse (Andersen 1990). Children seemed quite aware of some of the correlations of power or status with gender and age.

What is deemed polite in one culture doesn't always hold for another (Brown and Levinson 1987). Politeness is a matter of convention, and children have to learn what the relevant conventions are. Those acquiring Chinese or Japanese must learn to use the appropriate address terms for relatives for each occasion as well as any honorifics required (Clancy 1985, Erbaugh 1992, Nakamura 2001). Children learning Norwegian must learn to use hints in comments or remarks rather than the more elaborate requests conventional in Hungarian (Hollos and Beeman 1978). In all cultures, children have to learn how they are expected to speak as male or female participants in the society. And in each culture, children have to learn what counts as polite, and adopt prevailing norms for how to reiterate a request. Politeness is an important tool for achieving one's goals, and children appear to recognize this quite early.

9   Conclusion

By age six, children already know a lot about how to use language. They observe conventionality and contrast, and readily make inferences from what others do (and don't) say. And they have begun to master many of the details of how to participate in and manage conversations. They have also grasped when and where to use polite forms. They are guided in all this, in part, by the pragmatic directions adults offer on how to speak, when, and to whom (E. Clark 1998, E. Clark and Wong 2002). They are also guided early on by the information adults provide about words for objects and actions, and how these are related to other familiar words. But the pragmatic knowledge children have by age six really only marks the beginning. They must still learn how to put their knowledge of contrast to work in identifying speech acts, in deriving implicatures (e.g. McGarrigle et al. 1978, Noveck 2001), and in coining words (e.g. E. Clark 1993), to further their goals in conversation. And they still have much to learn about how to fine-tune their coordination of non-linguistic and linguistic options for communicating.

ACKNOWLEDGMENTS

Preparation of this chapter, and my own research, was supported in part by the National Science Foundation (SBR97-31781) and The Spencer Foundation (199900133). I am grateful to Michelle M. Chouinard and Barbara F. Kelly for much discussion of early communication.

NOTES

1   Data cited in this study are drawn from published sources, from the CHILDES Archive (MacWhinney and Snow 1990), from my own unpublished diary data, or data from ongoing studies. Citations from CHILDES are identified with the corpus name plus transcript and line numbers. Ages are given in years and months, e.g., 1;4 for one year and four months old.

2   These observations come from unpublished data (E. Clark and Chouinard, in preparation). Each episode begins at 0 secs, and the start of each gesture, gaze, or utterance is marked by how long after that it began. The duration of the child's gaze is given with start and stop times, also measured from the beginning of the episode as a whole.

3   Like younger one-year-olds, older ones then maintain their gaze on the target object as long as the adult talks about it.

4   Early on, there may be a one-to-one match of form and function for some linguistic structures in children's speech. For example, one two-year-old consistently used utterances like *more* + N as requests (demands), and utterances like *two* + N as assertions. Another child, in her first few weeks of multi-word utterances, used an invariant *see* to mark assertions and *want* to mark requests.

26 Pragmatics and Computational Linguistics

DANIEL JURAFSKY

1 Introduction

These days there's a computational version of everything. Computational biology, computational musicology, computational archaeology, and so on, ad infinitum. Even movies are going digital. This chapter, as you might have guessed by now, thus explores the computational side of pragmatics. Computational pragmatics might be defined as the computational study of the relation between utterances and context. Like other kinds of pragmatics, this means that computational pragmatics is concerned with indexicality, with the relation between utterances and action, with the relation between utterances and discourse, and with the relationship between utterances and the place, time, and environmental context of their being uttered.

As Bunt and Black (2000) point out, computational pragmatics, like pragmatics in general, is especially concerned with INFERENCE. Four core inferential problems in pragmatics have received the most attention in the computational community: REFERENCE RESOLUTION, the interpretation and generation of SPEECH ACTS, the interpretation and generation of DISCOURSE STRUCTURE AND COHERENCE RELATIONS, and ABDUCTION. Each of these four problems can be cast as an inference task, one of somehow filling in information that isn't actually present in the utterance at hand. Two of these tasks are addressed in other chapters of this volume; abduction in Hobbs (this volume), and discourse structure and coherence in Kehler (this volume). Reference resolution is covered in Kehler (2000b). I have therefore chosen the interpretation of speech acts as the topic of this chapter.

Speech act interpretation, a classic pragmatic problem, is a good choice for this overview chapter for many reasons. First, the early computational work drew very strongly from the linguistics literature of the period. This enables us to closely compare the ways that computational linguistic and non-computational linguistic approaches differ in their methodology. Second, there are two distinct computational paradigms in speech act interpretation: a logic-based approach and a probabilistic approach. I see these two approaches as good vehicles for motivating the two dominant paradigms in computational linguistics: one based on logic, logical inference, feature-structures, and unification, and the other based on probabilistic approaches. Third, speech act interpretation provides a good example of pragmatic inference: inferring a kind of linguistic structure which is not directly present in the input utterance. Finally, speech act interpretation is a problem that applies very naturally both to written and spoken genres. This allows us to discuss the computational processing of speech input, and in general talk about the way that computational linguistics has dealt with the differences between spoken and written inputs.

I like to think of the role of computational models in linguistics as a kind of musical conversation among three melodic voices. The base melody is the role of computational linguistics as a core of what we sometimes call "mathematical foundations" of linguistics, the study of the formal underpinnings of models such as rules or trees, features or unification, indices or optimality. The middle line is the attempt to do what we sometimes call language engineering. One futuristic goal of this research is the attempt to build artificial agents that can carry on conversations with humans in order to perform tasks like answering questions, keeping schedules, or giving directions. The third strain is what is usually called "computational psycholinguistics": the use of computational techniques to build processing models of human psycholinguistic perform-ance. All of these melodic lines appear in computational pragmatics, although in this overview chapter we will focus more on the first two roles; linguistic foundations and language engineering.

The problem with focusing on speech act interpretation, of course, is that we will not be able to address the breadth of work in computational pragmatics. As suggested above above, the interested reader should turn to other chapters in this volume (especially Kehler and Hobbs) and also to Jurafsky and Martin (2000), which covers a number of computational pragmatic issues from a ped-agogical perspective. Indeed, this chapter itself began as an expansion of, and meditation on, the section on dialogue act interpretation in Jurafsky and Martin (2000).

2   Speech Act Interpretation: the Problem, and a Quick Historical Overview

The problem of speech act interpretation is to determine, given an utterance, which speech act it realizes. Of course, some speech acts have surface cues to their form; some questions, for example, begin with *wh*-words or with aux-inversion. The Literal Meaning Hypothesis (Gazdar 1981), also called the Literal Force Hypothesis (Levinson 1983), is a strong version of this hypothesis, sug-gesting that every utterance has an illocutionary force which is built into its surface form. According to this hypothesis, aux-inverted sentences in English have QUESTION force; subject-deleted sentences have IMPERATIVE force, and so on (see Sadock, this volume).

But it has long been known that many or even most sentences do not seem to have the speech act type associated with their syntactic form. Consider two kinds of examples of this phenomenon. One example is INDIRECT REQUESTS, in which what looks on the surface like a question is actually a polite form of a directive or a request to perform an action. The sentence:

(1)   Can you pass the salt?

looks on the surface like a *yes-no* question asking about the hearer's ability to pass the salt, but functions actually as a polite directive to pass the salt.

There are other examples where the surface form of an utterance doesn't match its speech act form. For example, what looks on the surface like a statement can really be a question. A very common kind of question, called a CHECK question (Labov and Fanshel 1977, Carletta et al. 1997b) is used to ask the other participant to confirm something that this other participant has privileged knowledge about. These checks are questions, but they have declarative word order, as in the bold-faced utterance in the following snippet from a travel agent conversation:

(2)   A: I was wanting to make some arrangements for a trip that I'm going
            to be taking uh to LA uh beginning of the week after next.
      B: OK uh let me pull up your profile and I'll be right with you here.
            [pause]
      B: **And you said you wanted to travel next week?**
      A: Uh, yes.

There are two computational models of the interpretation of speech acts. The first class of models was originally motivated by indirect requests of the "pass the salt" type. Gordon and Lakoff (1971), and then Searle (1975a), proposed the seeds of this INFERENTIAL approach. Their intuition was that a sentence like *Can you pass the salt?* is unambiguous, having the literal meaning of a question: *Do you have the ability to pass me the salt?* The request speech act *Pass me the salt* is inferred by the hearer in a later step of understanding after processing the literal question. Computational implementations of this idea focus on using belief logics to model this inference chain.

The second class of models has been called CUE-BASED or PROBABILISTIC (Jurafsky and Martin 2000). The name CUE-BASED draws on the key role of cues in such psychological models as the Competition Model of Bates and MacWhinney (MacWhinney et al. 1984, MacWhinney 1987). These models are motivated more by indirect requests like CHECK questions. Here the problem is to figure out that what looks on the surface like a statement is really a question. Cue-based models think of the surface form of the sentence as a set of CUES to the speaker's intentions. Figuring out these intentions does require inference, but not of the type that chains through literal meanings.

These two models also differ in another important way. The inferential models are based on belief logics and use logical inference to reason about the speaker's intentions. The cue-based models tend to be probabilistic machine learning models. They see interpretation as a classification task, and solve it by training statistical classifiers on labeled examples of speech acts.

Despite their differences, these models have in common the use of a kind of abductive inference. In each case, the hearer infers something that was not contained directly in the semantics of the input utterance. That makes them an excellent pair of examples of these two different ways of looking at computational linguistics. The next section introduces a version of the inferential model called the PLAN INFERENCE or BDI model, and the following section the CUE-BASED model.

3   The Plan Inference (or BDI) Model of Speech Act Interpretation

The first approach to speech act interpretation we will consider is generally called the BDI (belief, desire, and intention) or PLAN-BASED model, proposed by Allen, Cohen, and Perrault and their colleagues (e.g. Allen 1995). Bunt and Black (2000: 15) define this line of inquiry as follows:

> to apply the principles of rational agenthood to the modeling of a (computer-based) dialogue participant, where a rational communicative agent is endowed not only with certain private knowledge and the logic of belief, but is considered to also assume a great deal of common knowledge/beliefs with an interlocutor, and to be able to update beliefs about the interlocutor's intentions and beliefs as a dialogue progresses.

The earliest papers, such as Cohen and Perrault (1979), offered an AI planning model for how speech acts are **generated**. One agent, seeking to find out some information, could use standard planning techniques to come up with the plan of asking the hearer to tell the speaker the information. Perrault and Allen (1980) and Allen and Perrault (1980) also applied this BDI approach to **comprehension**, specifically the comprehension of indirect speech effects.

Their application of the BDI model to comprehension draws on the plan-inference approach to dialogue act interpretation, first proposed by Gordon and Lakoff (1971) and Searle (1975a). Gordon, Lakoff, and Searle noticed that there was a structure to what kind of things a speaker could do to make an indirect request. In particular, they noticed that a speaker could mention or question various quite specific properties of the desired activity to make an indirect request. For example, the air travel request, *"Give me certain flight information"* can be realized as many different kinds of indirect requests. Here is a partial list from Jurafsky and Martin (2000) with examples from the ATIS[1] corpus of sentences spoken to a computerized speech understanding system for planning air travel:

1   The speaker can question the hearer's ability to perform the activity:
   - Can you give me a list of the flights from Atlanta to Boston?
   - Could you tell me if Delta has a hub in Boston?
   - Would you be able to, uh, put me on a flight with Delta?

2   The speaker can mention speaker's wish or desire about the activity:
   - I want to fly from Boston to San Francisco.
   - I would like to stop somewhere else in between.
   - I'm looking for one-way flights from Tampa to Saint Louis.
   - I need that for Tuesday.
   - I wonder if there are any flights from Boston to Dallas.

3   The speaker can mention the hearer's doing the action:
   - Would you please repeat that information?
   - Will you tell me the departure time and arrival time on this American flight?

4   The speaker can question the speaker's having permission to receive results of the action:
   - May I get a lunch on flight UA 21 instead of breakfast?
   - Could I have a listing of flights leaving Boston?

Based on the realization that there were certain systemic ways of making indirect requests, Searle (1975a: 73) proposed that the hearer's chain of reasoning upon hearing *Can you give me a list of the flights from Atlanta to Boston?* might be something like the following (Searle's sentence was actually different; I've modified it to this ATIS example):

1   X has asked me a question about whether I have the ability to give a list of flights.
2   I assume that X is being cooperative in the conversation (in the Gricean sense) and that his utterance therefore has some aim.
3   X knows I have the ability to give such a list, and there is no alternative reason why X should have a purely theoretical interest in my list-giving ability.
4   Therefore X's utterance probably has some ulterior illocutionary point. What can it be?
5   A preparatory condition for a directive is that the hearer have the ability to perform the directed action.
6   Therefore X has asked me a question about my preparedness for the action of giving X a list of flights.

7   Furthermore, X and I are in a conversational situation in which giving lists of flights is a common and expected activity.

8   Therefore, in the absence of any other plausible illocutionary act, X is probably requesting me to give him a list of flights.

The inferential approach thus explains why *Can you give me a list of flights from Boston?* is a reasonable way of making an indirect request in a way that *Boston is in New England* is not: the former mentions a precondition for the desired activity, and there is a reasonable inferential chain from the precondition to the activity itself.

As we suggested above, Perrault and Allen (1980) and Allen and Perrault (1980) applied this BDI approach to the comprehension of indirect speech effects, essentially cashing out Searle's (1975a) promissory note in a computational formalism.

I'll begin by summarizing Perrault and Allen's formal definitions of belief and desire in the predicate calculus. I'll represent "S believes the proposition P" as the two-place predicate $B(S,P)$. Reasoning about belief is done with a number of axiom schemas inspired by Hintikka (1969) (such as $B(A,P) \land B(A, Q) \Rightarrow B(A,P \land Q)$; see Perrault and Allen 1980 for details). Knowledge is defined as "true belief"; *S knows that P* will be represented as $KNOW(S,P)$, defined as follows:

$$KNOW(S,P) \equiv P \land B(S,P)$$

In addition to *knowing that*, we need to define *knowing whether*. *S knows whether* (KNOWIF) a proposition P is true if S KNOWs that P or S KNOWs that $\neg P$:

$$KNOWIF(S,P) \equiv KNOW(S,P) \lor KNOW(S, \neg P)$$

The theory of desire relies on the predicate WANT. If an agent S wants P to be true, we say $WANT(S,P)$, or $W(S,P)$ for short. P can be a state or the execution of some action. Thus if ACT is the name of an action, $W(S,ACT (H))$ means that S wants H to do ACT. The logic of WANT relies on its own set of axiom schemas just like the logic of belief.

The BDI models also require an axiomatization of actions and planning; the simplest of these is based on a set of ACTION SCHEMAS similar to the AI planning model STRIPS (Fikes and Nilsson 1971). Each action schema has a set of parameters with CONSTRAINTS about the type of each variable, and three parts:

- PRECONDITIONS: Conditions that must already be true in order to successfully perform the action.
- EFFECTS: Conditions that become true as a result of successfully performing the action.
- BODY: A set of partially ordered goal states that must be achieved in performing the action.

In the travel domain, for example, the action of agent *A* booking flight *F* for client *C* might have the following simplified definition:

BOOK-FLIGHT(A,C,F):

    Constraints: Agent(A) ∧ Flight(F) ∧ Client(C)

    Precondition: Know(A,departure-date(F)) ∧ Know(A,departure-time(F)) ∧ Know(A,origin-city(F)) ∧ Know(A,destination-city(F)) ∧ Know(A,flight-type(F)) ∧ Has-Seats(F) ∧ W(C,(Book(A,C,F))) ∧ . . .

    Effect: Flight-Booked(A,C,F)

    Body: Make-Reservation(A,F,C)

Cohen and Perrault (1979) and Perrault and Allen (1980) use this kind of action specification for speech acts. For example, here is Perrault and Allen's definition for three speech acts relevant to indirect requests. INFORM is the speech act of informing the hearer of some proposition (the Austin/Searle ASSERTIVE). The definition of INFORM is based on Grice's 1957 idea that a speaker informs the hearer of something merely by causing the hearer to believe that the speaker wants them to know something:

INFORM(S,H,P):

    Constraints: Speaker(S) ∧ Hearer(H) ∧ Proposition(P)

    Precondition: Know(S,P) ∧ W(S,INFORM(S,H,P))

    Effect: Know(H,P)

    Body: B(H,W(S,Know(H,P)))

INFORMIF is the act used to inform the hearer whether a proposition is true or not; like INFORM, the speaker INFORMIFs the hearer by causing the hearer to believe the speaker wants them to KNOWIF something:

INFORMIF(S,H,P):

    Constraints: Speaker(S) ∧ Hearer(H) ∧ Proposition(P)

    Precondition: KnowIf(S,P) ∧ W(S, INFORMIF(S,H,P))

    Effect: KnowIf(H,P)

    Body: B(H, W(S, KnowIf(H,P)))

REQUEST is the directive speech act for requesting the hearer to perform some action:

REQUEST(S,H,ACT):

    Constraints: Speaker(S) ∧ Hearer(H) ∧ ACT(A) ∧ H is agent of ACT

    Precondition: W(S,ACT(H))

    Effect: W(H,ACT(H))

    Body: B(H,W(S,ACT(H)))

Perrault and Allen's theory also requires what are called SURFACE-LEVEL ACTS. These correspond to the "literal meanings" of the imperative, interrogative, and declarative structures. For example the "surface-level" act S.REQUEST produces imperative utterances:

S.REQUEST(S,H,ACT):
  Effect: B(H,W(S,ACT(H)))

The effects of S.REQUEST match the body of a regular REQUEST, since this is the default or standard way of doing a request (but not the only way). This "default" or "literal" meaning is the start of the hearer's inference chain. The hearer will be given an input which indicates that the speaker is requesting the hearer to inform the speaker whether the hearer is capable of giving the speaker a list:

  S.REQUEST(S,H,InformIf(H,S,CanDo(H,Give(H,S,LIST))))

The hearer must figure out that the speaker is actually making a request:

  REQUEST(H,S,Give(H,S,LIST))

The inference chain from the request-to-inform-if-cando to the request-to-give is based on a chain of PLAUSIBLE INFERENCE, based on heuristics called PLAN INFERENCE (**PI**) rules. We will use the following subset of the rules that Perrault and Allen (1980) propose:

- **(PI.AE) Action–Effect Rule:** For all agents S and H, if Y is an effect of action X and if H believes that S wants X to be done, then it is plausible that H believes that S wants Y to obtain.
- **(PI.PA) Precondition–Action Rule:** For all agents S and H, if X is a precondition of action Y and if H believes S wants X to obtain, then it is plausible that H believes that S wants Y to be done.
- **(PI.BA) Body–Action Rule:** For all agents S and H, if X is part of the body of Y and if H believes that S wants X done, then it is plausible that H believes that S wants Y done.
- **(PI.KD) Know–Desire Rule:** For all agents S and H, if H believes S wants to KNOWIF(P), then H believes S wants P to be true:

$$B(H,W(S,KNOWIF(S,P))) \xrightarrow{\text{plausible}} B(H,W(S,P))$$

- **(EI.1) Extended Inference Rule:** if $B(H,W(S,X)) \xrightarrow{\text{plausible}} B(H,W(S,Y))$ is a PI rule, then

$$B(H,W(S,B(H,(W,(S,X))))) \xrightarrow{\text{plausible}} B(H,W(S,B(H,W(S,Y))))$$

is a PI rule (i.e. you can prefix $B(H,W(S))$ to any plan inference rule).

Let's see how to use these rules to interpret the indirect speech act in *Can you give me a list of flights from Atlanta?* Step 0 in the table below shows the speaker's initial speech act, which the hearer initially interprets literally as a question. Step 1 then uses Plan Inference rule ACTION-EFFECT, which suggests that if the speaker asked for something (in this case information), they probably want it. Step 2 again uses the ACTION-EFFECT rule, here suggesting that if the Speaker wants an INFORMIF, and KNOWIF is an effect of INFORMIF, then the speaker probably also wants KNOWIF.

(3)

Rule	Step	Result
	0	S.REQUEST(S,H,InformIf(H,S,CanDo(H,Give(H,S,LIST))))
PI.AE	1	B(H,W(S,InformIf(H,S,CanDo(H,Give(H,S,LIST)))))
PI.AE/EI	2	B(H,W(S,KnowIf(H,S,CanDo(H,Give(H,S,LIST)))))
PI.KP/EI	3	B(H,W(S,CanDo(H,Give(H,S,LIST))))
PI.PA/EI	4	B(H,W(S,Give(H,S,LIST)))
PI.BA	5	REQUEST(H,S,Give(H,S,LIST))

Step 3 adds the crucial inference that people don't usually ask about things they aren't interested in; thus if the speaker asks whether something is true (in this case CanDo), the speaker probably wants it (CanDo) to be true. Step 4 makes use of the fact that CanDo(ACT) is a precondition for (ACT), making the inference that if the speaker wants a precondition (CanDo) for an action (Give), the speaker probably also wants the action (Give). Finally, step 5 relies on the definition of REQUEST to suggest that if the speaker wants someone to know that the speaker wants them to do something, then the speaker is probably REQUESTing them to do it.

In summary, the BDI model of speech act interpretation is based on three components:

1 An axiomatization of belief, of desire, of action and of planning inspired originally by the work of Hintikka (1969)
2 A set of plan inference rules, which codify the abductive heuristics of the understanding system
3 A theorem prover

Given these three components and an input sentence, a plan-inference system can interpret the correct speech act to assign to the utterance by simulating the inference chain suggested by Searle (1975a).

The BDI model has many advantages. It is an explanatory model, in that its plan-inference rules explain why people make certain inferences rather than others. It is a rich and deep model of the knowledge that humans use in interpretation; thus in addition to its basis for building a conversational agent, the BDI model might be used as a formalization of a cognitive model of human interpretation. The BDI model also shows how linguistic knowledge can be integrated with non-linguistic knowledge in building a model of cognition. Finally, the BDI model is a clear example of the role of computational linguistics as a foundational tool in formalizing linguistic models.

In giving this summary of the plan-inference approach to indirect speech act comprehension, I have left out many details, including many necessary axioms, as well as mechanisms for deciding which inference rule to apply. The interested reader should consult Perrault and Allen (1980).

4   The Cue-based Model of Speech Act Interpretation

The plan-inference approach to dialogue act comprehension is extremely powerful; by using rich knowledge structures and powerful planning techniques the algorithm is designed to address even subtle indirect uses of dialogue acts. Furthermore, the BDI model incorporates knowledge about speaker and hearer intentions, actions, knowledge, and belief that is essential for any complete model of dialogue. But although the BDI model itself has crucial advantages, there are a number of disadvantages to the way the BDI model attempts to solve the speech act interpretation problem.

Perhaps the largest drawback is that the BDI model of speech act interpretation requires that each utterance have a single literal meaning, which is operated on by plan inference rules to produce a final non-literal interpretation. Much recent work has argued against this literal-first non-literal-second model of interpretation. As Levinson (1983) suggests, for example, the speech act force of *most* utterances does not match their surface form. Levinson points out, for example, that the imperative is very rarely used to issue requests in English. He also notes another problem: that indirect speech acts often manifest surface syntactic reflexes associated with their indirect force as well as their putative "literal force."

The psycholinguistic literature, similarly, has not found evidence for the temporal primacy of literal interpretation. Swinney and Cutler (1979), just to give one example, found that literal and figurative meanings of idioms are accessed in parallel by the human sentence processor.

Finally, for many speech act types that are less well studied than the "big three" (question, statement, request), it's not clear what the "literal" force would be. Consider, for example, utterances like *"yeah"* which can function as YES-ANSWERS, AGREEMENTS, and BACKCHANNELS. It's not clear why any one of these should necessarily be the literal speech act and the others be the inferred act.

An alternative way of looking at disambiguation is to downplay the role of a "literal meaning." In this alternate CUE model, we think of the listener as using different cues in the input to help decide how to build an interpretation. Thus the surface input to the interpretive algorithm provides clues to structure-building, rather than providing a literal meaning which must be modified by purely inferential processes. What characterizes a cue-based model is the use of different sources of knowledge (cues) for detecting a speech act, such as lexical, collocational, syntactic, prosodic, or conversational-structure cues.

The cue-based approach is based on metaphors from a different set of linguistic literature than the plan-inference approach. Where the plan-inference approach relies on Searle-like intuitions about logical inference from literal meaning, the cue-based approach draws from the conversational analytic tradition. In particular, it draws from intuitions about what Goodwin (1996) called MICROGRAMMAR (specific lexical, collocation, and prosodic features which are characteristic of particular conversational moves), as well as from the British pragmatics tradition on conversational games and moves (Power 1979). In addition, where the plan-inference model draws most heavily from analysis of written text, the cue-based literature is grounded much more in the analysis of spoken language. Thus, for example, a cue-based approach might use cues from many domains to recognize a true question, including lexical and syntactic knowledge like aux-inversion, prosodic cues like rising intonation, and conversational structure clues, like the neighboring discourse structure, turn boundaries, etc.

4.1   Speech acts and dialogue acts

Before I give the cue-based algorithm for speech act interpretation, I need to digress a bit to give some examples of the kind of speech acts that these algorithms will be addressing. This section summarizes a number of computational tag sets of possible speech acts. The next section chooses one such act, CHECK, to discuss in more detail.

While speech acts provide a useful characterization of one kind of pragmatic force, more recent work, especially computational work in building dialogue systems, has significantly expanded this core notion, modeling more kinds of conversational functions that an utterance can perform. The resulting enriched acts are often called DIALOGUE ACTS (Bunt 1994) or CONVERSATIONAL MOVES (Power 1979, Carletta et al. 1997b).

The phrase *dialogue act* is unfortunately ambiguous. As Bunt and Black (2000) point out, it has been variously used to loosely mean "speech act, in the context of a dialogue" (Bunt 1994), to mean a combination of the speech act and semantic force of an utterance (Bunt 2000), or to mean an act with internal structure related specifically to its dialogue function (Allen and Core 1997). The third usage is perhaps the most common in the cue-based literature, and I will rely on it here.

In the remainder of this section, I discuss various examples of dialogue acts and dialogue act structures. A recent ongoing effort to develop dialogue act tagging schemes is the DAMSL (Dialogue Act Markup in Several Layers) architecture (Walker et al. 1996, Allen and Core 1997, Carletta et al. 1997a, Core et al. 1999), which codes various kinds of dialogue information about utterances. As we suggested above, DAMSL and other such computational efforts to build practical descriptions of dialogue acts, like cue-based models in general, all draw on a number of research areas outside of the philosophical traditions that first defined speech acts. Perhaps the most important source has been work in conversation analysis and related fields. These include work on REPAIR (Schegloff et al. 1977), work on GROUNDING (Clark and Schaefer 1989), and work on the relation of utterances to the preceding and succeeding discourse (Schegloff 1968, 1988, Allwood et al. 1992, Allwood 1995).

For example, drawing on Allwood's work, the DAMSL tagset distinguishes between the FORWARD LOOKING and BACKWARD LOOKING function of an utterance. The forward looking function of an utterance corresponds to something like the Searle/Austin speech act. The DAMSL tag set is more complex in having a hierarchically structured representation that I won't discuss here and differs also from the Searle/Austin speech act in being focused somewhat on the kind of dialogue acts that tend to occur in task-oriented dialogue:

(4)

STATEMENT	a claim made by the speaker
INFO-REQUEST	a question by the speaker
CHECK	a question for confirming information
INFLUENCE-ON-ADDRESSEE	(= Searle's directives)
OPEN-OPTION	a weak suggestion or listing of options
ACTION-DIRECTIVE	an actual command
INFLUENCE-ON-SPEAKER	(= Austin's commissives)
OFFER	speaker offers to do something, (subject to confirmation)
COMMIT	speaker is committed to doing something
CONVENTIONAL	other
OPENING	greetings
CLOSING	farewells
THANKING	thanking and responding to thanks

The backward-looking function of DAMSL focuses on the relationship of an utterance to previous utterances by the other speaker. These include accepting and rejecting proposals (since DAMSL is focused on task-oriented dialogue), as well as acts involved in grounding and repair:

(5)

AGREEMENT	speaker's response to previous proposal
ACCEPT	accepting the proposal
ACCEPT-PART	accepting some part of the proposal
MAYBE	neither accepting nor rejecting the proposal
REJECT-PART	rejecting some part of the proposal
REJECT	rejecting the proposal
HOLD	putting off response, usually via subdialogue

ANSWER	answering a question
UNDERSTANDING	whether speaker understood previous
SIGNAL–NON–UNDER	speaker didn't understand
SIGNAL-UNDER	speaker did understand
ACKNOWLEDGEMENT	demonstrated via backchannel or assessment
REPEAT-REPHRASE	demonstrated via repetition or reformulation
COMPLETION	demonstrated via collaborative completion

DAMSL and DAMSL-like sets of dialogue acts have been applied both to task-oriented dialogue and to non-task-oriented casual conversational speech. We give examples of two dialogue act tagsets designed for task-oriented dialogue and one for casual speech.

The task-oriented corpora are the Map Task and Verbmobil corpora. The Map Task corpus (Anderson et al. 1991) consists of conversations between two speakers with slightly different maps of an imaginary territory. Their task is to help one speaker reproduce a route drawn only on the other speaker's map, all without being able to see each other's maps. The Verbmobil corpus consists of two-party scheduling dialogues, in which the speakers were asked to plan a meeting at some future date. Tables 26.1 and 26.2 show the most commonly used versions of the tagsets from those two tasks.

Switchboard is a large collection of 2,400 six-minute telephone conversations between strangers who were asked to informally chat about certain topics (cars, children, crime). The SWBD-DAMSL tagset (Jurafsky et al. 1997b) was developed from the DAMSL tagset in an attempt to label the kind of non-task-oriented dialogues that occur in Switchboard. The tagset was multidimensional, with approximately 50 basic tags (QUESTION, STATEMENT, etc.) and various diacritics. A labeling project described in Jurafsky et al. (1997b) labeled every utterance in about 1,200 of the Switchboard conversations; approximately 200,000 utterances were labeled. Approximately 220 of the many possible unique combinations of the SWBD-DAMSL codes were used by the coders. To obtain a system with somewhat higher inter-labeler agreement, as well as enough data per class for statistical modeling purposes, a less fine-grained tagset was devised, distinguishing 42 mutually exclusive utterance types (Jurafsky et al. 1998a; Stolcke et al. 2000). Table 26.3 shows the 42 categories with examples and relative frequencies.

None of these various sets of dialogue acts are meant to be an exhaustive list. Each was designed with some particular computational task in mind, and hence will have domain-specific inclusions or absences. I have included them here mainly to show the kind of delimited task that the computational modeling community has set for itself. As is clear from the examples above, the various tagsets do include commonly studied speech acts like QUESTION and REQUEST. They also, however, include acts that have not been studied in the speech act literature. In the next section, I summarize one of these dialogue acts, the CHECK, in order to give the reader a more in-depth view of at least one of these various "minor" acts.

Table 26.1 The 18 high-level dialogue acts used in Verbmobil-1, abstracted over a total of 43 more specific dialogue acts: examples are from Jekat et al. (1995)

Tag	Example
THANK	*Thanks*
GREET	*Hello Dan*
INTRODUCE	*It's me again*
BYE	*Allright bye*
REQUEST-COMMENT	*How does that look?*
SUGGEST	*from thirteenth through seventeenth June*
REJECT	*No Friday I'm booked all day*
ACCEPT	*Saturday sounds fine*
REQUEST-SUGGEST	*What is a good day of the week for you?*
INIT	*I wanted to make an appointment with you*
GIVE_REASON	*Because I have meetings all afternoon*
FEEDBACK	*Okay*
DELIBERATE	*Let me check my calendar here*
CONFIRM	*Okay, that would be wonderful*
CLARIFY	*Okay, do you mean Tuesday the 23rd?*
DIGRESS	*[we could meet for lunch] and eat lots of ice cream*
MOTIVATE	*We should go to visit our subsidiary in Munich*
GARBAGE	*Oops, I-*

Table 26.2 The 12 move types used in the Map Task: examples are from Taylor et al. (1998)

Tag	Example
INSTRUCT	*Go round, ehm horizontally underneath diamond mind*
EXPLAIN	*I don't have a ravine*
ALIGN	*Okay?*
CHECK	*So going down to Indian Country?*
QUERY-YN	*Have you got the graveyard written down?*
QUERY-W	*In where?*
ACKNOWLEDGE	*Okay*
CLARIFY	*{you want to go . . . diagonally} Diagonally down*
REPLY-Y	*I do.*
REPLY-N	*No, I don't*
REPLY-W	*{And across to?} The pyramid.*
READY	*Okay*

Table 26.3   The 42 dialogue act labels, from Stolcke et al. (2000): dialogue act frequencies are given as percentages of the total number of utterances in the corpus

Tag	Example	%
STATEMENT	*Me, I'm in the legal department.*	36
BACKCHANNEL/ACKNOWLEDGE	*Uh-huh.*	19
OPINION	*I think it's great.*	13
ABANDONED/UNINTERPRETABLE	*So, -/*	6
AGREEMENT/ACCEPT	*That's exactly it.*	5
APPRECIATION	*I can imagine.*	2
YES-NO-QUESTION	*Do you have to have any special training?*	2
NON-VERBAL	*⟨Laughter⟩, ⟨Throat_clearing⟩*	2
YES ANSWERS	*Yes.*	1
CONVENTIONAL-CLOSING	*Well, it's been nice talking to you.*	1
WH-QUESTION	*What did you wear to work today?*	1
NO ANSWERS	*No.*	1
RESPONSE ACKNOWLEDGMENT	*Oh, okay.*	1
HEDGE	*I don't know if I'm making any sense or not.*	1
DECLARATIVE YES-NO-QUESTION	*So you can afford to get a house?*	1
OTHER	*Well give me a break, you know.*	1
BACKCHANNEL-QUESTION	*Is that right?*	1
QUOTATION	*You can't be pregnant and have cats.*	0.5
SUMMARIZE/REFORMULATE	*Oh, you mean you switched schools for the kids.*	0.5
AFFIRMATIVE NON-YES ANSWERS	*It is.*	0.4
ACTION-DIRECTIVE	*Why don't you go first.*	0.4
COLLABORATIVE COMPLETION	*Who aren't contributing.*	0.4
REPEAT-PHRASE	*Oh, fajitas.*	0.3
OPEN-QUESTION	*How about you?*	0.3
RHETORICAL-QUESTIONS	*Who would steal a newspaper?*	0.2
HOLD BEFORE ANSWER/ AGREEMENT	*I'm drawing a blank.*	0.3
REJECT	*Well, no.*	0.2
NEGATIVE NON-NO ANSWERS	*Uh, not a whole lot.*	0.1
SIGNAL-NON-UNDERSTANDING	*Excuse me?*	0.1
OTHER ANSWERS	*I don't know.*	0.1
CONVENTIONAL-OPENING	*How are you?*	0.1
OR-CLAUSE	*or is it more of a company?*	0.1
DISPREFERRED ANSWERS	*Well, not so much that.*	0.1
3RD-PARTY-TALK	*My goodness, Diane, get down from there.*	0.1
OFFERS, OPTIONS and COMMITS	*I'll have to check that out.*	0.1
SELF-TALK	*What's the word I'm looking for?*	0.1
DOWNPLAYER	*That's all right.*	0.1
MAYBE/ACCEPT-PART	*Something like that.*	<0.1
TAG-QUESTION	*Right?*	<0.1
DECLARATIVE WH-QUESTION	*You are what kind of buff?*	<0.1
APOLOGY	*I'm sorry.*	<0.1
THANKING	*Hey thanks a lot.*	<0.1

4.2   The dialogue act check

We saw in previous sections that the motivating example for the plan-based approach was based on indirect requests (surface questions with the illocutionary force of a REQUEST). In this section we'll look at a different kind of indirect speech act, one that has motivated some of the cue-based literature. The speech act we will look at, introduced very briefly above, is often called a CHECK or a CHECK QUESTION (Labov and Fanshel 1977, Carletta et al. 1997b). A CHECK is a subtype of question which requests the interlocutor to confirm some information; the information may have been mentioned explicitly in the preceding dialogue (as in the example below), or it may have been inferred from what the interlocutor has said:

(6)

> A: I was wanting to make some arrangements for a trip that I'm going to be taking uh to LA uh beginning of the week after next.
> B: OK uh let me pull up your profile and I'll be right with you here. [pause]
> B: **And you said you wanted to travel next week?**
> A: Uh yes.

Here are some sample realizations of CHECKs in English from various corpora, showing their various surface forms:

(7)   As tag questions (example from the Trains corpus; Allen and Core 1997):

> U: **and it's gonna take us also an hour to load boxcars right?**
> S: Right

(8)   As declarative questions, usually with rising intonation (Quirk et al. 1985: 814) (example from the Switchboard corpus; Godfrey et al. 1992):

> A: and we have a powerful computer down at work.
> B: Oh (laughter)
> B: **so, you don't need a personal one (laughter)?**
> A: No

(9)   As fragment questions (subsentential unit, e.g. words, noun phrases, clauses) (Weber 1993) (example from the Map Task corpus; Carletta et al. 1997b):

> G: Ehm, curve round slightly to your right.
> F: **To my right?**
> G: Yes

The next section will discuss the kind of cues that are used to detect CHECKs and other dialogue acts.

4.3   Cues

A CUE is a surface feature that is probabilistically associated with some speech or dialogue act. Commonly studied features include lexical, syntactic, prosodic, and discourse factors, but cues may also involve more sophisticated and complex knowledge, such as speaker-specific or dyad-specific modeling.

4.3.1   Lexical or syntactic cues

Lexical and syntactic cues have been widely described, at least for the most commonly studied speech acts. In a useful typological study, Sadock and Zwicky (1985) mention the existence of such cues for DECLARATIVE acts as declarative particles (in Welsh or Hidatsa), or different inflectional forms used specifically in declarative acts (Greenlandic).

Cross-linguistically common lexical or syntactic cues for imperatives include sentence-initial or sentence-final particles, verbal clitics, special verb morphology in the verb stem, subject deletion, and special subject pronoun forms that are used specifically in the imperative (Sadock and Zwicky 1985).

A similar inventory of cue types applies to lexical or syntactic cues for *yes-no* QUESTIONS, including sentence-initial or sentence-final particles, special verb morphology, and word order.

In addition to these cross-linguistic universals for the major acts, more recent work has begun to examine lexical and syntactic cues for minor acts. Michaelis (2001) shows that EXCLAMATIVES, for example, are characterized cross-linguistically by anaphoric degree adverbs, as well as various surface cues associated with information questions. Michaelis and Lambrecht (1996) discuss the wide variety of surface syntactic features which can characterize EXCLAMATIVES in English, including extraposition, bare complements, and certain kinds of definite noun phrases.

I have seen these same kinds of cues in my own work and that of my colleagues. Studies of CHECKS, for example, have shown that, like the examples above, they are most often realized with declarative structure (i.e. no aux-inversion), and they often have a following question tag, usually *right* (Quirk et al. 1985: 810–14), as in example (7) above. They also are often realized as fragments, i.e. subsentential words or phrases (Weber 1993).

In the Switchboard corpus, a very common type of check is the REFORMULA-TION. A reformulation, by repeating back some summarized or rephrased version of the interlocutor's talk, is one way to ask "is this an acceptable summary of your talk?" Our examination of 960 reformulations in Switchboard (Jurafsky and Martin 2000) shows that they have a very specific micro-grammar. They generally have declarative word order, often with *you* as the subject (31 percent of the cases), often beginning with *so* (20 percent) or *oh*, and sometimes ending with *then*. Some examples:

(10)   Oh so you're from the Midwest too.

(11)   So you can steady it.

(12)   You really rough it then.

This kind of micro-grammar was originally noted by Goodwin (1996), in his discussion of ASSESSMENTS. Assessments are a particular kind of evaluative act, used to ascribe positive or negative properties:

(13)   That's good.

(14)   Oh that's nice.

(15)   It's great.

Goodwin (1996) found that assessments often display the following format:

(16)   *Pro Term + Copula + (Intensifier) + Assessment Adjective*

Jurafsky et al. (1998b) found an even more constrained, and more lexicalized, micro-grammar for the 1,150 assessments with overt subjects in Switchboard. They found that the vast majority (80 percent) of the Pro Terms were *that*, that only two types of intensifiers occurred (*really* and *pretty*), and that the range of assessment adjective was quite small, consisting only of the following: *great, good, nice, wonderful, cool, fun, terrible, exciting, interesting, wild, scary, hilarious, neat, funny, amazing, tough, incredible,* and *awful.*

4.3.2   *Prosodic cues*

Prosody is another important cue for dialogue act identity. The final pitch rise of *yes-no* questions in American English (Sag and Liberman 1975, Pierrehumbert 1980) as well as cross-linguistically (Sadock and Zwicky 1985) is well known. Similarly well studied is the realization of final lowering in declaratives and *wh*-questions in English (the H*L L% tune) (Pierrehumbert and Hirschberg 1990).

Prosody plays an important role in other dialogue acts. Shriberg et al. (1998) and Weber (1993), for example, found that CHECKS, like other questions, are also most likely to have rising intonation. Curl and Bell (2001) examined the dialogue-act coded portion of Switchboard for three dialogue acts which can all be realized by the word *yeah*: AGREEMENTS, YES-ANSWERS, and BACKCHANNELS. They found that *yeah* agreements are associated with high falling contour, and *yeah* backchannels with low falling or level contours.

Sadock and Zwicky (1985) mention various other types of prosodic cues that occur cross-linguistically, including special stress in the first word of a *yes-no* QUESTION in Hopi, and a glottal stop in the last word of a *yes-no* QUESTION in Hidatsa.

Pierrehumbert and Hirschberg (1990) offer a much more compositional kind of cue-based theory for the role of prosody in utterance interpretation in general. In their model, pitch accents convey information about such things as the status of discourse referents, phrase accents convey information about the semantic relationship between intermediate phrases, and boundary tones convey information about the directionality of interpretation. Presumably these kinds of intonational meaning cues, and others such as, for example, the rejection contour of Sag and Liberman (1975) or the uncertainty/incredulity contour of Ward and Hirschberg (1985, 1988), could be used to build a model of prosodic cues specifically for dialogue acts. (See also Hirschberg, this volume.)

4.3.3   *Discourse cues and summary*

Finally, discourse structure is obviously an important cue for dialogue act identity. A dialogue act which functions as the second part of an adjacency pair (for example the YES-ANSWER), obviously depends on the presence of the first part (in this case a QUESTION). This is even true for sequences that aren't clearly adjacency pairs. Allwood (1995) points out that the utterance "No it isn't" is an AGREEMENT after a negative statement like "It isn't raining" but a DISAGREEMENT after a positive statement like "It is raining."

The importance of this contextual role of discourse cues has been a main focus of the conversation analysis tradition. For example Schegloff (1988) focuses on the way that the changing discourse context and the changing understanding of the hearer affects his interpretation of the discourse function of the utterance. Schegloff gives the following example utterance:

(17)   Do you know who's going to that meeting?

which occurs in the following dialogue:

> *Mother*:   Do you know who's going to that meeting?
> *Russ*:   Who?
> *Mother*:   I don't kno:w
> *Russ*:   Oh:: Prob'ly Missiz McOwen . . .

Mother had meant her first utterance as a REQUEST. But Russ misinterprets it as a PRE-ANNOUNCEMENT, and gives an appropriate response to such pre-announcements, by asking the question word which was included in the pre-announcement ("Who?"). Mother's response ("I don't know") makes it clear that her utterance was a REQUEST rather than a PRE-ANNOUNCEMENT. In Russ's second utterance, he uses this information to reanalyze and re-respond to Mother's utterance.

This example shows that complex discourse information, such as the fact that an interlocutor has displayed a problem with a previous dialogue act interpretation, can play a role in future dialogue act interpretation.

In summary, we have seen three kinds of cues that can be used to help determine the dialogue act type of an utterance: prosodic cues, lexical and grammatical cues, and discourse structure cues. The next section discusses how cue-based algorithms make use of these cues to recognize dialogue acts.

4.4   The cue-based algorithms

The cue-based algorithm for speech act interpretation is given as input an utterance, and produces as output the most probable dialogue act for that utterance. In a sense, the idea behind the cue-based models is to treat every utterance as if it had no literal force. Determining the correct force is treated as a task of probabilistic reasoning, in which different cues at different levels supply the evidence.

In other words, I and other proponents of the cue-based model believe that the literal force hypothesis is simply wrong, i.e. that there is not a literal force for each surface sentence type. Certainly it is the case that some surface cues are more commonly associated with certain dialogue act types. But rather than model this commonality as a fact about literal meaning (the "Literal Force Hypothesis") the cue-based models treat it as a fact about a probabilistic relationship between cue and dialogue act; the probability of a given dialogue act may simply be quite high given some particular cue.

In discussing these cue-based approaches, I will draw particularly on research in which I have participated and hence with which I am familiar, such as Stolcke et al. (2000) and Shriberg et al. (1998). As we will see, these algorithms are mostly designed to work directly from input speech waveforms. This means that they are of necessity based on heuristic approximations to the available cues. For example, a useful prosodic cue might come from a perfect ToBI phonological parse of an input utterance. But the computational problem of deriving a perfect ToBI parse from speech input is unsolved. So we see very simplistic approximations to the syntactic, discourse, and prosodic knowledge that we will someday have better models of.

The models we will describe generally use supervised machine-learning algorithms, trained on a corpus of dialogues that is hand-labeled with dialogue acts for each utterance. That is, these algorithms are statistical classifiers. We train a QUESTION-classifier on many instances of QUESTIONS, and it learns to recognize the combination of features (prosodic, lexical, syntactic, and discourse) which suggest the presence of a question. We train a REQUEST-classifier on many instances of REQUESTS, a BACKCHANNEL-classifier on many instances of BACKCHANNELS, and so on.

Let's begin with lexical and syntactic features. The simplest way to build a probabilistic model which detects lexical and phrasal cues is simply to look at which words and phrases occur more often in one dialogue act than another. Many scholars, beginning with Nagata and Morimoto (1994), realized that simple statistical grammars based on words and short phrases could serve to detect local structures indicative of particular dialogue acts. They implemented this intuition by modeling each dialogue act as having its own separate N-gram grammar (see e.g. Suhm and Waibel 1994, Mast et al. 1996, Jurafsky et al. 1997a, Warnke et al. 1997, Reithinger and Klesen 1997, Taylor et al. 1998). An N-gram grammar is a simple Markov model which stores, for each word, what its probability of occurrence is given one or more particular previous words.

These systems create a separate mini-corpus from all the utterances which realize the same dialogue act, and then train a separate *N*-gram grammar on each of these mini-corpora. (In practice, more sophisticated *N*-gram models are generally used, such as backoff, interpolated, or class *N*-gram language models.) Given an input utterance consisting of a sequence of words *W*, they then choose the dialogue act *d* whose *N*-gram grammar assigns the highest likelihood to *W*. Technically, the formula for this maximization problem is as follows (although the non-probabilistic reader can safely ignore the formulas):

(18) $d^* = \underset{d}{\operatorname{argmax}} P(d|W)$

(19) $= \underset{d}{\operatorname{argmax}} P(d)P(W|d)$

Equation (18) says that our estimate of the best dialogue act *d** for an utterance is the dialogue act *d* which has the highest probability given the string *W*. By Bayes' Rule, that can be rewritten as equation (19). This says that the dialogue act which is most probable given the input is the one which maximizes the product of two factors: the prior probability of a particular dialogue act *P(d)* and the probability *P(W|d)*, which expresses, given that we had picked a certain dialogue act *d*, the probability it would be realized as the string of words *W*.

This *N*-gram approach, while only a local heuristic to more complex syntactic constraints, does indeed capture much of the micro-grammar. For example *yes-no* QUESTIONS often have bigram pairs indicative of aux-inversion (*do you*, *are you*, *was he*, etc.). Similarly, the most common bigrams in REFORMULATIONS are very indicative pairs like *so you*, *sounds like*, *so you're*, *oh so*, *you mean*, *so they*, and *so it's*.

While this *N*-gram model of micro-grammar has proved successful in practical implementations of dialogue act detection, it is obviously a gross simplification of micro-grammar. It is possible to keep the idea of separate, statistically trained micro-grammars for each dialogue act while extending the simple *N*-gram model to more sophisticated probabilistic grammars. For example Jurafsky et al. (1998b) show that the grammar of some dialogue acts, like APPRECIATIONS, can be captured by building probabilistic grammars of lexical category sequences. Alexandersson and Reithinger (1997) propose even more linguistically sophisticated grammars for each dialogue act, such as probabilistic context-free grammars. To reiterate this point: the idea of cue-based processing does not require that the cues be simplistic Markov models. A complex phrase-structural or configurational feature is just as good a cue. The model merely requires that these features be defined probabilistically.

Prosodic models of dialogue act micro-grammar rely on phonological features like pitch or accent, or their acoustic correlates like f0, duration, and energy. We mentioned above that features like final pitch rise are commonly used for questions and fall for assertions. Indeed, computational approaches to dialogue act prosody modeling have mostly focused on f0. Many studies have successfully shown an increase in the ability to detect *yes-no* questions by combining lexical cues with these pitch-based cues (Waibel 1988, Daly and Zue 1992, Kompe et al. 1993, Taylor et al. 1998).

One such system, Shriberg et al. (1998), trained CART-style decision trees on simple acoustically based prosodic features such as the slope of f0 at the end of the utterance, the average energy at different places in the utterance, and various duration measures. They found that these features were useful, for example, in distinguishing four broad clusters of dialogue acts, STATEMENTS (S), *yes–no* QUESTIONS (QY), DECLARATIVE-QUESTIONS like CHECKS (QD) and *wh*-QUESTIONS (QW), from each other. Figure 26.1 shows the decision tree which gives the posterior probability $P(d|F)$ of a dialogue act d type given a sequence of acoustic features F. Each node in the tree shows four probabilities, one for each of the four dialogue acts in the order S, QY, QW, QD; the most likely of the four is shown as the label for the node. Via Bayes' Rule, this probability can be used to compute the likelihood of the acoustic features given the dialogue act: $P(f|d)$.

In general, most such systems use phonetic rather than phonological cues, modeling f0 patterns with techniques such as vector quantization and Gaussian classifiers on acoustic input (Kießling et al. 1993, Kompe et al. 1995, Yoshimura et al. 1996). But some more recent systems actually attempt to directly model phonological cues such as pitch accent and boundary tone sequence (Taylor et al. 1997).

A final important cue for dialogue act interpretation is conversational structure. One simple way to model conversational structure, drawing on the idea of adjacency pairs (Schegloff 1968, Sacks et al. 1974) introduced above, is as a probabilistic sequence of dialogue acts. As first proposed by Nagata (1992), and in a follow-up paper (Nagata and Morimoto 1994), the identity of the previous dialogue acts can be used to help predict upcoming dialogue acts. For example, BACKCHANNELS or AGREEMENTS might be very likely to follow STATEMENTS. ACCEPTS or REJECTS might be more likely to follow REQUESTS, and so on. Woszczyna and Waibel (1994) give the dialogue automaton shown in figure 26.2, which models simple *N*-gram probabilities of dialogue act sequences for a Verbmobil-like appointment scheduling task.

Of course this idea of modeling dialogue act sequences as "*N*-grams" of dialogue acts only captures the effects of simple local discourse context. As I mentioned earlier in my discussion concerning syntactic cues, a more sophisticated model will need to take into account hierarchical discourse structure of various kinds. Indeed, the deficiencies of an *N*-gram model of dialogue structure are so great and so obvious that it might have been a bad idea for me to start this dialogue section of the chapter with them. But the fact is that the recent work on dialogue act interpretation that I describe here relies only on such simple cues. Once again, the fact that the examples we give all involve simple Markov models of dialogue structure should not be taken to imply that

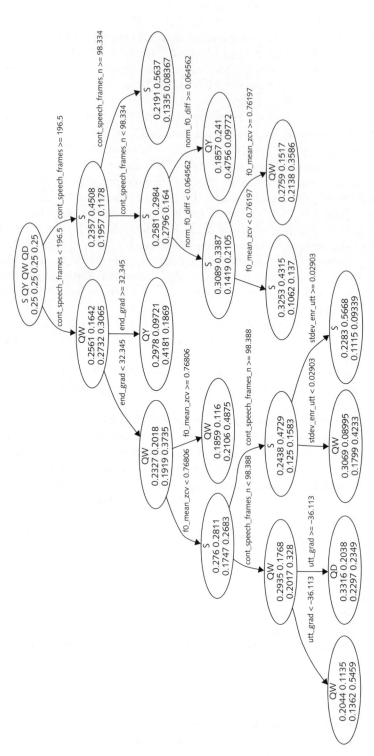

Figure 26.1 Decision tree for the classification of STATEMENT (S), *yes–no* QUESTIONS (QY), *wh*-QUESTIONS (QW) and DECLARATIVE QUESTIONS (QD), after Shriberg et al. (1998). Note that the difference between S and QY toward the right of the tree is based on the feature norm_f0_diff (normalized difference between mean f0 of end and penultimate regions), while the difference between QW and QD at the bottom left is based on utt_grad, which measures f0 slope across the whole utterance.

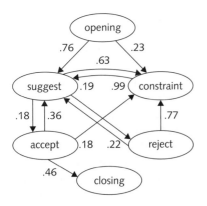

Figure 26.2 A dialogue act HMM for simple appointment scheduling conversations (after Woszczyna and Waibel 1994)

cue-based models of dialogue structure have to be simple. As the field progresses, presumably we will develop more complex probabilistic models of how speakers act in dialogue situations. Indeed, many others have already begun to enhance this *N*-gram approach (Nagata and Morimoto 1994, Suhm and Waibel 1994, Warnke et al. 1997, Stolcke et al. 1998, Taylor et al. 1998). Chu-Carroll (1998), for example, has shown how to model subdialogue structure in a cue-based model. Her model deals with hierarchical dialogue structures like insertion sequences (in which a question is followed by another question) and other kinds of complex structure. It's also important to note that a cue-based model doesn't disallow non-probabilistic knowledge sources; certainly not all dialogue structural information is probabilistic. For example, a REJECTION (a "no" response) is a *dispreferred* response to a REQUEST. I suspect this isn't a probabilistic fact; rejections may be always dispreferred. Studying how to integrate non-probabilistic knowledge of this sort into a cue-based model is a key problem that I return to in the conclusion.

I have now talked about simple statistical implementations of detectors for three kinds of cues for dialogue acts: lexical/syntactic, prosodic, and discourse structural. How can a dialogue act interpreter combine these different cues to find the most likely correct sequence of correct dialogue acts given a conversation?

One way to combine these statistical cues into a single probabilistic cue-based model is to treat a conversation as a Hidden Markov Model (HMM), an idea that seems to have been first suggested by Woszczyna and Waibel (1994) and Suhm and Waibel (1994). A Hidden Markov Model is a kind of probabilistic automaton in which a series of states in an automaton probabilistically generate sequences of symbols. Since the output is probabilistic, it is not possible to be certain from a given output symbol which state generated it; hence the states are "hidden." The intuition behind using an HMM for a dialogue is that the dialogue acts play the role of the hidden states. The words, syntax, and prosody act as observed output symbols.

HMMs can be viewed as generative or as interpretive models. As a generative model, given that the automaton is about to generate a particular dialogue act, the probabilistic cue-models give the probabilities of the different words, syntax, and prosody being produced. As an interpretive model, given a known sequence of words, syntax and prosody for an utterance, the HMM can be used to choose the single dialogue act which was most likely to have generated that sequence.

Stolcke et al. (2000) and Taylor et al. (1998) apply the HMM intuition of Woszczyna and Waibel (1994) to treat the dialogue act detection process as HMM-parsing. Given all available cues C about a conversation, the goal is to find the dialogue act sequence $D = \{d_1, d_2 \ldots, d_N\}$ that has the highest posterior probability $P(D|C)$ given those cues (here we are using capital letters to mean *sequences* of things). Applying Bayes' Rule we get:

$$(20) \quad D^* = \underset{D}{\arg\max} P(D|C)$$

$$= \underset{D}{\arg\max} \frac{P(D)P(C|D)}{P(C)}$$

$$= \underset{D}{\arg\max} P(D)P(C|D)$$

Equation (20) should remind the reader of equation (19). It says that we can estimate the best series of dialogue acts for an entire conversation by choosing that dialogue act sequence which maximizes the product of two probabilities, $P(D)$ and $P(C|D)$.

The first, $P(D)$, is the probability of a sequence of dialogue acts. Sequences of dialogue acts which are more coherent will tend to occur more often than incoherent sequences of dialogue acts, and will hence be more probable. Thus $P(D)$ essentially acts as a model of conversational structure. One simple way to compute an approximation to this probability is via the dialogue act N-grams introduced by Nagata and Morimoto (1994).

The second probability which must be considered is the likelihood $P(C|D)$. This is the probability, given that we have a particular dialogue act sequence D, of observing a particular set of observed surface cues C. This likelihood $P(C|D)$ can be computed from two sets of cues. First, the micro-syntax models (for example the different word-N-gram grammars for each dialogue act) can be used to estimate $P(W|D)$, the probability of the sequence of words W given a particular sequence of dialogue acts D. Next, the micro-prosody models (for example the decision tree for the prosodic features of each dialogue act) can be used to estimate $P(F|D)$, the probability of the sequence of prosodic features F. If we make the simplifying (but of course incorrect) assumption that the prosody and the words are independent, we can thus estimate the cue likelihood for a sequence of dialogue acts D as follows:

(21) $P(C|D) = P(F|D)P(W|D)$

We can compute the most likely sequence of dialogue acts D^* by substituting equation (21) into equation (20), thus choosing the dialogue act sequence which maximizes the product of the three knowledge sources (conversational structure, prosody, and lexical/syntactic knowledge):

(22) $D^* = \underset{D}{\mathrm{argmax}}\, P(D)P(F|D)P(W|D)$

Standard HMM-parsing techniques (like Viterbi) can then be used to search for this most-probable sequence of dialogue acts given the sequence of input utterances.

The HMM method is only one way of solving the problem of cue-based dialogue act identification. The link with HMM tagging suggests another approach, treating dialogue acts as tags, and applying other part-of-speech tagging methods based on various cues in the input. Samuel et al. (1998), for example, applied Transformation-Based Learning to dialogue act tagging.

As we conclude this section on the cue-based approach, it's worth taking a moment to distinguish the cue-based approach from what has been called the IDIOM or CONVENTIONAL approach. The idiom approach assumes that a sentence structure like *Can you give me a list?* or *Can you pass the salt?* is ambiguous between a literal meaning as a *yes–no* QUESTION and an idiomatic meaning as a REQUEST. The grammar of English would simply list REQUEST as one meaning of *Can you X?* The cue-based model does share some features of the idiom model; certain surface cues are directly linked to certain discourse functions. The difference is that the pure idiom model is by definition non-compositional and non-probabilistic. A certain surface sentence type is linked with a certain set of discourse functions, one of which must be chosen. The cue-based model can capture some generalizations which the idiom approach cannot; certain cues for questions, say, may play a role also in requests. We can thus capture the link between questions and requests by saying that a certain cue plays a role in both dialogue acts.

5   Conclusion

In summary, the BDI and cue-based models of computational pragmatics are both important, and both will continue to play a role in future computational modeling. The BDI model focuses on the kind of rich, sophisticated knowledge and reasoning that is clearly necessary for building conversational agents that can interact. Agents have to know why they are asking questions, and have to be able to reason about complex pragmatic and world-knowledge issues. But the depth and richness of this model comes at the expense of breadth; current models only deal with a small number of speech acts and situations. The cue-based model focuses on statistical examination of the surface cues to the realization of dialogue acts. Agents have to be able to make use of the rich lexical, prosodic, and grammatical cues to interpretation. But the breadth and coverage of this model come at the expense of depth; current algorithms are able to model only very simplistic and local heuristics for cues.

As I mentioned earlier, I chose speech act interpretation as the topic for this chapter because I think of it as a touchstone task. Thus this same dialectic between logical models based on knowledge-based reasoning and probabilistic models based on statistical interpretation applies in other computational pragmatic areas like reference resolution and discourse structure interpretation.

This dialectic is also important for the field of linguistics as well. Although linguistics has traditionally embraced the symbolic, structural, and philosophical paradigm implicit in the BDI model, it has only recently begun to flirt with the probabilistic paradigm. The cue-based model shows one way in which the probabilistic paradigm can inform our understanding of the relationship between linguistic form and linguistic function.

It is clear that both these models of computational pragmatics are in their infancy. I expect significant progress in both areas in the near future, and I look forward to a comprehensive and robust integration of the two methods.

ACKNOWLEDGMENTS

Work on this chapter was partially supported by NSF CAREER-IIS-9733067. I'm very grateful to the editors and to Andy Kehler, Laura Michaelis, Barbara Fox, Brad Miller, and Jim Martin for advice on and discussion about this material.

NOTE

1   ATIS, or Air Travel Information System, is a corpus of sentences spoken to a computerized speech understanding system for planning air travel. It is available as part of the Penn Treebank Project (Marcus et al. 1999).

Part IV Pragmatics and Cognition

27 Relevance Theory

DEIRDRE WILSON AND DAN SPERBER

1 Introduction

Relevance theory may be seen as an attempt to work out in detail one of Grice's central claims: that an essential feature of most human communication is the expression and recognition of intentions (Grice 1989: Essays 1–7, 14, 18; Retrospective Epilogue). In elaborating this claim, Grice laid the foundations for an inferential model of communication, an alternative to the classical code model. According to the code model, a communicator encodes her intended message into a signal, which is decoded by the audience using an identical copy of the code. According to the inferential model, a communicator provides evidence of her intention to convey a certain meaning, which is inferred by the audience on the basis of the evidence provided. An utterance is, of course, a linguistically coded piece of evidence, so that verbal comprehension involves an element of decoding. However, the decoded linguistic meaning is just one of the inputs to a non-demonstrative inference process which yields an interpretation of the speaker's meaning.

The goal of inferential pragmatics is to explain how the hearer infers the speaker's meaning on the basis of the evidence provided. The relevance-theoretic account is based on another of Grice's central claims: that utterances automatically create expectations which guide the hearer toward the speaker's meaning. Grice described these expectations in terms of a Cooperative Principle and maxims of Quality (truthfulness), Quantity (informativeness), Relation (relevance), and Manner (clarity), which speakers are expected to observe (Grice 1961, 1989: 368–72). We share Grice's intuition that utterances raise expectations of relevance, but question several other aspects of his account, including the need for a Cooperative Principle and maxims, the focus on pragmatic contributions to implicit (as opposed to explicit) content, the role of maxim violation in utterance interpretation, and the treatment of figurative utterances.[1] The central claim of relevance theory is that the expectations of relevance raised by an utterance are precise and predictable enough to guide the hearer toward the speaker's meaning.

The aim is to explain in cognitively realistic terms what these expectations amount to, and how they might contribute to an empirically plausible account of comprehension. The theory has developed in several stages. A detailed version was published in *Relevance: Communication and Cognition* (Sperber and Wilson 1986a, 1987a, b) and updated in Sperber and Wilson (1995, 1998a, 2002) and Wilson and Sperber (2002). Here, we will outline the main assumptions of the current version of the theory and discuss some of its implications.

2   Relevance and Cognition

What sort of things may be relevant? Intuitively, relevance is a potential property not only of utterances and other observable phenomena, but of thoughts, memories, and conclusions of inferences. According to relevance theory, any external stimulus or internal representation which provides an input to cognitive processes may be relevant to an individual at some time. Utterances raise expectations of relevance not because speakers are expected to obey a Cooperative Principle and maxims or some other communicative convention, but because the search for relevance is a basic feature of human cognition, which communicators may exploit. In this section, we will introduce the basic notion of relevance and the Cognitive Principle of Relevance, which lay the foundation for the relevance-theoretic approach.

When is an input relevant? Intuitively, an input (a sight, a sound, an utterance, a memory) is relevant to an individual when it connects with background information he has available to yield conclusions that matter to him: say, by answering a question he had in mind, improving his knowledge on a certain topic, settling a doubt, confirming a suspicion, or correcting a mistaken impression. According to relevance theory, an input is relevant to an individual when its processing in a context of available assumptions yields a POSITIVE COGNITIVE EFFECT. A positive cognitive effect is a worthwhile difference to the individual's representation of the world: a true conclusion, for example. False conclusions are not worth having; they are cognitive effects, but not positive ones (Sperber and Wilson 1995: §3.1–2).

The most important type of cognitive effect is a CONTEXTUAL IMPLICATION, a conclusion deducible from input and context together, but from neither input nor context alone. For example, on seeing my train arriving, I might look at my watch, access my knowledge of the train timetable, and derive the contextual implication that my train is late (which may itself achieve relevance by combining with further contextual assumptions to yield further implications). Other types of cognitive effect include the strengthening, revision, or abandonment of available assumptions. For example, the sight of my train arriving late might confirm my impression that the service is deteriorating, or make me alter my plans to do some shopping on the way to work. According to relevance theory, an input is RELEVANT to an individual when, and only when, its processing yields such positive cognitive effects.[2]

Relevance is not just an all-or-none matter but a matter of degree. There are potentially relevant inputs all around us, but we cannot attend to them all. What makes an input worth picking out from the mass of competing stimuli is not just that it is relevant, but that it is MORE relevant than any alternative input available to us at that time. Intuitively, other things being equal, the more worthwhile conclusions achieved by processing an input, the more relevant it will be. According to relevance theory, other things being equal, the greater the positive cognitive effects achieved by processing an input, the greater its relevance will be. Thus, the sight of my train arriving one minute late may make little worthwhile difference to my representation of the world, while the sight of it arriving half an hour late may lead to a radical reorganization of my day, and the relevance of the two inputs will vary accordingly.

What makes an input worth attending to is not just the cognitive effects it achieves. In different circumstances, the same stimulus may be more or less salient, the same contextual assumptions more or less accessible, and the same cognitive effects easier or harder to derive. Intuitively, the greater the effort of perception, memory, and inference required, the less rewarding the input will be to process, and hence the less deserving of attention. According to relevance theory, other things being equal, the greater the PROCESSING EFFORT required, the less relevant the input will be. Thus, RELEVANCE may be assessed in terms of cognitive effects and processing effort:

(1) **Relevance of an input to an individual**
   a. Other things being equal, the greater the positive cognitive effects achieved by processing an input, the greater the relevance of the input to the individual at that time.
   b. Other things being equal, the greater the processing effort expended, the lower the relevance of the input to the individual at that time.

Here is a brief and artificial illustration of how the relevance of alternative inputs might be compared. Mary, who dislikes most meat and is allergic to chicken, rings her host to find out what is on the menu. He could truly tell her any of three things:

(2) We are serving meat.

(3) We are serving chicken.

(4) Either we are serving chicken or $(7^2 - 3)$ is not 46.

According to the characterization in (1), all three utterances would be relevant to Mary, but (3) would be more relevant than either (2) or (4). It would be more relevant than (2) for reasons of cognitive effect: (3) entails (2), and therefore yields all the conclusions derivable from (2), and more besides. It would be more relevant than (4) for reasons of processing effort: although (3) and (4) are logically equivalent, and therefore yield exactly the same cognitive effects, these effects are easier to derive from (3) than from (4), which requires an additional effort of parsing and inference (in order to work out that the second disjunct is false and the first is therefore true). More generally, when similar amounts of effort are required, the effect factor is decisive, and when similar amounts of effect are achievable, the effort factor is decisive.

This characterization of relevance is comparative rather than quantitative: it allows clear comparisons in some cases, but not in all. While quantitative notions of relevance might be interesting from a formal point of view,[3] the comparative notion provides a better starting point for constructing a psychologically plausible theory. In the first place, only some aspects of effect and effort (e.g. processing time, number of contextual implications) are likely to be measurable in absolute numerical terms, while others (e.g. strength of implications, level of attention) are not. In the second place, even when absolute measures exist (for weight or distance, for example), we generally have access to more intuitive methods of assessment which are comparative rather than quantitative, and which are in some sense more basic. In therefore seems preferable to treat effort and effect (and relevance, which is a function of effort and effect) as **non-representational** dimensions of mental processes: they exist and play a role in cognition whether or not they are mentally represented; and when they are mentally represented, it is in the form of intuitive comparative judgments rather than absolute numerical ones.[4]

Within this framework, aiming to maximize the relevance of the inputs one processes is simply a matter of making the most efficient use of the available processing resources. No doubt this is something we would all want to do, given a choice. Relevance theory claims that humans do have an automatic tendency to maximize relevance, not because we have a choice in the matter – we rarely do – but because of the way our cognitive systems have evolved. As a result of constant selection pressures toward increasing efficiency, the human cognitive system has developed in such a way that our perceptual mechanisms tend automatically to pick out potentially relevant stimuli, our memory retrieval mechanisms tend automatically to activate potentially relevant assumptions, and our inferential mechanisms tend spontaneously to process them in the most productive way. This universal tendency is described in the First, or Cognitive, Principle of Relevance (Sperber and Wilson 1995: §3.1–2):

(5) **Cognitive Principle of Relevance**
     Human cognition tends to be geared to the maximization of relevance.

It is against this cognitive background that inferential communication takes place.

3 Relevance and Communication

The universal cognitive tendency to maximize relevance makes it possible (to some extent) to predict and manipulate the mental states of others. Knowing your tendency to pick out the most relevant inputs and process them so as to maximize their relevance, I may be able to produce a stimulus which is likely to attract your attention, activate an appropriate set of contextual assumptions and point you toward an intended conclusion. For example, I may leave my empty glass in your line of vision intending you to notice and conclude that I might like another drink. As Grice pointed out, this is not yet a case of inferential communication because, although I intended to affect your thoughts in a certain way, I gave you no evidence that I had this intention. When I quietly leave my glass in your line of vision, I am not engaging in inferential communication, but merely exploiting your natural cognitive tendency to maximize relevance.

Inferential communication – what relevance theory calls OSTENSIVE-INFERENTIAL COMMUNICATION, for reasons that will shortly become apparent – involves an extra layer of intention:

(6)   **Ostensive-inferential communication**
    a.   **The informative intention**:
        The intention to inform an audience of something.
    b.   **The communicative intention**:
        The intention to inform the audience of one's informative intention.[5]

Understanding is achieved when the communicative intention is fulfilled – that is, when the audience recognizes the informative intention. (Whether the informative intention itself is fulfilled depends on how much the audience trusts the communicator.)

How does the communicator indicate to an audience that she is trying to communicate in this overt, intentional way? Instead of covertly leaving my glass in your line of vision, I might touch your arm and point to my empty glass, wave it at you, ostentatiously put it down in front of you, stare at it meaningfully, or say, "My glass is empty." More generally, ostensive-inferential communication involves the use of an OSTENSIVE STIMULUS, designed to attract an audience's attention and focus it on the communicator's meaning. According to relevance theory, use of an ostensive stimulus may create precise and predictable expectations of relevance not raised by other inputs. In this section, we will describe these expectations and show how they may help to identify the communicator's meaning.

The fact that ostensive stimuli create expectations of relevance follows from the Cognitive Principle of Relevance. An ostensive stimulus is designed to attract the audience's attention. Given the cognitive tendency to maximize relevance, an audience will only pay attention to an input that seems relevant enough. By producing an ostensive stimulus, the communicator therefore encourages her audience to presume that it is relevant enough to be worth processing. This need not be a case of Gricean cooperation. Even a self-interested, deceptive, or incompetent communicator manifestly intends her audience to assume that her stimulus is relevant enough to be worth processing – why else would he

612 *Deirdre Wilson and Dan Sperber*

pay attention?[6] This is the basis for the Second, or Communicative, Principle of Relevance:

(7) **Communicative Principle of Relevance**
Every ostensive stimulus conveys a presumption of its own optimal relevance.

Use of an ostensive stimulus, then, creates a PRESUMPTION OF OPTIMAL RELEVANCE. The notion of optimal relevance is meant to spell out what the audience of an act of ostensive communication is entitled to expect in terms of effort and effect:

(8) **Presumption of optimal relevance**
   a. The ostensive stimulus is relevant enough to be worth the audience's processing effort.
   b. It is the most relevant one compatible with communicator's abilities and preferences.

According to clause (a), the audience can expect the ostensive stimulus to be at least relevant enough to be worth processing. Given the argument of section 2 that a stimulus is only worth processing if it is more relevant than any alternative input available at the time, this is not a trivial claim. Indeed, in order to satisfy the presumption of relevance, the audience may have to draw a stronger conclusion than would otherwise have been warranted. For example, if you just happen to notice my empty glass, you may be entitled to conclude that I *might* like a drink. If I deliberately wave it at you, you would generally be justified in concluding that I *would* like a drink.

According to clause (b), the audience of an ostensive stimulus is entitled to even higher expectations. The communicator wants to be understood. It is therefore in her interest – within the limits of her own capabilities and preferences – to make her ostensive stimulus as easy as possible for the audience to understand, and to provide evidence not just for the cognitive effects she aims to achieve but for further cognitive effects, which, by holding the audience's attention, will help her achieve her goal. For instance, the communicator's goal might be to inform her audience that she has started writing her paper. The most effective way of achieving this goal might be to offer more specific information and say, "I've already written a third of the paper." In the circumstances, her audience could then reasonably take her to mean that she has only written a third of the paper, because if she had written more, she should have said so, given clause (b) of the presumption of optimal relevance.

Of course, communicators are not omniscient, and they cannot be expected to go against their own interests and preferences. There may be relevant information that they are unable or unwilling to provide, and ostensive stimuli that would convey their intentions more economically, but that they are unwilling to produce, or unable to think of at the time. All this is allowed for in clause (b) of the presumption of optimal relevance, which states that the ostensive stimulus is the most relevant one that the communicator is WILLING AND ABLE to produce (Sperber and Wilson 1995: §3.3 and 266–78).

This approach explains some parallels between ostensive and non-ostensive behavior that the Gricean framework obscures. Suppose you ask me a question and I remain silent. My silence may or may not be an ostensive stimulus. When it is not, you will naturally take it as indicating that I am unable or unwilling to answer; if I am clearly willing, you can conclude that I am unable, and if I am clearly able, you can conclude that I am unwilling. Given the presumption of optimal relevance, an ostensive silence can be analyzed as merely involving an extra layer of intention, and hence as COMMUNICATING – or IMPLICATING – that the addressee is unable or unwilling to answer.[7] In Grice's framework, however, violation of the first Quantity maxim invariably implicates INABILITY – rather than UNWILLINGNESS – to provide the required information. Inability to make one's contribution "such as is required" is consistent with the Cooperative Principle as long as it results from a clash with the Quality maxims. Unwillingness to make one's contribution "such as is required" is a violation of the Cooperative Principle; and since conversational implicatures are recoverable only on the assumption that the Cooperative Principle is being observed, it is impossible in Grice's framework to implicate that one is unwilling to provide the required information.[8] While cooperation in Grice's sense is quite common, we have argued that it is not essential to communication or comprehension (see note 6).

This account of communication has practical implications for pragmatics. The overall task of inferring the speaker's meaning may be broken down into a variety of pragmatic subtasks. There may be ambiguities and referential ambivalences to resolve, ellipses to interpret, and other underdeterminacies of explicit content to deal with. There may be implicatures to identify, illocutionary indeterminacies to resolve, metaphors and ironies to interpret. All this requires an appropriate set of contextual assumptions, which the hearer must also supply. The Communicative Principle of Relevance and the presumption of optimal relevance suggest a practical procedure for performing these subtasks and constructing a hypothesis about the speaker's meaning. The hearer should take the decoded linguistic meaning; following a path of least effort, he should enrich it at the explicit level and complement it at the implicit level until the resulting interpretation meets his expectation of relevance:

(9) **Relevance-theoretic comprehension procedure**
   a. Follow a path of least effort in computing cognitive effects: Test interpretive hypotheses (disambiguations, reference resolutions, implicatures, etc.) in order of accessibility.
   b. Stop when your expectations of relevance are satisfied (or abandoned).

Given clause (b) of the presumption of optimal relevance, it is reasonable for the hearer to follow a path of least effort because the speaker is expected (within the limits of her abilities and preferences) to make her utterance as easy as possible to understand. Since relevance varies inversely with effort, the very fact that an interpretation is easily accessible gives it an initial degree of plausibility (an advantage specific to ostensive communication). It is also reasonable for the hearer to stop at the first interpretation that satisfies his expectations of relevance, because there should never be more than one. A speaker who wants her utterance to be as easy as possible to understand should formulate it (within the limits of her abilities and preferences) so that the first interpretation to satisfy the hearer's expectation of relevance is the one she intended to convey. An utterance with two apparently satisfactory competing interpretations would cause the hearer the unnecessary extra effort of choosing between them, and the resulting interpretation (if there were one) would not satisfy clause (b) of the presumption of optimal relevance.[9]

Thus, when a hearer following the path of least effort arrives at an interpretation that satisfies his expectations of relevance, in the absence of contrary evidence, this is the most plausible hypothesis about the speaker's meaning. Since comprehension is a non-demonstrative inference process, this hypothesis may well be false; but it is the best a rational hearer can do (on the role of the relevance-theoretic comprehension procedure in a modular approach to pragmatics, see section 5).

4   Relevance and Comprehension

In many non-verbal cases (e.g. pointing to one's empty glass, failing to answer a question), use of an ostensive stimulus merely adds an extra layer of intention recognition to a basic layer of information that the audience might have picked up anyway. In other cases (e.g. inviting someone out to a drink by miming the act of drinking), the communicator's behavior provides no direct evidence for the intended conclusion, and it is only the presumption of relevance that encourages the audience to spend the effort required to discover the communicator's meaning. In either case, the range of meanings that can be non-verbally conveyed is necessarily limited to those the communicator can evoke in her audience by drawing attention to observable features of the environment (whether pre-existing or produced specifically for this purpose).

In verbal communication, by contrast, speakers can convey a very wide range of meanings even though there is no independently identifiable basic layer of information for the hearer to pick up. What makes this possible is that utterances encode logical forms (conceptual representations, however fragmentary or incomplete) which the speaker has manifestly chosen to provide as input to the inferential comprehension process. As a result, verbal communication can achieve a degree of explicitness not available in non-verbal communication (compare pointing in the direction of a table containing glasses, ashtrays, plates, etc., and saying, "My glass is empty").

Although the decoded logical form of an utterance is an important clue to the speaker's intentions, it is now increasingly recognized that even the explicit content of an utterance may go well beyond what is linguistically encoded.[10] What is still open to debate is how these context-dependent aspects of explicit content are recovered. Grice invoked his Cooperative Principle and maxims mainly to explain the recovery of implicatures,[11] and many pragmatists have followed him on this. There has thus been a tendency, even in much of the recent pragmatic literature, to treat the "primary" processes involved in the recovery of explicit content as significantly different from – i.e. less inferential, or less directly dependent on speakers' intentions or pragmatic principles than – the "secondary" processes involved in the recovery of implicatures.[12]

In relevance theory, the identification of explicit content is seen as equally inferential, and equally guided by the Communicative Principle of Relevance, as the recovery of implicatures. The relevance-theoretic comprehension procedure applies in the same way to resolving linguistic underdeterminacies at both explicit and implicit levels. The hearer's goal is to construct a hypothesis about the speaker's meaning that satisfies the presumption of relevance conveyed by the utterance. As noted above, this overall task can be broken down into a number of subtasks:

(10) **Subtasks in the overall comprehension process**
   a. Constructing an appropriate hypothesis about explicit content (EXPLICATURES) via decoding, disambiguation, reference resolution, and other pragmatic enrichment processes.
   b. Constructing an appropriate hypothesis about the intended contextual assumptions (IMPLICATED PREMISES).
   c. Constructing an appropriate hypothesis about the intended contextual implications (IMPLICATED CONCLUSIONS).

These subtasks should not be seen as sequentially ordered: the hearer does not FIRST decode the logical form, THEN construct an explicature and select an appropriate context, and THEN derive a range of implicated conclusions. Comprehension is an on-line process, and hypotheses about explicatures, implicated premises, and implicated conclusions are developed in parallel against a background of expectations which may be revised or elaborated as the utterance unfolds.[13] In particular, the hearer may bring to the comprehension process not only a general presumption of relevance, but more specific expectations about how the utterance is intended to be relevant (what cognitive effects it is intended to achieve), and these may contribute, via backwards inference, to the identification of explicatures and implicated premises. Thus, each subtask in (10a–c) involves a non-demonstrative inference process embedded within the overall process of constructing a hypothesis about the speaker's meaning.

To illustrate, consider the exchange in (11):

(11)a. *Peter*: Did John pay back the money he owed you?
   b. *Mary*: No. He forgot to go to the bank.

Here is a schematic outline of how Peter might use the relevance-theoretic comprehension procedure in interpreting Mary's utterance, "He forgot to go to the bank":

(12)

(a)	Mary has said to Peter, "He$_x$ forgot to go to the BANK$_1$/BANK$_2$." [He$_x$ = uninterpreted pronoun] [BANK$_1$ = financial institution] [BANK$_2$ = river bank]	*Embedding of the decoded (incomplete) logical form of Mary's utterance into a description of Mary's ostensive behavior.*
(b)	Mary's utterance will be optimally relevant to Peter.	*Expectation raised by recognition of Mary's ostensive behavior and acceptance of the presumption of relevance it conveys.*
(c)	Mary's utterance will achieve relevance by explaining why John has not repaid the money he owed her.	*Expectation raised by (b), together with the fact that such an explanation would be most relevant to Peter at this point.*
(d)	Forgetting to go to the BANK$_1$ may make one unable to repay the money one owes.	*First assumption to occur to Peter which, together with other appropriate premises, might satisfy expectation (c). Accepted as an implicit premise of Mary's utterance.*
(e)	John forgot to go to the BANK$_1$.	*First enrichment of the logical form of Mary's utterance to occur to Peter which might combine with (d) to lead to the satisfaction of (c). Accepted as an explicature of Mary's utterance.*
(f)	John was unable to repay Mary the money he owes because he forgot to go to the BANK$_1$.	*Inferred from (d) and (e), satisfying (c) and accepted as an implicit conclusion of Mary's utterance.*
(g)	John may repay Mary the money he owes when he next goes to the BANK$_1$.	*From (f) plus background knowledge. One of several possible weak implicatures of Mary's utterance which, together with (f), satisfy expectation (b).*

Peter assumes in (12b) that Mary's utterance, decoded as in (12a), is optimally relevant to him. Since what he wants to know at this point is why John did not repay the money he owed, he assumes in (c) that Mary's utterance will achieve relevance by answering this question. One of the encoded logical forms provides easy access to the contextual assumption in (d) (that forgetting to go to the $BANK_1$ may prevent one repaying money one owes). This could be used as an implicit premise in deriving the expected explanation of John's behavior, as long as the utterance is interpreted on the explicit side (via disambiguation and reference resolution) as conveying the information in (e) (that John forgot to go to the $BANK_1$). By combining the implicit premise in (d) and the explicit premise in (e), Peter arrives at the implicit conclusion in (f), from which further, weaker implicatures, including (g) and others, follow. The resulting interpretation satisfies Peter's expectations of relevance. Thus, explicatures and IMPLICATURES (implicit premises and conclusions) are arrived at by a process of mutual parallel adjustment, with hypotheses about both being considered in order of accessibility.[14]

This schematic outline of the comprehension process is considerably over-simplified.[15] In particular, it omits a range of lexical-pragmatic processes involved in the construction of explicatures. Consider the word *bank* in (11b). Peter would probably take this to denote not just a banking institution but a specific type of banking institution: one that deals with private individuals, and in particular, with John. Unless it is narrowed in this way, the explicit content of Mary's utterance will not warrant the conclusion in (12f), which is needed to satisfy Peter's expectation of relevance. (It is hard to see how the fact that John had forgotten to go to the World Bank, say, might explain his failure to repay the money he owed.) Similarly, he would take the phrase *go to the bank* to mean not merely visiting the bank, but visiting it in order to get money, and to get money in the regular way (legally, rather than, say, by robbing the bank). Unless the explicit content is narrowed in this way, it will not warrant the conclusion in (12f), which is needed to satisfy Peter's expectation of relevance.

Such stereotypical narrowings have sometimes been analyzed as generalized conversational implicatures or default interpretations, derivable via default rules.[16] Despite the richness and subtlety of much of this literature, relevance theory takes a different approach, for two main reasons. First, as noted above, it treats lexical narrowing as a pragmatic enrichment process which contributes to explicatures rather than implicatures.[17] Like all enrichment processes, narrowing is driven by the search for relevance, which involves the derivation of cognitive effects, and in particular of contextual implications. By definition, a contextual implication must follow logically from the explicatures of the utterance and the context. Sometimes, as in (11b), the explicit content must be contextually enriched in order to warrant the expected conclusion. In any framework where implicated conclusions are seen as logically warranted by explicit content, there is good reason to treat lexical narrowing as falling on the explicit rather than the implicit side.[18]

Second, lexical narrowing is much more flexible and context-dependent than appeals to generalized implicature or default interpretations allow. Barsalou (1987, 1992) surveys a range of experimental evidence which shows that even "stereotypical" narrowings of terms such as *bird, animal, furniture, food,* etc. vary across situations, individuals, and times, and are strongly affected by discourse context and considerations of relevance. Barsalou sees his results as best explained by assuming that lexical items give access not to ready-made prototypes (assignable by default rules) but to a vast array of encyclopedic assumptions, with different subsets being selected ad hoc to determine the occasion-specific interpretation of a word. On this approach, *bank* in (11b) might be understood as conveying not the encoded concept BANK$_1$ but the ad hoc concept BANK*, with a more restricted encyclopedic entry and a narrower denotation.

According to Barsalou, the process of ad hoc concept construction is affected by a range of factors including context, accessibility of encyclopedic assumptions, and considerations of relevance. The relevance-theoretic comprehension procedure may be seen as a concrete hypothesis about how such a flexible, relevance-governed lexical interpretation process might go. The hearer treats the linguistically encoded concept (e.g. BANK$_1$ in (11b)) as no more than a clue to the speaker's meaning. Guided by expectations of relevance, and using contextual assumptions (e.g. (12d)) made accessible by the encyclopedic entry of the linguistically encoded concept, he starts deriving cognitive effects. When he has enough to satisfy his expectations of relevance, he stops. The results would be as in (12) above, except that the contextual assumption in (d), the explicature in (e), and the implicatures in (f) and (g) would contain not the encoded concept BANK$_1$ but the ad hoc concept BANK*, with a narrower denotation, which would warrant the derivation of the expected cognitive effects.

The effect of such a flexible interpretation process may be a loosening rather than a narrowing of the encoded meaning (resulting in a broader rather than a narrower denotation). Clear cases include generic uses of prominent brand name (e.g. *Hoover, Xerox, Kleenex*) and loose uses of well-defined terms such as *square, painless,* or *silent*; but the phenomenon is very widespread. Consider *bank* in (11b). Given current banking practice, the word is sometimes loosely used to denote a category containing not only banking institutions but also automatic cash dispensers. Indeed, in order to satisfy his expectations of relevance in (11b), Peter would probably have to take it this way (i.e. to mean, roughly, "bank-or-cash-dispenser"). (If John regularly gets his money from a cash dispenser, the claim that he forgot to go to the BANK$_1$, might be strictly speaking false, and in any case would not adequately explain his failure to repay Mary.) Thus, *bank* in (11b) might be understood as expressing not the encoded concept BANK$_1$, but an ad hoc concept BANK**, with a broader denotation, which shares with BANK$_1$ the salient encyclopedic attribute of being a place where one goes in order to access money from one's account. The interpretation of a quite ordinary utterance such as (11b) might then involve both a loosening and a narrowing of the encoded meaning.

Loose uses of language present a problem for Grice. Strictly speaking, faces are not square, rooms are generally not silent, and to describe them as such would violate his maxim of truthfulness ("Do not say what you believe to be false"). However, these departures from truthfulness do not fall into any of the categories of maxim-violation recognized by Grice (1989: 30). They are not covert violations, like lies, designed to deceive the hearer into believing what was said. They are not like jokes and fictions, which suspend the maxim entirely. Given their intuitive similarities to metaphor and hyperbole, it might be tempting to analyze them as overt violations (floutings), designed to trigger the search for a related implicature (in this case, a hedged version of what was said). The problem is that these loose uses are not generally perceived as violating the maxim of truthfulness at all. While we can all recognize on reflection that they are not strictly and literally true, these departures from truthfulness pass undetected in the normal flow of discourse. Grice's framework thus leaves them unexplained.[19]

Loose uses are not the only problem for a framework with a maxim of truthfulness. There are questions about how the maxim itself is to be understood, and a series of difficulties with the analysis of tropes as overt violations (cf. Wilson and Sperber 2002). Notice, too, that the intuitive similarities between loose talk, metaphor, and hyperbole cannot be captured as long as metaphor and hyperbole are seen as overtly violating the maxim of truthfulness, while loose uses are not. We have argued that the best solution is to abandon the maxim of truthfulness and treat whatever expectations of truthfulness arise in utterance interpretation as by-products of the more basic expectation of relevance. On this approach, loose talk, metaphor, and hyperbole are merely alternative routes to achieving optimal relevance. Whether an utterance is literally, loosely, or metaphorically understood will depend on the mutual adjustment of content, context, and cognitive effects in order to satisfy the overall expectation of relevance.[20]

To illustrate, consider the exchange in (13):

(13)a.   *Peter*:   What do you think of Martin's latest novel?
    b.   *Mary*:   It puts me to sleep.

Grice would treat Mary's utterance in (13b) as having three distinct interpretations: as a literal assertion, a hyperbole, or a metaphor. Of these, Peter should test the literal interpretation first, and consider a figurative interpretation only if the literal interpretation blatantly violates the maxim of truthfulness. Yet there is now a lot of experimental evidence suggesting that literal interpretations are not necessarily tested and rejected before figurative interpretations are considered;[21] indeed, in interpreting (13b), it would probably not even occur to Peter to wonder whether Mary literally fell asleep.

Our analysis takes these points into account. In the first place, there is no suggestion that the literal meaning must be tested first. As with *bank* in (11b), the encoded conceptual address is merely a point of access to an ordered array of encyclopedic assumptions from which the hearer is expected to select.

Whether the resulting interpretation is literal or loose will depend on which assumptions he selects. In processing (13b), Peter will be expecting to derive an answer to his question: that is, an evaluation of the book. In the circumstances, a highly salient assumption will be that a book that puts one to sleep is likely to be extremely boring and unengaging. Having used this assumption to derive an answer that satisfies his expectations of relevance, he should stop. Just as in interpreting *bank* in (11b), it does not occur to him to wonder whether John gets his money from a bank or a cash dispenser, so in interpreting (13b), it should not occur to him to wonder whether the book literally puts Mary to sleep, almost puts her to sleep, or merely bores her greatly. Thus, the mutual adjustment process for (13b) should yield an explicature containing the ad hoc concept PUT TO SLEEP*, which denotes not only literal cases of putting to sleep, but other cases that share with it the encyclopedic attribute of being extremely boring and unengaging. Only if such a loose interpretation fails to satisfy his expectations of relevance would Peter be justified in exploring further contextual assumptions, and moving toward a more literal interpretation.[22]

Generally, the explicit content of loose uses, and particularly of metaphors, is indeterminate to some degree. (Compare the concept SQUARE, SQUARE*, AND SQUARE** conveyed, respectively, by the literal phrase *square geometric figure*, the loose *square face*, and the metaphorical *square mind*.) This relative indeterminacy of explicatures is linked to the relative strength of implicatures.

A proposition may be more or less strongly implicated. It is STRONGLY IMPLICATED (or is a STRONG IMPLICATURE) if its recovery is essential in order to arrive at an interpretation that satisfies the addressee's expectations of relevance. It is WEAKLY IMPLICATED if its recovery helps with the construction of such an interpretation, but is not itself essential because the utterance suggests a range of similar possible implicatures, any one of which would do (Sperber and Wilson 1986a: 1.10–12, 4.6). For instance, (11b) strongly implicates (12f), since without this implication (or an appropriately narrowed-and-loosened variant), (11b) is not a relevant reply to (11a). (11b) also encourages the audience to derive a further implicature along the lines of (12g) (that John may repay Mary when he next goes to the bank), but here the audience must take some responsibility for coming to this conclusion rather than, say, the conclusion that John WILL repay Mary when he next goes to the bank, or some other similar conclusion.

Typically, loose uses, and particularly metaphorical uses, convey an array of weak implicatures. Thus, "John has a square mind" weakly implicates that John is somewhat rigid in his thinking, does not easily change his mind, is a man of principle, and so on. None of these implicatures is individually required for the utterance to make sense, but without some such implicatures, it will make no sense at all. If the word *square* is understood as expressing the concept SQUARE**, which combines with contextual information to yield these implications, then the concept SQUARE** itself will exhibit some indeterminacy or fuzziness, and the utterance as a whole will exhibit a corresponding weakness of explicature. Loose uses and metaphors typically exhibit such fuzziness, for which relevance theory provides an original account.

The distinction between strong and weak implicatures sheds light on the variety of ways in which utterance achieve relevance. Some utterances (e.g. technical instructions) achieve relevance by conveying a few strong implicatures. Others achieve relevance by weakly suggesting a wide array of possible implications, each of which is a weak implicature. This is typical of poetic uses of language, and has been discussed in relevance theory under the heading of POETIC EFFECT (Sperber and Wilson 1986a: 4.6–9, Pilkington 2000; for the related notions of STYLISTIC EFFECT and PRESUPPOSITIONAL EFFECT, see Sperber and Wilson 1986a: 4.5–6).

In Grice's framework (and indeed in all rhetorical and pragmatic discussions of irony as a figure of speech before Sperber and Wilson 1981) the treatment of verbal irony closely parallels the treatment of metaphor and hyperbole. For Grice, irony, like metaphor and hyperbole, is an overt violation of the maxim of truthfulness, differing only in the kind of implicature it conveys. We have argued not only against Grice's analysis of irony, but against the more general assumption that metaphor, hyperbole, and irony should be given parallel treatments.

Grice's account of irony is a variant of the classical rhetorical account on which an ironical utterance is seen as literally saying one thing and figuratively meaning the opposite. There are well-known arguments against this account. It is descriptively inadequate because ironical understatements, quotations, and allusions do not communicate the opposite of what is literally said. It is theoretically inadequate because saying the opposite of what one means is patently irrational; and this account does not explain why irony is universal and appears to arise spontaneously, without being taught or learned (Sperber and Wilson 1981, 1998b, Wilson and Sperber 1992).

According to relevance theory, verbal irony involves no special machinery or procedures not already needed to account for a basic use of language, INTERPRETIVE USE, and a specific form of interpretive use, ECHOIC USE.[23] An utterance may be interpretively used to (meta)represent another utterance or thought that it resembles in content. The best-known type of interpretive use is in reported speech or thought. An utterance is echoic when it achieves most of its relevance by expressing the speaker's attitude to views she tacitly attributes to someone else. Thus, suppose that Peter and Mary are leaving a party and one of the following exchanges occurs:

(14)   *Peter*:   That was a fantastic party.

(15)   *Mary*:   a.   [happily] Fantastic.
               b.   [puzzled] Fantastic?
               c.   [scornfully] Fantastic!

In (15a), Mary echoes Peter's utterance in order to indicate that she agrees with it; in (15b), she indicates that she is wondering about it; and in (15c) she indicates that she disagrees with it. The resulting interpretations might be as in (16):

(16)a. She believes I was right to say/think that the party was fantastic.
   b. She is wondering whether I was right to say/think that the party was fantastic.
   c. She believes I was wrong to say/think that the party was fantastic.

Here, the basic proposition expressed by the utterances in (15) (*the party was fantastic*) is embedded under an appropriate higher-order speech-act or propositional-attitude description indicating, on the one hand, that the basic proposition is being used to interpret views Mary attributes to someone else, and, on the other, Mary's attitude to these attributed views. To understand Mary, Peter has to recognize not only the basic proposition expressed but also the fact that it is being attributively used, and the attitude Mary intends to convey.

The attitudes conveyed by an echoic utterance may be very rich and varied. The speaker may indicate that she endorses or dissociates herself from the views she is echoing: that she is puzzled, angry, amused, intrigued, skeptical, etc., or any combination of these. We treat verbal irony as involving the expression of a tacitly dissociative attitude – wry, skeptical, bitter, or mocking – to an attributed utterance or thought. Consider Mary's utterance in (15c) above. This is clearly both ironical and echoic. We claim that it is ironical BECAUSE it is echoic: verbal irony consists in echoing a tacitly attributed thought or utterance with a tacitly dissociative attitude.[24]

This approach sheds light on some cases of irony not adequately handled by the classical or Gricean accounts. Consider Mary's utterance, "He forgot to go to the bank," in (11b) above. There are situations where this might well be ironically intended even though it is neither blatantly false nor used to convey the opposite of what was said. Suppose Peter and Mary both know that John has repeatedly failed to repay Mary, with a series of pitifully inadequate excuses. Then (11b) may be seen as an ironical echo in which Mary tacitly dissociates herself from the latest excuse in the series. Thus, all that is needed to make (11b) ironical is a scenario in which it can be understood as a mocking echo of an attributed utterance or thought.[25]

One implication of this analysis is that irony involves a higher order of metarepresentational ability than metaphor. As illustrated in (16) above, the hearer of an echoic utterance must recognize that the speaker is thinking, not directly about a state of affairs but about a thought or utterance that she attributes to someone else. This implication of our account is confirmed by experimental evidence showing that irony comprehension requires second-order metarepresentational abilities, while metaphor comprehension requires only first-order abilities.[26] This difference is unexplained on the classical or Gricean accounts.[27]

Metarepresentational abilities also play a role in the interpretation of illocutionary acts. Consider the exchange in (17):

(17)a.   *Peter*:   Will you pay back the money by Tuesday?
   b.   *Mary*:   I will pay it back by then.

Both (17a) and (17b) express the proposition that *Mary will pay back the money by Tuesday*. In the interrogative (17a), this proposition is expressed but not communicated (in the sense that Peter does not put it forward as true, or probably true):[28] it is not an explicature of Peter's utterance. Yet intuitively, (17a) is no less explicit an act of communication than (17b). According to relevance theory, what is explicitly communicated by (17a) is the HIGHER-ORDER EXPLICATURE in (18):

(18)   Peter is asking Mary whether she will pay back the money by Tuesday.

Like all explicatures, (18) is recovered by a mixture of decoding and inference based on a variety of linguistic and non-linguistic clues (e.g. word order, mood indicators, tone of voice, facial expression).[29] In (17b), by contrast, the explicatures might include both (19a), the BASIC EXPLICATURE, and higher-order explicatures such as (19b) and (19c):

(19)a.   Mary will pay back the money by Tuesday.
   b.   Mary is promising to pay back the money by Tuesday.
   c.   Mary believes she will pay back the money by Tuesday.

Thus, an utterance may convey several explicatures, each of which may contribute to relevance and warrant the derivation of implicatures.[30]

    On this approach, verbal irony has more in common with illocutionary and attitudinal utterances than it does with metaphor or hyperbole. As illustrated in (16c), the recognition of irony, like the recognition of illocutionary acts, involves the construction of higher-order explicatures, and therefore requires a higher degree of metarepresentational ability than the recognition of the basic proposition expressed by an utterance, whether literal, loose, or metaphorical.

    More generally, on both Gricean and relevance-theoretic accounts, the interpretation of EVERY utterance involves a high degree of metarepresentational capacity, since overt communication involves a complex, multi-levelled mental state attribution (see section 3 above). This raises the question of how pragmatic abilities are acquired, and how they fit into the overall architecture of the mind.

5   Relevance Theory and Mental Architecture

Grice's analysis of overt communication treats comprehension as a variety of MIND-READING, or THEORY OF MIND (the attribution of mental states to others in order to explain and predict behavior).[31] The link between mind-reading and communication is confirmed by a wealth of developmental and neuropsychological evidence.[32] However, mind-reading itself has been analyzed in rather different ways. Philosophers often describe it as an exercise in reflective reasoning (a central thought process, in Fodor's terms), and many of Grice's remarks about pragmatics are consistent with this. His rational reconstruction of how conversational implicatures are derived is a straightforward exercise in general-purpose "belief–desire" psychology:

> He said that P; he could not have done this unless he thought that Q; he knows (and knows that I know that he knows) that I will realise that it is necessary to suppose that Q; he has done nothing to stop me thinking that Q; so he intends me to think, or is at least willing for me to think, that Q.   (Grice 1989: 30–1)

In our own early work, we also treated pragmatic interpretation as a central, inferential process, albeit a spontaneous, intuitive rather than a conscious, reflective one (Sperber and Wilson 1986a: Chap. 2, Wilson and Sperber 1986b). More recently, there has been a tendency in the cognitive sciences to move away from Fodor's sharp distinction between modular input processes and relatively undifferentiated central processes and toward an increasingly modular view of the mind.[33] In this section, we will consider how the relevance-theoretic approach might fit with more modular accounts of inference, and in particular of mind-reading.[34]

One advantage of a domain-specific module is that it can contain special-purpose inferential procedures ("fast and frugal heuristics," in the terms of Gigerenzer et al. 1999) attuned to particular features of its own domain. In modular accounts of mind-reading, for example, standard "belief–desire" psychology is replaced by special-purpose inferential procedures justified by regularities existing only in this domain. Examples include an Eye Direction Detector, which infers perceptual and attentional states from direction of gaze, and an Intentionality Detector, which interprets self-propelled motion in terms of goals and desires (Leslie 1994, Premack and Premack 1994, Baron-Cohen 1995). This raises the question of whether there might be domain-specific communicative regularities to which a special-purpose comprehension module might be attuned.

Most approaches to mind-reading, whether modular or non-modular, assume that there is no need for special-purpose inferential comprehension procedures, because the mental-state attributions required for comprehension will be automatically generated by more general mechanisms which apply across the whole domain of intentional action (cf. Bloom 2000, 2002). However, there are problems with the view that speakers' meanings can be inferred from utterances by the same procedures used to infer intentions from actions. In the first place, the range of actions an agent can reasonably intend to perform in a given situation is in practice quite limited, and regular intention attribution is greatly facilitated by this. By contrast, the range of meanings a speaker can reasonably intend to convey in a given situation is virtually unlimited (cf. section 3 above). It is simply not clear how the standard procedures for intention attribution could yield attributions of speakers' meanings except in easy and trivial cases (Sperber 2000, Sperber and Wilson 2002).

In the second place, inferential comprehension typically involves several layers of metarepresentation (cf. sections 4 and 5 above), while in regular mind-reading a single level is generally enough. This discrepancy is particularly apparent in child development. It is hard to believe that two-year-old children, who fail, for instance, on regular first-order false belief tasks, can recognize and understand the peculiar multi-levelled representations involved in overt communication, using nothing more than a general-purpose "belief–desire" psychology. This makes the possibility of a special-purpose comprehension sub-module worth exploring (Sperber 1996, 2000, 2002, Origgi and Sperber 2000, Wilson 2000, Sperber and Wilson 2002).

We have argued (following Sperber 1996) that the regularity described in the Communicative Principle of Relevance (that acts of ostensive communication create presumptions of relevance) underpins the workings of a special-purpose inferential comprehension device. On this approach, the relevance-theoretic comprehension procedure in (9) should be seen not as a variant of Grice's working-out schema, but as a dedicated inferential mechanism, a "fast and frugal heuristic," which automatically computes a hypothesis about the speaker's meaning on the basis of the linguistic and other evidence provided.

This approach allows for varying degrees of sophistication in the hearer's expectations of relevance. In an unsophisticated version (presumably the one always used by young children), what is expected is actual optimal relevance. In a more sophisticated version (used by competent adult communicators who are aware that the speaker may be mistaken about what is relevant to the hearer, or in bad faith and merely intending to seem relevant), what is expected may be merely attempted or purported optimal relevance. Adult communicators may nevertheless expect actual optimal relevance by default (Sperber 1994, Bezuidenhout and Sroda 1998, Wilson 2000, Happé and Loth 2002).

The complexity of the inferences required by Grice's account of communication has sometimes been seen as an argument against the whole inferential approach. We are suggesting an alternative view on which, just as children do not have to learn their language but come with a substantial innate endowment, so they do not have to learn what ostensive-inferential communication is, but come with a substantial innate endowment.

6 Conclusion: An Experimentally Testable Cognitive Theory

Relevance theory is a cognitive psychological theory. Like other psychological theories, it has testable consequences: it can suggest experimental research, and is open to confirmation, disconfirmation, or fine-tuning in the light of experimental evidence. As with other theories of comparable scope, its most general claims can be tested only indirectly. For example, the Cognitive Principle of Relevance suggests testable predictions only when combined with descriptions of particular cognitive mechanisms (e.g. for perception, categorization, memory, or inference). Given a description of such a mechanism, it may be possible to test the relevance-theoretic claim that this mechanism contributes to a greater allocation of cognitive resources to potentially relevant inputs, by comparing it with some alternative hypothesis, or at least the null hypothesis.

The Communicative Principle of Relevance is a law-like generalization which follows from the Cognitive Principle of Relevance, combined with a broadly inferential view of communication. It could be falsified by finding genuine communicative acts which do not convey a presumption of optimal relevance (but rather, say, a presumption of literal truthfulness, or maximal informativeness, or no such presumption at all). When combined with descriptions of specific types and properties of communicative acts, it yields precise predictions, some of which have been experimentally tested.

In this survey, we have drawn attention to several cases where the predictions of relevance theory differ from those more or less clearly suggested by alternative frameworks, and where the relevance-theoretic analyses have been experimentally tested and their predictions confirmed. We will end with two further illustrations of how his approach yields testable predictions.

As noted in section 2 above, relevance theory does not provide an absolute measure of mental effort or cognitive effect, and it does not assume that such a measure is available to the spontaneous workings of the mind. What it does assume is that the actual or expected relevance of two inputs can quite often be compared. These possibilities of comparison help individuals to allocate their cognitive resources, and communicators to predict and influence the cognitive processes of others. They also enable researchers to manipulate the effect and effort factors in experimental situations.

For example, consider the conditional statement in (20), describing a series of cards with letters or numbers on both front and back:

(20)   If a card has a 6 on the front, it has an E on the back.

In the Wason selection task (the most famous experimental paradigm in the psychology of reasoning; cf. Wason 1966), participants are shown four cards with (say) a 6, a 4, an E, and an A on the front, and asked which ones they would have to turn over to check whether (20) is true or false. The correct response is to select the 6 and the A cards. By 1995, literally thousands of experiments with similar materials had failed to produce a majority of correct responses. Most people choose either the 6 card alone, or the 6 and the E. In "Relevance theory explains the selection task" (1995), Sperber, Cara, and Girotto argued that participants interpret conditional statement by deriving testable implications in order of accessibility, stop when their expectations of relevance are satisfied, and choose cards on the basis of this interpretation. Using this idea, Sperber et al. were able, by varying the content and context of (20), to manipulate the effort and effect factors so as to produce correct or incorrect selections at will.

Typically, a conditional statement of the form *If P then Q* achieves relevance by allowing the consequent *Q* to be derived whenever the antecedent *P* is satisfied. With (20), this leads to selection of the 6 card. Another common way for a conditional statement to achieve relevance is by creating the expectation that both *P* and *Q* are true. With (20), this leads to selection of the 6 and E cards. Of course, a conditional also implies that *P* and *not-Q* will not be true together. By choosing cards on this basis, participants would correctly select the 6 and A cards. However, in most contexts this implication is relatively costly to derive, leads to no further effects, and would not be derived by a hearer looking for optimal relevance. What Sperber et al. did was to manipulate the effort and effect factors (either separately or together), to make this implication easier and/or more rewarding to derive, and the correct cards correspondingly more likely to be chosen. In the most successful condition, (20) was presented as a statement made by an engineer who has just repaired a machine which was supposed to print cards according to the specification in (20), but which had malfunctioned and wrongly printed cards with a 6 on the front and an A on the back. Here, (20) achieved relevance by implying that there would be no more cards with a 6 on the front and an A rather than an E on the back, and a majority of participants made the correct selection. This experiment shows that performance on the selection task is determined not merely by general-purpose or special-purpose reasoning abilities (as had generally been assumed) but by pragmatic factors affecting the interpretation of conditional statements. It also confirms that the interpretation of conditionals is governed by the twin factors of effort and effect, either separately or in combination.[35]

Here is a second example of how the interaction of effort and effect can be experimentally investigated, this time in utterance production rather than interpretation. Suppose a stranger comes up and asks you the time. You look at your watch and see that it is 11:58 exactly. How should you reply? In Grice's framework, a speaker obeying the maxim of truthfulness should say "11:58." By saying "It's 12:00" (speaking loosely and thus violating the maxim of truthfulness), you would be understood as conveying that it was (exactly) 12:00. By contrast, a speaker aiming at optimal relevance has every reason to speak loosely (thus reducing her hearer's processing effort) unless this would (in her view) lead to some significant loss of cognitive effects. It should therefore be possible, by varying the scenario in which the question is asked, to produce stricter or looser answers depending on whether or not the stricter answer would carry relevant implications. This prediction has been experimentally tested, and the relevance-theoretic analysis confirmed: strangers in public places asked for the time tend to speak loosely or give strictly accurate answers depending on subtle clues as to what might make it relevant for the questioner to know the time (van der Henst et al. 2002).

So far, the main obstacle to experimental comparisons of relevance theory with other pragmatic theories has been that the testable consequences of these other theories have not always been explicitly spelled out. Most pragmatic research has been carried out in a philosophical or linguistic tradition, which places a higher priority on theoretical generality and reliance on intuitions than on the need for experimentation. Relevance theorists have been trying to combine theoretical generality with all the possibilities of testing provided by the careful use of linguistic intuitions, observational data, and the experimental methods of cognitive psychology. We see this as an important direction for future research.

ACKNOWLEDGMENTS

We are grateful to Larry Horn and Gregory Ward for valuable comments and suggestions, and to the many friends, colleagues, and students whose positive proposals and criticisms have contributed greatly to the development of the theory.

NOTES

1   For early arguments against these aspects of Grice's framework, see Sperber and Wilson (1981), and Wilson and Sperber (1981).

2   For early accounts of COGNITIVE (or CONTEXTUAL) EFFECTS, see Wilson and Sperber (1981, 1986b). For the standard definitions, see Sperber and Wilson (1986a: 2.7, especially note 26). On the deductive inferences involved, see Politzer (1990) and Sperber and Wilson (1990a). There may be still further types of positive cognitive effect (improvements in memory or imagination, for example; cf. Wilson and Sperber 2002).

3   For suggestions about how this might be done, see Sperber and Wilson (1986a: 124–32). Formal notions of relevance have been explored by Merin (1999), Blutner (1998) (which brings together ideas from Horn 1984a, 1992, Levinson 1987a, 2000a, Hobbs et al. 1993, and Sperber and Wilson 1986a); van Rooy (1999, 2001).

4   On COMPARATIVE and QUANTITATIVE concepts, see Sperber and Wilson (1986a: 79–81, 124–32). On factors affecting comparative and quantitative assessments of relevance, see Sperber and Wilson (1986a): 3.2, 3.5, 3.6.

5   This is the simpler of two characterizations of ostensive-inferential communication in Sperber and Wilson (1986a: 29, 58, 61). The fuller version involves the notions of MANIFESTNESS and MUTUAL MANIFESTNESS. We argue that for communication to be truly overt, the communicator's informative intention must become not merely manifest to the audience (i.e. capable of being recognized and accepted as true, or probably true), but mutually manifest to communicator and audience. On the communicative and informative intentions, see Sperber and Wilson (1986a): 1.9–12; on mutual manifestness, see Garnham and Perner (1990) and Sperber and Wilson (1990a).

6 On Gricean cooperation and communication, see Kasher (1976), Wilson and Sperber (1981), Sperber and Wilson (1986a: 161–2), Smith and Wilson (1992), Sperber (1994, 2000), Sperber and Wilson (2002).

7 On ostensive silences, see Morgan and Green (1987: 727) and Sperber and Wilson (1987b: 746–7).

8 The symmetry between unwillingness and inability to provide relevant information is also lost in Gricean analyses of scalar implicatures. See Sperber and Wilson (1995: 276–8), Green (1995), Matsumoto (1995), Carston (1995, 1998b), and section 6 below. For experimental work, see Noveck (2001), Papafragou (2002), Papafragou and Musolino (2002).

9 Puns and deliberate equivocations are sometimes seen as creating problems for this approach (e.g. Morgan and Green 1987: 726–7). We would analyze them as cases of layering in communication. Just as failure to provide relevant information at one level may be used as an ostensive stimulus at another, so production of an utterance which is apparently uninterpretable at one level may be used as an ostensive stimulus at another (Sperber and Wilson 1987b: 751, Tanaka 1992).

10 By "explicitly communicated content" (or EXPLICATURE), we mean a proposition recovered by a combination of decoding and inference, which provides a premise for the derivation of contextual implications and other cognitive effects (Sperber and Wilson 1986a: 176–93, Carston 2002b; this volume). Despite many terminological disagreements (see notes 17 and 18), the existence of pragmatic contributions at this level is now

widely recognized (Wilson and Sperber 1981, 1998, 2002, Kempson and Cormack 1982, Travis 1985, 2001, Sperber and Wilson 1986a: 4.2–3, Kempson 1986, 1996, Blakemore 1987, Carston 1988, 2000, 2002a, 2002b, Recanati 1989, 2002a, Neale 1992, Bach 1994a, 1994b, 1999a, Stainton 1994, 1997b, this volume, Bezuidenhout 1997, Levinson 2000a, Fodor 2001).

11 In his "Retrospective Epilogue," and occasionally elsewhere, Grice seems to acknowledge the possibility of intentional pragmatic contributions to "dictive content" (Grice 1989: 359–68). See Carston (2002b) and Wharton (in preparation).

12 On primary and secondary pragmatic processes, see Breheny (2002), Recanati (2002b), Carston (2002b, this volume), and Sperber and Wilson (2002). Some work on generalized conversational implicature and discourse pragmatics tacitly invokes a similar distinction (cf. Hobbs 1985b, Lascarides and Asher 1993, Lascarides et al. 1996, Levinson 2000a). See also notes 17 and 18.

13 See Sperber and Wilson (1986a): 4.3–5, esp. pp. 204–8, and Wilson and Sperber (2002).

14 For ease of exposition, we have used an example where preceding discourse creates a specific expectation of relevance, so that the interpretation process is strongly driven by expectations of effect. In an indirect answer such as (ib), where there are two possible implicatures (positive or negative), considerations of effort, and in particular the accessibility of contextual assumptions, play a more important role. In a discourse-initial utterance such as (ii), or in a questionnaire situation, considerations of effort are likely

to play a decisive role in choosing among possible interpretations:

(i)a. *Peter*: Did John pay back the money he owed?

  b. *Mary*: He forgot to go to the bank.

(ii) He forgot to go to the bank.

15 For one thing, the assumptions that Peter entertains in interpreting the utterance are presumably not represented in English but in some conceptual representation system or language of thought. We also ignore semantic issues such as the analysis of definite articles and definite descriptions (e.g. *the bank*).

16 See e.g. Horn (1984a, 1992), Levinson (1987a, 2000a), Hobbs et al. (1993), Lascarides et al. (1996), Lascarides and Copestake (1998), Blutner (1998, to appear).

17 As noted above (note 10), there is some debate about how the explicit–implicit distinction should be drawn (e.g. Horn 1992, Sperber and Wilson 1986a: 4.1–4, Wilson and Sperber 1993, Bach 1994a, 1994b, 1999a, Levinson 2000a, Carston 2002a, 2002b, this volume). The issue is partly terminological, but becomes substantive when combined with the claim that explicit and implicit communication involve distinct pragmatic processes (as in much of the literature on generalized implicatures, cf. Levinson 2000a).

18 Levinson (2000a: 195–6) rejects the explicature–implicature distinction on the ground that no criterion for distinguishing explicatures from implicatures is provided. Our notion of an explicature is motivated, among other things, by embedding tests which suggest that certain pragmatic processes contribute to truth-conditional content, while

others do not (Wilson and Sperber 1986b: 80; 2002, Ifantidou 2001). The allocation of pragmatically inferred material between explicatures and implicatures is constrained, on the one hand, by our theoretical definitions of explicature and implicature (Sperber and Wilson 1986a: 182, Carston 2002b), and, on the other, by the fact that implicated conclusions must be warranted by the explicit content, together with the context. See Sperber and Wilson (1986a: 4.3), Sperber and Wilson (1998a), Carston (1995, 1998b, 2000, 2002b, this volume), Wilson and Sperber (1998, 2002). For experimental evidence, see Gibbs and Moise (1997), Matsui (1998, 2000), Nicolle and Clark (1999), Wilson and Matsui (2000), Noveck (2001), Papafragou (2002), Papafragou and Musolino (2003).

19 Over time, lexical loosening may stabilize in a community and give rise to an extra sense, which may in turn be narrowed or loosened for occasion-specific pragmatic reasons. Typically, there are too many occasion-specific interpretations to allow a purely semantic or default-pragmatic account (Searle 1979, 1980, Horn 1984a, G. Lakoff 1987, Franks and Braisby 1990, Sweetser 1990, Hobbs et al. 1993, Bach 1994a, 1994b, 1999a, Recanati 1995, Carston 1997, 1998b, 2002b, this volume, Sperber and Wilson 1998a, Wilson 1998, Lasersohn 1999, Traugott 1999, Asher and Lascarides 2001, Papafragou 2000, Wilson and Sperber 2002).

20 For early arguments against the maxim of truthfulness, see Wilson and Sperber (1981). For a detailed critique, see Wilson and Sperber (2002). For experimental evidence, see Matsui (1998, 2000), Wilson and Matsui (2000), van der Henst et al. (2002).

21 See e.g. Gibbs (1994), Glucksberg (2001), Noveck et al. (2001). Glucksberg's claim that metaphor interpretation involves constructing a more inclusive category fits well with our account.

22 While the claim that metaphor is a variety of loose use has been part of the theory for some time (e.g. Sperber and Wilson 1985/6, 1986a: 4.7–8, 1990b), some details of this analysis are more recent. For discussion, see Recanati (1995), Carston (1997, 2002b, this volume), Sperber and Wilson (1998a), Wilson and Sperber (2002).

23 On interpretive use, see Sperber and Wilson (1986a: 4.7), Blass (1990), Gutt (1991), Sperber (1997), Papafragou (1998, 2000), Wilson (2000), Noh (2001). On the echoic use, see Sperber and Wilson (1986a: 4.9), Blakemore (1994), Carston (1996, 2002b), Noh (1998), Wilson (2000).

24 This account of irony was first proposed in Sperber and Wilson 1981, and extended in Sperber and Wilson (1986a: 4.7, 4.9), Sperber and Wilson (1990b, 1998b), Wilson and Sperber (1992), Curcò (1998). For critical discussion, see Clark and Gerrig (1984), Kreuz and Glucksberg (1989), Gibbs and O'Brien (1991), Martin (1992), Kumon-Nakamura et al. (1995), and the papers by Seto, Hamamoto, and Yamanashi in Carston and Uchida (1998). For responses, see Sperber (1984), Sperber and Wilson (1998b).

25 For experimental evidence, see Jorgensen et al. (1984), Happé (1993), Kreuz and Glucksberg (1989), Gibbs and O'Brien 1991, Gibbs (1994), Kumon-Nakamura et al. (1995), Langdon et al. (2002).

26 On the development of metaphor and irony, see Winner (1988).

On the relation between irony, metaphor, and metarepresentational abilities, see Happé (1993), Langdon et al. (2002). On communicative and metarepresentational, see section 5 below.

27 Levinson (2000a: 239), who interprets us (mistakenly) as claiming that irony does not contribute to explicatures, objects that we cannot account for the fact that ironical use of a referential expression may make a difference to truth conditions (as in his nice example "If you need a car, you may borrow my Porsche" [used to refer to the speaker's VW]). In fact, we treat irony as a variety of free indirect speech, which is closely related to metalinguistic use and contributes directly to explicatures. It is uncontroversial that free indirect speech and metalinguistic use may make a difference to truth conditions (Horn 1989, Sperber and Wilson 1981, 1986a: 4.7, Carston 1996, 2002b, Cappelen and Lepore 1997, Noh 2000, Wilson 2000), and Levinson's example fits well with our account.

28 See Sperber and Wilson (1986a): 1.9–12.

29 Mood indicators are among the items seen in relevance theory as carrying procedural rather than conceptual meaning. See Blakemore (1987, 2002, this volume), Wharton (2001, in press, in preparation), and Iten (2000b).

30 On higher-level explicatures, see Blakemore (1991), Wilson and Sperber (1993), and Ifantidou (2001). On non-declarative utterances, see Sperber and Wilson (1986a: 4.10), Wilson and Sperber (1988), Wilson (2000), and Noh (2001). For critical discussion, see Bird (1994) and Harnish (1994).

31 See Whiten (1991), Davies and Stone (1995a, 1995b), Carruthers and Smith (1996), and Malle et al. (2001).

32 See Perner et al. (1989), Happé (1993), Baron-Cohen (1995), Mitchell et al. (1999), Happé and Loth (2002), Papafragou (2002), and *Mind and Language* 17.1–2 (2002).

33 We use "module" in a somewhat broader sense than Fodor's, to mean a domain-specific autonomous computational mechanism (cf. Sperber 1996: Chapter 6, 2002).

34 See Leslie (1991), Hirschfeld and Gelman (1994), Barkow et al. (1995), Sperber (1996, 2002), and Fodor (2000).

35 For other experiments on the selection task, see Girotto et al. (2001), Sperber and Girotto (to appear). For other applications of relevance theory to the psychology of reasoning, see van der Henst (1999), Politzer and Macchi (2000), and van der Henst et al. (2002).

28 Relevance Theory and the Saying/Implicating Distinction

ROBYN CARSTON

1 Introduction

It is widely accepted that there is a distinction to be made between the explicit content and the implicit import of an utterance. There is much less agreement about the precise nature of this distinction, how it is to be drawn, and whether any such two-way distinction can do justice to the levels and kinds of meaning involved in utterance interpretation. Grice's distinction between what is said by an utterance and what is implicated is probably the best-known instantiation of the explicit/implicit distinction. His distinction, along with many of its post-Gricean heirs, is closely entwined with another distinction: that between semantics and pragmatics. Indeed, on some construals they are seen as essentially one and the same; "what is said" is equated with the truth-conditional content of the utterance, which in turn is equated with (context-relative) sentence meaning, leaving implicatures (conventional and conversational) as the sole domain of pragmatics.

This is emphatically not how the explicit/implicit distinction is drawn within the relevance-theoretic account of utterance understanding, a basic difference being that pragmatic processes play an essential role on both sides of the distinction. The relevance-theoretic account is rooted in a view of human cognitive architecture according to which linguistic semantics is the output of a modular linguistic decoding system and serves as input to a pragmatic processor. This "semantic" representation (or logical form) is typically not fully propositional, so does not have a determinate truth condition, but consists of an incomplete conceptual representation which functions as a schema or template for the pragmatic construction of propositional forms. The pragmatic system is in the business of inferring the intended interpretation (or "what is meant"); this is a set of propositional conceptual representations, some of which are developments of the linguistically provided template and others of which are not. The former are called EXPLICATURES, the latter IMPLICATURES; this is the explicit/implicit distinction made within relevance theory and it plainly does not coincide with the distinction between linguistically decoded meaning ("semantics") and pragmatically inferred meaning.

The title of this chapter notwithstanding, the terms "saying" and "what is said" do not feature in relevance theory, and the territory covered by the concept of explicature is significantly different from that of Grice's notion of "what is said" and other semantically oriented notions of saying. Necessarily, these differences entail corresponding differences in those aspects of utterance meaning that are taken to fall under the concept of implicature in the two frameworks. Some of what are taken to be conversational implicatures on Gricean accounts, specifically certain cases of "generalized" conversational implicatures, turn out to be pragmatic aspects of explicature.[1]

The structure of the chapter is as follows. In the next section, the two relevance-theoretic distinctions, that between semantics and pragmatics and that between explicature and implicature are set out. Then, in section 3, some of the different ways in which pragmatic inference may contribute to explicated assumptions (explicatures) are considered, and, in section 4, the conception of implicated assumptions (implicatures) that follows from this is outlined. The consequence mentioned above, that certain Gricean implicatures are reanalyzed as explicatures, is considered in section 5. Lastly, I compare the explicature/implicature distinction with some of the other ways of construing an explicit/implicit distinction, most of which are geared toward preserving a conception of "what is said" which is as close as possible to the semantics of the linguistic expression used.

2   Decoding/Inferring and the Explicature/Implicature Distinction

There are two distinctions which are central to the relevance-based account of utterance understanding. The first is the distinction between linguistically decoded meaning and pragmatically inferred meaning. This can be viewed as a semantics/pragmatics distinction though it is plainly not the only way, nor the most common way, of making such a distinction (for surveys of different ways of drawing the semantics/pragmatics distinction, see Bach 1999a and Carston 1999). Here "semantics" is a mapping between elements of linguistic form and certain kinds of cognitive information, rather than between linguistic expressions and truth conditions or real-world referents. It is type- rather than token-based in that it is context-free and invariant, entirely determined by principles and rules internal to the linguistic system. The "semantic" representation so generated provides input to the pragmatic processor, which is triggered by ostensive stimuli generally, that is, stimuli that are construed as indicating a communicative intention on the part of the agent who produced them. While the linguistic processor, or parser, employs a code (a natural language), the pragmatic processor does not. It has wide access to extralinguistic "contextual" information, including information gained from any perceptual inlet and from memory stores of various sorts. Its output (the set of assumptions that are derived as those communicated) is not determined by fixed rules, but is the result of inferential processes which are merely guided and constrained by a single general comprehension strategy (the relevance-theoretic procedure discussed in Wilson and Sperber, this volume). The interpretation that the system delivers for any given utterance is dependent on such variable factors as the degree of accessibility of relevant contextual assumptions.

The second distinction, the focal one for this chapter, concerns the two kinds of assumption communicated by a speaker: EXPLICATURE and IMPLICATURE. Sperber and Wilson's (1986a: 182) definitions are as follows:

(I)   An assumption communicated by an utterance U is EXPLICIT [hence an "explicature"] if and only if it is a development of a logical form encoded by U.
[*Note*: in cases of ambiguity, a surface form encodes more than one logical form, hence the use of the indefinite here, "**a** logical form encoded by U."]

(II) An assumption communicated by U which is not explicit is IMPLICIT [hence an "implicature"].

Let's consider a simple example:

(1)   X: How is Mary feeling after her first year at university?
      Y: She didn't get enough units and can't continue.

Suppose that, in the particular context, X takes Y to have communicated the following assumptions:

(2)a.   MARY$_x$ DID NOT PASS ENOUGH UNIVERSITY COURSE UNITS TO QUALIFY FOR ADMISSION TO SECOND-YEAR STUDY AND, AS A RESULT, MARY$_x$ CANNOT CONTINUE WITH UNIVERSITY STUDY.
   b.   MARY$_x$ IS NOT FEELING VERY HAPPY.

[*Note*:   Small caps are used throughout to distinguish propositions/assumptions/thoughts from natural language sentences; the subscripted x indicates that a particular referent has been assigned to the name "Mary."]

On the basis of the definitions above, it seems relatively clear that (2a) is an explicature of Y's utterance and (2b) is an implicature. The decoded logical form of Y's utterance, still more or less visible in (2a), has been taken as a template for the development of a propositional form, while (2b) is an independent assumption, inferred as a whole from (2a) and a further premise concerning the relation between Mary's recent failure at university and her current state of mind.

The representation in (2a) is much more specific and elaborated than the encoded meaning of the sentence type "She didn't get enough units and can't continue," which could be developed in any number of quite different ways, depending on context. A referent has been assigned to the pronoun (a concept of a particular person represented here as MARY$_x$), *get* and *units* have been assigned more specific meanings than those they encode, additional conceptual constituents have been supplied as arguments of *enough* and *continue*, and a cause – consequence connection has been taken to hold between the conjuncts. These are all the result of pragmatic processes, context-dependent and relevance-governed. I separate out some of these different processes and consider them in more individual detail in the next section.

It is clear from the definitions above that the conceptual content of an implicature is supplied wholly by pragmatic inference,[2] while the conceptual content of an explicature is an amalgam of decoded linguistic meaning and pragmatically inferred meaning. It follows that different token explicatures which have the same propositional content may vary with regard to the relative contributions made by each of these processes. According to the relevance-driven view of pragmatic inference, as discussed by Wilson and Sperber (this volume), the linguistically encoded element of an utterance is not generally geared toward achieving as high a degree of explicitness as possible. Taking account of the addressee's immediately accessible assumptions and the inferences he can readily draw, the speaker should encode just what is necessary to ensure that the pragmatic processor arrives as effortlessly as possible at the intended meaning.

The idea that linguistically encoded meaning is standardly highly underdetermining of the proposition explicitly expressed by an utterance distinguishes this view from Gricean conceptions of "what is said" by an utterance.[3] In fact, neither of the distinctions discussed in this section meshes with the traditional saying/implicating distinction: on the one hand, the meaning encoded in linguistic expression types falls short of "what is said" and, on the other hand, the content of explicatures goes well beyond "what is said," requiring for its recovery the exercise of pragmatic principles, just as much as implicatures do.[4] "What is said," then, falls somewhere between the two. Whether or not such an intermediate representational level is necessary is considered in section 6.

3   Pragmatic Aspects of Explicature

3.1   *Disambiguation and saturation*

I put these two apparently rather different processes together in a single section because, unlike the others to be discussed, there is general agreement that they play a crucial role in determining the explicit content of an utterance. In his brief discussion of "what is said" by an utterance of the sentence, "He is in the grip of a vice," Grice (1989: 25) explicitly mentions the need for a choice between the two senses of the phrase *in the grip of a vice* and for the identification of the referent of *he*. In the case of sense selection (or disambiguation), the candidates are supplied by the linguistic system itself. In the case of reference assignment, the candidates are not linguistically given but, rather, the linguistic element used – for instance, a pronoun – indicates that an appropriate contextual value is to be found, that is, that a given position in the logical form is to be saturated; see Recanati (1993, 2001) on this notion of "saturation."

Saturation is generally thought to be a much more widely manifest process than simply finding values for overt indexicals. Arguably, it is involved in those pragmatic developments of the logical forms of the following utterances that provide answers to the bracketed questions:

(3)a. Paracetamol is better. [than what?]
  b. It's the same. [as what?]
  c. He is too young. [for what?]
  d. It's hot enough. [for what?]
  e. I like Sally's shoes. [shoes in what relation to Sally?]

This "completion" process is obligatory on every communicative use of these sentences, since without it there is no propositional form, nothing that can be understood as the explicit content of the utterance. So, although there is no overt pronounced constituent in these sentences which indicates the need for contextual instantiation, the claim is that there is a slot in their logical form, a kind of covert indexical, which marks the saturation requirement. The lexical items *better*, *same*, *too*, *enough* and the genitive structure in *Sally's shoes* carry these imperceptible elements with them as part of their linguistic structure (Recanati 2002a).

While saturation (or linguistically mandated completion) is widely recognized across different frameworks as necessary in deriving the explicit content of an utterance, there is some disagreement about whether or not pragmatic principles (or conversational maxims) play a role in these processes. Grice seems to have thought not, seeing his maxims (truthfulness, informativeness, relevance, etc.) as coming into play only subsequently, in an assessment of the independently derived "what is said," and so responsible just for the derivation of conversational implicatures, those assumptions required in order to preserve the presumption that the speaker has observed the maxims, or at least the Cooperative Principle. See Grice (1967), where he introduces the maxims and shows their application, and Carston (2002b: chapter 2) for a discussion of the evidence that he excluded them from playing a role in the derivation of "what is said."

A similar view is held by many present-day truth-conditional semanticists. For instance, Segal (1994: 112) and Larson and Segal (1995: chapter 1) assume there is a specific performance system for identifying the referents of indexicals and assigning them to the relevant position in logical form. This system is located between the parser (which delivers structured linguistic meaning) and what they call "a pragmatics system," which, as in Grice's conception, assesses the conversational appropriateness of "what is said" and derives implicatures.

The obvious question, then, is: "What guides the highly context-sensitive processes of disambiguation, reference assignment, and other kinds of saturation?" The assumption seems to be that there is some sort of rule or procedure for matching the linguistic element with a contextual parameter and that the speaker's communicative intention need not be considered (hence that pragmatic maxims or principles are not involved in the process). What this procedure could be in cases such as those in (3) is a complete mystery. What it is thought to be in the case of overt pronouns and demonstratives is clear enough, but it simply doesn't work. The idea is that there is a set of objective contextual parameters that accompanies an utterance and each indexical element encodes a rule which ensures that it maps onto one of these. These contextual values include the speaker, the hearer, the time of utterance, the place of utterance, and certain designated objects in the perceptual environment. However, consider the two occurrences of the demonstrative pronoun *it* in the second utterance in the following exchange:

(4) A: Have you heard Alfred Brendel's version of *The Moonlight Sonata*?
     B: Yes. It made me realize I should never try to play it.

It's not difficult to see what B intends each of her uses of *it* to refer to, but the point is that the value of *it* is not assigned on the basis of objective features of the context but is dependent on what the speaker means (that is, on her communicative intention) and it is only through the employment of some pragmatic principle or other that the addressee is able to find the right value.

We can, of course, stipulate that *it* (or *this* or *that*) encodes a rule to the effect that it refers to what the speaker intends to refer to, and we can add to the set of contextual parameters a sequence of "speaker's intended referents," arranged in such a way that each demonstrative maps onto a referent as required. But, as Recanati (2002b: 111) says, while that may be fine from a formal point of view, "philosophically it is clear that one is cheating." To proceed in this formal way is to avoid dealing with an undeniable cognitive reality, which is that the assignment of referents to the vast range of linguistic referring expressions relies on a wide notion of context and requires the intervention of pragmatic principles or strategies that are geared to the recovery of the speaker's intended meaning.

As for disambiguation, it is generally ignored by the advocates of a non-pragmatic means of deriving the context-sensitive aspects of what is said. The evidence, again, though, is that generally this cannot be achieved independently of considerations of speaker intentions, hence of pragmatic principles or maxims (see, for instance, Walker 1975: 156, Bach and Harnish 1979: chapter 1, Asher and Lascarides 1995, Wilson and Matsui 2000: section 4). The relevance-theoretic position is that, given the decoded linguistic meaning, all aspects of utterance comprehension, including disambiguation and reference assignment, depend on the strategy of considering interpretive hypotheses in order of their accessibility and stopping when the criterion of optimal relevance is satisfied. See Wilson and Sperber (this volume) for extensive illustration of this process.

3.2   Free enrichment

There is a wide range of cases where it seems that pragmatics contributes to the proposition explicitly communicated by an utterance although there is no linguistic element indicating that a contextual value is required. That is, there is no overt indexical, and there is no compelling reason to suppose there is a covert element in the logical form of the utterance, and yet a contextually supplied constituent appears in the explicature.

Consider utterances of the following sentences, whose interpretation, in many contexts, would include the bracketed element which is provided on pragmatic grounds alone.

(5)a.   She has a brain.   [A HIGH-FUNCTIONING BRAIN]
  b.   It's going to take time for these wounds to heal.   [CONSIDERABLE TIME]
  c.   I've had a shower.   [TODAY]
  d.   It's snowing.   [IN LOCATION X]
  e.   Mary gave John a pen and he wrote down her address.   [AND THEN] [WITH THE PEN MARY GAVE HIM]
  f.   Sam left Jane and she became very depressed.   [AND AS A RESULT]

Given disambiguation and saturation, each of these would, arguably, express a proposition (hence be truth-evaluable) without the addition of the bracketed constituent, but in most contexts that minimal proposition would not be communicated (speaker-meant). One class of cases, represented here by (5a) and (5b), would express a trivial truth (every person has a brain, any process takes place over some time span or other), and it is easy to set up cases of obvious falsehoods (the negations of (5a) and (5b), for instance). Others, such as (5c) and (5d), are so vague and general as to be very seldom what a speaker would intend to communicate (they would not yield sufficient cognitive effects). Across most contexts in which these sentences might be uttered, obvious implicatures of the utterance would depend on the enriched proposition; for instance, in (5a), the implicature that she is a good candidate for an academic job; in (5c), the implicature that the speaker doesn't need to take a shower at that time. It is the enriched propositions that are communicated as explicatures and which function as premises in the derivation of implicatures; the uninformative, irrelevant, and sometimes truistic or patently false minimal propositions appear to play no role in the process of utterance understanding, which is geared to the recovery of just those propositional forms which the speaker intends to communicate. The pragmatic process at work here is known as FREE ENRICHMENT; it is "free" in that it is not under linguistic control. So, unlike saturation, it is an optional process, in the sense that there can be contexts in which it does not take place, though these tend to be somewhat unusual.

Let's briefly consider how the process of free enrichment is viewed outside relevance theory. While the issue with disambiguation and saturation processes is how they are brought about (whether with or without pragmatic principles geared to uncovering the speaker's meaning), the issue with free enrichment is more fundamental. It is whether or not there really is any such process, so whether or not there are such things as constituents of the explicit content of the utterance which do not occur in any shape or form in the linguistic representation. Philosophers of language who insist on the psychological reality of the process include Recanati (1993, 2001) and Bach (1994a, 2000). However, a current school of semantic thinking, represented by Stanley (2000, 2002), Stanley and Szabo (2000), and Taylor (2001), holds that if a contextually supplied constituent appears in the explicit content of an utterance then it must have been articulated in the logical form of the utterance, whether by an overt indexical or by a phonologically unrealized element. In other words, the only pragmatic processes at work at this level are disambiguation and saturation, and any other process of pragmatic inference involved in understanding an utterance results in an implicated proposition.[5]

Now, these deniers of free enrichment have their reasons. Their focus is on natural language semantics, which they take to be truth-conditional and compositional, so it is not too surprising that they would not want the meaning of a sentence to include elements that receive no mandate from the sentence itself. Relevance theorists have no quarrel with the view that pragmatically supplied constituents of explicature are not a matter for natural language semantics; in fact, it follows from the way in which the distinction between linguistic semantics and pragmatics is drawn in the theory, as discussed in section 2 above. Again, the underlying issue is whether there is any psychologically real level of representation between encoded linguistic semantics and explicature, a level of minimal propositionality at which saturation processes alone have taken place. This issue is picked up again in the last section.

Some neo-Gricean pragmaticists (such as Larry Horn and Stephen Levinson) treat as (generalized) conversational implicatures certain aspects of utterance meaning which, for relevance theorists, are pragmatic components of explicatures that have been derived by free enrichment. These include the enriched conjunct relations in examples (5e) and (5f) above and are discussed further in section 5. So, like the semanticists mentioned above, these Griceans deny the existence of a process of free enrichment of logical form. We see here two manifestations, one coming from semantics, the other from pragmatics, of the prevailing tenacious conviction that natural language semantics is essentially truth-conditional, hence minimally propositional, so that any pragmatic process other than disambiguation and saturation must take us into the realm of implicature.

However, there is an outstanding problem for all of these "saturation theorists," as we could call them, which is the existence of subsentential utterances; that is, the fact that single words or phrases can be used to express a proposition (or make an assertion). This provides perhaps the most compelling evidence for a process of free enrichment. Of course, many apparently subsentential utterances are cases of syntactic ellipsis, but there are many others that are not, as discussed by Stainton (1994, 1997b, this volume) and Elugardo and Stainton (2001b):

(6) Michael's dad. [uttered while indicating to the addressee a man who has just come into the room]

(7) Only 22,000 miles. Like new. [uttered by a used car salesman]

(8) In the fridge. [addressed to someone looking for coffee beans]

These have the following characteristics: they are (or, at least, can be) discourse-initial utterances, which is not a possibility for elliptical cases, there may be a degree of indeterminacy about the propositional content of the assertion, again not a property of ellipses, and they are bona fide assertions, hence explicitly communicated, as evidenced by the possibility of telling a lie with them (consider this possibility, in particular, in the case of the car salesman in (7)). Note that there does not seem to be an implicature option here, since any attempt to treat the recovered meaning as an implicature would entail that nothing propositional has been said, and so would preclude the (Gricean) derivation process from getting off the ground.

The significance of these cases is that, again, they show that, for many quite ordinary utterances, the pragmatic processes of disambiguation and saturation are not sufficient to derive the proposition explicitly communicated; rather, a pragmatic process of recovering conceptual material, without any linguistic mandate, is required.[6] The minimal linguistic form chosen by the speaker provides all the evidence necessary for the addressee to infer the speaker's informative intention and causes him no gratuitous processing effort. Stainton (1994) gives a relevance-theoretic account of the interpretation of an example like (6), according to which a speaker who utters "Michael's dad" is employing a noun phrase which occurs without any further linguistic structure (specifying slots to be contextually filled), and is thereby asserting the proposition THE MAN NEAR THE DOOR IS MICHAEL'S DAD.

3.3 *Ad hoc concept construction*

Free enrichment is a process which involves the addition of conceptual material to the decoded logical form (Bach's 1994a alternative term for the process, EXPANSION, captures this); for example, "it's snowing [IN ABERDEEN]." There are other cases where it seems that a better way of construing what is going on is that a lexical concept appearing in the logical form is pragmatically adjusted, so that the concept understood as expressed by the particular occurrence of the lexical item is different from, and replaces, the concept it encodes; it is narrower, looser, or some combination of the two, so that its denotation merely overlaps with the denotation of the lexical concept from which it was derived. Consider an utterance of the sentence in (9a) by a witness at the trial of X, who is accused of having murdered his wife; the utterance is a response to a question about X's state of mind at the time leading up to the murder:

(9)a.   He was upset but he wasn't upset.
   b.   X WAS UPSET* BUT X WASN'T UPSET**

As far as its linguistically supplied information goes, this is a contradiction, but it was not intended as, nor understood as, a contradiction. The two instances of the word *upset* were interpreted as expressing two different concepts of upsetness (as indicated in (9b) by the asterisks), at least one, but most likely both, involving a pragmatic narrowing of the encoded lexical concept UPSET. The second of the two concepts carries certain implications (e.g. that he was in a murdering state of mind) that the first one does not, implications whose applicability to X the witness is denying.

There are a vast number of other cases where any one of a wide range of related concepts might be expressed by a single lexical item; for instance, think of all the different kinds, degrees, and qualities of feeling that can be communicated by each of *tired, anxious, frightened, depressed, well, happy, satisfied, sweet*, etc. In one context, an utterance of *I'm happy* could communicate that the speaker feels herself to be in a steady state of low-key well-being, in another that she is experiencing a moment of intense joy, in yet another that she is satisfied with the outcome of some negotiation, and so on. The general concept HAPPY encoded by the lexical item *happy* gives access to an indefinite number of more specific concepts, recoverable in particular contexts by relevance-driven inference.

The examples considered so far have involved a narrowing or strengthening of the encoded concept, but there are others that seem to require some degree of widening or loosening (as well as narrowing). Consider what is most likely communicated by the highlighted lexical item in utterances of the following sentences:

(10)a.   There is a **rectangle** of lawn at the back.
    b.   This steak is **raw**.
    c.   On Classic FM, we play **continuous** classics.
    d.   Mary is a **bulldozer**.

The area of lawn referred to in (10a) is very unlikely to be truly a rectangle (with four right angles, opposite sides equal in length); rather it is approximately rectangular (so what is expressed is not the encoded concept RECTANGLE but a wider concept RECTANGLE*), and this holds for many other uses of geometrical terms: a "round" lake, a "square" cake, a "triangular" face, etc. In (10b), the steak, perhaps served in a restaurant, is not really raw but is much less cooked than the speaker wishes (it is RAW*); in (10c), the classical music played on the radio station is interspersed with advertisements and other announcements, so not strictly "continuous," and so on. In each case, a logical or defining feature of the lexically encoded concept is dropped in the process of arriving at the intended interpretation: "equal sides" in the case of *rectangle*, "uncooked" for *raw*, "uninterrupted" for *continuous*, "machinery" for *bulldozer*. According to recent developments within relevance theory, these ad hoc concepts, derived on-line in the process of understanding utterances, contribute to the proposition explicitly communicated; this includes cases of metaphor, like (10d), which have, of course, been treated quite differently within the Gricean tradition.[7]

What all these examples indicate is that there is a one-to-many relation between lexically encoded concepts and the concepts they can be used to express and communicate. This is to be expected on the relevance-theoretic view of communication, which entails that the linguistic expression used need only provide the addressee with skeletal evidence of the speaker's intended meaning, since the pragmatic processor is independently capable of forming quite rich hypotheses about the communicator's intentions on the basis of contextual clues alone; for discussion of this point, see Sperber and Wilson (1998a) and Wilson and Sperber (this volume).

While there are open disagreements and controversies of one sort or another in the current literature concerning the pragmatic processes discussed in the previous sections, there are none regarding the concept adjustment idea. This cannot be because it is an uncontentious issue but is, perhaps, because it is a relatively new player on the scene, one which has yet to be addressed by neo-Gricean pragmaticists or by truth-conditional semanticists. Without a doubt, though, such a process, like free enrichment, takes us well away from encoded linguistic meaning and has no linguistic mandate, so it cannot be construed as playing any part in the content of "what is said" where that is required to closely reflect (context-relative) truth-conditional linguistic meaning. Assuming there are pragmatic processes of ad hoc concept construction, they clearly belong in an account of linguistic communication rather than in a theory of natural language semantics. The issue, yet again, is whether there is a representational level that can do the double duty that seems to be required of a minimalist concept of "what is said": to be both the explicitly communicated content of an utterance and the semantics of a natural language sentence.

4   Conversational Implicatures

On the relevance-theoretic view, implicatures come in two sorts: implicated premises and implicated conclusions. Implicated premises are a subset of the contextual assumptions used in processing the utterance and implicated conclusions are a subset of its contextual implications. What distinguishes these subsets from other contextual assumptions and implications is that they are communicated (speaker-meant), hence part of the intended interpretation of the utterance. Consider B's response to A:

(11)   A: Let's go to a movie. I've heard *Sense and Sensibility* is good. Are you interested in seeing it?

B: Costume dramas are usually boring.

Understanding B's utterance requires deriving the following implicatures:

(12)a.   SENSE AND SENSIBILITY IS A COSTUME DRAMA.
   b.   SENSE AND SENSIBILITY IS LIKELY TO BE BORING.
   c.   B ISN'T VERY INTERESTED IN SEEING SENSE AND SENSIBILITY.

Once (12a) is derived, the other two follow fairly straightforwardly: (12b) follows deductively from premises consisting of the explicature of B's utterance and the assumption in (12a); then (12c) follows deductively from (12b) together with the further, easily accessible, assumption that people do not generally want to go to movies they expect to be boring. These are implicated conclusions. But what about (12a), an implicated premise, on which all this hinges? A assumes that B's response will meet his expectation of relevance, and the most obvious way it could do this is by supplying an answer to A's previous question. The presumption of optimal relevance licenses him to use the most accessible of the assumptions made available by the concepts encoded in B's response in interpreting the utterance. He may already know that *Sense and Sensibility* is a costume drama, but even if he doesn't, constructing this assumption will be relatively low cost, since it follows a well-worn comprehension route and is the most direct one for finding an answer to his yes/no question.

Notice that none of the inferred assumptions in (12) follows deductively from the basic explicature of B's utterance alone, though (12b) and (12c) are derived deductively (by modus ponens) once other particular assumptions have been accessed. So the overall picture is one of a non-demonstrative inference process, driven by the search for an optimally relevant interpretation.[8] Relevance-theorists and Griceans are in agreement on this sort of case: both those communicated assumptions described here as implicated premises and those described as implicated conclusions would qualify as (particularized) implicatures for Grice.

However, there are, inevitably, divergences between the two outlooks regarding other (putative) cases of implicature. One of these concerns the possibility of implicatures that are also entailments of the semantic content of the utterance. For Grice, entailments and implicatures were mutually exclusive, a view which remains widespread and which is a natural consequence of an account in which a notion of "what is said" is doing double duty as both semantics and explicitly communicated assumption (more on this in section 6). In my view, the concept of entailment and the concept of implicature belong to different explanatory levels, in fact different sorts of theory – the one a static semantic theory which captures knowledge of linguistic meaning, the other an account of the cognitive processes and representations involved in understanding utterances – so there is no reason at all why one and the same element of meaning should not fall into both categories. For discussion of this issue and of the relation between entailment and implicature, see Carston (2002b: chapter 2).

As mentioned earlier, disagreement also arises over certain cases treated by relevance-theorists as instances of pragmatic inference contributing to explicature and by Griceans as (generalized) implicatures. The differences in theoretical stance and basic aim that underlie these divergent predictions are discussed in the next section.

5 Explicature or "Generalized" Conversational Implicature?

Across a wide range of contexts, utterances of the sentences in (13a)–(15a) are likely to communicate the propositions given in (13b)–(15b) respectively:

(13) a. Bill drank a bottle of vodka and fell into a stupor.
   b. BILL DRANK A BOTTLE OF VODKA AND AS A RESULT HE FELL INTO A STUPOR.

(14) a. Sam and Jane moved the piano.
   b. SAM AND JANE MOVED THE PIANO TOGETHER.

(15) a. If Pat finishes her thesis by September she'll be eligible for the job.
   b. PAT WILL BE ELIGIBLE FOR THE JOB IF AND ONLY IF SHE FINISHES HER THESIS BY SEPTEMBER.

According to the relevance-theoretic account, these assumptions are explicatures; they are derived by pragmatically enriching the linguistically encoded logical form. According to various neo-Gricean accounts, they are generalized conversational implicatures, that is, default inferences that go through unless blocked by specific contextual assumptions (see Gazdar 1979, Horn 1984a, 1989, and Levinson 1987a, 1995, 2000a). So both camps are making a distinction between two kinds of communicated assumptions: explicatures and implicatures in relevance theory; generalized implicatures and particularized implicatures for the neo-Griceans. And, as the examples indicate, many cases of pragmatic inference which, according to the one account, develop the encoded meaning into explicatures, are, according to the other account, generalized conversational implicatures. However, there are substantive differences between the two conceptions, which the rest of this section will demonstrate: (a) the two distinctions do not coincide; (b) the Griceans recognize a level of "what is said" which is, very often at least, also communicated; and (c) the way in which the category of generalized conversational implicature works, as developed by Levinson (2000a) in particular, is directly at odds with relevance theory.

Let's focus briefly on what is perhaps the best known and most intensively studied class of generalized conversational implicatures, those involving scalar inference. Across a wide range of contexts, utterances of the sentences in (16a) and (17a) are likely to communicate the propositions in (16b) and (17b) respectively. Intuitively at least, the process looks quite similar to that in (13)–(15), that is, there is an enrichment (or strengthening) of the encoded content:

(16)a.   I've eaten three of your Swiss chocolates.
   b.   I'VE EATEN EXACTLY THREE OF YOUR SWISS CHOCOLATES.

(17)a.   Some of the children were sick.
   b.   SOME BUT NOT ALL OF THE CHILDREN WERE SICK.

These communicated assumptions are likely explicatures on a relevance-theoretic account, and one might suppose that the neo-Gricean account would treat them as generalized conversational implicatures. But this is not so; rather, on both Horn's and Levinson's accounts, "what is said" by an utterance of (a) in each case is as given in (c) below and the (generalized) implicature is as given in (d), the two together constituting what is communicated:

(16)c.   I'VE EATEN AT LEAST THREE OF YOUR SWISS CHOCOLATES.
   d.   I HAVEN'T EATEN MORE THAN THREE OF YOUR SWISS CHOCOLATES.

(17)c.   AT LEAST SOME (PERHAPS ALL) OF THE CHILDREN WERE SICK.
   d.   NOT ALL OF THE CHILDREN WERE SICK.

This is just one of many possible illustrations of the first two points of difference between the accounts: the distinctions made in the two theories do not line up neatly and, in fact, the Griceans distinguish three kinds of communicated assumptions: what is said and the two kinds of implicature (generalized and particularized).[9]

The relevance-theoretic view that the pragmatically inferred temporal and cause–consequence connections communicated by many *and*-conjunctions are elements of explicitly communicated content is supported by consideration of the following:

(18)a.   It's always the same at parties: either I get drunk and no one will talk to me or no one will talk to me and I get drunk.
   b.   If someone leaves a manhole uncovered and you break your leg, you can sue.

These examples come from Wilson and Sperber (1998: 3) and are based on ones developed by Cohen (1971) in his early argument against Grice's implicature analysis of the conjunction strengthenings. There seems to be a fairly general consensus that the truth-conditional content of (18a) consists of two genuinely distinct alternatives, rather than a redundant disjunction (P or P), which it should be if the inferred relations constitute implicatures (and, so, do not contribute to truth-conditional content). Similarly, the injunction to sue in (18b) is made on the condition that the leg-breaking is a consequence of the manhole having been left uncovered.[10]

Levinson (2000a: chapter 3) acknowledges these sorts of examples as cases of pragmatic inference contributing to "what is said," and he adds others, involving scalar inference, such as (19a) and (20a), which express the propositions given in (19b) and (20b) respectively:

(19)a.   If each side in the soccer game got three goals, then the game was a draw.

    b.   IF EACH SIDE IN THE SOCCER GAME GOT *EXACTLY* THREE GOALS, THEN THE GAME WAS A DRAW

(20)a.   Because the police have recovered some of the gold, they will no doubt recover the lot.

    b.   BECAUSE THE POLICE HAVE RECOVERED SOME *BUT NOT ALL* OF THE GOLD, THEY WILL NO DOUBT RECOVER THE LOT.

He labels the constructions in these examples (conditionals, disjunctions, comparatives, etc.) "intrusive constructions" because they have the property that "the truth conditions of the whole expression depend on the implicatures of some of its constituent parts" (Levinson 2000a: 213–14). His idea seems to be that while the unembedded scalar-containing clause and the unembedded conjunction each conversationally implicates the pragmatically inferred meaning, when they are embedded in one of the "intrusive constructions," that implicature gets composed into the semantics (the truth-conditional content) of the larger structure. (See Horn, this volume, for another view.)

Even if we could come up with a satisfactory explanation, which I doubt, of why an element of meaning should shift its status from implicature (hence non-truth-conditional) to truth condition in this way, the following argument seems to indicate that this is just not the right way to be thinking about what is going on:

(21)   Premise 1:   If someone leaves a manhole cover off and you break your leg, you can sue them.

      Premise 2:   Someone left a manhole cover off and Meg broke her leg.

      Conclusion: Meg can sue them.

I take it that this is an intuitively valid argument. But if Levinson's description of the phenomenon is correct, this should not be valid because the truth-conditional content of the antecedent of the conditional and the truth-conditional content of the second premise would not be the same, so the modus ponens deduction could not go through. On that sort of account, while the cause–consequence relation between the conjuncts is an element of what is said by the conditional (an "intrusive" construction), it is merely an implicature of what is said by the unembedded conjunction in the second premise. On the explicature account, on the other hand, the validity of the argument is explained, since the conclusion follows deductively from the premises, both of them having been pragmatically enriched in the same way.

I'll finish this section with a brief mention of what Levinson calls "Grice's circle," that is, the interdependence of what is said and what is implicated. On the basis of the examples just considered and a huge range of further cases that he has amassed of apparent "pragmatic intrusion" into truth-conditional content, Levinson points out that there is a pressing problem for the standard Gricean story: the derivation of implicatures depends on a prior determination of "what is said," but "what is said" itself depends on implicatures (Levinson 2000a: 186–7). This does seem to present an unworkable circularity if the standard Gricean assumptions are maintained: (a) any meaning derived via conversational principles constitutes an implicature, and (b) implicature calculation arises from the application of the maxims to "the saying of what is said." It is not, however, a problem for relevance theory, which makes neither of these assumptions. As demonstrated in Wilson and Sperber (2002, this volume), the pragmatic inferences involved in deriving explicatures and implicatures occur in parallel, the process being one of mutual adjustment until the propositional forms stabilize into an inferentially sound configuration which meets the expectation of relevance.

Levinson equates the saying/implicating circle with a semantic/pragmatic circle; that is, linguistic semantics is the input to pragmatic inference and semantics itself is dependent on, not autonomous from, pragmatic inference. But this is only so on the (widely held) assumption that "what is said" (the truth-conditional content of a linguistic utterance) is "the proper domain of a theory of **linguistic meaning**" (Levinson 2000a: 186, my emphasis). In the next and last section, I look at various versions of such a semantically oriented notion of "what is said" and conclude that, given a (context-independent) semantics for linguistic expression types, together with the concept of explicature, it is difficult to find any role for such a conception.

6   Semantics, "What is said," and Explicature

In Grice's theory, "what is said" takes part in two slightly different distinctions: what is said versus what is implicated, and what is said versus what is meant (that is, what falls under the speaker's communicative intention). The second distinction seems to allow, more obviously than the first, for the possibility that "what is said" is not meant, that it need not be part of what the speaker communicates but, rather, may be used as an instrument for the communication of something else. It is this possibility that certain truth-conditional semanticists call on when they invoke a "pragmatic" (= implicature-based) account for cases like the following:

(22)a.   Everyone screamed.
   b.   The door is locked.
   c.   There is milk in the fridge.
   d.   I've had breakfast.

The idea is that what is said by an utterance of (22a) is that everyone (in existence) screamed, but what is meant, hence implicated, on any given occasion of use will almost always be something more specific (e.g. everyone watching such and such a horror movie screamed). Similarly, for (22b), what is said is that there is one and only one door (in the universe) and it is locked, but what is meant concerns the lockedness of some specific door in the context. In both cases, what is said directly reflects the (alleged) semantics of the construction and is so patently false that it cannot be part of what is meant. In both (22c) and (22d), a very weak general proposition is what is said: for (22c), that there is some presence of milk in the fridge (perhaps just a stale drip or two on a shelf); for (22d), that the speaker's life is not entirely breakfastless. Something much more specific is understood in context (for instance, that there is milk usable for coffee in the fridge; that the speaker has had breakfast on the day of utterance) and, arguably, it is only these latter that are meant. See, for instance, Kripke (1977), Borg (2001), and Berg (2002), who explicitly take this position, and Larson and Segal (1995: 329), who assess its pros and cons for cases such as (22a) and (22b). In some discussions where this saying/meaning distinction is employed, there is a shift from talk of what the speaker says to "what the **sentence** says," thereby making it quite clear that "what is said" is a semantic notion to be kept distinct from what is communicated or meant.

Although Grice occasionally invoked this sort of distinction himself (for instance, in cases of misused definite descriptions; see Grice 1969: 142), when pressed it seems that he really wanted his concept of "what is said" to entail speaker meaning; that is, what the speaker said was to be taken as (part of) what the speaker meant (communicated). Evidence for this comes from his discussion of cases of non-literal language use, such as metaphor and irony. In such cases, it is clear that the proposition literally expressed is not something the speaker could possibly mean (e.g. "You are the cream in my coffee") and, tellingly, Grice moves to the locution "what the speaker made as if to say" (Grice 1989: 34). Furthermore, as Neale (1992) makes clear, the entailment from "U said that p" to "U meant that p" is an indispensable component of Grice's theory of (non-natural) meaning.

Grice seems to have wanted "what is said" to be both speaker meant and semantic – or at least, as he put it, "closely related to the conventional meaning of the words (the sentence) uttered . . ." Grice (1989: 25). But, as far as I can see, it's just not possible for these two properties to reside together. The problem is the (often considerable) gap between the meaning of the linguistic expression used and any of the propositions the speaker can be supposed to have meant/communicated. It's not just non-literal uses that force a prizing apart of these two properties, as the perfectly literal uses in (22), and those in section 3 above, illustrate. On the relevance-theoretic account, this particular tension doesn't arise because the domain of the distinction at issue is that of communicated assumptions (i.e. speaker meaning). The only linguistic semantic notion in play is that of the schematic logical form which is the output of context-immune linguistic decoding, not something that could be deemed to be "said" in any sense by the speaker.

Bach (1994a, 2001a, this volume) has an interesting response to this conflict in the Gricean conception. He develops a three-way distinction: what is said/ impliciture/implicature. The impliciture/implicature distinction is very similar to the explicature/implicature distinction: it is a distinction between communicated propositions, IMPLICITURES being the result of pragmatic processes of completion and expansion (i.e. enrichment) of the linguistic semantic content of the utterance. The third party in the distinction, "what is said," is intended to be an entirely semantic notion, albeit not the standard truth-conditional one since it may be subpropositional (a "propositional radical" – Bach 1994a: 127), as in the case of "Paracetamol is better" and the others in (3) above. He drops Grice's entailment from "what is said" to "what is meant" and imposes the strong requirement (which he takes to have been intended by Grice) of a "close syntactic correlation," constituent for constituent, between the linguistic expression used and "what is said" (Bach 1994a: 142). This move comes at the cost of an extra interpretive level in the overall picture since he seems to acknowledge context-free linguistic type meaning (schematic "logical form"), but this is distinct from "what is said," which is context-relative to some degree since it includes values for (certain) indexicals. Of course, economy considerations are overridden if the extra distinction can be shown to be required by the facts of linguistic communication. So let's consider whether or not that is the case.

A crucial feature of the account concerns the role played by context in determining what is said. Bach (1999a, 2001) assumes that there is a narrow semantic type of context which is quite distinct from the wide pragmatic context that comes into play in the derivation of implicitures and implicatures. This general idea was aired in section 3.1 in a discussion of the process of demonstrative pronoun saturation, where it was found to be unworkable. Bach is aware of that problem and insists that narrow context is restricted to just "a short list of variables, such as the identity of the speaker and the hearer and the time and place of an utterance" (Bach 1999a: 92), so that it applies only to "pure" indexicals such as *I, you, here,* and *now* which, it is claimed, can be contextually saturated without the need for consideration of the speaker's communicative intentions (hence without any guidance from pragmatic principles). In fact, the concept of a pure indexical is very dubious. With the possible exception of *I*, all the examples standardly cited are intention-dependent; for instance, *here* could refer to the spot on which the speaker is standing, the room she is in, the building, the city, etc. Furthermore, as noted earlier, disambiguation cannot be achieved by narrow context alone, but has to involve speaker intentions, which precludes it from any role in determining a purely semantic "what is said."

So what we seem to end up with as "what is said" is a set of propositions or propositional radicals with a few indexical values fixed but most not. What is this good for? According to Bach, it provides the linguistic basis for figuring out the implicitures and implicatures of the utterance (that is, what is communicated). But that's what decoded linguistic expression type meaning does, and, in fact, the two differ only in that "what is said" may have the odd referent filled in. Both are (or may be) subpropositional, so it's not as if "what is said" on this account can function in the way envisaged in the Gricean program, that is, as the truth-conditional content of the utterance and so the propositional basis for the calculation of implicatures. It looks very much as if this semantic notion of "what is said" is redundant. For a more extensive investigation of Bach's position, see Carston (2002b: section 2.5).

Any **semantic** notion of "what is said" is likely to endorse the view that: "the constituents of what is said must correspond to the constituents of the utterance" (Bach 1994a: 137). Coupling that with the widely held assumption that sentence semantics is propositional, and so truth-conditional, leads to the endorsement of a principle along the following lines, where "what is said" is to be understood as the proposition strictly and literally expressed by an utterance (see discussion in Reimer 1998c):

(23)   An adequate semantic theory T for a language L should assign p as the semantic content of a sentence S in L iff what is said by a speaker in uttering S is that p.

There are (at least) two ways to go in developing a linguistic semantics that adheres both to this principle and to the "syntactic correlation" requirement. One is to accept that sentences often express propositions which are trivially true or patently false, propositions which are seldom meant (communicated) by the speaker and are quite remote from the propositions that native speaker intuitions deliver. The other is to take intuitions about truth-conditional content to be the primary data of a semantic theory and, in order that the "syntactic correlation" requirement is met, to postulate the presence of a range of imperceptible constituents in the logical form of the sentence (or subsentential expression). Space precludes anything more than a brief word on each of these ways of marrying "what is said" and natural language semantics.

The second position – intuitive truth conditions and covert indexicals in logical form – has been given recent prominence by Stanley (2000). For instance, since an utterance of (24a) can be understood (in a particular context) as expressing the proposition in (24b), there must be a covert marker in the logical form of the sentence which indicates that a contextual value for a location is to be supplied. Similarly, *mutatis mutandis*, for the italicized elements in the propositions expressed by utterances of (24a)–(27a):

(24)a.   It's snowing.
    b.   IT'S SNOWING *IN ABERDEEN*.

(25)a.   On the table.
    b.   *THE MARMALADE IS* ON THE TABLE.

(26)a.   Every bottle is empty.
    b.   EVERY BOTTLE *IN THIS CRATE* IS EMPTY.

(27)a.   She seized the knife and stabbed her husband.
   b.   X SEIZED THE KNIFE AND *A FEW SECONDS LATER* X STABBED HER HUSBAND *WITH THE KNIFE*.

The cost of this approach is high – myriad hidden elements in logical form – and, if the view of relevance theorists and others (see notes 5 and 6) is right, it is an unnecessary cost, since these constituents can be recovered on pragmatic grounds alone by a process of free enrichment. On that view, the proposition explicitly communicated by an utterance may contain unarticulated constituents; that is, constituents which are not present in the logical form of the sentence or subsentential expression uttered. The italicized constituents in (24b)–(27b) are likely candidates. The conceptual semantics of the sentence is exhausted by the schematic, possibly subpropositional, decoded logical form, and it is at this level of encoded linguistic meaning, not at the level of the intuitive truth-conditional content or explicature, that the principle of semantic compositionality holds (for discussion of this point, see Powell 2000 and Carston 2002b: chapter 1).

The remaining truth-conditional semantic variant of "what is said" eschews both hidden elements in logical form and the possibility of unarticulated constituents in "what is said" by the utterance of a sentence. What you see or hear is what you get. Borg (2001) advocates a truth-conditional account that yields, for instance, the following truth statements:

(28)a.   "It is snowing" is true (in L) iff it is snowing.
   b.   "Mary can't continue" is true (in L) iff Mary can't continue.

The right-hand side specifies the semantic content of the sentence mentioned on the left, and that is what a speaker says when she utters the mentioned sentence. Semantic compositionality is satisfied since there is a one-to-one correlation between linguistic constituents and constituents of "what is said." These are very general, highly permissive truth-conditional specifications; for instance, (28b) is true provided there is something (anything) that Mary is unable to continue doing: running, staying up late, seeing John, pursuing university studies, etc. In fact, it seems likely that the sentence "Mary can't continue" is always true (since there is bound to be some activity or other that Mary cannot continue at any given moment). The strong intuition that this sentence is usually used to express something much more specific, which may be true or false, is an intuition about speaker meaning/communication, not about linguistic meaning/saying, and so is a matter for a theory of communication (or speech acts), not for semantics.

One might have qualms about the apparent prediction of this approach that sentences such as *Mary can't continue, John's book is on a shelf, It's night-time* are virtually always true (so what one "says" in uttering them is inevitably true), and that others, such as *Everyone was sick, The door is closed, It isn't night-time* are always false. One might also have qualms about the consequence that quite often every proposition the speaker communicates/means by uttering a linguistic expression is an implicature; that is, she communicates nothing explicitly. But where this picture really seems to come unstuck is, yet again, with indexicality.

Borg acknowledges that in order to accommodate overt indexicality the truth statements would have to be relativized to features of context, perhaps in the form of Higginbotham's (1988) CONDITIONALIZED truth statements, such as the following:

(29)   If U is an utterance of the sentence "she is happy," and the speaker of U refers with "she" to X, and X is female, then [U is true iff X is happy].

It may be that this does provide an adequate account of the semantics of the sentence type "she is happy."[11] But it certainly does not provide an adequate account of "what is said" by a particular utterance of the sentence, since that requires fixing the occasion-specific referent of the pronoun, a process which inevitably requires pragmatic work (hence consideration of speaker intention).

So there simply does not seem to be any wholly semantic notion of "what is said," a point which has also been argued forcefully by Recanati (2001). Of course, various minimalist notions of "what is said" can be defined; they are "minimalist" in that they keep pragmatic contributions to a minimum, for instance, allowing just reference assignment and disambiguation, or just saturation, or just whatever it takes to achieve truth-evaluability. But none of the results of these subtractions from the full range of pragmatic processes involved in explicature derivation has been shown to have any cognitive reality. Given decoded linguistic type meaning and a pragmatic processor which takes this as its input in deriving what is communicated (explicatures and implicatures), it is difficult to see a role for a further notion of "what is said," whether subpropositional or minimally propositional, which articulates a meaning that lies somewhere between linguistic meaning and explicature.

ACKNOWLEDGMENTS

I am very grateful to Larry Horn, Corinne Iten, Deirdre Wilson, and Vladimir Žegarac for their instructive and encouraging comments on an earlier draft of this chapter.

NOTES

1   I omit from this chapter any discussion of the Gricean notion of "conventional implicature," a category which simply does not arise within relevance theory and which is currently seen, across various pragmatic frameworks, to be in need of radical reworking. For instance, relevance theorists have reanalyzed most of the

linguistic devices allegedly
generating conventional implicatures
as encoding procedural constraints
on the inferential processes involved
in deriving conversational
implicatures (see, for instance,
Blakemore 1987, 2000, this volume,
and Iten 2000b). Bach (1999b), on
the other hand, sees certain of these
devices as contributing to "what
is said," where this is construed
as an entirely semantic notion (see
discussion of his concept of "what
is said" in section 6 of this chapter).
Note that, on both of these very
different accounts, the phenomenon
at issue is treated as falling on the
semantic side of a semantics/
pragmatics distinction.

2   The point is that decoded linguistic
meaning does not contribute
conceptual constituents to the
content of implicatures, not that it
never plays a role in shaping that
content. According to the relevance-
theoretic view, there are linguistic
expressions, including so-called
discourse connectives such as *but*,
so, *after all*, that encode procedural
meaning, which constrains the
derivation of implicated premises
and conclusions. See note 1 above
(and the references given there)
and Traugott (this volume).

3   Elsewhere, I have discussed in detail
the LINGUISTIC UNDERDETERMINACY
THESIS, that is, the position that the
linguistic form employed by a
speaker inevitably underdetermines
the proposition she explicitly
communicates. I have tried to
make a case for the view that this
is not just a matter of processing
convenience (saving of speaker
or hearer effort) but is, in fact,
an essential property of natural
language sentences, which do not
encode full propositions but merely
schemas for the construction of

(truth-evaluable) propositional forms
(see Carston 1998a, 2002b: chapter 1).

4   In the discussion of explicature in
this chapter, I am confining myself
to those of its properties that are
directly relevant when making
comparisons with dominant
construals of "what is said" in the
semantics and pragmatics literature.
I therefore omit discussion of so-
called "higher level explicatures,"
where the pragmatic development
of a logical form of the utterance
includes its embedding in
propositional attitude or speech act
descriptions, such as "The speaker
believes that . . ." or "The speaker is
asserting that. . . ." For discussion,
see Wilson and Sperber (1993) and
Ifantidou (2001). This subclass of
explicatures plays an important
part in the analysis of the content
explicitly communicated by non-
declarative utterances, another
matter which I cannot address in
this chapter. I also leave out any
discussion of the given definition of
"explicature" which, while adequate
for the cases to be discussed here,
needs some revision to cover the
full range of assumptions that fall
on the explicit side of what is
communicated. For discussion,
see Carston (2002b: chapter 2).

5   Stanley (2000) and Stanley and
Szabo (2000) present some
interesting arguments against
the existence of linguistically
unarticulated constituents of
content, hence against the need
for a process of free enrichment. In
different ways, Bach (2000), Carston
(2000), Breheny (2002), and Recanati
(2002a) address Stanley's and
Stanley and Szabo's arguments and
defend free enrichment as a crucial
pragmatic process in arriving at the
proposition explicitly communicated
by an utterance. In the next round

of this far-from-resolved dispute, Stanley (2002) addresses some of these arguments and raises a problem of possible overgeneration for the process of free enrichment.

6   Stanley (2000) disputes the position that there are non-sentential utterances which have propositional content; he argues that many cases, such as (6), are really elliptical and so, underlyingly, have a full sentential structure, and others are not genuine linguistic speech acts at all. Stainton (this volume) and Elugardo and Stainton (2001b) take issue with Stanley and defend the existence of non-sentential assertion; Clapp (to appear) also supports the existence of genuine non-sentential utterances and shows that these present a pressing problem for what he calls the "standard model of truth-conditional interpretation."

7   For arguments in support of the somewhat controversial view that loose uses, including metaphor, contribute to explicature, see Carston (1997, 1998a, 2002b: chapter 5). For further discussion of the role of ad hoc concept construction within the relevance-theoretic view of utterance understanding, see also Sperber and Wilson (1998a), Wilson and Sperber (2002, this volume), and Breheny (1999, 2001). For his related notions of "analogical transfer" and "metonymical transfer," pragmatic processes which contribute to the proposition explicitly communicated, see Recanati (1993: section 14.4, 1995, forthcoming).

8   The inferential process of deriving explicatures and implicatures follows a single comprehension strategy, based on the presumption of optimal relevance which is conveyed by all utterances. The strategy licenses the forming and

testing of interpretive hypotheses in order of their accessibility until an overall interpretation, which satisfies the current expectation of relevance, has been recovered. Hypotheses about explicatures and implicatures are made in parallel and "mutually adjusted" so that the result is a sound inference, such that any implicated conclusions are properly warranted by the explicature and contextual assumptions. For further discussion of this relevance-driven derivation process, with detailed worked examples involving the various different pragmatic processes discussed in this chapter, see Wilson and Sperber (2002, this volume).

9   Both Horn and Levinson develop pragmatic systems which feature two distinct, in fact conflicting, pragmatic principles, one of which accounts for the cases in (13)–(15), the other for the scalar cases. See Horn (1984a, 1989, this volume) and Levinson (1987a, 1995, 2000a), and, for some critical discussion of these approaches, Carston (1998b). There has been some acceptance in the neo-Gricean ranks of the role of pragmatic enrichment in determining "what is said" (or truth-conditional content): for instance, Horn (1992, 1996a, this volume) supports the enrichment analysis of the cardinal number cases, from an encoded "at least" semantics to an explicitly communicated "exactly" meaning, in many contexts, but does not believe it extends to the "inexact" scalar operators, such as partitive *some*. Geurts (1998), who is neither a neo-Gricean nor a relevance theorist, argues that all scalars can have a "bilateral" truth-conditional content in certain contexts. These developments shove a strong wedge

between the classic equation of linguistic semantics and "what is said" (the truth-conditional content of the utterance).

10   These observations about the truth conditions of complex constructions containing simple conjunctive (or scalar) sentences as a subpart have been used by a wide range of people in a wide range of ways. For Cohen (1971), they provided evidence against the Gricean view that the natural language counterparts of logical operators are semantically truth-functional and led to his proposal for a multi-featured non-truth-functional semantics for "and." A different possibility for accounting for the phenomenon arose in the early days of relevance theory: the non-truth-functional meaning conveyed by particular utterances involving "and" might constitute a PRAGMATIC contribution to the truth-conditional content of the conjunctive utterance. This idea was developed in Carston (1988), who claimed that the truth conditions that arise when key cases, such as conjunctions, are embedded in the scope of logical operators, such as negation and the conditional, provide crucial evidence for deciding when a pragmatically derived element of utterance meaning constitutes a component of the explicature of the utterance or is an implicature. Recanati (1989) elevated this embedding test to the status of a principle for distinguishing the two kinds of pragmatic inference (the SCOPE PRINCIPLE), though he subsequently demoted it in favor of a different principle for the same purpose

(see Recanati 1993: 269–74). Gazdar (1979: 167–8) briefly presents the idea that the truth conditions of certain constructions (conditionals, comparatives, etc.) "make reference to the pragmatic properties of their constituent clauses." As about to be discussed in the text, it is this latter position that Levinson (2000a) has adopted and elaborated. For more detailed consideration of the different approaches to these embedding data, see Carston (1998a: chapter 3, and 2002b: chapter 2, section 2.6.3).

11   A truth-conditional account of the semantics of a linguistic system is never going to be fully adequate because there is a range of linguistic devices (lexical and syntactic) whose encoded meaning does not affect truth conditions (this includes expressions whose meaning is analyzed by Griceans as cases of conventional implicature). Note also that communicated propositions (explicatures and implicatures) and all propositional thoughts have truth-conditional content. On the relevance-theoretic view, this is the appropriate domain for a truth-conditional semantics (a semantics that captures the relation between propositional representations and the world represented), with linguistic semantics being rather a mapping or translation from one kind of representation (linguistic) into another (conceptual). For discussion of these and other issues arising for a truth-conditional approach to natural language meaning, see Carston (2002b: chapter 1, section 1.5) and Iten (2000b).

29 Pragmatics and Cognitive Linguistics

GILLES FAUCONNIER

As we start a new century, rich and diverse evidence from the social and cognitive sciences continues to provide an ever sharper conception of the way we humans think. It is now widely understood that brains and cultures play a major role in constructing the world as we see it. They are not, and we are not, passive interpreters of that world. Distinctive and powerful cognitive capacities such as analogy, framing, metaphor, schematization, recursion, reference-point organization, and conceptual blending lie at the heart of perception, conception, and action, and suffuse our lives with rich meaning – sometimes unbearably rich meaning. For the most part, the operations and processes that correspond to those powerful capacities are carried out massively below the level of our consciousness.

Language, which we *do* experience consciously through sound, gesture, or writing, is a spectacular but far from transparent window into this backstage cognition of our minds. Conversely, many of the seemingly complicated, irregular, and "illogical" properties of language structures become intelligible when their cognitive underpinnings are discovered.

In everyday life, when we use or hear words in a language we know, in a culture we know, meanings form instantly. Consciously, we experience words, word combinations, and the automatic sensation of knowing what they mean. Quite naturally, we feel that the meanings are in the words and in their combinations.

Twentieth-century attempts to study meaning most often reflect this intuition by assigning to every form its "meaning" independently of context. But important work in pragmatics over several decades of the same century has shown the assumption of invariant meaning to be simplistic. Context matters. A popular scheme to emerge from work in pragmatics preserved the intuition that form had meaning *ex tempore*, but added to the arsenal of meaning theorists a very powerful pragmatic component that could use context and pragmatic principles to derive from the pristine meaning of a form in isolation the messier meaning of that form when mired in context.

In modern linguistic and philosophical research, the best-known efforts in this direction are the Gricean scheme of maxims and implicatures and the theory of speech acts developed by Austin and Searle. Interestingly, Grice's work was originally motivated by logical considerations – keeping the logic of semantic meanings simple and standard by accounting pragmatically for apparent complexities. Linguists in the late 1960s, and through the 1970s and beyond, noted many features of grammar that were associated with pragmatic properties, and that in turn led linguists to study pragmatics in its own right and for its own sake. There was a convergence of issues of common interest to philosophers, linguists, and others who ponder the mysteries of meaning. Pragmatics exploded into a rich, but not particularly well-defined, field of inquiry.

However, the very linguistic work that had contributed to an explosion of pragmatics was about to lead to its reassessment. It became clear to an ever-growing number of researchers (e.g. Ducrot 1972, Fillmore 1982, Jackendoff 1983, de Cornulier 1985, Fauconnier 1985, G. Lakoff 1987, Langacker 1987, Sweetser 1990) that the line in the sand between semantics and pragmatics was not an easy one to draw. The "meanings" spontaneously associated by informants with isolated forms were not the pristine core meanings that we yearned for; they were only defaults made extremely probable by culture, norms, and lack of imagination.

Just as a rigorous description of syntax in the 1950s, using the resources of computability theory, revealed its immense complexity, a rigorous description of meaning using the resources of cognitive science reveals far greater complexity than commonly assumed. Language is only the tip of a spectacular cognitive iceberg, and when we engage in any language activity, we draw unconsciously on vast cognitive and cultural resources, call up innumerable models and frames, set up multiple connections, coordinate large arrays of information, and engage in creative mappings, transfers, and elaborations.

Thus we find that language does not "represent" meaning: language prompts for the construction of meaning in particular contexts with particular cultural models and cognitive resources. To do so, it draws heavily on "backstage cognition" that is not accessible to our consciousness. When scientific analysis brings out backstage cognition explicitly, it highlights the contrast between the extreme brevity of the linguistic form and the spectacular wealth of the corresponding meaning construction. Very sparse grammar guides us along the same rich mental paths, by prompting us to perform complex cognitive operations.

Language forms do not "carry" information; they latch on to rich pre-existent networks in the subjects' brains and trigger massive sequential and parallel activations. Those activated networks are themselves in the appropriate state by virtue of general organization due to cognition and culture and local organization due to physical and mental context. Crucially, we have no awareness of this amazing chain of cognitive events that takes place as we talk and listen, except for the external manifestation of language (sounds, words, sentences) and the internal manifestation of meaning, experienced consciously with lightning speed. This is very similar to perception, which is also instantaneous and immediate, with no awareness of the extraordinarily complex intervening neural events.

Within cognitive frameworks for studying meaning construction, many standard issues of pragmatics remain as important as ever – we seek to account for scalar phenomena, speech acts and performatives, presupposition, referential opacity, so-called figurative speech, metonymic pragmatic functions, and implicature – but old problems are framed in novel ways.

There is a great wealth of recent work on these matters and there is not enough space in the present handbook entry to even remotely do it justice. I will proceed by giving some illustrative examples and pointing to larger bodies of work.

1   Language as a Prompt: Turner's *xyz* Constructions

In *Reading Minds*, Turner (1991) draws our attention to an extremely productive construction in English, *x* **is** *y* **of** *z*, as in:

- *Vanity is the quicksand of reason.*
- *Wit is the salt of conversation.*
- *Money is the root of evil.*

Turner notes insightfully that in the course of understanding such expressions, we build up a metaphorical mapping of the form (figure 29.1).

So, for example, in *Vanity is the quicksand of reason*, a plausible metaphorical source would have a traveler (*w*) who is sucked into quicksand (*y*), and that source would be mapped onto a target of human behavior containing vanity (*x*) and reason (*z*), in which vanity causes reason to falter and perhaps disappear. The grammatical construction "NP be NP of NP" licenses this mapping scheme, but tells us nothing about the domains themselves or the relevant inferences that will produce efficient understanding. In fact, the linguistic form has nothing that actually corresponds to the crucial fourth element *w* that must be mapped

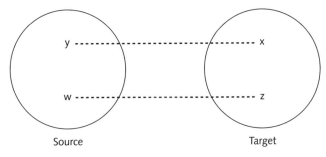

Source   Target

Figure 29.1   Metaphorical mapping for *xyz* constructions

onto *z* (in the quicksand example, this element could be the traveler who does not notice the quicksand and falls into it). In *Money is the root of evil*, the target domain is the complex social world of humans, money, greed, good and evil. The source is the domain of plants. *y* is "the root," the missing *w* is the plant; the counterpart of "the root" (*y*) (in the source) is "money" (*x*) in the target domain. The counterpart of the plant (*w*) is evil (*z*). Some inferences transfer from the source to the target:

> root "causes" plant ⇒ money causes evil
> without a root there is no plant ⇒ without money there is no evil
> we see the plant, not the root ⇒ we do not see the link between money and evil

There are two important points about the way in which the construction "NP be NP of NP" prompts for a systematic *xyz*(*w*) mapping scheme.

First, the grammar prompts us to look for two domains and a mapping between them, with a certain counterpart structure (e.g. *root* corresponds to *money*, and *something* (*w*) corresponds to *evil*). From this very minimal information, we are supposed to retrieve the right domains and the efficient inferential structure. Since the domains are not specified by language, their retrieval belongs to what is usually called pragmatics. But no meaning, even partial or schematic, except for the *xyz* mapping scheme itself, can possibly be constructed without the domains needed for the mapping. It follows that there cannot be a minimal, independent ("literal") meaning with truth conditions, linked solely to the linguistic form, from which the contextual meaning would be pragmatically derived. Rather, the form is a direct prompt to perform the pragmatic operations needed to satisfy the mapping scheme licensed by the linguistic construction. The truth conditions for the expression can only be computed after the connections and domains have been selected.

Second, the mapping scheme is not specialized in any particular type of surface phenomenon. One might think from the examples cited above that the *xyz* construction has the function of setting up metaphors, since indeed that is what it does in those examples. But in fact, the construction fits other kinds of mappings. So, if "NP is the NP of NP" is the English sentence *Paul is the father of Sally*, it will prompt for exactly the same *xyz* mapping scheme as in the other examples (see figure 29.2). This time, Paul and Sally (*x* and *z*) are mapped onto the kinship frame containing *father*, and the missing element *w* is *child* in the kinship frame.

Choosing a mapping from a kinship frame to individuals in this case is the default, but there are many other possibilities, all within the same mapping scheme, as in *Paul is the father of Sally for today* (as when a neighbor takes over some fatherly duties, e.g. taking Sally to school, reading her a story, cooking her lunch); *The Pope is the father of the church*; *Newton is the father of physics*; *Fear, father of cruelty*, etc. Constructing meaning in all these cases is a matter of finding domains and structure that best fit both the context and the mapping scheme. It is what used to be called pragmatics, but there is no longer an

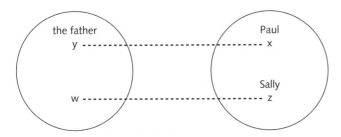

Figure 29.2   *xyz* mapping scheme used for *Paul is the father of Sally*

intermediate, core "semantic" content from which meaning in context is derived. Rather, the language form is a prompt to go directly to the context, using cognitive resources like memory, schemas, and cultural models (Fauconnier 2000). In fact, such examples highlight the often spurious nature of "core semantics" and the sometimes dubious application of Gricean maxims: why go to the trouble of trying to process a nonsensical "literal" meaning of *Money is the root of evil*, when the grammatical construction invites you to find and match separate domains directly, with *money* and *evil* in one, and *root* in the other? Strikingly, the grammatical construction makes no distinction between the case where the required matching is felt to be metaphorical (vanity and quicksand) and the case where it is not (father and Paul). The point is that the most elegant and general account of meaning construction in cases like this does not require, and in fact does not allow, an intermediate "literal" or "logical" or "core" meaning to intervene between the syntactic form and the intended meaning. It is useful to appreciate this, because in much of standard pragmatics, pragmatic principles apply to the semantic output of a grammar. The direct construction of meaning on the basis of (often minimal) prompting by grammatical constructions is not just an exotic property of *xyz* constructions; it is a pervasive, and arguably constitutive, property of language and meaning.

To achieve the desired generalizations, it is useful to forget notions like "meaning of an expression," "semantic representation," "truth function," and the like, and to think instead of the **meaning potential** of a language form. Meaning potential is the essentially unlimited number of ways in which an expression can prompt dynamic cognitive processes, which include conceptual connections, mappings, blends, and simulations. Such processes are inherently creative, and we recognize them as such when they are triggered or produced by art and literature. In everyday life, the creativity is hidden by the largely unconscious and extremely swift nature of the myriad cognitive operations that enter into the simplest of our meaning constructions. It is also hidden by the necessary folk-theory of our everyday behavior, which is based quite naturally on our conscious experience rather than on the less accessible components of our cognition. In doing away with distinct semantic and pragmatic components, cognitive theories actually highlight the centrality of pragmatic operations in meaning construction.

2   Opacity and Presuppositions

Opacity and presupposition projection are classical problems for the logic of language. A very general way of looking at these problems within a cognitive approach to meaning construction is to study the connections between the mental spaces that are set up in ongoing discourse.

Mental spaces are small conceptual packets constructed as we think and talk for purposes of local understanding and action. They are partial assemblies containing elements and are structured by frames and cognitive models. They are interconnected and can be modified as thought and discourse unfold.

Mental spaces proliferate in the unfolding of discourse, map onto each other in intricate ways, and provide abstract mental structure for shifting anchoring, viewpoint, and focus, allowing us to direct our attention at any time onto very partial and simple structures while maintaining an elaborate web of connections in working memory and in long-term memory.

Consider the following simple example of mental space construction prompted by sentence (1) coming at a certain point into a particular discourse in context (from Fauconnier 1998):

(1)   Max thought the winner received $100.

The language form prompts for setting up two mental spaces. One is the Base space, *B*, the initial space with partial structure corresponding to what has already been introduced at that point in the discourse or what may be introduced freely because it is pragmatically available in the situation. Another mental space, *M*, subordinate to this one, will contain partial structure corresponding to "what Max thinks." It is structured by *received $100*. That form evokes a general frame of receiving of which we may know a great number of more specific instances (receive money, a shock, a letter, guests, etc.). The expression *Max thought* explicitly sets up this second mental space. *Max* and *the winner* are noun phrases and will provide access to elements in the spaces. This happens as follows: the noun phrase is a name or description which either fits some already established element in some space or introduces a new element in some space. That element may, in turn, provide access to another element through a cognitive connection (a connector). In our example, the name *Max* accesses an element in the base space; the description *the winner* accesses a role in a frame of winning appropriate for the given context (winning a particular race, lottery, game, etc.). Roles can have values, and a role element can always access another element that is the value of that role. So we can say *The winner will get $10*, without pointing to any particular individual; this is the role interpretation. Or we can say *The winner is bald*, where being bald is a property of the individual who happened to win, not a condition for getting the prize; this is the value interpretation. The two mental spaces *B* and *M* are connected, and there can be counterparts of elements of *B* in *M*, as diagrammed in figure 29.3. The ACCESS PRINCIPLE defines a general procedure for accessing elements: If

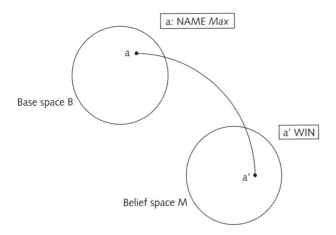

Figure 29.3 Mental space construction

two elements *a* and *a'* are linked by a connector *F* (*a'* = *F*(*a*)), then element *a'* can be identified by naming, describing, or pointing to its counterpart *a*.

What philosophers and linguists traditionally call the number of readings of a sentence like (1) is the number of accessing possibilities compatible with the explicit instructions of the linguistic form. But that number varies with the available types of connections between mental spaces and the available mental spaces in a particular discourse and pragmatic environment. So the number of "logical" readings of a particular language form is itself a **pragmatic** property, and constructing the appropriate reading in a particular context is itself a pragmatic exercise: finding a particular access path through a mental space configuration.

In Fauconnier (1998), several accessing possibilities for example (1) are outlined that are all equally sanctioned by the grammatical form. Typically, a particular context or discourse creates a strong bias for following a particular accessing path, and other paths formally possible for the single sentence form are not even considered consciously. These paths can remain available, however. Coulson (2001) has shown experimentally some neural correlates of frame-shifting and reactivation of accessing paths in the case of jokes. The punch line of a joke often forces a frame shift and a reconfiguration of the accessing path.

For a grammatical form like the *winner* example above, the accessing possibilities in the simplest contexts depend on whether the access principle is applied across spaces and from role to value. The grammatical form does not force a particular access path.

In a pure role interpretation within space *M* with no application of the access principle, we have readings in which Max thought there was a contest and thought it was a feature of that contest that $100 would be awarded to whoever won. This accessing strategy is noncommittal as to whether the speaker also assumes there was such a contest, whether an actual winner was ever selected, and whether Max thinks that a winner was selected. The sentence under this strategy would be appropriate in mini-discourses like the following:

(2)   The Boston Marathon will take place next week. Max thought the winner received $100, but it turns out there won't be any prize money.

(3)   My friends were under the impression that I was running a lottery in my garage. Max thought the winner received $100. But they were all wrong – there was no lottery.

Suppose now that the access principle operates, but only within the subordinate space *M*, linking the role "winner" to a value of that role. As before, Max believes that there was a contest and, moreover, that somebody won, and he has additional beliefs about the person who he assumes won. Although a likely default is that the $100 was prize money, this interpretation is no longer obligatory. Max may believe that something else happened, causing the person who had won to receive $100 independently.

In the two accessing possibilities just considered, a word (*winner*) simply evokes a script within a single space. but the access principle may also operate across spaces. The speaker may have a particular contest in mind, for which there is a role "winner," set up as an element *w* in the base *B*. That role can have a value (e.g. Harry) with a counterpart in mental space *M*. The access principle allows *the winner* to access the role, and then its value, and finally the counterpart of that value.

The interpretation, then, is that the speaker presents Harry as the winner, and says that Max thought Harry received $100. This is compatible with Max knowing nothing about the contest, or believing that someone other than Harry won and that Harry got the $100 for selling a used car or as a consolation prize in the contest.

Other accessing paths are available for this simple sentence if counterpart roles are considered, or if the extra space introduced by the past tense is taken into account, or if other spaces are accessible at that point in the discourse to provide counterparts. Typically, an understander does not have to consider all possibilities. The intended path will be favored by the space configuration in the discourse at the point at which the statement is made: we might already have the role "winner" in space *B*, or in space *M* but not in *B*; we might already have different values in *M* and *B* for the same role (*w* and its counterpart *w′*); and so on. In other cases, of course, the understander will lack sufficient information and may have to revise a space configuration or may simply misunderstand a speaker's intent.

Our example had a subordinate space corresponding to "belief." There are many other kinds of mental spaces, but they all share these complex accessing possibilities. For instance, time expressions are space-builders and set up new spaces in discourse. Consider (as part of a larger discourse) the following sentence: *In 1968, the winner received $100.* As before, we have a base *B* and a subordinate space *M*, corresponding to 1968 and set up by the space-builder *in 1968*. Also as before, the noun phrase *the winner* can access a role in *M*, or the counterpart role in *M* of a role in *B*, or the counterpart in *M* of a value in *B*, or a value of a role in *M*. Situations that fit these respective strategies might include:

- There was a certain type of game in 1968 (no longer played today) in which you got $100 for winning.
- There is a certain sports competition, say the Boston Marathon, that exists today (role *w* in space *B*) and also existed in 1968 (counterpart role *w'* in space *M*). In 1968 (as opposed to today), whoever won got $100.
- The winner of the chess championship held today is Susan. Back in 1968, in unrelated circumstances (e.g. selling her used car), Susan received $100.
- The winner back in 1968 of the contest we are talking about was Harry, and that year Harry received $100 (perhaps for selling his used car).

The access paths available in this example involving time (1968) are exactly the same as the access paths in the previous example involving belief. Even though time and belief are conceptually quite different, they give rise, at the level of discourse management considered here, to the same mental space configurations. More generally, we find that mental spaces are set up for a wide variety of conceptual domains that include time, belief, wishes, plays, movies, pictures, possibility, necessity, hypotheticals and counterfactuals, locatives, and reality. The connectors, the access principle, and the role/value distinctions work uniformly across this broad range of cases.

The study of accessing strategies is developed in great detail in Fauconnier (1985, 1997), Fauconnier and Sweetser (1996), and Fauconnier and Turner (2002). What we see is that phenomena traditionally viewed as logical, such as opacity, attributivity, and presupposition projection, and others traditionally viewed as literary, such as the *xyz* phenomena discussed in section 1, are all part of the same uniform and powerful prompting by language for connections across mental spaces.

Indeed, presupposition projection finds an elegant and general solution in these terms. The principle which guides presupposition projection can be formulated as:

(4) **Presupposition Float**
A presupposed structure Π in mental space *M* will propagate to the next higher space *N*, unless structure already in *M* or *N* is incompatible with Π or entails Π.

Informally, **a presupposition floats up until it meets itself or its opposite**. To say that a structure "propagates" from space *X* to another space *Y* is to say that if it is satisfied for elements *x*, *y*, . . . in *X*, it is satisfied for their counterparts *x'*, *y'*, . . . in *Y*, via some connector *C*. As usual, we find structure mappings involved in matching processes that transfer structure.

So, consider for example a familiar case like that presented in (5):

(5)   Sue believes Luke has a child and that Luke's child will visit her.

In this example, grammatical clues prompt for the construction of three spaces: the base B, a belief space M, and a future space W. The three spaces contain counterparts a, a', a'' for Sue and b, b', b'' for Luke. The presupposition in the future space W that ⟨b'' has a child⟩ meets itself in the form ⟨b' has a child⟩ in the higher belief space, and therefore does not float up. Because the presupposition does not float up to M, it cannot, a fortiori, float up to the base: it has been halted at the W level. This ensures that the piece of discourse does not globally presuppose (or entail) that Luke has children.

Notice that although the presupposition does not float all the way up, it is not canceled, but rather remains in force in the future space: a presupposition will float up into higher spaces until it is halted. It will then **remain** in force for the mental spaces into which it has floated. In other words, inheritance is not an "all or nothing" process. The general issue is: Which spaces inherit the presupposition? The vast literature on presupposition projection typically focuses on asking if the "whole sentence" inherits the presupposition, i.e. if the presupposition floats **all the way up**. To account for the full range of entailments, a more general question has to be answered: How far up does the presupposition float? The answer to the general question, given by the Presupposition Float Principle, subsumes the answer to the special question: Does it float to the base?

3   Word and Sentence Meanings

Sections 1 and 2 illustrate the fundamental but counterintuitive idea that language forms do not in themselves have core meanings that get modified, adjusted, or expanded through pragmatic elaboration. Rather, language forms steer the construction of meaning along certain paths in particular contexts. Thus there is no "autonomous" semantics separate from pragmatics, context, and cognition. The impossibility of drawing this line is well documented: detailed and forceful arguments are given in Haiman (1980b), Moore and Carling (1982), Sweetser (1999), and no doubt many others. Haiman finds that "the distinction between dictionaries and encyclopedias is . . . fundamentally misconceived" (1980b: 331). Langacker (1987) is unequivocal: "Certainly an autonomous semantics . . . can be formulated, but the account it offers of the meanings of linguistic expressions is apt to be so restricted and impoverished relative to the full richness of how we actually understand them that one can only question its utility and cognitive reality. Only limited interest attaches to a linguistic semantics that avoids most of the relevant phenomena and leaves recalcitrant data for an ill-defined 'pragmatic' component" (1987: 155). And he goes on to write: "The assumption that language (and in particular semantics) constitutes an autonomous formal system is simply gratuitous" (p. 156). He explains how entities have specifications that form a gradation in terms of their **centrality**, and how the notion of centrality in turn correlates with the notions of **conventional**, **generic**, **intrinsic**, and **characteristic**. Taking as an example the situation in which a wrestler triumphs over a tiger, so that the cat is on the mat, Langacker writes: "it is not that the expression [*the cat is on the mat*] intrinsically **holds** or **conveys** the contextual meaning, but rather, that conventional units **sanction** this meaning as falling within the open-ended class of conceptualizations they **motivate** through judgments of full or partial schematicity. These conceptualizations may draw on any facet of a speaker's conceptual universe."

Coulson (2001), Sweetser (1999), and Fauconnier and Turner (1998, 2002) explore many aspects of the on-line construction of meaning using conceptual blending theory. Conceptual blending is a very general cognitive operation that partially matches two (or more) input mental spaces and selectively projects from the matched spaces to create a **blended mental space** with emergent structure. This creates a conceptual integration network of the form shown in figure 29.4. The generic space represents the structure shared by the inputs. The square in the blended space stands here for the emergent structure which arises in the blending.

So, for example, one way to understand the counterfactual in (6):

(6) In France, Watergate wouldn't have done Nixon any harm.

is to build a conceptual integration network that partially matches two input spaces with prominent aspects of the American political system and the French political system, respectively, and develops an emergent blended space

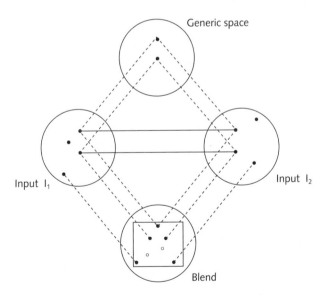

Figure 29.4   Diagram showing conceptual blending

framed by the French political and social system with Nixon as president and Watergate as a French scandal. In the selective projection, Nixon loses his American characteristics (English language, former vice-president, etc.). Watergate, similarly, loses most of its specific geographical and American characteristics. It becomes a French scandal with some properties analogous and others disanalogous to those of the American scandal. Emergent structure in the blended space includes the specification that Nixon is unharmed and the inferences (and emotions) that this may lead to. For most understanders, it projects back to the inputs, telling them something about the French mentality, or political system, and perhaps inviting value judgments in one direction or the other.

But of course, this is only one of the very many ways to construct a counterfactual blend licensed by example (6). Here are some other perfectly fine uses with completely different intended meanings, corresponding to different choices of selective projection:

(7)a.   In France, Watergate wouldn't have done Nixon any harm because Nixon is loved by the French.

   b.   In France, Watergate wouldn't have done Nixon any harm because French presidents are not affected by US scandals.

   c.   In France, Watergate wouldn't have done Nixon any harm because spying on American political parties is supported by public opinion.

   d.   In France, Watergate wouldn't have done Nixon any harm because he would never have been elected president in the first place.

Here again, we see that there is no single special meaning of the expression that would serve as a core and to which further pragmatic operations would apply to produce the other readings. Rather, the grammatical construction is from the outset an invitation to set up a counterfactual conceptual integration network, but it leaves highly underspecified much of the construction of that network – in particular, prominent aspects of the input mental spaces and selective projection (Mandelblit and Fauconnier 2000). Building the right network in context is clearly part of pragmatics; but there is no contentful meaning for the language form independent of the pragmatic construction. Fauconnier and Turner (2002) show that conceptual blending is highly constrained by numerous constitutive and governing principles. In addition to those cognitive principles, appropriate constructions of blends for a given context will be guided by pragmatic principles of the usual sort: goals and focus of the language activity, prior discourse, and general relevance.

Blending also plays a central role in constructing meanings for words in context, and once again it turns out that contextual meanings are not derived from prototypical or basic meanings. Rather, it is the other way around: what we take intuitively to be basic meanings are simply defaults for situations with minimum context. These defaults are not a basis for constructing the more elaborate meanings, rather they are special cases under special conditions (minimum, widely available context). They are psychologically real, but not theoretically fundamental.

Consider now the morphosyntactically simple forms of language that consist of putting two words together: e.g., noun-noun compounds like *boat house*, adjective-noun combinations like *angry man*, and noun-adjective combinations like *child-safe* or *sugar-free*.

Complicated integration networks lie behind these kinds of words. Take for example *dolphin-safe*, *shark-safe*, and *child-safe*: in all of these cases, one input has the abstract frame of DANGER and the other input has a more specific content, involving dolphins, sharks, or children. We build a specific counterfactual scenario of HARM in which *dolphin*, *shark*, or *child* is assigned to a role in the DANGER frame. In the counterfactual scenario, a victim is harmed. The word *safe* implies a disanalogy between the counterfactual blend and the specific input.

Dolphin-safe, as it is currently used on cans of tuna, means that measures were taken to avoid harming dolphins during the harvesting of the tuna. *Shark-safe*, as applied to, say, swimming, means conditions under which swimmers are not vulnerable to attack by sharks. *Child-safe* as applied to rooms can mean rooms that are free of typical dangers for children or rooms immune to children. In every case, the understander must construct elaborate counterfactual scenarios from simple forms.

How the understander does this mental work may differ from case to case. In *dolphin-safe tuna*, the role of the dolphin as potential victim is taken to be useful. In *dolphin-safe diving*, said of mine-seeking human divers who are protected by dolphins who are not themselves at risk, the blend uses dolphins in the role of agents of the safety. In *dolphin-safe diving*, said of diving that imitates the way dolphins swim and is therefore safe, the blend uses the manner of swimming associated with dolphins. If we assume that dolphins eat goldfish, then *dolphin-safe goldfish* casts dolphins in the role of predators. Genetic engineers who are concerned not to produce anything resembling a dolphin might refer to a technique that is known never to lead to a dolphin embryo as *dolphin-safe*. The dolphin this time does not fill the role of victim, victimizer, causal agent, or role model. And of course, a compositional theory of meaning immune to the dolphin examples would be hailed as *dolphin-safe*. There is a vast and insightful literature in linguistics dealing with compounds and the obvious fact that their meaning is not derivable from their form (e.g. Downing 1977, Ryder 1994). The deeper point, already made by Travis (1981), and Langacker (1987: 271–4) in his work on active zones, is that whatever operations are needed to construct meanings in such cases are also needed for the everyday cases like *black kettle*, *red pencil*, and *brown cow*. Fauconnier and Turner (2002: chapter 17) analyze in some detail the role of conceptual blending in understanding such simple forms.

Examples like *dolphin-safe* are useful because they highlight in a transparent and uncontroversial way the nature of the blending process. Furthermore, they abound. Think of *cruelty-free* on bottles of shampoo or the variety of non-compositional integration running across *waterproof*, *tamper-proof*, *foolproof*, and *child-proof* or *talent pool*, *gene pool*, *water pool*, *football pool*, and *betting pool*.

Sweetser (1999) considers the case in which *likely candidate*, in a political context, means not someone likely to become a candidate or succeed as a candidate but, for instance, a candidate likely to grant an interview. As she writes, "So long as we can think up a scenario relative to the candidate in question, and evaluate that scenario for likelihood, *likely candidate* can mean the candidate who figures in the scenario we have labeled as likely." On her analysis, conceiving of such a scenario and evaluating it consists of finding a blend of the frame for likelihood, conceived of as probability of occurrence in a sequence, and the frame for candidate. Like *safe* above, *likely* prompts for a conceptual blend. *Likely* requires the recruitment of a scenario of likelihood and another input space in which the noun prompts for a frame and an element filling a role in that frame. In the blend, the element must play a role in the specific scenario of likelihood, but there are many possibilities for the nature of this role. One general possibility is for the scenario evoked by the noun to already be a scenario of likelihood, as in *likely candidate*, meaning someone likely to become a candidate or a candidate likely to be chosen. *Likely suspect* is similar, meaning alternatively a person likely to be deemed a suspect or a suspect likely to be guilty or a suspect likely to be convicted. However, the scenario of likelihood in the blend need not be the one evoked by the noun. Sweetser's reading, "a candidate likely to grant an interview," does not use the likelihood of either becoming a candidate or being chosen. If every year the governor pardons someone in the jailhouse, we might bet on who is the "likely suspect."

Sweetser's examples make the point clearly that the scenario of likelihood need not be one evoked by the noun itself, as we see, for example, in the case in which *possible textbook* refers to a textbook that might possibly be chosen as the one to be used in a college course. Just as the different meanings of *safe* may go unnoticed, so the different meanings of *possible* and *likely* may go unnoticed. But a *possible textbook*, in the sense of one that may be adopted, is not the same as a *possible textbook* in the sense of one that might exist, or might be written, or a trade book that could double as a textbook. Humans have the crucial ability to construct the elaborate integration networks appropriate for each of these cases. This is not a special-purpose exotic capacity – it is the very foundation of meaning construction, and children master it early in their development. A semantic analysis that merely said that the meaning of *possible* ranges over unspecified elements would miss the heart of the problem.

Coulson has shown that *fake* is an adjective that carries an especially elaborate blending and mapping scheme (Coulson and Fauconnier 1999, Coulson 2001): it calls for two input spaces with a counterfactual connector, such that an element in one space is real, but in the other space its counterpart is not. For example, the *fake* of *fake gun* prompts a mapping between an actual scenario with an agent and an instrument and a counterfactual scenario in which the counterpart of that instrument is a real gun and some other participants, if there are any, react accordingly. In the blend, the reactions and beliefs of other participants are projected from the counterfactual scenario, while the nature of the object and the beliefs of the gunman are projected from the actual scenario.

In the case of *fake flowers* meant to decorate a dining table, there is an input space in which the object is flowers and a space in which it is not because it is, for example, silk or rubber. There is a counterfactual connector between the flowers in one space and the silk or rubber object in the other space. This counterfactual relation is compressed into a property of the object in the blend: it is now a fake flower. Note that there need be no indication that any of the participants believes the object is a flower. It can be treated as a flower, perhaps for aesthetic purposes, by projection from one space and as not a flower by projection from the other space. One might enjoy it but not have to water it. *Fake money* likewise requires two spaces: one in which the object is money and the other in which it is just, for example, paper. There are many possible projections to the blend. For example, the fake money might not be legal currency but still have monetary value since it is issued by a gambling house for in-house use; it cannot be stolen since it can only be redeemed by the in-house cashier. Alternatively, it could be used to fool someone by making them a worthless payment. In that case, the space where it is money is also the belief space of the person fooled, and the space where it is paper is the belief space of the crook. Whether the belief of the crook is shared by the speaker of the utterance depends on overall aspects of the discourse mental space configuration. In (8) it would be shared, but not in (9):

(8)   The crook paid them with fake money.

(9)   The crook thought he was paying them with fake money, but in fact it was the new European currency.

4   Performatives

The general finding that much of language and grammar is devoted to prompting for mapping schemes between mental spaces opens up an interesting way to rethink the key pragmatic questions raised by Austin (1962).

Sweetser (2001) develops a unified and elegant approach to performativity. Her general definition of performativity is that it involves a particular relation of fit between a mental space that is a representation and the corresponding represented space. If the representation is taken as fitting the represented space, then the relation between the spaces is depictive, or representational. It is the success or failure of depictive fit (of representation to world) which is described as *true* or *false, accurate* or *inaccurate.* If, on the other hand, the represented space is taken as fitting (being causally influenced or changed by) the representation, then the relation is performative. Sweetser's account maintains Searle's (1979, 1989) crucial distinctions between using a representation descriptively and using it performatively, and between performing an action by describing it and performing it by other means, but it generalizes the approach to non-linguistic phenomena and reveals that performativity is a special case of compression of vital relations in integration networks.

A non-linguistic example offered by Sweetser (2001) is that of a painting of a buffalo hunt on a cave wall, discovered by archaeologists who know from associated artifacts that the members of the social group that produced the paintings were also buffalo hunters. In the painting, buffalo fall prey to successful hunters: the painting could be depictive (describing a successful past hunt) or performative (made with the intention of bringing about success in a future hunt). (See Searle 1975b for a similar case, the "shopping-list parable.")

In both cases, we have a conceptual integration over two inputs, the mental space of the image and the mental space of the hunt (as it happened or as desired). In the depictive usage, the vital relation of representation is compressed into identity in the blended space. In the performative usage, it is the vital relation of cause–effect that is compressed into identity. These very compressions are widely attested independently of speech act phenomena (Fauconnier and Turner 2002), and so Sweetser's account places Austin's initial observations about performative vs. constative utterances in a significantly broader cognitive and cultural framework.

In particular, as Sweetser (2001) and Sorensen (2000) observe, non-linguistic performative examples abound in ritual and magic. An extreme example is voodoo death, in which manipulation of the representation produces a desired effect in reality. The belief in the efficacy of the conceptual integration network is basic for the community and for the victim, and so the effect of this deeply constitutive way of thinking is that the social body and the physiological body conspire to make the death happen.

Sweetser (2001) also notes that names, like other representations, are susceptible to referential use for either depictive or performative purposes. A name applied to an entity is depictive referentially if the entity is present, but names are also used as invocations or evocations of the named entity. Names of gods, for example, are powerful because they may invoke the presence of the deity. A second kind of performative use of names is the one that establishes a naming convention by using a name or a nickname.

Sweetser generalizes her analysis to include common types of rituals, such as that of a newborn baby being carried up the stairs of its parents' house as part of the celebration of its birth in a European ritual. The ritual is meant, symbolically, to promote the child's chances of rising in life and is supported by a conceptual integration network. One input in the network is the ordinary action of carrying a baby up the stairs. The other input is the schematic space of life, already structured so that living a life is metaphorically moving along a path, such that good fortune is up and misfortune is down. In a partial match between these inputs, the path up the stairs corresponds to the course of life, the baby is the person who will live this life, the manner of motion up the stairs corresponds to how the person goes through life, and so on. In the symbolic ritual, the two inputs are blended so that the ascent of the stairs is the course of life: an easy ascent signifies an easy rise in life for the person that the baby will become, and stumbling or falling might take on extraordinary significance. Vital relations hold within the network: cause–effect (success in climbing the stairs will (help to) cause success in life), part–whole (the ritual itself is a necessary part of the entire life), time (the short time it takes to climb the stairs is mapped onto the much longer time it takes to live a life), change (within the life input, the person will change considerably from birth till death), analogy (through metaphor, "going up" the stairs is similar to "going up" in life). In the blended space, these vital relations are compressed: cause–effect, part–whole, and change are all compressed into uniqueness – the cause (climbing the stairs) **is** the effect (leading a good life), the part (being carried up the stairs) **is** the whole (the entire life), and change becomes uniqueness. The baby doesn't change physically as it is carried up the stairs – there is a unique, unchanging person. Time is scaled down from the duration of life to the time it takes to climb the stairs. Such compressions are the rule in integration networks. The ritual of the newborn baby, although non-linguistic, is both metaphorical and performative.

Much religious ritual, notes Sweetser (2001), is both metaphorical and performative in this sense. The circular shape of a ring metaphorically represents the unending permanence of marriage, but its use in a wedding ceremony is to bring that permanence into social being, not just to describe it. The white dress worn by many Christian brides can metaphorically depict (truly or not) the bride's virgin status, but white ritual garments can also be worn by penitents for purification, thus metaphorically purporting to *bring about* purity, not to describe it. Sorensen (2000), in a similar vein, offers a detailed analysis of Catholic communion, which can be understood as describing spiritual union and also being intended to bring it about.

5 Cognitive Approaches to Some Other Classical Pragmatic Issues

Another topic that played a central role in the healthy development of modern pragmatics is the study of pragmatic scales, stemming from the pioneering work of Horn (1972) and Ducrot (1972). Horn discovered the exceptional importance of pragmatic scales for syntactic and semantic phenomena in language. Ducrot developed an elegant theory of argumentative force to explain a wide range of phenomena, including the meanings of notoriously difficult connectives such as *but*, *however*, French *puisque*, *parce que*, and scalar operators such as English *even*, and French *presque*, *à peine*. Fauconnier (1978b and elsewhere) introduced the powerful concept of implication reversal, proved a weak extension of De Morgan's laws for the general case of implication reversal, and showed that the extended De Morgan's law was one of the keys to a unified understanding of polarity phenomena of different stripes – grammatically entrenched, semantically marked, or pragmatically motivated. In his new book, Israel (to appear) explores the cognitive underpinnings of what he calls the rhetoric of grammar, extends previous analyses of scale reversal in a number of insightful directions, and achieves a unified cognitive semantic account of a broad spectrum of polarity phenomena.

Coulson (2001) is another cognitive scientist who takes pragmatic scales seriously and develops a realistic account of the power and hidden complexity of everyday human reasoning. As she explains early in her book, discourse participants, like paleontologists, "have the task of combining different sorts of information to derive the overall meaning of the discourse event, to exploit their imaginative capacities and derive the life of the organism from its grammatical bones" (2001: xii). Coulson emphasizes that, rather than compiling meanings, people use linguistic information to help them assemble cognitive models of the discourse event. Building pragmatic scales is part of the rhetorical strategies that participants deploy, often unconsciously, in constructing and manipulating cognitive and cultural models relevant to particular discourse events. This is not done **in addition** to the construction of some basic meaning, rather it is a necessary and central aspect of the construction of any meaning. Coulson shows how scales can be linked, forced upon participants, transformed into different scales, or rejected by switching frames and cultural models.

In the past ten years, cognitive linguistics has grown exponentially with findings and analyses that extend far beyond the usual boundaries of linguistics. Applications to many fields of human inquiry include musicology, art, literature, philosophy, political science, theology, and mathematics. To understand how classical pragmatic issues are re-evaluated, readers will want to add to the illustrative examples in the present entry the more general perspectives of seminal work on metaphor theory (Lakoff and Johnson 1999), cognitive semantics (Talmy 2000), cognitive grammar (Langacker 1987, vol. 1), and conceptual integration (Fauconnier and Turner 2002). The exemplary studies of anaphora by Van Hoek (1997), of signed languages by Liddell (1998), and of gesture by McNeill (2000) are also of exceptional importance. Coulson (1994) provides an excellent overview of the relevance of cognitive science to research in pragmatics. Mandelblit and Zachar (1998) explore the notion of dynamic unit in the conceptual developments of recent cognitive science.

The study of pragmatics in the second half of the twentieth century revealed many fascinating aspects of human thought and action that we take for granted in everyday life. We are not inclined to pay much conscious attention to pragmatics in everyday life, or even in the behavioral sciences, because pragmatics is largely part of invisible backstage cognition, with exceptionally sparse formal or symbolic marking. And so it belongs, like Erving Goffman's social framing (Goffman 1974), or Edwin Hutchins's distributed cognition (Hutchins 1995), to the realm of what is obvious and pervasive and yet invisible to its expert users and participants. A contribution of cognitive linguistics in recent years has been to show that this invisibility is a general feature of meaning construction, linguistic or not, pragmatic or not.

30 Pragmatic Aspects of Grammatical Constructions

PAUL KAY

1 Introduction: Constructions and Pragmatics

What do constructional approaches to grammar have to contribute to linguistic pragmatics? A careful answer to this question would require prior specification of which approaches should properly be called "constructional" and also what exactly is intended by "linguistic pragmatics." Conscientiously discharging these preparatory obligations could require a text longer than this chapter, as well as competence exceeding its author's. But a rough and ready answer might go something like this: Constructional approaches to grammar have shown that the interpretation of linguistic utterances can involve an interaction of grammar and context which vastly exceeds in complexity, formal structure and wealth of interpretive content the data discussed in the standard linguistic and philosophical literature on indexicals (pronouns, tenses, and other deictic elements). There are admirable exceptions. For example, Nunberg (1993) cites (1) (from a biology text) to illustrate the point that a referential use of a first person plural pronoun in English normally picks out some set of people, containing the speaker, whose further identity is left to the addressee to infer on the basis of the common conversational background and the rest of the utterance:

(1) *We* do not know much about this part of the brain, which plays such an important role in *our* lives, but *we* will see in the next chapter ...

The first italicized pronoun refers to the set comprised of the writer and other scientists, the second the writer and other humans, and the third the writer and the reader. Nunberg notes that indexicality includes deixis but goes beyond it in two respects. The first of these he calls classification; this includes information like number and gender. While the classificatory aspect of indexicals is generally recognized, little attention has been paid to how the classificatory information is used in identifying the referent. The second and subtler aspect of indexicals treated by Nunberg is the fact that often the entity pointed to by use of an indexical is distinct from the referent of the indexical. In each of the three cases of a first person plural pronoun in (1), the deictic target is the writer but the referent of the pronoun is a distinct set of people (each containing the writer). In general, the item pointed to by an indexical is not necessarily identical to the intended referent. Referential *we* means, roughly, "I and you-know-who else".[1]

A number of grammatical constructions have been described in which part or all of the meaning of the construction is analogous to the "you-know-who" part of the meaning of *we*, a virtual instruction to the addressee to examine the common ground of the conversation (along with the other interpretive content of the sentence) to fill in some partially specified part of the intended interpretation. An example involving the construction employing the expression *let alone* is given in (2):

(2)   Fred won't order shrimp, let alone Louise, squid.

The addressee of an utterance of (2) can only interpret it successfully if he can find in, or construct from, the conversational common ground a set of assumptions according to which Louise's willingness to order squid unilaterally entails Fred's willingness to order shrimp. This kind of background, comprising a matrix of propositions partially ordered by the relation of unilateral entailment, which we call a SCALAR MODEL (Fillmore et al. 1988), is discussed further below. Scalar models illustrate, first, the fact that the notional structures presupposed or imposed by constructions may be unrestricted or partially restricted in content and yet subject to precise formal conditions. For an utterance of (2) to succeed, it may be presupposed that squid is more exotic than shrimp and Louise is less adventurous than Fred, or that squid is less nutritious than shrimp and Louise is more health-conscious than Fred, or that squid is more expensive than shrimp and Louise is stingier than Fred, or . . . Successful interpretation of (2) requires only a presuppositional background in which anyone who will order squid will order shrimp and in which Fred will order anything Louise will order within some contextually determined set of possibilities; further substantive detail is not specified by the construction but it is presupposed to be available to the addressee in context. A distinct but closely related point is that presupposed material may come, not in the form simply of an unstructured set of propositions, but rather a highly structured set. In (2) a third interpretational phenomenon is illustrated as well: the fact that in addition to presupposition[2] the distinct matter of a proposition's being "on the floor" may be a pragmatic requirement of a construction. Felicitous utterance of (2) requires the proposition that Louise order squid to be – not necessarily taken for granted by speaker and addressee – but mutually accepted as having been posed in the conversation, as being on the floor. For example, someone may have just asked if Louise has ordered squid or suggested that she do so. Fillmore et al. call such a proposition a CONTEXT PROPOSITION (CP).

A different kind of contribution of constructional approaches to linguistic pragmatics is the recognition that a wide, perhaps unlimited, variety of illocutionary forces can attach to distinct constructions. A familiar chestnut (3) is discussed by Akmajian (1984) and Lambrecht (1990).

(3) Him be a doctor!?

The special morphosyntax of accusative subject and bare stem verb phrase, paired with a particular intonational contour,[3] is dedicated in this construction to the expression by the speaker of incredulity – or something like that – with regard to some proposition that has just been asserted (or otherwise posed).

Some constructions are devoted to metalinguistic comments, for example metalinguistic negation (Horn 1985) and metalinguistic comparatives, illustrated in (4a) and (4c), respectively.

(4)a. It's not good, but superb.
   b. #It's not good, but it is superb.
   c. He's more negligent than vicious.
   d. He's more negligent than he is vicious.
   e. His negligence exceeds his viciousness.

The metalinguistic negation in (4a) conveys that *superb* would have been a more apt descriptor than *good* in the context of utterance. The oddness of (4b), under the standard assumption that $\text{SUPERB}(x)$ implies $\text{GOOD}(x)$, highlights the fact that the metalinguistic understanding of (4a) is tied directly to its morphosyntactic form; the metalinguistic interpretation does not represent a conversational implicature. Similarly, the fact that (4d) is not a paraphrase of (4c), the former meaning something more like (4e), again points to the conventional relation between the morphosyntactic form of (4c) and its metalinguistic interpretation (that in the context of utterance *negligent* is a more apt predicator than *vicious*).

The final general point to be made about the contributions to pragmatics of constructional approaches to grammar is that a single construction can weave together a number of strands of the distinct interpretational types just listed in complex ways. Our discussion of (2) hinted at this point, which will be developed further below.[4]

This chaper is concerned with exemplifying some of the notional detail regarding all the matters touched on above, but also with displaying how such complex interpretational phenomena can be conventionally associated with a particular morphosyntax – that is, encoded in grammatical constructions, which, by conventionally associating formal and interpretational information, serve as the minimal building blocks of a grammar.[5] Sections 2–5 will take up constructions involving scalar models, non-scalar contextual operators, metalinguistic phenomena, and idiosyncratic illocutionary forces, respectively. Several of the constructions discussed exemplify more than one of these phenomena and some present additional interpretational[6] properties not fitting well into this classfication. Section 6 sums up.

2   Scalar Models

Scalar models represent one formal approach to the general phenomenon of interpretational scales. Seminal research on scalar phenomena within modern linguistics appears in the work of Horn (1972, 1973), Ducrot (1973, 1980), and Fauconnier (1975a, 1975b, 1976). Those early studies have led to a number of approaches to scalar phenomena which will not be covered in this section (e.g. Horn 1989, Hirschberg 1991, Koenig 1991, Lee and Horn 1994). The data to be discussed first involve the *let alone* construction, introduced in example (2); constructions similarly analyzed in terms of scalar models are discussed in Michaelis (1994) for Latin, Israel (1996, 1997, 1998), Kay (1991), and Michaelis (1994) for English, Schwenter (1999b, 2000) for Spanish, and Schwenter and Vasishth (2001) for Spanish and Hindi.

2.1   let alone

A simple *let alone* sentence, e.g. one like (2), repeated below, in which there is a single token of *let alone*, expresses two propositions.

(2)   Fred won't order shrimp, let alone Louise, squid.

In (2) the two propositions are that Fred won't order shrimp and that Louise won't order squid. The initial clause, which I will call the host, contains an overt negative element (*not, nobody,* . . .) or a covert negative element (*doubt, forbid* . . .). The host is followed by a fragment introduced by *let alone*, whose full meaning is restored by semantic copying from the host. In (2) the host is *Fred won't order shrimp*, the fragment is *let alone Louise, squid*, and the restored fragment proposition is that Louise won't order squid. The fragment contains one or more semantic (and prosodic) foci that are contrasted with corresponding foci in the host. Here the fragment foci are *Louise* and *squid*, which contrast with the host foci *Fred* and *shrimp*, respectively. A *let alone* sentence can be analyzed semantically as the conjunction of two negative propositions,[7] each consisting of the application of a single propositional function (here WON'T ORDER) to distinct, contrasting lists of arguments, possibly singleton (here ⟨Fred, shrimp⟩, ⟨Louise, squid⟩).[8] So far, we have as an approximate semantic translation of (2):

(5)   WON'T ORDER(Fred, shrimp) and WON'T ORDER(Louise, squid)

There are two things missing in (5). First is the idea that Fred's not ordering shrimp unilaterally entails (in the context of utterance) Louise's not ordering squid. Translation (5) can thus be improved as:

(6)   WON'T ORDER(Fred, shrimp) a fortiori WON'T ORDER(Louise, squid)

The second thing left out of (5), and (6), does not concern the semantic translation of (2) but rather its discourse status. Specifically, for an utterance of (2) to be felicitous, the fragment proposition, modulo negation and modality, viz. ORDER(Louise, squid), must be a CP.[9]

The combination of the unilateral entailment of the CP by the host or TEXT PROPOSITION (TP) and the fact that the fragment evokes a CP, invites a further interpretation of the discourse function of the *let alone* construction in Gricean terms. A typical conversational situation calling for the *let alone* construction might be something like (7):

(7)   A: Did Louise order squid?
      B: Are you kidding? Fred didn't (even) order shrimp, let alone Louise, squid.

Consider B's situation after A has posed her question. Relevance demands that B answer the question (and Quality that he answer it in the negative): Louise didn't order squid. But this response would not be maximally cooperative because B knows something relevant and equally succinctly expressible that is more informative, namely that Fred didn't order shrimp. Quantity enjoins B to express the more informative proposition. The *let alone* construction functions to reconcile the conflicting demands in situations like this of Relevance and Quantity. It enables the speaker economically to express both propositions in a form that indicates his awareness of the greater informativeness of the proposition answering to Quantity, the TP.

As noted, a scalar model is taken empirically to consist in a presupposed set of interrelated propositions. On the formal side, the nature of a scalar model (SM) can be sketched as follows.[10] One assumes the set of truth values $T = \{0, 1\}$ and a set of states of affairs S. The set F of functions from S to T is interpreted in the standard way as a set of propositions. What is special to a scalar model is the imposition of a particular structure on the set of propositions F. To form F in the desired way, we posit a finite set $D = \{D_1, \ldots, D_n\}$ ($n \geq 1$),[11] each member D_i of which is a set (not necessarily finite) on which a simple order exists. The members D_i of D are interpreted as semantic dimensions. Suppose one dimension is composed of a set of reindeer whose relative jumping abilities are established and another dimension is a set of obstacles whose relative heights are known. Since all our information is relative, we don't know whether any particular reindeer can jump any particular obstacle. We do know, however, a host of conditional facts. For example, we know that for any obstacle b, if *Rudolph*, a poor jumper, can jump b, *Prancer*, a good jumper, can jump b, and we also know that for any reindeer r, if r can clear a challenging obstacle like the *fence*, then r can clear a less challenging obstacle like the *bush*.

We are interested next in the Cartesian product of the members of D, i.e. the set of n-tuples the i_{th} member of which is a member of the i_{th} semantic dimension. We call this Cartesian product an ARGUMENT SPACE and represent it D_x. In the jumping reindeer example, D_x represents the set of all ordered pairs of which the first member is a reindeer and the second member is an obstacle.

Without loss of generality, we may think of the ordering of each semantic dimension D_i as being assigned so that the n-tuple consisting of the lowest numbered member of each semantic dimension is that point **o** in D_x such that for any state of affairs if the proposition corresponding to any point in D_x is true then the proposition corresponding to **o** is true. This unique point of the argument space is called the ORIGIN of D_x. In our example, the origin is the point that pairs the most athletic reindeer with the least challenging obstacle. We now define a propositional function P whose domain is D_x and whose range is F. In our example, P is a function from ⟨reindeer, obstacle⟩ pairs, e.g. ⟨Prancer, fence⟩, to propositions, e.g. CAN-JUMP(Prancer, fence), taking the propositional function P to be CAN-JUMP(x, y).

To capture the scalar property, we need now to constrain P appropriately. It is convenient first to define a binary relation on members of D_x. Given two members d_i, d_j of D_x, d_i is LOWER or equivalently CLOSER TO THE ORIGIN than d_j iff d_i has a lower value than d_j on at least one semantic dimension and a higher value than d_j on no semantic dimension. P is then constrained as follows:

(8)   For distinct d_i, d_j in D_x, $P(d_i)$ entails $P(_j)$ iff d_j is lower than d_i.[12]

We now define SCALAR MODEL as follows:

(9)   A four-tuple SM = ⟨S, T, D_x, P⟩ is a scalar model iff SM satisfies (8).

Further empirical justification for the full scalar model formulation comes from the observation that simple unilateral entailment of the CP by the TP does not justify use of *let alone*. The use of *let alone* in a sentence like (10) is distinctly odd, even though not having an odd number of books unilaterally entails not having 75 books.

(10)   #She doesn't have an odd number of books, let alone 75.

Consider now the context of a raffle in which every odd-numbered ticket wins at least a token prize and number 75 wins the grand prize.

(11)   She didn't get an odd-numbered ticket, let alone 75.

In the context of (11), since the foci "odd number" and "75" can be interpreted as points on the dimension size of prize in a scalar model, the oddness of (10) disappears. This example also exemplifies further the degree to which successful employment of scalar model constructions depends on the contextual inferencing abilities of the addressee. The size of prize dimension is not given by English grammar and lexicon; it is dependent on the particular raffle context.

A final observation on the *let alone* construction concerns a syntactic property that appears unique to this particular form of syntactic coordination (or subordination?). All the sentences in (12) are paraphrases of each other.

(12)a. You couldn't get a poor man to wash your car for $10 let alone a rich man to wax your truck for $5.
  b. You couldn't get a poor man to wash your car, let alone a rich man to wax your truck, for $10, let alone for $5.
  c. You couldn't get a poor man, let alone a rich man, to wash your car for $10, let alone wax your truck for $5.
  d. You couldn't get a poor man, let alone a rich man, to wash, let alone (to) wax, your car, let alone (your) truck, for $10, let alone (for) $5.

These four sentences are but a proper subset of the set of paraphrases of (12a) that can be constructed roughly as follows:

1. Starting from the left, place a token of *let alone* after any number of foci.
2. Move over from the fragment the stretch containing the corresponding foci (allowing certain "deletions" of otherwise repeated material).
3. Starting from the right end of what you have moved over, repeat step (1) if any of the fragment remains.

The combination of this extraordinary syntactic property[13] of the *let alone* conjunction and its pragmatics-intensive, scalar-model character of the interpretation of *let alone* sentences illustrates how much pragmatics can be built into the atomic elements of the grammar, i.e. the maximal grammatical constructions.

2.2   at least

The English expression *at least* corresponds to at least three distinct scalar modifiers. The first of these, simple scalar *at least*, is illustrated in the preceding sentence, as well as in (13):

(13)a. She has invited at least Sarah and James [if not others].
  b. At least five students passed [if not more than five].
  c. He'll be at least irritated [if not outraged].
  d. He's at least slightly depressed [if not seriously so].
  e. That will at least damage it [if not ruin it altogether].

In each case, *at least* modifies the focus of a sentence to be interpreted in a scalar model. In examples (13a–e), that focus is expressed as an NP, a QP, an AP, an ADVP, and a VP, respectively. We can think of simple scalar *at least* in all these cases as canceling the upper-bounding conversational implicature of a scalar predicate.[14] Another way to think about simple scalar *least* is to say that *at least* XP denotes the interval lower-bounded by the (possibly pragmatically inferred) intension of XP in a scalar model.[15]

Another *at least* construction, with different syntactic as well as interpretive properties, is illustrated in (14c, d):

(14)a. In that big trainwreck at least several people were saved.
   b. In that big trainwreck at least several people were killed.
   c. At least in that big trainwreck several people were saved.
   d. At least in that big trainwreck several people were killed.

Example (14d) requires an unusual presupposition, roughly that both speaker and addressee think it's good for people to be killed. Evaluative *at least*, which occurs unambiguously in (14c) and (14d), can occur initially and at a distance from the phrase in its scope, while simple scalar *at least* cannot.[16] Example (14d) cannot have the interpretation of (14b), even though normal background assumptions would conduce strongly to such an interpretation. Similarly (14c) does not share a reading with (14b). Again we see distinct peculiarities of interpretation – which would ordinarily be called pragmatic – conventionally attached to specific syntactic patterns.

From a scalar-model perspective, evaluative *at least* is interesting because it requires two context propositions, one denoting an event less desirable than the event denoted by the TP and one denoting a more desirable event. Often these will be furnished by accommodation. Example (15b) might be used to evoke the full interpretation of (15a):

(15)a. Well, I didn't get an A, but I didn't do too badly either. At least I got an A–.
   b. At least I got an A–.

The examples in (16) illustrate a third use of *at least*, which has been christened "rhetorical retreat" *at least*.[17]

(16)a. Mary is at home – at least John's car is in the driveway.
   b. Mary is at home – at least I think so.
   c. Mary is at home – at least that's what Sue said.
   d. Mary will help me – at least {on the first draft, if it doesn't rain, when I've finished the outline, . . . }   (examples from Kay 1992)

It is difficult to characterize with precision the illocutionary force, or other interpretive function, of rhetorical retreat *at least*. One wants to say that a sentence employing an adjunct introduced by this *at least* is somehow weaker or less forceful than the sentence would be without the adjunct, but it is difficult to specify just what one means here by "weaker" or "less forceful."[18]

Rhetorical retreat *at least* does not appear to be scalar in any straightforward way, but perhaps that observation reflects nothing more than our ignorance regarding the interpretational function of this expression. Simple scalar and evaluative *at least* are both scalar. There are, however, several differences, as we have seen. While simple scalar *at least* denotes an open interval on a dimension of a scalar model, evaluative *at least* appears to denote a point (or closed interval) between the two CPs. Simple scalar *at least* does not seem to carry with it any context proposition requirement; evaluative *at least* requires two CPs. The scale evoked by evaluative *at least* is, of course, one of assumed speaker and addressee attitude toward the events denoted, not one constituted by these events themselves, as is the case with simple scalar *at least* and most constructions evoking scalar models.

3 Non-Scalar Contextual Operators (NSCOs)

Expressions such as *let alone, even,* and *at least* constitute contextual operators of a specific type, namely scalar contextual operators. They require that any sentence in which they occur be interpreted in a contextually situated scalar model. Moreover, they specify the structural position that the interpretation of the sentence in which they occur will occupy in that scalar model. Characteristically, if not necessarily, much of the substantive material of the scalar model will be furnished by the common ground of the conversation. There are also contextual operators that place contextually analogous but non-scalar formal requirements on the common ground. Three examples are *respective, respectively,* and *vice versa*.[19]

In addition to the scalar/non-scalar difference, the two types of contextual operator provide a further contrast. While the scalar model requirement of the former operators pertains to the presuppositional aspect of the interpretation of a sentence, the NSCOs we will consider here affect a sentence's truth conditions. An utterance of (17) will be true just in case Mary collects neither Norwegian pottery nor Austrian prints and it is possible for speaker and addressee to agree in addition on a background scalar model in which anyone who collects Austrian prints collects Norwegian pottery.

(17) Mary doesn't collect Norwegian pottery, let alone Austrian prints.

If the scalar model background is not available, an utterance of (17) will suffer presupposition failure no matter what Mary does or doesn't collect. On the other hand, *respective* and *respectively* directly affect the truth conditions of the sentences in which they occur.

(18)a. Mr. Smith and Mr. Jones love Mrs. Jones and Mrs. Smith, respectively.
   b. Mr. Smith loves Mrs. Jones and Mr. Jones loves Mrs. Smith.
   c. Mr. Smith and Mr. Jones love their respective wives.
   d. Mr. Smith loves Mrs. Smith and Mr. Jones loves Mrs. Jones.

Sentence (18a) has the truth conditions of (18b), not those of (18d). Sentence (18c) has the truth conditions of (18d), not (18b).

Although the difference between *respective* and *respectively* may at first appear to be only a matter of morphology and syntax, there are interpretational differences as well. What these NSCOs have in common is that both can evoke a 1–1 mapping between two sets and distribute some predicate over the members of that mapping. In both (18a) and (18c), the sets are {Mr. Jones, Mr. Smith} and {Mrs. Jones, Mrs. Smith}. In both (18a) and (18c) the predicate is LOVE. In (18a) the mapping is {⟨Mr. Jones, Mrs. Smith⟩, ⟨Mr. Smith, Mrs. Jones⟩}; in (18c) the mapping is {⟨Mr. Jones, Mrs. Jones⟩, ⟨Mr. Smith, Mrs. Smith⟩}. So much for the common interpretational properties of *respective* and *respectively*. The difference is that in the case of *respectively* the mapping must be based on an independent linear ranking of the two sets. In (18a) the ranking principle is a metalinguistic one: order of mention. Mr. Jones is mentioned before Mr. Smith and Mrs. Smith is mentioned before Mrs. Jones. But this need not be the case; the ordering principle may be either metalinguistic, viz. order of mention, or purely conceptual, as in (19)

(19)a.   The three brightest students scored 95, 99, and 96, respectively.
   b.   Clarence, Florence, and Terrence got the three highest grades, respectively.
   c.   The three brightest students got the three highest grades, respectively.

In (19a) the subject NP is ordered conceptually, not metalinguistically, while the complement NP is ordered metalinguistically – and in a way that violates an available conceptual ordering. In (19b) the subject NP is ordered meta-linguistically and the complement NP is ordered conceptually. In (19c) both orderings are conceptual. The fact that *respectively* requires independent linear orderings but accepts either metalinguistic (order of mention) or conceptual orderings – even in the same sentence – illustrates the potential of grammatical constructions to mix and match pragmatic and semantic properties in quite idiosyncratic ways.[20]

When *respective* distributes a predicate it does not require any independent linear ordering of the sets constituting the mapping over which the predicate is distributed:

(20)a.   Many senators represent their respective states well.
   b.   *Many senators represent their states well, respectively.
   c.   Senators Jones and Smith represent their respective states well.
   d.   *Senators Jones and Smith represent their states well, respectively.

Unacceptable examples (20b) and (20d) show that *respectively* requires linear ordering, and does not merely permit it.[21] This ordering, however, may rely heavily on mutual background knowledge. If one knows that in horse racing the expression *finish in the money* means to come in either first, second, or third, winning a decreasing amount of money with lateness of finish, a sentence like (21a) is readily interpretable. We know that Augustus won, and so on.

(21)a.   The horses finishing in the money were Augustus, Brutus, and Cassius, respectively.
   b.   *The horses finishing out of the money were Xerxes, Yerkes, and Zippo, respectively.

Sentence (21b) is acceptable to no one, including those to whom the expression *finish out of the money* is familiar, since the finishing order of the horses who finish out of the money is not accorded any conventional significance.[22]

Respective often occurs in a noun phrase determined by a possessive pronoun, and, curiously, is often otiose in that context. Thus (22a) and (22b) are substitutable for (20a) and (20c), respectively, *salva veritate*.

(22)a.   Many senators represent their states well.
   b.   Senators Jones and Smith represent their states well.

The contextual character of the possessive construction (Kay and Zimmer 1976) seems to render the contextual job done by *respective* unnecessary in such cases.

It appears that when independent linear orderings of the sets constituting the mapping over which a predicate is to be distributed are available, *respective* is dispreferred, and perhaps for some speakers ungrammatical.

(23)   ??Clarence, Florence, and Terrence got the respective scores of 95, 99, and 96.

However, there appear to be some cases illustrating crucial linear rankings where *respective* is relatively acceptable, as in (24b).

(24)a.   Billy Martin and Tony La Russa are known for their volatility and charm, respectively.
   b.   ?Billy Martin and Tony La Russa are known for their respective volatility and charm.[23]

For speakers for whom (24)b is unexceptionable, one cannot say that *respective* requires that the mapping over which it distributes a predicate must not be based on a linear ranking of the sets being matched.

Respective, as indicated above, also has a non-distributive use. An attested example of this usage is:

(25)   Twelve generals and admirals from the United States, the Soviet Union and their respective allies . . . met for two days of discussions. (*New York Times*)

No predicate is distributed over the set of ordered pairs {⟨US, US allies⟩, ⟨USSR, USSR allies⟩}. Similarly in (26), no predicate is distributed over a relation pairing rock stars with entourages.

(26)   Two rock stars and their respective entourages can fill a small stadium.

In cases like (25) and (26) it appears that *respective* simply functions to denote a set of sets by naming, for each member set, an individual who stands in a certain constant, contextually determined relation to that set.

Vice versa has been said to interchange a pair of noun phrases (Fraser 1970) or "elements of [a] clause" (McCawley 1970). Presumably it was the denotata of these expressions that those authors had in mind as being interchanged. This emendation does not go far enough, however, because the items interchanged by *vice versa* are elements of a contextually determined interpretation, not necessarily denotata of linguistic expressions. The evidence for this claim lies in the observation that *vice versa* can be parasitic on a number of contextually determined disambiguations of potential ambiguities. One of these is the mapping induced by *respective*:

(27)   The secretaries emailed their respective mayors.

For (27), the mayors in question could be either the mayors of the towns where the secretaries live or the employers of the secretaries (or they might bear less obvious relations to the secretaries in other contexts). The interpetation of *vice versa* in a sentence like (28) will depend on the contextual diambiguation of (27).

(28)   The secretaries emailed their respective mayors, and vice versa.

In an utterance of (28), each secretary who sent email to a mayor is asserted to have received email from that mayor, whether the secretary for each mayor was picked out as an employee, a constituent, or by some other criterion.

Similarly, the interpretation of *vice versa* can depend on the prior, contextually determined decision whether a pronoun is given a bound variable or an anaphoric interpretation. In (29) *his* may be bound by *every boy* or it may refer anaphorically to a particular boy mentioned earlier:

(29)   [Every boy]$_i$ loves his$_{i,j}$ mother.

In (30) the interpretation of *vice versa* depends on the decision made with respect to the ambiguity of (29):

(30)   Every boy loves his mother, and vice versa.

On the bound variable reading each mother–son pair enjoys mutual love. On the anaphoric reading, there is one lucky mother and she shares mutual love with every boy.

Resolution of *vice versa* can also depend on an ambiguity based on anaphora of sense versus anaphora of reference.

(31) The Joneses don't like their next-door neighbors, but we do, and vice versa.

Depending on anaphora of sense or reference, an utterance of (31) says either that we like our neighbors or that we like the Jones's neighbors. Depending on whose neighbors it is determined contextually that we like, those people are claimed, by *vice versa*, to like us. Again the interpretation of *vice versa* is dependent on contextual disambiguation of a sentential ambiguity.

Neither *respective, respectively*, nor *vice versa* is indexical *sensu strictu*. None of these contextual operators point deictically to a participant or aspect of the utterance situation, as pronouns and tenses do. However, the processes that take indexicality beyond deixis, particularly the you-know-who-else kind of process operating in Nunberg's analysis of *we*, seem to be evoked by these operators. Whereas *we* is a true indexical, in which deixis gives the initial clue to the addressee for finding the referent, in these contextual operators there is no deixis, but instead other kinds of virtual instructions are given to the addressee regarding how to interrogate the common ground to find underspecified referents. We might call this kind of contextuality "indexicality without deixis," or, if that seems oxymoronic, we can call it more longwindedly a kind of grammatical pragmatics closely akin to indexicality but in which the constant character of the operator is not based on deixis but rather specifies some formal aspect of the relation between the context and the interpretation of an utterance.

4 Metalinguistic Constructions

Probably the best-known work on metalinguistic constructions deals with metalinguistic negation. Horn (1985) showed that the family of problems posed by the so-called "external negation" of a sentence like (32)

(32) The King of France is not bald . . . because there is no King of France.

cannot be dealt with satisfactorily either by defining natural language negation as a single propositional operator of great generality or by positing two distinct propositional negations for English (and for many other languages that operate in the relevant respects just like English).[24] The basic empirical evidence presented by Horn for the thesis that the negation in (32) is metalinguistic, not descriptive (i.e. propositional), comes from facts like those in (33), which show that the same metalinguistic negation that answers to presupposition failure in (32) answers to Quantity implicature cancelation, faulty pronunciation, disagreement regarding inflectional morphology, and register conflicts in (33a–d), respectively – more generally, to rejection and correction of a previous utterance for virtually any reason.

(33)a.   This is not tasty, it's delicious.
   b.   Her name's not [ændrij'], it's [andreèj'].
   c.   We're not dealing with a rare phenomena here, we're dealing with a rare phenomenon.
   d.   Your Aunt May is not taking a pee, she's going to the bathroom.

Metalinguistic negation is interesting from a constructional point of view because it has both the interpretational properties just mentioned and also idiosyncratic morphosyntactic properties. Horn points out that metalinguistic negation does not act as a negative polarity trigger, as illustrated in (34a). Not surprisingly, positive polarity items can occur in the scope of a metalinguistic negation (cf. 34b).

(34)a.   John didn't manage to solve *ANY/SOME of the problems, he managed to solve ALL of them.   (Horn 1985: 135)
   b.   I wouldn't RATHER walk, but I'm WILLING to.

It may reasonably be objected that polarity sensitivity is fundamentally a semantic property and only derivatively a syntactic one. There are, however, indisputably non-interpretational properties of metalinguistic negation. Horn observes that metalinguistic negation is not possible with incorporated negation, offering examples similar to (35):

(35)a.   That's *IMPOSSIBLE/NOT POSSIBLE, it's CERTAIN.
   b.   She's *UNLIKELY/NOT LIKELY to help you, she's BOUND to.

All of the metalinguistic negation examples Horn presents consist of two clauses or a clause and a fragment, the second clause (or fragment) providing a correction to the objectionable aspect of what is metalinguistically negated in the first clause. Horn does not say that such an overt rectification clause or fragment is required and in fact it may not be strictly required in cases where the rectification can be readily inferred.

(36)a.   ?He didn't break A FEW bottles. [intended inference: He broke many.]
   b.   He didn't break only/just A FEW bottles. [entailment: He broke many.]

Greater intonational support is required for (36a) to pass muster than (36b), but to the extent that (36a) is acceptable to express a metalinguistic negation, the construction imposes no requirement for an overt rectification clause or phrase. Sentence (36b) entails the rectification of (36a) and does not express a metalinguistic negation. So far as can be determined from examples like these, it is not possible to say with assurance whether or not an overt rectification clause or fragment is a morphosyntactic requirement of metalinguistic negation. What we can say with assurance is that a rectification or correction is a necessary part of the interpretation of the metalinguistic negation construction and that the rectification is usually, if not always, realized in an overt phrase or clause.

Horn observes a further morphosyntactic restriction on overt rectifications. The rectification can be introduced by *but*, and it can consist of a full finite clause, but it cannot both be introduced by *but* and consist of a full finite clause:

(37)a. It isn't hot, but scalding.
   b. It isn't hot – it's scalding.
   c. #It isn't hot, but it's scalding.[25]

We made an analogous observation with respect to the metalinguistic comparative in connection with the examples in (4).[26]

Horn discusses related metalinguistic use of logical operators, specifically disjunction, conditionals, and echo questions. As with negation, these metalinguistic constructions impose their own morphosyntactic signatures. Metalinguistic *or* rejects *either* (38); metalinguistic *if* rejects *then* (39); and echo questions, which exhibit a metalinguistic use of *wh*-words, neither front nor trigger inversion in main clauses (40):

(38)a. It may be hot, or scalding.
   b. #It may be either hot or scalding.

(39)a. If you're looking for a gas station, there's one around that corner.
   b. #If you're looking for a gas station, then there's one around that corner.

(40)   You spilled WHAT in my laptop?

A different kind of metalinguistic construction involves the grammar and interpretation of elements of the type originally termed *hedges* by Lakoff (1972), such as *strictly speaking, loosely speaking, technically,* and *kinda* (equivalently *kind of, sort of, sorta*).

> A hedged sentence, when uttered, often contains a comment on itself or on its utterance or on some part thereof. For example, when someone says, *Loosely speaking France is hexagonal,* part of what they have uttered is a certain kind of comment on the locution *France is hexagonal.* In this sort of metalinguistic comment, the words that are the subject of the comment occur both in their familiar role as part of the linguistic stream and in a theoretically unfamiliar role as part of the world the utterance is about. (Kay 1983: 129)

That paper argues further that certain metalinguistic operators tend to blur the boundary between knowledge of language and world knowledge. The point is not that we have folk knowledge (or beliefs) about language – no news there. The observation of interest is that when knowledge or belief about language is part of the interpretational potential of hedging constructions, it can happen that that conceptual material:

> becomes part of the combinatorial semantics of the sentence and utterance in which it occurs. A familiar (if probably vacuous) combinatorial semantic rule is (SR). If adjective *a* denotes a class A and noun *n* denotes a class N, then the denotation of the expression *an* is the intersection of the classes A and N. . . . the notion "loose speech" is part of the combinatorial semantics of sentences containing the expression *loosely speaking* in the same way in which the notion of class intersection is . . . part of the combinatorial semantics of an expression like *red chair*. (Kay 1984: 134)[27]

Assume (41a) to be spoken by anthropologist A. A may have decided to hedge the bald statement (41b) with *loosely speaking* for strikingly diverse reasons.

(41)a. A: Loosely speaking, the first human beings lived in Kenya.
  b. The first human beings lived in Kenya.

As a believer in gradual evolution, A may consider the expression *the first human beings* to be, strictly speaking, incoherent. Independently, A may consider that only a locution such as *the first human beings **known to science*** can be employed in this context by a careful speaker. Or it could be the approximate nature of Kenya as a location for the first humans that leads A to hedge. Or perhaps instead (or in addition) A is worried about using a modern political label to name a region that wasn't called Kenya, or probably anything else, at the time. What can the semantic value of *loosely speaking* be, which allows this expression to solicit absolution for such diverse locutional sins? It appears that *loosely speaking*, and its cousin, *strictly speaking*, are both based on a schematization or folk theory of language according to which words have inherent fit, because of their intensions or senses, to objects in the world and the meanings of words are combined according to rules of the language. When the words fit the facts and the rules are followed, one speaks strictly. Otherwise one speaks loosely. This view is, in shorthand, a folk version of the Fregean view, especially Frege's theory of reference, according to which a word refers via its intension or sense (*Sinn*).

A distinct, if not competing, philosophical theory of reference makes no use of the concept of intension or sense. This theory, associated primarily with the philosophers Kripke (1972) and Putnam (1975), holds that (some) words refer as a result of a two-stage process. There is an original act of baptism – the prototype is the naming of a person – and then through a series of causal events the association of the thing and the name is passed from speaker to speaker. When the process functions imperfectly – for example when we find ourselves unsure whether what we are holding in our hand really is gold – we can have recourse, according to Putnam, to a "linguistic division of labor," according to which certain individuals have become official keepers of the diagnostic flame, in this case, say, the proprietor of a jewelry store or an officer of the Federal Bureau of Standards. So *gold* means the stuff originally baptized *gold*, and which we can take a putative sample of to an accredited expert for authentication if necessary.

A folk theory that seems to correspond rather well to the Kripke–Putnam theory of reference is evoked by the locutions *technically* or *technically speaking*. When we say *Technically, a whale is a mammal*, we mean that whatever we ordinary folk may say, those scientists with a right to so stipulate have decreed that whales are mammals. Minimal pairs like those in (42) and (43) illustrate the point:

(42) a. Technically, that's a rodent. (order *Rodentia*)
    b. *Technically, that's a varmint.

(43) a. Technically, that's an insect. (order *Insecta*)
    b. *Technically, that's a bug.

Rodent and *insect* are technical terms, terms of art of socially recognized experts. *Varmint* and *bug* are not.[28]

The long stories about the notional values of *loosely speaking, strictly speaking*, and *technically (speaking)* briefly sketched above show that complex substantive beliefs about language or speech can furnish the basis of a hedging, or other metalinguistic, construction. This fact is significant because metalinguistic constructions don't merely effect incidental comments on the passing linguistic show. Employment by a speaker of a metalinguistic construction also helps constitute the message being commented on. For example, hedges can affect truth conditions. Against a shared background in which Sacco and Vanzetti were unjustly convicted (44a) is true and (44b) is false.[29]

(44) a. Technically, Sacco and Vanzetti were murderers.
    b. Strictly speaking, Sacco and Vanzetti were murderers.

While the metalinguistic hedges we have considered so far, *loosely speaking, strictly speaking*, and *technically (speaking)*, appear to behave syntactically like garden variety sentence adverbs, their cousins *kinda* and *sorta* have a syntax all their own. In particular, these items may appear as modifiers of any projection of any major lexical category. Examples with lexical nouns, adjectives, and verbs are commonplace:

(45) a. It's got a sorta halo over it.
    b. It was very kinda blustery that day. [Speaker's intent: The weather was extreme in a certain respect that day, but I'm somewhat hesitant to use the word *blustery* to decribe that respect, although I can't really think of a better word.]
    c. He was kinda ELECTED the hereditary ruler.

Attested examples (46a, b, c) illustrate modifications of a maximal NP, AP, and VP, respectively.[30]

(46)a. Crete is sort of an island.
  b. All the papers were kinda really interesting.
  c. I kinda have to get going now, because . . .

In (47) *sorta* modifies a non-maximal nominal phrase:

(47)   Marvin's a [sorta [self-made straw man]].

Various possibilities with other categories and levels of projection are shown in examples (48):

(48)a. He distributed the grapes kinda amongst the mangoes.
  b. while singing kinda in between the notes . . .
  c. Sort of all over the world, reports kept cropping up.
  d. She did it very kinda unfalteringly.
  e. It began to shake kinda very jerkily.
  f. I wonder sorta how many of the people he thinks he can fool how much of the time.
  g. Kinda twist it over the flange and under the casing.
  h. In trying kinda to outdo herself . . .

In (48a, b) the hedge forms a constituent with a preposition, in (48c) with a preposition phrase, in (d) with an adverb, in (e) with an adverb phrase, and in (f), (g), and (h) with a clause or sentence.[31]

5   Illocutionary Forces and Related Speaker Attitudes

According to a standard view – or perhaps a burlesque version of a standard view – there are three basic illocutionary forces, corresponding to the declarative, interrogative, and imperative syntactic modes, plus forces imposed by the semantics of the main verb in an explicitly performative sentence, as in (49a, b).[32]

(49)a. I (hereby) appoint you Assistant Principal of George Walker Shrub Elementary School.
  b. This court (hereby) finds in favor of the plaintiff.

Without trying to draw too fine a line between illocutionary force *sensu strictu* and closely related aspects of a speaker's attitude toward the content of his speech, we can recognize many cases in which a particular force or attitude is associated by grammatical convention with overt linguistic form. We have already considered the morphosyntax and force of the incredulity construction illustrated in (3), repeated below:

(3)   Him be a doctor!?

Sometimes the special forces attached to a particular grammatical form are quite difficult to describe, although immediately recognizable. A sentence like (50), said when picking up a tray laden with glasses and bottles, illustrates one such construction:

(50)   Watch me drop this:

Such a sentence does not have imperative force, the speaker doesn't really ask the addressee to watch anything. The force has been described as "conjuring fate, among other things, although what that means exactly and whether it is correct are both open questions."[33] Appearances to the contrary notwithstanding, the construction illustrated by (50), whose syntax is sketched in (51), is not an imperative morphosyntactically, either:

(51)   *Watch* NP[ACC] VP[BARE STEM]

The NP in this construction is not the object of the transitive verb *watch*. A second person object of a transitive imperative verb is realized with a reflexive pronoun, as illustrated in (52):

(52)   [Look in the mirror.] Now, when I tell you this joke watch yourself/*you blush.

In the *Watch* NP VP construction, however, a second person postverbal NP is realized with a free pronoun:

(53)   [I've finally taught you a proper backhand.] Now, watch *yourself/you beat me.[34]

Sometimes, straightforward syntactic process, which are normally associated with their own rules of semantic composition, are combined in a construction whose semantics is not that predicted from the separate syntaxes. In such a case, one must posit a new construction. Negative questions provide an example of this phenomenon. Thus, (54b) does not provide a paraphrase for (54a).

(54)a.   Didn't Fido eat the pizza?
    b.   Did Fido fail to eat the pizza?

Tagged question constructions can be classified into four types,[35] each, seemingly, with its particular force.[36] We can first distinguish same (semantic) polarity tags from opposite polarity tags. There are two subtypes of same polarity tags: positive same polarity tags and "fake negative" tags. Positive same polarity tags have positive semantic and syntactic polarity in both host and tag[37] and are pronounced with rising intonation.[38]

(55)a.   Fido ate the pizza, did he?
   b.   *Fido didn't eat the pizza, didn't he?

With regard to illocutionary force: "Same polarity tags are attached to sentences that the speaker is not putting forward as his own but is 'citing in order to ask the listener if it is his'" (McCawley 1988: 480, citing Cattell 1973). They can appear in utterances conveying either belligerence or docility:

(56)a.   So John has washed dishes, has he? Well I know for a fact that he hasn't.
      (McCawley 1988: 480)
   b.   Lucy can play the viola, can she? I didn't know that.   (McCawley 1988: 480)

McCawley also describes what he calls "fake negative" tags. These superficially have negation in the host (and not in the tag), but the host is nonetheless a positive polarity environment. Fake negative tagged sentences have a characteristic intonational contour with a falling tone at the end of the host (indicated by '\') and rising tone on the tag (indicated by '/').

(57)a.   You wouldn't rather go to the \movies, /would you?
   b.   *I wouldn't rather go to the movies.
   c.   *You wouldn't prefer to give me \a red cent, /would you?
   d.   You wouldn't prefer to give me \a penny, /would you?

Sentence (57a) represents a successful fake negative tag construct, containing the positive polarity item *rather*, whose positive polarity property is demonstrated in (57b). We might say that the force of sentences like (57a) is that of a timid suggestion: "Would you consider going to movies, instead?" Examples (57c) and (57d) show that the negative polarity item *a red cent* is not permissible in this construction, while the polarity neutral expression *a penny* is.

Opposite polarity tags are more straightforward in that morphosyntactic polarity always matches semantic polarity. The polarity of the host is part of the semantics of the proposition being asserted (or otherwise conveyed). Intonation on the tag, rising (/) or falling (\) affects illocutionary force.

(58)a.   They got caught, didn't they.   pol +   tone \
   b.   They got caught, didn't they?   pol +   tone /
   c.   They didn't get caught, did they.   pol −   tone \
   d.   They didn't get caught, did they?   pol −   tone /

Falling intonation polarity reversal tags (58a, c) seem to contribute a force akin to that of negative questions, perhaps expressing even greater confidence: "I think p is the case, but please confirm." Rising intonation polarity reversal tags (58b, d) sound less assertive. Thus, falling intonation tags are more fluently followed by "I told you so!," rising intonation tags by "I've been wondering."[39]

There are many constructions, like the one illustrated in (59), which combine a special force with a rich presuppositional background:

(59)a.   Sing away!
   b.   Talk away!
   c.   Eat away!

The morphosyntax of the construction illustrated in (59) is schematized in (60):

(60)   V[BARE STEM, – DIRECTIONAL] *away!*

The presuppositional background includes the idea that the addressee wishes to perform the action denoted by the verb but requires the speaker's permission to do so and the illocutionary force is that of granting this permission.

We have been considering examples where force is tied directly to morphosyntax. There are also cases, originally noted in Morgan (1978), where the illocutionary force, or other interpretational information, is conventionally associated with making a statement or asking a question of a very broadly defined type. For example, "it is more or less conventional to challenge the wisdom of a suggested course of action by questioning the mental health of the suggestor, by any appropriate linguistic means" (Morgan 1978: 277):

(61)a.   Are you crazy?   Morgan (1978: 277)
   b.   Have you lost your mind?   Morgan (1978: 278)
   c.   Are you out of your gourd? Morgan (1978: 278)
   d.   Is he out of his gourd?
   e.   Is that woman out of her gourd?

Morgan develops the useful concept of short-circuited implicature (SCI). Sometimes expressions of a certain form (e.g. [*Can you* VP?] in (62a)) that start out by conversationally implicating a certain kind of proposition (e.g. 62b) come over time to convey directly their erstwhile implicatum:

(62)a.   Can you pass the salt?
   b.   [Please] pass the salt.

In such cases, the association has become a construction. The construction can remain exclusively interpretational, lacking idiosyncratic pecularities of morphosyntax, as is the case with the construction exemplified in (61). Morgan (1978: 269ff.) termed that kind of strictly interpretational construction a *convention of usage*, following Searle (1975). Morgan makes the further point that over time interpretational constructions (conventions of usage) often become grammaticalized. Such is the case with the construction illustrated in (62). This construction allows preverbal *please*, a characteristic of direct, but not indirect, requests (cf. Sadock, this volume).

(63)a.   Can you please pass the salt?
   b.   *Are you able to please pass the salt.

The SCI of (62) and (63a) has become fully grammaticalized, having acquired its own morphosyntactic signature.

6   Conclusion

The purpose of this chapter has been to illustrate the remarkable diversity of ways in which pragmatic information of various types can be directly associated with linguistic form in irreducible grammatical constructions – that is, constructions whose form cannot be produced by combining smaller units of the grammar according to general principles.[40] I have presented these examples in terms of a rough, heuristic classification of types of pragmatic information: scalar models, non-scalar contextual operators, metalinguistic phenomena, and illocutionary forces. (The classification was created exclusively for the practical purpose of organizing this chapter.)

   If the reader were to go away with a single observation from this highly selective survey, perhaps the most characteristic one would be that made in connection with (19), repeated below for convenience:

(19)a.   The three brightest students scored 95, 99, and 96, respectively.
   b.   Clarence, Florence, and Terrence got the three highest grades, respectively.
   c.   The three brightest students got the three highest grades, respectively.

We saw in these examples that within a single sentence the linear ordering of argument sets required by *respectively* can be both metalinguistic (order of mention, e.g. *Clarence, Florence, and Terrence*) or conceptual (e.g. *the three highest grades*). That a single construction can mix diverse types of pragmatic information under a single formal constraint in this way suggests that we have almost everything to learn about the ways pragmatic information is incorporated into grammatical constructions.

NOTES

1   There is also a bound variable use of *we*. Nunberg (1993) adapts an example from Partee (1989):

>   (i)   Whenever a pianist comes to visit, we play duets.

In this case, the "I" part of the reference is constant, and the remainder of the set containing the speaker is specified by the language of the sentence to be, on each occasion, the visiting pianist.

2   "An utterance U presupposes P . . . iff one can reasonably infer from U that the speaker . . . accepts P and regards it as uncontroversial . . ." (Soames 1982: 486).

3   Roughly, the same as that of a yes/no question with subject focus, like

>   (i)   Did yóu catch that fish?

4   An important pragmatic aspect of grammatical constructions, namely information flow (involving notions like topic, focus, availability, activation, etc.), will not be discussed in this chapter, since that subject is treated fully in Gundel and Fretheim (this volume).

5   The full picture of a construction-based grammar is a bit more complex than this. Such a grammar takes the form of a multiple inheritance hierarchy of constructions, the leaves of which – the maximal constructions – form the atomic elements of what we might call the fully compiled grammar. Only the maximal constructions are the "minimal building blocks" referred to above. The maximal constructions represent the smallest set of conventional stipulations associating form and meaning a speaker-hearer must

control to produce and understand the sentences of the language. Non-maximal constructions represent generalizations across maximal constructions that are extracted by the linguist. Linguistic data in themselves cannot tell us whether non-maximal constructions represent psychologically real entities. The relevant obligation of the grammarian, under this view, is to abstract from the data of the language all the generalizations, in the form of non-maximal constructions, that a speaker-hearer *might* extract.

6   Here and elsewhere I use the term "interpretational" to avoid a theoretically fraught choice between "semantic" and "pragmatic."

7   This discussion is oversimplified in several respects, one of which is the generalization just offered asserting the unproblematically negative nature of *let alone* sentences. See Fillmore et al. (1988: 518–19).

8   We have not gone into the rather intricate detail of exactly which non-focused elements of the host can and cannot be absent in the fragment; these have a lot to do with the syntactic idiosyncracies of *let alone* as a coordinating conjunction and the consequent justification of treating it as the mark of an independent grammatical construction.

9   See Kay (1990: 70–81) for discussion regarding the role of accommodation in fulfilling the CP requirement in the related case of *even*. Note that *even* always goes naturally in the host clause of a *let alone* sentence:

>   (i)   Fred won't even order shrimp, let alone Louise, squid.

10   The following semiformal characterization of scalar model is adapted from Kay (1990: 64–7).

11   Fillmore et al. (1988) and Kay (1990) argue that scalar models necessarily have at least two dimensions (n > 1). In thinking about a scale we often have to think also about a set of objects being scaled, yielding a minimum of two dimensions, but the weaker position adopted here admits of one-dimensional scalar models (n ≥ 1).

12   It follows from the fact that we have defined a simple order on each D_i; D that entailment between two distinct propositions in F is unilateral.

13   Among others; see Fillmore et al. (1988) for further discussion.

14   In some cases, notably (13a), we are talking about a predicate, *invite Sarah and James*, which is interpreted as scalar only in context.

15   The first way of putting it reflects the traditional view (see e.g. Horn 1984a) that the literal meaning of (i) is (ii) and that the ordinary interpretation of (i) as meaning (iii) is due to an upper-bounding Quantity implicature acting on (ii).

   (i)   Sam has three children.
   (ii) Sam has at least three children.
   (iii) Sam has exactly three children.

The second way of putting it agrees with the analysis of Koenig (1991), for whom number names, and perhaps other scalar predicates, are literally punctual and it is the interval readings of scalar predications, e.g. (ii) as a reading of (i), that are derived by conversational implicature. (See Carston 1998b for yet another view of cardinals and scalars in general,

and Horn, this volume, for an overview of the issue.)

16   See Kay (1992) for a more careful characterization of the syntactic differences between simple scalar and evaluative *at least*.

17   Rather lamely, I fear, in Kay (1992).

18   For further, but equally inconclusive, discussion, see Kay (1992: 319–23).

19   Many other such examples could be cited, such as Clark and Clark (1979) on English denominal verbs, Downing (1977) and Kay and Zimmer (1976) on English nominal compounds and possessive constructions, and H. Clark (1983) on a wide variety of phenomena of English.

20   I'll have nothing to say here about the highly idiosyncratic syntax of *respectively*, for which see McCawley (1976); also Fillmore et al. (1988: n. 14).

21   *Respectively* also requires distribution of a predicate. We will see below that distribution of a predicate is not a requirement of *respective*, although *respective* does frequently function in this way.

22   To obviate an irrelevant objection, we assume a six-horse race, in which, necessarily, exactly three horses finish out of the money.

23   Example (24b) is due to George Lakoff (personal communication). Seemingly, opinions differ on the acceptability of sentences like (23) and (24b).

24   Horn (1985: 121) cites as precursors Ducrot (1972, 1973), Grice (1967, 1975), and Wilson (1975). Ducrot was the first to my knowledge both to employ the term metalinguistic negation (*négation métalinquistique*) and to extensively examine some of its properties, especially the implicature canceling property illustrated by (34a).

25 (Horn 1985: 166). Interestingly, the same is true in French:

> (i)a. Il n'est pas intelligent, il est très intelligent.
>   He isn't intelligent, he's very intelligent.
>   b. Il n'est pas intelligent, mais très intelligent.
>   He isn't intelligent, but very intelligent.
>   c. #Il n'est pas intelligent, mais il est très intelligent.
>   #He isn't intelligent, but he's very intelligent.

See Horn (1985: 167f.) and Anscombre and Ducrot (1977) for further discussion. See also the latter source for comparison of the two uses of French negation+*mais*, with the "but" doublets of Spanish (*pero/sino*) and German (*aber/sondern*).

26 McCawley (1991) points out that the same *not . . . but* syntax can be used simply contrastively, not metalinguistically.

> (i) John has drunk a quart not of beer but of whiskey. (McCawley 1991: 193)

From observations such as these, McCawley concludes: "Not X but Y . . . is not inherently metalinguistic, even if it is often used metalinguistically . . ." (1991: 189). To the extent that McCawley demonstrates a syntactic equivalence between metalinguistic and contrastive uses of *not X . . . but Y*, we should perhaps say instead that two distinct grammatical constructions share the same syntax. The impossibility of sentences like (37c) establishes the correlation of *not X . . . but Y* syntax with metalinguistic interpretation as a matter of grammar, not merely of usage.

27 The present discussion of the hedges *loosely speaking, strictly speaking,* and *technically* is condensed from Kay (1984 and 1996).

28 At least not to my knowledge. One sometimes discovers that words one thought were only members of a colloquial register have in fact been given a technical meaning. I once offered *weed* as an example of a botanical term with no technical denotation and was duly chastened.

29 Judgments vary on this example. Although most people I have questioned agree with the judgments expressed in the text, a minority hear *technically* and *strictly speaking* as synonymous in this context. For such speakers (44b) is true even under the assumption of factual innocence despite legal guilt. (Or perhaps the conflict in judgments is really about the word *murderer*, some taking it to require performance of an act satisfying the (legal) definition of murder and others taking it to require performance of an act judged to be a murder by a court.)

30 Attested examples of *kinda* and *sorta* are from Kay (1984) unless otherwise noted.

31 Kay (1984) discusses the syntax of *kinda/sorta* further. In particular it is argued that *kinda/sorta* does not behave like an ordinary deintensifying adverb, such as *slightly*.

> (i)a. a very slightly but unevenly worn tire
>   b. *a very sorta but surprisingly classical theory
>
> (ii)a. That tire is worn very slightly.
>   b. *That tire is worn very sorta.

(iii)a.   That tire is worn, but only very slightly.

   b.   *That tire is worn, but only very sorta.

(iv)a.   That [very slightly]$_i$ worn tire is proportionately$_i$ discounted.

   b.   *That [very sorta]$_i$ classical theory is correspondingly$_i$ admired.

The same paper also discusses the metalinguistic function of the *kinda/sorta* construction, usually indicating that the speaker is unsure of the aptness of the word or phrase focused by *kinda/sorta*. This usage is illustrated in the following attested examples:

(v)   Chomsky has a very . . . sorta CLASSICAL theory of syntax. (David Justice, personal communication)

(vi)   Those of us who grew up in the extremely sort of COMFORTING days of linguistics . . .

32   Levinson (1983: 263–5, 274–6 *et passim*). Levinson rejects this view, but not for the reasons we will reject it below. Levinson argues that there are no literal illocutionary forces, that is illocutionary forces conventionally associated with a particular morphosyntax. I will suggest, contrariwise, that such associations are legion.

33   The example is due to Charles Fillmore (personal communication).

34   This observation, incidentally, shows that the grammar of English contains an independent *Watch NP VP* construction, that is, that the "fate conjuring" force of a sentence like (50) is not derived by some form of conversational reasoning from the imperative sentence realized by the same string of words. Of course, this is not to say that imperative sentences of the form in question played no role in the historical origin of the construction.

35   This discussion is based on Kay (ms.).

36   As in the examples considered so far, I won't be able to gloss these forces with precision. I can only hope to indicate enough of their substance to persuade the reader that they are in fact distinct.

37   In a sentence like (55a), I will call *Fido ate the pizza* the **host** and *did he?* the **tag**.

38   Cf. Hirschberg (this volume).

39   I have benefited from discussions regarding the different forces of various species of tag with Charles Fillmore, who is not responsible for any errors made here.

40   This notion of the ultimate contents of a grammar leads constructionally oriented grammatical research in a direction distinct from that advocated by Chomsky:

> A look at the earliest work from the mid-1950s will show that many phenomena that fell within the rich descriptive apparatus then postulated, often with accounts of no little interest and insight, lack any serious analysis within the much narrower theories motivated by the search for explanatory adequacy and remain among the huge mass of constructions for which no principled explanation exists – again, not an unusual concomitant of progress.   (1995b: 435)

31 The Pragmatics of Polarity

MICHAEL ISRAEL

What part of "no" don't you understand?

Feminist slogan and song title

1 Polarity, Opposition, and Negation

Polarity and negation, more perhaps than any other grammatical phenomena, sprawl awkwardly along the messy border separating semantics and pragmatics. Depending on whom you ask, negation may be a logical operator or a type of speech act, a basic element of semantic representation or a pragmatically loaded form of communicative interaction. Each of these answers tells only part of the story. Polarity is, in essence, the relation between semantic opposites – between meanings (or expressions denoting meanings) which are fundamentally inconsistent with each other. As such polarity encompasses not just the logical relation between negative and affirmative propositions, but also the conceptual relations defining contrary pairs like *hot–cold*, *long–short*, and *good–bad*, and, most broadly, the rhetorical relation between arguments for and against a conclusion. The question is, how are these various and very different sorts of opposition represented in language and in the mind?

The grammar of polarity poses a paradox. What should in principle be a simple and symmetrical relation is in practice fraught with asymmetry. In principle, opposed terms must be equal in their opposition: one term cannot be more opposite than another. But in natural language opposites are never equal. There is a consistent imbalance between the unmarked expression of affirmation and the marked expression of negation; between the general utility of affirmative sentences and the pragmatically loaded uses of negative sentences; between the simple logic of double negation and the not uncomplicated pragmatics which insures that denying a negative is never quite the same as asserting a positive (cf. Horn 1991a). And it's not just that negative and affirmative sentences are unequal – they are also to some degree incommensurable: not every negative sentence has a direct affirmative counterpart, nor does every affirmative have a simple negation. Natural languages commonly (perhaps always) include what artificial languages never do: a class of constructions which do not themselves express negation or affirmation, but which are restricted to sentences of one or the other polarity. The existence (and indeed abundance) of such *polarity items* suggests that the resources which languages provide for negative and affirmative sentences can be surprisingly independent of one another.

From a logical point of view, these asymmetries seem arbitrary and unexpected; there are, however, good reasons why they are a constant feature of natural languages. This chapter explores the landscape of these asymmetries, and seeks their motivations in the pragmatic functions they may serve in actual language use.

2   Varieties of Polar Experience

For the purposes of this chapter I distinguish three basic types of polar opposition: CONTRADICTION, CONTRARIETY, and REVERSAL. All three feature prominently in natural language, and in human cognition generally. The first two are familiar from standard treatments of negation in logic and linguistics: CONTRADICTION is a relation in which one term must be true and the other false; CONTRARIETY is a relation in which only one term may be true, though both may be false. REVERSAL is somewhat special in that it involves an opposition, not between propositions or predicates per se, but rather between ordered sets of propositions or predicates – that is, between scales.

Contradiction is the most fundamental sort of opposition – the relation expressed by the one-place logical operator of propositional negation, and the prototypical (though by no means unique) meaning of natural language negation. Every human language includes at least one construction which can express the contradictory of an unmarked sentence. Such a device seems essential to the success of language as a representational system: in a deep sense, one cannot understand what a sentence means unless one also, and by the same token, understands what it would mean to contradict that sentence.

Contradiction is a pure binary opposition – the relation between two semantic values which between them exhaust the possibilities in a given domain. Most conceptual domains, however, include more than two possible values and in such cases entities stand in contrary opposition. Contrary propositions cannot be simultaneously true, but they can both be false. The sentences *Sally smiled* and *Sally didn't smile* express contradictory propositions, but *Sally smiled* and *Sally frowned* are contraries. One cannot, at the same time and in the same respect, both smile and frown, but one can perfectly well do neither. Of course, this makes for a rather weak notion of contrariety, as any given term or proposition might have an unlimited number of such contraries with which it is incompatible but which are not, strictly speaking, its opposite. While being white is contrary to being blue, red, green, or any other color, the true opposite of white is that unique color which differs from it more than all others, i.e. black. In the general spirit of Aristotle (e.g. *Metaphysics* 1055a, *Categories* 6a, cf. Horn 1989: 37), we may thus distinguish (mere) incompatibles from true polar contraries – entities which live at opposite ends of a common conceptual domain.

Polar contrariety requires a domain in which entities are, or can be, ordered along a scalar dimension, for only in such cases can one reasonably speak of a maximal opposition. As it turns out, many, if not all, of our most basic conceptual domains are scalar in nature: perceptual, emotional, and evaluative experiences of all sorts come in degrees, and the words we use to describe such experience reflect this scalarity. Not surprisingly then, polar contrariety is one of the basic semantic relations in the lexicon of any language. As Cruse (1986: 197) points out, the sense of oppositeness we feel in pairs like *hot–cold*, *happy–sad*, *good–bad*, *love–hate*, and *all–none* is probably the most salient and deeply felt of all lexical relations: the one most likely to have a non-technical name in any language (e.g. French *contraire*, German *Gegenteil*, Turkish *karşı*) and the one most likely to be understood by any three-year-old.

That said, the lexical semantics of antonymy and of scalar expressions in general is surprisingly complicated (cf. inter alia, Lyons 1977, Cruse 1986, Bierwisch 1989). For our purposes, the most important complication involves the inferential relations which hold among scalar predicates: in particular, the fact that polar antonyms denoting opposite regions in a scalar domain systematically give rise to opposite sorts of inferences. This is clear when one considers the logic of a HORN SCALE, where scalar expressions, $\langle e_1, e_2, \ldots e_n \rangle$, are ranked in terms of their entailments so that for an arbitrary sentence frame S and expressions $e_j > e_k$, $S(e_j)$ unilaterally entails $S(e_k)$ (Horn 1972, 1989: 231). The examples below illustrate Horn scales with expressions from the domains of quantity, epistemic modality, temperature, preference, and evaluation:

(1) ⟨all, most, many, some⟩   ⟨none, hardly any, few⟩
     ⟨necessary, likely, possible⟩   ⟨impossible, unlikely, uncertain⟩
     ⟨boiling, hot, warm⟩   ⟨freezing, cold, cool⟩
     ⟨adore, love, like⟩   ⟨loathe, hate, dislike⟩
     ⟨excellent, good, OK⟩   ⟨{terrible/awful}, bad, mediocre⟩

Each domain actually supports two distinct scales with opposite orderings at opposite ends of the domain. Thus for temperature there is both a "hot" scale, for which *hot* is stronger than *warm* (e.g. *the soup was warm, if not downright hot/*cool*) and a "cold" scale, where *cold* outranks *cool* (e.g. *her manner was cool, in fact it was cold/*warm*). Polar antonyms are thus not just far apart on a scalar dimension, they actually belong to distinct, in fact opposite, orderings (cf. Sapir 1944, Ducrot 1972).

The relation between scales like these, with opposite orderings over the same domain, is one of reversal. This, our third and final form of opposition, may seem rather different from contrariety or contradiction: scales, after all, are not propositions – they cannot be true or false. But scales can and do define inferential relations between propositions, and these inferences crucially depend on the way a scale is ordered. To appreciate this it will help to clarify just what scales are, and just what sorts of inferences they can support.

There are two basic kinds of scalar inferences – SCALAR ENTAILMENTS and SCALAR IMPLICATURES – but there are many kinds of scales, with Horn scales being a special, albeit an especially well-studied case (cf. Horn 1972, 1989, Gazdar 1979, Matsumoto 1995, Schwenter 1999a, Levinson 2000a, inter alia). In general, the ordered elements in a scale need not be linguistic expressions, and the relations between them need not be limited to semantic entailment. Fauconnier (1975a, 1975b, 1976) and Hirschberg (1991) showed that scalar inferences need not be strictly logical, but rather may reflect normal expectations about how the world works. Thus, foods can be ranked by their succulence, or problems by their complexity, and people can use these rankings to reason about what someone might eat, or what problems they might be able to solve. Normally, for example, we expect those who can solve hard problems to succeed with easier problems as well. Following Fauconnier, I will call such default inferences PRAGMATIC ENTAILMENTS. The logic which supports them reflects an idealized model of the world, so they do not hold in all possible worlds, and, like implicatures, they are defeasible; but within the idealized model in which they are normally interpreted these inferences are automatically valid, and so deserve the name *entailment*.

Within Construction Grammar (Fillmore et al. 1988, Kay 1990, 1997, this volume) the idealizations which support pragmatic entailments are formalized in the structure of a SCALAR MODEL. Basically, a scalar model consists of a set of propositions ordered in a way that supports inferences. The model is built from a propositional function with one or more variables, each of which is associated with a conceptual scale of some sort (e.g. foods ordered in terms of their succulence).[1] Just as a single conceptual domain may support the lexicalization of opposed Horn scales with reverse orderings, so too a single conceptual scale may combine with different propositional functions to form scalar models with inferences going in opposite directions (Fauconnier 1975a, 1975b, 1976). Consider the examples in (2), based on a scale of times for running a mile: with the affirmative proposition in (2a), scalar entailments (symbolized by "$\Rightarrow$") go from faster miles to slower miles, and scalar implicatures (symbolized by "$+>$") from slower to faster miles; under negation, in (2b), the direction of entailments and implicatures is exactly reversed.

(2)a.　Hank can run a five-minute mile.
　　　　$\Rightarrow$ he can run a slower mile; $+>$ he can't run a faster mile

　　b.　Hank can't run a five-minute mile.
　　　　$\Rightarrow$ he can't run a faster mile; $+>$ he can run a slower mile

Negation is but one of many constructions which reverse scalar inferences. Other reversing constructions, illustrated in (3), include the antecedent of a conditional, *before* clauses, the standard of a comparative, and the complement of an adversative predicate like *be surprised*:

(3)a. If Hank can run a five-minute mile, he'll be here on time.
   b. We'll have world peace before Hank runs a five-minute mile.
   c. Jackie reads Hittite more easily than Hank can run a five-minute mile.
   d. I'm surprised Hank can run a five-minute mile.

(3a) pragmatically entails that if Hank can run a four-minute mile then he will also be on time, and it allows the implicature that a six-minute mile will not guarantee a timely arrival. Similarly, (3d) suggests that any faster time would also be a surprise, but that a six-minute mile might not.

Scalar models may serve rhetorical functions that go beyond the immediate inferences which they support. Typically, in context, a sentence like (2a) will not just say how fast Hank can run, but will also provide an argument for some conclusion, for example that Hank is athletic, or that he has a chance of winning some race. Given such argumentative goals, the ordering in a scalar model effectively determines what counts as a strong or a weak argument for a given conclusion, while the opposition between reversing and non-reversing contexts effectively determines the rhetorical orientation of any given utterance.[2]

3   Asymmetries of Use: the Onus of Negativity

The basic asymmetry between negation and affirmation is readily apparent in the way negation dominates most discussions of polarity – so much so that polarity often seems to be virtually identified with negation alone. Affirmation, at least as a logical category, is taken for granted; it is negation, the marked member of the polar opposition, which cries out for explanation. Opinions on negation have been divided, but rarely impartial. Whether or not negation is the most fundamental of all logical relations, it is surely, as Horn notes (1989: 45), the most maligned. Negation, it seems, is always suspect – ontologically, epistemologically, and even morally. Philosophers have for centuries cast aspersions on its usefulness and integrity; more recently linguists and psycholinguists have joined the chorus with empirical evidence for the derivative and second-class nature of negation with respect to affirmation. My purpose here, however, is not to bury negation but to praise it – to identify the ways it is actually used, and so is useful, in natural language. The key to this usefulness, it turns out, lies precisely in its peculiar asymmetry with affirmation.

Of course, negation has never been without its supporters who insist on the basic symmetry inherent in any polar opposition. Typically, such symmetricalists have been concerned with negation primarily as a logical category: for them the essential fact is the purely symmetrical relation between contradictory propositions which negation makes possible (cf. Frege 1919). In this light, negation may occasionally even be recognized as the guarantor of meaning itself.

Thus Spinoza's famous dictum, *determinatio est negatio*, rests on the epistemological insight that one cannot know what something is unless one also, and by the same token, knows what it is not. Still, in the long history of ideas from Parmenides to the present, negation has generally been held in rather low esteem.

The basic thrust of the charges against negation is that it is, in one way or another, secondary to and parasitic on the more wholesome category of affirmation. Affirmation is associated with truth, presence, plenitude, and goodness; negation with falsity, absence, deprivation, and evil. Affirmation is essential and necessary; negation is contingent and eliminable. Affirmative sentences are objective and relate directly to the world; negative sentences are subjective and relate merely to the affirmative sentences which they deny. Philosophers regularly question the very existence of negative propositions, and many, from Bacon and Kant to Bergson and Morris, have seen negation as, at best, a necessary evil – "a tool for rejecting or warding off error which in an epistemically perfect state would simply wither away," as Horn sums up the position (1989: 61).

A variety of empirical observations support the philosophical suspicion that negation is less than an equal partner with affirmation. The most obvious point is that negation is (almost) always a marked category. Languages employ special devices to express negation (i.e. negative inflections, particles, adverbs, auxiliaries, etc.), while the expression of affirmation tends to involve the absence of any such devices.[3] And negative sentences are not just formally but also semantically marked, being generally less informative than their positive counterparts. As Plato succinctly put it (see also Leech 1981, 1983), "about each form there is much that it is, but an infinite amount that it is not" (*Sophist*, 256E, cited in Horn 1989: 60). Given this superabundance of negative facts, negative sentences tend not to tell us much: if I know that President Bush didn't eat a burrito for breakfast, I still do not know what, if anything, he did eat. Positive sentences can be uninformative as well: assertions like "Harry sleeps in his bed at night" or "Sally was raised by her biological parents" are odd, and unlikely to be uttered, because they say no more than what one might normally assume. But uninformativity appears to be a systematic danger with negative sentences. And since speakers generally do try to be informative, the appropriate use of a negative sentence tends to require a context in which the information it does convey is somehow particularly relevant.

As a marked category, negation thus has a marked distribution: it is the special case. The normal way to express an idea is to affirm it; negation is used primarily in "contexts of plausible denial" (Wason 1965). As Strawson puts it, "the standard and primary use of *not* is specifically to contradict or to correct; to cancel a suggestion of one's own or another's" (1952: 7). One does not normally deny something unless one thinks that someone might believe it. Givón (1978: 79–81) notes that it would be odd, at best, to begin a conversation by saying, "Oh, my wife's not pregnant." The felicity of such an assertion depends on the possibility that someone might have thought that she was. Denial in general seems to presuppose the possibility, if not the expectation, that what is denied might actually have been the case. And so in as much as negative sentences are associated with denial, their use is sharply distinguished from, and in a sense secondary to, the use of affirmative sentences.

As Givón (1978) points out, because negative sentences are more restricted and less frequent than positive sentences, they tend to mark fewer grammatical distinctions. For example, perfective tense and aspect constructions are often unmarked under negation (Schmid 1980: 101) – even in South Dravidian, where negation is sometimes expressed by the absence of a morpheme, the absent morpheme is a tense marker (Pederson 1993). In general, grammatical innovations spread from positive to negative clauses: Givón notes innovative tense-aspect constructions in Bemba, Swahili, and Chana which occur with affirmative but not negative verbs (1975: 92–3). Givón also notes that it is common to find restrictions on the scope of adverbs under negation, on the use of referential indefinites under negation, and on the use of negation in a range of complex constructions. Thus negation may be awkward, or worse, in information questions (4), restrictive relatives (5), comparatives (6), and focus constructions (7), among others.

(4)   What did you (??not) do yesterday?

(5)   The woman I (??don't) want to marry drives a red Miata.

(6)   Jasper can run faster than Sidney {can/*can't}.

(7)   I looked around and near the bar I {saw/??didn't see} Glynda.

As Givón argues, the source of the trouble in such cases is pragmatic: very roughly, the use of negation makes these sentences so vague that either they defy interpretation, as in (4–6), or they fail to introduce a discourse referent where one is needed, as in (7). The details here, while interesting, need not concern us; the basic point is clear enough – that the use of negation, both in discourse and in a range of syntactic contexts, is systematically and significantly restricted in comparison with affirmation.

It's not just that negation is subject to restrictions: it's also just plain hard to process. All things being equal, subjects respond more slowly to negative sentences, and have more trouble recalling and evaluating them than they do with their positive counterparts (Wason 1965, 1972, Clark 1974, Carpenter and Just 1975, Fodor et al. 1975). Thus, for example, subjects are quicker to judge a sentence like "The number 5 is odd" as true than they are to judge a sentence like "The number 5 is not even" as true, despite the fact that the two are truth-conditionally equivalent. This sort of result suggests that negative sentences are inherently more complicated than positive sentences, and that their comprehension depends in some way on the addition of a negative judgment to a positive proposition.[4]

Negation appears specially suited to mark the exception to a salient pattern: a dog with no fur will be described as such; a dog without earrings is just a dog. Negation is reactive: it is useful where it responds to and opposes what is, or what might have been, expected. This is why negation is so peculiarly suited for so-called "negative" speech acts – e.g. denial, rejection, refusal, etc. – whose basic function is to answer and oppose some other speech act. Such speech acts are not themselves inherently negative, for they can always be accomplished without the use of negation (e.g. A: Can I have a kiss? B: You can go to hell!); but the reactive nature of negation makes it inherently well-suited for their performance. Presumably, this is why such speech acts feel so "negative," and also perhaps why negation itself tends to carry such negative connotations.

The fact is, negation is often experienced as an unpleasant sort of construction, and this unpleasantness has important consequences for the ways it is used. On the one hand, speakers may employ various sorts of indirection to soften the ill effects of a negative utterance; contrariwise, hearers may systematically strengthen the interpretation of negation to compensate for such euphemism. In general, this strengthening takes the form of an inference from a formally contradictory negation **not-p** to a strong contrary assertion **q**, effectively ignoring the logical possibility of something being neither **p** nor **q**. Horn (1989: §5) explores this phenomenon of "contrary-negation-in-contradictory-clothing" as it appears with affixal negation (*unhappy* = "sad"), negative raising phenomena (*I don't think you should* = "I think you should not"), and sentential negations (*Elma doesn't like squid* = "Elma dislikes squid").

The question is under what conditions does negation allow such contrary readings? The facts are complicated, but part of the answer seems to be that they occur with evaluatively positive (e-positive) predicates, the denial of which may indirectly express an evaluatively negative (e-negative) judgment. Thus, for example, we find contrary readings available with (weakly) e-positive predicates, as in (8), but not with e-negative or strongly e-positive predicates, as in (9).

(8)a. He's not nice.   (= 'he's mean')
   b. She's not happy.   (= 'she's sad')

(9)a. He's not mean.   (≠ 'he's nice')
   b. She's not sad.   (≠ 'she's happy')
   c. She's not ecstatic.   (≠ 'she's miserable')

Similarly, with affixal negation, the English *un-* prefix in (10) yields contrary meanings in combination with e-positive roots, but tends not to combine at all with the contrary e-negative roots (Zimmer 1964).

(10) happy unhappy   sad   *unsad
      kind   unkind   cruel   *uncruel
      wise   unwise   foolish *unfoolish

A form like *unhappy* provides an oblique way of delivering the loaded content of *sad*; but *unsad* can serve no similar purpose, as one is normally happy to express the content of *happy*.

The pragmatics of contrary negation is clearest perhaps in the phenomenon of NEG(ATIVE)-RAISING, as in (11), where a matrix negation is interpreted as applying to an embedded constituent.

(11)a. I don't think you should do that.   (= 'I think you should not . . .')
    b. I don't suppose you expect to win.   (= 'I suppose you wouldn't . . .')

As many have noted (G. Lakoff 1969a, Prince 1976), neg-raised sentences are typically felt as weaker and more tentative than their otherwise synonymous counterparts with lower-clause negation, and the phenomenon appears to be motivated in large part by the need to hedge or mitigate the expression of a negative judgment. In this sense, although the grammar of neg-raising may seem lawlessly illogical, it is animated by the best pragmatic intentions.[5]

The same may be said for negation in general, whose simple semantics makes it ideally suited for rather complicated pragmatic functions. Polarity in natural language is inherently asymmetrical – not because it is illogical, but rather, and simply, because there is so much it has to do.

4 Asymmetric Distributions: the Pragmatics of Sensitivity

Perhaps the most surprising asymmetry in the expression of polarity is the phenomenon of POLARITY SENSITIVITY – the tendency for certain forms, POLARITY ITEMS, to be distributed unevenly across negative and affirmative contexts. Although the details vary from language to language, polarity items seem likely to occur in every human language. In many there are literally hundreds of such forms. This is actually rather odd: if one were to devise an artificial language, the idea of including forms which are systematically excluded from certain sentences might seem a perverse extravagance; however, it is an extravagance which natural languages commonly indulge.

Despite a large literature, there is actually no standard definition for polarity items (cf. van der Wouden 1994/1997, Tovena 1998). Intuitively, they are constructions whose use or interpretation is sensitive to polarity – that is, to the expression of contradiction, contrariety, or reversal. Such a broad formulation, of course, makes for a messy category: since polarity is itself so complex, there are many ways a construction can be sensitive to its expression. In the prototypical case, polarity items are best distinguished by their asymmetric behavior in minimal pairs of negative and affirmative sentences: NEGATIVE POLARITY ITEMS (NPIs) will occur in a negative sentence but not in its affirmative counterpart; POSITIVE POLARITY ITEMS (PPIs) will occur in an affirmative sentence but not (normally) in its negative counterpart. The examples in (12) illustrate the negative preferences of the English NPIs *sleep a wink*, *so much as*, and *all that*. The examples in (13) show the positive proclivities of three PPI constructions: predicative *some*, *a regular*, and *in the blink of an eye*.

(12)a.   Clarissa (*did/didn't) *sleep a wink* that night.
   b.   She (*would/wouldn't) *so much as* say hello to me.
   c.   She (*is/isn't) *all that* interested in seeing my stamp collection.

(13)a.   That guy Winthrop (is/*isn't) *some* mathematician.
   b.   He (is/*isn't) *a regular* Einstein.
   c.   He (can/*can't) calculate an eigen vector *in the blink of an eye*.

The full range of contexts in which NPIs may be licensed and PPIs inhibited corresponds roughly to the set of reversing constructions (cf. above, section 2). It includes, among others, the scope of negation, whether expressed by the adverbial *not*, by a negative quantifier such as *nobody*, *nothing*, or *never*, or by a weakly negative form like *hardly*, *few*, or *rarely*; the complements of adversative predicates like *be surprised*, *be amazed*, or *doubt*; the antecedent of a conditional; the restriction of a universal or a generic quantifier; the nuclear scope of *only* (and occasionally the restriction as well); the focus of a *yes–no* question; rhetorical information questions; comparative and equative constructions; and subordinate clauses marked by *before*, and occasionally, *long after*. The examples below illustrate a few of these contexts with the NPI *at all* and the PPI *considerably*.

(14)a.   **Are you** at all interested in what I'm saying?
   b.   ??**Are you** considerably interested in what I'm saying?

(15)a.   **If** Gladys is at all late, there may be trouble.
   b.   ??**If** Gladys is considerably late, there may be trouble.

(16)a.   She'd **sooner** die **than** appear at all drunk in public.
   b.   ??She'd **sooner** die **than** appear considerably drunk in public.

(17)a.   **Only** Hugo was at all impressed by her convoluted arguments.
   b.   ?**Only** Hugo was considerably impressed by her convoluted arguments.

(18)a.   I'm **amazed** that Elly is at all interested in birdwatching.
   b.   ?I'm **amazed** that Elly is considerably interested in birdwatching.

A comprehensive theory of polarity sensitivity must face (at least) three general problems (Israel 1996, cf. Ladusaw 1996):

Licensing: How are polarity items licensed? What makes polarity contexts a natural class?

Sensitivity: What makes polarity items sensitive to polarity? Are there features which all polarity items share and which might explain their sensitivities?

Diversity: Why do different polarity items, both within and across languages, often exhibit different sensitivities? Is polarity sensitivity a unified phenomenon?

Of these, the licensing problem is typically viewed as the most fundamental: since polarity items are defined in terms of their distributions, it makes sense to begin by clarifying just what these distributions are. Moreover, licensing has a certain allure for generative theories, as it lends itself to structural explanations; partly for this reason, polarity items have figured prominently in debates on the architecture of grammar, and especially on the existence and nature of a linguistic level of logical form (cf. Baker 1970, Ladusaw 1983, Linebarger 1987, 1991). However, as we shall see, polarity items tend to resist purely structural explanations, and the details of their sensitivities reveal a crucial role for pragmatics in the determination of grammaticality.

4.1 The semantics and pragmatics of licensing

Theories of polarity sensitivity divide into two major camps, one focused on syntax and the other on semantics, both of which find their roots in Klima's seminal paper "Negation in English" (1964). Klima clearly distinguished two basic questions (cf. Ladusaw 1996): what makes something a polarity licensor (Ladusaw's LICENSOR QUESTION)?; and what sort of relation must obtain for a licensor to license a polarity item (Ladusaw's LICENSING RELATION QUESTION)? Klima proposed that polarity licensors share a "grammatico-semantic property" he called AFFECTIVITY (1964: 313), and that NPIs are licensed if they occur "in construction with" (i.e. are c-commanded by) an appropriately affective licensor. These same questions still shape most modern accounts of polarity: semantic theories in general focus on the problem of how to cash out the notion of affectivity (Hoeksema 1983, 1986, Heim 1984, Kadmon and Landman 1993, Kas 1993, Dowty 1994, Zwarts 1996a, 1996b, van der Wouden 1994/1997, Giannakidou 1998); syntactic accounts, on the other hand, focus less on the variety of licensors and more on the syntactic relations which must hold between a licensor (usually negation) and a licensed polarity item (Laka 1990, Progovac 1994, Uribe-Etxebarria 1994, Kato 2000).

The modern semantic approach begins with Fauconnier's (1975a, 1975b, 1976, 1978b) work on pragmatic scales and implication reversal, but it is most famously associated with Ladusaw's (1980, 1983) proposal that NPIs are sensitive to logical monotonicity and can only be licensed in the scope of a DOWNWARD ENTAILING (DE) operator. Intuitively, a DE context licenses inferences from general properties to specific instances, from sets to subsets. Negation is a DE operator because it allows inferences as in (19) from the general, *a bird*, to the specific, *a penguin*:

(19)a.   Beth didn't see a bird in the garden. →
    b.   Beth didn't see a penguin in the garden.

Upward entailing contexts – for example, simple affirmatives – license inferences in the other direction, from specific instances to general cases, as in (20):

(20)a.   Beth saw a penguin in the garden. →
    b.   Beth saw a bird in the garden.

The advantage of a monotonicity-based theory is that it allows for a precise formulation of the constraints on polarity items in terms of a well-formedness condition on semantic representations. Thus Ladusaw defines the set of DE operators as in (21a) and offers (21b) as a necessary condition for licensing NPIs (1983: 383):

(21)a.   Given Boolean algebras A and B, a function d from A to B is downward entailing iff for any a_1, a_2 in the domain of d, if $a_1 \leq a_2$ then $d(a_2) \leq d(a_1)$.
    b.   A negative polarity item will be acceptable only if it is in the scope of a downward entailing expression.

It is worth emphasizing that the Monotonicity Thesis in (21), at least as Ladusaw originally conceived it, is a structural constraint on the form of semantic representations (specifically, on the composition structure of a sentence's truth conditions). The significance of Ladusaw's theory lies in its conception of linguistic semantics. For Ladusaw, polarity licensing depends on an algorithmically derived representation of a sentence's literal, truth-conditional meaning. The theory thus stands as an argument for including such representations in a theory of grammar. Polarity sensitivity is probably the clearest example of a grammatical phenomenon which depends on the logical properties of a sentence. The interesting claim here is that these logical properties require their own level of representation, distinct both from syntactic structure and from a pragmatically enriched sentence interpretation.

In fact, Fauconnier's original interpretation was radically different. Fauconnier argued that the scalar logic to which polarity items are sensitive is itself pragmatic in nature, and he concluded that polarity licensing does not depend on linguistic representations at all, but rather involves the interaction of linguistic and pragmatic knowledge in a dynamic process of meaning construction. As he put it, people "need not have extremely abstract *representations* of *sentences* in their heads, but they do need quite sophisticated and relatively abstract *processes* to interpret sentences in particular contexts" (Fauconnier 1978a: 49, emphasis in original).

Fauconnier may have underestimated the potential for a representational theory of polarity licensing, but he was surely right in emphasizing the importance of pragmatics. The fundamental advantage of Ladusaw's semantically driven theory is its formal precision; however, as Ladusaw concedes (1996: 328), this precision comes at a price. The monotonicity thesis makes categorical predictions about polarity licensing, but the behavior of polarity items is often far from categorical. For one thing, polarity items vary in their sensitivities, with some items occurring only in the scope of negation, some with all DE operators, and others with some subset of potential licensors. Several proposals account for these facts by ranking polarity contexts in terms of their licensing strength and polarity items in terms of their licensing needs (e.g. Horn 1970, Edmondson 1981, van der Wouden 1994, Zwarts 1996a, 1996b, Giannakidou 1998), although it is far from clear that the diversity of sensitivities can be reduced to a single hierarchy (cf. Hoeksema 1994, 2000, and Israel 1995, 1998). What is clear, however, is that a comprehensive theory of sensitivity must be attuned to the needs of individual polarity items. Even more troubling for a theory like Ladusaw's is the fact that polarity items are often sensitive to pragmatic properties of sentences (Lakoff 1969b, Smith 1975). This means that appearance in the scope of a DE operator may not be sufficient, and sometimes is not even necessary for licensing.

This point is emphasized in the work of Linebarger (1980, 1987, 1991). Like Ladusaw, Linebarger defines licensing in terms of constraints on grammatical representations; however, for her the constraints are essentially syntactic rather than semantic. As she puts it, "the distribution of [NPIs] in English reflects an interplay between syntax and pragmatics, with no apparent role for a level of 'pure' semantic representation" (1987: 326). Linebarger sees negation (that is, the abstract operator NOT) as the only true licensor. NPIs are taken to be "close associates of negation" (1991: 167), which must occur in the immediate scope of negation at Logical Form (LF – crucially, a syntactic level of representation). Building on the two-tiered licensing theory of Baker (1970), Linebarger suggests that NPIs which do not meet this condition can be licensed derivatively, by conveying a NEGATIVE IMPLICATURE (NI) which is itself associated with an appropriate LF representation: "the use of an NPI in a sentence whose LF does not license it represents an allusion, one might say, to some entailed or implicated proposition, the NI, in which the NPI does occur in the immediate scope of negation" (1991: 167).

Licensing by implicature allows Linebarger to explain why NPIs, like the italicized forms in (22), often fail to be licensed in the scope of a DE operator (cf. Heim 1984, Yoshimura 1994).

(22)a. Anyone who *gives a damn* about the environment enjoys recycling.
   b. ??Anyone who *gives a damn* about the environment shops at Ikea.

On Linebarger's account, (22a) works because it conveys the implicature that people who do not recycle do not give a damn about the environment, and (22b) fails because there is no natural connection between environmental friendliness and patronage of Ikea which might support similar negative implicature. The fact that (22b) begins to sound acceptable to the extent that one can make such a connection strongly suggests that implicature plays a crucial role here.

The examples in (23) illustrate the opposite problem, showing NPIs which are licensed even in the absence of a DE operator.

(23)a.   He kept dreaming of her long after he had *the slightest* desire to see her.

    b.   There are precisely four people in the whole world who would *so much as* consider *lifting a finger* to help that maniac.

Neither of these sentences contains an appropriate licensor, but they both generate negative implicatures: (23a) suggests that the dreams continued when he did NOT have the slightest desire, (23b) suggests that normal people would NOT lift a finger to help.

While Linebarger makes a compelling case for the role of implicature in licensing, a natural worry is how such a powerful mechanism might be constrained (cf. Krifka 1991, Kadmon and Landman 1993, Yoshimura 1994). Linebarger recognizes this problem and proposes three constraints on when a negative implicature can license NPIs (1991: 166): AVAILABILITY – the speaker must be actively attempting to convey the NI; STRENGTH – the truth of the NI "must virtually guarantee" the truth of the overtly expressed proposition; and FOREGROUNDING – neither the NPI nor the NI can occur as background information in the conversational context. These constraints are a promising start: for instance, they help explain (24), where *barely* licenses an NPI while *almost* does not, despite the fact that *barely* suggests that Clara did say at least something, and *almost* suggests that she did not. The difference is that *barely* introduces the NI "that Clara almost did not say a word" – a proposition which is both foregrounded and strong enough to guarantee the truth of (24a); with *almost*, however, the NI that *Clara didn't say a word* certainly cannot guarantee that Clara almost did say one: licensing thus fails due to a lack of strength.

(24)a.   Clara barely said a word to me at the party.

    b.   *Clara almost said a word to me at the party.

Unfortunately, as Horn (1996b) makes clear, the Strength Constraint cannot explain why certain other negative implicatures do not license NPIs. Following Atlas (1984), Horn notes that *almost* is truth-conditionally identical to *not quite*, so that the proposition "He didn't quite finish" should be available as an implicature which guarantees the truth of a sentence like *He almost finished*. This would seem to predict that *almost* in (25a) should be just as good a licensor for *any* as *not quite* is in (25b); clearly, however, it is not:

(25)a.   He almost finished {some/*any} of the essays.

    b.   He didn't quite finish any of the essays.

Clearly, Linebarger's theory faces some empirical problems in explaining just what can count as a negative implicature. And the theory clearly requires a more explicit account of how such implicatures are calculated. Still, given the wealth of data which the theory handles well, these might not be seen as fatal flaws but rather as goads to further refinement. There is, however, a more fundamental problem, and that is the peculiar role that implicatures play in this theory, and the particular relation between syntax and pragmatics that role presupposes.

Linebarger clearly demonstrates that polarity licensing can be context-sensitive, and she makes a compelling case that implicatures are crucial to the process. Still, licensing for her remains a structural condition on syntactic representations, and this has some odd consequences. Implicatures are assigned syntactic structures of their own, and although their calculation presumably depends on general cognitive processes, they are made subject to the constraints of an autonomous syntactic module. Furthermore, while the role of implicature poses problems for a theory of licensing based strictly on sentence meaning, it does not obviously support a theory based on syntactic structure either: on the contrary, it suggests that polarity items might be sensitive directly to speaker meaning rather than to semantic or syntactic representations alone. Indeed, licensing by implicature might supplement a monotonicity-based theory like Ladusaw's just as easily as it does Linebarger's LF-based theory. The real question then is whether polarity items have a special relationship with negation, as Linebarger suggests, or whether they are somehow attuned to the kinds of inferences that DE operators license (or perhaps both). One natural place to look for enlightenment, then, is in the lexical semantics of polarity items themselves.

4.2   The lexicon of sensitivity

The traditional focus on licensing and structural explanation has led to a certain neglect of empirical issues related to the sensitivity and diversity problems. The most basic of these issues are lexicographical in nature (cf. Hoeksema 2000: 116): What is the complete inventory of polarity items for a given language? Are there cross-linguistic regularities in these inventories? What sorts of meanings do polarity items typically encode? What sorts of meanings do they never encode? Although we still lack any really satisfactory answers to these questions, the little we do know poses some interesting theoretical challenges.

By far the most well-known and widely observed class of polarity items are the minimizers – NPIs in which a stereotypically minimal unit is used to render an emphatic negation (Borkin 1971, Schmerling 1971a, Fauconnier 1975a, Horn 1978a, 1989, Heim 1984). Minimizers typically take the form of an indefinite NP which either combines freely with different predicates (*a jot, an iota, a red cent, a soul, a stitch of clothing, a stick of furniture*) or else is incorporated in a VP idiom (*lift a finger, sleep a wink, bat an eyelid, breathe a word, miss a beat, crack a book*). Minimizers are without a doubt the most eye-catching of all polarity items: they are abundant within languages and widespread across languages, and their emphatic force is exemplary of an important trend found in many polarity items.

The role of NPIs as strengtheners of negation is often seen as the key to their distributions: if strengthening is part of NPIs' conventional meaning, then sensitivity may simply reflect a need to appear in contexts where they will be appropriately strong. The insight goes back at least to Pott (1859, cited in Horn 1989: 452) who viewed minimizer NPIs as incorporating the meaning of a scalar focus particle like *even*. Modern accounts of indefinite NPIs (Kadmon and Landman 1993, Lee and Horn 1994, Lee 1996, Haspelmath 1997, Lahiri 1998, Horn 2000b) regularly appeal to the work these forms perform in expressing informatively strong propositions. Krifka (1991, 1994, 1995) extends this sort of approach to a wide class of NPIs and PPIs. He notes that while many NPIs denote minimal units of some sort, PPIs typically involve maximal units: for example, high scalar degree adverbs – forms like *utterly, thoroughly, damnably,* and *as hell* – are chronically PPIs (cf. Hinds 1974, Klein 1997, 1998). Krifka proposes that polarity items are interpreted with respect to a set of alternatives, and that their sensitivity reflects a need to occur in contexts where they will be informative with respect to these alternatives – in effect, where they will yield strong speech acts rather than trivial ones.

But while many NPIs and PPIs do effectively strengthen a speech act, others work in just the opposite way, serving to hedge or mitigate the force of an expressed proposition. Such attenuating polarity items are in fact quite common: along with English NPIs like *all that, so very,* and *much,* one finds the French *grand chose* "much (stuff)" and *grand monde* "many people," the Dutch *bijster* "very", the Japanese *sonna-ni* "that much" and *anmari* lit., "too very" (Vasishth 1998), and the Persian *cœndan* "much" and *un-qœdrha* "that much" (Raghibdoust 1994).

There is in fact a reliable correlation between the pragmatic force of a polarity item (whether emphatic or attenuating) and its scalar semantics (Israel 1996, 1998), and the interaction between them divides polarity items into four basic classes. Roughly, and with some principled exceptions (cf. Israel 2001), EMPHATIC POLARITY items include NPIs denoting minimal scalar values and PPIs denoting maximal values, while ATTENUATING POLARITY ITEMS include NPIs with high scalar values and PPIs with low scalar values. The lists below give a hint of the variety of such forms in each of these classes in English.

Emphatic NPIs:	*any, ever, at all, the least bit, in the slightest, give a damn, have a chance in hell, can fathom, can possibly, would dream of*
Emphatic PPIs:	*tons of N, scads of N, constantly, utterly, insanely, in a flash, within an inch of N, be bound to V, gotta V*
Attenuating NPIs:	*be all that, any too, overmuch, long, much, great shakes, be born yesterday, trouble to V, mince words, need*
Attenuating PPIs:	*some, somewhat, rather, sorta, a fair bit, a tad, a whiff, a hint, a little, a smidgen, more or less, would just as soon*

This regular correlation suggests a principled relationship between polarity sensitivity and scalar semantics: I call this the scalar model of polarity sensitivity. The basic idea is that polarity items are SCALAR OPERATORS – forms which are construed within the structure of a scalar model (cf. Kay 1990, this volume). The scalar denotation of a polarity item determines its position within the model, its pragmatic force constrains its inferential relation with other propositions in the model, and the two together create the effect of sensitivity. For example, an item like *lift a finger* denotes a minimal effort and contrasts with the expression of any greater effort; as an emphatic item it contributes its meaning to a strong proposition, and so must unilaterally entail contrasting propositions in the model. The result is that *lift a finger* can only be used in scale reversing contexts, where inferences run from lesser to greater efforts: *she didn't lift a finger* is fine because it licenses the inference that "she didn't try very hard"; *she lifted a finger* yields no such inference: it fails because it expresses a weak proposition incompatible with its inherently emphatic nature.

A similar logic applies to attenuating polarity items. These forms require a construal in which they are entailed by, rather than themselves entailing, some default norm within a scalar model. Again, unlicensed polarity items are semantically incoherent: a sentence like *Her theory is all that complicated* simultaneously offers itself as a weak claim (due to the conventionally attenuating NPI *all that*) and yet makes a strong claim (i.e. "the theory is very complicated"). The sentence is bad because it allows no construal consistent with both its scalar denotation and its attenuating pragmatics.

A key feature of the scalar model is the idea that polarity items themselves conventionally express certain pragmatic functions, and that they are licensed precisely (and only) where they can successfully discharge these functions. This is rather different from, for example, Krifka's theory, in which the lexical meanings of polarity items are cashed out basically in terms of a semantic denotation plus a set of alternatives, and the pragmatic rules which limit their distributions are general properties of sentences rather than of the polarity items themselves. On the other hand, it is very much in the spirit of a theory like Kadmon and Landman's (1993), which attributes the distributional constraints on English *any* to the interaction of a semantic feature, WIDENING (analogous to the expression of a low scalar value) and a pragmatic requirement, STRENGTHENING (equivalent to emphasis in a scalar model).

What distinguishes the scalar model is its wide application to polarity items of all sorts. The theory seeks to explain why polarity items should exist at all, and it finds the reason precisely in their usefulness. The pragmatic functions which polarity items encode, emphasis and attenuation, reflect two antithetical ways in which scalar semantics may be deployed for rhetorical effect: emphatic expressions serve to mark commitment or emotional involvement in a communicative exchange, while attenuation both protects a speaker's credibility and shows deference to a hearer by minimizing any demands on his credulity. These complementary functions may thus be seen as tools for negotiating politeness (cf. Brown and Levinson 1987).

The scalar model receives circumstantial support from the fact that polarity items consistently come from semantic domains which are somehow inherently scalar. This is obviously true of the measure terms and degree adverbs which are so common among polarity items (von Bergen and von Bergen 1993, van der Wouden 1994/1997, Klein 1997), but it also holds for other major cross-linguistic sources of polarity items, among others, indefinite pronouns and determiners (Haspelmath 1997), modal verbs (Edmondson 1983, de Haan 1997), and temporal and aspectual adverbs (Tovena 1998, Hoeksema 2000). By the same token, the reason why color terms, for example, are probably never polarity sensitive (except, as with *a red cent*, as part of some idiom) may be that alternatives within the color domain are not easily construed as exhibiting scalar structure.

Still, the scalar model and its four-way taxonomy are at best just a first approximation of the forms polarity items may take and the ways they may differ: even if modal, aspectual, and indefinite polarity items are all fundamentally scalar, that doesn't mean they should all behave exactly the same. Every polarity item has its own story: the scalar model just makes some general predictions about what sorts of characters will appear in these stories. The scalar model does, however, take a strong view that sensitivity is a lexical property of polarity items, and that the varieties of sensitivity reflect the lexical details which distinguish different polarity items. The fine-grained study of such differences is still in its infancy (cf. van der Wouden 1994/1997, von Klopp 1998, Tovena 1998, Hoeksema 2000), but it may yet prove a growth industry in polarity studies.

4.3 *The scalar pragmatics of licensing*

The robust correlation between scalar semantics and polarity sensitivity suggests that, *pace* Linebarger, polarity items do have a special relationship to scalar inferencing: the question is, what sort of relationship is it? One possibility, as I suggested above, is that it is purely pragmatic, that licensing depends directly on the meanings of polarity items and their coherence with the contexts in which they occur. The more standard assumption, following Ladusaw (1980), is that polarity items are sensitive to logical properties of sentence grammar – to an algorithmically derived representation of a sentence's literal truth-conditional meaning. Indeed, polarity items are often seen as providing the best evidence there is for such representations. In this section I will argue to the contrary that the inferential properties which license polarity items are pragmatic in nature and cannot be reduced to logical properties of sentence meaning.

A variety of polarity contexts are not, strictly speaking, downward entailing. Non-rhetorical questions are perhaps the most notorious example of a non-monotonic polarity licensor (Fauconnier 1980, Krifka 1995). Similarly, the antecedent of a conditional usually licenses downward inferences, but as (26) suggests, not always; and, as Atlas (1996) notes, the status of *only* as

DE operator seems doubtful given the lack of entailment from examples like (27a) to (27b).

(26)a. If you work hard, you'll succeed ⇒?
  b. If you work hard and are incompetent, you'll succeed.

(27)a. Of all my sisters, only Gwendolyn keeps pets. ⇒?
  b. Of all my sisters, only Gwendolyn keeps a pet mongoose.

There are, however, various ways in which the logic of downward entailingness can be extended to accommodate these sorts of contexts (cf. Heim 1984, von Fintel 1999, Horn, to appear), and I will simply concede that such cases may be handled with a sufficiently sophisticated theory of semantic representations.

More interesting for my purposes are cases where the inferences which license a polarity item clearly depend on pragmatic assumptions that cannot be part of sentence meaning. In extreme cases it is difficult to discern any licensor at all. Examples like those in (28) involve what Horn (2001) calls FLAUBERT TRIGGERS since, "like God in the deist universe and the author in the Flaubertian novel, so is negation [in these examples]: everywhere present yet nowhere visible."

(28)a. It's nice to sit at a table with a candle <u>at all</u>.   [dinner conversation]
  b. The tone [of Germaine Greer's attack on manufacturers of vaginal deodorants] wasn't light-hearted, which might have justified touching the subject <u>at all</u>.   [C. McCabe, *S.F. Chronicle*, cited in Horn 1978a: 153]
  c. Sensitive Man as portrayed in popular culture was always a caricature, of course. But the signs of his discrediting have been building, along with male confusion. (We speak of those heterosexual men, mainly in their 30s, 40s, and 50s, who <u>ever gave a thought</u> to <u>any</u> of this.)   [*New York Times*, May 8, 1994; cited in Horn 2001]
  d. The reason one <u>ever bothers to</u> decant a wine is to leave the sediment . . . behind in the bottle.)   [*SouthWest Airlines Spirit* August 1994: 47]

Such uses are rare, but they are not random aberrations. Crucially, the NPIs work in these examples because they do function in context as emphatic scalar endpoints: thus in (28a), *at all* emphasizes the degree to which having a candle is in itself a treat, and in (28c) the NPIs underscore the exceptionality of a rare species of male.

The determiners *most* and *few* provide a more systematic example of a context in which licensing crucially depends on pragmatic rather than logical inferencing. Ladusaw finds *most* difficult to judge (1980: 151), but the examples below suggest that it is neither upward nor downward entailing on its first argument.

(29)a. [Most of the boys who ate an apple] got sick. −/→
  b. ←/−[Most of the boys who ate fruit] got sick.

(29a) does not entail (29b): it could be that all the boys ate some fruit, and that the apples were poisoned so that most of those who ate an apple got sick, but that really very few boys got sick because most just ate cherimoyas and blackberries and avoided the poisoned apples. This shows that *most* is not upward entailing on its first argument. Similarly, (29b) does not entail (29a): after all, it could be that the cherimoyas were poisoned, but that the apples contained an antidote, so that most of the boys who ate fruit got sick, but those lucky few who ate an apple were spared. This shows that *most* is not downward entailing on its first argument. Parallel examples may be constructed for *few* to show that it is also non-monotonic on its first argument.

Despite their non-monotonicity *most* and *few* do occasionally license NPIs (Heim 1984, Jackson 1994, Barker 1995, Israel 1995, 1998), including, at least marginally, strong NPIs like *lift a finger* and *the least bit*.

(30)a.   Most children with <u>any</u> sense steal candy.   [from Barker 1995: 117]
   b.   Most people who <u>would lift a finger</u> to help Bill now are either very foolish or very well paid.

(31)a.   Few children with <u>any</u> sense play Frisbee on freeways.
   b.   Few people with <u>the least bit</u> of human feeling could doubt her sincerity.

Apparently, under the right circumstances *most* and *few* do allow the limited downward entailments needed to license a polarity item (cf. Heim 1984: 102–4). For example, *any* is licensed in (30a) and (31a) by the inferences that most children with a lot of sense would also steal candy, and that few children with a lot of sense would play Frisbee on the highway. In other words, these forms license NPIs because, and precisely to the extent that, they trigger appropriate scalar inferences.

These inferences are crucially context sensitive. Because these forms are non-monotonic, they may trigger inferences in either direction in a scalar model. In (32), for example, given a scale of puzzles ranked by difficulty, *most* can license pragmatic inferences either from easy puzzles to harder puzzles, or from harder puzzles to easier puzzles, depending on what it is the inferences are about.

(32)a.   [Most students who could solve the easy puzzles] got a prize.
      → [Most students who could solve the hard puzzles] got a prize.
   b.   [Most students who could solve the hard puzzles] had trouble on the exam.
      → [Most who could solve the easy puzzles] had trouble on the exam.

The inference in (32a) follows from an assumption that major accomplishments, like solving a difficult puzzle, will be at least as well rewarded as minor accomplishments. The inference in (32b), on the other hand, depends on the assumption that those with modest abilities will have as much difficulty as those with greater abilities. Crucially, it is only in the first case, where inferences run from easy puzzles to hard ones, that *most* can license NPIs.

(33)a.   Most students who could solve even a single puzzle got a prize.
  b.   *Most students who could solve even a single puzzle had trouble on the exam.

It is worth noting here that this is not just an idiosyncratic fact about *most* and *few*: the same judgments hold in (30) and (32–3), a quasi-universal NP like *Almost every student*, or even with a generic bare plural subject, *Students*. I suggest that all of these forms license polarity items by virtue of their inferential properties, but that these are not logical properties of the forms themselves, nor even of the sentences they occur in. Rather they reflect the complex interaction of syntactic, semantic and especially pragmatic factors which determine the availability of an appropriate scalar construal.

The need for a coherent scalar construal also helps explain why NPIs sometimes fail to be licensed when they do occur in the scope of a DE operator. For example, Yoshimura (1994) shows that the use of NPIs in *before* clauses as in (34) (an unambiguously DE context) may depend on pragmatic assumptions about how the world works.

(34)a.   Miss Prism {spilled/??poured} her wine before she had drunk a drop.
  b.   The alarm clock was {ringing/??plugged in} before I could sleep a wink.

As Yoshimura argues, the felicity of the NPI in these examples depends on the availability of an implicit contrast between what is said and what might have been expected: at least in polite society, one does not expect wine to be drunk before it is poured; and one normally makes a point of plugging in the alarm clock before one even tries to go to sleep. Yoshimura formulates this need for an implicit contrast as a procedural semantic constraint on polarity licensing. Such a constraint is, in fact, implicit in the structure of a scalar model, since the key notions of emphasis and attenuation are defined by the contrast between different propositions in a model. Where normal assumptions about how the world works fail to make such a contrast available, as with the poured wine and the plugged-in alarm clock, a scalar construal is impossible, and so polarity items cannot be licensed.

The need for a scalar construal systematically limits the licensing potential of all polarity triggers, including even sentential negation.

(35)a.   Cecily didn't eat a bite of her food.
  b.   ??Cecily didn't stare at a bite of her food.

The contrast in (35) reflects the fact that while there are many activities for which a bite of food might count as a natural minimal unit, staring is not one of them: one can just as easily stare at a banquet as at a single bite. Since the expressed proposition does not seem to contrast with any weaker proposition, the NPI fails to express its emphatic force, and the sentence fails to be grammatical. Again, what counts for NPI licensing are not so much the logical properties of the licensor but the way those properties help the NPI to fulfill its inherent pragmatic functions.

Finally, I should acknowledge that even if polarity items are basically pragmatic operators, they still can be subject to syntactic constraints: they might, for instance, undergo processes of grammaticalization which narrow their use to certain syntactic constructions; or they might start off as negative idioms which for one reason or another never get generalized to other licensing contexts. In this sense, Linebarger is surely right that NPIs are (at least sometimes) "close associates of negation," and that they may be subject to constraints which are more structural than semantic.

The real question is how we should think of such constraints. My own (minority) view is that they reflect collocational dependencies between polarity items and licensing constructions – that polarity items are, in effect, idioms and that their distributions are learned on the basis of conventional usage.[6] On this view, part of what it means to know a polarity item is to know what contexts it occurs in, and so the use of a polarity item in a novel context (i.e. one where it has not previously been heard) will reflect the degree to which that context is felt to be similar (lexically, semantically, pragmatically, and syntactically) to contexts where it has previously occurred. The weakness of such a usage-based model, of course, is that it is grossly unconstrained: it begs the question of what similarities may be linguistically significant. On the other hand, this may be just the right question to beg at this point. A more constrained theory may come once we come to terms with the diverse sensitivities polarity items may exhibit,[7] and this can only be done through the detailed study of the idiomatic properties of a large range of examples.

5   Conclusions

Having said so much, and so quickly, I can do no more than return to the paradox with which I began. Polarity, the opposition between negation and affirmation, seems to be both simple and symmetrical, and yet its behavior in natural language is neither. There are many parts of "no" one might easily not understand. Negation, it seems, is simply too useful to be confined by the simplicity of its own logic. The question is, what is the relation between the logic of negation and the pragmatics of polarity? Is negation essentially a logical relation with many pragmatic uses? Or is it an argumentative device from whose uses we distill a logical essence? The answers to these questions must have radical implications for how we think about the relation between semantics and pragmatics, and the nature of language and thought. I will not presume to answer them myself, but I hope, if nothing else, that this essay may help us to pose them more clearly.

ACKNOWLEDGMENTS

I am grateful to Claudia Brugman, Larry Horn, Paul Kay, and Tess Wood for comments and discussions which have helped me in preparing this chapter. What inadequacies remain are entirely my own responsibility.

NOTES

1   Such scales come in a variety of forms, including taxonomies, meronomies, partonomies, and rank orders: Hirschberg (1991) in fact argues that any partial ordering can be used to generate scalar implicatures. Whether or not a more constrained theory of scalar reasoning is feasible (cf. Levinson 2000a), it is clear that the knowledge structures which underlie scalar models are remarkably diverse.

2   In Argumentation Theory (i.e. *La Théorie de l'Argumentation dans la Langue* – Ducrot 1973, 1980, Anscombre and Ducrot 1983) these sorts of argumentative relations are built directly into the structure of a scale. In this theory, sentences do not in fact convey truth-conditional content at all (at least not directly), but are seen rather as tools for orienting a discourse toward a conclusion of some sort. For a useful comparison of entailment-based and argumentational approaches to the scalar properties of *even* see Kalokerinos (1995).

3   Pederson (1993) discusses the origin of zero-marked negatives in South Dravidian languages. For details on the cross-linguistic expression of negation see Dahl (1979), Payne (1985), and Kahrel and van den Berg (1994).

4   Along these lines Langacker (1987, vol. 2: 134–9) analyzes negation as involving the conceptualization of a background entity and profiling the absence of that entity from the current discourse space.

5   I hasten to acknowledge that pragmatic motivations alone are not sufficient to explain the grammar of neg-raising. In particular, as Horn (1989) demonstrates, the set of matrix predicates in any language which allow neg-raising is, at least in part, a matter of convention. The point, in any case, is not that pragmatics can explain grammar away (it can't), but that it can explain why grammar takes the forms it does.

6   Similar views are found in Fillmore et al. (1988) and van der Wouden (1994/1997).

7   Haspelmath's (1997) cross-linguistic study of indefinite pronouns provides a particularly striking portrait of the many ways distributional constraints may vary.

32 Abduction in Natural Language Understanding

JERRY R. HOBBS

1 Language and Knowledge

We are able to understand language so well because we know so much. When we read the sentence

(1) John drove down the street in a car.

we know immediately that the driving and hence John are in the car and that the street isn't. We attach the prepositional phrase to the verb "drove" rather than to the noun "street." This is not syntactic knowledge, because in the syntactically similar sentence

(2) John drove down a street in Chicago.

it is the street that is in Chicago.

Therefore, a large part of the study of language should be an investigation of the question of how we use our knowledge of the world to understand discourse. This question has been examined primarily by researchers in the field of artificial intelligence (AI), in part because they have been interested in linking language with actual behavior in specific situations, which has led them to an attempt to represent and reason about fairly complex world knowledge.

In this chapter I describe how a particular kind of reasoning, called ABDUCTION, provides a framework for addressing a broad range of problems that are posed in discourse and that require world knowledge in their solutions. I first defend first-order logic as a mode of representation for the information conveyed by sentences and the knowledge we bring to the discourses we interpret, but with one caveat: Reasoning must be defeasible. I discuss several ways that defeasible inference has been formalized in AI, and introduce abduction as one of those methods. Then in successive sections I show:

- how various problems in LOCAL PRAGMATICS, such as reference resolution, metonymy, interpreting compound nominals, and word sense disambiguation can be solved via abduction;
- how this processing can be embedded in a process for recognizing the structure of discourse; and
- how these can all be integrated with the recognition of the speaker's plan.

I close with a discussion of the relation of this framework to Relevance Theory and of some of the principal outstanding research issues.

2   Logic as the Language of Thought

A very large body of work in AI begins with the assumptions that information and knowledge should be represented in first-order logic and that reasoning is theorem proving. On the face of it, this seems implausible as a model for people. It certainly doesn't seem as if we are using logic when we are thinking, and if we are, why are so many of our thoughts and actions so illogical? In fact, there are psychological experiments that purport to show that people do not use logic in thinking about a problem (e.g. Wason and Johnson-Laird 1972).

I believe that the claim that logic is the language of thought comes to less than one might think, however, and that thus it is more controversial than it ought to be. It is the claim that a broad range of cognitive processes are amenable to a high-level description in which six key features are present. The first three of these features characterize propositional logic and the next two first-order logic. I will express them in terms of "concepts," but one can just as easily substitute propositions, neural elements, or a number of other terms.

- **Conjunction**:   There is an additive effect $(P \wedge Q)$ of two distinct concepts (P and Q) being activated at the same time.
- **Modus ponens**:   The activation of one concept (P) triggers the activation of another concept (Q) because of the existence of some structural relation between them $(P \supset Q)$.
- **Recognition of obvious contradictions**:   The recognition of contradictions in general is undecidable, but we have no trouble with the easy ones, for example, that cats aren't dogs.
- **Predicate–argument relations**:   Concepts can be related to other concepts in several different ways. For example, we can distinguish between a dog biting a man $(bite(D, M))$ and a man biting a dog $(bite(M, D))$.
- **Universal instantiation (or variable binding)**:   We can keep separate our knowledge of general (universal) principles ("All men are mortal") and our knowledge of their instantiations for particular individuals ("Socrates is a man" and "Socrates is mortal").

Any plausible proposal for a language of thought must have at least these features, and once you have these features you have first-order logic.

Note that in this list there are no complex rules for double negations or for contrapositives (if P implies Q then not Q implies not P). In fact, most of the psychological experiments purporting to show that people don't use logic really show that they don't use the contrapositive rule or that they don't handle double negations well. If the tasks in those experiments were recast into problems involving the use of modus ponens, no one would think to do the experiments because it is obvious that people would have no trouble with the task.

As an aside, let me mention that many researchers in linguistics and in knowledge representation make use of **higher-order** logic. It is straightforward, through various kinds of reification, to recast these logics into first-order logic, and in view of the resulting simplification in characterizing the reasoning process, there are very good reasons to do so (Hobbs 1985a).

There is one further property we need of the logic if we are to use it for representing and reasoning about commonsense world knowledge – defeasibility or non-monotonicity.

3   Non-monotonic Logic

The logic of mathematics is monotonic, in that once we know the truth value of a statement, nothing else we learn can change it. Virtually all commonsense knowledge beyond mathematics is uncertain or defeasible. Whatever general principles we have are usually only true most of the time or true with high probability or true unless we discover evidence to the contrary. It is almost always possible that we may have to change what we believed to be the truth value of a statement upon gaining more information. Almost all commonsense knowledge should be tagged with "insofar as I have been able to determine with my limited access to the facts and my limited resources for reasoning." The logic of commonsense knowledge must be non-monotonic.

The development of non-monotonic logics has been a major focus in AI research (Ginsberg 1987). One early attempt involved "negation as failure" (Hewitt 1972); we assume that not P is true if we fail to prove that P. Another early non-monotonic logic (McDermott and Doyle 1980) had rules of the form "If P is true and Q is consistent with everything else we know, then take Q to be true."

Probably the most thoroughly investigated non-monotonic logic was that developed by McCarthy (1980). He introduced ABNORMALITY CONDITIONS which the reasoner then minimized. For example, the general fact that birds fly is expressed:

(3) $(\forall x)[bird(x) \land \neg ab_1(x) \supset fly(x)]$.

That is, if x is a bird and not abnormal in a way specific to this rule, then x flies. Further axioms might spell out the exceptions:

(4) $(\forall x)[penguin(x) \supset ab_1(x)]$.

That is, penguins are abnormal in the way specific to the "birds fly" rule.

Then to draw conclusions we minimize, in some fashion, those things we take to be abnormal. If all we know about Tweety is that he is a bird, then we assume he is not abnormal, and thus we conclude he can fly. If we subsequently learn that Tweety is a penguin, we retract the assumption that he is not abnormal in that way.

A problem arises with this approach when we have many axioms with different abnormality conditions. There may be many ways to minimize the abnormalities, each leading to different conclusions. This is illustrated by an example that is known as the NIXON DIAMOND (Reiter and Criscuolo 1981). Suppose we know that generally Quakers are pacifists. We can write this as:

(5) $(\forall x)[Quaker(x) \wedge \neg ab_2(x) \supset pacifist(x)]$.

Suppose we also know that Republicans are generally not pacifists:

(6) $(\forall x)[Republican(x) \wedge \neg ab_3(x) \supset \neg pacifist(x)]$.

Then what do we conclude when we learn that Nixon is both a Quaker and a Republican? Assuming both abnormality conditions results in a contradiction. If we take ab_2 to be false, we conclude Nixon is a pacifist. If we take ab_3 to be false, we conclude Nixon is not a pacifist. How do we choose between the two possibilities? Researchers have made various suggestions for how to think about this problem (e.g. Shoham 1987). In general, some scheme is needed for choosing among the possible combinations of assumptions.

In recent years there has been considerable interest in AI in the reasoning process known as abduction, or inference to the best explanation. As it is normally conceived in AI, it can be viewed as one variety of non-monotonic logic.

4 Abduction

The simplest way to explain abduction is by comparing it with two words it rhymes with – deduction and induction. In deduction, from P and $P \supset Q$, we conclude Q. In induction, from P and Q, or more likely a number of instances of P and Q together with other considerations, we conclude $P \supset Q$. Abduction is the third possibility. From an observable Q and a general principle $P \supset Q$, we conclude that P must be the underlying reason that Q is true. We assume P because it explains Q.

Of course, there may be many such possible P's, some contradictory with others, and therefore any method of abduction must include a method for evaluating and choosing among alternatives. At a first cut, suppose in trying to explain Q we know $P \wedge R \supset Q$ and we know R. Then R provides partial evidence that Q is true, making the assumption of P more reasonable. In addition, if we are seeking to explain two things, Q_1 and Q_2, then it is reasonable to favor assuming a P that explains both of them rather than a different explanation for each.

The conclusions we draw in this way are only assumptions and may have to be retracted later if we acquire new, contradictory information. That is, this method of reasoning is non-monotonic.

Abduction has a history. Prior to the late seventeenth century science was viewed as deductive, at least in the ideal. It was felt that, on the model of Euclidean geometry, one should begin with propositions that were self-evident and deduce whatever consequences one could from them. The modern view of scientific theories, probably best expressed by Lakatos (1970), is quite different. One tries to construct abstract theories from which observable events can be deduced or predicted. There is no need for the abstract theories to be self-evident, and they usually are not. It is only necessary for them to predict as broad a range as possible of the observable data and for them to be "elegant," whatever that means. Thus, the modern view is that science is fundamentally abductive. We seek hidden principles or causes from which we can deduce the observable evidence.

This view of science, and hence the notion of abduction, can be seen first, insofar as I am aware, in some passages in Newton's *Principia* (1934 [1686]). At the end of *Principia*, in a justification for not seeking the cause of gravity, he says, "And to us it is enough that gravity does really exist, and act according to the laws which we have explained, and abundantly serves to account for all the motions of the celestial bodies, and of our sea" (Newton 1934: 547). The justification for gravity (P) and its laws ($P \supset Q$) is not in their self-evidential nature but in what they account for (Q).

In the eighteenth century, the German philosopher Christian Wolff (1963 [1728]) shows, to my knowledge, the earliest **explicit** awareness of the importance of abductive reasoning. He presents almost the standard Euclidean account of certain knowledge, but with an important provision in his recognition of the inevitability and importance of hypotheses:

> Philosophy must use hypotheses insofar as they pave the way to the discovery of certain truth. For in a philosophical hypothesis certain things which are not firmly established are assumed because they provide a reason for things which are observed to occur. Now if we can also deduce other things which are not observed to occur, then we have the opportunity to either observe or experimentally detect things which otherwise we might not have noticed. In this way we become more certain as to whether or not anything contrary to experience follows from the hypothesis. If we deduce things which are contrary to experience, then the hypothesis is false. If the deductions agree with experience, then the probability of the hypothesis is increased. And thus the way is paved for the discovery of certain truth.   (Wolff 1963: 67)

He also recognizes the principle of parsimony: "If one cannot necessarily deduce from a hypothesis the things for which it is assumed, then the hypothesis is spurious" (Wolff 1963: 68). However, he views hypotheses as only provisional, awaiting deductive proof.

The term "abduction" was first used by C. S. Peirce (e.g. 1955). His definition of it is as follows:

(7)   The surprising fact, Q, is observed;
       But if P were true, Q would be a matter of course,
       Hence, there is reason to suspect that P is true.   (Peirce 1955: 151)

(He actually used A and C for P and Q.) Peirce says that "in pure abduction, it can never be justifiable to accept the hypothesis otherwise than as an interrogation," and that "the whole question of what one out of a number of possible hypotheses ought to be entertained becomes purely a question of economy." That is, there must be an evaluation scheme for choosing among possible abductive inferences.

The earliest formulation of abduction in artificial intelligence was by C. Morgan (1971). He showed how a complete set of truth-preserving rules for generating theorems could be turned into a complete set of falsehood-preserving rules for generating hypotheses.

The first use of abduction in an AI application was by Pople (1973), in the context of medical diagnosis. He gave the formulation of abduction sketched above and showed how it can be implemented in a theorem-proving framework. Literals (or propositions) that are "abandoned by deduction in the sense that they fail to have successor nodes" (Pople 1973: 150) are taken as the candidate hypotheses. That is, one tries to prove the symptoms and signs exhibited and the parts of a potential proof that cannot be proven are the candidate hypotheses. Those hypotheses are best that account for the most data, and in service of this principle, he introduced factoring or synthesis, which attempts to unify goal literals. Hypotheses where this is used are favored. That is, that explanation is best that minimizes the number of causes.

Work on abduction in artificial intelligence was revived in the 1980s at several sites. Reggia and his colleagues (e.g. Reggia et al. 1983, Reggia 1985) formulated abductive inference in terms of parsimonious covering theory. Charniak and McDermott (1985) presented the basic pattern of abduction and then discussed many of the issues involved in trying to decide among alternative hypotheses on probabilistic grounds. Cox and Pietrzykowski (1986) present a formulation in a theorem-proving framework that is very similar to Pople's, though apparently independent. It is especially valuable in that it considers abduction abstractly, as a mechanism with a variety of possible applications, and not just as a handmaiden to diagnosis.

Josephson and Josephson (1994) provide a comprehensive treatment of abduction, its philosophical background, its computational properties, and its utilization in AI applications.

I have indicated that the practice of science is fundamentally abductive. The extension of abduction to ordinary cognitive tasks is very much in line with the popular view in cognitive science that people going about in the world trying to understand it are scientists in the small. This view can be extended to natural language understanding – interpreting discourse is coming up with the best explanation for what is said.

The first appeal to something like abduction that I am aware of in natural language understanding was by Grice (1967, 1989), when he introduced the notion of CONVERSATIONAL IMPLICATURE to handle examples like the following:

(8)   A: How is John doing on his new job at the bank?
     B: Quite well. He likes his colleagues and he hasn't embezzled any money yet.

Grice argues that in order to see this as coherent, we must assume, or draw as a conversational implicature, that both A and B know that John is dishonest. Although he does not say so, an implicature can be viewed as an abductive move for the sake of achieving the best interpretation.

Lewis (1979) introduces the notion of ACCOMMODATION in conversation to explain the phenomenon that occurs when you "say something that requires a missing presupposition, and straightaway that presupposition springs into existence, making what you said acceptable after all." The hearer accommodates the speaker.

Thomason (1990) argued that Grice's conversational implicatures are based on Lewis's rule of accommodation. We might say that implicature is a procedural characterization of something that, at the functional or interactional level, appears as accommodation. Implicature is the way we do accommodation.

In the middle 1980s researchers at several sites began to apply abduction to natural language understanding (Norvig 1983, 1987; Wilensky 1983; Wilensky et al. 1988; Charniak and Goldman 1988, 1989; Hobbs et al. 1988, 1993). At least in the last case the recognition that implicature was a use of abduction was a key observation in the development of the framework.

Norvig, Wilensky, and their associates proposed an operation called CON-CRETION, one of many that take place in the processing of a text. It is a "kind of inference in which a more specific interpretation of an utterance is made than can be sustained on a strictly logical basis" (Wilensky et al. 1988: 50). Thus, "to use a pencil" generally means to write with a pencil, even though one could use a pencil for many other purposes.

Charniak and his associates also developed an abductive approach to interpretation. Charniak (1986) expressed the fundamental insight: "A standard platitude is that understanding something is relating it to what one already knows. . . . One extreme example would be to prove that what one is told must be true on the basis of what one already knows. . . . We want to prove what one is told *given certain assumptions*" (Charniak 1986: 585).

Charniak and Goldman developed an interpretation procedure that incrementally built a belief network (Pearl 1988), where the links between the nodes, representing influences between events, were determined from axioms expressing world knowledge. They felt that one could make not unreasonable estimates of the required probabilities, giving a principled semantics to the numbers. The networks were then evaluated and ambiguities were resolved by looking for the highest resultant probabilities.

Stickel invented a method called WEIGHTED ABDUCTION (Stickel 1988, Hobbs et al. 1993) that builds the evaluation criteria into the proof process. Briefly, propositions to be proved are given an assumption cost – what you will have to pay to assume them. When we backchain over a rule of the form $P \supset Q$, the cost is passed back from Q to P, according to a weight associated with P. Generally, P will cost more to assume than Q, so that short proofs are favored over long ones. But if partial evidence is found, for example, if $P \wedge R \supset Q$ and we can prove R, then it will cost less to assume P than to assume Q, and we get a more specific interpretation. In addition, if we need to prove Q_1 and Q_2 and P implies both, then it will cost less to assume P than to assume Q_1 and Q_2. This feature of the method allows us to exploit the implicit redundancy inherent in natural language discourse.

Weighted abduction suggests a simple way to incorporate the uncertainty of knowledge into the axioms expressing the knowledge. Propositions can be assumed at a cost. Therefore, we can have propositions whose only role is to be assumed and to levy a cost. For example, let's return to the rule that birds fly. We can express it with the axiom

(9) $(\forall x)[bird(x) \wedge etc_1(x) \supset fly(x)]$

That is, if x is a bird and some other unspecified conditions hold for x ($etc_1(x)$), then x flies. The predicate etc_1 encodes the unspecified conditions. There will never be a way to prove it; it can only be assumed at cost. The cost of etc_1 will depend inversely on the certainty of the rule that birds fly. It will cost to use this rule, but the lowest-cost proof of everything we are trying to explain may nevertheless involve this rule and hence the inference that birds fly. We know that penguins don't fly:

(10) $(\forall x)[penguin(x) \supset \neg fly(x)]$

If we know Tweety is a penguin, we know he doesn't fly. Thus, to assume etc_1 is true of Tweety would lead to a contradiction, so we don't. The relation between the etc predicates and the abnormality predicates of McCarthy's nonmonotonic logic is obvious: etc_1 is just $\neg ab_1$.

The framework of "Interpretation as Abduction" (IA) (Hobbs et al. 1993) follows directly from this method of abductive inference, and it is the IA framework that is presented in the remainder of this chapter. Whereas in Norvig and Wilensky's work, abduction or concretion was one process among many involved in natural language understanding, in the IA framework abduction is the whole story. Whereas in Charniak and Goldman's work, specific procedures involving abduction are implemented to solve specific interpretation problems, in the IA framework there is only one procedure – abduction – that is used to explain or prove the logical form of the text, and the solutions to specific interpretation problems fall out as by-products of this process.

It should be pointed out that in addition to what is presented below there have been a number of other researchers who have used abduction for various natural language understanding problems, including Nagao (1989) for resolving syntactic ambiguity, Dasigi (1988) for resolving lexical ambiguity, Rayner (1993) for asking questions of a database, Ng and Mooney (1990) and Lascarides and Oberlander (1992) for recognizing discourse structure, McRoy and Hirst (1991) for making repairs in presupposition errors, Appelt and Pollack (1990) for recognizing the speaker's plan, and Harabagiu and Moldovan (1998) for general text understanding using WordNet as a knowledge base.

5   Interpretation as Abduction

In the IA framework we can describe very concisely what it is to interpret a sentence:

(11)   Prove the logical form of the sentence,
            together with the selectional constraints that predicates impose on
               their arguments,
            allowing for coercions,
        Merging redundancies where possible,
        Making assumptions where necessary.

By the first line we mean "prove, or derive in the logical sense, from the predicate calculus axioms in the knowledge base, the logical form that has been produced by syntactic analysis and semantic translation of the sentence."

In a discourse situation, the speaker and hearer both have their sets of private beliefs, and there is a large overlapping set of mutual beliefs. An utterance lives on the boundary between mutual belief and the speaker's private beliefs. It is a bid to extend the area of mutual belief to include some private beliefs of the speaker's. It is anchored referentially in mutual belief, and when we succeed in proving the logical form and the constraints, we are recognizing this referential anchor. This is the given information, the definite, the presupposed. Where it is necessary to make assumptions, the information comes from the speaker's private beliefs, and hence is the new information, the indefinite, the asserted. Merging redundancies is a way of getting a minimal, and hence a best, interpretation.

Merging redundancies and minimizing the assumptions result naturally from the method of weighted abduction.

6 Abduction and Local Pragmatics

Local pragmatics encompasses those problems that are posed within the scope of individual sentences, even though their solution will generally require greater context and world knowledge. Included under this label are the resolution of coreference, resolving syntactic and lexical ambiguity, interpreting metonymy and metaphor, and finding specific meanings for vague predicates such as in the compound nominal.

Consider a simple example that contains three of these problems:

(12)   The Boston office called.

This sentence poses the problems of resolving the reference of "the Boston office," expanding the metonymy to "[Some person at] the Boston office called," and determining the implicit relation between Boston and the office. Let us put these problems aside for the moment, however, and interpret the sentence according to the IA characterization. We must prove abductively the logical form of the sentence together with the constraint "call" imposes on its agent, allowing for a coercion. That is, we must prove abductively that there is a calling event by a person who may or may not be the same as the explicit subject of the sentence, but it is at least related to it, or coercible from it, and that there is an office bearing some unspecified relation to Boston.

The sentence can be interpreted with respect to a knowledge base of mutual knowledge that contains the following facts and rules, expressed as axioms:

There is a city of Boston.
There is an office in Boston.
John is a person who works for the office.
The "in" relation can be represented by a compound nominal.
An organization can be coerced into a person who works for it.

Given these rules, the proof of all of the logical form is straightforward except for the existence of the calling event. Hence, we assume that it is the new information conveyed by the sentence.

Now notice that the three local pragmatics problems have been solved as a by-product. We have resolved "the Boston office" to the specific office we know about. We have determined the implicit relation in the compound nominal to be "in." And we have expanded the metonymy to "John, who works for the Boston office, called."

For an illustration of the resolution of lexical ambiguity, consider an example from Hirst (1987):

(13)   The plane taxied to the terminal.

The words "plane," "taxied," and "terminal" are all ambiguous.

Suppose the knowledge base consists of axioms with the following content:

An airplane is a plane.
A wood smoother is a plane.
For an airplane to move on the ground is for it to taxi.
For a person to ride in a cab is for him or her to taxi.
An airport terminal is a terminal.
A computer terminal is a terminal.
An airport has airplanes and an airport terminal.

To prove the logical form of the sentence, we need to prove abductively the existence of a plane, a terminal, and a taxi-ing event. The minimal proof of this will involve assuming the existence of an airport, deriving from that an airplane, and thus the plane, and an airport terminal, and thus the terminal, assuming that a plane is moving on the ground, and recognizing the identity of the airplane at the airport with the one in that reading of "taxi."

Another possible interpretation would be one in which we assumed that a wood smoother, a ride in a cab, and a computer terminal all existed. It is because weighted abduction favors merging redundancies that the correct interpretation is the one chosen. That interpretation allows us to minimize the assumptions we make.

7   Recognizing Discourse Structure

Syntax can be incorporated into this framework (Hobbs 1998) by encoding the rules of Pollard and Sag's (1994) Head-driven Phrase Structure Grammar in axioms. The axioms involve predications asserting that strings of words describe entities or situations. Parsing a sentence is then proving that there is a situation that the sentence describes. This proof bottoms out in the logical form of the sentence, and proving this is the process of interpretation described in the previous section. We have recast the process of interpreting a sentence from the problem of proving the logical form into the problem of proving the string of words is a grammatical, interpretable sentence, where "interpretable" means we can prove the logical form.

When two segments of discourse are adjacent, that very adjacency conveys information. Each segment, insofar as it is coherent, conveys information about a situation or eventuality, and the adjacency of the segments conveys the suggestion that the two situations are related in some fashion, or are parts of larger units that are related. Part of what it is to understand a discourse is to discover what that relation is.

Overwhelmingly, the relations that obtain between discourse segments are based on causal, similarity, or figure–ground relations between the situations they convey. We can thus define a number of COHERENCE RELATIONS in terms of the relations between the situations. This will not be explored further here, but it is described in greater detail in Kehler (this volume). Here it will be shown how this aspect of discourse structure can be built into the abduction framework.

The two rules defining coherent discourse structure are as follows:

- A grammatical, interpretable sentence is a coherent segment of discourse.
- If two coherent segments of discourse are concatenated and there is a coherence relation between the situations they describe, then the concatenation is a coherent segment of discourse, and the situation it describes is determined by the coherence relation.

That is, when we combine two coherent segments of discourse with a coherence relation we get a coherent segment of discourse. By applying this successively to a stretch of discourse, we get a tree-like structure for the whole discourse. Different structures result from different choices in ordering the concatenation operations.

Now interpreting a text is a matter of proving that it is a coherent segment of discourse conveying some situation.

Consider an example. Explanation is a coherence relation, and a first approximation of a definition of the Explanation relation would be that the eventuality described by the second segment causes the eventuality described by the first. That is, if what is described by the second segment could cause what is described by the first segment, then there is a coherence relation between the segments.

Consider a variation on a classic example of pronoun resolution difficulties from Winograd (1972):

(14) The police prohibited the women from demonstrating.
      They feared violence.

How do we know "they" in the second sentence refers to the police and not to the women?

As in section 6, we will not attack the coreference problem directly, but we will proceed to interpret the text by abduction. To interpret the text is to prove abductively that the string of words comprising the whole text is a coherent segment of discourse describing some situation. This involves proving that each sentence is a segment, by proving they are grammatical, interpretable sentences, and proving there is a coherence relation between them. The proof that they are sentences would bottom out in the logical forms of the sentences, thus requiring us to prove abductively those logical forms.

One way to prove there is a coherence relation between the sentences is to prove there is an Explanation relation between them by showing there is a causal relation between the eventualities they describe. Thus, we must prove abductively the existence of the police, their prohibition of the demonstrating by the women, the fearing by someone of violence, and a causal relation between the fearing and the prohibition.

Suppose, plausibly enough, we have in our knowledge base axioms with the following content:

> If you fear something, that will cause you not to want it.
> Demonstrations cause violence.
> If you don't want the effect, that will cause you not to want the cause.
> If those in authority don't want something, that will cause them to prohibit it.
> The police are in authority.
> Causality is transitive.

From such axioms, we can prove all of the logical form of the text except the existence of the police, the demonstrating, and the fearing, which we assume. In the course of doing the proof, we unify the people doing the fearing with the police, thus resolving the problematic pronoun reference that originally motivated this example. "They" refers to the police.

One can imagine a number of variations on this example. If we had not included the axiom that demonstrations cause violence, we would have had to assume the violence and the causal relation between demonstrations and violence. Moreover, other coherence relations might be imagined here by constructing the surrounding context in the right way. It could be followed by the sentence "But since they had never demonstrated before, they did not know that violence might result." In this case, the second sentence would play a subordinate role to the third, forcing the resolution of "they" to the women. Each example, of course, has to be analyzed on its own, and changing the example changes the analysis. In Winograd's original version of this example,

(15)   The police prohibited the women from demonstrating, because they feared violence.

the causality was explicit, thus eliminating the coherence relation as a source of ambiguity. The causal relation would be part of the logical form.

Winograd's contrasting text, in which "they" is resolved to the women, is

(16)   The police prohibited the women from demonstrating, because they advocated violence.

Here we would need the facts that when one demonstrates one advocates and that advocating something tends to bring it about. Then showing a causal relation between the clauses will result in "they" being identified with the demonstrators.

8 Recognizing the Speaker's Plan

As presented so far, understanding discourse is seeing the world of the text as coherent, which in turn involves viewing the content of the text as observables to be explained. The focus has been on the information conveyed explicitly or implicitly by the discourse. We can call this the INFORMATIONAL account of a discourse.

But utterances are embedded in the world as well. They are produced to realize a speaker's intention, or, more generally, they are actions in the execution of a speaker's plan to achieve some goal. The description of how a discourse realizes the speakers' goals may be called the INTENTIONAL account of the discourse.

Consider the intentional account from the broadest perspective. An intelligent agent is embedded in the world and must, at each instant, understand the current situation. The agent does so by finding an explanation for what is perceived. Put differently, the agent must explain why the complete set of observables encountered constitutes a coherent situation. Other agents in the environment are viewed as intentional, that is, as planning mechanisms, and this means that the best explanation of their observable actions is most likely to be that the actions are steps in a coherent plan. Thus, making sense of an environment that includes other agents entails making sense of the other agents' actions in terms of what they are intended to achieve. When those actions are utterances, the utterances must be understood as actions in a plan the agents are trying to effect. That is, the speaker's plan must be recognized – the intentional account.

Generally, when a speaker says something it is with the goal of the hearer believing the content of the utterance, or thinking about it, or considering it, or taking some other cognitive stance toward it. Let us subsume all these mental terms under the term "cognize." Then we can summarize the relation between the intentional and informational accounts succinctly in the following formula:

(17) **intentional-account** = $goal(A, cognize(B, $ **informational-account**$))$

The speaker ostensibly has the goal of changing the mental state of the hearer to include some mental stance toward the content characterized by the informational account. Thus, the informational account is embedded in the intentional account. When we reason about the speaker's intention, we are reasoning about how this goal fits into the larger picture of the speaker's ongoing plan. We are asking why the speaker seems to be trying to get the hearer to believe this particular content. The informational account explains the situation described in the discourse; the intentional account explains why the speaker chose to convey this information.

Both the intentional and informational accounts are necessary. The informational account is needed because we have no direct access to the speaker's plan. We can only infer it from history and behavior. The content of the utterance is often the best evidence of the speaker's intention, and often the intention is no more than to convey that particular content. On the other hand, the intentional account is necessary in cases like pragmatic ellipsis, where the informational account is highly underdetermined and the global interpretation is primarily shaped by our beliefs about the speaker's plan.

Perhaps most interesting are cases of genuine conflict between the two accounts. The informational account does not seem to be true, or it seems to run counter to the speaker's goals for the hearer to come to believe it, or it ought to be obvious that the hearer already does believe it. Tautologies are an example of the last of these cases – tautologies such as "boys will be boys," "fair is fair," and "a job is a job." Norvig and Wilensky (1990) cite this figure of speech as something that should cause trouble for an abduction approach that seeks minimal explanations, since the minimal explanation is that they just express a known truth. Such an explanation requires no assumptions at all.

In fact, the phenomenon is a good example of why an informational account of discourse interpretation has to be embedded in an intentional account. Let us imagine two parents, A and B, sitting in the playground and talking.

(18)   A: Your Johnny is certainly acting up today, isn't he?
       B: Boys will be boys.

In order to avoid dealing with the complications of plurals and tense in this example, let us simplify B's utterance to

(19)   B: A boy is a boy.

Several informational accounts of this utterance are possible. The first is the Literal Extensional Interpretation. The first "a boy" introduces a specific, previously unidentified boy and the second says about him that he is a boy. The second informational account is the Literal Intensional Interpretation. The sentence expresses a trivial implicative relation between two general propositions – $boy(x)$ and $boy(x)$. The third is the Desired Interpretation. The first "a boy" identifies the typical member of a class of which Johnny is a member and the second conveys a general property, "being a boy," as a way of conveying a specific property, "misbehaving," which is true of members of that class.

Considering the informational account alone, the Literal Extensional Interpretation is minimal and hence would be favored. The Desired Interpretation is the worst of the three.

But the Literal Extensional and Intensional Interpretations leave the **fact** that the utterance **occurred** unaccounted for. In the intentional account, this is what we need to explain. The explanation would run something like this:

B wants A to believe that B is not responsible for Johnny's misbehaving.
Thus, B wants A to believe that Johnny misbehaves necessarily.
Thus, given that Johnny is necessarily a boy, B wants A to believe that
    Johnny's being a boy implies that he misbehaves.

Thus, B wants to convey to A that being a boy implies misbehaving.
Thus, given that boy-ness implies misbehaving is a possible interpretation
of a boy being a boy, B wants to say to A that a boy is a boy.

The content of the utterance under the Literal Extensional and Intensional
Interpretations do not lend themselves to explanations for the fact that the
utterance occurred, whereas the Desired Interpretation does. The requirement for the **globally** minimal explanation in an intentional account, that is,
the requirement that both the content and the fact of the utterance must be
explained, forces us into an interpretation of the content that would not be
favored in an informational account alone. We are forced into an interpretation
of the content that, while not optimal locally, contributes to a global interpretation that **is** optimal.

9   Relation to Relevance Theory

One of the other principal contenders for a theory of how we understand
extended discourse is Relevance Theory (RT) (Sperber and Wilson 1986a). In
fact, the IA framework and RT are very close to each other in the processing
that would implement them.

In RT, the agent is in the situation of having a knowlege base K and hearing a
sentence with content Q. From K and Q a new set R of inferences can be drawn:

(20) $K, Q \vdash R$

RT says that the agent strives to **maximize** R in an appropriately hedged sense.
An immediate consequence of this is that insofar as we are able to pragmatically
strengthen Q by means of axioms of the form

(21) $P \supset Q$

then we are getting a better R, since P implies anything that Q implies, and
then some. In the IA framework, we begin with pragmatic strengthening. The
task of the agent is to explain the general Q with the more specific P.

This means that anything done in the IA framework ought to carry over
without change into RT. Much of the work in RT depends primarily or solely
on pragmatic strengthening, and where this is the case, it can immediately be
incorporated into the IA framework.

From the point of view of IA, people are going through the world trying
to figure out what is going on. From the point of view of RT, they are going
through the world trying to learn as much as they can, and figuring out what
is going on is in service of that.

The IA framework has been worked out in greater detail formally and, I
believe, has a more compelling justification – explaining the observables in our

environment. But a great deal of excellent work has been done in RT, so it is useful to know that the two frameworks are almost entirely compatible.

10 Research Issues

In the examples given in this chapter, I have cavalierly assumed the most convenient axioms were in the knowledge base that was being used. But of course it is a serious research issue how to construct a knowledge base prior to seeing the discourses it will be used for interpreting. I believe there is a principled methodology for deciding what facts should go into a knowledge base (Hobbs 1984), and there are previous and ongoing efforts to construct a knowledge base of the required sort. For example, WordNet (Miller 1995), while shallow and lacking the required formality, is very broad, and attempts have been made to employ it as a knowledge base in text understanding (Harabagiu and Moldovan 1998). FrameNet (Baker et al. 1998) is a more recent effort aimed at deeper inference, but it is not yet as broad. The efforts of Hobbs et al. (1986), recently resumed, are deeper yet but very much smaller in scope. Cyc (Guha and Lenat 1990) is both broad and deep, but it is not clear how useful it will be for interpreting discourse (e.g. Mahesh et al. 1996). In any case, progress is being made on several fronts.

Another issue I was silent about in presenting the examples was exactly what the measure is that decides among competing interpretations. In some of the examples, factors such as redundancy in explanation and the coverage of the explanations were appealed to as criteria for choosing among them. But this was not made precise. Charniak and Shimony (1990) went a long way in setting the weighting criteria on a firm mathematical foundation, in terms of probabilities. But we still do not have very much experience in seeing how the method works out in practice. My feeling is that now the task is to build up a large knowledge base and do the necessary empirical studies of attempting to process a large number of texts with respect to the knowledge base. That of course requires the knowledge base.

I have written in this chapter only about interpretation, not about generation. It is an interesting question whether generation can be done in the same framework. At the most abstract level, it seems it should be possible. Interpreting a string of words was described as proving the existence of a situation that the string describes. It should be possible correspondingly to characterize the process of describing a situation as the process of proving the existence of a string of words that describes it. Preliminary explorations of this idea are described in Thomason and Hobbs (1997), but these are only preliminary.

The investigation of quantity implicatures should probably be located at the level of interactions between interpretation and generation. The sentence

(22) John has three children.

is usually not said when John has more than three children, even though it is still true in those circumstances. The hearer's reasoning would go something like this: The speaker said U_1, which could mean either M_1 or M_2. But she probably means M_1, because if she had meant M_2, she probably would have said U_2.

Also located in this area is the problem of how speakers are able to co-construct a single coherent segment of discourse, and sometimes a single sentence, across several conversational turns (e.g. Wilkes-Gibbs 1986).

Learning is another important research issue. Any framework that has ambitions of being a serious cognitive model must support an approach to learning. In the IA framework, what is learned is axioms. A set of axioms can be augmented incrementally via the following incremental changes: introducing a new predicate which is a specialization of an old one, increasing the arity of a predicate, adding a proposition to the antecedent of an axiom, and adding a proposition to the consequent of an axiom. But the details of this idea, e.g., when an axiom should be changed, have not yet been worked out.

Finally, there should be a plausible realization of the framework in some kind of neural architecture. The SHRUTI architecture developed by Shastri and his colleagues (e.g. Shastri and Ajjanagadde 1993) looks very promising in this regard. The variable binding required by first-order logic is realized by the synchronized firing of neurons, and the weighting scheme in the abduction method is realized by means of variable strengths of activation. But again, details remain to be worked out.

ACKNOWLEDGMENTS

This material is based in part on work supported by the National Science Foundation and Advanced Research Projects Agency under Grant Number IRI-9304961 (Integrated Techniques for Generation and Interpretation), and by the National Science Foundation under Grant Number IRI-9619126 (Multimodal Access to Spatial Data). Any opinions, findings, and conclusions or recommendations expressed in this chapter are those of the author and do not necessarily reflect the views of the National Science Foundation.

Bibliography

BLS n = *Proceedings of the nth Annual Meeting of the Berkeley Linguistics Society*. Berkeley, CA: Berkeley Linguistics Society.

CLS n = *Papers from the Chicago Linguistic Society, nth Regional Meeting*. Berkeley, CA: Berkeley Linguistics Society.

Similarly for the annual proceedings of rotating conferences for NELS (= North East Linguistic Society), WCCFL (West Coast Conference on Formal Linguistics), and SALT (= Semantics and Linguistic Theory).

Abbott, Barbara. (1993). A pragmatic account of the definiteness effect in existential sentences. *Journal of Pragmatics* 19: 39–55.

Abbott, Barbara. (1994). Referentiality, specificity, strength, and individual concepts. *West Coast Conference on Formal Linguistics* 12: 473–84. Stanford, CA: CSLI.

Abbott, Barbara. (1996). Doing without a partitive constraint. In J. Hoeksema (ed.), *Partitives: Studies on the Syntax and Semantics of Partitive and Related Constructions*, 25–56. Berlin: Mouton de Gruyter.

Abbott, Barbara. (1999). Support for a unique theory of definite descriptions. *Semantics and Linguistic Theory* IX: 1–15. Ithaca, NY: CLC Publications.

Abbott, Barbara. (2000). Presuppositions as non-assertions. *Journal of Pragmatics* 32: 1419–37.

Abbott, Barbara. (2001). Definiteness and identification in English. In E. Németh (ed.), *Pragmatics in 2000: Selected Papers from the 7th International Pragmatics Conference*, vol. 2, 1–15. Antwerp: International Pragmatics Association.

Abney, Steven. (1995). *Chunks and Dependencies: Bringing Processing Evidence to Bear on Syntax*. Stanford, CA: CSLI.

Aissen, Judith. (1975). Presentational *there*-insertion: a cyclic root transformation. *CLS* 11: 1–14.

Aissen, Judith. (2000). Differential object marking: iconicity vs. economy. Unpublished manuscript, University of California, Santa Cruz.

Akimoto, Minoji and Laurel J. Brinton. (1999). The origin of the composite predicate in Old English. In Brinton and Akimoto (eds.), 21–58.

Akmajian, Adrian. (1984). Sentence types and the form–function fit. *Natural Language and Linguistic Theory* 2: 1–23.

Alexandersson, Jan and Norbert Reithinger. (1997). Learning dialogue structures from a corpus. *EUROSPEECH-97* 4: 2231–4. Rhodes, Greece.

Allan, Keith. (1998). Meaning and speech acts. Available online at http://www.arts.monash.edu.au/ling/speech_acts_allan.shtml

Allen, James. (1995). *Natural Language Understanding.* Menlo Park, CA: Benjamin Cummings.

Allen, James and Mark Core. (1997). Draft of DAMSL: Dialog Act Markup in Several Layers. Unpublished manuscript, University of Rochester. Available online at http://www.cs.rochester.edu/research/cisd/resources/damsl/RevisedManual/RevisedManual.html

Allen, James and C. Raymond Perrault. (1980). Analyzing intention in utterances. *Artificial Intelligence* 15: 143–78. Reprinted in Grosz et al. (eds.) (1986), 441–58.

Allen, Shanley E. M. (2000). A discourse-pragmatic explanation for argument representation in child Inuktitut. *Linguistics* 38: 483–521.

Allen, Shanley E. M. and Heike Schroder (to appear). Preferred argument structure in early Inuktitut speech data. In J. DuBois, L. Kumpf and W. Ashby (eds.), *Preferred Argument Structure: Grammar as Architecture for Function.* Amsterdam: Benjamins.

Allerton, David John and Alan Cruttenden. (1979). Three reasons for accenting a definite subject. *Journal of Linguistics* 15: 49–53.

Allwood, Jens. (1995). *An Activity-Based Approach to Pragmatics.* Gothenburg Papers in Theoretical Linguistics 76, University of Göteborg.

Allwood, Jens, Joakim Nivre, and Elisabeth Ahlsen. (1992). On the semantics and pragmatics of linguistic feedback. *Journal of Semantics* 9: 1–26.

Alston, William P. (1964). *Philosophy of Language.* Englewood Cliffs, NJ: Prentice-Hall.

Alston, William P. (1994). Illocutionary acts and linguistic meaning. In Tsohatzidis (ed.), 29–49.

Altenberg, Bengt. (1987). *Prosodic Patterns in Spoken English: Studies in the Correlation between Prosody and Grammar for Text-to-Speech Conversion.* Lund: Lund University Press.

Andersen, Elaine S. (1990). *Speaking with Style: The Sociolinguistic Skills of Children.* London: Routledge.

Andersen, Henning. (1973). Abductive and deductive change. *Language* 49: 765–93.

Anderson, Anne H., Miles Bader, Ellen G. Bard, Elizabeth H. Boyle, Gwyneth M. Doherty, Simon C. Garrod, Stephen D. Isard, Jacqueline C. Kowtko, Jan M. McAllister, Jim Miller, Catherine F. Sotillo, Henry S. Thompson, and Regina Weinert. (1991). The HCRC Map Task Corpus. *Language and Speech* 34: 351–66.

Anderson, Stephen R. (1971a). On the Linguistic Status of the Performative/Constative Distinction. Bloomington: Indiana University Linguistics Club.

Anderson, Stephen R. (1971b). On the role of deep structure in semantic interpretation. *Foundations of Language* 6: 197–219.

Anderson, Stephen R. and Edward L. Keenan. (1985). Deixis. In T. Shopen (ed.), *Language Typology and Syntactic Description,* vol. 3: *Grammatical Categories and the Lexicon,* 259–308. Cambridge: Cambridge University Press.

Annamalai, E. (2000). Lexical anaphors and pronouns in Tamil. In Lust et al. (eds.), 169–216.

Anscombre, Jean-Claude and Oswald Ducrot. (1976). L'argumentation dans la langue. *Langages* 42: 5–27.

Anscombre, Jean-Claude and Oswald Ducrot. (1977). Deux *mais* en francais? *Lingua* 43: 23–40.

Anscombre, Jean-Claude and Oswald Ducrot. (1983). *L'Argumentation dans la Langue*. Brussels: Mardaga.

Anscombre, Jean-Claude and Oswald Ducrot. (1989). Argumentativity and informativity. In M. Meyer (ed.), *From Metaphysics to Rhetoric*, 71–87. Dordrecht: Kluwer.

Anttila, Arto and Vivienne Fong. (2000). The partitive constraint in optimality theory. Paper available from the Rutgers Optimality Archive. ROA 416-09100.

Anttila, Raimo. (1992). Historical explanation and historical linguistics. In G. W. Davis and G. K. Iverson (eds.), *Explanation in Historical Linguistics*, 17–39. Amsterdam: Benjamins.

Appelt, Douglas E. and Martha E. Pollack. (1990). Weighted abduction for plan ascription. Technical Note 491, SRI International. Menlo Park, CA.

Apresjan, Jurij. (1973). Regular polysemy. *Linguistics* 142: 5–32.

Ariel, Mira. (1988). Referring and accessibility. *Journal of Linguistics* 24: 65–87.

Ariel, Mira. (1990). *Accessing Noun Phrase Antecedents*. London: Routledge.

Arnold, Jennifer, Thomas Wasow, Anthony Losongco, and Ryan Ginstrom. (2000). Heaviness vs. newness: The effects of complexity and information structure on constituent ordering. *Language* 76: 28–55.

Arnovick, Leslie K. (1999). *Diachronic Pragmatics: Seven Case Studies in English Illocutionary Development*. Amsterdam: Benjamins.

Aronoff, Mark. (1976). *Word Formation in Generative Grammar*. Cambridge, MA: MIT Press.

Asher, Nicholas and Alex Lascarides. (1994). Intentions and information in discourse. *ACL-94*, 34–41, Las Cruces, NM.

Asher, Nicholas and Alex Lascarides. (1995). Lexical disambiguation in a discourse context. *Journal of Semantics* 12: 69–108.

Asher, Nicholas and Alex Lascarides. (1998a). Questions in dialogue. *Linguistics and Philosophy* 21: 237–309.

Asher, Nicholas and Alex Lascarides. (1998b). The semantics and pragmatics of presupposition. *Journal of Semantics* 15: 239–300.

Asher, Nicholas and Alex Lascarides. (2001). The semantics and pragmatics of metaphor. In P. Bouillon and F. Busa (eds.), *The Language of Word Meaning*, 262–89. Cambridge: Cambridge University Press.

Asher, Nicholas and Hajime Wada. (1988). A computational account of syntactic, semantic and discourse principles for anaphora resolution. *Journal of Semantics* 6: 309–44.

Atkinson, J. Maxwell and John Heritage. (1984). *Structures of Social Action*. Cambridge: Cambridge University Press.

Atlas, Jay David. (1974). Presupposition, ambiguity, and generality: a coda to the Russell–Strawson debate on referring. Unpublished manuscript, Pomona College, Claremont, CA.

Atlas, Jay David. (1975). Frege's polymorphous concept of presupposition and its role in a theory of meaning. *Semantikos* 1: 29–44.

Atlas, Jay David. (1977a). Presupposition revisited. *Pragmatics Microfiche* II.5: D5–D11.

Atlas, Jay David. (1977b). Negation, ambiguity, and presupposition. *Linguistics and Philosophy* 1: 321–36.

Atlas, Jay David. (1978a). Presupposition and Grice's pragmatics: Some foundational questions. Colloquium Lecture, University College London.

Atlas, Jay David. (1978b). On presupposing. *Mind* 87: 396–411.

Atlas, Jay David. (1979). How linguistics matters to philosophy: Presupposition, truth, and meaning. In Oh and Dinneen (eds.), 265–81.

Atlas, Jay David. (1983). Comments on "Metalinguistic negation and pragmatic ambiguity" by Larry Horn. Unpublished manuscript, Institute for Advanced Study, Princeton, NJ.

Atlas, Jay David. (1984). Comparative adjectives and adverbials of degree. *Lingustics Philosophy* 7: 347–77.

Atlas, Jay David. (1988). What are negative existence statements about? *Linguistics and Philosophy* 11: 373–94.

Atlas, Jay David. (1989). *Philosophy without Ambiguity*. Oxford: Clarendon Press.

Atlas, Jay David. (1991). Topic/comment, presupposition, logical form, and focus stress implicatures: The case of focal particles *only* and *also*. *Journal of Semantics* 8: 127–47.

Atlas, Jay David. (1995). G. E. Moore's paradox, Wittgenstein's philosophy of mind, and the grammar of first-person belief. Unpublished paper, University of Groningen.

Atlas, Jay David. (1996). "Only" noun phrases, pseudo-negative generalized quantifiers, negative polarity items, and monotonicity. *Journal of Semantics* 13: 265–332.

Atlas, Jay David. (2001). A note on pragmatic ambiguity and the myth of presupposition cancelation. Unpublished manuscript, Pomona College, Claremont, CA.

Atlas, Jay David (to appear). Descriptions, linguistic topic/comment, and negative existentials: A case study in the application of linguistic theory to problems in the philosophy of language. In Bezuidenhout and Reimer (eds.).

Atlas, Jay David (in press). *Logic, Meaning, and Conversation*. New York: Oxford University Press.

Atlas, Jay David and Stephen C. Levinson. (1973). What is an implicature? Part 1: Kenny Logic. Unpublished manuscript, Mathematical and Social Sciences Board Workshop on the Pragmatics of Natural Language, University of Michigan.

Atlas, Jay David and Stephen C. Levinson. (1981). It-clefts, informativeness, and logical form. In Cole (ed.), 1–51.

Auer, Peter. (1996). On the prosody and syntax of turn-continuations. In E. Couper-Kuhlen and M. Selting (eds.), *Prosody in Conversation*, 57–100. Cambridge: Cambridge University Press.

Austin, J. L. (1962). *How to Do Things with Words*. Oxford: Oxford University Press.

van der Auwera, Johan. (1997). Pragmatics in the last quarter century: The case of conditional perfection. *Journal of Pragmatics* 27: 261–74.

van der Auwera, Johan. (2001). On the typology of negative modals. In Hoeksema et al. (eds.), 23–48.

Avesani, Cinzia and Mario Vayra. (1988). Discorso, segmenti di discorso e un' ipotesi sull' intonazione. *Corso di stampa negli Atti del Convegno Internazionale Sull'Interpunzione*, 8–53. Florence: Vallecchi.

Axia, Giovanna and Maria Baroni. (1985). Linguistic politeness at different age levels. *Child Development* 56: 918–27.

Ayers, Gayle M. (1992). Discourse functions of pitch range in spontaneous and read speech. Presented at the annual meeting of the Linguistic Society of America, San Diego, CA.

Baart, Joan L. G. (1987). Focus, Syntax and Accent Placement. PhD thesis, University of Leiden.

Bach, Emmon. (1986). The algebra of events. *Linguistics and Philosophy* 9: 5–16.

Bach, Kent. (1987a). On communicative intentions: A reply to Recanati. *Mind and Language* 2: 141–54.

Bach, Kent. (1987b). *Thought and Reference*. Oxford: Oxford University Press. (Expanded edition, 1994.)

Bach, Kent. (1992). Paving the road to reference. *Philosophical Studies* 67: 295–300.

Bach, Kent. (1994a). Conversational impliciture. *Mind and Language* 9: 124–62.

Bach, Kent. (1994b). Semantic slack: What is said and more. In Tsohatzidis (ed.), 267–91.

Bach, Kent. (1995). Standardization vs. conventionalization. *Linguistics and Philosophy* 18: 677–86.

Bach, Kent. (1998). Review of Fretheim and Gundel (eds., 1996). *Pragmatics and Cognition* 8: 335–8.

Bach, Kent. (1999a). The semantics–pragmatics distinction: What it is and why it matters. In Turner (ed.), 65–84.

Bach, Kent. (1999b). The myth of conventional implicature. *Linguistics and Philosophy* 22: 327–66.

Bach, Kent. (2000). Quantification, qualification and context: A reply to Stanley and Szabó. *Mind and Language* 15: 262–83.

Bach, Kent. (2001a). You don't say? *Synthese* 127: 11–31.

Bach, Kent. (2001b). Speaking loosely: Sentence nonliterality. *Midwest Studies in Philosophy* 25: 249–63.

Bach, Kent. (2002). "Giorgione was so-called because of his name." *Philosophical Perspectives* 16: 73–103.

Bach, Kent (to appear a). Descriptions: Points of reference. In Bezuidenhout and Reimer (eds.).

Bach, Kent (to appear b). Context *ex machina*. In Z. Szabó (ed.), *Semantics vs. Pragmatics*. Oxford: Oxford University Press.

Bach, Kent and Robert M. Harnish. (1979). *Linguistic Communication and Speech Acts*. Cambridge, MA: MIT Press.

Bach, Kent and Robert M. Harnish. (1992). How performatives really work: A reply to Searle. *Linguistics and Philosophy* 15: 93–110.

Bachenko, Joan and Eileen Fitzpatrick. (1990). A computational grammar of discourse-neutral prosodic phrasing in English. *Computational Linguistics* 16: 155–70.

Baker, C. L. (1970). Double negatives. *Linguistic Inquiry* 1: 169–86.

Baker, C. L. (1995). Contrast, discourse prominence, and intensification, with special reference to locally free reflexives in British English. *Language* 71: 63–101.

Baker, Collin F., Charles J. Fillmore, and John B. Lowe. (1998). The Berkeley FrameNet project. *ACL-98*, 86–90. Montreal.

Bakhtin, M. M. (1981). *The Dialogic Imagination: Four Essays by M. M. Bakhtin*, trans. C. Emerson and M. Holquist. Austin: University of Texas Press.

Baldwin, Dare A. (1993). Infants' ability to consult the speaker for clues to word reference. *Journal of Child Language* 20: 395–418.

Ball, Catherine N. (1991). The Historical Development of the It-cleft. PhD dissertation, University of Pennsylvania.

Ball, Catherine N. and Ellen F. Prince. (1977). A note on stress and presupposition. *Linguistic Inquiry* 8: 585.

Ballmer, Thomas. (1972). Einführung und Kontrolle von Diskurswelter. In D. Wunderlich (ed.), *Linguistische Pragmatik*, 183–206. Frankfurt-am-Main: Athenäum-Verlag.

Ballmer, Thomas. (1978). *Logical Grammar: With Special Consideration of Topics in Context Change*. Amsterdam: North-Holland.

Ballmer, Thomas and Waltraud Brennenstuhl. (1981). *Speech Act Classification: A Study in the Lexical Analysis of English Speech Activity Verbs*. Berlin: Springer Verlag.

Barcan Marcus, Ruth. (1963). Modalities and intensional languages. In W. Wartofsky (ed.), *Boston Studies in the Philosophy of Science*, vol. 1, 77–116. Dordrecht: Reidel.

Barcelona, Antonio. (2000). Introduction: The cognitive theory of metaphor and metonymy. In A. Barcelona (ed.), *Metaphor and Metonymy at the Crossroads: A Cognitive Perspective*, 1–28. Berlin: Mouton de Gruyter.

Bard, Ellen. (1999). The dissociation of deaccenting, givenness, and syntactic role in spontaneous speech. *Proceedings of ICPhS99 (International Congress of Phonetic Sciences)*, 1753–6. San Francisco, CA.

Bardovi-Harlig, Kathleen. (1983a). Pronouns: When "given" and "new" coincide. *CLS 18*, 15–26.

Bardovi-Harlig, Kathleen. (1983b). A Functional Approach to English Sentence Stress. PhD dissertation, University of Chicago.

Bar-Hillel, Yehoshua. (1954). Indexical expressions. *Mind* 63: 359–79.

Bar-Hillel, Yehoshua. (1970). *Aspects of Language*. Jerusalem: Magnes Press.

Bar-Hillel, Yehoshua. (1971). Out of the pragmatic wastebasket. *Linguistic Inquiry* 2: 401–7.

Barker, Chris. (1995). *Possessive Descriptions*. Stanford, CA: CSLI.

Barker, Chris. (1998). Partitives, double genitives and anti-uniqueness. *Natural Language and Linguistic Theory* 16: 679–717.

Barker, Chris. (2000). Definite possessives and discourse novelty. *Theoretical Linguistics* 26: 211–27.

Barkow, John, Leda Cosmides, and John Tooby. (1995). *The Adapted Mind: Evolutionary Psychology and the Generation of Culture*. Oxford: Oxford University Press.

Baron-Cohen, Simon. (1995). *Mindblindness: An Essay on Autism and Theory of Mind*. Cambridge, MA: MIT Press.

Baroni, Maria R. and Giovanna Axia. (1989). Children's meta-pragmatic abilities and the identification of polite and impolite requests. *First Language* 9: 285–97.

Barsalou, Lawrence. (1987). The instability of graded structure: implications for the nature of concepts. In U. Neisser (ed.), *Concepts and Conceptual Development: Ecological and Intellectual Factors in Categorization*, 101–40. Cambridge: Cambridge University Press.

Barsalou, Lawrence. (1992). Frames, concepts, and conceptual fields. In E. Kittay and A. Lehrer (eds.), *Frames, Fields, and Contrasts: New Essays in Semantic and Lexical Organization*, 21–74. Hillsdale, NJ: Lawrence Erlbaum.

Barton, Ellen. (1990). *Nonsentential Constituents*. Philadelphia, PA: Benjamins.

Barwise, Jon and Robin Cooper. (1981). Generalized quantifiers and natural language. *Linguistics and Philosophy* 4: 159–219.

Barwise, Jon and John Etchemendy. (1987). *The Liar: An Essay in Truth and Circularity*. Oxford: Oxford University Press.

Barwise, Jon and John Perry. (1983). *Situations and Attitudes*. Cambridge, MA: MIT Press.

Bates, Elizabeth. (1976). *Language and Context: The Acquisition of Pragmatics*. New York: Academic Press.

Bates, Elizabeth, Luigia Camaioni, and Virginia Volterra. (1975). The acquisition of performatives prior to speech. *Merrill–Palmer Quarterly* 21: 205–26.

Bates, Elizabeth and Louise Silvern. (1977). Social adjustment and politeness in preschoolers. *Journal of Communication* 27: 104–11.

Bauer, Laurie. (1983). *English Word-Formation*. Cambridge: Cambridge University Press.

Bavelas, Janet B. (1994). Gestures as part of speech: Methodological implications. *Research on Language and Social Interaction* 27: 201–21.

Bavelas, Janet B., Nicole Chovil, Douglas Lawrie, and Allan Wade. (1992). Interactive gestures. *Discourse Processes* 15: 469–89.

Beach, Cheryl. (1991). The interpretation of prosodic patterns at points of syntactic structure ambiguity: Evidence for cue trading relations. *Journal of Memory and Language* 30: 644–63.

Beaver, David. (1997). Presupposition. In J. van Benthem and A. ter Meulen (eds.), *Handbook of Logic and Language*, 939–1008. Amsterdam: Elsevier Science.

Beaver, David. (2000). Centering and the Optimization of Discourse. Unpublished manuscript, Stanford University, CA.

van Benthem, Johan and Alice G. B. ter Meulen (eds.). (1985). *Generalized Quantifiers in Natural Language*. Dordrecht: Foris Publications.

Benveniste, Emile. (1958). Subjectivity in language. In *Problems in General Linguistics*, 223–30. (M. E. Meek, trans.) Coral Gables, FL: University of Miami Press. (Originally published in *Journal de psychologie* 55, 1958.)

Berg, Jonathan (2002). Is semantics still possible? *Journal of Pragmatics* 34: 349–59.

von Bergen, Anke and Karl von Bergen. (1993). *Negative Polarität im Englischen*. Tübingen: Gunter Narr Verlag.

Berlin, Brent and Paul Kay. (1969). *Basic Color Terms: Their Universality and Evolution*. Berkeley, CA: University of California Press.

Berman, Steve and Arild Hestvik (eds.). (1992). *Proceedings of the Stuttgart Ellipsis Workshop*. Bericht no. 29. Arbeitspapiere des Sonderforschungsbereichs 340. Stuttgart: Institute of Computational Linguistics, University of Stuttgart.

Bernicot, Josie. (1992). *Les actes de langage chez l'enfant*. Paris: Presses Universitaires de France.

Bertolet, Rod. (1984). Reference, fiction, and fictions. *Synthèse* 60: 413–37.

Bertolet, Rod. (1994). Are there indirect speech acts? In Tsohatzidis (ed.), 335–49.

Bezuidenhout, Anne. (1997). Pragmatics, semantic underdetermination and the referential–attributive distinction. *Mind* 106: 375–409.

Bezuidenhout, Anne and Marga Reimer (eds.) (to appear). *Descriptions and Beyond: An Interdisciplinary Collection of Essays on Definite and Indefinite Descriptions and Other Related Phenomena*. Oxford: Oxford University Press.

Bezuidenhout, Anne and Mary Sue Sroda. (1998). Children's use of contextual cues to resolve referential ambiguity: An application of relevance theory. *Pragmatics and Cognition* 6: 265–99.

Bierwisch, Manfred. (1989). The semantics of gradation. In M. Bierwisch and E. Lang (eds.), *Dimensional Adjectives*, 71–261. Berlin: Springer Verlag.

Bing, Janet. (1979). Aspects of English Prosody. PhD dissertation, University of Massachusetts.

Birch, Stacey and Charles Clifton. (1995). Focus, accent, and argument structure: Effects on language comprehension. *Language and Speech* 38: 365–91.

Bird, Graham. (1994). Relevance theory and speech acts. In Tsohatzidis (ed.), 292–311.

Birner, Betty J. (1989). On the "referential–attributive" distinction. *Northwestern University Working Papers in Linguistics* 2: 1–12.

Birner, Betty J. (1992). The Discourse Function of Inversion in English. PhD dissertation, Northwestern University.

Birner, Betty J. (1994). Information status and word order: An analysis of English inversion. *Language* 70: 233–59.

Birner, Betty J. (1996). Form and function in English *by*-phrase passives. *CLS* 32: 23–31.

Birner, Betty J. and Gregory Ward. (1994). Uniqueness, familiarity, and the definite article in English. *BLS* 20: 93–102.

Birner, Betty J. and Gregory Ward. (1998). *Information Status and Noncanonical Word Order in English*. Amsterdam/Philadelphia: Benjamins.

Blackburn, William K. (1988). Wettstein on definite descriptions. *Philosophical Studies* 53: 263–78.

Blackwell, Sarah E. (2000). Anaphora interpretations in Spanish utterances and the neo-Gricean pragmatic theory. *Journal of Pragmatics* 32: 389–424.

Blackwell, Sarah E. (2001). Testing the neo-Gricean pragmatic theory of anaphora: The influence of consistency constraints on interpretations of coreference in Spanish. *Journal of Pragmatics* 33: 901–41.

Blakemore, Diane. (1987). *Semantic Constraints on Relevance*. Oxford: Blackwell.

Blakemore, Diane. (1989). Denial and contrast: a relevance-theoretic analysis of "but." *Linguistics and Philosophy* 12: 15–37.

Blakemore, Diane. (1991). Performatives and parentheticals. *Proceedings of the Aristotelian Society* 91: 197–214.

Blakemore, Diane. (1992). *Understanding Utterances*. Oxford: Blackwell.

Blakemore, Diane. (1994). Echo questions: A pragmatic account. *Lingua* 4: 197–211.

Blakemore, Diane. (1995). Relevance theory. In J. Verschueren, J.-O. Östman, and J. Blommaert (eds.), *Handbook of Pragmatics*, 443–52. Amsterdam: Benjamins.

Blakemore, Diane. (1996). Are apposition markers discourse markers? *Journal of Linguistics* 32: 325–47.

Blakemore, Diane. (1997). Non-truth-conditional meaning. *Linguistische Berichte* 8: 103–27.

Blakemore, Diane. (1998). On the context for so-called discourse markers. In J. Williams and K. Malmkjaer (eds.), *Context in Language Understanding and Language Learning*, 44–60. Cambridge: Cambridge University Press.

Blakemore, Diane. (2000). Procedures and indicators: *nevertheless* and *but*. *Journal of Linguistics* 36: 463–86.

Blakemore, Diane. (2001). Discourse and relevance. In D. Schiffrin, D. Tannen, and H. E. Hamilton (eds.), *Handbook of Discourse Analysis*, 100–18. Oxford: Blackwell.

Blakemore, Diane (2002). *Relevance and Linguistic Meaning: The Semantics and Pragmatics of Discourse Connectives*. Cambridge: Cambridge University Press.

Blakemore, Diane and Robyn Carston (1999). The pragmatics of *and* conjunctions: the non-narrative cases. *UCL Working Papers in Linguistics* 11: 1–20.

Bland, Susan R. K. (1980). Topic/comment sentences in English. *Cornell Working Papers in Linguistics* 2: 32–49.

Blank, Andreas and Peter Koch (eds.). (1999). *Historical Semantics and Cognition*. Berlin: Mouton de Gruyter.

Blass, Regina. (1990). *Relevance Relations in Discourse: A Study with Special Reference to Sissala*. Cambridge: Cambridge University Press.

Bloom, Lois. (1970). *Language Development: Form and Function in Emerging Grammars*. Cambridge, MA: MIT Press.

Bloom, Lois, Cheryl Margulis, Erin Tinker, and Naomi Fujita. (1996). Early conversations and word learning: contributions from child and adult. *Child Development* 67: 3154–75.

Bloom, Paul. (2000). *How Children Learn the Meanings of Words.* Cambridge, MA: MIT Press.

Bloom, Paul. (2002). Mindreading, communication and the learning of names for things. *Mind and Language* 17: 37–54.

Blutner, Reinhard. (1998). Lexical pragmatics. *Journal of Semantics* 15: 115–62.

Blutner, Reinhard. (1999). Some aspects of optimality in natural language interpretation. In de Hoop and de Swart (eds.), 1–21.

Blutner, Reinhard (2002). Lexical semantics and pragmatics. *Linguistische Berichte* 10: 27–58.

Blutner, Reinhard and Torgrim Solstad. (2000). Dimensional designation: a case study in lexical pragmatics. In R. Blutner and G. Jäger (eds.), *Studies in Optimality Theory*, 30–40. Potsdam: University of Potsdam.

Bock, J. Kathryn and R. K. Warren. (1985). Conceptual accessibility and syntactic structure in sentence formulation. *Cognition* 21: 47–67.

Boër, Steven E. and William G. Lycan. (1976). *The Myth of Semantic Presupposition.* Bloomington, IN: Indiana University Linguistics Club.

Boër, Steven E. and William G. Lycan. (1980). A performadox in truth-conditional semantics. *Linguistics and Philosophy* 4: 1–46.

Boersma, Paul. (1998). *Functional Phonology.* The Hague: Holland Academic Graphics.

Boersma, Paul and Bruce Hayes. (2001). Empirical tests of the gradual learning algorithm. *Linguistic Inquiry* 32: 45–86.

Bohnemeyer, Jürgen. (1998). Temporal reference from a radical pragmatics perspective: Why Yucatec does not need to express "after" or "before." *Cognitive Linguistics* 9: 239–82.

Bolinger, Dwight. (1961). Contrastive accent and contrastive stress. *Language* 37: 87–96.

Bolinger, Dwight. (1972a). *That's That.* The Hague: Mouton de Gruyter.

Bolinger, Dwight. (1972b). Accent is predictable (if you're a mindreader). *Language* 48: 633–44.

Bolinger, Dwight. (1977). "There." In *Meaning and Form*, 90–123. London: Longman.

Bolinger, Dwight. (1982). Nondeclaratives from an intonational standpoint. *Papers from the Parasession on Nondeclaratives*, 1–22. Chicago, IL: Chicago Linguistic Society.

Bolinger, Dwight. (1986). *Intonation and Its Parts: Melody in Spoken English.* Stanford, CA: Stanford University Press.

Bolinger, Dwight. (1989). *Intonation and Its Uses: Melody in Grammar and Discourse.* London: Edward Arnold.

Borg, Emma. (2001). Saying what you mean: unarticulated constituents and communication. Unpublished manuscript, University of Reading.

Borkin, Ann. (1971). Polarity items in questions. *CLS 7*, 53–62.

Borkin, Ann. (1974). Raising to Object Position. PhD dissertation, University of Michigan. Published as *Problems in Form and Function*, Norwood, NJ: Ablex, 1984.

Bosanquet, Bernard. (1911). *Logic*, vol. 1. Oxford: Clarendon. (First edition, 1888.)

Bosch, Peter and Rob van der Sandt (eds.) (1999). *Focus: Linguistic, Cognitive, and Computational Perspectives.* Cambridge: Cambridge University Press.

Boula de Mareüil, Philippe and Christophe d'Alessandro. (1998). Text chunking for prosodic phrasing in French. *The Third ESCA/COCOSDA Workshop on Speech Synthesis*, 127–31. Jenolan Caves Mountain House, Blue Mountains, Australia.

Bouton, Lawrence F. (1982). Stem polarity and tag intonation in the derivation of the imperative tag. *Papers from the Parasession on Nondeclaratives*, 23–42. Chicago, IL: Chicago Linguistic Society.

Braun, David. (1994). Structured characters and complex demonstratives. *Philosophical Studies* 74: 193–219.

Braun, David. (1998). Understanding belief reports. *Philosophical Review* 107: 555–95.

Bréal, Michel. (1900). *Semantics*. (Mrs. H. Cust, trans.) New York: Henry Holt. (Original work published 1898.)

Breheny, Richard. (1999). Context-dependence and Procedural Meaning: the Semantics of Definites. PhD dissertation, University College London.

Breheny, Richard. (2001). Maximality, negation and plural definites. Unpublished manuscript, University of Cambridge.

Breheny, Richard. (2002). The current state of (radical) pragmatics in the cognitive Sciences. *Mind and Language* 17: 169–87.

Brennan, Susan E., Marilyn W. Friedman, and Carl J. Pollard. (1987). A centering approach to pronouns. *ACL-25*, 155–62. Stanford, CA.

Bresnan, Joan. (1971). Sentence stress and syntactic transformations. *Language* 47: 257–81.

Bresnan, Joan. (2001). The emergence of the unmarked pronoun. In Legendre et al. (eds., 2001), 113–42.

Bresnan, Joan and Sam A. Mchombo (1986). Topic, pronoun, and agreement in Chichewa. *Language* 63: 741–82.

Brinton, Laurel J. (1988). *The Development of English Aspectual Systems*. Cambridge: Cambridge University Press.

Brinton, Laurel J. (1996). *Pragmatic Markers in English: Grammaticalization and Discourse Functions*. Berlin: Mouton de Gruyter.

Brinton, Laurel J. (2001). Historical discourse analysis. In Schiffrin et al. (eds., 2001), 138–60.

Brinton, Laurel J. and Minoji Akimoto. (1999). Introduction. In Brinton and Akimoto (eds.), 1–20.

Brinton, Laurel J. and Minoji Akimoto (eds.). (1999). *Collocational and Idiomatic Aspects of Composite Predicates in the History of English*. Amsterdam: Benjamins.

Briscoe, Ted and Ann Copestake. (1996). Controlling the application of lexical rules. *Proceedings of the ACL SIGLEX Workshop on Breadth and Depth of Semantic Lexicons*, 7–19. Santa Cruz, CA.

Brown, Gillian. (1983). Prosodic structure and the given/new distinction. In D. R. Ladd and A. Cutler (eds.), *Prosody: Models and Measurements*, 67–78. Berlin: Springer Verlag.

Brown, Gillian, Karen Currie, and Joanne Kenworthy. (1980). *Questions of Intonation*. Baltimore, MD: University Park Press.

Brown, Penelope (to appear). Verb specificity and argument realization in Tzeltal child language. In M. Bowerman and P. Brown (eds.), *Crosslinguistic Perspectives on Argument Structure: Implications for Language Acquisition*. Norwood, NJ: Lawrence Erlbaum.

Brown, Penelope and Stephen C. Levinson (1987). *Politeness*. Cambridge: Cambridge University Press.

Brown, Roger W. and Albert Gilman. (1960). The pronouns of power and solidarity. In T. Sebeok (ed.), *Style in Language*, 253–76. Cambridge, MA: MIT Press.

Bruner, Jerome S. (1975). The ontogenesis of speech acts. *Journal of Child Language* 2: 1–20.

Buchler, Justus (ed.). (1940). *Philosophical Writings of Peirce*. London: Routledge & Kegan Paul.

Bühler, Karl. (1934). The deictic field of language and deictic words. Reprinted in Jarvella and Klein (eds., 1982), 9–30.

Bunt, Harry. (1994). Context and dialogue control. *Think* 3: 19–31.

Bunt, Harry. (2000). Dynamic interpretation and dialogue theory. In M. M. Taylor, F. Neel, and D. G. Bouwhuis (eds.), *The Structure of Multimodal Dialogue*, vol. 2, 139–66. Amsterdam: Benjamins.

Bunt, Harry and Bill Black. (2000). The ABC of computational pragmatics. In H. C. Bunt and W. Black (eds.), *Computational Pragmatics: Abduction, Belief and Context*, 1–46. Amsterdam: Benjamins.

Burge, Tyler (1974). Demonstrative constructions, reference, and truth. *Journal of Philosophy* 71: 205–23.

Büring, Daniel. (1999). Topic. In Bosch and van der Sandt (eds.), 142–65.

Burt, Susan M. (1994). Where does sociopragmatic ambiguity come from? Paper presented at the 8th International Conference on Pragmatics and Language Learning, Urbana, Illinois.

Burzio, Luigi. (1991). The morphological basis of anaphora. *Journal of Linguistics* 27: 81–105.

Burzio, Luigi. (1996). The role of the antecedent in anaphoric relations. In R. Friedin (ed.), *Current Issues in Comparative Grammar*, 1–45. Dordrecht: Kluwer.

Butt, Miriam and Tracy H. King (to appear). Null elements in discourse structure. In K. V. Subbarao (ed.), *Papers from the NULLS Seminar*. New Delhi: Moti Lal Banarsi Das.

Butterworth, Brian. (1975). Hesitation and semantic planning in speech. *Journal of Psycholinguistic Research* 4: 75–87.

Butterworth, George. (1998). What is special about pointing in babies. In F. Simion and G. Butterworth (eds.), *The Development of Sensory, Motor and Cognitive Capacities in Early Infancy*, 171–90. Hove: Psychology Press.

Bybee, Joan, Revere Perkins, and William Pagliuca. (1994). *The Evolution of Grammar: Tense, Aspect, and Modality in the Languages of the World.* Chicago, IL: University of Chicago Press.

Cacoullous, Rena Torres and José Estaban Hernandez. (1999). *A trabajarle*: La construccion intensiva en el español. *Southwest Journal of Linguistics* 18: 79–100.

Cahn, Janet E. (1989). Generating Expression in Synthesized Speech. Master's thesis, MIT.

Cahn, Janet E. (1995). The effect of pitch accenting on pronoun referent resolution. *ACL-33 (Student Session)*, 290–92.

Cahn, Janet E. (1998). Generating pitch accent distributions that show individual and stylistic differences. *The Third ESCA/COCOSDA Workshop on Speech Synthesis*, 121–6. Jenolan Caves Mountain House, Blue Mountains, Australia.

Campbell, Jeremy. (2001). *The Liar's Tale*. New York: W. W. Norton.

Campbell, Nick and Mary Beckman. (1997). Stress, prominence, and spectral tilt. In A. Botinis, G. Kouroupetroglou, and G. Carayiannis (eds.), *Intonation: Theory, Models and Applications*, 67–70. Athens: ESCA.

Cappelen, Herman and Ernie Lepore. (1997). Varieties of quotation. *Mind* 106: 429–50.

Carberry, Sandra. (1989). A pragmatics-based approach to ellipsis resolution. *Computational Linguistics* 15: 75–96.

Carletta, Jean, Nils Dahlbäck, Norbert Reithinger, and Marilyn A. Walker. (1997a). Standards for dialogue coding in natural language processing. Report no. 167, Dagstuhl seminar number 9706.

Carletta, Jean, Amy Isard, Stephen Isard, Jacqueline C. Kowtko, Gwyneth Doherty-Sneddon, and Anne H. Anderson. (1997b). The reliability of a dialogue structure coding scheme. *Computational Linguistics* 23: 13–32.

Carlson, Gregory. (1977). A unified analysis of the English bare plural. *Linguistics and Philosophy* 1: 413–56.

Carlson, Lauri. (1983). *Dialogue Games: An Approach to Discourse Analysis*. Dordrecht: Reidel.

Carnap, Rudolf. (1937). *The Logical Syntax of Language*. London: Routledge & Kegan Paul.

Carnap, Rudolf. (1942). *Introduction to Semantics*. Cambridge, MA: Harvard University Press.

Carpenter, Malinda, Nameera Akhtar, and Michael Tomasello. (2000). Fourteen through 18-month-old infants differentially imitate intentional and accidental actions. In D. Muir and A. Slater (eds.), *Infant Development: The Essential Readings*, 295–318. Oxford: Blackwell.

Carpenter, Patricia A. and Marcel A. Just. (1975). Sentence comprehension: A psycholinguistic processing model of verification. *Psychological Review* 82: 45–73.

Carroll, John and Michael Tanenhaus. (1975). Prolegomena to a functional theory of word formation. *Papers from the Parasession on Functionalism*, 47–62. Chicago, IL: Chicago Linguistic Society.

Carruthers, Peter and Peter Smith (eds.) (1996). *Theories of Theories of Mind*. Cambridge: Cambridge University Press.

Carstairs-McCarthy, Andrew. (1999). *The Origins of Complex Language: An Inquiry into the Evolutionary Beginnings of Sentences, Syllables, and Truth*. Oxford: Oxford University Press.

Carston, Robyn. (1988). Implicature, explicature, and truth-theoretic semantics. In R. Kempson (ed.), *Mental Representations: The Interface Between Language and Reality*, 155–81. Cambridge: Cambridge University Press. Reprinted in S. Davis (ed., 1991), 33–51 and (with 1995 postscript) in Kasher (ed., 1998), vol. IV: 436–79.

Carston, Robyn. (1993). Conjunction, explanation and relevance. *Lingua* 90: 27–48.

Carston, Robyn. (1995). Quantity maxims and generalized implicature. *Lingua* 96: 213–44.

Carston, Robyn. (1996). Metalinguistic negation and echoic use. *Journal of Pragmatics* 25: 309–30.

Carston, Robyn. (1997). Enrichment and loosening: complementary processes in deriving the proposition expressed? *Linguistische Berichte* 8: 103–27.

Carston, Robyn. (1998a). Pragmatics and the Explicit/Implicit Distinction. PhD dissertation, University College London.

Carston, Robyn. (1998b). Informativeness, relevance, and scalar implicature. In Carston and Uchida (eds.), 179–236.

Carston, Robyn. (1999). The semantics/pragmatics distinction: a view from relevance theory. In K. Turner (ed., 1999), 85–125.

Carston, Robyn. (2000). Explicature and semantics. *UCL Working Papers in Linguistics* 12: 1–44.

Carston, Robyn. (2002a). Linguistic meaning, communicated meaning and cognitive pragmatics. *Mind and Language* 17: 127–48.

Carston, Robyn (2002b). *Thought and Utterances: The Pragmatics of Explicit Communication*. Oxford: Blackwell.

Carston, Robyn and Seiji Uchida (eds.) (1998). *Relevance Theory: Applications and Implications*. Amsterdam: Benjamins.

Carter, Anne L. (1978). From sensori-motor vocalizations to words: a case study of the evolution of attention-directing communication in the second year. In A. Lock (ed.), *Action, Gesture, and Symbol: The Emergence of Language*, 309–49. London: Academic Press.

Caspers, Johanneke. (1998). Who's next? The melodic marking of question vs. continuation in Dutch. *Language and Speech* 41: 375–98.

Cassell, Justine and David McNeill. (1991). Gesture and the poetics of prose. *Poetics Today* 12: 375–404.

Cattell, Ray. (1973). Negative transportation and tag questions. *Language* 49: 612–39.

Chafe, Wallace L. (1974). Language and consciousness. *Language* 50: 111–33.

Chafe, Wallace L. (1976). Givenness, contrastiveness, definiteness, subjects, topics, and point of view. In C. N. Li (ed.), *Subject and Topic*, 25–55. New York: Academic Press.

Chafe, Wallace L. (1980). The deployment of consciousness in the production of a narrative. In W. L. Chafe (ed., 1980), 9–50.

Chafe, Wallace L. (ed.). (1980). *The Pear Stories*. Norwood, NJ: Ablex.

Chafe, Wallace L. (1987). Cognitive constraints on information flow. In R. S. Tomlin (ed.), *Coherence and Grounding in Discourse*, 21–51. Amsterdam: Benjamins.

Chafe, Wallace L. (1994). *Discourse, Consciousness, and Time*. Chicago, IL: University of Chicago Press.

Chao, Wynn. (1988). *On Ellipsis*. New York: Garland.

Chao, Y. R. (1968). *A Grammar of Spoken Chinese*. Berkeley, CA: University of California Press.

Charniak, Eugene. (1986). A neat theory of marker passing, *Proceedings, AAAI-86, Fifth National Conference on Artificial Intelligence*, 584–8. Philadelphia.

Charniak, Eugene and Robert Goldman. (1988). A logic for semantic interpretation. *ACL-88*, 87–94. Buffalo.

Charniak, Eugene and Robert Goldman. (1989). A semantics for probabilistic quantifier-free first-order languages, with particular application to story understanding. *Proceedings of the Eleventh International Joint Conference on Artificial Intelligence*, 1074–79. Detroit.

Charniak, Eugene and Drew McDermott. (1985). *Introduction to Artificial Intelligence*. Reading, MA: Addison-Wesley.

Charniak, Eugene and Solomon E. Shimony. (1990). Probabilistic semantics for cost based abduction. Technical Report CS-90-02, Department of Computer Science, Brown University.

Chastain, Charles. (1975). Reference and context. In K. Gunderson (ed.), *Minnesota Studies in the Philosophy of Science*, vol. 7: *Language, Mind and Knowledge*, 194–269. Minneapolis: University of Minnesota Press.

Chierchia, Gennaro. (1995). *Dynamics of Meaning: Anaphora, Presupposition, and the Theory of Grammar*. Chicago, IL: University of Chicago Press.

Chierchia, Gennaro. (2001). Scalar implicatures, polarity phenomena, and the syntax/pragmatics interface. Unpublished MS., University of Milan.

Chierchia, Gennaro, Stephen Crain, Maria Teresa Guasti, Andrea Gualmini, and Luisa Meroni. (2001). The acquisition of disjunction: Evidence for a grammatical view of scalar implicatures. *BUCLD 25 Proceedings*, 157–68. Somerville, MA: Cascadilla Press.

Chierchia, Gennaro and Sally McConnell-Ginet. (2000). *Meaning and Grammar*, 2nd edn. Cambridge, MA: MIT Press.

Chomsky, Noam. (1965). *Aspects of the Theory of Syntax*. Cambridge, MA: MIT Press.

Chomsky, Noam. (1971). Deep structure, surface structure, and semantic interpretation. In Steinberg and Jakobovits (eds.), 183–216.

Chomsky, Noam. (1976). Conditions on rules of grammar. *Linguistic Analysis* 2: 303–51.

Chomsky, Noam. (1981). *Lectures on Government and Binding*. Dordrecht: Foris.

Chomsky, Noam. (1982a). *Some Concepts and Consequences of the Theory of Government and Binding*. Cambridge, MA: MIT Press.

Chomsky, Noam. (1982b). *On the Generative Enterprise: A Discussion with Riny Huybregts and Henk van Riemsdijk*. Dordrecht: Foris.

Chomsky, Noam. (1992). Language and interpretation: Philosophical reflections and empirical inquiry. In J. Earman (ed.), *Inference, Explanation, and Other Frustrations: Essays in the Philosophy of Science*, 99–128, Berkeley, CA: University of California Press.

Chomsky, Noam. (1993). A minimalist program for linguistic theory. In Kenneth Hale and Samuel K. Keyser (eds.), *The View from Building 20*, 1–52. Cambridge, MA: MIT Press.

Chomsky, Noam. (1995a). Language and nature. *Mind* 104: 1–61.

Chomsky, Noam. (1995b). Bare phrase structure. In G. Webelhuth (ed.), *Government and Binding Theory and the Minimalist Program: Principles and Parameters in Syntactic Theory*, 428–46. Oxford: Blackwell.

Chomsky, Noam. (1995c). *The Minimalist Program*. Cambridge, MA: MIT Press.

Chouinard, Michelle M. and Eve V. Clark. (2003). Adult reformulations of child errors as negative evidence. *Journal of Child Language* 30.

Christophersen, Paul. (1939). *The Articles: A Study of Their Theory and Use in English*. Copenhagen: Munksgaard.

Chu, Jennifer-Carroll. (1998). A statistical model for discourse act recognition in dialogue interactions. In J.-C. Chu and N. Green (eds.), *Applying Machine Learning to Discourse Processing: Papers from the 1998 AAAI Spring Symposium*, 12–17. Technical Report SS-98-01. Menlo Park, CA: AAAI Press.

Church, Alonzo. (1943). Review of Carnap's *Introduction to Semantics. Philosophical Review* 52: 298–304.

Clancy, Patricia M. (1985). The acquisition of Japanese. In D. I. Slobin (ed.), *The Cross-linguistic Study of Language Acquisition*, vol. 1, 373–524. Hillsdale, NJ: Lawrence Erlbaum.

Clancy, Steven J. (1999). The ascent of *guy. American Speech* 74: 282–97.

Clapp, Lenny. (2001). What unarticulated constituents could not be. In J. C. Campbell, M. O'Rourke, and D. Shier (eds.), *Meaning and Truth: Investigations in Philosophical Semantics*, 231–56. New York: Seven Bridges Press.

Clapp, Lenny. (to appear). On the interpretation and performance of non-sentential assertions. In R. Elugardo and R. Stainton (eds.), *Ellipsis and Non-Sentential Speech*. Dordrecht: Kluwer.

Clark, Billy. (1991). Relevance Theory and the Semantics of Non-declaratives. PhD dissertation, University College London.

Clark, Eve V. (1978). From gesture to word: On the natural history of deixis in language acquisition. In J. Bruner and A. Garton (eds.), *Human Growth and Development: Wolfson College Lectures 1976*, 85–120. Oxford: Clarendon Press.

Clark, Eve V. (1983). Meanings and concepts. In J. H. Flavell and E. M. Markman (eds.), *Handbook of Child Psychology*, vol. 3: *Cognitive Development*, 787–840. New York: John Wiley and Sons.

Clark, Eve V. (1987). The principle of contrast: A constraint on language acquisition. In B. MacWhinney (ed.), *Mechanisms of Language Acquisition*, 1–33. Hillsdale, NJ: Lawrence Erlbaum.

Clark, Eve V. (1990). The pragmatics of contrast. *Journal of Child Language* 17: 417–31.

Clark, Eve V. (1993). *The Lexicon in Acquisition.* Cambridge: Cambridge University Press.

Clark, Eve V. (1997). Conceptual perspective and lexical choice in acquisition. *Cognition* 64: 1–37.

Clark, Eve V. (1998). Lexical structure and pragmatic directions in acquisition. *CLS 34, Part 2, The Panels*, 437–46.

Clark, Eve V. (1999). Conceptual perspectives and lexical choice in acquisition. *Cognition* 64: 1–37.

Clark, Eve V. (2001). Grounding and attention in the acquisition of language. *CLS 37, Part 1*, 95–116.

Clark, Eve V. (2002). Making use of pragmatic inferences in the acquisition of meaning. In D. Beaver, S. Kaufmann, B. Clark, and L. Casillas (eds.), *The Construction of Meaning*, 45–58. Stanford, CA: CSLI.

Clark, Eve V. (2003). *First Language Acquisition.* Cambridge: Cambridge University Press.

Clark, Eve V. and Michelle M. Chouinard. (2000). Enoncés enfantins, formules adultes dans l'acquisition du langage. *Langages* 140: 9–23.

Clark, Eve V. and Michelle M. Chouinard (in preparation). Coordinating attention as a precondition for offering new words.

Clark, Eve V. and Herbert H. Clark. (1979). When nouns surface as verbs. *Language* 55: 767–811.

Clark, Eve V. and James B. Grossman. (1998). Pragmatic directions and children's word learning. *Journal of Child Language* 25: 1–18.

Clark, Eve V. and Andrew D.-W. Wong. (2002). Pragmatic directions about language use: words and word meanings. *Language in Society* 31: 181–212.

Clark, Herbert H. (1974). Semantics and comprehension. In T. Sebeok (ed.), *Current Trends in Linguistics*, vol. 12, 1291–1428.

Clark, Herbert H. (1977). Bridging. In P. N. Johnson-Laird and P. C. Wason (eds.), *Thinking: Readings in Cognitive Science*, 411–20. Cambridge: Cambridge University Press.

Clark, Herbert H. (1983). Making sense of nonce sense. In G. B. Flores D'Arcais and R. J. Jarvella (eds.), *The Process of Language Understanding*, 297–332. New York: John Wiley.

Clark, Herbert H. (1993). Making sense of nonce sense. In H. Clark, *Arenas of Language Use*, 305–40. Stanford, CA: CSLI.

Clark, Herbert H. (1996). *Using Language.* Cambridge: Cambridge University Press.

Clark, Herbert H. (1999). On the origins of conversation. *Verbum* 21: 147–61.

Clark, Herbert H. and Susan A. Brennan. (1991). Grounding in communication. In L. B. Resnick, J. M. Levine, and S. D. Teasley (eds.), *Perspective on Socially Shared Cognition*, 127–49. Washington, DC: APA Books.

Clark, Herbert H. and Jean E. Fox Tree. (2002). Using *uh* and *um* in spontaneous speaking. *Cognition* 84: 73–111.

Clark, Herbert and Richard Gerrig. (1984). On the pretense theory of irony. *Journal of Experimental Psychology: General* 113: 121–6.

Clark, Herbert H. and Catherine R. Marshall. (1981). Definite reference and mutual knowledge. In Joshi et al. (eds.), 10–63.

Clark, Herbert H. and Edward F. Schaefer. (1987). Collaborating on contributions to conversations. *Language and Cognitive Processes* 2: 19–41.

Clark, Herbert H. and Edward F. Schaefer. (1989). Contributing to discourse. *Cognitive Science* 13: 259–94.

Clark, Herbert H. and Thomas Wasow. (1998). Repeating words in spontaneous speech. *Cognitive Psychology* 37: 201–42.

Clark, Herbert H. and Deanna Wilkes-Gibbs. (1986). Referring as a collaborative process. *Cognition* 22: 1–39.

Cohen, L. Jonathan. (1971). Some remarks on Grice's views about the logical particles of natural language. In Y. Bar-Hillel (ed.), *Pragmatics of Natural Language,* 50–68. Dordrecht: Reidel.

Cohen, Philip R. and Hector J. Levesque. (1990). Rational interaction as the basis for communication. In Cohen et al. (eds.), 221–56.

Cohen, Philip R. and Hector J. Levesque. (1991). Teamwork. *Nous* 25: 487–512.

Cohen, Philip R., Jerry Morgan, and Martha E. Pollack. (1990). Introduction. In Cohen et al. (eds.), 1–13.

Cohen, Philip R., Jerry Morgan, and Martha E. Pollack (eds.). (1990). *Intentions in Communication.* Cambridge, MA: MIT Press.

Cohen, Philip R. and C. Raymond Perrault. (1979). Elements of a plan-based theory of speech acts. *Cognitive Science* 3: 177–212. Reprinted in Grosz et al. (1986): 423–40.

Cole, Peter (ed.). (1978). *Syntax and Semantics 9: Pragmatics.* New York: Academic Press.

Cole, Peter (ed.). (1981). *Radical Pragmatics.* New York: Academic Press.

Cole, Peter, Gabriella Hermon, and C.-T. James Huang (eds.). (2001). *Syntax and Semantics 33: Long-distance Reflexives.* London: Academic Press.

Cole, Peter and Jerry Morgan (eds.). (1975). *Syntax and Semantics 3: Speech Acts.* New York: Academic Press.

Comrie, Bernard. (1985). *Tense.* Cambridge: Cambridge University Press.

Comrie, Bernard. (1989). *Aspect.* Cambridge: Cambridge University Press.

Cooke, Joseph. (1968). *Pronominal Reference in Thai, Burmese and Vietnamese.* Berkeley, CA: University of California Press.

Cooper, William E. and Jeanne Paccia-Cooper. (1980). *Syntax and Speech.* Cambridge, MA: Harvard University Press.

Copestake, Ann and Ted Briscoe. (1995). Semi-productive polysemy and sense extension. *Journal of Semantics* 12: 15–67. Reprinted in J. Pustejovsky and B. Boguraev (eds.), *Lexical Semantics: The Problem of Polysemy,* 15–67. Oxford: Oxford University Press, 1996.

Core, Mark, Masato Ishizaki, Johanna D. Moore, Christine Nakatani, Norbert Reithinger, David Traum, and Syun Tutiya. (1999). *The Report of the Third Workshop of the Discourse Resource Initiative.* No. 3 CC-TR-99-1, Chiba Corpus Project, Chiba, Japan.

de Cornulier, Benoît. (1985). *Effets de sens.* Paris: Éditions de Minuit.

Corsaro, William A. (1977). The clarification request as a feature of adult interactive styles with young children. *Language in Society* 6: 183–207.

Coulson, Seana. (1994). Cognitive science. Entry in J. Blommaert (ed.), *Handbook of Pragmatics.* Amsterdam: Benjamins.

Coulson, Seana. (2001). *Semantic Leaps.* New York: Cambridge University Press.

Coulson, Seana and Gilles Fauconnier. (1999). Fake guns and stone lions: conceptual blending and privative adjectives. In B. Fox, D. Jurafsky, and L. Michaelis (eds.), *Cognition and Function in Language,* 143–58. Stanford, CA: CSLI.

Cox, P. T. and T. Pietrzykowski. (1986). Causes for events: their computation and applications. *Proceedings of the Eighth International Conference on Automated Deduction (CADE-8),* 608–21. Oxford, UK.

Creider, Chet A. and Jane T. Creider. (1983). Topic–comment relations in a verb-initial language. *Journal of African Languages and Linguistics* 5: 1–15.

Cresswell, Max. (1973). *Logics and Languages*. London: Methuen.

Croft, William. (1994). Speech act classification, language typology and cognition. In Tsohatzidis (ed.), 460–77.

Croft, William. (1995). Intonation units and grammatical structure. *Linguistics* 33: 839–82.

Croft, William. (2000). *Explaining Language Change: An Evolutionary Approach*. Harlow, Essex: Pearson Education.

Cruse, D. Alan. (1986). *Lexical Semantics*. Cambridge: Cambridge University Press.

Cruse, D. Alan. (2000). Aspects of the micro-structure of word meanings. In Ravin and Leacock (eds.), 30–51.

Crystal, David. (1969). *Prosodic Systems and Intonation in English*. Cambridge: Cambridge University Press.

Culicover, Peter and Louise McNally (eds.). (1998). *Syntax and Semantics 29: The Limits of Syntax*. New York: Academic Press.

Culicover, Peter and Michael Rochemont. (1983). Stress and focus in English. *Language* 59: 123–65.

Culy, Christopher. (1994). Aspects of logophoric marking. *Linguistics* 32: 1055–94.

Curcó, Carmen. (1998). Indirect echoes and verbal humour. In V. Rouchota and A. Jucker (eds.), *Current Issues in Relevance Theory*, 305–25. Amsterdam: Benjamins.

Curl, Traci S. and Alan Bell. (2001). Yeah, yeah, yeah: Prosodic differences of pragmatic functions. Unpublished manuscript, University of Colorado.

Cutler, Anne. (1974). On saying what you mean without meaning what you say. *CLS 10*, 117–27.

Cutler, Anne. (1977). The context dependence of "intonational meanings." *CLS 13*, 104–15.

Cutler, Anne and Donald Foss. (1977). On the role of sentence stress in sentence processing. *Language and Speech* 20: 1–10.

Cysouw, Michael. (2001). The Paradigmatic Structure of Person Marking. PhD dissertation, University of Nijmegen.

Dahl, Östen. (1979). The typology of sentence negation. *Linguistics* 17: 79–106.

Dahl, Östen. (1985). *Tense and Aspect Systems*. Oxford: Blackwell.

Dahl, Östen. (1988). The role of deduction rules in semantics. *Journal of Semantics* 6: 1–18.

Dalrymple, Mary. (1991). Against reconstruction in ellipsis. Technical Report SSL-91-114, Xerox Corporation.

Dalrymple, Mary, Stuart M. Shieber, and Fernando Pereira. (1991). Ellipsis and higher-order unification. *Linguistics and Philosophy* 14: 399–452.

Daly, Nancy A. and Victor W. Zue. (1992). Statistical and linguistic analyses of f0 in read and spontaneous speech. *Proceedings of the International Conference on Spoken Language Processing (ICSLP-92)* 1: 763–6.

Daneš, František. (1970). One instance of Prague School methodology: Functional analysis of utterance and text. In P. Garvin (ed.), *Method and Theory in Linguistics*, 132–56. The Hague: Mouton de Gruyter.

Daneš, František. (1974). *Papers on Functional Sentence Perspective*. The Hague: Mouton de Gruyter.

Dasigi, Venu R. (1988). Word Sense Disambiguation in Descriptive Text Interpretation: A Dual-route Parsimonious Covering Model. PhD dissertation, University of

Maryland. Also published as Technical Report TR-2151, Department of Computer Science, University of Maryland.

Davidson, Donald. (1967). Truth and meaning. *Synthèse* 17: 304–23.

Davidson, Donald. (1984). *Inquiries into Truth and Interpretation*. Oxford: Clarendon Press.

Davidson, Donald. (1986). A nice derangement of epitaphs. In E. Lepore (ed.), *Truth and Interpretation: Perspectives on the Philosophy of Donald Davidson*, 433–46. Oxford: Blackwell.

Davidson, Donald and Gilbert Harman (eds.). (1972). *Semantics of Natural Language*. Dordrecht: Reidel.

Davies, Martin. (1981). *Meaning, Quantification, Necessity*. London: Routledge & Kegan Paul.

Davies, Martin and Tony Stone (eds.). (1995a). *Mental Simulation: Philosophical and Psychological Essays*. Oxford: Blackwell.

Davies, Martin and Tony Stone (eds.). (1995b). *Folk Psychology*. Oxford: Blackwell.

Davis, Steven (ed.). (1991). *Pragmatics: A Reader*. Oxford: Oxford University Press.

Davis, Wayne A. (1998). *Implicature: Intention, Convention and Principle in the Failure of Gricean Theory*. Cambridge: Cambridge University Press.

Davison, Alice. (1973). Performative Verbs, Adverbs, and Felicity Conditions: an Inquiry into the Nature of Performative Verbs. PhD dissertation, University of Chicago.

Davison, Alice. (1980). Peculiar passives. *Language* 56: 42–66.

Davison, Alice. (1984). Syntactic markedness and the definition of sentence topic. *Language* 60: 797–846.

Deane, Paul D. (1988). Polysemy and cognition. *Lingua* 75: 325–61.

van Deemter, Kees and Stanley Peters (eds.). (1996). *Semantic Ambiguity and Underspecification*. Stanford, CA: CSLI.

Dekker, Paul. (1996). The values of variables in dynamic semantics. *Linguistics and Philosophy* 19: 211–57.

Dekker, Paul. (1998). Speaker's reference, descriptions and information structure. *Journal of Semantics* 15: 305–34.

Dekker, Paul and Robert van Rooy. (1999). Optimality theory and game theory: Some parallels. In de Hoop and de Swart (eds.), 22–45.

Delin, Judy. (1995). Presupposition and shared knowledge in *it*-clefts. *Language and Cognitive Processes* 10: 97–120.

Demirci, Mahide. (2001). Acquisition of binding of English reflexives by Turkish L2 learners: a neo-Gricean pragmatic account. *Journal of Pragmatics* 33: 753–75.

De Morgan, Augustus. (1847). *Formal Logic*. London: Taylor and Walton.

Derbyshire, Desmond C. (1979). Hixkaryana Syntax. PhD dissertation, University of London.

Diesing, Molly. (1992). *Indefinites*. Cambridge, MA: MIT Press.

Diessel, Holger. (1999). *Demonstratives: Form, Function and Grammaticalization*. Amsterdam: Benjamins.

van Dijk, Teun. (1977). *Text and Context*. London: Longman.

van Dijk, Teun. (1985). *Handbook of Discourse Analysis*, vol. 3: *Discourse and Dialogue*. London: Academic Press.

van Dijk, Teun and Walter Kintsch. (1983). *Strategies of Discourse Comprehension*. New York: Academic Press.

Dik, Simon C. (1978). *Functional Grammar*. Amsterdam: North-Holland.

Dik, Simon C. (1997). *The Theory of Functional Grammar*, part 1: *The Structure of the Clause*. Berlin: Mouton de Gruyter.

Dinsmore, John. (1981). *Pragmatics, Formal Theory and the Analysis of Presupposition.* Bloomington, IN: Indiana University Linguistics Club.

Dirksen, Arthur. (1992). Accenting and deaccenting: A declarative approach. *Proceedings of COLING-92*, 865–9.

Dirksen, Arthur and Hugo Quené. (1993). Prosodic analysis: The next generation. In V. J. van Hueven and L. C. W. Pols (eds.), *Analysis and Synthesis of Speech: Strategic Research towards High-Quality Text-to-Speech Generation*, 131–44. Berlin: Mouton de Gruyter.

Dixon, Robert M. W. (1972). *The Dyirbal Language of North Queensland.* Cambridge: Cambridge University Press.

Dixon, Robert M. W. (1980). *The Languages of Australia.* Cambridge: Cambridge University Press.

Dixon, Robert M. W. (1991). *A New Approach to English Grammar, on Semantic Principles.* Oxford: Clarendon Press.

Donaldson, Margaret. (1971). Preconditions of inference. In J. K. Cole (ed.), *Nebraska Symposium on Motivation*, 81–106. Lincoln, NB: University of Nebraska Press.

Donnellan, Keith. (1966). Reference and definite descriptions. *Philosophical Review* 77: 281–304. Reprinted in S. Davis (ed., 1991), 52–64, and in Kasher (ed., 1998), vol. V: 5–23.

Donnellan, Keith. (1972). Proper names and identifying descriptions. In Davidson and Harman (eds.), 356–79.

van Donzel, Monique. (1999). Prosodic Aspects of Information Structure in Discourse. PhD dissertation, University of Amsterdam.

Dooley, Robert A. (1982). Options in the pragmatic structuring of Guarani sentences. *Language* 58: 307–31.

Downing, Bruce T. (1970). Syntactic Structure and Phonological Phrasing in English. PhD dissertation, University of Texas, Austin.

Downing, Pamela. (1977). On the creation and use of English compound nouns. *Language* 53: 810–42.

Dowty, David. (1979). *Word Meaning and Montague Grammar.* Dordrecht: Kluwer.

Dowty, David. (1980). Comments on the paper by Bach and Partee. *CLS 16, Part 2: Papers from the Parasession on Pronouns and Anaphora*, 29–40.

Dowty, David. (1994). The role of negative polarity and concord marking in natural language reasoning. *SALT IV*, 114–44.

Dowty, David. (2000). "The Garden Swarms with Bees" and the fallacy of "Argument Alternation." In Ravin and Leacock (eds.), 111–28.

Dowty, David, Robert E. Wall, and Stanley Peters. (1981). *Introduction to Montague Semantics.* Dordrecht: Kluwer.

Doyle, John J. (1951). In defense of the square of opposition. *The New Scholasticism* 25: 367–96.

Dretske, Fred. (1972). Contrastive statements. *Philosophical Review* 81: 411–37.

Dryer, Matthew S. (1986). Primary objects, secondary objects and antidative. *Language* 62: 808–45.

Du Bois, John W. (1980). Beyond definiteness: The trace of identity in discourse. In W. L. Chafe (ed.), *The Pear Stories: Cognitive, Cultural, and Linguistic Aspects of Narrative Production*, 203–74. Norwood, NJ: Ablex.

Du Bois, John W. (1987). The discourse basis of ergativity. *Language* 63: 805–55.

Ducrot, Oswald. (1969). Présupposés et sous-entendus. Reprinted in Ducrot (1984), 13–31.

Ducrot, Oswald. (1972). *Dire et ne pas dire: Principes de sémantique linguistique*. Paris: Hermann.

Ducrot, Oswald. (1973). *La preuve et le dire*. Paris: Maison Mame.

Ducrot, Oswald. (1980). *Les échelles argumentatives*. Paris: Minuit.

Ducrot, Oswald. (1984). *Le dire et le dit*. Paris: Minuit.

Dummett, Michael. (1973). *Frege: Philosophy of Language*. Cambridge, MA: Harvard University Press.

Dummett, Michael. (1975). What is a theory of meaning? In S. Guttenplan (ed.), *Mind and Language*, 97–138. Oxford: Clarendon Press.

Dummett, Michael. (1981). *The Interpretation of Frege's Philosophy*. London: Duckworth.

Dummett, Michael. (1993). *Origins of Analytical Philosophy*. Cambridge, MA: Harvard University Press.

Eady, Stephen J. and William E. Cooper. (1986). Speech intonation and focus location in matched statements and questions. *Journal of the Acoustical Society of America* 80: 402–15.

Eckert, Penelope. (1999). *Linguistic Variation and Social Practice*. Oxford: Blackwell.

Edmondson, Jerry A. (1981). Affectivity and gradient scope. *CLS 17*, 38–44.

Edmondson, Jerry A. (1983). Polarized auxiliaries. In F. Heny and B. Richards (eds.), *Linguistic Categories: Auxiliaries and Related Puzzles*, vol. I, 49–68. Dordrecht: Reidel.

Edmondson, Jerry A. and Frans Plank. (1978). Great expectations: an intensive *self* analysis. *Linguistics and Philosophy* 2: 373–413.

Elugardo, Reinaldo and Robert Stainton. (2001a). Logical form and the vernacular. *Mind and Language* 16: 393–424.

Elugardo, Reinaldo and Robert Stainton. (2001b). Non-sentential assertions: A reply to Stanley. Unpublished manuscript, Carleton University, Ottawa.

Elugardo, Reinaldo and Robert Stainton (in press). Grasping objects and contents. In A. Barber (ed.), *The Epistemology of Language*. Oxford: Oxford University Press.

Enç, Mürvet. (1981). Tense without Scope: An Analysis of Nouns as Indexicals. PhD dissertation, University of Wisconsin-Madison.

Enç, Mürvet. (1991). The semantics of specificity. *Linguistic Inquiry* 22: 1–25.

Enfield, N. J. (2002). "Lip-pointing" – a discussion with special reference to data from Laos. *Gesture* 1: 185–212.

England, Nora C. (1983). Mamean voice: syntactic and narrative considerations. Unpublished manuscript, University of Iowa.

Enkvist, Nils Erik. (1979). Marked focus: Functions and constraints. In S. Greenbaum, G. Leech, and J. Svartvik (eds.), *Studies in English Linguistics for Randolph Quirk*, 134–52. London: Longman.

Erbaugh. Mary S. (1992). The acquisition of Mandarin. In D. I. Slobin (ed.), *The Cross-linguistic Study of Language Acquisition*, vol. 3, 373–455. Hillsdale, NJ: Lawrence Erlbaum.

Erman, Britt. (1987). *Pragmatic Expressions in English: A Study of* you know, you see, *and* I mean *in Face-to-Face Conversation*. Stockholm: Almqvist and Wiksell.

Ernst, Thomas. (1984). *Towards an Integrated Theory of Adverb Position in English*. Bloomington, IN: Indiana University Linguistics Club.

Errington, Joseph. (1988). *Structure and Style in Javanese: A Semiotic View of Linguistic Etiquette*. Philadelphia, PA: University of Pennsylvania Press.

Erteschik-Shir, Nomi. (1979). Discourse constraints on dative movement. In T. Givón (ed.), *Syntax and Semantics 12*, 441–67. New York: Academic Press.

Erteschik-Shir, Nomi. (1997). *The Dynamics of Focus Structure*. Cambridge: Cambridge University Press.

Erteschik-Shir, Nomi. (1998). The syntax–focus structure interface. In Culicover and McNally (eds.), 211–40.

Erteschik-Shir, Nomi and Shalom Lappin. (1983). Under stress: A functional explanation of English sentence stress. *Journal of Linguistics* 19: 419–53.

Ervin-Tripp, Susan. (1970). Discourse agreement: How children answer questions. In J. R. Hayes (ed.), *Cognition and the Development of Language*, 79–107. New York: Wiley and Son.

Ervin-Tripp, Susan. (1977). Wait for me, roller-skate! In S. Ervin-Tripp and C. Mitchell-Kernan (eds.), *Child Discourse*, 165–88. New York: Academic Press.

Ervin-Tripp, Susan. (1979). Children's verbal turn-taking. In E. Ochs and B. B. Schieffelin (eds.), *Developmental Pragmatics*, 391–414. New York: Academic Press.

Evans, Gareth. (1973). The causal theory of names. *Proceedings of the Aristotelian Society*, suppl. vol. 47: 187–208.

Evans, Gareth. (1980). Pronouns. *Linguistic Inquiry* 11: 337–62.

Faltz, Leonard M. (1985). *Reflexivization: A Study in Universal Syntax*. New York: Garland.

Faltz, Leonard M. (1989). A role for inference in meaning change. *Studies in Language* 13: 317–31.

Farmer, Ann K. and Robert M. Harnish. (1987). Communicative reference with pronouns. In Verschueren and Bertuccelli-Papi (eds.), 547–65.

Farrell, Patrick. (1990). Null objects in Brazilian Portuguese. *Natural Language and Linguistic Theory* 8: 325–46.

Fauconnier, Gilles. (1975a). Polarity and the scale principle. *CLS 11*, 188–99.

Fauconnier, Gilles. (1975b). Pragmatic scales and logical structure. *Linguistic Inquiry* 6: 353–75.

Fauconnier, Gilles. (1976). Etude de certains aspects logiques et grammaticaux de la quantification et de l'anaphore en français et en anglais. Doctorat d'État, Université de Paris VII. Paris: Champion.

Fauconnier, Gilles. (1978a). Is there a linguistic level of logical representation? *Theoretical Linguistics* 5: 31–49.

Fauconnier, Gilles. (1978b). Implication reversal in a natural language. In F. Guenthner and S. J. Schmidt (eds.), *Formal Semantics and Pragmatics for Natural Languages*, 289–301. Dordrecht: Reidel.

Fauconnier, Gilles. (1980). Pragmatic entailment and questions. In J. R. Searle, F. Kiefer, and M. Bierwisch (eds.), *Speech Act Theory and Pragmatics*, 57–71. Dordrecht: Reidel.

Fauconnier, Gilles. (1985). *Mental Spaces*. Cambridge, MA: MIT Press. (Reissued New York: Cambridge University Press, 1994.)

Fauconnier, Gilles. (1997). *Mappings in Thought and Language*. Cambridge: Cambridge University Press.

Fauconnier, Gilles. (1998). Mental spaces, language modalities, and conceptual integration. In M. Tomasello (ed.), *The New Psychology of Language: Cognitive and Functional Approaches to Language Structure*, 251–79. Hillsdale, NJ: Lawrence Erlbaum.

Fauconnier, Gilles. (2000). Methods and generalizations. In T. Janssen and G. Redeker (eds.), *Scope and Foundations of Cognitive Linguistics*, 95–127. The Hague: Mouton de Gruyter.

Fauconnier, Gilles and Eve Sweetser (eds.). (1996). *Spaces, Worlds, and Grammar*. Chicago, IL: University of Chicago Press.

Fauconnier, Gilles and Mark Turner. (1998). Conceptual integration networks. *Cognitive Science* 22: 133–87.

Fauconnier, Gilles and Mark Turner. (2002). *The Way We Think*. New York: Basic Books.

Fellbaum, Christiane. (1985). *On the Middle Construction in English*. Bloomington, IN: Indiana University Linguistics Club.

Fiengo, Robert and Robert May. (1994). *Indices and Identity*. Cambridge, MA: MIT Press.

Fiengo, Robert and Robert May. (1996). Anaphora and identity. In Lappin (ed., 1996), 117–44.

Fikes, Richard E. and Nils J. Nilsson. (1971). STRIPS: A new approach to the application of theorem proving to problem solving. *Artificial Intelligence* 2: 189–208.

Fillmore, Charles J. (1967). On the syntax of preverbs. *Glossa* 1: 91–125.

Fillmore, Charles J. (1968). The case for case. In E. Bach and R. T. Harms (eds.), *Universals in Linguistic Theory*, 1–88. New York: Holt, Rinehart and Winston.

Fillmore, Charles J. (1973). May we come in? *Semiotica* 9: 97–116.

Fillmore, Charles J. (1975). *Santa Cruz Lectures on Deixis*. Bloomington, IN: Indiana University Linguistics Club.

Fillmore, Charles J. (1977). Topics in lexical semantics. In R. W. Cole (ed.), *Current Issues in Linguistic Theory*, 76–138. Bloomington, IN: Indiana University Press.

Fillmore, Charles J. (1978). On the organization of semantic information in the lexicon. *Parasession on the Lexicon*, 148–73. Chicago, IL: Chicago Linguistics Society.

Fillmore, Charles J. (1982). Frame semantics. In P. Kiparsky (ed.), *Linguistics in the Morning Calm*, 111–37. Seoul: Hanshin.

Fillmore, Charles J. (1986). Pragmatically controlled zero anaphora. *BLS 12*, 95–107.

Fillmore, Charles J. (1997). *Lectures on Deixis*. Stanford, CA: CSLI.

Fillmore, Charles J. and B. T. S. Atkins. (2000). Describing polysemy: The case of "crawl." In Ravin and Leacock (eds.), 91–110.

Fillmore, Charles J., Paul Kay, and Mary Catherine O'Connor. (1988). Regularity and idiomaticity in grammatical constructions: The case of *let alone*. *Language* 64: 501–38.

von Fintel, Kai. (1999). NPI-licensing, Strawson-entailment, and context-dependency. *Journal of Semantics* 16: 1–44.

von Fintel, Kai (to appear). Would you believe it? The King of France is back! (Presuppositions and truth-value intuitions.) In Bezuidenhout and Reimer (eds.).

Firbas, Jan. (1964). On defining the theme in functional sentence perspective. *Travaux linguistiques de Prague* 1: 267–80.

Firbas, Jan. (1966). Non-thematic subjects in contemporary English. *Travaux linguistiques de Prague* 2: 239–56.

Fleischman, Suzanne. (1982). *The Future in Thought and Language*. Cambridge: Cambridge University Press.

Fleischman, Suzanne. (1990). *Tense and Narrativity: From Medieval Performance to Modern Fiction*. Austin, TX: University of Texas Press.

Fodor, Janet Dean. (1977). *Semantics: Theories of Meaning in Generative Grammar*. New York: Crowell.

Fodor, Janet Dean, Jerry Fodor, and Merrill F. Garrett. (1975). The psychological unreality of linguistic representations. *Linguistic Inquiry* 6: 515–31.

Fodor, Janet Dean and Ivan A. Sag. (1982). Referential and quantificational indefinites. *Linguistics and Philosophy* 5: 355–98.

Fodor, Jerry. (1983). *The Modularity of Mind*. Cambridge, MA: MIT Press.

Fodor, Jerry. (2000). *The Mind Doesn't Work That Way*. Cambridge, MA: MIT Press.

Fodor, Jerry. (2001). Language, thought and compositionality. *Mind and Language* 16: 1–15.

Fodor, Jerry and Zenon W. Pylyshyn. (1988). Connectionism and cognitive architecture: A critical analysis. *Cognition* 28: 3–71.

Fogelin, Robert. (1967). *Evidence and Meaning*. New York: Humanities Press.

Fortescue, Michael. (1984). *West Greenlandic*. London: Croom Helm.

Fowler, Carol A. and Jonathan Housum. (1987). Talkers' signaling of new and old words in speech and listeners' perception and use of the distinction. *Journal of Memory and Language* 26: 489–504.

Fox Tree, Jean E. (2001). Listeners' uses of *um* and *uh* in speech comprehension. *Memory and Cognition* 29: 320–6.

Fox Tree, Jean E. and Herbert H. Clark. (1997). Pronouncing "the" as "thee" to signal problems in speaking. *Cognition* 62: 151–67.

Fox Tree, Jean E. and Josef C. Schrock. (2002). Basic meanings of *you know* and *I mean*. *Journal of Pragmatics* 34: 727–47.

van Fraassen, Bas C. (1971). *Formal Semantics and Logic*. New York: Macmillan.

Frajzyngier, Zygmunt. (1985). Logophoric systems in Chadic. *Journal of African Languages and Linguistics* 7: 23–37.

Frajzyngier, Zygmunt and Traci S. Curl (eds.). (2000). *Reflexives: Forms and Functions*. Amsterdam: Benjamins.

Francis, Hartwell S., Michelle L. Gregory, and Laura A. Michaelis. (1999). Are lexical subjects deviant? *CLS 35, Part 1*, 85–97.

Francis, W. Nelson. (1964). A standard sample of present-day English for use with digital computers. Report to the US Office of Education on Cooperative Research. Project No. E-007, Brown University, Providence, RI.

Franks, Bradley and Nicholas Braisby. (1990). Sense generation or how to make a mental lexicon flexible. *Proceedings of the 12th Annual Conference of the Cognitive Science Society*. Cambridge, MA.

Fraser, Bruce. (1970). A note on *vice versa*. *Linguistic Inquiry* 1: 277–8.

Fraser, Bruce. (1974a). An analysis of vernacular performative verbs. R. W. Shuy and C.-J. Bailey (eds.), *Towards Tomorrow's Linguistics*, 139–58. Washington, DC: Georgetown University Press.

Fraser, Bruce. (1974b). An examination of the performative analysis. *Papers in Linguistics* 7: 1–40.

Fraser, Bruce. (1975). Hedged performatives. In Cole and Morgan (eds.), 187–210.

Fraser, Bruce. (1988). Types of English discourse markers. *Acta Linguistica Hungarica* 38: 19–33.

Fraser, Bruce. (1990). An approach to discourse markers. *Journal of Pragmatics* 14: 383–95.

Fraser, Bruce. (1996). Pragmatic markers. *Pragmatics* 6: 167–90.

Frege, Gottlob. (1879). Begriffsschrift. Reprinted in M. Beaney (ed.), *The Frege Reader*, 47–78. Oxford: Blackwell, 1997.

Frege, Gottlob. (1884). *The Foundations of Arithmetic*. (J. L. Austin, trans.) 2nd rev. edn. Oxford: Basil Blackwell, 1978.

Frege, Gottlob. (1892). Über Sinn und Bedeutung. *Zeitschrift für Philosophie und Philosophische Kritik* NF 100: 25–50. Trans. as "On sense and reference" in Frege (1970), 56–78.

Frege, Gottlob. (1918). The thought: A logical enquiry. Reprinted in P. F. Strawson (ed.), *Philosophical Logic*, 17–38. Oxford: Oxford University Press, 1967.

Frege, Gottlob. (1919). Negation. *Beiträge zur Philosophie des Deutschen Idealismus.* 1: 143–57. Reprinted in Frege (1970), 117–35.

Frege, Gottlob. (1970). *Translations from the Philosophical Writings of Gottlob Frege.* (P. Geach and M. Black, eds. and trans.) Oxford: Basil Blackwell.

Freidin, Robert. (1986). Fundamental issues in theory of binding. In B. Lust (ed.), *Studies in the Acquisition of Anaphora,* 151–88. Dordrecht: Reidel.

Freidin, Robert. (1994). Generative grammar: Principles and parameters framework. In R. E. Asher (ed.), *Language and Linguistics,* vol. 3, 1370–85. London: Pergamon Press.

Freidin, Robert. (1997). Binding theory on minimalist assumptions. *Proceedings of the Fourth Seoul International Conference on Linguistics,* 133–42. Seoul: The Linguistic Society of Korea.

Fretheim, Thorstein. (1987). Pragmatics and intonation. In Verschueren and Bertuccelli-Papi (eds.), 395–420.

Fretheim, Thorstein. (1992a). Grammatically underdetermined theme-rheme articulation. *ROLIG* No. 49, Roskilde University Center, Denmark.

Fretheim, Thorstein. (1992b). Themehood, rhemehood and Norwegian focus structure. *Folia Linguistica* XXVI: 111–50.

Fretheim, Thorstein. (1995). Why Norwegian right-dislocation phrases are not after-thoughts. *Nordic Journal of Linguistics* 18: 31–54.

Fretheim, Thorstein. (2001). The interaction of right-dislocated pronominals and intonational phrasing in Norwegian. In W. van Dommelen and T. Fretheim (eds.), *Nordic Prosody: Proceedings of the VIIIth Conference,* 61–76. Frankfurt-am-Main: Peter Lang.

Fretheim, Thorstein and Jeanette K. Gundel (eds.). (1996). *Reference and Referent Accessibility.* Amsterdam/Philadelphia: Benjamins.

Fu, Jingqi, Thomas Roeper, and Hagit Borer. (2001). The VP within process nominals: Evidence from adverbs and the VP anaphor *do-so. Natural Language and Linguistic Theory* 19: 549–82.

Fuchs, Anna. (1980). Accented subjects in "all-new" utterances. In G. Brettschneider and C. Lehmann (eds.), *Wege zur Universalienforschung: Sprachwissenschaftliche Beiträge zum 60.* Tübingen: Narr.

Fuchs, Anna. (1984). Deaccenting and default accent. In D. Gibbon and H. Richter (eds.), *Intonation, Accent and Rhythm,* 134–64. Berlin: Walter de Gruyter.

Fujio, Shigeru, Yoshinori Sagisaka, and Norio Higuchi. (1997). Prediction of major phrase boundary location and pause insertion using a stochastic context-free grammar. In Y. Sagisaka, N. Campbell, and N. Higuchi (eds.), *Computing Prosody: Computational Models for Processing Spontaneous Speech,* 271–83. New York: Springer.

Fukada-Karlin, Atsuko (in preparation). Pragmatic Functions of Attitudinal Discourse Markers in Japanese. PhD dissertation, University of Illinois, Urbana.

Fukada, Atsushi. (1986). Pragmatics and Grammatical Description. PhD dissertation, University of Illinois, Urbana.

von der Gabelentz, Georg. (1868). Ideen zur einer vergleichenden Syntax: Wort- und Satzstellung. *Zeitschrift für Völkerpsychologie und Sprachwissenschaft* 6: 376–84.

Gallagher, Tanya M. (1977). Revision behaviors in the speech of normal children developing language. *Journal of Speech and Hearing Research* 20: 303–18.

Gärdenfors, Peter. (1993). The emergence of meanings. *Linguistics and Philosophy* 16: 285–309.

Gärdenfors, Peter. (2000). *Conceptual Spaces: The Geometry of Thought.* Cambridge, MA: MIT Press.

Garnham, Alan. (1985). *Psycholinguistics: Central Topics.* London: Methuen.

Garnham, Alan and Josef Perner. (1990). Does manifestness solve problems of mutuality? *Behavioral and Brain Sciences* 13: 178–9.

Garrod, Simon C. and Anthony J. Sanford. (1994). Resolving sentences in a discourse context. In M. A. Gernsbacher (ed.), *Handbook of Psycholinguistics*, 675–98. New York: Academic Press.

Garvey, Catherine. (1975). Requests and responses in children's speech. *Journal of Child Language* 2: 41–63.

Garvey, Catherine. (1979). Contingent queries and their relations in discourse. In E. Ochs and B. B. Schiefflin (eds.), *Developmental Pragmatics*, 363–72. New York: Academic Press.

Gawron, Mark and Andrew Kehler. (2000). Respective readings and gaps. Paper presented at the Annual Meeting of the Linguistic Society of America, Chicago.

Gazdar, Gerald. (1979). *Pragmatics: Implicature, Presupposition and Logical Form.* New York: Academic Press.

Gazdar, Gerald. (1981). Speech act assignment. In Joshi et al. (eds.), 64–83.

Gazdar, Gerald, Ewan Klein, Geoffrey Pullum and Ivan Sag (1985). *Generalized Phrase. Structure Grammar.* Cambridge, MA: Harvard University Press.

Geach, Peter T. (1962). *Reference and Generality: An Examination of Some Medieval and Modern Theories.* Ithaca, NY: Cornell University Press.

Geach, Peter T. (1967). Intentional identity. *Journal of Philosophy* 64: 627–32.

Gee, James P. and François Grosjean. (1983). Performance structure: A psycholinguistic and linguistic appraisal. *Cognitive Psychology* 15: 411–58.

van Geenhoven, Veerle and Natasja Warner (eds.). (1999). *Annual Report 1998*, MPI for Psycholinguistics, Nijmegen, The Netherlands.

Geeraerts, Dirk. (1997). *Diachronic Prototype Semantics: A Contribution to Historical Lexicology.* Oxford: Clarendon Press.

Geis, Michael and Arnold M. Zwicky. (1971). On invited inferences. *Linguistic Inquiry* 2: 561–6.

Gelman, Rochel. (1969). Conservation acquisition: A problem of learning to attend to relevant attributes. *Journal of Experimental Child Psychology* 7: 167–87.

Geluykens, Ronald. (1987). Tails (right-dislocations) as a repair mechanism in English conversation. In J. Nuyts and G. de Schutter (eds.), *Getting One's Words into Line: On Word Order and Functional Grammar*, 119–29. Dordrecht: Foris.

Geluykens, Ronald. (1988). The interactional nature of referent-introduction. *CLS 24*, 151–64.

Geluykens, Ronald. (1992). *From Discourse Process to Grammatical Construction: On Left-Dislocation in English.* Amsterdam: Benjamins.

Geluykens, Ronald and Marc Swerts. (1994). Prosodic cues to discourse boundaries in experimental dialogues. *Speech Communication* 15: 69–77.

Geurts, Bart. (1998). Scalars. In P. Ludewig and B. Geurts (eds.), *Lexicalische Semantik aus kognitiver Sicht*, 95–117. Tübingen: Gunter Narr Verlag.

Giannakidou, Anastasia. (1998). *Polarity Sensitivity as (Non)Veridical Dependency.* Amsterdam: Benjamins.

Gibbs, Ray. (1994). *The Poetics of Mind: Figurative Thought, Language and Understanding.* Cambridge: Cambridge University Press.

Gibbs, Ray and Jessica Moise. (1997). Pragmatics in understanding what is said. *Cognition* 62: 51–74.

Gibbs, Ray and Jennifer O'Brien. (1991). Psychological aspects of irony understanding. *Journal of Pragmatics* 16: 523–30.

Gigerenzer, Gerd, Peter M. Todd, and the ABC Research Group. (1999). *Simple Heuristics That Make Us Smart*. Oxford: Oxford University Press.

Ginsberg, Matthew L. (ed.). (1987). *Readings in Nonmonotonic Reasoning*. Los Altos, CA: Morgan Kaufmann.

Ginzburg, Jonathan. (1996a). Dynamics and the semantics of dialogue. In J. Seligman and D. Westerstahl (eds.), *Language, Logic and Computation*, 221–38. Stanford, CA: CSLI.

Ginzburg, Jonathan. (1996b). Interrogatives: Questions, facts, and dialogue. In Lappin (ed.), 385–422.

Giora, Rachel. (1997). Discourse coherence and theory of relevance: stumbling blocks in search of a unified theory. *Journal of Pragmatics* 27: 17–34.

Giora, Rachel. (1998). Discourse coherence is an independent notion: a reply to Deirdre Wilson. *Journal of Pragmatics* 29: 75–86.

Girotto, Vittorio, Markus Kemmelmeir, Dan Sperber, and Jean-Baptiste van der Henst. (2001). Inept reasoners or pragmatic virtuosos? Relevance and the deontic selection task. *Cognition* 81: 69–76.

Givón, Talmy. (1975). Focus and the scope of assertion: some Bantu evidence. *Studies in African Linguistics* 6: 185–205.

Givón, Talmy. (1978). Negation in language: pragmatics, function, ontogeny. In Cole (ed.), 69–112.

Givón, Talmy. (1979). *On Understanding Grammar*. New York: Academic Press.

Givón, Talmy. (1984). *Syntax: A Functional-Typological Introduction*. Amsterdam: Benjamins.

Glucksberg, Sam. (2001). *Understanding Figurative Language*. Oxford: Oxford University Press.

Gödel, Kurt. (1944). Russell's mathematical logic. In P. Schilpp (ed.), *The Philosophy of Bertrand Russell*, 123–53. New York: Tudor.

Godfrey, John J., Edward C. Holliman, and Jane McDaniel. (1992). SWITCHBOARD: Telephone speech corpus for research and development. *Proceedings of the IEEE International Conference on Acoustics, Speech, and Signal Processing (IEEE ICASSP-92)*, 517–20. San Francisco, CA.

Goffman, Erving. (1974). *Frame Analysis: An Essay on the Organization of Experience*. New York: Harper and Row.

Goffman, Erving. (1981). Radio talk. In E. Goffman (ed.), 197–327.

Goffman, Erving. (ed.). (1981). *Forms of Talk*. Philadelphia, PA: University of Pennsylvania Press.

Gogate, Lakshmi J., Lorraine E. Bahrick, and Jilayne D. Watson. (2000). A study of multimodal motherese: the role of temporal synchrony between verbal labels and gestures. *Child Development* 71: 878–94.

Goldberg, Adele E. (1995). *Constructions: A Construction Grammar Approach to Argument Structure*. Chicago, IL: University of Chicago Press.

Goldberg, Adele E. (2000). Patient arguments of causative verbs can be omitted: The role of information structure in argument distribution. *Language Sciences* 34: 503–24.

Goldberg, Adele E. and Farrell Ackerman. (2001). The pragmatics of obligatory adjuncts. *Language* 77: 798–814.

Goldberg, Jo Ann. (1975). A system for the transfer of instructions in natural settings. *Semiotica* 14: 269–96.

Goldman, Alvin I. (1970). *A Theory of Human Action*. Princeton, NJ: Princeton University Press.

Goldsmith, John. (1985). A principled exception to the coordinate structure constraint. *CLS 21*, 133–43.

Golinkoff, Roberta M. (1983). The preverbal negotiation of failed messages: insights into the transition period. In R. M. Golinkoff (ed.), *The Transition from Prelinguistic to Linguistic Communication*, 57–78. Hillsdale, NJ: Lawrence Erlbaum.

Goodall, Grant. (1987). *Parallel Structures in Syntax*. Cambridge: Cambridge University Press.

Goodwin, Charles. (1981). *Conversational Organization: Interaction between Speakers and Hearers*. New York: Academic Press.

Goodwin, Charles. (1987). Forgetfulness as an interactive resource. *Social Psychology Quarterly* 50: 115–31.

Goodwin, Charles. (1996). Transparent vision. In E. Ochs, E. A. Schegloff, and S. A. Thompson (eds.), *Interaction and Grammar*, 370–404. Cambridge: Cambridge University Press.

Goodwin, Marjorie Harness and Charles Goodwin. (1986). Gesture and coparticipation in the activity of searching for a word. *Semiotica* 62: 51–75.

Goossens, Louis. (1995). Metaphtonymy: The interaction of metaphor and metonymy in figurative expressions for linguistic action. In L. Goossens, P. Pauwels, B. Rudzka-Ostyn, A.-M. Simon-Vandenbergen, and J. Vanparys (eds.), *By Word of Mouth: Metaphor, Metonymy and Linguistic Action in a Cognitive Perspective*, 159–74. Amsterdam: Benjamins.

Gordon, David and George Lakoff. (1971). Conversational postulates. *CLS 7*, 63–84. Reprinted in Cole and Morgan (eds., 1975), 83–106.

Gordon, Peter C., Barbara J. Grosz, and Laura A. Gillion. (1993). Pronouns, names, and the centering of attention in discourse. *Cognitive Science* 17: 311–48.

Grabe, Esther, Carlos Gussenhoven, Judith Haan, Erwin Marsi, and Brechte Post. (1997). The meaning of intonation phrase onsets in Dutch. In A. Botinis, G. Kouroupetroglou, and G. Carayiannis (eds.), *Intonation: Theory, Models and Applications*, 161–4. Athens: ESCA.

Graff, Delia. (2001). Descriptions as predicates. *Philosophical Studies* 102: 1–42.

Grandy, Richard. (1973). Reference, meaning, and belief. *Journal of Philosophy* 70: 439–52.

Green, Georgia M. (1968). On *too* and *either*, and not just on *too* and *either*, either. *CLS 4*, 22–39.

Green, Georgia M. (1973). The lexical expression of emphatic conjunction. *Foundations of Language* 10: 197–248.

Green, Georgia M. (1974). *Semantics and Syntactic Regularity*. Bloomington, IN: Indiana University Press.

Green, Georgia M. (1980). Some wherefores of English inversion. *Language* 56: 582–601.

Green, Georgia M. (1981). Pragmatics and syntactic description. *Studies in the Linguistic Sciences* 11: 27–37.

Green, Georgia M. (1982a). Linguistics and the pragmatics of language use. *Poetics* 11: 45–76.

Green, Georgia M. (1982b). Colloquial and literary uses of inversions. In D. Tannen (ed.), *Spoken and Written Language*, 119–53. Norwood, NJ: Ablex.

Green, Georgia M. (1985). The description of inversions in generalized phrase structure grammar. *BLS 11*, 117–45.

Green, Georgia M. (1990). The universality of Gricean interpretation. *BLS 16*, 411–28.

Green, Georgia M. (1993a). Rationality and Gricean inference. Cognitive Science Technical Report UIUC-BI-CS-93-09 (Language Series). Urbana, IL: Beckman Institute, University of Illinois.

Green, Georgia M. (1993b). You gotta have *wa*. Unpublished manuscript, available at http://mccawley.cogsci.uiuc.edu/~green.

Green, Georgia M. (1994). The structure of CONTEXT: The representation of pragmatic restrictions in HPSG. In J. H. Yoon (ed.), *Proceedings of the Fifth Annual Conference of the Formal Linguistics Society of Mid-America. Studies in the Linguistic Sciences* 24: 215–32.

Green, Georgia M. (1996a). *Pragmatics and Natural Language Understanding*, 2nd edition. Hillsdale, NJ: Lawrence Erlbaum.

Green, Georgia M. (1996b). Ambiguity resolution and discourse interpretation. In K. van Deemter and S. Peters (eds.), *Semantic Ambiguity and Underspecification*, 1–26. Stanford, CA: CSLI Publications.

Green, Georgia M. (2000). The nature of pragmatic information. In R. Cann, C. Grover, and P. Miller (eds.), *Grammatical Interfaces in HPSG*, 113–36. Stanford, CA: CSLI.

Green, Georgia M. (2001). Discourse particles in natural language processing. Unpublished manuscript, University of Illinois, Urbana.

Green, Georgia M. and Jerry L. Morgan. (2001). *Practical Guide to Syntactic Analysis*, 2nd edition. Stanford, CA: CSLI.

Green, Mitchell. (1995). Quantity, volubility, and some varieties of discourse. *Linguistics and Philosophy* 18: 83–112.

Gregory, Michelle L. and Laura A. Michaelis (to appear). Topicalization and left dislocation: A functional opposition revisited. *Journal of Pragmatics*.

Grice, H. P. (1957). Meaning. *Philosophical Review* 66: 377–88. Reprinted as Chapter 14 of Grice (1989).

Grice, H. P. (1961). The causal theory of perception. *Proceedings of the Aristotelian Society*, Supplementary Volume 35, 121–52.

Grice, H. P. (1967). *Logic and Conversation*. The William James lectures, Harvard University. Published as Part 1 of Grice (1989).

Grice, H. P. (1969). Vacuous names. In D. Davidson and J. Hintikka (eds.), *Words and Objections*, 118–45. Dordrecht: Reidel.

Grice, H. P. (1981). Presupposition and conversational implicature. In Cole (ed.), 183–98. (An earlier unpublished version was presented at the University of Illinois in 1970.)

Grice, H. P. (1989). *Studies in the Way of Words*. Cambridge, MA: Harvard University Press.

Grimm, Hannelore. (1975). Analysis of short-term dialogues in 5–7-year-olds: Encoding of intentions and modifications of speech acts as a function of negative feedback. Paper presented at the Third International Child Language Symposium, London.

Grimshaw, Jane. (1997). Projection, heads, and optimality. *Linguistic Inquiry* 28: 373–422.

Groenendijk, Jeroen and Martin Stokhof. (1984). Studies on the Semantics of Questions and the Pragmatics of Answers. PhD dissertation, University of Amsterdam.

Groenendijk, Jeroen and Martin Stokhof. (1989). Dynamic Montague Grammar: A first sketch. Amsterdam: ITLI/Department of Philosophy, University of Amsterdam.

Groenendijk, Jeroen and Martin Stokhof. (1990). Dynamic Montague Grammar. In L. Kálman and L. Pólos (eds.), *Papers from the Second Symposium on Logic and Language*, 3–48. Budapest: Adakémiai Kiadó.

Grosjean, François, Lysiane Grosjean, and Harlan Lane. (1979). The patterns of silence: Performance structures in sentence production. *Cognitive Psychology* 11: 58–81.

Grosu, Alexander. (1973). On the nonunitary nature of the coordinate structure constraint. *Linguistic Inquiry* 4: 88–92.

Grosz, Barbara J. (1977). The Representation and Use of Focus in Dialogue Understanding. PhD dissertation, University of California, Berkeley. (Technical Report 151, SRI International, Menlo Park, CA.)

Grosz, Barbara J. (1981). Focusing and description in natural language dialogues. In Joshi et al. (eds.), 84–105.

Grosz, Barbara J. (1997). Discourse and dialogue. In H. Uszkoreit, A. Zaenen and V. Zue (eds.), *Survey of the State of the Art in Human Language Technology*, 227–54. Cambridge: Cambridge University Press.

Grosz, Barbara J. and Julia Hirschberg. (1992). Some intonational characteristics of discourse structure. *Proceedings of ICSLP-92*, 429–32. Banff.

Grosz, Barbara J., Karen Sparck Jones, and Bonnie Lynn Webber (eds.). (1986). *Readings in Natural Language Processing*. Los Altos, CA: Morgan Kaufmann.

Grosz, Barbara J., Aravind K. Joshi, and Scott Weinstein. (1983). Providing a unified account of definite noun phrases in discourse. *ACL-21*, 44–50. Cambridge, MA.

Grosz, Barbara J., Aravind K. Joshi, and Scott Weinstein. (1995). Centering: A framework for modelling the local coherence of discourse. *Computational Linguistics* 21: 203–25.

Grosz, Barbara J. and Candace L. Sidner. (1986). Attention, intentions, and the structure of discourse. *Computational Linguistics* 12: 175–204.

Grosz, Barbara J. and Candace L. Sidner. (1990). Plans for discourse. In Cohen et al. (eds.), 417–44.

Guha, R. V. and Douglas B. Lenat. (1990). Cyc: A midterm report. *AI Magazine* 11: 32–59.

Guindon, R. and Walter Kintsch. (1984). Priming macropropositions: Evidence for the primacy of macropropositions in the memory for text. *Journal of Verbal Learning and Verbal Behavior* 23: 508–18.

Gumperz, John. (1976). Code switching in conversation. *Pragmatics Microfiche* 1.4, A2–D4.

Gundel, Jeanette K. (1974). The Role of Topic and Comment in Linguistic Theory. PhD dissertation, University of Texas, Austin.

Gundel, Jeanette K. (1978). Stress, pronominalization and the given-new distinction. *University of Hawaii Working Papers in Linguistics* 10: 1–13.

Gundel, Jeanette K. (1980). Zero NP-anaphora in Russian: a case of topic-prominence. *Parasession on Anaphora, Chicago Linguistic Society* 10, Part 2: 139–46.

Gundel, Jeanette K. (1985). "Shared knowledge" and topicality. *Journal of Pragmatics* 9: 83–107.

Gundel, Jeanette K. (1988). Universals of topic–comment structure. In M. Hammond, E. Moravcsik and J. Wirth (eds.), *Studies in Syntactic Typology*, 209–39. Amsterdam: Benjamins.

Gundel, Jeanette K. (1999a). On different kinds of focus. In Bosch and van der Sandt (eds.), 293–305.

Gundel, Jeanette K. (1999b). Topic, focus and the grammar pragmatics interface. *Penn Working Papers in Linguistics* 6: 185–200.

Gundel, Jeanette K., Nancy Hedberg, and Ron Zacharski. (1990). Givenness, implicature, and the form of referring expressions in discourse. *BLS 16*, 442–53.

Gundel, Jeanette K., Nancy Hedberg, and Ron Zacharski. (1993). Cognitive status and the form of referring expressions in discourse. *Language* 69: 274–307.

Gundel, Jeanette K., Nancy Hedberg, and Ron Zacharski. (2001). Definite descriptions and cognitive status in English: Why accommodation is unnecessary. *English Language and Linguistics* 5: 273–95.

Gussenhoven, Carlos. (1983). *On the Grammar and Semantics of Sentence Accents*. Dordrecht: Foris.

Gussenhoven, Carlos and Toni Rietveld. (1997). Empirical evidence for the contrast between L* and H* in Dutch rising contours. In A. Botinis, G. Kouroupetroglou, and G. Carayiannis (eds.), *Intonation: Theory, Models and Applications*, 18–20. Athens: ESCA.

Gutt, Ernst-August. (1988). Towards an analysis of pragmatic connectives in Silt'i. *Proceedings of the Eighth International Conference of Ethiopian Studies*, 26–30. Addis Adaba University.

Gutt, Ernst-August. (1991). *Translation and Relevance: Cognition and Context*. Oxford: Basil Blackwell.

de Haan, Ferdinand. (1997). *The Interaction of Modality and Negation: A Typological Study*. New York: Garland.

Haïk, Isabelle. (1987). Bound variables that need to be. *Linguistics and Philosophy* 10: 503–30.

Haiman, John. (1980a). The iconicity of grammar. *Language* 56: 515–40.

Haiman, John. (1980b). Dictionaries and encyclopedias. *Lingua* 50: 329–57.

Haiman, John. (1985). *Natural Syntax*. Cambridge: Cambridge University Press.

Hajičova, Eva, Petr Kubon, and Vladislav Kubon. (1990). Hierarchy of salience and discourse analysis and production. *Papers Presented to the 13th International Conference on Computational Linguistics*, 144–8. Helsinki.

Hale, Kenneth and Jay Keyser. (1987). A view from the middle. Lexicon Project Working Papers 10. Center for Cognitive Science, MIT.

Halle, Morris. (1964). Phonology in generative grammar. In J. A. Fodor and J. J. Katz, (eds.), *The Structure of Language: Readings in the Philosophy of Language*, 334–52. Englewood Cliffs, NJ: Prentice-Hall.

Halliday, Michael A. K. (1967). Notes on transitivity and theme in English, Part 2. *Journal of Linguistics* 3: 199–244.

Halliday, Michael A. K. and Ruquaiya Hasan. (1976). *Cohesion in English*. London: Longman.

Hamilton, Sir William (1860). *Lectures on Logic*, vol. 1. Edinburgh: Blackwood.

Han, Chung-Hye. (2000). *The Structure and Interpretation of Imperatives: Mood and Force in Universal Grammar*. New York: Routledge.

Hankamer, Jorge. (1971). Constraints on Deletion in Syntax. PhD dissertation, Yale University.

Hankamer, Jorge. (1978). On the nontransformational derivation of some null VP anaphors. *Linguistic Inquiry* 9: 66–74.

Hankamer, Jorge and Ivan Sag. (1976). Deep and surface anaphora. *Linguistic Inquiry* 7: 391–428.

Hanks, William. (1990). *Referential Practice: Language and Lived Space in a Maya Community*. Chicago, IL: University of Chicago Press.

Hanks, William. (1996). Language form and communicative practices. In J. J. Gumperz and S. C. Levinson (eds.), *Rethinking Linguistic Relativity*, 232–70. Cambridge: Cambridge University Press.

Hansen, Maj-Britt Mosegaard. (1996). Discourse particles in spoken French. In Hansen and Skytte (eds.), 105–49.

Hansen, Maj-Britt Mosegaard. (1997). *Alors* and *donc* in spoken French: A reanalysis. *Journal of Pragmatics* 28: 153–87.

Hansen, Maj-Britt Mosegaard and Gunver Skytte (eds.). (1996). *Le discours: Cohérence et connexion. Actes du Colloque international Copenhague le 7 Avril 1995*. Copenhagen: Museum Tusculanum Press.

Happé, Francesca. (1993). Communicative competence and theory of mind in autism: A test of relevance theory. *Cognition* 48: 101–19.

Happé, Francesca and Eva Loth. (2002). "Theory of mind" and tracking speakers' intentions. *Mind & Language* 17: 24–36.

Harabagiu, Sanda and Dan Moldovan. (1998). Knowledge processing on an extended WordNet. In C. Fellbaum (ed.), *WordNet: An Electronic Lexical Database*, 379–405. Cambridge, MA: MIT Press.

Hardt, Daniel. (1992). VP ellipsis and contextual interpretation. In *Proceedings of the International Conference on Computational Linguistics (COLING-92)*, 303–9.

Hardt, Daniel. (1993). Verb Phrase Ellipsis: Form, Meaning, and Processing. PhD dissertation, University of Pennsylvania.

Hardt, Daniel. (1999). Dynamic interpretation of verb phrase ellipsis. *Linguistics and Philosophy* 22: 187–221.

Harman, Gilbert. (1986). *Change in View: Principles of Reasoning*. Cambridge, MA: MIT Press.

Harnish, Robert M. (1976). Logical form and implicature. In T. G. Bever, J. J. Katz, and D. T. Langendoen (eds.), *An Integrated Theory of Linguistic Ability*, 464–79. New York: Crowell. Reprinted in S. Davis (ed., 1991), 316–64 and in Kasher (ed., 1998), vol. IV: 230–314.

Harnish, Robert M. (1994). Mood, meaning and speech acts. In Tsohatzidis (ed.), 407–59.

Harris, Alice C. and Lyle Campbell. (1995). *Historical Syntax in Cross-Linguistic Perspective*. Cambridge: Cambridge University Press.

Harris, Zellig. (1951). *Methods in Structural Linguistics*. Chicago, IL: University of Chicago Press.

Haspelmath, Martin. (1993). *Lezgian Grammar*. New York: Mouton de Gruyter.

Haspelmath, Martin. (1997). *Indefinite Pronouns*. Oxford: Oxford University Press.

Haspelmath, Martin. (1999a). Explaining article-possessor complementarity: Economic motivation in noun phrase syntax. *Language* 75: 227–43.

Haspelmath, Martin. (1999b). Optimality and diachronic adaptation. *Zeitschrift für Sprachwissenschaft* 18: 180–205.

Hauser, Marc. (1997). *The Evolution of Communication*. Cambridge, MA: MIT Press.

Haviland, John. (1979). How to talk to your brother-in-law in Guugu Yimithirr. In T. Shopen (ed.), *Languages and Their Speakers*, 161–239. Cambridge, MA: Winthrop.

Haviland, John (in press). How to point in Zinacantán. In Kita (ed.).

Hawkins, John A. (1978). *Definiteness and Indefiniteness*. Atlantic Highlands, NJ: Humanities Press.

Hawkins, John A. (1984). A note on referent identifiability and co-presence. *Journal of Pragmatics* 8: 649–59.

Hawkins, John A. (1991). On (in)definite articles: implicatures and (un)grammaticality prediction. *Journal of Linguistics* 27: 405–42.

Hedberg, Nancy. (1990). Discourse Pragmatics and Cleft Sentences in English. PhD dissertation, University of Minnesota.

Hedberg, Nancy. (2000). The referential status of clefts. *Language* 76: 891–920.

Hedberg, Nancy and Juan Manuel Sosa. (2001). The prosodic structure of topic and focus in spontaneous English dialogue. Presentation at Workshop on Intonation and Meaning, University of California, Santa Barbara.

Heim, Irene. (1982). The Semantics of Definite and Indefinite Noun Phrases. PhD dissertation, University of Massachusetts.

Heim, Irene. (1983a). File change semantics and the familiarity theory of definiteness. In R. Bauerle, C. Schwarze, and A. von Stechow (eds.), *Meaning, Use and the Interpretation of Language*, 164–89. Berlin: Walter de Gruyter.

Heim, Irene. (1983b). On the projection problem for presuppositions. *WCCFL 2*, 114–25.

Heim, Irene. (1984). A note on negative polarity and downward entailingness. *NELS 14*, 98–107.

Heim, Irene. (1990). E-type pronouns and donkey anaphora. *Linguistics and Philosophy* 13: 137–78.

Heim, Irene. (1992). Presupposition projection and the semantics of attitude verbs. *Journal of Semantics* 9: 183–221.

Henderson, Jim. (1995). Phonology and the grammar of Yele, Papua New Guinea. *Pacific Linguistics*, Series B-112.

Hendriks, Petra and Helen de Hoop (2001). Optimality theoretic semantics. *Linguistics and Philosophy.* 24: 1–32

van der Henst, Jean-Baptiste. (1999). The mental model theory and spatial reasoning re-examined: The role of relevance in premise order. *British Journal of Psychology* 90: 73–84.

van der Henst, Jean-Baptiste, Laure Carles, and Dan Sperber (2002). Truthfulness and relevance in telling the time. *Mind & Language* 17: 457–60.

van der Henst, Jean-Baptiste, Dan Sperber, and Guy Politzer. (2002). When is a conclusion worth deriving? A relevance-based analysis of indeterminate relational problems. *Thinking and Reasoning* 8: 1–20.

Hestvik, Arild. (1995). Reflexives and ellipsis. *Natural Language Semantics* 3: 211–37.

Hewitt, Carl E. (1972). Description and theoretical analysis (using schemas) of PLANNER: a language for proving theorems and manipulating models in a robot. Technical Report TR-258, AI Laboratory, MIT.

Higashimori, Isao. (1994). A relevance-theoretic analysis of *even, sae/sura/mo/remo/ddemo/ datte/made*. *English Literature Review* 38: 51–80. Kyoto Women's University.

Higginbotham, James. (1988). Contexts, models, and meanings: a note on the data of semantics. In R. Kempson (ed.), *Mental Representations: The Interface between Language and Reality*, 29–48. Cambridge: Cambridge University Press.

Himmelmann, Nikolaus. (1997). *Deiktikon, Artikel, Nominalphrase*. Tübingen: Niemeyer.

Hinds, Marilyn. (1974). Doubleplusgood polarity items. *CLS 10*, 259–68.

Hinrichs, Erhard. (1986). Temporal anaphora in discourses of English. *Linguistics and Philosophy* 9: 63–82.

Hintikka, Jaakko. (1962). *Knowledge and Belief*. Ithaca, NY: Cornell University Press.

Hintikka, Jaakko. (1968). Logic and philosophy. In R. Klibansky (ed.), *La Philosophie Contemporaine, 1: Logique et Fondements des Mathématiques*, 3–30. Florence: La Nuova Italia.

Hintikka, Jaakko. (1969). Semantics for propositional attitudes. In J. W. Davis, D. J. Hockney, and W. K. Wilson (eds.), *Philosophical Logic*, 21–45. Dordrecht: Reidel.

Hintikka, Jaakko. (1973). *Logic, Language-Games, and Information*. Oxford: Clarendon Press.

Hintikka, Jaakko. (1976). *The Semantics of Questions and the Questions of Semantics*. Amsterdam: North Holland.

Hintikka, Jaakko. (1981). On the logic of an interrogative model of scientific inquiry. *Synthèse* 47: 69–83.

Hintikka, Jaakko. (1983). Situations, possible worlds, and attitudes. *Synthèse* 54: 153–62.

Hintikka, Jaakko and Esa Saarinen. (1979). Information-seeking dialogues: Some of their logical properties. *Studia Logica* 32: 355–63.

Hirschberg, Julia. (1991). *A Theory of Scalar Implicature*. New York: Garland.

Hirschberg, Julia. (1993). Pitch accent in context: Predicting intonational prominence from text. *Artificial Intelligence* 63: 305–40.

Hirschberg, Julia and Cinzia Avesani. (1997). The role of prosody in disambiguating potentially ambiguous utterances in English and Italian. *ESCA Tutorial and Research Workshop on Intonation: Theory, Models and Applications*, 189–92. Athens.

Hirschberg, Julia and Cinzia Avesani. (2000). Prosodic disambiguation in English and Italian. In A. Botinis (ed.), *Intonation: Analysis, Modelling and Technology*, 87–95. Dordrecht: Kluwer.

Hirschberg, Julia and Barbara J. Grosz. (1992). Intonational features of local and global discourse structure. *Proceedings of the DARPA Speech and Natural Language Workshop*, 441–6, Harriman, NY. San Mateo: Morgan Kaufmann.

Hirschberg, Julia and Diane Litman. (1987). Now let's talk about "now": Identifying cue phrases intonationally. *ACL-87*, 163–71. Stanford, CA.

Hirschberg, Julia and Diane Litman. (1993). Empirical studies on the disambiguation of cue phrases. *Computational Linguistics* 19: 501–30.

Hirschberg, Julia and Christine Nakatani. (1996). A prosodic analysis of discourse segments in direction-giving monologues. *ACL-34*, 286–93. Santa Cruz, CA.

Hirschberg, Julia and Janet Pierrehumbert. (1986). The intonational structuring of discourse. *ACL-24*, 136–44. New York.

Hirschberg, Julia and Pilar Prieto. (1996). Training intonational phrasing rules automatically for English and Spanish text-to-speech. *Speech Communication* 18: 281–90.

Hirschberg, Julia and Gregory Ward. (1991). Accent and bound anaphora. *Cognitive Linguistics* 2: 101–21.

Hirschberg, Julia and Gregory Ward. (1992). The influence of pitch range, duration, amplitude, and spectral features on the interpretation of L*+H L H%. *Journal of Phonetics* 20: 241–51.

Hirschfeld, Laurence and Susan Gelman (eds.). (1994). *Mapping the Mind: Domain Specificity in Cognition and Culture*. Cambridge: Cambridge University Press.

Hirst, Graeme. (1987). *Semantic Interpretation and the Resolution of Ambiguity*. Cambridge: Cambridge University Press.

Hobbs, Jerry R. (1978). Why is discourse coherent? In F. Neubauer (ed.), *Coherence in Natural Language Texts*, 29–70. Hamburg: Buske.

Hobbs, Jerry R. (1979). Coherence and coreference. *Cognitive Science* 3: 27–90.

Hobbs, Jerry R. (1984). Sublanguage and knowledge. Technical Note 329, Artificial Intelligence Center, SRI International, Menlo Park, CA.

Hobbs, Jerry R. (1985a). Ontological promiscuity. *ACL-85*, 61–69. Chicago, IL.

Hobbs, Jerry R. (1985b). On the coherence and structure of discourse. CSLI Report 85–37. Menlo Park, CA: CSLI.

Hobbs, Jerry R. (1990). *Literature and Cognition*. CSLI Lecture Notes 21.

Hobbs, Jerry R. (1997). On the relation between the informational and intentional perspectives on discourse. In E. H. Hovy and D. R. Scott (eds.), *Computational and Conversational Discourse*, 139–57. Berlin: Springer Verlag.

Hobbs, Jerry R. (1998). The syntax of English in an abductive framework. Unpublished manuscript, available at http://www.isi.edu/~hobbs/discourse-inference/chapter4.pdf

Hobbs, Jerry R., William Croft, Todd Davies, Douglas Edwards, and Kenneth Laws. (1986). Commonsense metaphysics and lexical semantics. *ACL-86*, 231–40. New York.

Hobbs, Jerry R. and Andrew Kehler. (1997). A theory of parallelism and the case of VP ellipsis. *ACL-97*, 394–401. Madrid.

Hobbs, Jerry R., Mark E. Stickel, Douglas E. Appelt, and Paul Martin. (1993). Interpretation as abduction. *Artificial Intelligence* 63: 69–142.

Hobbs, Jerry R., Mark E. Stickel, Paul Martin, and Douglas Edwards. (1988). Interpretation as abduction. *ACL-88*, 95–103. Buffalo, NY.

Hockett, Charles. (1958). *A Course in Modern Linguistics.* New York: Macmillan.

Hockett, Charles. (1961). The problem of universals in language. In J. H. Greenberg (ed.), *Universals of Language*, 1–29. Cambridge, MA: MIT Press.

Hockett, Charles and S. A. Altmann. (1968). A note on design features. In T. Sebeok (ed.), *Animal Communication*, 61–72. Bloomington, IN: Indiana University Press.

Hoeksema, Jack. (1983). Negative polarity and the comparative. *Natural Language and Linguistic Theory* 1: 403–34.

Hoeksema, Jack. (1986). Monotonicity phenomena in natural language. *Linguistic Analysis* 16: 25–40.

Hoeksema, Jack. (1994). On the grammaticalization of negative polarity items. *BLS 20*, 273–82.

Hoeksema, Jack. (2000). Negative polarity items: triggering, scope and c-command. In Horn and Kato (eds.), 115–46.

Hoeksema, Jack, Hotze Rullmann, and Victor Sánchez-Valencia (eds.). (2001). *Perspectives on Negation and Polarity Items.* Amsterdam: Benjamins.

Hoffmann, Maria (1987). *Negatio Contrarii: A Study of Latin Litotes.* Assen: Van Gorcum.

Hofstadter, Douglas (1997). *Le Ton beau de Marot: In Praise of the Music of Language.* New York: Basic Books.

Hollos, Marida and William Beeman. (1978). The development of directives among Norwegian and Hungarian children: An example of communicative style in culture. *Language in Society* 7: 345–55.

de Hoop, Helen. (1991). Restrictions on existential sentence and object-scrambling: Some facts from Dutch. *West Coast Conference on Formal Linguistics* 9: 277–88.

de Hoop, Helen. (1996). *Case Configuration and Noun Phrase Interpretation.* New York: Garland.

de Hoop, Helen. (2000). Optimal scrambling and interpretation. In H. Bennis, M. Everaert, and E. Reuland (eds.), *Interface Strategies*, 153–68. Amsterdam: KNAW.

de Hoop, Helen and Henriëtte de Swart. (1998). Temporal adjunct clauses in optimality theory. Unpublished manuscript, Utrecht Institute of Linguistics OTS.

de Hoop, Helen and Henriëtte de Swart (eds.). (1999). *Papers on Optimality Theoretic Semantics.* Utrecht Institute of Linguistics OTS.

Hopper, Paul J. (1979). Aspect and foregrounding in discourse. In T. Givón (ed.), *Syntax and Semantics 12: Discourse and Syntax*, 213–41. New York: Academic Press.

Hopper, Paul J. (1988). Emergent grammar and the a priori grammar postulate. In D. Tannen (ed.), *Linguistics in Context*, 117–34. Norwood, NJ: Ablex.

Hopper, Paul J. and Elizabeth Closs Traugott. (1993). *Grammaticalization.* Cambridge: Cambridge University Press.

Horn, Laurence R. (1970). Ain't it hard anymore. *CLS 6*, 318–27.

Horn, Laurence R. (1971). Negative transportation: Unsafe at any speed? *CLS 7*, 120–33.

Horn, Laurence R. (1972). On the Semantic Properties of Logical Operators in English. PhD dissertation, UCLA. Distributed by the Indiana University Linguistics Club, 1976.

Horn, Laurence R. (1973). Greek Grice: a brief survey of proto-conversational rules in the history of logic. *CLS 9*: 205–14.

Horn, Laurence R. (1978a). Some aspects of negation. In J. Greenberg et al. (eds.), *Universals of Human Language*, vol. 4, 127–210. Stanford, CA: Stanford University Press.

Horn, Laurence R. (1978b). Remarks on neg-raising. In Cole (ed.), 129–220.

Horn, Laurence R. (1981). Exhaustiveness and the semantics of clefts. *NELS 11*, 125–42.

Horn, Laurence R. (1984a). Toward a new taxonomy for pragmatic inference: Q-based and R-based implicature. In D. Schiffrin (ed.), *Meaning, Form, and Use in Context: Linguistic Applications (GURT '84)*, 11–42. Washington, DC: Georgetown University Press. Reprinted in Kasher (ed., 1998), vol. IV: 389–418.

Horn, Laurence R. (1984b). Ambiguity, negation, and the London School of Parsimony. *NELS 14*, 108–31.

Horn, Laurence R. (1985). Metalinguistic negation and pragmatic ambiguity. *Language* 61: 121–74.

Horn, Laurence R. (1986). Presupposition, theme and variations. *CLS 22, Part 2: Papers from the Parasession on Pragmatics and Grammatical Theory*, 168–92.

Horn, Laurence R. (1988). Pragmatic theory. In Newmeyer (ed.), vol. 1, 113–45.

Horn, Laurence R. (1989). *A Natural History of Negation.* Chicago, IL: University of Chicago Press. (Expanded reissue, Stanford, CA: CSLI, 2001.)

Horn, Laurence R. (1990). Hamburgers and truth: Why Gricean inference is Gricean. *BLS 16*, 454–71.

Horn, Laurence R. (1991a). *Duplex negatio affirmat . . .* : The economy of double negation. *CLS 27, Part 2: Papers from the Parasession on Negation*, 80–106.

Horn, Laurence R. (1991b). Given as new: When redundant affirmation isn't. *Journal of Pragmatics* 15: 305–28.

Horn, Laurence R. (1992). The said and the unsaid. *Semantics and Linguistic Theory II*, 163–92. Columbus: Ohio State University Department of Linguistics.

Horn, Laurence R. (1993). Economy and redundancy in a dualistic model of natural language. In S. Shore and M. Vilkuna (eds.), *SKY 1993: 1993 Yearbook of the Linguistic Association of Finland*, 33–72.

Horn, Laurence R. (1996a). Presupposition and implicature. In Lappin (ed.), 299–320.

Horn, Laurence R. (1996b). Exclusive company: *Only* and the dynamics of vertical inference. *Journal of Semantics* 13: 1–40.

Horn, Laurence R. (1997). All John's children are as bald as the king of France: Existential import and the geometry of opposition. *CLS 33*, 155–79.

Horn, Laurence R. (2000a). From *if* to *iff*: Conditional perfection as pragmatic strengthening. *Journal of Pragmatics* 32: 289–326.

Horn, Laurence R. (2000b). Pick a theory (not just *any* theory): Indiscriminatives and the free choice indefinite. In Horn and Kato (eds.), 147–92.

Horn, Laurence R. (2001). Flaubert triggers, squatitive negation, and other quirks of grammar. In Hoeksema et al. (eds.), 173–200.

Horn, Laurence R. (to appear). Assertoric inertia and NPI licensing. *CLS 38, Part 2: The Panels.*

Horn, Laurence R. and Samuel Bayer (1984). Short-circuited implicature: A negative contribution. *Linguistics and Philosophy* 7: 397–414. Reprinted with new postscript in Kasher (ed., 1998), vol. IV, 658–81.

Horn, Laurence and Yasuhiko Kato (eds.) (2000). *Negation and Polarity: Syntactic and Semantic Perspectives.* Oxford: Oxford University Press.

Horne, Merle. (1985). English sentence stress, grammatical functions and contextual coreference. *Studia Linguistica* 39: 51–66.

Horne, Merle. (1987). Towards a discourse-based model of English sentence intonation. *Lund University Department of Linguistics Working Papers* 32.

Horne, Merle. (1991a). Accentual patterning in "new" vs "given" subjects in English. *Department of Linguistics Working Papers* 36, Lund University.

Horne, Merle. (1991b). Phonetic correlates of the new/given parameter. *Proceedings of the Twelfth International Congress of Phonetic Sciences*, 230–3. Aix-en-Provence.

Hornstein, Norbert. (1984). *Logic as Grammar*. Cambridge, MA: MIT Press.

Householder, Fred W. (1971). *Linguistic Speculations*. New York: Cambridge University Press.

Householder, Fred W. (1992). Semantic and lexical change. In W. Bright (ed.), *International Encyclopedia of Linguistics*, vol. 3, pp. 387–9. New York: Oxford University Press.

Hovy, Eduard H. (1990). Parsimonious or profligate approaches to the question of discourse structure relations. *Proceedings of the 5th International Workshop on Natural Language Generation*, 128–36. Dawson, PA.

Hovy, Eduard H. (1991). Approaches to the planning of coherent text. In C. L. Paris, W. R. Swartout, and W. C. Mann (eds.), *Natural Language Generation in Artificial Intelligence and Computational Linguistics*, 83–102. Dordrecht: Kluwer.

Hovy, Eduard H. (1993). Automated discourse generation using discourse structure relations. *Artificial Intelligence* 63: 341–84.

Huang, Yan. (1989). Anaphora in Chinese: Toward a Pragmatic Analysis. PhD dissertation, University of Cambridge.

Huang, Yan. (1991). A neo-Gricean pragmatic theory of anaphora. *Journal of Linguistics* 27: 301–35.

Huang, Yan. (1994). *The Syntax and Pragmatics of Anaphora: A Study with Special Reference to Chinese*. Cambridge: Cambridge University Press.

Huang, Yan. (1995). On null subjects and null objects in generative grammar. *Linguistics* 33: 1081–1123.

Huang, Yan. (1996). A note on the head-movement analysis of long-distance reflexives. *Linguistics* 34: 833–40.

Huang, Yan. (2000a). *Anaphora: A Cross-Linguistic Study*. Oxford: Oxford University Press.

Huang, Yan. (2000b). Discourse anaphora: Four theoretical models. *Journal of Pragmatics* 32: 151–76.

Huang, Yan. (2002). Logophoric marking in East Asian languages. In T. Güldemann and M. von Roncador (eds.), *Reported Speech*, 211–24. Amsterdam: Benjamins.

Hume, David (1955) [1748]. *An Inquiry Concerning Human Understanding*. Reprinted, New York: The Liberal Arts Press.

Hungerland, Isabel (1960). Contextual implication. *Inquiry* 3: 211–58.

Hunter, J. F. M. (1990). *Wittgenstein on Words as Instruments: Lessons in Philosophical Psychology*. Edinburgh: Edinburgh University Press.

Hutchins, Edwin. (1995). *Cognition in the Wild*. Cambridge, MA: MIT Press.

Hyams, Nina. (1986). *Language Acquisition and the Theory of Parameters*. Dordrecht: Reidel.

Hyman, Larry and Bernard Comrie. (1981). Logophoric reference in Gokana. *Journal of African Languages and Linguistics* 3: 19–37.

Ifantidou-Trouki, Elly. (1993). Sentential adverbs and relevance. *Lingua* 90: 69–90.

Ifantidou, Elly. (2001). *Evidentials and Relevance*. Amsterdam: Benjamins.

Israel, Michael. (1995). Negative polarity and phantom reference. *BLS 21*, 162–73.

Israel, Michael. (1996). Polarity sensitivity as lexical semantics. *Linguistics and Philosophy* 19: 619–66.

Israel, Michael. (1997). The scalar model of polarity sensitivity: The case of the aspectual operators. In D. Forget, P. Hirschbühler, F. Martineau, and M-L. Rivero (eds.), *Negation and Polarity: Syntax and Semantics*, 209–29. Amsterdam/Philadelphia: Benjamins.

Israel, Michael. (1998). The Rhetoric of Grammar: Scalar Reasoning and Polarity Sensitivity. PhD dissertation, University of California, San Diego.

Israel, Michael. (1999). *Some* and the pragmatics of indefinite construal. *BLS 25*, 169–82.

Israel, Michael. (2001). Minimizers, maximizers and the rhetoric of scalar reasoning. *Journal of Semantics* 18: 297–331.

Israel, Michael (to appear). *The Rhetoric of Grammar*. Cambridge: Cambridge University Press.

Iten, Corinne. (2000a). The relevance of Argumentation Theory. *Lingua* 110: 665–701.

Iten, Corinne. (2000b). "Non-truth-conditional" Meaning, Relevance and Concessives. PhD dissertation, University College London.

Iwasaki, Shoichi. (1985). The "Given A Constraint" and the Japanese particle *ga*. *Proceedings of the First Annual Pacific Linguistics Conference*, 152–67.

Iwata, Shoichi. (1999). On the status of implicit arguments in middles. *Journal of Linguistics* 35: 527–53.

Jackendoff, Ray. (1971). Gapping and related rules. *Linguistic Inquiry* 2: 21–35.

Jackendoff, Ray. (1972). *Semantic Interpretation in Generative Grammar*. Cambridge, MA: MIT Press.

Jackendoff, Ray. (1983). *Semantics and Cognition*. Cambridge, MA: MIT Press.

Jackendoff, Ray. (1992). Mme. Tussaud meets the Binding Theory. *Natural Language and Linguistic Theory* 10: 1–32.

Jackendoff, Ray. (1999). Possible stages in the evolution of the language capacity. *Trends in Cognitive Sciences* 3: 272–9.

Jackson, Eric. (1994). Negative Polarity, Definites under Quantification and General Statements. PhD dissertation, Stanford University, CA.

Jacobs, Andreas and Andreas H. Jucker. (1995). The historical perspective in pragmatics. In Jucker (ed.), 3–33.

Jaeggli, Osvaldo and Nina Hyams. (1988). Morphological uniformity and the setting of the null-subject parameter. *NELS 18*, 238–53.

Jäger, Gerhard. (2000). Some notes on the formal properties of bidirectional optimality theory. In R. Blutner and G. Jäger. (eds.), *Studies in Optimality Theory*, 41–63. Potsdam: Linguistics in Potsdam.

Jakobson, Roman. (1957). Shifters, verbal categories, and the Russian verb. Reprinted in *Selected Writings II*, 130–47. The Hague: Mouton, 1971.

James, Sharon L. (1978). Effect of listener age and situation on the politeness of children's directives. *Journal of Psycholinguistic Research* 7: 307–17.

Jarvella, Robert and Wolfgang Klein (eds.). (1982). *Speech, Place and Action: Studies of Deixis and Related Topics*. New York: John Wiley.

Jefferson, Gail. (1972). Side sequences. In D. Sudnow (ed.), *Studies in Social Interaction*, 294–338. New York: Free Press.

Jefferson, Gail. (1978). Sequential aspects of storytelling in conversation. In J. Schenkein (ed.), *Studies in the Organization of Conversational Interaction*, 219–48. New York: Academic Press.

Jekat, Susanne, Alexandra Klein, Elisabeth Maier, Ilona Maleck, Marion Mast, and Joachim Quantz. (1995). Dialogue Acts in VERBMOBIL. *April 1995 Verbmobil Report*, 65–95. Saarbrücken: DFKI GmbH.

Jespersen, Otto. (1922). *Language: Its Nature, Development and Origin.* London: Allen & Unwin.

Johannessen, Janne Bondi. (1998). *Coordination.* Oxford: Oxford University Press.

Johnson, Mark. (1987). *The Body in the Mind: The Bodily Basis of Meaning, Imagination and Reason.* Chicago, IL: University of Chicago Press.

de Jong, Franciska. (1987). The compositional nature of (in)definiteness. In Reuland and ter Meulen (eds.), 286–317.

de Jong, Franciska and Henk Verkuyl. (1985). Generalized quantifiers: The properness of their strength. In van Benthem and ter Meulen (eds.), 21–43.

de Jonge, C. C. (2001). *Natura artis magistra*: Ancient rhetoricians, grammarians, and philosophers on natural word order. *Linguistics in the Netherlands 2001*, 159–66.

Jorgensen, Julia, George Miller, and Dan Sperber. (1984). Test of the mention theory of irony. *Journal of Experimental Psychology: General* 113: 112–20.

Josephson, John R. and Susan G. Josephson (eds.). (1994). *Abductive Inference: Computation, Philosophy, Technology.* Cambridge: Cambridge University Press.

Joshi, Aravind, Bonnie L. Webber, and Ivan A. Sag (eds.). (1981). *Elements of Discourse Understanding.* Cambridge: Cambridge University Press.

Jucker, Andreas. (1993). The discourse marker *well*: a relevance-theoretic account. *Journal of Pragmatics* 19: 435–52.

Jucker, Andreas H. (ed.). (1995). *Historical Pragmatics: Pragmatic Developments in the History of English.* Amsterdam: Benjamins.

Jucker, Andreas H. (1997). The discourse marker *well* in the history of English. *English Language and Linguistics* 1: 91–110.

Jucker, Andreas and Yael Ziv (eds.). (1998). *Discourse Markers: Descriptions and Theory.* Amsterdam: Benjamins.

Jurafsky, Daniel, Rebecca Bates, Noah Coccaro, Rachel Martin, Marie Meteer, Klaus Ries, Elizabeth Shriberg, Andreas Stolcke, Paul Taylor, and Carol Van Ess-Dykema. (1997a). Automatic detection of discourse structure for speech recognition and understanding. In *Proceedings of the 1997 IEEE Workshop on Speech Recognition and Understanding*, 88–95. Santa Barbara, CA.

Jurafsky, Daniel, Rebecca Bates, Noah Coccaro, Rachel Martin, Marie Meteer, Klaus Ries, Elizabeth Shriberg, Andreas Stolcke, Paul Taylor, and Carol Van Ess-Dykema. (1998a). *Switchboard Discourse Language Modeling Project Report*, Research Note 30. Center for Speech and Language Processing, Johns Hopkins University.

Jurafsky, Daniel and James H. Martin. (2000). *Speech and Language Processing: An Introduction to Natural Language Processing, Computational Linguistics, and Speech Recognition.* Englewood Cliffs, NJ: Prentice-Hall.

Jurafsky, Daniel, Elizabeth Shriberg, and Debra Biasca. (1997b). Switchboard SWBD-DAMSL Labeling Project Coder's Manual, Draft 13. 97-02, University of Colorado Institute of Cognitive Science. Also available as http://www.colorado.edu/ling/jurafsky/manual.august1.html

Jurafsky, Daniel, Elizabeth E. Shriberg, Barbara Fox, and Traci Curl. (1998b). Lexical, prosodic, and syntactic cues for dialog acts. In *Proceedings of ACL/COLING-98 Workshop on Discourse Relations and Discourse Markers*, 114–20.

Kadmon, Nirit. (1990). Uniqueness. *Linguistics and Philosophy* 13: 273–324.

Kadmon, Nirit. (2000). *Formal Pragmatics: Semantics, Pragmatics, Presupposition, and Focus.* Oxford: Blackwell.

Kadmon, Nirit and Fred Landman. (1993). Any. *Linguistics and Philosophy* 16: 353–422.

Kahrel, Peter and René van den Berg. (1994). *Typological Studies in Negation.* Amsterdam: Benjamins.

Kalokerinos, Alexis. (1995). *Even*: How to make theories with a word. *Journal of Pragmatics* 24: 77–98.

Kameyama, Megumi. (1986). A property-sharing constraint in centering. *ACL-86*, 200–6. New York.

Kamp, Hans. (1975). Two theories about adjectives. In E. L. Keenan (ed.), 123–55.

Kamp, Hans. (1981). A theory of truth and semantic representation. In J. Groenendijk, T. M. V. Janssen, and M. Stokhof (eds.), *Formal Methods in the Study of Language*, 277–321. Amsterdam: Mathematische Centrum.

Kamp, Hans and Uwe Reyle. (1993). *From Discourse to Logic*. Dordrecht: Kluwer.

Kanazawa, Makoto. (1994). Weak vs. strong readings of donkey sentences and monotonicity inference in a dynamic setting. *Linguistics and Philosophy* 17: 109–58.

Kaplan, David. (1972). What is Russell's theory of descriptions? In D. F. Pears (ed.), *Bertrand Russell: A Collection of Critical Essays*, 227–44. New York: Doubleday.

Kaplan, David. (1978). Dthat. In Cole (ed., 1978), 221–43.

Kaplan, David. (1979). On the logic of demonstratives. *Journal of Philosophical Logic* 8: 81–9. Reprinted in S. Davis (ed., 1991), 137–45.

Kaplan, David. (1989a). Demonstratives. In J. Almog, H. Wettstein, and J. Perry (eds.), *Themes from Kaplan*, 481–563. New York: Oxford University Press.

Kaplan, David. (1989b). Afterthoughts. In J. Almog, H. Wettstein, and J. Perry (eds.), *Themes from Kaplan*, 565–614. New York: Oxford University Press.

Karttunen, Lauri. (1969). Problems of Reference in Syntax. PhD dissertation, Indiana University.

Karttunen, Lauri. (1973). Presuppositions of compound sentences. *Linguistic Inquiry* 4: 169–93.

Karttunen, Lauri. (1974). Presupposition and linguistic context. *Theoretical Linguistics* 1: 182–94.

Karttunen, Lauri. (1976). Discourse referents. In McCawley (ed.), 363–85.

Karttunen, Lauri. (1977). The syntax and semantics of questions. *Linguistics and Philosophy* 1: 3–44.

Karttunen, Lauri and Stanley Peters. (1979). Conventional implicature. In Oh and Dinneen (eds.), 1–56.

Kas, Mark. (1993). *Essays on Boolean Functions and Negative Polarity*. Groningen: Groningen Dissertations in Linguistics 11.

Kasher, Asa. (1976). Conversational maxims and rationality. In A. Kasher (ed.), *Language in Focus: Foundations, Methods and Systems*, 197–211. Dordrecht: Reidel. Reprinted with next paper in Kasher (ed., 1998), vol. IV: 181–214.

Kasher, Asa. (1982). Gricean inference revisited. *Philosophica* 29: 25–44.

Kasher, Asa. (1984). Pragmatics and the modularity of mind. *Journal of Pragmatics* 8: 539–57. Reprinted in S. Davis (ed., 1991), 567–82.

Kasher, Asa (ed.). (1998). *Pragmatics: Critical Concepts*. London: Routledge.

Kasher, Asa and Dov M. Gabbay. (1976). On the semantics and pragmatics of specific and non-specific indefinite expressions. *Theoretical Linguistics* 3: 145–90.

Kasper, Robert T., Craige Roberts, and Paul C. Davis. (1999). An integrated approach to reference and presupposition resolution. Paper presented at ACL-99 Workshop on the Relationship between Discourse/Dialogue Structure and Reference, University of Delaware.

Kato, Yasuhiko. (2000). Interpretive asymmetries in negation. In Horn and Kato (eds.), 62–87.

Katz, Jerrold J. (1972). *Semantic Theory*. New York: Harper & Row.

Katz, Jerrold J. (1975). Logic and language: An examination of recent criticisms of intensionalism. In K. Gunderson (ed.), *Language, Mind, and Knowledge*, 36–130. Minneapolis, MN: University of Minnesota Press.

Katz, Jerrold J. (1977). *Propositional Structure and Illocutionary Force*. New York: Crowell.

Katz, Jerrold J. and Jerry A. Fodor. (1963). The structure of a semantic theory. *Language* 39: 170–210.

Katz, Jerrold J. and Paul M. Postal. (1964). *An Integrated Theory of Linguistic Descriptions*. Cambridge, MA: MIT Press.

Kay, Paul. (1984). The *kind of/sort of* construction. *BLS 10*, 128–37.

Kay, Paul. (1990). Even. *Linguistics and Philosophy* 13: 59–111.

Kay, Paul. (1991). Constructional modus tollens and level of conventionality. *CLS 27, Part 2: Parasession on Negation*, 107–24.

Kay, Paul. (1992). *At least*. In A. Lehrer and E. F. Kittay (eds.), *Frames, Fields, and Contrasts: New Essays in Semantic and Lexical Organization*, 309–32. Hillsdale, NJ: Lawrence Erlbaum.

Kay, Paul. (1997). *Words and the Grammar of Context*. Stanford, CA: CSLI.

Kay, Paul. (2002). English subjectless tagged sentences. *Language* 78: 453–81.

Kay, Paul and Karl Zimmer. (1976). On the semantics of compounds and genitives in English. *Proceedings of the Sixth California Linguistic Association Conference*, 29–35. San Diego, CA: San Diego State University.

Keating, Elizabeth. (1998). Honor and stratification in Pohnpei, Micronesia. *American Ethnologist* 25: 399–411.

Keenan, Edward L. (1974). The functional principle: Generalizing the notion of "subject of." *CLS 10*, 298–310.

Keenan, Edward L. (ed.). (1975). *Formal Semantics for Natural Language*. Cambridge: Cambridge University Press.

Keenan, Edward L. (1987). A semantic definition of "indefinite NP." In Reuland and ter Meulen (eds.), 286–318.

Keenan, Edward L. (to appear). *Creating Anaphors: The History of Reflexive Pronouns in English*. Cambridge, MA: MIT Press.

Keenan, Elinor Ochs. (1974). Conversational competence in children. *Journal of Child Language* 1: 163–83.

Keenan, Elinor Ochs. (1976). The universality of conversational postulates. *Language in Society* 5: 67–80. Reprinted in Kasher (ed., 1998), vol. IV: 215–29.

Keenan, Janice M., George R. Potts, J. M. Golding, and T. M. Jennings. (1990). Which elaborative inferences are drawn during reading? A question of methodologies. In D. A. Balota, G. B. Flores d'Arcais, and K. Rayner (eds.), *Comprehension Processes in Reading*, 377–402. Hillsdale, NJ: Lawrence Erlbaum.

Kehler, Andrew. (1993a). The effect of establishing coherence in ellipsis and anaphora resolution. *ACL-93*, 62–9.

Kehler, Andrew. (1993b). A discourse copying algorithm for ellipsis and anaphora resolution. In *Proceedings of the Sixth Conference of the European Chapter of the Association for Computational Linguistics (EACL-93)*, 203–12. Utrecht.

Kehler, Andrew. (2000a). Coherence and the resolution of ellipsis. *Linguistics and Philosophy* 23: 533–75.

Kehler, Andrew. (2000b). Discourse. In Jurafsky and Martin (eds.), 669–718.

Kehler, Andrew. (2002). *Coherence, Reference, and the Theory of Grammar*. Stanford, CA: CSLI.

Kehler, Andrew and Gregory Ward. (1999). On the semantics and pragmatics of "identifier *so*." In Ken Turner (ed.), *The Semantics/Pragmatics Interface from Different Points of View*, 233–56. Amsterdam: Elsevier.

Keller, Rudi. (1994). *On Language Change: The Invisible Hand in Language*. London: Routledge. (B. Nerlich, trans.) Originally published as *Sprachwandel: Von der unsichtbaren Hand in der Sprache*. Tübingen: Francke, 1990.

Kemmer, Suzanne. (1993). *The Middle Voice*. Amsterdam: Benjamins.

Kempson, Ruth. (1975). *Presupposition and the Delimitation of Semantics*. Cambridge: Cambridge University Press.

Kempson, Ruth. (1980). Ambiguity and word meaning. In S. Greenbaum, G. Leech, and J. Svartvik (eds.), *Studies in English Linguistics for Randolph Quirk*, 1–66. London: Longman.

Kempson, Ruth. (1986). Ambiguity and the semantics–pragmatics distinction. In C. Travis (ed.), *Meaning and Interpretation*, 77–103. Oxford: Basil Blackwell.

Kempson, Ruth. (1988). Grammar and conversational principles. In Newmeyer (ed.), vol. 2, 139–63.

Kempson, Ruth. (1996). Semantics, pragmatics and deduction. In S. Lappin (ed.), *Handbook of Contemporary Semantic Theory*, 561–98. Oxford: Blackwell.

Kempson, Ruth and Annabel Cormack. (1982). Ambiguity and quantification. *Linguistics and Philosophy* 4: 259–309.

Kendon, Adam. (1980). Gesticulation and speech: Two aspects of the process of utterance. In M. R. Key (ed.), *Relationship of Verbal and Nonverbal Communication*, 207–27. Amsterdam: Mouton de Gruyter.

Kennedy, Christopher. (1997). VP deletion and "nonparasitic gaps." *Linguistic Inquiry* 28: 697–707.

Kennedy, Christopher (in press). Ellipsis and syntactic representation. In K. Schwabe and S. Winkler (eds.), *The Syntax–Semantics Interface: Interpreting (Omitted) Structure*. Amsterdam: Benjamins.

Kenyon, Tim. (1999). Non-sentential assertions and the dependence thesis of word meaning. *Mind & Language* 14: 424–40.

Keyser, Samuel J. and Thomas Roeper. (1984). On the middle and ergative constructions in English. *Linguistic Inquiry* 15: 381–416.

Kiessling, Andreas, Ralf Kompe, Heinrich Niemann, Elmar Noeth, and Anton Batliner. (1993). Roger, sorry, I'm still listening: Dialog guiding signals in informational retrieval dialogs. In D. House and P. Touati (eds.), *ESCA Workshop on Prosody*, 140–3. Lund, Sweden.

Kim, Nam-Kil. (1990). Korean. In B. Comrie (ed.), *The World's Major Languages*, 881–98. New York: Oxford University Press.

Kim, Sun-Hee. (1993). Division of Labor between Grammar and Pragmatics: The Distribution and Interpretation of Anaphora. PhD dissertation, Yale University.

King, Jeffrey C. (1988). Are indefinite descriptions ambiguous? *Philosophical Studies* 53: 417–40.

King, Jeffrey C. (2001). *Complex Demonstratives*. Cambridge, MA: MIT Press.

Kintsch, Walter. (1974). *Representation of Meaning in Memory*. Hillsdale, NJ: Lawrence Erlbaum.

Kintsch, Walter. (1988). The role of knowledge in discourse comprehension: A construction-integration model. *Psychological Review* 95: 163–82.

Kintsch, Walter and Teun van Dijk. (1978). Toward a model of text comprehension and production. *Psychological Review* 85: 363–94.

Kiparsky, Paul. (1982). Lexical morphology and phonology. In P. Kiparsky (ed.), *Linguistics in the Morning Calm*, 3–91. Seoul: Hanshin.

Kiparsky, Paul. (1983). Word-formation and the lexicon. In F. Ingemann (ed.), *Proceedings of the 1982 Mid-America Linguistic Conference*, 47–78.

Kiparsky, Paul and Carol Kiparsky. (1970). Fact. In M. Bierwisch and K. E. Heidolph (eds.), *Progress in Linguistics*, 143–73. The Hague: Mouton. Reprinted in Steinberg and Jakobovits (eds., 1971), 345–69.

Kiss, Katalin É. (1998). Identificational focus versus information focus. *Language* 74: 245–73.

Kita, Sotaro (ed.) (in press). *Pointing: Where Language, Cognition, and Culture Meet.* Mahwah, NJ: Lawrence Erlbaum.

Kitagawa, Yoshihisa. (1991). Copying identity. *Natural Language and Linguistic Theory* 9: 497–536.

Kitis, Eliza. (1995). Connectives and ideology. Paper delivered at the 4th International Symposium on Critical Discourse Analysis: Language, Social Life and Critical Thought, University of Athens.

Klein, Henny. (1997). *Adverbs of Degree in Dutch.* Groningen: Groningen Dissertations in Linguistics 21.

Klima, Edward S. (1964). Negation in English. In J. Fodor and J. Katz (eds.), *The Structure of Language: Readings in the Philosophy of Language*, 246–323. Englewood Cliffs, NJ: Prentice-Hall.

von Klopp, Ana. (1998). An alternative view of polarity items. *Linguistics and Philosophy* 21: 393–432.

Knott, Alastair and Robert Dale. (1994). Using linguistic phenomena to motivate a set of coherence relations. *Discourse Processes* 18: 35–62.

Knott, Alistair and Chris Mellish. (1996). A feature-based account of the relations signalled by sentence and clause connectives. *Language and Speech* 39: 143–83.

Knott, Alastair and Ted Sanders. (1998). The classification of coherence relations and their linguistic marker: an exploration of two languages. *Journal of Pragmatics* 30: 135–75.

Koenig, Jean-Pierre. (1991). Scalar predicates and negation: Punctual semantics and interval interpretations. *CLS 27, Part 2: Parasession on Negation*, 140–54.

Koike, Kazuhito, Hirotaka Suzuki, and Hiroaki Saito. (1998). Prosodic parameters in emotional speech. *Proceedings of ICSLP-98*, 679–82. Sydney.

Koiso, Hanae, Yasuo Horiuchi, Syun Tutiya, Akira Ichikawa, and Yasuharu Den. (1998). An analysis of turn-taking and backchannels based on prosodic and syntactic features in Japanese map task dialogs. *Language and Speech* 41: 292–321.

Koiso, Hanae, Atsushi Shimojima, and Yasuhiro Katagiri. (1998). Collaborative signaling of informational structures by dynamic speech rate. *Language and Speech* 41: 323–50.

Kompe, Ralf, Andreas Kiessling, Thomas Kuhn, Marion Mast, Heinrich Niemann, Elmar Nöth, K. Ott, and Anton Batliner. (1993). Prosody takes over: A prosodically guided dialog system. *EUROSPEECH-93* 3: 2003–6. Berlin.

Kompe, Ralf, Andreas Kiessling, Heinrich Niemann, Elmar Noeth, E. Guenther Schukat-Talamazzini, A. Zottmann, and Anton Batliner. (1995). Prosodic scoring of word hypothesis graphs. *EUROSPEECH-95* 3: 1333–6. Madrid.

König, Ekkehard. (1985). On the history of concessive connectives in English: diachronic and synchronic evidence. *Lingua* 66: 1–19.

König, Ekkehard and Peter Siemund. (2000). Intensifiers and reflexives: A typological perspective. In Frajzyngier and Curl (eds.), 41–74.

Kose, Yuriko Suzuki. (1997). The Pragmatics of Japanese Sentence-final Particles. PhD dissertation, University of Illinois, Urbana.

Kövecses, Zoltán and Günter Radden. (1998). Metonymy: Developing a cognitive linguistic view. *Cognitive Linguistics* 9: 37–77.

Kreuz, Roger and Sam Glucksberg. (1989). How to be sarcastic: The echoic reminder theory of irony. *Journal of Experimental Psychology: General* 118: 374–86.

Krifka, Manfred. (1991). Some remarks on polarity items. In D. Zaefferer (ed.), *Semantic Universals and Universal Semantics*, 150–89. Dordrecht: Foris.

Krifka, Manfred. (1994). The semantics of weak and strong polarity items in assertion. *SALT IV*, 195–219.

Krifka, Manfred. (1995). The semantics and pragmatics of polarity items. *Linguistic Analysis* 25: 209–57.

Kripke, Saul. (1972). Naming and necessity. In Davidson and Harman (eds.), 253–355 and 763–9.

Kripke, Saul. (1977). Speaker's reference and semantic reference. *Midwest Studies in Philosophy* 2: 255–76. Reprinted in S. Davis (ed., 1991), 77–96.

Kripke, Saul. (1980). *Naming and Necessity*. Cambridge, MA: Harvard University Press.

Krug, Manfred G. (2000). *Emerging English Modals: A Corpus-Based Study of Grammaticalization*. Berlin: Mouton de Gruyter.

Kruyt, J. Geertruida. (1985). Accents from Speakers to Listeners: An Experimental Study of the Production and Perception of Accent Patterns in Dutch. PhD thesis, University of Leiden.

Kumon-Nakamura, Sachi, Sam Glucksberg, and Mary Brown. (1995). How about another piece of pie: the allusional pretense theory of discourse irony. *Journal of Experimental Psychology: General* 124: 3–21.

Kuno, Susumu. (1972). Functional sentence perspective: A case study from Japanese and English. *Linguistic Inquiry* 3: 269–320.

Kuno, Susumu. (1975). Three perspectives in the functional approach to syntax. *Papers from the Parasession on Functionalism*, 276–336. Chicago, IL: Chicago Linguistic Society.

Kuno, Susumu. (1976a). Gapping: A functional analysis. *Linguistic Inquiry* 7: 300–18.

Kuno, Susumu. (1976b.) Subject, theme, and the speaker's empathy – a reexamination of the relativization phenomena. In C. Li (ed.), *Subject and Topic*, 419–44. New York: Academic Press.

Kuno, Susumu. (1987). *Functional Syntax – Anaphora, Discourse and Empathy*. Chicago, IL: University of Chicago Press.

Kuno, Susumu. (1990). Passivization and thematization. In O. Kamada and W. M. Jacobsen (eds.), *On Japanese and How to Teach It*, 43–66. Tokyo: The Japan Times.

Kuno, Susumu. (1997). Binding theory in the minimalist program. Unpublished manuscript, Harvard University.

Kuno, Susumu and Etsuko Kaburaki. (1977). Empathy and syntax. *Linguistic Inquiry* 8: 627–72.

van Kuppevelt, Jan (1996). Inferring from topics: Scalar implicature as topic-dependent inferences. *Linguistics and Philosophy* 19: 393–443.

Kuroda, S.-Y. (1965). Generative Grammatical Studies in the Japanese Language. PhD dissertation, MIT.

Kuroda, S.-Y. (1972). The categorical and the thetic judgment. *Foundations of Language* 2: 153–85.

Kuroda, S.-Y. (1973). Where epistemology, style, and grammar meet: A case study from Japanese. In Stephen R. Anderson and Paul Kiparsky (eds.), *A Festschrift for Morris Halle*, 377–91. New York: Holt, Rinehart and Winston.

Kuroda, S.-Y. (1977). Description of presuppositional phenomena from a non-presuppositionist point of view. *Lingvisticae Investigationes* 1: 63–162.

Kutik, Elanah J., William E. Cooper, and Suzanne Boyce. (1983). Declination of fundamental frequency in speaker's production of parenthetical and main clauses. *Journal of the Acoustical Society of America* 73: 1731–8.

Labov, William and David Fanshel. (1977). *Therapeutic Discourse*. New York: Academic Press.

Ladd, D. Robert. (1977). The function of the A-rise accent in English. Bloomington, IN: Indiana University Linguistics Club.

Ladd, D. Robert. (1978). Stylized intonation. *Language* 54: 517–40.

Ladd, D. Robert. (1979). Light and shadow: A study of the syntax and semantics of sentence accents in English. In L. Waugh and F. van Coetsem (eds.), *Contributions to Grammatical Studies: Semantics and Syntax*, 93–131. Baltimore, MD: University Park Press.

Ladd, D. Robert. (1980). *The Structure of Intonational Meaning: Evidence from English*. Bloomington, IN: Indiana University Press.

Ladd, D. Robert. (1996). *Intonational Phonology*. Cambridge: Cambridge University Press.

Ladd, D. Robert, Kim E. A. Silverman, Frank J. Tolkmitt, Guenther Bergmann, and Klaus R. Scherer. (1985). Evidence for the independent function of intonation contour type, voice quality, and f0 range in signaling speaker affect. *Journal of the Acoustical Society of America* 78: 435–44.

Ladusaw, William. (1980). *Polarity Sensitivity as Inherent Scope Relations*. New York: Garland.

Ladusaw, William A. (1982). Semantic constraints on the English partitive construction. *West Coast Conference on Formal Linguistics* 1: 231–42.

Ladusaw, William A. (1983). Logical form and conditions on grammaticality. *Linguistics and Philosophy* 6: 373–92.

Ladusaw, William A. (1994). Thetic and categorical, stage and individual, weak and strong. *Semantics and Linguistic Theory* IV, 220–9.

Ladusaw, William A. (1996). Negation and polarity items. In Lappin (ed.), 321–41.

Lahav, Ran. (1989). Against compositionality: the case of adjectives. *Philosophical Studies* 55: 111–29.

Lahav, Ran. (1993). The combinatorial–connectionist debate and the pragmatics of adjectives. *Pragmatics and Cognition* 1: 71–88.

Lahiri, Utpal. (1998). Focus and negative polarity in Hindi. *Natural Language Semantics* 6: 57–123.

Laka, Itziar. (1990). Negation in Syntax: On the Nature of Functional Categories and Projections. PhD dissertation, MIT.

Lakatos, Imre. (1970). Falsification and the methodology of scientific research programmes. I. Lakatos and A. Musgrave (eds.), *Criticism and the Growth of Knowledge*, 91–195, Cambridge: Cambridge University Press.

Lakoff, George. (1965). On the Nature of Syntactic Irregularity. PhD dissertation, Indiana University. (Published as *Irregularity in Syntax*, New York: Holt, Rinehart and Winston, 1970.)

Lakoff, George. (1968). Pronouns and reference. Bloomington, IN: Indiana University Linguistics Club. Reprinted in McCawley (ed., 1976), 275–335.

Lakoff, George. (1971a). On generative semantics. In Steinberg and Jakobovits (eds.), 232–96.

Lakoff, George. (1971b). Presuppositions and relative well-formedness. In Steinberg and Jakobovits (eds.), 329–40.

Lakoff, George. (1972). Hedges: A study in meaning criteria and the logic of fuzzy concepts. *CLS 8*, 183–228.

Lakoff, George. (1986). Frame semantic control of the coordinate structure constraint. *CLS 22, Part 2: Papers from the Parasession on Pragmatics and Grammatical Theory*, 152–67.

Lakoff, George. (1987). *Women, Fire, and Dangerous Things: What Categories Reveal about the Mind*. Chicago, IL: University of Chicago Press.

Lakoff, George and Mark Johnson. (1999). *Philosophy in the Flesh*. New York: Basic Books.

Lakoff, George and John Robert Ross. (1966). Criterion for verb phrase constituency. Technical Report NSF-17, Aiken Computation Laboratory, Harvard University.

Lakoff, George and Mark Turner. (1989). *More than Cool Reason: A Field Guide to Poetic Metaphor*. Chicago, IL: University of Chicago Press.

Lakoff, Robin. (1968). *Abstract Syntax and Latin Complementation*. Cambridge, MA: MIT Press.

Lakoff, Robin. (1969a). A syntactic argument for negative transportation. *CLS 5*, 140–7.

Lakoff, Robin. (1969b). Some reasons why there can't be any *some-any* rule. *Language* 45: 608–15.

Lakoff, Robin. (1971a). Passive resistance. *CLS 7:* 141–62.

Lakoff, Robin. (1971b). If's, and's, and but's about conjunction. In C. J. Fillmore and D. T. Langendoen (eds.), *Studies in Linguistic Semantics,* 114–49. New York: Holt, Rinehart, and Winston.

Lakoff, Robin. (1977). What you can do with words: Politeness, pragmatics, and performatives. In Rogers et al. (eds.), 79–106.

Lambert, William and Gordon Tucker. (1976). *Tu, Vous, Usted*. Rawley, MA: Newbury Press.

Lambrecht, Knud. (1987). On the status of SVO sentence in French discourse. In R. Tomlin (ed.), *Coherence and Grounding in Discourse,* 217–62. Amsterdam: Benjamins.

Lambrecht, Knud. (1990). What, me worry? *Mad Magazine* sentences revisited. *BLS 16*, 215–28.

Lambrecht, Knud. (1994). *Information Structure and Sentence Form: Topic, Focus and the Mental Representation of Discourse Referents*. Cambridge: Cambridge University Press.

Lambrecht, Knud. (1995). The pragmatics of case: On the relationship between semantic, grammatical and pragmatic roles in English and French. In M. Shibatani and S. A. Thompson (eds.), *Essays in Semantics and Pragmatics*, 145–91. Amsterdam: Benjamins.

Lambrecht, Knud. (2001). A framework for the analysis of cleft constructions. *Linguistics* 39: 463–516.

Langacker, Ronald. (1984). Active zones. *BLS 10*, 172–88.

Langacker, Ronald. (1987). *Foundations of Cognitive Grammar*, vol. 1. Stanford, CA: Stanford University Press. (Volume 2 published 1991.)

Langacker, Ronald. (1990). *Concept, Image, and Symbol: The Cognitive Basis of Grammar*. Berlin: Mouton de Gruyter.

Langacker, Ronald W. (1999). Losing control: Grammaticalization, subjectification, and transparency. In Blank and Koch (eds.), 147–75.

Langdon, Robyn, Martin Davies, and Max Coltheart. (2002). Understanding minds and understanding communicated meanings in schizophrenia. *Mind & Language* 17: 68–104.

Lappin, Shalom. (1993). The syntactic basis of ellipsis resolution. In S. Berman and A. Hestvik (eds.), *Proceedings of the Stuttgart Workshop on Ellipsis*. Arbeitspapiere des Sonderforschungsbereich 340, Bericht Nr. 29-1992, SFB 340. University of Stuttgart, University of Tübingen, and IBM Germany.

Lappin, Shalom. (1996). The interpretation of ellipsis. In Lappin (ed.), 145–75.

Lappin, Shalom (ed.). (1996). *The Handbook of Contemporary Semantic Theory*. Oxford: Blackwell.

Lappin, Shalom. (1999). An HPSG account of antecedent-contained ellipsis. In S. Lappin and E. Benmamoun (eds.), *Fragments: Studies in Ellipsis and Gapping*. 68–97. New York: Oxford University Press.

Lappin, Shalom and Elabbas Benmamoun. (1999). *Fragments: Studies in Ellipsis and Gapping*. Oxford: Oxford University Press.

Lappin, Shalom and Nissim Francez. (1994). E-type pronouns, i-sums, and donkey anaphora. *Linguistics and Philosophy* 17: 391–428.

Larson, Richard and Gabriel Segal. (1995). *Knowledge of Meaning: An Introduction to Semantic Theory*. Cambridge, MA: MIT Press.

Lascarides, Alex and Nicholas Asher. (1993). Temporal interpretation, discourse relations, and common sense entailment. *Linguistics and Philosophy* 16: 437–93.

Lascarides, Alex, Ted Briscoe, Nicholas Asher, and Ann Copestake. (1995). Order independent and persistent typed default unification. *Linguistics and Philosophy* 19: 1–89.

Lascarides, Alex and Anne Copestake. (1998). Pragmatics and word meaning. *Journal of Linguistics* 34: 387–414.

Lascarides, Alex, Anne Copestake, and Ted Briscoe. (1996). Ambiguity and coherence. *Journal of Semantics* 13: 41–65.

Lascarides, Alex and Jon Oberlander. (1992). Abducing temporal discourse. In R. Dale, E. Hovy, D. Rosner, and O. Stock (eds.), *Aspects of Automated Natural Language Generation*, 167–82. Berlin: Springer Verlag.

Lasersohn, Peter. (1999). Pragmatic halos. *Language* 75: 522–51.

Lasnik, Howard. (1989). *Essays on Anaphora*. Dordrecht: Kluwer.

Lasnik, Howard. (1992). Case and expletives: notes toward a parametric account. *Linguistic Inquiry* 23: 381–405.

Lebeaux, David. (1988). Language Acquisition and the Form of the Grammar. PhD dissertation, University of Massachusetts.

Lebeaux, David. (1992). Relative clauses, licensing, and the nature of the derivation. In S. Rothstein and M. Speas (eds.), *Syntax and Semantics 25: Perspectives on Phrase Structure*, 209–39. New York: Academic Press.

Lebeaux, David. (1995). Where does the binding theory apply? *University of Maryland Working Papers in Linguistics* 3: 63–88.

Lee, Chungmin. (1996). Negative polarity items in English and Korean. *Language Sciences* 18: 505–23.

Lee, Young-Suk and Laurence Horn. (1994). *Any* as indefinite + *even*. Unpublished manuscript, Yale University.

Leech, Geoffrey. (1974). *Semantics*. Harmondsworth: Penguin.

Leech, Geoffrey. (1976). Metalanguage, pragmatics, and performatives. Semantics: Theory and application. In C. Rameh (ed.), *Georgetown University Roundtable on Languages and Linguistics*, 81–98. Washington, DC: Georgetown University Press.

Leech, Geoffrey. (1981). Pragmatics and conversational rhetoric. In H. Parret, M. Sbisà, and J. Verschueren (eds.), *Possibilities and Limitations of Pragmatics*, 413–42. Amsterdam: Benjamins.

Leech, Geoffrey. (1983). *Principles of Pragmatics*. London: Longman.

Lees, Robert B. and Edward Klima. (1963). Rules for English pronominalization. *Language* 39: 17–28.

Legendre, Géraldine, Jane Grimshaw, and Sten Vikner (eds.). (2001). *Optimality-Theoretic Syntax*. Cambridge, MA: MIT Press.

Lehiste, Ilse. (1975). The phonetic structure of paragraphs. In A. Cohen and S. G. Nooteboom (eds.), *Structure and Process in Speech Perception*, 195–203. Heidelberg: Springer Verlag.

Lehiste, Ilse. (1979). Perception of sentence and paragraph boundaries. In B. Lindblom and S. Oehman (eds.), *Frontiers of Speech Research*, 191–201. London: Academic Press.

Lehiste, Ilse. (1980). Phonetic characteristics of discourse. Paper presented at the Meeting of the Committee on Speech Research, Acoustical Society of Japan. S80: 25–38. Tokyo.

Lehman, Christina. (1977). A re-analysis of givenness: Stress in discourse. *CLS 13*, 316–24.

Lemmens, Maarten. (1998). *Lexical Perspectives on Transitivity and Ergativity: Causative Constructions in English*. Amsterdam: Benjamins.

de León, Lourdes. (1998). The emergent participant: Interactive patterns in the socialization of Tzotzil (Mayan) infants. *Journal of Linguistic Anthropology* 8: 131–61.

Leslie, Alan. (1991). The theory of mind impairment in autism: Evidence for a modular mechanism of development? In A. Whiten (ed.), *Natural Theories of Mind: Evolution, Development and Simulation of Everyday Mindreading*, 63–78. Oxford: Basil Blackwell.

Leslie, Alan. (1994). ToMM, ToBy, and Agency: Core architecture and domain specificity. In Hirschfeld and Gelman (eds.), 119–48.

Levelt, Willem J. M. (1983). Monitoring and self-repair in speech. *Cognition* 14: 41–104.

Levelt, Willem J. M. (1989). *Speaking*. Cambridge, MA: MIT Press.

Levin, Beth. (1993). *English Verb Classes and Alternations*. Chicago, IL: University of Chicago Press.

Levin, Nancy and Ellen F. Prince. (1986). Gapping and causal implicature. *Papers in Linguistics* 19: 351–64.

Levinson, Stephen C. (1979a). Pragmatics and social deixis: Reclaiming the notion of conventional implicature. *BLS 5*, 206–23.

Levinson, Stephen C. (1979b). Activity types and language. *Linguistics* 17: 365–99.

Levinson, Stephen C. (1983). *Pragmatics*. Cambridge: Cambridge University Press.

Levinson, Stephen C. (1987a). Minimization and conversational inference. In Verschueren and Bertuccelli-Papi (eds.), 61–129. Reprinted in Kasher (ed., 1998), vol. IV: 545–612.

Levinson, Stephen C. (1987b). Pragmatics and the grammar of anaphora: A partial pragmatic reduction of binding and control phenomena. *Journal of Linguistics* 23: 379–434.

Levinson, Stephen C. (1988). Generalized Conversational Implicature and the semantics/pragmatics interface. Unpublished manuscript, Stanford University, CA.

Levinson, Stephen C. (1991). Pragmatic reduction of the binding conditions revisited. *Journal of Linguistics* 27: 107–61.

Levinson, Stephen C. (1995). Three levels of meaning. In F. Palmer (ed.), *Grammar and Meaning: Essays in Honour of Sir John Lyons*, 90–115. Cambridge: Cambridge University Press.

Levinson, Stephen C. (1996). Frames of reference and Molyneux's question: Cross-linguistic evidence. In P. Bloom, M. Peterson, L. Nadel, and M. Garrett (eds.), *Language and Space*, 109–69. Cambridge, MA: MIT Press.

Levinson, Stephen C. (2000a). *Presumptive Meanings: The Theory of Generalized Conversational Implicature*. Cambridge, MA: MIT Press.

Levinson, Stephen C. (2000b). Yélî Dnye and the theory of basic color terms. *Journal of Linguistic Anthropology* 10: 3–55.

Lewis, David. (1969). *Convention: A Philosophical Study*. Cambridge, MA: Harvard University Press.

Lewis, David. (1972). General semantics. In Davidson and Harman (eds.), 169–218.

Lewis, David. (1979). Scorekeeping in a language game. *Journal of Philosophical Logic* 8: 339–59.

Lewis, David. (1983). Languages and language. In *Philosophical Papers*, vol. 1, 163–88. New York: Oxford University Press.

Li, Charles N. and Sandra A. Thompson. (1976). Subject and topic: a new typology of language. In C. N. Li (ed.), *Subject and Topic*, 457–89. New York: Academic Press.

Liberman, Mark and Ivan A. Sag. (1974). Prosodic form and discourse function. *CLS 10*, 416–27.

Liberman, Mark and Richard Sproat. (1992). The stress and structure of modified noun phrases in English. In I. Sag (ed.), *Lexical Matters*, 131–82. Chicago, IL: University of Chicago Press.

Liddell, Scott. (1998). Grounded blends, gestures, and conceptual shifts. *Cognitive Linguistics* 9: 283–314.

Lidz, Jeffrey. (1996). Dimensions of Reflexivity. PhD dissertation, University of Delaware.

Lightfoot, David. (1979). *Principles of Diachronic Syntax*. Cambridge: Cambridge University Press.

Lindblom, Björn. (1983). Economy of speech gestures. In P. MacNeilage (ed.), *The Production of Speech*, 217–45. New York: Springer-Verlag.

Lindblom, Björn, Peter MacNeilage, and Michael Studdert-Kennedy. (1984). Self-organizing processes and the explanation of phonological universals. In B. Butterworth, B. Comrie, and Ö. Dahl (eds.), *Explanations for Language Universals*, 182–203. Berlin: Mouton.

Lindblom, Björn, Peter MacNeilage, and Michael Studdert-Kennedy (to appear). *The Evolution of Spoken Language*. Orlando, FL: Academic Press.

Linebarger, Marcia. (1980). The Grammar of Negative Polarity. PhD dissertation, MIT.

Linebarger, Marcia. (1987). Negative polarity and grammatical representation. *Linguistics and Philosophy* 10: 325–87.

Linebarger, Marcia. (1991). Negative polarity as linguistic evidence. *CLS 27, Part 2: Papers from the Parasession on Negation*, 165–88.

Linsky, Leonard. (1963). Reference and referents. In C. Caton (ed.), *Philosophy and Ordinary Language*, 74–89. Champaign, IL: University of Illinois Press.

Litman, Diane and James Allen. (1990). Discourse processing and commonsense plans. In Cohen et al. (eds.), 365–88.

Lobeck, Anne. (1995). *Ellipsis: Functional Heads, Licensing, and Identification*. New York: Oxford University Press.

Lobeck, Anne. (1999). VP ellipsis and the minimalist program: Some speculations and proposals. In Shalom Lappin and Elabbas Benmamoun (eds.), *Fragments: Studies in Ellipsis and Gapping*, 98–123. New York: Oxford University Press.

Löbner, Sebastian. (1985). Definites. *Journal of Semantics* 4: 279–326.

Lochbaum, Karen. (1993). *A Collaborative Planning Approach to Discourse Understanding.* Cambridge, MA: Harvard University Center for Research in Computing Technology.

Lochbaum, Karen. (1994). A model of plans to support inter-agent communication. In *Proceedings of the AAAI Workshop on Planning for Inter-agent Communication*, 26–32. Seattle.

Longacre, Robert E. (1983). *The Grammar of Discourse.* New York: Plenum Press.

Longuet-Higgins, Christopher. (1976). . . . And out walked the cat. *Pragmatics Microfiche* 1.7: G10–G14.

Ludlow, Peter. (2003). Referential semantics for I-languages? In L. Antony and N. Hornstein (eds.), *Chomsky and his Critics*, 140–61. Oxford: Blackwell.

Ludlow, Peter and Stephen Neale. (1991). Indefinite descriptions: In defense of Russell. *Linguistics and Philosophy* 14: 171–202.

Lumsden, Michael. (1988). *Existential Sentences: Their Structure and Meaning.* London: Croom Helm.

Lust, Barbara, Kashi Wali, James Gair, and K. V. Subbarao (eds.). (2000). *Lexical Anaphors and Pronouns in Selected South Asian Languages.* Berlin: Mouton de Gruyter.

Lyons, Christopher. (1999). *Definiteness.* Cambridge: Cambridge University Press.

Lyons, John. (1975). Deixis as the source of reference. In E. Keenan (ed.), 61–83.

Lyons, John. (1977). *Semantics.* Cambridge: Cambridge University Press.

Lyons, John. (1982). Deixis and subjectivity: *Loquor, ergo sum*? In Jarvella and Klein (eds.), 101–24.

MacWhinney, Brian. (1987). The competition model. In B. MacWhinney (ed.), *Mechanisms of Language Acquisition*, 249–308. Hillsdale, NJ: Lawrence Erlbaum.

MacWhinney, Brian, Elizabeth Bates, and R. Kliegl. (1984). Cue validity and sentence interpretation in English, German, and Italian. *Journal of Verbal Learning and Verbal Behavior* 23: 127–50.

MacWhinney, Brian and Catherine Snow. (1990). The Child Language Data Exchange System: an update. *Journal of Child Language* 17: 457–72.

Mahesh, Kavi, Sergei Nirenburg, Jim Cowie, and David Farwell. (1996). An assessment of Cyc for natural language processing. Technical Report MCSS-96-302, Computing Research Laboratory, New Mexico State University.

Makino, Reiko. (2001). The Japanese Nouns *koto* and *no.* PhD dissertation, University of Illinois, Urbana.

Malinowski, Bronislaw. (1935). *Coral Gardens and their Magic.* New York: American Book Co.

Malle, Bertram, Louis Moses, and Dare Baldwin (eds.). (2001). *Intentions and Intentionality: Foundations of Social Cognition.* Cambridge, MA: MIT Press.

Mandelblit, Nili and Gilles Fauconnier. (2000). Underspecificity in grammatical blends as a source for constructional ambiguity. In A. Foolen and F. van der Leek (eds.), *Constructions*, 167–89. Amsterdam: Benjamins.

Mandelblit, Nili and Oron Zachar. (1998). The notion of dynamic unit: Conceptual developments in cognitive science. *Cognitive Science* 22: 229–68.

Mann, William and Sandra Thompson. (1986). Relational propositions in discourse. *Discourse Processes* 9: 57–90.

Mann, William and Sandra Thompson. (1988). Rhetorical Structure Theory: towards a functional theory of text organization. *Text* 8: 243–81.

Maratsos, Michael P. (1976). *The Use of Definite and Indefinite Reference in Young Children: An Experimental Study in Semantic Acquisition.* Cambridge: Cambridge University Press.

Marcu, Daniel. (2000). *The Theory and Practice of Discourse Parsing and Summarization.* Cambridge, MA: MIT Press.

Marcus, Mitchell P. and Donald Hindle. (1990). Description theory and intonation boundaries. In G. Altmann (ed.), *Computational and Cognitive Models of Speech,* 1–23. Cambridge, MA: MIT Press.

Marcus, Mitchell P., Beatrice Santorini, Mary Ann Marcinkiewicz, and Ann Taylor. (1999). Treebank-3, Catalog #LDC99T42. Linguistic Data Consortium, University of Pennsylvania.

Martin, James R. (1992). *English Text: Systems and Structure.* Amsterdam: Benjamins.

Martin, Robert. (1992). Irony and universe of belief. *Lingua* 87: 77–90.

Martinich, A. P. (1980). Conversational maxims and some philosophical problems. *Philosophical Quarterly* 30: 215–28.

Marty, Anton. (1918). *Gesammelte Schriften,* vol. II, part 1. Halle: Niemeyer.

Mast, Marion, Ralf Kompe, Stefan Harbeck, Andreas Kiessling, Heinrich Niemann, Elmar Nöth, E. Guenther Schukat-Talamazzini, and Volker Warnke. (1996). Dialog act classification with the help of prosody. *Proceedings of the International Conference on Spoken Language Processing (ICSLP-96)* 3: 1732–5. Philadelphia.

Mates, Benson. (1968). Leibniz on possible worlds. In B. van Rootselaar and J. F. Staal (eds.), *Logic, Methodology and the Philosophy of Science III,* 507–29. Amsterdam: North-Holland.

Mathesius, Vilém. (1928). On linguistic characterology with illustrations from modern English. Reprinted in J. Vachek (ed.), *A Prague School Reader in Linguistics,* 59–67. Bloomington, IN: Indiana University Press, 1967.

Mathesius, Vilém. (1939). O tak zvaném aktuálním clenení veti. *Slovo a slovenost* 5: 171–4.

Matsui, Tomoko. (1998). Pragmatic criteria for reference assignment: A relevance-theoretic account of the acceptability of bridging. *Pragmatics and Cognition* 6: 47–97.

Matsui, Tomoko. (2000). *Bridging and Relevance.* Amsterdam: Benjamins.

Matsumoto, Yo. (1995). The conversational condition on Horn scales. *Linguistics and Philosophy* 18: 21–60.

Mazuka, Reiko, Barbara Lust, Toshiro Wakayama, and William Snyder. (1986). Distinguishing effects of parameters in early syntax acquisition: A cross-linguistic study of Japanese and English. *Papers and Reports on Child Language Development* 25: 73–82.

McCafferty, Andrew S. (1987). Reasoning about Implicature. PhD dissertation, University of Pittsburgh.

McCarthy, John. (1980). Circumscription – a form of non-monotonic reasoning. *Artificial Intelligence* 13: 27–39. Reprinted in M. Ginsberg (ed.), *Readings in Nonmonotonic Reasoning,* 145–52. Los Altos, CA: Morgan Kaufmann.

McCawley, James D. (1968). The role of semantics in a grammar. In E. Bach and R. T. Harms (eds.), *Universals in Linguistic Theory,* 124–69. New York: Holt, Rinehart and Winston.

McCawley, James D. (1970). On the applicability of *vice versa. Linguistic Inquiry* 1: 278–80.

McCawley, James D. (1971). Interpretive semantics meets Frankenstein. *Foundations of Language* 7: 285–96.

McCawley, James D. (1976). The annotated respective. In J. D. McCawley (ed.), *Grammar and Meaning: Papers on Syntactic and Semantic Topics,* 121–32. New York: Academic.

McCawley, James D. (ed.). (1976). *Syntax and Semantics,* vol. 7: *Notes from the Linguistic Underground.* New York: Academic Press.

McCawley, James D. (1977). Remarks on the lexicography of performative verbs. In Rogers et al. (eds.), 13–26.

McCawley, James D. (1978). Conversational implicature and the lexicon. In Cole (ed., 1978), 245–59. Reprinted in Kasher (ed., 1998), vol. IV: 332–46.

McCawley, James D. (1979). Presupposition and discourse structure. In Oh and Dinneen (eds.), 371–88.

McCawley, James D. (1981). *What Linguists Have Always Wanted to Know about Logic but Were Ashamed to Ask*. Chicago, IL: University of Chicago Press. (2nd edition, 1993.)

McCawley, James D. (1985). What price the performative analysis? *University of Chicago Working Papers in Linguistics* 1: 43–64.

McCawley, James D. (1988). *The Syntactic Phenomena of English*. Chicago, IL: University of Chicago Press.

McCawley, James D. (1991). Contrastive negation and metalinguistic negation. *CLS 27, Part 2: Parasession on Negation*, 189–206.

McConnell-Ginet, Sally. (1982). Adverbs and logical form: A linguistically realistic theory. *Language* 58: 144–84.

McDermott, Drew and John Doyle. (1980). Non-monotonic logic I. *Artificial Intelligence* 13: 41–72.

McDowell, John. (1977). On the sense and reference of a proper name. *Mind* 86: 159–85.

McGarrigle, James and Margaret Donaldson. (1975). Conservation accidents. *Cognition* 3: 341–50.

McGarrigle, James, Robert Grieve, and Martin Hughes. (1978). Interpreting inclusion: A contribution to the study of the child's cognitive and linguistic development. *Journal of Experimental Child Psychology* 26: 528–50.

McGinn, Colin (1981). The mechanism of reference. *Synthèse* 49: 157–86.

McKoon, Gail and Roger Ratcliff. (1992). Inferences during reading. *Psychological Review* 99: 440–66.

McNeill, David. (1992). *Hand and Mind*. Chicago, IL: University of Chicago Press.

McNeill, David. (2000). *Language and Gesture*. Cambridge: Cambridge University Press.

McRoy, Susan and Graeme Hirst. (1991). An abductive account of repair in conversation. *Working Notes, AAAI Fall Symposium on Discourse Structure in Natural Language Understanding and Generation*, 52–7. Asilomar, CA.

Meillet, Antoine. (1912). L'évolution des formes grammaticales. *Scientia (Rivista di scienza)* XII. Reprinted in *Linguistique historique et linguistique générale*, 130–48. Paris: Champion, 1958.

Meinong, Alexius. (1904). *Untersuchungen zur Gegenstandstheorie und Psychologie*. Leipzig: Johann Ambrosius Barth.

Merchant, Jason. (2001). *The Syntax of Silence: Sluicing, Islands, and the Theory of Ellipsis*. Oxford: Oxford University Press.

Merin, Arthur. (1994). Algebra of elementary social acts. In Tsohatzidis (ed.), 234–66.

Merin, Arthur. (1999). Information, relevance, and social decisionmaking: some principles and results of decision-theoretic semantics. In L. S. Moss, J. Ginzburg, and M. de Rijke (eds.), *Logic, Language, and Computation* 2: 179–221. Stanford, CA: CSLI.

Mervis, Carolyn B. and Cynthia A. Mervis. (1988). Role of adult input in young children's category evolution. I: An observational study. *Journal of Child Language* 15: 257–72.

Mey, Jacob L. (ed.). (1998). *Concise Encyclopedia of Pragmatics*. Amsterdam: Elsevier.

Meyer, Ralf. (1993). *Compound Comprehension in Isolation and in Context*. Tübingen: Max Niemeyer Verlag.

Michaelis, Laura A. (1994). A case of constructional polysemy in Latin. *Studies in Language* 18: 45–70.

Michaelis, Laura A. (2001). Exclamative constructions. In M. Haspelmath, W. Österreicher, and Wolfgang Raible (eds.), *Language Typology and Universals: An International Handbook*, 1038–50. Berlin: Walter de Gruyter.

Michaelis, Laura A. and Knud Lambrecht. (1996). Toward a construction-based theory of language function: the case of nominal extraposition. *Language* 72: 215–47.

Mill, John Stuart. (1843). Of names. In *A System of Logic*, Book I, Ch. 2. New York: Harper.

Mill, John Stuart (1867). *An Examination of Sir William Hamilton's Philosophy* (3rd edn.). London: Longman.

Mill, John Stuart. (1872). *A System of Logic*, definitive 8th edn. London: Longmans, Green, 1949.

Miller, George. (1995). WordNet: A lexical database for English. *Communications of the ACM* 38: 39–41.

Miller, George and Philip Johnson-Laird. (1976). *Language and Perception*. Cambridge, MA: Harvard University Press.

Miller, Philip. (1990). Pseudogapping and *do so* substitution. *CLS 26*, 293–305.

Miller, Philip. (2001). Discourse constraints on (non-)extraposition from subject in English. *Linguistics* 39: 683–701.

Milsark, Gary. (1974). Existential Sentences in English. PhD dissertation, MIT. Distributed by the Indiana University Linguistics Club, 1976.

Milsark, Gary. (1977). Toward an explanation of certain peculiarities of the existential construction in English. *Linguistic Analysis* 3: 1–29.

Mitchell, Jonathan. (1986). The Formal Semantics of Point of View. PhD dissertation, University of Massachusetts.

Mitchell, Peter, Elizabeth Robinson, and D. E. Thompson. (1999). Children's understanding that utterances emanate from minds: Using speaker belief to aid interpretation. *Cognition* 72: 45–66.

Mithun, Marianne. (1999). *The Languages of Native North America*. Cambridge: Cambridge University Press.

Mittwoch, Anita. (1976). Grammar and illocutionary force. *Lingua* 40: 21–42.

Mittwoch, Anita. (1977). How to refer to one's own words. *Journal of Linguistics* 13: 177–89.

Moeschler, Jacques. (1989). Pragmatic connectives, argumentative coherence and relevance. *Argumentation* 3: 321–39.

Moeschler, Jacques (1999). Economy and pragmatic optimality: the case of directional inferences. Paper delivered at the International Symposium on Economy in Language Design, Computation and Use, Lyons.

Moeschler, Jacques and Anne Reboul. (1994). *Dictionnaire encyclopédique de pragmatique*. Paris: Seuil.

Mohanan, K. P. (1983). Functional and anaphoric control. *Linguistic Inquiry* 14: 641–74.

Montague, R. (1968). Pragmatics. Reprinted in Montague (1974), 95–118, and in Kasher (ed., 1998), vol. V: 24–42.

Montague, Richard. (1970). Universal grammar. *Theoria* 36: 373–98. Reprinted in Montague (1974), 222–46.

Montague, Richard. (1973). The proper treatment of quantification in ordinary English. In J. Hintikka, J. Moravcsik, and P. Suppes (eds.), *Approaches to Natural Language: Proceedings of the 1970 Stanford Workshop on Grammar and Semantics*, 221–42. Dordrecht: Reidel. Reprinted in Montague (1974), 247–70.

Montague, Richard. (1974). *Formal Philosophy: Selected Papers*, R. Thomason (ed.). New Haven, CT: Yale University Press.

Moore, Chris and Philip J. Dunham (eds.). (1995). *Joint Attention: Its Origins and Role in Development*. Hillsdale, NJ: Lawrence Erlbaum.

Moore, G. E. (1942). A reply to my critics. In P. A. Schilpp (ed.), *The Philosophy of G. E. Moore*, 535–677. Evanston and Chicago, IL: Northwestern University Press.

Moore, Johanna D. (1995). *Participating in Explanatory Dialogues: Interpreting and Responding to Questions in Context*. Cambridge, MA: MIT Press.

Moore, Johanna D. and Cecile L. Paris. (1993). Planning text for advisory dialogues: Capturing intentional and rhetorical information. *Computational Linguistics* 19: 651–94.

Moore, Johanna D. and Martha E. Pollack. (1992). A problem for RST: The need for multi-level discourse analysis. *Computational Linguistics* 18: 537–44.

Moore, Terrence and Christine Carling. (1982). *Language Understanding: Towards a Post-Chomskyan Linguistics*. New York: St. Martin's Press.

Morgan, Charles G. (1971). Hypothesis generation by machine. *Artificial Intelligence* 2: 179–87.

Morgan, Jerry L. (1968). Some strange aspects of *it*. *CLS 4*, 81–93.

Morgan, Jerry L. (1969). On the treatment of presupposition in transformational grammar. *CLS 5*, 167–77.

Morgan, Jerry L. (1970). On the criterion of identity for noun phrase deletion. *CLS 6*, 380–9.

Morgan, Jerry L. (1972a). Verb agreement as a rule of English. *CLS 8*, 278–86.

Morgan, Jerry L. (1972b). Some problems of verb agreement. *Studies in the Linguistic Sciences* 2: 84–90.

Morgan, Jerry L. (1973a). How can you be in two places at once when you're not anywhere at all? *CLS 9*, 410–17.

Morgan, Jerry L. (1973b). Presupposition and the Representation of Meaning: Prolegomena. PhD dissertation, University of Chicago.

Morgan, Jerry. (1973c). Sentence fragments and the notion "sentence". In B. B. Kachru, R. B. Lees, Y. Malkier, D. Pietrangeli, and S. Saporta (eds.), *Issues in Linguistics: Papers in Honor of Henry and Renée Kahane*, 719–51. Urbana, IL: University of Illinois Press.

Morgan, Jerry L. (1975a). On the nature of sentences. *Papers from the Parasession on Functionalism*, 433–49. Chicago, IL: Chicago Linguistic Society.

Morgan, Jerry L. (1975b). Some interactions of syntax and pragmatics. In Cole and Morgan (eds.), 289–304.

Morgan, Jerry L. (1978). Two types of convention in indirect speech acts. In Cole (ed., 1978), 261–80. Reprinted in Kasher (ed., 1998), vol. IV: 639–57.

Morgan, Jerry and Georgia Green. (1987). On the search for relevance. *Behavioral and Brain Sciences* 10: 726–7.

Morris, Charles. (1938). *Foundations of the Theory of Signs*. (*International Encyclopedia of Unified Science*, vol. 1, no. 2.) Chicago, IL: University of Chicago Press.

Moser, Megan and Johanna D. Moore. (1996). Toward a synthesis of two accounts of discourse structure. *Computational Linguistics* 22: 403–19.

Moulton, Janice. (1981). The myth of the neutral "man." In M. Vetterling-Braggin (ed.), *Sexist Language: A Modern Philosophical Analysis*, 100–16. Totowa, NJ: Littlefield, Adams.

Mozziconacci, Silvie J. L. (1998). Speech Variability and Emotion: Production and Perception. PhD thesis, University of Leiden.

Murray, Iain R. and Mohn L. Arnott. (1993). Toward the simulation of emotion in synthetic speech: A review of the literature on human vocal emotion. *Journal of the Acoustical Society of America* 93: 1097–1108.

Nagao, Katashi. (1989). Semantic interpretation based on the multi-world model. *Proceedings of the Eleventh International Conference on Artificial Intelligence*, 1467–73. Detroit.

Nagata, Masaaki. (1992). Using pragmatics to rule out recognition errors in cooperative task-oriented dialogues. In *Proceedings of the International Conference on Spoken Language Processing (ICSLP-92)*, 647–50. Banff.

Nagata, Masaaki and Tsuyoshi Morimoto. (1994). First steps toward statistical modeling of dialogue to predict the speech act type of the next utterance. *Speech Communication* 15: 193–203.

Nakamura, Keiko. (2001). The acquisition of polite language by Japanese children. In K. E. Nelson and A. Aksu-Koç (eds.), *Children's Language: Developing Narrative and Discourse Competence*, vol. 10, 93–112. Mahwah, NJ: Lawrence Erlbaum.

Nakatani, Christine. (1997). The Computational Processing of Intonational Prominence: A Functional Prosody Perspective. PhD dissertation, Harvard University.

Napoli, Donna Jo. (1982). Initial material deletion in English. *Glossa* 16: 85–111.

Napoli, Donna Jo and Emily Rando. (1978). Definites in *there*-sentences. *Language* 54: 300–13.

Neale, Stephen. (1990). *Descriptions*. Cambridge, MA: MIT Press.

Neale, Stephen. (1992). Paul Grice and the philosophy of language. *Linguistics and Philosophy* 15: 509–59.

Neale, Stephen. (1993). Term Limits. *Philosophical Perspectives* 7: 89–123.

Neale, Stephen. (to appear). This, that, and the other. In Bezuidenhout and Reimer (eds.).

Neijt, Anneke. (1979). *Gapping: A Contribution to Sentence Grammar*. Dordrecht: Foris.

Neijt, Anneke. (1981). Gaps and remnants – sentence grammar aspects of gapping. *Linguistic Analysis* 8: 69–93.

Nerbonne, John. (1986). Reference time and time in narration. *Linguistics and Philosophy* 9: 83–95.

Nerlich, Brigitte and David Clarke. (1992). Outline of a model for semantic change. In G. Kellermann and M. D. Morrissey (eds.), *Diachrony within Synchrony: Language History and Cognition. Papers from the International Symposium at the University of Duisburg, 26–28 March 1990*, 125–41. Frankfurt-am-Main: Peter Lang.

Nerlich, Brigitte and David D. Clarke. (1999). Synecdoche as a cognitive and communicative strategy. In Blank and Koch (eds.), 197–213.

Nespor, Marina and Irene Vogel. (1983). Prosodic structure above the word. In A. Cutler and D. R. Ladd (eds.), *Prosody: Models and Measurements*, 123–32. Heidelberg: Springer Verlag.

Newcombe, Nora and Martha Zaslow. (1981). Do 2½-year-olds hint? A study of directive forms in the speech of 2½-year-old children to adults. *Discourse Processes* 4: 239–52.

Newton, Isaac. (1934). *Mathematical Principles of Natural Philosophy*, vol. 1: *The Motion of Bodies*, and vol. 2: *The System of the World*. (A. Motte and F. Cajori, trans.) Berkeley, CA: University of California Press. (Originally published 1686.)

Newmeyer, Frederick J. (ed.). (1988). *Linguistics: The Cambridge Survey*. Cambridge: Cambridge University Press.

Ng, Hwee Tou and Raymond J. Mooney. (1990). The role of coherence in abductive explanation. *Proceedings of the Eighth National Conference on Artificial Intelligence*, 337–42. Boston, MA.

Nichols, Johanna. (2001). Long-distance reflexivization in Chechen and Ingush. In Cole et al. (eds.), 255–78.

Nickerson, Jill S. and Jennifer Chu-Carroll. (1999). Acoustic-prosodic disambiguation of direct and indirect speech acts. *Proceedings of the XIV International Congress of Phonetic Sciences*, 1309–12. San Francisco, CA.

Nicolle, Steven. (1998). A relevance theory perspective on grammaticalization. *Cognitive Linguistics* 9: 1–35.

Nicolle, Steven and Billy Clark. (1999). Experimental pragmatics and what is said: A response to Gibbs and Moise. *Cognition* 66: 337–54.

Noh, Eun-ju. (1998). Echo questions: Metarepresentation and pragmatic enrichment. *Linguistics and Philosophy* 21: 603–28.

Noh, Eun-ju. (2000). *Metarepresentation: A Relevance-Theory Approach*. Amsterdam: Benjamins.

Nølke, Henning. (1992). Semantic constraints on argumentation: From polyphonic microstructure to argumentative macro-structure. In F. H. van Eemeren, R. Grootendorst, J. A. Blair, and C. A. Willard (eds.), *Argumentation Illuminated*, 189–200. Amsterdam: SICSAT.

Nooteboom, Sieb G. and Jacques Terken. (1982). What makes speakers omit pitch accents? An experiment. *Phonetica* 39: 317–36.

Norvig, Peter. (1983). Frame activated inferences in a story understanding program. *Proceedings of the 8th International Joint Conference on Artificial Intelligence*, 624–6. Karlsruhe, Germany.

Norvig, Peter. (1987). Inference in text understanding. *Proceedings of AAAI-87, Sixth National Conference on Artificial Intelligence*, 561–5. Seattle.

Norvig, Peter and George Lakoff. (1987). Taking: A study in lexical network theory. *BLS 13*, 195–205.

Norvig, Peter and Robert Wilensky. (1990). A critical evaluation of commensurable abduction models for semantic interpretation. In H. Karlgren (ed.), *Proceedings of the Thirteenth International Conference on Computational Linguistics* 3: 225–30. Helsinki.

Nöth, Elmar, Anton Batliner, Volke Warnke, et al. (2002). On the use of prosody in automatic dialogue understanding. *Speech Communication* 36: 45–62.

Noveck, Ira. (2001). When children are more logical than adults: Experimental investigations of scalar implicature. *Cognition* 78: 165–88.

Noveck, Ira, Maryse Bianco, and Alain Castry. (2001). The costs and benefits of metaphor. *Metaphor and Symbol* 16: 109–21.

Nunberg, Geoffrey D. (1977). The Pragmatics of Reference. PhD dissertation, City University of New York. Distributed Bloomington, IN: Indiana University Linguistics Club, 1978.

Nunberg, Geoffrey. (1979). The non-uniqueness of semantic solutions: Polysemy. *Linguistics and Philosophy* 3: 143–84.

Nunberg, Geoffrey. (1993). Indexicality and deixis. *Linguistics and Philosophy* 16: 1–44. Reprinted in Kasher (ed., 1998), vol. V: 145–84.

Nunberg, Geoffrey. (1995). Transfers of meaning. *Journal of Semantics* 12: 109–32.

Nunberg, Geoffrey and Annie Zaenen. (1992). Systematic polysemy in lexicology and lexicography. In *Proceedings of Euralex II*, 2: 387–98. Tampere, Finland.

O'Connor, J. D. and Gordon F. Arnold. (1961). *Intonation of Colloquial English*. London: Longman.

Oehrle, Richard T. (1981). Common problems in the theory of anaphora and the theory of discourse. In H. Parret, M. Sbisà, and J. Verschueren (eds.), *Possibilities and Limitations of Pragmatics*, 509–30. Amsterdam: Benjamins.

Oehrle, Richard T. (1991). Prosodic constraints on dynamic grammar analysis. In S. Bird (ed.), *Declarative Perspectives on Phonology*, vol. 7, 167–95. Edinburgh: Centre for Cognitive Science, University of Edinburgh.

Oh, Choon-Kyu and David A. Dinneen (eds.). (1979). *Syntax and Semantics 11: Presupposition*. New York: Academic Press.

O'Hair, S. G. (1969). Implication and meaning. *Theoria* 35: 38–54.

Ojeda, Almerindo E. (1993). New evidence for a more general theory of singularity. *ESCOL '93*, 247–58.

Olsen, Margaret. (1986). Some Problematic Issues in the Study of Intonation and Sentence Stress. PhD dissertation, University of Illinois, Urbana.

O'Neill, Daniela K. (1996). Two-year-olds' sensitivity to the parent's knowledge when making requests. *Child Development* 67: 659–77.

van Oosten, Jeanne. (1984). The Nature of Subjects, Topics and Agents: a Cognitive Explanation. PhD dissertation, University of California, Berkeley.

Origgi, Gloria and Dan Sperber. (2000). Evolution, communication and the proper function of language. In P. Carruthers and A. Chamberlain (eds.), *Evolution and the Human Mind: Language, Modularity and Social Cognition*, 140–69. Cambridge: Cambridge University Press.

Osgood, Charles E. (1980). *Lectures on Language Performance*. New York: Springer-Verlag.

Ostendorf, Mari and Nanette Veilleux. (1994). A hierarchical stochastic model for automatic prediction of prosodic boundary location. *Computational Linguistics* 20: 27–54.

Ostertag, Gary (ed.). (1998). *Definite Descriptions: A Reader*. Cambridge, MA: MIT Press.

Ostler, Nicholas and B. T. S. Atkins. (1991). Predictable meaning shift: Some linguistic properties of lexical implication rules. Paper presented at SIGLEX 1, Berkeley, CA.

Özyürek, Asli and Sotaro Kita. (2002). Interacting with demonstratives: Encoding of joint attention as a semantic contrast in the Turkish and Japanese demonstrative systems. Unpublished MS., MPI Nijmegen.

Pander Maat, Henk and Ted Sanders. (2000). Domains of use or subjectivity? The distribution of three Dutch discourse markers explained. In E. Cooper-Kuhlen and B. Kortmann (eds.), *Cause, Condition, Concession, Contrast: Cognitive and Discourse Perspectives*, 57–82. Berlin: de Gruyter.

Papafragou, Anna. (1998). The acquisition of modality: Implications for theories of semantic representation. *Mind & Language* 13: 370–99.

Papafragou, Anna. (2000). *Modality: Issues in the Semantics–Pragmatics Interface*. Amsterdam: Elsevier Science.

Papafragou, Anna. (2002). Mindreading and verbal communication. *Mind & Language* 17: 55–67.

Papafragou, Anna and Julien Musolino. (2003). Scalar implicatures: Experiments at the semantics–pragmatics interface. *Cognition* 86: 253–82.

Park, Yong-Yae. (1998). A discourse analysis of contrastive connectives in English, Korean and Japanese conversations: with special reference to the context of disreferred responses. In A. Jucker and Y. Ziv (eds.), 277–300.

Parsons, Terence. (1980). *Nonexistent Objects*. New Haven, CT: Yale University Press.

Partee, Barbara H. (1965). *Subject and Object in Modern English*. New York: Garland.

Partee, Barbara H. (1972). Opacity, coreference, and pronouns. In Davidson and Harman (eds.), 415–41.

Partee, Barbara H. (1984a). Compositionality. In F. Landman and F. Veltman (eds.), *Varieties of Formal Semantics*, 281–311. Dordrecht: Foris.

Partee, Barbara H. (1984b). Nominal and temporal anaphora. *Linguistics and Philosophy* 7: 243–86.

Partee, Barbara H. (1989). Binding implicit variables in quantified contexts. *CLS 25, Part 2: Parasession on Language in Context*, 342–65.

Partee, Barbara H. (1991). Topic, focus and quantification. *SALT I*, 159–87.

Passoneau, Rebecca and Diane Litman. (1993). Intention-based segmentation: Human reliability and correlation with linguistic cues. *ACL-31*, 148–55. Columbus.

Paul, Hermann. (1880). *Prinzipien der Sprachgeschichte*. Tübingen: Niemeyer.

Payne, Doris L. (1987). Information structuring in Papago narrative discourse. *Language* 63: 783–804.

Payne, John R. (1985). Negation. In T. Shopen (ed.), *Language Typology and Linguistic Description*, vol. 1: *Clause Structure*, 197–242. Cambridge: Cambridge University Press.

Peacocke, Christopher. (1975). Proper names, reference, and rigid designation. Reprinted in Ostertag (ed., 1998), 201–24.

Pearl, Judea. (1988). *Probabilistic Reasoning in Intelligent Systems: Networks of Plausible Inference*. San Mateo, CA: Morgan Kaufmann.

Pederson, Eric. (1993). Geographic and manipulable space in two Tamil linguistic systems. In A. U. Frank and I. Campari (eds.), *Spatial Information Theory*, 294–311. Berlin: Springer Verlag.

Peirce, Charles Sanders. (1955). Abduction and induction. In Justus Buchler (ed.), *Philosophical Writings of Peirce*, 150–6. New York: Dover Books.

Pereira, Cecile and Catherine Watson. (1998). Some acoustic characteristics of emotion. *Proceedings of ICSLP-98*, 927–30. Sydney.

Perner, Josef, Uta Frith, Alan Leslie, and Sue Leekam. (1989). Explorations of the autistic child's theory of mind: Knowledge, belief, and communication. *Child Development* 60: 689–700.

Perrault, C. Raymond. (1990). An application of default logic to speech act theory. In Cohen et al. (eds.), 161–86.

Perrault, C. Raymond and James Allen. (1980). A plan-based analysis of indirect speech acts. *American Journal of Computational Linguistics* 6: 167–82.

Perry, John. (1977). Frege on demonstratives. *Philosophical Review* 86: 474–97. Reprinted in S. Davis (ed., 1991), 146–59.

Pick, Herbert and Anne Pick. (1999). James Jerome Gibson. In R. Wilson and F. Keil (eds.), *The MIT Encyclopedia of the Cognitive Sciences*, 349–51. Cambridge, MA: MIT Press.

Pierrehumbert, Janet. (1980). The Phonology and Phonetics of English Intonation. PhD dissertation, MIT.

Pierrehumbert, Janet and Julia Hirschberg. (1990). The meaning of intonational contours in the interpretation of discourse. In Cohen et al. (eds.), 271–312.

Pilkington, Adrian. (2000). *Poetic Effects: A Relevance Theory Perspective*. Amsterdam: Benjamins.

Pitrelli, John, Mary Beckman, and Julia Hirschberg. (1994). Evaluation of prosodic transcription labeling reliability in the ToBI framework. *Proceedings of ICSLP-94* 2: 123–6. Yokohama.

Polanyi, Livia. (1985). Conversational storytelling. In T. van Dijk (ed.), *Handbook of Discourse Analysis*, vol. 3: *Discourse and Dialogue*, 183–202. New York: Academic Press.

Politzer, Guy. (1990). Characterizing spontaneous inferences. *Behavioral and Brain Sciences* 13: 177–8.

Politzer, Guy and Laura Macchi. (2000). Reasoning and pragmatics. *Mind and Society* 1: 73–93.

Pollack, Martha E. (1986). Inferring Domain Plans in Question-answering. PhD dissertation, University of Pennsylvania.

Pollard, Carl M. and Ivan A. Sag. (1994). *Head-driven Phrase Structure Grammar*. Chicago, IL: University of Chicago Press.

Pople, Harry E., Jr. (1973). On the mechanization of abductive logic. *Proceedings of the Third International Joint Conference on Artificial Intelligence*, 147–52. Stanford, CA.

Postal, Paul M. (1966). On so-called "pronouns" in English. Reprinted in D. A. Reibel and S. A. Schane (eds.), *Modern Studies in English: Readings in Transformational Grammar*, 201–24. Englewood Cliffs, NJ: Prentice-Hall, 1969.

Postal, Paul M. (1967). Linguistic anarchy notes. Reprinted in McCawley (ed., 1976), 203–25.

Postal, Paul M. (1974). *On Raising*. Cambridge, MA: MIT Press.

Postal, Paul M. (1998). *Three Investigations of Extraction*. Cambridge, MA: MIT Press.

Pott, A. F. (1859). *Etymologicshe Forschungen auf dem Gebiete der Indo-Germanischen Sprachen*. Vol. 1. Lemgo and Detmold: Meyer.

Povinelli, Daniel, Jesse Bering, and Steve Giambrone (in press). Chimpanzee "pointing." Another error of the argument by analogy? In Kita (ed.), 35–68.

Powell, George. (2000). Compositionality, innocence and the interpretation of NPs. *UCL Working Papers in Linguistics* 12: 123–44.

Powell, M. J. (1992). The systematic development of correlated interpersonal and meta-linguistic uses in stance adverbs. *Cognitive Linguistics* 3: 75–110.

Power, R. (1979). The organization of purposeful dialogs. *Linguistics* 17: 105–52.

Premack, David and Ann James Premack. (1994). Moral belief: Form versus content. In Hirschfeld and Gelman (eds.), 149–68.

Prevost, Scott. (1995). A Semantics of Contrast and Information Structure for Specifying Intonation in Spoken Language Generation. PhD dissertation, University of Philadelphia.

Prevost, Scott and Mark Steedman. (1994). Specifying intonation from context for speech synthesis. *Speech Communication* 15: 139–53.

Price, Patricia J., Mari Ostendorf, Stephanie Shattuck-Hufnagel, and Cynthia Fong. (1990). The use of prosody in syntactic disambiguation. *Journal of the Acoustical Society of America* 90: 2956–70.

Prince, Alan and Paul Smolensky. (1993). *Optimality Theory: Constraint Interaction in Generative Grammar*. Report RuCCS-TR-2. New Brunswick, NJ: Rutgers University Center for Cognitive Science.

Prince, Ellen F. (1976). The syntax and semantics of neg-raising, with evidence from French. *Language* 52: 404–26.

Prince, Ellen F. (1978). A comparison of *wh*-clefts and *it*-clefts in discourse. *Language* 54: 883–906.

Prince, Ellen F. (1981a). Toward a taxonomy of given/new information. In Cole (ed., 1981), 223–55.

Prince, Ellen F. (1981b). On the inferencing of indefinite-*this* NPs. In Joshi et al. (eds.), 231–50.

Prince, Ellen F. (1981c). Topicalization, Focus-movement, and Yiddish-movement: a pragmatic differentiation. *BLS 7*, 249–64.

Prince, Ellen F. (1982). The simple futurate: not simply progressive futurate minus progressive. *CLS 18*, 453–65.

Prince, Ellen F. (1983). Grice and universality. Unpublished MS., University of Pennsylvania, available at http://babel.ling.upenn.edu/~ellen/grice.ps.

Prince, Ellen F. (1984). Topicalization and left-dislocation: a functional analysis. In S. J. White and V. Teller (eds.), *Discourses in Reading and Linguistics. Annals of the New York Academy of Sciences* 433: 213–25.

Prince, Ellen F. (1985). Fancy syntax and shared knowledge. *Journal of Pragmatics* 9: 65–81.

Prince, Ellen F. (1992). The ZPG Letter: subjects, definiteness, and information-status. In S. A. Thompson and W. C. Mann (eds.), *Discourse Description: Diverse Analyses of a Fundraising Text*, 295–325. Amsterdam/Philadelphia: Benjamins.

Prince, Ellen F. (1997). On the functions of left-dislocation in English discourse. In A. Kamio (ed.), *Directions in Functional Linguistics*, 117–43. Philadelphia: Benjamins.

Prince, Ellen F. (1998). On the limits of syntax, with reference to left-dislocation and topicalization. In Culicover and McNally (eds.), 261–302.

Progovac, Ljiljana. (1994). *Negative and Positive Polarity*. Cambridge: Cambridge University Press.

Pustejovsky, James. (1991). The generative lexicon. *Computational Linguistics* 17: 409–41.

Pustejovsky, James. (1995). *The Generative Lexicon*. Cambridge, MA: MIT Press.

Putnam, Hilary. (1975). The meaning of "meaning." In K. Gunderson (ed.), *Language, Mind, and Knowledge*, 131–93. Minneapolis, MN: University of Minnesota Press.

Putnam, Hilary. (1976). "Two Dogmas" revisited. In G. Ryle (ed.), *Contemporary Aspects of Philosophy*, 202–13. Stocksfield, UK: Oriel Press.

Quine, W. V. (1940). *Mathematical Logic*. Cambridge, MA: Harvard University Press. (Revised edition, 1951.)

Quine, W. V. (1960). *Word and Object*. Cambridge, MA: MIT Press.

Quine, W. V. (1961). *From a Logical Point of View*. New York: Harper.

Quirk, Randolph, Sidney Greenbaum, Geoffrey Leech, and Jan Svartvik. (1985). *A Comprehensive Grammar of the English Language*. New York: Longman.

Raghibdoust, Shahla. (1994). The semantic–pragmatic nature of the Persian polarity items. Unpublished manuscript, University of Ottawa.

Ravid, Dorit Diskin. (1995). *Language Change in Child and Adult Hebrew: A Psycholinguistic Perspective*. New York: Oxford University Press.

Ravin, Yael and Claudia Leacock. (2000). Overview. In Ravin and Leacock (eds.), 1–29.

Ravin, Yael and Claudia Leacock (eds.). (2000). *Polysemy: Theoretical and Computational Approaches*. Oxford: Oxford University Press.

Ray, Tapas S. (2000). Lexical anaphors and pronouns in Oriy. In Lust et al. (eds.), 575–636.

Rayner, Manny. (1993). Abductive Equivalential Translation and its Application to Natural Language Database Interfacing. PhD thesis, Royal Institute of Technology, Stockholm.

Read, Barbara K. and Louise J. Cherry. (1978). Preschool children's production of directive forms. *Discourse Processes* 1: 233–45.

Recanati, François. (1986). On defining communicative intentions. *Mind & Language* 1: 213–42.

Recanati, François. (1989). The pragmatics of what is said. *Mind & Language* 4: 295–329. Reprinted in S. Davis (ed., 1991), 97–120.

Recanati, François. (1993). *Direct Reference: From Language to Thought*. Oxford: Blackwell.

Recanati, François. (1995). The alleged priority of literal interpretation. *Cognitive Science* 19: 207–32.

Recanati, François. (1996). Domains of discourse. *Linguistics and Philosophy* 19: 445–75.

Recanati, François. (2000). *Oratio Obliqua, Oratio Recta: The Semantics of Metarepresentations*. Cambridge, MA: MIT Press.

Recanati, François. (2001). What is said. *Synthèse* 125: 75–91.

Recanati, François. (2002a). Unarticulated constituents. *Linguistics and Philosophy* 25: 299–345.

Recanati, François. (2002b). Does linguistic communication rest on inference? *Mind & Language* 17: 105–26.

Recanati, François (forthcoming). *Literal Meaning*. Cambridge: Cambridge University Press.

Redeker, Gisela. (1986). Language Use in Informal Narratives: Effects of Social Distance and Listener Involvement. PhD dissertation, University of California, Berkeley.

Redeker, Gisela. (1990). Ideational and pragmatic markers of discourse structure. *Journal of Pragmatics* 14: 367–81.

Redeker, Gisela. (1991). Linguistic markers of discourse structure. *Linguistics* 29: 1139–72.

Reed, Irene, Osahito Miwaoke, Pascal Ascan, and Michael Krauss. (1977). *Yup'ik Eskimo Grammar*. Fairbanks: Alaska Native Language Center.

Reeder, Kenneth. (1980). The emergence of illocutionary skills. *Journal of Child Language* 7: 13–28.

Reggia, James A. (1985). Abductive inference. In K. N. Karna (ed.), *Proceedings of the Expert Systems in Government Symposium*, 484–9. New York: IEEE Computer Society Press.

Reggia, James A., Dana S. Nau, and Pearl Y. Wang. (1983). Diagnostic expert systems based on a set covering model. *International Journal of Man–Machine Studies* 19: 437–60.

Reichenbach, Hans. (1947). *Elements of Symbolic Logic*. London: Macmillan.

Reichman, Rachel. (1978). Conversational coherency. *Cognitive Science* 2: 283–327.

Reimer, Marga. (1991). Do demonstrations have semantic significance? *Analysis* 51: 177–83.

Reimer, Marga. (1998a). Quantification and context. *Linguistics and Philosophy* 21: 95–115.

Reimer, Marga. (1998b). The Wettstein/Salmon debate: Critique and resolution. *Pacific Philosophical Quarterly* 79: 130–51.

Reimer, Marga. (1998c). What is meant by "what is said"? A reply to Cappelen and Lepore. *Mind & Language* 13: 598–604.

Reinhart, Tanya. (1976). The Syntactic Domain of Anaphora. PhD dissertation, MIT.

Reinhart, Tanya. (1981). Pragmatics and linguistics: an analysis of sentence topics. *Philosophica* 27: 53–94.

Reinhart, Tanya. (1983). *Anaphora and Semantic Interpretation*. London: Croom Helm.

Reinhart, Tanya. (1995). Interface strategies. *OTS Working Papers* (OTS-WP-TL-95-002), Research Institute for Language and Speech, Utrecht University.

Reinhart, Tanya and Eric Reuland. (1993). Reflexivity. *Linguistic Inquiry* 24: 657–720.

Reiter, Raymond and Giovanni Criscuolo. (1981). On interacting defaults. *Proceedings of the Seventh International Joint Conference on Artificial Intelligence,* 270–6. Vancouver.

Reithinger, Norbert and Martin Klesen. (1997). Dialogue act classification using language models. *EUROSPEECH-97* 4: 2235–8. Rhodes, Greece.

Reuland, Eric and Alice ter Meulen (eds.). (1987). *The Representation of (In)definiteness.* Cambridge, MA: MIT Press.

Riddle, Elizabeth. (1975). Some pragmatic conditions on complementizer choice. *CLS 11,* 467–74.

Riddle, Elizabeth. (1978). Sequence of Tenses in English. PhD dissertation, University of Illinois, Urbana.

Rieber, Stephen. (1997). Conventional implicatures as tacit performatives. *Linguistics and Philosophy* 20: 50–72.

Roberts, Craige. (1996a). Information structure: Towards an integrated theory of formal pragmatics. *OSU Working Papers in Linguistics,* vol. 49: *Papers in Semantics,* 91–136.

Roberts, Craige. (1996b). Information structure, plans, and implicature. Paper presented at *AAAI Symposium on Computational Implicature: Computational Approaches to Interpreting and Generating Conversational Implicature,* Stanford University, CA.

Roberts, Craige. (1998a). The place of Centering in a general theory of anaphora resolution. In Walker et al. (eds.), 359–400.

Roberts, Craige. (1998b). Focus, the flow of information, and universal grammar. In Culicover and McNally (eds.), 109–60.

Roberts, Craige (2002). Demonstratives as definites. In K. van Deemter and R. Kibble (eds.), *Information Sharing,* 89–136. Stanford, CA: CSLI.

Roberts, Craige (to appear). Uniqueness in definite noun phrases. *Linguistics and Philosophy.*

Roberts, Ian. (1985). The Representation of Implicit and Dethematized Subjects. PhD dissertation, University of Southern California.

Roberts, Jane. (2001). *Robbares and reuares þat ryche men despoilen*: Some competing forms. In I. Taavitsainen, T. Nevalainen, P. Pahta, and M. Rissanen (eds.), *Placing Middle English in Context,* 235–53. Berlin: Mouton de Gruyter.

Rochemont, Michael. (1978). A Theory of Stylistic Rules in English. PhD dissertation, University of Massachusetts.

Rochemont, Michael. (1986). *Focus in Generative Grammar.* Amsterdam/Philadelphia: Benjamins.

Rochemont, Michael S. and Peter W. Culicover. (1990). *English Focus Constructions and the Theory of Grammar.* Cambridge: Cambridge University Press.

Rodman, Robert. (1974). On left dislocation. *Papers in Linguistics* 7: 437–66.

Rogers, Andy. (1971). Three kinds of physical perception verbs. *CLS 7,* 206–22.

Rogers, Andy, John Murphy, and Bob Wall (eds.). (1977). *Proceedings of the Texas Conference on Performatives, Presuppositions, and Implicatures.* Austin, TX: Center for Applied Linguistics.

Rooth, Mats. (1981). A comparison of three theories of verb phrase ellipsis. *University of Massachusetts Occasional Papers in Linguistics* 7: 212–44.

Rooth, Mats. (1985). Association with Focus. PhD dissertation, University of Massachusetts, Amherst.

Rooth, Mats. (1992). A theory of focus interpretation. *Natural Language Semantics* 1: 75–116.

van Rooy, Robert. (1999). Questioning to resolve decision problems. In P. Dekker (ed.), *Proceedings of the Twelfth Amsterdam Colloquium*. Amsterdam: ILLC.

van Rooy, Robert (2000). Comparing questions and answers: A bit of logic, a bit of language, and some bits of information. Unpublished manuscript, University of Amsterdam. Available from http://turing.wins.uva.nl/~vanrooy/papers.html

van Rooy, Robert. (2001). Relevance of communicative acts. *Proceedings of Tark 2001*.

van Rooy, Robert (2004a). Signalling games select Horn strategies. *Linguistics and Philosophy*. 27: 493–527

van Rooy, Robert. (2004b). Relevance and bidirectional OT. In R. Blutner and H. Zeevat (eds.), *Optimality Theory and Pragmatics*,11–22. Basingstoke : Palgrave Macmillan.

Ross, John Robert. (1967). Constraints on Variables in Syntax. PhD dissertation, MIT.

Ross, John Robert. (1970a). On declarative sentences. In R. Jacobs and P. S. Rosenbaum (eds.), *Readings in English Transformational Grammar*, 222–72. Waltham, MA: Ginn.

Ross, John Robert. (1970b). Gapping and the order of constituents. In M. Bierwisch and K. E. Heidolph (eds.), *Progress in Linguistics*, 249–59. The Hague: Mouton.

Ross, John Robert. (1975). Where to do things with words. In Cole and Morgan (eds.), 233–56.

Rossari, Corinne. (1994). *Les opérations de reformulation: Analyse du processus et des marques dans une perspective contrastive français–italien*. Bern: Peter Lang.

Rossari, Corinne. (1996). Considérations sur la méthodologie contrastive français–italien: À propos de locutions adverbiales fonctionnant comme connecteurs. In Hansen and Skytte (eds.), 55–68.

Rosta, Alla. (1995). How does this sentence interpret? The semantics of English mediopassives. In B. Aarts and C. F. Meyer (eds.), *The Verb in Contemporary English: Theory and Description*, 123–44. Cambridge: Cambridge University Press.

Rouchota, Villy. (1996). Discourse connectives: What do they link? *UCL Working Papers in Linguistics* 8: 199–214.

Rouchota, Villy. (1998). Procedural meaning and parenthetical discourse markers. In Jucker and Ziv (eds.), 97–126.

Roulet, Eddy. (1984). Speech acts, discourse structure, and pragmatic connectives. *Journal of Pragmatics* 8: 31–47.

Roulet, Eddy. (1990). Et si, *après tout*, ce connecteur pragmatique n'était pas un marqueur d'argument ou de prémise impliquée? *Cahiers de linguistique française* 11: 329–43.

Rudolph, Elisabeth. (1996). *Contrast: Adversative and Concessive Relations and their Expressions in English, German, Spanish, Portuguese on Sentence and Text Level*. Berlin: Walter de Gruyter.

Russell, Bertrand. (1905). On denoting. *Mind* 14: 479–93.

Russell, Bertrand. (1910–11). Knowledge by acquaintance and knowledge by description. *Proceedings of the Aristotelian Society* 8: 108–28.

Russell, Bertrand. (1919). *Introduction to Mathematical Philosophy*. London: George Allen & Unwin.

Russell, Bertrand. (1956). *Logic and Knowledge: Essays 1901–1950*. (R. Marsh, ed.) London: George Allen & Unwin.

Ryder, Mary Ellen. (1994). *Ordered Chaos: The Interpretation of English Noun–Noun Compounds*. Berkeley, CA: University of California Press.

Ryle, Gilbert. (1954). *Dilemmas*. Cambridge: Cambridge University Press.

Sachs, Jacqueline and Judith Devin. (1976). Young children's use of age-appropriate speech styles in social interaction and role playing. *Journal of Child Language* 3: 81–98.

Sacks, Harvey and Emanuel A. Schegloff. (1979). Two preferences in the organization of reference to persons in conversation and their interaction. In G. Psathas (ed.), *Everyday Language: Studies in Ethnomethodology*, 15–21. New York: Irvington.

Sacks, Harvey, Emanuel A. Schegloff, and Gail Jefferson. (1974). A simplest systematics for the organization of turn-taking for conversation. *Language* 50: 696–735. Reprinted in J. Schenkein (ed.), *Studies in the Organization of Conversational Interaction*, 7–55. New York: Academic Press, 1978.

Sadock, Jerrold M. (1969). Hypersentences. *Papers in Linguistics* 1: 283–371.

Sadock, Jerrold M. (1970). Whimperatives. In J. M. Sadock and A. L. Vanek (eds.), *Studies Presented to R. B. Lees by his Students*, 223–39. Edmonton: Linguistic Research.

Sadock, Jerrold M. (1972). Speech act idioms. *CLS 8*, 329–39.

Sadock, Jerrold M. (1974). *Toward a Linguistic Theory of Speech Acts.* New York: Academic Press.

Sadock, Jerrold M. (1977). Aspects of linguistic pragmatics. In Rogers et al. (eds.), 67–78.

Sadock, Jerrold M. (1978). On testing for conversational implicature. In P. Cole (ed.), *Syntax and Semantics 9: Pragmatics*, 281–97. New York: Academic Press.

Sadock, Jerrold M. (1981). Almost. In Cole (ed., 1981), 257–72.

Sadock, Jerrold M. (1985). On the performadox, or a semantic defense of the performative hypothesis. *University of Chicago Working Papers in Linguistics* 1: 160–9. Chicago, IL: Department of Linguistics, University of Chicago.

Sadock, Jerrold M. (1994). Toward a grammatically realistic typology of speech acts. In Tsohatzidis (ed.), 393–406.

Sadock, Jerrold M. and Arnold M. Zwicky. (1985). Sentence types. In T. Shopen (ed.), *Language Typology and Syntactic Description*, vol. 1: *Clause Structure*, 155–96. Cambridge: Cambridge University Press.

Safir, Kenneth. (1985). *Syntactic Chains.* Cambridge: Cambridge University Press.

Sag, Ivan A. (1976). Deletion and Logical Form. PhD dissertation, MIT.

Sag, Ivan A. (1981). Formal semantics and extralinguistic context. In Cole (ed., 1981), 273–94.

Sag, Ivan and Jorge Hankamer. (1977). Syntactically vs. pragmatically controlled anaphora. In R. W. Fasold and R. W. Shuy (eds.), *Studies in Language Variation*, 121–35. Washington, DC: Georgetown University Press.

Sag, Ivan and Jorge Hankamer. (1984). Toward a theory of anaphoric processing. *Linguistics and Philosophy* 7: 325–45.

Sag, Ivan A. and Mark Liberman. (1975). The intonational disambiguation of indirect speech acts. *CLS 11*, 487–98.

Sainsbury, R. M. (1979). *Russell.* London: Routledge & Kegan Paul.

Sakakibara, Sonoko. (1995). The Pragmatics and Distribution of the Japanese Reflexive Pronoun *zibun*. PhD dissertation, University of Illinois, Urbana.

Salmon, Nathan. (1981). *Reference and Essence.* Oxford: Basil Blackwell.

Salmon, Nathan. (1986). *Frege's Puzzle.* Cambridge, MA: MIT Press.

Salmon, Nathan. (1989). Reference and information content: names and descriptions. In D. Gabbay and F. Guenthner (eds.), *Handbook of Philosophical Logic*, 409–61. Dordrecht: Reidel.

Salmon, Nathan. (1991). The pragmatic fallacy. *Philosophical Studies* 63: 83–97.

Samet, Jerry and Roger Schank. (1984). Coherence and connectivity. *Linguistics and Philosophy* 7: 57–82.

Samuel, Ken, Sandra Carberry, and K. Vijay-Shanker. (1998). Dialogue act tagging with transformation-based learning. *COLING/ACL-98* 2: 1150–6. Montreal.

Sanders, Ted. (1997). Semantic and pragmatic sources of coherence: On the categorization of coherence relations in context. *Discourse Processes* 24: 119–47.

Sanders, Ted and Leo G. M. Noordman. (2000). The role of coherence relations and their linguistic markers in text processing. *Discourse Processes* 29: 37–60.

Sanders, Ted and Wilbert P. M. Spooren. (1999). Communicative intentions are coherence relations. In W. Bublitz and U. Lenk (eds.), *Coherence in Spoken and Written Discourse*, 235–50. Amsterdam: Benjamins.

Sanders, Ted, Wilbert P. M. Spooren, and Leo G. M. Noordman. (1992). Towards a taxonomy of discourse relations. *Discourse Processes* 15: 1–35.

Sanders, Ted, Wilbert P. M. Spooren, and Leo G. M. Noordman. (1993). Coherence relations in a cognitive theory of discourse representation. *Cognitive Linguistics* 4: 93–133.

Sapir, Edward. (1944). Grading: a study in semantics. *Philosophy of Science* 11: 93–116. Reprinted in D. G. Mandelbaum (ed.), *Edward Sapir: Selected Writings in Language, Culture, and Personality*, 122–49. Berkeley, CA: University of California Press.

Sasse, Hans-Jurgen. (1987). The thetic/categorical distinction revisited. *Linguistics* 25: 511–80.

Sauerland, Uli. (2001). Scalar implicatures in complex sentences. *Semantics and Linguistic Theory XI*.

Saul, Jennifer. (2002). What is said and psychological reality: Grice's project and relevance theorists' criticisms. *Linguistics and Philosophy* 25: 347–72.

Saul, Jennifer. (to appear). Review of W. Davis (1998). *Nous*.

Schachter, Paul. (1977a). Does she or doesn't she? *Linguistic Inquiry* 8: 762–7.

Schachter, Paul. (1977b). Constraints on coordination. *Language* 53: 86–103.

Schafer, Amy J., Shari R. Speer, Paul Warren, and S. David White. (2000). Intonational disambiguation in sentence production and comprehension. *Journal of Psycholinguistic Research* 29: 169–82.

Schegloff, Emanuel A. (1968). Sequencing in conversational openings. *American Anthropologist* 70: 1075–95.

Schegloff, Emanuel A. (1972). Notes on a conversational practice: Formulating place. In D. Sudnow (ed.), *Studies in Social Interaction*, 75–119. New York: Free Press.

Schegloff, Emanuel A. (1979). Identification and recognition in telephone conversational openings. In G. Psathas (ed.), *Everyday Language: Studies in Ethnomethodology*, 23–78. New York: Irvington.

Schegloff, Emanuel A. (1982). Discourse as an interactional achievement: Some uses of "uh huh" and other things that come between sentences. In D. Tannen (ed.), *Analyzing Discourse: Text and Talk*, 71–93. Georgetown University Roundtable on Languages and Linguistics 1981. Washington, DC: Georgetown University Press.

Schegloff, Emanuel A. (1984). On some gestures' relation to talk. In J. M. Atkinson and J. Heritage (eds.), *Structures of Social Action: Studies in Conversation Analysis*, 262–96. Cambridge: Cambridge University Press.

Schegloff, Emanuel A. (1987). Recycled turn beginnings: A precise repair mechanism in conversation's turn-taking organization. In G. Button and J. R. E. Lee (eds.), *Talk and Social Organization*, 70–85. Clevedon: Multilingual Matters.

Schegloff, Emanuel A. (1988). Presequences and indirection: Applying speech act theory to ordinary conversation. *Journal of Pragmatics* 12: 55–62.

Schegloff, Emanuel A., Gail Jefferson, and Harvey Sacks. (1977). The preference for self-correction in the organization of repair in conversation. *Language* 53: 361–82.

Schegloff, Emanuel A. and Harvey Sacks. (1973). Opening up closings. *Semiotica* 8: 289–327.

Schelling, Thomas. (1960). *The Strategy of Conflict*. Oxford: Oxford University Press.

Schiffer, Stephen. (1972). *Meaning*. Oxford: Oxford University Press.

Schiffrin, Deborah. (1987). *Discourse Markers*. Cambridge: Cambridge University Press.

Schiffrin, Deborah. (1990). Between text and context: Deixis, anaphora, and the meaning of *then*. *Text* 10: 245–70.

Schiffrin, Deborah. (1994). *Approaches to Discourse*. Oxford: Blackwell.

Schiffrin, Deborah, Deborah Tannen, and Heidi E. Hamilton (eds.). (2001). *Handbook of Discourse Analysis*. Oxford: Blackwell.

Schladt, Mathias. (2000). The typology and grammaticalization of reflexives. In Frajzyngier and Curl (eds.), 103–24.

Schmerling, Susan F. (1971a). A note on negative polarity. *Papers in Linguistics* 4: 200–6.

Schmerling, Susan F. (1971b). Presupposition and the notion of normal stress. *CLS 7*, 242–53.

Schmerling, Susan F. (1973). Subjectless sentences and the notion of surface structure. *CLS 9*, 577–86.

Schmerling, Susan F. (1974). A re-examination of the notion NORMAL STRESS. *Language* 50: 66–73.

Schmerling, Susan F. (1976). *Aspects of English Sentence Stress*. Austin, TX: University of Texas Press.

Schmerling, Susan F. (1978). Synonymy judgments as syntactic evidence. In Cole (ed., 1978), 299–314.

Schmid, Maureen A. (1980). Co-occurence Restrictions in Negative, Interrogative, and Conditional Clauses: A Cross-linguistic Study. PhD Dissertation, SUNY, Buffalo.

Schmidt, Chris L. (1996). Scrutinizing reference: how gesture and speech are coordinated in mother–child interaction. *Journal of Child Language* 23: 279–305.

Schourup, Lawrence. (1985). *Common Discourse Particles in English Conversation*. New York: Garland.

Schourup, Lawrence. (1999). Discourse markers. *Lingua* 107: 227–65.

Schuetze-Coburn, Stephan. (1987). Topic management and the lexicon: a discourse profile of three-argument verbs in German. Unpublished manuscript, UCLA.

Schwarzschild, Roger. (1999). GIVENness, Avoid F and other constraints on the placement of accent. *Natural Language Semantics* 7: 141–77.

Schwenter, Scott A. (1996). Some reflections on *o sea*: a discourse marker in Spanish. *Journal of Pragmatics* 25: 855–74.

Schwenter, Scott A. (1999a). *Pragmatics of Conditional Marking: Implicature, Scalarity, and Exclusivity*. New York: Garland.

Schwenter, Scott A. (1999b). Two types of scalar particles: Evidence from Spanish. In J. Gutiérrez-Rexach and F. Martínez-Gil (ed.), *Advances in Hispanic Linguistics*, 546–61. Somerville, MA: Cascadilla Press.

Schwenter, Scott A. (2000). Lo absoluto y lo relativo de las partículas escalares *incluso* y *hasta*. *Oralia* 3: 169–97.

Schwenter, Scott and Elizabeth Closs Traugott. (2000). Invoking scalarity: the development of *in fact*. *Journal of Historical Pragmatics* 1: 7–26.

Schwenter, Scott A. and Shravan Vasishth (2001). Absolute and relative scalar particles in Spanish and Hindi. *BLS 26*, 225–33.

Searle, John. (1965). What is a speech act? In M. Black (ed.), *Philosophy in America*, 221–39. Ithaca, NY: Cornell University Press.

Searle, John. (1969). *Speech Acts: An Essay in the Philosophy of Language*. Cambridge: Cambridge University Press.

Searle, John. (1975a). Indirect speech acts. In Cole and Morgan (eds.), 59–82. Reprinted in S. Davis (ed., 1991), 255–77, and in Kasher (ed., 1998), vol. IV: 617–38.

Searle, John. (1975b). A taxonomy of speech acts. In K. Gunderson (ed.), *Minnesota Studies in the Philosophy of Science*, vol. 9: *Language, Mind and Knowledge*, 344–69. Minneapolis: University of Minnesota Press. Reprinted in Searle (1979), 1–29.

Searle, John. (1979). *Expression and Meaning*. Cambridge: Cambridge University Press.

Searle, John. (1980). The background of meaning. In J. Searle, F. Keifer, and M. Bierwisch (eds.), *Speech Act Theory and Pragmatics*, 221–32. Dordrecht: Reidel.

Searle, John. (1989). How performatives work. *Linguistics and Philosophy* 15: 535–58.

Searle, John and Daniel Vanderveken. (1985). *Foundations of Illocutionary Logic*. Cambridge: Cambridge University Press.

Segal, Gabriel. (1994). Priorities in the philosophy of thought. *Aristotelian Society Supplementary Volume* LXVIII: 107–30.

Selkirk, Elizabeth O. (1984). *Phonology and Syntax: The Relation between Sound and Structure*. Cambridge, MA: MIT Press.

Selkirk, Elizabeth. (1995). Sentence prosody: Intonation, stress and phrasing. In J. Goldsmith (ed.), *Handbook of Phonological Theory*, 550–69. Oxford: Blackwell.

Sellars, Wilfred. (1954). Presupposing. *Philosophical Review* 63: 197–215.

Sells, Peter. (1987). Aspects of logophoricity. *Linguistic Inquiry* 18: 445–79.

Selting, Margret. (1996). On the interplay of syntax and prosody in the constitution of turn-constructional units and turns in conversation. *Pragmatics* 6: 371–89.

Sgall, Petr, Eva Hajičova, and Eva Benešova. (1973). *Topic, Focus, and Generative Semantics*. Kronberg: Scriptor Verlag GmbH.

Sgall, Petr, Eva Hajičova and Jarmila Panevová. (1986). *The Meaning of the Sentence in its Semantic and Pragmatic Aspects*. Dordrecht: Reidel.

Shapley, Marian. (1983). Some Constraints on Fragments. MA thesis, UCLA.

Shastri, Lokendra and Venkat Ajjanagadde. (1993). From simple associations to systematic reasoning: A connectionist representation of rules, variables and dynamic bindings using temporal synchrony. *Behavioral and Brain Sciences* 16: 417–94.

Shatz, Marilyn. (1978). Children's comprehension of their mothers' question-directives. *Journal of Child Language* 5: 39–46.

Shatz, Marilyn and Rochel Gelman. (1973). The development of communication skills: Modifications in the speech of young children as a function of listener. *Monograph of the Society for Research in Child Development* 38 (Serial No. 152).

Sheintuch, Gloria and Kathleen Wise. 1976. On the pragmatic unity of the rules of Neg-raising and Neg-attraction. *CLS 12*, 548–57.

Shibatani, Masayoshi (ed.). (1976). *Syntax and Semantics 6: The Grammar of Causative Constructions*. New York: Academic.

Shibatani, Masayoshi. (1999). Honorifics. In K. Brown and J. Miller (eds.), *Concise Encyclopedia of Grammatical Categories*, 192–201. Amsterdam: Elsevier.

Shimojima, Atsushi, Yasuhiro Katagiri, Hanae Koiso, and Marc Swerts. (2001). An experimental study on the informational and grounding functions of prosodic features of Japanese echoic responses. *Speech Communication* 36: 113–32.

Shoham, Yoav. (1987). Nonmonotonic logics: meaning and utility. *Proceedings of the International Joint Conference on Artificial Intelligence*, 388–93. Milan.

Shoham, Yoav. (1988). *Reasoning About Change*. Cambridge, MA: MIT Press.

Shopen, Tim. (1973). Ellipsis as grammatical indeterminacy. *Foundations of Language* 10: 65–77.

Shriberg, Elizabeth, Rebecca Bates, Paul Taylor, Andreas Stolcke, Daniel Jurafsky, Klaus Ries, Noah Coccaro, Rachel Martin, Marie Meteer, and Carol Van Ess-Dykema. (1998). Can prosody aid the automatic classification of dialog acts in conversational speech? *Language & Speech* 41: 439–87.

Sidner, Candace. (1979). Towards a Computational Theory of Definite Anaphora Comprehension in English Discourse. PhD dissertation, MIT.

Sidner, Candace. (1983). Focusing in the comprehension of definite anaphora. In M. Brady and R. Berwick (eds.), *Computational Models of Discourse*, 267–330. Cambridge, MA: MIT Press.

Siegal, Michael. (1997). *Knowing Children: Experiments in Conversation and Cognition* (2nd edn.). Hove, UK: Lawrence Erlbaum.

Siewierska, Anna. (1984). *The Passive: A Comparative Linguistic Analysis*. London: Croom Helm.

Siewierska, Anna. (1988). *Word Order Rules*. London: Croom Helm.

Silverman, Kim. (1987). The Structure and Processing of Fundamental Frequency Contours. PhD dissertation, Cambridge University.

Silverman, Kim, Mary Beckman, Janet Pierrehumbert, Mari Ostendorf, Colin Wightman, Patti Price, and Julia Hirschberg. (1992). ToBI: A standard scheme for labeling prosody. *Proceedings of ICSLP-92*, 867–79. Banff.

Singer, Murray. (1994). Discourse inference processes. In M. A. Gernsbacher (ed.), *Handbook of Psycholinguistics*, 479–515. New York: Academic Press.

Slobin, Dan I. (1994). Talking perfectly: Discourse origins of the present perfect. In William Pagliuca (ed.), *Perspectives on Grammaticalization*, 119–33. Amsterdam: Benjamins.

Smith, Benjamin. (1999). Conversation and rationality. Unpublished MS., Yale University.

Smith, Wendy. (1996). Spoken narrative and preferred clause structure: Evidence from modern Hebrew discourse. *Studies in Language* 20: 163–89.

Smith, Neil and Deirdre Wilson. (1992). Introduction to the special issue on relevance theory. *Lingua* 87: 1–10.

Smith, Steven (1975). *Meaning and Negation*. The Hague: Mouton.

Snow, Catherine E. (1977). The development of conversation between mothers and babies. *Journal of Child Language* 4: 1–22.

Soames, Scott (1982). How presuppositions are inherited. *Linguistic Inquiry* 13, 483–545.

Soames, Scott (1986). Incomplete definite descriptions. *Notre Dame Journal of Formal Logic* 27: 349–75. Reprinted in Ostertag (ed., 1998), 275–308.

Soames, Scott. (1989). Presupposition. In D. Gabbay and F. Guenthner (eds.), *Handbook of Philosophical Logic*, vol. 4, 553–616. Dordrecht: Reidel.

Soames, Scott. (2001). *Beyond Rigidity: The Unfinished Semantic Agenda of Naming and Necessity*. Oxford: Oxford University Press.

Sorensen, Jesper. (2000). Essence, Schema, and Ritual Action: Towards a Cognitive Theory of Magic. PhD thesis, Faculty of Theology, University of Aarhus.

Sperber, Dan. (1984). Verbal irony: pretense or echoic mention? *Journal of Experimental Psychology: General* 113: 130–6.

Sperber, Dan. (1994). Understanding verbal understanding. In J. Khalfa (ed.), *What Is Intelligence?*, 179–98. Cambridge: Cambridge University Press.

Sperber, Dan. (1996). *Explaining Culture: A Naturalistic Approach.* Oxford: Blackwell.

Sperber, Dan. (1997). Intuitive and reflective beliefs. *Mind & Language* 12: 67–83.

Sperber, Dan. (2000). Metarepresentations in an evolutionary perspective. In Sperber (ed.), 117–37.

Sperber, Dan (ed.) (2000). *Metarepresentations: An Interdisciplinary Perspective.* New York: Oxford University Press.

Sperber, Dan. (2002). In defense of massive modularity. In E. Dupoux (ed.), *Language, Brain and Cognitive Development: Essays in Honor of Jacques Mehler,* 47–57. Cambridge, MA: MIT Press.

Sperber, Dan, Francisco Cara, and Vittorio Girotto. (1995). Relevance theory explains the selection task. *Cognition* 57: 31–95.

Sperber, Dan and Vittorio Girotto (to appear). Does the selection task detect cheater detection? *Cognition.*

Sperber, Dan and Deirdre Wilson. (1981). Irony and the use–mention distinction. In Cole (ed., 1981), 295–318. Reprinted in S. Davis (ed., 1991), 550–63.

Sperber, Dan and Deirdre Wilson. (1985/6). Loose talk. *Proceedings of the Aristotelian Society* LXXXVI: 153–71. Reprinted in S. Davis (ed., 1991), 540–9.

Sperber, Dan and Deirdre Wilson. (1986a). *Relevance: Communication and Cognition.* Cambridge, MA: Harvard University Press. (2nd edn., 1995, Oxford: Blackwell.)

Sperber, Dan and Deirdre Wilson (1986b). On defining relevance. In R. Grandy and R. Warner (eds.), *Philosophical Grounds of Rationality: Intentions, Categories, Ends,* 143–58. Oxford: Oxford University Press.

Sperber, Dan and Deirdre Wilson. (1987a). Précis of *Relevance. Behavioral and Brain Sciences* 10: 697–710. Reprinted in Kasher (ed., 1998), vol. V: 82–115.

Sperber, Dan and Deirdre Wilson. (1987b). Presumptions of relevance. *Behavioral and Brain Sciences* 10: 736–53.

Sperber, Dan and Deirdre Wilson. (1990a). Spontaneous deduction and mutual knowledge. *Behavioral and Brain Sciences* 13: 179–84.

Sperber, Dan and Deirdre Wilson. (1990b). Rhetoric and relevance. In J. Bender and D. Wellbery (eds.), *The Ends of Rhetoric: History, Theory, Practice,* 140–56. Stanford, CA: Stanford University Press.

Sperber, Dan and Deirdre Wilson. (1995). Postface to the second edition of *Relevance: Communication and Cognition.* Oxford: Blackwell.

Sperber, Dan and Deirdre Wilson. (1996). Fodor's frame problem and relevance theory: A reply to Chiappe and Kukla. *Behavioral and Brain Sciences* 19: 530–2.

Sperber, Dan and Deirdre Wilson. (1998a). The mapping between the mental and the public lexicon. In P. Carruthers and J. Boucher (eds.), *Language and Thought: Interdisciplinary Themes,* 184–200. Cambridge: Cambridge University Press.

Sperber, Dan and Deirdre Wilson. (1998b). Irony and relevance: A reply to Seto, Hamamoto and Yamanashi. In Carston and Uchida (eds.), 283–93.

Sperber, Dan and Deirdre Wilson. (2002). Pragmatics, modularity and mind-reading. *Mind & Language* 17: 3–23.

Sproat, Richard. (1994). English noun-phrase accent prediction for text-to-speech. *Computer Speech and Language* 8: 79–94.

Stainton, Robert J. (1994). Using non-sentences: An application of relevance theory. *Pragmatics and Cognition* 2: 269–84.

Stainton, Robert J. (1995). Non-sentential assertions and semantic ellipsis. *Linguistics and Philosophy* 18: 281–96.

Stainton, Robert J. (1997a). What assertion is not. *Philosophical Studies* 85: 57–73.

Stainton, Robert J. (1997b). Utterance meaning and syntactic ellipsis. *Pragmatics and Cognition* 5: 49–76.

Stainton, Robert J. (1998a). Quantifier phrases, meaningfulness "in isolation," and ellipsis. *Linguistics and Philosophy* 21: 311–40.

Stainton, Robert J. (1998b). Unembedded definite descriptions and relevance. *Revista Alicantina de Estudios Ingleses* (special issue on Relevance Theory) 11: 231–9.

Stainton, Robert J. (2000). The meaning of "sentences." *Nous* 34: 441–54.

Stainton, Robert J. (to appear). In defense of non-sentential assertion. In Z. G. Szabo (ed.), *Semantics vs. Pragmatics*. Oxford: Oxford University Press.

Stallard, Dave. (1993). Two kinds of metonymy. Paper presented at 31st Annual Meeting of the Association for Computational Linguistics, Columbus.

Stalnaker, Robert C. (1968). A theory of conditionals. In N. Rescher (ed.), *Studies in Logical Theory*, 98–112. Oxford: Basil Blackwell.

Stalnaker, Robert C. (1972). Pragmatics. In Donald Davidson and Gilbert Harman (eds.), *Semantics of Natural Language*, 380–97. Dordrecht: Reidel.

Stalnaker, Robert C. (1974). Pragmatic presuppositions. In M. K. Munitz and P. K. Unger (eds.), *Semantics and Philosophy*, 197–214. New York: New York University Press. Reprinted in Davis (ed., 1991), 471–82, in Stalnaker (1999), 47–62, and in Kasher (ed., 1998), vol. IV: 16–31.

Stalnaker, Robert C. (1978). Assertion. In Cole (ed., 1978), 315–22.

Stalnaker, Robert C. (1997). Reference and necessity. In B. Hale and C. Wright (eds.), *A Companion to the Philosophy of Language*, 534–54. Oxford: Blackwell.

Stalnaker, Robert C. (1999). *Context and Content*. Oxford: Oxford University Press.

Stanley, Jason. (2000). Context and logical form. *Linguistics and Philosophy* 23: 391–434.

Stanley, Jason. (2002). Making it articulated. *Mind & Language* 17: 149–68.

Stanley, Jason and Zoltán Gendler Szabó. (2000). On quantifier domain restriction. *Mind & Language* 15: 219–61.

Steedman, Mark. (1985). Dependency and coordination in the grammar of Dutch and English. *Language* 61: 523–68.

Steedman, Mark. (1990). Gapping as constituent coordination. *Linguistics and Philosophy* 13: 207–63.

Steedman, Mark. (1991). Structure and intonation. *Language* 67: 260–96.

Steedman, Mark. (2000). *The Syntactic Process*. Cambridge, MA: MIT Press.

Steele, Shirley and Julia Hirschberg. (1987). Unpublished findings, Murray Hill, NJ.

Steever, Sanford. (1977). Raising, meaning, and conversational implicature. 12: 590–602.

Stein, Dieter and Susan Wright (eds.). (1995). *Subjectivity and Subjectivisation in Language*. Cambridge: Cambridge University Press.

Steinberg, Danny D. and Leon A. Jakobovits (eds.). (1971). *Semantics: An Interdisciplinary Reader in Philosophy, Linguistics, and Psychology*. Cambridge: Cambridge University Press.

Stevenson, Rosemary J., Rosalind A. Crawley, and David Kleinman. (1994). Thematic roles, focus, and the representation of events. *Language and Cognitive Processes* 9: 519–48.

Stickel, Mark E. (1988). A Prolog-like inference system for computing minimum-cost abductive explanations in natural-language interpretation. *Proceedings of the International Computer Science Conference-88*, 343–50. Hong Kong. (Also published as Technical Note 451, Artificial Intelligence Center, SRI International, Menlo Park, CA, September 1988.)

Stillings, Justine T. (1975). The formulation of gapping in English as evidence for variable types in syntactic transformations. *Linguistic Analysis* 1: 247–73.

Stirling, Lesley. (1993). *Switch-Reference and Discourse Representation*. Cambridge: Cambridge University Press.

Stockwell, Robert P., Paul Schachter, and Barbara Hall Partee. (1973). *The Major Syntactic Structures of English*. New York: Holt, Rinehart and Winston.

Stolcke, Andreas, Klaus Ries, Noah Coccaro, Elizabeth Shriberg, Rebecca Bates, Daniel Jurafsky, Paul Taylor, Rachel Martin, Marie Meteer, and Carol Van Ess-Dykema. (2000). Dialog act modeling for automatic tagging and recognition of conversational speech. *Computational Linguistics* 26: 339–71.

Stolcke, Andreas, Elizabeth Shriberg, Rebecca Bates, Noah Coccaro, Daniel Jurafsky, Rachel Martin, Marie Meteer, Klaus Ries, Paul Taylor, and Carol Van Ess-Dykema. (1998). Dialog act modeling for conversational speech. In J. Chu-Carroll and N. Green (eds.), *Applying Machine Learning to Discourse Processing: Papers from the 1998 AAAI Spring Symposium*, 98–105. Technical Report SS-98-01. Menlo Park, CA: AAAI Press.

Strawson, P. F. (1950). On referring. *Mind* 59: 320–44.

Strawson, P. F. (1952). *Introduction to Logical Theory*. London: Methuen.

Strawson, P. F. (1964a). Intention and convention in speech acts. *Philosophical Review* 73: 439–60. Reprinted in S. Davis (ed., 1991), 290–302.

Strawson, P. F. (1964b). Identifying reference and truth values. *Theoria* 30: 96–118. Reprinted in Steinberg and Jakobovits (eds., 1971), 86–99.

Strawson, P. F. (1971). Intention and convention in speech acts. In J. R. Searle (ed.), *The Philosophy of Language*, 23–38. London: Oxford University Press.

Suhm, Bernhard and Alex Waibel. (1994). Toward better language models for spontaneous speech. *Proceedings of the International Conference on Spoken Language Processing (ICSLP-94)* 2: 831–4. Yokohama.

Svartvik, Jan and Randolph Quirk (eds.). (1980). *A Corpus of English Conversation*. Lund: Gleerup.

Sweetser, Eve. (1990). *From Etymology to Pragmatics: Metaphorical and Cultural Aspects of Semantic Structure*. Cambridge: Cambridge University Press.

Sweetser, Eve. (1999). Compositionality and blending: Working towards a fuller understanding of semantic composition in a cognitively realistic framework. In T. Janssen and G. Redeker (eds.), *Scope and Foundations of Cognitive Linguistics*, 129–62. The Hague: Mouton de Gruyter.

Sweetser, Eve. (2001). Blended spaces and performativity. *Cognitive Linguistics* 11: 305–34.

Swerts, Marc. (1997). Prosodic features at discourse boundaries of different strength. *Journal of the Acoustical Society of America* 22: 25–41.

Swerts, Marc, Rene Collier, and Jacques Terken. (1994). Prosodic predictors of discourse finality in spontaneous monologues. *Speech Communication* 15: 79–90.

Swerts, Marc, Ronald Geluykens, and Jacques Terken. (1992). Prosodic correlates of discourse units in spontaneous speech. *Proceedings of ICSLP-92* (International Conference on Spoken Language Processing), 421–28. Banff.

Swinney, David A. and Anne Cutler. (1979). The access and processing of idiomatic expressions. *Journal of Verbal Learning and Verbal Behavior* 18: 523–34.

Szabó, Zoltán Gendler. (2000). Descriptions and uniqueness. *Philosophical Studies* 101: 29–57.

Takahara, Paul. (1998). Pragmatic functions of the English discourse marker *anyway* and its corresponding Japanese discourse markers. In Jucker and Ziv (eds.), 327–52.

Talmy, Leonard. (2000). *Toward a Cognitive Semantics*. Cambridge, MA: MIT Press.

Tanaka, Keiko. (1992). The pun in advertising: A pragmatic approach. *Lingua* 87: 91–102.

Tanz, Christine. (1980). *Studies in the Acquisition of Deictic Terms*. Cambridge: Cambridge University Press.

Tarski, Alfred. (1930). Fundamentale Begriffe der Methodologie der deduktiven Wissenschaften I. *Monatshefte für Mathematik und Physik* 37: 361–404.

Tarski, Alfred. (1935). Grundzüge des Systemkalküls I, *Fund. Math.* 25: 503–26.

Taylor, Kenneth. (2001). Sex, breakfast, and descriptus interruptus. *Synthèse* 128: 45–61.

Taylor, Paul, Simon King, Stephen Isard, and Helen Wright. (1998). Intonation and dialog context as constraints for speech recognition. *Language and Speech* 41: 489–508.

Taylor, Paul, Simon King, Stephen Isard, Helen Wright, and Jacqueline Kowtko. (1997). Using intonation to constrain language models in speech recognition. *EUROSPEECH-97*, 2763–66. Rhodes, Greece.

Terken, Jacques. (1984). The distribution of pitch accents in instructions as a function of discourse structure. *Language and Speech* 27: 269–89.

Terken, Jacques. (1985). Use and Function of Accentuation: Some Experiments. PhD thesis, University of Leiden.

Terken, Jacques. (1993). Accessibility, prominence, pronouns and accents. Paper presented at the Workshop on Centering Theory in Naturally Occurring Discourse, University of Pennsylvania, Philadelphia, 1993.

Terken, Jacques. (1997). Variation of accent prominence within the phrase: Models and spontaneous speech data. In Y. Sagisaka, N. Campbell, and N. Higuchi (eds.), *Computing Prosody: Computational Models for Processing Spontaneous Speech*, 95–116. New York: Springer.

Terken, Jacques and Julia Hirschberg. (1994). Deaccentuation of words representing "given" information: Effects of persistence of grammatical function and surface position. *Language and Speech* 37: 125–45.

Terken, Jacques and Sieb G. Nooteboom. (1987). Opposite effects of accentuation and deaccentuation on verification latencies for given and new information. *Language and Cognitive Processes* 2: 145–63.

Tesar, Bruce and Paul Smolensky. (2000). *Learnability in Optimality Theory*. Cambridge, MA: MIT Press.

Thomason, Richmond H. (1973). Philosophy and formal semantics. In H. Leblanc (ed.), *Truth, Syntax and Modality*, 294–307. Amsterdam: North Holland.

Thomason, Richmond H. (1984). Accommodation, conversational planning, and implicature. Unpublished MS., University of Pittsburgh, Pennsylvania.

Thomason, Richmond H. (1990). Accommodation, meaning, and implicature: Interdisciplinary foundations for pragmatics. In Cohen et al. (eds.), 325–63.

Thomason, Richmond H. and Jerry R. Hobbs. (1997). Interrelating interpretation and generation in an abductive framework. *Proceedings of the AAAI Fall Symposium Workshop on Communicative Action in Humans and Machines*, 97–105. Cambridge, MA.

Thomason, Richmond H., Jerry R. Hobbs, and Johanna D. Moore. (1996). Communicative goals. Paper presented at *ECAI 96: 12th European Conference on Artificial Intelligence*.

Thomason, Richmond H. and Johanna D. Moore. (1995). Discourse context. Paper presented at AAAI Fall Symposium on Formalizing Context, Menlo Park, CA.

Thompson, Sandra A. (1990). Information flow and Dative Shift in English discourse. In J. Edmondson, C. Feagin, and F. Mühlhäusler (eds.), *Development and Diversity: Linguistic Variation across Time and Space*, 239–53. Dallas: SIL.

Tobler, Adolf. (1882). "Il ne faut pas que tu meures 'du darfst nicht sterben.'" Reprinted in *Vermischte Beiträge zur französischen Grammatik 1*, 3rd edn., 201–5. Leipzig: S. Hirzel, 1921.

Tomasello, Michael and Michelle Barton. (1994). Learning words in nonostensive contexts. *Developmental Psychology* 30: 639–50.

Tomlin, Russell S. (1995). The cognitive bases of functional interaction. Paper presented at the Colloquium on Discourse: Linguistic, Philosophical and Computational Perspectives, University of Pittsburgh.

Tomlin, Russell S. and Richard Rhodes. (1979). The distribution of information in Ojibwa Texts. *Journal of Pragmatics* 15: 307–20.

Tomlin, Russell S. and Richard Rhodes. (1992). Information Distribution in Ojibwa. In D. L. Payne (ed.), *Pragmatics of Word Order Flexibility*, 117–35. Amsterdam/Philadelphia: Benjamins.

Tovena, Lucia. (1998). *The Fine Structure of Polarity Items*. New York: Garland.

Traugott, Elizabeth Closs. (1982). From propositional to textual and expressive meanings: Some semantic–pragmatic aspects of grammaticalization. In W. P. Lehmann and Y. Malkiel (eds.), *Perspectives on Historical Linguistics*, 245–71. Amsterdam: Benjamins.

Traugott, Elizabeth Closs. (1985). Conditional markers. In J. Haiman (ed.), *Iconicity in Syntax*, 289–308. Amsterdam: Benjamins.

Traugott, Elizabeth Closs. (1988). Pragmatic strengthening and grammaticalization. *BLS 14*, 406–16.

Traugott, Elizabeth Closs. (1989). On the rise of epistemic meanings in English: An example of subjectification in semantic change. *Language* 57: 33–65.

Traugott, Elizabeth Closs. (1995). Subjectification in grammaticalization. In D. Stein and S. Wright (eds.), *Subjectivity and Subjectification: Linguistic Perspectives*, 31–54. Cambridge: Cambridge University Press.

Traugott, Elizabeth Closs. (1996). Subjectification and the development of epistemic meaning: The case of *promise* and *threaten*. In T. Swan and O. Jansen Westvik (eds.), *Modality in Germanic Languages*, 185–210. Berlin: Mouton de Gruyter.

Traugott, Elizabeth Closs. (1999). The role of pragmatics in semantic change. In J. Verschueren (ed.), *Pragmatics in 1998: Selected Papers from the 6th International Pragmatics Conference*, vol. II, 93–102. Antwerp: International Pragmatics Association.

Traugott, Elizabeth Closs (in press). A critique of Levinson's view of Q- and M-inferences in historical pragmatics. *Journal of Historical Pragmatics*.

Traugott, Elizabeth Closs and Richard B. Dasher (2002). *Regularity in Semantic Change*. Cambridge: Cambridge University Press.

Traugott, Elizabeth Closs and Ekkehard König. (1991). The semantics–pragmatics of grammaticalization revisited. In E. C. Traugott and B. Heine (eds.), *Approaches to Grammaticalization*, I: 189–218. Amsterdam: Benjamins.

Travis, Charles. (1981). *The True and the False: The Domain of the Pragmatic*. Amsterdam: Benjamins.

Travis, Charles. (1985). On what is strictly speaking true. *Canadian Journal of Philosophy* 15: 187–229.

Travis, Charles. (2001). *Unshadowed Thought: Representation in Thought and Language*. Cambridge, MA: Harvard University Press.

Tsohatzidis, Savas L. (ed.). (1994). *Foundations of Speech Act Theory: Philosophical and Linguistic Perspectives*. London: Routledge.

Turner, Ken (ed.). (1999). *The Semantics–Pragmatics Interface from Different Points of View*. Oxford: Elsevier.

Turner, Mark. (1991). *Reading Minds: The Study of English in the Age of Cognitive Science.* Princeton, NJ: Princeton University Press.

Turner, Mark. (1996a). Conceptual blending and counterfactual argument in the social and behavioral sciences. In P. E. Tetlock and A. Belkin (eds.), *Counterfactual Thought Experiments in World Politics*, 291–5. Princeton, NJ: Princeton University Press.

Turner, Mark. (1996b). *The Literary Mind.* New York: Oxford University Press.

Ullmann, Stephen. (1959). *The Principles of Semantics*, 2nd edn. Oxford: Blackwell.

Unger, Christoph. (1996). The scope of discourse connectives: implications for discourse organization. *Journal of Linguistics* 32: 403–38.

Uribe-Etxebarria, María. (1994). Interface Licensing Conditions on Negative Polarity Items: A Theory of Polarity and Tense Interactions. PhD dissertation, University of Connecticut.

Urmson, J. O. (1956). *Philosophical Analysis: Its Development Between the Two Wars.* Oxford: Clarendon Press.

Urmson, J. O. (1977). Performative utterances. *Midwest Studies in Philosophy* 2: 120–7.

Uziel-Karl, Sigal and Ruth A. Berman (2000). Where's ellipsis? Whether and why there are missing arguments in Hebrew child language. *Linguistics* 38: 457–82.

Vallduví, Enric. (1992). *The Informational Component.* New York: Garland.

Vallduví, Enric and Maria Vilkuna. (1998). On rheme and kontrast. In Culicover and McNally (eds.), 79–108.

Vallduví, Enric and Ron Zacharski. (1994). Accenting phenomena, association with focus, and the recursiveness of focus-ground. In P. Dekker and M. Stokhof (eds.), *Proceedings of the Ninth Amsterdam Colloquium*, 683–702. Amsterdam: ILLC.

Vanderveken, Daniel. (1994). In Tsohatzidis (ed.), 99–131.

Van Hoek, Karen. (1997). *Anaphora and Conceptual Structure.* Chicago, IL: University of Chicago Press.

Van Valin, Robert D. Jr. and Randy J. LaPolla. (1997). *Syntax: Structure, Meaning and Function.* Cambridge: Cambridge University Press.

Vasishth, Shravan (1998). Monotonicity constraints on negative polarity in Hindi. *Ohio State University Working Papers in Linguistics* 151: 201–20.

Veilleux, Nanette. (1994). Computational Models of the Prosody/Syntax Mapping for Spoken Language Systems. PhD dissertation, Boston University, MA.

Vendler, Zeno. (1972). *Res Cogitans: An Essay in Rational Psychology.* Ithaca, NY: Cornell University Press.

Verschueren, Jef and Maria Bertuccelli-Papi (eds.). (1987). *The Pragmatic Perspective.* Amsterdam: Benjamins.

Verschueren, Jef, Jan-Ola Östman, and Jan Blommaert (eds.). (1995). *Handbook of Pragmatics: Manual.* Amsterdam: Benjamins.

Wagner, Peter Alan. (2000). Default Reasoning and Sense Extension: Using Hypothetical Models to Account for Polysemy in Noun Denotations. MA thesis, Ohio State University.

Waibel, Alex. (1988). *Prosody and Speech Recognition.* San Mateo, CA: Morgan Kaufmann.

van der Wal, Sjoukje. (1996). *Negative Polarity Items and Negation: Tandem Acquisition.* Groningen: Groningen Dissertations in Linguistics 17.

Wald, Benji. (1983). Referents and topic within and across discourse units: Observations from current vernacular English. In F. Klein-Andreu (ed.), *Discourse Perspectives of Syntax*, 91–116. New York: Academic Press.

Wales, Roger. (1986). Deixis. In P. Fletcher and M. Garman (eds.), *Language Acquisition*, 2nd edn., 401–28. Cambridge: Cambridge University Press.

Wales, Roger and Hugh Toner. (1979). Intonation and ambiguity. In W. E. Cooper and E. C. Walker (eds.), *Sentence Processing: Psycholinguistic Studies Presented to Merrill Garrett*, 135–58. New York: Halsted Press.

Walker, Marilyn A. (1993). Informational Redundancy and Resource Bounds in Dialogue. PhD dissertation, University of Pennsylvania.

Walker, Marilyn A. (1994). Rejection by implicature. *BLS 20*, 563–74.

Walker, Marilyn A. (1996). Inferring acceptance and rejection in dialog by default rules of inference. *Language and Speech* 39: 265–304.

Walker, Marilyn A., Elisabeth Maier, James Allen, Jean Carletta, Sherri Condon, Giovanni Flammia, Julia Hirschberg, Steve Isard, Masato Ishizaki, Lori Levin, Susann Luperfoy, David Traum, and Steve Whittaker. (1996). *Penn Multiparty Standard Coding Scheme: Draft Annotation Manual*. Available at http://www.cis.upenn.edu/~ircs/discourse-tagging/newcoding.html.

Walker, Marilyn A. and Ellen F. Prince. (1996). A bilateral approach to givenness: A Hearer-Status algorithm and a Centering algorithm. In Fretheim and Gundel (eds.), 291–306.

Walker, Marilyn A., Aravind K. Joshi, and Ellen F. Prince (eds.). (1998). *Centering Theory in Discourse*. Oxford: Oxford University Press.

Walker, Ralph. (1975). Conversational implicatures. In S. Blackburn (ed.), *Meaning, Reference, and Necessity*, 133–81. Cambridge: Cambridge University Press.

Ward, Gregory. (1988). *The Semantics and Pragmatics of Preposing*. New York: Garland.

Ward, Gregory. (1990). The discourse functions of VP preposing. *Language* 66: 742–63.

Ward, Gregory and Betty J. Birner. (1995). Definiteness and the English existential. *Language* 71: 722–42.

Ward, Gregory and Betty J. Birner. (2002). Information structure. In G. Pullum and R. Huddleston (eds.), *The Cambridge Grammar of English*, Chapter 14, 1363–1447. Cambridge: Cambridge University Press.

Ward, Gregory and Julia Hirschberg. (1985). Implicating uncertainty: The pragmatics of fall–rise intonation. *Language* 61: 747–76.

Ward, Gregory and Julia Hirschberg. (1988). Intonation and propositional attitude: The pragmatics of L*+H L H%. In *Proceedings of the Fifth Eastern States Conference on Linguistics (ESCOL '88)*, 512–22.

Ward, Gregory and Ellen F. Prince. (1991). On the topicalization of indefinite NPs. *Journal of Pragmatics* 16: 167–77.

Warnke, Volker, Ralf Kompe, Heinrich Niemann, and Elmar Noeth. (1997). Integrated dialog act segmentation and classification using prosodic features and language models. *EUROSPEECH-97* 1: 207–10. Rhodes, Greece.

Warnock, G. J. (1973). Some types of performative utterance. In I. Berlin (ed.), *Essays on J. L. Austin*, 69–89. Oxford: Oxford University Press.

Wason, P. C. (1961). Response to affirmative and negative binary statements. *British Journal of Psychology* 52: 133–42.

Wason, P. C. (1965). The contexts of plausible denial. *Journal of Verbal Learning and Verbal Behavior* 4: 7–11.

Wason, P. C. (1966). Reasoning. In B. M. Foss (ed.), *New Horizons in Psychology*, 135–51. Harmondsworth: Penguin.

Wason, P. C. (1972). In real life negatives are false. *Logique et Analyse* 15: 17–38.

Wason, P. C. and Philip Johnson-Laird. (1972). *Psychology of Reasoning: Structure and Content*. Cambridge, MA: Harvard University Press.

Watts, Richard, Sachiko Ide, and Konrad Ehlich (eds.). (1992). *Politeness in Language: Studies in its History, Theory and Practice.* Berlin: Mouton de Gruyter.

Webber, Bonnie Lynn. (1978). A Formal Approach to Discourse Anaphora. PhD dissertation, Harvard University. Reprinted New York: Garland, 1979.

Webber, Bonnie Lynn. (1986). Two steps closer to event reference. Technical Report CIS-86-75, Department of Computer and Information Science, University of Pennsylvania.

Webber, Bonnie Lynn. (1988). Tense as discourse anaphor. *Computational Linguistics* 14: 61–73.

Webber, Bonnie Lynn. (1991). Structure and ostension in the interpretation of discourse deixis. *Language and Cognitive Processes* 6: 107–35.

Webber, Bonnie Lynn, Alistair Knott, Matthew Stone, and Aravind Joshi. (1999). Discourse relations: A structural and presuppositional account using Lexicalized TAG. In *Proceedings of the 37th Annual Meeting of the Association for Computational Linguistics (ACL-99)*, 41–8.

Weber, Elizabeth G. (1993). *Varieties of Questions in English Conversation.* Amsterdam: Benjamins.

Weinreich, Uriel, William Labov, and Marvin I. Herzog. (1968). Empirical foundations for a theory of language change. In W. P. Lehmann and Y. Malkiel (eds.), *Directions for Historical Linguistics: A Symposium*, 97–195. Austin, TX: University of Texas Press.

Weissenborn, Jürgen and Wolfgang Klein. (1982). *Here and There: Cross-linguistic Studies on Deixis and Demonstration.* Amsterdam: Benjamins.

Welker, Kate. (1994). Plans in the Common Ground: Toward a Generative Account of Implicature. PhD dissertation, Ohio State University.

Werner, Heinz and Bernard Kaplan. (1963). *Symbol Formation.* New York: John Wiley.

Westerståhl, Dag. (1985). Determiners and context sets. In van Benthem and ter Meulen, (eds.), 45–72.

Wettstein, Howard. (1981). Demonstrative reference and definite descriptions. *Philosophical Studies* 40: 241–57. Reprinted in Ostertag (ed.), 256–73.

Wettstein, Howard. (1984). How to bridge the gap between meaning and reference. *Synthèse* 58: 63–84. Reprinted in S. Davis (ed., 1991), 160–74.

Wharton, Tim. (2001). Natural pragmatics and natural codes. *UCL Working Papers in Linguistics* 13: 109–58.

Wharton, Tim (in press). Interjections, language and the "showing"/"saying" continuum. *Pragmatics and Cognition.*

Wharton, Tim (in preparation). Pragmatics and the Showing–Saying Distinction. PhD dissertation, University College London.

Whitehead, Alfred North and Bertrand Russell. (1910). *Principia Mathematica.* Reprinted (in part) as *Principia Mathematica to *56.* Cambridge: Cambridge University Press, 1964.

Whiten, Andrew (ed.). (1991). *Natural Theories of Mind: Evolution, Development and Simulation of Everyday Mindreading.* Oxford: Basil Blackwell.

Wierzbicka, Anna. (1986). The semantics of "internal dative" in English. *Quaderni di semantica* 7: 121–35.

Wierzbicka, Anna. (1987). *English Speech Act Verbs: A Semantic Dictionary.* Sydney: Academic Press.

Wilcock, Graham. (1999). Lexicalization of context. In G. Webelhuth, J.-P. Koenig, and A. Kathol (eds.), *Lexical and Constructional Aspects of Linguistic Explanation*, 373–87. Stanford, CA: CSLI.

Wilensky, Robert. (1983). *Planning and Understanding: A Computational Approach to Human Reasoning.* Reading, MA: Addison-Wesley.

Wilensky, Robert. (1991). Extending the lexicon by exploiting subregularities. Unpublished manuscript. EECS, Computer Science Division, University of California at Berkeley.

Wilensky, Robert, David N. Chin, Marc Luria, James Martin, James Mayfield, and Dekai Wu. (1988). The Berkeley UNIX Consultant Project. *Computational Linguistics* 14: 35–84.

Wilkes-Gibbs, Deanna. (1986). Collaborative Processes of Language Use in Conversation. PhD dissertation, Stanford University, CA.

Wilkins, David. (1992). Interjections as deictics. *Journal of Pragmatics* 17: 119–58.

Wilkins, David. (1996). Natural tendencies of semantic change and the search for cognates. In M. Durie and M. Ross (eds.), *The Comparative Method Revisited*, 264–304. New York: Oxford University Press.

Wilkins, David and Deborah Hill. (1995). When "GO" means "COME": Questioning the basicness of basic motion verbs. *Cognitive Linguistics* 6: 209–59.

Wilkins, David, Deborah Hill, and Stephen C. Levinson. (1995). Bedeutet KOMMEN und GEHEN in verschiedenen Sprachen immer dasselbe? *Max-Planck-Gesellschaft Jahrbuch*, 307–12. Munich: Max-Planck-Gesellschaft.

Wilkinson, Louise C., Steven Calculator, and Christine Dollaghan. (1982). Ya wanna trade – just for awhile: children's requests and response to peers. *Discourse Processes* 5: 161–76.

Williams, Edwin. (1977). Discourse and logical form. *Linguistic Inquiry* 8: 103–39.

Williams, Edwin. (1997). Blocking and anaphora. *Linguistic Inquiry* 28: 577–628.

Wilson, Deirdre. (1975). *Presupposition and Non-Truth-Conditional Semantics.* New York: Academic Press.

Wilson, Deirdre. (1994a). Relevance and understanding. In G. Brown, K. Malmkjær, A. Pollitt, and J. Williams (eds.), *Language and Understanding*, 35–58. Oxford: Oxford University Press.

Wilson, Deirdre. (1994b). Discourse markers: social and cognitive approaches. Paper delivered at conference on Linguistic Processes in Communication, University of Wales, Bangor.

Wilson, Deirdre. (1998a). Discourse, coherence and relevance: a reply to Rachel Giora. *Journal of Pragmatics* 29: 57–74.

Wilson, Deirdre. (1998b). Linguistic structure and inferential communication. In B. Caron (ed.), *Proceedings of the 16th International Congress of Linguists* (25 July 1997). Amsterdam: Elsevier Sciences.

Wilson, Deirdre. (2000). Metarepresentation in linguistic communication. In Sperber (ed.), 411–48.

Wilson, Deirdre and Tomoko Matsui. (2000). Recent approaches to bridging: Truth, coherence, relevance. In J. de Bustos Tovar, P. Charaudeau, J. Alconchel, S. Iglesias Recuero and C. Lopez Alonso (eds.), *Lengua, Discurso, Texto*, vol. 1: 103–32. Madrid: Visor Libros.

Wilson, Deirdre and Dan Sperber. (1979). Ordered entailments: An alternative to presuppositional theories. In Oh and Dinneen (eds.), 299–323.

Wilson, Deirdre and Dan Sperber. (1981). On Grice's theory of conversation. In P. Werth (ed.), *Conversation and Discourse*, 155–78. London: Croom Helm. Reprinted in Kasher (ed., 1998), vol. IV: 347–68.

Wilson, Deirdre and Dan Sperber. (1986a). Inference and implicature. In C. Travis (ed.), *Meaning and Interpretation*, 45–75. Oxford: Basil Blackwell. Reprinted in S. Davis (ed., 1991), 377–93.

Wilson, Deirdre and Dan Sperber. (1986b). Pragmatics and modularity. *CLS 22, Part 2: Parasession on Pragmatics and Grammatical Theory*, 68–74. Reprinted in S. Davis (ed., 1991), 583–95.

Wilson, Deirdre and Dan Sperber. (1988). Mood and the analysis of non-declarative sentences. In J. Dancy, J. Moravcsik, and C. Taylor (eds.), *Human Agency: Language, Duty and Value*, 77–101. Stanford, CA: Stanford University Press. Reprinted in Kasher (ed., 1998), vol. II: 262–89.

Wilson, Deirdre and Dan Sperber. (1992). On verbal irony. *Lingua* 87: 53–76.

Wilson, Deirdre and Dan Sperber. (1993). Linguistic form and relevance. *Lingua* 90: 1–25.

Wilson, Deirdre and Dan Sperber. (1998). Pragmatics and time. In Carston and Uchida (eds.), 1–22.

Wilson, Deirdre and Dan Sperber. (2002). Truthfulness and relevance. *Mind* 111: 583–632.

Wilson, George M. (1978). On definite and indefinite descriptions. *Philosophical Review* 87: 48–76.

Wilson, George M. (1984). Pronouns and pronominal descriptions: A new semantical category. *Philosophical Studies* 45: 1–30.

Wilson, George M. (1991). Reference and pronominal descriptions. *Journal of Philosophy* 88: 359–87.

Winner, Ellen. (1988). *The Point of Words: Children's Understanding of Metaphor and Irony.* Cambridge, MA: Harvard University Press.

Winograd, Terry. (1972). *Understanding Natural Language.* New York: Academic Press.

Winter, Yoad and Mori Rimon. (1994). Contrast and implication in natural language. *Journal of Semantics* 11: 365–406.

Wittgenstein, Ludwig. (1953). *Philosophical Investigations.* Oxford: Basil Blackwell.

Woisetschlaeger, Erich. (1983). On the question of definiteness in "an old man's book." *Linguistic Inquiry* 14: 137–54.

Wolff, Christian. (1963). *Preliminary Discourse on Philosophy in General.* (R. J. Blackwell, trans.) Indianapolis: Bobbs-Merrill. (Originally published 1728.)

Woodbury, Anthony C. (1987). Rhetorical structure in a central Alaskan Yupik Eskimo traditional narrative. In J. Sherzer and A. Woodbury (eds.), *Native American Discourse: Poetics and Rhetoric*, 176–239. Cambridge: Cambridge University Press.

Woszczyna, Monika and Alex Waibel. (1994). Inferring linguistic structure in spoken language. *Proceedings of the International Conference on Spoken Language Processing (ICSLP-94)*, 847–50. Yokohama.

van der Wouden, Ton. (1994). *Negative Contexts.* Groningen: Groningen Dissertations in Linguistics 12. (Published in revised form as *Negative Contexts: Collocation, Polarity and Multiple Negation.* London: Routledge, 1997.)

Wu, Dejai. (1990). Probabilistic unification-based intergration of syntactic and semantic preferences for nominal compounds. *Proceedings of the 13th International Conference on Computational Linguistics (COLING 90)*, 413–18. Helsinki.

Wurzel, Wolfgang U. (1998). On markedness. *Theoretical Linguistics* 24: 53–71.

Yanofsky, Nancy. (1978). NP utterances. *CLS 14*, 491–502.

Yngve, Victor H. (1970). On getting a word in edgewise. *CLS 6*, 567–78.

Yoshimura, Akiko. (1994). A cognitive constraint on negative polarity phenomena. *BLS* *20*, 599–610.

Yoshimura, Takashi, Satoru Hayamizu, Hiroshi Ohmura, and Kazuyo Tanaka. (1996). Pitch pattern clustering of user utterances in human–machine dialogue. *Proceedings of the International Conference on Spoken Language Processing (ICSLP-96)* 2: 837–40. Philadelphia, PA.

Zacharski, Ron. (1992). Generation of accent in nominally premodified noun phrases. *Papers Presented to the 15th International Conference on Computational Linguistics*, 253–9. Nantes.

Zacharski, Ron. (1993). A Discourse Pragmatics Model of English Accent. PhD dissertation, University of Minnesota.

Zaenen, Annie. (1982). Subjects and other subjects. Bloomington, IN: Indiana University Linguistics Club.

Zeevat, Henk. (1999a). Explaining presupposition triggers. Manuscript AC99. University of Amsterdam, available at http://www.hum.uva.nl/computerlinguistiek/henk/.

Zeevat, Henk. (1999b). Semantics in optimality theory. In de Hoop and de Swart (eds.), 76–87.

Zimmer, Karl. (1964). *Affixal Negation in English and Other Languages*. Supplement to *Word*, monograph no. 5.

Zimmermann, T. Ede. (1991). Kontextabhängigkeit. In D. Wunderlich and A. von Stechow (eds.), *Semantik: Ein internationales Handbuch der zeitgenössischen Forschung*, 156–229. Berlin: Walter de Gruyter.

Zipf, George Kingsley. (1949). *Human Behavior and the Principle of Least Effort*. Cambridge: Addison-Wesley.

Ziv, Yael. (1976). On the Communicative Effect of Relative Clause Extraposition in English. PhD dissertation, University of Illinois, Urbana.

Ziv, Yael. (1998). Hebrew *kaze* as discourse marker and lexical hedge: Conceptual and procedural properties. In Jucker and Ziv (eds.), 203–23.

Ziv, Yael and Barbara Grosz. (1994). Right dislocation and attentional state. *Israeli Association for Theoretical Linguistics* 9: 184–99.

Zribi-Hertz, Anne. (1989). Anaphor binding and narrative point of view: English reflexive pronouns in sentence and discourse. *Language* 65: 695–727.

Zukow, Patricia G. (1986). The relationship between interaction with the caregiver and the emergence of play activities during the one-word period. *British Journal of Developmental Psychology* 4: 223–34.

Zwarts, Frans. (1996a). Three types of polarity. In F. Hamm and E. Hinrichs (eds.), *Plural Quantification*, 177–238. Dordrecht: Foris.

Zwarts, Frans. (1996b). A hierarchy of negative expressions. In H. Wansing (ed.), *Negation: A Notion in Focus*, 169–94. Berlin: Walter de Gruyter.

Zwicky, Arnold M. and Jerrold M. Sadock. (1975). Ambiguity tests and how to fail them. In J. P. Kimball (ed.), *Syntax and Semantics 4*, 1–35. New York: Academic Press.

Index

a, 377
Abbott, B., 125, 136, 148 n6
abduction, 724–41
  coherence, 244
  context, 217
  explanations, 549, 727–32
  interpretation as abduction (IA),
    731–40
  language and knowledge, 724–5
  logic as language of thought, 725–6
  non-monotonic logic, 726–7
  relevance theory, 739–40
  weighted abduction, 731
abnormality conditions, 726–7
aboutness, 74–5
accepts, 599
access principle, 662–3
accommodation,
  context, 214, 478
  presupposition, 36, 41, 45–6, 47, 50, 51,
    134–5, 730
Ackerman, F., 438
acknowledgments, 64, 372, 467, 484 n4
action schemas, 583–4
activated referents, 388
adjacency pairs, 370
adjective phrase preposing, 417
adjectives, 492, 495–7, 499–500, 501
adverb preposing, 417
adverbs, "subcategorized," 439–40
affective dimension, 65
affectivity, 711

affordances, 106
after all, 553–60
  diachronic development, 556–60
  present-day situation, 554–6
agreements, 587, 595, 596, 599
AI *see* artificial intelligence
AIS *see* Algorithm Is Sufficient
Ajjanagadde, V., 741
Akan, 294
Akmajian, A., 677
Alexandersson, J., 598
Algorithm Is Sufficient (AIS), 280–3,
  287 n18
Allan, K., 56
Allen, J., 581, 583, 584, 593
Allen, S., 437
Allwood, J., 596
Alston, W., 62–3
ambiguity, 36–8
  avoidance, 300–1
anaphora, 288–314, 313 n1
  deep and surface anaphora, 385–6,
    402–3 nn4–5
  definition, 288–9
  Dowty–Reinhart analysis, 300–1
  generative approaches to binding,
    289–96
  indexicality, 101, 103, 119
  Levinson–Huang analysis, 301–4
  neo-Gricean pragmatic theory, 296–300
  pitch accent and, 528–9
  revised theory, 304–10, 312–13

so, 383, 384, 394–7, 403 n11
  unexpectedness, 310–12
  verb-phrase ellipsis, 391–4
and, 18–19, 232, 236, 479–80
Andersen, E., 573
Anderson, A., 590, 591*t*, 593
Anderson, S., 116, 117
Annamalai, E., 296
anomaly, 495, 502–3, 506
Anscombre, J.-C., 227–9, 699 n25
antonymy, 703
Anttila, A., 507
Anttila, R., 550
any, 414–15, 717, 720
applied pragmatics, 478–84
  assertion fallacy, 479
  logical expressions, 479–84, 486 nn23–4
  speech act fallacy, 478–9
appreciations, 598
Apresjan, J., 350, 353
argument structure, 427–41
  argument omission, 434–7, 441 n8
  information structure, 429–30, 433–4,
    441 nn3–6
  obligatory adjuncts, 437–40, 441 n10
  Preferred Argument Structure, 430–2
  sentence focus (SF) constructions,
    432–3
  terminology, 427–8
Argumentation Theory (AT), 227–9,
  240 n9, 723 n2
Ariel, M., 122, 123, 137
Aristotle, 14
Arnold, J., 433, 441 n3
Arnovick, L., 538
Aronoff, M., 501
artificial intelligence (AI), 73, 724, 725,
  726–7, 729
  see also computational linguistics
Asher, N., 210, 216, 245, 263 n4
asides, 375–6
assertion, 26 n5, 31–3, 37, 46–7, 50,
  51–2 n3
assertion fallacies, 479
assessments, 595
AT *see* Argumentation Theory
at all, 710, 719
at least, 681–3, 698 n15
Atkins, B., 350, 362 n15

Atlas, J., 18, 34–8, 39, 40, 41–2, 44, 45, 48,
  51, 52 n5, 503, 714, 718–19
attention, 102, 106, 180, 193 n8, 563–5
Austin, J., 54–8, 59, 62, 64, 66, 443,
  462 n2, 463, 464, 466, 469, 484 n4,
  671
Van der Auwera, J., 545
Avesani, C., 531
Avoid Synonymy, 501
avoidance ambiguity, 300–1
Axia, G., 575
Ayers, G., 531

Bach, E., 402 n1
Bach, K., 6, 8, 21, 22, 28 n15, 28 n17,
  63–4, 70, 73, 92, 131, 226–7, 229,
  452, 482, 484 n2, 484–5 n4,
  485–6 nn14–15, 640, 641, 650–1,
  654 n1, 654 n5
back-channels, 587, 595, 599
Baker, C., 311, 713, 740
Ball, C., 195 n21
Ballmer, T., 65
Ban on Conflicting Empathy Foci, 316,
  317, 318
Bar-Hillel, Y., xi, 445, 446
Barcan Marcus, R., 85
Barcelona, A., 550
Bard, E., 530
Baroni, M., 575
Barsalou, L., 618
Barton, E., 267, 276
Barwise, J., 130, 139, 140–1, 142–3,
  149 n10, 160, 452
basic markers, 223
Bates, E., 574–5
BDI model *see* plan inference (BDI)
  model of speech act interpretation
because, 229, 232
behabitives, 64, 467, 484 n4
Bell, A., 595
Benveniste, E., 550
Berg, J., 649
Berlin, B., 72
Bertolet, R., 70, 95
binding theory, 327, 332–6, 342–3 n9
  condition A, 289, 290–2, 293–5, 302,
    391–2
  condition B, 289, 292–5, 302, 308

binding theory (*cont'd*)
  condition C, 289, 295–6, 302, 391–2
  principle A, 338
  principle B, 338, 339
  principle C, 331, 332–40
  problems, 290–6
  semantic/argument-structure
    approach, 289–90
  syntactic/geometric approach, 289,
    314 n5
Birner, B., 93, 122, 131, 136, 158, 165, 171,
  185
Black, B., 578, 581, 588
Blackburn, W., 129–30
Blakemore, D., 223, 224, 227, 230, 231,
  237, 238–9, 554
Bland, S., 180
Blass, R., 238, 554, 559
Blutner, R., 496, 505, 507
Boër, S., 39, 68, 477
Boersma, P., 512
Bohnemeyer, J., 115
Bolinger, D., 73, 136–7, 184, 518, 533
Borg, E., 649, 652–3
bottom-up process, 459–60
boundary tones, 516
Brazilian Portuguese, 435, 436
break index tier, 516
break indices, 516, 516*f*, 517*f*
Bréal, M., 539, 550
Breheny, R., 654 n5
Brennenstuhl, W., 65
bridging, 135
Brinton, L., 539
Briscoe, T., 350, 352, 356, 362 n20,
  503
Bromberger, S., 274
Brown, G., 530, 531, 532
Brown, P., 71, 436
Buchler, J., 367
Bühler, K., 102, 103, 111
Bunt, H., 578, 581, 588
Burge, T., 128, 129
Büring, D., 182, 194 n17
Burzio, L., 293, 294, 295, 309, 310
but, 223, 224, 225–8, 231, 233, 235, 236,
  458–9
Butterworth, B., 531
by, 169–70

Cacoullous, R., 441 n8
Cahn, J., 529
Campbell, J., 8
cancelability, 38–9
Carberry, S., 286 n9
Carletta, J., 593
Carlson, G., 139
Carlson, L., 209
Carnap, R., 444–6
Carroll, J., 14
Carston, R., 14, 230, 237, 455, 457, 480,
  654 n5, 656 n10
categorical statements, 144
causal theory of names, 86–7
Centering Theory, 180, 202
CG *see* common ground
Chafe, W., 177, 378, 382 n8, 436
Chao, W., 253
Chao, Y. R., 175
charity, 451
Charniak, E., 729, 730, 731, 732, 740
Chastain, C., 145
checks, 580, 593, 594, 595, 598
Chierchia, G., 13
Chinese, 372
  anaphora, 290, 291, 295, 303, 304, 312
  argument ellipsis, 436
  definiteness, 148 n2
  language acquisition, 576
  tense, 115
  topic, 175, 186
Chomsky, N., 60, 75, 96, 158, 176, 236,
  288, 289, 312, 313 n2, 314 n5, 327,
  332, 336, 421, 700 n40
Chouinard, M., 564, 565
Christophersen, P., 131, 132
Chu-Carroll, J., 536, 601
Church, A., 88
circumscriptive reference, 399
Clark, E., 349, 350, 564, 565
Clark, H., 132, 349, 350
Clarke, D., 561 n8
cleft, 417
Clines, F., 12
cognitive linguistics, 657–74
  cognitive dimensions, 65
  cognitive status, 137, 387–8, 403 n8
  deferred interpretation, 359 n1
  opacity and presuppositions, 661–6

performatives, 671–3
pragmatic scales, 673–4
relevance theory, 608–10, 625–8
Turner's *xyz* constructions, 659–61, 659*f*, 661*f*
word and sentence meanings, 666–71
Cognitive Principle of Relevance, 610, 625–6
Cohen, L. J., 19, 480, 646, 656 n10
Cohen, P., 73, 260, 581, 584
coherence *see* discourse coherence; discourse markers: and coherence
coherence constraint, 241
coherence relations, 234, 244–5, 734–6
  Cause–Effect relations, 247–8, 391, 392
  Contiguity relations, 250–1
  descriptive adequacy, 244
  extraction from conjoined clauses, 254–6, 264–5 nn13–15
  neo-Humean classification, 246–51
  Occasion, 242–3, 246, 250
  Parallel, 242, 246, 248, 263 n6, 391
  pronominal reference, 257–60
  psychological plausibility, 244
  Resemblance relations, 248–50, 263 nn6–7, 390–1, 392–3
  Result, 241–2, 246, 247, 391
cohesion, 232–4
come, 117–18
comment *see* topic and focus: terminology
commentary markers, 223
commissives, 64, 467
common ground (CG),
  context, 205, 208, 209, 214, 215, 219 n18
  implicature, 504
  language acquisition, 563–4, 565–6
  language performance, 371–2
  presupposition, 41, 42, 43, 44–8
  questions, 209, 219 n14
communication,
  aboutness, 74–5
  collateral system, 366, 381
  communicative intentions, 53, 469–70, 485 nn7–8
  communicative speech acts, 63, 469, 485 n6
  indexicality, 97–9

intention, inference, and relevance, 470–2
language acquisition, 562–3
non-literal, 269–70
ostensive-inferential, 611, 628 n5
presumption of optimal relevance, 230, 612, 613
primary system, 366
relevance theory, 472, 485 n12, 610–14, 629 n9
silence, 613
communicative presumption, 63–4
Communicative Principle of Relevance, 612, 613, 626
comparatives, 677, 689
complementizer choice, 410
composition, transfer in, 354–6, 362–3 nn19–21
compositionality, 492, 495–8, 506
comprehension,
  relevance and, 226, 614–23
  semantic/pragmatic distinction, 634–5
  subtasks, 615
computational linguistics, 578–604
  coherence relations, 244–5
  computational models, 579
  cue-based model of speech act interpretation, 580–1, 587–603, 604
  cues, 594–6
  plan inference (BDI) model of speech act interpretation, 580, 581–7, 603–4
  Rhetorical Structure Theory (RST), 245
  speech act interpretation, 578–81
Comrie, B., 116, 311
conceptual blending, 667–8, 667*f*
concomitants, 379–81
concretion, 730
conditional perfection, 498
conjoined clauses, 254–6, 264–5 nn13–15
conjunct constraint, 254
conjunctions, 233–4
  see also and; but; so
considerably, 710
consistency, 41
constatives, 54, 55, 56–7, 464
constitutive rules, 60–1, 465
content, 366, 367
  presupposed, 209
  proferred, 209

content (*cont'd*)
  reference, 94–6
  see also context/content distinction
context, 197–220
  abduction, 217
  affordances, 106
  common ground, 205, 208, 209, 214,
    215, 219 n18
  context, semantics, and pragmatics,
    197–9, 476–7, 486 n20
  de dicto contexts, 78, 79, 80, 82, 83
  de re contexts, 78, 81
  dynamic interpretation, 203–7
  felicity, 199–202, 206
  indexicality, 90
  intentions in interpretation (language
    game), 207–17
  narrow context, 477
  relevance, 216, 219 n20
  role in interpretation, 90, 197–8, 452–3,
    476–7, 486 n20
  situational context, 384
  update, 199, 201, 202
  wide context, 477
  see also context/content distinction
context change potential, 204, 206, 478
Context Change Semantics, 205, 206, 478
context/content distinction, 46, 48–50, 51
context propositions, 676
context set, 130, 208
contextual implication, 608
contextual parameters, 280–3
continuers, 372
contradiction, 702
contradictories, 11
contraries, 11
contrariety, 702–3
contrast, 211–12, 213, 311–12, 567–9
convention, 567–9
conventional implicature *see under*
    implicature
conventional pragmatics, 428
conversational implicature,
  and abduction, 730
  definition, 50
  exploitation, 8
  generalized/particularized dichotomy,
    4–6, 25–6 n2, 26 n4, 477, 486 n22
  and lexical pragmatics, 490, 503–6, 507

maxims, 7–8, 9, 13, 27 nn7–8, 34, 201,
    208–9, 471, 540–1
  pragmatic licensing, 505, 507
  presupposition, 41–4
  relevance-theoretic view, 643–8
  short-circuited, 13
  speaker meaning and inference, 6–8,
    424
  see also explicit/implicit distinction;
    implicature
conversational pragmatics, 428
Cooper, R., 139, 140–1, 142–3, 149 n10
Cooper, W., 525
Cooperative Principle, 7, 8, 24, 28 n17,
    297, 471, 613
Coordinate Structure Constraint (CSC),
    254–6, 264 n13
Copestake, A., 350, 352, 356, 362 n20, 503
Core, M., 593
Corrective Sentence Pattern
    Requirement, 321–2, 340 n2
correspondence theory of meaning, 74
Coulson, S., 663, 667, 670, 674
Cox, P., 729
Criscuolo, G., 727
Cruse, A., 703
CSC *see* Coordinate Structure Constraint
cue-based model of speech act
    interpretation, 580–1, 587–603, 604
  cue-based algorithms, 597–603, 600f,
    601f
  cues, 594–6
  dialogue acts, 588–90, 591–2t, 593
  speech acts, 588
cue markers *see* discourse markers
cues, 594–6
Culy, C., 311
Curl, T., 595
Cutler, A., 587

Dale, R., 234, 244
Dalrymple, M., 251, 252, 383, 392, 395
DAMSL (Dialogue Act Markup in
    Several Layers), 588–90
Dative Incorporation, 326, 342 n7
Davidson, D., 280
Davies, M., 130
Davis, W., 26 n4, 28 n19
Davison, A., 67, 68

De Morgan, A., 9
declarative sentences, 417
deferred interpretation (deference),
    344–64, 359 n1
  conceptual relations, 345–6, 359–60 n3
  deferred indexical reference, 361 n7,
    361 n10
  definition, 344
  figuration, 344–5, 359 n2, 549–50, 561 n8
  meaning transfer, 346–8, 360–1 nn5–8
  noteworthiness, 349–50, 353, 354, 355,
    361 n9, 362 nn11–12, 363 nn22–3
  as pragmatic phenomenon, 344–5
  predicate transfer in systematic
    polysemy, 350–1, 357, 362 n15
  semantics or pragmatics?, 351–4
  "sortal crossings," 357–9, 363–4 n24
  transfer in composition, 354–6,
    362–3 nn19–21
deferred ostension, 105
definiteness and indefiniteness, 122–49,
    148 nn1–3
  accessibility, 137
  definites, 110–11, 112, 122–3
  existential sentences, 138–44
  false definites, 165, 166
  familiarity, 132–7, 148 n7
  grammatical definiteness, 136
  indefinites, 122, 123–4, 145
  novelty, 134
  specificity, 144–7, 149 n17
  uniqueness, 125–32, 135–7, 148 n4
definites, 110–11, 112, 122–3
deictic origo, 102, 103, 111, 112
deixis, 97–121
  demonstrative systems, 107–11, 108*f*
  expressions, 103–7, 112
  fields, 111–21
  and indexicality, 97, 100–1, 675–6, 687,
    697 n1
  terminology, 97
  see also discourse markers; indexicality
Dekker, Paul, 147, 508, 513 n10
demonstratives, 98–9, 102–3, 107–11,
    108*f*, 112, 116–17, 128, 453–4
described situation, 104
descriptions, theory of, 82–4
  de dicto contexts, 82, 83
  incomplete descriptions, 128–31, 148 n5

"non-unique" definite descriptions,
    131–2, 148 n6
  presuppositionality, 126–7
  quantificational phrases, 482–3
  reference, 92, 127–8, 486 n25
  uniqueness, 125–6, 148 n4
descriptive meaning, 457–8
descriptive semantics, 444–5
Descriptor Empathy Hierarchy, 316,
    317
determiners, 110–11, 112, 142
Devin, J., 573
diachronic pragmatics, 538–9
dialogue acts, 588–90, 591–2*t*, 593
dictionaries, 345, 351, 362 n15
Diesing, M., 143, 145
Diessel, H., 107, 108–9, 112, 117
van Dijk, T., 245–6
Dionysius of Halicarnassus, 18–19
direct discourse perspective, 329–40
direct entailment, 31
direction of fit, 65
directives, 467
discourse coherence, 241–65, 263 n1
  coherence relations, 234, 243–6, 390–1,
    734–6
  computational linguistics perspectives,
    244–5
  discourse markers, 232–9
  informational coherence, 260–1
  intentional coherence, 260–1
  linguistic case studies, 251–60
  neo-Humean classification, 246–60
  psycholinguistics perspectives, 245–6
  theoretical linguistics perspectives,
    243–4
discourse connectives *see* discourse
    markers
discourse cues, 596
discourse deixis, 118–19
discourse entities, xii, 96
discourse function of gapping, 390
discourse markers (DM), 221–40
  Argumentation Theory, 227–9, 240 n9,
    723 n2
  and coherence, 232–9
  as conventional implicatures, 222–7
  intonation and accent, 532
  meaning, 222–32

discourse markers (DM) (*cont'd*)
  Relevance Theory, 229–31, 237, 238, 239
  terminology, 221–2, 223, 239
discourse model, 384
discourse-new, 386–7, 429
discourse-old, 132, 386–7, 429
discourse operators *see* discourse markers
discourse particles *see* discourse markers
discourse referents, 205–6, 215, 216
Discourse Representation Theories, 205, 206, 216, 219 n21
discourse segments, 399
discourse-status, 386–7
discourse structure, 416–20, 425 n8, 734–7
disjoint reference presumption, 303
display, 367–9
Division of Pragmatic Labor, 16–17, 27 n12, 509, 510, 542
Dixon, R., 113, 430, 439
DM *see* discourse markers
doctrine of infelicities, 56–7
dolphin-safe etc., 669
domain goals, 210, 215
donkey sentences, 132–4, 148 n8, 203–5
Donnellan, K., 85, 86, 92–3, 127–8, 129–30, 146, 482
Donno So, 311
Downing, P., 349
Dowty, D., 300–1, 354
Doyle, J., 9, 726
Dretske, F., 190
Du Bois, J., 131, 132, 430, 431, 436, 441 n1
Ducrot, O., 227–9, 459, 673, 698 n24, 699 n25
Dummett, M., 80
Dutch, 235, 291, 307, 716
dynamic interpretation, 203–7
Dynamic Montague Grammar, 205, 267, 287 n15

Eady, S., 525
echoic use, 621
effective dimension, 65
effectives, 467
elaboration/set-member, 213
element constraint, 254

ellipsis,
  argument omission, 436–7, 441 n8
  non-sentences, 272–9
  semantic, 274, 275, 277–9, 287 n15
  syntactic, 273–4, 275–9, 286–7 nn11–14, 640–1
  verb phrase ellipsis, 251–4, 263–4 nn8–12, 276, 383, 384, 391–4, 403 n10
elliptically speaking, 272–3, 275, 286 n9
Elugardo, R., 276, 287 n16, 641, 655 n6
emblems, 380
empathy, 316
empathy perspective, 315–28
  principles, 315–25
  and reflexive pronouns, 326–8
emphaticness, 311–12
Enç, M., 106, 116, 145
entailment, 6, 26n5, 34, 41
  direct entailment, 31
  first background entailment (FBE), 390
  ordered entailment, 390
  pragmatic entailments, 704
  presupposition, 31–3, 34, 41, 43, 52 n4
  scalar, 704
Erteschik-Shir, N., 180, 193–4 n8, 434
Ervin-Tripp, S., 563, 574
Evans, G., 86, 87, 296
even, 4, 697 n9, 716, 723 n2
event reference, 383–402
  constraints in discourse, 384–8
  eventualities, 383, 388–401, 402 n1
  terminology, 383, 402 n1
Ewe, 118
exclamatives, 594
exercitives, 64
existential sentences, 138
  generalized quantifier approach, 140–1
  Keenan's analysis, 142
  presuppositionality, 142–4, 149 nn13–14
  weak/strong distinction, 138–40
explicature, 19–21, 473–4
  ad hoc concept construction, 641–3
  comprehension, 614–15, 617, 620, 623, 629 n10, 630 n18
  definition, 635, 654 n4
  disambiguation, 636–8, 733–4
  free enrichment, 639–41, 654–5 n5

saturation, 636–8
semantics, and "What is said," 648–53,
    656 n11
explicit/implicit distinction, 633–56
    conversational implicatures, 643–5,
        655 n8
    decoding/inferring, 634–6, 654 n2,
        654 n4
    explicature or "generalized"
        conversational implicature?, 645–8,
        655–6 nn9–10
    see also explicature
exploitation, 8
expositives, 64
expression types, 269, 448
extraposition, 166–8, 173, 413, 417,
    420

factive presuppositions, 34–6
fake, 670–1
falsity, 57
Faltz, L., 294
familiar referents, 388
familiarity, 132, 148 n7
    assumed familiarity, 154, 155–6
    donkey sentences, 132–4, 148 n8
    unfamiliar definites and
        accommodation, 134–5
    and uniqueness, 135–7
Farley, P., 255
Farmer, A., 303
Fauconnier, G., 12, 350, 360 n6, 663, 667,
    668, 669, 670, 673, 704, 711, 712–13
FBE (first background entailment), 390
felicity, 199–202, 206
Fellbaum, C., 439
few, 719, 720, 721
Fiengo, R., 264 n12
figuration, 344–5, 359 n2, 549–50, 561 n8,
    587, 619, 621, 738
Fijian, 113, 292
File Change Semantics, 133–4
fillers, 376
Fillmore, C., 103, 114, 144, 145, 354,
    362 n15, 697 n2, 698 n11, 700 n33
final lowering, 532
Finnish, 183, 185
first background entailment (FBE), 390
Flaubert triggers, 719

focus, 176, 193 n3, 428
    information structure, 157–8
    information vs. contrastive, 181–3,
        194 n14
    interpretation, 213, 219 n15
    and intonation, 161, 182, 183–5,
        194 n16, 195 n18, 530–2
    preposing, 160–1, 173–4 nn4–5
    see also topic and focus
Fodor, Janet, 145, 146, 147
Fodor, Jerry, 281, 488–9, 491, 492, 624
Fogelin, R., 15
Fong, V., 507
force indicators, 268, 269
formal semantics, 222, 442–3
foundational semantics, 445
Van Fraassen, B., 31, 32
Frajzyngier, Z., 311
Francis, W. N., 163, 166, 169, 392
Fraser, B., 65, 222, 223–4, 232, 555, 686
free enrichment, 460, 639–41, 654–5 n5
free variable view, 496–7
Frege, G., 29–33, 51–2 n3, 76–82, 99,
    126–7, 442, 474, 487 n25, 492
Freidin, R., 336
French,
    acknowledgments, 372
    anaphora, 295
    après tout, 554
    argument structure, 430, 432
    discourse markers, 227
    negation, 699 n25
    polarity, 703, 716
    polysemy, 353, 362 n17
Fretheim, T., 183, 188, 195 n23, 196 n25
Frisian, 308
From-Old-To-New Principle, 326, 342 n5,
    342 n7
functional view, 496
fundamental frequency, 516

Gabbay, D., 147
Von der Gabelentz, G., 175
gapping, 262, 383, 384, 388–91, 402 n2
Gawron, M., 265 n15
Gazdar, G., 424, 425, 446, 656 n10
Geach, P., 85, 133, 203
Geis, M., 498, 499, 513 n4, 540, 552
generalized quantifiers, 139–41

German,
 aber/sondern, 699 n25
 acknowledgments, 372
 anaphora, 292
 argument structure, 430
 deixis, 116, 120
 ellipsis, 277
 polarity, 72, 703
 weil, 553
gesture,
 collateral gestures, 379–81
 iconic gestures, 380
 indexicality, 91–2, 96 n1, 98, 102–3,
  108–10, 108*f*, 111
 language acquisition, 98–9, 102, 110,
  569–70
 pointing, 91–2, 96 n1, 98, 102–3, 111,
  226, 569–70
Geurts, B., 655 n9
Gibson, J., 106, 121 n1
Gigerenzer, G., 624
Ginzburg, J., 208
Given A generalization, 430–2
Givenness Hierarchy, 137, 177, 387–8
given–new distinctions, 176–9, 529–30
Givón, T., 436, 706–7
Glucksberg, S., 631 n21
go, 118
Gödel, K., 88
Godfrey, J., 593
Goffman, E., 373–4
Goldberg, A., 435, 438
Goldman, R., 731, 732
Goldsmith, J., 255
Golinkoff, R., 562
Goodwin, C., 380, 588, 595
Goodwin, M., 380
Gordon, D., 69, 422, 580, 581
gradable adjectives, 499–501
Graff, D., 148 n3
grammar, 407–26, 441 n1
 belief/attitude/value cases, 412–16
 constructional approaches, 675, 697 n5,
  700 n40; *see also* grammatical
  constructions
 discourse structure, 416–20, 425 n8
 extraposition, 420
 heavy NP shift, 420–1
 illustrative phenomena, 408–12, 425 n5

microgrammar, 588, 595
 pragmatic information, 407–8, 409*f*,
  476
 speech acts and, 66–8
 syntactic constructions, 421–5,
  426 nn14–16
 Transformational Grammar (TG), 66
 universal grammar, 254
grammatical constructions, 675–700
 illocutionary forces and speaker
  attitudes, 677, 692–6, 700 n34
 metalinguistic constructions, 687–92
 non-scalar contextual operators
  (NSCOs), 683–7
 and pragmatics, 675–8, 696, 697 n5,
  700 n40
 scalar models, 676, 678–83, 698 n11,
  704, 723 n1
grammaticalization, 441 n1
Green, G., 424
Greenlandic Eskimo, 353
 see also West Greenlandic
Gregory, M., 430
Grice, H. P.,
 on implicature, 3–4, 6, 7, 10, 14, 15, 18,
  24, 25, 26–7 n6, 26 n3, 28 n15, 43, 91,
  224, 269, 297, 458, 468, 474, 476, 540,
  621, 623–4, 636–7, 648–9, 730
 logic and conversation, 422, 479–80,
  498
 on metaphor, 344–5
 philosophy of language, 462 n2
 on presupposition, xi, 33, 34, 36–9,
  42–5, 47, 48
 on speech act theory, 58–62, 470–1,
  472–3, 485 n7, 551, 607
 theory of meaning, 102, 197, 207–8,
  297, 443, 463, 479, 484 n1
Grimm, Hannelore, 571
grinding, 350, 352, 353–4, 362 n17, 502–3
Groenendijk, J., 205, 210
Grosu, A., 254
Grosz, B., 216, 257, 261, 532
ground *see* topic and focus: terminology
grounding, 371–2, 565
Guha, R. V., 740
Guindon, R., 246
Gundel, J., 137, 148 n2, 176, 177, 178–9,
  180, 182, 185, 187–8, 190, 192,

194 n15, 195 n22, 387–8, 397, 399, 400–1, 403 n8

Haiman, J., 666
Halliday, M., 176, 190, 232–4, 243, 428, 525, 526
Hamilton, W., 9
Han, C.-H., 73
Hankamer, J., 286 n12, 385–6, 389, 391, 393, 394, 402 n4
Hardt, D., 392
Harnish, R., 8, 15, 63–4, 65, 70, 73, 303, 484 n2, 484–5 n4, 486 n23
Harris, Z., 236
Hasan, R., 232–4, 243
Haspelmath, M., 123, 145, 148 n2, 723 n7
Hawkins, J., 126, 130, 136
Hayes, B., 512
hearer-new, 386–7
hearer-old, 386–7
hearer-status, 386–7
heavy NP shift, 417, 420–1
Hebrew, 307, 430, 435
Hedberg, N., 186
hedges, 689–90, 691–2, 699 n29, 699–700 n31
Heim, I., 132–4, 135, 136, 148 n8, 203, 204, 205, 206
Henderson, J., 117
Hernandez, J., 441 n8
Hewitt, C., 726
hiatus, 375
Hidden Markov Models (HMMs), 601–3
Higginbotham, J., 653
Hill, D., 117
Himmelmann, N., 116
Hindi, 435, 441 n9
Hindle, D., 524
Hintikka, J., 73, 95, 462 n3, 583
Hirschberg, J., 12, 173–4 n4, 530, 531–2, 536, 595–6, 723 n1
Hirst, G., 733
historical discourse analysis, 539
historical pragmatics, 538–61
  case study: *after all*, 553–60
  language change perspective, 548–52
  synchronic perspective, 540–8, 560
HMMs *see* Hidden Markov Models

Hobbs, J., 217, 229, 238, 241, 244, 246, 250, 257, 263 nn4–5, 730, 731, 740
Hockett, C., 98, 112
Hoffmann, M., 3
holism, 451
honorifics, 119–21, 547, 548
de Hoop, H., 145
Horace, 14
Horn, L., 3, 45, 52 nn4–5, 143–4, 149 n15, 237, 305, 409, 414, 416, 499, 503–4, 510, 541–5, 552, 655 n9, 673, 687–9, 698–9 nn24–25, 703, 705, 706, 708, 714, 723 n5
Horn scales, 703, 704
Hornstein, N., 75
Householder, F., 501
Hovy, E., 234
Huang, Y., 291, 301–4, 306
Huddleston, R., 167
Humanness Empathy Hierarchy, 316
Hume, D., 246
Hungarian, 576
Hyman, L., 311

I principle, 298, 299, 300, 302–4, 305–10, 546–8
IA *see under* abduction
Ideal Language Philosophy, 442–3, 462 n1
identity sentences, 78–9, 80–1
if, 498–9
illocutionally charged expressions, 393
illocutionary act potential, 62–6, 71
illocutionary acts, 54–6, 57, 58, 59, 60–2, 368, 464, 465, 466, 467
  classification, 64–6, 466–7
  direct/indirect, 468
  explicit/inexplicit, 468–9
  literal/non-literal, 468
illocutionary effects, 59, 68, 69–70
illocutionary forces, 465
  "conjuring fate," 693
  conventions of usage, 695–6
  negative questions, 693
  and speaker attitudes, 677, 692–6, 700 n34
  tagged questions, 694–5
imperative mood, 209, 447
implicated conclusions, 615

implicated premises, 615
implicature, 3–28
    comprehension, 615, 620–1
    conventional implicature, 4, 6,
        222–7, 269, 458, 474–5, 490,
        653–4 n1
    conversational implicature *see*
        conversational implicature
    Cooperative Principle, 7, 8, 24–5,
        28 n17, 297, 471, 613
    definitions, 3, 635
    Division of Pragmatic Labor, 16–17,
        27 n12, 509, 510, 542
    I principle *see* I principle
    vs. impliciture, 21–4, 469, 473,
        485–6 n14, 650
    negative implicature, 713–15
    pragmatic intrusion, 17–21, 22–3
    presupposition and, 36–8
    Q principle *see* Q principle
    R principle *see* R principle
    rationality, 24–5
    scalar implicature, 6, 8–10, 12–13,
        645–6, 655–6 n9
    subtypes, 3–4
    two-sided understanding, 10
    see also explicature; explicit/implicit
        distinction
impliciture, 21–4, 469, 473, 485–6 n14,
    650
indefiniteness *see* definiteness and
    indefiniteness
indefinites, 122, 123–4, 145
indexical expressions, 369, 447–8
indexicality, 97–121
    attentional phenomenon, 102
    character, 90
    in communication, 97–9
    context, 90
    deferred reference, 361 n7, 361 n10
    deixis, 97, 100–1, 675–6, 687, 697 n1
    display, 367–9
    gesture, 91–2, 96 n1, 98, 102–3, 108–10,
        108f, 111
    and imperative mood, 447
    intentional phenomenon, 102
    pure indexicals, 453–4
    and reference, 90, 99
    terminology, 97, 100–1

    in thought, 99–100
    token-reflexivity, 99
    see also deixis
indirect requests, 580, 581–3
indirect speech acts, 68–71
    mood, 73
    and politeness, 71, 580
    sentence type, 71–3
inertness, assertorical, 26 n5
infelicities, doctrine of, 56–7
inference, 4, 6–8, 424, 470–2, 578
inform, 584
information status, 387, 403 n8
information structure, 153–74, 194 n12
    argument reversal, 169–72
    and argument structure, 429–30,
        433–4, 441 nn3–6
    assumed familiarity, 154, 155–6
    focus, 157–8
    left-dislocation (LD), 162–3, 174 n7,
        186–7
    and non-canonical syntax, 153–5,
        172–3
    open propositions (OPs), 156–8
    postposing, 154, 155, 163–8, 173
    preposing, 154, 155, 158–62, 173
    right-dislocation, 168–9, 187, 188–9,
        195 n23, 196 n25
    see also topic and focus
informational account, 737–8
informational uniqueness, 131
Ingush, 294
inserts, 374–6
intention,
    deictic expressions, 102, 106
    discourse coherence, 260–1
    inference and relevance, 470–2
    language acquisition, 208, 218 n10,
        571–2
    reference, 92–3
    speech acts, 53, 469–70, 485 nn7–8
intentional account, 737–9
intentions in interpretation (language
    game), 207–17
intermediate phrase, 516
internal dative construction, 413
interpretive use, 621
intersective adjectives, 495
intersectivity, 142

intonation, 515–37
  discourse phenomena, 527–36
  focus and, 161, 182, 183–5, 194 n16,
    195 n18, 530–2
  questions, 73
  semantic phenomena, 525–7
  syntactic phenomena, 520–1,
    523–5
  ToBI system, 516–20
  try markers, 376–7
intonational phrase, 516
intrinsic connections, 367
Inuktitut, 430, 436
inversion, 417
Invited Inference Theory of Semantic
  Change, 552–3
irony, 621–2, 623, 631 n27
Israel, M., 673
Italian, 117, 118, 295, 360 n5, 436
Iten, C., 226, 227, 228, 231, 240 n10,
  240 n19

Jackendoff, R., 98, 176, 184, 349, 357,
  362 n11
Jacobs, A., 538–9
Jäger, G., 509, 510
James, S., 575
Japanese,
  acknowledgments, 372
  anaphora, 291, 303, 304
  argument ellipsis, 436
  definiteness, 144, 148 n2
  demonstratives, 110
  honorifics, 120, 551, 576
  language acquisition, 576
  main verb inversion, 420
  polarity, 716
  speaker beliefs, 416
  subjectification, 550
  topic, 179, 180, 186, 187
Jennings, P., 160
Jesperson, O., 112
joint attention, 563–5
joint commitments, 370
de Jong, F., 142, 143
de Jonge, C., 19
Josephson, J., 729
Josephson, S., 729
Journal of Broadcasting, 419

Jucker, A., 221, 538–9
Jurafsky, D., 579, 582, 590, 593, 594, 595,
  598
Justice, David, 700 n31
juxtapositions, 378–9

Kaburaki, E., 316
Kabuverdiano, 307
Kadmon, N., 219 n15, 717
Kalkatungu, 306
Kalokerinos, A., 723 n2
Kameyama, M., 258
Kamp, H., 96, 203, 205, 496
Kannada, 307, 308
Kant, I., 314 n6
Kaplan, D., 85, 90–1, 104, 106, 160, 444,
  452, 453
Karttunen, L., 6, 33, 34, 73, 133, 144, 145,
  147, 483
Kasher, A., 24, 147
Kasper, R., 218 n4
Katz, J., 66, 446–7, 448, 488–9
Kay, P., 72, 682, 689, 690, 698 n11,
  698 nn16–18, 699–700 n31
Keenan, E. L., 116, 117, 141–2, 496
Keenan, E. O., 8, 27 n8
Kehler, A., 246, 253, 256, 258, 262,
  265 n15, 384, 389, 390–1, 392, 396
Kempson, R., 36, 40
Kennedy, C., 264 nn11–12
Kim, N.-K., 72
kinda/sorta, 691–2, 699–700 n31
King, J., 145
Kintsch, W., 245–6
Kiparsky, C., 34
Kiparsky, P., 34, 501
Kita, S., 110
Kitis, E., 240 n16
Klima, E., 300, 711
Knott, A., 234, 235, 244
knowledge of hearer, 384
knownness *see* familiarity
Koenig, J.-P., 698 n15
König, E., 307, 308, 558
Korean,
  anaphora, 291, 303, 304, 309
  argument ellipsis, 436–7
  honorifics, 120
  non-sentential speech, 277

Korean (*cont'd*)
  sentence types, 72
  topic, 179, 187
Kose, Y., 416
Kövecses, Z., 550
Krifka, M., 716
Kripke, S., 83–4, 85–7, 94, 128, 218 n5,
    482, 486–7 n25, 649, 690–1
Kukla, R., 285 n5
Kuno, S., 132, 176, 256, 264–5 n14, 316,
    330, 337–8, 341 n3
Kuroda, S.-Y., 38, 144, 176, 550
Kwakwa'la, 117

Ladd, D. R., 534
Ladusaw, W., 711–12, 713, 718, 719
Lahav, R., 496
Lakatos, I., 728
Lakoff, G., 69, 190, 255, 264 n13, 350, 421,
    422, 580, 581, 689, 698 n23
Lakoff, R., 414
Lambrecht, K., 177, 184–5, 428, 430, 432,
    594, 677
Landman, F., 717
Langacker, R., 363 n23, 666–7, 669, 723 n4
language acquisition, 562–77
  abduction, 549
  anaphora, 288
  argument ellipsis, 437
  common ground, 563–4, 565–6
  contrast, 567–9
  convention, 567–9
  gesture, 98–9, 102, 110, 569–70
  intention, 208, 218 n10, 571–2
  joint attention, 563–5
  politeness, 574–6
  speech acts, 569–71
  taking account of addressee, 573
  taking turns, 574
language and languages, 462 n4
  preplanned, non-interactive, 365
  spontaneous, interactive, 365–6
language change *see* historical
    pragmatics
language performance, 365–82, 382 n1
  coordinating on use of language,
    369–73
  saying and displaying, 366–9
  signals, 366–7, 368, 373–81, 382 n5

Larson, R., 637, 649
Lascarides, A., 210, 216, 245, 263 n4
Lasnik, H., 295
Leacock, C., 345
Lebeaux, D., 332, 334–5, 336
Leech, G., 71, 354
Lees, R., 300
left-dislocation (LD), 162–3, 174 n7,
    186–7, 417
Lehiste, I., 531
Leibniz's law, 77
Lenat, D., 740
let alone, 676, 678–81, 697 n2, 697 n9
levels of meaning, 457
levels of representation, 384–5
Levesque, H., 73
Levin, N., 389–90
Levinson, S., 6, 13, 21–2, 23, 27 n9,
    27 n12, 35, 36, 37, 39, 40–2, 43, 44,
    45, 48, 50, 51, 68, 71, 107, 118, 222,
    292, 297–300, 301–4, 456–7, 486 n19,
    486 n22, 500, 503–4, 510, 542, 545–8,
    587, 630 n18, 631 n27, 647–8, 655 n9,
    656 n10, 700 n32
Lewis, D., xii, 7, 33, 36, 45, 131, 134–5,
    198, 207, 209, 450, 455, 456, 478, 730
lexical blocking, 501–3, 506
lexical cues, 594–5
lexical loosening, 618–19, 620, 630 n19
lexical meaning, 488–514
  cognition, 666–71
  conversational implicature, 490, 503–6
  lexicon vs. encyclopedia, 489–90
  optimality theory, 506–12
  standard view, 491–5; challenges,
    495–503
lexical narrowing, 617–18
lexical projections, 267, 285 n3
Lezgian, 307, 437
Liberman, M., 535
licensing,
  affectivity, 711
  downward entailing (DE), 712, 718–19
  Flaubert triggers, 719
  Monotonicity Thesis, 712, 713, 715
  negative implicature (NI), 713–15
  polarity licensing, 711–15
  pragmatic, 505, 507
  scalar pragmatics, 718–22

Lidz, J., 306, 308
likely, 670
Linebarger, M., 713–14, 715, 722
linguistic semantics, 455–6, 457
linguistic structure, 214
Linsky, L., 84
Literal Force/Meaning Hypothesis, 579–80, 597
Litman, D., 531
litotes, 3, 511
Löbner, S., 148 n5
local pragmatics, 725, 733–4
locative preposing, 417
Lochbaum, K., 395
locutionary acts, 54, 55, 56, 59, 466
logic,
    as language of thought, 725–6
    non-monotonic, 726–7
    square of opposition, 10–12
logical expressions, 479–84
    and, 18–19, 232, 236, 479–80
    or, 18, 480–1, 486 n23
    quantificational phrases and descriptions, 481–3, 486 n24
logical forms, 455
logophoric NP constraint, 331
logophoricity, 310–11, 329–39
Longacre, R., 243
Longgu, 117, 118
Ludlow, P., 75, 145, 147, 482
Lycan, W., 39, 68, 477
Lyons, C., 136, 148 n2
Lyons, J., 550

M principle, 298, 299–300, 302–4, 305–10, 546–8
Malagasy, 116
Malay, 115, 293, 430
Malinowski, B., 562
Mandelblit, N., 674
Mann, W., 212–13, 233, 245
Mapun, 311
Marcus, M., 524
Markedness Principle for Discourse Rule Violations, 316, 317–18, 321, 325–6
Marshall, C., 132
Martin, J. H., 579, 582, 594
Martin, J. R., 243
Martinich, A., 14, 27 n11

Marty, A., 184
Mathesius, V., 175–6, 342 n5
Matsumoto, Y., 503
Mauritian Creole, 436
Maxim of Quantity-Quality, 15
maximal projection, 267
Maxims of Conversation, 7–8, 9, 13, 27 nn7–8, 34, 201, 208–9, 471, 540–1
Maxims of Relativity, 41
May, R., 264 n12
MCBs (mutual contextual beliefs), 63
McCarthy, J., 506, 726
McCawley, J., 65, 67, 131, 426 n15, 502, 686, 694, 699 n26
McDermott, D., 726, 729
McDowell, J., 80
McGinn, C., 76, 88–9
McKenna, G., 161
meaning, 657–9
    Argumentation Theory, 227–9
    correspondence theory, 74
    descriptive meaning, 457–8
    discourse markers, 222–32
    Grice's theory, 102, 197, 207–8, 297, 443, 463, 479, 484 n1
    imparted via usage, 93–4
    inference and speaker meaning, 6–8, 424
    levels of meaning, 457
    lexical meaning, 488–514, 666–71
    literal vs. speaker's, 450–3
    potential, 661
    pragmatic meaning, 457–8
    procedural, 223
    representational, 223
    and speech acts, 446–50, 449f, 462 n5
    transfer, 346–8, 360–1 nn5–8
    and truth-conditional effects, 189–91
    varieties of meaning, 457–61
    see also semantics
Meinong, A., 82
mental architecture, 623–5
mental spaces, 662–3, 663f, 667
Merin, A., 73
metalinguistic constructions, 687–92
    comparatives, 677, 689
    hedges, 689–90, 691–2, 699 n29, 699–700 n31
    negation, 10, 677, 687–9, 698 n24

metaphor, 344–5, 359 n2, 550, 619, 622,
     631 nn21–2, 659–60
  see also deferred interpretation
metasemantics, 444
metonymy, 345, 348, 550, 733
  see also deferred interpretation
Mexican Spanish, 441 n8
Michaelis, L., 430, 594
Mill, J. S., 9, 76, 98, 102, 486–7 n25
Miller, G., 740
Miller, P., 166, 167
Milsark, G., 138–40, 141, 144, 145,
     148 n11, 187
miscellaneous tier, 516
Mithun, M., 116
Mittwoch, A., 67
Modesty Principle, 325, 342 n4
modifications, 376–8
Modified Occam's Razor principle, 10
Moeschler, J., 229, 240 n9
monotonicity,
  inferential competence, 492–3, 513 n2
  invited inferences, 498–501, 506
  lexical system, 493–4, 494f, 501–2, 506
  licensing, 712, 713, 715
  non-monotonic logic, 726–7
Montague, R., 80, 88, 104, 139, 140,
     148 n4, 197, 496
mood, 65, 71–3, 209, 268, 447
mood indicators, 623, 631 n29
Moore, G. E., 478–9
Moore, J., 260, 261
Moore's paradox, 463–4
moreover, 224, 225
Morgan, C., 71, 729
Morgan, J., 70–1, 422, 424, 425, 426 n15,
     695–6
Morimoto, T., 597, 602
Morris, C., xi, 443–4
most, 719–21
motivation, 214
mutual contextual beliefs (MCBs), 63

Nagata, M., 597, 599, 602
naïve theory of reference, 76
Nakatani, C., 529, 532
names, causal theory of, 86–7
Napoli, D., 287 n14
narrow context, 477

Neale, S., 130, 145, 147, 482, 649
negation,
  ambiguity, 36–8
  contrary readings, 708–9
  marked category, 706–7
  metalinguistic negation, 10, 677, 687–9,
     698 n24
  negative implicature, 713–15
  negative polarity items (NPIs), 710,
     711–12, 713–14, 715–16, 719–22
  neg(ative)-raising, 709, 723 n5
  negative strengthening, 499–501, 500f,
     510–12, 708
  negative transportation, 414
  and polarity, 415, 701–2, 705–9, 722
  presupposition, 31–3, 34–5, 36–8,
     51–2 n3
  processing, 707–8, 723 n4
  questions, 693
  reactive nature, 708
Neijt, A., 394
Nerlich, B., 561 n8
Newcombe, N., 575
Newton, I., 728
Nichols, J., 294
Nickerson, J., 536
Nixon diamond, 727
Nølke, H., 555
non-canonical syntax, 153–74
non-controversiality, 41–2, 45, 46–7, 50,
     51
non-conventional pragmatics, 428
non-detachability, 40–1
non-literality, 13
non-monotonic logic, 726–7
non-monotonicity, 451, 498–502, 506
non-scalar contextual operators (NSCOs),
     683–7
non-sentences, 266–87
  appearances, 266–70
  ellipsis, 272–9
  not a genuine speech act, 271–2, 665 n6
  pragmatic explanation, 279–80, 283–5
  type, 267–8
Noordman, L., 235, 236, 237
Norvig, P., 350, 730, 731, 738
Norwegian,
  anaphora, 291, 307
  language acquisition, 576

topic and focus, 183–4, 185, 188–9, 195 n23, 196 n25
noteworthiness, 349–50, 353, 354, 355, 356–7, 361 n9, 362 nn11–12, 363 nn22–3
Nöth, E., 536
noun phrases, 122–4, 148 nn1–3
  cardinal, 138
  heavy NP shift, 417, 420–1
  logophoric NP constraint, 331
  quantificational, 138
  stage-level properties, 139
  see also definiteness and indefiniteness
novelty, 134
NPIs *see* polarity items: negative
NSCOs *see* non-scalar contextual operators
nuclear accent/stress, 517
Nunberg, G., 105, 350, 361 n7, 503, 675–6

offers, 570–1
O'Hair, S., 15
Ojeda, A., 131
O'Neill, D., 573
only, 718–19
opacity and presuppositions, 661–6
open propositions (OPs), 156–8
opposition, 701–2
optimal relevance, 230
optimality theory and lexical pragmatics, 506–12
or, 18, 480–1, 486 n23
ordered entailment, 390
Ordinary Language philosophy, 442, 443, 462 n2, 478
Oriya, 294
orthographic tier, 516
ostensive stimulus, 611
Ostler, N., 350
overlap, 379
Özyürek, A., 110

parallel markers, 223
parcel of speaking, 375
Parsons, T., 95
Partee, B., 146, 190
passive constructions, 409–10, 417
Passoneau, R., 531
Paul, H., 175

Peacocke, C., 129
Pederson, E., 723 n3
Peirce, C., 99, 102, 103, 367, 729
perception verbs, 489
performance, 366
performance indexes, 367–8, 369, 372, 373
performative hypothesis, 67–8
performatives, 54, 55, 56–7, 464, 484 nn2–3, 671–3
  formula, 57–8
  and illocutionary force, 465
  tacit, 225
Perkins, E., 161
perlocutionary acts, 55–6, 368, 466
perlocutionary effects, 68, 69, 70
Perrault, C. R., 73, 581, 583, 584
Perry, J., 106, 130, 160, 452
Persian, 716
person deixis, 112–14
perspective, 310–11
Peters, S., 6
philosophy of language, 463–87
  applied pragmatics, 478–84
  semantic–pragmatic distinction, 475–8, 486 nn19–20, 486 n22
  speech acts and communication, 469–75
phonetic acts, 368
phrase accents, 516, 517
phrase-final lengthening, 517
Piedmontese, 293
Pierrehumbert, J., 161, 184, 516, 531–2, 537 n3, 595–6
Pietrzykowski, T., 729
pitch accents, 516, 517, 518–19, 519*f*, 520*f*, 521*f*, 528–9
plan inference (BDI) model of speech act interpretation, 580, 581–7, 603–4
Plato, 706
poetic effect, 621
Pohnpei, 120
pointing, 91–2, 96 n1, 98, 102–3, 111, 226, 569–70
polarity, 701–23
  negation, 415, 701–2, 705–9, 722
  sensitivity, 709–22
  types, 702–5
  see also polarity items

polarity items, 709–10, 711
   lexicon, 715–18
   minimizers, 715–16
   negative (NPIs), 710, 711–12, 713–14,
      715–16, 719–22
   positive (PPIs), 710, 716
   pragmatic force, 716
   scalar operators, 717
   sensitivity, 709, 711
   syntactic constraints, 722
politeness, 71, 574–6, 580, 717
Pollack, M., 260, 261
Pollard, C., 423, 424, 734
polysemy, 345, 350–1, 357, 359 n2,
   362 n15, 498, 543
Pople, H., Jr., 729
portioning, 351, 352
posets, 159–60
positive cognitive effect, 608
possible, 670
Postal, P., 66, 139, 265 n15, 426 n15
postposing, 154, 155, 163–8, 173
Pott, A. F., 716
PPIs *see* polarity items: positive
pragmaphilology, 538, 539
pragmatic entailments, 704
pragmatic information, 407–8, 409f, 476
pragmatic interpretation, 451–3
pragmatic intrusion, 17–21, 22–3, 40–1,
   48, 51
pragmatic licensing, 505, 507
pragmatic markers, 221, 223
pragmatic meaning, 457–8
pragmatic presupposition, xii, 33, 477
pragmatic scales, 673–4, 703, 704
pragmatic sets, 130
pragmatics,
   definitions, xi, xii, 197, 222
   goals, xi
   types, 428
pre-announcements, 596
predicate transfer in systematic
   polysemy, 350–1, 357, 362 n15
Preferred Argument Structure, 430–2
preposing, 154, 155, 158–62, 173, 417–18,
   426 n9
   focus preposing, 160–1, 173–4 nn4–5
   topicalization, 160, 161–2, 174 n5, 183,
      185, 195 n19

presupposed content, 209
presupposition, 29–52
   accommodation, 36, 41, 45–6, 47, 50,
      51, 134–5, 730
   assertion, 31–3, 37, 46–7, 50, 51–2 n3
   cognitive approach, 662–6
   common ground, 41, 42, 43, 44–8
   context/content distinction, 46, 48–50,
      51
   conversational implicata, 41–4
   definiteness and indefiniteness, 126–7,
      142–4, 149 nn13–14
   entailment, 31–3, 34, 41, 43, 52 n4
   factive presuppositions, 34–6
   Frege on, 29–33, 51–2 n3
   Grice on, xi, 33, 34, 36–9, 42–5, 47, 48
   negation, 31–3, 34–5, 36–8, 51–2 n3
   non-controversiality, 41–2, 45, 46–7, 50,
      51
   non-detachability, 40–1
   non-specificity, 37, 48, 50–1
   opacity and, 661–6
   pragmatic intrusion, 40–1, 48, 51
   pragmatic presupposition, xii, 33, 477
   referential presupposition, 29, 33, 38–9
   semantical presupposition, xii, 29–30,
      477
presupposition float, 665–6
Price, P., 516
Prince, E., 122, 132, 137, 148 n7, 154,
   155–6, 162, 163, 177, 180–1, 186, 187,
   386, 387, 389–90, 396–7, 403 n8, 416,
   434
Principle of Effective Means, 24
Principle of Relevance, 17–18, 28 n13, 472
procedural markers, 553
procedural meaning, 223
processing effort, 609
proferred content, 209
projection properties, 106–7
projective pairs, 370
prolongations, 378
pronominal reference, 257–60, 383, 384,
   397–401
pronouns, 112, 326–8, 528–9, 723 n5, 735
propositional acts, 59
propositional forms, 455
propositions, xiii, 156–8, 676
prosodic cues, 595–6

pseudo-cleft, 417
Pustejovsky, J., 350, 353, 354–5, 356, 357
Putnam, H., 48, 85, 86, 95, 690–1
Pylyshyn, Z., 491, 492

Q principle, 13–17, 25, 27 n10, 27 n12,
    297–9, 300, 302–10, 503–6, 541–8
quantificational phrases and
    descriptions, 481–3, 486 n24
quantity generalization, 430–2
QUDs *see* questions: questions under
    discussion
questions,
    check questions, 580, 593, 594, 595, 598
    and common ground, 209, 219 n14
    as imperative, 209
    intonation, 73
    negative questions, 693
    polarity questions, 72–3
    questions under discussion (QUDs),
        208–16, 219 n17
    superquestions and subquestions, 210
    tagged questions, 694–5
    wh-questions, 599
    yes–no questions, 595, 598, 603
Quileute, 109
Quine, W. V., 102, 105, 130, 495–6
Quintilian, 14
Quirk, R., 149 n16

R principle, 16–17, 25, 541–5
Radden, G., 550
raised subject construction, 413–14
rationality, 24–5
Ravin, Y., 345
Ray, T., 294
Recanati, F., 28 n16, 287 n18, 473, 485 n7,
    486 n15, 638, 640, 653, 654 n5,
    656 n10
Redeker, G., 233
Reed, I., 117
Reeder, K., 570
reference, xii–xiii, 74–96
    aboutness, 74–5
    circumscriptive reference, 399
    content, 94–6
    descriptions, 92, 127–8, 486 n25
    indexicality, 90, 99
    intentions, 92–3

    Kaplan's analysis, 90–1
    meaning imparted via usage, 93–4
    naïve theory of reference, 76
    phenomenon of, 74–6
    pointing, 91–2, 96 n1, 98, 102–3, 111,
        226, 569–70
    as pragmatic, 84–7
    pronominal reference, 257–60, 383, 384,
        397–401
    referential properties of topic, 179–81
    semantic theory, 76–84, 88–9
    terminology, 87–8, 94
    see also deferred interpretation;
        definiteness and indefiniteness;
        deixis; event reference
referential givenness–newness, 176–9
referential presupposition, 29, 33, 38–9
referential semantics, 456–7
reflexivity, 289–90, 291–3, 309, 312,
    314 nn3–4, 326–8, 342–3 n9, 547
reformulations, 594, 598
Reggia, J., 729
Reichenbach, H., 99, 462 n1
Reimer, M., 91
Reinhart, T., 176, 180, 191, 192, 195 n22,
    289–90, 291, 292–3, 301, 312,
    314 nn3–4, 333
Reiter, R., 727
Reithinger, N., 598
rejections, 599, 601
relational givenness–newness, 177–9
relevance, 216, 219 n20
relevance theory, 607–32, 633–56
    abduction and, 739–40
    cognition, 608–10, 625–8
    Cognitive Principle of Relevance, 610,
        625–6
    coherence, 237, 238, 239
    communication, 230, 472, 485 n12,
        610–14
    Communicative Principle of Relevance,
        612, 613, 626
    comprehension, 226, 614–23
    definition, 607–8
    discourse markers, 229–31, 237, 238,
        239
    explicature, 636–43
    explicit/implicit distinction, 633–56
    implicature, 643–8

relevance theory (*cont'd*)
  mental architecture, 623–5
  Principle of Relevance, 17–18, 28 n13, 472
Rembarrnga, 113
repetition, 379
replacement, 378
representational dimension, 65
representational meaning, 223
requests, 570–1, 580, 581–3, 584–5, 596, 599, 601, 603
resource situation, 104, 130
respective, 683–4, 685–6, 687
respectively, 683–5, 687, 696
Reuland, E., 289–90, 291, 292–3, 312, 314 nn3–4
reversal, 702, 703–5
Reyle, U., 96, 205
rheme *see* topic and focus: terminology
Rhetorical Structure Theory (RST), 245
Rieber, S., 223–4, 225–6
right-dislocation, 168–9, 187, 188–9, 195 n23, 196 n25, 417
Roberts, C., 130, 136, 208, 213, 219 n15, 219 n21
Rooth, M., 181, 253
Van Rooy, R., 508, 513, 513 n10
Ross, J., 66–7, 185, 186, 254, 255
Rouchota, V., 231, 238–9
Roulet, E., 554
RST (Rhetorical Structure Theory), 245
rule of strength, 15
Russell, B., 81, 82–4, 85, 98, 125, 126, 128–9, 148 n4, 442, 482, 486 n25
Russian, 148 n2, 307, 309, 353
Ryle, G., 18

Sacapultec Maya, 430
Sachs, J., 573
Sacks, H., 376
Sadock, J., 25–6 n2, 47, 56, 65, 67, 68, 69, 70, 72, 353, 594, 595
Sag, I., 145, 146, 147, 286 n12, 286 n13, 385–6, 389, 391, 393, 394, 402 n4, 423, 424, 535, 734
Sainsbury, R., 130
Sakakibara, S., 416
salience, 387–8, 403 n8
Salmon, N., 85, 93–4, 482

Samuel, K., 603
Sanders, T., 234, 235, 236, 237, 244, 247
SAS (speech act schema), 63
Saul, J., 22
saying, 366–9, 472–5
  conventional implicature, 474–5
  syntactic correlation constraint, 473
  what is said and what isn't, 472–4
scalar entailments, 704
scalar implicature, 6, 8–13, 645–6, 655–6 n9
scalar inferences, 704, 718–22
scalar models, 704, 705, 723 n1
  grammatical constructions, 676, 678–83, 698 n11, 704, 723 n1
  polarity sensitivity, 717–18
scales, pragmatic, 673–4, 703, 704
Scandinavian languages, 188, 307
Schachter, P., 393
Schegloff, E., 376, 596
Schiffer, S., 33
Schiffrin, D., 233, 235–6, 555
Schladt, M., 306
Schmerling, S., 184, 287 n14
Schourup, L., 221, 232, 240 n2
Schwenter, S., 239
Searle, J., 14, 56, 59–62, 63, 65, 68, 70, 73, 465, 470, 479, 484 n2, 484 n4, 535, 580, 581, 582, 696
Segal, G., 637, 649
Sellars, W., 130
semantic ellipsis, 274, 275, 277–9, 287 n15
semantical determinants, 30
semantical interpretation, 450–1, 453
semantical presupposition, xii, 29–30, 477
semantic–pragmatic distinction, 442–3, 447, 475–6
  Carnapian approach, 443–6, 462 nn3–4
  comprehension, 634–5
  consequences of, 477–8, 486 n22
  context, 476–7, 486 n20
  information, 476
  prototypicality effects, 461
  terminology, 476, 486 n19
semantics, 442–62
  Context Change Semantics, 205, 206, 478
  correspondence theory of meaning, 74–5

definitions, 197, 222
descriptive semantics, 444–5
File Change Semantics, 133–4
formal semantics, 222, 442–3
foundational semantics, 445
linguistic semantics, 455–6, 457
literal meaning vs. speaker's meaning, 450–3
meaning and speech acts, 446–50, 449*f*, 462 n5
metasemantics, 444
referential semantics, 456–7
Situation Semantics, 104
underdetermination, 453–7, 654 n3
varieties of meaning, 457–61
see also lexical meaning; meaning; semantic–pragmatic distinction
sense, 79–80, 87, 94
sensitivity, 709–22
diversity, 711
lexicon, 715–18
licensing, 711–15
scalar model, 717–18
sentence focus (SF) constructions, 432–3
sentences,
declarative, 417
donkey sentences, 132–4, 148 n8, 203–5
existential, 138–44
identity sentences, 78–9, 80–1
setting, 488–9
types, 65, 71–3
setting, 488–9
Sgall, P., 178
Shastri, L., 741
Shimony, S., 740
Shoham, Y., 506
Shopen, T., 271, 286 n13
Shriberg, E., 536, 595, 597, 599, 600*f*
Sidner, C., 216, 257, 258, 261, 532
Siemund, P., 307, 308
signals, 366–7, 368
collateral, 373–81, 382 n5
primary, 373
Silverman, K., 531
Situation Semantics, 104
situational context, 384
slifting, 413
sluicing, 415–16
Smith, B., 24, 27 n8

so, 223, 224, 236, 238, 239, 383, 384, 394–7, 403 n11
Soames, S., 697 n2
social deixis, 119–21
some, 9–10, 414–15
Sorensen, J., 672, 673
sortal crossings, 357–9, 363–4 n24
source clauses, 383
South Dravidian, 707, 723 n3
Southeast Asian languages, 112, 119–20
Spanish, 109, 148 n2, 307, 441 n8, 699 n25
spatial deixis, 116–18
specificity, 144–7, 149 n17
Speech Act Empathy Hierarchy, 316, 318
speech act fallacy, 478–9
speech act schema (SAS), 63
speech acts, xii, 53–73
and assertion fallacies, 479
Austin's view, 54–8, 59, 62, 64, 66
central vs. non-central, 224
communication and, 464–75, 485 nn6–8
constitutive rules, 60–1, 465
doctrine of infelicities, 56–7
formal approaches, 73
generation, 581
and grammar, 66–8
Grice's influence, 58–62
ground floor vs. higher level, 224–5
illocutionary act potential, 62–6, 71
illocutionary acts, 54–6, 57, 58, 59, 60–2, 64–6, 368, 464, 465, 466–9
indirect speech acts, 68–73, 580
intonation, 532–6
language acquisition, 569–71
locutionary acts, 54, 55, 56, 59, 466
meaning and, 446–50, 449*f*, 462 n5
performatives, 54, 55, 56–8, 464, 465, 484 nn2–3
perlocutionary acts, 55–6, 368, 466
Searle's view, 59–62, 63
Strawson's view, 59, 63
see also cue-based model of speech act interpretation; non-sentences; plan inference (BDI) model of speech act interpretation; saying
Sperber, D., 6, 43, 219 n20, 224, 226, 228, 229, 230, 231, 287 n18, 390, 454, 470, 472, 473, 485 n12, 626, 635, 646, 648

Spinoza, B., 706
square of opposition, 10–12
Stainton, R., 276, 287 n16, 641, 655 n6
Stallard, D., 358
Stalnaker, R., xii, xiii, 33, 34, 36, 44,
  45–6, 47–50, 208, 444–5, 477, 478,
  486 n20
Standard American English contours, 522*t*
Standard Picture (SP), 452
standardized non-literality, 13
Stanley, J., 130–1, 271, 279, 486 n24, 640,
  651, 654–5 nn5–6
statements, 144, 599
Steele, S., 536
Stevenson, R., 259–60
Stickel, M., 731
Stokhof, M., 205, 210
Stolcke, A., 592*t*, 597, 602
Strawson, P., 15, 18, 45, 59, 83, 84–5, 126,
  127, 129, 189–90, 287 n18, 462 n2,
  465, 469, 470, 706
structural description features, 421
subalterns, 11
subcontraries, 11
Subject Preference for Characterizing
  Sentences, 323
Suhm, B., 601
Surface Structure Empathy Hierarchy,
  316, 317
Sweetser, E., 489, 667, 670, 671–3
Swerts, M., 531
Swinney, D., 587
symmetry, 132
synecdoche, 345, 561 n8
syntactic constructions, 421–5,
  426 nn14–16
syntactic correlation constraint, 28 n15,
  473
syntactic cues, 594–5
syntactic ellipsis, 273–4, 275–9,
  286–7 nn11–14, 640–1
Syntactic Prominence Empathy
  Hierarchy, 323
syntax, 185–9, 195 n22, 444, 448
  non-canonical, 153–74
systematic polysemy, 350–1, 357,
  362 n15, 498
systematicity, 491–2
Szabó, Z., 130–1, 136, 486 n24, 640, 654 n5

tagged questions, 694–5
Tamil, 113, 118, 120, 296
Tanenhaus, M., 14
Tanz, C., 99
target clauses, 383
Tarski, A., 455–6, 493, 513 n2
Taylor, K., 22, 640
Taylor, P., 536, 591*t*, 602
tense, 411–12, 422
Terken, J., 173–4 n4, 529, 530
text macrostructure, 245
textual units, 232
TG (Transformational Grammar), 66
the, 377, 382 n7
theme *see* topic and focus: terminology
theory of mind, 623, 625
there, 164–5, 166, 417
thetic statements, 144
thinking face, 380
Thomason, R., 730, 740
Thompson, S., 212–13, 233, 245
thought, 99–100, 725–6
time deixis, 114–16
to, 377
ToBI system: intonation, 516–20
  break indices, 516, 516*f*, 517*f*
  pitch accents, 517, 518–19, 519*f*, 520*f*,
    521*f*
  Standard American English contours,
    522*t*
token-reflexivity, 99
Tomlin, R., 180, 193 n8
tonal tier, 516
too, 4, 200–1, 218 n5
topic and focus, 175–96
  conceptual issues, 176–83
  given–new distinctions, 176–9, 529–30
  information structure, 157–8, 175–6,
    191, 428–9
  meaning and truth-conditional effects,
    189–91
  phenomena, 183–91
  pragmatic effects, 191–2
  syntactic structure, 185–9, 195 n20,
    195 n22
  terminology, 175, 176, 180, 182,
    193–4 n8
topic, 176, 179–81, 182, 191, 193–4 n8,
  194 n17, 428

topic/focus identification, 192–3
topicalization, 160, 161–2, 174 n5, 183,
    185, 195 n19, 417
    topichood, 256, 264–5 n14
    see also focus
Topic Empathy Hierarchy, 316, 318,
    324
tough-movement, 417
Transformational Grammar (TG), 66
Traugott, E., 239
Travis, C., 669
truth, 57, 76–7, 80–1, 88, 89–90
truth conditions,
    discourse markers, 222, 223
    formal semantics, 222, 442–3
    implicature, 4, 6, 25 n1
    interpretation, 280
    meaning, 189–91
    pragmatics, 222, 453, 454, 456, 457
    topic and focus, 189–91
try markers, 376–7
Turkish, 110, 307, 308, 703
turn-taking, 201–2, 574
Turner, M., 659, 667, 668, 669
two-sided understanding, 10
type, 267
type identifiability, 137
Tzeltal, 430, 436

Ullman, S., 539
unarticulated constituent, 460
underdetermination, 453–7, 654 n3
unexpectedness, 310–12
uniquely identifiable referents, 388
uniqueness, 125–32, 135–7, 148 n4
Urmson, J., 18, 59
utterance situation, 104

Vallduví, E., 183, 194 n10
Vanderveken, D., 73
Vayra, M., 531
Vendler, Z., 65
verb phrase ellipsis, 251–4,
    263–4 nn8–12, 276, 383, 384, 391–4,
    403 n10
verb phrase preposing, 417
Verbmobil corpus, 590, 591*t*
verbs, perception, 489
verdictives, 64, 467

Verkuyl, H., 142, 143
vice versa, 686–7
Vilkuna, M., 183, 194 n10
vowels, non-reduced, 377

Waibel, A., 599, 601, 601*f*, 602
Walker, M., 12, 94
Ward, G., 27 n11, 96 n2, 122, 131, 136,
    158, 165, 185, 194 n13, 360 n6, 384,
    396, 417–18
Warnock, G., 59
Warrwa, 109
Washington, George, 8, 27 n7
Wason, P., 706
we, 675–6, 697 n1
Webber, B., 391, 398–400, 403 n13
Weber, E., 595
West Greenlandic, 117
    see also Greenlandic Eskimo
Westerståhl, D., 122, 130
wh-questions, 599
"what is said," 224, 472–4, 648–53,
    656 n11
wide context, 477
Wierzbicka, A., 65, 413
Wilcock, G., 424
Wilensky, R., 350, 730, 731, 738
Wilkins, D., 117, 118
Wilkinson, L., 575–6
Williams, E., 286 n11
Wilson, D., 6, 19, 43, 219 n20, 224, 226,
    228, 229, 230, 231, 236, 237, 287 n18,
    390, 454, 470, 472, 473, 485 n12, 635,
    646, 648
Wilson, G., 145
Winograd, T., 257, 735, 736
Wittgenstein, L., 75, 102, 462 n2, 463
Wolff, C., 728–9
Woodbury, A., 531
Word Order Empathy Hierarchy, 323,
    324
Woszczyna, M., 599, 601, 601*f*, 602

xyz constructions, 659–61, 659*f*, 661*f*

yeah, 587, 595
Yélî Dnye, 121 n3
    discourse deixis, 119
    person deixis, 112, 113

Yélî Dnye (*cont'd*)
  social deixis, 120
  spatial deixis, 109–10, 117, 118
  time deixis, 114, 115
yes-answers, 587, 595
yes–no questions, 595, 598, 603
Yokoyama, O., 342 n7
Yoshimura, A., 721
you-tense deletion, 422

Yucatec, 115
Yup'ik, 116, 117

Zachar, O., 674
Zaenen, A., 503
Zaslow, M., 575
Zipf, G., 13, 14, 541
Zwicky, A., 72, 498, 499, 513 n4, 540, 552, 594, 595

THE LEADING REFERENCE SERIES IN LINGUISTICS

Offering original, state-of-the-art essays by an international collection of leading scholars, the outstanding Blackwell Handbooks in Linguistics series covers all the major subdisciplines within linguistics today.

THE HANDBOOK OF APPLIED LINGUISTICS
Edited by Alan Davies and Catherine Elder

THE HANDBOOK OF PRAGMATICS
Edited by Laurence R. Horn and Gregory Ward

THE HANDBOOK OF BILINGUALISM
Edited by Tej K. Bhatia and William C. Ritchie

THE HANDBOOK OF SECOND LANGUAGE ACQUISITION
Edited by Catherine J. Doughty and Michael H. Long

THE HANDBOOK OF HISTORICAL LINGUISTICS
Edited by Brian D. Joseph and Richard D. Janda

THE HANDBOOK OF LANGUAGE AND GENDER
Edited by Janet Holmes and Miriam Meyerhoff

THE HANDBOOK OF LANGUAGE VARIATION AND CHANGE
Edited by J. K. Chambers, Peter Trudgill, and Natalie Schilling-Estes

THE HANDBOOK OF DISCOURSE ANALYSIS
Edited by Deborah Schiffrin, Deborah Tannen, and Heidi E. Hamilton

THE HANDBOOK OF LINGUISTICS
Edited by Mark Aronoff and Janie Rees-Miller

THE HANDBOOK OF CONTEMPORARY SYNTACTIC THEORY
Edited by Mark Baltin and Chris Collins

THE HANDBOOK OF JAPANESE LINGUISTICS
Edited by Natsuko Tsujimura

THE HANDBOOK OF MORPHOLOGY
Edited by Andrew Spencer and Arnold Zwicky

THE HANDBOOK OF PHONETIC SCIENCES
Edited by William J. Hardcastle and John Laver

THE HANDBOOK OF SOCIOLINGUISTICS
Edited by Florian Coulmas

THE HANDBOOK OF CONTEMPORARY SEMANTIC THEORY
Edited by Shalom Lappin

THE HANDBOOK OF PHONOLOGICAL THEORY
Edited by John A. Goldsmith

THE HANDBOOK OF CHILD LANGUAGE
Edited by Paul Fletcher and Brian MacWhinney

FORTHCOMING:

THE HANDBOOK OF PIDGINS AND CREOLES
Edited by Silvia Kouwenberg and John Victor Singler

THE HANDBOOK OF SPEECH PERCEPTION
Edited by David B. Pisoni and Robert E. Remez

Blackwell
Publishing

For more information about all these titles, visit www.blackwellpublishing.com/reference